# THE ROUTLEDGE INTER]
# HANDBOOK OF DOMESTIC
# VIOLENCE AND ABUSE

This book makes an important contribution to the international understanding of domestic violence and shares the latest knowledge of what causes and sustains domestic violence between intimate partners, as well as the effectiveness of responses in working with adult and child victims, and those who act abusively towards their partners.

Drawing upon a wide range of contemporary research from across the globe, it recognises that domestic violence is both universal, but also shaped by local cultures and contexts. Divided into seven parts:

- Introduction.
- Theoretical perspectives on domestic violence and abuse.
- Domestic violence and abuse across the life-course.
- Manifestations of domestic violence and abuse.
- Responding to domestic violence and abuse.
- Researching domestic violence and abuse.
- Concluding thoughts.

It will be of interest to all academics and students working in social work, allied health, sociology, criminology and gender studies as well as policy professionals looking for new approaches to the subject.

**John Devaney** is Professor and Centenary Chair of Social Work at the University of Edinburgh, United Kingdom.

**Caroline Bradbury-Jones** is Professor of Gender-Based Violence and Health at the University of Birmingham, United Kingdom.

**Rebecca J. Macy** is Professor and Associate Dean for Research and Faculty Development at the University of Northern Carolina at Chapel Hill School of Social Work, USA.

**Carolina Øverlien** is a Research leader at Norwegian Center for Violence and Traumatic Stress Studies (NKVTS) in Oslo, Norway, and Professor at Stockholm University, Sweden.

**Stephanie Holt** is Associate Professor in the School of Social Work and Social Policy, Trinity College Dublin, Republic of Ireland.

# THE ROUTLEDGE INTERNATIONAL HANDBOOK OF DOMESTIC VIOLENCE AND ABUSE

*Edited by John Devaney, Caroline Bradbury-Jones,*
*Rebecca J. Macy, Carolina Øverlien*
*and Stephanie Holt*

LONDON AND NEW YORK

First published 2021
by Routledge
2 Park Square, Milton Park, Abingdon, Oxon OX14 4RN

and by Routledge
52 Vanderbilt Avenue, New York, NY 10017

*Routledge is an imprint of the Taylor & Francis Group, an informa business*

*British Library Cataloguing-in-Publication Data*
A catalogue record for this book is available from the British Library

*Library of Congress Cataloging-in-Publication Data*
*Names: Devaney, John (Senior lecturer) editor.*
*Title: The Routledge international handbook of domestic violence and abuse/edited by John Devaney, Caroline Bradbury-Jones, Rebecca J. Macy, Carolina Øverlien and Stephanie Holt.*
*Description: Abingdon, Oxon; New York, NY: Routledge, 2021. | Includes bibliographical references and index.*
*Identifiers: LCCN 2020041414 (print) | LCCN 2020041415 (ebook) | ISBN 9780367334857 (hbk) | ISBN 9780429331053 (ebk)*
*Subjects: LCSH: Family violence. | Intimate partner violence—Prevention. | Spousal abuse.*
*Classification: LCC HV6626 .R69 2021 (print) | LCC HV6626 (ebook) | DDC 362.82/92—dc23*
*LC record available at https://lccn.loc.gov/2020041414*
*LC ebook record available at https://lccn.loc.gov/2020041415*

ISBN: 978-0-367-33485-7 (hbk)
ISBN: 978-0-367-68625-3 (pbk)
ISBN: 978-0-429-33105-3 (ebk)

Typeset in Bembo
by Apex CoVantage, LLC

MIX
Paper | Supporting
responsible forestry
FSC
www.fsc.org  FSC® C013985

Printed in the United Kingdom
by Henry Ling Limited

# CONTENTS

Contents

Contents

Contents

*Contents*

# EDITORIAL TEAM

**Caroline Bradbury-Jones**, PhD, is Professor of Gender-Based Violence and Health at the University of Birmingham, United Kingdom. She has a clinical background in nursing, midwifery and health visiting. She has extensive experience of working directly with families, particularly those with high levels of need. Her research work focuses broadly within the scope of addressing inequalities and more specifically on issues of family violence.

**John Devaney**, PhD, is Professor and Centenary Chair of Social Work at the University of Edinburgh, United Kingdom. He spent nearly 20 years in social work practice and policy making before moving into academia, and his research over the past 20 years primarily relates to domestic violence, child maltreatment and the impact of adversity across the life-course.

**Stephanie Holt**, PhD, is Associate Professor in the School of Social Work and Social Policy, Trinity College Dublin, where she is currently Head of School and Director of the Postgraduate Diploma in Child Protection and Welfare. Stephanie's research interest and expertise focuses on domestic violence, with a particular emphasis on the impact of domestic violence on children and young people. This is interdisciplinary in its appeal, relating to the work of a range of health, social care and justice professionals.

**Rebecca J. Macy**, MSW, PhD, is Professor, the Associate Dean for Research and Faculty Development, and the L. Richardson Preyer Distinguished Chair for Strengthening Families at the University of North Carolina at Chapel Hill School of Social Work. Her research comprises 18 years' experience conducting community-based studies that focus on intimate partner violence, sexual violence, human trafficking, and improving services for survivors of violence and trafficking.

**Carolina Øverlien**, PhD, is a research leader at Norwegian Centre for Violence and Traumatic Stress Studies (NKVTS) in Oslo, Norway, and Professor at the Department of Social Work, Stockholm University, Sweden. She has conducted numerous studies on children and youth living in difficult life situations, in particular children experiencing domestic violence and youth intimate partner violence. Her research interests include children's rights, resilience and strength-based approaches, research ethics, and qualitative methods. She has published extensively in international peer-reviewed journals as well as writing and editing several books. Øverlien is Associate Editor of the *Journal of Family Violence*.

# ABOUT THE CONTRIBUTORS

**Helene Flood Aakvaag**, PhD, is a clinical psychologist and a researcher at the Norwegian Centre for Violence and Traumatic Stress Studies. Dr Aakvaag has worked with and published on various topics within the fields of domestic violence, sexual abuse, child maltreatment and traumatic stress. Among her research interests are trauma-related shame, social processes after violence and trauma, and revictimisation. Currently, Dr Aakvaag is the principal investigator on a population study of the prevalence of violence and abuse in Norway.

**Sundari Anitha** is Professor of Gender, Violence and Work at the School of Social and Political Sciences, University of Lincoln, UK. Her research interests lie in two areas: (1) the problem of violence against women and girls (VAWG); and (2) labour market experiences of migrant women workers in the UK. She has published widely on both these themes. In between academic jobs, she has previously managed a Women's Aid refuge and has been active in campaigning and policy making on VAWG for over two decades.

**Loraine J. Bacchus**, BSc, MA, PhD, is Associate Professor of Social Science at the London School of Hygiene and Tropical Medicine, and Co-Director of the National Institute for Health Research Global Health Group on Health System Responses to Violence Against Women. She focuses on the development and evaluation of complex interventions within health systems that address violence against women and men in same-sex relationships. She is co-investigator on a trial of a psychoeducational intervention for children exposed to domestic violence and a Global Research Challenges Interdisciplinary Hub on Gender, Justice and Security. Her work spans high-, low- and middle-income countries.

**Laura Badenes-Ribera**, PhD, currently works as Assistant Professor at the University of Valencia, Spain and is Head of the MSc in Health and Social Attention to Dependency of the same university. She has a degree in psychology, criminology and law, and a master's degree in psychology and criminology. Her research areas include meta-analysis and their application to the fields of psychology and criminology, including sexual prejudice, violence and LGBTIQ+ studies. She has several publications in prestigious journals, such as *Trauma, Violence and Abuse*; *Sexuality Research and Social Practice*; *Clinical Psychology: Science and Practice*; *Psicothema* and *Social Indicators Research*.

**Betty Jo Barrett**, PhD is Associate Professor of Women's and Gender Studies and Social Work. She is a founding member of the Animal and Interpersonal Abuse Research Group at the University of Windsor, the first research group in Canada dedicated to knowledge creation and mobilisation about the intersection of violence against humans and animals. Her research focuses on intimate partner violence in heterosexual and LGBTQ relationships, with a specific focus on survivors' help-seeking and interactions with sources of support in the aftermath of violence.

**Stål Bjørkly** is Professor of Clinical Psychology at Molde University College, Norway. He is also research consultant at the Forensic Centre, Oslo University Hospital. His main work concerns violence among mentally ill patients. He has published several books on the psychology of aggression and over 100 international publications in journals and books in the fields of clinical psychology/psychiatry. Intimate partner violence (IPV) is his second largest research topic with almost 20 publications. His research on IPV is based on interactional perspectives with focus on dynamic factors that increase or decrease the risk of IPV.

**Margunn Bjørnholt** is a sociologist and Research Professor at the Norwegian Centre for Violence and Traumatic Stress Studies (NKVTS) in Oslo, Norway. Her research interests include sexual and gender-based violence, migrants and refugees, gender equality, men and masculinities, organisation and policy studies; she is currently involved in research projects on violence against women migrants and refugees, violence in indigenous Sámi communities and intimate partner violence. Her most recent book is *Men, Masculinities and Intimate Partner Violence* (Routledge, 2021), co-edited with L. Gottzén and F. Boonzaier.

**Amparo Bonilla-Campos**, PhD, is Full Professor of Psychology at the University of Valencia, Spain and she is a member of the University Institute of Women's Studies at this institution. She focuses her teaching and research on gender studies and LGBTIQ+ studies. Her areas of interest include gender stereotypes, sexual prejudice, violence against women and intimate partner violence, health, feminist epistemologies, narrative methodologies and review studies. She has several publications in journals such as *Trauma, Violence and Abuse*; *Sexuality Research and Social Practice* and *Frontiers in Psychology*.

**Recheal Silvia Bonsuk** is a community, social and youth activist. She is a social worker with Hangout Foundation, a youth-led network in Uganda empowering young people through Entrepreneurship, Leadership and Sustainable Development, where she serves as a founding member, Finance and Project Manager. Recheal is a former Global Ambassador for The Better Tomorrow Movement (Sri Lanka) and a member of the World Youth Forum (Egypt). She holds a bachelor of science in finance from Makerere University with additional trainings from the Institute of Chartered Secretaries and Administrators-Uganda (Professional Mentorship Programme) and Commonwealth Secretariat (Faith in the Commonwealth Programme).

**Floretta Boonzaier** is Professor at the Department of Psychology, University of Cape Town, South Africa and Co-Director of the Hub for Decolonial Feminist Psychologies in Africa. She is noted for her work in feminist, critical and decolonial psychologies with emphasis on subjectivity, race, gender, sexuality, gendered and sexual violence as well as feminist decolonial methodologies.

**Caroline Bradbury-Jones** is Professor of Gender-Based Violence and Health at the University of Birmingham, United Kingdom. She is a registered nurse, midwife and health visitor and has extensive experience of working directly with families, particularly those with high levels of need. Her research work focuses broadly within the scope of addressing inequalities and more specifically on issues of family violence.

**Ana Maria Buller**, PhD, is Associate Professor in Social Sciences and Deputy Director of the Gender, Violence and Health Centre (www.lshtm.ac.uk/research/centres-projects-groups/gender-violence-health-centre) at the London School of Hygiene and Tropical Medicine. Her main research interests lay on the intersection of gender-based violence health and development with a focus on gender-based violence prevention in low- and middle-income countries. She is currently principal investigator of the Learning Initiative on Norms, Exploitation and Abuse (LINEA), a multi-partner collaboration exploring the association of romantic jealousy and intimate partner violence.

**Wendy Bunston**, PhD, is a senior social worker, infant mental health practitioner and family therapist who currently works as a private consultant, trainer and reflective practice supervisor in addition to her role as an adjunct lecturer at La Trobe University, Victoria, Australia. She has developed multiple award-winning group work interventions for infants, children and their parents, to address the impacts of family violence. Wendy is also the author of numerous international articles, chapters and books. She continues to work directly with infants, children and families through her consultancy role within specialist children's agencies and women's refuges.

**Lynne Cahill**, PhD, works for the Service Reform Fund which implements social service improvements at a national level, across addiction, disability, mental health and homelessness programmes in Ireland. She is Adjunct Assistant Professor at the School of Social Work and Social Policy at Trinity College Dublin, where she lectures in the Applied Social Research Masters. Lynne is highly motivated to work across research domains that focus on social justice and has worked in areas such as disability, domestic violence, homelessness and LGBT equality. Lynne holds a PhD and a MSc from Trinity College Dublin, and a BA in anthropology and sociology from the National University of Ireland, Maynooth.

**Margaret I. Campe** is Director of the Jean Nidetch Women's Center at the University of Nevada, Las Vegas. She received her PhD in sociology from the University of Kentucky in 2019. Margaret has worked on several federally funded research projects, published peer-reviewed journal articles, and book chapters related to college campus sexual assault, the experiences of marginalised populations with gender-based violence, domestic violence programming, and research methods. She is also co-editing a forthcoming textbook, *Substance Use and Family Violence*, with Drs Carrie Oser and Kathi Harp (Cognella, anticipated 2021).

**Alison C. Cares** is Associate Professor of Sociology and member of the Violence Against Women Cluster at the University of Central Florida in Orlando, Florida, US. Her career started as a community educator in a sexual assault and domestic violence services agency. Dr Cares's research focuses on violence against women, primarily intimate partner violence and campus sexual assault. Her recent work has appeared in *Journal of Criminal Justice Education*, *Journal of Interpersonal Violence*, *Violence & Victims* and *Violence Against Women*. She enjoys teaching undergraduate and graduate courses including victimology, sexual violence, domestic violence, and research methods.

**Maria T. Clark** is Programme Lead/Senior Lecturer in Safeguarding at Birmingham City University, UK. She holds a PhD in sociology and a BSc (Hons) in community health studies. A public health nurse by background she has long-standing experience in responding to domestic abuse in community contexts. She has published articles on protecting women and children from abuse and led co-research with the Anti-Domestic Violence and Abuse Center (ADOVIC) in Uganda. Maria is Associate Editor for the journal *Child Abuse Review* and Affiliate of the Risk, Abuse and Violence research group at the University of Birmingham.

**Hannah E. Cole**, BS, is currently pursuing a doctoral degree in clinical psychology at the University of Memphis. She received her BS in Psychology at the University of Tulsa. Prior to attending graduate school, she worked alongside Dr Casey Taft as a research assistant at the National Center for PTSD at VA Boston Healthcare System. The overarching aims of her research are to (1) explore the complex relationships between trauma, PTSD and violence in gender and sexual minority populations; (2) reduce violence and its consequences; and to (3) increase access to competent, sensitive care for these historically underserved communities.

**Maxine Davis**, PhD, serves as Assistant Professor at The University of Texas at Arlington School of Social Work. She earned her PhD in social work from Washington University in St. Louis. Her research focuses on people who act abusively within intimate relationships and interventions to help them change. Davis is guided by former work in batterer/partner abuse intervention programmes and her lived experiences. A primary aim of her scholarly work is to improve intervention outcomes and service delivery. Dr Davis is unapologetically and especially committed to work that helps Black/African and Latino men end violence/abuse in their romantic relationships.

**Myrna Dawson** is Professor of Sociology and Director of the Centre for the Study of Social and Legal Responses to Violence (www.violenceresearch.ca), University of Guelph. She is Director of the Canadian Femicide Observatory for Justice and Accountability (www.femicideincanada.ca) and Co-Director of the Canadian Domestic Homicide Prevention Initiative with Vulnerable Populations (www.cdhpi.ca). She has spent over two decades researching social and legal responses to violence with emphasis on violence against women and femicide. She is the author/co-author of numerous publications, including *Domestic Homicides and Death Reviews: An International Perspective* (Palgrave Macmillan, 2017).

**Ashwini Deshmukh**, MD, MPH, is a Public Health Researcher who has worked on research studies related to patient care, non-communicable diseases in the Middle East and North Africa Region, while she was residing in Qatar. She has also studied the cultural impact on healthcare and diet and nutrition in adolescent children in Qatar. She is currently involved in a project related to domestic violence in the United Kingdom.

**John Devaney**, PhD, is Professor and Centenary Chair of Social Work at the University of Edinburgh. He has nearly 20 years' experience in social work practice and management, and his research mostly relates to domestic violence, child maltreatment and the impact of adversity across the life-course. He is a past chair of the British Association for the Study and Prevention of Child Abuse and Neglect, and convenor of the inaugural European Conference on Domestic Violence.

**Marc Dones** is a social entrepreneur, policy strategist and social justice activist with over ten years of experience in equitable systems transformation across local, state and federal governmental systems. Prior to launching National Innovation Service, Marc held various roles in social impact, specialising in policy, programme design, and continuous improvement. This includes leadership roles at The Future Company and Center for Social Innovation (C4). Outside of direct systems transformation, Marc is a faculty member at the School of Visual Arts (SVA) and leverages their experience as a keynote and panellist. Marc holds a BA from NYU in psychiatric anthropology and is a highly qualified equity trainer.

**Ketty Fernandez** is Doctoral Candidate in the Sociology Department at the University of Central Florida. Her research interests include violence against women, with an emphasis on sexual assault and rape, human trafficking, and racial/ethnic inequalities. She is currently working on her dissertation and aspires to work in academia.

**Amy J. Fitzgerald**, PhD, is Professor in the Department of Sociology, Anthropology and Criminology, and is cross-appointed to the Great Lakes Institute for Environmental Research at the University of Windsor. She is a founding member of the University of Windsor's Animal and Interpersonal Abuse Research Group. Her research focuses on the intersection of harms (criminal and otherwise) perpetrated against people, non-human animals and the environment. The co-occurrence of animal abuse and intimate partner violence is one of her substantive areas of research focus. She has authored several articles and books.

**Larissa Fogden** is Associate Lecturer and Researcher in the Department of Social Work at the University of Melbourne. Her research is focused on the experiences of children and young people living with domestic and family violence. Larissa is also a qualified social worker and has worked in specialist family violence services in crisis, refuge and justice settings supporting infants, children and young people.

**Diane R. Follingstad**, PhD, is Full Professor in the Department of Psychiatry at the University of Kentucky. She serves as Executive Director and Endowed Chair in the Center for Research on Violence Against Women. This appointment follows her career as Distinguished Professor Emeritus at the University of South Carolina. She has been a past President both for the ABPP Forensic Psychology Board and the South Carolina Psychological Association. As a clinical and forensic psychologist, her research has focused on battered women, dating violence, measurement of psychological maltreatment, campus climate violence/harassment, and factors impacting jury verdicts in battered women's cases.

**Molly R. Franz**, PhD, is currently a NIMH T32-funded postdoctoral research fellow at the Boston University School of Medicine, affiliated with the National Center for PTSD at the VA Boston Healthcare System. She received her doctoral degree in clinical psychology from the University of Nebraska-Lincoln. The overarching aims of her research are to (1) understand the effects of PTSD and trauma-related psychopathology on survivors' family relationships, particularly intimate partner and parent-child relationships and (2) reinforce and strengthen family support networks to aid in the prevention and treatment of trauma-related psychopathology and comorbid family dysfunction.

**Jane Freedman** is Professor at the Université Paris 8 and Director of the Centre de Recherches Sociologiques et Politiques de Paris (CRESPPA). Her research focuses on issues of gender, violence and migration. Previous publications include *Gendering the International Asylum Debate* (Palgrave, 2015) and *A Gendered Approach to the Syrian Refugee Crisis* (Routledge, 2017). She is currently leading an international research project on Violence against Women Migrants and Refugees (https://gbvmigration.cnrs.fr/).

**Christine Friestad**, PhD, is a psychologist and researcher at the Center for Research and Education in Forensic Psychiatry, Oslo University Hospital, Norway and Associate Professor at the University College of Norwegian Correctional Service. Her research focuses on mental health among prison populations, focusing especially on perpetrators of violent and sexual crimes.

**Aisha K. Gill**, PhD, CBE, is Professor of Criminology at University of Roehampton, UK. Her main areas of interest and research focus on health and criminal justice responses to violence against black, minority ethnic and refugee women in the UK, Iraqi Kurdistan, India, Pakistan and Yemen. She has been involved in addressing the problem of violence against women and girls, 'honour' crimes and forced marriage at the grassroots/activist level for the past 20 years. Her recent publications include articles on crimes related to the murder of women/femicide, 'honour' killings, coercion and forced marriage, child sexual exploitation and sexual abuse in South Asian/Kurdish and Somali communities, female genital mutilation, sex selective abortions, intersectionality and women who kill, domestic violence and Covid-19. In 2019, she was appointed Co-Chair of End Violence Against Women Coalition (EVAW).

**Kristin Alve Glad**, PhD, is a clinical psychologist. She holds a bachelor of arts (psychology) from Trinity College Dublin, and did her master's degree and PhD in psychology at the University of Oslo. Dr Glad has been affiliated with the Norwegian Centre on Violence and Traumatic Stress since 2005 and has published a number of reports and a research papers. She is currently working as a researcher on a study exploring the psychological reactions among survivors directly exposed to the terrorist attack on Utøya island in Norway in 2011 and their caregivers.

**Lisa A. Goodman** is a clinical-community psychologist and Professor of Counseling Psychology at Boston College. She uses a community-based participatory research approach to explore the unintended harms of systems designed to support intimate violence survivors, and how survivors use their social networks for healing and safety. Her research highlights the strengths and needs of marginalised survivors, including those from homeless, BIPOC, and queer communities. Dr Goodman consults to multiple domestic violence organisations, and is co-coordinator of the Domestic Violence Program Evaluation and Research Collaborative. She has received national awards for teaching and mentoring excellence, including the Elizabeth Hurlock Beckman Award.

**Helen P. Hailes** received her MSc in psychiatry from the University of Oxford and her MA in counseling theory from Boston College. She is Doctoral Candidate in Counseling Psychology at Boston College and Clinical Fellow at the Brookline Center for Community Mental Health. Her research focuses on the intersection of gender, violence, trauma and systemic oppression. She is particularly interested in collaborative, community-based approaches to research and understanding the experiences of intimate partner violence survivors with multiple marginalised identities.

**Laurie Cook Heffron**, PhD, LMSW, is Assistant Professor and the Social Work Program Director at St. Edward's University in Austin, Texas, USA. Her research focuses on intimate partner and sexual violence and intersections of violence and migration. Laurie draws from social work practice with refugees, asylum-seekers, trafficked persons, and detained immigrants and regularly provides assessments and serves as an expert in asylum cases, T visas and U visas. Laurie completed an undergraduate degree from Georgetown University and graduate work at the University of Texas at Austin.

**Marianne Hester**, OBE FacSS, holds the Chair in Gender, Violence and International Policy at the University of Bristol, UK, where she heads the Centre for Gender and Violence Research. She is Editor-in-Chief of the *Journal of Gender-Based Violence*. She is a leading researcher of gender-based violence in its many forms, with work on sexual violence, domestic abuse and 'honour'-related violence, in relation to the UK, Scandinavia and Europe. Her research and theoretical models are used extensively in other research, and by practitioners in the GBV, criminal justice, health and child welfare fields, and influence practice to tackle GBV.

**Petula Sik Ying Ho** is Professor in the Department of Social Work and Social Administration at the University of Hong Kong. Her recent work includes *Women Doing Intimacy: Gender, Family and Modernity in Britain and Hong Kong* (2020) co-authored with Stevi Jackson; *Love and Desire in Hong Kong*, co-authored with Ka Tat Tsang. She is also author of *I Am Ho Sik Ying, 55 Years Old* (2013) and *Everyday Life in the Age of Resistance* (2015). Her documentary films and multi-media theatre call for the imagination of new modalities of social activism to include various forms of cultural interventions.

**Stephanie Holt**, PhD, is Associate Professor in the School of Social Work and Social Policy, Trinity College Dublin, where she is currently Head of School and Director of the Postgraduate Diploma in Child Protection and Welfare. Stephanie's research interest and expertise focuses on domestic violence, with a particular emphasis on the impact of domestic violence on children and young people. This is interdisciplinary in its appeal, relating to the work of a range of health, social care and justice professionals.

**Yu Te Huang** is Assistant Professor in the Department of Social Work and Social Administration at the University of Hong Kong. His research interests cover adolescent mental health, sexual and gender minority youth, and immigrants' cross-cultural experiences. His research is marked by the integration of intersectionality perspective and methodological plurality with a view to understanding and promoting mental health among Chinese sexual minority populations. He has received grants to implement and evaluate the effectiveness of innovative interventions including a mentoring programme and an arts-based cognitive behavioural therapy for LGB communities in Hong Kong.

**Cathy Humphreys** is Professor of Social Work at the University of Melbourne. She is Co-Chair of the University of Melbourne Research Alliance to End Violence Against Women and Their Children (MAEVe). She specialises in applied research working with co-design and participatory action research. Her research specialisation has been in the intersections between child abuse, domestic violence, mental health and problematic substance use. Her more recent work has focused on strategies for the participation of young people in research and the attention to men who use violence as fathers. She is a well-published author of more than 120 journal articles primarily focused on domestic violence and abuse.

**Andrew Irish**, MSW, is a PhD candidate at the University at Buffalo where he was the recipient of a presidential fellowship and serves as a graduate research assistant and adjunct instructor. He is currently completing his dissertation on the longitudinal relationship between wealth distribution and measures of mental health in the United States. He has previously authored articles in the areas of mental health, substance use and violence related to socioeconomic and other disadvantages.

**Gabrielle Johnson** is a recent honours graduate of the Psychological and Brain Sciences Department at Boston University. She received her BA in psychology. Johnson's research interests include trauma-informed therapeutic approaches to treatment, attachment systems and developmental psychology. Currently, Johnson is working as a clinical research coordinator for the OCD and Related Disorders Program at Massachusetts General Hospital under the principal investigator, Daniel Geller MD, where an investigative drug is being tested for efficacy against Tourette Syndrome.

**Laura Johnson** is Assistant Professor in the School of Social Work at Temple University. She holds a PhD and MSW in social work from Rutgers, The State University of New Jersey. The goal of her research is to support the mental and physical health of survivors of interpersonal violence, as well as their safety and empowerment, through the development and adaptation of measures and interventions. She is also interested in community-based evaluations, and research focused on intervention implementation and strengthening interagency collaborations.

**Ernest N. Jouriles**, PhD, is the Dale McKissick Endowed Professor of Psychology at Southern Methodist University. His research interests include sexual and relationship violence among adolescents and young adults; children's exposure to interparent conflict and violence; and interventions for preventing violence and assisting victims of violence. His research is published in academic journals in the fields of psychology and interpersonal violence, and it has been sponsored by the National Institutes of Health, The Centers for Disease Control and Injury Prevention, and the US Department of Justice (National Institute of Justice; Office of Juvenile Justice and Delinquency Prevention).

**Åsa Källström (previously Cater)**, PhD, is Professor and Chair of Social Work at Örebro University, Sweden. Her research and teaching focuses on children's and young people's experiences of conflict, violence and abuse, primarily in the family, but includes also what exposure to neglect and crime means for children and how society can meet their needs of support. Recent books (in Swedish) include *Etiska reflektioner i forskning med barn* (with Kjerstin Andersson Bruck; Gleerups, 2017) and *Barns och ungas utsatthet – Våld och kränkningar i barns och ungas relationer* (with Björn Johansson et al.; Liber, 2019).

**Anuj Kapilashrami** is an interdisciplinary social scientist trained in sociology and public health and Professor in Global Health Policy and Equity in the School of Health and Social Care at University of Essex. Her work lies at the intersections of health policy and development praxis, and advances a gender intersectional approach in understanding health inequalities and structural determinants of health and gender-based violence. She has widely published on these topics in eminent journals including *Lancet*, *BMJ* and others and serves on the Gender Advisory Panel for the WHO's Human Reproduction programme. Her research interest and experience spreads over two decades and spans both academia and the development sector in the UK, Europe and

South Asia. Her passion and commitment to human rights and social justice informs her long-standing association with the People's Health Movement and other civil society initiatives.

**Angie C. Kennedy** is Associate Professor in the School of Social Work at Michigan State University. Her work focuses on cumulative victimisation and intimate partner violence (IPV) among adolescents and young adults, particularly those who are poor or low-income. Current projects include a study of young women's experiences with co-occurring IPV (coercive control, physical and sexual) across adolescence, beginning with their first relationship, and a study of economic abuse and coerced debt among women who have divorced abusive partners. Additional research interests include IPV-related stigma and stigmatisation, disclosure and help attainment, and mental health, educational and economic outcomes.

**Margaret Kertesz** is a senior research fellow at the University of Melbourne, and has worked in the child and family welfare sector for 25 years. Her research over the last decade has focused on evaluation, practice development and knowledge translation, with specific interests in the impact on children of domestic violence and approaches that promote recovery post-violence, and women who use force in the context of domestic violence. Recent research outputs have included evaluations of group work interventions.

**Jeongsuk Kim**, MSW, PhD, is Preyer Postdoctoral Scholar for Strengthening Families at the School of Social Work at the University of North Carolina at Chapel Hill. She received her doctoral degree in social work from the University of South Carolina in Columbia. Her programme of research focuses on examining the underlying causes and mechanisms that increase the risk of interpersonal violence victimisation and perpetration including intimate partner violence, sexual violence, human trafficking and school-based violence. Kim has been selected as an Early Career Reviewer for the *Journal of the Society for Social Work and Research*.

**Tanja Koivula**, PhD, is Senior Specialist in the Finnish Institute for Health and Welfare. She focuses her work and research on shelters, domestic violence and violence towards children. Currently, Koivula is working on a research project that aims to pilot a domestic violence risk assessment method in the Finnish shelters. This risk assessment method is called iRiSk and it has been developed by the University of Gothenburg, Sweden.

**Sui-Ting Kong** is Assistant Professor in the Department of Sociology and the Deputy Director of the Centre for Social Justice and Community Action at Durham University (UK). Her research interests are in the areas of violence against women, innovative feminist methods and social work practice research. Innovative methodologies co-developed by her and other colleagues include *Cooperative Grounded Inquiry* and *Collaborative Focus Group Analysis*. She has also applied and published on visual arts and theatres in feminist research.

**Sibel Korkmaz** is a PhD student in the Department of Social Work at Stockholm University, Sweden. She is part of a mixed methods research project on Youth Intimate Partner Violence in a Swedish context, drawing upon survey data as well as qualitative interviews in her thesis. Of particular interest is how specific cultural and social conditions of youth may be important to consider when discussing IPV in young people's own romantic relationships.

**Alison Krauss** is a PhD student in the Clinical Psychology programme at Southern Methodist University. Her research interests include sexual and relationship violence among adolescents and emerging adults, as well as measurement and methodological considerations in the study of interpersonal violence.

**Lawrence L. Kupper**, PhD, is Emeritus Alumni Distinguished Professor and former Associate Chair, Department of Biostatistics, Gillings School of Global Public Health at the University of North Carolina at Chapel Hill. His primary research efforts concern the development of novel statistical methods for the design and analysis of public health research studies. His areas of research collaboration include environmental and occupational health, epidemiology, toxicology and teratology, medicine and dentistry, genetics, and women's and children's health. He is an elected Fellow of the American Statistical Association, and he has received several university, national and international awards for his research, teaching and mentorship of students and younger colleagues.

**Bugonzi Margaret Kyemba Kulaba** is a woman human rights defender and activist. She holds a bachelor's degree in business administration and a diploma in gender studies from MASHAV Israel, alongside many trainings in GBV, Human Rights and Women and Girls Empowerment. She is the Chair of the Women Human Rights Defenders Network Uganda and the founder and Executive Director of Anti Domestic Violence Center (Uganda).

**Katie Lamb**, PhD, has a background in criminology, a master's in public policy and a PhD in social work. She is Research Fellow at the University of Melbourne and an independent consultant and family violence trainer. Her research interests include issues that sit at the interface between the criminal justice and child and family welfare systems.

**Simon Lapierre**, PhD, is Full Professor in the School of Social Work at the University of Ottawa, and a founding member of the Feminist Anti-Violence (FemAnVi) Research Collective. Dr Lapierre's work has investigated women's and children's experiences and perspectives on domestic violence, with a focus on mothering and mother-child relationships in this context. His work has also investigated policies and practices in child protection services, family courts and the criminal justice system. His recent work has provided a critical perspective on the 'parental alienation' discourse and its implications for abused women and their children.

**Rebecca J. Macy**, MSW, PhD, is Professor, the Associate Dean for Research and Faculty Development, and the L. Richardson Preyer Distinguished Chair for Strengthening Families at the UNC at Chapel Hill School of Social Work. She also serves as the editor-in-chief for the *Journal of Family Violence*. Macy is Fellow of the American Academy of Social Work and Social Welfare and Guest Professor at Jinan University in Guangdong, China. Her research comprises 18 years' experience conducting community-based studies that focus on intimate partner violence, sexual violence, human trafficking, and improving services for survivors of violence and trafficking.

**Sandra L. Martin**, PhD, is Professor in Maternal and Child Health at the Gillings School of Global Public Health at the University of North Carolina at Chapel Hill. Her research focuses on violence prevention, with recent investigations on sex trafficking prevention among school children and prevention of sexual violence on US college campuses and in the military. Her research has been funded by NIH, CDC, DOD, WHO and US state governments, and she has authored more than 130 scientific papers plus book chapters/reports, with her work often cited in scientific manuscripts and government reports, including those by the US Congress and White House.

**Heather L. McCauley**, ScD, is Assistant Professor in the School of Social Work at Michigan State University. A scholar trained in global health and social epidemiology at Harvard University, Dr McCauley's research portfolio focuses on the prevention of sexual violence, intimate partner violence, reproductive coercion and sex trafficking, with emphasis on sexual and gender minorities. She has authored or co-authored 80 journal articles and book chapters on these topics in outlets spanning a variety of health and social science disciplines. She is Associate Editor of *Psychology of Violence* and is on the editorial board of *Journal of Family Violence*.

**Renee McDonald**, PhD, is Professor of Psychology at Southern Methodist University. Her research comprises two primary foci. The first is understanding interpersonal violence, including developmental, family and social factors that give rise to it, and the effects on children and adolescents of exposure to caregiver intimate partner conflict and violence. The second is the development and evaluation of interventions, including online programmes, to prevent and ameliorate the effects of violence exposure and victimisation. Her research has been sponsored by the National Institutes of Health, The Centers for Disease Control and Injury Prevention, and the US Department of Justice (National Institute of Justice; Office of Juvenile Justice and Delinquency Prevention).

**Elizabeth Meier** is a PhD student in the School of Social Work at Michigan State University. She has experience as an LMSW working with survivors and perpetrators of domestic violence, sexual assault and child sexual abuse, in both community settings and at a maximum-security men's prison. Her research interests include institutional trust and betrayal, moral injury and the deradicalisation of social movement organisations over time. Current projects include studies into economic abuse among recently divorced women with abusive ex-partners, perceived vulnerabilities of people engaging in civil court services, and combat veterans' experiences of trust and betrayal across the deployment cycle.

**Patricia Melgar**, PhD, is Professor at the University of Girona. She is the principal researcher of the project SOL-NET, "Solidarity networks with an impact on the recovery processes of women victims of gender violence". Melgar's research on the preventive socialisation of gender violence and education that overcomes social inequalities has been published in top-ranked journals. Melgar is co-editor of the journal *GÉNEROS: The Multidisciplinary Journal of Gender Studies*, and a member of the editorial board of the journal *Violence Against Women*.

**Guiomar Merodio**, PhD in sociology from the University of Barcelona, is Assistant Professor at the Department of Education at Nebrija University. She has been a visiting scholar at the Office of Sex Trafficking Intervention Research at the School of Social Work, Arizona State University. Some of her work on gender-based violence and sex trafficking of youth has been published in *Frontiers in Psychology* and *Qualitative Inquiry*.

**Ada R. Miltz**, PhD, is Research Fellow in Epidemiology at University College London. Dr Miltz received an MRC studentship for her PhD thesis on the role of depression in sexual behaviour linked to STI/HIV transmission among gay and bisexual men. She continues to research the psychosocial determinants of health among gay and bisexual men, in particular intimate partner violence (IPV). She combines epidemiology and complex statistical methodology with psychological and social theories. She contributes to teaching on causation in epidemiology and gender and health. She is passionate about improving the healthcare response to IPV within male same-sex relationships.

**Sarah Morton**, PhD, is Director of the Community Drugs Programme and Assistant Professor in the School of Social Policy, Social Work and Social Justice at University College Dublin. Her research and teaching interests include drug policy and intervention, the intersection of substance use and domestic violence and creative research methodologies. Sarah has a particular interest in responses and interventions to inter-generational experiences of trauma and exclusion. In 2020 she was the joint recipient of the European Award for Teaching Excellence in the Social Sciences and Humanities for her work successfully supporting students who have experienced lifelong educational disadvantage.

**Nadine Shaanta Murshid**, MPP, PhD, is Associate Professor and Interim Associate Dean of Diversity, Equity and Inclusion at the School of Social Work, University at Buffalo. She studies economic institutions and policies, structural violence including intimate partner violence, and health disparities primarily in the global South.

**Andy Myhill**, PhD, is Evidence and Evaluation Advisor at the UK College of Policing. He has published both academic papers and government reports on topics including domestic violence, public attitudes to the police, community engagement and procedural justice.

**Shiella Nabunya** holds a degree in ethics and human rights. She is currently working as a data clerk at Family Search International and she is an established social worker with the Anti Domestic Violence Center in Uganda.

**Nkiru Nnawulezi**, PhD, is an Assistant Professor at the University of Maryland, Baltimore County. She utilises transformative, participatory research methods to improve the material and social conditions for gender-based violence survivors who experience structural marginalisation and stigmatisation. Her work primarily examines the ecological factors that enhance equity within and across housing systems that serve survivors. She also develops and evaluates community-led interventions that serve as alternatives to mainstream social service systems.

**Siobán O'Brien Green**, PhD, has worked in academic, research, non-profit and government sectors. Her research and teaching interests include gender-based violence (GBV), female genital mutilation (FGM), sexual and reproductive health, substance use and gender equality, in particular how these issues intersect and impact in women's lives. Siobán has worked on many Irish and European GBV research studies. Siobán holds a Master's from University College Dublin in social policy and was awarded an Ussher Postgraduate Fellowship by Trinity College Dublin in 2015 where she undertook her PhD. Her PhD research explored help, support and safety seeking by women who have experienced domestic violence during pregnancy in Ireland.

**Eija Paavilainen**, PhD, has worked as Professor (Nursing Science) at the Faculty of Social Sciences/Health Sciences in Tampere University, Finland since 2001. She also has had a research position in Etelä-Pohjanmaan Hospital District, Finland since 2002. Her main areas of research and expertise concern families with children in challenging life situations. Her largest research projects concern family violence, child maltreatment, family risks and services for families with children. Those research projects are or have been funded by the Academy of Finland, Boards of Hospital Districts, Ministry for Social Affairs and Health, Finland, and the European Union. She has over 200 conference presentations and over 200 scientific and other publications.

**Esther Oliver**, PhD, is Professor of Sociology at the University of Barcelona, former Ramon y Cajal Research Chair at the University of Barcelona and Postdoctoral Fellow at the University of Warwick (2006–2008) with research on gender violence in universities. She was a member of the research team of FP7 IMPACT-EV (2014–2017) and principal researcher of the project, "The mirage of upward mobility and the socialization on gender violence" funded by the Spanish National Plan I+D+I (2010–2012). Her research on preventive socialisation of gender violence has been published in the *Qualitative Inquiry* and PLOS One among other top-ranked peer-reviewed journals.

**Carolina Øverlien**, PhD, is a Research leader at Norwegian Center for Violence and Traumatic Stress Studies (NKVTS) in Oslo, Norway, and Professor at the Department of Social Work, Stockholm University, Sweden. She has conducted numerous studies on children and youth living in difficult life situations, in particular children experiencing domestic violence and youth intimate partner violence. Her research interests include children's rights, resilience, research ethics, and qualitative methods. She has published extensively in international peer-reviewed journals as well as writing and editing several books.

**Amy Reckdenwald**, PhD, is Associate Professor in the Sociology Department and member of the Violence Against Women Cluster at the University of Central Florida. Her primary research and teaching interests focus on domestic violence and intimate partner homicide. Much of her recent research examines severe forms of violence including non-fatal strangulation as well as the importance of geographical place, gender inequality, economic disadvantage and the availability of domestic violence services in the study of domestic violence and homicide. Her work appears in journals such as *Trauma, Violence and Abuse*; *Criminology*; *Homicide Studies*; *Feminist Criminology*; *Journal of Criminal Justice*; *Violence Against Women* and *Violence and Victims*.

**Taylor A. Reid**, BA in Human Development and Family Studies, is a doctoral student in HDFS at Michigan State University. Her area of research focuses on intimate partner violence as experienced by sexual minority women, with added emphasis on the resilience these women display. She is particularly interested in understanding the power dynamics that occur in women's same-sex relationships. Through mixed-methods research, Taylor strives to provide a platform for marginalised communities to tell their stories. She was previously awarded the Dean's Assistantship in 2017 and has since served on multiple committees aimed at diversity as a representative for the LGBT community.

**Claire M. Renzetti**, PhD, is the Judi Conway Patton Endowed Chair for Studies of Violence Against Women, and Professor and Chair of Sociology at the University of Kentucky. Her work focuses on the violent victimisation experiences of socially and economically marginalised women and girls. She is Editor of the international, interdisciplinary journal *Violence Against Women*, as well as three book series. She has written or edited 26 books as well as numerous book chapters and journal articles based on her research, which currently includes an evaluation of a therapeutic horticulture programme at a battered women's shelter, studies that explore religiosity and religious self-regulation as protective and risk factors for intimate partner violence perpetration, and studies of students' perceptions of justice in campus sexual assault cases.

**Sarah Richards-Desai**, MSW, is a PhD candidate at the University at Buffalo School of Social Work. Using a critical transnational feminist lens, her research areas include refugee women in resettlement, the economic adjustment of refugee women, and social capital among refugees. Richards-Desai has experience in qualitative and quantitative research methods. Richards-Desai has experience among refugee and immigrant communities through community engagement in Toronto, ON; Ithaca, NY and Buffalo, NY. As a member of community-led advocacy groups and planning committees for refugee-centred events and workforce development programmes, she has engaged with individuals from Burma, Iraq, Somalia, Nepal and other countries.

**Emma Ritch** is a gender expert and feminist leader who has worked on policy advocacy in Scotland for 15 years. She has been Executive Director of Engender since 2013, and has led initiatives on women's labour market equality and women's human rights. Emma is particularly interested in gender mainstreaming, economic policy and feminist governance. She is a member of Scotland's National Advisory Council on Women and Girls and sits on a number of boards of feminist and human rights organisations, including that of the European Women's Lobby and Rape Crisis Scotland.

**Cynthia Fraga Rizo**, PhD, MSW, is Assistant Professor at the School of Social Work at the University of North Carolina at Chapel Hill (UNC). Prior to joining the faculty in 2013, she received her MSW from Florida International University and her doctoral degree in social work from UNC. Dr Rizo has also worked on and led a number of projects in the area of interpersonal violence, including intimate partner violence, human trafficking and sexual assault. Overall, Dr Rizo's programme of research focuses on developing and evaluating community-based interventions and services aimed at preventing and responding to interpersonal violence.

**Amanda Robinson** is Professor of Criminology at Cardiff University (UK), where she has worked since 2001. Amanda's research focuses on violence and the individual, agency, community and societal responses to it, with a particular emphasis on domestic violence. Her research in this area has helped to set the policy and practice agenda both in the UK and abroad. Notable examples include MARACs (multi-agency risk assessment conferences), IDVAs (independent domestic violence advisors), police use of risk assessment tools, and new approaches to working with perpetrators. Amanda was directly involved in producing the Welsh Government's White Paper that led to the Violence against Women, Domestic Abuse and Sexual Violence (Wales) Act 2015. She is Editor of the *British Journal of Criminology*.

**Michaela Rogers**, PhD, is Senior Lecturer in Social Work at the University of Sheffield. Her research primarily focuses on interpersonal and gender-based violence and abuse; gender, trans and gender diversity; hidden and marginalised communities; and multiple social exclusion, using a range of qualitative and narrative methods.

**Anupama Roy** is Professor at the Centre for Political Studies in Jawaharlal Nehru University, New Delhi, India. Her research interests are in the domain of citizenship, political institutions, gender and constitutional democracy. Her recent books are *Citizenship in India* (OUP, 2016) and a co-authored volume on the Election Commission of India (OUP, 2019). She has co-edited a volume on *Dimensions of Constitutional Democracy: India and Germany* (Springer, 2020).

**Jessica Saba** is a doctoral student in the School of Social Work at Michigan State University. Her research interests include participatory methods, critical consciousness, and resilience particularly as it pertains to marginalised youth in the United States and Palestine.

**Lorena Saletti-Cuesta** is a psychologist with a PhD in health, anthropology and history, with more than 12 years of professional experience in the field of gender, health and healthcare services. Since 2016 she has been a researcher of the National Scientific and Technical Research Council of Argentina, leading projects regarding gender-based violence. She has participated as a teacher in a number of courses organised by universities, health services and women's associations. Moreover, she contributed to the implementation of protocols to strengthen responses to violence against women in different sectors (educational, academic and health sectors) and countries.

**Kelli S. Sargent** is a PhD student in the Clinical Psychology programme at Southern Methodist University. Her research focuses on intervention evaluation, specifically targeting violence prevention among adolescents and young adults. Her research interests also include adolescent risk factors that render teens more susceptible to negative consequences of violence and adverse experiences.

**Katreena Scott**, PhD, is Psychologist, Professor and incoming Director of the Centre for Research and Education on Violence Against Women and Children at Western University. She held the Canada Research Chair in Family Violence Prevention and Intervention between 2008 and 2018. Dr Scott leads an applied research programme aimed at ending violence in family relationships, with specific expertise on addressing violence perpetration in men. The *Caring Dads* programme that she developed is offered in many sites across North American and Europe. She is a contributor to international networks including the DV@Work Network and the Safer Families Centre of Excellence.

**Dr Marsha Scott** is a feminist activist, researcher and practitioner and has advocated, volunteered, researched and worked in gender and violence against women sectors in Europe, the United Kingdom and the United States for 30+ years. She has been CEO of Scottish Women's Aid since 2015. Scott has a particular interest in the intersections of economic policy, women's poverty and violence against women and has worked with colleagues across Europe, including serving on the European Women's Lobby Board of Directors and as the UK Expert on the European Observatory on Violence against Women.

**Dr Sonali Shah** is Research Fellow in the School of Nursing at the University of Birmingham where she works on the Eternal project, a qualitative study exploring access to sexual and reproductive healthcare for girls and women with cerebral palsy, from menarche to menopause. Sonali has a PhD in occupational psychology and disability. She has developed a series of innovative projects and published widely on disability and life-course issues and uses different methods to allow disabled people to speak for themselves. Sonali moderates an international Facebook group for women with cerebral palsy and identifies as a British Indian disabled woman.

**Rochelle Stevenson**, PhD, is Assistant Professor in the Department of Sociology and Anthropology at Thompson Rivers University. Her core research interest is domestic violence, concentrating on the intersection of violence against humans and animals. Her research has included an evaluation of safe pet programmes in Western Canada, national surveys of residents and staff of domestic violence shelters about animal abuse and mistreatment, as well as interviews with men who had committed abuse against their partners. Rochelle's research takes an intersectional and anti-oppression approach, that violence in any form needs to be named, understood and stopped.

**Karlie E. Stonard**, PhD, is Senior Lecturer in Criminology at the University of Wolverhampton, UK, and a member of the Violence Against Women and Girls Research Cluster at the university. Her past and current research interests are in the area of domestic violence and its impact on children and young people, the role of technology in adolescent dating violence (PhD) and gender-based violence more broadly. She has published several articles on the topic of her PhD research and presented at a number of national and international conferences.

**Casey T. Taft**, PhD, is a staff psychologist at the National Center for PTSD in the VA Boston Healthcare System, and Professor of Psychiatry at Boston University School of Medicine. He was the 2009 Linda Saltzman Memorial Intimate Partner Violence Researcher Award winner from the Institute on Violence, Abuse and Trauma. He has been Principal Investigator on several funded grants focusing on understanding and preventing partner violence, is on the editorial boards of five journals, and has published over 100 peer-reviewed academic articles and an American Psychological Association book on trauma-informed partner violence intervention.

**Julie Taylor** is Professor of Child Protection and Director of Research in the College of Medical and Dental Sciences, University of Birmingham. She holds a joint appointment with Birmingham Women's and Children's Hospital. Julie is a nurse scientist specialising in child maltreatment, with extensive research experience with vulnerable populations using a wide range of qualitative and participative methods. Her research programme is concentrated at the interface between health and social care and is largely underpinned by the discourse of cumulative harm and the exponential effects of living with multiple adversities (domestic abuse, parental mental ill health, substance misuse, disabilities, etc.).

**Patti A. Timmons Fritz**, PhD, is Associate Professor in the Department of Psychology at the University of Windsor in Ontario, Canada. Dr Fritz's research interests include the aetiology, developmental course, correlates and measurement of various forms of family violence, including intimate partner violence (IPV). She is also interested in the relation between intimate partner violence and animal abuse. Some of her recent research has focused on how and when dating violence first begins in emerging adults' relationships and partner aggression that occurs through electronic means (e.g., via cell phones, social networking websites).

**Taryn van Niekerk** recently completed her Postdoctoral Fellowship in the Department of Psychology at the University of Cape Town, South Africa. Her primary research and teaching areas include decolonial feminist theories and approaches for engaging with issues of gender and race, critical psychological theories of identity, and intersectional studies related to masculinities and partner violence against women. She has published in these related areas, including her co-edited volume *Decolonial Feminist Community Psychology* (Springer, 2019).

**Solveig Karin Bø Vatnar**, PhD, is a Specialist in Clinical Psychology at the Centre for Research and Education in Forensic Psychiatry, Oslo University Hospital, Norway. She also holds a position as Professor of Clinical Psychology at the Molde University College, Norway. Her expertise is in the field of intimate partner violence (IPV) with a special focus on the interactional perspective of IPV, risk assessment, and intimate partner homicide. She has authored more than 20 international publications in journals and books in the fields of clinical psychology/psychiatry.

**Karin Wachter**, PhD, MEd, is Assistant Professor in the School of Social Work at Arizona State University in Phoenix, Arizona, USA. Rooted in extensive international experience in humanitarian assistance, her research focuses on the intersection of forced migration, violence against women, and social support. Drawing from feminist and postcolonial theories, and a practice-oriented perspective, Karin's research seeks to address the psychosocial consequences of war, displacement and resettlement among women who have survived extreme loss and violence, and to develop social-relational interventions that promote health and well-being.

**Kyemba Rosemary Wakesho** is a social worker with ADOVIC Uganda, which strives to see families free from domestic violence. She holds a diploma in social work and social administration (2015). She is a certified Master Trainer in the Peace Program for youth and adults. She is passionate about community work, especially with young people. Rosemary is also an activist for the girl child in Africa.

**Christopher J. Wretman**, PhD, is Senior Data Analyst at The Cecil G. Sheps Center for Health Services Research, and a Faculty Research Associate at the School of Social Work, both at the University of North Carolina at Chapel Hill. His work focuses on the quantitative analysis of health and well-being outcomes to inform services for vulnerable populations, with primary expertise in the management and analysis of data from cross-sectional and longitudinal studies.

**Sarah Wydall** is Principal Investigator on Dewis Choice and Director of the Centre for Age, Gender and Social Justice at Aberystwyth University, Wales. Sarah's research uses inclusive and participatory methods to co-produce solutions that tackle gendered harms. In the last five years her research has focused on justice responses to domestic abuse and violence in later life. As a feminist and LGBTQ activist Sarah has worked to raise the profile of domestic abuse in later life by co-producing the bespoke service for older people – Dewis Choice, co-producing short LGBTQ films, and developing survivor, volunteer and practitioner forums, training and guidance drawn from the longitudinal findings of Dewis Choice. For further information about the work of the Centre see https://dewischoice.org.uk/.

**Harshita Yalamarty** is a PhD candidate in Gender, Feminist and Women's Studies at York University, Toronto (Tkaronto) Canada. Her doctoral work examines the experiences of marriage of migrant women from India to Canada. She holds an MPhil and MA in political studies from Jawaharlal Nehru University, India. Her previous research has looked at the role of law in women's lives in India through the multiple constructions of public/private spheres. She is a teaching assistant at York University and has also taught at the University of Delhi.

# FOREWORD

I am honoured to have been invited to write a foreword to this much needed and very comprehensive publication. I come to this as an academic and an activist, with violence against women, gender-based violence and domestic violence and abuse as my main areas of activism and of research/teaching. I also come to this with the experience of having had the opportunity of contributing to policy, both at a national and European/international level. And finally I come to this also with my experience of having been a practitioner.

I have always held that there is a clear link between research (data), (evidence-informed) policy and (evidence-based) practice – in other words: undertaking the research/collecting the data to identify the issues, to raise awareness and apply pressure, so, together, we can tackle the problem (policies), and work towards prevention (practice). As demonstrated in this Handbook, the interconnection between research, policy and practice means that each is stronger if the other two are also strong. If one of these is weak, then this will be felt in the other two.

Whilst we have made some good progress in this field, sadly, researchers and practitioners tell us that the women survivors often raise the same issues, the same problems, the same complaints. And still we have women being killed as a result. Notwithstanding a bottom-up/grassroots movement that has fought, resisted and persisted, the changes and results we hoped for have not fully come about. And we know things cannot happen overnight. But, the tragedy is that we do need things to happen NOW – not next year, or next decade – we need action. Women have been waiting and fighting and crying and dying long enough. We need to see things implemented, and we need to see the results on the ground.

The Council of Europe Convention on the prevention and combatting of violence against women and domestic violence (the Istanbul Convention), which is often referred to as the gold standard in the field, seeks to make this happen. This is the first legally binding instrument to provide for comprehensive measures addressing the prevention of violence against women, the protection of victims, the prosecution of perpetrators and integrated policies. And at heart, it is a renewed call for greater equality between women and men. The underlying message of the Convention is that every single form of gender-based violence against women must be responded to in a swift and professional manner that puts the rights and needs of victims, their safety and their empowerment, at the centre.

The Convention therefore also requires a change in harmful attitudes, stereotypes, behaviours – it requires us all to act and to change; attitudes towards women and men, their role in society and what we think is appropriate, all these need to change to ensure women are considered fully equal to men in both the public and private sphere – including in intimate relationships. We need to open our eyes and acknowledge the abuse that exists around us – all of us, the researchers, the person on the street, the politicians and policy makers, the professionals, etc. We also need to call out men who abuse women and children. The focus is all too often on what society or what women can do when really we should also be talking about why there are so many men who think they can control and abuse women and children.

GREVIO published its first activity report in April 2020 covering its first four years of operation and setting out some of the trends and challenges that emerged from the monitoring of the implementation of the Istanbul Convention. The report does demonstrate the dedication of several States towards preventing and combating violence against women. It also highlights several gaps, such as lack of adequately segregated and harmonised data, insecure and/or insufficient funding for women's and children's specialised services, among others. Governments are under an obligation to find ways of improving these situations, and to do this they need to listen to researchers, frontline workers, non-governmental organisations, specialist services, and women and children.

This is why a publication such as this is so important – it gives us the theory, presents us with the situation as it is, the problems experienced, it describes some of the responses to the problems, and goes on to demonstrate good practices in research. The various chapters are grounded in a feminist understanding of the structural causes of domestic violence and abuse, and what continues to sustain it, weaving in an ecological understanding of the issues, but simultaneously acknowledging that gender is the significant factor in terms of victimisation. Through the various chapters a wide range of contemporary research from across the globe is presented, exploring the issue of gender inequality and its manifestation through oppression, coercion, power and control and violence, demonstrating the universality of domestic violence and abuse, whilst also recognising that it is affected by local cultures and contexts.

Another important issue running through both this publication and the Convention is intersectionality with other issues – such as race, sexual orientation, poverty, disability, age, etc. GREVIO has found that, generally, services offered for the mainstream population are not always as easily accessible to women who are further disadvantaged by and within our societies. Hence GREVIO country rapporteurs are constantly asking: What about disabled women? What about migrant women? What about women in prostitution? LB and trans women? Roma? Indigenous women (e.g. Sami)? etc. It is therefore good to see that some of these issues are specifically tackled in this Handbook.

I have to add that there has also been a worrying trend in some of the signatories to the Convention of misrepresenting the aims of the Istanbul Convention. The fact that it defines gender as "socially constructed roles, behaviours, activities and attributes that a given society considers appropriate for women and men" is being used to deflect from its original aims, that is the protection of women from violence by men, and is used to present it as a document that would radically alter sexuality, family life and education. The objective of the Convention is not to regulate family life and/or family structures. The Convention requires governments to ensure the safety of victims who find themselves in dangerous situations at home or are threatened by family members, spouses or intimate partners, which unfortunately is the most common form of violence.

As long as women are perceived/seen/considered as property – submissive, objectified, dismissed, then we will continue to have violence against women and domestic violence.

For women to leave an abusive relationship they need to be assured that they will find the help and support they need – and this means research, policy, practice! We need sufficient specialist services as well as general services, knowledgeable and empathic police officers, and other helping professionals, courts that understand the gendered nature of violence against women and gives them justice (including in custody decisions), coordinated policies, with everyone pulling the same rope.

We're on our way – but we're certainly not there yet. But this publication will help us get there.

Dr Marceline Naudi

**Dr Marceline Naudi** (B.A., M.A. (Bradford), Ph.D. (Manchester)) is a social worker by profession and Senior Lecturer and Head of Department of Gender and Sexualities at the University of Malta. She contributes to teaching and supervision of student research on gender issues, violence against women and other anti-oppressive issues at the diploma, bachelor, master and doctoral levels. She acts as Regional Editor of the *Journal on Gender-Based Violence*. Marceline is active on the issues of gender equality and violence against women, LGBTIQ, as well as wider human rights issues, both in Malta and in Europe. She is President of GREVIO, the Council of Europe monitoring body of the Istanbul Convention and has led EU-funded research projects in Malta on the Bystanders Approach to Sexual Harassment, and on Barriers to Reporting for victims of Violence against Women. Marceline is also a member of the WAVE Advisory Board.

# TABLES

# FIGURES

# PART 1

# Introduction

# 1

# INTRODUCTION

*Rebecca J. Macy, Caroline Bradbury-Jones, Carolina Øverlien,*
*Stephanie Holt and John Devaney*

Domestic violence and abuse is a significant global concern, with almost one-third of women worldwide reporting that they have experienced some form of physical and/or sexual violence by their current or former intimate partner in their lifetime (World Health Organization (WHO), 2013a). Globally, research show that 40–70% of female murder victims were killed by their partners (WHO, 2013a). Moreover, mounting evidence shows that domestic violence and abuse has serious consequences for victims' and victims' children's health and social well-being (e.g., Ansara & Hindin, 2011; Black et al., 2011; Ellsberg, Jansen, Heise, Watts, & Garcia-Moreno, 2008; Evans, Davies, & DiLillo, 2008; Sharps, Laughon, & Giangrande, 2007; Vives-Cases, Ruiz-Cantero, Escribà-Agüir, & Miralles, 2011), as well as tremendous economic costs for individuals, families, communities, and countries (Coker, Williams, Follingstad, & Jordan, 2011; Holmes, Richter, Votruba, Berg, & Bender, 2018; Peterson et al., 2018).

Given the pervasiveness and seriousness of domestic violence and abuse, national and international bodies, such as the Council of Europe, the Centers for Disease Control and Prevention, and the WHO, have sought to address both the causes and consequences of domestic violence and abuse through the development and implementation of a range of strategies to support victims and to hold to account those who behave abusively towards their current or former partners and their children (e.g., Niolon et al., 2017; WHO, 2013b).

Because domestic violence and abuse continues to be a pressing and important challenge to all our global nations, this Handbook aims to foster an exchange of the latest knowledge concerning what causes and sustains violence between intimate partners, the effectiveness of responses in working with adult and child victims, as well as the effectiveness of responses in working with those who act abusively towards their partners or close family members. By ensuring that each section and chapter provides an authoritative reference, this Handbook seeks to provide a comprehensive compendium and resource concerning domestic violence evidence that can be used valuably by practitioners, policymakers, researchers, and students worldwide. To meet these aims, while also recognising that domestic violence is both universal and shaped by local cultures and contexts, this book includes a diverse group of global experts and draws upon a wide range of contemporary research.

With a total of 50 chapters and 101 authors involved in contributing, we realise that the Handbook might initially appear overwhelming or unwieldy. Here, in this introduction, we offer a guide to help readers understand the overall goals, frameworks, organisation, and structure of the Handbook. With this guiding introduction, we aim to offer readers ways forward through the Handbook, whether they read every chapter in the Handbook cover to cover in a short time frame or whether they read selected chapters over time.

## The Handbook's guiding frameworks

Given the complex, dynamic, and widespread nature of domestic violence and abuse, the editors chose four key guiding perspectives for this Handbook, including (1) the social ecological framework, (2) intersectionality, (3) interdisciplinarity, and (4) a global point of view.

### *Ecological*

Overall, the handbook frames domestic violence and abuse as an ecological issue while also recognising that gender is a significant factor in victimisation. Specifically, a social ecological framework represents the phenomenon of domestic violence as developing and dynamically existing within the context of four nested environments representing the individual's context, the interpersonal and relational context, the community context, as well as the larger social environment (Heise & Kotsadam, 2015; Krug et al., 2002). According to a social ecological framework, violence dynamically and reciprocally manifests through factors across all four levels. In turn, such an understanding of violence requires that that we acknowledge and address the social, community, and relationship levels – as well as the individual level – when we aim to address, prevent, and understand violence.

### *Intersectionality*

As noted, while recognising that domestic violence and abuse is a universal problem, the handbook also aims to highlight and underscore how domestic violence and abuse is also shaped by local cultures and contexts as well as by the overlapping and interconnecting identities of the people who experience abuse and victimisation, as well as those who use domestic violence and abuse (Carbado, Crenshaw, Mays, & Tomlinson, 2013; Crenshaw, 1990). Increasingly, those concerned with domestic violence and abuse emphasise how such abuse is experienced by and impacts diverse people in diverse ways, in particular, how a person's positions of disadvantage and/or privilege might intersect with experiences of victimisation, as well as domestic violence and abuse perpetration (e.g., Chiu, 2017; Etherington & Baker, 2018; Lippy, Jumarali, Nnawulezi, Williams, & Burk, 2020). Accordingly, all authors were invited to consider the topics within their respective chapters using an intersectionality perspective.

### *Interdisciplinarity*

Domestic violence and abuse is known to affect individuals and families at multiple levels and the health and social impacts are well-recognised. No single discipline can understand or tackle the problem alone and it takes multi-disciplinary and multi-agency approaches to enact primary, secondary, and tertiary responses. The need for such interdisciplinarity is a fundamental framework for the book. Not only are the editors drawn from different disciplinary backgrounds, the author contributors have been purposively selected for their contrasting but complementary expertise within diverse settings. They offer insights on how domestic violence and abuse is addressed within a multitude of disciplines, highlighting in particular the specifics within disciplines, but crucially, the commonalities that underpin meaningful efforts in relation to interdisciplinary approaches to tackling domestic violence and abuse.

## *A global point of view*

In the same way that domestic violence and abuse cannot be addressed from within one discipline, it cannot be tackled within one country or region. We have already highlighted the global significance of the problem and although the specific nature and manifestation of violence and abuse may vary across settings, it is important to recognise that domestic violence and abuse knows no boundaries. It is a pervasive, pernicious problem that happens across the globe. We have been keen to include contributions from authors from a range of countries in order to capture some of the geographical diversity relating to domestic violence and abuse. We are aware that despite our best efforts, there is under-representation from some regions and this needs to be borne in mind when reading the Handbook. That said, the volume of contributors has resulted in a comprehensive text that captures the global nature of the problem. Moreover, just as the interdisciplinary element captures both difference and commonality, so too does the global viewpoint. Each chapter provides a contextually rich account of domestic violence and abuse in terms of geography and context that may capture the specifics of a particular country, but the roots of the abuse, its consequences, and the mechanisms through which it may be tackled are likely to transcend geographical demarcations.

## Why the phrase domestic violence and abuse?

In the early stages of planning the book, we deliberated over the title. There is a plethora of terms that are often used synonymously and this can be incredibly confusing for those who are new to the field. We regard Gender-Based Violence as being an overarching umbrella term that encompasses a range of abuses perpetrated against someone based on their gender. The term tends to be understood as Violence against Women, although it is important to recognise that abuse happens to boys, men, as well as to non-binary and transgender people. Then there are the terms domestic violence and domestic abuse. People use them variously, but these are understood to be all abuse that takes place within a domestic setting. Many people prefer the term 'abuse' rather than 'violence' because it encourages a wider view and avoids focusing overly on the physical connotations of violence. After all, we know that abuse takes many forms including coercion, control, and emotional abuse – physical violence is not the most prevalent form. Readers from Australia and New Zealand may be more familiar with 'family violence' which is used as the preferred term in recognition of the interpretations of the meaning of family in those countries, and the intersection between abuse of intimate partners and children within the same family group. Then there are intimate partner violence and interpersonal violence that again are used synonymously, particularly in North America. These refer to abuse that takes place between current or recent intimate partners and is the most widespread form of domestic violence and abuse. So why our term 'domestic violence and abuse'? We have selected this term as it is the one that has currency from a political perspective, particularly in the United Kingdom, where this Handbook is published. We see value in using the terms violence *and* abuse side by side, as a reminder that they are not necessarily the same.

## The Handbook's structure

This Handbook is organised into five major sections, including: (1) theoretical perspectives on domestic violence and abuse, (2) domestic violence and abuse across the life-course,

3) manifestation of domestic violence and abuse, (4) responding to domestic violence and abuse, and (5) researching domestic violence and abuse. These topics and sections were selected to provide a comprehensive overview of the topic of domestic violence as a whole and to convey helpful information and evidence to readers concerning how domestic violence may be theoretically conceived, how domestic violence differs across the life-course and how domestic violence expresses itself in different ways, as well as how we can best address and conduct studies on domestic violence.

Within each section, key topics related to each of the sections' themes are divided into chapters. In turn, each chapter delves into a key aspect of a facet of domestic violence. For each chapter, our editorial team invited global experts to develop a robust and meaningful summary of the latest thinking and research on the various topics. Each chapter also includes attention – as relevant – to issues of intersectionality, differences in domestic violence which may present due to context and/or culture, and key debates concerning the chapter topic. In addition, each chapter includes a description of the evidence and/or research on which the chapter is based, including the limits of such knowledge.

## *Theoretical perspectives*

There are different and sometimes competing ways of understanding what causes and sustains violence and abuse within the context of current or former intimate relationships. How we understand an issue can influence how we respond, and to what degree we see the response as needing to be directed primarily at the level of the individual or society. This section provides an introduction to a number of theoretical perspectives, all of which are helpful, but also have been critiqued for providing an incomplete way of accounting for the varied presentations and motivations underpinning domestic violence and abuse. Throughout the remainder of the Handbook these core theoretical perspectives can be seen in the way different contributors present and discuss various issues.

## *Life-course*

Over recent decades there has been mounting evidence for the intergenerational impacts of domestic violence and abuse, with understandings about how its harmful impacts have potential to be carried from one generation to the next. The evidence around this points to the need for understanding domestic violence and abuse from a life-course perspective. This means that it is necessarily viewed as a problem that spans all ages. Although there are sections of the population who may be more at risk (adolescents for example), there needs to be mindfulness that domestic violence and abuse occurs across the lifespan, from cradle to grave. This section of the book then includes rich insights into the problem of domestic violence and abuse from infanthood, childhood, mid-life, and into later life.

## *Manifestation*

We are now more aware of the many different presentations of domestic violence, and how abuse may present in different forms, and vary depending on a range of issues. In this section each contribution explores a particular form of violence or abuse, such as coercive control, economic abuse, wife abandonment, or sexual violence within intimate relationships, focusing on the particular presentation and the underlying dynamics. In doing so the contributors discuss the intersection of domestic violence with a range of other important issues, exploring how abuse may present in same-sex relationships or when one or both partners are transgender or non-binary, the added complexities of experiencing domestic violence when disabled, the particularities of intimate partner homicide and honour killings, the relationship between domestic violence and animal abuse, and the use of technology to facilitate harassment, abuse, and violence.

### *Responding to domestic violence and abuse*

This section of the Handbook presents the best available evidence, as well as practice and policy innovations, concerning responses to domestic violence and abuse. Responses to domestic violence can include interventions, policies, programmes, services, and strategies. Accordingly, all such responses are described throughout this section and in the chapters. Guided by the social ecological model, this section's chapters underscore how responses may be directed at individuals, relationships, families, communities, and the greater social context. Likewise, responses include helping address the needs of domestic violence victims and survivors, as well as the needs of those who are actively abusive toward their partners. Accordingly, this section overviews approaches to helping all of those who may be involved with and impacted by domestic violence and abuse.

### *Research*

Representing the broad methodologies of qualitative and quantitative research, this final section presents on select aspects of both the principles and practices underpinning research on domestic violence and abuse. In doing so, the ten chapters in this section offer a methodological road map of the myriad of approaches that have been utilised to engage with the experiences of increasingly diverse populations who live with domestic violence and abuse. Grounded in a commitment to hearing the voices of those less heard, this section also focuses on research with those considered marginalised or vulnerable populations while simultaneously arguing for the critical importance of inclusive yet ethically sound research practices to underscore evidence-informed policy and practice. Both the challenges to conducting such research and the innovative methods that have developed in response to these challenges, are outlined.

### Conclusion

In concluding this chapter, we – the editorial team – send you – the reader – off with our sincere and strong belief that domestic violence and abuse is not intractable, nor is it inevitable. Although domestic violence and abuse has proven to be pervasive, pernicious, and universal, the writings in this Handbook also show that domestic violence and abuse can be prevented, ended, and ameliorated. We hope that the contributions which follow will advance, develop, further, and inspire global efforts to end domestic violence and abuse once and for all.

### References

Ansara, D. L., & Hindin, M. J. (2011). Psychosocial consequences of intimate partner violence for women and men in Canada. *Journal of Interpersonal Violence, 26*(8), 1628–1645. doi:10.1177%2F0886260510370600

Black, M. C., Basile, K. C., Breiding, M. J., Smith, S. G., Walters, M. L., Merrick, M. T., . . . Stevens, M. R. (2011). *The national intimate partner and sexual violence survey (NISVS): 2010 summary report.* Atlanta, GA: National Center for Injury Prevention and Control, Centers for Disease Control and Prevention. Retrieved from www.cdc.gov/violenceprevention/pdf/nisvs_executive_summary-a.pdf

Carbado, D. W., Crenshaw, K. W., Mays, V. M., & Tomlinson, B. (2013). Intersectionality: Mapping the movements of a theory. *Du Bois Review: Social Science Research on Race, 10*(2), 303–312.

Chiu, T. Y. (2017). Marriage migration as a multifaceted system: The intersectionality of intimate partner violence in cross-border marriages. *Violence Against Women, 23*(11), 1293–1313. doi:10.1177/1077801216659940

Coker, A. L., Williams, C. M., Follingstad, D. R., & Jordan, C. E. (2011). Psychological, reproductive and maternal health, behavioral, and economic impact of intimate partner violence. In J. W. White, M. P. Koss, & A. E. Kazdin (Eds.), *Violence against women and children, Vol. 1. Mapping the terrain* (p. 265–284). American Psychological Association. doi:10.1037/12307-012

Crenshaw, K. (1990). Mapping the margins: Intersectionality, identity politics, and violence against women of color. *Stanford Law Review, 43*, 1241.

Ellsberg, M., Jansen, H. A., Heise, L., Watts, C. H., & Garcia-Moreno, C. (2008). Intimate partner violence and women's physical and mental health in the WHO multi-country study on women's health and domestic violence: An observational study. *The Lancet, 371*(9619), 1165–1172. doi:10.1016/S0140-6736(08)60522-X

Etherington, N., & Baker, L. (2018). From "buzzword" to best practice: Applying intersectionality to children exposed to intimate partner violence. *Trauma, Violence, & Abuse, 19*(1), 58–75. doi:10.1177/1524838016631128

Evans, S. E., Davies, C., & DiLillo, D. (2008). Exposure to domestic violence: A meta-analysis of child and adolescent outcomes. *Aggression and Violent Behavior, 13*(2), 131–140. doi:10.1016/j.avb.2008.02.005

Heise, L. L., & Kotsadam, A. (2015). Cross-national and multilevel correlates of partner violence: An analysis of data from population-based surveys. *The Lancet Global Health, 3*(6), e332–e340.

Holmes, M. R., Richter, F. G., Votruba, M. E., Berg, K. A., & Bender, A. E. (2018). Economic burden of child exposure to intimate partner violence in the United States. *Journal of Family Violence, 33*(4), 239–249. doi:10.1007/s10896-018-9954-7

Krug, E. G., et al. (Eds.). (2002). *World report on violence and health.* Geneva: World Health Organization. Retrieved from https://apps.who.int/iris/bitstream/handle/10665/42495/9241545615_eng.pdf

Lippy, C., Jumarali, S. N., Nnawulezi, N. A., Williams, E. P., & Burk, C. (2020). The impact of mandatory reporting laws on survivors of intimate partner violence: Intersectionality, help-seeking and the need for change. *Journal of Family Violence, 35*, 255–267. doi:10.1007/s10896-019-00103-w

Niolon, P. H., Kearns, M., Dills, J., Rambo, K., Irving, S., Armstead, T., & Gilbert, L. (2017). *Preventing intimate partner violence across the lifespan: A technical package of programs, policies, and practices.* Atlanta, GA: National Center for Injury Prevention and Control, Centers for Disease Control and Prevention. Retrieved from www.cdc.gov/violenceprevention/pdf/ipv-technicalpackages.pdf

Peterson, C., Kearns, M. C., McIntosh, W. L., Estefan, L. F., Nicolaidis, C., McCollister, K. E., . . . Florence, C. (2018). Lifetime economic burden of intimate partner violence among U.S. adults. *American Journal of Preventive Medicine, 55*(4), 433–444. doi:10.1016/j.amepre.2018.04.049

Sharps, P. W., Laughon, K., & Giangrande, S. K. (2007). Intimate partner violence and the childbearing year: Maternal and infant health consequences. *Trauma, Violence, & Abuse, 8*(2), 105–116. doi:10.1177/1524838007302594

Vives-Cases, C., Ruiz-Cantero, M. T., Escribà-Agüir, V., & Miralles, J. J. (2011). The effect of intimate partner violence and other forms of violence against women on health. *Journal of Public Health, 33*(1), 15–21. doi:10.1093/pubmed/fdq101

World Health Organization. (2013a). *Global and regional estimates of violence against women: Prevalence and health effects of intimate partner violence and non-partner sexual violence.* World Health Organization. Retrieved from http://apps.who.int/iris/bitstream/10665/85239/1/9789241564625_eng.pdf

World Health Organization. (2013b). *Responding to intimate partner violence and sexual violence against women: WHO clinical and policy guidelines.* World Health Organization. Retrieved from www.who.int/iris/handle/10665/8524

# PART 2

# Theoretical perspectives on domestic violence and abuse

# 2

# DOMESTIC VIOLENCE AND ABUSE THROUGH A FEMINIST LENS

*Margunn Bjørnholt*

## Introduction

Very broadly speaking, feminist perspectives on domestic violence (DV) see DV as caused by and constitutive of gendered patterns of power and privilege in society (Dobash & Dobash, 1979; Schechter, 1982; Yllö & Bograd, 1988). In seeing DV as socially produced within and part of a gender order, feminist scholars focus on the complex social processes that produce both gender and DV, developing epistemologies as well as methodologies to study and explain these processes. Feminist research and theorisations of DV originate in and are shaped within different disciplines and cover a range of topics. These include how victims' and perpetrators' gendered subjectivities and embodiment shape gendered relations and structures, including gendered patterns and experiences of DV victimization (Young, 1990; Cahill, 2001, 2016) and perpetration (Hearn, 1998), the gendered effects and harms of DV on selfhood (Walker, 1979; Lundgren, 2004; Anderson, 2005), the role of culture and everyday interactions and experiences of DV (MacKinnon, 1987; Kelly, 1987, 1988a; Smart; Alcoff, 2014; Gavey, 2005; Gunnarsson, 2018) and the intersection of gender, race, class and other forms of domination and the consequences for the lived experience as well as institutional responses to DV (Crenshaw, 1989; Hill-Collins, 2000). Another strain of research focusses on the politicisation of DV at the national and international level, including the role of the state in tolerating, facilitating and responding to DV (MacKinnon, 1989; Walby, 1990), gendered institutional responses to DV (Stanko, 2013 [1985]) and ongoing struggles between the feminist perspective and other perspectives on DV in international bodies like the UN (Merry, 2003, 2006, 2016). Social movement research focusses on the importance of activism for state responses to DV (Schechter, 1982; Htun & Weldon, 2012) as well as the need for and failure of legal reforms to prevent DV and support victims (Stark, 2007, 2009, 2013; Salter, 2012; Burman & Brooks-Hay, 2018; Barlow, Johnson, Walklate, & Humphreys, 2019; Walklate & Fitz-Gibbon, 2019). Finally, there is a stream of studies focussing on the effectiveness of interventions such as perpetrator programmes and initiatives to engage men against DV (Hester & Newman, 2021; Flood, 2021).

The feminist perspective is often presented as the hegemonic or even mainstream perspective on DV. However, from the outset, the feminist framing of DV has been contested academically as well as politically. In the UN, the feminist perspective on DV has been continually challenged by competing perspectives, the health perspective in particular (Merry, 2016). Academic controversies over prevalence and gendered patterns of perpetration and victimisation (Straus, Gelles, & Steinmetz, 1980; Dobash & Dobash, 1979; Kimmel, 2002; Loseke & Kurz, 2005; Straus, 2005; Johnson, 1995, 2008) have been essential – and productive – in the methodological and theoretical development of the field. This controversy still resonates in contemporary struggles over definitions and methodologies for measuring DV.

Although feminist perspectives have been highly influential in theorising, researching and politicising DV – somewhat paradoxically – DV has been more or less ignored in mainstream feminist theory (if one can talk of such). There is for instance no mention of DV in the comprehensive Sage handbook on feminist theory (Evans et al., 2014). Feminist perspectives on DV reflect the theoretical developments in feminist theory and contribute to the increasing theoretical diversity and methodological sophistication of studies of violence and sexual violence (McPhail, Busch, Kulkarni, & Rice, 2007; Brown & Walklate, 2011). This chapter makes no claim of presenting a coherent story nor a full picture of the diverse and evolving feminist perspectives on DV. Rather, the chapter will mimic the multiplicity of the field by highlighting some formative and ongoing controversies. The ambition of this chapter is to elucidate how feminist perspectives on DV may be seen as an ongoing practice of simultaneously theorising and politicising DV.

## Discussion and analysis

### *Co-development of practices and theories*

The feminist perspective on DV was formed in opposition to previous psychological and criminological explanations that linked violence to perpetrators' psychopathology and substance abuse – and masochist traits in the victim (Gelles, 1976). It sprang out of the feminist movement that, under the slogan the private is political, brought forward a range of experiences that had been hidden and silent, seen as belonging to the private realm.

The framing of violence as 'men's violence against women' and a 'women's issue' was pivotal in transforming DV from a marginal phenomenon which was perceived to affect only a few, to a general issue being caused by and constitutive of a patriarchal social structure in which women's subordination was systematic and institutionalised. According to Walby (1990) violence is an institution in itself and a central and relatively independent pillar of gender orders. The conceptualisation of DV as rooted in the core of the social structure, potentially affecting all women, was important for mobilisation of solidarity and support for victims of DV, for making DV a criminal offence and the development of perpetrator programmes, as well as for the inclusion of women's rights among the human rights and the recognition of DV as a violation of women's human rights, all of which are the result of the women's movement's persistent struggles over several decades. In a cross-country analysis, the strength of the women's movement was found to be the key factor of success in states' responses and policies related to DV (Htun & Weldon, 2012).

Advocacy has been an important element of feminist practice, and this is particularly true in the field of domestic violence (Bjørnholt, 2018; Malbon, Carson, & Yates, 2018). The importance of practical activism and institution building, most notably the shelter movement, as part of the feminist response to DV cannot be ignored. The first domestic violence shelter was created in London by Erin Pizzey in the early 1970s (Pizzey, 1974). As soon as they were in place, the shelters demonstrated the magnitude and pervasiveness of violence and sexual abuse in women's lives. However, it is also important to note how activism and practice have not only been important for policies but have also been at the core in the development of feminist research and theory, including the theorisation of violence (Cho, Crenshaw, & McCall, 2013; Ross, 2017; Bjørnholt, 2018), as part of a wider feminist ambition of problematising the gendered assumptions in the mainstream disciplines, redefining what constitutes knowledge, the relations between researcher and researched, as well as the methods of producing scientific knowledge and the theories that guide research. In line with other liberation movements, theorising from experience, giving voice to hitherto silenced subjects were at the root of feminist theory in general as well as in theorisations of DV.

An example of the co-development of feminist practice and theory is the development of treatment programmes, starting with the initiative to develop a comprehensive community response to perpetrators in Duluth, Minnesota, and the simultaneous conceptualisation of the 'power and control wheel': a theoretical model that links a variety of violent and abusive behaviours to power and control. The 'power and control wheel' was created by the founders of the Duluth batterer programme, Ellen Pence, Michael Paymar and Coral McDonald, in close consultation with battered women's groups in Duluth, and they credit the women's input as being the sole basis for the concept (Pence, 2010).

Increasingly, the theoretical and political legacy of black and queer feminism has been recognised also in the field of DV. The Combahee River Collective (CRC) was one of the most important organisations to develop out of the antiracist and women's liberation movements in the US of the 1960s and '70s (Harris, 2001; Ross, 2017; Taylor, 2017). Combining activism and theoretical innovation, the collective mobilised against violence and murder of black women as well as for reproductive rights. They challenged the racism and class-based oppression in American society including the lack of understanding of race and class-based oppression – and implicit racism – in the white women's movement, as well as the male leadership in the civil rights movement and black men's sexism and violence against black women. Based on their analysis of the experiences of black, lesbian women in American society, they introduced terms such as 'interlocking oppression' and 'identity politics'. The CRC (1997 [1977]) thus provided an analysis based on the idea that multiple oppressions reinforce each other to create new categories of suffering, as captured in the concept of intersectionality, that was later coined by Crenshaw (1989). Hill-Collins (2000) used the concept a 'matrix of domination' to describe how intersecting oppressions are organised.

The travelling and appropriation of theories and concepts, as well as interventions in new contexts may raise new problems. The Duluth model has been very influential in the design of perpetrator programmes all over the world. However, it has also been criticised along with other theories and models originating in the Global North, for not sufficiently taking into consideration the specific social context, such as the reality of racism, colonial oppression and inequality and its consequences for perpetrators as well as victims of DV in the Global South (Boonzaier and van Niekerk, this volume; van Niekerk, 2021). Such critiques can be seen as part of a wider trend towards de-colonising knowledge production (Smith, 2013 [1999]. However, in contrast, the popularity and appropriation of the concept intersectionality by European scholars has also been criticised for erasing its origin in black feminist thought (Bilge, 2013).

## *Prevalence, definitions and methods of measurement*

Framing DV as men's violence against women rests on the assumption that DV is predominantly perpetrated by men against women. This claim has been challenged by sociological survey research framing DV within a family conflict model, relying on a particular scale of measurement, the Conflict Tactics Scale (CTS), developed by Straus et al. (1980) for the first national survey on DV in the US which concluded that DV was gender symmetrical: men and women were equally represented both as victims and perpetrators of partner violence. The CTS has been widely used in survey research – and has been widely criticised from a feminist perspective. The main critique has been that the definition of violence, counting incidents alone, ignores context as well as issues of power and control (Dobash & Dobash, 1979; Kimmel, 2002; Walby & Towers, 2017). Another critique is that surveys with their reliance on physical violence may count some incidents that are not experienced as violence, which might affect the gendered distribution of reported violence (Johnson, 1995, 2008; Myhill, 2017; Ackerman, 2015, 2018). Finally, feminist research links DV to its consequences in terms of harm (Walby & Towers, 2017) and homicide (Dobash & Dobash, 2015; Monckton Smith, 2019).

The 'gender symmetry controversy' has been formative in the development of theories and concepts, and has continued to inform methodological and epistemological work in the field of DV over several decades (Straus, 2005; Loseke & Kurz, 2005; Walby, Towers, & Francis, 2016; Walby & Towers, 2017, 2018; Ackerman, 2015, 2018; Myhill, 2017; Myhill & Kelly, 2019). Johnson (1995, 2008) developed a typology of different forms of violence as an attempt to explain why feminist research based on research on victims, came to the conclusion that DV was mainly perpetrated by men against women, while representative population studies based on the CTS concluded that DV was gender symmetrical. Johnson's typology distinguishes between severe forms of repeated violence in combination with control and power asymmetry: 'patriarchal terrorism'/'intimate terrorism', which is predominantly perpetrated by men against female partners; and incidents of physical violence between couples, 'common couple violence', which are not part of a pattern of power and control, and which are gender symmetrical. Johnson argued that surveys will predominantly measure the latter, while clinical studies of victimised populations will measure the severe forms. However, Johnson's typology has been criticised for being static (Walby & Towers, 2017), for its lack of empirical basis and for the recent use of the typology in court, where, contrary to Johnson's intention, the concept 'common couple violence' is increasingly used to minimise violence as part of the defence of perpetrators (Lapierre & Côté, 2014).

Recently, the controversy has moved beyond the 'gender symmetry' debate between feminist and non-feminist researchers. Today, different feminist researchers place themselves on different sides in an ongoing debate over definitions and methods of measurement; on one hand, those who promote relying on and improving survey methodology, focussing on physical violence, and on the other hand, those who focus on coercive control.

Drawing on data from the Crime Survey for England and Wales (CSEW), Walby and colleagues (Walby et al., 2016; Walby &Towers, 2017) suggest a narrower definition of violence with the aim of harmonising the definitions of DV in research and criminal law. Based on a definition of DV as incident plus harm, they launch the concept Domestic Violent Crime, along with other proposals aimed at improving methods of measurement to more accurately represent gendered patterns of exposure to violence in surveys. Walby and Towers' argument is that adding harm changes the gendered pattern of exposure, as the same act will have different consequences in terms of harm if it is carried out by a man against a woman or a woman against a man. While this assumption is supported by Walby and Towers' analysis of data from the CSEW, when tested on a Norwegian survey, adding harm did not change the gender distribution of DV (Bjørnholt & Hjemdal, 2018) – but fear of being injured or killed did.

Donovan and Barnes (2019) who have for decades been studying DV in same-sex and gender-non-conforming couples using feminist perspectives, are also concerned that a too strong emphasis on gender in survey studies may reinforce the 'public story of IPV' as limited to (heterosexual) men's violence against heterosexual women as well as perpetuate sex and gender stereotypes, ignoring non-conforming victims' experiences. Donovan and Barnes conclude that there is still a need for typologies of different kinds of violence and for more inclusive methodologies and theories.

## Coercive control

Coercive control has been an important and indeed main frame of understanding in feminist conceptualisations of DV (Stark & Hester, 2019), although the definitions and methods of measurement vary (Hamberger, Larsen, & Lehrner, 2017). It is an important aspect of Johnson's concept 'patriarchal terrorism', and Stark (2007, 2009, 2013) argues that coercive control is indeed the defining aspect of DV and that DV should be understood as a liberty crime. Kelly has argued along similar lines that DV limits women's space for action (2003). Sharp-Jeffs, Kelly and Klein (2018) have developed a scale of measuring for coercive control, focussing on space for action. According to Stark, the concept 'coercive control' was developed to describe the experiences of women who contacted shelters and health services for victims of violence, as an effort to overcome the shortcomings of both research and societies' responses to DV, resulting from an incident-based understanding of DV (Stark, 2009).

Although the concept of coercive control and the related typologies were developed with cis-, heterosexual, adult and married or cohabiting couples in mind, the concept and related typologies, such as those of Johnson and Stark, have also inspired research on the dynamics of power and control in same-sex and non-gender-conforming couples (Donovan & Hester, 2014; Donovan & Barnes, 2019) and in studies of DV in relation to motherhood (Katz, 2019). Recently, Johnson's typology has also been used in studies of violence among adolescents (Överlien, Hellevik, & Korkmaz, 2019).

Walby and Towers (2018) have further developed their argument in favour of improved survey methodology focussing on physical violence and harm, arguing that the main assumption underlying the gender symmetry controversy – that surveys do not reveal gendered patterns of exposure – has now been debunked. Subsequently, surveys using more precise methodologies may give an accurate picture of gendered patterns of DV. As a result, they argue, there is no need for focussing on coercive control, including typologies such as that of Johnson.

Myhill and Kelly (2019) and Donovan and Barnes (2019) challenge this argument and raise concerns over Walby and colleagues' privileging of physical violence, arguing that the feminist focus on power and control as defining characteristics of DV is still crucial in describing the lived experience of DV and being able to identify those most at risk of escalation, fear and a closing down of 'space for action'. They conclude that there is still a need for the concept coercive control and for typologies to distinguish between different forms of violence, and emphasise the role of qualitative research on victims in the development of concepts and theory in the field. In Donovan and Barnes' words it is 'important to (re-)state the critical contribution of qualitative research to the field of IPV in its own right and in informing the design, the analysis and interpretation of quantitative data' (2019, p. 10).

Recently, coercive control has also increasingly made its way into legal jurisdictions. However, as it has been taken up in legislation as a crime in itself, it turns out to be difficult to translate into legal practice, and critiques have argued that it may indeed harm the women it was intended to help (Hanna, 2009; Burman & Brooks-Hay, 2018; Walklate & Fitz-Gibbon, 2019).

## States' role

Placing men's violence against women in a larger social context also include research and theorisation of institutions and states' complicity in violence. Stanko (2013 [1985]) examined the male bias in institutional responses to women's complaints of DV in the decision-making process of the criminal justice system and of administrative personnel. MacKinnon (1989) and Walby (1990) have argued that the lack of or inadequate responses to men's violence against women conveys that the state is condoning it. In Walby's words, 'Only when inter-personal violence against women and minorities is effectively criminalized can it be said that the state does not condone it' (2009, p. 201).

On the other hand, demanding state action and holding states to account, in terms of legal reforms and formal obligations and policies, has been a major focus of feminist activism against DV. Nevertheless, feminist scholarship has also demonstrated that the law largely fails to produce justice for the majority of victims of DV, that women's experiences of DV do not necessarily fit with the legal definitions of DV, and that laws alone are not very effective in protecting victims or reducing DV (Burman & Brooks-Hay, 2018; Walklate, 2019). According to Salter, 'Legal responses to GBV often employ the language of perpetrators of GBV, and this vocabulary is used in a similar fashion in order to over-write the victim's own experiences' (2012, pp. 6–7).

Different strands of feminist theorising and research offer different solutions to this dilemma. While Walby and colleagues have proposed to define DV more narrowly to fit with the criminal definition of DV by launching the term Domestic Violent Crime (DVC) (Walby et al., 2016; Walby & Towers, 2017, 2018), another strand is the trend towards expanding the concept of DV to criminalise behaviours such as economic abuse, and stalking, as well as criminalising coercive control as a crime in itself. Critiques of the strong reliance on legal solutions to DV and sexual violence have also spurred new developments towards transformative justice (Kim, 2018).

The theorisation of DV in relation to states has been revitalised in indigenous and postcolonial feminist studies (Kuokkanen, 2015, 2019), exploring how collective trauma resulting from histories of oppression and the complex and gendered relations with states and state apparatuses in the past and today, may influence levels of DV as well as gendered patterns and responses to DV in indigenous populations, and indigenous victims' access to justice.

### *Agency and victim positions*

The power and control wheel was developed as a contrast to the 'cycle of violence' model, developed by Walker (1979), a model that explains how the victim is trapped and her self-esteem is undermined in the abusive relationship, leaning heavily on Seligman's psychological theory of 'learned helplessness'. Similarly, Eva Lundgren coined the concept 'the normalisation process' (2004) to describe how victims gradually come to take the perpetrators' perspective and to accept the violence as normal. Walkers' reliance on this psychological model with its lack of agency has posed problems for (other) feminists (van Schalkwyk, Boonzaier, & Gobodo-Madikizela, 2014). Hydén (1994) challenged Lundgren's 'normalisation theory', focussing on victims' resistance and agency, which led to a deep disunity among feminist scholars on DV in Scandinavia.

The theorisation of victim positions in relation to political agency remains important in feminist theorisations of DV. Recently, as a reaction to the increasing professionalisation and subsequent depoliticisation of the field, there has also been a renewed involvement with second-wave feminist theorists with the aim of reclaiming the victim position as a position for political agency in contrast to the passive role as a client to be acted on by the victim services. Mardorossian (2014) invokes Brownmiller's (1975) argument that women are the victims only of patriarchal oppression, offering a victim position to act from and a victim role that evades the notions of passivity, helplessness and shame that are often associated with it. However, the politicisation of the victim role is not without its problems. Brown (1995) has warned against the reliance on the state for adjudication of social injury, as it may also spur state responses targeting the groups identified as victims in ways that also imply control and governance.

As DV is increasingly criminalised and seen as non-acceptable, and not compatible with contemporary ideals of masculinity and femininity, being a victim as well as being a perpetrator of DV are stigmatised. In presumed gender-equal Sweden, Hydén (1994) found that her informants felt ashamed over violence-induced bruises as signs of not being loved. A Swedish study of male perpetrators (Gottzén, 2016) found that expressing shame while distancing themselves from the category of 'violent men' was important in the self-presentation of men who had been violent to an intimate partner. In racist and inequal South Africa, Boonzaier found that bruises from DV were seen as signs of wrongdoing on the female victim's part, as the husband's right to punish her was not questioned. For the black and coloured South African women in her study, the feelings of shame were both related to self-worth and to the position of being abused women vis-à-vis white people (2008; Boonzaier, Lafrance, & McKenzie-Mohr, 2014). Juggling racialised shame and respectability also figures prominently in South African perpetrators' narratives (van Niekerk, 2019).

Social institutions may both support and undermine victims' experiences and agency in the context of DV. Salter (2012) argues that the invalidation of female victim's experiences in a number of institutional contexts, ranging from families to the judicial system, is an important and unrecognised aspect of the gender dynamics of DV. Stark (2007, 2009, 2013), on a more positive note, links victims' agency to the empowering aspects of the social and cultural context. Trying to explain how the women he met in shelters and forensic contexts had drawn on 'reservoirs of courage and faith in self-emancipation for which I could find no objective correlate in their situations', Stark (2009, p. 1524) emphasises the role of the women's movement and the framework of universal human rights, arguing that these women

> were in touch with a larger social context in which their right to dignity, freedom, and safety was affirmed. It is this link between the particular predicament they faced and the political movement that allowed them to speak while silenced that Coercive Control tried to strengthen.
>
> (2009, p. 1524)

He proposes 'to retell the "story" of surviving abuse as part of the larger liberty narrative that goes back to the War of Independence, the U.S. Constitution, and the Universal Declaration of Human Rights' (2009, p. 1524).

## *Sexual violence as part of DV*

On one hand, sexual violence has been part of feminist understandings of DV from the outset (Kelly, 1988a). On the other hand, sexual violence and DV are often studied and theorised separately, and despite sexual violence being an important and highly gendered part of DV, it is not routinely included in studies and categories of DV. This is the reason why Walby and Towers (2017) propose that any sexual aspect or sexual motivation should be measured routinely in relation to all acts of violence as part of their proposal to improve survey methodology. The concept of a continuum of sexual violence (Sheffield, 1987; Kelly, 1987, 1988a, 1988b; Smart, 1995) links minor sexual harassment and micro-aggressions in the public sphere which are part of women's everyday experiences of living in a sexist and patriarchal culture, with other forms of sexual violence, arguing that they shade into each other, creating an atmosphere of fear. The continuum approach also captures how in the victim's experience different acts of violence in the context of DV may form one coherent experience, rather than being experienced as separate events. Sørensen (2013) argues that for the victims, distinguishing between sexual violence and other forms of DV did not necessarily make sense: the sexual violence was just part of the whole.

## Emerging themes

### Mothers and children

Feminist conceptualisation of DV originally focussed on women, but increasingly, children were also brought into the picture, in research that focussed on mothers in the context of custody and visiting arrangements after divorce in the context of DV (Hester & Radford, 1992; Eriksson & Hester, 2001). Increasingly, children were brought into the frame as subjects in their own right (Överlien & Hydén, 2009) and witnessing violence against a caregiver has come to be recognised as harmful and as violence towards the child, even if the child is not directly targeted.

Recently, children's relations with their mothers in the context of DV have been centred in research (Lapierre et al., 2018; Katz, 2015, 2019). This strand of research presents a picture of complex, varied and often fraught mother-child relations, but also a more positive view of mother-child bonds and children's agency in the context and aftermath of DV than in previous research which tends to juxtapose mothers' and children's interests (Överlien, 2011).

In contrast, research and advocacy regarding custody and visiting arrangements is an important area of anti-feminist backlash, with father's rights' advocates mobilising concepts like 'false memories' and 'parental alienation syndrome', with the aim of invalidating mothers and children's accounts of violence and abuse. Challenging these concepts and the way they are used has become an increasingly important part of the ongoing struggles regarding DV, gender and parenting (see for instance Thomas & Richardson, 2015).

## Reproductive coercion – re-tangling sexual violence and reproductive violence

Violence in pregnancy was first documented by Gelles (1976), and the fact that violence occurs in pregnancy and that pregnancy may represent a heightened risk of DV is now widely recognised (Grace & Anderson, 2018). Over the last few years, the concept reproductive coercion conceptualises a more comprehensive approach to a range of abusive behaviours related to sexuality and reproduction which may take place within an intimate relation, but which are not restricted to intimate relations. States may also be seen as responsible for reproductive coercion, as Kevin and Agutter (2018) have demonstrated in the Australian state's relations to refugees in the past and today.

## Male victims of DV

Male victims – and even more so, female perpetrators – of DV have been a contentious issue in feminist research on DV (Gilbert, 2002; Abrams, 2015). The struggle over numbers in the 'gender symmetry' controversy that so long dominated the field may have hampered a more nuanced approach to male victims, and research on male victims tends to be framed in opposition to the feminist perspective, the existence of male victims often routinely taken as evidence of the insufficiency of the feminist perspective or even proving it wrong (see for example Migliaccio, 2002; Kestell, 2019). In recent years, however, male victims are increasingly studied from a variety of feminist perspectives (Nybergh, Enander, & Krantz, 2016; Venäläinen, 2019; Bjørn-holt & Rosten, 2021), acknowledging that there is no antagonism between seeing (hetero-sexual) men as a minority among victims of DV on one hand, and studying male victims from feminist perspectives.

### Transcending the gender and species boundaries

Feminist perspectives also inform recent developments in research and theorising of DV that problematise the gender binary, moving from studying DV in 'same-sex' relations to studying DV in a whole range of LBGTI relations (Donovan & Barnes, 2020). Further, studies and theo-risations of DV increasingly also encompass non-human family animals. Fitzgerald, Barrett, Ste-venson and Cheung (2019) for instance study animal abuse as part of coercive control. Recently, there has also been a rapprochement between these two research strains, as demonstrated by Riggs, Taylor, Fraser, Donovan, and Signal's study (2018) of DV against non-human animals in LGBTI intimate relations. This widening of the scope of DV research is consistent with feminist research and theorising as an evolving and expanding liberatory project.

### How are DV and gender equality related?

An important assumption following from a feminist perspective on DV is that there is a link between DV and gender equality. Subsequently, DV should be expected to decrease with decreasing levels of gender inequality. However, the correlation between levels of DV and lev-els of gender equality has not been clearly demonstrated in research. The fact that the Nordic countries, despite their high ranking in international gender equality comparisons, still have high levels of DV has recently spurred debates over a possible 'Nordic paradox' (Gracia & Merlo, 2016; Gracia, Martín-Fernández, Lila, Merlo, & Ivert, 2019). Although the data on which such claims are based have been criticised (Walby & Towers, 2017), it is still an undisputable fact that DV remains a problem also in the Nordic countries, which may challenge claims of a simple causal relation between the level of gender equality and DV. Another recent approach theorises the relation between gender relations, domination and policy, developing the concept of violence regimes that conceptualises violence as an inequality in its own right (Hearn, Strid, Humbert, Balkmar, & Delauney, 2020).

### Anti-feminist backlash

The contemporary illiberal, anti-gender movement also represents a new challenge for feminist perspectives on DV, which have become the target of anti-feminist critiques which include the contestation of DV as an issue, claims of false allegations of DV in the context of custody cases, and contestations of states' responsibilities to address DV, a revitalisation of the gender symmetry debate and claims of men being equally the victims of DV. When these issues are linked to the political contestation of gender as a concept and gender studies as an academic discipline in many countries, there is reason to worry that the feminist victories in institutionalising states' responsibilities to address DV as part of a gender equality agenda may be under threat (Walby, 2018; Verloo & Paternotte, 2018).

## Conclusion

This chapter elucidates how feminist perspectives on DV may be seen as an ongoing practice of simultaneously theorising and politicising of DV. By highlighting the multiple origins, as well as some formative controversies and emerging themes, spurred by the theoretical and political contributions from black, postcolonial, queer and indigenous feminisms, this chapter presents the feminist perspective on DV as an unfinished project and a work in progress. The chapter, rather than attempting to give an exhaustive overview, mimics the fluidity and multiplicity of the field.

## *Postscript*

As this chapter was being finalised, the Covid-19 pandemic struck, acutely demonstrating the importance and relevance of studying and theorising DV, and the feminist perspective on DV in particular, illustrating and extending several of the topics that have been discussed in this chapter.

DV emerged as one among several factors contributing to the gendered, racial and classed shape of the pandemic, reflecting and elucidating pre-existing social inequalities such as gendered patterns of employment, risk and valuation (Wanqing, 2020; Godin, 2020; the United Nations, 2020a, 2020b). The virus itself and the lockdown strategies also provided perpetrators with new pandemic-specific means of coercive control and threatening behaviours (Gearin & Knight, 2020). The interaction between DV, the infection control measures, and services for victims of DV in the pandemic epitomises the relation between DV and the state. The pandemic had the effect of raising awareness, nationally and internationally to DV as a 'shadow pandemic'.

With the prospect of a severe economic downturn (the International Monetary Fund, 2020), levels of DV are likely to increase, as Walby and Towers (2012) and Walby et al. (2016) demonstrated in their studies of the effects on DV after the 2009 financial crisis. On a more optimistic tone, the pandemic also revealed the critical and essential importance and value of care and other low-paid and underestimated – gendered, classed and minoritised – work. Further, the unprecedented response to the pandemic, shutting down large parts of the formal economy to save lives, forcefully demonstrated what feminist economists have long argued: people are more important than money (Benaria, Berik, & Floro, 2015), and the aim of the economy is not to maximise monetary value but social provisioning to sustain people (Power, 2004).

The Covid-19 pandemic has reiterated the importance and relevance of feminist, intersectional analyses of various sectors of society and from different disciplinary perspectives, thereby creating new contexts and opportunities for future theorisations and politicisation of DV.

## Critical findings

- In the feminist perspective, DV is constituted in and constitutive of gender orders. DV is seen as one among other pillars underpinning and reproducing gender inequality in society.
- Power and control figure prominently in feminist theorisations and research on DV. DV is seen as a liberty crime. Another strain of feminist research on DV focusses on physical violence. In both strains, the attention is directed towards the totality of violence that the victim experiences and consequences for the victim, rather than the individual violent acts.
- The co-development of knowledge and activism has been pivotal in the development of feminist theory, community responses and policies of DV. The feminist theorisation of DV relies on theorising from experience, placing victim's voices at the core of theory and

practice. Black feminism, queer, postcolonial and indigenous feminisms have played and play crucial roles in the theorisation, critique, dialogue, expansion and research on DV. The feminist theorisation of DV is an ongoing and evolving practice.

- Feminist perspectives on DV have influenced policies and legislation, but the feminist perspective on DV as well as states' responsibilities to address DV are also contested. On one hand, international and state actors have adopted responsibility for addressing DV. On the other hand, political backlashes in some countries and growing resistance against gender equality and gender theory have also led to contestations of states' responsibility to address DV.

## Implications for policy, practice and research

- Researchers on DV need to recognise the multiplicity of past and contemporary feminist perspectives on DV.
- There is a need for policymakers and researchers to recognise the legacy and the continued importance of feminist theorisations, advocacy and practical activism in community responses to DV.
- In the contemporary context of political backlashes against gender equality, gender theory and state responsibility to address DV, it is important to politically defend and consolidate past feminist victories in terms of legislation and institutions addressing DV.

## References

Abrams, J. R. (2015). The feminist case for acknowledging women's acts of violence. *Yale Journal of Law & Feminism, 27*, 287–329.

Ackerman, J. M. (2015). Over-reporting intimate partner violence in Australian survey research. *British Journal of Criminology, 56*(4), 646–667.

Ackerman, J. M. (2018). Assessing conflict tactics scale validity by examining intimate partner violence overreporting. *Psychology of Violence, 8*(2), 207–217.

Alcoff, L. M. (2014). Sexual violations and the question of experience. *New Literary History, 45*(3), 445–462.

Anderson, K. L. (2005). Theorizing gender in intimate partner violence research. *Sex Roles, 52*(11–12), 853–865.

Barlow, C., Johnson, K., Walklate, S., & Humphreys, L. (2019). Putting coercive control into practice: Problems and possibilities. *The British Journal of Criminology, 60*(1), 160–179.

Benería, L., Berik, G., & Floro, M. (2015). *Gender, development and globalization: Economics as if all people mattered.* New York, NY and London: Routledge.

Bilge, S. (2013). Intersectionality undone: Saving intersectionality from feminist intersectionality studies. *Du Bois Review: Social Science Research on Race, 10*(2), 405–424.

Bjørnholt, M. (2018). How to make what really matters count in economic decision-making: Care, domestic violence, gender-responsive budgeting, macroeconomic policies and human rights. In V. Giorgino & Z. D. Walsh (Eds.), *Co-designing economies in transition* (pp. 135–159). London: Palgrave Macmillan.

Bjørnholt, M., & Hjemdal, O. K. (2018). Measuring violence, mainstreaming gender: Does adding harm make a difference? *Journal of Gender-Based Violence, 2*(3), 465–479.

Bjørnholt, M., & Rosten, M. (2021). Male victims of violence and men's rights struggles: A perfect match? In L. Gottzén, M. Bjørnholt, & F. Boonzaier (Eds.), *Men, masculinities and intimate partner violence* (pp. 126–140). London and New York, NY: Routledge.

Boonzaier, F. (2008). If the man says you must sit, then you must sit': The relational construction of woman abuse: Gender, subjectivity and violence. *Feminism & Psychology, 18*(2), 183–206.

Boonzaier, F., Lafrance, M. N., & McKenzie-Mohr, S. (2014). South African women resisting dominant discourse in narratives of violence. *Women Voicing Resistance: Discursive and Narrative Explorations,* 102–120.

Brown, J. M., & Walklate, S. L. (Eds.). (2011). *Handbook on sexual violence*. London and New York, NY: Routledge.

Brown, W. (1995). *States of injury: Power and freedom in late modernity*. Princeton, NJ: Princeton University Press.

Brownmiller, S. (1975). *Against our will: Rape, women, and men*. New York: Simon u. Schuster.

Burman, M., & Brooks-Hay, O. (2018). Aligning policy and law? The creation of a domestic abuse offence incorporating coercive control. *Criminology & Criminal Justice, 18*(1), 67–83. doi:10.1177%2F1748895817752223

Cahill, A. J. (2001). *Rethinking rape*. Ithaca and London: Cornell University Press.

Cahill, A. J. (2016). Unjust sex vs. rape. *Hypatia, 31*(4), 746–761.

Cho, S., Crenshaw, K., & McCall, L. (2013). Toward a field of intersectionality studies: Theory, applications, and praxis. *Signs, 38*(4), 785–810. doi:10.1086/669608.

Crenshaw, K. (1989). Demarginalizing the intersection of race and sex: A black feminist critique of antidiscrimination doctrine, feminist theory and antiracist politics. *University of Chicago Legal Forum*, 139–167.

Dobash, R. E., & Dobash, R. (1979). *Violence against wives: A case against the patriarchy*. New York, NY: The Free Press.

Dobash, R. E., & Dobash, R. (2015). *When men murder women*. Oxford: Oxford University Press.

Donovan, C., & Barnes, R. (2019). Re-tangling the concept of coercive control: A view from the margins and a response to Walby and Towers (2018). *Criminology & Criminal Justice*. doi:10.1177/1748895819864622

Donovan, C., & Barnes, R. (2020). *Queering narratives of domestic violence and abuse*. Cham: Palgrave Macmillan, Springer Nature.

Donovan, C., & Hester, M. (2014). *Domestic violence and sexuality: What's love got to do with it?* Bristol: Policy Press.

Eriksson, M., & Hester, M. (2001). Violent men as good-enough fathers? A look at England and Sweden. *Violence Against Women, 7*(7), 779–798.

Evans, M., Hemmings, C., Henry, M., Johnstone, H., Madhok, S., Plomien, A., & Wearing, S. (Eds.). (2014). *The SAGE handbook of feminist theory*. London: Sage.

Fitzgerald, A. J., Barrett, B. J., Stevenson, R., & Cheung, C. H. (2019). Animal maltreatment in the context of intimate partner violence: A manifestation of power and control. *Violence Against Women, 25*(15), 1806–1828.

Flood, M. (2021). Engaging men and boys in violence prevention. In L. Gottzén, M. Bjørnholt, & F. Boonzaier (Eds.), *Men, masculinities and intimate partner violence* (pp. 155–170). London and New York, NY: Routledge.

Gavey, N. (2005). Just sex. In *The cultural scaffolding of rape*. Hove, Brighton: Routledge.

Gearin, M., & Knight, B. (2020, March 29). Family violence perpetrators using COVID-19 as 'a form of abuse we have not experienced before'. *ABC News*. Retrieved from www.abc.net.au/news/2020-03-29/coronavirus-family-violence-surge-in-victoria/12098546

Gelles, R. J. (1976). Abused wives: Why do they stay. *Journal of Marriage and the Family, 38*(4), 659–668.

Gilbert, P. R. (2002). Discourses of female violence and societal gender stereotypes. *Violence Against Women, 8*(11), 1271–1300.

Godin, M. (2020, March 18). As cities around the world go on lockdown, victims of domestic violence look for a way out. *Time*. Retrieved from https://time.com/5803887/coronavirus-domestic-violence-victims/

Gottzén, L. (2016). Displaying shame: Men's violence towards women in a culture of gender equality. In M. Hydén, A. Wade, & D. Gadd (Eds.), *Response based approaches to the study of interpersonal violence* (pp. 156–175). London: Palgrave Macmillan.

Grace, K. T., & Anderson, J. C. (2018). Reproductive coercion: A systematic review. *Trauma, Violence, & Abuse, 19*(4), 371–390.

Gracia, E., Martín-Fernández, M., Lila, M., Merlo, J., & Ivert, A. K. (2019). Prevalence of intimate partner violence against women in Sweden and Spain: A psychometric study of the 'Nordic paradox'. *PLoS One, 14*(5), e0217015.

Gracia, E., & Merlo, J. (2016). Intimate partner violence against women and the Nordic paradox. *Social Science & Medicine, 157*, 27–30.

Gunnarsson, L. (2018). "Excuse me, but are you raping me now?" Discourse and experience in (the grey areas of) sexual violence. *NORA-Nordic Journal of Feminist and Gender Research, 26*(1), 4–18.

Hamberger, K., Larsen, S. E., & Lehrner, A. (2017). Coercive control in intimate partner violence. *Aggression and Violent Behavior, 37*, 1–11. doi:10.1016/j.avb.2017.08.003

Hanna, C. (2009). The paradox of progress: Translating Evan Stark's coercive control into legal doctrine for abused women. *Violence Against Women, 15*(12), 1458–1476.

Harris, D. (2001). From Kennedy to Combahee: Black feminist activism from 1960 to 1980. In V. P. Franklin & B. Collier-Thomas (Eds.), *Sisters in the struggle: African-American women in the civil rights-black power movement.* New York, NY: New York University Press.

Hearn, J. (1998). *The violences of men: How men talk about and how agencies respond to men's violence to women.* London, Thousand Oaks, CA and New Delhi: Sage.

Hearn, J., Strid, S., Humbert, A. L., Balkmar, D., & Delaunay, M. (2020). From gender regimes to violence regimes: Re-thinking the position of violence. *Social Politics: International Studies in Gender, State & Society.* doi:10.1093/sp/jxaa022.

Hester, M., & Newman, C. (2021). Evaluating IPV programs. In L. Gottzén, M. Bjørnholt, & F. Boonzaier (Eds.), *Men, masculinities and intimate partner violence* (pp. 140–155). London and New York, NY: Routledge.

Hester, M., & Radford, L. (1992). Domestic violence and access arrangements for children in Denmark and Britain. *The Journal of Social Welfare & Family Law, 14*(1), 57–70.

Hill-Collins, P. (2000). *Black feminist thought: Knowledge, consciousness, and politics of empowerment.* New York, NY: Routledge.

Htun, M., & Weldon, S. L. (2012). The civic origins of progressive policy change: Combating violence against women in global perspective, 1975–2005. *American Political Science Review,* 548–569.

Hydén, M. (1994). *Woman battering as marital act: The construction of a violent marriage.* Oslo: Scandinavian University Press.

International Monetary Fund. (2020, April). *IMF world economic outlook, The great lockdown;* 1/37. Retrieved from www.imf.org/en/Publications/WEO/Issues/2020/04/14/World-Economic-Outlook-April-2020-The-Great-Lockdown-49306

Johnson, M. P. (1995). Patriarchal terrorism and common couple violence: Two forms of violence against women. *Journal of Marriage and the Family,* 283–294.

Johnson, M. P. (2008). *A typology of domestic violence: Intimate terrorism, violent resistance, and situational couple violence.* Lebanon, NH: Northeastern University Press.

Katz, E. (2015). Domestic violence, children's agency and mother – Child relationships: Towards a more advanced model. *Children & Society, 29*(1), 69–79.

Katz, E. (2019). Coercive control, domestic violence, and a five-factor framework: Five factors that influence closeness, distance, and strain in mother – Child relationships. *Violence Against Women.* doi:10.1177/1077801218824998.

Kelly, L. (1987). The continuum of sexual violence. In J. Hanmer & M. Maynard (Eds.), *Women, violence and social control* (pp. 46–60). London: Palgrave Macmillan.

Kelly, L. (1988a). *Surviving sexual violence.* Cambridge, UK: Polity Press.

Kelly, L. (1988b). How women define their experiences of violence. In K. Yllö & M. Bograd (Eds.), *Feminist perspectives on wife abuse* (pp. 114–132). Thousand Oaks, CA: Sage.

Kelly, L. (2003). The wrong debate: Reflections on why force is not the key issue with respect to trafficking in women for sexual exploitation. *Feminist Review, 73,* 139–144.

Kestell, B. (2019). Against me(n): *Accounting for oneself as a male victim of intimate partner abuse in a discrediting context* (PhD dissertation). The School of Nursing and Human Sciences, Dublin City University.

Kevin, C., & Agutter, K. (2018). Failing 'Abyan', 'Golestan' and 'the Estonian mother': Refugee women, reproductive coercion and the Australian state. *Immigrants & Minorities, 36*(2), 87–104.

Kim, M. E. (2018). From carceral feminism to transformative justice: Women-of-color feminism and alternatives to incarceration. *Journal of Ethnic & Cultural Diversity in Social Work, 27*(3), 219–233. doi: 10.1080/15313204.2018.1474827.

Kimmel, M. S. (2002). "Gender symmetry" in domestic violence: A substantive and methodological research review. *Violence Against Women, 8*(11), 1332–1363.

Kuokkanen, R. (2015). Gendered violence and politics in indigenous communities: The cases of aboriginal people in Canada and the Sami in Scandinavia. *International Feminist Journal of Politics, 17*(2), 271–288.

Kuokkanen, R. (2019). *Restructuring relations: Indigenous self-determination, governance, and gender.* Oxford: Oxford University Press.

Lapierre, S., & Côté, I. (2014). La typologie de la violence conjugale de Johnson. *L'encadrement juridique de la pratique professionnelle,* 69–79.

Lapierre, S., Côté, I., Lambert, A., Buetti, D., Lavergne, C., Damant, D., & Couturier, V. (2018). Difficult but close relationships: Children's perspectives on relationships with their mothers in the context of domestic violence. *Violence Against Women, 24*(9), 1023–1038. doi:10.1177/1077801217731541.

Loseke, D., & Kurz, D. (2005). Men's violence toward women is the serious social problem. In D. R. Loseke, R. J. Gelles, & M. M. Cavanaugh (Eds.), *Current controversies on family violence* (pp. 79–96). Thousand Oaks, CA: SAGE.

Lundgren, E. (2004). *Våldets normaliserings-process*. Stockholm: Riksorganisationen för kvinnojourer och tjejjourer i Sverige.

MacKinnon, C. A. (1987). *Feminism unmodified: Discourses on life and law*. Cambridge, MA: Harvard University Press.

MacKinnon, C. A. (1989). *Toward a feminist theory of the state*. Cambridge, MA: Harvard University Press.

Malbon, E., Carson, L., & Yates, S. (2018). What can policymakers learn from feminist strategies to combine contextualised evidence with advocacy? *Palgrave Communications, 4*(1), 104. doi:10.1057/s41599-018-0160-2

Mardorossian, C. M. (2014). *Framing the rape victim: Gender and agency reconsidered*. New Brunswick, NJ and London: Rutgers University Press.

McPhail, B. A., Busch, N. B., Kulkarni, S., & Rice, G. (2007). An integrative feminist model: The evolving feminist perspective on intimate partner violence. *Violence Against Women, 13*(8), 817–841.

Merry, S. E. (2003). Rights talk and the experience of law: Implementing women's human rights to protection from violence. *Human Rights Quarterly, 25*(2), 343–381.

Merry, S. E. (2006). Transnational human rights and local activism: Mapping the middle. *American Anthropologist, 108*(1), 38–51.

Merry, S. E. (2016). The seductions of quantification: Measuring human rights, gender violence, and sex trafficking. Chicago, IL and London: University of Chicago Press.

Migliaccio, T. A. (2002). Abused husbands: A narrative analysis. *Journal of Family Issues, 23*(1), 26–52.

Monckton Smith, J. (2020). Intimate partner femicide: Using Foucauldian analysis to track an eight stage progression to homicide. *Violence Against Women, 26*(11), 1267–1285. doi:10.1177/1077801219863876

Myhill, A. (2017). Measuring domestic violence: Context is everything. *Journal of Gender-Based Violence, 1*(1), 33–44.

Myhill, A., & Kelly, L. (2019). Counting with understanding? What is at stake in debates on researching domestic violence. *Criminology & Criminal Justice*, 1748895819863098. doi:10.1177/1748895819863098

Nybergh, L., Enander, V., & Krantz, G. (2016). Theoretical considerations on men's experiences of intimate partner violence: An interview-based study. *Journal of Family Violence, 31*(2), 191–202. doi:10.1007/s10896-015-9785-8.

Överlien, C. (2011). Abused women with children or children of abused women? A study of conflicting perspectives at women's refuges in Norway. *Child & Family Social Work, 16*(1), 71–80.

Överlien, C., Hellevik, P. M., & Korkmaz, S. (2019). Young women's experiences of intimate partner violence – Narratives of control, terror, and resistance. *Journal of Family Violence*, 1–12.

Överlien, C., & Hydén, M. (2009). Children's actions when experiencing domestic violence. *Childhood, 16*(4), 479–496.

Pence, E. (2010). Interview transcript. *Power and control. Domestic violence in America*. Media resource for the documentary *Power and control. Domestic violence in America*, directed by Cohn, P. Retrieved from www.powerandcontrolfilm.com/wp-content/uploads/2010/04/transcript-ellen-pence.pdf

Pizzey, E. (1974). *Scream quietly or the neighbours will hear*. Harmondsworth: Penguin.

Power, M. (2004). Social provisioning as a starting point for feminist economics. *Feminist Economics, 10*(3), 3–19.

Riggs, D. W., Taylor, N., Fraser, H., Donovan, C., & Signal, T. (2018). The link between domestic violence and abuse and animal cruelty in the intimate relationships of people of diverse genders and/or sexualities: A binational study. *Journal of Interpersonal Violence*. doi:10.11770886260518771681.

Ross, L. J. (2017). Reproductive justice as intersectional feminist activism, *Souls, 19*(3), 286–314. doi:10.1080/10999949.2017.1389634.

Salter, M. (2012). Invalidation: A neglected dimension of gender-based violence and inequality. *International Journal for Crime, Justice and Social Democracy, 1*(1), 3–13.

Schechter, S. (1982). *Women and male violence: The visions and struggles of the battered women's movement*. Boston, MA: South End Press.

Sharp-Jeffs, N., Kelly, L., & Klein, R. (2018). Long journeys toward freedom: The relationship between coercive control and space for action – Measurement and emerging evidence. *Violence Against women*, *24*(2), 163–185.

Sheffield, C. J. (1987). Sexual terrorism: The social control of women. In B. B. Hess & M. M. Ferree (Eds.), *Analyzing gender: A handbook of social science research* (pp. 171–189). Thousand Oaks, CA: Sage.

Smart, C. (1995). *Law, crime and sexuality: Essays in feminism*. London, Thousand Oaks, CA and New Delhi: Sage.

Smith, L. T. (2013 [1999]). *Decolonizing methodologies: Research and indigenous peoples* (2nd ed.). London and New York, NY: Zed Books Ltd.

Sørensen, B. W. (2013). Voldens kontinuum og kvinders voldserfaringer [The continuum of violence and women's experiences of violence]. *Sosiologi i dag [Sociology Today]*, *43*(4), 69–93.

Stanko, E. A. (2013 [1985]). *Intimate intrusions women's experience of male violence*. Abingdon and New York, NY: Routledge [London, Boston, Melbourne & Henley: Routledge & Kegan Paul].

Stark, E. (2007). *Coercive control: The entrapment of women in personal life*. New York: Oxford University Press.

Stark, E. (2009). Rethinking coercive control. *Violence Against Women*, *15*(12), 1509–1525.

Stark, E. (2013). Coercive control. In N. Lombard & L. McMillan (Eds.), *Violence against women: Current theory and practice in domestic abuse, sexual violence and exploitation* (pp. 17–33). London and Philadelphia: Jessica Kingsley Publishers.

Stark, E., & Hester, M. (2019). Coercive control: Update and review. *Violence Against Women*, *25*(1), 81–104. doi:10.1177/1077801218816191

Straus, M. (2005). Women's violence toward men is a serious social problem. In D. R. Loseke, R. J. Gelles, & M. M. Cavanaugh (Eds.), *Current controversies on family violence* (pp. 55–78). Thousand Oaks, CA: SAGE.

Straus, M., Gelles, R., & Steinmetz, S. K. (1980). *Behind closed doors: A survey of family violence in America*. New York, NY: Doubleday.

Taylor, K.-Y (Ed.). (2017). *How we get free: Black feminism and the Combahee river collective*. Chicago, IL: Haymarket Books.

Taylor, K.-Y. (2019). Black feminism and the Combahee river collective. *Monthly Review*, *70*(8). Retrieved from https://monthlyreview.org/2019/01/01/black-feminism-and-the-combahee-river-collective/

The Combahee River Collective. (1997). A Black feminist statement. In L. Nicholson (Ed.), *The second wave: A reader in feminist theory* (pp. 63–70). New York, NY: Routledge.

Thomas, R. M., & Richardson, J. T. (2015). Parental alienation syndrome: 30 years on and still junk science. *Judges Journal*, *54*(3), 25.

United Nations. (2020a). Gender and data resources related to COVID-19. *Data2X*. Retrieved from nde-sourhttps://data2x.org/resource-center/gender-and-data-resources-related-to-covid-19/

United Nations. (2020b, April 9). Put women and girls at centre of COVID-19 recovery: UN Secretary-General. *UN News*. Retrieved from https://news.un.org/en/story/2020/04/1061452

van Niekerk, T. J. (2019). Silencing racialised shame and normalising respectability in "coloured" men's discourses of partner violence against women in Cape Town, South Africa. *Feminism & Psychology*, *29*(2), 177–194.

van Niekerk, T. J. (2021). Programme facilitators' discourses of masculinity and intimate partner violence. In L. Gottzén, M. Bjørnholt, & F. Boonzaier (Eds.), *Men, masculinities and intimate partner violence* (pp. 184–200). London and New York, NY: Routledge.

van Schalkwyk, S., Boonzaier, F., & Gobodo-Madikizela, P. (2014). 'Selves' in contradiction: Power and powerlessness in South African shelter residents' narratives of leaving abusive heterosexual relationships. *Feminism & Psychology*, *24*(3), 314–331. doi:10.1177/0959353513514245

Venäläinen, S. (2019). Reversing positions: Constructions of masculine victimhood in online discussions about intimate partner violence committed by women. *Men and Masculinities*. doi:1097184X18824374

Verloo, M., & Paternotte, D. (2018). The feminist project under threat in Europe. *Politics and Governance*, *6*(3), 1–5.

Walby, S. (1990). *Theorizing patriarchy*. Oxford: Basil Blackwell.

Walby, S. (2009). *Globalization and inequalities: Complexity and contested modernities*. London, Thousand Oaks, CA, New Delhi and Singapore: Sage.

Walby, S. (2018). Is Europe cascading into fascism? Addressing key concepts including gender and violence. *Politics and Governance*, *6*(3), 67–77.

Walby, S., & Towers, J. (2012). Measuring the impact of cuts in public expenditure on the provision of services to prevent violence against women and girls. *Safe: The Domestic Abuse Quarterly, 41*, 14–17.

Walby, S., & Towers, J. (2017). Measuring violence to end violence: Mainstreaming gender. *Journal of Gender-Based Violence, 1*(1), 11–31.

Walby, S., & Towers, J. (2018). Untangling the concept of coercive control: Theorizing domestic violent crime. *Criminology and Criminal Justice, 18*, 7–28.

Walby, S., Towers, J., & Francis, B. (2016). Is violent crime increasing or decreasing? A new methodology to measure repeat attacks making visible the significance of gender and domestic relations. *British Journal of Criminology, 56*(1), 1203–1234.

Walker, L. E. (1979). *The battered woman.* New York: Harper & Row.

Walklate, S., & Fitz-Gibbon, K. (2019). The criminalisation of coercive control: The power of law? *International Journal for Crime, Justice & Social Democracy, 8*(4).

Wanqing, Z. (2020, March 2). Domestic violence cases surge during COVID-19 epidemic. *Sixth Tone. Fresh Voices from today's China.* Retrieved from www.sixthtone.com/news/1005253/domestic-violence-cases-surge-during-covid-19-epidemic

Yllö, K., & Bograd, M. (Eds.). (1988). *Feminist perspectives on wife abuse.* Beverly Hills, CA: Sage.

Young, I. M. (1990). *Throwing like a girl.* Bloomington, IN, Indiana Press.

3

# PSYCHOLOGY AND DOMESTIC VIOLENCE AGAINST WOMEN[1]

*Floretta Boonzaier and Taryn van Niekerk*

## Introduction

The war on women's bodies continues unabated across the globe. Following the declaration of violence as a serious and fast-growing public health problem worldwide at the 1996 World Health Assembly, the first World Report on Violence and Health was published in 2002. The report provided descriptions of the breadth, typology, the impact and key risk factors for violence as well as key interventionist strategies and recommendations for action (Krug, Dahlberg, Mercy, Zwi, & Lozano, 2002). Within the well-established base of psychological literature on domestic violence and abuse, the ecological framework often employed in mainstream community psychological research has been central to the mapping of global violence and addressing its causes and consequences. Emerging within the first wave of violence research (Bowman et al., 2015), the shift towards an epidemiological, public health and ecological approach has been propelled by global public health imperatives and has largely taken an interventionist stance.

Psychological researchers across the global South and North committed to the ecological framework have taken to conceptualising domestic violence, and more broadly, violence against women as "a complex outcome of intersecting risk factors across the human lifespan and within the different tiers of the ecological systems that shape it" (Bowman et al., 2015, p. 243). Framed through a perspective of 'risk', this body of work foregrounds the ecological model to understand the multifaceted aspects of violence and to identify who is *most* at risk of perpetrating violence and who is *most* at risk of becoming victims, varying across different populations and contexts (Heise, 1998). Although acknowledging the importance of this line of enquiry in gaining more holistic insight into the problem of domestic violence, we reiterate our own (Boonzaier, 2018; van Niekerk & Boonzaier, 2019) as well as other scholars' (Hydén, Gadd, & Wade, 2015) arguments that critically interrogate and problematise this 'risk' language, and the implications thereof. More specifically, we argue that much psychological work on domestic violence centres discourses of 'risk' that tend to individualise and decontextualise the problem of violence. This kind of 'risk' language aligns with neoliberalist ideologies that foreground individual agency, choice and empowerment. However, it fails to acknowledge how social injustices are shaped within complex systems and structures, such as racism, capitalism, patriarchy, and globalisation (Rutherford, 2018). Importantly, these critiques additionally bring into view debates on psychology's relevance for sufficiently centring social justice issues.

The debate on psychology's relevance has been a recurring issue, evoked to critically assess the discipline's complicity in maintaining the status quo, while arguing for the importance of centring a liberatory and social justice agenda. Critiques of psychology include, for example, unequal access to mental health services and policies (Pillay & Freeman, 1996), stigmatising questions and engagements with race (Kessi & Boonzaier, 2018), stereotypical engagement with questions of sex, sexuality and gender (Shefer, Boonzaier, & Kiguwa, 2006) as well as the silencing and marginalisation of black women scholars and gender research in mainstream psychological journals (Boonzaier & Shefer, 2006; Kiguwa & Langa, 2011). This latter critique is particularly driven by the peripheral positioning of feminist psychological activism and engagements in mainstream psychological professionalisation. As noted by Kessi and Boonzaier (2018),

> despite the advances made in theorising gendered and other forms of subjectivity, a cursory reading of any mainstream psychological journal will evidence the ways in which the discipline of psychology continues to discipline and reproduce essentialising and stigmatising tropes – especially of those who are already marginalised.
>
> (p. 303)

Despite the establishment of alternative forms and practices of psychology – such as critical community psychologies, critical and feminist psychologies for example – that aim to address political agendas with greater social relevance, we illustrate in this chapter how this discourse of (ir)relevance continues to pervade much mainstream psychological research and practice on domestic violence and abuse, illustrating that further labour is necessary.

In this chapter, we focus on the discipline of psychology and the ways in which it has (dis)engaged with questions of violence against women and the attendant challenges and implications, with a particular focus on the ways in which it reproduces individualised discourses that decontextualise the problem of domestic violence. We illustrate how some psychological discourse on domestic violence and abuse may close down possibilities for knowledge production in the service of ending violence against women and non-normative persons, leaving silences and complexities unattended. More specifically, we ask what discourses will lead us closer to equality and a world free of violence, and which ones will take us further away? Some recognition has been given to the role of the discipline and its complicity in the perpetuation of racism and the maintenance of the racialised status quo but little proportional attention has been paid to the ways in which it has advanced heteronormative, essentialist, damaging and stereotypical thinking on gender-entanglements. Through our interrogation of the implications of individualising and pathologising language in psychological discourse and how it shapes power and oppressions experienced by various identities exposed to domestic violence, we adopt an intersectional approach to our analysis of discourses – a concept developed by second-wave black feminists, and explains the complex ways in which social identities related to sexuality, ethnicity, gender, class, race, disability and so forth, intersect and experience oppressions and power based on their positioning within the social strata (Collins, 2010; Crenshaw, 1994). This intersectional analysis is conducted through the interrogation of the following discourses broadly emerging across the psychological literature on domestic violence: risk and representation; trauma and pathologisation; and heteronormativity. Importantly, as decolonial feminist psychologists we engage with these discourses to comment on the possibilities for future research and practice in psychology.

## 'Risk' and representation

This discourse on gendered and racialised 'risk' offers a critical reflection on how the 'other' is represented in psychological work attempting to explain domestic violence and abuse. Some of the key global themes emerging from psychological scholarship are mapped according to the ecological levels of individual, relationship, community and societal risk factors. These include: poverty; low education; substance abuse; history of aggression and abuse; cultural norms that make violence permissible; and patriarchal practices and belief systems that support men's domination over women and children, economic and social power imbalances, disease, and death of family members (Babalola, 2014; Berg et al., 2010; Burlaka, Grogan-Kaylor, Savchuk, & Graham-Bermann, 2017; Dahlberg & Krug, 2002; De Puy, Abt, & Romain-Glassey, 2017; Kelmendi & Baumgartner, 2017; Mootz, Stabb, & Mollen, 2017; Ní Raghallaigh, Morton, & Allen, 2017). Within studies that examined associations between pre-determined risk factors and domestic violence, several examined associations between such violence and alcohol use (Berg et al., 2010; Pitpitan et al., 2013), place of residence (urban versus rural; Ayotunde, Akintoye, & Adefunke, 2014), physical disability (del Río Ferres, Megías, & Expósito, 2013), mental illness (Khalifeh, Oram, Trevillion, Johnson, & Howard, 2015) and partner's gender role beliefs and levels of general violence (Herrero, Torres, Rodríguez, & Juarros-Basterretxea, 2017) were found. For example, Burlaka and colleagues (2017) looked at the possible associations between domestic violence and family, parent and child characteristics in a group of Ukrainian mothers. They found lower maternal education, unemployment, separate living arrangements and residing in an urban area to be significantly associated with domestic abuse.

In this literature on who is most at risk of experiencing violence, discourses of helplessness are often present and can be described as scripts that position women as inevitable victims of future violence, especially if they had been victimised in the past. Studies of re-victimisation and multiple victimisations abound in the scholarly literature with a history of child abuse or witnessing a mother being abused being described as a risk factor for later revictimisation. The discourse of learning victimisation locates itself in findings that experiences of childhood trauma contribute to women becoming later victims of men's violence (Stith, Smith, Penn, Ward, & Tritt, 2004). While both women and men may have been victims of violence in childhood, women are described as being groomed for further victimisation, while men are groomed for further perpetration of violence. A ten-year longitudinal study found that women with mothers who suffered abuse from their husbands were (1) more likely to experience sexual abuse as a child, (2) more likely to enter abusive relationships as an adult and (3) more likely to have daughters who experienced sexual abuse as a child (McCloskey, 2013). Moreover, childhood sexual abuse among third-generation daughters was related to anxiety around romantic relationships, dating violence and increased sexual risk-taking (McCloskey, 2013). This is important work that at the very least manages to provide evidence of how pervasive and normalised gender-based violence is. However, careful attention must be paid to how this research is framed and where our focus is placed in order to avoid configuring violence as inevitable and positioning women as perpetual victims at risk for men's violence. If not, we run the risk of further entrenching long-standing narratives about women being to blame for their own victimisation, and absolving men of their culpability, thus setting up a circular, reinforcing loop of inevitable violence that women invite onto themselves.

This 'risk' language also feeds into a racialised discourse on domestic violence in the psychological literature. Categories that position 'perpetrator' and 'victim' along the male/female gender binary also tend to reinforce stigmatising discourses on race. In psychological literature that interrogates domestic violence in marginalised, 'vulnerable' and low-income settings, it is largely the case that the risk profiles generated from this work point primarily to poor, black and marginalised men who are constructed as perpetrators and poor, black and marginalised women who are constructed as 'victims'. Through recurring themes in psychological literature that highlight high levels of poverty, income inequality and unemployment that oftentimes occur along racialised divisions and are positioned as risk factors for victimisation and perpetration of this violence, it unequivocally labels black and marginalised people and communities as products of and at risk for violence. This pattern is amplified in the context of psychological literature that repetitively seeks out low-income, 'disadvantaged' communities to study risky sexual behaviours; substance abuse, including problematic alcohol consumption and HIV risk. This kind of racialised discourse positions black men and women's very racialised identities as risk factors for violence but also problematically serves to only locate such violence in poor, black and marginalised spaces. This is not to say that gendered and sexual violence does not exist in these contexts, but rather that they are not the only contexts within which such violence occurs. This kind of discourse is not only stigmatising and problematic, but also a form of violence against black people and communities, especially in the context of heteropatriarchal, capitalist systems that keep poor black people subjugated, and that position black men in particular as threatening (see Boonzaier & van Niekerk, 2019).

It is commonly argued, especially amongst scholars located in the global South, that psychology has reinforced a Euro-American approach that centres knowledge production from the North, and colonial ways of representing people and communities (Kessi & Boonzaier, 2018). These forms of knowledge depict marginalised peoples in dehumanising and pathologising ways, and reflect problematic ways of working with the 'other'. Depictions of black and marginalised peoples and communities in the scholarship on violence do not depart significantly from problematic colonial representations.

Research emerging from this 'risk' and interventionist approach to domestic violence research has made important strides in providing patterned understandings of violence. However, we argue that the full complexity of this violence cannot be accounted for by a language of *risk factors* and *cause and effect* alone. It appears that the hegemonic focus on risk factors has hindered theoretical advancement on how and why violence has become normative and has the inadvertent outcome of making individuals responsible for their exposure to domestic violence.

Scholars, such as Bowman and colleagues (2015), have called for more nuanced studies of how forms of violence are enacted to make layers of complexity more evident. They argue that psychology's incorporation of the public health framework and its predominant use of survey data fails to engage adequately with the tracing of historical patterns, and the links between subjectivities and contexts that provide depth of insight into violent enactments. In foregrounding 'why' questions, they envision comprehensive insights into the psychological study of violence, which involve interrogating a range of factors "from the socio-structural to the individual, the immediate and background factors, the subject and the context, the subjective and the objective, and the systemic and symbolic" (Bowman et al., 2015, p. 245). In redirecting the focus of enquiry, a shift in language might also invite us to think differently about this violence. Questions that, for example, centre enquiries into the intergenerational cycling of domestic violence and the manifestations and effects thereof may allow us to decentre discourses that position women as always at risk and as inevitable victims, just by virtue of their being positioned as women. In addition it allows for a critical perspective on how black, poor and marginalised communities are represented in the scholarship on violence.

We thus argue for the centring of alternative, resistant forms of psychology that take the "psychology of the oppressed as the starting point" (Kessi & Boonzaier, 2018) while centring a social justice approach. Some of these alternate forms of psychology emerging from postcolonial contexts, include but are not limited to, liberation psychology in Latin America (e.g., Jiménez-Domínguez, 2009; Montero & Sonn, 2009), black consciousness movements in South Africa (Manganyi, 1973), indigenous psychologies from the Australasian region (e.g., Groot, Rua, Masters-Awatere, Dungeon, & Garvey, 2012) or decolonial feminist and postcolonial psychologies (e.g., Kessi & Boonzaier, 2017, 2018). These approaches include reflections on the politics of location and practice in psychology and take questions of racism, sexism, homophobia and oppression seriously. They draw on intersectional approaches to domestic violence enquiries that move beyond a sole focus on gender towards acknowledging how poverty, unemployment, race and class relations, whiteness and cultural tradition shape men's violence against women (Boonzaier & van Niekerk, 2019; Moolman, 2013; van Niekerk, 2019). This work suggests that an intersectional lens is central to intervening with men who are violent towards intimate partners but who are themselves marginalised at the intersection of their race and class identities and who have "little stake in the patriarchal dividend" (Boonzaier & van Niekerk, 2018, p. 2). Despite the importance of broadening the scope of critical psychological enquiry, these theories and methodologies have not necessarily been centred in mainstream psychological teaching and research in psychology (Kessi & Boonzaier, 2018). A further limitation to psychological theorising on domestic violence against women is the perpetuation of individualism and the pathologisation of 'victims'.

## Discourses of trauma and 'pathology'

In the vast body of psychological research on gender-based violence (GBV) – featuring women who have been victimised through sexual and physical assault, domestic and partner violence – a key focus is on the psychosocial and diagnostic outcomes for women victims. Much of this work cultivates discourses around psychopathology, whilst furthermore foregrounding psychological practice that 'treats' the trauma of abuse through biomedical models that individualise experiences and recovery from domestic violence. These kinds of circulating discourses, we argue, work to individualise not only the outcomes of such violence, but also the 'treatment' thereof.

While many studies consider the broader psychosocial outcomes of being exposed to gender-based violence, others look more specifically at the associations between gender-based violence and the diagnosis of one or more mental disorders. These studies examining specific diagnostic outcomes in women who have experienced domestic violence have found associations with depression, anxiety, post-traumatic stress disorder and substance abuse (Rees et al., 2011; Schwartz et al., 2014; Vázquez, Torres, & Otero, 2012; Walsh, Hasin, Keyes, & Koenen, 2016). For example, one study looked at the relationship between gender-based violence and diagnosis of a mental disorder in a demographically representative sample of Australian women (Rees et al., 2011). They found that experiences of intimate partner violence, non-partner physical violence, rape and sexual assault and stalking were significantly associated with a range of mental health disorders, as well as overall impaired quality of life. Another examined the association between lifetime experiences of partner and non-partner physical or sexual assault or stalking and personality disorders in a demographically representative sample of women living in the United States (Walsh et al., 2016). They found lifetime experiences of these forms of violence to be associated with greater odds of meeting criteria for a personality disorder. Moreover, they found that women who had experienced multiple instances of such violence were at greater risk for meeting criteria for more than one personality disorder. Similarly, another study found significant associations between experiences of gender-based violence and symptoms of depression as well as current and previous drug use (Schwartz et al., 2014).

These are just a few examples of the kinds of questions that continue to occupy psychologists in the study of gender-based violence more broadly, but also more specifically domestic violence. It is no coincidence that a large body of psychological work on victims of domestic violence has examined the incidence of psychopathology amongst women who have been victimised. To a large degree, psychology has failed to counter individualising discourses in relation to women's experiences of violence from men (Haaken, 2010). The social and political implications of the diagnostic labelling of abused women has largely been overlooked in this body of work, framing women's victimisation in individualising and pathologising ways, and paying little attention to the multiplicity of modes of power, inequities and its range of intersections. As expressed by Ussher (2010),

> Stripping accounts of women's misery of any acknowledgement of the historical and political context of women's lives, whilst paying lip service to sociocultural or psychological influences, thus serves to shore up the very structural factors that lead to distress in the first place, through making gender inequality an invisible issue.
>
> (p. 20)

The discourse of pathology is also apparent in the literature related to psychological intervention for trauma. Biomedical approaches for trauma are commonly referenced within the psychological literature and are used to trace the ways in which emotional memories generate certain biological responses in the brain (Mannell, Ahmad, & Ahmad, 2018). Central to biomedical psychotherapeutic approaches – as well as cognitive behavioural and exposure therapies – are the therapeutic practices of allowing survivors of trauma to tell their stories with the purpose of assessing the reconstructed stories (Hofmann, Asnaani, Vonk, Sawyer, & Fang, 2012). This biomedical approach to psychological intervention for trauma therefore requires that therapy serves to identify the traumatic event, with the aim of retelling the narrative to arrive at a more positive cognition (Mannell et al., 2018). However, some scholars have shown the limitations of the biomedical approach to psychological therapeutic intervention, especially in the case of women experiencing domestic violence in high prevalence and low-income settings. These limitations include the biomedical approach's (1) capacity to pathologise, (2) limited use and applicability in marginalised settings and (3) potential breaches in ethics (Mannell et al., 2018).

It has been argued that psychoanalytic therapies are challenging to implement as they require specialised resources, many of which are not readily available in marginalised, poor communities (Mannell et al., 2018). Furthermore, the biomedical approach raises important ethical concerns through survivors' retelling and re-enacting stories of trauma, especially in spaces where domestic violence is ongoing and where there is the very pervasive threat of continuing violence (Mannell et al., 2018). The approach's construction of trauma as an individualised pathology furthermore obscures larger systems of power, such as heteropatriarchy, that keep gendered inequality and domestic violence in place.

Kessi and Boonzaier (2018) and Segalo (2015) argue that the discipline of psychology although positioned as the appropriate point of enquiry for traumatic histories has done little to attend to questions that centre historically contextualised, gendered, raced and localised understandings of trauma and its responses. Attention to transgenerational trauma in psychological work is central to engaging with the high levels of gendered violence we see persisting across the globe and particularly in global southern contexts with protracted histories of colonialism (Kessi & Boonzaier, 2018).

A feminist psychological study with women living in safe houses in Afghanistan called for socially transformative interventions that challenge this discourse of individualised pathology present in biomedical psychological approaches to trauma amongst women survivors (Mannell and colleagues, 2018). The study also incorporated storytelling not only to reduce particular symptoms but as a tool to begin a process of conscientisation, empowerment and advocacy. The authors concluded that for many of the women, the opportunity to share their stories without moral judgement or blame, and in socially supportive environments had a significant impact on their well-being. Additionally, they argued that narrative storytelling incorporates a shift from addressing what are deemed as problematic thoughts in the biomedical approach, towards giving women the opportunity to imagine more positive identities and outcomes for themselves. Storytelling spaces established as part of interventionist practices that address domestic violence against women are growing in utilisation, to advance empowerment and personal expression for women survivors of violence.

Importantly, this focus on 'whose knowledge matters' is one that raises critical engagements around 'expertise' and how certain forms of 'knowledge' are regarded as more valuable than others. We need to keep asking ourselves what constitutes expertise on violence against women in ongoing critical psychological work, as well as who decides this, and with what criteria. Importantly, do these criteria reflect women's lived experience? To answer these questions and craft new stories about recovery from sexual, physical and verbal assault, we have to listen to the survivors themselves as they are always the first experts. Feminist psychological research is grounded in political commitment to women's equality and the value of women's experiential knowledge, and it must be reclaimed and reasserted by us as researchers and practitioners, in research projects, at women's centres and in the courtroom. When we listen, we hear stories about women who find meaning in collective sharing and support that helps them find their own voice and challenge the stigma and silence that surrounds their experiences of domestic violence and abuse. The next discourse furthers this dialogue around the exclusion and silencing of some 'voices' in psychological scholarship.

## Heteronormativity

The literatures on domestic violence, across disciplines including psychology as well as government, policy, justice and practice-based responses globally have overwhelmingly assumed a heteronormative framework in which women feature as victims and men as perpetrators, and which adheres to heteronormative sexuality and gendered boundaries.

Psychology as a discipline has also been argued to maintain and reinforce heteropatriarchal structures whilst experiences that challenge the normative – such as work on gender and sexual diversity – are marginalised and silenced (Kessi & Boonzaier, 2018). Mainstream psychological knowledge production has often been framed through the lens of white, heterosexual, middle-class, able-bodied, cis-gendered men's experiences whilst decentring women's issues (Kessi & Boonzaier, 2018).

A recent report (Human Rights Campaign Foundation, 2018a) and tracking efforts by advocates (Human Rights Campaign Foundation, 2017, 2018b) illustrate that fatal violence disproportionately affects transgender women of colour in the United States and globally and that intersections of racism, sexism, homophobia and transphobia conspire to make this group vulnerable to disproportionate barriers in the help-seeking aftermath of a violent incident. However, we need more work in this area to understand the violence and more complete representation of the experiences of transgender survivors of domestic and partner violence.

Along the lines of sexuality, a study by the Centers for Disease Control and Prevention's latest *National Intimate Partner and Sexual Violence Survey* (Black et al., 2011) breaks down its data along the lines of sexual orientation to illustrate that not only heterosexual men and women are involved in situations of domestic violence at high rates. In fact, lesbian-, gay- and bisexual-identifying women, according to this report, experience some of the highest rates of intimate partner violence: "43.8% of self identified lesbians reported to have been physically victimized, stalked, or raped by an intimate partner in their lifetime, compared to 35.0% of heterosexual women, 29.0% of heterosexual men, and 26.0% of gay men" (ibid., p. 66). Cannon and Buttell (2015) remark that "same-sex relationships are rendered deviant and invisible" (p. 69) by the very same "patriarchal system that legitimizes male violence, as a bid for control, against women" (ibid., p. 69).

Limited empirical research is a reason why subsequent policy and intervention proposals may not effectively be accessible to, target or assist (even help-seeking) queer individuals who are either offenders or victims in domestic violence situations. This lack of research sustains the urgent need for psychology as a discipline to establish knowledge on the experiences of such violence amongst queer and trans women, and its implications for service providers and practice.

The language of psychology provides an important resource through which gender-based violence can be framed, by both victims, perpetrators, bystanders and others who encounter violence. Psychological discourse in particular has been extremely influential in shaping representations of victims and perpetrators of domestic violence. We need to be mindful of the ways in which mainstream psychological discourse has produced and reproduced heteronormativity by setting women up as helpless victims and men as inevitable perpetrators – allowing no room for challenging normative, restrictive and binary notions of gender that produce violence in the first place (Shefer, 2016). These limited ways of being and seeing additionally offer little opportunity to understand the complexities around identities as well as the complex ways in which domestic violence and abuse function.

## Implications and conclusions

This chapter traces dominant psychological discourse on domestic violence and abuse and illustrates some of the challenges, silences and problematics delivered in current critiques of psychological theories and approaches. Although we highlight the importance of various approaches to psychological knowledge production on domestic violence, we also interrogate what it means to develop a 'relevant' psychology – one that speaks more holistically to the needs of people located in marginalised historical, social and cultural contexts and that is sensitive to contextual nuances that shape experiences of domestic violence. In contexts where histories of slavery and colonialism have shaped ongoing violences against its inhabitants, various forms of violence – not only interpersonal forms, but also those at the structural level – ought to be viewed as deeply interrelated, rather than distinct from domestic violence (Bowman, Stevens, Eagle, & Matzopoulos, 2014). This involves acknowledging the broader links between poverty, unemployment and domestic violence, and other forms of violence to unsettle discourses that individualise, pathologise and that make some marginalised identities risk factors for their own victimisation and perpetration of violence. As psychological researchers, we need to be critical about how these 'risk factors' are associated with violence or we will be in danger of producing simplistic explanations that continue to marginalise those individuals and communities who are already on the margins.

It is also worthwhile for scholars of psychology – in both mainstream and critical camps – to caution against other individualising discourses, such as those related to 'agency' and 'empowerment'. Some have challenged this notion of 'empowerment' that involves the assumption that conscientising marginalised communities to consider their circumstances differently may help to mobilise them towards community and social change (Barnes, 2015); while ignoring the larger forces and structures of social injustice – such as capitalism, globalisation, patriarchy – that impede individualised practices of becoming active agents and 'empowered' (Barnes, 2018). The traditional notion of 'agency' is highly dependent on an individual's positioning, where those who find themselves in positions of power within the social hierarchy are likely to have more access to choice and autonomy in the context of existing structures that support this (Rutherford, 2018). Understanding the discourse of individualisation in the context of systems of globalisation and capitalism provides more insight into the ways in which marginalised people – especially those located in global southern contexts – and their experiences cannot be packaged in individualising, decontextualising ways, and especially through approaches to psychological intervention tailored for those in the global North and imposed on those in global southern contexts.

In conclusion, we need to ask ourselves: what is the purpose of this work? What are the new and alternative stories that we want to see? We must produce counter-stories that resist, disrupt and challenge our current ways of making sense of domestic violence against women if we are to ever tackle the ways in which it continues to persist. It is important that psychologists think through their research practices and what this means for the process of knowledge production as well as the ethics and politics thereof. We need to think about what kinds of psychological research can be useful in centring a social justice agenda (Barnes, 2018) that advances equity and non-violence. It is important that as psychologists we ensure that dialogue around power and critical reflexivity and positionality surfaces in our research on domestic violence to better reflect on how people and communities are represented (Kessi & Boonzaier, 2018). We need more imaginative and relevant psychological research on gendered and sexual violence. There is an urgent need for this work to be undertaken in earnest.

## Critical findings

- Within the well-established database of psychological literature on domestic violence and abuse, the ecological framework often employed in mainstream community psychological research has been central to the 'mapping' of global violence and addressing its causes and consequences.
- Much psychological work on domestic violence centres discourses of 'risk' that tend to individualise and decontextualise the problem of violence. The hegemonic focus on risk factors has hindered theoretical advancement on how and why violence has become normative, and has the inadvertent outcome of leaving individuals responsible for their own exposure to domestic violence.
- Racialised 'risk' discourse positions black men and women's very racialised identities as risk factors for violence but also problematically serves to only locate violence in poor, black and marginalised spaces.
- Women's victimisation and trauma has largely been framed in individualising and pathologising ways, paying little attention to the multiplicity of modes of power, inequities and its range of intersections.

- The literatures on domestic violence, across disciplines including psychology as well as government, policy, justice and practice-based responses globally have assumed a heter-onormative framework in which women feature as victims and men as perpetrators, and which adheres to sexuality and gender boundaries.

## Implications for policy, practice and research

- Ensure that dialogue around power, critical reflexivity and positionality surfaces in psycho-logical research on domestic violence to better reflect on how people and communities are represented.
- Centre alternative, resistance forms of psychology that take the "psychology of the oppressed as the starting point" (Kessi & Boonzaier, 2018) while centring a social justice approach.
- Incorporate methodologies that are likely to be instrumental in impacting social justice. For example, intersectional approaches to the study of domestic violence that move beyond a sole focus on gender towards acknowledging how poverty, unemployment, race and class relations, whiteness and cultural tradition shape men's violence against women are critical.
- We need to regard survivors themselves as the first experts. Feminist psychological research is grounded in political commitment to women's equality and the value of women's expe-riential knowledge, and it must be reclaimed and reasserted by us as researchers and practi-tioners, in research projects, at women's centres and in the courtroom.
- Psychologists ought to ensure that dialogue around power and critical reflexivity and posi-tionality surfaces in our research on domestic violence to better reflect on how people and communities are represented.
- We need more imaginative and relevant psychological work on domestic, gendered and sexual violence.

## Note

1  We would like to gratefully acknowledge funding from the University of Cape Town's Vice Chancel-lor's Advancing Womxn Fund for the project titled 'Unsettling Knowledge Production on Gendered and Sexual Violence' as well as research assistance provided by Amalie Ravn and Kara Engelbrecht.

## References

Ayotunde, T., Akintoye, O., & Adefunke, E. S. (2014). Influence of women's attitude on the perpetration of gender-based domestic violence in Nigeria. *Gender & Behaviour, 12*(2), 6420–6429.

Babalola, S. O. (2014). Dimensions and correlates of negative attitudes toward female survi-vors of sexual violence in Eastern DRC. *Journal of Interpersonal Violence, 29*(9), 1679–1697. doi:10.1177/0886260513511531

Barnes, B. R. (2015). Critiques of health behaviour change programmes. *South African Journal of Psychol-ogy, 45*, 430–438.

Barnes, B. R. (2018). Decolonising research methodologies: Opportunity and caution. *South African Jour-nal of Psychology, 48*(3), 379–387. doi:10.1177/00812463187982

Berg, M. J., Kremelberg, D., Dwivedi, P., Verma, S., Schensul, J. J., Gupta, K., . . . Singh, S. K. (2010). The effects of husband's alcohol consumption on married women in three low-income areas of greater Mumbai. *AIDS and Behavior, 14*(S1), 126–135. doi:10.1007/s10461-010-9735-7

Black, M. C., Basile, K. C., Breiding, M. J., Smith, S. G., Walters, M. L., Merrick, M. T., . . . Stevens, M. R. (2011). *National intimate partner and sexual violence survey: 2010 summary report.* Atlanta, GA: National Center for Injury Prevention and Control, Centers for Disease Control and Prevention. Retrieved August 25, 2019, from www.cdc.gov/violenceprevention/pdf/nisvs_report2010-a.pdf#page=47

Boonzaier, F. (2018). Challenging risk: The production of knowledge on gendered violence in South Africa. In K. Fitz-Gibbon, S. Walklate, J. McCulloch, & J. Maree Maher (Eds.), *Intimate partner violence, risk and security: Securing women's lives in a global world*. London: Routledge.

Boonzaier, F., & Shefer, T. (2006). Gendered research. In T. Shefer, F. Boonzaier, & P. Kiguwa (Eds.), *The gender of psychology* (pp. 3–11). Cape Town: UCT Press.

Boonzaier, F., & van Niekerk, T. (2018). "I'm here for abusing my wife": South African men constructing intersectional subjectivities through narratives of their own violence. *African Safety Promotion: A Journal of Injury and Violence Prevention, 16*(1), 2–19.

Boonzaier, F., & van Niekerk, T. (2019). Discursive trends in research on masculinities and interpersonal violence in Africa. In L. Gottzén, U. Mellström, & T. Shefer (Eds.), *The Routledge international handbook of masculinity studies*. Oxfordshire and New York: Routledge.

Bowman, B., Stevens, G., Eagle, G., Langa, M., Kramer, S., Kiguwa, P., & Nduna, M. (2015). The second wave of violence scholarship: South African synergies with a global research agenda. *Social Science & Medicine, 146*, 243–248.

Bowman, B., Stevens, G., Eagle, G., & Matzopoulos, R. (2014). Bridging risk and enactment: The role of psychology in leading psychosocial research to augment the public health approach to violence in South Africa. *South African Journal of Psychology*, 1–15.

Burlaka, V., Grogan-Kaylor, A., Savchuk, O., & Graham-Bermann, S. A. (2017). The relationship between family, parent, and child characteristics and intimate-partner violence (IPV) among Ukrainian mothers. *Psychology of Violence, 7*(3), 469–477. doi:10.1037/vio0000085

Cannon, C., & Buttell, F. (2015). Illusion of inclusion: The failure of the gender paradigm to account for intimate partner violence in LGBT relationships. *Partner Abuse, 6*(1), 65–77.

Collins, P. H. (2010). *Black feminist thought: Knowledge, consciousness and the politics of empowerment* (2nd ed.). New York, NY: Routledge.

Crenshaw, K. (1994). Mapping the margins: Intersectionality, identity politics, and violence against women of color. In M. A. Fineman & R. Mykitiuk (Eds.), *The public nature of private violence* (pp. 93–118). New York, NY: Routledge.

Dahlberg, L. L., & Krug, E. G. (2002). Violence – A global public health problem. In E. G. Krug, L. L. Dahlberg, J. A. Mercy, A. B. Zwi, & R. Lozano (Eds.), *World report on violence and health* (pp. 1–22). Geneva: World Health Organization.

del Río Ferres, E., Megías, J. L., & Expósito, F. (2013). Gender-based violence against women with visual and physical disabilities. *Psicothema, 25*, 67–72.

De Puy, J., Abt, M., & Romain-Glassey, N. (2017). Coping with multiple adversities: Men who sought medico-legal care because of physical violence from a partner or ex-partner. *Psychology of Violence, 3*(7), 428–439. doi:10.1037/vio0000101

Groot, S., Rua, M., Masters-Awatere, B., Dudgeon, P., & Garvey, D. (2012). Editorial special issue. Indigenous Psychologies. *The Australian Community Psychologist, 24*, 5–10.

Haaken, J. (2010). *Hard knocks. Domestic violence and the psychology of storytelling*. London: Routledge.

Heise, L. L. (1998). Violence against women: An integrated, ecological framework. *Violence Against Women, 4*(3), 262–290.

Herrero, J., Torres, A., Rodríguez, F. J., & Juarros-Basterretxea, J. (2017). Intimate partner violence against women in the European Union: The influence of male partners' traditional gender roles and general violence. *Psychology of Violence, 7*(3), 385–394. doi:10.1037/vio0000099

Hofmann, S. G., Asnaani, A., Vonk, I. J. J., Sawyer, A. T., Fang, A. (2012). The efficacy of cognitive behavioral therapy: A review of meta-analyses. *Cognitive Therapy and Research, 36*, 427–440. doi:10.1007/s10608-012-9476-1.

Human Rights Campaign Foundation. (2017). *Violence against the transgender community in 2016*. Retrieved from www.hrc.org/resources/violence-against-the-transgender-community-in-2017

Human Rights Campaign Foundation. (2018a). *A national epidemic: Fatal anti-transgender violence in America in 2018*. Retrieved from https://assets2.hrc.org/files/assets/resources/AntiTransViolence-2018Report-Final.pdf?_ga=2.96721052.2053660276.1569325411–1419845433.1569325411

Human Rights Campaign Foundation. (2018b). *Violence against the transgender community in 2017*. Retrieved from www.hrc.org/resources/violence-against-the-transgender-community-in-2018

Hydén, M., Gadd, D., & Wade, A. (2015). Introduction to response based approaches to the study of interpersonal violence. In M. Hydén, D. Gadd, & A. Wade (Eds.), *Response based approaches to the study of interpersonal violence* (pp. 1–16). London: Palgrave Macmillan. doi:10.1057/9781137409546_1

Jiménez-Domínguez, B. (2009). Ignacio Martín-Baró's social psychology of liberation: Situated knowledge and critical commitment against objectivism. In M. Montero & C. Sonn (Eds.), *Psychology of liberation: Theory and applications* (pp. 37–50). New York, NY: Springer Science + Business Media.

Kelmendi, K., & Baumgartner, F. (2017). A mixed-method evidence of intimate partner violence victimization among female students in Kosovo and its correlates. *Psychology of Violence, 7*(3), 440–449. doi:10.1037/vio0000098

Kessi, S., & Boonzaier, F. (2017). Resistance and transformation in postcolonial contexts. In C. Howarth & E. Andreouli (Eds.), *The Social psychology of everyday politics* (pp. 116–130). London: Routledge.

Kessi, S., & Boonzaier, F. (2018). Centre/ing decolonial feminist psychology in Africa. *South African Journal of Psychology, 48*(3), 299–309.

Khalifeh, H., Oram, S., Trevillion, K., Johnson, S., & Howard, L. M. (2015). Recent intimate partner violence among people with chronic mental illness: Findings from a national cross-sectional survey. *The British Journal of Psychiatry: The Journal of Mental Science, 207*(3), 207–212. doi:10.1192/bjp.bp.114.144899

Kiguwa, P., & Langa, M. (2011). South African psychology and gender: An analysis of the SAJP and PINS journals 1994–2009. In A. Rutherford, R. Capdevila, V. Undurti, & I. Palmary (Eds.), *Handbook of international feminisms: Perspectives on psychology, women, culture and rights* (pp. 247–267). New York, NY: Springer.

Krug, E. G., Dahlberg, L. L., Mercy, J. A., Zwi, A. B., & Lozano, R. (2002). *World report on violence and health*. Geneva: World Health Organization.

Manganyi, N. (1973). *Being black in the world*. Johannesburg, South Africa: Sprocas.

Mannell, J., Ahmad, A., & Ahmad, L. (2018). Narrative storytelling as mental health support for women experiencing gender-based violence in Afghanistan. *Social Science & Medicine, 214*, 91–98. doi:10.1016/j.socscimed.2018.08.011

McCloskey, L. A. (2013). The intergenerational transfer of mother – Daughter risk for gender-based abuse. *Psychodynamic Psychiatry, 41*(2), 303–328. doi:10.1521/pdps.2013.41.2.303

Montero, M., & Sonn, C. (2009). *Psychology and liberation: Theory and applications*. New York, NY: Springer Science + Business Media.

Moolman, B. (2013). Rethinking 'masculinities in transition' in South Africa considering the 'intersectionality' of race, class, and sexuality with gender. *African Identities, 11*(1), 93–105. doi:10.1080/14725843.2013.775843

Mootz, J. J., Stabb, S. D., & Mollen, D. (2017). Gender-based violence and armed conflict. *Psychology of Women Quarterly, 41*(3), 368–388. doi:10.1177/0361684317705086

Ní Raghallaigh, M., Morton, S., & Allen, M. (2017). HIV transmission as a form of gender-based violence: Experiences of women in Tigray, Ethiopia. *International Social Work, 60*(4), 941–953. doi:10.1177/0020872815594224

Pillay, Y., & Freeman, M. (1996). Mental health policy and planning: Continuing the debates. *Psychology in Society, 21*, 60–72.

Pitpitan, E., Kalichman, S., Eaton, L., Cain, D., Sikkema, K., Skinner, D., . . . Pieterse, D. (2013). Gender-based violence, alcohol use, and sexual risk among female patrons of drinking venues in Cape Town, South Africa. *Journal of Behavioral Medicine, 36*(3), 295–304. doi:10.1007/s10865-012-9423-3

Rees, S., Silove, D., Chey, T., Ivancic, L., Steel, Z., Creamer, M., . . . Forbes, D. (2011). Lifetime prevalence of gender-based violence in women and the relationship with mental disorders and psychosocial function. *JAMA, 306*(5), 513–521. doi:10.1001/jama.2011.1098

Rutherford, A. (2018). Feminism, psychology, and the gendering of neoliberal subjectivity: From critique to disruption. *Theory & Psychology, 28*(5), 619–644. doi:10.1177/0959354318797194

Schwartz, R. M., Weber, K. M., Schechter, G. E., Connors, N. C., Gousse, Y., Young, M. A., & Cohen, M. H. (2014). Psychosocial correlates of gender-based violence among HIV-infected and HIV-uninfected women in three US cities. *AIDS Patient Care and STDs, 28*(5), 26–267. doi:10.1089/apc.2013.0342

Segalo, P. (2015). Trauma and gender. *Social and Personality Psychology Compass, 9*, 447–454.

Shefer, T. (2016). Resisting the binarism of victim and agent: Critical reflections on 20 years of scholarship on young women and heterosexual practices in South Africa. *Global Public Health, 11*, 211–223.

Shefer, T., Boonzaier, F., & Kiguwa, P. (Eds.). (2006). *The gender of psychology*. Juta: Cape Town.

Stith, S. M., Smith, D. B., Penn, C. E., Ward, D. B., & Tritt, D. (2004). Intimate partner physical abuse perpetration and victimization risk factors: A meta-analytic review. *Aggression and Violent Behavior, 10*, 65–98.

Ussher, J. M. (2010). Are we medicalizing women's misery? A critical review of women's higher rates of reported depression. *Feminism & Psychology, 20,* 9–35.

van Niekerk, T. J. (2019). Silencing racialised shame and normalising respectability in 'coloured' men's discourses of partner violence against women in Cape Town, South Africa. *Feminism & Psychology, 29*(2), 177–194. doi:10.1177/0959353519841410

van Niekerk, T. J., & Boonzaier, F. A. (2019). An intersectional analysis of responses to intimate partner violence in two marginalised South African communities. *International Journal of Child, Youth and Family Studies, 10*(1), 26–48.

Vázquez, F. L., Torres, A., & Otero, P. (2012). Gender-based violence and mental disorders in female college students. *Social Psychiatry and Psychiatric Epidemiology, 47*(10), 1657–1667. doi:10.1007/s00127-012-0472-2

Walsh, K., Hasin, D., Keyes, K. M., & Koenen, K. C. (2016). Associations between gender-based violence and personality disorders in U.S. women. *Personality Disorders, 7*(2), 205–210. doi:10.1037/per0000158

# 4

# DOMESTIC VIOLENCE AND ABUSE THROUGH A SOCIOLOGICAL LENS

*Alison C. Cares, Amy Reckdenwald and Ketty Fernandez*

## Introduction

Quite simply, sociology is the study of the social or human world, which is quite broad. Primary concerns of sociologists include the study of social norms and culture, inequality and stratification, social issues and problems, and social institutions (such as family, government, churches, and schools), as well as the commitment to use findings to contribute to social change, particularly reductions in inequality. That commitment is the hallmark of public sociology (Burawoy, 2005). What guides this is the Sociological Imagination (Mills, 2000). This is, when engaging in research, breaking through the false consciousness that one "knows" why things happen, not taking what is as given or natural, and stepping outside one's own experiences to understand the experiences of others, from their own perspective and without applying value judgements.

The application of the Sociological Imagination is crucial to understanding how experiences with domestic violence and responses to it differ according to an individual's location in the social structure. Social location is not just based on gender, sexual orientation, race, ethnicity, age, and class identities individually. Instead, it is based on the interaction of these identities (i.e., intersectionality) and is influenced by community and societal level factors. How social location and domestic violence interact varies by context, including differences across nations, with different social norms and cultural traditions. However, to understand how domestic violence intersects with other social problems, such as immigration, poverty, racism, war, and oppression of all kinds, we must practice the non-judgemental open-mind advocated for by the Sociological Imagination. This is particularly important since the field of researchers studying domestic violence remains dominated by those of privilege, drawing heavily from English-speaking Western countries (particularly the United States) and those who are white, highly educated, female (typically cis-gender female), straight, and middle and upper class.

Sociologists have made important contributions to the study of domestic violence, dating back nearly four decades to the nascent period of studying the issue. Sociologists have studied domestic violence and reactions to it from many angles, but this chapter focuses on contributions in three areas: first, historical contributions, including early studies of the nature and extent of domestic violence, the development of a widely employed measure of domestic violence, and the relationship of gender to domestic violence and the related gender symmetry debate; second, the role of social norms, particularly related to gender and acceptance of domestic violence, in facilitating domestic violence; and third, how inequality conditions experiences of domestic violence, and the important contributions of an intersectional approach, building on the work of Black feminists, in understanding the diversity of experiences of domestic violence.

## Discussion and analysis

### *Historical contributions*

### *Initial studies of nature and extent*

Sociology as a discipline was early to the study of domestic violence. This began in the early 1970s in the United States with the first National Family Violence Survey (NFVS) and its 1985 follow up (Straus, Gelles, & Steinmetz, 1980; Straus & Gelles, 1990). The NFVSs generated the first national estimates of domestic violence in the U.S., providing evidence of widespread physical domestic violence; 16% of couples in both surveys reported physical violence in the past year (Straus & Gelles, 1986). The results also uncovered that physical violence was not limited to married couples, but happened among those cohabiting (which was important to highlight, given the rapidly increasing rates of pre-marital cohabitation in the US and elsewhere) and dating (Stets & Straus, 1990).

### *Measurement of domestic violence and abuse*

Murray Straus (1979) created the Conflict Tactics Scale (CTS) as part of the NFVS. The CTS and its revision (often referred to as the CTS-R or CTS2; Straus, Hamby, Boney-McCoy, & Sugarman, 1996) are multi-item scales for use in surveys and interviews to measure physical abuse, psychological abuse, and sexual coercion among couples. The CTS has been subject to extensive criticism for decades particularly by feminist sociologists (e.g., DeKeseredy & Schwartz, 1998; Dobash, Dobash, Wilson, & Daly, 1992). While the CTS revision addressed some criticisms (e.g., that the original CTS did not include sexual assault or injury), remaining criticisms include that the CTS fails to account for the motives behind, meanings of, context of, and consequences of domestic violence (Ackerman, 2018; DeKeseredy & Schwartz, 1998; Dobash et al., 1992; Kimmel, 2002). All of these differ by gender, and relying on the CTS as designed can lead to over-reporting of victimisation of men and perpetration by women, a belief that domestic violence is perpetrated equally between genders, and a failure to include violent acts perpetrated in an effort to wield control over a partner (Ackerman, 2018; DeKeseredy & Schwartz, 1998; Dobash et al., 1992). In spite of ongoing criticism, the CTS has endured and remains the most widely used measure of physical domestic violence. For example, a recent check (as of July 16, 2020) on the citation website Google Scholar reflected the seminal articles for the CTS (Straus, 1979) and CTS2 (Straus et al., 1996) had been cited 8133 and 7160 times respectively.

### *The gender symmetry debate and Johnson's typology-based solution*

The ongoing controversy originally grounded in the findings and framing of the NFVS (Steinmetz, 1978) and criticisms of the CTS undergird the ongoing debate about the role of gender in domestic violence and led to another major sociological contribution to the study of domestic violence: the creation of Johnson's Typology of Partner Violence (Johnson, 1995, 2008; Johnson & Ferraro, 2000). Findings of equal or higher female-to-male than male-to-female rates of partner violence from the NFVS (Straus & Gelles, 1986) did not reflect the experiences of those who worked with and did research on victims of domestic violence, who saw much higher rates of male-to-female than female-to-male partner violence. This led to a decades-long academic debate about the relationship between gender and perpetration of domestic violence, often referred to as the gender symmetry debate (e.g., Archer, 2000; Kimmel, 2002; Straus, 1999). Simply described, family violence scholars argue that domestic violence is perpetrated at equal rates between genders and feminist scholars argue men perpetrate domestic violence at higher rates than women (Johnson, 1995).

In a seminal paper for the field, Johnson (1995) argued both groups were right, that there are multiple types of domestic violence, and the balance by gender differs between types of domestic violence. Although Johnson argues for more than two types of domestic violence (e.g., violent resistance, familial intimate terrorism, Johnson, 2017), this summary focuses on the two main types key to understanding his solution to the gender symmetry debate. General population survey samples, such as those typically used by family violence scholars (e.g., the NFVS), disproportionately include a type of domestic violence called situational couple violence. Agency samples, like those from criminal justice systems and domestic violence services typically used by feminist scholars, disproportionately include a type of domestic violence referred to as coercive controlling violence (formerly referred to as patriarchal terrorism (Johnson, 1995) and intimate terrorism (Johnson & Ferraro, 2000)). Situational couple violence is the most common type of domestic violence. It is the result of a pattern of escalating conflict in a partnership that is not related to trying to exert power and control, but occurs in the context of a specific conflict when at least one partner uses physical violence. It is equally likely to be perpetrated by men and women. Coercive controlling violence is violence embedded in a larger effort at what had been traditionally conceived of as power and control (Pence & Paymar, 1993), where physical violence is just one tactic a perpetrator will employ to control their partner. This type of violence is less common and is more likely to be perpetrated by men against women. Those who have experienced coercive controlling violence may not participate in general population surveys due to concerns about personal safety if their abuser discovered their participation. However, they may be heavily represented in agency samples, which are often relied on for studies by those coming from a feminist perspective, as they are more likely to need and seek help.

A considerable body of research has tested Johnson's predictions related to types of sample and types of domestic violence, as well as differences between the types. Studies have found differences in the proportion of situational couple violence and coercive controlling violence by type of sample as predicted (Frye, Manganello, Campbell, Walton-Moss, & Wilt, 2006; Graham-Kevan & Archer, 2003). Studies have also found coercive controlling violence is correlated with poorer outcomes for women such as higher levels of injury, poorer mental health, and higher levels of fear (Hardesty et al., 2015; Johnson & Leone, 2005; Leone, Johnson, Cohan, & Lloyd, 2004; Tiwari et al., 2015). Physical violence was more frequent in coercive controlling violence (Hardesty et al., 2015) and women who experienced coercive controlling violence were more likely to engage in formal help-seeking, but were equally or less likely to seek help from informal sources than those who experienced situational couple violence (Leone, Johnson, & Cohan, 2007). Not all studies have found support for differentiation between coercive controlling and situational couple violence on all outcomes (e.g., Anderson, 2008), and it is unclear if patterns hold across race and ethnicity (Bubriski-McKenzie & Jasinski, 2013). The typology has been successfully applied in non-heterosexual partnerships (e.g., Frankland & Brown, 2014) and international contexts (Brown & Chew, 2018; Tiwari et al., 2015).

In spite of this research support, the gender symmetry debate, likened by Johnson (2017) to a zombie, continues (e.g., Hines, Straus, & Douglas, 2020). Those citing empirical evidence of gender symmetry continue to rely predominantly on general population-based surveys, many with college samples, using the CTS or similar measures (e.g., Bates, Graham-Kevan, & Archer, 2014; Straus, 2008). In spite of the ongoing debate, considerable work by sociologists centres on the role of gender, particularly norms about gender, in domestic violence.

## Contemporary contributions

### *Social norms: gender, family, and domestic violence*

Sociology highlights that social norms, which are written and unwritten shared expectations for behaviour, strongly influence behaviour and social interaction. In the case of domestic violence, there is ample evidence of the influence of social norms related to gender and family. Gender norms have important implications for the roles and expectations of men and women in families (most of which remain built upon male-female partnerships) and their interactions, including those that are violent and abusive. Gender is more than a way to distinguish male and female roles. Hegemonic cultural beliefs (the dominant cultural beliefs of a society based on the norms of the group in power, whether that group is in the minority or majority) related to gender maintain a gendered system of inequality in relationships, families, communities, and society. This is achieved by defining behavioural expectations of men and women, which impacts how individuals behave in families and intimate relationships, and translates to gender inequality in distributions of resources at the macro level, organisational practices at the interactional level, and selves and identities at the individual level (Ridgeway & Correll, 2004, pp. 510–511).

While we have witnessed dramatic changes to the social institution of family over the last half century in many countries (e.g., decline in marriage rates, increase in divorce rates, increase of non-married partners living together, differing family structures), which have impacted the role of women within the household (the private sphere) and in the workplace (the public sphere) and vice versa, traditional gender norms and gender inequality remain regarding women's place within the family (e.g., Hochschild, 1989, 1997). Patriarchy, "a system of social structures, and practices in which men dominate, oppress and exploit women" (Walby, 1989, p. 214), remains a key contributor to gender norms and ongoing inequality by gender in private (institutional structures of home and family) and public spheres. Feminist sociologists have argued this includes patriarchy functioning as the primary contributor to domestic violence – where patriarchal norms of male dominance over women gets translated to control and violence (DeKeseredy & Dragiewicz, 2007; Dobash & Dobash, 1979, 1998; Yllo, 1993, 2005). Family violence scholars challenge the role of patriarchy as the main reason behind domestic violence and argue it is only one of many contributing factors, along with sociodemographic variables and cultural acceptance of violence (e.g., Straus & Gelles, 1986).

Research on gender norms and domestic violence in various countries and cultural contexts has largely supported the arguments advanced by feminist sociologists. In other words, patriarchal norms justify men using violence against women in relationships, particularly within marriage, as a general principle. For instance, husbands in Zimbabwe with patriarchal beliefs perpetrated violence against their wives more often than those with less patriarchal beliefs (Fidan & Bui, 2016). Men in Bangladesh who desired to control their wives' lives were far more abusive than those who did not desire such control (Akhter & Wilson, 2016).

The association between patriarchal beliefs and holding gender norms related to gender inequality is not limited to men and husbands – these are also characteristics of women and are related to experiencing domestic violence. Among women in Jordan, it was found that 98% experienced at least one form of domestic violence, more than a quarter believed husbands had the right to control wives' behaviour, and 93% believed wives should obey their husbands (Al-Badayneh, 2012). In rural Bangladesh, men and women equally supported norms that "support strict, traditional, and unequal gender roles and violence against women" (Fattah & Camellia, 2020, p. 776). Women justify domestic violence through a process which involves internalising norms even though it is at their expense (Fattah & Camellia, 2020). This phenomenon is not relegated to countries in the Global South. Research with US samples shows that men use domestic violence as a means of control and a way to maintain traditional masculinity (Peralta & Tuttle, 2013), and African American women with higher acceptance of patriarchal views are more likely to experience domestic violence (Wright & Benson, 2010).

Kinship norms governing gender relationships and power within the household are strongly influential as well with patrilineal societies experiencing more domestic violence. In Ghana, which contains both matrilineal and patrilineal societies, although women experienced domestic violence in matrilineal societies, it was higher for women in patrilineal societies, including higher likelihood of experiencing a continuous pattern of abuse and violent sexual attacks, and, if they retaliated, they were more likely to face increased violence and abandonment (Sedziafa, Tenkorang, & Owuso, 2018).

Violations of gender norms, either in beliefs or behaviours, is associated with increased experience of domestic violence. For example, in a US national sample, gender role incompatibility, such as when a non-traditional woman and traditional man were partnered, resulted in a higher likelihood of male violence (DeMaris, Benson, Fox, Hill, & Wyk, 2003). This carries over to actual violations of gender roles, such that when females earned more money than their male partners, those male partners were more likely to perpetrate domestic violence (Anderson, 1997). Anderson argues that in these cases men use violence as a way to accomplish a masculine image/identity when they were not able to do so through employment and income – thus finding an alternate (albeit maladaptive) manner of maintaining or re-establishing traditional gender roles with male dominance or as some term it, asserting hegemonic masculinity (Connell & Messerschmidt, 2005).

The mismatch of norms in the public or private sphere may be related to domestic violence. At least in some nations in the Global South, violations of gender expectations in the public sphere, represented by increased women's achievement in public endeavours, is related to greater violence in the private sphere, represented by a higher likelihood of experiencing domestic violence. For example, in rural northern India, women experienced more abuse when they achieved a higher status outside of the home (through employment and education) and experienced less abuse when their status was higher in the household (through decision making and mobility) (Mogford, 2011). In Zimbabwe, women's employment was related to increased domestic violence, although gender equality in education and decision making within the household was associated with less domestic violence (Fidan & Bui, 2016). In Malawi, when women's level of education and income exceeded their husband's they were at greater risk for domestic violence (Bonnes, 2016). In short, women experienced less violence when they comported to gendered norms of women having status in the home, but not in public, which is the realm of men.

Although sociologists have done important work on gender norms in general, they also have made key contributions regarding within-culture (or country) variations in gender norms and domestic violence by place – specifically focused on experiences in rural areas, where traditional gender norms may be more likely to have persisted. Reviews of international research show high levels of domestic violence occur in rural areas and women in rural areas are at an increased risk of domestic violence (DeKeseredy, 2019; DeKeseredy, Hall-Sanchez, Dragiewicz, & Rennison, 2016). The structure of patriarchy may be different in rural and urban areas (Websdale & Johnson, 1998). Rural patriarchy (similar to manifestation in urban areas, but different based on social context of rural life) relegates men and women to "separate spheres" and this along with strong patriarchal religious beliefs (and also, characteristics of rural life; i.e., geographic and social isolation, everyone knows everyone, ineffective response of police, availability of guns used for hunting, economic issues), may cause differences in violence between rural and urban areas, at least in the US context. Among rural and urban shelter women in Kentucky the frequency of physical abuse was similar; however, hair pulling, torture, and being shot were more common among rural women (Websdale & Johnson, 1998). Rural and urban women reported similar levels of sexual abuse, with the exception that rural women were more likely to report coercion into sexual relations to prevent abuse towards other household members.

## Social norms: norms about domestic violence

Gender norms are not the only norms related to domestic violence – norms specific to acceptability or justification of domestic violence are also related to domestic violence behaviour. As attitudes about domestic violence have been shown to influence many aspects of domestic violence victimisation and perpetration (Flood & Pease, 2009), considerable research has focused on norms regarding justification or acceptance of domestic violence within and across countries. In reviewing the literature Waltermaurer (2012) found notable differences between countries in overall justification of domestic violence based on ten scenarios (e.g., victim's fault, neglects child, argues back, infidelity, refuses sex, disobeys). Support for domestic violence due to infidelity, for example, varied from a low of 3% justifying it in Cyprus to 63% justifying it in Iran and 66% in Nigeria. Variability by country may depend on other societal level differences, as highlighted by a study of norms regarding justification of domestic violence across 49 low- and middle-income countries (Sardinha & Catalán, 2018). Norms justifying domestic violence varied widely (ranging from 3% to 80% of the population justifying use of domestic violence in at least some situations). Domestic violence justification was lower in countries with more economic equality for women and higher in countries experiencing political conflict. Beyond that, there were differences between men and women overall and in how aspects of society influenced acceptance of domestic violence. Specifically, women were more likely than men to support attitudes justifying domestic violence in 36 of 49 countries, which echoes Waltermaurer's (2012) finding that women held norms more supportive of domestic violence than men in a review of studies from over 60 countries. Women in countries with high female literacy had lower acceptance of domestic violence. Norms accepting of domestic violence were lower for men in more democratic societies and higher for women in countries with more women represented in government.

Much of the research across countries, such as that just reviewed, focuses on justification of domestic violence by men against women. But there is also the issue of norms justifying domestic violence varying according to whether the domestic violence is perpetrated by a male or a female. Both feminist and family violence sociologists have long argued that Americans are more accepting of violence within marriage than other types of violence (Straus et al., 1980), with male violence against women being commonly accepted (Dobash & Dobash, 1998). Yet, research generally finds that domestic violence is viewed as unacceptable by both men and women (Copp, Giordano, Longmore, & Manning, 2019).

Finally, a considerable body of research has honed in on women's attitudes towards domestic violence, perhaps due to the findings in many countries that more women than men subscribe to norms justifying domestic violence. Research with women in four countries revealed high levels of approval of domestic violence against women (Bangladesh: Jesmin, 2015, 2017; India: Kimuna, Djamba, Ciciurkaite, & Cherukuri, 2013; Nigeria: Kunnuji, 2015; Turkey: Marshall & Furr, 2010) – ranging from approximately one in three to 78% identifying at least one type of situation that justifies domestic violence against a woman (Jesmin, 2015, 2017; Kunnuji, 2015; Marshall & Furr, 2010). Approval of domestic violence was common in a number of situations across those studies: neglecting children (18% to 55%), going out without a husband's permission or knowledge (17% to 30%), arguing (23% to 31%), burning food (4% to 29%), and refusing sex (8% to 17%). Research in a number of countries has shown women who believe wife abuse is justified or acceptable are more likely to experience it (India: Kimuna et al., 2013; Nigeria: Kunnuji, 2015; Nwabunike & Tenkorang, 2017; China: Lin, Sun, Liu, & Chen, 2018; Ghana: Tenkorang, Owusu, & Yeboah, 2013; Georgia: Waltermaurer, Butsashvili, Avaliani, Samuels, & McNutt, 2013). A study in China of married and divorced women found that justifying domestic violence (e.g., acceptance of traditional gender roles by justifying abuse for refusing to do housework, going out without telling husband, refusing sex, failing to care for children, disrespecting in-laws, failing to birth a boy, or fighting with husband) was related to experiencing psychological and moderate physical violence, controlling behaviours, and sexual abuse (Lin et al., 2018). Out-of-school adolescent girls in Nigeria who had experience with at least one type of abuse (i.e., emotional/psychological, physical, sexual) were more likely to approve of violence under certain situations (i.e., when a wife did not make food for her husband on time or burnt food) (Kunnuji, 2015).

Research examining the global diffusion of norms regarding domestic violence is not universally focused on negative norms. From 2000 to 2010, women's views in 23 of 26 countries examined became less accepting of domestic violence (Pierotti, 2013). Demographics or socio-economic factors did not have an impact on this trend, suggesting that dissemination efforts of global norms against domestic violence had a wide reach. Limited sociological research does examine cultural differences within countries (e.g., Jiao, Sun, Farmer, & Lin, 2016; Kimuna et al., 2013). For instance, college students' views of gender roles and domestic violence had similarities and differences across three Chinese societies (China, Hong Kong, and Taiwan; Jiao et al., 2016). Students varied by society in how they defined domestic violence. Taiwanese students were most likely to endorse a broad definition, while students in China were most likely to endorse a narrow definition. However, across the three societies, students who were supportive of gender roles related to male dominance had narrow definitions of domestic violence. Students who were less supportive of gender role attitudes and viewed domestic violence as a criminal behaviour endorsed a much broader definition of domestic violence.

## Inequality, intersectionality, and domestic violence

As a field, sociology is concerned with how inequality in communities and societies structures individual experiences. This extends to the relationship between inequality and domestic violence, with studies generally finding that those subject to greater inequality are more likely to perpetrate and experience domestic violence, and are less likely to access formal resources for help and support. For example, Black and Latina/x women in the US have been found to be less likely to access formal resources than white women when experiencing domestic violence (Crisafi & Jasinski, 2016). US women who are low income (earning less than $25,000), have less than a high school education, or are unemployed are more likely to experience domestic violence (Lacey, West, Matusko, & Jackson, 2016).

Sociologists often study the relation of single factors of inequality (e.g., race, gender, income) to domestic violence. Black feminist scholars and activists, notably legal scholar Kimberlé Crenshaw (1989), developed what they termed an intersectional approach. They highlighted the problems with considering only single dimensions of identity in studying people's lived experiences. Approaches that focus on a single dimension exclude those who experience multiple forms of oppression in concert, leading to an incomplete and inaccurate understanding of social problems, including domestic violence (Crenshaw, 1991), which precludes effective solutions. An intersectional approach advocates focusing on "the interaction between gender, race, and other categories of difference in individual lives, social practices, institutional arrangements, and cultural ideologies and the outcomes of these interactions in terms of power" (Davis, 2008, p. 68).

Although not developed by sociologists, many sociologists have taken an intersectional approach to the study of domestic violence which has expanded our understanding of what it means to experience domestic violence. In one heralded example, Richie (1996) focused on Black female domestic violence victims in the US. Using data gathered from life-history interviews of incarcerated women, Richie found Black women's privileged status in the family as children led them to success expectations that were hard to fulfill as adults. When discouraged by barriers and failures in education, work, and the larger social world, they focused on success in the private sphere in the form of having a traditional nuclear family with a male head of household. This rendered them particularly vulnerable to abuse, because all of their success was riding on making their relationship work, even though they had little faith in Black men's ability to meet that ideal. These women avoided seeking support in order to keep their elevated status within their family of origin and they avoided reporting the abuse as a way to protect the Black family (and the Black male) and because of a lack of trust in the police given the history of abuse towards Black males. Others have done important work to highlight experiences at the intersection of race and culture of origin, rather than assuming a uniform experience by race, such as finding that African American women had higher rates of violence than US Caribbean Black women (Lacey et al., 2016).

Although intersectional work on domestic violence by sociologists has focused heavily on the intersections of gender, race, and class (Sokoloff & Dupont, 2005), there has been controversy over how much an intersectional approach should go beyond or include different structural issues from these three intersecting oppressions (Davis, 2008). That said, intersectional approaches have explored other structural marginalities, such as the intersection of gender or gender, race, and class, with immigration and citizenship. For example, gender, immigration status, and country of origin (along with race, sexual orientation, and class) intersect to impact how immigrant women in the United States view domestic violence and access resources for support, where there are commonalities across immigrants but also important differences (Erez, Adelman, & Gregory, 2009). Experiences of immigrant women enduring domestic violence are conditioned by the issues immigrants face in the host country including limited (or no) proficiency in the host country's language, isolation from family and related support systems, changes in economic status, particularly vis-à-vis a male partner, and legal status, all of which can interact differently by country, depending in part on the host country responses to domestic violence and immigrants (Menjívar & Salcido, 2002).

Intersectional work has been important in expanding the definitional boundaries of gender, pushing sociologists to be more inclusive in their studies and challenging traditional theorising of the relationship between gender and domestic violence by highlighting its heteronormative and cis-gendered perspective (Rogers, 2017), as well as identifying related barriers to accessing support and help (Guadalupe-Diaz & Jasinksi, 2016). This negatively impacts the ability of trans survivors to identify what they are experiencing as domestic violence (Guadalupe-Diaz & Jasinski, 2016), and, in concert with experiences coloured by race, can reduce comfort in disclosing domestic violence to the police. For example, non-white and male gay and bisexual individuals who had previously reported same-sex domestic violence to the police reported lower comfort in future reporting (Guadalupe-Diaz, 2015).

Intersecting inequalities can also be used as a tool of domestic violence. In this case, sociologists have worked to root the psychological abuse tactic of gaslighting (making victims feel like they are crazy or imagining an event happened) to social inequalities. Sweet (2019) argues gaslighting is predominantly a sociological phenomenon, made possible by gender and other inequalities. In intimate heterosexual relationships men can leverage ongoing stereotypes and beliefs of women as emotional and irrational to sow seeds of self-doubt and convince women of an alternate reality constructed by the male partner. Successful use of gaslighting depends on multiple facets of inequality. First, due to gender norms and societal gender inequality that gives more power to men, men wield power over women within intimate relationships. Second, due to the larger structure of inequality in society, intersecting inequalities of gender with other identities (due to factors including race, ethnicity, and immigration status) give power to men in relationships. This power emanates from men's ability to take advantage of the reduced likelihood that women with marginalised identities will seek help from formal sources in anticipation of the negative reaction they may encounter. Additionally, due to stereotypes, men hold the advantage of being able to successfully convince outside sources that their female partner is crazy, emotional, and irrational (thereby neutralising avenues for help-seeking). As an example of how intersecting inequality matters for gaslighting, abusers exploit stereotypes of immigrants as being ignorant (e.g., constantly telling a partner she was insane and would be deported because of it if he reported her), and of Black women as being aggressive (e.g., a perpetrator capitalising on stereotypes of Black women as aggressors to convince police she was the aggressor) to discourage help-seeking.

## Conclusions

This chapter has drawn attention to the contributions sociologists made in the early history of studying domestic violence, from conducting the first studies in the US leading to the development of the Conflict Tactics Scale and estimations of prevalence, to advancing the field near the turn of the century with a typology highlighting different types of domestic violence, to more contemporary study of the influence of norms, such as those related to gender and approval of domestic violence, on experiences of domestic violence to transitioning to an intersectional approach to the study of domestic violence. These last two represent hallmarks of sociology – the study of norms and considering how an individual's social location conditions their lived experiences.

## *Limitations*

One chapter cannot include the broad swath of contributions sociology has made to the study of domestic violence and we had to make hard choices regarding what to highlight. While we focused largely on experiences of domestic violence with adult male perpetrators and female victims, excellent work in sociology has extended beyond that focus (e.g., Jasinski, Blumenstein, &

Morgan, 2014). We focused heavily on differences in experiences of domestic violence without looking at how norms and cultural contexts impact other outcomes, such as help-seeking and reporting to police. Others may have chosen to highlight sociological contributions regarding evaluation of policies related to domestic violence, such as that of mandatory arrest laws (Berk, Campbell, Klap, & Western, 1992; Sherman & Berk, 1984), which represent a case of research findings being linked quickly and directly to widespread policy change (although we acknowledge the controversy of the roll-out of the findings (Lempert, 1989; Sherman & Cohn, 1989), and of mandatory arrest policies in general (Chesney-Lind, 2002; DeLeon-Granados, Wells, & Binsbacher, 2006)). We did not, but could have included the influence of neighbourhood, community, and societal contexts (besides patriarchy, gender norms, and norms about domestic violence) where important work has been done (e.g., Benson, Wooldredge, Thistlethwaite, & Fox, 2004; Wright & Benson, 2010). In the end, even with its exclusions and limitations, we trust this chapter has highlighted important contributions of sociology.

## *Final closing remarks*

Sociology as a discipline helped to lay the early foundation of the study of domestic violence (e.g., Straus, 1979; Straus & Gelles, 1986), developing approaches that continue to contribute to its study today. As we embark on a new decade, we look forward to the contributions that intersectional scholarship by sociologists and others in the study of domestic violence can make to understanding societal-level structural contributors to domestic violence, how domestic violence is experienced by women and men with varying lived experiences, and how those different lived experiences impact experiences with help-seeking. We believe in sociology as a discipline, with its practice of the Sociological Imagination. We challenge sociologists to better engage in public sociology – partnering with victims and survivors, with those who work in the field with domestic violence victims and survivors, and with those working to prevent domestic violence to ensure that research and practice inform each other as part of the iterative practice called for in the practice of public sociology. This would represent sociology's greatest contribution to the study of domestic violence – using what we have found to end domestic violence and to lead to better support for survivors.

## Critical findings

* *There are different types of domestic violence.* Domestic violence is not a unitary phenomenon, but rather there are different types of domestic violence with different prevalence by gender, antecedents, and outcomes. Women who experience violence embedded in a larger pattern of control (coercive controlling violence) experience violence that is more serious, frequent, and injurious. These same women have poorer mental health and higher levels of fear.
* *Patriarchal and traditional gender norms matter.* The more strongly a man endorses patriarchal and traditional gender norms, the more likely he is to perpetrate domestic violence. Acceptance of these norms is also widespread among women, and the more strongly a woman endorses those same norms, the more likely she is to have experienced domestic violence.
* *Behaviour violating patriarchal and traditional gender norms matters.* In many countries, when women achieve more than they are "supposed" to in the public sphere or more than their male partner does (such as in terms of education or income), it is more likely that they have experienced domestic violence.

- *Norms regarding acceptance of domestic violence matter.* The more strongly a man accepts norms approving of domestic violence, the more likely he is to perpetrate domestic violence. Acceptance of these norms is also widespread among women, and the more strongly a woman endorses those same norms, the more likely she is to have experienced domestic violence.
- *Lived realities at the intersection of multiple identities matter.* Again, domestic violence is not a unitary phenomenon in that there are important differences in how individuals define and experience domestic violence, and how they engage in seeking help and support (or how they do not).

## Implications for policy, practice, and research

The findings reviewed in this chapter identify a number of shared implications for policy, practice, and research.

- *Attention to intersectionality.* A one-size-fits-all approach to research, policy, and practice is unlikely to yield satisfactory solutions for many, if not most, of those who experience domestic violence. Instead, research can lead the way in understanding the diversity of experiences with domestic violence and help-seeking to identify the different risk factors and needs. Ideally, this research should be done in partnership with victims/survivors and practitioners, many of whom have recognised the diverse needs of survivors, but do not always have the resources to meet all the different needs. Researcher-practitioner partnerships taking an intersectional approach hold the potential to push for policies that will meet the needs of a wider range of victims.
- *Attention to social norms.* Research by sociologists and others has identified patriarchal and traditional gender norms and norms about domestic violence at the individual and societal levels as risk factors for domestic violence. Without detracting from the needed intervention programs aimed at survivors of domestic violence, we need to develop prevention programs aimed at the level of communities and societies. Perhaps these primary prevention efforts can start by taking aim at norms regarding acceptability of domestic violence, which already have evidenced movement in the direction of less acceptance of domestic violence in many countries. This could be guided by work done in the United States, Canada, and Australia targeting norms regarding acceptability of sexual assault.

## References

Ackerman, J. (2018). Assessing conflict tactics scale validity by examining intimate partner violence over-reporting. *Psychology of Violence, 8*(2), 207–217. doi:10.1037/vio0000112

Akhter, R., & Wilson, J. K. (2016). Using an ecological framework to understand men's reasons for spousal abuse: An investigation of the Bangladesh demographic and health survey 2007. *Journal of Family Violence, 31*, 27–38. doi:10.1007/s10896-015-9741-7

Al-Badayneh, D. M. (2012). Violence against women in Jordan. *Journal of Family Violence, 27*(5), 369–379. doi:10.1007/s10896-012-9429-1

Anderson, K. L. (1997). Gender, status, and domestic violence: An integration of feminist and family violence approaches. *Journal of Marriage and the Family, 59*, 655–669. doi:10.2307/353952

Anderson, K. L. (2008). Is partner violence worse in the context of control? *Journal of Marriage and Family, 70*(5), 1157–1168. doi:10.1111/j.1741-3737.2008.00557.x

Archer, J. (2000). Sex differences in aggression between heterosexual partners: A meta-analytic review. *Psychological Bulletin, 126*(5), 651–680. doi:10.1037/0033-2909.126.5.651

Bates, E. A., Graham-Kevan, N., & Archer, J. (2014). Testing predictions from the male control theory of men's partner violence. *Aggressive Behaviour, 40*(1), 42–55. doi:10.1002/ab.21499

Benson, M. L., Wooldredge, J., Thistlethwaite, A. B., & Fox, G. R. (2004). The correlation between race and domestic violence is confounded with community context. *Social Problems, 51*(3), 326–342. doi:10.1525/sp.2004.51.3.326

Berk, R. A., Campbell, A., Klap, R., & Western, B. (1992). The deterrent effect of arrest in incidents of domestic violence: A Bayesian analysis of four field experiments. *American Sociological Review, 57*(5), 698–708.

Bonnes, S. (2016). Education and income imbalances among married couples in Malawi as predictors for likelihood of physical and emotional intimate partner violence. *Violence & Victims, 31*(1), 51–70. doi:10.1891/0886-6708.VV-D-14-00016

Brown, J., & Chew, D. (2018). Prevalence of types of perpetration: Gender and patterns of intimate partner violence within a prison sample in Singapore. *Journal of Aggression, Maltreatment & Trauma, 27*(8), 883–901. doi:10.1080/10926771.2017.1410744

Bubriski-McKenzie, A., & Jasinski, J. L. (2013). Mental health effects of intimate terrorism and situational couple violence among Black and Hispanic women. *Violence Against Women, 19*(12), 1429–1448. doi:10.1177/1077801213517515

Burawoy, M. (2005). For public sociology. *American Sociological Review, 70*(1), 4–28. doi:10.1177/000312 240507000102

Chesney-Lind, M. (2002). Criminalizing victimization: The unintended consequences of pro-arrest policies for girls and women [Reaction Essay]. *Criminology & Public Policy, 2*(1), 81–90.

Connell, R. W., & Messerschmidt, J. W. (2005). Hegemonic masculinity rethinking the concept. *Gender & Society, 19*(6), 829–859. doi:10.1177/0891243205278639

Copp, J. E., Giordano, P. C., Longmore, M. A., & Manning, W. D. (2019). The development of attitudes toward intimate partner violence: An examination of key correlates among a sample of young adults. *Journal of Interpersonal Violence, 34*(7), 1357–1387. doi:10.1177/0886260516651311

Crenshaw, K. (1989). Demarginalizing the intersection of race and sex: A black feminist critique of anti-discrimination doctrine, feminist theory and antiracist politics. *University of Chicago Legal Forum, 14*, 538–554.

Crenshaw, K. (1991). Mapping the margins: Intersectionality, identity politics, and violence against women of color. *Stanford Law Review, 43*(6), 1241–1299. doi:10.2307/1229039

Crisafi, D. N., & Jasinski, J. L. (2016). Within the bounds: The role of relocation on intimate partner violence help-seeking for immigrant and native women with histories of homelessness. *Violence Against Women, 22*(8), 986–1006. doi:10.1177/1077801215613853

Davis, K. (2008). Intersectionality as buzzword: A sociology of science perspective on what makes a feminist theory successful. *Feminist Theory, 9*(1), 67–85. doi:10.1177/1464700108086364

DeKeseredy, W. S. (2019). Intimate violence against rural women: The current state of sociological knowledge. *International Journal of Rural Criminology, 4*(2), 312–331.

DeKeseserdy, W. S., & Dragiewicz, M. (2007). Understanding the complexities of feminist perspectives on woman abuse: A commentary on Donald G. Dutton's rethinking domestic violence. *Violence Against Women, 13*(8), 874–884. doi:10.1177/1077801207304806

DeKeseredy, W. S., Hall-Sanchez, A., Dragiewicz, M., & Rennison, C. M. (2016). Intimate violence against women in rural communities. In J. F. Donnermeyer (Ed.), *The Routledge international handbook of rural criminology* (pp. 171–179). London: Routledge.

DeKeseredy, W. S., & Schwartz, M. D. (1998). *Measuring the extent of woman abuse in intimate heterosexual relationships: A critique of the conflict tactics scales.* US Department of Justice Violence Against Women Grants Office Electronic Resources, Issue.

DeLeon-Granados, W., Wells, W., & Binsbacher, R. (2006). Arresting developments: Trends in female arrests for domestic violence and proposed explanations. *Violence Against Women, 12*(4), 355–371. doi:10.1177/1077801206287315

DeMaris, A., Benson, M. L., Fox, G. L., Hill, T., & Wyk, J. V. (2003). Distal and proximal factors in domestic violence: A test of an integrated model. *Journal of Marriage and Family, 65*, 652–667.

Dobash, R. E., & Dobash, R. P. (1979). *Violence against wives – A case study against the patriarchy.* New York, NY: The Free Press.

Dobash, R. E., & Dobash, R. P. (1998). Violent men and violent contexts. In R. E. Dobash & R. P. Dobash (Eds.), *Rethinking violence against women* (pp. 141–168). Sage. doi:10.4135/9781452243306.n6

Dobash, R. P., Dobash, R. E., Wilson, M., & Daly, M. (1992). The myth of sexual symmetry in marital violence. *Social Problems, 39*(1), 71–91.

Erez, E., Adelman, M., & Gregory, C. (2009). Intersections of immigration and domestic violence: Voices of battered immigrant women. *Feminist Criminology, 4*(1), 32–56. doi:10.1177/1557085108325413

Fattah, K. N., & Camellia, S. (2020). Gender norms and beliefs, and men's violence against women in rural Bangladesh. *Journal of Interpersonal Violence, 35*(3–4), 771–793. doi:10.1177/0886260517690875

Fidan, A., & Bui, H. N. (2016). Intimate partner violence against women in Zimbabwe. *Violence Against Women, 22*(9), 1075–1096. doi:10.1177/1077801215617551

Flood, M., & Pease, B. (2009). Factors influencing attitudes to victims against women. *Trauma, Violence, & Abuse, 10*(2), 125–142. doi:10.1177/1524838009334131

Frankland, A., & Brown, J. (2014). Coercive control in same-sex intimate partner violence. *Journal of Family Violence, 29*(1), 15–22. doi:10.1007/s10896-013-9558-1

Frye, V., Manganello, J., Campbell, J. C., Walton-Moss, B., & Wilt, S. (2006). The distribution of and factors associated with intimate terrorism and situational couple violence among a population-based sample of urban women in the United States. *Journal of Interpersonal Violence, 21*(10), 1286–1313. doi:10.1177/0886260506291658

Graham-Kevan, N., & Archer, J. (2003). Physical aggression and control in heterosexual relationships: The effect of sampling. *Violence and Victims, 18*(2), 181–196.

Guadalupe-Diaz, X. L. (2015). Disclosure of same-sex intimate partner violence to police among lesbians, gays, and bisexuals. *Social Currents, 3*(2), 160–171. doi:10.1177/2329496515604635

Guadalupe-Diaz, X. L., & Jasinski, J. (2016). "I wasn't a priority, I wasn't a victim": Challenges in help seeking for transgender survivors of intimate partner violence. *Violence Against Women, 23*(6), 772–792. doi:10.1177/1077801216650288

Hardesty, J. L., Crossman, K. A., Haselschwerdt, M. L., Raffaelli, M., Ogolsky, B. G., & Johnson, M. P. (2015). Toward a standard approach to operationalizing coercive control and classifying violence types. *Journal of Marriage and Family, 77*(4), 833–843. doi:10.1111/jomf.12201

Hines, D. A., Straus, M. A., & Douglas, E. M. (2020). Using dyadic concordance types to understand frequency of intimate partner violence. *Partner Abuse, 1*, 76–97. doi:10.1891/1946-6560.11.1.76

Hochschild, A. R. (1997). *The time bind: When work becomes home and home becomes work.* New York, NY: Metropolitan Books.

Hochschild, A. R., & Machung, W. A. (1989). *The second shift: Working parents and the revolution at home.* New York, NY: Viking.

Jasinski, J., Blumenstein, L., & Morgan, R. (2014). Testing Johnson's typology: Is there gender symmetry in intimate Terrorism? *Violence & Victims, 29*(1), 73–88. doi:10.1891/0886-6708.VV-D-12-00146

Jesmin, S. S. (2015). Married women's justification of intimate partner violence in Bangladesh: Examining community norm and individual-level risk factors. *Violence and Victims, 30*(6), 984–1003. doi:10.1891/0886-6708.

Jesmin, S. S. (2017). Social determinants of married women's attitudinal acceptance of intimate partner violence. *Journal of Interpersonal Violence, 32*(21), 3226–3244. doi:10.1177/0886260515597436

Jiao, Y., Sun, I. Y., Farmer, A. K., & Lin, K. (2016). College students' definitions of intimate partner violence: A comparative study of three Chinese societies. *Journal of Interpersonal Violence, 31*(7), 1208–1229. doi:10.1177/0886260514564162

Johnson, M. P. (1995). Patriarchal terrorism and common couple violence: Two forms of violence against women. *Journal of Marriage and the Family, 57*(2), 283–294.

Johnson, M. P. (2008). *A typology of domestic violence: Intimate terrorism, violent resistance, and situational couple violence.* Lebanon, NH: University Press of New England.

Johnson, M. P. (2017). A personal social history of a typology of intimate partner violence. *Journal of Family Theory & Review, 9*(2), 150–164. doi:10.1111/jftr.12187

Johnson, M. P., & Ferraro, K. J. (2000). Research on domestic violence in the 1990s: Making distinctions [Review]. *Journal of Marriage and the Family, 62*, 948–963.

Johnson, M. P., & Leone, J. M. (2005). The differential effects of intimate terrorism and situational couple violence: Findings from the national violence against women survey. *Journal of Family Issues, 26*(3), 322–349. doi:10.1177/0192513X04270345

Kimmel, M. S. (2002). "Gender symmetry" in domestic violence: A substantive and methodological research review. *Violence Against Women, 8*(11), 1332–1363. doi:10.1177/107780102237407

Kimuna, S. R., Djamba, Y. K., Ciciurkaite, G., & Cherukuri, S. (2013). Domestic violence in India: Insights from the 2005–2006 national family health survey. *Journal of Interpersonal Violence, 28*(4), 773–807. doi:10.1177/0886260512455867

Kunnuji, M. O. N. (2015). Experience of domestic violence and acceptance of intimate partner violence among out-of-school adolescent girls in Iwaya community, Lagos State. *Journal of Interpersonal Violence, 30*(4), 543–564. doi:10.1177/0886260514535261

Lacey, K. K., West, C. M., Matusko, N., & Jackson, J. S. (2016). Prevalence and factors associated with severe physical intimate partner violence among U.S. Black women: A comparison of African American and Caribbean Blacks. *Violence Against Women, 22*(6), 651–670. doi:10.1177/1077801215610014

Lempert, R. (1989). Humility is a virtue: On the publicization of policy-relevant research. *Law and Society Review, 23*(1), 145–161.

Leone, J. M., Johnson, M. P., & Cohan, C. L. (2007). Victim help seeking: Differences between intimate terrorism and situational couple violence. *Family Relations, 56*(5), 427–439. doi:10.1111/j.1741-3729.2007.00471.x

Leone, J. M., Johnson, M. P., Cohan, C. L., & Lloyd, S. E. (2004). Consequences of male partner violence for low-income minority women. *Journal of Marriage and Family, 66*, 471–489.

Lin, K., Sun, I. Y., Liu, J., & Chen, X. (2018). Chinese women's experience of intimate partner violence: Exploring factors affecting various types of IPV. *Violence Against Women, 24*(1), 66–84. doi:10.1177/1077801216671221

Marshall, G. A., & Furr, L. A. (2010). Factors that affect women's attitudes toward domestic violence in Turkey. *Violence and Victims, 25*(2), 265–277. doi:10.1891/0886–6708.25.2.265

Menjívar, C., & Salcido, O. (2002). Immigrant women and domestic violence: Common experiences in different countries. *Gender & Society, 16*(6), 898–920. doi:10.1177/089124302237894

Mills, C. W. (2000). *The sociological imagination* (Fortieth Anniversary Edition ed.). New York, NY: Oxford University Press, 1959.

Mogford, E. (2011). When status hurts: Dimensions of women's status and domestic abuse in rural Northern India. *Violence Against Women, 17*(7), 835–857. doi:10.1177/1077801211412545

Nwabunike, C., & Tenkorang, E. Y. (2017). Domestic and marital violence among three ethnic groups in Nigeria. *Journal of Interpersonal Violence, 32*(18), 2751–2776. doi:10.1177/0886260515596147

Pence, E., & Paymar, M. (1993). *Education groups for men who batter: The Duluth model.* New York, NY: Springer Publishing Company.

Peralta, R. L., & Tuttle, L. A. (2013). Male perpetrators of heterosexual-partner-violence: The role of threats to masculinity. *The Journal of Men's Studies, 21*(3), 255–276. doi:10.3149/jms.2103.255

Pierotti, R. S. (2013). Increasing rejection of intimate partner violence: Evidence of global cultural diffusion. *American Sociological Review, 78*(2), 240–265. doi:10.1177/0003122413480363

Richie, B. E. (1996). *Compelled to crime: The gender entrapment of battered black women.* New York, NY: Routledge.

Ridgeway, C. L., & Correll, S. J. (2004). Unpacking the gender system: A theoretical perspective on gender beliefs and social relations. *Gender & Society, 18*(4), 510–531. doi:10.1177/0891243204265269

Rogers, M. (2017). Challenging cisgenderism through trans people's narratives of domestic violence and abuse. *Sexualities, 22*(5–6), 803–820. doi:10.1177/1363460716681475

Sardinha, L., & Nájera Catalán, H. E. (2018). Attitudes towards domestic violence in 49 low- and middle-income countries: A gendered analysis of prevalence and country-level correlates. *PLoS One, 13*(10), 1–18. doi:10.1371/journal. pone.0206101

Sedziafa, A. P., Tenkorang, E. Y., & Owuso, A. Y. (2018). Kinship and intimate partner violence against married women in Ghana: A qualitative exploration. *Journal of Interpersonal Violence, 33*(14), 2197–2224. doi:10.1177/0886260515624213

Sherman, L. W., & Berk, R. A. (1984). The specific deterrent effects of arrest for domestic assault. *American Sociological Review, 49*(2), 261–272.

Sherman, L. W., & Cohn, E. G. (1989). The impact of research on legal policy: The Minneapolis Domestic Violence Experiment. *Law and Society Review, 23*(1), 117–144.

Sokoloff, N. J., & Dupont, I. (2005). Domestic violence at the intersections of race, class, and gender: Challenges and contributions to understanding violence against marginalized women in diverse communities. *Violence Against Women, 11*(1), 38–64. doi:10.1177/1077801204271476

Steinmetz, S. K. (1978). The Battered Husband Syndrome. *Victimology: An International Journal, 2*, 499–509.

Stets, J. E., & Straus, M. A. (1990). The marriage license as a hitting license: A comparison of assaults in dating, cohabiting, and married couples. In M. A. Straus & R. J. Gelles (Eds.), *Physical violence in*

*American families: Risk factor and adaptation to violence in 8,145 families* (pp. 227–244). New Brunswick, NJ: Transaction Publishers.

Straus, M. A. (1979). Measuring intrafamily conflict and violence: The conflict tactics (CT) Scales. *Journal of Marriage and the Family, 41*(1), 75–88.

Straus, M. A. (1999). The controversy over domestic violence by women. In X. B. Arriaga & S. Oskamp (Eds.), *Violence in intimate relationships* (pp. 17–44). Thousand Oaks, CA: Sage.

Straus, M. A. (2008). Dominance and symmetry in partner violence by male and female university students in 32 nations. *Children and Youth Services Review, 30*(3), 252–275. doi:10.1016/j.childyouth.2007.10.004

Straus, M. A., & Gelles, R. J. (1986). Society change and change in family violence from 1975 to 1985 as revealed by two national surveys. *Journal of Marriage and the Family, 48*(3), 465–479. doi:10.2307/352033

Straus, M. A., & Gelles, R. J. (Eds.). (1990). *Physical violence in American families: Risk factors and adaptations to violence in 8,145 families.* New Brunswick, NJ: Transaction Publishers.

Straus, M. A., Gelles, R. J., & Steinmetz, S. K. (1980). *Behind closed doors: Violence in the American family.* Garden City, NY: Anchor Press/Doubleday.

Straus, M. A., Hamby, S. L., Boney-McCoy, S., & Sugarman, D. B. (1996). The revised conflict tactics scale (CTS2): Development and preliminary psychometric data. *Journal of Family Issues, 17*(3), 283–316.

Sweet, P. L. (2019). The sociology of gaslighting. *American Sociological Review, 84*(5), 851–875. doi:10.1177/0003122419874843

Tenkorang, E. Y., Owusu, A. Y., & Yeboah, E. H. (2013). Factors influencing domestic and marital violence against women in Ghana. *Journal of Family Violence, 28*, 771–781. doi:10.1007/s10896-013-9543-8

Tiwari, A., Chan, K. L., Cheung, D. S. T., Fong, D. Y. T., Yan, E. C. W., & Tang, D. H. M. (2015). The differential effects of intimate terrorism and situational couple violence on mental health outcomes among abused Chinese women: A mixed-method study. *BMC Public Health, 15*(1), 314. doi:10.1186/s12889-015-1649-x

Walby, S. (1989). Theorizing patriarchy. *Sociology, 23*(2), 213–234.

Waltermaurer, E. (2012). Public justification of intimate partner violence: A review of the literature. *Trauma, Violence, & Abuse, 13*(3), 167–175. doi:10.1177/1524838012447699

Waltermaurer, E., Butsashvili, M., Avaliani, N., Samuels, S., & McNutt, L. (2013). An examination of domestic partner violence and its justification in the Republic of Georgia. BMC *Women's Health, 13*(44), 1–9. doi:10.1186/1472-6874-13-44

Websdale, N., & Johnson, B. (1998). An ethnostatistical comparison of the forms and levels of woman battering in urban and rural areas of Kentucky. *Criminal Justice Review, 23*(2), 161–196.

Wright, E. M., & Benson, M. L. (2010). Immigration and intimate partner violence: Exploring the immigrant paradox. *Social Problems, 57*(3), 480–503. doi:10.1525/sp.2010.57.3.480

Yllo, K. A. (1993). Through a feminist lens: Gender, power and violence. In R. J. Gelles & D. R. Loseke (Eds.), *Current controversies on family violence* (pp. 47–62). Newbury Park, CA: Sage.

Yllo, K. A. (2005). Through a feminist lens: Gender, diversity, and violence. In D. R. Loseke, R. J. Gelles, & M. M. Cavanaugh (Eds.), *Current controversies on family violence* (pp. 19–34). Thousand Oaks, CA: Sage.

# 5

# DOMESTIC VIOLENCE AND ABUSE THROUGH A CRIMINOLOGICAL LENS

*Marianne Hester*

## Introduction

This chapter looks at what it means to look at domestic violence and abuse (DVA) through a criminological lens. It begins with a brief look at the uneasy relationship between criminology and DVA in the history and theory of criminology and the related topic of victimology. Then it goes on to discuss DVA as a crime, and the application of criminal (procedural) justice processes to DVA, ending up with a wider discussion of a criminological approach to DVA that includes risk assessment and wider understanding of 'justice' for victim-survivors.

Criminology is the study of crime and societies' responses. Criminology developed alongside the increasing use of laws as a means of social organisation. Important questions in criminology thus include how crime is defined, and of particular importance to looking at DVA and criminology: who defines and frames what a crime is. As Heidensohn points out: "crime is not merely socially constructed, it is in part socially concernedly constructed, and this has always had a bearing on its study" (Heidensohn, 1989, p. 5).

While modern criminology may be considered to have its roots in the nineteenth century, the topic of DVA within criminology has been largely omitted until quite recently. There are a number of reasons for this, mainly to do with the wider omission of gendered analyses in criminology. It was not until the late 1970s and '80s that DVA began to be considered within criminology, and the development of feminist scholarship was especially crucial in thus "expanding the gaze and the domains of criminology" to include domestic violence and abuse, as well as others forms of violence against women (Burman & Gelsthorpe, 2017, p. 218). By contrast 'race' or ethnicity has had more consideration in criminology (see Phillips & Bowling, 2003). It should also be noted that intersection of race/ethnicity and gender in DVA was the starting point in Kimberly Crenshaw's (1989) development of the notion of 'intersectionality'. Other intersectional concerns, for instance related to people identifying as LGBTQ or with disabilities, have had much less focus in criminology and in research on DVA.

Criminology draws on other disciplines such as sociology, psychology, history, law, anthropology and psychiatry. Various sub-categories are also important, such as victimology, punishment and penology and profiling of perpetrators. Since its inception, criminology can be broadly characterised as developing around two main axes: the collation and analysis of administrative data on offenders (and later also on victims) and a more questioning approach to societal use of criminal approaches.

Early use of administrative data, such as prison records, showed men to be offending and incarcerated to a much greater extent than women. The Italians Lombroso and Ferrero (1895), writing in the late nineteenth century, explained such differences from biological and psychological approaches, seeing individuals who committed crimes as 'born criminal' and defective and backward in evolutionary terms. Moreover, women's biology and childcare responsibilities would normally render them more conservative and passive. Thus while men committed more crime, Lombroso and Ferrero argued that female criminals were indeed more defective and backward in evolutionary terms than male criminals.

Theorists providing a more questioning approach in criminology such as Durkheim (1952) or Merton (1938), and other influential theorists such Cohen (1972), identified that societies have rules and regulations and were concerned with reasons for and forms of deviation from such rules or norms. But the focus (if not always obvious) was on men and boys behaving criminally in the public realm, to the exclusion of what was happening to women in the 'private' realm.

Also relevant to the emerging criminological lens on DVA were the development of the newer strands of criminology that involve deviance and labelling, social control, critical criminology and feminism. Becker (1963), for instance, in his interactionist approach, suggests two ways of looking at deviance. On the one hand the deviant is the focus and problem, or on the other it is the societal reaction that is problematic rather than the individual deviant (Heidensohn, 1989, pp. 68–69) and the use of 'deviant' thereby labels the individual as problematic (see also Cohen, 1972, regarding moral panics). In terms of domestic violence and abuse we can see such approach reflected where it is the victim who is situated as the problem (the deviant woman who caused the violence) rather than the perpetrator. Critical criminology adds power to the mix, that is, the powerful control the powerless (Quinney, 1973), where the tools of the 'powerful' in this respect is deemed the criminal law. We thus have hints of the impunity that tends to be the outcome for perpetrators in DVA cases (especially if they are from a white rather than Black or minority ethnic community).

The 'new victimology' and work on 'fear of crime' in the 1970s were particularly important to shift the focus of criminology to include DVA. The 'new victimology' that emerged from the victim movement of the 1970s in the US and UK, including the women's movement, involved a more critical approach. The generation of victim surveys, initially in the US, from the 1960s (established partly as a means of obtaining better data than that recorded by the police), also opened the window on who was experiencing what crimes and that there appeared to be social differences in this respect. Feminists began to question why women were not carrying out as much crime as men, and why they were committing lesser crimes and less repetitively.

However, victimology also tended to invoke 'victim-blaming', viewing victims as in some way causing violence to themselves. Feminists began to question such victim blaming in DVA, situating the reason instead with the male perpetrator and society. The work of Rebecca and Russell Dobash (1979) in the late 1970s was especially important in placing DVA within the criminological domain, and to bring a critical lens that situated female victims as survivors, and within the wider social context of male power and patriarchy. They showed DVA was not deviant or pathological but normalised within a patriarchal society. The Dobashes, while concluding that few victims of domestic violence ever contacted the police, none the less found that 25% of all violent crimes reported to the police authorities in England and Wales actually took place in the home.

Victim surveys and interviews have thus helped to convey a much clearer picture of the possible criminal victimisation or domestic violence and abuse that goes on in private, behind closed doors, largely from men to women. Crime surveys also began to show that fear of crime was reported to a greater extent by women, even if women were not the group at highest risk of experiencing some of the crime. Women were especially concerned with walking on their own after dark or being raped. One of the early examples, a detailed local survey in 1990 in the UK (Crawford, Jones, Woodhouse, & Young, 1990) found that nearly one in two women felt unsafe in their own homes. Stanko's (1995) work on the fear of crime found that while policy makers advised women to adopt precautionary strategies to minimise violence against them, "Confronting women's fear means confronting the danger women face at the hands of their partners, acquaintances, clients, and co-workers, as well as other potential violence from men inside and outside the home" (Stanko, 1995, p. 49).

## Discussion and analysis

### *DVA as crime*

So is DVA a crime? During the past 30 years in particular there have been significant shifts towards seeing domestic violence as a social and public problem in many countries, including Europe, North America and the UK. Feminists have partly driven this agenda, within a 'culture of control' (Garland, 2001) that has been receptive to increasing criminalisation and recognition of domestic violence as a crime. However, there are only a few countries where DVA is a specific crime, even if the behaviour associated with DVA (such as physical and sexual violence and harassment) may be deemed criminal and other offences applied instead, such as offences of 'violence against the person'. Criminalisation of domestic violence has provided a symbolic and normative condemnation of domestic violence. In the UK for instance this has resulted in a move away from emphasising a woman's own responsibility to solve the problem towards a view of DVA as an unacceptable crime which both state and non-governmental agencies should try to prevent. Pressure from feminists and women's organisations were important in creating this shift.

However, the criminalisation of DVA is a very recent phenomenon. The reason is that patriarchal or male-dominant cultures have generally sanctioned physical punishment of wives by husbands as well as expecting wives to comply with sex or marital rape. Historically, in patriarchal societies, women have been seen as the property of their husbands, and the husband as duty bound to punish wives who transgressed perceived norms. Such approach was exemplified in the nineteenth century by Sir William Blackstone (1895) in his *Commentaries on the Laws of England*. He stated, "the very being or legal existence of the woman is suspended during the marriage, or at least is incorporated and consolidated into that of the husband" (Blackstone, 1895, Book 1 Chapter 15). This allowed the husband to chastise his wife, although this should be 'moderate' and husbands could beat their wives with sticks which were no thicker than their own thumb. Thus, historically DVA was not by any means deemed a crime, but accepted as a means of men controlling 'their' women.

Many countries have of course moved beyond the sanctioning of DVA in marriage and in other intimate partner and family relationships. One approach has been to frame such behaviour as gender-based violence, that is, disproportionately affecting women, and also within a human rights framework. Spain has some of the earliest of such legislation, with DVA behaviour such as physical or psychological violence, threats, coercion and the arbitrary deprivation of liberty, deemed criminal as part of the comprehensive *Organic Act* 1/2004. This Act aims to tackle the type of violence which is

> the manifestation of discrimination, inequality and power of men over women, (which) is perpetrated against the latter by those who are or used to be their spouses or by those to whom they have or used to have an affectionate relationship which has not necessarily involved cohabitation.
>
> (Artículo 1)

As far as female victims of violence are concerned, the law guarantees women's right to have access to information, comprehensive social assistance from the emergency care services, free legal assistance and protection measures in society and the workplace (Bodelon, 2008).

However, the most developed legislation using a human rights framework is the Council of Europe Convention on preventing and combating violence against women and domestic violence (the 'Istanbul Convention', 2011). This is the first such international instrument, and perceives gender-based violence as both a cause and a consequence of inequalities between women and men. To date 34 countries have ratified the Convention and a further 12 countries have signed it. Two of the four pillars that form the Convention, on protection and prosecution, encourage the criminalisation of DVA and enhancement of procedural justice. For instance, Article 52 urges that states legislate for and implement emergency barring orders where the police may be granted the power to order a perpetrator of DVA to vacate the victim's home for a period of time and prohibit the perpetrator from re-entering or contacting the victim. Such barring order may sit between a criminal and civil approach. The implementation of the Convention is also overseen by a formidable inspection framework, the GREVIO, which has resulted in states developing new legislation on DVA. For example, following a GREVIO report, the Danish government have implemented a law on psychological violence, as an element of DVA.

While an important aspect of the debate for criminalisation of DVA included the argument that DVA is 'a crime like any other', in reality DVA is different from other crimes in that DVA perpetrators will use a range of abusive behaviours and over time in order to exert power and control over the victim-survivor. Other crimes not in the context of DVA, whether assault or criminal damage, tend to be largely discrete and one-off incidents. Thus, using existing 'violence against the person' offences to criminalise DVA is limited and does not capture the patterns of coercion and control that a growing body of research and personal testimony have shown that DVA victim-survivors experience. A number of studies have highlighted this problem of repeated incidents of DVA being reported to the police, and the lack of legal means of linking these into the patterns of abuse that they exemplify. In their study of policing in England, Hester (2006) and Hester and Westmarland (2006) reported rates of attrition of more than 96% from police calls for offences related to domestic abuse to conviction or punishment for any crime. A large proportion of the male offenders (but not the female offenders) were 'repeaters'. But because police responded to each complaint anew, criminal sanctions were no more likely after a man's 50th offence than his first (Hester, 2006). As Stark and Hester conclude:

> Offenders were seen through the prism of their offenses. But since, taken alone, these seemed relatively minor, the offenders themselves drew scant notice.
>
> (Stark & Hester, 2019, p. 82)

Following pressure on the UK government, the result was the creation of a new criminal offence of 'coercive and controlling behaviour' in England in 2015. This was followed by consideration of similar laws elsewhere, with a more comprehensive offence of partner abuse in Scotland in 2018 (Burnam & Brooks-Hay, 2018), and the passing or consideration of similar laws by The Irish Republic in 2018, Northern Ireland in 2019 and in Tasmania and Australia (Douglas, 2015). Such legislation has the potential to move beyond merely 'psychological violence' (as specified in the Istanbul Convention), because 'coercive control' may include any form of coercive and controlling behaviour.

## Who are the DVA offenders?

Profiling of perpetrators formed an element of classical criminology, such as the work of Lombroso and Ferrero (1895) referred to earlier. More recent approaches in criminology focused on 'criminogenic' factors, thought to be strongly correlated with criminal reoffending, such as antisocial personality traits, pro-criminal attitudes, criminal associates, substance use, poor marital and family relationships, employment or school problems. Non-criminogenic needs (e.g., major mental disorder, low self-esteem) tend to be seen as less relevant to recidivism than criminogenic needs – but have been found to be important in DVA. While there are numerous empirical studies on the criminogenic needs of offenders more generally, this has not been replicated to the same extent for DVA offenders.

In a US study (Hilton & Radatz, 2018) the authors compared the criminogenic and non-criminogenic needs of 99 DVA offenders, 233 non-DVA violent offenders, and 103 nonviolent offenders, all of whom were men who had undergone institutional forensic assessment. Results indicated that the DVA offenders had more needs than the other two offender groups, and the authors conclude that this supports the increasing focus in perpetrator interventions or programmes on criminogenic treatment needs.

In a study in the UK of DVA offender characteristics, similar characteristics were observed across the sample, especially personality psychopathology, negative early experiences, unemployment and alcohol dependence (Gilchrist et al., 2003). The authors again suggest that these offenders could benefit from intervention which addresses these criminogenic needs, and in particular anger, self-efficacy and perspective-taking and cognitive distortions surrounding masculinity. Moreover, they identified two distinct types of DVA offenders: borderline/emotionally dependent offenders, who were primarily characterised by high levels of interpersonal dependency, high levels of anger and low self-esteem, and antisocial/narcissistic offenders, who were primarily characterised by hostile attitudes towards women, low empathy and had the highest rate of alcohol dependence and previous convictions. Interviews with their partners showed that the types lead to differing patterns of abusive behaviour.

Another UK study, Hester et al. (2006) with a different approach to profiling, defined DVA perpetrators by type of offence recorded by the police, including DVA or non-DVA offences. Perpetrators were tracked through police records over three years. The majority were men (92%) and most of their victims were women (91%). The perpetrators could be placed in one of four groups depending on whether they were repeat offenders: the 'one incident' group, with one DVA incident recorded by the police (n=112); the 'mainly non-domestic violence' group, with one DVA incident but also arrested for other, non-DVA, offences (n=62); those who were 'dedicated repeat domestic violence' perpetrators, who had the highest proportion of male offenders, with numerous DVA incidents but no non-DVA offences (n=62); and finally those who were 'all-round repeat offenders' with a number of DVA incidents as well as non-DVA offences (n=120). It was apparent that the criminal justice system deemed non-DVA offences as more serious, even though the DVA offenders often used extreme violence against their partners. Those in the 'mainly non-DVA' group were thus most likely to be convicted and to receive custodial sentences. Yet, criminal justice interventions appeared to be most effective in relation to the lesser DVA of 'one incident' group but tended not to be effective with the offenders in the other groups, who continued to repeat their behaviour.

## Victims or perpetrators/offenders?

One of the problems with identifying DVA perpetrators within a criminal justice setting is that processes of gendering play into the procedural aspects of the criminal justice system and decisions that police and other criminal justice actors make. The legal system can be understood as a gender regime (Connell, 1987) where distinct norms and assumptions about gender coalesce. Previous research in Britain has identified a range of gendered attitudes and approaches of the police to domestic violence (Hoyle, 1998; Stanko, 1989). Research on police interactions with domestic violence victims and suspects in the United States has shown that male domestic violence suspects were able to influence decisions made by officers at the scene of the crime, minimising their own role as primary aggressors and making women who were the victims appear as perpetrators (Anderson & Umberson, 2001; DeLeon-Granados, Wellsa, & Binsbacher, 2006).

Violence by women may also be minimised by some professionals who do not perceive women as capable of 'doing such a thing' (Fitzroy, 2001), while others perceive violence by women as especially abhorrent and treat it more severely, also because it does not fit the female stereotype (Hester, 2012). One of the classic criminologists, Manheim, first suggested that "the female offender – if punished – meets on the whole with greater leniency on the part of the courts than the male" (Mannheim, 1940, p. 343), what he termed the 'chivalry' approach. But this is not necessarily borne out in practice. Overall there is little evidence of Manheim's 'chivalry' approach, and instead women may actually be treated more harshly by the criminal justice system, for instance where women kill partners they tend to receive harsher sentences than men doing likewise, because women are more likely to be seen as using intent (Wykes, 2001).

In her work on 'Who Does What to Whom', Hester (2012, 2013) explored the differences in approach by the criminal justice system to men and women who had been deemed perpetrators. The study tracked 96 DVA cases through the criminal justice system over six years and compared aspects such as arrest, prosecution and conviction. Gender differences were found relating to the nature of cases, forms of violence recorded, frequency of incidents and levels of arrest. Men were significantly more likely to be repeat perpetrators (Chi-Square 43.619, p=< .000). As expected from previous literature on service samples (Johnson, 2006), the intensity and severity of violence and abusive behaviours from the men was much more extreme. Reflecting the nature and severity of the domestic violence incidents, there were more arrests overall of men than of women. However, women were arrested to a disproportionate degree and were three times more likely to be arrested per incident than were the men. One reason was women's use of weapons, seemingly in situations where they were protecting themselves and their children, but where the police considered that they were the main or primary aggressor. As Miller has also pointed out regarding criminal justice approaches in the US, "Gender neutrality offered by arrest policies may become gendered injustice as women who are not batterers get arrested under laws designed for men who are" (Miller, 2001, p. 104). Even so, it appeared that at least some of the police in the English study were using a gender-sensitive approach to determining the primary aggressor. Such an approach relied on consideration of context and pattern of incidents over time, differentiating between initiator and retaliator, and thus pointing to a primary aggressor.

Of direct relevance here are also other intersectional aspects. Research has found that individuals identifying as LGB or T are less likely to access the criminal justice system due to concerns about discrimination, although GB and T individuals may experience higher rates of DVA than heterosexuals (Donovan & Hester, 2014). Other aspects, such as mental health impacts for the victim-survivors, have also been found to impact especially negatively on the progression of DVA cases through the justice system, with such cases rarely proceeding beyond arrest or to conviction (McPhee, Hester, Bates, Lilley-Walker, & Patsios, in press). Women from Black and minority ethnic communities have also reported experiencing DVA and the justice process differently from white women, with impacts of structural inequality, immigration status and community and faith institutions playing into and complicating the picture to different extents for different individuals (Gangoli, Bates, & Hester, 2019).

## Risk and identifying victims and perpetrators

Risk is a key issue in criminology. Who is at risk of offending, and how risk is mitigated are important questions.

The criminal justice system as such is of course also about risk, the argument being that by arresting and convicting perpetrators and imposing sanctions, risk of further DVA will be reduced – even if that is not necessarily what the evidence indicates, as shown earlier. Walklate (1995) argues that criminology has largely accepted a conventional scientific agenda and thus an understanding of risk as something to be avoided, also leading to problematic links between fear of crime and risk that are gendered but without this being explicit – exemplified by the victim-blaming notion 'why does she not just leave' rather than an emphasis on 'why does he not stop' regarding DVA. One aspect has related to profiling and ascertaining of criminogenic needs of offenders (as outlined previously), involving assessment of the factors that may increase and therefore reduce risk of offending. The fear of crime data and debate referred to earlier also leads to issues of how to reduce risk for the victim-survivors concerned, by perhaps appeasing the perpetrator – that is, acting according to what he wants and when he wants it.

Beck (1992) has suggested that we are now living in a 'risk society' where technology has led to increasing multitudes of and focus on risk. The issue of risk is also echoed in criminological work on DVA. Since the 1990s a whole 'risk industry' has developed with regard to DVA, evident across Europe, whereby the police (and often other agencies) are expected to assess the level of risk a DVA victim-survivor is facing and intervene accordingly. The Council of Europe Istanbul Convention also specifically addresses risk assessment and risk management as a strategy for the prevention of violence against women, with Article 51 outlining risk assessment as an "assessment of the lethality risk, the seriousness of the situation and the risk of repeated violence", including access to firearms.

The European Institute for Gender Equality (EIGE) has recently compiled an overview of risk assessment policies and processes across Europe (EIGE, 2019). The work defines risk assessment as a "decision-making process through which we determine the best course of action by estimating, identifying, qualifying or quantifying risk" and its purpose is to reduce harm to female victims of intimate partner violence and their children. Different approaches to risk assessment in DVA cases were found across Europe, the main approaches involving unstructured clinical decision-making, the actuarial approach and the structured professional judgement approach. In the UK, for instance, use of risk assessment by the police has had a strong actuarial base, using a schema to grade risk for victim-survivors as for instance low (or standard), medium and high, with high-risk victims most likely to be provided with protection and support. Alongside risk assessment there has also in the UK been development of Multi-Agency Risk Assessment Conferences (MARACs) where representatives from a number of relevant agencies, usually led by the police, will make decisions as to what is required to make victim-survivors safe. Only high risk cases tend to be referred to MARAC. There is evidence, however, that if victim-survivors do not comply with the decisions of MARAC, which may be difficult if decisions are not developed with victim-survivors' needs and wishes in mind, then it is victim-survivors who are blamed for 'non-compliance' rather than the shortcomings in professional approaches (Rogerson, 2015).

The EIGE overview identified a number of challenges in relation to risk assessment. One aspect was the tendency to focus mainly on the 'violence incident model' of reoffending and revictimisation that reflects physical assault and risk of physical injury, underestimating the impacts of psychological violence or coercive control. Thus the tools being used cannot adequately pick up the patterns of behaviour that underpin DVA. Also a gender perspective is missing from most countries' risk assessment instruments. One example regards Slovakia, where the police are required to pose the same questions to each victim, regardless of gender (or other characteristics). In another example, in Ireland, the law is gender neutral, focusing on the victims while "strategies for controlling abusive behaviour of the perpetrator are noticeably absent". EIGE conclude that:

> elements such as the victim-centred approach, inclusion of gender and intersectionality aspects, as well as the estimation of coercive control, are embedded in risk assessment instruments, to enable the improvement of their predictive validity and effectiveness. It is also important that police officers who are going to apply and develop more accurate procedures receive the relevant training.
>
> (EIGE, 2019, p. 36)

## DVA and criminal justice system

So should we even consider using criminal justice approaches in relation to DVA?

Applying a criminological lens shows us that criminalisation of DVA is by no means straightforward. Neither formal nor informal justice systems are, or can, be independent of the culture and social mores within which they develop and through which they are administered. As Walklate (2008) observes, even when policy makers harness the progressive or symbolic function of law, for example promoting equalities and (de-)criminalising particular acts, its translation through the criminal justice system is not assured. The prevailing social and cultural context is implicated at each point: from the victim-survivor's interpretation of what has happened, to their decision whether or not to disclose their experience of GBV, to the assessment of police and prosecutors on whether there is sufficient evidence to proceed, to the response in court of juries and/or magistrates/judges.

Criminalisation has therefore been contested as an effective approach to tackling DVA. Feminists have highlighted the tension between a focus on often individualised criminal justice interventions and the potential detriment to women's empowerment and understandings of gender inequality that may result (Mills, 2003; Stark, 2007). Women's right to protection may have increased but the power and control she experiences from her partner may have merely transferred to the criminal justice system. As Walklate suggests, this results in a central tension regarding engagement with the criminal justice system: "The potential for such transformation [shift of control from partner to police] in the guise of protection strikes at the very heart of the policing dilemma with respect to 'domestic' violence" (Walklate, 1995, p. 112). The contradictions have also led to more generic criticism about the appropriateness of criminal and legal remedies to DVA more widely and raised questions about how and why individual victim-survivors access such sources of help, whether they achieve their intentions, let alone whether victim-survivors see them as 'just'. This is especially problematic for Black and minority ethnic women where the relationship to the criminal justice system involves race as well as gender.

There are also specific questions about the outcomes of using a criminal justice approach, and the difficulties for victim-survivors of DVA to obtain what they would consider to be justice. Theoretical and empirical analyses of 'justice', whether in relation to the response of the police or the wider criminal or civil justice systems, or in relation to victim-survivors' perspectives, have been at the forefront of research about domestic and sexual violence since the 1970s (e.g. Radford, 1987). Alongside the provision of emergency refuge services, campaigners and researchers sought to improve the police and court responses to both protect women and children and to increase the effectiveness of justice agencies. The past decades have seen considerable changes in the policies and practices of police and prosecutors in relation to these crimes, including provision of information and support for victims, and the introduction of specialist domestic violence courts and dedicated police units for domestic and sexual violence across a number of countries.

Research in the 1980s in the United States initially indicated that use of arrest helped to reduce repeat offending in relation to domestic violence (Sherman, 1993). Later work was less clear-cut, and has increasingly shown that, while arrest may act as a deterrent for some domestic violence perpetrators, it does not appear to have such an effect on the more chronic domestic violence offenders (e.g. Buzawa & Buzawa, 2003). The more limited research on court outcomes appears to indicate that conviction, especially where it involves jail or probation rather than fines, may reduce repeat offending. However, the proportion of domestic violence cases resulting in conviction tends to be very small (Hester, 2006; McPhee et al., in press). Generally, research indicates that criminal justice interventions are unlikely to be effective on their own, and are most effective when carried out in a context of wider support and advocacy for those victimised (Buzawa & Buzawa, 2003; Hester et al., 2020).

One aspect of relevance using a criminological lens, also alluded to earlier, is the large rate of attrition of DVA cases in criminal justice systems, that is the dropping out of cases, so that they do not result in prosecution let alone conviction. Both underreporting and attrition is a problem identified in relation to a number of crimes but has particular characteristics in DVA cases. Violence Against Women Surveys and Victim Surveys conducted in many European countries have identified the high percentage of women victims of their partners' violence who do not want to press charges and the poor responses to women who report crime apparent in attrition rate studies (see Hester, 2006; WOSAFEJUS, 2008). In the UK a series of government reports have highlighted the problem of the 'justice gap' that exists between reporting and prosecuting DVA (HMICFRS, 2017).

A study comparing criminal justice processes in DVA cases in Italy, Spain, Romania and the UK found that, while the legal and policy contexts in the four countries differed in important respects, the major issues for the women who attempted to use the system in response to DVA were in many ways similar (WOSAFEJUS, 2008). Attrition in England was especially high, with only about 4% of DVA cases reported to the police resulting in conviction. In Spain attrition was much less, with more than a third of cases resulting in conviction, partly because a wider range of abusive behaviours were taken into account, and because the courts would consider cases more readily even if victim-survivors withdrew. However, women were generally concerned that engagement with the criminal justice system would not provide safety, that they would not be taken seriously, and that it would not stop the perpetrator from using further violence and abuse against them; they were influenced by their children in decisions of whether to contact the police or support charges. Across the four countries there were differences in women's engagement with the criminal justice system linked to socio-economic status and ethnicity or nationality: in England, for instance, they were less likely to use the criminal justice system if they were immigrants or from Black and minority ethnic communities, but the opposite was the case in Italy. Across the four countries professional responses revealed similarities, with instances of professionals minimising women's experiences and blaming them for lack of engagement with the criminal justice system. Women were generally more likely to remain engaged with the system where they were offered good support. However, differences in responses were also apparent, and England and Spain, with more developed and 'progressive' policies, saw fewer instances of cases being trivialised as 'just domestics'. Bodelon (2008) notes, however, resistance to the Spanish Act 1/2004 concerning the underpinning approach to intimate partner or ex-partner violence, which involved a focus on inequalities between men and women. A Spanish judge interviewed in the research explained that, in general, his colleagues did not subscribe to the theoretical approach underpinning this law "because they do not agree with it. I am critical, not about the existence [of the Act] but about the way it has been developed" (Judge interview – EP14).

Reviews of criminal justice practices, for instance in England and Wales, have also continued to highlight serious problems in the response to victims of DVA. An All Party Parliamentary Group hearing on domestic and sexual violence and justice in the UK Parliament (Women's Aid, 2014) indicated that 90% of respondents felt there were barriers in place preventing women from accessing justice. An audit of police force responses to DVA found that while many forces had good policies on paper, this was often not translated into effective practice on the ground, concluding that policing was "not good enough" and was putting victims at "unnecessary risk" (HMIC, 2014).

Individuals may be deemed to be acquainted, even tacitly, with the 'rules' of different gender regimes. As such, victim-survivors of DVA understand that they may need to bridge the gap between the formal promise of law and the subjective reality of the criminal and other justice systems if they are to achieve justice. Thus, withdrawing from the criminal justice system process, for example, could indicate positive, self-protective choices by victim-survivors who recognise the type of 'justice' on offer is not what they want or how they want it, and it may simultaneously be an indictment of the prevailing formal systems, raising the question of what alternatives are available. That was evident in the four-country WOSAFEJUS study, and also in recent research in the UK where 251 victim-survivors were asked about their perceptions and experience of 'justice'. The latter research indicates what a 'victim-focused justice' could look like, with emphasis on accountability by perpetrators for what they have done, acknowledgement by others that it has happened (family, friends, community, agencies and services), empowerment through support (The Justice, Inequality and GBV project, https://research-information.bris.ac.uk/en/projects/justice-inequality-and-gender-based-violence).

## Conclusion

The chapter has provided an insight into what it means to apply a criminological lens to DVA, that such perspective is relatively recent and has relied heavily on input from feminist criminologists. While criminologists have looked at DVA and crime from a number of perspectives, including individual and social approaches, particularly important questions have emerged from looking at DVA through a criminological lens with regard to gender, power and criminal justice systems, and how these issues shape what is seen as crime, how such crimes are treated by the criminal justice system and the importance of engaging with victim perspectives. It is also clear that wider intersectional issues, for instance related to minority ethnic communities, for those identifying as LGBT and/or Q, or regarding those with disabilities, are important in shaping the experiences and outcomes of the individuals and communities concerned, and need greater focus in deepening criminological approaches to DVA.

## Critical findings

- DVA is a relatively new area to be looked at through a criminological lens, brought to the fore by the work of feminists and their focus on gender and crime.
- There is a lack of work on intersectionality in relation to DVA through a criminological lens.
- In many countries DVA is not a specific crime, but behaviours associated with DVA (e.g. physical violence, rape) may be deemed crimes.
- Different country contexts lead to different engagement by women with criminal justice systems in DVA cases. For instance, women who were immigrants or from Black and minority ethnic communities contacted the police less than other women in England, but the opposite was the case in Italy.
- Processes of gendering play into the procedural aspects of the criminal justice system and decisions that police and other criminal justice actors make. This can make it more difficult to identify DVA perpetrators within a criminal justice setting and lead to minimising of DVA by male perpetrators.
- Assessing risk is a key concern in criminal justice systems and may be challenging in relation to DVA unless patterns of DVA behaviours and gender are taken into account.
- Criminal justice approaches may not provide just outcomes, and victim-survivors look to other forms of 'justice' that include accountability and empowerment.

## Implications for policy, practice and research

- To ensure victim-survivors obtain just outcomes, there is need to look beyond criminal justice systems and to focus on wider notions of justice such as accountability and empowerment. DVA services are more likely to provide such wider 'justice' for victim-survivors.
- To be effective, risk assessment needs to move beyond the 'violence incident model' of reoffending and revictimisation that tends to reflect merely physical assault and risk of physical injury, and should include impacts of psychological violence or coercive control.
- Legislation that criminalises DVA needs to take into account that DVA involves patterns of behaviours over time rather than a single incident.
- There is a gap in research on DVA through a criminological lens regarding intersectional issues (for instance intersections involving ethnicity, LGBTQ identity and/or disability).

## References

Anderson, K., & Umberson, D. (2001). Gendering violence: Masculinity and power in men's accounts of domestic violence. *Gender & Society, 15*, 358–380.

Beck, U. (1992). *Risk and society: Towards a new modernity*. London: Sage.

Becker, H. (1963). *The outsiders: Studies in the sociology of deviance* (pp. 1–18). New York: Free Press.

Blackstone, Sir W. (1895). *Commentaries on the laws of England*. Retrieved from https://oll.libertyfund.org/titles/blackstone-commentaries-on-the-laws-of-england-in-four-books

Bodelon, E. (2008). *In WOSAFEJUS*. Retrieved from http://ec.europa.eu/justice/grants/results/daphne-toolkit/content/wosafejus---why-doesn't-she-press-charges-understanding-and-improving-women's-safety-and_en

Burman, M., & Brooks-Hay, O. (2018). Aligning policy and law? The creation of a domestic abuse offence incorporating coercive control. *Criminology & Criminal Justice, 18*, 67–84.

Burman, M., & Gelsthorpe, L. (2017). Feminist criminology: Inequalities, powerlessness, and justice. In A. Liebling, S. Maruna, & L. McAra(Eds.), *The Oxford handbook of criminology* (pp. 213–238). Oxford: Oxford University Press.

Buzawa, E. S., & Buzawa, C. G. (2003). *Domestic violence: The criminal justice response*. London: Sage.

Cohen, S. (1972). *Folk devils and moral panics*. London: Routledge.

Connell, R. W. (1987). *Gender and power*. Sydney, Australia: Allen and Unwin.

Council of Europe. (2011). *Council of Europe Convention on preventing and combating violence against women and domestic violence*, CETS No.:210. Geneva: Council of Europe.

Crawford, A., Jones, T., Woodhouse, T., & Young, J. (1990). *The second Islington crime survey*. London: Middlesex University, Centre for Criminology.

Crenshaw, K. (1989). Demarginalizing the intersection of race and sex: A black feminist critique of anti-discrimination doctrine, feminist theory and antiracist politics. *University of Chicago Legal Forum, 1989*, Article 8. Retrieved from http://chicagounbound.uchicago.edu/uclf/vol1989/iss1/8

DeLeon-Granados, W., Wellsa, W., & Binsbacher, R. (2006). Arresting developments, trends in female arrests for domestic violence and proposed explanations. *Violence Against Women, 12*(4), 355–371.

Dobash, R. E., & Dobash, R. P. (1979). *Violence against wives: A case against the patriarchy*. New York, NY: The Free Press.

Donovan, C., & Hester, M. (2014). *Domestic violence and sexuality: What's love got to do with it?* Bristol: Policy Press.

Douglas, H. (2015). Do we need a specific domestic violence offence? *Melbourne University Law Review, 39*, 434–471.

Durkheim, E. (1952). *Suicide: A study in sociology*. London: Routledge & Kegan.

EIGE. (2019). Retrieved from https://eige.europa.eu/gender-based-violence/risk-assessment-risk-management

Fitzroy, L. (2001). Violent women: Questions for feminist theory, practice and policy. *Critical Social Policy, 21*, 7–34.

Gangoli, G., Bates, L., & Hester, M. (2019). What does justice mean to black and minority ethnic (BME) victims/survivors of gender-based violence? *Journal of Ethnic and Migration Studies*. doi:10.1080/1369183X.2019.1650010

Garland, D. (2001). *The culture of control: Crime and social order in contemporary society*. Oxford: Oxford University Press.

Gilchrist, E., Johnson, R., Takriti, R., Weston, S., Beech, B., & Kebbell, M. (2003). *Domestic violence offenders: Characteristics and offending related needs*. London: Home Office.

Heidensohn, F. (1989). *Women and crime*. London: Palgrave Macmillan.

Hester, M. (2006). Making it through the criminal justice system: Attrition and domestic violence. *Social Policy and Society, 5*(1), 79–90.

Hester, M. (2012). Portrayal of women as intimate partner domestic violence perpetrators. *Violence Against Women, 18*(9), 1067–1082.

Hester, M. (2013). Who does what to whom? Gender and domestic violence perpetrators in English police records. *European Journal of Criminology, 10*, 623–637.

Hester, M., Eisenstadt, N., Morgan, K., Ortega Avia, A., Walker, S.-J., & Bell, J. (2020). *Evaluation of the drive project – A three-year pilot to address high-risk, high-harm perpetrators of domestic abuse*. Bristol: SafeLives. Retrieved from http://driveproject.org.uk/wp-content/uploads/2020/02/DriveYear3_UoBEvaluationReport_Final.pdf

Hester, M., & Westmarland, N. (2006). Domestic violence perpetrators. *Criminal Justice Matters, 66*, 34–35.

Hester, M., Westmarland, N., Gangoli, G., Wilkinson, M., O'Kelly, C., Kent, A., & Diamond, A. (2006). *Domestic violence perpetrators: Identifying needs to inform early intervention*. Bristol: University of Bristol in association with the Northern Rock Foundation and the Home Office.

Hilton, N. Z., & Radatz, D. L. (2018). The criminogenic and non-criminogenic treatment needs of intimate partner violence offenders. *International Journal of Offender Therapy and Comparative Criminology*, *62*(11), 3247–3259.

HMIC. (2014). *Everyone's business: Improving the police response to domestic abuse*. London: HMIC. Retrieved from www.hmic.gov.uk/wp-content/uploads/2014/04/improving-the-police-response-to-domesticabuse.pdf

HMICFRS. (2017). *A progress report on the police response to domestic abuse*. London: HMICFRS. Retrieved from www.justiceinspectorates.gov.uk/hmicfrs

Hoyle, C. (1998). *Negotiating domestic violence*. Oxford: Clarendon.

Johnson, M. (2006). Conflict and control: Gender symmetry and asymmetry in domestic violence. *Violence Against Women, 12*(11), 1003–1018.

The Justice, Inequality and GBV project. Retrieved from https://research-information.bris.ac.uk/en/projects/justice-inequality-and-gender-based-violence

Lombroso, C., & Ferrero, W. (1895). *The female offender*. London: T Fisher Unwin.

Mannheim, H. (1940). *Social Aspects of Crime in England between the Wars*. London: Routledge

McPhee, D., Hester, M., Bates, L., Lilley-Walker, S. J., & Patsios, D. (in press). Criminal justice responses to domestic violence and abuse in England and Wales: An analysis of case attrition and inequalities using police data. *Policing and Society*.

Merton, R. K. (1938). Social structure and anomie. *American Sociological Review*, *3*(5), 672–682.

Miller, S. L. (2001). The paradox of women arrested for domestic violence. *Violence Against Women, 7*(12), 1339–1376.

Mills, L. (2003). *Insult to injury: Rethinking our responses to intimate abuse*. Princeton, NJ: Princeton University Press.

Phillips, C., & Bowling, B. (2003). Racism, ethnicity and criminology. Developing minority perspectives. *The British Journal of Criminology*, *43*(2), 269–290. doi:10.1093/bjc/43.2.269

Quinney, R. (1973). Crime control in capitalist society: A critical philosophy of legal order. *Issues in Criminology*, *8*(1), 75–99.

Radford, J. (1987). Policing male violence – Policing women. In J. Hanmer & M. Maynard (Eds.), *Women, violence, and social control*. London: Palgrave Macmillan.

Rogerson, B. (2015). How a needs-led approach to MARAC cases delivers effective outcomes: The evidence. *Safe: The Domestic Abuse Quarterly*, *52*, 10–14.

Sherman, L. W. (1993). *Policing domestic violence: Experiments and dilemmas*. New York, NY: The Free Press.

Stanko, A. E. (1989). Missing the mark? Policing battering? In J. Hanmer, J. Radford, & E. Stanko (Eds.), *Women, policing and male violence*. London: Routledge.

Stanko, B. (1995). Women, crime and fear. *The Annals of the American Academy of Political and Social Science*, *539*(1). doi:10.1177/0002716295539001004

Stark, E. (2007). *Coercive control: How men entrap women in personal life*. Oxford: Oxford University Press.

Stark, E., & Hester, M. (2019). Coercive control: Update and review. *Violence Against Women*, *25*(1), 81–104.

Walklate, S. (1995). *Gender and crime*. London: Prentice Hall Harvester Wheatsheef.

Walklate, S. (2008). What is to be done about violence against women? Gender, violence, cosmopolitanism and the law. *British Journal of Criminology*, *48*(1), 39–54.

Women's Aid. (2014). *Women's access to justice, from reporting to sentencing*. All-Party Parliamentary Group on Domestic and Sexual Violence. Bristol: Women's Aid (England). Retrieved from www.womensaid.org.uk/page.asp?section=0001000100100029&sectionTitle=APPG+on+Domestic+and+Sexual+Violence

WOSAFEJUS. (2008). Retrieved from http://ec.europa.eu/justice/grants/results/daphne-toolkit/content/wosafejus---why-doesn't-she-press-charges-understanding-and-improving-women's-safety-and_en

Wykes, M. (2001). *News, crime and culture*. London: Pluto Press.

# 6

# DOMESTIC VIOLENCE THROUGH A HUMAN RIGHTS LENS

*Jane Freedman*

## Introduction

Whilst it might seem clear to many today that domestic violence is an abuse of the human rights of its victims, for a long time, international human rights law was deemed inappropriate for dealing with domestic violence cases. The principal reason for this was the supposed incompatibility between the "public" sphere of international human rights, and the "private" sphere of the home or family in which domestic violence occurs. Whilst human rights law was developed to protect individuals from abuses by the State (Thomas & Beasley, 1995), domestic violence as a manifestation of abuse not by the State but by another individual was thus outside the remit of human rights law (Bettinger-Lopez, 2008). Today, in great part thanks to feminist mobilizations, domestic violence has been recognized as a human rights issue and is explicitly addressed in various international human rights laws and conventions. There has thus been a clear advance in the international normative framework for protecting victims of domestic violence (Joachim, 2007). However, despite this recognition in international human rights laws and norms, we can argue that women's human rights to be free from domestic violence are still not being realized due to a range of factors, including both a continuing reticence by States to acknowledge domestic violence as a human rights issue, especially when this comes into conflict with other political priorities and policies, and by procedural and other barriers that prevent victims of domestic violence from accessing justice through the mobilization of human rights law. Further, it can be argued that the move itself to place the issue of domestic violence at the centre of universal human rights discourse can lead to the de-historicization and de-territorialization of this violence by imposing a universal model drawn from the experience of women in the Global North, and that the universalist tendencies of human rights can also mask inequalities between women within States. In this chapter we will first trace the way in which domestic violence came to be considered an issue for human rights, before addressing some of the issues which arise from the use of human rights norms and discourse to tackle domestic violence, and some of the barriers which still exist to the protection of victims of domestic violence under human rights law. We will use the case studies of domestic violence in conflict and post-conflict, and domestic violence as a form of gender-based persecution in asylum claims to illustrate some of the limits to the human rights framework for claiming protection for victims of domestic violence.

## Discussion and analysis

### *Putting domestic violence on the human rights agenda*

The recognition that domestic violence is a human rights issue arrived relatively late within the institutionalization and globalization of normative human rights instruments. In fact, we can argue that the recognition of domestic violence as a breach of human rights has only been assured since the early 1990s as a result of widespread feminist mobilizations and lobbying of international human rights bodies. The reasons for this late adoption of domestic violence (or more widely violence against women or gender-based violence) as an international human rights issue can be attributed to three interlinked factors. Firstly, the widely entrenched division between the public and the private, and the belief that international human rights law should deal with public relations amongst States, and protection of citizens from public breaches of rights carried out by the State. Within this framework, domestic violence which by definition occurs in the private or domestic sphere was not considered a proper object for human rights laws or conventions. Secondly, human rights law has traditionally granted a privileged position to civil and political rights, at the expense of economic, social and cultural rights (although there is a formal recognition that all of these rights are interdependent). And as Sullivan explains:

> The liberal ideology underlying much of civil and political rights discourse views the law, principally as a means of regulating State intervention in private life, generally without acknowledging the role of the State itself in constructing the separation of public from private life.
>
> (Sullivan, 1995, p. 127)

The privileging of civil and political rights thus leads human rights law to focus more on con-straining the power of the State than on affirming its duties to ensure rights (Sullivan, 1995). Thirdly, we can point to the importance of norms regarding the family and the protection of the family and its privacy. This centrality of the family as a unit, which should be protected, leads to the ignoring or neglecting of abuses which are committed within the family itself. To quote Sullivan again, "Because the family is the site of many of the most egregious violations of women's physical and mental integrity, any blanket deference to the institution of the family or privacy rights within the family has disastrous consequences for women" (Sullivan, 1995, p. 127). These three constraints meant that it took a large-scale feminist mobilization to put women's rights onto the human rights agenda, and in particular to argue for the recognition of domestic violence as a human rights issue.

From the 1990s onwards the recognition that domestic violence is a breach of human rights has been substantiated by the adoption of a range of international norms and standards around violence against women including domestic violence. Feminist mobilizations around interna-tional conferences gradually led to the acknowledgement that violence against women, includ-ing domestic violence, is an international human rights issue. To gain this recognition, activists used the argument that States' failure to protect women from violence is in itself a human rights violation, and that States must exercise "due diligence" not only in not perpetrating vio-lence against their citizens, but in actively protecting these citizens from abuse (Bunch, 1990; Thomas & Beasley, 1995). Due diligence can be explained as the principle that a State "bears the duty of preventing, protecting, investigating, and compensating for wrongs committed by the state, its agents, and more recently nonstate actors" (McWilliams & Ni Aolain, 2016). Led by the Center for Women's Global Leadership, based in the USA, a massive mobilization around the 1993 UN Conference on Human Rights in Vienna was organized. This mobilization involved a worldwide petition calling for violence against women to be considered as a central issue of the conference (Friedman, 1995), and for the recognition of "gender violence as a universal phenomenon which takes many forms across culture, race and class . . . as a violation of human rights requiring immediate action" (Cited in Bunch & Frost, 2000). The Vienna Declaration issued at the conclusion of the Conference was hailed as a milestone in recognizing violence against women as a breach of human rights. Article 18 of the Declaration states that:

> The human rights of women and the girl child are an inalienable, integral and indivisible part of human rights. . . . Gender-based violence and all forms of sexual harassment and exploitation, including those resulting from cultural prejudice and international trafficking, are incompatible with the dignity and worth of the human person, and must be eliminated.

As Kelly remarks, the use of the strongest human rights language was a sign that gender-based violence including domestic violence was finally being taken seriously as a human rights issue (Kelly, 2005).

The Vienna Conference also called for the appointment of a special rapporteur on violence against women, and the drafting of a declaration on the elimination of violence against women (Engle Merry, 2006). The UN Declaration on the Elimination of Violence Against Women (DEVAW) was duly adopted in 1993 and the following year, in 1994, the UN Commission on Human Rights appointed a special rapporteur as requested. The role of the Special Rapporteur is to investigate the issue of violence against women and to suggest measures to be taken by governments, regional and international organizations to prevent such violence and bring remedies to victims.

International feminist mobilization meant that the issue of violence against women was also introduced into other international human rights conventions. Whilst the issue of violence against women was a notable omission from the original CEDAW Convention (1979), "this glaring omission was arguably the impetus behind the committee responsible for supervising the treaty's implementation to issue two general recommendations on violence against women" (Edwards, 2011, p. 8). The CEDAW Committee's General Recommendation No. 19 (1992) thus states that violence against women constitutes discrimination against women and impairs or nullifies women's enjoyment of human rights and fundamental freedoms. General Recommendation No. 19 also underlined States' active responsibility for protecting women, affirming that:

> Discrimination under the Convention is not restricted to action by or on behalf of Governments. . . . Under general international law and specific human rights covenants, States may be responsible for private acts if they fail to act with due diligence to prevent violations of rights or to investigate and punish acts of violence, and for providing compensation.

And more recently, General Recommendation No. 35 (2017) updates the previous recommendation and includes a recognition of the structural causes of violence and notably "the ideology of men's entitlement and privilege over women". General Recommendation No. 35 also calls for recognition of the impacts of multiple and intersecting forms of discrimination on women's experiences of violence.

In addition to these international commitments on violence against women, there are also regional conventions including the 1994 Inter-American Convention on the Prevention, Punishment, and Eradication of Violence Against Women (also known as the Belem Convention), and the Protocol to the African Charter on Human and People's Rights on the Human Rights of Women of 2003 (also known as the Maputo Protocol). Most recently, in 2011, the Convention on Preventing and Combating Violence Against Women and Domestic Violence (the Istanbul Convention) was adopted by the Council of Europe. The Istanbul Convention has been seen as particularly significant by women's rights activists because unlike other soft law conventions, it is legally binding on States (McQuigg, 2017). A monitoring mechanism called the GREVIO (the Group of Experts on Action Against Violence Against Women) has been set up to monitor States' adherence to the Convention and to report regularly on this. Perhaps most significantly the Istanbul Convention has been praised for the way in which it links violence against women to underlying structures of gender inequality and defines violence against women as both a cause and a consequence of gendered power relations. The Convention thus states explicitly that the elimination of violence against women requires a holistic approach, incorporating the attainment of gender equality. And whilst other Conventions have tended to subsume the question of domestic violence in the wider issue of violence against women or gender-based violence, the Istanbul Convention has a specific definition of domestic violence in its Article 3 which affirms that:

> "Domestic violence" shall mean all acts of physical, sexual, psychological or economic violence that occur within the family or domestic unit or between former or current spouses or partners, whether or not the perpetrator shares or has shared the same residence with the victim.
>
> (Council of Europe, 2011, Article 3b)

There has thus been great progress made in enshrining the issue of domestic violence within human rights laws and norms. However, the fact that much of this remains in soft law is problematic in that it relies on the will of individual States to implement international human rights norms at the national level. As McWilliams and Ni Aolain argue,

> Norm development is merely a starting point. The contemporary challenge clearly lies in enforcement, preventing a backlash to the normative rules, and closing off avenues for cultural relativism to be used as a rationale at the national level to prevent these rules from becoming operative.
>
> (McWilliams & Ni Aolain, 2016, p. 10)

The non-binding nature of much of this normative framework means that national governments may feel free to ignore it when other political priorities arise. In a report for the UN, for example, it was found that out of a sample of twenty States, none had fulfilled their obligations of timely submission of reports to the international treaty monitoring bodies (McQuigg, 2011). International human rights norms can be used for "naming and shaming" to attempt to force national governments to take action on certain issues, and they are also a useful tool for local activists to help them put the issue of domestic violence on the national political agenda, and to claim international legitimacy in doing so. But barriers still remain. In the following section we will explore the question of universalism of international human rights, and whether this undermines the legitimacy and efficacy of these norms.

## *Problems of universalism*

Whilst the acceptance that domestic violence is a human rights issue, and its incorporation into international human rights law has been widely welcomed, this use of international laws and norms could also be argued to be problematic, in that it has led in some cases to the imposition of a universalist framework which is in fact based on norms from the Global North, into other contexts where this framework may not in fact be suitable. Engle Merry (2006) has discussed at length the problems of vernacularization of international human rights norms into local and national settings and the difficulties that this engenders. Amongst several "conundrums" she highlights in "applying human rights to local places", is the problem that "human rights law is committed to setting universal standards using legal rationality, yet this stance impedes adapting those standards to the particulars of local context" (Engle Merry, 2006, p. 5).

Some post-colonial feminist activists contend that feminists from the Global North arguing from a position of supposed "universalism" are in fact guilty of "othering" women in the Global South, painting them as "victims" of essentialized gendered and cultural models (Razack, 1995; Kapur, 2002). These universal models are applied without consideration of how varying local cultures construct their norms and ideas on family, marriage, law or violence, for example (Morgaine, 2007). As Razack argues, the issue of violence against women has played a central role in the "women's rights are human rights" campaign by providing a universal signifier of woman, often de-historicized and de-territorialized, and neglecting the various systems and forms of oppression, violence and inequality which exist between North and South (Razack, 1995). Proponents of universal rights have in some cases portrayed their defence of women's human rights and the fight against domestic violence as a struggle against cultural relativism which they argue justifies impunity for perpetrators of domestic violence on the grounds of the defence of culture or tradition. But in doing so there is a risk of essentializing "other" cultures as bad for women, whilst ignoring the aspects of cultures in countries of the Global North which also facilitate or exacerbate the incidence of domestic violence.

Concerns about the universalizing nature of human rights discourse on violence against women are explored in Hajjar's analysis of the interactions of Islamic family law and human rights discourse on violence against women in Muslim societies (2004). She argues that contrary to some feminist arguments, engaging seriously with religious beliefs and practices does not equate with condoning cultural relativism and thus justifying violence against women. Instead she advocates a comparative analysis which focuses on the central role the State plays in struggles over religion and women's rights as they come to bear on issues of domestic violence. This type of comparative analysis allows us to escape from the dichotomy between universalism and cultural relativism, and to perceive that in all States there are to different degrees struggles over these issues, and that in each case local contextualization is important to understand how the struggle against domestic violence can be understood as part of a wider struggle to ensure that the State protects the rights of all of its citizens.

Linked to the already mentioned concerns with the pretend universalism of human rights norms, and the need for contextualization, is the way in which States may discriminate between citizens not only on the basis of gender, but on that of race, religion, social class, etc. In particular, there are questions to be asked about whether or not States guarantee the right to protection from domestic violence to all women equally, or whether indigenous and migrant women are in general less protected than others (Kelly, 2016). Grewal, for example, points to the importance of the critique by black feminists in the US who have challenged the mainstream women's human rights movement for their failures to employ a comprehensive and culturally sensitive framework and analysis which would consider the situation of black women (Grewal, 1999).

Similarly, research on domestic violence against indigenous women has shown the necessity of not assuming a universal rights framework, and of considering the violence not only of gender, but of race, post-colonialism, and of being a minority with less access to all social, economic and political resources (Andrews, 1996). These critiques do not completely negate the importance and role of international human rights in fighting domestic violence but do show the necessity of a nuanced and complex view which understands the way in which global rights must be contextualized within different national and local contexts.

## *Domestic violence in conflict and post-conflict*

A focus of international human rights interventions concerning violence against women in recent years has been on the prevalence of violence in conflict and post-conflict. In 2000 the UN Security Council passed Resolution 1325 on Women, Peace and Security, a move that was hailed by the transnational feminist community as a great step forward in addressing gender issues and gender-based violence in international policies as it was in fact the first time that the Security Council had discussed and passed a resolution on women's rights and gender issues. As with previous international conventions and declarations on the elimination of violence against women, the placing of the question of gender-based violence on the international agenda must be welcomed (especially considering its long absence). However, there have also been criticisms of the way in which the question of gender-based violence has been framed in international political discussion, as well as some of the ways in which States and international organizations have designed programmes and activities on the ground to prevent violence and support "victims". One of the issues which arises is that the focus on sexual violence during conflict and post-conflict, and specifically sexual violence committed by armed groups, might obscure the question of domestic violence which is also prevalent in conflict and post-conflict settings. The widespread prevalence of rape and sexual violence during the Rwandan genocide or during ongoing conflicts in the Democratic Republic of Congo or Sudan, for example, have drawn international attention and have led to the creation of initiatives such as the Preventing Sexual Violence in Conflict Initiative (PSVI) launched by the UK Government in 2013, an initiative which has been criticized for the ways in which it has framed the issue of sexual violence in conflict (Kirby, 2015). Although this global public and political attention to the issue of sexual violence and rape in conflict can be welcomed if it brings a greater response to the problem, it can also be argued that the focus has been switched entirely to this sub-section of the range of different forms of violence against women which has diverted attention and action away from the fight against other forms of violence including domestic violence in the countries concerned. Targeting the elimination of rape in conflict has narrowed the focus of actions even further to target rape and sexual violence committed as a direct result of armed conflict, that is committed by soldiers or armed groups, ignoring other forms of violence which result from or are exacerbated by conflict. Research in the Democratic Republic of Congo, for example, has shown that increased attention to and funding for initiatives to prevent rape and sexual violence and to support victims of such violence, have resulted in a decrease in attention paid to other forms of violence such as domestic violence (Douma & Hilhorst, 2012; Freedman, 2015a). This neglect is particularly worrying as domestic violence has been shown to have increased during the conflict and post-conflict period in the country.

Thus, although there has been much research on sexual violence in conflict, there is far less that explores other forms of gender-based violence such as domestic violence which occurs during or as a result of conflicts. As a result, there is very little evidence about the ways in which conflicts may cause or exacerbate different forms of violence such as domestic violence.

Incidents of domestic violence, for example, may thus be masked by the high attention paid to sexual violence in conflict situations (Stark & Ager, 2011; Hossain et al., 2014) although there is evidence that conflict increases rates of perpetration of violence against women in the home (Stark & Ager, 2011; Horn et al., 2014). Sexual violence by non-combatants may also be overlooked although there is evidence that this also increases during times of armed conflict (Kaufman & Williams, 2015). Existing research suggests that those working to prevent violence against women need to spend more time advocating at legal and policy levels for stronger mechanisms for the prevention of violence within the home (Stark & Ager, 2011).

## Public versus private violence: domestic violence in refugee law and policy

An illustrative example of the barriers that exist to the utilization of human rights for protection of victims of domestic violence is that of the consideration of domestic violence as a grounds for protection under international refugee law. The 1951 Convention on the Status of Refugees, like many international conventions of its time, does not consider gender as a grounds for granting refugee status. A refugee is defined under the 1951 Convention, Article 1(A)2 as a person who

> owing to a well-founded fear of being persecuted for reasons of race, religion, nationality, membership of a particular social group or political opinion, is outside the country of his nationality and is unable, or owing to such fear is unwilling to avail himself of the protection of that country; or who, not having a nationality or being outside the country of his former habitual residence as a result of such events, is unable, or owing to such fear is unwilling to return to it.

Whilst there have been ongoing debates on whether gender should be added as a sixth ground of persecution under the Convention, the favoured solution advanced by the United Nations High Commission for Refugees (UNHCR) is that in States' application and interpretation of the Convention they should take gender-related forms of persecution, including domestic violence, into account under one of the other five grounds of persecution. In practice, this means that most cases related to gender-based violence including domestic violence are currently treated under the category of a "particular social group", and that women who flee from domestic violence and seek asylum in another country have to prove that they are members of such as "particular social group". As argued earlier, one of the main reasons for the late integration of domestic violence into international human rights conventions was the belief that this was a "private" matter which was not a suitable domain of intervention for international laws or norms. This belief that domestic violence is a private or family matter persists in many States with regard to their application of refugee laws and constitutes a barrier to women's claims for this reason (Freedman, 2015b).

As domestic violence is considered as a private or family matter in many countries and frequently remains invisible, even if it is reported to the police, no action is taken (Boyd, 2018). Many women do not, therefore, even contemplate seeking protection from their own national authorities, let alone fleeing to seek international protection in another State. But for those that do try and claim asylum on the grounds of domestic violence, there are many obstacles. These are exacerbated by the fact that in all of the States which grant asylum, domestic violence is also widespread, and in these States as well there may be a lack of effective action to protect women nationals from this type of violence. The normalization of domestic violence is thus so pervasive that it is often not registered as being a proper ground for claiming asylum. One of the most famous cases in which a woman attempted to claim asylum on the grounds of domestic violence was that of Rodi Alvarado, a Guatemalan woman, who sought asylum in the US to escape brutal beatings and violence from her husband. The immigration authorities in the US admitted that the violence she had suffered was "heinous" and acknowledged that although she had sought protection from the Guatemalan police, she had received no help from them. They found, however, that because her husband's actions were "private" and "independent", her treatment could not be qualified as persecution under the terms of the Geneva Convention (Heyman, 2005).

This evocation of a public-private division means that in practice domestic violence is a type of violence often dismissed as "irrelevant" to asylum claims, even when the women who experience domestic violence can expect no help or protection from the police or State authorities in their country of origin. Because this type of violence takes place within the family, and is indeed perpetrated by family members, it is somehow perceived as less severe than other types of violence which are experienced in the public sphere (Copelon, 1994). A woman who is severely beaten by her husband or father can thus expect less recognition from immigration officials and judges than one who is beaten by the police in her country of origin. Crawley, for example, recounts the experience of two women from Ghana who sought asylum in the UK. They had both suffered severe domestic violence at the hands of their husbands. One of the women recounts the violence thus:

> My husband started chasing girls after my son was born. He wouldn't come home. If I said something about it he would beat me, with his hands, his belt. I had a very swollen face. He beat me for three years. He said if I tried to stop him he would cut me with knives and kill me. He didn't want me to divorce and his family has to divorce me.
>
> (Ghanaian woman, cited in Crawley, 2001, p. 318)

Although the abuse this woman and her compatriot suffered was so severe that they both fled the country without their children, their asylum claims were described as "frivolous". The adjudicator at the appeal hearing of one of the women claimed that as far as he understood the law, "being beaten up by your husband is not a ground for asylum however deplorable it might be" (cited in Crawley, 2001, p. 319). This type of official reaction shows the way in which violence which takes place within the home is still considered less "serious" and less worthy of official attention by immigration officials than other forms of violence, even though a woman who is beaten in her home every day by her husband or intimate partner may under other criteria of judgement be considered just as much a victim of "persecution" as a political prisoner who is beaten by a guard in his prison cell. The continuing failure of States to interpret refugee law in a way which gives adequate protection to victims of domestic violence can be seen as a result of the "securitization" of migration policy and the general reluctance of richer States in the Global North to admit refugees. The idea of widening protection to victims of domestic violence goes against this political will to limit migration, including asylum and refugee migration. Thus, the advances in international law recognizing the "due diligence" of States to offer adequate protection against violence have not been fully incorporated into the area of refugee law. This remains one area where the human rights of victims of domestic violence are not fully respected, and the international protection that is offered remains weak.

## Conclusions

The previous examples show that despite progress in ensuring that domestic violence is recognized as an international human rights issue, the fact of including domestic violence in international human rights laws and conventions has not in itself guaranteed greater protection for the victims of such violence. Moreover, it seems clear that some victims of domestic violence are far more able to avail themselves of international human rights norms in this respect than others, depending on their geographical location, and their social, economic and political situation. One of the ongoing problems is the non-binding nature of much of the normative human rights framework, and the difficulties in ensuring the implementation of human rights law, meaning that as Copelon remarks: "the international human rights system still operates more in rhetoric than in reality" (Copelon, 2003). This is evident in the example of the (non)protection of women claiming asylum when fleeing domestic violence as discussed earlier.

To make human rights norms effective in fighting domestic violence and in seeking redress for victims, it is thus necessary to push national governments to take more responsibility for protecting the human rights of their citizens. It is also vital that the issue of domestic violence be considered in a wider context of gender inequalities which are situated within an unequal global system, and to realize that victims of domestic violence are situated within specific local contexts which must be taken into account when thinking about their human rights. When thinking about domestic violence it is thus necessary to theorize about its place within wider structural gender inequalities – economic, political and social. Therefore, to make any real inroads into combating and eventually eliminating domestic violence, it is vital to tackle the basic structural gender inequalities which underlie it, and to analyze and take action on institutionalized forms of economic and gender inequality at national and international levels. Measures such as land reform to allow women access to and ownership of land, economic and employment opportunities to reduce economic inequalities between men and women, and measures to increase women's political participation and representation, can reduce these structural gender inequalities and provide the basis for a more gender equal society. Recognition that women's experiences of physical and sexual violence are inextricably linked to these other forms of social, economic and political inequality, means that to be effective, responses to violence must also be holistic and address all of these forms of gender inequality. This focus on wider structural gender inequalities, including global inequalities based on relations of violence and domination between the Global North and South, should allow for a more situated vision of domestic violence and of the way in which universal human rights discourse can be challenged to take into account the lived situations of women in their local contexts. Reilly argues for forms of cosmopolitan feminism which are at once committed to international human rights laws, but at the same time take into account the "intersectionality of different forms of oppression, across economic, social, cultural, and political domains" (Reilly, 2007, p. 194). This is a prerequisite for harnessing the full power of human rights in the global struggle to eliminate domestic violence and to seek justice for victims of this violence.

## Critical findings

- Despite progress in ensuring that domestic violence is recognized as an international human rights issue, the fact of including domestic violence in international human rights laws and conventions has not in itself guaranteed greater protection for the victims of such violence.

- Campaigning and implementation of human rights norms for victims of domestic violence has sometimes been hampered by the dichotomies created by the debates over universalism versus cultural relativism.
- The ability to benefit from international human rights norms and conventions as a protection from domestic violence depends to a great extent on the identity and the location of the person concerned. Asylum seekers, refugees and migrants, indigenous women, women living in conflict zones, for example, find it much harder to access justice.

## Implications

- The main challenge that exists today is ensuring that global norms recognizing domestic violence as a human rights violation are enforced at local and national levels.
- To do so it is important to overcome oppositions between feminists over universalism versus cultural relativism and to understand the ways in which global rights must be contextualized within different national and local contexts.
- It is also vital to recontextualize debates over domestic violence within the wider global context of gender inequalities, including global inequalities based on relations of violence and domination between the Global North and South.
- International human rights laws and conventions can only be effectively implemented locally if they take account of the intersectionality of various forms of oppression and violence.

## References

Andrews, P. (1996). Violence against Aboriginal women in Australia: Possibilities for redress within the international human rights framework. *Albany Law Review, 60*, 917.

Bettinger-Lopez, C. (2008). Human rights at home: Domestic violence as human rights violation. *Columbia Human Rights Law Review, 40*(1), 19–78.

Boyd, M. (2018). Refuge from violence: A global comparison of the treatment of domestic violence asylum claims. *Berkeley La Raza LJ, 29*, 1.

Bunch, C. (1990). Women's rights as human rights: Toward a re-vision of human rights. *Human Rights Quarterly, 12*(4), 486–498.

Bunch, C., & Frost, S. (2000). Women's human rights: An introduction. In *Routledge international encyclopaedia of women global women's issues and knowledge*. New York: Routledge. Retrieved from http://www.cwgl.rutgers.edu/globalcenter/whr.Html

Copelon, R. (1994). Surfacing gender: Re-engraving crimes against women in humanitarian law. *Hastings Women's LJ, 5*, 243–266.

Copelon, R. (2003). International human rights dimensions of intimate violence: Another strand in the dialectic of feminist lawmaking. *American University Journal of Gender, Social Policy and the Law, 11*, 865–876.

Council of Europe. (2011). *Convention on preventing and combating violence against women and domestic violence*. Strasbourg: Council of Europe. Retrieved from https://www.coe.int/en/web/conventions/full-list/-/conventions/rms/090000168008482e

Crawley, H. (2001). *Refugees and gender: Law and process*. Bristol: Jordan Publishing Limited.

Douma, N., & Hilhorst, D. (2012). *Fond de commerce? Assistance aux victims de violences sexuelles en République Démocratique du Congo*. University of Wageningen, Netherlands: Occasional Papers No. 03.

Edwards, A. (2011). *Violence against women under international human rights law*. Cambridge: Cambridge University Press.

Engle Merry, S. (2006). *Human rights and gender violence: Translating international law into local justice*. Chicago and London: University of Chicago Press.

Freedman, J. (2015a). *Gender, violence and politics in the Democratic Republic of the Congo*. Aldershot: Ashgate.

Freedman, J. (2015b). *Gendering the international asylum and refugee debate*. Basingstoke: Palgrave Macmillan.

Friedman, E. (1995). Women's human rights: The emergence. In J. Peters & A. Wolper (Eds.), *Women's rights, human rights: International feminist perspectives* (pp. 18–35). New York and London: Routledge.

Grewal, I. (1999). 'Women's rights as human rights': Feminist practices, global feminism, and human rights regimes in transnationality. *Citizenship Studies, 3*(3), 337–354.

Hajjar, L. (2004). Religion, state power, and domestic violence in Muslim societies: A framework for comparative analysis. *Law & Social Inquiry, 29*(1), 1–38.

Heyman, M. G. (2005). Domestic violence and asylum: Toward a working model of affirmative state obligations. *International Journal of Refugee Law, 17*(4), 729–748.

Horn, R., Puffer, E. S., Roesch, E., & Lehman, H. (2014). Women's perceptions of the effects of war on intimate partner violence and gender roles in two post-conflict West African Countries. *Conflict and Health, 8*(12).

Hossain, M., Zimmerman, C., Kiss, L., Kone, D., Bakayoko-Topolska, M., David Mannan, K. A., . . . & Watts, C. (2014). Men's and women's experiences of violence and traumatic events in rural Côte d'Ivoire before, during and after a period of armed conflict. *BMJ Open, 4*(2).

Joachim, J. (2007). *Agenda setting, the UN and NGOs: Gender violence and reproductive rights*. Washington, DC: Georgetown University Press.

Kapur, R. (2002). Un-veiling women's rights in the 'War on Terrorism'. *Duke Journal of Gender Law and Policy, 9*, 211–225.

Kaufman, J. P., & Williams, K. P. (2015). Women, DDR and post-conflict transformation: Lessons from the cases of Bosnia and South Africa. *Journal of Research in Gender Studies, 5*(2), 11–53.

Kelly, L. (2005). Inside outsiders: Mainstreaming violence against women into human rights discourse and practice. *International Feminist Journal of Politics, 7*(4), 471–495.

Kelly, L. (2016). *Moving in the shadows: Violence in the lives of minority women and children*. London and New York: Routledge.

Kirby, P. (2015). Ending sexual violence in conflict: The preventing sexual violence initiative and its critics. *International Affairs, 91*(3), 457–472.

McQuigg, R. J. (2011). *International human rights law and domestic violence: The effectiveness of international human rights law*. London and New York, NY: Routledge.

McQuigg, R. J. (2017). *The Istanbul convention, domestic violence and human rights*. London and New York, NY: Routledge.

McWilliams, M., & Ni Aolain, F. (2016). Moving slowly to regulate and recognize: Human rights meets intimate partner sexual violence. In Kersti Yllö & M. Gabriela Torres (Eds.), *Marital rape: Consent, marriage, and social change in global context* (pp. 187–199). Oxford: Oxford University Press.

Morgaine, K. (2007). Domestic violence and human rights: Local challenges to a universal framework. *Journal of Sociology and Social Welfare, 34*(1), 109–130.

Razack, S. (1995). Domestic violence as gender persecution: Policing the borders of nation, race, and gender. *Canadian Journal of Women and the Law, 8*(1), 45–88.

Reilly, N. (2007). Cosmopolitan feminism and human rights. *Hypatia, 22*(4), 180–196.

Stark, L., & Ager, A. (2011). A systematic review of prevalence studies of gender-based violence in complex emergencies. *Trauma, Violence and Abuse, 12*(3), 127–134.

Sullivan, D. (1995). The public/private distinction in international human rights law. In J. Peters & A. Wolpe (Eds.), *Women's rights human rights: International feminist perspectives* (pp. 126–134). London and New York, NY: Routledge.

Thomas, D. Q., & Beasley, M. E. (1995). Domestic violence as human rights issue. *Albany Law Review, 58*(4), 1119–1148.

# 7

# TACKLING DOMESTIC VIOLENCE AND ABUSE USING A RIGHTS-ORIENTED PUBLIC HEALTH LENS

*Anuj Kapilashrami*

## Introduction

The framing of gender-based violence (GBV) as a 'public health' problem is relatively nascent, with earliest developments in the field dating back to the 1990s. Scholarship and policy debates in this period emphasised the 'epidemic' proportion that GBV had risen to; justifying a societal and systemic response. Such attention from the international health community was a result of the long-standing efforts of women's movements and human rights advocates in highlighting the significant health burden imposed by GBV at both international and national levels (Mitra, 2011; Bhate-Deosthali, Rege, & Prakash, 2013). Internationally, a series of declarations on violence against women[1] (VAW), developed in the UN Commission on the Status of Women and UN General Assemblies in 1991 and 1993, highlighted the resulting physical, psychological, reproductive harms and morbidities among women. In some countries, this trend was marked by the establishment of specific institutions as well as legislative and constitutional reforms, for example, the formation of the National Centre for Injury Prevention and Control in the UK as part of the Centres for Disease Control and Prevention in 1991. However, it was only in 1996 at the World Health Assembly in Geneva when member states adopted a resolution declaring violence a leading worldwide public health problem and placed VAW as a core priority on the international agenda (Resolution WHA49.25: Preventing violence: a public health priority). It regarded the elimination of VAW as a prerequisite for women's holistic health and instructed member states to implement a "comprehensive national strategy to promote women's health throughout their lifespan" with due attention to "prevention and treatment of diseases and conditions affecting women, as well as responding to VAW" (CEDAW, 1999). Subsequently, the first World Report on Violence and Health brought out by the World Health Organization (WHO) in 2002 made a compelling case for adopting a public health approach. It critiqued the hitherto "reactive and therapeutic" response of the health sector, calling for a more comprehensive and holistic approach to tackle the complex phenomenon of violence.

A public health perspective on GBV, and more specifically on Domestic Violence and Abuse[1] (DVA), is predicated on its widespread health and social consequences as well as the growing acknowledgement of the role of healthcare institutions (e.g. health facilities) and professionals in timely recognition and response. However, in comparison to other approaches for example, human rights, criminal justice or family violence (see the other chapters in this section of the Handbook), a public health perspective is much less understood (Nakray, 2013). Consequently, there are few empirical studies and insights on what a public health approach entails, not least how comprehensive health systems and strategies can be designed to effectively address DVA. Attending to this gap begs an important question: does classifying violence as a public health issue mark a shift in our approach to tackling violence and, if so, what does a public health response to DVA entail?

This chapter attempts to respond to this question by elucidating a public health perspective to examine DVA and its determinants and approaches that can prevent further occurrence and mitigate its consequences. The analysis presented in this chapter is structured around three objectives addressed in three corresponding parts. I first establish a public health imperative for attending to DVA by presenting the health burden resulting from it, as well as its wider socio-economic and societal burdens. For this purpose, I draw on existing population level studies and analysis on scale, magnitude, nature and consequences of DVA, and comment on the forms and types of victimisation that are omitted from the estimates and burden of disease measures. I then elaborate what a public health approach entails and the principles that could inform design of effective policies and programmes. Adopting a socio-ecological framework, I critically review the evidence base on risk factors of DVA and outline pathways to effectively tackle these risks, thereby preventing domestic violence. In the final section, I present examples of integrated health systems' response to DVA, reviewing evidence on their effectiveness and highlighting promising areas for wider societal and institutional changes.

The chapter combines evidence from my research that examined health systems' response to GBV in India and extensive review of scholarship and evidence in this field. It also draws on experiential learnings from my long-standing engagement with women's movements and women's health and rights advocacy on VAW. Central to this engagement were appraisals of interventions and policy advocacy in India around a range of DVA issues including sex-selection, inclusion/recognition of marital rape in rape laws, medical violence in delivering sexual and reproductive health services among others.

At the outset, however, it is important to note that the term 'domestic violence' remains contested and variously defined. Of particular relevance here is the Southern feminist critique of the dominant discourse that rests on a Western conceptualisation of DVA that involves an 'intimate partner' and a unified understanding of context as 'nuclear household', heteronormative institutions or that of stable political economies (Mirza, 2017; Kapilashrami, 2017; Alsaba & Kapilashrami, 2016). Elsewhere, I have argued that such framing overlooks the complex nature of 'family' in non-Western societies, the specificities (of culture and transitory contexts) in patterns of abuse and help-seeking, and the deep-rooted patriarchal norms and institutions within which such practices are embedded (Kapilashrami, 2017). Consequently, policy and institutional responses to DVA tend to focus primarily on presence of laws, availability of legal aid and counsel services, and processes of adjudication, assuming that the availability of these material goods/resources guarantees uptake by those most in need. Such perspective disregards any differences in social position of women (with regards to ethnicity, legal status, age, etc.) that prevent uptake of these provisions by some communities and in certain contexts (ibid.). Critiquing this perspective, in this chapter, I also discuss how public health approaches must go beyond such a restrictive paradigm that renders dimensions of diversity and structural inequalities invisible.

From such standpoint, I view DVA as rooted in unequal gender-power relations at the household and societal level that get mediated by multiple, interacting structures of inequalities and oppression (race/ethnicity, caste, sexual orientation, religion). I also emphasise the centrality of a life cycle approach that sees violence as much wider, cutting across all life stages to include violence faced by children (e.g. excess child mortality among girls, sex-selective abortions, child marriage), adolescents and adults before and once married, as well as the aged in the domestic sphere. DVA is therefore not restricted to physical, emotional and psychosocial abuse experienced by women in hetero-sexual marital relationships but also those forms that place young girls, children and the aged at increased threat or incidence of such abuse.

## DVA – a public health 'pandemic'

The case for recognising DVA as a public health issue rests on recognition of two fundamental aspects: its pervasiveness (widespread prevalence) and its health and wider societal burden (i.e. DVA being a significant cause of morbidity and mortality, affecting not only individuals but households and communities). Cumulatively, these aspects have resulted in an indiscriminate use of public health terminologies such as 'pandemic', 'epidemic' for DVA (Knaul et al., 2020). I explore these two aspects next.

*Violence as a pervasive threat* relates to the public health understanding of population exposure and risk. According to this perspective, violence is viewed not as individual threats but as a pervasive, cyclical phenomenon with intergenerational effects, suggesting that no society and population group is immune.

While there are considerable regional and country variations, as per available statistics, the lifetime prevalence of violence in the domestic sphere (measured primarily in relation to intimate partner violence in ten countries) varies between 15% and 71% (Garcia-Moreno et al., 2006). A study examining prevalence of violence in marriage in five countries in South Asia (Jeejebhoy, Santhya, & Acharya, 2014) from 2000–2013 found 10–38% women reporting severe violence that included being hit, kicked, choked, burned, threatened with a weapon or forced to have sex over the course of their marital life. It's noteworthy however that country-level statistical evidence on prevalence of DVA is scant, and varies substantially across studies due to differences in populations and settings, inadequate adaptation of tools and methodological challenges of standardisation and validation (Kalokhe et al., 2017). Moreover, these focus largely on physical beating and/or sexual abuse. Feminist research and advocacy agenda in Southern contexts brought to fore other forms of abuse in the private sphere including sex determination and termination, forced desertion on grounds of infertility, dowry-related torture and deaths, marital rape among others. Though small scale, these qualitative studies were critical in revealing the everyday nature of violence experienced by women across their life cycle (see Mitra, 2011) and establishing the imperative for state action. Scholars also highlight paucity of studies examining the experiences of elderly women (over 50), and those in live-in, same-sex relationships and also among indigenous women (Kalokhe et al., 2017).

*The health consequences* of DVA are manifold and widely recognised (WHO, 2013). Violence not only affects the physical, mental and emotional health and well-being of the individual woman survivor but has significant impact on their children, on families, households and communities and other institutions such as healthcare systems. **Three distinct levels** at which such impact is felt can be discerned.

*At the individual level, most visible and direct effects on health and well-being* are physical injuries ranging from cuts, bruises, aches and pains to broken bones and dislocations, burns among others (Garcia-Moreno et al., 2006). Although scant, evidence also indicates a strong association between DVA and poor mental health including higher risk of depression and suicide (Dutton et al., 2006; Kumar, Jeyaseelan, Suresh, & Ahuja, 2005; Rose et al., 2010). While immediate effects (visible injuries) are more effectively and frequently captured by large-scale national and multi-country surveys, there's mounting evidence on the longer-term and indirect adverse health outcomes of violence as it impacts on wider determinants of health (e.g. nutritional status, economic productivity, behaviours and practices).

In relation to sexual and reproductive health (SRH), a global review by WHO (2013) revealed that women who have experienced partner violence are at 16% greater odds of having a low birthweight baby, more than twice as likely to have an induced abortion and depression, and 1.5–1.6 times more likely to acquire HIV or syphilis in comparison to women who have not experienced violence (Jejeebhoy, Santhya, & Acharya, 2013). Associations between the experience of violence and reproductive health outcomes such as unwanted pregnancy, induced abortions and other obstetric and perinatal complications, pregnancy loss as well as infant and maternal mortality are reported in studies from both developing and developed countries (Bacchus, Mezey, & Bewley, 2004; Nasir & Hyder, 2003). These adverse outcomes result from both the direct but also indirect effects of DVA as it leads to, for instance, poor nutrition and higher levels of malnourishment, anaemia (Ackerson & Subramanian, 2008) and pre- and postnatal depression (Tiwari et al., 2008) among abused pregnant women. Studies also report how the experience of violence pushes individuals to high-risk behaviours and environments (e.g. decline in use of contraceptives, uptake of family planning using wider SRH services), resulting in adverse SRH outcomes such as teen pregnancy and higher incidence of HIV (Dunkle et al., 2006; Decker et al., 2009; Jejeebhoy, Santhya, & Acharya, 2010). The evidence suggests that DVA can considerably impact the progress made in SRH policy, truncating any possibilities of attaining SRH goals by 2030.

DVA also has considerable impact on *families and households*. Studies confirm the intergenerational effects of DVA that can lead to long-term suffering and affect the ability to develop positive relationships. A study examining risk factors for men's perpetration of physical violence across eight low- and middle-income countries found witnessing parental violence was the strongest risk factor. Boys who witnessed their mother being beaten were 2.5 times more likely to abuse their partner (Fleming et al., 2015).

A second set of arguments that strengthened advocacy in favour of health programmes/services on DVA emphasises the **wider societal costs** of DVA and its growing burden on economic and social development. DVA places increased demands on overstretched health systems, and reinforces poverty by limiting educational attainment and economic productivity of the survivor and family (Duvvury, Callan, Carney, & Raghavendra, 2013). The impact of direct and indirect health consequences of violence on women's workforce participation is now well established (World Development Report, 2012). While focus on economic costs (and the efficiency argument it is underpinned by) has been criticised for its departure from the focus on human rights, it has indeed facilitated the wider uptake and development of public health approach. Using varied methodologies, researchers successfully demonstrated the direct and indirect burden of violence; for example, a prominent UK study estimated the costs of DVA to the National Health Service and the criminal justice system at £1.2billion and £1billion respectively (Walby, 2004, 2009). The World Bank estimates the economic consequences of GBV at 1.2–3.7% of GDP in some countries as a result of lost productivity. This figure is greater than the average public spending of low-income countries on health as a proportion of GDP, which stood at 1.5% in 2016 (WHO, 2018).

The significance of documenting the impact of DVA on health notwithstanding, it is important to establish the bi-directional relationship between violence and health, and how it perpetuates a cycle of ill-health, poverty and deprivation, and further violence. Pregnancy, ill-health and disclosure of illness increase women's exposure to and experience of violence (Hegarty, 2011). For instance, women living with tuberculosis, HIV/AIDS and poor mental health in large parts of the global South are unlikely to get married, or if married, are threatened with abandonment and desertion. Disclosure in these circumstances has resulted in increased violence (Gupte, 2013), exacerbating their experience of (post-natal) depression, isolation and detachment, and vulnerability to further abuse.

## What does a public health approach to violence entail?

I answer this question by first laying out the key principles or core premises of a public health approach to DVA. Drawing on these, I then propose a framework that can guide the development of a public health response to DVA.

## Population level focus

The fundamental goal of public health is to promote, maintain and improve health of populations. Thus, by definition, public health moves away from the individual and targets communities and populations as a whole. Consequently, public health interventions are based on assessment of risks and focus on populations that are at greatest risk of ill-health or injury. A range of risk factors and environments associated with DVA have been identified in literature. Deriving from a socio-ecological framework, these can be identified as individual and interpersonal/relational factors, economic factors and factors related to the social, cultural and physical environment (see Figure 7.1). However, much less is understood about the distribution of these risks in society and differentiated vulnerabilities in relation to gender, ethnicity/race or migration status. I discuss these knowledge gaps in the next section.

## Preventive focus

It is concerned as much with preventing violence, as with mitigating the harms associated with it. This demands attention to the 'upstream' determinants (i.e. the social, economic, political and structural) of DVA that must be tackled to reduce the consequences that can be observed 'downstream'. Prevention strategies may target three levels: *primary*, which concerns efforts to prevent violence from happening by targeting risk environments; *secondary*, developed in immediate response to instance of violence and therefore needing a strong referral system to support services; while *tertiary* focuses on long-term care and rehabilitation needs in the wake of violence (Dahlberg & Krug, 2002). In view of the specific contexts and resource availability, policy and programme-level responses need to carefully consider which of these are universal and aimed at the wider population, and which should be targeted at populations most at risk.

## Multisectoral

Affecting these wider (distal and proximal) determinants of DVA calls for a multisectoral and integrated approach that involves creating safe public spaces and establishing appropriate referrals and links with other public sector agencies (such as health services, police, shelter, judiciary, employment, and the information, education and communication sectors).

## Evidence-informed policy and planning

An effective public health response requires a clear definition of violence (form, sites) and a robust evidence base that can inform the development, implementation and monitoring of violence prevention policies and programmes. Absence of data also limits the advocacy space necessary to demand responsiveness and hold governments accountable for inaction. Such evidence base must provide evidence on what works, with what resources, and in what contexts (i.e. the enabling conditions in which certain programmes tend to have greater uptake and impact).

Notably, since DVA is a result of deep-rooted patriarchal norms and gender power relations operating at multiple levels in society (household, community, public and private institutions), any response developed to reduce or eliminate it must go beyond tackling its symptoms and affect the multi-dimensional and complex pathways in which these forms present themselves and the multifactorial risks underlying them. Measuring effectiveness of such responses may not therefore be amenable to randomised controlled trials and experimental research designs but require more complex mixed-methods approaches and qualitative insights to capture the short-, mid- and long-term effects of interventions on norms, perceptions, attitudes and behaviours.

## Risk-based (rights-oriented) public health approach to tackling DVA: framework

Development of effective response strategies necessitates a detailed assessment of risk factors and 'environments' that heighten women's vulnerability to (or to protect them from) DVA. However, such understanding of risk environments/factors is inadequate, supported by few empirical assessments and micro-level studies. Among these, only a few factors are more commonly reported and strongly evidenced across contexts and there is no overall consistency (Flury & Nyberg, 2010). The most expansive review of evidence on the risk and protective factors provided by Heise (2011) and subsequently updated (Heise & Fulu, 2014; Fulu, Jewkes, Roselli, Garcia-Moreno, & on behalf of the UN Multi-country Cross-sectional Study on Men and Violence research team, 2013) concludes that the evidence base is highly skewed towards Western high-income contexts. It is also deficient in accounting for the peculiarities of 'Southern' contexts and family structures in which violence takes place.

Empirical studies have tended to focus more on individual and interpersonal factors; much less on the impact of wider socio-economic, cultural, environmental and institutional factors or environments that place women at increased likelihood of DVA and the pathways through which they shape individual risks and vulnerabilities. Evidence is particularly deficient in situating violence amid the wider shifts and transformations brought about by globalisation, urbanisation, climate change, war and conflict and large-scale population movements resulting from these trends. The challenge, in part, is the diversity of contexts and populations to be studied, failure of research methods to capture more contextualised yet large population-level studies on a sensitive subject as DVA, and the absence of a broader socio-ecological framework guiding these studies.

Methodological limitations notwithstanding, evidence suggests that no single factor causes DVA. A socio-ecological model, first proposed by Bronfenbrenner (1979), considers the interaction of multiple factors incorporated into different levels of the "social ecology" (individual, interpersonal, community, societal). Its application to DVA studies therefore allows for a multi-dimensional and holistic understanding of DVA to emerge and effectively inform interventions, behaviours and attitudes for social change (Heise, 1998). Taking a socio-ecological approach, and adapting the framework to incorporate a more explicit focus on institutional and structural influences, in Figure 7.1, I present a framework to guide the development of a public health

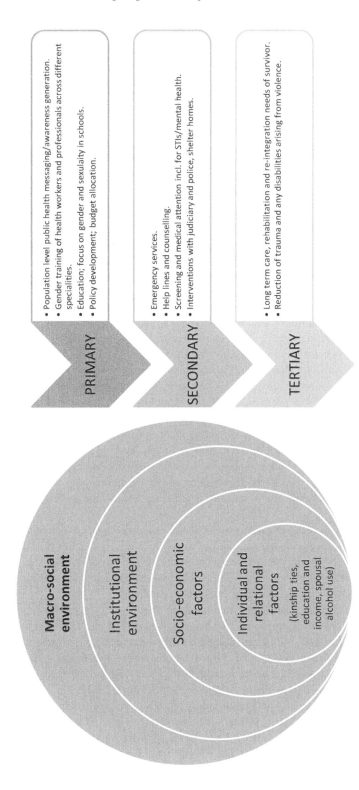

*Figure 7.1* A public health framework for tackling DVA

approach to tackle the multiple, interacting risk factors of DVA. As a departure from the earlier models, which identify the levels or sites in which the determinants operate (e.g. individual, interpersonal, community and societal), I focus primarily on categories of determinants. This allows examination of the nature of risk and enables development of strategies that can effectively address these.

*Individual and relational factors* concern women's individual and familial context, which are often mediated by other gradients of social disadvantage. Commonly reported risk factors for DVA include low income, illiteracy or having no further education, prior history of abuse experienced/witnessed in childhood (Jewkes, Levin, & Penn-Kekana, 2002) and men's harmful use of alcohol, drugs and problem gambling and multiple sexual relationships (Jeyaseelan et al., 2007; Mahapatro, Gupta, & Gupta, 2012; Muelleman, DenOtter, Wadman, Tran, & Anderson, 2002; WHO, 2012, 2019). Much less attention is given to kinship norms and ties and particular context in which marital arrangements are formed (for example, dowry, son-preference in family) when examining risks and considering protection mechanisms. A qualitative study in Ghana (Sedziafa & Tenkorang, 2016) contrasted experience of DVA in patrilineal and matrilineal societies and found the experience of emotional, physical, and sexual abuse was more continuous, pervasive and aggressive in patrilineal society as compared to matrilineal society. Here, it is important to highlight the variations in the forms of families and interpersonal relationships that characterise different contexts (Ghosh, 2004) but are often omitted in the dominant discourse on DVA. Women from diverse ethnicities and patriarchal cultures are subjected to abuse by not only the spouse but also members of extended family, especially female kin such as the mother-in-law and sister-in-law (Mirza, 2017). While older women in these families are subject to the authority of men, they are also delegated authority over younger daughters-in-law to ensure conformity to patriarchal social norms (Kapilashrami, 2017). Violence in this case takes the form of everyday abuse exercised in domains of the economic, social and political (freedom of movement and other liberties), also referred to as 'coercive control' (Stark, 2009). Studies from India and other South Asian countries expand our understanding in this regard; identifying co-relations between wife beating and abuse and factors such as social isolation, lack of resources, early age at marriage, type of marriage/habitation, strained relations with in-laws, absence of children (in general or especially a male child) and other factors such as social stress and illiteracy (see Mitra, 2011).

Drawing from the earlier points, a public health approach to tackle individual and interpersonal factors must therefore not only improve women's access to education, social and vocational skills, but simultaneously work with women, girls, men and boys to promote gender-equitable attitudes and behaviours and healthy and pleasurable relationship skills, and target behaviours involving harmful drinking, gambling, etc. in the household.

*Economic factors* demand particular attention here. While occurrence of DVA cuts across class/economic divisions in society, poverty is identified as a critical risk factor for violence (Evans, 2005; Heise et al., 1994). Not disregarding this evidence, Southern feminist scholars have questioned the link between poverty and domestic violence, arguing against seeing this as a phenomenon occurring only in socio-economically deprived class and calling out the invisibility of other classes in assessments of violence (Vindhya, 2005; Mitra, 2011). The relationship between economic independence and violence is more complex. On the one hand, there is evidence to suggest that poverty determines women's vulnerability to violence limiting access to and control over income, assets and entitlements (housing, employment) – resources necessary to seek help, justice or exit abusive relationships. On the other hand, women's acquisition of financial independence may place them at greater risk of violence from spouse and families as evident from reports of abuse among women who are sole earners of the family and seen as transgressing gender norms (Jewkes et al., 2002). The mixed evidence on the impacts of micro-finance programmes aimed at women's economic empowerment concurs with the previous point. While loan holdings and employment opportunities are shown to improve women's bargaining position in the family, it may also act as a precursor to violence. Studies reporting household-level impact of programmes such as *Grameen* bank suggest an increase in DVA resulting from the changes in power relations brought about by shifting gender roles (see Kabeer, 2005 for more detailed examination of evidence on micro-finance). These differences notwithstanding, evidence suggests that the protective mechanism in such income- and employment-generating programmes is a greater degree of social capital (networks, non-material resources including information) and self-confidence and self-worth that are affected through these (Jewkes et al., 2002; Nakray, 2013).

*Socio-cultural factors* concern the norms, values, expectations and rules around which a society is structured and governed, and which shape the conditions in which people live, work and thrive. Among these, the system of gender – and its constituent patriarchal norms, relations, expectations around roles, division of labour – is prominent in sanctioning social control and legitimising violence in cases of transgression from these norms by women. Such a system, on one hand, sanctions practices such as dowry, son-preference and forced marriage that place women at greater risk of DVA (e.g. bride-burning, sex-selective abortion and infanticide, desertion and punishment for not fulfilling their 'duties') and limits opportunities and capabilities of women to break the cycle of violence. For example, withdrawing girls from schools, denying opportunities for education and earning a secure livelihood and income are known to increase women's risk to violence (Bates, Schuler, Islam, & Islam, 2004). On the other hand, it privileges male power and normalises ideas of aggressive masculinity and passive femininities that are linked to women's submission and tacit acceptance of violence to ensure conformity to societal norms.

Here, I bring to scrutiny the nomenclature and artificial dichotomy created in violence scholarship between certain forms of DVA framed in terms of 'culture' (e.g. 'honour' killings or female genital mutilation) and that which are perpetrated within families in the West (e.g. spousal murder/hate and domestic violence homicides or femicide). While notions of honour, shame and social control underpin all the aforementioned acts of violence, explanations for the latter often centre on perpetrators' characteristics. Such representation marks a false distinction between 'Southern' and Western values and creates racialised imagery of victims. Dismissing such dichotomy, feminist scholars (Gupte, 2013; Shier & Shor, 2016) demand attention to the unequal gender norms that underpin all forms of violence in the 'domestic' sphere and the weak community and societal sanctions that allow their occurrence.

A public health approach needs to go beyond strong enforcement of legislation (for example, against dowry, sex-selective abortions, female genital mutilation) to simultaneously tackle social norms (related to education, employment, marriage) through comprehensive gender and sexuality education across institutions and mass-media public awareness campaigns. Such campaigns should be aimed at creating a zero-tolerance for DVA among the public and promoting gender-sensitive stances in the community, health sector, judiciary and with law-enforcing officials.

Institutional factors relate to laws, formal rules and institutions that are in place (or not) to intervene and break the cycle of violence. Core social institutions such as schools/educational institutions, family, religion and state institutions such as legislature, judiciary among others are sites where disadvantage is accumulated over the life-course. Attention to these is crucial as they foster a social environment that reinforces disadvantage and allows abuse to occur with impunity. For instance, while education is seen as a critical protective factor for DVA, the environment in schools and the absence of an empowerment approach in educational programmes (including sex-education programmes) may reinforce gender stereotypes and continue to place women and girls at greater risk (Haberland & Rogow, 2015; Le Mat, 2017). Institutional analysis in DVA studies is restricted to the responses of the police and education sector, overlooking their role in perpetuating the cycle of violence and re-victimisation. Absence of laws, lack of gender-sensitive policies and women-friendly spaces may result in re-victimising women and increasing their risk to DVA. For example, 'no recourse to public funds in the UK' disregards the familial context of abuse that migrant brides find themselves in and limits their recourse to legal and financial support and justice systems, trapping them in abusive relationships (Graca, 2017). A similar disregard for the upstream determinants of violence was seen in early proposals to address sex-selective abortions in India that penalised women for termination of pregnancy; failing to address the commercial determinants of this practice and hold healthcare providers, especially in the unregulated private sector, to account. This was subsequently amended in the pre-conception and pre-natal diagnostic test act that was adopted in India.

From an institutional perspective, a public health intervention to DVA must therefore bring attention to school, youth settings, work places as well as other institutions such as police, judiciary and healthcare systems, and target gender and sexuality norms that underpin social attitudes that may condone and re-victimise survivors. Such attempts can not only help reduce aggressive incidents in intimate relationships and families as a whole (by changes in gender norms and attitudes) but also offer a supportive environment to survivors of abuse.

*Macro-environmental factors* concern broader conditions of living and working and encompass the natural, social, geo-political and the physical environment, which create heightened risk of DVA. While violence is pervasive and women in a variety of contexts are vulnerable to incidence of abuse, certain contexts and environments exacerbate these risks and grossly undermine women's access to support and justice systems. These include, for example, 'upstream' determinants such as political conflicts, state repression, climate disasters, all of which may lead to forced displacement and migration, which impact the 'downstream' or more 'proximate' determinants of violence (e.g. changes in family and kinship structures, income and livelihood opportunities), yet remain under studied in DVA research. Women living in conflict situations or as refugees and asylum seekers in transit and host countries experience cumulative risks that increase their vulnerability to DVA (Pittaway & Rees, 2006). My research in transit contexts of Serbia and the Balkans and in Scotland revealed that migrant women experience a greater burden of silence and get deterred from justice-seeking because reporting DVA in the wider context of racism and a growing anti-migrant sentiment is viewed as adding to the family's suffering and community's honour.

Scholars are beginning to draw attention to this major lacuna in DVA studies that fail to consider the relationship between the macro processes of globalisation, transitions in climate and population movements, and the community and individual experiences of DVA (Fulu & Miedema, 2015). A nascent but growing body of work is highlighting the gendered nature of these forces and how they produce sexualised and racialised bodies, and masculinised institutions and identities (Ferguson, 2008; Andrijasevic, 2009; Alsaba & Kapilashrami, 2016), with complex and contradictory effects on women in areas of labour, livelihoods, sexuality (see Doyal, 2002; Rege, 2003; Kabeer, 2001). Feminist scholars have thus focused on flows of violence between states, local communities and individuals (Das & Kleinman, 2001; Mitra, 2011), placing DVA in a continuum of violence inextricably linked to the wider socio-political and economic developments. Yet, such understanding has not translated to empirical investigation of these links to examine the nature of risks produced and how such risk is distributed in society across different axes of marginalisation (e.g. race/ethnicity, religion, sexuality) (Kapilashrami & Hankivsky, 2018). Critical questions remain unanswered: who are most at-risk population groups in these contexts; what is the current status of legal protection and other support services; how can their access be enhanced? Such assessment exacts explicit adoption of an intersectionality framework that, as emphasised elsewhere, integrates a feminist political economy perspective for more in-depth examination of how these broader shifts in ecology and political economy re-structure gender power relations in households/families and communities and create distinct risk environments (Alsaba & Kapilashrami, 2016). This empirical gap renders DVA interventions that do not consider the changing context of vulnerabilities ineffective.

Having explored the value added by a public health lens to the work on DVA and outlined its core premise, I now turn to evidence on effective strategies and interventions. The purpose of this chapter is not to offer a comprehensive review of that evidence; rather I highlight key messages from available international and regional reviews.

## Evidence on effective public health strategies and health systems' response to DVA

Global and regional evidence on what works to prevent and effectively respond to DVA point to a dearth of rigorous evaluations and report mixed evidence (Heise, 2011; Solotaroff & Pande, 2014 for South Asia). Limitations notwithstanding, these evaluations suggest the importance of interventions that are multisectoral, have an explicit gender focus and simultaneously target risk factors at multiple levels of society – individual, household, community, institutional and structural (Solotaroff & Pande, 2014). Furthermore, campaigns that target and change underlying attitudes and gender norms are regarded effective in bringing DVA to public attention if using established community networks, change agents and applying innovative media with bold messaging (ibid.).

While there is little evaluation of services targeting specific needs of survivors, integrated health systems' responses are gaining popularity as a promising response to the multiple needs of survivors and also as preventative approaches. The UN Framework to underpin action to prevent violence (UN Women, 2015) presents a comprehensive systems approach to eliminating violence, suggesting a continuum of interdependent and mutually reinforcing interventions. Three foci of such action identified in the framework are:

| | |
|---|---|
| Prevention | Focusing at the population level and on the range of settings in which gender relations and violent behaviour are shaped. |
| Early intervention | Focusing on individuals and groups at a higher risk of experiencing/perpetrating violence and the factors contributing to that risk. |
| Response | Focusing on building systemic, organisational and community capacity to respond to those affected by violence. |

Several health system interventions have been implemented in the last few decades on the premise that healthcare facilities are a key entry point for women seeking treatment for a variety of physical, sexual, psychological and reproductive morbidities resulting from violence, though they may not disclose as such. This arguably places the health system in a unique position to offer women "a safe environment where they can confidentially disclose experiences of violence and receive a supportive response" (Garcia-Moreno et al., 2015, p. 1567) that attends to its diverse health consequences.

Reviewing international evidence on their effectiveness, Spangaro (2017) identifies specific interventions – for example, first-line responses, routine screening, counselling women, child protection notification, training and system-level responses – as effective in reducing the extent of harm from DVA. Scholars also identify healthcare systems' ability to go beyond addressing the health consequences to enhance access to justice by facilitating responses of other sectors such as criminal justice, social work (Temmerman, 2015). In doing so, they may be effective in breaking the cycle of abuse and preventing further recurrence.

Among comprehensive systems responses, an approach that holds promise is 'one-stop crisis centres' (OSCC) established in tertiary-level hospitals in several countries in South Asia. For example, the Multi-Sectoral Programme on VAW in Bangladesh with the Ministry of Women and Children Affairs, the OSC Management Centres in Nepal under the Ministry of Health and Population, the *Dilaasa* programme offered in partnership with a women's health non-government organisation and the Municipal Hospital in Mumbai and *Bhoomika* implemented by the government of Kerala in India. By linking with other departments and critical services, these centres facilitate access to a range of services needed by survivors of violence including medical attention, shelter, rehabilitation, psychosocial and legal counselling (including individual and family counselling) and crisis management. Studies examining the functioning and impact of OSCC report promising results; for example, growing uptake of services and acceptance in local communities, improvements in women's access to support services and their potential to empower women in situations of abuse (Kapilashrami, 2018; Kirk, Terry, Lokuge, & Watterson, 2017; Jewkes, 2014). Services were found particularly responsive and sensitive to women's complex needs when these interventions were embedded in feminist approaches to counselling women survivors (for example, the *Dilaasa* model in Mumbai) and offered routine and refresher gender trainings for counsellors, wider hospital staff as well as other service providers (e.g. police).

Yet, significant barriers to their effective implementation exist. Prominent among these are 'organisational constraints' including lack of trained and specialised staff, budget, and varied success in integrating support services (e.g. linking women with lawyers for legal guidance, NGOs for rehabilitation, police for security) (Colombini, Mayhew, Ali, Shuib, & Watts, 2012; Jewkes, 2014), poor working conditions including physical space and infrastructure, short-term contracts as well as wider hostility and low prioritisation of abuse cases among wider medical staff (Kapilashrami, 2018; Solotaroff & Pande, 2014). In the study in India, I found the OSCCs operated in a very hierarchical healthcare system where counsellors were entrusted with increased administrative demands of keeping records and entering data for other services, doctors and managers (ibid.). Coordination of OSCC and counselling was mediated by gender-power relations (between counsellor and other medical staff; between counsellor, survivor, and their families) and embedded in the formal and informal rules, norms, and an organisational culture resistant to change (Kapilashrami, 2018). The absence of training and supportive supervision of counsellors not only increased staff burnout from isolation, secondary trauma or 'compassion fatigue' but also prevented development of trusting relationships with abused women (Kapilashrami, 2018).

These challenges are less accounted for in literature and signal an absence of a critical and comprehensive understanding of healthcare systems as social institutions and sites of pervasive systemic violence. Studies examining health-seeking experiences among women survivors of abuse report service providers' attitudes and view of domestic violence as a 'private' matter (Jejeebhoy et al., 2014; Colombini, Mayhew, & Watts, 2008). Similarly, as argued elsewhere, historical experiences of coercive sterilisation programmes, obstetric violence, invasive medico-legal examination to determine "habituation" to sexual intercourse in case of sexual violence (Pitre & Lingam, 2013) reflect the deep-seated gender bias prevalent in attitudes and practices of healthcare professionals (Kapilashrami, 2018). In these contexts, interface with the healthcare system may result in further victimisation, violate women's right to privacy and dignity, and reinforce a culture of silence and impunity that hinders women's access to help-seeking and justice.

These system-wide deficits notwithstanding, there is growing optimism on the impact of integrated health-sector interventions, supported by process documentations that reveal critical learnings and promising practices (Bhate-Deosthali, Ravindran, & Vindhya, 2012; Kapilashrami, 2018; Solotaroff & Pande, 2014). Acknowledging this potential, Garcia-Moreno et al. (2015) highlight three levels and pathways of prevention where healthcare systems can play a crucial role: *primary* prevention to detect risk environments and raise awareness; *secondary* prevention requiring early identification, referrals for legal aid, acute care and long-term support services; and *tertiary level* intervention involving support for mental and physical rehabilitation of the survivor.

## Conclusion

DVA is a complex phenomenon driven by multiple interrelated risk factors that operate at different levels of social ecology, though ultimately, DVA results from gender and sexual norms that patriarchal societies are deeply entrenched in. Therefore, responding to it requires a multi-pronged approach and the participation of multiple sectors and institutions.

Different theoretical and conceptual frameworks have been utilised to understand and effectively respond to DVA. While criminal justice, human rights and family violence have contributed significantly to our understanding of DVA and informed interventions, the magnitude of DVA, its pervasive psychosocial, health and wider societal burdens render it a public health priority. A public health approach to DVA focuses at population-level risk factors and environments and proposes a *multisectoral* and *integrated* approach aimed at reducing risks and enhancing protecting factors. Such approach is premised on establishing links with other public sector agencies (such as law enforcement/prosecution, health services, forensic laboratories, social welfare, shelter, employment) and creating safe public spaces. Integrating rights and feminist principles within a public health approach has the potential to go beyond a siloed response to DVA, and offers sector-wide intervention that address the systemic nature of gender power relations, socio-cultural norms, and wider inequalities that impede effective responses.

Such an ambitious goal of eliminating DVA also demands implementation of laws and policies that promote gender equality, appropriate resource allocation to prevention efforts, alignment of interventions with evidence on risk and protective factors, close monitoring, and above all, political commitment and leadership to bring about change. As illustrated in the above example of integrated health-sector interventions, a rights-based public health response can not only facilitate early identification of signs of abuse and offer support services to women, but it also has the potential to be a vehicle for women's access to justice.

## Note

1 The interchangeable use of terminologies to denote GBV in this section illustrates the evolving discourse on gender-based violence. The author views GBV as an all-encompassing and appropriate terminology to refer to violence that is rooted in gender inequality and directed against a person, in

majority cases women, due to their gender. However, the term violence against women was of common usage in international policy developments and milestones in the '90s that brought to fore the violence experienced by women and placed the unequal gender power relations and status of women on the global agenda. Domestic violence and abuse (DVA), the focus of this book, refers to a form or sub-set of GBV that is defined with respect to the particular domain in which violence is exercised. As described on earlier, the author considers DVA to be a broader construct than intimate partner violence as it is applicable to diverse contexts and kinship formations.

# References

Ackerson, L. K., & Subramanian, S. V. (2008). Domestic violence and chronic malnutrition among women and children in India. *American Journal of Epidemiology, 167*(10), 1188–1196.

Alsaba, K., & Kapilashrami, A. (2016). Understanding women's experience of violence and the political economy of gender in conflict: The case of Syria. *Reproductive Health Matters, 24*(47), 5–17.

Andrijasevic, R. (2009). Sex on the move: Gender, subjectivity and differential inclusion. *Subjectivity, 29*(1), 389–406.

Bacchus, L., Mezey, G., & Bewley, S. (2004). Domestic violence: Prevalence in pregnant women and associations with physical and psychological health. *European Journal of Obstetrics & Gynecology and Reproductive Biology, 113*(1), 6–11.

Bates, L. M., Schuler, S. R., Islam, F., & Islam, M. K. (2004). Socioeconomic factors and processes associated with domestic violence in rural Bangladesh. *International Family Planning Perspectives*, 190–199.

Bhate-Deosthali, P., Ravindran, T. K. S., & Vindhya, U. (2012). Addressing domestic violence within healthcare settings. The Dilaasa model. *Economic & Political Weekly, XLVII*, 66–75.

Bhate-Deosthali, P., Rege, S., & Prakash, P. (Eds.). (2013). *Feminist counselling and domestic violence* (p. 352). New Delhi: Routledge. ISBN 978-04-158-3206-9

Bronfenbrenner, U. (1979). *The ecology of human development: Experiments by design and nature.* Cambridge, MA: Harvard University Press.

CEDAW. (1999). The Committee on the Elimination of Discrimination against Women, General Recommendation No. 24, 20th Session.

Colombini, M., Mayhew, S. H., Ali, S. H., Shuib, R., & Watts, C. (2012). An integrated health sector response to violence against women in Malaysia: Lessons for supporting scale up. *BMC Public Health, 12*, Article 548.

Colombini, M., Mayhew, S., & Watts, C. (2008). Health-sector responses to intimate partner violence in low-and middle-income settings: A review of current models, challenges and opportunities. *Bulletin of the World Health Organization, 86*, 635–642.

Dahlberg, L. L., & Krug, E. G. (2002). Violence – A global public health problem. In E. G. Krug et al. (Eds.), *World report on violence and health* (pp. 3–21). Geneva: World Health Organization.

Das, V., & Kleinman, A. (2001). Introduction. In V. Das, A. Kleinman, M. Ramphele, & P. Reynolds (Eds.), *Violence and subjectivity*. New Delhi: Oxford University Press.

Decker, M. R., Seage III, G. R., Hemenway, D., Raj, A., Saggurti, N., Balaiah, D., & Silverman, J. G. (2009). Intimate partner violence functions as both a risk marker and risk factor for women's HIV infection: Findings from Indian husband-wife dyads. *Journal of Acquired Immune Deficiency Syndromes (1999), 51*(5), 593.

Doyal, L. (2002). Putting gender into health and globalization debates: New perspectives and old challenges. *Third World Quarterly, 23*, 233–250.

Dunkle, K. L., Jewkes, R. K., Nduna, M., Levin, J., Jama, N., Khuzwayo, N., . . . Duvvury, N. (2006). Perpetration of partner violence and HIV risk behaviour among young men in the rural Eastern Cape, South Africa. *Aids, 20*(16), 2107–2114.

Dutton, M. A., Green, B. L., Kaltman, S. I., Roesch, D. M., Zeffiro, T. A., & Krause, E. D. (2006). Intimate partner violence, PTSD, and adverse health outcomes. *Journal of Interpersonal Violence, 21*, 955–968. doi:10.1177/0886260506289178 PMID:16731994

Duvvury, N., Callan, A., Carney, P., & Raghavendra, S. (2013). *Intimate partner violence: Economic costs and implications for growth and development.* Retrieved from http://documents.worldbank.org/curated/en/412091468337843649/Intimate-partner-violence-economic-costs-and-implications-for-growth-and-development

Evans, S. (2005). Beyond gender: Class, poverty and domestic violence. *Australian Social Work, 58*(1), 36–43.

Ferguson, S. (2008). Canadian contributions to social reproduction feminism, race and embodied labor. *Race, Gender & Class*, 42–57.

Fleming, P. J., McCleary-Sills, J., Morton, M., Levtov, R., Heilman, B., & Barker, G. (2015). Risk factors for men's lifetime perpetration of physical violence against intimate partners: Results from the international men and gender equality survey (IMAGES) in eight countries. *PLoS One, 10*(3), e0118639.

Flury, M., & Nyberg, E. (2010). Domestic violence against women: Definitions, epidemiology, risk factors and consequences. *Swiss Medical Weekly, 140*(3536).

Fulu, E., Jewkes, R., Roselli, T., Garcia-Moreno, C., & on behalf of the UN Multi-country Cross-sectional Study on Men and Violence research team. (2013). Prevalence of and factors associated with male perpetration of intimate partner violence: Findings from the UN Multi-country cross-sectional study on men and violence in Asia and the Pacific. *Lancet Global Health, 1*, e187–se207.

Fulu, E., & Miedema, S. (2015). Violence against women: Globalizing the integrated ecological model. *Violence Against Women, 21*(12), 1431–1455.

García-Moreno, C., Hegarty, K., d'Oliveira, A. F. L., Koziol-McLain, J., Colombini, M., & Feder, G. (2015). The health-systems response to violence against women. *The Lancet, 385*(9977), 1567–1579.

Garcia-Moreno, C., Jansen, H. A., Ellsberg, M., Heise, L., & Watts, C. H. (2006). Prevalence of intimate partner violence: Findings from the WHO multi-country study on women's health and domestic violence. *The Lancet, 368*(9543), 1260–1269. doi:10.1016/S0140-6736(06)69523-8 PMID:17027732

Ghosh, S. V. (2004). Contextualising domestic violence: Family, community, state. In Rinki Bhattacharya (Ed.), *Behind closed doors. Domestic violence in India* (pp. 51–66). New Delhi: Sage.

Graca, S. (2017). Domestic violence policy and legislation in the UK: A discussion of immigrant women's vulnerabilities. *European Journal of Current Legal Issues, 22*(1).

Gupte, M. (2013). Why feminism should inform our routine interventions in domestic violence. In P. Bhate-Deosthali, S. Rege, & P. Praksah (Eds.), *Feminist counselling and domestic violence in India* (pp. 48–92). New Delhi: Routledge.

Haberland, N., & Rogow, D. (2015). Sexuality education: Emerging trends in evidence and practice. *Journal of Adolescent Health, 56*(1), S15–S21.

Hegarty, K. (2011). Domestic violence: The hidden epidemic associated with mental illness. *British Journal of Psychiatry, 198*(3), 169–170.

Heise, L. (1998). Violence against women: An integrated, ecological framework. *Violence Against Women, 4*(3), 262–290.

Heise, L. (2011). *What works to prevent partner violence? An evidence overview.* Working Paper version 2.0). STRIVE Research Consortium, London School of Hygiene and Tropical Medicine, London. Retrieved from http://researchonline.lshtm.ac.uk/21062/

Heise, L., & Fulu, E. (2014). What works to prevent violence against women and girls. *State of the field of violence against women and girls: What do we know and what are the knowledge gaps.* Annex D. Retrieved from https://assets.publishing.service.gov.uk/media/57a089b640f0b6497400021a/What_Works_Inception_Report_June_2014_AnnexD_WG1_paper_State_of_the_field.pdf

Heise, L. L., Raikes, A., Watts, C. H., & Zwi, A. B. (1994). Violence against women: A neglected public health issue in less developed countries. *Social Science & Medicine, 39*(9), 1165–1179.

Jejeebhoy, S. J., Santhya, K. G., & Acharya, R. (2010). *Health and social consequences of marital violence: A synthesis of evidence from India.* New Delhi. PopCouncil. Retrieved from https://knowledgecommons.popcouncil.org/cgi/viewcontent.cgi?article=1016&context=departments_sbsr-pgy

Jejeebhoy, S. J., Santhya, K. G., & Acharya, R. (2013). Physical and sexual violence and symptoms of gynaecological morbidity among married young women in India. *Global Public Health, 8*(10), 1151–1167.

Jejeebhoy, S. J., Santhya, K. G., & Acharya, R. (2014). Violence against women in South Asia: The need for the active engagement of the health sector. *Global Public Health, 9*(6), 678–690. doi:10.1080/1744 1692.2014.916736

Jewkes, R. (2014). *What works to prevent violence against women and girls? Evidence review of the effectiveness of response mechanisms in preventing violence against women and girls.* London: Department for International Development.

Jewkes, R., Levin, J., & Penn-Kekana, L. (2002). Risk factors for domestic violence: Findings from a South African cross-sectional study. *Social Science & Medicine, 55*(9), 1603–1617.

Jeyaseelan, L., Kumar, S., Neelakantan, N., Peedicayil, A., Pillai, R., & Duvvury, N. (2007). Physical spousal violence against women in India: Some risk factors. *Journal of Biosocial Science, 39*(5), 657–670.

Kabeer, N. (2005). Is microfinance a 'magic bullet' for women's empowerment? Analysis of findings from South Asia. *Economic and Political Weekly*, 4709–4718.

Kabeer, N. (2001). Conflicts over credit: Re-evaluating the empowerment potential of loans to women in rural Bangladesh. *World Development, 29*, 63–84.

Kalokhe, A., del Rio, C., Dunkle, K., Stephenson, R., Metheny, N., Paranjape, A., & Sahay, S. (2017). Domestic violence against women in India: A systematic review of a decade of quantitative studies. *Global Public Health, 12*(4), 498–513.

Kapilashrami, A. (2017, December 5). Southern perspectives on domestic violence: Contesting universalisations and reconceptualising social and lived realities of migrant women experiencing multiple marginalisation. *Blog Post.*16 Days of Activism against Gender based violence. Retrieved from https://genderpoliticsatedinburgh.wordpress.com/2017/12/05/southern-perspectives-on-domestic-violence-contesting-universalisations-and-reconceptualising-social-and-lived-realities-of-migrant-women-experiencing-multiple-marginalisation/

Kapilashrami, A. (2018). Transformative or functional justice? Examining the role of health care institutions in responding to violence against women in India. *Journal of Interpersonal Violence.* doi:10.1177/0886260518803604.

Kapilashrami, A., & Hankivsky, O. (2018). Intersectionality and why it matters to global health. *The Lancet, 391*(10140), 2589–2591.

Kirk, L., Terry, S., Lokuge, K., & Watterson, J. L. (2017). Effectiveness of secondary and tertiary prevention for violence against women in low and low-middle income countries: A systematic review. *BMC Public Health, 17*(1), 622.

Knaul, F. M., Bustreo, F., Horton, R., Lehmann, V., Kutteh, W. H., Sparrow, C. K., . . . Baer, J. (2020). Countering the pandemic of gender-based violence and maltreatment of young. *The Lancet, 395*(10218), 98.

Kumar, S., Jeyaseelan, L., Suresh, S., & Ahuja, R. C. (2005). Domestic violence and its mental health correlates in Indian women. *British Journal of Psychiatry, 187*(1), 62–67.

Le Mat, M. L. (2017). (S) exclusion in the sexuality education classroom: Young people on gender and power relations. *Sex Education, 17*(4), 413–424.

Mahapatro, M., Gupta, R. N., & Gupta, V. (2012). The risk factor of domestic violence in India. *Indian Journal of Community Medicine*: Official publication of Indian Association of Preventive & Social Medicine, 37(3), 153.

Mirza, N. (2017). South Asian women's experience of abuse by female affinal kin: A critique of mainstream conceptualisations of 'domestic abuse'. *Families, Relationships and Societies, 6*(3), 393–409.

Mitra, N. (2011). Domestic violence research: Expanding understandings but limited perspective. *Feminist Review, 98*(1_suppl), e62–e78.

Muelleman, R. L., DenOtter, T., Wadman, M. C., Tran, T. P., & Anderson, J. (2002). Problem gambling in the partner of the emergency department patient as a risk factor for intimate partner violence. *The Journal of Emergency Medicine, 23*(3), 307–312.

Nakray, K. (Ed.). (2013). *Gender-based violence and public health: International perspectives on budgets and policies.* London: Routledge.

Nasir, K., & Hyder, A. A. (2003). Violence against pregnant women in developing countries: Review of evidence. *The European Journal of Public Health, 13*(2), 105–107.

Pitre, A., & Lingam, L. (2013). Rape and medical evidence gathering systems. *Economic & Political Weekly, 48*(3), 17.

Pittaway, E., & Rees, S. (2006). Multiple jeopardy: Domestic violence and the notion of cumulative risk for women in refugee camps. *Women Against Violence: An Australian Feminist Journal,* (18), 18.

Rege, S. (2003). More than just tacking women on to the "macropicture": Feminist contributions to globalisation discourses. *Economic & Political Weekly, 38*, 4555–4563.

Rose, L., Alhusen, J., Bhandari, S., Soeken, K., Marcantonio, K., Bullock, L., & Sharps, P. (2010). Impact of intimate partner violence on pregnant women's mental health: Mental distress and mental strength. *Issues in Mental Health Nursing, 31*(2), 103–111.

Sedziafa, A. P., & Tenkorang, E. Y. (2016). Kin group affiliation and marital violence against women in Ghana. *Violence and Victims, 31*(3), 486–509.

Shier, A., & Shor, E. (2016). "Shades of foreign evil": "Honour killings" and "family murders" in the Canadian press. *Violence Against Women, 22*(10), 1163–1188. ISSN 1077–8012. doi:10.1177/1077801215621176

Solotaroff, J. L., & Pande, R. P. (2014). *Violence against women and girls: Lessons from South Asia.* Washington, DC: World Bank Group, South Asia Development Forum. https://openknowledge.worldbank.org/handle/10986/20153

Spangaro, J. (2017). What is the role of health systems in responding to domestic violence? An evidence review. *Australian Health Review, 41,* 639–645.

Stark, E. (2009). *Coercive control: The entrapment of women in personal life.* New York, NY: Oxford University Press.

Temmerman, M. (2015). Research priorities to address violence against women and girls. *The Lancet, 385*(9978), e38–e40.

Tiwari, A., Chan, K. L., Fong, D., Leung, W. C., Brownridge, D. A., Lam, H., . . . Cheung, K. B. (2008). The impact of psychological abuse by an intimate partner on the mental health of pregnant women. *BJOG: An International Journal of Obstetrics & Gynaecology, 115*(3), 377–384.

UN Women. (2015). *A framework to underpin action to prevent violence against women.* Retrieved from https://www.unwomen.org/-/media/headquarters/attachments/sections/library/publications/2015/prevention_framework_unwomen_nov2015.pdf?la=en&vs=5223

Vindhya, U. (2005). Battered conjugality: The psychology of domestic violence against women. In K. Kannabiran (Ed.), *Violence in normal times: Women's life worlds.* New Delhi: Women Unlimited and London and Zed Books.

Walby, S. (2004). *The cost of domestic violence.* London: Women and Equality Unit (DTI). Retrieved from https://openaccess.city.ac.uk/id/eprint/21681/1/The%20Cost%20of%20Domestic%20Violence.pdf

Walby, S. (2009). *The cost of domestic violence: Up-date 2009.* Lancaster: Lancaster University. Retrieved from https://openaccess.city.ac.uk/id/eprint/21695/1/

World Development Report. (2012). *Gender equality and development.* Washington, DC: The World Bank.

WHO. (2012). *Understanding and addressing violence against women: Intimate partner violence* (No. WHO/RHR/12.36). Geneva: World Health Organization.

WHO. (2013). *Global and regional estimates of violence against women: Prevalence and health effects of intimate partner violence and non-partner sexual violence.* Geneva: Authors: García-Moreno, C., Pallitto, C., Devries, K., Stöckl, H., Watts, C., & Abrahams, N. Geneva: World Health Organization.

WHO. (2018). *Public spending on health: A closer look at global trends* (No. WHO/HIS/HGF/HFWorkingPaper/18.3). Geneva: World Health Organization.

WHO. (2019). *Violence against women intimate partner and sexual violence against women. Evidence brief.* (No. WHO/RHR/19.16). Geneva: World Health Organization.

# 8

# DOMESTIC VIOLENCE AND ABUSE THROUGH A PSYCHOLOGICAL LENS

*Helene Flood Aakvaag and Kristin Alve Glad*

## Introduction

Psychology is the study of the mind and behaviour (American Psychological Association, 2020). As such, it focuses on the scientific study of a broad scope of themes, from a neural level to a societal level. Subjects of focus include neural processes, group processes, mental health problems, human development, and the impact and consequences of adversity, including violence and abuse. Psychologists have in some way concerned themselves with the consequences of domestic violence and abuse since the profession's early years, but in a systematic, scientific perspective, domestic violence entered into psychology in the seventies. The impact of the women's liberation movement prompted researchers to investigate issues that bore particular importance to women, including violence in the home. Psychologist Leonore Walker studied women who had experienced violence from their male partners, and she was one of the first to describe the symptoms of the battered women and the violence they suffered (Walker, 1977, 1979). The scientific focus on domestic violence led to such terms as 'the battered woman syndrome' (Appleton, 1980) and, taking children's experiences into account, 'the battered child syndrome' (Hicks, 1987; Kempe, Silverman, Droegemueller, & Silver, 1962). As these terms imply, much of the psychological literature on this subject focuses on the detrimental consequences violence and abuse may have on victims' health, particularly on their mental health. The decades that followed these publications have seen great development in theory and research on domestic violence, which has given us a deeper understanding of the mechanisms involved in, potential risk factors for, and the health consequences of, domestic violence victimization, as well as advances in treatment models.

Psychological research on domestic violence and abuse often takes a perspective of trauma psychology, focusing on the risk for trauma-related mental health problems and treatment of such problems. In the current chapter, we will therefore discuss the psychological angle of domestic violence research, with a focus on psychotraumatology. When considering violence against children, we will take perspectives from developmental psychology. With a background in theory and research from these perspectives, we will consider the phenomenology of domestic violence, risk and protective factors in terms of health problems, with a specific focus on social relationship factors, and briefly describe models of psychological treatment of victims suffering from the health consequences of domestic violence. Although psychology may inform the study of violence perpetration, we will limit this chapter to research on victims, and not discuss psychological perspectives on perpetrator behaviour.

## Discussion and analysis

### *Domestic violence as a trauma*

The word 'trauma' (derived from the Greek word for 'wound') originally referred to an injury caused by an external factor. Using this term in the context of psychological trauma implies that an external event can cause psychological injury, much like a blow to the head can cause physiological injury. A traumatic event is defined as exposure to actual or threatened death, serious injury, or sexual violence, either directed towards the person her-/himself or indirectly, such as when a person witnesses a traumatic event happening to someone else (American Psychiatric Association, 2013). Using *trauma* as an overarching term for events as diverse as exposure to a natural disaster, being imprisoned in a concentration camp, experiencing a sexual assault, and being abused by one's parent or partner, entails an acknowledgement that while these events differ in important ways, there are many similarities in the mental health consequences that they may have.

*Psychotraumatology* is the study of psychological trauma, hereunder factors occurring before, during, and after the traumatic event. Whereas certain instances of domestic violence may not fall under the definition of trauma (e.g., some forms of low-intensity physical violence would perhaps not entail actual or threatened serious injury), domestic violence is generally considered a potential trauma, and because it may cause considerable psychological damage, it has been extensively studied within the field of psychotraumatology.

### *Characteristics of the traumatic event*

Domestic violence has some characteristics that can make it a particularly damaging form of trauma. Interpersonal traumatic events are frequently found to be more severe than non-interpersonal trauma in terms of mental health outcomes (Alisic et al., 2014). Violence is interpersonal in character, and the notion that someone wilfully inflicted the traumatic event upon them can make it harder for victims to cope with the trauma. Further, violence committed in families is often part of a pattern that persists over time, as the victim is bound to the perpetrator in ways that are not easily escapable. Children depend on their parents to meet their needs for a home, food, and clothes, as well as for safety, love, and support. If parents are abusive, the chances of escape are often few and risky. Children are at the mercy of their parents, and child maltreatment in many cases continues for large parts of childhood, meaning that it is a repeated and persistent form of trauma. While adults in comparison may appear freer to leave a violent romantic relationship, adult victims of partner violence are also bound to the perpetrator, and often remain with the abusive partner over time. The various ways in which adult victims of domestic violence are constrained within the relationship is covered in more detail elsewhere in the Handbook.

Psychologist Judith Herman (1992) describes how victims of domestic violence are captive in the abusive situation, and compares this captivity to that of political prisoners and prisoners in concentration camps. While there are fewer physical barriers to escape domestic violence, there are still extremely powerful barriers, she writes, but these barriers are invisible, and the domestic captivity of victims of violence is often unseen. Domestic violence is thus often protracted, and victims stay in close contact with their abuser over time, with acts of violence repeated, sometimes on an almost daily basis, creating what Herman describes as a relationship dominated by *coercive control* (Herman, 1992). Further, in some violent families, the victim may care deeply for the perpetrator. Jennifer Freyd has described how traumatic experiences may involve betrayal, that is, the violation of trust or well-being by people or institutions upon which the individual depends (Freyd, 2008). One can argue that betrayal is part of all violence, as violent acts go against underlying assumptions of how people behave towards each other. However, the closer the relationship to the perpetrator is, the higher the level of betrayal will presumably be, and domestic violence is clearly a high-betrayal trauma.

Further, domestic violence often consists of multiple violence types. For example, it is difficult to imagine severe physical abuse of a child without there being some component of emotional abuse as well. Michael Johnson's description of 'intimate terrorism' in relationships covers multiple forms of abuse, including physical, sexual, emotional and economic abuse (Johnson, 2010). Studies tend to find that the number of violence types is associated with negative consequences; the more types, the worse the health outcome, for example (Thoresen, Myhre, Wentzel-Larsen, Aakvaag, & Hjemdal, 2015). For survivors living in violent families over years, it may not make sense to count the number of events, or even consider each violent episode a specific event. Rather, the violence may be experienced as ever-present, with patterns of control, threat, and violent assaults influencing almost every aspect of life.

In sum, while cases of domestic violence may vary in severity, they often contain several qualities indicating trauma severity, such as being protracted and inescapable, interpersonal, as well as often involving betrayal and multiple types of violence. With this in mind, we will turn to the potential mental health consequences of violence.

## Domestic violence and mental health

Exposure to violence and abuse can have devastating effects on health, including severe physical injuries, heart disease, cancer, and obesity (Campbell, 2002; Felitti et al., 2019). Importantly, domestic violence may also result in death. It is estimated that between 40 and 60% of murdered women in North America are killed by their intimate partners (Campbell, 2002; see chapter 4.10 for a fuller discussion of intimate partner homicide). For psychologists, the mental health aspects of such violence have been of particular interest. Experiences of domestic violence, in childhood and adulthood, increase the risk for a wide variety of mental health problems, including (but not limited to) posttraumatic stress disorder (PTSD), depression, suicidal behaviour, and substance abuse disorders. All of these can have a large impact on the individual's life and well-being. They may persist long after the abuse has ended, and can be one way in which survivors carry with them experiences of violence through life.

Posttraumatic stress disorder (PTSD) can only be diagnosed in the presence of a traumatic event, for example violence, accidents, or terrorist attacks. The disorder entails symptoms of re-experiencing the trauma, avoiding things that remind the person of the trauma, and exhibiting alterations in arousal and in cognitions and mood (American Psychiatric Association, 2013). Rape, often a component of domestic violence (see Chapter 4, this volume), is the trauma type most strongly associated with PTSD among women (Kessler, Sonnega, Bromet, Hughes, & Nelson, 1995). A review of the literature found that a significant proportion (31% to 84%) of women who had experienced domestic violence showed symptoms of PTSD (Jones, Hughes, & Unterstaller, 2001). Studies find that the more traumatic events a person experiences, the higher the risk for PTSD (Vrana & Lauterbach, 1994). Domestic violence survivors may have a particularly high risk of PTSD symptoms, as this type of violence often persists over time, with multiple traumatic events, and is severe in various ways, as described earlier. Many psychologists researching domestic violence, or working clinically with victims, have argued that the full impact of this prolonged, inescapable violence is not sufficiently captured within the framework of PTSD (e.g., Herman, 1992). A group of trauma psychologists suggested that the exposure to complex trauma, where a person experiences repeated or multiple forms of trauma they cannot escape, might result in a more complex symptom picture than that of PTSD (Cloitre, Garvert, Brewin, Bryant, & Maercker, 2013). A suggestion of a separate Complex PTSD diagnosis[1] resulted in much debate, but critics also recognized that prolonged trauma might result in a more complex constellation of symptoms than single traumas (Resick et al., 2012).

Taking into account the complexity of symptoms displayed by survivors, it is not surprising that a variety of mental health problems are associated with domestic violence victimization. Depressive symptoms, including feelings of worthlessness, markedly diminished interest in activities, and recurrent thoughts of death, are not uncommon among victims (Campbell, Kub, Belknap, & Templin, 1997; R. Gilbert et al., 2009). Depression is a debilitating disorder, estimated to be among the most common causes of disability worldwide (Ferrari et al., 2013). Women are at particular risk for depression, and some researchers hypothesize that gender differences in depressive disorders may in part be explained by intimate partner violence (Campbell, 2002).

It is also a consistent finding that victims of domestic violence have an increased risk of substance abuse disorders, including problems with alcohol (Strøm, Birkeland, Aakvaag, & Thoresen, 2019; Testa, Livingston, & Leonard, 2003; White & Chen, 2002). This may be understood as a type of self-medication strategy, in which a person is using alcohol or drugs to ease trauma symptoms, such as flashbacks, nightmares, or feelings of sadness, shame, or guilt. It can also be a way of escaping in a literal sense, where a violence-exposed teenager may gravitate towards social groups where substance use is encouraged because these groups provide an alternative to going home (Finkelhor & Browne, 1985). Survivors of intimate partner violence also have an elevated risk for suicidal behaviour (Ellsberg, Jansen, Heise, Watts, & Garcia-Moreno, 2008).

Many symptoms of mental health problems may be seen as a form of adaptation to a very distressing situation, prompting the question of at what point a normal response to an abnormal situation becomes pathological. While there is no easy, all-encompassing answer to this question, the diagnostic manuals give guidelines for how intense and long-lasting symptoms should be, and how much they should interfere with functioning, before the criteria to a given diagnosis are met. Additionally, the notion that symptoms are painful and disruptive at a diagnostic level, does not mean that they cannot be understood as a form of adaptation. For a child who is severely abused by his or her parents, PTSD-symptoms such as hyper-alertness and dissociation may help the child predict and endure the violent events. At the same time, these symptoms can be deeply problematic for the child, possibly persisting long after escape from the parents.

## Mental health in children who have experienced domestic violence

There is much evidence that experiencing domestic violence in childhood and adolescence can have severe mental health consequences (Edwards, Holden, Felitti, & Anda, 2003; R. Gilbert et al., 2009). A complicating factor is that violence experienced in childhood may adversely influence development, meaning that not only is the child exposed to something highly negative; violence may also disrupt a natural processes, and deprive the child of positive and necessary conditions for development. Developmental psychology is the scientific study of how humans develop from birth, through childhood, and into adulthood. Often focusing primarily on infancy and childhood, the field has expanded to include the entire lifespan. Childhood in particular is a period with rapid development, and experiences of violence, especially violence within the family, may interfere with natural development in various ways; for example, it may entail neurodevelopmental consequences, negative physical health outcomes, conduct and behavioural problems (including substance abuse), mental health challenges, delinquency, and academic problems (for a review, see Artz et al., 2014).

A central subject in developmental psychology has been the importance of the child-caregiver relationship, and theory and research has focused on the attachment between the child and its caregivers. Attachment theory focuses on a child's predisposition to form an emotional bond with their caregivers, and the behaviour that goes along with this predisposition (Bowlby, 1958; Cassidy, 2008). At the core of attachment theory is the notion that fear or distress in an infant or toddler activates the attachment system, whereby the child exhibits a set of behaviours aimed at seeking physical proximity to and attention from the caregiver. An important aspect of the caregiver as an attachment figure is his or her function as *a safe base* for the child. For example, if a child becomes frightened by a loud noise while the mother is in the next room, she will cry for the mother, crawl in her direction, and raise her arms to be picked up. The parent serves as a source of safety and comfort for the child. If parents are the source of fear, stress and anxiety, for example because they are violent, the safe-base function is compromised. Consequently, the child is placed in the dilemma of depending upon the source of danger for protection they are biologically prewired to seek (Kobak & Madsen, 2008). Ainsworth, Blehar, Waters, and Wall (1978) originally identified three patterns of attachment behaviours: secure, anxious-avoidant, and anxious-ambivalent. Further categorization has included the category of *disorganized attachment*, a sub-type of anxious attachment where the infant, among other behaviours, displays apprehension and contradictory behaviour in relation to the caregiver, overt signs of disorientation, and/or freeze (Main & Solomon, 1986; Reisz, Duschinsky, & Siegel, 2018). While it is stressed in the literature that disorganized attachment should not be used as an indicator of abuse, studies have found that abused children display disorganized attachment behaviour far more often than non-abused children (Baer & Martinez, 2006; Van Ijzendoorn, Schuengel, & Bakermans-Kranenburg, 1999).

Another important perspective on how domestic violence in childhood may influence development comes from the field of neuropsychology. Studies of children, as well as animal studies with primates, show that early maltreatment may involve alterations in hormonal and neurotransmitter systems. Such alterations may involve the hypothalamic pituitary adrenal axis (HPA-axis), which mediates the neural and hormonal response to stress, as well as the immune system (Pollak, 2008). Childhood maltreatment may alter the trajectories of brain development, and is associated with reduced volume of specific brain structures (Teicher, Samson, Anderson, & Ohashi, 2016). Taken together, findings on attachment problems and neurobiological changes after childhood maltreatment may help explain how family violence in childhood is associated with a wide variety of psychiatric, somatic, and social problems. It also demonstrates the previous point that violence in childhood may interfere with important developmental tasks, making it particularly devastating for those who experience it.

Much research on mental health problems after childhood experiences with violence has focused on adult survivors. The mental health problems children suffer may not manifest in the same way as they do in adulthood. Dante Cicchetti is a psychologist who has been influential in describing how a variety of developmental progressions may result in a given disorder (this is referred to as *equifinality*) (Cicchetti & Rogosch, 1996; Cicchetti & Toth, 2009); for example, ADHD may have biological roots, but may also be diagnosed based on behaviour that originates from problems in the family, such as domestic violence. At the same time, one risk factor may be associated with different outcomes (this is called *multifinality*) (Cicchetti & Rogosch, 1996).

The problems of a child that experiences severe abuse may have many expressions. There are PTSD criteria adapted for children, but exposure to violence may serve as a risk factor for a variety of child mental health problems.

## Cross-cultural aspects of mental health after domestic violence

Much research on the health consequences of violence and abuse has been conducted in the global North, with a heavy focus on North American populations (for example the National Comorbidity Study, Kessler et al., 1995). Knowledge about prevalence, risk factors, and mental health consequences is not necessarily transferable from one region to the next; violence occurs in social situations within a given culture, and the way it is talked about, accepted, or even justified is enmeshed in the culture in which it occurs. Thus, critics have noted the need for cross-cultural research on violence and abuse (Kulwicki, 2002). The World Health Organization (WHO) conducted a large multi-country study on women's health and domestic violence against women (Garcia-Moreno, Jansen, Ellsberg, Heise, & Watts, 2005, 2006). In this study, household interviews were conducted with more than 24 000 women from ten different countries (Bangladesh, Brazil, Ethiopia, Japan, Peru, Namibia, Samoa, Serbia and Montenegro, Thailand, and the United Republic of Tanzania), including, in some countries, both urban and rural settings. Findings showed that prevalence estimates varied widely; for example, estimates of the amount of ever-partnered women who had experienced physical or sexual abuse or both in a relationship varied from varied from 15% to 71%. However, women were abused by their intimate partners in all countries studied, indicating that this problem is not specific to a certain culture, or to countries with certain characteristics. The researchers reflect that taking the great variation in prevalence estimates into account, violence does not appear to be inevitable (Garcia-Moreno et al., 2005, p. xii). Across countries and sites, having experience with intimate partner violence was associated with increased risk for a range of health problems, including problems with mental health (Garcia-Moreno et al., 2005, p. 85). Coping strategies varied greatly among countries, and cultural beliefs on domestic violence may affect service responses (Fernandez, 2006; Garcia-Moreno et al., 2005), highlighting the importance of a cross-cultural focus for research and practice.

## Risk factors for mental health problems

The potential effects of violence and abuse on mental health underscore the importance of a mental health response to domestic violence. However, not all victims experience such consequences. When discussing risk and protective factors, it is important to note that while certain factors relating to the event, the person, or the surroundings may increase vulnerability, domestic violence in and of itself makes a person vulnerable for range of health problems. However, knowledge about risk and protective factors may help us identify those at particular risk, as well as prevent health problems.

Risk factors for negative consequences after exposure to domestic violence can take many forms. One way of sub-categorizing them is based on when they occur, relative to the trauma: before, during, or after. *Pre-trauma risk factors* include gender, age, previous mental health problems, and poverty. It is, for example, a consistent finding that women are at higher risk for PTSD after trauma than men, even after controlling for trauma type (Olff, Langeland, Draijer, & Gersons, 2007).

*Peri-trauma risk factors* include high levels of stress during the trauma, as well as particular characteristics of the violent event. While trauma is often discussed as a singular concept, there are large variations in the experiences that fall under this category. For example, was it a single event, or multiple events? How grave was the threat to life? Was it an accident, or something that another person did intentionally? If the trauma was interpersonal, what relationship did the victim have to the perpetrator? Was the traumatic event over in an instant, or protracted over time? Did physical injury occur? Was the event particularly degrading or invasive, for example including sexual penetration? These are some of the characteristics on which a traumatic event can vary, and although it is not given in all cases, there is no doubt that much domestic violence tends to fall on the severe end of the scale.

*Post-trauma risk factors* can include life stress following trauma and lack of social support post-trauma, including the response of services, or the availability and quality of social support (see more about this later). A meta-study of risk factors for PTSD found that any one single risk factor had limited effect on PTSD, but that peri- and post-trauma risk factors showed stronger effects than pre-trauma factors (Brewin, Andrews, & Valentine, 2000).

## Risk and protection in the social environment

The social environment of a person may help or complicate recovery after trauma. Among social factors that have received much research attention is social support. Social support may be instrumental (e.g., having someone to help with practical tasks) or emotional (e.g., having someone who can listen, offer advice and comfort) (Santini, Koyanagi, Tyrovolas, Mason, & Haro, 2015). It is a consistent finding that social support protects against mental health problems after adverse events (see for example Thoits, 2011, for a review). A meta-analysis found lack of social support to be among the strongest risk factors for PTSD (Brewin et al., 2000). One way to sub-categorize social support is to separate perceived support from received support. Perceived social support can be seen as a sort of fund from which the person can make a withdrawal in times of need, and this perception that you have support available should you need it seems to be more consistently related to health than actually received support (Thoits, 2011). For trauma victims, it may be of high importance to perceive the people around them as support-ive. However, many survivors may find it difficult to use this support when they need it. Such barriers to seeking social support may involve perceptions that others have enough with their own problems or that survivors worry about overburdening their friends (Thoresen, Jensen, Wentzel-Larsen, & Dyb, 2014). A study of young survivors of a terrorist attack found that social support barriers were associated with symptoms of PTSD. Further, when controlling for barri-ers, social support was no longer significantly associated with PTSD symptoms (Thoresen et al., 2014). Another study found that adults with experiences of violence in childhood scored lower on social support and higher on support-seeking barriers (Aakvaag & Strøm, 2019), indicating a double negative; not only did they have less support available, they also had trouble utilizing the support that they had.

In addition, many survivors of domestic violence feel shame after their victimization. Trauma-related shame is associated with symptoms of PTSD, and symptoms of anxiety and depression (Aakvaag et al., 2016; La Bash & Papa, 2014), making it a risk factor for mental health problems. Shame is a painful emotion, connected to perceptions that some part of oneself is unattractive to others, and may lead to rejection or devaluation (P. Gilbert, 2000). Thus, shame is closely con-nected to an individual's social surroundings, and is for this reason sometimes referred to as a 'social emotion' (P. Gilbert, 1997). Shame after violence is not uncommon, and experiencing multiple types of violence is associated with more shame (Aakvaag et al., 2016; Andrews, Brewin, Rose, & Kirk, 2000). This association may be puzzling, because, after all, why should a person feel shame for having been a victim of violence? The evolutionary psychologist Paul Gilbert sees shame as motivating defensive behaviour, where the individual attempts to protect her- or himself from social devaluation (P. Gilbert, 2000). If shame has as its purpose to protect the individual's social standing, this should also be the case for violence-related shame. The question, then, is whether victims are justified to worry that others will look down on them or reject them. In the case of shame after sexual violence, researchers have found that stereotypical beliefs about rape and so-called rape myths (for example that rape only happens to women who are careless or deserving; Payne, Lonsway, & Fitzgerald, 1999) are quite common. Domestic violence myths have been researched to a lesser degree, but studies find that they, too, are more common than we would like to think (Policastro & Payne, 2013). One study found that participants ascribed more blame to a woman who returned to her abusive partner than to a woman in a scenario with no such information (Yamawaki, Ochoa-Shipp, Pulsipher, Harlos, & Swindler, 2012). Participants who believed domestic violence myths tended to blame the abused woman more, and men tended to minimize the violence more than female participants did. Further, a meta-study on disclosure after domestic violence found that while women generally reported more positive than negative responses, a mixture of the two appeared to be more common (Sylaska & Edwards, 2013). Negative responses could involve pressuring the victim to act in a certain way, expressing disbelief, blaming the victim, or minimizing the violence. Negative social responses after abuse have been found to be closely linked to poor mental health outcomes (Ullman, Townsend, Filipas, & Starzynski, 2007), and one study found that negative social responses had a stronger effect on mental health than social support (Andrews, Brewin, & Rose, 2003).

Based on this, domestic violence survivors who fear rejection and devaluation from others, may be somewhat realistic in their expectations. Shame may be understood as protecting the individual from harmful social consequences; a woman who is abused by her partner may feel shame based on expectations that friends, family and colleagues would think less of her if they knew about the abuse. These feelings of shame may motivate her not to disclose the abuse, thereby avoiding the social devaluation. However, secrecy may have severe negative consequences. If nobody knows about the abuse, it is more likely to continue. On a societal level, secrecy may mean that the problem is silenced, and does not get the political attention needed. Importantly, secrecy also protects the abuser. For the individual, there may be valuable social support available that victims cannot utilize when they do not share their experiences. It is perhaps not surprising, then, that shame is associated with loneliness (Thoresen, Aakvaag, Strøm, Wentzel-Larsen, & Birkeland, 2018).

In sum, violence may damage victims' social lives through different pathways. Non-supportive social networks, barriers to support-seeking, and trauma-related shame are risk factors for mental health problems, but can also be negative consequences of violence in and of themselves. Social relationships are important for people's well-being. The findings discussed here imply that in order to diminish violence-related shame, and improve victims' social support, there is a need to change social perceptions of domestic violence and its victims, not only those of perpetrators and survivors, but of their social surroundings and society at large as well.

### *Psychological treatment of mental health problems after violence*

The devastating impact violence and other types of trauma can have on survivors' mental health points to the need for psychological treatment of trauma-related mental problems. To date, a variety of such treatment models exist, for example trauma-focused cognitive behavioural therapy (TF-CBT), narrative exposure therapy, eye-movement desensitization and reprocessing (EMDR), and brief eclectic therapy (for an overview, see Schnyder et al., 2015). While these approaches differ in a number of ways, the following six key interventions have been identified by pioneers in the field: psychoeducation; emotion regulation and coping skills; imaginal exposure; cognitive processing, restructuring, and/or meaning making; targeting emotions; and memory processing (Schnyder et al., 2015). The current recommendation in international clinical guidelines is that adults suffering from PTSD should be offered TF-CBT or EMDR (National Institute for Health and Care Excellence, 2018). TF-CBT programmes include psychoeducation about reactions to trauma, strategies for managing arousal and flashbacks, processing the trauma memory and trauma-related emotions, and restructuring the meaning of the trauma. EMDR includes many of the same interventions, but also repeated exposure combined with in-session bilateral eye-movement stimulation for specific target memories. For children and adolescents, clinicians are also recommended to provide TF-CBT or, for children older than seven years of age, EMDR (National Institute for Health and Care Excellence, 2018). Given the potential detrimental effects domestic violence may have on attachment, several researchers have emphasized the need to target the parent-child relationship in treatment (Borrego, Gutow, Reicher, & Barker, 2008; Humphreys, Mullender, Thiara, & Skamballis, 2006). Strategies towards this end have been developed for various disciplines, and include treatment approaches used not only by psychologists, but also by other professionals, such as social workers and family therapists (Humphreys et al., 2006; Thomas, Abell, Webb, Avdagic, & Zimmer-Gembeck, 2017).

Evidence-based psychological treatment has been found to be effective in treatment of PTSD symptomatology (Kline, Cooper, Rytwinksi, & Feeny, 2018). This gives reason to some optimism for the health and well-being of those affected by domestic violence. However, importantly, many people never seek treatment, and among those who do, some do not recover and some only achieve moderate improvement. Furthermore, for many people exposed to trauma, including domestic violence, health services are unavailable (e.g., too costly). Current innovation in the field of trauma treatment addresses some of these issues; for example, technological advances have made it possible to administer psychological treatment modules online. This is an emerging field, and much is still unknown, but promising results may mean that trauma treatment can be made available for people who would otherwise not have access (Olff et al., 2019).

## Conclusion

Traditionally, psychologists who study violence and abuse have tended to focus on mental health consequences. However, the field is moving towards a more comprehensive understanding of how such experiences may influence victims' lives. Studies on how experiences with violence and abuse influence survivors' social lives underscore that the psychological impact of violence and abuse go well beyond symptoms of mental health problems. Other areas that violence exposure may influence include work-life participation, financial status, closeness in relationships, and quality of life.

The monumental health effects of violence and abuse combined with evidence that it is prevalent all around the globe imply that violence should be considered a public health issue. Societal efforts are needed to prevent its occurrence, and also to diminish the risk of problems (mental health and otherwise) after exposure. Shame after trauma is pervasive and is one example of a violence-related issue that warrants a societal response. While shame is an emotion within the person him- or herself, it is highly contingent on the social surroundings of the individual, including myths and perceptions in society at large. Advances in areas such as legislation and law enforcement, as well as political movements like #metoo, may work in a shame-reducing way. While the recent decades have seen important advances in de-shaming various types of violence and abuse, findings discussed in this chapter imply that there is still a way to go to reduce shame after violence, in specific cultures and sub-cultures, but also across cultures.

## Critical findings

- Exposure to domestic violence can be considered a trauma. There is a large literature on how traumatic events can impact victims' psychological functioning.
- Mental health consequences of domestic violence and abuse can be devastating. These can include symptoms of posttraumatic stress disorder (PTSD) and depression, suicidal behaviour, and substance abuse.
- An additional problem for children who experience domestic violence and abuse is that the trauma may disrupt their natural development, including the child-caregiver relationship.
- Social relationships bear importance for how violence impacts a person. Non-supportive social networks, barriers to social support-seeking, and trauma-related shame have all been found to negatively affect mental health after trauma.
- There are several evidence-supported models for the treatment of trauma-related mental health problems.

## Implications for policy, practice, and research

- Prevalence estimates imply that domestic violence and abuse affect people all over the world. Domestic violence is often considered a severe trauma, and health consequences can be long-lasting, severe, and complex. Consequently, domestic violence should be considered a public health issue.
- The potential effects of violence and abuse on mental health underscore the importance of a mental health response to domestic violence.
- While there are effective ways to treat mental health problems after trauma, many victims do not have access to treatment. Emerging innovations may help meet this challenge; for example, online treatment modules may make treatment more accessible.
- Shame after violence is pervasive. As shame closely reflects other people's view, the reduction of shame after violence must entail society at large playing a big part.

## Note

1 Complex PTSD is included in the World Health Organization's diagnostic manual ICD-11 (WHO, 2019), but not in the American Psychiatric Association's diagnostic manual DSM-5 (APA, 2013).

## References

Aakvaag, H. F., & Strøm, I. F. (2019). *Vold i oppveksten: Varige spor? En longitudinell undersøkelse av reviktimisering, helse, rus og sosiale relasjoner hos unge utsatt for vold i barndommen.* Retrieved from Oslo.

Aakvaag, H. F., Thoresen, S., Wentzel-Larsen, T., Dyb, G., Røysamb, E., & Olff, M. (2016). Broken and guilty since it happened: A population study of trauma-related shame and guilt after violence and sexual abuse. *Journal of Affective Disorders, 204,* 16–23. doi:10.1016/j.jad.2016.06.004

Ainsworth, M. D. S., Blehar, M. C., Waters, E., & Wall, S. N. (1978). *Patterns of attachment. A Psychological study of the strange situation*. New York: Routledge.

Alisic, E., Zalta, A. K., van Wesel, F., Larsen, S. E., Hafstad, G. S., Hassanpour, K., & Smid, G. E. (2014). Rates of post-traumatic stress disorder in trauma-exposed children and adolescents: Meta-analysis. *British Journal of Psychiatry, 204*(5), 335–340. doi:10.1192/bjp.bp.113.131227

American Psychiatric Association. (2013). *Diagnostic and statistical manual of mental disorders* (5th ed). Arlington, VA: American Psychiatric Association.

American Psychological Association. (2020). *About APA*. Retrieved from www.apa.org/support/about-apa

Andrews, B., Brewin, C., & Rose, S. (2003). Gender, social support, and PTSD in victims of violent crime. *Journal of Traumatic Stress, 16*(4), 421–427. doi:10.1023/A:1024478305142

Andrews, B., Brewin, C. R., Rose, S., & Kirk, M. (2000). Predicting PTSD symptoms in victims of violent crime: The role of shame, anger, and childhood abuse. *Journal of Abnormal Psychology, 109*(1), 69–73. doi:10.1037/0021-843X.109.1.69

Appleton, W. (1980). The battered woman syndrome. *Annals of Emergency Medicine, 9*(2), 84–91. doi:10.1016/S0196-0644(80)80336-2

Artz, S., Jackson, M. A., Rossiter, K. R., Nijdam-Jones, A., Géczy, I., & Porteous, S. (2014). A comprehensive review of the literature on the impact of exposure to intimate partner violence for children and youth. *International Journal of Child, Youth and Family Studies, 5*(4). Retrieved from http://dspace.library.uvic.ca/bitstream/handle/1828/6611/Artz_Sibylle_IJCYFS_2014.pdf?sequence=1&isAllowed=y

Baer, J. C., & Martinez, C. D. (2006). Child maltreatment and insecure attachment: A meta-analysis. *Journal of Reproductive and Infant Psychology, 24*(3), 187–197. doi:10.1080/02646830600821231

Borrego, J., Gutow, M. R., Reicher, S., & Barker, C. H. (2008). Parent – Child interaction therapy with domestic violence populations. *Journal of Family Violence, 23*(6), 495–505.

Bowlby, J. (1958). The nature of the child's tie to his mother. *International Journal of Psycho-Analysis, 39*, 350–373.

Brewin, C. R., Andrews, B., & Valentine, J. D. (2000). Meta-analysis of risk factors for posttraumatic stress disorder in trauma-exposed adults. *Journal of Consulting and Clinical Psychology, 68*(5), 748–766. doi:10.1037/0022-006X.68.5.748

Campbell, J. C. (2002). Health consequences of intimate partner violence. *The Lancet, 359*(9314), 1331–1336. doi:10.1016/S0140-6736(02)08336-8

Campbell, J. C., Kub, J., Belknap, R. A., & Templin, T. N. (1997). Predictors of depression in battered women. *Violence Against Women, 3*(3), 271–293. doi:10.1177/1077801297003003004

Cassidy, J. (2008). The nature of the child's ties. In J. Cassidy & P. R. Shaver (Eds.), *Handbook of attachment* (pp. 3–22). New York, NY: The Guilford Press.

Cicchetti, D., & Rogosch, F. A. (1996). Equifinality and multifinality in developmental psychopathology. *Development and Psychopathology, 8*(4), 597–600. doi:10.1017/S0954579400007318

Cicchetti, D., & Toth, S. L. (2009). The past achievements and future promises of developmental psychopathology: The coming of age of a discipline. *Journal of Child Psychology and Psychiatry, 50*(1–2), 16–25. doi:10.1111/j.1469-7610.2008.01979.x

Cloitre, M., Garvert, D. W., Brewin, C. R., Bryant, R. A., & Maercker, A. (2013). Evidence for proposed ICD-11 PTSD and complex PTSD: A latent profile analysis. *European Journal of Psychotraumatology, 4*. doi:10.3402/ejpt.v4i0.20706

Edwards, V. J., Holden, G. W., Felitti, V. J., & Anda, R. F. (2003). Relationship between multiple forms of childhood maltreatment and adult mental health in community respondents: Results from the adverse childhood experiences study. *American Journal of Psychiatry, 160*(8), 1453–1460. doi:10.1176/appi.ajp.160.8.1453

Ellsberg, M., Jansen, H. A. F. M., Heise, L., Watts, C. H., & Garcia-Moreno, C. (2008). Intimate partner violence and women's physical and mental health in the WHO multi-country study on women's health and domestic violence: An observational study. *The Lancet, 371*(9619), 1165–1172. doi:10.1016/S0140-6736(08)60522-X

Felitti, V. J., Anda, R. F., Nordenberg, D., Williamson, D. F., Spitz, A. M., Edwards, V., . . . Marks, J. S. (2019). REPRINT OF: Relationship of childhood abuse and household dysfunction to many of the leading causes of death in adults: The adverse childhood experiences (ACE) study. *American Journal of Preventive Medicine, 56*(6), 774–786. doi:10.1016/j.amepre.2019.04.001

Fernandez, M. (2006). Cultural beliefs and domestic violence. *Annals of the New York Academy of Sciences, 1087*, 250–260. doi:10.1196/annals.1385.005

Ferrari, A. J., Charlson, F. J., Norman, R. E., Patten, S. B., Freedman, G., Murray, C. J. L., . . . Whiteford, H. A. (2013). Burden of depressive disorders by country, sex, age, and year: Findings from the global burden of disease study 2010. *PLoS Med, 10*(11), e1001547. doi:10.1371/journal.pmed.1001547

Finkelhor, D., & Browne, A. (1985). The traumatic impact of child sexual abuse: A conceptualization. *American Journal of Orthopsychiatry, 55*(4), 530–541. doi:10.1111/j.1939-0025.1985.tb02703.x

Freyd, J. J. (2008). Betrayal trauma. In G. Reyes, J. D. Elhai, & J. D. Ford (Eds.), *The encyclopedia of psychological trauma* (p. 76). Hoboken, NJ: John Wiley & Sons.

Garcia-Moreno, C., Jansen, H. A. F. M., Ellsberg, M., Heise, L., & Watts, C. H. (2005). *WHO Multi-country Study on women's health and domestic violence against women – Initial results on prevalence, health outcomes and women's responses.* Geneva: World Health Organization.

Garcia-Moreno, C., Jansen, H. A. F. M., Ellsberg, M., Heise, L., & Watts, C. H. (2006). Prevalence of intimate partner violence: Findings from the WHO multi-country study on women's health and domestic violence. *The Lancet, 368*(9543), 1260–1269. doi:10.1016/S0140-6736(06)69523-8

Gilbert, P. (1997). The evolution of social attractiveness and its role in shame, humiliation, guilt and therapy. *British Journal of Medical Psychology, 70*(2), 113–147. doi:10.1111/j.2044-8341.1997.tb01893.x

Gilbert, P. (2000). The relationship of shame, social anxiety and depression: The role of the evaluation of social rank. *Clinical Psychology and Psychotherapy, 7*, 174–189.

Gilbert, R., Widom, C. S., Browne, K., Fergusson, D., Webb, E., & Janson, S. (2009). Burden and consequences of child maltreatment in high-income countries. *The Lancet, 373*(9657), 68–81. doi:10.1016/S0140-6736(08)61706-7

Herman, J. L. (1992). *Trauma and recovery: From domestic abuse to political terror.* New York, NY: Basic Books.

Hicks, S. R. (1987). Admissibility of expert testimony on the psychology of the battered child. *Law & Psychology Review, 11*, 103–143.

Humphreys, C., Mullender, A., Thiara, R., & Skamballis, A. (2006). 'Talking to my mum' developing communication between mothers and children in the aftermath of domestic violence. *Journal of Social Work, 6*(1), 53–63.

Johnson, M. P. (2010). *A typology of domestic violence. Intimate terrorism, violent resistance, and situational couple violence.* Lebanon, NH: University Press of New England.

Jones, L., Hughes, M., & Unterstaller, U. (2001). Post-traumatic stress disorder (PTSD) in victims of domestic violence: A review of the research. *Trauma, Violence, & Abuse, 2*(2), 99–119. doi:10.1177/1524838001002002001

Kempe, C., Silverman, F. N., Steele, B. F., Droegemueller, W., & Silver, H. K. (1962). The battered-child syndrome. *JAMA, 181*(1), 17–24.

Kessler, R. C., Sonnega, A., Bromet, E., Hughes, M., & Nelson, C. B. (1995). Posttraumatic stress disorder in the national comorbidity survey. *Archives of General Psychiatry, 52*(12), 1048–1060. doi:10.1001/archpsyc.1995.03950240066012

Kline, A. C., Cooper, A. A., Rytwinksi, N. K., & Feeny, N. C. (2018). Long-term efficacy of psychotherapy for posttraumatic stress disorder: A meta-analysis of randomized controlled trials. *Clinical Psychology Review, 59*, 30–40. doi:10.1016/j.cpr.2017.10.009

Kobak, R., & Madsen, S. (2008). Disruptions in attachment bonds. In J. Cassidy & P. R. Shaver (Eds.), *Handbook of attachment* (pp. 23–47). New York, NY: The Guilford Press.

Kulwicki, A. D. (2002). The practice of honor crimes: A glimpse of domestic violence in the Arab world. *Issues in Mental Health Nursing, 23*(1), 77–87. doi:10.1080/01612840252825491

La Bash, H., & Papa, A. (2014). Shame and PTSD symptoms. *Psychological Trauma: Theory, Research, Practice, and Policy, 6*(2), 159–166. doi:10.1037/a0032637

Main, M., & Solomon, J. (1986). Discovery of an insecure-disorganized/disoriented attachment pattern. In *Affective development in infancy* (pp. 95–124). Westport, CT: Ablex Publishing.

National Institute for Health and Care Excellence. (2018). *Post-traumatic stress disorder.* Retrieved from www.nice.org.uk/guidance/ng116

Olff, M., Amstadter, A., Armour, C., Birkeland, M. S., Bui, E., Cloitre, M., . . . Thoresen, S. (2019). A decennial review of psychotraumatology: What did we learn and where are we going? *European Journal of Psychotraumatology, 10*(1), 1672948. doi:10.1080/20008198.2019.1672948

Olff, M., Langeland, W., Draijer, N., & Gersons, B. P. R. (2007). Gender differences in posttraumatic stress disorder. *Psychological Bulletin, 133*(2), 183–204. doi:10.1037/0033-2909.133.2.183

Payne, D. L., Lonsway, K. A., & Fitzgerald, L. F. (1999). Rape myth acceptance: Exploration of its structure and its measurement using the Illinois rape myth acceptance scale. *Journal of Research in Personality, 33*(1), 27–68. doi:10.1006/jrpe.1998.2238

Policastro, C., & Payne, B. K. (2013). The blameworthy victim: Domestic violence myths and the criminalization of victimhood. *Journal of Aggression, Maltreatment & Trauma, 22*(4), 329–347. doi:10.1080/10926771.2013.775985

Pollak, S. D. (2008). Mechanisms linking early experience and the emergence of emotions: Illustrations from the study of maltreated children. *Current Directions in Psychological Science, 17*(6), 370–375. doi:10.1111/j.1467-8721.2008.00608.x

Reisz, S., Duschinsky, R., & Siegel, D. J. (2018). Disorganized attachment and defense: Exploring John Bowlby's unpublished reflections. *Attachment & Human Development, 20*(2), 107–134. doi:10.1080/14616734.2017.1380055

Resick, P. A., Bovin, M. J., Calloway, A. L., Dick, A. M., King, M. W., Mitchell, K. S., . . . Wolf, E. J. (2012). A critical evaluation of the complex PTSD literature: Implications for DSM-5. *Journal of Traumatic Stress, 25*(3), 241–251. doi:10.1002/jts.21699

Santini, Z. I., Koyanagi, A., Tyrovolas, S., Mason, C., & Haro, J. M. (2015). The association between social relationships and depression: A systematic review. *Journal of Affective Disorders, 175,* 53–65. doi:10.1016/j.jad.2014.12.049

Schnyder, U., Ehlers, A., Elbert, T., Foa, E. B., Gersons, B. P. R., Resick, P. A., . . . Cloitre, M. (2015). Psychotherapies for PTSD: What do they have in common? *European Journal of Psychotraumatology, 6*(1), 28186. doi:10.3402/ejpt.v6.28186

Strøm, I. F., Birkeland, M. S., Aakvaag, H. F., & Thoresen, S. (2019). Trajectories of alcohol use and alcohol intoxication in young adults exposed to childhood violence and later problematic drinking behavior. *Journal of Family Violence.* doi:10.1007/s10896-019-00094-8

Sylaska, K. M., & Edwards, K. M. (2013). Disclosure of intimate partner violence to informal social support network members: A review of the literature. *Trauma, Violence, & Abuse, 15*(1), 3–21. doi:10.1177/1524838013496335

Teicher, M. H., Samson, J. A., Anderson, C. M., & Ohashi, K. (2016). The effects of childhood maltreatment on brain structure, function and connectivity. *Nature Reviews Neuroscience, 17*(10), 652–666. doi:10.1038/nrn.2016.111

Testa, M., Livingston, J. A., & Leonard, K. E. (2003). Women's substance use and experiences of intimate partner violence: A longitudinal investigation among a community sample. *Addictive Behaviors, 28*(9), 1649–1664. doi:10.1016/j.addbeh.2003.08.040

Thoits, P. A. (2011). Mechanisms linking social ties and support to physical and mental health. *Journal of Health and Social Behavior, 52*(2), 145–161. doi:10.1177/0022146510395592

Thomas, R., Abell, B., Webb, H. J., Avdagic, E., & Zimmer-Gembeck, M. J. (2017). Parent-child interaction therapy: A meta-analysis. *Pediatrics, 140*(3). doi:10.1542/peds.2017-0352.

Thoresen, S., Aakvaag, H. F., Strøm, I. F., Wentzel-Larsen, T., & Birkeland, M. S. (2018). Loneliness as a mediator of the relationship between shame and health problems in young people exposed to childhood violence. *Social Science & Medicine, 211,* 183–189. doi:10.1016/j.socscimed.2018.06.002

Thoresen, S., Jensen, T. K., Wentzel-Larsen, T., & Dyb, G. (2014). Social support barriers and mental health in terrorist attack survivors. *Journal of Affective Disorders, 156,* 187–193. doi:10.1016/j.jad.2013.12.014

Thoresen, S., Myhre, M., Wentzel-Larsen, T., Aakvaag, H. F., & Hjemdal, O. K. (2015). Violence against children, later victimisation, and mental health: A cross-sectional study of the general Norwegian population. *European Journal of Psychotraumatology, 6.* doi:10.3402/ejpt.v6.26259

Ullman, S. E., Townsend, S. M., Filipas, H. H., & Starzynski, L. L. (2007). Structural models of the relations of assault severity, social support, avoidance coping, self-blame, and PTSD among sexual assault survivors. *Psychology of Women Quarterly, 31*(1), 23–37. doi:10.1111/j.1471-6402.2007.00328.x

Van Ijzendoorn, M. H., Schuengel, C., & Bakermans-Kranenburg, M. J. (1999). Disorganized attachment in early childhood: Meta-analysis of precursors, concomitants, and sequelae. *Development and Psychopathology, 11*(2), 225–250. doi:10.1017/S0954579499002035

Vrana, S., & Lauterbach, D. (1994). Prevalence of traumatic events and post-traumatic psychological symptoms in a nonclinical sample of college students. *Journal of Traumatic Stress, 7*(2), 289–302. doi:10.1007/BF02102949

Walker, L. E. (1977). Who are the battered women? *Frontiers: A Journal of Women Studies, 2*(1), 52–57. doi:10.2307/3346107

Walker, L. E. (1979). *Battered woman.* New York, NY: Harper and Row.

White, H. R., & Chen, P.-H. (2002). Problem drinking and intimate partner violence. *Journal of Studies on Alcohol*, *63*(2), 205–214. doi:10.15288/jsa.2002.63.205

World Health Organization. (2019). *International statistical classification of diseases and related health problems* (11th ed.). Geneva: WHO.

Yamawaki, N., Ochoa-Shipp, M., Pulsipher, C., Harlos, A., & Swindler, S. (2012). Perceptions of domestic violence: The effects of domestic violence myths, victim's relationship with her abuser, and the decision to return to her abuser. *Journal of Interpersonal Violence*, *27*(16), 3195–3212. doi:10.1177/0886260512441253

# PART 3

# Domestic violence and abuse across the life-course

# 9

# THE IMPACT OF DOMESTIC VIOLENCE AND ABUSE ON INFANT MENTAL HEALTH

*Wendy Bunston*

## Introduction

Infant Mental Health (IMH) is concerned with beginnings. First and foremost, beginning with the infant's birth and early years. This includes understanding the parents/carers' early beginnings, relationally and contextually, and how this has shaped who they are; and how the evolving infant-parents/carers' relationship, with all the potential it holds, effects them in return. These threads then weave together to influence the developing infant and their caregiving world and intersect powerfully with multiple contextual factors such as race, culture, ideology, religion, gender and socio-economic considerations. Specific to this chapter is how domestic violence and abuse (DVA) within the primary caregiving relationship impacts the mental health of the infant.

Research has unequivocally demonstrated that DVA impacts the infant's mental health and wellbeing (Schechter, Willheim, Suardi, & Serpa, 2019). The repetition of early relational trauma in the caregiving world lays the foundation for all subsequent development (Stern, 1985/2003). As yet without words, the preverbal infant communicates volumes about their world, psychosomatically, relationally and emotionally. Holding the infants' experience of DVA in mind calls for adults to resist the impulse to minimise or disappear this trauma, as

> fully engaging with an infant or young child's psychological distress is often too confronting and too painful . . . if we are not prepared to go there, we leave the very small child alone to manage this by themselves, something they are neurologically, emotionally and physiologically ill-equipped to do.
>
> (Bunston, 2017, p. 15)

## Chapter overview

An overview of what is known about the developing infant begins this chapter. This will be followed by describing what IMH is and does, with prevailing research and thinking into the impacts of trauma on infants explained. The available research on the impacts of DVA on IMH will then be described in more detail and a critique of this research provided. Next will be a consideration of how to approach researching, as well as purposefully intervening with infants and mothers, and how fathers who use violence are included in this space. The final area explored involves hope, and the under-conceptualised, under-researched and underestimated hope infants hold for changing the future.

## The developing infant

Infants demonstrate their ability for engaging with others, exploring their environment and demonstrating self-agency soon after birth (Zeanah Jr, 2009). The infant possesses a sense of self as separate to, but in relationship with others, and attempts to create connectedness, building their social and emotional competencies as they discover "ways-of-being-with-others" (Stern, 1985/2003, p. xii). This is "how communication begins and develops in infancy, how it influences the individual subject's movement, perception, and learning, and how the infant's biologically grounded self-regulation of internal state and self-conscious purposefulness is sustained through active engagement with sympathetic others" (Trevarthen & Aitken, 2001, p. 3).

The sensate, embodied and physiological processes experienced by the newborn are shaped by how their caregiving system responds to and/or initiates each relational exchange. Such exchanges have been described as a neural "mapping of the other onto the self" (Ammaniti & Gallese, 2014, p. 8). This exchange is reciprocal, particularly with the mother, who, as the likely primary caregiver (DESA, 2011), is most significantly impacted by the experience of giving birth (Stern, 1998), and most vulnerable to experiencing DVA at the hands of men (WHO, 2013).

Essentially, the infant is neurologically 'wired to connect' and will innately seek out proximity with others, occurring even when those others may also be a source of harm (Main, Hesse, & Hesse, 2011). A major developmental task for the first years of life is the infant beginning to emotionally and physically regulate, internalising the outside experience of being held 'well enough' physically, emotionally and relationally by their caregiving context (Winnicott, 2002). Emotional affect regulation, that of being able to manage internal feeling states, occurs in the context of safety and active reassurance, as does the capacity to experience relational repair when things do not immediately go well (Tronick, 2007). "Feeling felt" is an important validation of the emerging sense of self and throughout one's lifetime, as "empathy soothes us and makes us feel safe" (Fishbane, 2007, p. 403).

It is the caregiving context enveloping the infant which directly shapes their attachment/s and "the functional origins of the bodily-based implicit self" (Schore & Schore, 2008, p. 10). Further, the quality of the attachment the infant develops in their primary caregiving relationships directly impacts the infant's neurological, physiological, psychological and emotional development (Schore, 2016; Siegel, 2012). It is the reciprocity the infant is capable of which seems extraordinary to many adults: their demonstrated ability to show empathy for others, to initiate social engagement, and the evidence of implicit relational perceptiveness beginning in their first year of life (Liddle, Bradley, & McGrath, 2015).

## Infant mental health

IMH focuses on the infant, their parent/s and the relational health of the caregiving system. Traditionally targeting the prenatal stage to age 3 (WAIMH, 2019), some now extend this to age 5. Zeanah Jr and Zeanah (2019, p. 6), quoting ZeroToThree (2001) explains that IMH is concerned with:

> the young child's capacity to experience, regulate and express emotions, form close and secure relationships, and explore the environment and learn. All of these capacities

will be best accomplished within the context of the caregiving environment that includes family, community and cultural expectations for young children.

In 2016 the World Association for Infant Mental Health (WAIMH) developed a "position paper on the rights of infants" (WAIMH, 2016, p. 4) declaring:

> The infant's status as a person is to include equal value for life regardless of gender or any individual characteristics such as those of disability . . . the right to be given nurturance that includes love, physical and emotional safety, adequate nutrition and sleep . . . the right to be protected from neglect, physical, sexual, and emotional abuse, including infant trafficking.

IMH is concerned with the overall welfare of infants, including adequate access to food, shelter and clothing as well as love, attention, protection and care (Weatherston, 2000). The infant is fully dependent on others for their survival and "cannot exist alone but is essentially part of a relationship" (Winnicott, 1964, p. 88).

As a field of enquiry, IMH began in the UK and US in the 1960s, drawing on developmental psychology and psychoanalysis (Harman, 2003; Zeanah Jr, 2019). Today, it is a large international, multidisciplinary, theoretically diverse, clinically based, scientific and research-informed field with most knowledge derived from research with infants from high-income countries (Bornstein, Putnick, Park, Suwalsky, & Haynes, 2017). As such, IMH knowledge has largely been formulated by white, Western, upper middle-class practitioners, researchers and academics, using a heteronormative lens and concerned with the influence of the early years across the lifespan. However, Western childrearing practices have been charged with being ethnocentric, posing challenges for differing cultural practices and what determines a beneficial start in life (Quinn & Mageo, 2013).

The mainstays of thinking within IMH includes attachment theory (Salter-Ainsworth & Bowlby, 1991), psychoanalytic and object relations concepts (Winnicott, 2002) and the transgenerational transmission of trauma (Fraiberg, Adelson, & Shapiro, 1975). Research into the brain throughout the 1990s laid the foundation for what is now a scientific agenda influencing IMH research and practice (Jones & Mendell, 1999), along with more recent explorations into epigenetics (Zeanah Jr, 2019). Current research into the cognitive and sensory-perceptual capacities of infants has definitively demonstrated that infants are not passive participants in the parent/infant relationship but competent and sentient beings in and of themselves, impacted by as well as impacting their caregiving environment (Ammaniti & Gallese, 2014).

Absent from IMH research and infant development generally, is a comprehensive examination of the effects of systemic racism, war, famine, ill-health, oppressive regimes and ideologies and the complexities facing low-income countries. The impacts of disease, poverty, malnutrition and lack of health care are conspicuous and measurable, receiving considerably more attention in the literature (Lu, Black, & Richter, 2016). Giving space to the experience of infants and their caregivers in low-income countries, their experience of violence and oppression, and the equally strong bonds and determination of mothers to protect and see their infants thrive, remains a challenge for this sector.

## Impacts of relational, emotional, physical trauma and abuse on the infant

Infants are at the greatest risk of harm, neglect and death than any other time in childhood (UNICEF, 2015) with DVA identified as a significant associated factor (Menon, 2014). Within high-income countries where DVA is present, infants and young children are at a heightened risk of being removed from families by state-based child protection services and placed in kinship or non-familial care (Alaggia, Gadalla, Shlonsky, Jenney, & Daciuk, 2015). Less common, poorly understood and responded to are incidences of filicide, murder-suicide and familicide, and the immediate and long-term impacts and consequences for surviving infants and siblings (Eyre, Milburn, & Bunston, 2020). Of concern for this chapter is what occurs for the infant when the caregiving environment is impacted by DVA such that the provision of 'good enough parenting' is thwarted or severely jeopardised.

Early childhood maltreatment has been linked to symptoms of anxiety and depression during adolescence (Harpur, Polek, & van Harmelen, 2015); increased risk of developing cancer, cardiovascular difficulties and immune system deficiencies (Cicchetti, Hetzel, Rogosch, Handley, & Toth, 2016); and reduced cerebral volume, verbal memory retrieval, attention and cognitive deficits (Carrion, Wong, & Kletter, 2013). The Adverse Childhood Experiences (ACE) study involving 17,337 adults, including some who reported experiences of DV (Anda et al., 2006, p. 174), found a correlation between ACEs and substance abuse, neuropsychiatric syndromes, numerous health problems and relational difficulties.

To some extent the impacts of exposure to early infant trauma are inferred (Schechter & Willheim, 2009). This is not to argue that they are not real, but that direct and time-specific correlates are hard to measure given much relational trauma impacting infants and young children occurs behind closed doors. Such trauma is infrequently reported, difficult to substantiate and too often minimised (Gilbert et al., 2009). Abuse may not be evident in infancy until a baby requires urgent medical attention, dies or impacts become apparent through longitudinal or retrospective studies (Enlow, Egeland, Blood, Wright, & Wright, 2012).

During pregnancy the foetal brain is vulnerable to acute maternal hormone expression resulting from trauma and stress and can leave enduring impacts (Berens & Nelson, 2019). Postnatally, the developing brain is 'experience dependent', shaped by their caregiving environment and with exposure to ongoing stress or trauma believed to significantly increase cortisol levels and the release of flight/fight hormones, epinephrine and norepinephrine, saturating the rapidly developing but immature brain. This is detrimental to cognitive development, affect regulation and optimal growth of the brain (Carpenter & Stacks, 2009). Ongoing and significant early relational trauma and maltreatment has been demonstrated to impinge hippocampal, cerebellar and corpus callosum volume; impair synaptic growth; and risk damage to the prefrontal cortex and limbic regions (Teicher & Samson, 2013). Such functional losses are consistent with the classification of paediatric posttraumatic stress disorder (Carrion et al., 2013).

Early implicit memories, particularly those created through trauma, are believed to remain operating throughout our lives, acting as the foundation upon, and intimately linked with later developing explicit memories and a sense of self (Van der Kolk, 2014). The right brain, responsible for the emotional, non-verbal self is dominant in the first 24 months of life and is highly vulnerable to cumulative, traumatic events "which are imprinted into the neurobiological structures that are maturing during the brain growth spurt of the first two years of life, and therefore have far-reaching effects" (Schore, 2001, p. 208).

Poor emotional development in the preverbal period impacts later developing, left hemisphere language, cognition and social capabilities (Schore, 2016; Van der Kolk, 2014). Teicher, Samson, Polcari and McGreenery (2006) in their research into the various effects of childhood maltreatment found that the "combined exposure to verbal abuse and witnessing of DV was associated with extraordinarily large adverse effects, particularly on dissociation" (p. 997), an outcome which has profound implications for future interpersonal relationships, skill acquisition and learning.

## Research into the impacts of DVA in the early years

Infants born to mothers who were assaulted whilst pregnant are twice as likely to have lower birth weights, and more likely to suffer foetal death or die within the first year of life with infant mortality higher amongst females in some developing countries (Menon, 2014). Research specifically targeting DVA exposure in the early years points to difficulties in three substantive and intimately interconnected areas:

- Forming healthy attachments.
- Affect regulation.
- Developmental pathways.

## Forming healthy attachments

The infant develops within the context of their caregiving environment, forming a significant attachment to a specific caregiver/s which largely endures across time (Van Ryzin, Carlson, & Sroufe, 2011). Four basic categories describe the type of attachment the infant develops through organising themselves in response to what they come to expect from each caregiver interaction (Crittenden & Ainsworth, 1989).

*Secure Attachment*: the infant is supported over time to develop a healthy and autonomous sense of self, engaging in play and discovery, experiencing their caregiver as a safe haven, finding continuity in this relationship and congruence in how to read and respond to the cues of others.

*Anxious Ambivalent*: an infant or young child is excessively clingy and loath to separate from their caregiver, yet does not appear to gain sufficient comfort from their closeness.

*Anxious Avoidant*: the infant appears to seldom use their caregiver as an emotional anchor yet will not stray too far. Proximity is desired but past experience has taught them that to express this need risks rejection.

*Disorganised Attachment*: the infant does not find sanctuary in their relationship with their primary caregiver/s. They experience a paradox of wanting to seek safety with, but feel frightened of approaching their caregiver/s, exhibiting complex, contradictive, inexplicable and disorientated behaviours.

DVA reflects a 'disorder of an attachment' within a caregiving system according to (Bowlby, 1984). He believed violence, from male to female, or parent to child, tended to be transmitted across generations. The excessive and distorted use of anger was used to prevent the threat of abandonment, maintain proximity or assert control over another. Bowlby (1984) was appalled that "family violence as a casual factor in psychiatry should have been so neglected by clinicians" (p. 9). A comprehensive meta-analysis of the literature found attachment styles which are classified as insecure, strongly correlate with violent offending behaviours (Ogilvie, Newman, Todd, & Peck, 2014). Lieberman, Chu, Van Horn and Harris (2011) argue that, where children are exposed to DVA, it is the child 5 years and under who are most likely to experience DVA yet are least likely to be provided with a service response.

## *The infant in utero and DVA*

The circumstances surrounding an infant's conception also has potential implications for their mental health. This includes, for example, where infants are conceived through rape or coercion, a mother experiences increasing violence targeted at herself and the unborn foetus, a mother is prevented from seeking an abortion or is accused of infidelity. Such circumstances impact a mother's feelings and ideas about the baby growing inside of her. "Maternal representations" describes how a mother comes to imagine what their baby is like, in character, temperament and personality, and the influence of her own current circumstances, and early experiences of being parented (Benoit, Zeanah, Parker, Nicholson, & Coolbear, 1997). For the infant to find security in their attachment with their caregiver, their caregiver requires a healthy "awareness of mental processes in the self and other" (Fonagy, Steele, Steele, Moran, & Higgitt, 1991, p. 203). Ongoing threat and/or presence of harm impinges the capacity for healthy awareness of others in favour of survival.

Envisioning the infant and the impact of their arrival becomes very potent during pregnancy, for the mother, father or co-parent, as their own implicit and explicit childhood experiences and memories of how they were parented are activated. "Caregivers who have unresolved mourning or trauma" (Crawford & Benoit, 2009, p. 132) and who themselves were exposed to DVA as infants and children risk carrying states of mind which may inhibit the infant forming a close and healthy attachment (Malone, Levendosky, Dayton, & Bogat, 2010).

## *Attachment difficulties*

Exposure to DVA during pregnancy and in the early years has significant impacts on the infant's ability to attach securely to their mother and father. The Michigan "Mother-Infant Study" with 150 pregnant women experiencing DV (Levendosky, Leahy, Bogat, Davidson, & von Eye, 2006) found the quality of the attachment of the infant with their mother was negatively impacted where mothers experienced DV during the pregnancy and their first years of life. In part, this was caused by the DV interrupting the maternal capacity to positively hold in mind a sense of themselves becoming a mother and their growing sense of their infant. However, where a mother had left a violent relationship post the birth and before age 1, the child by age 4 was more likely to be securely attached (Levendosky, Bogat, Huth-Bocks, Rosenblum, & Von Eye, 2011).

Research from the Lehigh Longitudinal Study recruited 457 toddlers from 18 months up to children aged 6 (average age 4) and their primary caregivers, from both child welfare services and community day care centres (Herrenkohl & Herrenkohl, 2007). Attempts to strengthen their attachments to parents post their early childhood experience of violence and abuse was hypothesised to be insufficient to ameliorate the impacts of this early trauma (Sousa et al., 2011).

## *Attachment behaviours*

An infant's attachment behaviour emerges from their relational exchange with their caregiver/s. Inherent in creating security is a reciprocity of engagement, with the mother and/or father/carer able to offer the infant responsive and attuned caregiving. This effectively provides the infant with external relational responses which help them to manage their own, overwhelming, internal emotional states; something they cannot do alone. If these states are co-managed with their mother's, father's or primary caregiver's help, albeit not always perfectly but consistently enough; over time the infant internalises these neurophysiological competencies which allows the foundation for the developing child's own increasing capacity for affect regulation. When faced with unpredictable or frightening responses an infant will initially exhibit proximity-seeking behaviours. However, if these prove futile and occur repeatedly, "the younger the child, the less internal capacities they have at their disposal and the more likely they will be to dissociate. All of these defences serve to anaesthetise feelings of fear" (Bunston, 2017, p. 33). Maternal sensitivity decreases with DV, impacts maternal mental health and increases aggression and externalising difficulties in infants by age 1 as a result of maternal dysregulation (Levendosky et al., 2006).

## *Criticism*

Attachment theory is a dominant prism through which infant development and the impacts of DVA are understood. This includes using standardised and quantitative research approaches which (Lapierre, 2008) argues places "the problem primarily with women and their mothering" (p. 456) rather than the violent behaviour of men and serves to "obscure the variability of children's individual experiences" (p. 455). Main et al. (2011) acknowledges that "all present methods of assessing attachment were designed for research purposes . . . and have yet to be sufficiently tested for their predictive powers with respect to the assessment of individuals" (p. 428). The ethics of using standardised procedures which force separations between mothers and infants to assess attachment profiles have been called into question (Bunston, 2016), whilst (White, Gibson, Wastell, & Walsh, 2019) argue that the dominance of attachment theory in research and practice needs to be challenged by a more realistic view of the complexities and power of human connections.

Buchanan, Power and Verity (2013) argue that the ascendancy of attachment thinking has precluded an appreciation of gendered violence and failed to acknowledge the role fear plays in a mother's protectiveness of her infant and the developing infant/mother relationship. Attachment theory has promoted "mother blaming" contends Jackson & Mannix, (2004) and "failed to acknowledge the gendered nature of the social world" (p. 157).

Research with a large USA sample of low income and ethnically diverse mothers and pre-school children, Starting Early, Starting Smart, found a relational "spill-over" effect of living with DVA. They found that harsher maternal discipline was associated with inter-partner conflict, negatively impacted child development, but did not lessen maternal warmth, and situated the negative impacts of DVA with the violence, and not the mother (Whiteside-Mansell, Bradley, McKelvey, & Fussell, 2009). Letourneau et al. (2013) in a smaller Canadian study found that whilst there was some level of spill-over in caregiving practices resulting from DV, mothers and infants exhibited compensatory behaviours within their interactions in response to living with violence. Missing from the research is how compensatory relationships formed with others, such as extended family members, siblings, childcare personnel and others who may provide relational reparation. Nor has an appreciation of children's own resilience been adequately explored. Furthermore, the interplay between other significant variables such as social, economic, racial and gender inequality seldom receive due attention in the research and practice space.

## Affect regulation

The newborn, infant or very young child is reliant on their caregiver/s to manage their emotional wellbeing. "This process is internalized and over time builds the capacity for effective self-regulation" (Arvidson et al., 2011, p. 38). However, when a mother herself is overwhelmed by DVA, past traumatic memories and the struggle to survive; the capacity to manage her own dysregulation, let alone her infant's is severely diminished. Levendosky, Bogat and Martinez-Torteya (2013) found that "in the youngest children, affective dysregulation is the most dominant response to witnessing IPV" (p. 196). Internalising (withdrawal, shutting down) and externalising (oppositional behaviour, settling problems) difficulties are the most reported symptoms resulting from exposure to DV in infancy. Children at age 3 who had experienced DV across their lifetime exhibited arousal and avoidance symptoms which by school age were more likely to measure within the subclinical range for disturbances in internalising and externalising difficulties (Briggs-Gowan, Carter, & Ford, 2012).

## Developmental pathways

DVA impacts the infant's ability to find a secure attachment and safe haven to help organise heightened emotional states, impeding development. Early experiences matter. In their small-scale study, Letourneau et al. (2013) found "effects of exposure to IPV even on children younger than 3 years of age". Whilst their study suggested that infants counteracted the effects of Interpersonal Family Violence in their interactions with their mothers, "children in the sample scored significantly lower on the Ages and Stages Questionnaire (ASQ) Fine Motor and Problem Solving subscales and the means of the remaining ASQ subscales were lower (although not significantly) than the norm" (Letourneau et al., 2013, p. 582).

Levendosky et al. (2013) found that as children's ages increased so too did their traumatic symptoms. Where infants struggle with affect regulation young children start to exhibit "more cognitive and behavioural dysregulation as a response to witnessing IPV" (p. 196). Kitzmann, Gaylord, Holt and Kenny (2003) in their meta-analytic review of 118 studies into child witnesses to DV suggested that pre-schoolers were at greater risk of problems in social competence and sensitivity to anticipated parental conflict. Osofsky (2003) reported on the ripple effect of children exposed to DV and child maltreatment, observing "disturbances in school behaviour, mixed feelings toward parents with positive affect being mingled with anger, and difficulties in forming later relationships" (p. 166).

A study of 206 children in the USA from infancy to early school years measured intelligence quotient, language and academic progress across three points with delays becoming increasingly evident as children grew older (Enlow et al., 2012). DVA was associated with decreased cognitive capacity, and most evident in the cohort exposed to family violence from birth to 2 years. Similarly, a study involving 47 children (7–16 years) used multiple standardised measures to assess their cognitive functioning concluded that family violence inhibited executive functioning, and increased impulsivity and distractibility (Samuelson, Krueger, & Wilson, 2012). DVA impacts IMH over generations, and shapes developmental trajectories as does "consideration of the ways in which historically informed systemic inequities intersect to create social conditions that increase risks for negative experiences such as IPV . . . and the compounded hardship that families face" (Grady, Hinshaw-Fuselier, & Friar, 2019, p. 634).

## Practice interventions which start with the infant's inclusion

Interventions targeting the impacts of DVA traditionally focus on children only, mothers only, or have used conjoint models, with separate concurrent groups for children and their mothers, and with some combined time (Graham-Bermann, Miller-Graff, Howell, & Grogan-Kaylor, 2015; McWhirter, 2011). Interventions have tended to include verbal children from 4 upwards, leaving mothers responsible for attending to the resulting impacts of the trauma.

Approaches often emphasise education, behavioural change or enhancing maternal sensitivity (Letourneau et al., 2015).

However, the need to intervene earlier is clearly indicated. Interventions with the infant in mind, particularly in relation to DVA, have been scarce. This reflects a generalised belief that infants do not remember, are not impacted or are too young to understand what is happening. Furthermore, anxiety abounds in misguided attempts to ensure that the relational, emotional and psychological safety of infants is not further exacerbated by their inclusion in therapeutic interventions, resulting in infants being excluded from service responses. Unwittingly, this failure to actively involve the infant in therapeutic work risks disappearing their experience altogether.

The infant's experience is relevant in dyadic and familial exchanges yet is made meaningless if they are not directly invited to participate and add their perspective to research, thinking and interventions which directly concern them (Bunston & Jones, 2020). Infants occupy the space where language has less meaning than action, participation, reciprocity and engagement. Infants are more than capable of letting others know their feeling states and to be active participants in therapeutic interventions should others take care to observe, reflect and intuitively listen to them.

Interventions which are 'infant inclusive' (Bunston, 2017) are likely to see rapid changes. Such work includes *Child-Parent Psychotherapy* (Bernstein, Timmons, & Lieberman, 2019; Lieberman & Van Horn, 2009) which undertakes comprehensive dyadic work with the infant and parent. *The Peek a Boo Club* offers an 'infant-led' approach for infants from birth to 4 years and their mothers within a group work setting (Bunston, 2015). *Mothers in Mind* uses a trauma informed, strengths-based group work intervention which caters for vulnerable infants under 4 and their mothers (Jenney, 2020).

Such work recognises the infant's right to participate, and as the newest, least stuck and most receptive member of a family, the infant is often quickest to engage, ready to adapt and most amenable to change. The infant's inclusion brings immediate interactional meaning into the research and treatment space as they bring their feeling states authentically to the fore. The infant's interactions with their caregiver brings multifarious opportunities for intervention and reflection and presents evocative and immediate opportunities for revisiting parents' own past experiences.

## Involving fathers

Controversy surrounds developing interventions for fathers who use violence and evaluation of such programmes remain limited (Labarre, Bourassa, Holden, Turcotte, & Letourneau, 2016); however, there is increasing recognition that infants and young children often remain living with or remain in contact with fathers who use violence. For better or for worse, infants and young children form attachments with their fathers which are meaningful, often complex, may be different to what others experience, deserve to be acknowledged and allowed space to be safely recognised and made sense of (Jones & Bunston, 2012). "As the product of both parents, the infant needs something good to take from both, helping them to grow their sense of identity as connected to, but also separate from, both their mother and father" (Bunston, 2017, p. 156). However, working with fathers who have used violence should by no means place the infant at risk. To the contrary, it is imperative to make blatant the safety of infants and young children as the centrepiece in any work which concerns them.

Amongst the small number of programmes available approaches vary. For example, *Caring Dads* works solely with the fathers through what is largely a group-based motivational intervention to enhance men's capacity for child sensitive parenting (McConnell, Barnard, & Taylor, 2017). *Fathers for Change* piloted an intervention which combined attachment, systems and cognitive approaches, and provided individual treatment, co-parenting sessions and targeted interactional change through videotaped sessions of fathers engaged in free play (Stover, 2015). The *Bubs on Board* pilot programme worked with fathers post a men's behaviour change programme, working directly with the infant/young child and their father in a group setting (Bunston, 2013). *For Baby's Sake* commences their work with mothers and fathers during pregnancy, remains involved for the first two years and uses a 'whole of family' trauma and attachment-based approach (Domoney et al., 2019). *Changing Futures* tailored their work to flexibly meet the needs of the family and affect wider systems change (Stanley & Humphreys, 2017).

Labarre et al. (2016) argue that "it is vital to support fathers who wish to eliminate their violent behaviour and become positively engaged in their children's lives" (p. 3). Analysing ten intervention programmes, Labarre et al. (2016) state that fathers need to take responsibility for their children, be accountable for their violence, need support to change and, as many remain involved in their children's lives, use their motivation for wanting a relationship with their children as leverage for change.

## Hope

Neuro-biologically, the birthing process "allows for mutual regulation of vital endocrine, autonomic, and central nervous systems of both mother and infant by elements of their interaction with each other" (Schore, 2005, p. 207). Oxytocin, associated with building trust and bonding can be activated during pregnancy and birth (Clark et al., 2013; Kimura, Tanizawa, Kensaku, J, & Hiroto, 1992) and a sensitivity to environmental impacts is heightened (Luijk et al., 2011). This early stage of infancy is their most vulnerable, but most expectant, with services, support, engagement and openness to possibilities ripe. Newborns actively seek and invite their parents to connect with them and can bring something new to the lives of their caregivers.

Young children exposed to DV have been shown to exhibit higher than usual sensitivity and clearer cues to their mothers than the norm, suggesting that the child actively participates in compensatory interactions with their mothers (Letourneau et al., 2013). Possibilities of change and wanting better for their children is a strong motivation for a mother to leave a violent relationship: "Infants and small children can represent hope for parents. This is in the form of repairing hurts from the past and creating something new. This is about capitalising on hope" (Bunston, 2017, p. 27).

## Conclusion

This chapter has provided an overview of infant development, IMH and the deleterious impacts of DV on the infant's ability to find security within their attachments, and subsequent developmental trajectories. How the DVA sector responds to the challenges of bringing the infants' experiences of trauma and abuse into the forefront of this work will have implications for generations to come.

This chapter returns to where it began: with the evolving possibilities that the infant-parent relationship holds. The restorative hopefulness and receptivity of infants to change and healing, and the motivation many parents possess to grow a safe, different and healthy relationship with, and future for, their infants has yet to be fully recognised in DVA work. Not least because the infant and very young child is entitled, deserves and craves safe, respectful inclusion in all matters which concern them.

## Acknowledgement

Many thanks to Associate Professor Brigid Jordan for her time and feedback on early sections of this chapter.

## Critical findings

- From birth the infant possesses subjectivity, demonstrates reciprocity and engages with their relational world.
- The infant's mental health, general development and quality of attachment is adversely impacted by DVA.
- Keeping infants safe from harm does not prevent 'infant inclusive practice' nor their experiences of DVA to be kept in mind.
- Infants, as the newest members of families, can provide an entry point for engaging in change and hold hope for the future.

## Implications for policy, practice, and research

- The infant's experience can, and is entitled to be included in DVA practice, policies and research which concern them.
- The vulnerability of the infant to DVA calls for a greater service response.
- Recognition of wider social, gender and cultural inequalities for infants and their families experiencing DVA requires attention.
- The experience of the infant can bring something new to DVA research and service responses.

## References

Alaggia, R., Gadalla, T. M., Shlonsky, A., Jenney, A., & Daciuk, J. (2015). Does differential response make a difference: Examining domestic violence cases in child protection services. *Child & Family Social Work*, *20*(1), 83–95.

Ammaniti, M., & Gallese, V. (2014). *The birth of intersubjectivity: Psychodynamics, neurobiology, and the self*. New York, NY: W.W. Norton & Company.

Anda, R. F., Felitti, V. J., Bremner, J. D., Walker, J. D., Whitfield, C., Perry, B. D., . . . Giles, W. H. (2006). The enduring effects of abuse and related adverse experiences in childhood. A convergence of evidence from neurobiology and epidemiology. *European Archives of Psychiatry and Clinical Neuroscience*, *256*(3), 174–186. doi:10.1007/s00406-005-0624-4

Arvidson, J., Kinniburgh, K., Howard, K., Spinazzola, J., Strothers, H., Evans, M., . . . Blaustein, M. E. (2011). Treatment of complex trauma in young children: Developmental and cultural considerations in application of the arc intervention model. *Journal of Child & Adolescent Trauma*, *4*(1), 34–51. doi:10.1080/19361521.2011.545046

Benoit, D., Zeanah, C. H., Parker, K. C., Nicholson, E., & Coolbear, J. (1997). "Working model of the child interview": Infant clinical status related to maternal perceptions. *Infant Mental Health Journal*, *18*(1), 107–121.

Berens, A. E., & Nelson, C. A. (2019). Neurobiology of fetal and infant development: Implications for infant mental health. In J. Charles & H. Zeanah (Eds.), *Handbook of infant mental health* (4th ed., pp. 41–80). New York, NY: The Guilford Press.

Bernstein, R. E., Timmons, A. C., & Lieberman, A. F. (2019). Interpersonal violence, maternal perception of infant emotion, and child-parent psychotherapy. *Journal of Family Violence*, *34*(4), 309–320. doi:10.1007/s10896-019-00041-7

Bornstein, M. H., Putnick, D. L., Park, Y., Suwalsky, J. T. D., & Haynes, O. M. (2017). Human infancy and parenting in global perspective: Specificity. *Proceedings of the Royal Society B*, *284*, 20172168. doi:10.1098/rspb.2017.2168

Bowlby, J. (1984). Violence in the family as a disorder of the attachment and caregiving systems. *American Journal of Psychoanalysis, 44*(1), 9–27.

Briggs-Gowan, M. J., Carter, A. S., & Ford, J. D. (2012). Parsing the effects violence exposure in early childhood: Modeling developmental pathways. *Journal of Pediatric Psychology, 37*(1), 11–22. doi:10.1093/jpepsy/jsr063

Buchanan, F., Power, C., & Verity, F. (2013). Domestic violence and the place of fear in mother/baby relationships: "What was I afraid of? Of making it worse.". *Journal of Interpersonal Violence, 28*(9), 1817–1838. doi:10.1177/0886260512469108

Bunston, W. (2013). "What about the fathers?" bringing "Dads on Board™" with their infants and toddlers following violence. *Journal of Family Studies, 19*(1), 70–79.

Bunston, W. (2015). Infant-led practice: Responding to infants and their mothers (and fathers) in the aftermath of domestic violence. In N. Stanley & C. Humphreys (Eds.), *Domestic violence and protecting children: New thinking and approaches*. London, UK: Jessica Kingsley Publishers.

Bunston, W. (2016). *How refuge provides 'refuge' to Infants: Exploring how 'refuge' is provided to infants entering crisis accommodation with their mothers after fleeing family violence* (PhD thesis). La Trobe University, Melbourne. Retrieved from http://hdl.handle.net/1959.9/559171

Bunston, W. (2017). *Helping babies and children (0–6) to heal after family violence: A practical guide to infant- and child-led practice*. London, UK: Jessica Kingsley Publishers.

Bunston, W., & Jones, S. J. (2020). *Supporting vulnerable babies and young children: Interventions for working with trauma, mental health, illness and other complex challenges*. London, UK: Jessica Kingsley Publishers.

Carpenter, G. L., & Stacks, A. M. (2009). Developmental effects of exposure to intimate partner violence in early childhood: A review of the literature. *Children and Youth Services Review, 31*(8), 831–839.

Carrion, V., Wong, S., & Kletter, H. (2013). Update on neuroimaging and cognitive functioning in maltreatment-related pediatric PTSD: Treatment implications. *Journal of Family Violence, 28*(1), 53–61. doi:10.1007/s10896-012-9489-2

Cicchetti, D., Hetzel, S., Rogosch, F. A., Handley, E. D., & Toth, S. L. (2016). An investigation of child maltreatment and epigenetic mechanisms of mental and physical health risk. *Development and Psychopathology, 28*(4pt2), 1305–1317. doi:10.1017/S0954579416000869

Clark, C. L., St. John, N., Pasca, A. M., Hyde, S. A., Hornbeak, K., Abramova, M., . . . Penn, A. A. (2013). Neonatal CSF oxytocin levels are associated with parent report of infant soothability and sociability. *Psychoneuroendocrinology, 38*(7), 1208–1212.

Crawford, A., & Benoit, D. (2009). Caregivers' disrupted representations of the unborn child predict later infant – Caregiver disorganized attachment and disrupted interactions. *Infant Mental Health Journal, 30*(2), 124–144. doi:10.1002/imhj.20207

Crittenden, P. M., & Ainsworth, M. D. S. (1989). Child maltreatment and attachment theory. In D. Cicchetti & V. Carlson (Eds.), *Child maltreatment: Theory and research on the causes and consequences of child abuse and neglect* (pp. 432–463). Cambridge, UK: Cambridge University Press.

DESA. (2011). *Men in families and family policy in a changing world*. New York, NY: United Nations. Retrieved from www.un.org/esa/socdev/family/docs/men-in-families.pdf

Domoney, J., Fulton, E., Stanley, N., McIntyre, A., Heslin, M., Byford, S., . . . Trevillion, K. (2019). For baby's sake: Intervention development and evaluation design of a whole-family perinatal intervention to break the cycle of domestic abuse. *Journal of Family Violence, 34*(6), 539–551. doi:10.1007/s10896-019-00037-3

Enlow, M. B., Egeland, B., Blood, E. A., Wright, R. O., & Wright, R. J. (2012). Interpersonal trauma exposure and cognitive development in children to age 8 years: A longitudinal study. *Journal of Epidemiology and Community Health, 66*(11), 1005–1010. doi:10.1136/jech-2011-200727

Eyre, K., Milburn, N., & Bunston, W. (2020). 'Murder in their family': Making space for the experience of the infant impacted by familial murder. In W. Bunston & S. J. Jones (Eds.), *Supporting vulnerable babies and young children: Interventions for working with trauma, mental health, illness and other complex challenges* (pp. 107–123). UK: Jessica Kingsley Publishers.

Fishbane, M. D. (2007). Wired to connect: Neuroscience, relationships, and therapy. *Family Process, 46*(3), 395–412.

Fonagy, P., Steele, M., Steele, H., Moran, G. S., & Higgitt, A. C. (1991). The capacity for understanding mental states: The reflective self in parent and child and its significance for security of attachment. *Infant Mental Health Journal, 12*(3), 201–218. doi:10.1002/1097-0355(199123)12:3<201::aid-imhj2280120307>3.0.co;2-7

Fraiberg, S., Adelson, E., & Shapiro, V. (1975). Ghosts in the nursery. *Journal of the American Academy of Child Psychiatry, 14*(3), 387–421.

Gilbert, R., Kemp, A., Thoburn, J., Sidebotham, P., Radford, L., Glaser, D., & MacMillan, H. L. (2009). Recognising and responding to child maltreatment. *The Lancet, 373*(9658), 167–180. doi:10.1016/S0140-6736(08)61707-9

Grady, G., Hinshaw-Fuselier, S., & Friar, N. (2019). Expanding perspectives: A social inequities lens on intimate partner violence, reproductive justice, and infant mental health. *Infant Mental Health Journal, 40*(5), 624–639. doi:10.1002/imhj.21809

Graham-Bermann, S. A., Miller-Graff, L. E., Howell, K. H., & Grogan-Kaylor, A. (2015). An efficacy trial of an intervention program for children exposed to intimate partner violence. *Child Psychiatry and Human Development, 46*(6), 928–939. doi:10.1007/s10578-015-0532-4

Harman, R. J. (2003). Thirty years in infant mental health. *Zero-To-Three, 24*(1), 22–28.

Harpur, L. J., Polek, E., & van Harmelen, A. L. (2015). The role of timing of maltreatment and child intelligence in pathways to low symptoms of depression and anxiety in adolescence. *Child Abuse & Neglect, 47*, 24–37.

Herrenkohl, T. I., & Herrenkohl, R. C. (2007). Examining the overlap and prediction of multiple forms of child maltreatment, stressors, and socioeconomic status: A longitudinal analysis of youth outcomes. *Journal of Family Violence, 22*(7), 553–562. doi:10.1007/s10896-007-9107-x

Jackson, D., & Mannix, J. (2004). Giving voice to the burden of blame: A feminist study of mothers' experiences of mother blaming. *International Journal of Nursing Practice, 10*(4), 150–158. doi:10.1111/j.1440-172X.2004.00474.x

Jenney, A. (2020). Keeping the child in mind when thinking about violence in families. In W. Bunston & S. J. Jones (Eds.), *Supporting vulnerable babies and young children: Interventions of working with trauma, mental health, illness and other complex challenges* (pp. 91–123). London, UK: Jessica Kingsley Publishers.

Jones, E. G., & Mendell, L. M. (1999). Assessing the decade of the brain. *Science, 284*(5415), 739. doi:10.1126/science

Jones, S., & Bunston, W. (2012). The "original couple": Enabling mothers and infants to think about what destroys as well as engenders love, when there has been intimate partner violence. *Couple and Family Psychoanalysis, 2*(2), 215–232.

Kimura, T., Tanizawa, O., Kensaku, M., J, B. M., & Hiroto, O. (1992). Structure and expression of a human oxytocin receptor. *Nature, 356*(6369), 526–529.

Kitzmann, K. M., Gaylord, N. K., Holt, A. R., & Kenny, E. D. (2003). Child witnesses to domestic violence: A meta-analytic review. *Journal of Consulting and Clinical Psychology, 71*(2), 399–352.

Labarre, M., Bourassa, C., Holden, G. W., Turcotte, P., & Letourneau, N. (2016). Intervening with fathers in the context of intimate partner violence: An analysis of ten programs and suggestions for a research agenda. *Journal of Child Custody, 13*(1), 1–29. doi:10.1080/15379418.2016.1127793

Lapierre, S. (2008). Mothering in the context of domestic violence: The pervasiveness of a deficit model of mothering. *Child & Family Social Work, 13*(4), 454–463. doi:10.1111/j.1365-2206.2008.00563.x

Letourneau, N., Morris, C. Y., Secco, L., Stewart, M., Hughes, J., & Critchley, K. (2013). Mothers and infants exposed to intimate partner violence compensate. *Violence and Victims, 28*(4), 571–586.

Letourneau, N., Tryphonopoulos, P., Giesbrecht, G., Dennis, C. L., Bhogal, S., & Watson, B. (2015). Narrative and meta-analytic review of interventions aiming to improve maternal – Child attachment security. *Infant Mental Health Journal, 36*(4), 366–387. doi:10.1002/imhj.21525

Levendosky, A. A., Bogat, G. A., Huth-Bocks, A. C., Rosenblum, K., & Von Eye, A. (2011). The effects of domestic violence on the stability of attachment from infancy to preschool. *Journal of Clinical Child & Adolescent Psychology, 40*(3), 398–410. doi:10.1080/15374416.2011.563460

Levendosky, A. A., Bogat, G. A., & Martinez-Torteya, C. (2013). PTSD symptoms in young children exposed to intimate partner violence. *Violence Against Women, 19*(2), 187–201.

Levendosky, A. A., Leahy, K. L., Bogat, G. A., Davidson, W. S., & von Eye, A. (2006). Domestic violence, maternal parenting, maternal mental health, and infant externalizing behavior. *Journal of Family Psychology, 20*(4), 544–552.

Liddle, M.-J. E., Bradley, B. S., & McGrath, A. (2015). Baby empathy: Infant distress and peer prosocial responses. *Infant Mental Health Journal, 36*(4), 446–458. doi:10.1002/imhj.21519

Lieberman, A. F., Chu, A., Van Horn, P., & Harris, W. W. (2011). Trauma in early childhood: Empirical evidence and clinical implications. *Development and Psychopathology, 23*(2), 397–410. doi:10.1017/S0954579411000137

Lieberman, A. F., & Van Horn, P. (2009). Child-parent psychotherapy. In C. H. Zenah Jr (Ed.), *Handbook of infant mental health* (3rd ed., pp. 439–449). New York, NY: The Guilford Press.

Lu, C., Black, M. M., & Richter, L. M. (2016). Risk of poor development in young children in low-income and middle-income countries: An estimation and analysis at the global, regional, and country level. *The Lancet Global Health, 4*(12), e916–e922. doi:10.1016/S2214-109X(16)30266-2

Luijk, M. P. C. M., Roisman, G. I., Haltigan, J. D., Tiemeier, H., Booth-LaForce, C., van Ijzen-doorn, M. H., . . . Bakermans-Kranenburg, M. J. (2011). Dopaminergic, serotonergic, and oxy-tonergic candidate genes associated with infant attachment security and disorganization? In search of main and interaction effects. *Journal of Child Psychology and Psychiatry, 52*(12), 1295–1307. doi:10.1111/j.1469-7610.2011.02440.x

Main, M., Hesse, E., & Hesse, S. (2011). Attachment theory and research: Overview with suggested applications to child custody. *Family Court Review, 49*(3), 426–463.

Malone, J. C., Levendosky, A. A., Dayton, C. J., & Bogat, G. A. (2010). Understanding the "ghosts in the nursery" of pregnant women experiencing domestic violence: Prenatal maternal representations and histories of childhood maltreatment. *Infant Mental Health Journal, 31*(4), 432–454.

McConnell, N., Barnard, M., & Taylor, J. (2017). Caring dads safer children: Families' perspectives on an intervention for maltreating fathers. *Psychology of Violence, 7*(3), 406–416.

McWhirter, P. T. (2011). Differential therapeutic outcomes of community-based group interventions for women and children exposed to intimate partner violence. *Journal of Interpersonal Violence, 26*(12), 2457–2482.

Menon, S. (2014). *Unfinished lives: The effect of domestic violence on neonatal and infant mortality* (No. 2014–27). Retrieved from http://hdl.handle.net/10419/126472

Ogilvie, C. A., Newman, E., Todd, L., & Peck, D. (2014). Attachment & violent offending: A meta-analysis. *Aggression and Violent Behavior, 19*(4), 322–339. doi:10.1016/j.avb.2014.04.007

Osofsky, J. D. (2003). Prevalence of children's exposure to domestic violence and child maltreatment: Implications for prevention and intervention. *Clinical Child and Family Psychology Review, 6*(3), 161–170.

Quinn, N., & Mageo, J. (Eds.). (2013). *Attachment reconsidered: Cultural perspectives on a western theory.* New York, NY: Palgrave Macmillan.

Salter-Ainsworth, M. D., & Bowlby, J. (1991). An ethological approach to personality development. *American Psychologist, 46*(4), 333–341.

Samuelson, K. W., Krueger, C. E., & Wilson, C. (2012). Relationships between maternal emotion regulation, parenting, and children's executive functioning in families exposed to intimate partner violence. *Journal of Interpersonal Violence, 27*(17), 3532–3550. doi:10.1177/0886260512445385

Schechter, D. S., & Willheim, E. (2009). The effects of violent experiences on infants and young children. In C. H. Zenah Jr (Ed.), *Handbook of infant mental health* (pp. 197–213). New York, NY: The Guilford Press.

Schechter, D. S., Willheim, E., Suardi, F., & Serpa, S., Rusconi. (2019). The effects of violent experiences on infants and young children. In C. H. Zeanah Jr (Ed.), *Handbook of infant mental health* (4th ed., pp. 219–238). New York, NY: The Guilford Press.

Schore, A. N. (2001). The effects of early relational trauma on the right brain development, affect regulation, and infant mental health. *Infant Mental Health Journal, 22*(1–2), 201–269.

Schore, A. N. (2005). Back to basics attachment, affect regulation, and the developing right brain: Linking developmental neuroscience to pediatrics. *Pediatrics in Review, 26*(6), 204–217.

Schore, A. N. (2016). *Affect regulation and the origin of the self: The neurobiology of emotional development.* New York, NY: Routledge.

Schore, J. R., & Schore, A. N. (2008). Modern attachment theory: The central role of affect regulation in development and treatment. *Clinical Social Work Journal, 36*(1), 9–20.

Siegel, D. J. (2012). *Developing Mind: How relationships and the brain interact to shape who we are* (2nd ed.). New York, NY: The Guilford Press.

Sousa, C., Herrenkohl, T. I., Moylan, C. A., Tajima, E. A., Klika, J. B., Herrenkohl, R. C., & Russo, M. J. (2011). Longitudinal study on the effects of child abuse and children's exposure to domestic violence, parent-child attachments, and antisocial behavior in adolescence. *Journal of Interpersonal Violence, 26*(1), 111–136. doi:10.1177/0886260510362883

Stanley, N., & Humphreys, C. (2017). Identifying the key components of a 'whole family' intervention for families experiencing domestic violence and abuse. *Journal of Gender-Based Violence, 1*(1), 99–115. doi:10.1332/239868017X14913081639164

Stern, D. N. (1985/2003). *The interpersonal world of the infant: A view from psychoanalysis and developmental psychology.* London: Karnac Books.

Stern, D. N. (1998). Mothers' emotional needs. *Pediatrics, 102*(5), 1250–1252.

Stover, C. S. (2015). Fathers for change for substance use and intimate partner violence: Initial community pilot. *Family Process*, *54*(4), 600–609. doi:10.1111/famp.12136.

Teicher, M. H., & Samson, J. A. (2013). Childhood maltreatment and psychopathology: A case for ecophenotypic variants as clinically and neurobiologically distinct subtypes. *American Journal of Psychiatry*, *170*(10), 1114–1133. doi:10.1176/appi.ajp.2013.12070957

Teicher, M. H., Samson, J. A., Polcari, A., & McGreenery, C. E. (2006). Sticks, stones, and hurtful words: Relative effects of various forms of childhood maltreatment. *American Journal of Psychiatry*, *163*(6), 993–1000.

Trevarthen, C., & Aitken, K. (2001). Infant intersubjectivity: Research, theory, and clinical applications. *Journal of Child Psychology and Psychiatry*, *42*(1), 3–48.

Tronick, E. Z. (2007). *The neurobehavioral and social-emotional development of infants and children*. New York, NY: W.W. Norton & Company.

UNICEF. (2015). *Committing to child survival: A promise renewed*. New York, NY: UNICEF. Retrieved from www.unicef.org/publications/index_83078.html

Van der Kolk, B. (2014). *The body keeps the score: Brain, mind, and body in the healing of trauma*. London: Penguin Books.

Van Ryzin, M. J., Carlson, E. A., & Sroufe, L. A. (2011). Attachment discontinuity in a high-risk sample. *Attachment & Human Development*, *13*(4), 381–401. doi:10.1080/14616734.2011.584403

WAIMH. (2016). WAIMH position paper on the rights of infants. *Perspectives in Mental Health*, *1–2*, 3–5. Retrieved from https://perspectives.waimh.org/2016/06/15/waimh-position-paper-on-the-rights-of-infants/

WAIMH. (2019). *Overview*. Retrieved September 27, 2019, from https://waimh.org/page/about_waimh

Weatherston, D. J. (2000). The infant mental health specialist. *Zero to Three*(October/November), 3–10.

White, S., Gibson, M., Wastell, D., & Walsh, P. (Eds.). (2020). *Reassessing attachment theory in child welfare*. Bristol, UK: Policy Press.

Whiteside-Mansell, L., Bradley, R. H., McKelvey, L., & Fussell, J. J. (2009). Parenting: Linking impacts of interpartner conflict to preschool children's social behavior. *Journal of Pediatric Nursing*, *24*(5), 389–400. doi:10.1016/j.pedn.2007.08.017

WHO. (2013). *Global and regional estimates of violence against women*. Geneva: World Health Organization.

Winnicott, D. W. (1964). *The child, the family, and the outside world*. Harmondsworth, UK: Penguin Books.

Winnicott, D. W. (2002). *Winnicott on the child*. Cambridge, MA: Perseus Publishing.

Zeanah Jr, C. H. (2009). *Handbook of infant mental health*. New York, NY: The Guilford Publication.

Zeanah Jr, C. H. (2019). *Handbook of infant mental health* (4th ed.). New York, NY: The Guilford Press.

Zeanah Jr, C. H., & Zeanah, P. D. (2019). Infant mental health: The clinical science of early experience. In J. Charles & H. Zeanah (Eds.), *Handbook of infant mental health*. New York, NY: The Guilford Press.

ZeroToThree. (2001). *Definition of infant mental health*. Washington, DC: Zero-to-Three Infant Mental Health Steering Committee.

# 10

# DOMESTIC VIOLENCE AND THE IMPACT ON CHILDREN

*Margaret Kertesz, Larissa Fogden and Cathy Humphreys*

## Introduction

The vulnerability of infants is palpable. From day one, parents are tasked with keeping wobbly little heads, floppy limbs and tiny fingers and toes out of danger, and translating their baby's cries into requests for food, sleep or nappy changes. The tiredness of parents as they seek to respond to their infants can feel for some like a permanent state of jetlag. It highlights the need for emotional and physical support which all mothers and fathers require from family, friends and service systems. Many will feel as vulnerable as their infants as they come to terms with their role as a mother or father. As children grow into the toddler years their developing independence presents fresh challenges for parents. For women, mothering through domestic and family violence (DV) creates mountains that will need to be climbed for both herself and her infant (and other children) to survive. It is a time which may be characterised more by isolation than support (Buchanan, 2018; Radford & Hester, 2006).

This chapter outlines the impact of DV on young children, with a specific focus on pre-school children. The research evidence in this space is paradoxically both limited and wide ranging. The meta-syntheses in this area point to the extent of research on children under 5 (Lourenço et al., 2013; Romano, Weegar, Gallitto, Zak, & Saini, 2019; Stanley, 2011), while the analysis of their findings also points to the limitations of our knowledge and specifically the directions for good practice that will make a difference to the lives of these infants and young children (Howarth et al., 2015).

An initial diversion is required to clarify language and terminology. Throughout the chapter, gendered terminology is used, referring to women as victim survivors of DV and men as perpetrators of DV. This terminology reflects dominant patterns of interpersonal violence (Cox, 2015), although we acknowledge that people of all sexual orientations and gender identities can be victim survivors and perpetrators of DV. We also note that we have used the contested term 'domestic violence' throughout this chapter. In Australia, research suggests that Aboriginal families may prefer 'family violence', as this term acknowledges that violence is not limited to intimate partner violence (Andrews et al., 2018). However, within the broader violence against women movement, domestic violence, intimate partner violence or domestic abuse may be the preferred terminology. We respect these different perspectives and recognise that our terminology has limitations, while trying to include an easily recognisable international term.

## The context of abuse for children living with domestic violence

The evidence about children living with DV has been growing since the early nineties when publications in the UK (Mullender & Morley, 1994) and the US (Jaffe, Wolfe, & Wilson, 1990) drew attention to the plight of these children. Since that time, there has been growing interest in the impact that living with DV has on children. The consequences of children's exposure to DV across all studies show detrimental effects on the emotional and behavioural adjustment of a significant number of children (McTavish, MacGregor, Wathen, & MacMillan, 2016; Stanley, 2011). However, children live in different contexts of vulnerability and protection, issues which will be explored further in this chapter. It is also noteworthy that in any sample of children living with DV, one-third or more are doing as well as other children when compared with community samples (Laing, Humphreys, & Cavanagh, 2013).

There are a number of ways in which children may experience or get caught up in DV. Taxonomies have been developed to assist practitioners in identifying the possible experiences of children living with DV (Holden, 2003; McGee, 1997). However, these may be limited in scope given the myriad ways in which coercive control can be exerted by one person over another (Stark, 2012). Experiences include children being directly assaulted, directly observing or overhearing violence, witnessing the outcome of an assault, being involved in the violence through 'joining in', being used to intimidate the mother, being used as a shield or intervening, or being impacted by psychological and physical abuse (Holt, Buckley, & Whelan, 2008; Lourenço et al., 2013). Young children are particularly affected by the ways in which the perpetrator's abuse may harm their mother's physical and mental health, which may in turn impact upon her parenting (Carpenter & Stacks, 2009).

## Domestic violence as an attack on the mother-child relationship

Children are profoundly affected when the violence and abuse directed at their mothers interferes with the mothers' ability to be available to children and to care for their physical and emotional well-being. In this sense, DV represents a direct attack on the mother-child relationship, which is crucial to the safety and well-being of infants and small children, as they are dependent on adults for physical safety and survival. The younger and more dependent the child, the more profound the impact of the abuse of their mothers (Bunston, 2008; Jordan & Sketchley, 2009).

In fact, abuse may be evident even in the conception of the child through various forms of reproductive coercion in which women's reproductive choices are controlled through manipulation or violence. This could occur when a woman is prevented from using contraceptives or through rape (Clark, Allen, Goyal, Raker, & Gottlieb, 2014; Willie, Alexander, Amutah-Onukagha, & Kershaw, 2019). Pregnancy is a time of particular vulnerability, with some studies suggesting that violence and abuse may commence in pregnancy and that pregnant women are more vulnerable than women who are not pregnant (Burch & Gallup, 2004).

The abuse during pregnancy may continue following the birth of the child, significantly impacting the physical and mental health of the child's mother (Woolhouse, Gartland, Hegarty, Donath, & Brown, 2012), as well as the physical health of the infant (Rivara et al., 2007). The perpetrator's undermining of the mother's parenting can interfere with the attachment process between both mother and child, and father and child, impacting the infant's development (Cunningham & Baker, 2007). Young children look to their caregivers when they feel distressed, sick or scared (Bowlby, 1982). When a caregiver comforts their child, their actions teach the child how to soothe their nervous system and manage their emotions after a period of arousal. From these interactions, the infant eventually learns the necessary skill of emotional self-regulation (Carpenter & Stacks, 2009). As such, when a young child is faced with a father whose actions not only frighten them, but prevent their mother from providing comfort, the infant has little opportunity to learn this skill.

However, as Buchanan (2018) notes, the protective measures many women take to preserve their relationship with their babies and young children can be easily overlooked by professionals. There is evidence that mothers strive to provide good parenting and protect their children from the effects of DV. In a number of studies, women describe the strategies and tactics they use to ensure children's good behaviour to avoid annoying the perpetrator, shield them from the violence and compensate for the perpetrator's abusive behaviour (Lapierre, 2010; Levendosky, Lynch, & Graham-Bermann, 2000). In addition, for those mothers whose parenting is compromised by the experience of DV, their pre-violence capacity for nurturing for their children will often re-emerge once the violence is absent (Stanley, 2011).

## Addressing fathering issues for men who use violence

Emphasising support for women and their mothering, particularly those with very young children, is entirely appropriate. However, the focus on mothering has tended to overshadow the parenting choices of men who use violence (Mandel, 2009).

Emerging evidence suggests that these fathers are a heterogenous group. Some are highly dysregulated and volatile in their use of abuse, and others are highly controlled and controlling (Heward-Belle, 2017). A number of studies suggest that these fathers expect children to meet their needs, rather than vice versa (Bancroft & Silverman, 2002; Harne, 2004). There is a clear message from women abused in pregnancy, and ongoing into the post-natal period, that the self-centredness or sense of entitlement of fathers who use violence means that they are unable to tolerate the woman paying attention to the developing infant (Scott & Crooks, 2007). In particular, abusive men use the high societal expectations of mothers to undermine their partners (Buchanan, 2018), attacking their self-esteem and their struggles with early mothering (Heward-Belle, 2017).

Paradoxically, while a great vulnerability for children is created by having a father who uses DV, there is also evidence to suggest that fathering may be the strongest point of engagement around attitudinal and behavioural change (Holt, 2015; Stanley, Graham-Kevan, & Borthwick, 2012). Programmes such as Caring Dads (McConnell, Barnard, Holdsworth, & Taylor, 2016; Scott & Lishak, 2012) are emerging, which address fathering in the context of DV. Programmes for fathers who use violence seek to increase fathers' parenting skills and understanding of child development, whilst also inviting fathers to reflect on the impacts of their use of violence, and teaching more appropriate ways of relating to their children, partners or ex-partners. Broady, Gray, Gaffney, and Lewis (2017) found that fathers' desire to improve and maintain relationships with their children was the main motivating factor for attending programmes such as these.

## Children's perspectives

Much of the research about children living with DV is reliant upon adult measures and predetermined outcomes to assess the impact of DV on children (Howarth et al., 2015; Noble-Carr, Moore, & McArthur, 2019). However, there is a growing body of research which focuses on children and young people's accounts of their experience of DV (Eriksson & Nasman, 2012; Katz, 2016; Lamb, Humphreys, & Hegarty, 2018). While most of this evidence is gleaned from qualitative research from children and young people of school age, there is also a body of work based on infant observation or 'infant-led practice' which attempts to 'hear and see' what babies are saying about their experiences (Bunston, 2008).

The accounts and experiences of infants, children and young people are important in so far as they give an indication of what living with DV can be like for children. In an international meta-synthesis of qualitative research about children's experiences, Noble-Carr and colleagues (2019) report that the complex and diverse nature of the violence they witnessed and experienced meant that children's understanding of what was happening (violence, sexual abuse, coercive control, etc.) took time to develop and was sometimes very difficult for them to understand. For the children and young people in these studies, the unpredictable and chronic nature of the DV they experienced created a continuous sense of fear and worry, not just in the home but pervading all arenas of their lives. A sense of powerlessness to change their circumstances or to keep people safe was commonly felt, as was an enduring sadness that outlasted their exposure to DV. Children and young people spoke of being left to deal with these pervasive feelings of fear, powerlessness and sadness on their own, without having anyone to talk to, or from whom they could seek help.

The experience of DV creates mixed and complex family relationships which are challenging for children to understand and negotiate. Some fathers, while violent, also have positive relationships with their children. Relationships with mothers can be strained even when she is a child's primary protective and caring relationship. Many children also speak of the disruption and loss they have experienced due to DV, particularly related to moving house, and leaving behind important friendships or possessions. It is also clear that children's experiences are very diverse, and influenced by a range of factors such as the nature and longevity of the DV, the level of disruption to their lives, family circumstance and children's position in the family and individual coping styles (Holt et al., 2008; Stanley, 2011). Interviews with children have additionally highlighted factors which have contributed to children's resilience, including geographical distance from fathers who use abuse, the ability and opportunities to talk about and name the domestic violence they were living with, and having non-violent role models (with their mothers and other family members) (Morris, Humphreys, & Hegarty, 2015).

## Child development in the context of domestic violence

In addition to the importance of understanding every child's experience and needs on an individual basis, it is also important to think about the impact of DV on infants and children in the context of what we know about milestones and child development.

Unborn children, infants and toddlers are at highest risk of death and serious harm from a father or mother using violence (Holt et al., 2008). This is partly due to their physical vulnerability and dependence. They are also at greater risk of exposure to DV. A major American study found that children under 5 years were disproportionately present in homes where DV occurred compared with homes without DV. This age group was also more likely than older children to be exposed to multiple incidents of DV (Fantuzzo & Mohr, 1999).

Children develop in different ways and at different paces, but development is sequential. Disruption of developmental tasks may also affect future developmental tasks (Rossman, 2001). Impacts of DV may be manifested differently at different ages. Exposure to DV also affects children both in ways that are easy for others to discern and in more subtle ways (Baker & Cunningham, 2009).

Studies from the US have provided much of the evidence we have for the impact of DV on infants, toddlers and pre-school children (Stanley, 2011). In addition to physical injuries, impacts include sleep disturbance, emotional distress, a fear of being left alone, delayed language and toilet training (Osofsky, 2003; Lundy & Grossman, 2005). Nutrition and health may be compromised if finances are controlled so that basic necessities are not available (Cunningham & Baker, 2007).

## *Infancy*

Infants and toddlers are learning about the world through all five senses. They cannot understand what is occurring, but they feel the tension. Trauma symptoms such as hyperarousal, numbing or aggression are common among infants, particularly when their mothers also show these symptoms (Bogat, DeJonghe, Levendosky, Davidson, & von Eye, 2006). They may be distressed by loud noises such as banging and yelling, particularly when these are sudden and unpredictable. They may also be too fearful to explore and play, an important developmental task for this age group (Cunningham & Baker, 2007).

Unable to protect themselves or leave a stressful situation, infants and toddlers depend on adults to keep them safe and healthy. In DV situations, the mother may be distracted by the violence, socially isolated and traumatised to the point that her parenting abilities are compromised, and the father may also provide inconsistent or neglectful parenting which does not focus on a child's needs.

Significant attention has been given to the impact of DV on the developing brains of infants. The infant brain is formed through experience, and as such, infants are acutely sensitive to their environment and the relationships they develop with their caregivers (Schore, 2016; Siegel, 1999). The brain of an infant who is experiencing stress, and whose attachment figures are unavailable, becomes survival-focused. Under these circumstances, the infant brain directs its energy towards activating the parts of the brain that respond to immediate threat (Rifkin-Graboi, Borelli, & Enlow, 2009). The brain begins to produce an array of chemicals, including stress hormones cortisol, epinephrine and norepinephrine, to physiologically cope with the infant's overwhelming sense of fear and distress (Carpenter & Stacks, 2009).

If a caregiver steps in to provide comfort at the point when the infant is experiencing fear or distress, the brain secretes serotonin and other hormones that help with emotional regulation (Perry, 2001). If a caregiver is unable to step in, and the child is regularly exposed to unmanageable levels of stress, these chronically high levels of stress-related chemicals begin to impact cognitive, behavioural and emotional development (Streeck-Fischer & van der Kolk, 2000). Of particular importance, research suggests that the development of the Hypothalamus-Pituitary-Adrenal (HPA) axis, a critical stress response system enabling the body to return to homeostasis after stress, is greatly impeded by chronic stress in infancy (Mueller & Tronick, 2019). Developments in neuroscience have taught us that the brain develops in a 'use-dependent' way; that is, connections between parts of the brain increase and strengthen through repeated use, or diminish through disuse (Perry, 2001). Therefore, an infant who has been exposed to DV from an early age will continue to struggle under stress as they move into childhood and beyond.

## *Pre-school*

It is common for pre-schoolers who have been exposed to DV to exhibit behaviours that may be described as 'problematic'. They may respond less appropriately to situations, be more aggressive with peers and have more difficult relationships with teachers than children unaffected by DV (Levendosky, Huth-Bocks, Shapiro, & Semel, 2003).

Still learning how to verbalise strong emotions, pre-schoolers may express these through aggressive behaviour, temper tantrums, anxiety and sadness (Baker & Cunningham, 2009; Lundy & Grossman, 2005). Furthermore, the extreme fear generated by witnessing violence may generate psychosomatic problems such as headaches, stomach aches and asthma, as well as nightmares, sleep disturbances and bed-wetting (Martin, 2002; see Table 10.1). Pre-schoolers are concrete and egocentric in their thinking. They are too young to make sense of the contradictions between what they are told and what they see or experience, and may blame themselves (Baker & Cunningham, 2009).

## School-aged children

School-aged children have a more sophisticated understanding of DV than pre-schoolers, being more aware of how it affects themselves and others. They may worry about their mother's safety and notice her being sad or upset between incidents. Depending on their relationship with their father, there may be a need to preserve an image of him as a good person, and they may worry about negative consequences, such as arrest. They may also understand the violence in terms of causes such as alcohol, stress, finances or somebody's bad behaviour (Cunningham & Baker, 2007).

Developmentally, peers and the school environment become more important. However, school performance may be compromised by distraction and anxiety, or lack of sleep

*Table 10.1* Risks and observable impacts of domestic violence on children

| Risks of domestic violence | Some observable impacts |
| --- | --- |
| *Infants and toddlers* | |
| • DV prevents non-offending parent from responding consistently, leading to disrupted attachment and poor physical health.<br>• Fear inhibits exploration and play.<br>• Physical injuries. | • Excessive irritability.<br>• Underweight, sleep and eating difficulties.<br>• Frequent illness.<br>• Distress at loud noises.<br>• Inability to play. |
| *Pre-schoolers* | |
| • Fear of being hurt.<br>• Learning unhealthy ways to express anger.<br>• Attributing violence to something they did.<br>• Instability may inhibit the growth of independence.<br>• Physical injuries. | • Frequent illness.<br>• Nightmares and significant sleeping difficulties.<br>• Inability to play.<br>• Extreme clinginess.<br>• Aggression towards others.<br>• Problems adjusting to change in routine. |
| *Primary school-aged children* | |
| • School learning may be compromised.<br>• Susceptibility to rationalisations justifying violence.<br>• Anxiety may affect school learning and social skills.<br>• Physical injuries. | • Frequent illness.<br>• Bed-wetting.<br>• Defiant and aggressive behaviour.<br>• Limited tolerance and poor impulse control.<br>• Overly compliant behaviour.<br>• Poor social competence. |

(Cunningham & Baker, 2007). Alternatively, the school environment may be experienced as a respite from the violence at home (Holt et al., 2008). The messages about gender roles and interpersonal behaviour witnessed at home may result in poor social skills and problems with peer relationships. There is an increased risk of bullying or being bullied (Cunningham & Baker, 2007). A UK study found that witnessing DV was associated with conduct disorders in children (Meltzer, Doos, Vostanis, Ford, & Goodman, 2009).

Few longitudinal studies have been undertaken to examine the long-term impact of differing levels of exposure to DV (Graham-Bermann, Gruber, Howell, & Girz, 2009; Rossman, Hughes, & Rosenberg, 2013). Rossman et al. (2013) found that behavioural problems and post-traumatic symptoms were considerably worse for those children who had had the longest exposure to DV over their lifetime. While there have been few longitudinal studies that examine the effects of differing levels of exposure to DV (Stanley, 2011), there is evidence that outcomes for children are worst when the violence is chronic, the conflict between parents is severe and there are few mediating influences (McIntosh, 2003).

Whatever the age of the child, their responses to DV are immediate and cumulative, whether these are obvious responses such as distress or aggression, or less visible depressive or dissociative responses which may not be easily recognised. It is essential that children are assisted to deal with the impact of DV. Without this, the child's experience is fragmented – the child may be able to talk about what happened but not be able to describe the associated thoughts or feelings – and post-traumatic symptoms will continue to occur, such as chronic tension, arousal, numbing, avoidance and intrusive thoughts about the violence itself.

## The impact of direct abuse and living with DV

Children exposed to DV are much more likely to be physically or sexually abused or neglected as well (Finkelhor, Ormrod, Turner, & Holt, 2009). A significant amount of research has investigated the impact of this 'double whammy' on children, but the evidence is unclear about whether there is a compounding effect of the combined impacts of DV along with physical and/or sexual abuse. While some studies indicate that this occurs (Cyr, Fortin, & Lachance, 2006), the meta-analysis by Kitzmann and colleagues of 118 studies showed no difference in behavioural and emotional adjustment for those exposed to DV alone compared with those who experienced both direct abuse and DV (Kitzmann, Gaylord, Holt, & Kenney, 2003). This is a similar finding to Silverman and Gelles (2001). These studies suggest that it is the fear induced through living with violence and abuse, combined with the physical and emotional undermining of the child's mother, that creates the impact on children's emotional, behavioural and cognitive functioning (Lourenço et al., 2013).

However, the studies of poly-victimisation also shed light on the complexities of child abuse in the context of DV. Finkelhor et al. (2009) suggest that there are vulnerable children who are subjected to many forms of abuse. The literature on poly-victimisation shows a linear relationship between the number of childhood adversities (domestic violence, peer bullying, property crime, child physical and sexual abuse) and the level of adverse outcomes for children (Finkelhor et al., 2009, p. 404). Domestic violence leads to the largest increase in lifetime victimisation scores for children under 18, though issues such as child sexual abuse are weighted more heavily in terms of their impact on the child's future emotional well-being.

## Intersecting adversities

Children's vulnerabilities may be compounded by the intersection with issues of poverty, racism and disability. For example, the report by the Australian Aboriginal Children's Commissioner highlights not only the over-representation of Aboriginal children in care, but the fact that for 88% of these children in care, DV was a feature of their lives (Commission for Children and Young People, 2016). Separating the influence of culture, disability, poverty and temperament is a difficult but important task and may affect the way distress is expressed. However, the evidence suggests that there are features of the experience of DV that are common to children of all cultures (McIntosh, 2003). It may be that the issues of poverty are the intervening variable. The studies of children coming into care aligned with the low socio-economic areas in which they are located is indicative of the added stress, often on already vulnerable parents, created through poverty (Morris et al., 2018).

A significant difference between Anglo-Celtic cultures and Asian and Indigenous cultures often lies in the attention and embedded nature of extended family connections (Commission for Children and Young People, 2016). Migration and dislocation may interfere with these ties. However, there is evidence that too much emphasis may be placed by child protection practitioners on the nuclear family without 'safe places' being searched for in the family network. The Family Group Conference model with its roots in Maori extended family culture formalised the processes through which these networks could be explored and utilised to support and protect infants, children and young people when DV was present in their nuclear family (Corwin et al., 2019). The trial by Corwin and colleagues (2019) highlighted the significant difference to social support provided through the Family Group Conferencing process when compared to a control group.

The literature highlights the many forms of coercive control and abuse that constitute DV, and the diverse ways in which DV affects children. At one extreme, children die (Commission for Children and Young People, 2016) or their mothers are killed (Alisic, Krishna, Groot, & Frederick, 2015). Other children's lives are severely disrupted by the impacts of violence that undermine the functioning of their mothers and create an atmosphere of fear which heightens anxiety in children and impedes the development of their behaviour, emotional well-being and their neurological development (Holt et al., 2008). It is the child's perception and reaction to abuse and other stresses, and the protective factors they have around them, that influences the degree of trauma suffered. In short, the literature is not able to make predictions about which children under what circumstances will continue to thrive, and those for whom outcomes will be poor (Stanley, 2011).

## Intervention and debates

The form that helpful interventions should take and the debates in the area are interconnected, particularly when discussing antenatal care, infants and children under 5 years old. Some of these issues include strategies for intervening with pregnant women, the role of fathers who use violence and appropriate interventions, and grappling with levels of risk, particularly given the vulnerability of infants.

The vulnerability of infants and their mothers when men are violent and abusive during pregnancy suggest that these men have little positive to offer the family. Data from Canadian prevalence surveys show women attacked when pregnant, over time, were three times more likely than other women suffering domestic abuse to report serious violence (attack with weapons, strangulation and hospitalisation) (Jamieson & Hart, 1999). These men respond to vulnerability with violence and abuse rather than protection and are therefore an ongoing risk to women and children. Evidence such as this suggests that efforts should be made to support, in every way possible, women who wish to separate during their pregnancy and when their children are infants.

However, many women for a wide range of reasons do not want to, or are not in a position to separate (Humphreys & Campo, 2017). There are also a group of men who want to father differently and can be responsive to invitations to change their behaviour. A range of programmes have been established, some of which specialise in the period early in the infant's life, providing information, support and counselling. For example, For Baby's Sake (www.stefanoufoundation.org/copy-of-for-professionals) and Dads on Board (Bunston, 2013) exemplify the approach of attending to safety while providing support. Programmes may also begin during the antenatal period (Solmeyer, Feinberg, Coffman, & Jones, 2014) focusing on early intervention, including programmes customised for Indigenous men and their families such as Wondering from the Womb (Crouch, 2017). The early evidence from these programmes show mixed results, though clearly a group of men within them are responsive and engaged. Piloting of these programmes is at an early stage as decisions are made about assessment, risk and safety and the extent to which they are 'all of family' programmes (in which each family member receives a service though not necessarily together) or group work programmes focused primarily on men, but with an adjunct partner support programme.

A further debate arises in relation to the role of statutory child protection and the level of risk to children under 5 which can be held before places of safety outside the nuclear family need to be found. This chapter has outlined the significant vulnerabilities for infants and young children living with DV. The work of David Mandel and colleagues from the Safe and Together Institute (www.safeandtogetherinstitute.com) provide a framework for intervening where there is domestic violence, customised for statutory child protection workers. Central to the model is partnering with women (rather than placing them under surveillance) and intervening much more directly and fully with fathers who use violence (Humphreys, Healey, & Mandel, 2018; Mandel, 2014;). Much greater attention is placed on assessment, risk management of men and engaging them in relation to their fathering.

There are no easy answers to the debate around 'rescue' versus 'family support' for infants in these families. Assessment should be customised to each family. Protective factors need to be assessed and explored as extensively as risk factors. This includes whether the isolation of many of the women living with domestic violence can be addressed. The dangers for infants living with mothers and fathers who often have drug and alcohol and mental health problems in a context of domestic violence will be dependent upon the demonstrated capacity for change and the places in the family where safety and protection can be found (Commission for Children and Young People, 2016).

## Conclusions

Intervening early, preventing the abuse of women during pregnancy and beyond is the most obvious strategy for protecting young children from DV. It indicates that a public health approach is required which engages young people early in understanding the harm to children created by violence and abuse in relationships (Jordan & Sketchley, 2009). The risks to the developing infant and the undermining of women in their role as mothers create significant harms which go beyond individual women and highlight the need to address 'the wicked problem' of domestic violence.

The range of strategies to intervene early are contested, particularly in relation to the role of fathers who use violence and the actions to be taken when domestic violence occurs early in the lives of children. A customised approach is required that recognises that infants and young children live in different contexts of vulnerability and protection and that these nuanced assessments will require highly differentiated responses.

# Critical findings

- Children under 5 years old are the most vulnerable to the impacts of domestic violence.
- Infants are particularly susceptible to the undermining of their mothers by violence and abuse due to their high dependency needs.
- The neurological development of infants and small children occurs through relationships with their primary carer/s. Debilitating the infant's mother through abuse may have profound impacts on the cognitive, behavioural and emotional development of the child.
- Many women seek to mother in circumstances of violence in ways that resist the abuse they are experiencing and seek to compensate with protective action towards their children.
- Listening to children, observing infants and seeking to hear what they are telling us are important practices for professionals working with children living with domestic violence.
- Children live in different contexts of protection and vulnerability. Blanket assertions that all children are equally harmed by violence are inaccurate.
- Repeated exposure over time produces worse outcomes for children.
- Mothers' parenting is often undermined by DV. Parenting capacity can be further compromised by poor mental health, substance misuse and lack of social supports.

# Implications for policy, practice and research

- Early intervention in the life-course of infants and young children to prevent the harmful effects of violence and abuse is critical.
- Recognising that infants and young children are safe if their mothers are safe is a foundational concept.
- Fathers who use violence and abuse do not magically become good parents on separation.
- It is incumbent upon professionals to ensure that men who use violence are assessed, and attempts made to engage them in strategies to address their behaviour and attitudes.
- Women who are abused during pregnancy and beyond will need ongoing support from health visitors/maternal and child health nurses and other professionals to decrease their isolation and address the ways in which their safety and well-being can be supported. This will directly affect the well-being of infants and young children in their care.

# References

Alisic, E., Krishna, R., Groot, A., & Frederick, J. (2015). Children's mental health and well-being after parental intimate partner homicide: A systematic review. *Clinical Child and Family Psychology Review, 18*, 328–345. doi:10.1007/s10567-015-0193-7

Andrews, S., Gallant, D., Humphreys, C., Ellis, D., Bamblett, A., Briggs, R., & Harrison, W. (2018). Holistic program developments and responses to Aboriginal men who use violence against women. *International Social Work*. doi:10.1177/0020872818807272

Baker, L., & Cunningham, A. (2009). Inter-parental violence: The pre-schooler's perspective and the educator's role. *Early Childhood Education Journal, 37*(3), 199–207. doi:10.1007/s10643-009-0342-z

Bancroft, L., & Silverman, J. G. (2002). *The batterer as parent: Assessing the impact of domestic violence on family dynamics*. New York, NY: Sage.

Bogat, G. A., DeJonghe, A. A., Levendosky, A. A., Davidson, W. S., & von Eye, A. (2006). Trauma symptoms among infants exposed to intimate partner violence. *Child Abuse and Neglect, 30*(2), 109–125. doi:10.1016/j.chiabu.2005.09.002

Bowlby, J. (1982). *Attachment and loss volume 1: Attachment* (2nd ed.). New York, NY: Basic Books.

Broady, T. R., Gray, R., Gaffney, I., & Lewis, P. (2017). 'I miss my little one a lot': How father love motivates change in men who have used violence. *Child Abuse Review, 26*, 328–338. doi:10.1002/car.2381

Buchanan, F. (2018). *Mothering babies in domestic violence: Beyond attachment theory*. London: Routledge.

Bunston, W. (2008). Baby lead the way: Mental health group work for infants, children and mothers affected by family violence. *Journal of Family Studies, 14*, 334–341. doi:10.5172/jfs.327.14.2-3.334

Bunston, W. (2013). 'What about the fathers?' Bringing 'Dads on Board' with their infants and toddlers following violence. *Journal of Family Studies, 19*, 70–79. doi:10.5172/jfs.2013.19.1.70

Burch, R. L., & Gallup, G. G., (2004). Pregnancy as a stimulus for domestic violence. *Journal of Family Violence, 19*(4), 243–247. doi:10.1023/B:JOFV.0000032634.40840.48

Carpenter, G. L., & Stacks, A. M. (2009). Developmental effects of exposure to intimate partner violence in early childhood: A review of the literature. *Children and Youth Services Review, 31*, 831–839. doi:10.1016/j.childyouth.2009.03.005

Clark, L. E., Allen, R. H., Goyal, V., Raker, C., & Gottlieb, A. S. (2014). Reproductive coercion and co-occurring intimate partner violence in obstetrics and gynaecology patients. *American Journal of Obstetrics and Gynaecology, 210*(1), 42.e1–8. doi:10.1016/j.ajog.2013.09.019

Commission for Children and Young People. (2016). *'Always was, always will be Koori children': Systemic inquiry into services provided to Aboriginal children and young people in out-of-home care in Victoria.* Melbourne: Commission for Children and Young People.

Corwin, T., Mayer, E., Merkel-Holguin, L., Allan, H., Hollinshead, D., & Fluke, J. (2019). Increasing social support for child welfare-involved families through family group conferencing. *British Journal of Social Work*, bcz036. doi:10.1093/bjsw/bcz036

Cox, P. (2015). *Violence against women: Additional analysis of the Australian bureau of statistics' personal safety survey.* Horizons Research Paper No. 1. Sydney, Australia's National Research Organisation for Women's Safety Limited (ANROWS).

Crouch, K. (2017). Wondering from the womb: Antenatal yarning in rural Victoria. *Children Australia, 42*, 75–78. doi:10.1017/cha.2017.15

Cunningham, A. J., & Baker, L. L. (2007). *Little eyes, little ears: How violence against a mother shapes children as they grow.* London: Centre for Children & Families in the Justice System.

Cyr, M., Fortin, A., & Lachance, L. (2006). Children exposed to domestic violence: Effects of gender and child physical abuse on psychosocial problems. *International Journal of Child and Family Welfare, 9*(3), 114.

Eriksson, M., & Nasman, E. (2012). Interviews with children exposed to violence. *Children & Society, 26*(1), 63–73. doi:10.1111/j.1099-0860.2010.00322.x

Fantuzzo, J. W., & Mohr, W. K. (1999). Prevalence and effects of child exposure to domestic violence. *The Future of Children, 9*(3), 21–32. doi:10.2307/1602779

Finkelhor, D., Ormrod, R., Turner, H., & Holt, M. (2009). Pathways to poly-victimization. *Child Maltreatment, 14*(4), 316–329. doi:10.1177/1077559509347012

Graham-Bermann, S. A., Gruber, G., Howell, K. H., & Girz, L. (2009). Factors discriminating among profiles of resilience and psychopathology in children exposed to intimate partner violence (IPV). *Child Abuse & Neglect, 33*(9), 648–660.

Harne, L. (2004). *Violence, power and meanings of fatherhood in issues of child contact* (Doctoral dissertation). University of Bristol. Retrieved from https://ethos.bl.uk/OrderDetails.do?uin=uk.bl.ethos.404185

Heward-Belle, S. (2017). Exploiting the 'good mother' as a tactic of coercive control: Domestically violent men's assaults on women as mothers. *Affilia, 32*(3), 374–389. doi:10.1177/0886109917706935

Holden, G. W. (2003). Children exposed to domestic violence and child abuse: Terminology and taxonomy. *Clinical Child and Family Psychology Review, 6*(3), 151–160. doi:10.1023/A:1024906315255

Holt, S. (2015). Post-separation fathering and domestic abuse: Challenges and contradictions. *Child Abuse Review, 24*(3), 210–222. doi:10.1002/car.2264

Holt, S., Buckley, H., & Whelan, S. (2008). The impact of exposure to domestic violence on children and young people: A review of the literature. *Child Abuse & Neglect, 32*(8), 797–810. doi:10.1016/j.chiabu.2008.02.004

Howarth, E., Moore, T. H. M., Shaw, A. R. G., Welton, N. J., Feder, G. S., Hester, M., . . . Stanley, N. (2015). The effectiveness of targeted interventions for children exposed to domestic violence: Measuring success in ways that matter to children, parents and professionals. *Child Abuse Review, 24*(4), 297–310. doi:10.1002/car.2408

Humphreys, C., & Campo, M. (2017). *Fathers who use violence: Options for safe practice where there is ongoing contact with children.* CFCA Paper no. 43. Melbourne, Australian Institute of Family Studies. Retrieved from https://aifs.gov.au/cfca/publications/fathers-who-use-violence

Humphreys, C., Healey, L., & Mandel, D. (2018). Case reading as a practice and training intervention in domestic violence and child protection. *Australian Social Work, 71*, 277–291. doi:10.1080/0312407X.2017.1413666

Jaffe, P., Wolfe, D., & Wilson, S. (1990). *Children of battered women: Issues in child development and intervention planning*. Newbury Park, CA: Sage.

Jamieson, B., & Hart, L. (1999). *A handbook for health and social service professionals responding to abuse during pregnancy*. Ottawa: Health Canada.

Jordan, B., & Sketchley, R. (2009). *A stitch in time saves nine: Preventing and responding to the abuse and neglect of infants*. National Child Protection Clearinghouse Issues Paper No. 30. Melbourne, Australian Institute of Family Studies. Retrieved from https://aifs.gov.au/cfca/publications/stitch-time-saves-nine-preventing-and-responding-th

Katz, E. (2016). Beyond the physical incident model: How children living with domestic violence are harmed by and resist regimes of coercive control. *Child Abuse Review, 25*(1), 46–59. doi:10.1002/car.2422

Kitzmann, K. M., Gaylord, N. K., Holt, A. R., & Kenney, E. D. (2003). Child witnesses to domestic violence: A meta-analytic review. *Journal of Consulting and Clinical Psychology, 71*(2), 339–352. doi:10.1037/0022-006X.71.2.339

Laing, L., Humphreys, C., & Cavanagh, K. (2013). *Social work and domestic violence: Developing critical and reflective practice*. London: Sage.

Lamb, K., Humphreys, C., & Hegarty, K. (2018). "Your behaviour has consequences": Children and young people's perspectives on reparation with their fathers after domestic violence. *Child and Youth Services, 88*, 164–169. doi:10.1016/j.childyouth.2018.03.013

Lapierre, S. (2010). Striving to be 'good' mothers: Abused women's experiences of mothering. *Child Abuse Review, 19*(5), 342–357. doi:10.1002/car.1113

Levendosky, A. A., Huth-Bocks, A. C., Shapiro, D. L., & Semel, M. A. (2003). The impact of domestic violence on the maternal-child relationship and preschool-age children's functioning. *Journal of Family Psychology, 17*(3), 275. doi:10.1037/0893-3200.17.3.275

Levendosky, A. A., Lynch, S. M., & Graham-Bermann, S. A. (2000). Mothers' perceptions of the impact of woman abuse on their parenting. *Violence Against Women, 6*(3), 247–271. doi:10.1177/10778010022181831

Lourenço, L. M., Baptista, M. N., Senra, L. X., Almeida, A. A., Basílio, C., & Bhona, F. M. C. (2013). Consequences of exposure to domestic violence for children: A systematic review of the literature. *Paideia, 23*(55), 263–271. doi:10.1590/1982-43272355201314

Lundy, M., & Grossman, S. F. (2005). The mental health and service needs of young children exposed to domestic violence: Supportive data. *Families in Society, 86*(1), 17–29. doi:10.1606/1044-3894.1873

Mandel, D. (2009). Batterers in the lives of their children. In E. Stark & E. S. Buzawa (Eds.), *Violence against women in families and relationships* (Vol. 2, pp. 67–93). Santa Barbara, CA: ABC-CLIO.

Mandel, D. (2014). Beyond domestic violence perpetrator accountability in child welfare systems. *The No to Violence Journal, 1*(Spring), 50–85.

Martin, S. G. (2002). Children exposed to domestic violence: Psychological considerations for health care practitioners. *Holistic Nursing Practice, 16*(3), 7–15.

McConnell, N., Barnard, M., Holdsworth, T., & Taylor, J. (2016). *Caring dads: Safer children evaluation report*. London: NSPCC. Retrieved from www.nspcc.org.uk/globalassets/documents/evaluation-of-services/caring-dads-safer-children-evaluation-report.pdf

McGee, C. (1997). Children's experiences of domestic violence. *Child and Family Social Work, 2*, 13–23. doi:10.1046/j.1365-2206.1997.00037.x

McIntosh, J. (2003). Children living with domestic violence: Research foundations for early intervention. *Journal of Family Studies, 9*(2), 219–234. doi:10.5172/jfs.9.2.219

McTavish, J. R., MacGregor, J. C. D., Wathen, C. N., & MacMillan, H. L. (2016). Children's exposure to intimate partner violence: An overview. *International Review of Psychiatry*. doi:10.1080/09540261.2016.1205001

Meltzer, H., Doos, L., Vostanis, P., Ford, T., & Goodman, R. (2009). The mental health of children who witness domestic violence. *Child and Family Social Work, 14*(4), 491–501. doi:10.1111/j.1365-2206.2009.00633.x

Morris, A., Humphreys, C., & Hegarty, K. (2015). Children's views of safety and adversity when living with domestic violence. In C. Humphreys & N. Stanley (Eds.), *Domestic violence and protecting children: New thinking and approaches* (pp. 18–33). London: Jessica Kingsley Publishers.

Morris, K., Mason, W., Bywaters, P., Featherstone, B., Daniel, B., Brady, G., . . . Webb, C. (2018). Social work, poverty, and child welfare interventions. *Child and Family Social Work, 23*, 364–372. doi:10.1111/cfs.12423

Mueller, I., & Tronick, E. (2019). Early life exposure to violence: Developmental consequences on brain and behaviour. *Frontiers in Behavioural Neuroscience, 13*, 1–7. doi:10.3389/fnbeh.2019.00156

Mullender, A., & Morley, R. (1994). *Preventing domestic violence to women.* London: Home Office Police Department.

Noble-Carr, D., Moore, T., & McArthur, M. (2019). Children's experiences and needs in relation to domestic and family violence: Findings from a meta-synthesis. *Child & Family Social Work.* doi:10.1111/cfs.12645

Osofsky, J. D. (2003). Prevalence of children's exposure to domestic violence and child maltreatment: Implications for prevention and intervention. *Clinical Child and Family Psychology Review, 6*(3), 161–170. doi:10.1023/A:1024958332093

Perry, B. D. (2001). The neurodevelopmental impact of violence in childhood. In D. Schetky & E. P. Benedek (Eds.), *Textbook of child and adolescent forensic psychiatry* (pp. 221–238). Washington, DC: American Psychiatric Press.

Radford, L., & Hester, M. (2006). *Mothering through domestic violence.* London: Jessica Kingsley Publishers.

Rifkin-Graboi, A., Borelli, J. L., & Enlow, M. B. (2009). Neurobiology of stress in infancy. In C. H. J. Zeanah & J. C. H. Zeanah (Eds.), *Handbook of infant mental health.* New York, NY: The Guilford Press.

Rivara, F. P., Anderson, M. L., Fishman, P., Bonomi, A. E., Reid, R. J., Carrell, D., & Thompson, R. S. (2007). Intimate partner violence and health care costs and utilization for children living in the home. *Pediatrics, 120*(6), 1270–1277. doi:10.1542/peds.2007-1148

Romano, E., Weegar, K., Gallitto, E., Zak, S., & Saini, M. (2019). Meta-analysis on interventions for children exposed to intimate partner violence. *Trauma, Violence & Abuse.* doi:10.1177/1524838019881737

Rossman, B. B. (2001). Longer term effects of children's exposure to domestic violence. In S. A. Graham-Bermann & J. L. Edleson (Eds.), *Domestic violence in the lives of children: The future of research, intervention and social policy.* Washington, DC: American Psychological Association.

Rossman, B. R., Hughes, H. M., & Rosenberg, M. S. (2013). *Children and interparental violence: The impact of exposure.* New Yok, NY: Routledge.

Schore, A. (2016). *Affect regulation and the origin of the self: The neurobiology of emotional development.* New York, NY: Psychology Press.

Scott, K. L., & Crooks, C. V. (2007). Preliminary evaluation of an intervention program for maltreating fathers. *Brief Treatment and Crisis Intervention, 7*(3), 224–238. doi:10.1093/brief-treatment/mhm007

Scott, K. L., & Lishak, V. (2012). Intervention for maltreating fathers: Statistically and clinically significant change. *Child Abuse and Neglect, 36*(9), 680–684. doi:10.1016/j.chiabu.2012.06.003

Siegel, D. (1999). *The developing mind: Toward a neurobiology of interpersonal experience.* New York, NY: The Guilford Press.

Silverman, A., & Gelles, R. J. (2001). The double whammy revisited: The impact of exposure to domestic violence and being a victim of parent to child violence. *Indian Journal of Social Work, 62*, 305–327.

Solmeyer, A., Feinberg, M., Coffman, D., & Jones, D. (2014). The effects of the family foundations prevention program on co-parenting and child adjustment: A mediation analysis. *Prevention Science, 15*, 213–223. doi:10.1007/s11121-013-0366-x

Stanley, N. (2011). *Children experiencing domestic violence: A research review.* Dartington: Research in Practice.

Stanley, N., Graham-Kevan, N., & Borthwick, R. (2012). Fathers and domestic violence: Building motivation for change through perpetrator programmes. *Child Abuse Review, 21*(4), 264–274. doi:10.1002/car.2222

Stark, E. (2012). Looking beyond domestic violence: Policing coercive control. *Journal of Police Crisis Negotiations, 12*(2), 199–217. doi:10.1080/15332586.2012.725016

Streeck-Fisher, A., & van der Kolk, B. (2000). Down will come baby, cradle and all: Diagnostic and therapeutic implications of chronic trauma on child development. *Australian and New Zealand Journal of Psychiatry, 34*, 903–918. doi:10.1080/000486700265

Willie, T. C., Alexander, K. A., Amutah-Onukagha, N., & Kershaw, T. (2019). Effects of reproductive coercion on young couples' parenting behaviors and child development: A dyadic perspective. *Journal of Family Psychology, 33*(6), 682–689. doi:10.1037/fam0000546

Woolhouse, H., Gartland, D., Hegarty, K., Donath, S., & Brown, S. J. (2012). Depressive symptoms and intimate partner violence in the 12 months after childbirth: A prospective pregnancy cohort study. *BJOG, 119*(3), 315–323. doi:10.1111/j.1471-0528.2011.03219.x

# 11

# PREVENTIVE SOCIALISATION OF INTIMATE PARTNER VIOLENCE THROUGH THE ANALYSIS OF FAMILY INTERACTIONS AND PREVIOUS INTIMATE RELATIONSHIPS

*Esther Oliver, Guiomar Merodio and Patricia Melgar*

## Introduction

This chapter is based on previous research on preventive socialisation (analysis of those elements that involve learning – socialisation into – models of attraction linked to violence or, contrary, linked to equality and freedom) and on the intergenerational transmission of violence (ITV) to contribute to the understanding of IPV (Black, Sussman, & Unger, 2010; Eriksson & Mazerolle, 2014; Fang & Corso, 2007; Hou, Yu, Fang, & Epstein, 2015). When we mention the ITV concept, we use the definition of Angèle Fauchier (Renzetti & Edleson, 2008), who mentions that children learn to be perpetrators and/or victims of violence through exposure to their parents' expression of violence. Regarding IPV, we start from the definition of Bonnie E. Carlson (Renzetti & Edleson, 2008), who establishes that IPV consists of physical, emotional, sexual, or psychological abuse or violence committed by an intimate partner or acquaintances. While Carlson highlights that IPV is also called domestic violence or wife abuse, throughout this chapter we will only use the term domestic violence (DV) when we refer to violence in the context of families.

Therefore, the main aim of this chapter is to provide qualitative evidence based on testimonies of different life trajectories to fill a gap in the academic literature, which largely considers only perpetrators' or victims' families of origin as an explanatory factor of IPV. Previous scientific contributions on preventive socialisation have already highlighted the relevance of a person's first sexual and affective relationships as key elements of socialisation towards a model of attraction to violent or non-violent relationships (Valls, Puigvert, & Duque, 2008; Racionero-Plaza, Ugalde-Lujambio, Puigvert, & Aiello, 2018; Rios-González, Peña Axt, Duque Sánchez, & De Botton Fernández, 2018; Puigvert, Gelsthorpe, Soler-Gallart, & Flecha, 2019). This chapter is based on contributions that address violence that is not necessarily learnt from intimate partner relationships but before, and not in the family during childhood but afterwards. In this chapter, three contributions are highlighted, not to establish deterministic suppositions but to add to the current debate and stress the relevance of first sexual and/or affective interactions or relationships during childhood, early adolescence and youth (from the first kiss to the first instance of sexual intercourse) for both violent and non-violent life trajectories.

## Recent research

Over the past few decades, substantial research has been conducted on IPV with the purpose of offering useful explanations for male perpetration of violence and for understanding women's victimisation. Definitions of DV have also evolved and the focus of study has broadened to consider how women experience violence in different types of intimate relationships (e.g., while dating, cohabiting, or married) (Renzetti & Edleson, 2008; Stanley & Devaney, 2017).

Studies have increasingly considered important variables, such as the gender of the perpetrator or of direct or indirect victims, and the direction of the violence perpetrated. The analysis of such variables reveals with greater detail those elements that can be risk factors for being a perpetrator or victim of violence. However, many questions remain opened for instance, does having witnessed or suffered direct violence during childhood influence subsequent involvement in adulthood IPV? Is subsequent victimisation or perpetration influenced more when violence witnessed in childhood was perpetrated by a parent of the same gender? Do other relationships beyond the family of origin influence the socialisation of violence in relationships?

### *Influence of the family*

The intergenerational transmission of violence builds on social learning theory, which assumes that children who witness violence learn to engage in interpersonal violence via observation, imitation, and modelling (Bandura, 1977). Following this view, witnessing DV might increase children's likelihood of either becoming a victim of IPV or of committing DV crimes during adulthood. From this perspective, children who witness violence in the family or who are direct victims of family violence may grow up believing that violence serves as an acceptable means of resolving conflicts and that violent adults can positively reinforce their violent attitudes (Black et al., 2010). In this regard, some studies have found significant associations between children who witness interparental violence and IPV victimisation in early adulthood (Black et al., 2010). Another study on the relationship quality of parent victims of IPV, abusive behaviours and youths' histories of abuse indicates that children are more likely to reproduce abusive patterns in their partnerships (Liu, Mumford, & Taylor, 2017). A study of 1099 adult males arrested for battering in the US also found that men witnessing DV as children commit IPV more frequently while those abused as children are more likely to later abuse other children (Murrell, Christoff, & Henning, 2007). A more complex approach to the victimisation experiences of children points out that children are more than witnesses, they are victims of DV (Callaghan, Alexander, Sixsmith, & Fellin, 2018).

Other studies adopting an ecological approach to the study of DV consider both environmental and individual factors. These studies point to the coexistence of risk factors, especially to forms of maltreatment that additionally contribute to DV perpetration or victimisation. Following this approach, Bevan and Higgins (2002) found, for a sample of abuser men with a history of DV, that childhood neglect predicts physical partner abuse, whereas witnessing family violence influences psychological spouse abuse. Similarly, most of the focus has been placed on family dysfunction itself in seeking DV predictors linked to adverse childhood experiences, such as physical, psychological, or sexual abuse, and childhood family characteristics. Recent studies have considered coercive control as an important element for understanding how children victims of DV are affected and how it disturbs children and mothers' relationships (Katz, 2019). Another study suggests that child maltreatment and neglect increase risks for physical IPV and particularly for neglected girls during childhood, who are more likely to eventually report being victimised by an intimate partner (Widom, Czaja, & Dutton, 2014). Another study also shows that child maltreatment influences future IPV perpetration more than victimisation affects youth violence or IPV (Fang & Corso, 2007).

However, most studies have focused on violent men's childhood experiences of witnessing violence or being victimised. Therefore, there is limited information on child victims of DV who may later not become perpetrators of IPV. Additionally, other studies have found weak evidence for the transmission of family violence hypothesis (Renner & Slack, 2006). Indeed, a meta-analysis on the intergenerational transmission of family violence shows that despite the extended premise of a link between exposure to family violence and future IPV, the literature is actually not completely consistent with this association with various studies not finding significant links (Smith-Marek et al., 2015). At the same time, other recent findings also highlight the influence of having experienced multiple vulnerabilities at the mesosocial level in the ecological conceptual model (De Puy, Radford, Le Fort, & Romain-Glassey, 2019).

## Influence of gender

Studies have also analysed the importance of gender for the intergenerational transmission for IPV. These studies are based on the premise that children learn violent behaviours from same-gender role models. Girls whose mothers are victims of DV might be predisposed to future victimisation through modelling. Likewise, according to social learning theory, boys who witness their fathers' perpetrating violence tend to be more aggressive in adulthood (Milletich, Kelley, Doane, & Pearson, 2010). Another study stressed the relevance of gender role-specific modelling to the intergenerational transmission of violence, rather than experiencing child abuse, which was not found to be predictive of IPV perpetration (Eriksson & Mazerolle, 2014). These studies also examine differences in associations between exposure to the gender of the perpetrator in the family and the directionality of violence. A study of 917 adolescent female and male students shows that adolescent girls might be more influenced by exposure to father-to-mother and mother-to-father violence and IPV perpetration, while for boys, only mother-to-father violence has an impact (Temple, Shorey, Tortolero, Wolfe, & Stuart, 2013). In contrast, other studies have not found gender-specific social learning models to predict the intergenerational transmission of DV (Kwong, Bartholomew, Henderson, & Trinke, 2003; Hou et al., 2015).

## Peer group

Other studies have started to focus on elements other than the family (e.g., prosocial attitudes and beliefs among peer and friend groups and positive parenting practices) as moderators and key protective factors of the association between DV exposure and IPV involvement (Garrido & Taussig, 2013). There are also emerging questions on how peer contexts influence IPV, as having tolerant attitudes towards IPV in peer groups has been found to be associated with higher levels of psychological, physical, and sexual DV perpetration among boys exposed to wife-perpetrated spousal violence in their families (Gage, 2016). In this regard, attitudes towards the acceptance and normalisation of violence among peers might increase risks of DV perpetration more than witnessing violence in the family of origin. Additionally, regarding the influence of contexts, experiencing community violence is an important predictor of youth IPV victimisation and of developing an acceptance of IPV perpetration among youth (Black et al., 2014).

## Intimate relationship socialisation

Recent studies have broadened potential risk factors for violence perpetration in intimate partner relationships among adolescents and young adults beyond factors traditionally associated with family violence. A longitudinal study conducted in the US to identify the strongest risk factors for vulnerability to IPV perpetration with a sample of 1031 high school students found that having a violent dating history and acceptance of IPV are the strongest predictors of IPV perpetration above family violence (Cohen, Shorey, Menon, & Temple, 2018).

Previous studies have largely focused on the family environment itself and on its influence on later involvement in adulthood IPV without considering other social relationships and experience. Relationship contexts are sources of socialisation. It is important to consider the socialisation experiences of children and teens, not only from their families of origin and later when they create their own families but also from other affective and sexual socialising experiences that occur between these periods and that may influence DV victimisation or perpetration. Research adopting theoretical approaches to the preventive socialisation of gender violence helps address this gap by providing explanatory elements for IPV (Valls et al., 2008; Gómez, 2015; Racionero-Plaza et al., 2018; Puigvert et al., 2019).

## Social promotion of violent attractiveness models

Research on the preventive socialisation of gender violence has stressed the existence of a link between aggressiveness and attractiveness that promotes models of attractiveness linked to violence, shaping adolescents' sexual-affective relationship preferences, choices, and desires (Valls et al., 2008; Díez-Palomar, Capllonch, & Aiello, 2014; Puigvert, 2016; Ruiz-Eugenio et al., 2020). Importantly, these studies have also identified the existence of a coercive dominant discourse that portrays violent attitudes and behaviours as attractive and exciting as the main agents of socialisation: visual and popular media, teen magazines, social networks, and peer interactions with others (Puigvert, 2014; Gómez, 2015; Racionero-Plaza et al., 2018; Racionero-Plaza et al. 2020; Torras-Gómez, Puigvert, Aiello, & Khalfaoui, 2020). Adolescents' and young adults' sexual-affective socialisation patterns are influenced by this coercive dominant discourse. Evidence also suggests that adolescents' first affective-sexual relationships (particularly hook-up relationships) have a strong impact on their future intimate partner relationships, as they serve as key aspects in the socialisation of both girls and boys towards a model of attraction to violent or non-violent relationships. First affective-sexual experiences can even render girls socialised into this coercive dominant discourse, which associates attractiveness and desire with masculine models that are dominant and violent, more vulnerable to IPV (Bukowski, Sippola, & Newcomb, 2000; Valls et al., 2008; Puigvert, 2016; Torras-Gómez et al., 2020). Coercive socialisation attraction patterns are based on unequal gender power relations that reproduce a double standard whereby boys who exhibit violent behaviours are socially perceived as exciting and sexually desired, particularly for sporadic relationships, while boys with non-violent attitudes are considered less exciting but "convenient" and preferred for stable relationships (Puigvert et al., 2019). Social interactions among peers and everyday interactions and dialogues within families are also important among socialisation patterns that either prevent or perpetuate the coercive model of socialisation (Rios-González et al., 2018). The approach to the preventive socialisation of gender violence also contributes to the understanding of the transformative elements that socialise in egalitarian romantic relationships free of violence (Torras-Gómez et al., 2020).

## Research study

We adopted a qualitative research approach to develop a nuanced understanding of complex phenomena of IPV from individual life trajectories (Denzin & Lincoln, 2011). Our use of qualitative methods provided us with insight into the family and previous intimate relationships of our study participants. This chapter is based on empirical data obtained from two qualitative sources. We employed purposive sampling to select participants with different life trajectories, having experienced the phenomenon studied in this chapter and willing to share their experiences in a reflective manner (Creswell & Plano Clark, 2011). The purposive sample is consistent with the aims of the study, as the participants' experiences are considered relevant to our focus. To identify diverse participants' profiles to respond to the studied aims we used snowball sampling. We first collected the oral testimonies[1] of six women of different socio-economic backgrounds who have suffered any form of gender violence. We then conducted seven additional in-depth interviews. In these interviews, informants were encouraged to reflect on the impact of different interactions they had experienced. With quotes of the interviewees, this chapter provides elements for reflection on significant interactions that can lead to life moments and lives with and without violence. Characteristics of the respondents were established before entering the field to meet the following criteria: (1) a man who had experienced violence in his family of origin and who does not experience violence in his affective and sexual relationships (Gerard); (2) a woman who has had violent affective and sexual relationships without having experienced violence in her family of origin (Yolanda); (3) men who did not experience violence in their families of origin and who have been perpetrators of violence in their affective and sexual relationships (data on these life trajectories were collected indirectly from interviews held by a professional working with 35–45 perpetrators every year) (Alicia); (4) a woman who experienced violence in her family of origin and does not have violent affective and sexual relationships (Clara); and (5) three women who have experienced violence or abuse in their families of origin and who have had violent affective and sexual relationships in their first relationships but not in their later relationships (Paula, Carolina, and Raquel).

Participants were informed of the study's purpose and of the sensitive focus of the research. The confidentiality of information given was ensured, and all participants have been kept anonymous. The interviewers posed broad, open-ended questions about the participants' life trajectories with a focus on family and intimate relationship experiences. Interviews were conducted in locations that guaranteed confidentiality and that fostered trust between the researchers and participants. Informed consent was obtained prior to the interviews. The interviews were transcribed and coded for analysis.

## Discussion and analysis

The approach to the preventive socialisation of gender violence, on which this study is framed, broadens the scope of elements and social interactions that influence affective-sexual socialisation patterns to both peers and family interactions. Following this perspective, we analyse and discuss the life trajectories of adults who were victims of violence in their families of origin and later did not become victims or perpetrators of DV, and of adults who were not victims of DV in childhood but ended up experiencing IPV in adulthood. The findings suggest the relevance of violent and non-violent first sexual-affective experiences and relationships in later intimate relationships, either violent or non-violent. Their different life paths can help us better understand complex risks and protective and preventive elements/relationships related to DV.

## 1 First sexual and affective interactions studied have a deep impact on later intimate relationships

From the evidence collected we observe different impacts on the feelings and life trajectories of both men and women depending on their experiences with first affective and sexual relationships. The studied life trajectories demonstrate the influence of being involved in stable or sporadic first affective and sexual relationships based on positive feelings, such as passionate love, respect, and esteem, or in contrast, based on feeling despised, deceived, or any form of maltreatment.

The women participating in our study, whether they have experienced violence in their families or not, agreed that for them the most decisive element has been socialisation in their first relationships. In the cases studied, being involved in violent relationships and suffering physical, emotional, or sexual abuse in initial sexual and affective interactions or intimate relationships has a tremendous impact and is linked to patterns of attraction to violence in adolescence and young adulthood. The life trajectory of Carolina, who experienced violence in her family of origin and grew up in a violent and deprived neighbourhood, shows that more than these previous negative experiences in childhood, interactions with her peer group and her first sexual-affective relationships have been critical in shaping her sexual-affective preferences. Carolina's closest female friend pressured her to become involved with a boy who exhibited a pattern of a dominant traditional masculinity, resulting in her first intimate relationship. The boy violently forced Carolina to kiss him without her consent:

> The first boy I dated . . . he treated girls very badly . . . he was the womaniser of town and I liked him because of that, because everybody was saying he was cool. A friend of mine talked to him and he asked me on a date . . . and I said yes. Just a few minutes later, we were having drinks with friends and suddenly he kissed me in front of everybody, which was very rude. I remember it being forceful. I found it disgusting.

Carolina reflects on the circumstances of her first kiss, on the role of the coercive dominant discourse on it and on the impact it had in her later violent relationships. From this first violent episode others followed over the following four years, which Carolina identifies as rooted in an attraction to violent attitudes and behaviours. Her first sexual-affective experience and peer pressure rendered Carolina more vulnerable to eventually being involved in sporadic or stable relationships with men with violent and despising attitudes. She also held negative views of men who treated her well.

Yolanda, another participant who did not experience a violent family context, reflects on her own sexual and affective trajectory after leaving a violent relationship in early adulthood. Similar to Carolina, Yolanda points to adolescence and first sexual-affective relationships as key experiences. When her group of female friends started flirting with boys who followed a dominant traditional model of masculinity, she decided not to do the same despite being subjected to peer pressure. As a result, Yolanda was left alone, and she soon became very sad without other role models of friendship for support in a vital period of her life, resulting in a profound crisis of meaning. For Yolanda, this initial period of loneliness and lack of connections was crucial to later starting to flirt with the ex-partner (who had toxic attitudes) of a close friend who experienced psycho-logical problems after ending her relationship with him due to his despising attitudes. Yolanda's female friend suffered considerably from the experience. Yolanda recounts:

> he continued flirting with me and I never stopped him. I never had a relationship with him but I never stopped it because it was not having a negative effect on me even when I knew what my friend was suffering. She of course ended our friendship. . . . Two or three months after that I started a relationship with a boy with whom I suf-fered all kinds of violence.

After this first harmful relationship, Yolanda started a violent relationship with a boy who exhibited patterns of violent masculinity. As she reflects on her trajectory, she realises how in her adolescence and early youth the dominant coercive discourse influenced the relationships and the way she has been socialised (Torras-Gómez et al., 2020).

By contrast, some of our informants highlighted how important it was for them to find someone who showed them true love, respect, honesty, or friendship in their first intimate and romantic stable or sporadic relationships. These first positive interactions proved crucial in guiding what they wanted to experience from then on. Gerard's life trajectory demonstrates the relevance of friendship and positive first affective relationships in preventing experiences of violence despite suffering DV in childhood. Gerard refused to accept violent intimidation from his father and complicity with his father's abuse of his mother, even confronting him at the age of 13 or 14. Feelings of love and friendship he developed in his first "platonic" relationship with a girl in childhood served as a guide for what he wanted for in his life and helped him develop an alternative understanding of egalitarian masculinity with self-esteem and a strong sense of his own attractiveness. This confidence encouraged him to reject peer pressure and not give up on his search for freedom and positive feelings in his later sexual and affective relationships:

> I had memories of such intense feelings from my childhood. When I was around 16 or 17, I didn't need to be with anybody, but I was pressured by my parents, as they thought I was gay, and by my friends. I remember one who was not really a friend but a colleague. He called me a rough diamond and said that if he polished me, I would be very successful because I would attract lots of girls. . . . But I told him I didn't need to do that because I already knew I was liked by many of them.

Gerard stressed his need to avoid reproducing attitudes similar to those of his father and to develop a sense of his masculinity based on an understanding of his attractiveness and security in seeking positive and passionate egalitarian feelings free of violence.

## 2  *In some cases, people have violent relationships in adolescence or adulthood without having experienced a violent family context*

Other informants stress the non-violent nature of their family contexts. Alicia, for example, reflects on the fact that while many male perpetrators of violence have a previous history of violence in their childhoods, others have not suffered major problems or difficulties in their childhoods. Sara, who suffered physical, psychological, and sexual violence in one of her rela-tionships, explained: "My father hated that we shouted. We could argue but I never hit my sisters. There was always a level of respect . . . and my friends always maintained a stable environ-ment". Yolanda similarly described growing up in a family built on trust and positive feelings of love and mutual respect even with extended family members: "My family relationships were always very good and very positive, too. . . . It was never a violent family; quite the contrary. . . . I have very nice memories of my childhood". Despite this positive family upbringing, Yolanda was trapped in a violent relationship in her youth. It is thus relevant to note that socialisation based on positive interactions with one's family of origin can also be interrupted by the coercive discourse of the society, which can take the form of peer pressure that results in men and women becoming victims or perpetrators of IPV.

Other informants described how their family members' or close friends' attitudes did not accept or normalise their violent relationships. This stand against violence helped the victims reflect and promoted a change in their own models of intimate relationships. Emma, for example, who suffered a violent relationship, noted how violence fell outside of the frame of acceptable behaviours for her parents:

> The last thing I wanted was for my mother or father to see that my partner was treating me like this, that he was doing such things to me . . . eventually, with time, I realised that it was not normal, that it is not normal for your partner to cause you to panic.

### 3 Positive social interactions (friendship and love relationships) can serve as protective factors in overcoming past DV and IPV experiences

Some of our informants described experiencing family and community contexts with many violent or abusive interactions. Raquel came from a family in which her father perpetrated psychological and sexual violence towards her mother. Raquel was not only exposed to DV but was also sexually abused by a health professional at the age of 10. This episode had a very damaging impact in her life:

> I left the medical examination room hysterical and my mum asked me what had happened, but people are not prepared to confront these situations and I knew I could not say anything . . . but at that moment something broke inside of me. The trust was broken, as those who were expected to protect me didn't, but I am proud of myself because I said I didn't want to return to that examination room.

Some years later, Raquel was again a victim of repeated sexual abuse by a person very close to her extended family. These abusive encounters were kept secret for a long time until she decided to break the silence after receiving the support of friends who encouraged her to confront her family. After some initial moments of rejection and re-victimisation from some members of her family, she finally received the support of the whole family and the family rejected the perpetrator. Raquel identifies one specific relationship that helped her cope with these difficult life experiences. What helped her maintain hope in her most difficult moments were memories of positive feelings of love and friendship that she experienced when she was only four or five years old:

> Yes, I was 4 or 5, I felt "platonic" love for a boy in my class who took care of me and who defended me from a bullying attack. . . . I remember four or five older boys insulting me, and he confronted them and said that I was his friend and asked them to stop annoying me. In the winter, he gave me his cap to protect me from the cold weather . . . if you asked me if it was my first love, I would say yes. It involved this union of friendship and feelings of affection.

Raquel explains how despite several abusive interactions she experienced in her life, she also experienced kind and meaningful interactions:

> In my childhood and adolescence I also attended a Christian youth club and it became like a counterpoint to the abusive situations because we talked about profound feelings and friendship. There were people who loved me a lot and who I loved a lot, but all the other stuff was there also, and that weighed on me . . . those destructive interactions. I felt both, but without that counterpoint things would have been worse.

Raquel currently enjoys positive and healthy friendships and relationships.

Gerard, as described earlier, suffered DV in his family of origin in childhood. His father was violent toward both his mother and him. This victimisation deeply damaged his self-esteem in early childhood:

> With my mother, there was emotional violence; he controlled and despised her in public spaces. With me, he looked down on me; he created embarrassing situations for me. . . . I remembered one day when I was around 13 or 14, we were having dinner, and he took my plate, opened the window, threw the plate out the window and said that while I was living there, he was in charge, and if I didn't want that, I could leave home.

Gerard describes his current romantic relationship as passionate and happy. He has neither had violent relationships nor experienced violence in his current family. We should also mention that there are no data on men like Gerard who are raised in violent family contexts but never become perpetrators of violence, as there are no official records on their links to such behaviours.

Another participant, Clara, when asked about her childhood and experiences with her family of origin, described a familial context with physical violence directed from her mother to herself and her sister throughout her childhood and early adolescence but with no physical violence between her parents, though they had an unhappy relationship. The violence she suffered was never stopped by her father, though it was not perpetrated in front of him or anyone in her extended family. Clara's first sexual-affective interaction was with a boy with whom she was in love for a long time before the relationship started. Over a number of months, she nurtured platonic, romantic, and positive feelings towards him even though they barely knew each other. Later, Clara finally started an intimate relationship with him. Contrary to what Clara expected and had imagined for a long time, this boy cheated on her and used the relationship to get close to her best friend and flirt with her. While this deception left Clara disappointed and less hopeful about the possibility of having satisfactory and positive intimate relationships, she did not give up on her desire to find other partners who would treat her with love and respect. For Clara and Gerard it was important to not repeat the violent attitudes and behaviours they had experienced at home. For Clara, anticipating future ideal romantic relationships free of violence provided her with hope.

As described earlier, Carolina grew up in a family context with physical, verbal, and psychological violence from her father to her mother as well as towards her and her sister. She also grew up in a neighbourhood where community violence, drugs, and drug dealers were present at schools and in the streets, which was normalised. Carolina also notes that her first sexual and affective sporadic relationships in early adolescence and later stable relationships during her youth were violent. She reflects on how these violent relationships influenced her sexual-affective socialisation in developing a pattern of attraction towards boys with violent attitudes and behaviours. However, she identifies a crucial shift in her life upon having conversations with female friends who helped her understand that she was a victim of gender-based violence such as her mother:

> Once, female friends told me very clearly that I was suffering gender-based violence in that relationship . . . and I said: "What?! Why are you saying that I have suffered gender-based violence?" . . . Then, I realised. . . . Until that moment I thought I had only experienced violence in my family home.

Carolina is currently involved in a stable sexual and affective relationship with a man. She describes this intimate relationship as having two key elements that she considers very important, respect and passion:

> I like it mainly because it is passionate, as I used to be bored when I was not fighting. . . . In our relationship, in addition to treating each other well, is important that we have passion and sex . . . because if I had to live with a friend instead of a romantic partner, I'd prefer to live with a female friend.

Finally, strengthening the argument about the relevance of the peers' role in the overcoming of abusive situations, Yolanda decided to end her violent intimate relationship after finding new friends at her university who helped her critically think about her relationship and question the violence she was suffering: "There were conversations with people who did not stay at the surface of what happened. Friends told me that I was not happy and asked me to take steps to improve my situation".

## Conclusions

This chapter aimed to shed light on new approaches to the problem of DV based on the scientific contributions of research on the preventive socialisation of gender violence and on qualitative testimonies of different life trajectories. To scientifically comprehend DV, we should consider more explanatory and analytical elements beyond associations between victimisation in the family of origin and current intimate or family violence. In this regard, studies note the importance of being cautious of results that attempt to predict future victimisation or perpetrations of IPV based on experiences of DV in childhood since in some cases, causal interpretations are inferred when most investigations are correlational (Tolman & Bennett, 1990 in Bevan & Higgins, 2002). Additionally, violent and abusive familial and community contexts are not always related to having violent relationships in adulthood, as the attitudes and beliefs of one's peer group and positive parenting can protect against the association between IPV exposure and IPV involvement (Garrido & Taussig, 2013).

The scientific literature on the approach of preventive socialisation shows that involvement in IPV adulthood is also influenced by processes of socialisation into different models and patterns of attraction (Valls et al., 2008; Racionero-Plaza et al., 2018; Rios-González et al., 2018; Puigvert et al., 2019). The qualitative research presented in this chapter offers greater understanding of a range of first-person accounts of individuals who suffered DV during childhood and those who were not victims as children but experienced IPV in early adulthood. Although the results are based on a small sample, they confirm that first sexual and affective interactions and/or relationships have a deep impact on both men and women. Our evidence highlights the relevance of relationship contexts as sources of socialisation from adolescence to early adulthood that influence ways of viewing relationships and violence in intimate relationships. This applies to both the influence it has on socialisation processes linked to an attraction to violence (when first interactions are dominated by hostile, violent, or disrespectful attitudes) or to non-violence and passionate and positive feelings (when these features are predominant in first sexual and affective interactions in childhood, adolescence, or early adulthood). This learning is not exclusive to socialisation in childhood in the bosom of the family nor to socialisation in adult intimate relationships, but it is rather mediated by first affective experiences and relationships that happen in between.

Future studies on this issue might use mixed methods by integrating quantitative and qualitative methodologies to advance knowledge on IPV, including new ways to analyse the incidence of socialisation experiences in the family and in first intimate relationships as done in this work. Mixed methods in the study of gender violence can facilitate scholarly work that provides a platform for the voices of survivors to be heard and to explore in depth their experiences (Puigvert, Valls, García-Yeste, Aguilar, & Merrill, 2017; Shorten & Smith, 2017).

## Critical findings

- Positive social interactions (friendship and love) serve as protective factors in overcoming DV experiences, fostering the search for egalitarian, free, and passionate intimate relationships throughout life.
- DV in childhood is not the unique possible explanation for the subsequent experience of DV. First sexual and affective interactions and relationships are sources of socialisation into future intimate relationships. In some cases, people have violent relationships in adolescence or adulthood without having experienced a violent family context. When first sexual and affective relationships have violent connotations, these relationships can contribute to socialise into violent sexual and affective relationships in adulthood. When first sexual and affective relationships have non-violent connotations, these experiences can contribute to socialise into experiences of satisfactory sexual and affective relationships in adulthood.

## Implications for policy, practice, and research

- As highlighted by previous scientific research on preventive socialisation (Puigvert et al., 2019; Puigvert et al., 2019), experiences of true love and friendship are central in: (1) reinforcing the self-esteem and sense of security needed to reject peer pressure to engage in violent interactions or sexual and affective relationships and (2) empowering victims of violence to overcome violent situations and experiences.
- A refusal to accept and normalise violent relationships among family members and close friends promotes change in violent relationships. Encouraging families and communities to take a stand against violence and support victims of DV is critical to developing bystander and active interventions and strong relationships and networks.
- Friends and family interactions that encourage victims to end violent relationships are based in honesty (clear statements on not tolerating violent attitudes) and a commitment to the wellbeing of victims (encouraging deep reflection on violent situations rather than examining them on a more superficial level).
- Children who witness or suffer violence in their families of origin are victims of DV. Regarding implications for practitioners, deeming such victimisation a predictor of future DV victimisation or perpetration may stigmatise children who are already victims and may

prevent the identification of other protective factors that can serve as a counterpoint in these difficult experiences. Narrowly using the intergenerational transmission of violence to explain future DV or IPV experiences can also limit the prevention of DV and understanding of cases in which children and youth who do not suffer or witness violence in their families of origin become victims in adolescence or adulthood due to other factors.

- DV prevention strategies should consider the relevance of first sexual-affective interactions and relationships to socialising and shaping future patterns of attraction linked to violence or to egalitarian relationships free of violence.

## Note

1 Some of the interview transcripts presented here were collected as part of the PhD dissertation of one of the authors of this chapter.

## References

Bandura, A. (1977). *Social learning theory*. Englewood Cliffs, NJ: Prentice Hall.

Bevan, E., & Higgins, D. J. (2002). Is domestic violence learned? The contribution of five forms of child maltreatment to men's violence and adjustment. *Journal of Family Violence, 17*(3), 223–245. doi:10.1023/a:1016053228021

Black, B. M., Chido, L. M., Preble, K. M., Weisz, A. N., Yoon, J. S., Delaney-Black, V., Kernsmith, P., & Lewandowski, L. (2014). Violence exposure and teen dating violence among African American youth. *Journal of Interpersonal Violence, 30*(12), 2174–2195. doi:10.1177/0886260514552271

Black, D. S., Sussman, S., & Unger, J. B. (2010). A further look at the intergenerational transmission of violence: Witnessing interparental violence in emerging adulthood. *Journal of Interpersonal Violence, 25*(6), 1022–1042. doi:10.1177/0886260509340539

Bukowski, W. M., Sippola, L. K., & Newcomb, A. F. (2000). Variations in patterns of attraction of same and other sex peers during early adolescence. *Developmental Psychology, 36*(2), 147. doi:10.1037/0012-1649.36.2.147

Callaghan, J. E. M., Alexander, J. H., Sixsmith, J., & Fellin, L. C. (2018). Beyond "witnessing": Children's experiences of coercive control in domestic violence and abuse. *Journal of Interpersonal Violence, 33*, 1551–1581. doi:10.1177/0886260515618946

Cohen, J. R., Shorey, R. C., Menon, S. V., & Temple, J. R. (2018). Predicting teen dating violence perpetration. *Pediatrics, 141*(4). doi:10.1542/peds.2017-2790

Creswell, J. W., & Plano Clark, V. L. (2011). *Designing and conducting mixed methods research* (2nd ed.). Los Angeles: Sage.

Denzin, N. K., & Lincoln, Y. S. (2011). *The SAGE handbook of qualitative research*. Thousand Oaks, CA: Sage.

De Puy, J., Radford, L., Le Fort, V., & Romain-Glassey, N. (2019). Developing assessments for child exposure to intimate partner violence in Switzerland – A study of medico-legal reports in clinical settings. *Journal of Family Violence, 34*(5), 371–383. https://doi.org/10.1007/s10896-019-00047-1

Díez-Palomar, J., Capllonch, M., & Aiello, E. (2014). Analyzing male attractiveness models from a communicative approach: Socialisation, attraction, and gender-based violence. *Qualitative Inquiry, 20*(7), 844–849. doi:10.1177/1077800414537205

Eriksson, L., & Mazerolle, P. (2014). A cycle of violence? Examining family-of-origin violence, attitudes, and intimate partner violence perpetration. *Journal of Interpersonal Violence, 30*(6), 945–964. doi:10.1177/0886260514539759

Fang, X., & Corso, P. S. (2007). Child maltreatment, youth violence, and intimate partner violence. *American Journal of Preventive Medicine, 33*(4), 281–290. doi:10.1016/j.amepre.2007.06.003

Gage, A. J. (2016). Exposure to spousal violence in the family, attitudes and dating violence perpetration among high school students in Port-au-Prince. *Journal of Interpersonal Violence, 31*(14), 2445–2474. doi:10.1177/0886260515576971

Garrido, E. F., & Taussig, H. N. (2013). Do parenting practices and prosocial peers moderate the association between intimate partner violence exposure and teen dating violence? *Psychology of Violence, 3*(4), 354–366. doi:10.1037/a0034036

Gómez, J. (2015). *Radical love: A revolution for the 21st century*. New York, NY: Peter Lang.

Hou, J., Yu, L., Fang, X., & Epstein, N. B. (2015). The intergenerational transmission of domestic violence: The role that gender plays in attribution and consequent intimate partner violence. *Journal of Family Studies*, *22*(2), 121–139. doi:10.1080/13229400.2015.1045923

Katz, E. (2019). Coercive control, domestic violence, and a five-factor framework: Five factors that influence closeness, distance, and strain in mother – Child relationships. *Violence Against Women*, 1–25.

Kwong, M. J., Bartholomew, K., Henderson, A. J. Z., & Trinke, S. J. (2003). The intergenerational transmission of relationship violence. *Journal of Family Psychology*, *17*(3), 288–301. doi:10.1037/0893-3200.17.3.288

Liu, W., Mumford, E. A., & Taylor, B. G. (2017). The relationship between parents' intimate partner victimization and youths' adolescent relationship abuse. *Journal of Youth and Adolescence*, *47*(2), 321–333. doi:10.1007/s10964-017-0733-1

Milletich, R. J., Kelley, M. L., Doane, A. N., & Pearson, M. R. (2010). Exposure to interparental violence and childhood physical and emotional abuse as related to physical aggression in undergraduate dating relationships. *Journal of Family Violence*, *25*(7), 627–637. doi:10.1007/s10896-010-9319-3.

Murrell, A., Christoff, K., & Henning, K. (2007). Characteristics of domestic violence offenders: Associations with childhood exposure to violence. *Journal of Family Violence*, *22*, 523–532. doi:10.1007/s10896-007-9100-4

Puigvert, L. (2014). Preventive socialisation of gender violence moving forward using the communicative methodology of research. *Qualitative Inquiry*, *20*(7), 839–843. doi:10.1177/1077800414537221

Puigvert, L. (2016). Female university students respond to gender violence through dialogic feminist gatherings. *International and Multidisciplinary Journal of Social Sciences*, *5*(2), 183. doi:10.17583/rimcis.2016.2118

Puigvert, L., Gelsthorpe, L., Soler-Gallart, M., & Flecha, R. (2019). Girls' perceptions of boys with violent attitudes and behaviours, and of sexual attraction. *Palgrave Communications*, *4*(25). doi:10.1057/s41599-019-0262-5

Puigvert, L., Valls, R., Garcia Yeste, C., Aguilar, C., & Merrill, B. (2017). Resistance to and transformations of gender-based violence in Spanish universities: A communicative evaluation of social impact. *Journal of Mixed Methods Research*. doi:10.1177/1558689817731170

Racionero-Plaza, S., Ugalde-Lujambio, L., Puigvert, L., & Aiello, E. (2018). Reconstruction of autobiographical memories of violent sexual-affective relationships through scientific reading on love: A psycho-educational intervention to prevent gender violence. *Frontiers in Psychology*, *9*, 1996. doi:10.3389/fpsyg.2018.01996

Racionero, S., Ugalde, L., Merodio, G., & Gutiérrez, N. (2020). Architects of their own brain. Social impact of an intervention study for the prevention of gender-based violence in adolescence. *Frontiers in Psychology*. https://10.3389/fpsyg.2019.03070

Renner, L. M., & Slack, K. S. (2006). Intimate partner violence and child maltreatment: Understanding intra- and intergenerational connections. *Child Abuse & Neglect*, *30*(6), 599–617. doi:10.1016/j.chiabu.2005.12.005

Renzetti, C. M., & Edleson, J. L. (Eds.). (2008). *Encyclopedia of interpersonal violence* (Vols. 1–2). Thousand Oaks, CA: Sage.

Rios-González, O., Peña Axt, J. C., Duque Sánchez, E., & De Botton Fernández, L. (2018). The language of ethics and double standards in the affective and sexual socialisation of youth. communicative acts in the family environment as protective or risk factors of intimate partner violence. *Frontiers in Sociology*, *3*. doi:10.3389/fsoc.2018.00019

Ruiz-Eugenio, L., Puigvert, L., Ríos, O., & Cisneros, R. M. (2020). Communicative Daily Life Stories: Raising Awareness About the Link Between Desire and Violence. *Qualitative Inquiry*. https://doi.org/10.1177/1077800420938880

Shorten, A., & Smith, J. (2017). Mixed methods research: Expanding the evidence base. *Evidence-Based Nursing*, *20*(3), 74–75. doi:10.1136/eb-2017-102699

Smith-Marek, E. N., Cafferky, B., Dharnidharka, P., Mallory, A. B., Dominguez, M., High, J., . . . Mendez, M. (2015). Effects of childhood experiences of family violence on adult partner violence: A meta-analytic review. *Journal of Family Theory & Review*, *7*(4), 498–519. doi:10.1111/jftr.12113

Stanley, N., & Devaney, J. (2017). Gender-based violence: Evidence from Europe. *Psychology of Violence*, *7*(3), 329–332. http://dx.doi.org/10.1037/vio0000120

Temple, J. R., Shorey, R. C., Tortolero, S. R., Wolfe, D. A., & Stuart, G. L. (2013). Importance of gender and attitudes about violence in the relationship between exposure to interparental violence and the perpetration of teen dating violence. *Child Abuse & Neglect*, *37*(5), 343 352. doi:10.1016/j.chiabu.2013.02.001

Torras-Gómez, E., Puigvert, L., Aiello, E., & Khalfaoui, A. (2020). Our right to the pleasure of falling in love. *Frontiers in Psychology*. doi:10.3389/fpsyg.2019.03068

Valls, R., Puigvert, L., & Duque, E. (2008). Gender violence amongst teenagers: Socialisation and prevention. *Violence Against Women, 14*(7), 759–785. doi:10.1177/1077801208320365

Widom, C. S., Czaja, S., & Dutton, M. A. (2014). Child abuse and neglect and intimate partner violence victimization and perpetration: A prospective investigation. *Child Abuse & Neglect, 38*(4), 650–663. doi:10.1016/j.chiabu.2013.11.004

# 12

# YOUTH INTIMATE PARTNER VIOLENCE

*Sibel Korkmaz*

## Introduction

A body of research confirms that many youth are subjected to physical, psychological and/ or sexual violence by a partner, challenging our previous understanding of intimate partner violence (IPV) as primarily an adult problem (Barter, 2011). This phenomenon, generally described as 'dating' violence, or adolescent/teenage/youth intimate partner violence,[1] sheds light on violence that occurs within youths' own intimate romantic relationships. The severity of such violence may vary, as well as its impact. Nevertheless, it is clear that this social and public health problem is important to address, not least from a life-course perspective, as it has been shown that the strongest predictor of adult IPV victimisation and perpetration includes earlier forms of exposure and peer approval of dating violence in adolescence (Herrenkohl & Jung, 2016). Hence, victimisation during youth is strongly associated with recurrent episodes of victimisation later in life (cf. Arriaga & Foshee, 2004).

Moreover, a number of scholars have observed that youth IPV differs from adult IPV in certain ways (Cutter-Wilson & Richmond, 2011; Murray & Azzinaro, 2019), arguing for the need to specifically focus on youth and IPV. Building on this, this chapter will present research on youth IPV, aiming to discuss what it is like to be subjected to, as well as perpetrate, IPV during youth. Theoretically, this chapter departures from social constructivism theory, and the social studies of childhood and youth, drawing upon the notion that how youth and IPV are understood and constructed, is dependent on the societal and social contexts (Burr, 2015; James, Jenks & Prout, 1998; Furlong, Woodman, & Wyn, 2011). Further, thus, age, or more specifically youth, is viewed as a construed social position (Krekula, Närvänen, & Näsman, 2005). Moreover, societal, social and individual aspects of youth (Furlong et al., 2011) will be acknowledged, addressing how they may affect IPV (cf. Korkmaz & Överlien, 2020; Gottzén & Korkmaz, 2013). This approach follows scholars who have argued for the need to focus on IPV and youths' conditions specifically. For example, Murray and Azzinaro (2019) present teen dating violence as an 'old disease in a new world' (article title), arguing that it is critical to identify the key differences between adolescent and adult victims of IPV, since adolescent victims have unique features that affect their victimisation, such as experiences, anatomy, attitudes and their use of technology (Murray & Azzinaro, 2019). The contextual, situational and relational aspects of IPV among youth have also been the focus of additionally recent research in order to further the understanding of such violence (Överlien, Hellevik, & Korkmaz, 2019).

Furthermore, through an intersectional lens, the chapter aims to point out how youth are a heterogeneous group (Wood, Barter, & Berridge, 2011; Barter & Stanley, 2016; Pentaraki, 2017), proposing that their vulnerability is influenced by the interactions of different social positions (e.g. ethnicity, socioeconomic status, age, gender, sexuality) (Crenshaw, 1991; Donovan & Hester 2015). Firstly, the chapter will focus on terminology and definitions, followed by a discussion on the challenges to understanding youth IPV. Thereafter, youth and IPV will be examined, drawing upon existing research and literature. Lastly, prevention and implications for policy, practice and research will be addressed.

## A few words on terminology and definitions

Most definitions of violence in youths' relationships incorporate all prevalent violence typologies: physical, psychological and/or sexual violence (e.g. Stonard, Bowen, Lawrence, & Price, 2014). In recent years, it has been acknowledged that violence can also be perpetrated online, using technologies, such as smartphone applications or a computer (Stonard et al., 2014; Lucero, Weisz, Smith-Darden, & Lucero, 2014; Barter et al., 2015; Cutbush, Williams, Miller, Gibbs, & Clinton-Sherrod, 2018; Överlien, 2018; Hellevik, 2019). However, there is no common terminology or overall internationally accepted definition used to capture violence in youths' intimate relationships, with numerous terms seemingly aiming to identify this phenomenon. In North America, where the research field regarding violence in young people's romantic relationships was originally established, such violence is commonly termed 'dating violence' or 'teen dating abuse'. These concepts, or variations of them (e.g. 'dating aggression'), are to some extent also used in Europe; however, their applicability outside North America has been questioned (Barter, 2009). Instead, in Europe, English terms such as 'teenage intimate partner violence and abuse' or 'youth intimate partner violence' are additionally used to underline intimate partner violence in young people's romantic relationships. In a non-English speaking context, there are a few examples of youth-specific terms (to the best of the author's knowledge), similar to 'dating violence'. Overall, the lack of a common terminology and definition may give rise to challenges in investigating this phenomenon, which will be discussed further in the next section.

## Violence in youths' relationships: challenges in understanding the phenomenon

In the following, some challenges when conducting research on youth IPV will be addressed, specifically the factors to consider when interpreting research results. Further, the question of gender with regards to understanding and unpacking youth IPV as a phenomenon will be presented.

### *Challenges when conducting research on youth IPV*

A substantial body of quantitative evidence on youths' experiences of IPV show an extensive social problem deserving our attention. Many studies present rates of perpetration and victimisation, widening our understanding of how common these experiences are. These rates are often divided by gender (occasionally gender identity and sexuality, too), and usually distinguish between physical, psychological and sexual violence. However, measurements, definitions (i.e. broad or narrow), the age of sample and populations studied vary greatly, making it a challenge to compare research results and policy initiatives across the globe.

Cultural factors may also make it hard to compare studies and interpret and use research results (Barter & Stanley, 2016; Stanley, Ellis, Farrelly, Hollinghurst, & Downe, 2015; Hamby, Nix, De Puy, & Monnier, 2012; Nocentini et al., 2011). For example, external cultural factors may influence informants' willingness to report, as addressed by Lysova and Douglas (2008) when they discuss the significant differences in IPV perpetration rates between men and women in their sample of Russian university students. The authors suggest that the difference might be explained by the deterrent effect of the Russian army, as in Russia, if found to abuse a woman, a male student may be expelled from the university and instead enlisted into military service. Moreover, cultural factors may also affect what expressions of violence are culturally accepted or not, since, for example, mild expressions of violence may be more culturally accepted in some countries but unacceptable in others (Viejo, Monks, Sanchez, & Ortega-Ruiz, 2016). Further, it has been argued that teenagers do not always identify their experiences with equivalent definitions of violence used in research (Karlsson, Calvert, Rodriguez, Weston, & Temple, 2018), proposing that it is challenging to examine the phenomenon of youth IPV. Overall, these factors are important to consider when reading and interpreting studies on youth IPV; nevertheless, it is also vital to acknowledge that experiences of IPV might in fact vary across countries and samples.

With regard to reported prevalence rates, studies do show a great variation. For example, Stonard et al.'s (2014) review revealed a broad range of estimates when looking at studies investigating prevalence and impact of adolescent dating violence. Similarly, in their data synthesis on sexual and physical forms of teen dating violence (TDV), Wincentak, Connolly and Card (2017) found a great variation. Conducting a meta-analysis of 101 studies with samples consisting of teens between the ages of 13 and 18, they estimated a 20 % overall prevalence rate of being subjected to physical TDV, irrespective of gender. Regarding perpetration of physical TDV, gender differences were significant, suggesting that girls perpetrate more violence when compared with boys (girls 25 % vs. boys 13 %). The authors note that these findings appear to support previous research that indicates that female youth are equally or even more disposed to report perpetrating physical violence within a romantic relationship. However, regarding sexual TDV, it was observed that girls reported lower rates of perpetration compared to boys (3 % vs. 10 %), and higher rates of victimisation (14 % vs. 8 %). Overall, these rates suggest some gendered implications; however, studies have explored the factor of gender further (Arriaga & Foshee, 2004; Barter et al., 2015; Gadd, Fox, Corr, Alger, & Butler, 2015; Barter & Lombard, 2019).

## *The question on gender*

Gendered patterns concerning rates of victimisation and perpetration respectively, are the focus for a number of researchers conducting work on youth IPV. Some studies have presented data on reciprocal involvement, suggesting that both boys and girls involved in aggressive behaviour are generally aggressors as well as victims (Viejo, 2014). Nevertheless, it has also been shown that a greater proportion of girls and young women report more severe forms of IPV victimisation compared to young men (Foshee, 1996). Related, it has also been shown that young men are involved in more severe physical aggression (Muñoz-Rivas, Graña, O'Leary, & González, 2007) and perpetrate more sexual violence and aggression than young women (Fernández-González,

O'Leary, & Muñoz-Rivas, 2013; Sebastían, Verdugo, & Ortiz, 2014; Stanley et al., 2016). Overall, undisputable, gendered patterns are a central debate within the research field.

Over two decades ago, Jackson (1999) reviewed the existing literature on dating violence and concluded that it is essential to describe violence as a gender issue. Jackson argued that this required an extension of the parameters of the research 'beyond measuring acts of violence to a more extensive investigation of consequences, context, motivation and meaning' (p. 241). Nevertheless, arguably, there are challenges to extensively investigate the role of gender in relation to IPV victimisation as well as perpetration. Hamby and Turner (2013) assert that 'IPV may be particularly hard to assess in ways that are equally valid for males and females' (p. 335), and that teen dating violence (TDV) may be an even more challenging violence phenomenon to assess, due to its unique developmental and relational aspects. Further, Hamby and Turner underline the need to consider aspects of the context of TDV, similar to the arguments of Jackson a decade earlier. In 1999, Jackson addressed methodological limitations in the studies reviewed that have led to the suggestion that men and women are equally violent. As a conceivable solution to these limitations, Jackson highlighted the need for qualitative research methods to elicit rich contextual data, providing understanding from the perspective of participants.

Today, largely, it is possible to point out two different standpoints within the research field on youth IPV, whereas it is sometimes framed as a more or less gender-neutral phenomenon, and at other times considered in relation to unequal gender and power relationships (Jackson, 1999; Gadd et al., 2015; Korkmaz, 2017; Barter & Lombard, 2019). This distinction has also been described as a turn within the field. Baker and Stein (2016) describe how the lack of a gender-based analysis reflects a shift from a feminist framing of violence, to a more conservative and individualistic focus. Nevertheless, considering all data on the importance and significance of gender, gender is unquestionably a key variable when investigating youth IPV and will therefore be examined throughout in this chapter.

## Analysis and discussion

In the following section, existing research and literature are drawn upon and structured thematically on a societal, social and individual level (Bronfenbrenner, 1977; see Hagemann-White, Kelly, & Römkens, 2010 for a similar approach), in order to discuss aspects of youth on each level that arguably affect victimisation as well as perpetration of IPV for young people (Korkmaz & Överlien, 2020; Överlien et al., 2019; Gottzén & Korkmaz, 2013; Gadd et al., 2015). This approach takes its stance within the social constructionist theory, underlining that how we understand a phenomenon is bound to historical and cultural specificity, as well as social processes (Burr, 2015). Furthermore, this approach also departures from the social studies of childhood and youth (James et al., 1998), which offer the notion of youth as socially constructed. Youth is not just an age attribute, but dependent on both social and societal contexts (Jones, 2011), and thus also a social position (Krekula et al., 2005; Staunæs, 2003).

Thereby, through a social constructionist lens, an examination of a societal level of IPV will highlight the cultural and societal context (Furlong et al., 2011). Moreover, social processes will be in focus on a social level, as the focus is on youths' social networks and their responses to youth IPV (Hydén, Gadd, & Wade, 2016). Here, youths' everyday life will also be addressed, as this level also includes the immediate social context (Överlien et al., 2019). Lastly, on the individual level, individual aspects of youth IPV will be highlighted, focusing on childhood risk factors, the impact of victimisation, and young perpetrators of IPV. Overall, the aim is to broadly portray what it is like to be young and be subjected to, or perpetrate, IPV.

## Societal aspects

Societal aspects of youth IPV vary, naturally, due to how it is constructed within a specific cultural and societal contextual setting (Burr, 2015).[2] In this chapter, societal aspects refer to the cultural and societal norms that govern young people's lives. Beliefs about IPV, gendered power relations, gendered behavioural expectations, gendered (in)equality, and norms on youth can affect the notion of *who is a potential victim* (cf. Christie, 2001) *and perpetrator of IPV*, as well as influence which acts that are defined as violence (Chung, 2005, 2007; Gadd et al., 2015; Överlien et al., 2019). Overall, these societal aspects can affect the experience of IPV for young people.

Alongside, governmental awareness of youth IPV play an important role. In 2015, an extensive five-country European study, 'Safeguarding teenagers' intimate relationships' (STIR) (Barter et al., 2015), showed that legislation, public policy and action plans disregard teenage intimate partner violence (online and offline) or acknowledge it to only a limited degree. The lack of governmental awareness arguably connects to the notion of *who is a potential victim and perpetrator of IPV*, making teenage and youth invisible from a governmental point of view. However, there are examples of governmental acknowledgement of youth IPV as a genuine problem as well. For example, in the UK in 2013, the government implemented a new definition of domestic violence and abuse as follows: 'Any incident or pattern of incidents of controlling, coercive or threatening behaviour, violence or abuse between those aged 16 or over who are or have been intimate partners or family members regardless of gender or sexuality' (Home Office, 2013). The Home Office aimed that this revision would encourage young people to come forward and seek support, since, prior to that point, the definition had not included young people aged 16–17 years. Thus, the change reflects a governmental awareness that this age group can be victims as well as perpetrators of IPV. Similarly, in Sweden in 2014, the Swedish National Board of Health and Welfare introduced binding regulations (SOSFS, 2014:4) for the social services on domestic violence, including partner violence among youth under the age of 18. These binding regulations mean that the children's services are mandated to assess the need for help and support when a young person under the age of 18 has been subjected to partner violence. Furthermore, with regards to the prevention of youth IPV, there are some examples of governmental actions. For example, in the state of Ohio, USA, age-appropriate dating violence prevention education is incorporated into the curriculum for grades 7 through 12 (involving 12–18 year olds), education which includes instruction in recognising dating violence warning signs and the characteristics of healthy relationships (Ohio Substitute House Bill 19).

These examples highlight governmental awareness and societal aspects of youth IPV. These examples of governmental awareness can indicate how norms on youth are conceptualised. It can show how youth are regarded legally as children and thereby formally (more) protected by the governmental system due to their status as a child. However, even though youth are positioned as potential victims or perpetrators of IPV and formally protected, there can still be societal prejudices regarding these experiences.

A body of research reveals numerus prejudices regarding youth and IPV, prejudices that may prevent youth from seeking help. Some prejudices are on youth and their intimate relationships, reflecting a belief *that youth do not have 'serious relationships'* (Carlson, 2003; Chung, 2005; Hellevik & Överlien, 2016). Related, there are prejudices that *it would be easier for youth to end an abusive relationship*, since they may not have children or live together with the abuser (Chung, 2007). Regarding the perpetration of IPV, stereotypes of the *'domestic violence perpetrator' as a shameful man who is not identifiable nor relatable*, may also hinder young men who are at risk of being abusive, to get support (Gadd, Fox, Corr, Butler, & Bragg, 2013; Gadd et al., 2015). Moreover, certain prejudices might mark some youth even more. For example, lesbian, gay and bisexual (LGB) youth may be even more affected by societal prejudices since there are heteronormative views on IPV; in other words, beliefs exist that *violence does not occur in same-sex relationships* (Gillum & DiFulvio, 2012).

In summary, the societal and cultural contexts convey certain aspects that are important to consider when focusing on youth IPV. Through a social constructionist lens, these aspects reveal how youth IPV is constructed within a society, whether it is considered as a social problem, or not. Related, the mentioned prejudices can also reflect a distinction between youth IPV and 'adult' IPV, and how they are constructed as two separate phenomena. Furthermore, governments may acknowledge youth as potential victims as well as perpetrators of IPV, providing help and support due to their status as children (James et al., 1998), and thus address youth IPV as a social problem. Conversely, a lack of societal awareness can reflect that youth IPV is not considered as a serious issue. It is noteworthy that societal aspects and how youth IPV is constructed can arguably vary within countries, and even cities as well as neighbourhoods, since an area's concentration of disadvantage can inflict local cultural norms (e.g. acceptance of violence) (Garthe, Gorman-Smith, Gregory, & Schoeny, 2018). Furthermore, the period of youth may also reflect prejudices that affect how a young person is supported and helped. Thereby, through an intersectional lens, it is important to acknowledge that youth are not a homogeneous group (Wood et al., 2011; Barter & Stanley, 2016), and that societal aspects may vary due to youths' societal positions (e.g. socioeconomic status, sexuality).

## Social aspects

The social aspects of youth intimate partner violence (IPV) refer to youths' social network and immediate familial context. In the following discussion, research that investigates these aspects will be presented, focusing on parents, the role of schools and friends, and digital means. Overall, the aim in this section is to address the social sphere of youth IPV, including social and familial relationships (cf. Överlien et al., 2019).

### *Parents*

Having a youth's social network and immediate context in view, parents arguably are present since youth are often cared by and still live with their parents. The role of parents in relation to youth intimate partner violence (IPV) seems to have been examined extensively within the field of developmental research, aiming to explore parental roles with respect to children's subsequent victimisation. A body of knowledge suggests that violence in young people's intimate relationships has its origins in childhood externalising behaviour, and that parents play an important role in the development and maintenance of such behaviour (Morris, Mrug, & Windle, 2015; Livingston et al., 2018). For instance, *maternal warmth and sensitivity* in early childhood is presented as a protective factor against involvement in teen dating violence (Livingston et al., 2018). Further, 'positive parenting practices' has been highlighted as a key protective factor that may attenuate teen dating violence involvement for adolescents who have been exposed to IPV (Garrido & Taussig, 2013).

Parents may also have the opportunity, as well as the responsibility, to detect when their children are subject to, or are perpetrating, violence within an intimate romantic relationship. Concerning this, communication is essential. Corona, Gomes, Pope, Shaffer and Yaros (2016) showed in their study on maternal caregivers' strategies to discussing dating violence with their young adolescents, how 'healthier' messages about risky dating behaviours (e.g. focus on the meaning of love, identifying red flags in the relationships), increased parent–youth communication in this respect. Nevertheless, youth with experiences of dating violence have been found to report lower overall communication with their parents, and more problematic communication (Ombayo, Black, & Preble, 2019).

Further, parents are shown to respond to youth IPV in different ways (Preble, Black, & Weisz, 2018; Weisz, Black, & Hawley, 2017). In a study drawing upon qualitative interviews with IPV victimised youth, questions were asked regarding the parents' (their own as well as the abuser's) responses when they found out about the informants' IPV victimisation. The youth described different kinds of parental responses: some that helped bring an end to the violence they were experiencing, where, for example, parents broke up the abusive relationship; and some responses which enabled the abuse to continue, for example forms of responses that best can be described as a lack of response where the parents did not act upon the violent situation (Korkmaz & Överlien, 2020). Overall, it is found that parents play an important role and have a unique opportunity to interact and respond to their children's IPV experiences.

## Schools

Schools are important arenas for many youths' everyday lives: they spend most of their day on school premises and largely interact with their social networks within the school setting. Further, schools can provide opportunities for psychosocial interventions that can improve children's resilience (Ungar, Connelly, Liebenberg, & Theron, 2017). Nevertheless, schools can also be a setting where youth experience different forms of violence (Klein, 2006; Carlson, 2003). For example, it is described how many girls experience sexual harassment by male peers at school, and, further, how this is linked to sexual dating violence victimisation (Gagné, Lavoie, & Hébert, 2005).

Regarding IPV, schools have been identified as important when it comes to safeguarding youths' wellbeing through challenging the normalisation of IPV, as well as addressing instigation and supporting victims (Barter, 2014). Arguably, the schools' role is highly relevant as youth may attend the same school, or even belong to the same class, as their abusive partner. In the school setting, adults are also present (i.e. teachers), making them part of youths' social network and a possible resource for help, depending on their responses (Korkmaz & Överlien, 2020; Weisz et al., 2007). Classmates and peers can also intervene to help victims of IPV. Nevertheless, teachers play an important role in encouraging the reporting of dating violence, and it is crucial that youth perceive them, rather than fellow students, to have more expertise to respond effectively (Storer, Casey, & Herrenkohl, 2017). This places considerable responsibility on teachers, as their responses may affect whether a victim approaches them, as well as if a bystander acts to help. Overall, the schools' potential as an arena where youth IPV can take place, as well as an arena where youth can get help and support, is clear.

## Friends

Friends also play an important role in relation to social aspects of youth intimate partner violence (IPV). Youth see their friends every day at school, and as they are starting to distance themselves from their parents, friends arguably become a key part of youths' social network. Thereby, friends are often present to witness relationships interaction, and may have the opportunity to intervene (Landor et al., 2017). Further, it is shown that youth are more likely to disclose dating violence or romantic relationship problems to friends rather than others (Weisz et al., 2007; Black, Tolman, Callahan, Saunders, & Weisz, 2008). In addition, support from friends is associated with significantly less dating violence perpetration and victimisation, but only for girls (Richards & Branch, 2012).

Moreover, friends seem to influence what is considered as acceptable dating behaviours or not, underlining the meaning of friends' perception of relationships and behaviours. In addition, Arriaga and Foshee (2004) found that having friends who were in violent relationships was one important predictor of dating violence. Overall, when focusing on social aspects of youth IPV, the role of friends seems to be highly important and many prevention programs involve an active response from friends and peers (Weisz & Black, 2008). However, as Barter (2014) points out, peer networks can also be involved in violence perpetration, as a means to extend control and surveillance.

## Digital social aspects

The digital revolution plays an important role regarding youths' everyday lives and represents a new and significant aspect of youths' social context. Regarding youths' use of technology and digital media, a number of studies focus on violence perpetrated 'online' (e.g. Barter et al., 2017; Van Ouytsel, Ponnet, Walrave, & Temple, 2016; Reed, Tolman, & Ward, 2016; Stonard, Bowen, Walker, & Price, 2015). For example, Hellevik and Överlien (2016) present how 29.1 % of their sample of Norwegian teenagers had experienced 'digital violence'. Overall, it is shown how new technology offers new ways of perpetrating violence, where controlling behaviours and surveillance are common features (Barter et al., 2017). The phenomenon of 'sexting' (sending and receiving sexual images and text messages) has also been linked to IPV among youth (Wood & Barter, 2015; Bianchi, Morelli, Nappa, Baiocco, & Chirumbolo, 2018; Kernsmith, Victor, & Smith-Darden, 2018). This offers an insight into the social conditions youth live in (Furlong et al., 2011), showing how the digital revolution needs to be acknowledged in relation to youth IPV.

In summary, these social aspects of youth IPV – the presence of parents, the role of friends, school as an arena, as well as the digital sphere – highlight youth-specific factors (Korkmaz & Överlien, 2020) that need to be taken into consideration when addressing youth IPV. Thus, these aspects reflect the construction of youth IPV (Burr, 2015), as well as underline youths' societal position as children (James et al., 1998; cf. Gottzén & Korkmaz, 2013).

## Individual aspects

In this section, individual aspects of youth intimate partner violence (IPV) are presented, focusing on risk factors as well as gendered aspects, which will be discussed mainly when addressing impact and perpetration of IPV. Overall, some general individual aspects arguably are present by the time that youth might experience violence in their first intimate relationship. Further, individual aspects also refer to the vulnerability of particular groups of young people who are more at risk of being subjected to or perpetrating IPV.

## Relationship inexperience

Firstly, it is relevant to highlight young people's presumed relationship inexperience. Youth might be subjected to, or perpetrate, violence in their very first intimate romantic relationship, having no reference point regarding what it is like to have a healthy relationship. This inexperience may affect how they manage to navigate and detect what is an abusive relationship and what is not (Överlien et al., 2019; Gadd et al., 2013; Gadd et al., 2015; Toscano, 2014; Davies, 2019). For victims, the challenge to navigate and detect may be even more prominent if the abusive partner is older and the distribution of power thereby is uneven, making it easier for the older partner to control the younger (Barter, McCarry, Berridge, & Evans, 2009; Vézina & Hébert, 2007). Furthermore, Toscano (2014) describes in her study how college students with histories of high school dating violence felt popularity was gained by dating older, rebellious and popular boys as this type of partner meet their ideal image. This idea of the 'perfect older partner' arguably adds to the uneven power distribution and the challenge to navigate an abusive relationship.

## Childhood risks

The question whether there is a cycle of violence has received considerable attention among researchers. If you experience violence as a child, will you be at greater risk experiencing violence in later life and possibly pass this risk on to future generations? Several studies have shown an association between experiencing parental IPV/domestic violence and being subjected to IPV in a romantic relationship as a teenager (e.g. Hellevik & Överlien, 2016; Ruel et al., 2017). Nevertheless, it is challenging to single out individual factors that predict youth IPV since they may be mediated by numerous unobserved variables. Drawing upon prospective and retrospective longitudinal data on a community sample, Maas, Fleming, Herrenkohl and Catalano (2010) show how childhood risks (e.g. experiencing parental IPV/domestic violence) and protective factors (e.g. bonding to parents) interplay with early teen externalising and internalising behaviours and provide a conceptual model of possible paths predicting TDV victimisation. Overall, this model shows complex and reciprocal links among different factors that inflict a child's life and possible teen dating victimisation.

## 'High-risk' youth

It is possible to identify some individual aspects of youth intimate partner violence (IPV) that make youth 'high risk', or especially vulnerable. In several studies, high-risk behaviours, such as consuming alcohol at a relatively young age or use of addictive substances, are associated with dating violence victimisation (Van Ouytsel, Ponnet, & Walrave, 2017; Leen et al., 2013; Ihongbe & Masho, 2018). Low academic achievements have also been found to be associated with experiencing teenage IPV (Hellevik & Överlien, 2016); nevertheless conversely, it has also been shown that low academic achievements do not seem to affect the risk of being subjected to IPV (Korkmaz, Överlien, & Lagerlöf, 2020). Moreover, pregnant teenagers and teenage mothers have been identified as especially vulnerable (Brown, Brady, & Letherby, 2011; Edirne et al., 2010; Wood & Barter, 2015). Further, it has been shown that LGB youth report significantly higher rates of all types of victimisation and perpetration experiences in comparison to heterosexual youth (Dank, Lachman, Zweig, & Yahner, 2014), suggesting that sexual minorities may be at a greater risk for teen dating violence than their heterosexual peers (Reuter, Sharp, & Temple, 2015).

## Impact of victimisation

A body of evidence suggests that being subjected to intimate partner violence (IPV) may result in severe consequences for young people, as well as negatively affecting the transition from adolescence to adulthood (Wiklund, Malmgren-Olsson, Bengs, & Öhman, 2010). Studies have shown that victimisation can predict increased alcohol and cigarette use, as well as increased internalising symptoms (e.g. feelings of depression or anxiety), and fewer close friends (Foshee, Reyes, Gottfredson, Chang, & Ennett, 2013). A link between reporting physical dating violence victimisation and perpetration, and suicidal ideation has also been found (Nahapetyan, Orpinas, Song, & Holland, 2014; cf. Unlu & Cakaloz, 2016).

Even though IPV victimisation may result in adverse consequences for youth irrespective of gender, an extensive body of research convincingly shows gender differences regarding impact. It has been shown that boys report fewer, less serious impacts compared to girls, which is especially the case in relation to sexual violence (Barter et al., 2009; Barter & Stanley, 2016; Barter et al., 2017). Adolescent girls exposed to IPV report more severe impacts, such as depression, panic attacks, eating problems and suicidal ideation compared to boys (Romito, Beltramini, & Escribà-Agüir, 2013). This does not suggest that boys' experiences of IPV are not worthy of attention, but rather, it emphasises how important it is to acknowledge that impact may vary by gender (Barter et al., 2017; Barter & Lombard 2019).

## Young perpetrators of IPV

As presented, some studies on dating violence suggest that youth are involved in violent acts reciprocally, that they are simultaneously perpetrators and victims. However, it is also shown that young women's violence tends to be in reaction to male violence and, consistently, that men tend to initiate violence leading to violent responses from their partners (Allen, Swan, & Raghavan, 2009). Overall, this contributes to the complex discussion on perpetrators of violence, also implicating gendered patterns in terms of motives behind perpetration.

Concerning boys' perpetration of IPV, gendered scripts seem to play an important role. It has been shown that violent boys more often seek to justify male dominance and IPV against women, as well as receiving more dominant and violent messages from adults in their family, compared to non-violent boys (Diaz-Aguado & Martinez, 2015). Further, drawing upon data from focus groups with 23 Latino male adolescents, Haglund et al. (2019) present how the participants argued that the pressure to display masculinity might lead some young men to perpetrate teen dating violence. Nevertheless, Gadd et al. (2015) point out how the problem is not only about boys and their masculinities, but also a relational one that exists between boys and girls, showing how societal and social aspects are intertwined.

Besides findings that show how young women's violence tends to be in response to male violence (Allen et al., 2009), a number of studies show some additional aspects of female youth perpetration. For example, Joly and Connolly (2016) showed in their meta-synthesis of qualitative studies on dating violence among high-risk young women, how these women report perpetrating dating violence to gain power and respect. Further, it has been suggested that adolescent females who are identified as non-white, belonging to an ethnic minority, have an increased risk of perpetrating physical dating violence, compared to adolescent females who are identified as white (Moultrie King, Smith Hatcher, & Bride, 2017). Overall, female youth IPV perpetration seems to be a complex phenomenon that needs to be investigated further (King, Hatcher, & Bride, 2015; Shaffer, Adjei, Viljoen, Douglas, & Saewyc, 2018).

## Conclusion: youth IPV – through an intersectional lens

Even though youth IPV surpasses socioeconomic status, gender, sexuality, etc., it is possible to argue that some youth are especially vulnerable and more likely to experience or perpetrate IPV. By taking an intersectional lens, it is possible to highlight that youth is not a homogenous group, showing how youths' vulnerability is impacted by the interaction of different social positions (Donovan & Hester, 2015). For example, as presented earlier, adolescent females who belong to an ethnic minority are at increased risk of perpetrating physical dating violence, compared to adolescent females who belong to the majority ethnic group. Further, it is shown that victimised girls seem to experience more negative consequences compared to victimised boys. Additionally, LGB youth report significantly higher rates of all types of victimisation and perpetration experiences, in comparison to heterosexual youth. Thus, the social position of 'youth' interact with other positions, influencing their vulnerability. A young person is, for example, not solely a girl, but belongs to other social categories too. Moreover, these social categories are constructed within a societal and social context (cf. Staunæs, 2003), meaning that a holistic approach to a young person's experience of IPV is necessary. In other words, a young girl lives within a specific society that may or may not show societal awareness of youth IPV, has a specific social network that may respond in different ways (Korkmaz & Överlien, 2020), which thus will affect her experience of IPV. This needs to be taken into consideration in preventive work (Fox, Hale, & Gadd, 2014; Gadd, Fox, & Hale, 2014; cf. Ravi, Black, Mitschke, & Pearson, 2019), as different vulnerabilities may need to be specifically targeted. As this chapter has proposed, youth IPV need to be examined on a societal, social as well as an individual level. Furthermore, this holistic approach also arguably stands true for how this social problem should be tackled; by involving youth, parents, practitioners, researchers and policy-makers, representing all levels. It seems important that we all work together, by sharing information and influencing each other's work, to fully understand and prevent youth IPV.

## Critical findings

- Gender seems to be a significant factor in relation to understanding youth IPV.
- By taking a holistic approach to youth IPV, we can harvest important knowledge to inform practical work, as well as policy-making.
- An intersectional lens is needed to fully unpack the phenomenon of youth IPV.

## Implications for policy, practice and research

- The contextual aspects of youth IPV need to be taken into consideration in policy and practical work.
- Preventative work, including a focus on youth IPV warning signs and characteristics of healthy relationships, should be a priority in societal and political agendas.
- Future research studies should benefit from using youths' own voices as empirical data, as well as looking at contextual aspects of IPV to fully unpack how, for example, gender may impact the experience of being subjected to IPV.

## Notes

1  The concept 'youth intimate partner violence' will primarily be used in this chapter. However, when citing a study, the authors' choice of violence concept will be used (e.g. teen dating violence), as well as their description of their sample (e.g. 'adolescents', 'teenagers', etc.) When not citing a study, 'youth' and 'young people' will be used interchangeably.
2  It is acknowledged the cultural and societal context vary greatly and that the following discussion is from a 'Western society' perspective.

# References

Allen, C. T., Swan, S. C., & Raghavan, C. (2009). Gender symmetry, sexism, and intimate partner violence. *Journal of Interpersonal Violence, 24*(11), 1816–1834.

Arriaga, X. B., & Foshee, V. A. (2004, February). Adolescent dating violence do adolescents follow in their friends', or their parents', footsteps? *Journal of Interpersonal Violence, 19*(2), 162–184.

Baker, C., & Stein, N. (2016). Obscuring gender-based violence: Marriage promotion and teen dating violence research. *Journal of Women, Politics & Policy, 37*(1), 87–109.

Barter, C. (2009). In the name of love: Partner abuse and violence in teenage. *The British Journal of Social Work, 30*(2), 211–233.

Barter, C. (2011). Domestic violence: Not just an adult problem. *Criminal Justice Matters, 85*(1), 22–23.

Barter, C. (2014). Responding to sexual violence in girls' intimate relationships: The role of schools In J. Ellis & R. K. Thiara (red.), *Preventing violence against women and girls: Educational work with children and young people*. Bristol: Polity Press.

Barter, C., & Lombard, N. (2019). 'Thinking and doing' Children's and young people's understandings and experiences of intimate partner violence and abuse (IPVA). In N. Lombard (Ed.), *The Routledge handbook of gender and violence*. London: Routledge.

Barter, C., McCarry, M., Berridge, D., & Evans, K. (2009). *Partner exploitation and violence in teenage intimate relationships*. London: NSPCC.

Barter, C., & Stanley, N. (2016). Inter-personal violence and abuse in adolescent intimate relationships: Mental health impact and implications for practice. *International Review of Psychiatry, 28*(5), 485–503.

Barter, C., Stanley, N., Wood, M., Lanau, A., Aghtaie, N., Larkins, C., & Överlien, C. (2017). Young people's online and face-to-face experiences of interpersonal violence and abuse and their subjective impact across five European countries. *Psychology of Violence*. Advance online publication. doi:10.1037/vio0000096

Barter, C., Wood, M., Aghtaie, N., Stanley, N., Pavlou, S., Apostolov, G., . . . & Overlien, C. (2015). *Safeguarding Teenage Intimate Relationships (STIR): Connecting online and offline contexts and risks. Briefing paper 2: Incidence rates and impact of experiencing interpersonal violence and abuse in young people's relationships*. Retrieved from http://stiritup.eu

Bianchi, D., Morelli, M., Nappa, M. R., Baiocco, R., & Chirumbolo, A. (2018). A bad romance: Sexting motivations and teen dating violence. *Journal of Interpersonal Violence*. doi:10.1177/0886260518817037.

Black, B. M., Tolman, R. M., Callahan, M., Saunders, D. G., & Weisz, A. N. (2008). When will adolescents tell someone about dating violence victimization?. *Violence Against Women, 14*(7), 741–758.

Bronfenbrenner, U. (1977). Toward an experimental ecology of human development. *American Psychologist, 32*(7), 513.

Brown, G., Brady, G., & Letherby, G. (2011). Young mothers' experiences of power, control and violence within intimate and familial relationships. *Child Care in Practice, 17*(4), 359–374.

Burr, V. (2015). *Social constructionism*. New York: Routledge.

Carlson, C. N. (2003). Invisible victims: Holding the educational system liable for teen dating violence at school. *Harvard Women's Law Journal, 26*, 351–393.

Christie, N. (2001). Det idealiska offret. In M. Åkerström & Sahlin (Eds.), *Det motspänstiga offret*. Lund: Studentlitteratur.

Chung, D. (2005). Violence, control, romance and gender equality: Young women and heterosexual relationships. *Women's Studies International Forum, 28*.

Chung, D. (2007). Making meaning of relationships: Young women's experiences and understandings of dating violence. *Violence Against Women, 13*(12), 1274–1295.

Corona, R., Gomes, M. M., Pope, M., Shaffer, C., & Yaros, A. (2016). Love shouldn't hurt: What do African American maternal caregivers tell their daughters about dating violence? *The Journal of Early Adolescence, 36*(4), 465–489.

Crenshaw, K. W. (1991). Mapping the margins: Intersectionality, identity politics, and violence against women of color. *Stanford Law Review, 43*(6), 1241–1299.

Cutbush, S., Williams, J., Miller, S., Gibbs, D., & Clinton-Sherrod, M. (2018). Longitudinal patterns of electronic teen dating violence among middle school students. *Journal of Interpersonal Violence*, 1–21. doi:10.1177/0886260518758326

Cutter-Wilson, E., & Richmond, T. (2011). Understanding teen dating violence: Practical screening and intervention strategies for pediatric and adolescent healthcare providers. *Current Opinion in Pediatrics, 23*, 373–383.

Dank, M., Lachman, P., Zweig, J. M., & Yahner, J. (2014). Dating violence experiences of lesbian, gay, bisexual, and transgender youth. *Journal of Youth and Adolescence, 43*(5), 846–857.

Davies, C. T. (2019). This is abuse: Young women's perspectives of what's 'OK' and 'not OK' in their intimate relationships. *Journal of Family Violence, 34*(5), 479–491.

Donovan, C., & Hester, M. (2015). *Domestic violence and sexuality. What's love got to do with it?* Bristol, UK: Policy Press.

Diaz-Aguado, M. J., & Martinez, R. (2015). Types of adolescent male dating violence against women, self-esteem, and justification of dominance and aggression. *Journal of Interpersonal Violence, 30*(15), 2636–2658.

Edirne, T., Can, M., Kolusari, A., Yildizhan, R., Adali, E., & Akdag, B. (2010). Trends, characteristics, and outcomes of adolescent pregnancy in eastern Turkey. *International Journal of Gynecology and Obstetrics, 110*, 105–108.

Fernández-González, L., O'Leary, D. K., & Muñoz-Rivas, M. J. (2013). We are not joking: Need for controls in reports of dating violence. *Journal of Interpersonal Violence, 28*(3), 602–620.

Foshee, V. A. (1996). Gender differences in adolescent dating abuse prevalence, types, and injuries *Health Education Research, 11*(3), 275–286.

Foshee, V. A., Reyes, H. L. M., Gottfredson, N. C., Chang, L. Y., & Ennett, S. T. (2013). A longitudinal examination of psychological, behavioral, academic, and relationship consequences of dating abuse victimization among a primarily rural sample of adolescents. *Journal of Adolescent Health, 53*(6), 723–729.

Fox, C. L., Hale, R., & Gadd, D. (2014). Domestic abuse prevention education: Listening to the views of young people. *Sex Education, 14*(1), 28–41.

Furlong, A., Woodman, D., & Wyn, J. (2011). Changing times, changing perspectives: Reconciling 'transition' and 'cultural' perspectives on youth and young adulthood. *Journal of Sociology, 47*, 355.

Gadd, D., Fox, C. L., Corr, M. L., Alger, S., & Butler, I. (2015). *Young men and domestic abuse.* New York, NY: Routledge.

Gadd, D., Fox, C. L., Corr, M. L., Butler, I., & Bragg, J. (2013). *From boys to men: Overview and recommendations.* Report No. 4. Manchester: University of Manchester.

Gadd, D., Fox, C. L., & Hale, R. (2014). Preliminary steps towards a more preventative approach to eliminating violence against women in Europe. *European Journal of Criminology, 11*(4), 464–480.

Gagné, M. H., Lavoie, F., & Hébert, M. (2005). Victimization during childhood and revictimization in dating relationships in adolescent girls. *Child Abuse & Neglect, 29*(10), 1155–1172.

Garrido, E. F., & Taussig, H. N. (2013). Do parenting practices and prosocial peers moderate the association between intimate partner violence exposure and teen dating violence? *Psychology of Violence, 3*(4), 354.

Garthe, R. C., Gorman-Smith, D., Gregory, J. E., & Schoeny, M. (2018). Neighborhood concentrated disadvantage and dating violence among urban adolescents: The mediating role of neighborhood social processes. *American Journal of Community Psychology, 61*(3–4), 310–320.

Gillum, T. L., & DiFulvio, G. (2012). "There's so much at stake" sexual minority youth discuss dating violence. *Violence Against Women, 18*(7), 725–745.

Gottzén, L., & Korkmaz, S. (2013). *Killars våld mot tjejer i nära relationer: Familjers och vänners responser.* Stockholm: Ungdomsstyrelsen.

Hagemann-White, C., Kelly, E., & Römkens, R. (2010). *Feasibility study to assess the possibilities, opportunities and needs to standardise national legislation on violence against women, violence against children and sexual orientation violence.* Brussels: European Union.

Haglund, K., Belknap, R. A., Edwards, L. M., Tassara, M., Hoven, J. V., & Woda, A. (2019). The influence of masculinity on male Latino adolescents' perceptions regarding dating relationships and dating violence. *Violence Against Women, 25*(9), 1039–1052.

Hamby, S., Nix, K., De Puy, J., & Monnier, S. (2012). Adapting dating violence prevention to francophone Switzerland: A story of intra-Western cultural differences. *Violence and Victims, 27*, 1.

Hamby, S., & Turner, H. (2013). Measuring teen dating violence in males and females: Insights from the national survey of children's exposure to violence. *Psychology of Violence, 3*(4), 323.

Hellevik, P. (2019). Teenagers' personal accounts of experiences with digital intimate partner violence and abuse. *Computers in Human Behavior, 92*, 178–187.

Hellevik, P., & Överlien, C. (2016). Teenage intimate partner violence: Factors associated with victimization among Norwegian youths. *Scandinavian Journal of Public Health*, 1–7.

Herrenkohl, T. I., & Jung, H. (2016). Effects of child abuse, adolescent violence, peer approval and proviolence attitudes on intimate partner violence in adulthood. *Criminal Behaviour and Mental Health, 26*, 304–314.

Home Office. (2013). *Domestic violence and abuse*. Retrieved from www.gov.uk/guidance/domestic-violence-and-abuse

Hydén, M., Gadd, D., & Wade, A. (2016). Introduction to response based approaches to the study of interpersonal violence. In M. Hydén, G. Gadd, & A. Wade (Eds.), *Response based approaches to the study of interpersonal violence* (pp. 1–16). London: Palgrave Macmillan.

Ihongbe, T. O., & Masho, S. W. (2018). Gender differences in the association between synthetic cannabinoid use and teen dating violence victimization. *Violence and Gender, 5*(2), 103–109.

Jackson, S. M. (1999). Issues in the dating violence research. A review of the literature. *Aggression and Violent Behavior, 4*(2), 233–247.

James, A., Jenks, C., & Prout, A. (1998). *Theorizing childhood*. Cambridge, MA: Polity Press.

Joly, L. E., & Connolly, J. (2016). Dating violence among high-risk young women: A systematic review using quantitative and qualitative methods. *Behavioral Sciences, 6*(1), 7.

Jones, G. (2011). *Youth*. Cambridge, MA: Polity Press.

Karlsson, M. E., Calvert, M., Rodriguez, J. H., Weston, R., & Temple, J. R. (2018). Changes in acceptance of dating violence and physical dating violence victimization in a longitudinal study with teens. *Child Abuse & Neglect, 86*, 123–135.

Kernsmith, P. D., Victor, B. G., & Smith-Darden, J. P. (2018). Online, offline, and over the line: Coercive sexting among adolescent dating partners. *Youth & Society, 50*(7), 891–904.

King, D. M., Hatcher, S. S., & Bride, B. (2015). An exploration of risk factors associated with dating violence: Examining the predictability of adolescent female dating violence perpetration. *Journal of Human Behavior in the Social Environment, 25*(8), 907–922.

King, D. M., Hatcher, S. S., & Bride, B. (2017). Adolescent predictors of female dating violence perpetration. *Vulnerable Children and Youth Studies, 12*(1), 17–32.

Klein, J. (2006). An invisible problem: Everyday violence against girls in schools. *Theoretical Criminology, 10*(2), 147–177.

Korkmaz, S. (2017). Research on teenage intimate partner violence within a European context: Findings from the literature. In S. Holt, C. Överlien, & J. Devaney (Eds.), *Responding to domestic violence. Emerging Challenges for policy, practice and research in Europe*. London: Jessica Kingsley Publishers.

Korkmaz, S., & Överlien, C. (2020). Responses to youth intimate partner violence: The meaning of youth-specific factors and interconnections with resilience. *Journal of Youth Studies, 23*(3), 371–387.

Korkmaz, S., Överlien, C., & Lagerlöf, H. (2020). Youth intimate partner violence: Prevalence, characteristics, associated factors and arenas of violence. *Nordic Social Work Research*. DOI: 10.1080/2156857X.2020.1848908

Krekula, C., Närvänen, A., & Näsman, E. (2005). Ålder i intersektionell analys. *Kvinnovetenskaplig tidskrift*, (2–3).

Landor, A. M., Hurt, T. R., Futris, T., Barton, A. W., McElroy, S. E., & Sheats, K. (2017). Relationship contexts as sources of socialization: An exploration of intimate partner violence experiences of economically disadvantaged African American adolescents. *Journal of Child and Family Studies, 26*(5), 1274–1284.

Leen, E., Sorbring, E., Mawer, M., Holdsworth, E., Helsing, B., & Bowen, E. (2013). Prevalence, dynamic risk factors and the efficacy of primary interventions for adolescent dating violence: An international review. *Aggression and Violent Behavior, 18*, 159–174.

Livingston, J. A., Eiden, R. D., Lessard, J., Casey, M., Henrie, J., & Leonard, K. E. (2018). Etiology of teen dating violence among adolescent children of alcoholics. *Journal of Youth and Adolescence, 47*(3), 515–533.

Lucero, J. L., Weisz, A. N., Smith-Darden, J., & Lucero, S. M. (2014). Exploring gender differences: Socially interactive technology use/abuse among dating teens. *Journal of Women and Social Work 2014, 29*(4), 478–491.

Lysova, V. A., & Douglas, E. M. (2008). Intimate partner violence among male and female Russian University students. *Journal of Interpersonal Violence, 23*(11), 1579–1599.

Maas, C. D., Fleming, C. B., Herrenkohl, T. I., & Catalano, R. F. (2010). Childhood predictors of teen dating violence victimization. *Violence and Victims, 25*(2), 131.

Morris, A. M., Mrug, S., & Windle, M. (2015). From family violence to dating violence: Testing a dual pathway model. *Journal of Youth and Adolescence, 44*(9), 1819–1835.

Muñoz-Rivas, M. J., Graña, J. L. O'Leary, D. K., & González, M. P. (2007). Aggression in adolescent dating relationships: Prevalence, justification, and health consequences. *Journal of Adolescent Health, 40*, 298–304.

Murray, A., & Azzinaro, I. (2019). Teen dating violence: Old disease in a new world. *Clinical Pediatric Emergency Medicine, 20*(1).

Nahapetyan, L., Orpinas, P., Song, X., & Holland, K. (2014). Longitudinal association of suicidal ideation and physical dating violence among high school students. *Journal of Youth and Adolescence, 43*(4), 629–640.

Nocentini, A., Menesini, E., Pastorelli, C., Connolly, J., Pepler, D., & Craig, W. (2011). Physical dating aggression in adolescence. Cultural and gender invariance. *European Psychologist, 16*(4), 278–287.

Ohio Substitute House Bill 19. Retrieved from www.legislature.ohio.gov/legislation/legislation-documents?id=GA132-HB-19

Ombayo, B., Black, B., & Preble, K. M. (2019). Adolescent – Parent communication among youth who have and have not experienced dating violence. *Child and Adolescent Social Work Journal, 36*(4), 381–390.

Överlien, C. (2018). Våld mellan ungdomar i nära relationer. Digitala medier och utövande av kontroll. *Socialvetenskaplig tidskrift, 2018*(1).

Överlien, C., Hellevik, P. M., & Korkmaz, S. (2019). Young women's experiences of intimate partner violence–narratives of control, terror, and resistance. *Journal of Family Violence,* 1–12.

Pentaraki, M. (2017). Fear of double disclosure and other barriers to help seeking: An intersectional approach to address the needs of LGBT teenagers experiencing teenage relationship abuse. In S. Holt, C. Överlien, & J. Devaney (Eds.), *Responding to domestic violence: Emerging challenges for policy, practice and research in Europe* (Chapter 7). London: Jessica Kingsley Publishers.

Preble, K. M., Black, B. M., & Weisz, A. N. (2018). Teens' and parents' perceived levels of helpfulness: An examination of suggested "things to say" to youth experiencing Teen Dating Violence. *Children and Youth Services Review, 85,* 326–332.

Ravi, K. E., Black, B. M., Mitschke, D. B., & Pearson, K. (2019). A pilot study of a teen dating violence prevention program with Karen refugees. *Violence Against Women, 25*(7), 792–816.

Reed, L. A., Tolman, R. M., & Ward, L. M. (2016). Snooping and sexting: Digital media as a context for dating aggression and abuse among college students. *Violence Against Women, 22*(13), 1556–1576.

Reuter, T. R., Sharp, C., & Temple, J. R. (2015). An exploratory study of teen dating violence in sexual minority youth. *Partner Abuse, 6*(1), 8–28.

Richards, T. N., & Branch, K. A. (2012). The relationship between social support and adolescent dating violence: A comparison across genders. *Journal of Interpersonal Violence, 27*(8), 1540–1561.

Romito, P., Beltramini, L., & Escribà-Agüir, V. (2013). Intimate partner violence and mental health among Italian adolescents: Gender similarities and differences. *Violence Against Women, 19*(1), 89–106.

Ruel, C., Lavoie, F., Hébert, M., & Blais, M. (2017). Gender's role in exposure to interparental violence, acceptance of violence, self-efficacy, and physical teen dating violence among quebec adolescents. *Journal of Interpersonal Violence.* doi:10.1177/0886260517707311

Sebastían, J., Verdugo, A., & Ortiz, B. (2014). Jealousy and violence in dating relationships: Gender-related differences among a Spanish sample. *Spanish Journal of Psychology, 17,* 1–12.

Shaffer, C. S., Adjei, J., Viljoen, J. L., Douglas, K. S., & Saewyc, E. M. (2018). Ten-year trends in physical dating violence victimization among adolescent boys and girls in British Columbia, Canada. *Journal of Interpersonal Violence.* 1–18. Retrieved from https://doi-org.ezp.sub.su.se/10.1177/0886260518788367

SOSFS. (2014). *Våld i nära relationer.* Stockholm: Socialstyrelsens författningssamling. [Regulations and general advice on violence in intimate relationships].

Stanley, N., Barter, C., Wood, M., Aghtaie, N., Larkins, C., Lanau, A., & Överlien, C. (2016). Pornography, sexual coercion and abuse and sexting in young people's intimate relationships: A European study. *Journal of Interpersonal Violence,* 1–26.

Stanley, N., Ellis, J., Farrelly, N., Hollinghurst, S., & Downe, S. (2015). Preventing domestic abuse for children and young people: A review of school-based interventions. *Children and Youth Services Review, 59,* 120–131.

Staunæs, D. (2003). Where have all the subjects gone? Bringing together the concepts of intersectionality and subjectification. *Nordic Journal of Feminist and Gender Research, 11*(2).

Stonard, K. E., Bowen, E., Lawrence, T. R., & Price, S. A. (2014). The relevance of technology to the nature, prevalence and impact of adolescent dating violence and abuse: A research synthesis. *Aggression and Violent Behavior, 19,* 390–417.

Stonard, K. E., Bowen, E., Walker, K., & Price, S. A. (2015). "They'll always find a way to get to you": Technology use in adolescent romantic relationships and its role in dating violence and abuse. *Journal of Interpersonal Violence,* 1–35.

Storer, H. L., Casey, E. A., & Herrenkohl, T. I. (2017). Developing "whole school" bystander interventions: The role of school-settings in influencing adolescents responses to dating violence and bullying. *Children and Youth Services Review, 74*, 87–95.

Toscano, S. E. (2014). "My situation wasn't that unique": The experience of teens in abusive relationships. *Journal of Pediatric Nursing, 29*(1), 65–73.

Ungar, M., Connelly, G., Liebenberg, L., & Theron, L. (2019). How schools enhance the development of young people's resilience. *Social Indicators Research, 145*(2), 615–627.

Unlu, G., & Cakaloz, B. (2016). Effects of perpetrator identity on suicidality and nonsuicidal self-injury in sexually victimized female adolescents. *Neuropsychiatric Disease and Treatment, 12*, 1489–1497.

Van Ouytsel, J., Ponnet, K., & Walrave, M. (2017). The association of adolescents' dating violence victimization, well-being and engagement in risk behaviors. *Journal of Adolescence, 55*, 66–71.

Van Ouytsel, J., Ponnet, K., Walrave, M., & Temple, J. R. (2016). Adolescent cyber dating abuse victimization and its associations with substance use, and sexual behaviors. *Public Health, 135*, 147–151.

Vézina, J., & Hébert, M. (2007). Risk factors for victimization in romantic relationships of young women: A review of empirical studies and implications for prevention. *Trauma Violence Abuse, 8*, 33–66.

Viejo, C. (2014). Physical dating violence: Towards a comprehensible view of the phenomenon. *Journal for the Study of Education and Development, 37*(4), 785–815.

Viejo, C., Monks, C. P., Sanchez, V., & Ortega-Ruiz, R. (2016). Physical dating violence in Spain and the United Kingdom and the importance of relationship quality. *Journal of Interpersonal Violence, 31*(8), 1453–1475.

Weisz, A. N., & Black, B. M. (2008). Peer intervention in dating violence: Beliefs of African-American middle school adolescents. *Journal of Ethnic & Cultural Diversity in Social Work, 17*(2), 177–196.

Weisz, A. N., Black, B. M., & Hawley, A. C. (2017). What would they do? Parents' responses to hypothetical adolescent dating violence situations. *Violence and Victims, 32*(2), 311–325.

Weisz, A. N., Tolman, R. M., Callahan, M. R., Saunders, D. G., & Black, B. M. (2007). Informal Helpers' responses when adolescents tell them about dating violence or romantic relationship problems. *Journal of Adolescence, 30*(5), 853–868.

Wiklund, M., Malmgren-Olsson, E-B., Bengs, C., & Öhman, A. (2010). "He messed me up": Swedish adolescent girls' experiences of gender-related partner violence and its consequences over time. *Violence Against Women, 16*, 2.

Wincentak, K., Connolly, J., & Card, N. (2017). Teen dating violence: A meta-analytic review of prevalence rates. *Psychology of Violence, 7*(2), 224.

Wood, M., & Barter, C. (2015). Hopes and fears: Teenage mothers' experiences of intimate partner violence. *Children & Society, 29*, 558–568.

Wood, M., Barter, C., & Berridge, D. (2011). *'Standing on my own two feet': Disadvantaged teenagers, intimate partner violence and coercive control.* London: NSPCC.

# 13

# THE MIDDLE YEARS

## A neglected population regarding domestic violence and abuse?

*Eija Paavilainen and Tanja Koivula*

### Introduction

DV is a complex issue perpetrated by and against both men and women, often occurring bidirectionally (i.e. perpetrated by both intimate [ex-]partners), although the dynamics of violence can vary significantly across genders. The same men and women as parents may also maltreat their children, either by way of neglect, exposure to parental violence, or even direct physical, emotional, or sexual abuse (Keiski, Helminen, Lindroos, Kommeri, & Paavilainen, 2018). DV causes suffering to individuals and families, sometimes resulting in the intergenerational transmission of violence (Hughes et al., 2017), while also resulting in an economic burden for societies (Peterson et al., 2018). DV is generally considered to be an adverse childhood experience (ACE) with a sustained impact throughout the life-course of those affected (McGavock & Spratt, 2017).

For the purposes of our discussion, DV will be used to refer specifically to the issue of intimate partner violence (IPV) and its variants, although we acknowledge that the term can encompass many wider forms of abuse (for example, certain definitions include so-called 'honour' violence, female genital mutilation/cutting, and forced marriage; Crown Prosecution Service, 2017). The aim of this chapter is to bring DV in the middle years (from about 30 to 65) into the discussion and explore the experiences and perspectives of this age group. Due to a limited focus in the literature on the unique characteristics of this age group, we argue that it is important to explore issues pertaining to the prevalence and impact of DV among this demographic in more depth, in addition to professionals' identification of and responses to the issue. In a recent analysis of longitudinal records in the UK, focusing on childhood maltreatment and DV against women, Chandan et al. (2020a) concluded that maltreatment and abuse continue to be significantly under-recorded within primary care records. The study found that the incidence rate of DV was highest among those aged 18–34, with incidence gradually declining with age. That said, given the study's focus on recording, its figures may serve to indicate a reduced recognition and/or reporting of abuse which coincides with increasing age, rather than a decrease in actual incidence.

The Middle year person (MYP) may be busy at work, having and raising children, and possibly taking care of their own parents who require additional help and care. Acting as an official caregiver to family members may even directly cause or exacerbate DV (Latomäki, Runsala, Koivisto, Kylmä, &

Paavilainen, 2020). Individuals in this age group also frequently utilise health and social care services, as clients or patients in different settings, with a multitude of health problems of their own. It is important therefore that their experiences of DV as a (very diverse) group are not neglected by researchers and policy-makers.

As already noted, DV researchers and service providers often focus their attention on specific perpetrator/victim subgroups, including children, pregnant women, or the elderly as victims, and men as perpetrators. However, violence perpetrated towards men (by both male and female intimate partners or family members) continues to be an issue and, as with violence against women, often goes unreported (Bradbury-Jones, Appleton, Clark, & Paavilainen, 2017). The National Intimate Partner Violence Victimization Survey notes that

> any focus on differences between men and women should not obscure the fact that nearly 16 million men [in the USA] have experienced some form of severe physical violence by an intimate partner during their lifetimes and over 13 million men have experienced intimate partner violence during their lifetimes that resulted in a negative impact.
>
> (Breiding et al., 2014)

In Finland, we undertook a survey in one large hospital (across different clinics and wards) to ask adult patients whether they had been victims or perpetrators of DV at some point during their lifetime. Twenty-two percent reported having been victims and 11% reported perpetrating DV on at least one occasion (Leppäkoski & Paavilainen, 2015). These mostly middle-aged patients had been hospitalised for various reasons *not* connected to their current hospital stay, indicating that adults among this age group could be found across all settings of a hospital, many of them potentially suffering from long-term effects of DV. Yet the issue of DV would likely be overlooked in most cases.

This chapter, based on our experiential knowledge and theoretical understanding of DV, will present an exploration of current literature and ideas. Eija Paavilainen has for a long time worked with a family violence research team focusing on various DV issues, particularly child maltreatment and IPV as perpetrated by both men and women, and together with colleagues has written a national guideline concerning the identification of child maltreatment. Tanja Koivula has studied violence perpetrated against children by mothers. She is currently piloting a domestic violence risk assessment model from Sweden called iRiSk in Finnish shelters. Earlier in her career, Tanja worked as a nurse on a child psychiatric ward with children who had experienced DV, and alongside her research continues to work as a part-time psychotherapist. Together we have noticed that certain aspects of DV have been studied to very different extents among different disciplines. However, the incidence of DV continues to be high despite ongoing research and public health efforts to address it. Much is known about the risk factors for DV and methods to facilitate identification, yet interventions to reduce its prevalence have not been so effective. A review of the literature has shown us that the MYP as a specific group has not received much research attention, with these individuals often being included among (and hidden behind) other specific subgroups. We present here an example of DV in the MYP.

## Scenario: Terry's story

Terry is a 35-year-old woman living in a small city. She has recently divorced Michael, her husband of 15 years, with whom she has three children (two of school age and one of preschool age). Terry has a lower-level degree and previously worked in a traditional 'woman's occupation' which paid a low income, though she has been out of work for several years in order to look after her children. Michael has a high income, high social status, and a senior position at work. Terry doesn't have close friends and only remains in touch with a few former colleagues from her previous workplace. After several years of consideration she decided to divorce her husband, though her parents were against her decision and no longer support her in any way. One of the main reasons behind the decision was Michael's behaviour towards the children, and Terry's recognition of its negative effects on the children's wellbeing. Michael often outwardly blamed the children for various perceived wrongdoings, and even began using physical violence against their eldest child, Thomas. This included pushing, slapping, or hitting Thomas with a belt when he came to Terry's defence during Michael's violent episodes.

Terry often thinks that she is unworthy because of Michael's sustained affront to her confidence and sense of self. After a diagnosis of depression, Terry began using alcohol as a coping mechanism. Michael's abuse extended to denying Terry access to their shared finances throughout the marriage, forcing her to have sex with him against her will, and openly having affairs with other women. He also insisted on knowing her whereabouts at all times, both before and after their divorce, which involved digitally stalking her via her mobile phone.

Terry has never disclosed this abuse to anybody. She is in a precarious financial situation post-divorce, requiring expensive legal support from a lawyer because of Michael's aggressive affronts to her freedom. This has recently involved attempts to alienate the children from their mother, telling them that Terry does not love them, and threatening to take them permanently away from her. Terry now suffers with insomnia and has begun to experience panic attacks. However, she has started wondering whether she should go back to Michael who continues to tell Terry that he loves her and that she will not be able to cope without him. He also insists that he is going to change and will be a better husband and father.

While reading this chapter, we would like you to pay attention to two things: firstly, consider how gender inequality impacts on the incidence of DV, and secondly, consider the association between DV and other physical and mental health problems. Once you have read Terry's story, consider your own attitudes or preconceptions about DV and how these might manifest when discussing the issue with others. Do you anticipate any differences in your approach to talking about DV with women and men? The chapter will also discuss DV services and consider how reporting and recording of DV might be improved. We will start with an overview of DV, as experienced by the MYP, and then continue with suggestions for the actions required for addressing DV among this group.

## Overview of DV as experienced by the middle years population

A 2018 multilevel study across 28 European Union (EU) countries by Sanz-Barbero et al. found that 4.2% of ever-partnered women (aged 18 and older) had experienced DV within the last year. The study's objective was to establish whether a relationship exists between a country's gender equality (measured by Gender Equality Index [GEI] score) and political responses to women who experience physical and/or sexual DV. The authors concluded that countries with *higher* gender equality and with anti-gender-based violence legislation had an overall decreased prevalence of recent DV. Women who had suffered abuse by an adult before the age of 15 were the most likely to have experienced recent DV. However, other recent studies (see Alsaker, Moen, Morken, & Baste, 2018) have discovered what is now termed the 'Nordic paradox', a phenomenon seen in Nordic countries, where gender equality is typically high, and where paradoxically women are known to suffer from DV at a disproportionality high level compared with other countries with comparable levels of gender equality.

In the USA, the association between DV and gender inequality has been explored by Willie and Kershaw (2019). Their study found that the lifetime prevalence of DV ranged between 28–45% for women and between 18–39% for men. Across states, high Gender Inequality Index values (note this is a different index to the GEI mentioned earlier; United Nations Development Programme, 2018) correlated positively with the prevalence of any form of either physical or psychological DV among women. In a cross-sectional study focusing on the relationship between DV and quality of life, Alsaker et al. (2018) found that quality of life (as measured by a 12-item questionnaire called the SF-12) among abused women was significantly lower than the norm for the female Norwegian population.

Associations between DV and mental health problems have been widely studied across the MYP. Nationally representative data have been collected in Korea by Soyeon Oh, Kim, Jang, and Park (2019) from women (n=3732) and men (n=1040), with the aim of studying associations between DV and depression. In this study, 40% (n=415) of men and 23% (n=866) of women had suffered from DV, and both groups also suffered significantly more from depression both in terms of prevalence and severity. Furthermore, Miltz et al. (2019) explored DV among a group (n=410) of gay, bisexual, and other men who have sex with men, and found a 40.2% lifetime prevalence of DV, with a past-year DV prevalence of 14.7%. As with the findings from Oh, a history of DV was strongly associated with recent depressive symptoms.

Ruiz-Perez, Rodriguez-Barranco, Cervilla, and Ricci-Cabello (2018) explored the associations between DV and 'mental disorders' (MD) (as diagnosed via the 'Mini-International Neuropsychiatric Interview') in Spain, from the perspective of both women and men. In their community-based study (n=4507) the prevalence of DV was 9.4%, and the prevalence of MD cooccurring with DV was 4.4%. Poor health status (measured via the SF-12) was associated with MD and with DV-MD in both men and women. Their paper concludes that there is a strong association between DV and MD in both women and men, although the prevalence is typically higher in women than in men, which has a relevance in terms of long-term health inequalities (this will be discussed later on). Van Deinse, Wilson, Macy, and Cuddeback (2019) similarly found that severe mental illness and DV are connected: women with severe mental illness who experience DV face additional challenges that perpetuate behavioural ill-health and DV issues, ultimately putting these women at greater risk for continued victimisation.

DV and physical illnesses such as cardiovascular disease and type 2 diabetes are also connected. This link has been described in a retrospective cohort study from the UK where a large group (n=18547) of women with experience of DV were matched to women without such experiences (n=72231) by age and lifestyle factors (Chandan et al., 2020b). The paper describes how women with a history of DV suffer higher incidence rate ratios (IRR) for cardiac events (IRR=1.31), type 2 diabetes (IRR=1.51) and all-cause mortality (IRR=1.44). These numbers demonstrate that women exposed to DV have a disproportionate risk for adverse health outcomes across the lifespan. There are considerations surrounding the directionality of violence in intimate relationships, as this has a bearing on the severity of violence that women suffer. According to Behnken, Duan, Temple, and Wu (2018), in their study focusing on low-income women (n=763), women in relationships with bidirectional DV were more likely to experience severe physical violence and severe DV-related injury compared with women in the unidirectional DV relationships. These findings highlight the importance of approaching the issue of DV with a non-judgemental attitude so that all involved parties can access the support they need in order to remain safe.

Gibson et al. (2019) collected data from women between 40 and 80 years of age (n=2016). The authors undertook a cross-sectional analysis to examine the association between lifetime experience of DV, sexual assault, and post-traumatic stress disorder (PTSD) and the development of menopausal symptoms (difficulty sleeping, hot flushes, night sweats as well as vaginal symptoms). The authors conclude that individuals with a history of DV are statistically *more* likely to experience more menopausal symptoms than those without exposure, with the number rising more steeply in those with diagnosed PTSD. Seeking medical care for menopausal symptoms is common, and the findings from this study present an argument for DV screening among women reporting menopausal symptoms in primary care settings.

Hughes et al. (2017) discuss how the presence of multiple ACEs leads to an increased risk of developing long-term health conditions: for example, obesity, diabetes, numerous cancers, heart conditions, respiratory disease, and mental health issues. Their systematic review and meta-analysis also found that individuals with multiples ACEs have worse self-reported health scores. Again, these findings have a relevance across multiple health and social care settings, and highlight the importance of holistic professional assessment.

Despite the negative impact of DV, many couples in relationships characterised by violence remain together, and to date we know little about the factors affecting violence desistance (i.e. how individuals come to abstain from violence within their relationship). Using grounded theory methods, Merchant and Whiting (2017) aimed to find out more about the process of desistance in formerly violent couples. The authors describe three stages in the process of desistance: (1) the 'Turning Point', described as a 'conscious decision to change'; (2) the 'Decision to Change', where both partners become committed to improving their relationships or overall lifestyles; and (3) 'Doing Things Differently', which involved a multicomponent change in the participants' lives. An awareness of these three stages might enable professionals to have a more nuanced understanding of the desistance process, and thus allow for more targeted and optimised treatment for individuals experiencing *and* perpetrating DV.

To conclude this section, we argue that taking steps to address gender inequality at a societal level is important to meeting the goal of reduced overall prevalence of DV. In turn, these efforts can lead to improved physical and mental health outcomes across populations. Given that ACEs are known to transmit intergenerationally, together with accumulating evidence which suggests that violence is likely to cooccur with multiple ACEs (see Hughes et al., 2017), reducing DV on a wider scale can contribute to an overall reduction in the prevalence of certain health problems for future generations.

## Actions needed to tackle DV in the MYP

Healthcare services often provide the first formal support opportunities for many individuals experiencing DV. However, in addition to addressing immediate healthcare needs, professionals are required to signpost service users to other specialist services who can meet their needs appropriately. These can be both professional services or voluntary organisations. Emergency departments are important points of contact for many individuals experiencing DV, particularly those currently suffering (or with a history of) physical abuse. DiVietro et al. (2018) tested a dual screening method for DV, which involved the combination of a tablet-based questionnaire and a face-to-face assessment, and found that the combined methods were more successful in identifying DV than either method in isolation.

In a retrospective cohort study across two Hong Kong hospitals, Choi et al. (2018) found that of 980 DV victims (157 male, 823 female), 69.9% accepted on-site counselling when offered during visits to the emergency department (following a confirmed incident of DV). The authors also explored associations between help-seeking and demographic- and injury-related factors. Rates of acceptance of on-site counselling were significantly lower for victims with mental illness, while victims who had experienced more than two abuse incidents were *more* likely to seek and/or accept help than those visiting for the first and second time. Rates of help acceptance were also lower among those who attended the emergency department alone, with the authors suggesting that the presence of family, friends, or professionals (such as police officers or paramedics) may increase the motivation to seek help. The article concludes by stating that healthcare professionals require formal training on how to promote help-seeking behaviour, and specifically, on how to provide individualised support for both male and female victims of abuse. Chandan et al. (2020a, 2020b) similarly argue that clinicians should have a good awareness of DV in order to improve physical and mental health outcomes for patients, in addition to enabling better recognition and management of risk factors for abuse. DiVietro et al. (2018) stress the importance of utilising various different techniques and approaches to asking patients about DV, rather than relying solely on a single method.

A study of 42,000 women across the EU (European Union Agency for Fundamental Rights; FRA, 2019) found that only one-third of individuals experiencing DV contacted either the police or other formal support services following the most serious incident of violence. Reasons for not reporting violence are similar across different contexts: these include fear of retaliation from abusers, pressure from families to maintain privacy, lack of awareness of rights or available support, economic dependency, and a perception that authorities will fail to take adequate action. It is clear that more effort is needed to facilitate access to legal remedies and justice in the case of DV. Lack of coordination between agencies and organisations responding to DV, including health and social services, the police, forensic services, and the judicial system, is also a common problem globally. Some countries have established specific structures to increase coordination, such as cross-sectoral taskforces operating with specific protocols for case referrals. However, more efforts are needed to make sure that individuals' safety is not compromised due to the failure of agencies to coordinate with one another (United Nations; UN, 2019).

Previous studies have shown that many parents who are subjected to DV contact social services without talking about the violence they experience (Stanley, 2011). In Finland in 2019, 1052 adults (attending shelters) came without children compared to 1825 who brought children with them. The typical age of those seeking refuge from DV is 25–34 years, with an overwhelming majority being women (males represented only 267 [9%]; Finnish institution for health and welfare (THL 2020). In contrast, individuals over the age of 45 are less likely to seek refuge at a shelter when compared to 25–34-year-olds Finnish institutution for health and welfare (THL 2020). Evidence also suggests that women with younger children are often in contact with social services more regularly than childless individuals in the MYP Finnish institution for health and welfare (THL 2020). After the age of 29, IPV prevalence rates begin to decrease according to data for 53 countries. Sixteen and a half percent of women in the oldest age group analysed (aged 45–49) reported a history of some form of IPV within the year preceding the survey, compared with 22.8% among the age group of 20–24-year-olds. Unfortunately, data on violence experienced by women above the age of 50 are limited because most population-based surveys use the 15–49 age range (UN, 2019). We argue that it is important to fill this data gap given the MYP's underrepresentation in DV literature, in addition to the fact that older women are more susceptible to abuse and neglect than their male counterparts (United Nations Department of Economic and Social Affairs, 2013). In the 2002 Madrid International Plan of Action on Ageing, the increased susceptibility of older women to abuse and neglect was acknowledged:

> Older women face greater risk of physical and psychological abuse due to discriminatory societal attitudes and the nonrealization of the human rights of women. Some harmful traditional practices and customs result in abuse and violence directed at older women, often exacerbated by poverty and lack of access to legal protection.
>
> (UN, 2003; para. 108)

Again, this points to the wider issue of gender inequality on a societal level.

When it comes to supporting male individuals experiencing DV, many professionals' lack of knowledge and experience are compounded by the overwhelming 'female focus' of the majority of models designed to facilitate health and social care responses to DV. Shelter programmes have also historically been gender-specific, and in many areas are still segregated by gender identity in an effort to protect the safety and security of women and girls. Males can typically be accommodated in off-site hotels or partner shelters (for example, homeless shelters). These options likely intensify feelings of isolation, potentially even exposing individuals to further harm or resulting in limited access to additional supportive services. Hotel stays are generally short term and lack the constant staff presence and support needed to help male DV victims fully process their experiences, ultimately resulting in heightened feelings of loneliness and vulnerability (Stiles, Ortiz, & Keene, 2017).

The accessibility of services for women who experience multiple and intersecting forms of violence also remains a major challenge. Significant gaps exist, for example, in the accessibility and reach of violence against women (VAW) services for rural and remote areas (UN, 2013). Older women, indigenous women, immigrant women, lesbian, bisexual, and transgender women or women with disabilities may also face additional barriers to accessing mainstream services. These can include language barriers, cultural discrimination, physical barriers, or a lack of competency from service providers to respond appropriately to particular circumstances. In response, many countries have established group-specific services (UN, 2019).

Previous research has mainly focused on men as perpetrators of violence within intimate relationships. As such, the majority of DV risk assessment instruments assume a male perpetrator and female victim. Additionally, Axberg, Broberg, Eriksson, Hultmann, and Iversen's (2018) review of the literature showed that there were no domestic violence risk assessment instruments which focused on a male perpetrator's role as a father. Therefore, these instruments fail to take into account some important perspectives, for example, the feelings of remorse or abusers' understanding of how their own behaviour is affecting the victim or the child (Hultmann, 2020). Hultmann and his team are currently undertaking a study to test the structured iRiSk interview for use by professionals within child welfare investigations, focusing on fathers who have used DV and who are in contact with crisis centres and child welfare. Their project is being funded by the Swedish National Board of Health and Welfare.

Use of ICD-10 coding (International Classification of Disease) for domestic violence injuries in healthcare settings is problematic for a number of reasons. This coding system was developed by the World Health Organization (WHO) and is used internationally for statistical purposes to monitor diseases, injuries, symptoms, and other issues which impact health status across populations (WHO, 2020a). Partner- or spouse-related perpetrator coding has been shown to be particularly poor, with a 2019 Finnish study finding that only 11% of DV-related hospital visits were coded appropriately (Kivelä, Leppäkoski, Ruohoniemi, Puolijoki, & Paavilainen, 2019). The insufficient (or inappropriate) use of perpetrator codes contributes to an underestimation of the incidence of DV and reduces the coding system's usefulness for DV monitoring. Similar results have also been found in other countries (see Btoush, Campbell, & Gebbie, 2008; Schafer, Drach, Hedberg, & Kohn, 2008). This is a huge problem for international researchers and policy-makers who seek to compare DV prevalence across different countries.

Sanz-Barbero, Corradi, Otero-Garcia, Ayala, and Vives-Cases (2018) argue that the introduction of a consolidated legislative framework to address VAW, together with the assumption of state responsibility for responding to VAW, could decrease overall prevalence of DV in Europe. The authors also suggest that responses to DV in Europe require an integrated approach which protects women during their youth. Bradbury-Jones et al. (2017) conclude in their focused mapping review and synthesis on VAW research in Europe that researchers should be explicit about the gendered nature of violence, for both women and men, and that more research should be conducted between countries. This could contribute to addressing the enduring gendered inequalities across Europe and worldwide, and may also draw needed attention to the perspectives of men who experience DV. Writing from the USA perspective, Willie and Kershaw (2019) recently concluded that structural changes to gender inequality may help to reduce the overall incidences of DV and improve women's overall wellbeing. To illustrate this, they suggest: "Creating an egalitarian environment that supports the wellbeing of women may weaken gender power dynamics and reduce the incidence of IPV" (p. 262).

Lilley-Walker, Hester, and Turner (2018) reviewed 60 evaluation studies relating to DV perpetrator programmes across Europe, involving over 7000 participants across 12 countries. The study assessed the design, methods, input, output, and outcome measures used across the evaluations in order to identify the possibilities and challenges of a Europe-wide evaluation methodology that could be used to assess future perpetrator programmes. The authors conclude that a standardised approach to evaluating DV perpetrator programmes would facilitate smoother comparisons across countries. They suggest that a standardised approach should include the following:

> A mix of quantitative and qualitative methodologies; larger and more varied participant samples; some form of control group design; a wider range of potential outcome measures (including perpetration of controlling and coercive behaviours as well as all other types of domestic abuse) assessed over a longer period postintervention; a focus on the role and quality of programme facilitation; and outcome data triangulation (e.g., including reports of those women/partners in a position to reliably assess change).
>
> (p. 879)

In a Finnish follow-up study, the effectiveness of a psychodynamic group intervention developed for female perpetrators of family violence was evaluated (Keiski et al., 2018). The participants (n=134) voluntarily sought help after perpetrating violence against a partner, child, or both. The study, whose sample included only women *without* acute mental health or substance abuse problems, concluded that the intervention led to an improvement in women's knowledge and a reduction in violent behaviour. The study also discovered that both of these positive outcomes continued after six months. However, given that perpetrator programmes are mostly utilised in situations where participation is mandatory, it is important to consider that motivation to engage will likely be quite different when participation is voluntary, as it was in Keiski et al.'s study.

According to Dias et al. (2019), social support may safeguard individuals against some of the negative effects of violence on physical and mental health. They conducted a cross-sectional study across eight European countries to assess the association between social support (referring to support from friends, family, or other reciprocal networks) and DV victimisation. The study found a statistically significant association between low levels of social support and DV victimisation. The authors conclude that although further research is needed, the presence of both formal and informal networks seems to correlate positively with a reduction in prevalence of DV.

In a systematic review, Tol et al. (2019) examined the relationship between 'mental health treatments' (referring to a range of interventions designed specifically for individuals experiencing mental health problems) and rates of DV perpetration and victimisation in middle-income countries. The authors concluded that the existing literature is too limited in scope for reliable conclusions to be drawn. They propose that future research should maintain a strong theoretical focus, particularly with a view to exploring which specific mechanisms of DV (both perpetration and victimisation) are impacted by mental health interventions. Other research suggests that individuals who disclose their abuse and receive appropriate support are at a significantly reduced risk of experiencing mental ill-health (e.g. Dias et al., 2019). However, these positive outcomes are to an extent dependent on a prevailing 'informed' or non-judgemental attitude towards DV among formal and informal support networks. For example, professionals, friends, and other reciprocal networks who endorse the belief that DV is a private or family matter are unlikely to offer the same level of support as those who would encourage a disclosure. According to Dias et al. (2019), women seek support more easily than men. However, another important finding from their cross-sectional study was that most individuals who reported being victims of violence *also* reported having perpetrated violence at some point. This echoes an earlier finding from a study by Leppäkoski and Paavilainen (2015), and reiterates the importance of asking about DV in a non-judgemental and open-minded manner.

According to Peterson et al. (2018), DV prevalence can only be reduced if prevention is prioritised and if prevention strategies are also evaluated and continuously improved. In addition, as highlighted by Bellis et al. (2019), millions of adults across Europe and North America are living with the burden of multiple ACEs. In their study, the authors suggest that a 10% reduction in ACE prevalence could result in annual savings of 3 million DALYs (Disability-Adjusted Life Years, which represent "the loss of the equivalent of one year of full health"; WHO, 2020b). Programmes for reducing the prevalence of ACEs are already available (e.g. Chen & Chan, 2016). One possible intervention would be to implement routine ACE-history-taking to identify those who are at risk of poor health outcomes. Alternatively, universal implementation of trauma-informed approaches (e.g. fostering trust, transparency, and empathy with families) may be sufficient (see Sweeney, Filson, Kennedy, Collinson, & Gillard, 2018). Ereyi-Osas, Racine, and Madigan (2020) argue that professionals in health and social care services should be more aware of the potential for adversity such as DV to transmit intergenerationally. Adequate resources, multidisciplinary collaborative work, and adequate trauma training are undoubtedly needed for professionals. Furthermore, as noted earlier in the chapter, checklist approaches such as ICD-10 coding can cause more harm than good if not used appropriately.

## Conclusions

In conclusion, we argue that actions are needed to educate professionals of different fields to appropriately discuss, identify, and support individuals experiencing DV in their middle years. Current evidence suggests that multi-professional collaboration lacks coordination and is ineffective. For example, in social services, the topic of DV is seldom discussed (Stanley, 2011). Documentation and recording of DV requires development, and DV perpetrator programmes similarly require ongoing improvement. Due to inconsistent professional training, both women and men experiencing DV often go unidentified and therefore unsupported.

DV is common among the MYP and often impacts children, perpetuating the intergenerational transmission of adversity. Multiple ACEs (including those which manifest as a direct result of DV) are a major risk factor for many health conditions, regardless of the type of violence experienced. The true prevalence of DV on a global scale is unclear for a number of reasons, including (but not limited to) underreporting and poor documentation and/or monitoring methods. This also makes it difficult to compare statistics relating to the prevalence of DV across different countries.

A number of long-term conditions such as heart disease, diabetes, cancer, respiratory conditions, and mental health problems can be directly linked to exposure to DV. Moreover, DV often correlates with heavy alcohol use, smoking, poor self-rated health, and sexual risk taking. Quality of life among abused women has been found to be significantly lower when compared to women who have not suffered DV, and there is ample evidence linking exposure to DV with mental ill-health in both men and women. Although this link is stronger for women, men who experience DV are also at a heightened risk of depression, PTSD, and other mood disorders. It is important for health and social care professionals to bear these issues in mind when working with individuals who have experienced violence of any sort.

DV causes significant suffering to individuals and families, and incurs vast costs for societies worldwide. Systemic improvements in training for health and social care professionals are required to enable them to better advocate for victims and develop a more tailored and individualised response. Formal and informal social support may buffer the negative effects of violence on physical and mental health, while the provision of better treatment for mental health conditions may likewise contribute to a reduced prevalence of DV across populations. Structural changes to gender inequality are also incredibly important in tackling this issue at its roots. Researchers and policy-makers should be explicit about the gendered nature of violence, though a focus should also be maintained on improving research into and opportunities for men who suffer DV. Furthermore, an increased effort to conduct research cross-nationally is needed to ensure a more coordinated response to tackling gender-based inequalities on the global scale.

## Critical findings

- DV among the MYP is common and often impacts on children. Children can be affected directly by witnessing or overhearing violent episodes, becoming injured while intervening, or may themselves become the targets of abuse. Children also suffer indirectly by way of the intergenerational transmission of ACEs.
- The association between DV and gender (in)equality requires more global attention.
- The MYP have been included in a great deal of DV research, yet as a group they are rarely singled out for the purposes of analysis.
- DV causes suffering to individuals and families and incurs significant costs for societies worldwide.
- DV among the MYP causes innumerable short- and long-term health problems, regardless of the type of violence experienced.
- The specific needs of the MYP experiencing DV are not sufficiently well established or studied. This group experiences multiple burdens due to competing demands on time and energy from work, childcare, and, in many cases, acting as an official caregiver to older family members.
- DV continues to be poorly identified, documented, and responded to across health and social care settings.

## Implications for policy, practice, and research

- DV among the MYP requires an improved research focus across all levels of society.
- Global action is needed to improve gender equality.
- Individuals experiencing DV often don't disclose their abuse for a number of reasons, including (but not limited to) fear of retaliation from abusers, economic dependency, and

lack of awareness of the support services available. Asking about DV, particularly by those working in health and social care settings, is important.

- The needs of individuals experiencing abuse can be addressed by multiple different services, and professionals across sectors (including health and social care and police services) should have a good awareness of DV.
- While approaches to identifying and responding to DV have been well studied, further research, evaluation, and dissemination are required to continue improving our understanding of what 'best practice' looks like.

# References

Alsaker, K., Moen, B., Morken, T., & Baste, V. (2018). Intimate partner violence associated with low quality of life-a-cross-sectional study. *BMC Women's Health.* doi:10.1186/s123905-018-0638-5

Axberg, U., Broberg, A., Eriksson, M., Hultmann, O., & Iversen, C. (2018). *Utveckling av bedömnings-metoder för barn som utsatts för våls i sin familj – Rapport från en fortsättningsstudie.* Göteborgs Uviversitet, Report.

Behnken, M., Duan, Y., Temple, J., & Wu, Z. (2018). Injury and psychiatric disorder in low-income women experiencing bidirectional intimate partner violence. *Violence and Victims, 33,* 259–274.

Bellis, M., Hughes, K., Ford, K., Ramos Rodriguez, G., Sethi, D., & Passmore, J. (2019, October). Life course health consequences and associated annual costs of adverse childhood experiences across Europe and North America: A systematic review and meta-analysis. *The Lancet, 4.* Retrieved from www.thelancet.com/public-health

Bradbury-Jones, C., Appleton, J., Clark, M., & Paavilainen, E. (2017). A profile of gender-based violence research in Europe: Findings from a focused mapping review and synthesis. *Trauma, Violence, & Abuse.* doi:10.1177/1524838017719234

Breiding, M., Smith, S., Basile, K., Walters, M., Chen, J., Merrick, M., & Division of Violence Prevention, National Center for injury Prevention and Control CDC. (2014). Prevalence and characteristics of sexual violence, stalking, and intimate partner violence victimization – National Intimate Partner and Sexual Violence Survey, United States, 2011. *MMWR, 1014,* 63. Retrieved from www.cdc.gov/mmwr/pdf/ss/ss6308.pdf

Btoush, R., Campbell, J., & Gebbie, K. (2008). Visits coded as intimate partner violence in emergency departments: Characteristics of the individuals and the system as reported in a national survey of emergency departments. *Journal of Emergency Nursing, 34,* 419–427.

Chandan, J. S., Gokhale, K., Bradbury-Jones, C., Niranthakumar, K., & Bandyopadhuay, S., & Taylor, J. (2020a). Exploration of trends in the incidence and prevalence of childhood maltreatment and domestic abuse recording in UK primary care: A retrospective cohort study using "the health improvement network" database. *BMJ Open,* 10e036949. doi:10.1136/bmjopen-2020-036949

Chandan, J. S., Thomas, T., Bradbury-Jones, C., Taylor, J., Bandyopadhuay, S., & Nirantharakumar, K. (2020b). Risk of cardiometabolic disease and all-cause mortality in female survivors of domestic abuse. *Journal of American Heart Association JAHA.* doi:10.1161/JAHA.119.014580

Chen, M., & Chan, K. L. (2016). Effects of parenting programs on child maltreatment prevention: A meta-analysis. *Trauma, Violence, & Abuse, 17,* 88–104.

Choi, A., Wong, J., Lo, R., Chan, P., Wong, J., Lau, C., & Kam, C. (2018). Intimate partner violence victims' acceptance and refusal of on-site counseling in emergency departments: Predictors of help-seeking behavior explored through a 5-year medical chart review. *Preventive Medicine, 108,* 86–92.

Dias, N., Costa, D., Soares, J., Hatzidimitriadou, E., Ioannidi-Kapolou, E., Lindert, J., . . . Fraga, S. (2019). Social support and the intimate partner violence victimization among adults from six European countries. *Family Practice, 36,* 117–124.

DiVietro, S., Beebe, R., Grasso, D., Green, C., Joseph, D., & Lapidus, G. (2018). A dual-method approach to identifying intimate partner violence within a level 1 trauma center. *Journal of Trauma and Acute Care Surgery, 85,* 766–772.

Ereyi-Osas, W., Racine, N., & Madigan, S. (2020, February 14). Asking about adverse childhood experiences (ACEs) in prenatal and pediatric primary care: A narrative review and critique. *Perspectives in Infant Mental Health.* Retrieved from https://perspectives.waimh.org/category/peer-reviewed

European Union Agency for Fundamental Rights (FRA). (2019). *Women as victims of partner violence. Justice for victims of violent crime Part IV*. Retrieved from https://fra.europa.eu/en/publication/2019/women-victims-partner-violence-justice-victims-violent-crime-part-iv

Gibson, C., Huang, A., McCaw, B., Subak, L., Thom, D., & Van Den Eeden, S. (2019). Associations of intimate partner violence, sexual assault, and posttraumatic stress disorder with menopause symptoms among midlife and older women. *JAMA Internal Medicine, 179*, 80–87.

Hughes, K., Bellis, M., Hardcastle, K., Sethi, D., Butchart, A,. Mikton, C., Jones, L., & Dunne, M. (2017, August). The effect of multiple adverse childhood experiences on health: Systematic review and meta-analysis. *The Lancet, 2*. Retrieved from www.thelancet.com/public-health

Hultmann, O. (2020). Talking to parents who have abused: Enhancing the child focus in social child welfare investigations about intimate partner violence and child abuse. Conference paper.

Keiski, P., Helminen, M., Lindroos, M., Kommeri, H., & Paavilainen, E. (2018). Female-perpetrated family violence – Effectiveness of a psychodynamic group intervention. *Health Care for Women International.* doi:10.1080/07399332.2018.1548622

Kivelä, S., Leppäkoski, T., Ruohoniemi, J., Puolijoki, H., & Paavilainen, E. (2019). The documentation and characteristics of hospitalized IPV patients using electronic medical records data: A follow-up descriptive study. *Journal of Family Violence, 34*(7), 611–619. doi:10.1007/s10896-019-00081-z

Latomäki, M., Runsala, E., Koivisto, A. M., Kylmä, J., & Paavilainen, E. (2020). Associations between care burden and abuse experienced by caregivers within home care (in Finnish, English abstract. *Journal of Social Medicine* (accepted for publication).

Leppäkoski, T., & Paavilainen, E. (2015). Prevalence of family violence and its impact on family functioning experienced by patients in a hospital. (In Finnish, English abstract). *Tutkiva Hoitotyö, 13*(3), 32–43.

Lilley-Walker, S., Hester, M., & Turner, W. (2018). Evaluation of European domestic violence perpetrator programmes: Toward a model for designing and reporting evaluations related to perpetrator treatment interventions. *International Journal of Offender Therapy and Comparative Criminology, 62*, 868–884.

McGavock, L., & Spratt, T. (2017). Children exposed to domestic violence: Using adverse childhood experience scores to inform service response. *British Journal of Social Work, 47*(4), 1128–1146.

Merchant, L., & Whiting, J. (2017). A grounded theory study of how couples desist from intimate partner violence. *Journal of Marital and Family Therapy, 44*, 590–605.

Miltz, A., Lampe, F., Bacchus, L., McCormack, S., Dunn, D., White, E., . . . Gafos, M. (2019). Intimate partner violence, depression, and sexual behavior among guy, bisexual and other men who have sex with men in the PROUD trial. *BMC Public Health.* doi:10.1186/s12889-019-6757-6

Peterson, C., Kearns, M., McIntosh, W., Estefan, L., Nicolaidis, C., McCollister, K., . . . Florence, C. (2018). Lifetime economic burden of intimate partner violence among U.S. adults. *American Journal of Preventive Medicine, 55*, 433–444.

Ruiz-Perez, I., Rodriguez-Barranco, M., Cervilla, J., & Ricci-Cabello, I. (2018). Intimate partner violence and mental disorders: Co-occurrence and gender differences in a large cross-sectional population based study in Spain. *Journal of Affective Disorders, 229*, 69–78.

Sanz-Barbero, B., Corradi, C., Otero-Garcia, L., Ayala, A., & Vives-Cases, C. (2018). The effect of macrosocial policies on violence against women: A multilevel study in 28 European countries. *International Journal of Public Health, 63*, 901–911.

Schafer, S., Drach, L., Hedberg, K., & Kohn, M. (2008). Using diagnostic codes to screen for intimate partner violence in Oregon emergency departments and hospitals. *Public Health Reports, 123*(5), 628–635.

Soyeon Oh, S., Kim, W., Jang, S., & Park, E. (2019). The association between intimate partner violence onset and gender-specific depression: A longitudinal study of a nationally representative sample. *Journal of Affective Disorders, 250*, 79–84. doi:10.1016/j.jad.2019.02.065

Stanley, N. (2011). *Children experiencing domestic violence: A research review*. Dartington: Research in Practice.

Stiles, E., Ortiz, I., & Keene, C. (2017). *Serving male-identified survivors of intimate partner violence. technical assistance guidance.* National Resource Center on Domestic Violence. Retrieved from https://vawnet.org/sites/default/files/assets/files/2017-07/NRCDV_TAG-ServingMaleSurvivors-July2017.pdf

Sweeney, A., Filson, B., Kennedy, A., Collinson, L., & Gillard, S. (2018). A paradigm shift: Relationships in trauma-informed mental health services. *BJPsych Advances, 24*(5), 319–333.

The Crown Prosecution Service (CPS). (2017). *Domestic abuse*. Retrieved August 15, 2020, from www.cps.gov.uk/domestic-abuse#:~:text=Domestic%20abuse%2C%20or%20domestic%20violence,of%20their%20gender%20or%20sexuality

THL. (2020). Turvakotipalvelut 2019 [Shelter services]. Tilastoraportti [Statistic report] 17/2020. Retrieved from www.julkari.fi/bitstream/handle/10024/139988/Tr_17_2020_Korjattu%201.6.2020. pdf?sequence=5&isAllowed=y

Tol, W., Murray, S., Lund, C., Bolton, P., Murray, L., Davies, T., . . . Bass, J. (2019). Can mental health treatments help prevent or reduce intimate partner violence in low- and middle-income countries? A systematic review. *BMC Women's Health*. doi:10.1186/s2905-019-0782-z

UN DESA (United Nations Department of Economic and Social Affairs). (2013). Neglect, abuse and violence against older women. ST/ESA/351. In *Progress of the world's women 2019–2020*. UN WOMEN. 2020. Retrieved from https://reliefweb.int/sites/reliefweb.int/files/resources/Progress-of-the-worlds-women-2019–2020-en.pdf

United Nations. (2003). *Political declaration and Madrid international plan of action on ageing [online]*. New York, NY: Department of Public Information. Retrieved August 16, 2020, from www.un.org/esa/socdev/documents/ageing/neglect-abuse-violence-older-women.pdf

United Nations Development Programme. (2018). *Human development data (1990–2018)*. Retrieved August 15, 2020, from http://hdr.undp.org/en/data

UN Women. (2019). *Families in a changing world's*. Progress of the World's Women 2019–2020. Retrieved from https://reliefweb.int/sites/reliefweb.int/files/resources/Progress-of-the-worlds-women-2019–2020-en.pdf

Van Deinse, T., Wilson, A., Macy, R., & Cuddeback, G. (2019). Intimate partner violence and women with severe mental illness: Needs and challenges from the perspectives of behavioral health and domestic violence service providers. *Journal of Behavioral Health Services & Research, 46*, 283–293.

Willie, T., & Kershaw, T. (2019). An ecological analysis of gender inequality and intimate partner violence in the United States. *Preventive Medicine, 118*, 257–263.

World Health Organization. (2020a). *International classification of diseases (ICD) revision*. Retrieved August 15, 2020, from www.who.int/classifications/icd/revision/icd11faq/en

World Health Organization. (2020b). *Disability-adjusted life years (DALYs)*. Retrieved August 16, 2020, from www.who.int/gho/mortality_burden_disease/daly_rates/text/en/

# 14

# INTIMATE PARTNER VIOLENCE

## Transforming the response to older victim-survivors in later life

*Sarah Wydall*

### Why domestic abuse and not elder abuse?

Stereotypical views of old age, along with ageist discourses associated with 'decline' and 'disengagement', have served to marginalise older people from mainstream society (Biggs & Powell, 2001; Cumming & Henry, 1961). A pervasive structural ageism places less value on older people in comparison to their younger counterparts and has in part, contributed to the systemic invisibility of older people as victim-survivors[1] of domestic abuse. As a consequence, when compared to other age groups, there is a paucity of knowledge about the lived experiences of older victim-survivors of intimate partner violence (IPV)[2] and their help-seeking experiences (Wydall & Zerk, 2017; McGarry & Ali, 2019; Wydall, Clarke, Williams, & Zerk, 2019).

As Mansell and Beadle-Brown (2009, p. 34) note, although 'older people dominate the abuse landscape', there is evidence that theory, methodology, policy and practice are significantly underdeveloped when it comes to tackling abuse within domestic settings in later life. Unfortunately, there has been a tendency to view abuse in this context as 'elder abuse' and not 'domestic abuse', with the result that domestic abuse practice and policy responses are largely inadequate when tackling IPV in later life (Wydall, Clarke, Williams, & Zerk, 2018).

Although domestic abuse occurs across the lifespan, its occurrence in later life is a largely neglected area. Research, policy, guidance, specialist service development, professional training and consultancy appears to have focussed on victim-survivors at earlier stages of the life-course. One explanation why domestic abuse in later life has received such limited attention, is the ongoing conceptual ambiguity between domestic abuse and elder abuse, which has contributed to practitioners under-recording incidences of domestic abuse involving older people. Indeed, as noted by the Welsh Government, 'confusion between domestic abuse in later life and "elder abuse" . . . can result in victims of abuse falling between systems which are designed to offer them protection' (Welsh Government, 2016, p. 11). There are definitional constraints when framing domestic abuse as elder abuse, as there is no universally accepted definition of elder abuse and definitions are in a 'constant state of flux' (Phelan, 2013, p. 7). The World Health Organization (2008, p. 15), adopting a definition originally formulated by Action on Elder Abuse (UK), defines elder abuse as 'a single or repeated act, or lack of appropriate action, occurring within any relationship where there is an expectation of trust, which causes harm or distress to an older person'. Notwithstanding the definitional confusion, there is a consensus regarding the multi-dimensional nature of abuse, which includes the following types: financial/material, physical, psychological/emotional, sexual, neglect (intentional or unintentional) and discriminatory abuse (Penhale, 2008). Although the general term 'elder abuse' helps to identify the type and nature of certain forms of abuse, the definition is too broad and all-encompassing to give clarity to fully inform policy and service development in cases of intimate partner violence.

Ironically, while disciplines such as gerontology, psychology, and health have helped to draw attention to systemic age discrimination (Biggs & Powell, 2001), an over-emphasis on 'difference', combined with an ageist, welfare-led, medical gaze, has influenced the type of agency response to abuse in later life, leading to age discrimination (Townsend, 1981; Clarke, Wydall, Williams, & Boaler, 2012; Wydall et al., 2018). What is evident when reviewing the research literature, is that using the term 'elder abuse' to describe domestic abuse in later life is disadvantageous, by default it heuristically separates older people from those at other stages in the life-course.

Rather than adopting a wider socio-ecological perspective that recognises extrinsic vulnerabilities, factors external to the individual, and how they impact on individual decision-making and help-seeking, many of the disciplines and sub fields that use elder abuse terminology tend to lean towards a response that individualises 'the problem' of abuse. This is clearly acknowledged by Dow and Joosten (2012, p. 853) when they assert that:

> Defining elder abuse as the occurrence of specific acts has encouraged better regulation and, in many cases, more direct support, but it risks limiting responses to being only interventions at an individual or family level. . . . the focus is mainly on carer stress or family dysfunction and thereby fails to address the systemic context in which abuse is allowed to occur. This . . . encourages an acceptance of the victim-perpetrator dichotomy, and does not take into account the complexity of the relationships between two adults, or the societal pressures and assumptions that affect individuals.

Simply individualising the nature of abuse by focussing largely on age-related intrinsic vulnerabilities, such as physical frailty and mental vulnerability, is inherently victim-blaming.

Elder abuse is a gender-neutral term that fails to sufficiently acknowledge the gendered dynamics of power and control, where women are more likely to be victims and men perpetrators (Penhale, 2003). Consequently, there is a need to make a case for rejecting the term elder abuse in the context of IPV, not only because there is a lack of conceptual clarity about how elder abuse is defined, measured and understood (Hightower, 2002) but also because of gender neutral and victim blaming assumptions (Whittaker, 1995).

## Domestic abuse in later life: the research deficit

It is difficult to determine the true prevalence of domestic abuse in later life, when older people's experiences are rarely captured, or only partly captured by researchers (Harbison, 2008; De Donder et al., 2016). This is particularly apparent when research methodologies designed to measure prevalence, discount domestic abuse in people over the age of 59 years. Indeed, it is only since 2017 that the largest self-report victimisation survey in Europe, the Crime Survey for England and Wales conducted by the Office of National Statistics, increased the upper age limit for recording domestic abuse from 59 to 74 years. The ageist rationale behind neglecting to capture victimisation of those aged 59 years and over was that older people would experience technical difficulties completing a computer-assisted personal interviewing (CAPI) process.

Prevalence studies of older people's experiences of domestic abuse often do not encompass the more marginalised groups of victim-survivors (De Donder et al., 2016; Pathak, Dhairyawan, & Tariq, 2019). Thus quantitative and qualitative research data about the impact of domestic abuse (Stöckl & Penhale, 2015), help-seeking activity (Beaulaurier, Seff, & Newman, 2008), engagement with criminal justice (Clarke, Williams, & Wydall, 2016) and adult protection services and effective recovery (Brandl, Herbert, Rozwadowski, & Spangler, 2003), often only presents a partial picture. Studies involving older people invariably tend to focus on white, heterosexual women under 74 years of age, who have experienced long-term intimate partner abuse. Consequently, late onset intimate partner relationships, older male victim-survivors (Pritchard, 2007; Wydall, Freeman, & Zerk, 2020), older LGBTQ+ survivors of domestic abuse (Subhrajit; 2014; Wydall et al., 2020) and victims of intimate partner sexual violence (Bows, 2018) are under-researched, and as a result largely overlooked in policy and practice spheres.

The scant data that exists highlights that domestic abuse in later life is an under-recognised phenomenon that has considerable impact on the lives of older people (McGarry & Simpson, 2011; McGarry & Ali, 2019). However, as there is significant under-reporting and under-recording of domestic abuse, the extent of the problem remains largely unknown (McGarry & Simpson, 2011; Wydall & Zerk, 2017). A lack of knowledge about the nature of intimate partner violence particularly within certain groups of older men and women continues to restrict the development of a coherent theory, effective legislation and service provision.

In England and Wales, a non-statutory cross-government definition is in place, which defines domestic abuse as,

> Any incident of pattern of incidents of controlling, coercive, threatening behaviour, violence or abuse between those aged 16 or over who are, or have been, intimate partners or family members regardless of gender of sexuality. The abuse can encompass, but it not limited to psychological, physical, sexual, financial and emotional abuse.
>
> (Home Office, 2016, p. 1)

Coercive and controlling behaviour, as a pattern of abuse used to regulate the everyday activities of victim-survivors and isolate them from social support systems is a significant feature of perpetrator behaviour (Dutton & Goodman, 2005). The inclusion of coercive and controlling behaviours in policy has been largely welcomed by academics, activists, policy-makers and service providers internationally (Candela, 2016; Stark & Hester, 2019). However, as Lagdon, Armour and Stringer (2014) note, the Home Office definition is not without its shortcomings. For example, the definition has been criticised for being 'gender-blind', as women are more likely to be victims of domestic abuse and men are more likely to be perpetrators (Kelly & Westmarland, 2016). The definition does, however, include abusers who are not intimate partners and this serves to widen the lens to encompass other family members; this is particularly relevant when considering cases involving older people. Whilst adult family violence is not the focus of this chapter, it is important to note that older people are as likely to be abused by other family members as they are by current intimate partners (Safelives, 2016; Wydall & Zerk, 2017).

How we define abuse will undoubtedly determine how we respond to it: definitions have consequences and will influence the nature and content of intervention programmes and prevention strategies. A victim-survivor can experience multiple types of abuse at any one time or over the life-course. Furthermore, there are significant and meaningful differences across the types of abuse, particularly in relation to the nature of victim–perpetrator dynamics. As noted by Dixon et al. (2010, p. 418) 'definitions will need to be provisional, flexible and pragmatic'. They also need to reflect the perceptions of older people themselves. As qualitative research suggests, older people's understanding of what constitutes abuse or mistreatment may differ from that of policy-makers, practitioners and researchers (Erlingsson, Carlson, & Saveman, 2006; Mowlam, Tennant, Dixon, & McCreadie, 2007).

To develop a greater understanding of older victim-survivors' experiences of abuse, and how age, gender, disability and victimhood influence their decision-making and help-seeking behaviour, the author, along with colleagues John Williams and Alan Clarke, secured funding through the National Communities Fund in 2015 to launch the Dewis Choice Initiative in 2015. 'Dewis' is Welsh for 'choice'. The name was adopted to emphasise the relevance of facilitating autonomy and informed choice for older people experiencing harm and abuse by intimate partners and other family members. The next section will draw on Dewis Choice as a case study to provide insights into older victim-survivors' perceptions of their help-seeking experiences.

## Dewis Choice (2015–20)

Dewis Choice was a co-produced initiative comprising both service and research elements, aimed at promoting a 'sense of justice' and empowerment in later life. It was established in two locations in Wales: one rural and one urban (see Wydall, Clarke, Williams, & Zerk, 2019). The initiative was designed over a five-month period and involved in-depth and ongoing consultation with older people to ensure a holistic client-led, rights-based response, which integrated both justice and wellbeing provision. For five years, the service provided crisis intervention, intensive support and wellbeing strategies to help client recovery. The initiative operated within a multi-agency, adult safeguarding infrastructure to ensure clients received appropriate protection and support for a wide range of needs. Referrals to Dewis Choice were made by the police, local authorities, and health and third sector practitioners. The referral process is illustrated in Figure 14.1.

The research component of the initiative featured a longitudinal study to capture the lived experiences of older victim-survivors of domestic abuse. A key objective was to explore how prioritising informed choice influenced decision-making for people aged 60 years and over. To ensure all participants, including those living with dementia, had the opportunity to share their experiences, Health Research Authority Approval was granted through the NHS Research Ethics Committee. Of a sample of 89 older victim-survivors who engaged with the service, 46 (52%) were experiencing IPV, whereas the remainder experienced abuse by other family members. Sixty-seven older survivors talked about their experiences in a series of narrative interviews conducted before, during and after their engagement with Dewis Choice. All 46 survivors of IPV agreed to participate in the qualitative element of the research. Participants in this sub-group engaged in three or more narrative interviews over a three-year period. Participants chose the location of the interview, reviewed any previous transcripts and directed the content of the discussion. Counselling support was offered after each interview, with a follow-up meeting with the Wellbeing Practitioner, within five days after the research interview. Data were fully anonymised, encrypted and coded. Following Charmaz (2006), constructivist grounded theory was employed in the analysis of the data. This method was adopted as it accepts that knowledge is co-constructed, subjective and relativist. In comparison to other forms of analysis, Charmaz's approach offers a more reflexive and collaborative process between the researcher and those researched. A prospective longitudinal design was chosen to gain rich insights into the dynamic contextual factors influencing help-seeking.

The development of the initiative was informed by research that drew attention to the systematic invisibility of older victim-survivors within justice-seeking domains (Wydall & Zerk,

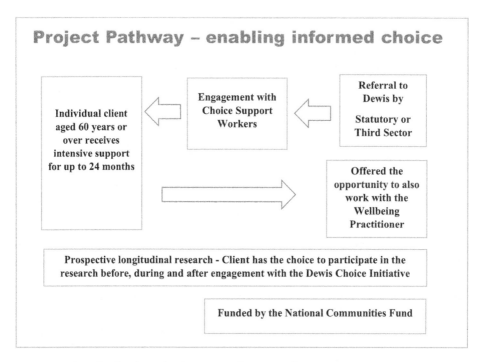

*Figure 14.1*  The referral pathway for clients using the Dewis Choice service

2017; Clarke, Williams, & Wydall, 2016). The research suggested that people aged 60 years and over experienced 'welfarisation', when in comparison to their younger counterparts, practitioners diverted them away from domestic abuse resources and access to criminal and civil justice responses (Clarke et al., 2012; Clarke et al., 2016). Although it has been widely accepted that the majority of victims of domestic abuse may not want to criminalise perpetrators (Kelly, 1999; Mirrlees-Black, 1999), older victim-survivors should not be denied the opportunity to sense justice and pursue civil and/or criminal justice options. Failing to address the issue of criminality denies citizens their ordinary civil or human rights (Fitzgerald, 2006). This begs the question as to whether older adults experiencing a crime are denied access to justice as a consequence of pervasive ageist assumptions, paternalism and a particular social construction of older age.

For example, a research study that highlighted the invisibility of older adults' involvement in decision-making was the evaluation of the 'Access to Justice' study in Wales (Clarke et al., 2016; Williams, Wydall, & Clarke, 2013), which involved the analysis of 131 cases of domestic abuse of people aged 60 years and over. In two-thirds of the sample, there was no evidence that older people were asked what their preferences were, nor was there any indication that civil or criminal options had been discussed with them. In addition, older people were 'welfareised', that is, diverted away from domestic abuse resources, which included specialist key workers, IPV risk assessment, access to legal protection, and civil and criminal justice sanctions. Interviews with practitioners, as to why older people's views and justice options were not explored, revealed that practitioners felt the process of justice-seeking would impact negatively on the health and wellbeing of older adults. As Holder and Daly (2017, p. 788) note, 'there has been a tendency by researchers, policy-makers and activists to assume the aspirations for justice of victims of domestic violence'; the process of decision-making 'on behalf of others' particularly resonates with the research findings that informed the development of Dewis Choice. A core ethos of the initiative was to explore *all options* throughout the help-seeking process and ensure help-giving was client-led and non-directive.

The next section provides an insight into the individual impact of IPV. The section will also examine how factors external to the individual influenced not only the experience of help-seeking but also the outcomes for the victim-survivors supported by Dewis Choice.

## The lived experiences of older victim-survivors of IPV

Of the 46 older survivors experiencing IPV, 34 identified as female and 12 as male. Forty-three percent of this sample reported having a disability. All 46 participants were in heterosexual relationships, with two-thirds having lived with long-term abuse over more than two decades, and one-third experiencing abuse over a period of less than ten years. The demographic characteristics of this sample are presented in Table 14.1.

During their initial discussions with the researchers, over 85% of the clients experiencing IPV stated that their physical and mental health was poor. For the proportion of the sample that had experienced long-term IPV, many older victim-survivors said they had suffered abuse and coercive and controlling behaviours over many years and spent long periods 'reframing' their experiences as a form of coping.

> I think I've walked on egg-shells for most of my married life, so the adrenaline is constantly pumping. I know I look a lot older than I am, I certainly feel old, older than my years. . . . The stress, the fear, it's all been too much. I just couldn't cope anymore and I know now it has taken its toll on me.
>
> (Client, female, 69 years old)

*Table 14.1* Demographic breakdown of clients who experienced IPV

|  | *Male* | *Female* | *Total* |
| --- | --- | --- | --- |
|  | 12 | 34 | 46 |
| Long-term abuse | 8 | 22 | 30 |
| White British | 10 | 30 | 40 |
| White Welsh | 2 | 3 | 5 |
| Black African | 0 | 1 | 1 |
| Disability | 5 | 15 | 20 |
| Coercive control | 12 | 34 | 46 |
| Sexual abuse+ | 0 | 20 | 20 |
| Insomnia | 4 | 7 | 11 |
| Eating disorder | 0 | 10 | 10 |
| CJS engagement | 1 | 21 | 22 |
| Civil justice | 1 | 6 | 7★ |
| % who left abuser | 17 (8) | 70 (32) | 87(40) |

Intimate Partner Violence (Individuals aged between 60–91 years on referral)

★ All seven clients also engaged with the CJS
+ Disclosed sexual abuse

Research shows that older victim-survivors of IPV are more likely to experience poorer physical and mental health outcomes than those in mature adulthood who have not experienced IPV (McGarry, 2011; Stockl & Penhale, 2015). A national longitudinal study in Australia (Loxton, Dolja-Gore, Anderson, & Townsend, 2017) examined the impact of IPV on women's physical and mental health for three birth cohorts (1973–78, 1946–51 and 1921–26). Across all three generations, women who had experienced IPV reported to be in a worse state of physical and mental health for their age than their non-abused counterparts.

Disclosures of long-term sexual abuse and the resultant chronic urinary and gynaecological and gastro-intestinal problems took place after many months of engagement with the Choice Support Worker. Other studies have reported similar effects of long-term sexual abuse (Morgan Disney & Associates, 2000). As with other age groups, insomnia (Abath Leal, Melo Filho, & Marques, 2010; Matud, 2005) and eating disorders (Bundock et al., 2013) were present. For those engaging with Dewis, a third of female victim-survivors of long term IPV experienced both conditions.

Some interesting patterns emerged from the longitudinal data that challenged assumptions about domestic abuse in later life. For example, previous research findings suggest that emotional abuse is more frequently reported by older adults, whereas physical abuse is less common (Band-Witterstein & Eisikovits, 2009; Roberto, 2016; Stockl & Penhale, 2015); however the longitudinal research undertaken at Dewis Choice did not show a reduction in physical abuse. In the series of narrative interviews, participants all stated that as a consequence of retirement and an increase in time spent together, the levels of physical abuse had not changed. Furthermore physical abuse would intensify, as would other forms of abuse if the perpetrator was ill, about to be admitted to hospital for surgery or had been diagnosed with a terminal illness.

Establishing a rapport and building trust with researchers throughout the longitudinal study may have facilitated a more private and intimate view of the nature and forms of abuse, than with a cross-sectional research design. Furthermore, consent had been given to access the case files, and these data helped to confirm the presence of physical abuse and when there was escalation in this form of abuse, which occurred especially when the perpetrator sensed a real or symbolic loss of control. As with much contextual qualitative data, whilst the sample size is relatively small compared to quantitative approaches, the consistency of this theme across the narratives as to the presence of physical abuse is worthy of further investigation.

### Being given 'the run around'

On accessing Dewis Choice, those clients, both women and men, who had been exposed to prolonged coercive and controlling behaviour, felt that their self-confidence and self-belief had been severely undermined. Like victim-survivors in other age groups, they experienced a restricted 'space for action' (Kelly, Sharp-Jeffs, & Klein, 2014) whilst help-seeking. In addition to this, as described later, they also encountered constraints imposed by wider social conditions and stereotypical perceptions of ageing, that at times limited what may be termed their 'scope for action'.

Although clients' sense of agency fluctuated across service settings, thus influencing their capacity to act on their decisions, over time a growing sense of independence and self-belief helped to build 'help-seeking resilience'. Dewis Choice clients felt that prior to receiving support, they were rarely in a position to execute decision-making; however their sense of agency increased when professionals from Dewis Choice empowered clients by providing accurate information on their rights and the resources available to them.

When clients were asked about the barriers to help-seeking, many said that prior to accessing the support offered by Dewis Choice, a significant barrier was the lack of information about where to find help and whether, as older women or men, they were eligible to receive support. They felt that because of their age they did not necessarily 'fit' into the perceptions of domestic abuse victimhood subscribed to by statutory bodies, specialist agencies and prevalent in the wider society. In this sense, the exclusion of older people from mainstream discourse is similar to Donovan and Hester's (2014) observations regarding LGBTQ groups and their exclusion from the 'public story' of domestic abuse.

Clients who had previously contacted service providers, described in research interviews how these agencies had either failed to act or had taken inappropriate action at each stage in the help-seeking journey. A major source of frustration, particularly within criminal and civil justice domains, was poor communication, and the sense that the process of fair, procedural justice had not taken place. Age discrimination, and being made to feel that they were not behaving in a way victim-survivors were expected to behave, were commonly cited by participants as contributory factors in the breakdown in relations with some of the professionals with whom they came into contact. As one client noted:

> as a victim you're not supposed to get angry . . . sorry I'm getting angry now . . . the months I've waited by the phone in that chair, then they [solicitors] they don't ring. Then they [the police] come around without notice, demanding, then they [the CPS] can't even get your name right on the form . . . you are taken from pillar to post, and then dropped like a stone, because they [the police] didn't get *their result* [emphasis added]. I was completely given the run-around, then they [the police] get arsey with me, as if I should be grateful . . . for what? because I'm doing all the work for them, the tax payer should pay me! It's arghhhh, . . . you try . . . until you feel like you lost everything . . . it's [the experience of seeking justice] really opened my eyes . . . there's just no . . . dignity.
>
> (Client, female, 61 years old)

Of the 22 clients who chose to pursue either a criminal or civil justice option, only two, both of whom were involved in civil cases, reported a satisfactory experience throughout each stage of the process. For others, there was evidence of victim-blaming responses. For example, if victim-survivors were perceived as being 'non-compliant', and challenged misinformation and/or communication processes, some professionals withdrew their support. While for some participants this withdrawal of support was only temporary, for others it was permanent: in both instances, this resulted in victim-survivors feeling a sense of helplessness and isolation if an alternative option was not available. For the seven clients who were involved in criminal or civil justice proceedings for eight months or longer, any expectation that they would be treated well diminished over time.

Among the 46 clients, there was a general awareness that the agencies they encountered in the help-seeking process had their own organisational objectives. In describing their individual experiences of interacting with representatives of these agencies, clients felt they were more likely to receive the help requested if they assisted agencies in fulfilling their organisational goals. Both female and male clients likened the process to brokering a deal. While this was particularly the case when statutory agencies were involved, the majority of clients felt all services treated them differently, in a negative sense, than younger victim-survivors at some point in the help-seeking process. As one client commented:

> I am not a priority. I know that I don't fit the type of work they do (domestic abuse service). I know what I ask for is different to what younger women with kiddies ask

for and I know there have been days when I've rang the office terrified, they promise to ring right back, . . . I know she (the Independent Domestic Violence Advisor) is there because they told me she was, she was, and the call hasn't come. I know I'm not on her list . . . that frightens me.

(Client, female 69 years old, living with a disability)

The sudden absence of professional support in the aftermath of a negative court process commonly led to re-traumatisation, depression and in rare cases suicide ideation. Some clients felt harmed by the experience because the unequal power differential was not dissimilar to the actions of perpetrators. Even in cases where court outcomes were more positive, clients felt exposed and resented having to repeatedly justify their decision-making. Participants were clear and unanimous about what would improve the experience. Central to these suggestions were fair and dignified treatment, consistent communication, debunking legal jargon and the appropriate management of expectations.

Providing older people with the time and space to act on decisions was not only influenced by intersecting prejudices about age, gender and also disability, but also about how little was known by practitioners about contextual factors influencing help-seeking. Common gaps in help-providers' knowledge were the impact of coercive control, the co-existence of dementia and domestic abuse, socio-cultural factors and an understanding of older people's rights, benefits and pensions.

### Intersections that impact on help-seeking behaviours in later life

Using the concept of triple jeopardy, Penhale (2016) draws attention to older women's feelings of difference and marginalisation on account of intersections of age, abuse and gender. In the Dewis Choice study, the women's narratives provided examples of similar marginalisation; being 'othered', feeling 'different', was an ever-present dynamic experience, which fluctuated over time and within different organisational settings. Female participants saw ageism and ageist stereotypes as significant discriminatory features when they disclosed intimate partner abuse, engaged with statutory and third sector agencies, and during recovery. Whilst sexism was present and mentioned by all research participants at some point, negative references to gender were perceived by the women in the sample to be less frequently overt and far less explicit than references to age. For the 12 older men, being male and being an older male compounded their feelings of isolation and the experience of discrimination. As one male victim-survivor commented:

Domestic abuse services, the police, everyone so far treats me with suspicion. I am made to feel like I'm odd, like I'm not 'a man' because somehow I can't cope. I'm older now and I don't have the strength to cope . . . so I think being a man and being old . . . it has made it really hard for me to find someone to talk to . . . who treats me like a human being.

(Client, male, 76 years old)

Irrespective of gender, participants stated that practitioners across criminal, civil and support services frequently commented on older victim-survivors' behaviour if it did not conform to ageist stereotypical norms and social expectations about intimate partner relationships.

My age seems to be an issue, not for me but for other people . . . the fact I wanted a divorce in my eighties didn't go down at all well with her [the solicitor] and I'm the one paying! 'What do you want a divorce for . . . at your age' she said. 'Well' I thought, 'I'm not over the hill yet!'

(Client, female, 81 years old)

There was a general feeling among interviewees that practitioners assumed that an older person, because of their age and stage in the life-course, would not want to consider leaving a perpetrator or seeking a divorce. Consequently, this was rarely, if ever, raised as a possible option with older victim-survivors.

As regards gender, interestingly, one woman attributed the lack of reference to her gender as a sign that her identity as a woman disappeared as she aged because she was no longer perceived as sexually attractive.

> You disappear as a woman when you age, your ageing takes over. You lose part of yourself. So I may be 'a just silly old woman', but I'm made to feel 'less than' they [the police] are, by being 'silly' and 'old' and also the 'woman' in me is somehow used differently now. . . . I dunno . . . perhaps I am not seen as a sexual women because I'm well past the menopause. It is really patronising.
>
> (Client, female, 83 years old)

For both women and men, the degrees of intersectionality limited the sense of leverage they felt they had to ask for more help. This was particularly the case for men, given the gendered nature of much service provision that is geared to dealing with female victim-survivors who form the majority of cases. One of the main barriers reported by male clients was that many professionals they encountered were seen to be either unwilling or unable to 'do more'.

In some instances, the lack of awareness agencies and practitioners had about needs, rights and entitlements on account of age, gender, sexuality, victimhood and disability, led to clients feeling unvalued and worthless. Chrisler, Barney and Palatino (2016) have reported similar age-related issues in relation to help-seeking in healthcare domains.

## The co-existence of domestic abuse and dementia

Where older victim-survivors had a disability, they felt that any reference to this was avoided by the professionals they encountered in their help-seeking journeys. Many interviewees felt their disability was 'the elephant in the room', alongside other aspects of their identity, which professionals were unfamiliar with discussing. One client who was diagnosed with dementia whilst attempting to leave her coercive and controlling partner of ten years, discussed how isolated she felt prior to referral to her Dewis Choice. The diagnosis also led to an escalation in a range of controlling behaviours by the perpetrator:

> He [the perpetrator] couldn't stand it, the attention I was getting. There's no advice out there [for women like me]. They are lovely [domestic abuse services]. I was told they could not help me no more. I was very sad . . . the council said you [Dewis Choice] would help me and you have.
>
> (Client, female, 71 years old, living with dementia)

Dewis Choice practitioners worked extensively with health and social care professionals to support this client over several years. It was evident that there was a considerable divide between health and third sector organisations working in the field of dementia, and third sector domestic abuse specialists and statutory agencies with a knowledge of IPV and coercive control. A 'rule of optimism' appeared to apply in cases of dementia, whereby professionals assumed intimate partners were supportive care-givers. Similar misconceptions about the nature of the relationship between care-givers and care-receivers have been found in previous studies where domestic abuse has been masked by age-related factors (Straka & Montminy, 2006; Williams, Wydall, & Clarke, 2013). One health professional commented how joint working with Dewis Choice had changed how she perceived the abuse, and how this influenced her practice:

> It is bringing a whole new area of work to me, coercive control, here in health we work to a family model. So in a sense I have until now just thought 'oh bless', he [the perpetrator] is just struggling to adapt to her diagnosis: cleaning and cooking, not men's roles. We just talked to them both, you tend to think the whole family will muck in and be supportive. Now I take more time to talk with her [the client] alone, I see his actions very, very differently, it has really opened my eyes to the risks where there is domestic abuse.
>
> (Health professional, 4)

Thus, for this client, the initial response of health professionals to the husband was sympathetic, as they were not aware of coercive and controlling tactics, particularly the use of gaslighting by the husband to further confuse the client. As noted by Bergeron (2001) and Brandl and Raymond (2012), health and social work professionals may not always recognise IPV and instead frame the harm as care-giver stress.

There is evidence that a complex interplay of intersections, such as disability, gender and age, can mask IPV and neutralise agency responses, thus producing an inequality of opportunity for older victim-survivors to engage meaningfully with services (Mattsson, 2014). Discriminatory responses led to clients lacking a voice and having limited choices, both of which had a profound negative effect not only on their sense of wellbeing but also on their own perceptions of *their value* as equal citizens in society.

### The invisibility of older victim-survivors

Many clients claimed that help-seeking was hampered by the fact that specialist domestic abuse services did not effectively market themselves to meet the needs of people aged 60 years and over. As one interviewee commented:

> I have had nowhere to go until now [Dewis Choice]. Services say they support you, but their website, photos, don't show people like me. I'm now in my eighties, and even when I thought to knock on their door, I hesitated, many, many times. . . . I thought this [the domestic abuse service] is for younger people with families and I carried on walking. Years on, still so few services. . . . Older people don't matter, they are invisible, I'm invisible as a victim. It is only now I can get the help, now I know what I'm entitled to, I can leave, I feel I've wasted years because I didn't know who would help me as an older women. . . . I often wonder how many there are out there like me, older people, not knowing where to go for help.
>
> (Client, female, 83 years old)

It was common for older clients to state there were very few other services available to them in Wales; this was not only the case for older women, but also true for older men, older

LGBTQ victim-survivors and for those living with dementia or recovering from cancer treatment. Whilst domestic abuse providers are becoming more aware of the need to support older victim-survivors, efforts to resource and market their services vary considerably (McGarry, Simpson, & Hinsliff-Smith, 2014).

## *Starting over*

While a number of studies show that older victim-survivors tend to choose to stay in an intimate partner relationship (Safelives, 2016), the majority of clients (87%) in the Dewis Choice sample chose to leave their abusive partners. This may be attributed to a number of reasons. First, Dewis Choice was a bespoke initiative, co-produced by older people, with a goal to be client-led and age-sensitive. Consequently, it was able to provide long-term, individually tailored intensive support, which would be unsustainable for other service providers. Clients, in the evaluation of the programme rated this aspect of the initiative very positively. Second, effective inter-agency working may have helped older victim-survivors to make more fully informed choices as services worked well to provide a co-ordinated community response. Collectively, these enabling factors may have had an influence on decision-making by clients and provide some explanation as to why a high proportion of clients chose to leave their abusive partner.

When viewing help-seeking from an ecological perspective, it would appear that extrinsic vulnerabilities inherent in service provision, such as 'welfarisation', an inability to support clients with additional needs, and discriminatory practices played a more significant role in inhibiting help-seeking than individual factors. However, adopting a non-judgemental, victim-led ethos and providing clients with the necessary time and space to explore a range of options probably helped to address these barriers to some extent. As noted earlier, the resources available provided practitioners with the ability to move beyond crisis intervention and look in more depth and detail at recovery processes.

## Discussion and conclusion

Interestingly, from a longitudinal research perspective, researchers noted how that by engaging in a series of narrative interviews, over time victim-survivors began to attribute greater responsibility for the IPV to the wrong-doer. It became increasingly noticeable how a moral dimension emerged and developed as the narratives of victimisation unfolded in the series of interviews. The narrative technique also allowed the individual to uncover and explore in depth the impact of experiencing wrong-doing on their sense of identity and wellbeing. The process of collaboration and autonomy in the qualitative research appeared to create an empowering sense of authorship when re-constructing this period of victimisation in participant's life story. Many individual survivors reported that they felt a therapeutic benefit from sharing their lived experience with the researchers. As non-judgemental receivers of the narratives, researchers felt they provided a safe space for participants to explore temporally the experience of victimisation and its aftermath. The extent to which the use of collaborative research methodologies that involve a series of narrative interviews can also contribute towards wellbeing is well-documented (Laslett & Rapoport, 1975; Olson, 2016). For participants, the process of sharing their experience and making themselves more visible as victim-survivors of domestic abuse was very important. As one client stated: 'If this [research] helps just one person, just one, I know I will have made a difference, and that really matters to me' (Client, female, 72 years old).

In conclusion, research about older people's 'lived experiences' of domestic abuse still only exists in the margins and this has led to limited theory and policy development. This, in turn, has restricted opportunities to resource responses that provide 'expanded space for action' to meet the needs, rights and entitlements of a diverse group of older victim-survivors. The findings from Dewis Choice highlight how intersections of age, disability and gender act as a barrier to help-giving. A lack of knowledge about older victim-survivors' needs has a significant impact on the experience of help-seeking and this can inhibit older victim-survivors' ability to make informed choices and limit their scope for action.

Despite an increase in public interest about age and ageing, the discourse around domestic abuse continues to 'other' older women and men by reframing and de-gendering the experience under individualised victim-blaming discourses. Systemic ageism has resulted in 'welfarisation' and discriminatory practices leading to the underdevelopment of policy and practice aimed at supporting older victim-survivors especially within domestic abuse sectors. Whilst there are some signs that services are becoming more age-sensitive in cases of older IPV, there is still a significant gaps in the 'public story' of domestic abuse. The absence of resources committed to tackling IPV in later life by policy-makers, practitioners and researchers serves to legitimise domestic violence and abuse against older women and men in society. A transformative rights-based approach is required to raise the awareness about the nature and extent of IPV in later life. Domestic abuse occurs across the life-course, and societal responses to help-seeking should not diminish with age.

## Acknowledgements

I would like to thank Professor John Devaney and Professor Caroline Bradbury-Jones for inviting me to submit a chapter on this topic area and for their fantastic support and feedback in such a challenging year. I would also like to thank Rebecca Zerk and Emeritus Professor Alan Clarke for their very constructive comments; they are wonderful colleagues and very dear friends.

## Critical findings

- Including older people in service design, implementation and governance of domestic abuse services will assist in making the response to tackling domestic abuse more age-sensitive.
- Paternalism, acting on behalf of older people, rather than allowing them the opportunity to make informed choices, is ageist.
- Stereotypical views about ageing, lifestyle choices and sexuality may not only mask the presence of intimate partner violence, it may also lead to discriminatory policy, practice and research.
- Accessing justice is a basic human right; current responses to older victim-survivors aged 60 years are discriminatory when compared against the service responses to victim-survivors aged 59 and under.
- Where care-giving is a feature, coercive and controlling behaviours by perpetrators can lead to further isolation and an increased risk of harm. Practitioners should avoid a 'rule of optimism' especially where dementia has been diagnosed.

## Implications for policy, practice and research

### *Policy implications*

- This research, and others, has highlighted how domestic abuse policy and feminist discourse on this subject needs to be more inclusive of older victim-survivors of intimate partner violence and adult family violence.

- Policy guidance needs to explore in more depth the intersection of age in relation to males, LGBTQ groups and those living with a disability.
- Safeguarding policy and domestic abuse policy is not sufficiently integrated to address the needs, rights and entitlements of older victim-survivors of domestic abuse; this results in 'welfarisation' whereby older people are diverted from domestic abuse practice including domestic abuse risk assessment, specialist resources and access to justice options. Diversion away from specialist support increases the risk of serious harm and denies older people their basic human rights.

## Practice implications

- Imagery used by services providing specialist domestic abuse support needs to better reflect the diversity of three generations of older people, so that all victim-survivors know the service is inclusive of their needs. Language also needs to be age-sensitive, and include reference to LGBTQ victim-survivors and older men.
- Training is required to incorporate the needs of all older individuals, particularly those who experience intersections of disability and age; training on legal guidance that protects older victim-survivors' rights and entitlements is a significant gap, especially where there is a co-existence of domestic abuse and dementia.
- As disclosures of abuse, particularly sexual violence and abuse may take longer, further consideration needs to be given to training dedicated workers to support older victim-survivors, and providing longer-term support where possible.

## Research implications

- Prospective longitudinal qualitative research has helped to capture the dynamic and complex circumstances in which older people experience abuse, and highlight the numerous barriers they face when help-seeing. Further qualitative research is required to capture older LGBTQ groups, and older men in particular.
- Quantitative and qualitative studies should include all age ranges to capture the experience of domestic abuse along the life-course. This requires factoring in time to reach more victim-survivors who may exist on the margins.

## Notes

1 The majority of male and female research participants who shared their lived experiences with the researchers preferred to use the term 'victim-survivor'. (See also Donovan & Hester, 2010.) However, the use of terminology was complex and transitory; for example, most participants felt that on their first disclosure to professionals, they were not recognised as victims *per se*, and that external validation of their victim status was important. More generally, participants felt the term 'victim-survivor' was more positive than the term 'victim', as this signified movement along an often non-linear continuum from victim to survivor. Formal and informal responses after a disclosure impacted significantly on individual interpretations of terms used. For the purpose of this chapter, the term victim-survivor or client will be used interchangeably.
2 Intimate partner violence (IPV) is domestic abuse by a current or former spouse or partner in an intimate relationship against the other spouse or partner.

## References

Abath, M. D. B., Leal, M. C. C., Melo Filho, D. A. D., & Marques, A. P. D. O. (2010). Physical abuse of older people reported at the Institute of Forensic Medicine in Recife, Pernambuco State, Brazil. *Cadernos de Saúde Pública*, *26*, 1797–1806. doi:10.1590/s0102-311x2010000900013

Band-Winterstein, T., & Eisikovits, Z. (2009). "Aging out" of violence: The multiple faces of intimate violence over the life span. *Qualitative Health Research, 19*(2), 164–180. doi:10.1177/1049732308329305

Beaulaurier, R. L., Seff, L. R., & Newman, F. L. (2008). Barriers to help-seeking for older women who experience intimate partner violence: A descriptive model. *Journal of Women & Aging, 20*(3–4), 231–248. doi:10.1080/08952840801984543

Bergeron, L. R. (2001). An elder abuse case study: Caregiver stress or domestic violence? You decide. *Journal of Gerontological Social Work, 34*(4), 47–63. doi:10.1300/j083v34n04_05

Biggs, S., & Powell, J. L. (2001). A Foucauldian analysis of old age and the power of social welfare. *Journal of Aging and Social Policy, 12*(2), 1–20. doi:10.1300/J031v12n02_06

Bows, H. (2018). Sexual violence against older people: A review of the empirical literature. *Trauma, Violence, & Abuse, 19*(5), 567–583. doi:10.1177/1524838016683455

Brandl, B., Hebert, M., Rozwadowski, J., & Spangler, D. (2003). Feeling safe, feeling strong: Support groups for older abused women. *Violence Against Women, 9*(12), 1490–1503. doi:10.1177/1077801203259288

Brandl, B., & Raymond, J. (2012). Policy implications of recognizing that caregiver stress is not the primary cause of elder abuse. *Generations, 36*(3), 32–39. doi:10.1300/j084v01n02_04

Bundock, L., Howard, L. M., Trevillion, K., Malcolm, E., Feder, G., & Oram, S. (2013). Prevalence and risk of experiences of intimate partner violence among people with eating disorders: A systematic review. *Journal of Psychiatric Research, 47*(9), 1134–1142. doi:10.1016/j.jpsychires.2013.04.014

Candela, K. (2016). Protection the invisible victim: Incorporating coercive control in domestic violence statutes. *Family Court Review, 54*(1), 112–125. doi:10.1111/fcre.12208

Charmaz, K. (2006). *Constructing grounded theory: A practical guide through qualitative analysis.* London: Sage.

Chrisler, J. C., Barney, A., & Palatino, B. (2016). Ageism can be hazardous to women's health: Ageism, sexism, and stereotypes of older women in the healthcare system. *Journal of Social Issues, 72*(1), 86–104. doi:10.1111/josi.12157

Clarke, A., Williams, J., & Wydall, S. (2016). Access to justice for victims/survivors of elder abuse: A qualitative study. *Social Policy and Society, 15*(2), 207–220. doi:10.1017/s1474746415000202

Clarke, A., Wydall, S., Williams, J., & Boaler, R. (2012). *An evaluation of the 'access to justice' pilot project Welsh government.* Retrieved from https://gov.wales/sites/default/files/statistics-and-research/2019-08/121220accesstojusticeen.pdf

Cumming, E., & Henry, W. E. (1961). *Growing old, the process of disengagement.* New York, NY: Basic Books. doi:10.1017/s0144686x00004025

De Donder, L. D., Lang, G., Ferreira-Alves, J., Penhale, B., Tamutiene, I., & Luoma, M. L. (2016). Risk factors of severity of abuse against older women in the home setting: A multinational European study. *Journal of Women & Aging, 28*(6), 540–554. doi:10.1080/08952841.2016.1223933

Dixon, J., Manthorpe, J., Biggs, S., Mowlam, A., Tennant, R., Tinker, A., & Mccreadie, C. (2010). Defining elder mistreatment: Reflections on the United Kingdom study of abuse and neglect of older people. *Ageing & Society, 30*(3), 403–420. doi:10.1017/s0144686x0999047x

Donovan, C., & Hester, M. (2010). 'I hate the word "victim"': An exploration of recognition of domestic violence in same sex relationships. *Social Policy and Society, 9*(2), 279. doi:10.1017/S1474746409990406

Donovan, C., & Hester, M. (2014). *Domestic violence and sexuality: What's love got to do with it?* Policy Press. doi:10.1332/policypress/9781447307433.001.0001

Dow, B., & Joosten, M. (2012). Understanding elder abuse: A social rights perspective. *International Psychogeriatrics, 24*(6), 853–855. doi:10.1017/s1041610211002584

Dutton, M. A., & Goodman, L. A. (2005). Coercion in intimate partner violence: Toward a new conceptualization. *Sex Roles, 52*(11–12), 743–756. doi:10.1007/s11199-005-4196-6

Erlingsson, C., Carlson, S., & Saveman, B.-I. (2006). Perceptions of elder abuse: Voices of professionals and volunteers in Sweden- an exploratory study. *Scandinavian Journal of Caring Sciences, 20*, 151–159. Retrieved from http://umu.diva-portal.org/smash/record.jsf?searchId=1&pid=diva2:140861; doi:10.1111/j.1471-6712.2006.00392.x

Fitzgerald, G. (2006). The realities of elder abuse. In A. Wahidin & M. Cain (Eds.), *Ageing, crime and society.* Cullompton, Devon: Willan Publishing.

Harbison, J. (2008). Stoic heroines or collaborators: Ageism, feminism and the provision of assistance to abused old women. *Journal of Social Work Practice, 22*(2), 221–234. doi:10.1080/02650530802099890

Hightower, J. (2002, April). *Violence and abuse in the lives of older women: Is it elder abuse or violence against women? Does it make any difference?* Paper for INSTRAW Electronic Discussion Forum Gender Aspects of Violence and Abuse of Older Persons.

Holder, R. L., & Daly, K. (2017). Sequencing justice: A longitudinal study of justice goals of domestic violence victims. *The British Journal of Criminology, 58*(4), 787–804. doi:10.1093/bjc/azx046

Home Office. (2016). *Domestic violence and abuse. Guidance: Domestic violence and abuse.* Retrieved from www.gov.uk/guidance/domestic-violence-andabuse.

Kelly, L. (1999). *Domestic violence matters. An evaluation of a development project.* Home Office Research Study 188. The Stationary Office. London. doi:10.1037/e452632008-001

Kelly, L., Sharp-Jeffs, N., & Klein, R. (2014). *Finding the costs of freedom: How women and children rebuild their lives after domestic violence.* London: Solace Women's Aid.

Kelly, L., & Westmarland, N. (2016). Naming and defining 'domestic violence': Lessons from research with violent men. *Feminist Review, 112*(1), 113–127. doi:10.1057/fr.2015.52

Lagdon, S., Armour, C., & Stringer, M. (2014). Adult experience of mental health outcomes as a result of intimate partner violence victimisation: A systematic review. *European Journal of Psycho-traumatology, 5*(1), 1–12. doi:10.3402/ejpt.v5.24794

Laslett, B., & Rapoport, R. (1975). Collaborative interviewing and interactive research. *Journal of Marriage and the Family,* 968–977. doi:10.2307/350846

Loxton, D., Dolja-Gore, X., Anderson, A. E., & Townsend, N. (2017). Intimate partner violence adversely impacts health over 16 years and across generations: A longitudinal cohort study. *PLoS One, 12*(6), e0178138. doi:10.1371/journal.pone.0178138

Mansell, J., & Beadle-Brown, J. (2009). *Dispersed or clustered housing for disabled adults: A systematic review.* Tizard Centre. doi:10.3109/13668250903310701

Mattsson, T. (2014). Intersectionality as a useful tool: Anti-oppressive social work and critical reflection. *Affilia, 29*(1), 8–17. doi:10.1177/0886109913510659

Matud, M. P. (2005). The psychological impact of domestic violence on Spanish women. *Journal of Applied Social Psychology, 35*(11), 2310–2322. doi:10.1111/j.1559-1816.2005.tb02104.x

McGarry, J., & Ali, P. (2019). The invisibility of older women and survivors of intimate partner violence. In H. Bows (Ed.), *Violence against older women, volume 1, nature and extent* (pp. 41–55). Cham: Palgrave Macmillan. doi:10.1108/jap-08-2013-0036

McGarry, J., & Simpson, C. (2011). Domestic abuse and older women: Exploring the opportunities for service development and care delivery. *The Journal of Adult Protection, 13*(6), 294–301. doi:10.1108/14668201111194203

McGarry, J., Simpson, C., & Hinsliff-Smith, K. (2014). An exploration of service responses to domestic abuse among older people: Findings from one region of the UK. *The Journal of Adult Protection, 16*(4), 202–212. doi:10.1108/JAP-08-2013-0036

Mirrlees-Black, C. (1999). *Domestic violence: Findings from a new British crime survey self completion questionnaire.* Research Study 191, London: Home Office. doi:10.1037/e452652008-001

Morgan Disney & Associates with Cupitt, L., & Associates. (2000). *Two lives – Two worlds: Older people and domestic violence* (Vol. 1, 2). Council on Ageing. Canberra, Australia: Partnerships against Domestic Violence.

Mowlam, A., Tennant, R., Dixon, J., & McCreadie, C. (2007). UK study of abuse and neglect of older people: Qualitative findings. *London: National Centre for Social Research, 90.*

Olson, K. (2016). *Essentials of qualitative interviewing.* Routledge. doi:10.4324/9781315429212

Pathak, N., Dhairyawan, R., & Tariq, S. (2019). The experience of intimate partner violence among older women. A narrative review. *Maturitas, 121*, 63–75. doi:10.1016/j.maturitas.2018.12.011

Penhale, B. (2003). Older women, domestic violence, and elder abuse: A review of commonalities, differences, and shared approaches. *Journal of Elder Abuse & Neglect, 15*(3–4), 163–183. doi:10.1300/j084v15n03_10

Penhale, B. (2008). Elder abuse in the United Kingdom. *Journal of Elder Abuse & Neglect, 20*(2), 151–168. doi:10.1080/08946560801974653

Penhale, B. (2016). *The nature, extent and impact of abuse against older women.* AVA Conference: Improving the support for older women. Retrieved from https://avaproject.org.uk/wp/wp-content/uploads/2016/12/The-Nature-Extent-Impact-of-Abuse-Against-Older-Women.pdf

Phelan, A. (2013). Elder abuse: An introduction. In A. Phelan (Ed.), *International perspectives on elder abuse* (pp. 1–31), Abingdon, Oxfordshire: Routledge.

Pritchard, J. (2007). Identifying and working with older male victims of abuse in England. *Journal of Elder Abuse & Neglect, 19*(1–2), 109–127. doi:10.1300/j084v19n01_08

Roberto, K. A. (2016). The complexities of elder abuse. *American Psychologist, 71*(4), 302. doi:10.1037/a0040259

SafeLives. (2016). *Safe later lives: Older people and domestic abuse*. Spotlights report.

Stark, E., & Hester, M. (2019). Coercive control: Update and review. *Violence Against Women, 25*(1), 81–104. doi:10.1177/1077801218816191

Stöckl, H., & Penhale, B. (2015). Intimate partner violence and its association with physical and mental health symptoms among older women in Germany. *Journal of Interpersonal Violence, 30*(17), 3089–3111. doi:10.1177/0886260514554427

Straka, S. M., & Montminy, L. (2006). Responding to the needs of older women experiencing domestic violence. *Violence Against Women, 12*(3), 251–267. doi:10.1177/1077801206286221

Subhrajit, C. (2014). Problems faced by LGBT people in the mainstream society: Some recommendations. *International Journal of Interdisciplinary and Multidisciplinary Studies, 1*(5), 317–331.

Townsend, P. (1981). The structured dependency of the elderly: A creation of social policy in the twentieth century. *Ageing & Society, 1*(1), 5–28. doi:10.1017/s0144686x81000020

Welsh Government. (2016). *National strategy on violence against women, domestic abuse and sexual violence – 2016–2021*. Cardiff. Retrieved from https://gov.wales/sites/default/files/consultations/2018-01/160815-national-strategy-consultation-en.pdf May 2020

Whittaker, T. (1995). Violence, gender and elder abuse: Towards a feminist analysis and practice. *Journal of Gender Studies, 4*(1), 35–45. doi:10.1080/09589236.1995.9960591

Williams, J., Wydall, S., & Clarke, A. (2013). Protecting older victims of abuse who lack capacity: The role of the independent mental capacity advocate. *Elder Law Journal, 2*(3), 167–174.

World Health Organization. (2008). *A global response to elder abuse and neglect: Building primary health care capacity to deal the problem worldwide*. Geneva. Retrieved from www.who.int/ageing/publications/elder_abuse2008/en/ May 2020.

Wydall, S., Clarke, A., Williams, J., & Zerk, R. (2018). Domestic abuse and elder abuse in Wales: A tale of two initiatives. *British Journal of Social Work, 48*(4), 962–981. doi:10.1093/bjsw/bcy056

Wydall, S., Clarke, A., Williams, J., & Zerk, R. (2019). Dewis choice: A Welsh initiative promoting justice for older victim-survivors of domestic abuse. In H. Bows (Ed.), *Violence against older women, volume II responses* (pp. 13–36). Cham: Palgrave Macmillan. doi:10.1007/978-3-030-16597-0_2

Wydall, S., Freeman, E., & Zerk, R. (2020) *Transforming the response to domestic abuse in later life*: Dewis Choice Practitioner Guidance. Llandysul: Gomer Press.

Wydall, S., & Zerk, R. (2017). Domestic abuse and older people: Factors influencing help-seeking. *The Journal of Adult Protection, 19*(5), 247–260. doi:10.1108/JAP-03-2017-0010

# PART 4

# Manifestations of domestic violence and abuse

# 15

# SEXUAL VIOLENCE WITHIN INTIMATE RELATIONSHIPS

*Angie C. Kennedy, Elizabeth Meier and Jessica Saba*

## Introduction

Sexual intimate partner violence (sexual IPV) is a significant social problem that affects millions of adolescent and adult women across the globe (Black et al., 2011; Decker et al., 2015). Though sexual IPV is experienced by women as particularly humiliating, degrading, and shameful, it has been under-researched in comparison to physical and psychological IPV (Kennedy & Prock, 2018; Logan, Walker, & Cole, 2015; Temple, Weston, Rodriguez, & Marshall, 2007; Weiss, 2010). Why might this be? Sexuality and sexual behavior – especially among young, unmarried women – are typically perceived as private, even taboo topics (Chillag et al., 2006; Montemurro, Bartasavich, & Wintermute, 2015). Additionally, male partners' sexual aggression has been normalized as innate and inevitable, with girls' and women's endurance of forced sex understood as part of their natural role (Hlavka, 2014; Tang & Lai, 2008). For example, only in the last 30 years has the United States outlawed rape within marriage, while marital rape remains legal in over 100 countries (Bennice & Resick, 2003; Decker et al., 2015). Finally, IPV researchers have too often ceded the study of sexual violence to sexual assault (SA) researchers, who frequently do not differentiate between partners and non-partners as perpetrators, thus rendering sexual IPV largely invisible within the sexual assault literature (Bagwell-Gray, Messing, & Baldwin-White, 2015).

Sexual victimization within intimate relationships takes many forms, including unwanted but consensual sex, coerced sex, and rape or attempted rape as a result of force, threat of force, or inability to give consent due to intoxication (Hamby & Koss, 2003; Logan et al., 2015). Additionally, technology-facilitated sexual violence (e.g., non-consensual sharing of sexually explicit images via social media, revenge pornography) is an emergent form of IPV, particularly among young people (see Stanley et al., 2018; Walker & Sleath, 2017). In order to focus our review and obtain consistency across global studies of women's experiences with sexual IPV, which is typically measured by two items on partner-forced sex from the World Health Organization's (WHO) Demographic and Health Survey (Decker et al., 2015; Kidman, 2017), we limit the inclusion of studies to those that assess for partner rape or attempted rape, unless otherwise noted. We take an intersectional feminist approach both to highlight social location factors (e.g., class, race/ethnicity/cultural context), and to bring marginalized voices to the center (Collins & Bilge, 2016; Crenshaw, 1991; Hancock, 2016; Sokoloff, 2005). We draw on qualitative, quantitative, and mixed methods studies that have been published since 2000. Because most of the research has been within the US, we separate US studies from those conducted in other countries. Given that even first relationships begun in early adolescence may involve sexual IPV, we include studies across women's life-course (Kennedy, Bybee, McCauley, & Prock, 2018a; Kidman, 2017). We first provide detailed estimates of the prevalence of sexual IPV; then turn to a discussion of sexual IPV in co-occurrence with other forms of IPV; predictors of sexual IPV; outcomes associated with sexual IPV, including acknowledgment and labeling, self-blame, shame, and anticipatory stigma, and mental health and health; and the process of disclosing sexual IPV, including seeking and attaining help. We highlight critical findings as well as research, practice, and policy implications.

## Prevalence of sexual IPV

### *United States estimates*

Data from the National Intimate Partner and Sexual Violence Survey (NISVS) indicate that just over half of rape survivors (51%) report that their perpetrator was a current or former intimate partner. Nearly one in ten women (9%) have been raped by a partner in their lifetime, with multiracial women experiencing the highest rate (20%), in comparison to Black (12%), White (9%), and Latina women (8%) (Black et al., 2011). Adolescence and young adulthood are highly vulnerable periods: a majority of female IPV and SA survivors (69% and 80%, respectively) report that their first victimization occurred before the age of 25 (Black et al., 2011). Among female adolescents aged 12–17 who have been in a relationship, 3% have experienced attempted rape by a partner (Hamby & Turner, 2013), while 12% of female high school students who have ever dated have been forced to do sexual things they did not want to do by a dating partner within the last year, including kissing, touching, or forced sex (Vagi, Olsen, Basile, & Vivolo-Kantor, 2015). Results from a diverse sample of young women (39% Black, 39% White, 10% Latina, 7% biracial, 5% Asian, 1% Native American) indicate that within girls' abusive first relationships, begun when they were just under 15 years old on average, sexual IPV occurred 29% of the time, with 37% of the sexual IPV occurring more than five times during the relationship (Kennedy et al., 2018a). Alice, a Chinese American adolescent who was 16 at the start of her first relationship, describes repeated rapes by her boyfriend:

> towards the end I was just not really feeling it anymore. I just didn't enjoy it with him anymore. And, it was just the same things over and over again but towards the end it was pretty much rape every time. Because it was, it would just be like, he'd start touching me and stuff and I'd be like "Stop." Wouldn't stop. And then he would, we'd be on the couch and he'd literally pick me up and then take me to his bedroom and I'd be like, like this on the door frame [acts out pulling on the door frame] "Stop." And "I don't want to do this." And he'd throw me on the bed and take off all my clothes. And then do whatever. And the entire time I'd be like "Stop, no." And then, [he] wouldn't.
>
> (Kennedy, Meier, & Prock, under review)

In a national sample of young women aged 18–24 (some of whom were in college, some not in college), 6% of both groups had been physically forced to have sex by a partner within the past year (Coker, Follingstad, Bush, & Fisher, 2016), while results from the National College Women Sexual Victimization Study indicate that 2% of participants had been raped since the beginning of the academic year, with nearly a quarter of the rapes (24%) committed by a partner or ex-partner (Fisher, Daigle, & Cullen, 2010). In a representative sample of adult women, 10% had been forced by a partner to have sex, either via threats of violence or physical force (Basile, 2002). Within samples of adult IPV survivors in shelters or seeking formal help from law enforcement (LE), the rate of sexual IPV is much higher, ranging from 26% to 68% (McFarlane et al., 2005a; Messing, Thaller, & Bagwell, 2014; Weaver et al., 2007). For example, McFarlane and colleagues (2005a) interviewed 148 African American, Latina, and White women seeking a protection order: over two-thirds (68%) had been raped by their partner, with 62% of sexual IPV occurring four or more times during the relationship. Repeated partner rape can be especially brutal, as a woman named Linda attests:

> Then he started getting rougher and rougher and then doing things I didn't want him to do against my will there towards the end. And I didn't want him to touch me. He touched me anyway, when I said no, he did it anyway. So he just more or less raped me, repeatedly over and over. He generally never asked, toward the end. It was either have sex or get beat to death and then have sex, that's just how it was.
>
> (Logan, Cole, & Shannon, 2007, p. 87)

## Global estimates

While US researchers tend to narrowly focus on either adolescent, young adult (typically college student), or adult sexual IPV, research outside of the US has relied on sexual IPV data gathered as part of the WHO Demographic and Health Survey, which surveys a representative sample of adolescent and adult women of childbearing age (aged 15–49) who are cohabiting or currently/ever married. Drawing on these WHO survey data, across five African countries the lifetime rate of sexual IPV ranged from 10% in Ethiopia, to 27–29% in Uganda, to 34% in urban Nigeria (Barzargan-Hejazi, Medeiros, Mohammadi, Lin, & Dalal, 2013; Ebrahim & Atteraya, 2019; Ogland, Xu, Bartkowski, & Ogland, 2014; Onigbogi, Odeyemi, & Onigbogi, 2015; Tlapek, 2015; Wandera, Kwagala, Ndugga, & Kabagenyi, 2015). There are within-country regional differences, however: a representative sample of women in southwest, predominantly rural Ethiopia reported a lifetime prevalence of sexual IPV of 50% (Deribe et al., 2012). Data from six Asian countries indicate a lifetime prevalence ranging from 5% in Sri Lanka, to 10% in China, to 37–46% in urban Pakistan and rural Bangladesh, respectively (Ali, Asad, Mogren, & Krantz, 2011; Dalal & Lindqvist, 2012; Jayasuriya, Wijewardena, & Axemo, 2011; Naved, 2013; Pandey, 2016; Tang & Lai, 2008). Across a region stretching from eastern Europe to the Middle East, the rate of lifetime sexual IPV ranged from 3% in Azerbaijan and Ukraine, to 6% in the West Bank/Gaza Strip, to 21% in the Kurdistan region of Iraq (Al-Atrushi, Al-Tawil, Shabila, & Al-Hadithi, 2013; Barrett, Habibov, & Chernyak, 2012; Haj-Yahia & Clark, 2013; Ismayilova & El-Bassel, 2013).

Turning to particular groups of survivors, a meta-analysis of WHO Demographic and Health Survey data from adolescent and young adult women across 30 low- and middle-income nations revealed that 12% were raped during their first sexual experience, ranging from 2% in Timor-Leste, to 13% in Kenya, to 29% in Nepal (Decker et al., 2015). Within a sample of Norwegian high school students, 19% of those who had been in a relationship had experienced sexual IPV (including both forced and pressured sex), while the lifetime prevalence of sexual IPV among young women attending college in Nigeria was 7% (Hellevik & Överlien, 2016; Umana, Fawole, & Adeoye, 2014). Finally, the pregnancy and postpartum period may be a time of increased vulnerability to IPV in general (Taillieu & Brownridge, 2010). In two studies that assessed sexual IPV during a recent pregnancy, prevalence ranged from 17% among Iranian women to 30% of Ethiopian women (Abate, Wossen, & Degfie, 2016; Farrokh-Eslamlou, Oshnouei, & Haghighi, 2014).

## The co-occurrence of sexual IPV with other forms of IPV

### United States studies

Researchers have determined that sexual IPV oftentimes occurs in relationships characterized by other forms of IPV, such as physical and psychological abuse, coercive control, and stalking. State-level results from the Youth Risk Behavior Survey (YRBS), which assessed lifetime partner rape along with physical IPV over two years among US high school students, indicate that sexual and physical IPV are strongly correlated (Kim-Godwin, Clements, McCuiston, & Fox, 2009); one in ten girls (9–10%) experienced physical IPV only, 4% sexual IPV only, and 5–6% both physical and sexual IPV (Silverman, Raj, Mucci, & Hathaway, 2001). More recent national YRBS data echo these results: 7% of girls experienced physical IPV only during the past year, 8% sexual IPV only (defined as forced sexual things such as kissing, touching, or being physically forced to have sexual intercourse), and 6% both physical and sexual IPV (Vagi et al., 2015). Finally, within a diverse sample of young women with a history of partner violence, the co-occurrence of sexual and physical IPV plus coercive control was the most common pattern across adolescence (19–29% of abusive relationships) (Kennedy et al., 2018a).

Among a sample of female college students (80% White, 12% African American, 6% Asian, 2% Latina), 79% had experienced some type of IPV (physical, sexual, or psychological abuse), with 25% of survivors enduring sexual IPV, either in combination with physical IPV (8%) or with both physical and psychological IPV (17%) (Eshelman & Levendosky, 2012). In one of the few longitudinal studies of co-occurring IPV among young women (71% White, 25% Black, with sexual IPV defined to include unwanted or coerced sex, attempted rape, and rape), 64% reported lifetime experience with both physical and sexual IPV, vs. 14% sexual IPV only and 11% physical IPV only (Smith, White, & Holland, 2003). Using NISVS data on adult women's lifetime experiences with physical, sexual, and psychological IPV, as well as stalking, Krebs and colleagues (2011) found that sexual IPV was associated with an average of three types of IPV; in a random sample of insured women, 28% of those who experienced IPV reported both physical and sexual IPV, vs. 62% physical IPV only and 11% sexual IPV only (Bonomi, Anderson, Rivara, & Thompson, 2007).

In samples of IPV survivors in shelters or seeking formal help from LE, the rate of sexual IPV in combination with physical IPV ranges from 20–58% (Cole, Logan, & Shannon, 2005; Weaver et al., 2007). In a longitudinal study of IPV cluster patterns among survivors in shelter or seeking a personal protection order, African American and employed women were more likely to be in the first cluster (moderate physical and psychological abuse and stalking, low sexual IPV) vs. the second (high physical and psychological abuse, high stalking, low sexual IPV) or third cluster (high across all four types) (Dutton, Kaltman, Goodman, Weinfurt, & Vankos, 2005). Notably, co-occurring sexual and physical IPV has been associated with greater violence severity and lethality threat appraisal (Cole et al., 2005; Dutton et al., 2005). Sexual IPV in combination with both physical IPV and coercive control may be especially brutal, as Molly describes:

> I think that's how he got off. You know I think he got hard from beating me and physical fighting, you know what I mean? And it was a way for him to overpower and

I would just hush sometimes and – the control. It was the control thing. . . . And it seemed like the harder I rebelled the harder he controlled and it always led into sex and I think sex became a way of controlling me.

(Logan et al., 2007, p. 79)

## Global studies

There have been a handful of studies that have examined co-occurring IPV among adult women who were married or cohabiting. In Norway, within a sample of female IPV survivors seeking help, 36% had experienced sexual IPV, almost exclusively in combination with physical and psychological IPV (Vatnar & Bjørkly, 2008). In Bangladesh, 35% of urban women and 46% of rural women reported ever being raped by an intimate partner; for the majority of participants (60–63%), sexual IPV co-occurred with either physical IPV or both physical and emotional IPV, rather than alone (17–31%) (Naved, 2013). In two studies with Pakistani women, recruited at either a hospital or in a large city, lifetime prevalence of sexual IPV ranged from 21–34%, with sexual IPV co-occurring with both physical and psychological/emotional IPV the most common pattern, reported by 50–58% of survivors (Ali et al., 2011; Kapadia, Saleem, & Karim, 2009). Lastly, within a randomly selected sample of pregnant women in Ethiopia, 30% had been raped during their pregnancy by their husband or cohabiting partner, with 56% reporting co-occurring sexual, physical, and psychological IPV (Abate et al., 2016).

## What predicts sexual IPV?

### United States studies

In a mixed methods study of sexual victimization (including sexual IPV) during adolescence, lack of parental supervision or guardianship, inexperience with sex and dating, substance use, social and relationship concerns (e.g., peer pressure), and powerlessness were all noted as contributors to heightened risk of sexual IPV within the sample of young women (76% White, 16% Black, 3% Latina) (Livingston, Hequembourg, Testa, & VanZile-Tamsen, 2007). Kennedy and colleagues (2018b) used multilevel modeling to examine risk factors for sexual IPV across young women's relationships, beginning with their first. The sample was recruited from a university, a two-year community college, and community sites serving low-income young women, and was diverse: 39% Black, 39% White, 10% Latina, 7% biracial, 5% Asian, and 1% Native American. During participants' first relationships, begun when they were just under 15 years old on average, socio-economic status (SES) and age were inversely related to sexual IPV, physical IPV plus coercive control was positively related, and two-year college and community participants had significantly lower sexual IPV than university participants (after controlling for covariates). Two-year college participants' trajectory of sexual IPV increased significantly over the course of relationships, in comparison to university participants' sexual IPV trajectory, which declined significantly. Across relationships, age difference (between participants and their partners) and physical IPV plus coercive control both positively co-varied with sexual IPV. Shondra, a poor African American woman who was HIV+ as a result of sexual IPV, illustrates this age difference dynamic:

He forced me to have sex. If I didn't want it, he'd say I was giving it to someone else. He was real jealous because he was 20 years older and thought I'd go off with someone younger. He'd lock me up and take the keys.

(Lichtenstein, 2005, p. 709)

In contrast, results from a longitudinal study with high school students revealed being depressed or having a friend who had been a victim of IPV – but not SES – as significant predictors of sexual IPV among female participants. (Foshee, Benefield, Ennett, Bauman, & Suchindran, 2004).

Among adult women, data from the National Crime Victimization Survey indicate that older age (age 50+) and household income are inversely related to the odds of sexual IPV, while living alone, rural residency (vs. urban), household crime, and being never married, separated, or divorced (vs. married) are all positively related to sexual IPV (Siddique, 2016). Graham-Bermann and colleagues (2011) found that sexual IPV was significantly associated with physical IPV in conjunction with other adversity (e.g., childhood victimization, serious illness), in comparison to physical IPV alone, within their diverse sample of female community residents (48% White, 37% African American). In a related vein, co-occurring sexual and physical IPV (vs. physical IPV only or no IPV) was associated with childhood sexual abuse, physical victimization, and witnessing IPV in two samples of women (Bonomi et al., 2007; Cole et al., 2005). Finally, in a two-year longitudinal study with a community sample of women aged 18–30 (78% White, 17% African American, 33% in college), being married or cohabiting (vs. being single), Time 1 sexual IPV, additional sexual victimization, and drug use all predicted increased odds of sexual IPV at Time 3, while Time 1 sexual refusal assertiveness predicted decreased odds of sexual IPV at Time 3 (Testa, VanZile-Tamsen, & Livingston, 2007).

## Global studies

Risk factors for sexual IPV have been studied extensively across the globe. In the lone study involving high school students, being bullied, being female, having an older partner, and witnessing IPV in the family were all predictors of sexual IPV within a sample of Norwegian adolescents (Hellevik & Överlien, 2016). After controlling for a variety of SES factors, Kidman (2017) found that child marriage (i.e., a girl marrying before she turned 18) was associated with heightened risk of sexual IPV across 34 low- and middle-income countries. Across multiple countries in Africa (Democratic Republic of Congo, Ethiopia, Ghana, Malawi, Nigeria, Rwanda, and Uganda), Asia (Bangladesh, India, Nepal, and Pakistan), and Eastern Europe (Azerbaijan, Moldova, and Ukraine), as well as the West Bank/Gaza Strip region and Haiti, risk factors for sexual IPV are quite consistent, with a few exceptions. Overall, lower SES, his and her lower education level, his and her reduced employment and income level, his and her history of witnessing IPV in their family of origin, a higher number of children, her lower age and decision-making, his use of coercive control, and his drinking are associated with increased odds of sexual IPV in Africa (Adebowale, 2018; Bazargan-Hejazi et al., 2013; Deribe et al., 2012; Ebrahim & Atteraya, 2019; Issahaku, 2017; Onigbogi et al., 2015; Tlapek, 2015; Umubyeyi et al., 2014; Wandera et al., 2015), in Asia (Ali et al., 2011; Dalal & Lindqvist, 2012; Hadi, 2000; Naved, 2013; Kapadia et al., 2009; Pandey, 2016), in Moldova and Ukraine (Barrett et al., 2012; Ismayilova & El-Bassel, 2013), in the West Bank/Gaza Strip (Haj-Yahia & Clark, 2013), and in Haiti (Gage & Hutchinson, 2006). On a positive note, Hadi (2000) found that women's participation in a micro-credit program reduced the odds of sexual IPV, indicating that anti-poverty approaches aimed at women might be an effective prevention strategy.

## Outcomes associated with sexual IPV

Most of the research in this area has been conducted in the United States, with a few exceptions, so our review is organized by outcome: acknowledgment and labeling; self-blame, shame, and anticipatory stigma; and mental health and health. When global studies are available, we have included them and noted the country or region.

## Acknowledgment and labeling

When a girl or woman has been raped (based on the behavioral definition of being forced to have sexual intercourse), she may or may not acknowledge the experience and label it as a rape or sexual assault. Indeed, a recent meta-analysis found that 60% of rapes among adolescent and adult women were unacknowledged, with college students more likely to resist labeling in comparison to non-college students (Wilson & Miller, 2016). There are many reasons why a survivor would not acknowledge her experience as rape. One key factor is the extent to which her experience conforms to societal notions about "real rape," understood as a violent, one-time traumatic incident perpetrated by a stranger, during which she fought back (Harned, 2005; Johnstone, 2016; Kahn, Jackson, Kully, Badger, & Halvorsen, 2003; Littleton, Axsom, Breit-kopf, & Berenson, 2006; Littleton, Breitkopf, & Berenson, 2008; Logan et al., 2015). Sexual IPV does not conform to this standard, and thus, girls and women who have been raped by their intimate partners may have greater difficulty labeling their experience as rape or assault: in a recent study on sexual assault with young women from community settings (73% White, 27% African American, 7% Latina), participants who had been raped by their spouses or partners were significantly less likely to label their experience as rape, compared to women who had been raped by a non-partner (Jaffe, Steel, DiLillo, Messman-Moore, & Gratz, 2017). Several studies have similarly found that partner-perpetrated rapes are less likely to be acknowledged and labeled (Kahn et al., 2003; Littleton, Axsom, & Grills-Taquechel, 2009; Littleton et al., 2008), though others have revealed no differences in women's acknowledgment by perpetrator type (Fisher, Daigle, Cullen, & Turner, 2003; Littleton et al., 2006).

Girls and women in an ongoing relationship with a partner who is raping them may minimize or deny what is happening because they want to avoid upsetting him, they do not want to acknowledge it to themselves, they see it as part of their role as a girlfriend or wife, or because they are committed to enduring it in order to maintain the relationship. Sarah, an 18-year-old European Canadian who was forced to have sex by her boyfriend, states: "Well, I said, I don't think I used the word 'rape' 'cause I think it would have . . . like sounded harsh to him" (Johnstone, 2016, p. 281). Cultural values such as *machismo* and *marianismo* may also play a role, as illustrated by this Mexican American survivor describing forced sex by her husband as an important sacrifice she made as a wife:

> I think a woman needs to take care of her husband's needs so he can be happy in the relationship so he will not go find other women that are around. As husband and wife, we sometimes need to sacrifice certain things in the relationship for it to function. If not, we can't live together.
>
> (Valdovinos & Mechanic, 2017, p. 336)

Similarly, an IPV survivor named Judith understood sexual IPV as part of her role as a Christian wife: "Lot of times I felt like I had to because I keep going back to that Scripture in the Bible, where it says the wife is supposed to be submissive to her husband". (Logan et al., 2007, p. 78)

Acknowledging and labeling sexual IPV experiences may best be understood as a process that unfolds over time, as women grapple with what happened (rather than avoiding or denying it), disclose to others, leave the relationship, and enter into new relationships (Harned, 2005;

Johnstone, 2016). A college student describes how her previous experience with sexual IPV was unexpectedly influencing her new relationships:

> [A]s I entered into other relationships, it almost haunted me . . . it is hard to even be able to realize that something wrong has happened, until it starts to affect other relationships and parts of life. It can be very difficult and scary.
>
> (Harned, 2005, p. 292)

A Mexican American woman reflects on her new, critical understanding of what she – and others she knew – had experienced:

> As women being with them, we do not call it sexual abuse because we feel we need to satisfy them because we are the wives and we have to satisfy them regardless if we want to or not, so we don't call it sexual abuse. Now that I look back I realize that it was sexual abuse what they would do to us because it was not an intimate relationship that we wanted to have.
>
> (Valdovinos & Mechanic, 2017, p. 337)

## Self-blame, shame, and anticipatory stigma

Adolescent and adult women who experience sexual IPV may blame themselves, feel ashamed, and anticipate that others will judge them harshly or disbelieve them if they share what happened (Kennedy & Prock, 2018). Though these sequelae have been studied extensively by SA researchers and IPV researchers focused on *physical* IPV, they have received limited attention by those examining sexual IPV specifically. In a quantitative study with IPV survivors seeking formal help from LE (45% White, 33% African American, 13% Native American, 7% Latina), women who had experienced sexual IPV along with physical IPV reported significantly higher levels of shame, compared to those with physical IPV only (Messing et al., 2014). Additionally, Vatnar and Bjørkly's (2008) study with Norwegian IPV survivors seeking help revealed that sexual IPV was associated with significantly more shame than psychological IPV. However, Jaffe and colleagues (2017) found that women who had been raped by a partner were less likely to blame themselves in comparison to women who were raped by a non-partner, in part because they were less likely to acknowledge their experience as rape. Qualitative findings reveal that women raped by their partners may blame themselves for their "poor judgment" and failure to protect themselves (Weiss, 2010). Amanda, a young woman attending college, stated: "I often have flashbacks and find myself crying. I feel unsafe and scared. I feel weird and guilty about being raped, therefore, I don't really like telling people about it (i.e., counselors)" (Amar & Alexy, 2005, p. 166). An African American woman who was HIV+ as a result of sexual IPV characterizes herself as weak:

> The guy I was going out with introduced me to drugs. He had me out there selling my body to get all the drugs and stuff for us, you know? He got to beating on me because I didn't want to get out there no more in the streets doing it, and that's when he broke my cheekbone and everything. That's when I got infected by him because he kept forcing me to have sex. I felt bad about myself, weak-minded, you know? Because I got into drugs and prostitution and then I got myself infected.
>
> (Lichtenstein, 2005, p. 707)

Finally, a Mexican American woman describes her self-blame and shame:

> You feel like you are the worst, very bad because you feel abused. It is no longer a rela-
> tionship; it is not pleasing to be with him if you have to satisfy him forcefully because
> you get beaten and you have to comply because of the fear you have. Then you feel
> bad within yourself because you have to take it.
>
> (Valdovinos & Mechanic, 2017, p. 336)

Blaming yourself, feeling ashamed, or anticipating that others will judge, blame, or disbelieve
you can be a powerful barrier to disclosure and attaining help, as well as exacerbate mental
health and health outcomes (Kennedy & Prock, 2018; Weiss, 2010).

## Mental health and health

Among female adolescents in high school in the US, sexual IPV has been linked to mental
health issues such as sadness, hopelessness, suicidality, and suicide attempts, and poor health
outcomes including unhealthy weight control, heavy alcohol use, drug use, fighting, and pregnancy (Kim-Godwin et al., 2009; Silverman et al., 2001; Vagi et al., 2015). One study with
female college students demonstrated an association between sexual IPV and depression, anxiety, and posttraumatic stress (PTSD) symptoms, as well as body shape concerns, substance use,
and school withdrawal (Harned, 2004). A second found that sexual IPV, in combination with
physical and psychological IPV, predicted depression and PTSD symptoms, as well as injuries (Eshelman & Levendosky, 2012). Among adult IPV survivors, researchers have examined
co-occurring sexual and physical IPV, vs. physical IPV only, as a predictor of mental health
and health outcomes: compared to physical IPV only, sexual and physical IPV are linked to
depression, anxiety, PTSD symptoms, suicidal ideation (as mediated by PTSD and depression),
and suicide attempts (Bonomi et al., 2007; Cole et al., 2005; Dutton et al., 2005; McFarlane
et al., 2005b; Weaver et al., 2007). Negative health outcomes include poor health symptoms,
increased daily health limitations, lower quality of life and social functioning, injury, sexually
transmitted infections (STIs), and substance use (Bonomi et al., 2007; Cole et al., 2005; McFarlane et al., 2005a; McFarlane et al., 2005b). Dana, an IPV survivor in recovery, illustrates one
connection between sexual IPV and substance use:

> He knew a little bit about my past. I explained to him that I do have an addiction
> to alcohol and drugs and that I black out easily and I pretty much do anything and
> everything in those blackouts. And I guess that's what really [encouraged] him to try
> to [get] me to go there. So that he could get me to do just what I didn't want to do.
>
> (Logan et al., 2007, p. 82)

Women who are raped repeatedly by partners (who are themselves having unprotected sex
with multiple partners) are at heightened risk of contracting HIV, given that the vaginal tears
and abrasions that women experience during forced sex appear to heighten the risk of infection
(Lichtenstein, 2005). Ilene, a Black woman who was pregnant and HIV+ as a result of sexual
IPV, describes her depression and isolation:

> I became so depressed that I asked him to come back and look after me. That's how
> desperate I was. I took to my bed and cried for three months. It just made me more

dependent on him, you know? And I guess him coming back was just an open door to say, "I'll treat you any way I want to."

(Lichtenstein, 2005, p. 710)

A handful of studies on sexual IPV and related outcomes have been conducted around the world. Beginning with mental health issues, Tiwari and colleagues (2014) used a mixed methods approach and found that sexual IPV predicted depression and PTSD symptoms, after controlling for physical IPV, in a sample of Chinese women residing in Hong Kong. A graduate student in her 30s described her experiences with sexual and physical IPV during her five years of marriage: "Whenever my husband wanted sex, I had to let him have it. Otherwise he would hurt me . . . just like that time when he bit my nipple so badly that I had to go to the hospital" (Tiwari et al., 2014, p. 7). Research in Bangladesh, India, Nepal, and Ethiopia has demonstrated a link between sexual IPV and health outcomes among married or cohabiting women (aged 15–49), including unintended or unwanted pregnancy and childbirth, STIs, and injuries (Acharya, Paudel, & Silwal, 2019; Anand, Unisa, & Singh, 2017; Deribe et al., 2012; Shabnam, 2017; Tiwari et al., 2014). Lastly, in a Canadian study involving women who had been raped and were seeking care from a hospital, sexual IPV was associated with greater violence severity and injury, in comparison to women who were raped by an acquaintance (Stermac, Del Bove, & Addison, 2001).

## Disclosure, help-seeking, and help attainment

Adolescent and adult women who have experienced IPV may disclose what they have experienced, most often to friends and family members, and seek out the attainment of formal help in meeting their needs, including mental health and health services, LE involvement, housing, and legal advice (Bundock, Chan, & Hewitt, 2018; Kennedy et al., 2012; Sabina & Ho, 2014; Sylaska & Edwards, 2014). Unfortunately, empirical research on disclosure and seeking and attaining help related specifically to sexual IPV is very limited: researchers have almost exclusively focused on sexual assault (with sexual IPV obscured) or IPV in general (again, with sexual IPV obscured), predominantly with college or adult samples of women. Kennedy and colleagues examined disclosure of sexual or physical IPV across adolescent abusive relationships within a diverse sample of young women. They found that disclosure of sexual IPV was much less common than disclosure of physical IPV across relationships, and relationships characterized by sexual IPV only (vs. those characterized by physical IPV alone or in combination with sexual IPV) predicted reduced disclosure (Kennedy, Bybee, Adams, Moylan, & Prock, under review). In a study with New Zealand high school students, girls were most likely to disclose emotional abuse (90%), followed by unwanted sexual activity (defined as unwanted kissing, hugging, genital contact, and sex; 54%), and then physical IPV victimization (45%, Jackson et al., 2000).

Among US college students, being more acquainted with the perpetrator was associated with significantly reduced disclosure of sexual assault over time, in comparison to being less acquainted (Orchowski & Gidycz, 2012). Results from the National College Women Sexual Victimization Study revealed that only 2% of female college students who had been raped by a partner reported it to LE (Fisher et al., 2010). Melissa, a 23 year old from Montreal who experienced sexual IPV, illustrates the desire to avoid disclosing, so as not to risk being exposed and potentially blamed: "I would not want to talk about things where the person could judge me or the situations. How could I? It's because I know I'll see the person often, if they judge me" (Fernet, Hébert, Couture, & Brodeur, 2019, p. 46).

Among adult women, rape acknowledgment (which was less likely among those who experienced partner rape vs. other perpetrators) was linked to increased disclosure within a sample of low-income women (51% Latina, 33% White, 12% African American) (Littleton et al., 2008). Results from the National Violence Against Women Survey indicate that sexual IPV in combination with physical IPV, vs. physical IPV alone, predicted reduced odds of seeking help (Flicker et al., 2011). In contrast, Cattaneo and colleagues (2008) drew on data from eight states to examine sexual and physical IPV within a sample of women seeking formal help from various providers (86% White); they found that women who had experienced both forms of IPV (vs. those experiencing only physical IPV) were simultaneously more likely to seek help and more likely to state that they had *not* sought help in the past even though they needed it. In a community sample with women from New England (66% Black, 20% White, 10% Latina), sexual IPV was associated with social support coping as well as negative social reactions upon disclosure (Sullivan, Schroeder, Dudley, & Dixon, 2010). Finally, female IPV survivors in Norway seeking formal help disclosed sexual IPV significantly less than physical or psychological IPV (Vatnar & Bjørkly, 2008).

## Conclusion

Nearly one in ten women (9%) in the United States has experienced sexual IPV in their lifetime (Black et al., 2011); global lifetime estimates range from 3% in Azerbaijan and Ukraine (Ismayilova & El-Bassel, 2013), to 50% in rural Ethiopia (Deribe et al., 2012). Sexual IPV is likely to co-occur with other forms of IPV, including physical and psychological IPV, coercive control, and stalking (Krebs et al., 2011; Vagi et al., 2015; Vatnar & Bjørkly, 2008). Predictors of sexual IPV include lower socioeconomic status, her low age, and his drinking, physical IPV, or coercive control (Dalal & Lindqvist, 2012; Kennedy et al., 2018b). Associated outcomes among girls and women include lack of acknowledgment or labeling of the experience as rape; shame, self-blame, and anticipatory stigma; and mental and physical health problems such as depression and posttraumatic stress disorder symptoms, suicidality, unintended pregnancy and birth, and sexually transmitted infections, including HIV (Acharya et al., 2019; Dutton et al., 2005; Jaffe et al., 2017; Kennedy & Prock, 2018; Lichtenstein, 2005; McFarlane et al., 2005a). Disclosing sexual IPV and seeking and attaining help appears to be less common, in comparison to other forms of IPV, though research in this area is only beginning (Flicker et al., 2011; Kennedy et al., under review).

## Critical findings

- Sexual IPV is relatively common among women, with one in ten US women and 3–50% of women around the globe reporting rape or attempted rape by an intimate partner, though there is great variability across nations.
- Sexual IPV is likely to co-occur with other forms of IPV, such as physical or psychological IPV, coercive control, and stalking.
- Key predictors include lower SES (including education level, income, and employment), her young age at the beginning of the relationship or marriage, and his drinking, physical abuse, and use of coercive control.
- Girls and women who have been raped by their partner may have difficulty acknowledging the experience or labeling it as rape or sexual assault; additionally, they may feel self-blame, shame, and anticipatory stigma.

- Sexual IPV has been linked to a host of negative mental health and health outcomes, such as depression and PTSD symptoms, unintended pregnancy and childbearing, and STIs, including HIV.
- Though research on sexual IPV disclosure, help-seeking, and help attainment is just beginning, it appears that sexual IPV may be associated with reduced levels of disclosure and seeking/attaining help, in comparison to other forms of IPV.

## Implications for policy, practice, and research

- The high rate of co-occurrence of sexual IPV with other forms of IPV means that researchers must take this into account when examining the effects of sexual assault on outcomes: for example, in a study of PTSD among women who have experienced SA (which will automatically include a sizable percentage of women who have experienced sexual IPV, perhaps repeatedly), researchers must be able to disentangle the effects of the sexual assault(s) from the effects of other forms of co-occurring IPV.
- Given the gaps in our knowledge, researchers should qualitatively and quantitatively explore sexual IPV (including predictors, associated outcomes, acknowledgment, self-blame and shame, and disclosure/help attainment) during adolescence as well as among young adults who are not attending four-year universities and colleges.
- Globally, we know very little about acknowledgment and labeling of sexual IPV, or the disclosure and help attainment process; researchers should prioritize these areas.
- Practitioners must proactively assess for sexual IPV along with physical and psychological IPV, especially given that girls and women may be less likely to disclose sexual IPV in comparison to other forms of IPV.
- Prevention and intervention programming for SA and IPV needs to be integrated so sexual IPV – which may be less visible as both a form of SA *and* a form of IPV – can be addressed and prevented, especially among adolescents just beginning to form relationships or enter marriage.
- Health providers may be effective, non-stigmatizing screeners for sexual IPV, among girls and women both in the US and around the globe.
- Given that marriage before the age of 18 is common globally and predicts sexual IPV, and that marital rape is still legal in more than 100 countries, anti-violence activism should center on addressing these at the policy level.
- With lower SES such a strong predictor of sexual IPV, anti-poverty initiatives, especially aimed at women (e.g., micro-credit programs), may be an effective prevention approach.

## References

Abate, B. A., Wossen, B. A., & Degfie, T. T. (2016). Determinants of intimate partner violence during pregnancy among married women in Abay Chomen district, Western Ethiopia: A community based cross sectional study. *BMC Women's Health, 16*, 1–8. doi:10.1186/s12905-016-0294-6

Acharya, K., Paudel, Y. R., & Silwal, P. (2019). Sexual violence as a predictor of unintended pregnancy among married young women: Evidence from the 2016 Nepal demographic and health survey. *BMC Pregnancy and Childbirth, 19*, 1–10. doi:10.1186/s12884-019-2342-3

Adebowale, A. S. (2018). Spousal age difference and associated predictors of intimate partner violence in Nigeria. *BMC Public Health, 18*, 1–15. doi:10.1186/s12889-018-5118-1

Al-Atrushi, H. H., Al-Tawil, N. G., Shabila, N. P., & Al-Hadithi, T. S. (2013). Intimate partner violence against women in the Erbil city of the Kurdistan region, Iraq. *BMC Women's Health, 13*, 1–9. doi:10.1186/1472-6874-13-37

Ali, T. S., Asad, N., Mogren, I., & Krantz, G. (2011). Intimate partner violence in urban Pakistan: Prevalence, frequency, and risk factors. *International Journal of Women's Health*, *3*, 105–115. doi:10.2147/IJWH.S17016

Amar, A. F., & Alexy, E. M. (2005). "Dissed" by dating violence. *Perspectives in Psychiatric Care*, *41*, 162–171. doi:10.1111/j.1744-6163.2005.00032.x

Anand, E., Unisa, S., & Singh, J. (2017). Intimate partner violence and unintended pregnancy among adolescent and young adult married women in South Asia. *Journal of Biosocial Science*, *49*, 206–221. doi:10.1017/S0021932016000286

Bagwell-Gray, M. E., Messing, J. T., & Baldwin-White, A. (2015). Intimate partner sexual violence: A review of terms, definitions, and prevalence. *Trauma, Violence, & Abuse*, *16*, 316–335. doi:10.1177/1524838014557290

Barrett, B. J., Habibov, N., & Chernyak, E. (2012). Factors affecting prevalence and extent of intimate partner violence in Ukraine: Evidence from a nationally representative survey. *Violence Against Women*, *18*, 1147–1176. doi:10.1177/1077801212464387

Basile, K. C. (2002). Prevalence of wife rape and other intimate partner sexual coercion in a nationally representative sample of women. *Violence and Victims*, *17*, 511–524. doi:10.1891/vivi.17.5.511.33717

Bazargan-Hejazi, S., Medeiros, S., Mohammadi, R., Lin, J., & Dalal, K. (2013). Patterns of intimate partner violence: A study of female victims in Malawi. *Journal of Injury & Violence*, *5*, 38–50. doi:10.5249/jivr.v5i1.139

Bennice, J. A., & Resick, P. A. (2003). Marital rape: History, research, and practice. *Trauma, Violence, & Abuse*, *4*, 228–246. doi:10.1177/1524838003252486

Black, M. C., Basile, K. C., Breiding, M. J., Smith, S. G., Walters, M. L., Merrick, M. T., . . . Stevens, M. R. (2011). *The national intimate partner and sexual violence survey (NISVS): 2010 summary report*. Atlanta, GA: National Center for Injury Prevention and Control, Centers for Disease Control and Prevention.

Bonomi, A. E., Anderson, M. L., Rivara, F. P., & Thompson, R. S. (2007). Health outcomes in women with physical and sexual intimate partner violence exposure. *Journal of Women's Health*, *16*, 987–997. doi:10.1089/jwh.2006.0239

Bundock, K., Chan, C., & Hewitt, O. (2018). Adolescents' help-seeking behavior and intentions following adolescent dating violence: A systematic review. *Trauma, Violence, & Abuse*. Advance online publication. doi:10.1177/1524838018770412

Cattaneo, L. B., DeLoveh, H. L. M., & Zweig, J. M. (2008). Sexual assault within intimate partner violence: Impact on helpseeking in a national sample. *Journal of Prevention & Intervention in the Community*, *36*, 137–153. doi:10.1080/10852350802022415

Chillag, K., Guest, G., Bunce, A., Johnson, L., Kilmarx, P. H., & Smith, D. K. (2006). Talking about sex in Botswana: Social desirability bias and possible implications for HIV-prevention research. *African Journal of AIDS Research*, *5*, 123–131. doi:10.2989/16085900609490372

Coker, A. L., Follingstad, D. R., Bush, H. M., & Fisher, B. S. (2016). Are interpersonal violence rates higher among young women in college compared to those never attending college? *Journal of Interpersonal Violence*, *31*, 1413–1429. doi:10.1177/0886260514567958

Cole, J., Logan, T. K., & Shannon, L. (2005). Intimate sexual victimization among women with protective orders: Types and associations of physical and mental health problems. *Violence and Victims*, *20*, 695–715. doi:10.1891/088667005780927430

Collins, P. H., & Bilge, S. (2016). *Intersectionality*. Malden, MA: Polity Press.

Crenshaw, K. (1991). Mapping the margins: Intersectionality, identity politics, and violence against women of color. *Stanford Law Review*, *43*, 1241–1299. doi:10.2307/1229039

Dalal, K., & Lindqvist, K. (2012). A national study of the prevalence and correlates of domestic violence among women in India. *Asia-Pacific Journal of Public Health*, *24*, 265–277. doi:10.1177/1010539510384499

Decker, M. R., Latimore, A. D., Yasutake, S., Haviland, M., Ahmed, S., Blum, R. W., . . . Astone, N. M. (2015). Gender-based violence against adolescent and young adult women in low- and middle-income countries. *Journal of Adolescent Health*, *56*, 188–196. doi:10.1016/j.jadohealth.2014.09.003

Deribe, K. Beyene, B. K., Tolla, A., Memiah, P., Biadgilign, S., & Amberbir, A. (2012). Magnitude and correlates of intimate partner violence against women and its outcome in southwest Ethiopia. *PLoS One*, *7*, e36189. doi:10.1371/journal.pone.0036189

Dutton, M. A., Kaltman, S., Goodman, L. A., Weinfurt, K., & Vankos, N. (2005). Patterns of intimate partner violence: Correlates and outcomes. *Violence and Victims*, *20*, 483–497. doi:10.1891/088667005780927430

Ebrahim, N. B., & Atteraya, M. S. (2019). Women's household decision-making and intimate partner violence in Ethiopia. *Academic Journal of Interdisciplinary Studies, 8*, 285–292. doi:10.2478/ajis-2019-0041

Eshelman, L., & Levendosky, A. A. (2012). Dating violence: Mental health consequences based on type of abuse. *Violence and Victims, 27*, 215–228. doi:10.1891/0886-6708.27.2.215

Farrokh-Eslamlou, H., Oshnouei, S., & Haghighi, N. (2014). Intimate partner violence during pregnancy in Urmia, Iran in 2012. *Journal of Forensic and Legal Medicine, 24*, 28–32. doi:10.1016/j.jflm.2014.03.007

Fernet, M., Hébert, M., Couture, S., & Brodeur, G. (2019). Meeting the needs of adolescent and emerging adult victims of sexual violence in their romantic relationships: A mixed-methods study exploring barriers to help-seeking. *Child Abuse & Neglect, 91*, 41–51. doi:10.1016/j.chiabu.2019.01.019

Fisher, B. S., Daigle, L. E., & Cullen, F. T. (2010). *Unsafe in the ivory tower: The sexual victimization of college women.* Thousand Oaks, CA: Sage.

Fisher, B. S., Daigle, L. E., Cullen, F. T., & Turner, M. G. (2003). Acknowledging sexual victimization as rape: Results from a national-level study. *Justice Quarterly, 20*, 535–574. doi:10.1080/07418820300095611

Flicker, S. M., Cerulli, C., Zhao, X., Tang, W., Watts, A., Xia, Y., & Talbot, N. L. (2011). Concomitant forms of abuse and help-seeking behavior among White, African American, and Latina women who experience intimate partner violence. *Violence Against Women, 17*, 1067–1085. doi:10.1177/1077801211414846

Foshee, V. A., Benefield, T. S., Ennett, S. T., Bauman, K. E., & Suchindran, C. (2004). Longitudinal predictors of serious physical and sexual dating violence victimization during adolescence. *Preventive Medicine, 39*, 1007–1016. doi:10.1016/j.ypmed.2004.04.014

Gage, A. J., & Hutchinson, P. L. (2006). Power, control, and intimate partner sexual violence in Haiti. *Archives of Sexual Behavior, 35*, 11–24. doi:10.1007/s10508-006-8991-0

Graham-Bermann, S., Sularz, A. R., & Howell, K. H. (2011). Additional adverse events among women exposed to intimate partner violence: Frequency and impact. *Psychology of Violence, 1*, 136–149. doi:10.1037/a0022975

Hadi, A. (2000). Prevalence and correlates of the risk of marital sexual violence in Bangladesh. *Journal of Interpersonal Violence, 15*, 787–805. doi:10.1177/088626000015008001

Haj-Yahia, M. M., & Clark, C. J. (2013). Intimate partner violence in the occupied Palestinian territory: Prevalence and risk factors. *Journal of Family Violence, 28*, 797–809. doi:10.1007/s10896-013-9549-2

Hamby, S. L., & Koss, M. P. (2003). Shades of gray: A qualitative study of terms used in the measurement of sexual victimization. *Psychology of Women Quarterly, 27*, 243–255. doi:10.1111/1471-6402.00104

Hamby, S. L., & Turner, H. (2013). Measuring teen dating violence in males and females: Insights from the national survey of children's exposure to violence. *Psychology of Violence, 3*, 323–339. doi:10.1037/a0029706

Hancock, A. (2016). *Intersectionality: An intellectual history.* New York, NY: Oxford University Press.

Harned, M. S. (2004). Does it matter what you call it? The relationship between labeling unwanted sexual experiences and distress. *Journal of Consulting and Clinical Psychology, 72*, 1090–1099. doi:10.1037/0022-006X.72.6.1090

Harned, M. S. (2005). Understanding women's labeling of unwanted sexual experiences with dating partners. *Violence Against Women, 11*, 374–413. doi:10/1177/10778012042772240

Hellevik, P., & Överlien, C. (2016). Teenage intimate partner violence: Factors associated with victimization among Norwegian youths. *Scandinavian Journal of Public Health, 44*, 702–708. doi:10.1177/1403494816657264

Hlavka, H. R. (2014). Normalizing sexual violence: Young women account for harassment and abuse. *Gender & Society, 28*, 337–358. doi:10.1177/089124526468

Ismayilova, L., & El-Bassel, N. (2013). Prevalence and correlates of intimate partner violence by type and severity: Population-based studies in Azerbaijan, Moldova, and Ukraine. *Journal of Interpersonal Violence, 28*, 2521–2556. doi:10.1177/0886260513479026

Issahaku, P. A. (2017). Correlates of intimate partner violence in Ghana. *SAGE Open, 7*, 1–14. doi:10.1177/2158244017709861

Jackson, S. M., Cram, F., & Seymour, F. W. (2000). Violence and sexual coercion in high school students' dating relationships. *Journal of Family Violence, 15*, 23–36. doi:10.1023/A:1007545302987

Jaffe, A. E., Steel, A. L., DiLillo, D., Messman-Moore, T. L., & Gratz, K. L. (2017). Characterizing sexual violence in intimate relationships: An examination of blame attributions and rape acknowledgment. *Journal of Interpersonal Violence.* Advance online publication. doi:10.1177/0886260517726972

Jayasuriya, V., Wijewardena, K., & Axemo, P. (2011). Intimate partner violence against women in the capital province of Sri Lanka: Prevalence, risk factors, and help seeking. *Violence Against Women, 17*, 1086–1102. doi:10.1177/1077801211417151

Johnstone, D. J. (2016). A listening guide analysis of women's experiences of unacknowledged rape. *Psychology of Women Quarterly, 40*, 275–289. doi:10.1177/0361684315624460

Kahn, A. S., Jackson, J., Kully, C., Badger, K., & Halvorsen, J. (2003). Calling it rape: Differences in experiences of women who do or do not label their sexual assault as rape. *Psychology of Women Quarterly, 27*, 233–242. doi:10.1111/1471-6402.00103

Kapadia, M. Z., Saleem, S., & Karim, M. S. (2009). The hidden figure: Sexual intimate partner violence among Pakistani women. *European Journal of Public Health, 20*, 164–168. doi:10.1093/eurpub/ckp110

Kennedy, A. C., Adams, A., Bybee, D., Campbell, R., Kubiak, S. P., & Sullivan, C. (2012). A model of sexually and physically victimized women's process of attaining effective formal help over time: The role of social location, context, and intervention. *American Journal of Community Psychology, 50*, 217–228. doi:10.1007/s10464-012-9494-x

Kennedy, A. C., Bybee, D., Adams, A. E., Moylan, C. A., & Prock, K. A. (under review). Social location and situational predictors of young women's disclosure of physical and sexual intimate partner violence victimization. Manuscript submitted for review.

Kennedy, A. C., Bybee, D., McCauley, H. L., & Prock, K. A. (2018a). Young women's intimate partner violence victimization patterns across multiple relationships. *Psychology of Women Quarterly, 42*, 430–444. doi:10.1177/0361684318795880

Kennedy, A. C., Bybee, D., Moylan, C. A., McCauley, H. L., & Prock, K. A. (2018b). Predictors of sexual violence across young women's relationship histories. *Journal of Interpersonal Violence*. Advance online publication. doi:10.1177/0886260518811439

Kennedy, A. C., Meier, E., & Prock, K. A. (under review). A qualitative study of young women's abusive first relationships: What factors shape their process of disclosure? Manuscript submitted for review.

Kennedy, A. C., & Prock, K. A. (2018). "I still feel like I am not normal": A review of the role of stigma and stigmatization among female survivors of child sexual abuse, sexual assault, and intimate partner violence. *Trauma, Violence, & Abuse, 19*, 512–527. doi:10.1177/1524838016673601

Kidman, R. (2017). Child marriage and intimate partner violence: A comparative study of 34 countries. *International Journal of Epidemiology, 46*, 662–675. doi:10.1093/ije/dyw225

Kim-Godwin, Y. S., Clements, C., McCuiston, A. M., & Fox, J. A. (2009). Dating violence among high school students in southeastern North Carolina. *Journal of School Nursing, 25*, 141–151. doi:10.1177/1059840508330679

Krebs, C., Breiding, M. J., Browne, A., & Warner, T. (2011). The association between different types of intimate partner violence experienced by women. *Journal of Family Violence, 26*, 487–500. doi:10.1007/s10896-011-9383-3

Lichtenstein, B. (2005). Domestic violence, sexual ownership, and HIV risk in women in the American deep south. *Social Science & Medicine, 60*, 701–714. doi:10.1016/j.socscimed.2004.06.021

Littleton, H. L., Axsom, D., Breitkopf, C. R., & Berenson, A. (2006). Rape acknowledgment and postassault experiences: How acknowledgment status relates to disclosure, coping, worldview, and reactions received from others. *Violence and Victims, 21*, 761–778. doi:10.1891/0886-6708.21.6.761

Littleton, H. L., Axsom, D., & Grills-Taquechel. (2009). Sexual assault victims' acknowledgment status and revictimization risk. *Psychology of Women Quarterly, 33*, 34–42. doi:10.1111/j.1471-6402.2008.01472.x

Littleton, H. L., Breitkopf, C. R., & Berenson, A. (2008). Beyond the campus: Unacknowledged rape among low-income women. *Violence Against Women, 14*, 269–286. doi:10.1177/1077801207313733

Livingston, J. A., Hequembourg, A., Testa, M., & VanZile-Tamsen, C. (2007). Unique aspects of adolescent sexual victimization experiences. *Psychology of Women Quarterly, 31*, 331–343. doi:10.1111/j.1471-6402.2007.00383.x

Logan, T. K., Cole, J., & Shannon, L. (2007). A mixed-methods examination of sexual coercion and degradation among women in violent relationships who do and do not report forced sex. *Violence and Victims, 22*, 71–94. doi:10.1891/088667007780482874

Logan, T. K., Walker, R., & Cole, J. (2015). Silenced suffering: The need for a better understanding of partner sexual violence. *Trauma, Violence, & Abuse, 16*, 111–135. doi:10.1177/1524838013517560

McFarlane, J., Malecha, A., Gist, J., Watson, K., Batten, E., Hall, I., & Smith, S. (2005b). Intimate partner sexual assault against women and associated victim substance use, suicidality, and risk factors for femicide. *Issues in Mental Health Nursing, 26*, 953–967. doi:10.1080/01612840500248262

McFarlane, J., Malecha, A., Watson, K., Gist, J., Batten, E., Hall, I., & Smith, S. (2005a). Intimate partner sexual assault against women: Frequency, health consequences, and treatment outcomes. *Obstetrics & Gynecology, 105,* 99–108. doi:10.1097/01.AOG.0000146641.98665.b6

Messing, J. T., Thaller, J., & Bagwell, M. (2014). Factors related to sexual abuse and forced sex in a sample of women experiencing police-involved intimate partner violence. *Health & Social Work, 39,* 181–191. doi:10.1093/hsw/hlu026

Montemurro, B., Bartasavich, J., & Wintermute, L. (2015). Let's (not) talk about sex: The gender of sexual discourse. *Sexuality & Culture, 19,* 139–156. doi:10.1007/s12119-014-9250-5

Naved, R. T. (2013). Sexual violence towards married women in Bangladesh. *Archives of Sexual Behavior, 42,* 595–602. doi:10.1007/s10508-012-0045-1

Ogland, E. G., Xu, X., Bartkowski, J. P., & Ogland, C. P. (2014). Intimate partner violence against married women in Uganda. *Journal of Family Violence, 29,* 869–879. doi:10.1007/s10896-014-9640-3

Onigbogi, M. O., Odeyemi, K. A., & Onigbogi, O. O. (2015). Prevalence and factors associated with intimate partner violence among married women in an urban community in Lagos State, Nigeria. *African Journal of Reproductive Health, 19,* 91–100.

Orchowski, L. M., & Gidycz, C. A. (2012). To whom do college women confide following sexual assault? A prospective study of predictors of sexual assault disclosure and social reactions. *Violence Against Women, 18,* 264–288. doi:10.1177/1077801212442917

Pandey, S. (2016). Physical or sexual violence against women of childbearing age within marriage in Nepal: Prevalence, causes, and prevention strategies. *International Social Work, 59,* 803–820. doi:10.1177/0020872814537857

Sabina, C., & Ho, L. Y. (2014). Campus and college victim responses to sexual assault and dating violence: Disclosure, service utilization, and service provision. *Trauma, Violence, & Abuse, 15,* 210–226. doi:10.1177/1524838014521322

Shabnam, S. (2017). Sexually transmitted infections and spousal violence: The experience of married women in India. *Indian Journal of Gender Studies, 24,* 24–46. doi:10.1177/0971521516678530

Siddique, J. A. (2016). Age, marital status, and risk of sexual victimization: Similarities and differences across victim-offender relationships. *Journal of Interpersonal Violence, 31,* 2556–2575. doi:10.1177/0886260515579507

Silverman, J. G., Raj, A., Mucci, L. A., & Hathaway, J. E. (2001). Dating violence against adolescent girls and associated substance use, unhealthy weight control, sexual risk behavior, pregnancy, and suicidality. *JAMA, 286,* 572–579. doi:10.1001/jama.286.5.572

Smith, P. H., White, J. W., & Holland, L. J. (2003). A longitudinal perspective on dating violence among adolescent and college-age women. *American Journal of Public Health, 93,* 1104–1109. doi:10.2105/AJPH.93.7.1104

Sokoloff, N. J. (Ed.). (2005). *Domestic violence at the margins: Readings on race, class, gender, and culture.* New Brunswick, NJ: Rutgers University Press.

Stanley, N., Barter, C., Wood, M., Aghtaie, N., Larkins, C., Lanau, A., & Överlien, C. (2018). Pornography, sexual coercion and abuse and sexting in young people's intimate relationships: A European study. *Journal of Interpersonal Violence, 33,* 2919–2944. doi:10.1177/0886260516633204

Stermac, L., Del Bove, G., & Addison, M. (2001). Violence, injury, and presentation patterns in spousal sexual assaults. *Violence Against Women, 7,* 1218–1233. doi:10.1177/10778010122183838

Sullivan, T. P., Schroeder, J. A., Dudley, D. N., & Dixon, J. M. (2010). Do differing types of victimization and coping strategies influence the type of social reactions experienced by current victims of intimate partner violence? *Violence Against Women, 16,* 638–657. doi:10.1177/1077801210370027

Sylaska, K. M., & Edwards, K. M. (2014). Disclosure of intimate partner violence to informal social support network members: A review of the literature. *Trauma, Violence, & Abuse, 15,* 3–21. doi:10.1177/152483801349335

Taillieu, T. L., & Brownridge, D. A. (2010). Violence against pregnant women: Prevalence, patterns, risk factors, theories, and directions for future research. *Aggression and Violent Behavior, 15,* 14–35. doi:10.1016/j.avb.2009.07.013

Tang, C. S., & Lai, B. P. (2008). A review of empirical literature on the prevalence and risk markers of male-on-female intimate partner violence in contemporary China, 1987–2006. *Aggression and Violent Behavior, 13,* 10–28. doi:10.1016/j.avb.2007.06.001

Temple, J. R., Weston, R., Rodriguez, B. F., & Marshall, L. L. (2007). Differing effects of partner and non-partner sexual assault on women's health. *Violence Against Women, 13,* 285–297. doi:10.1177/1077801206297437

Testa, M., VanZile-Tamsen, C., & Livingston, J. A. (2007). Prospective prediction of women's sexual victimization by intimate and nonintimate male perpetrators. *Journal of Consulting and Clinical Psychology*, *75*, 52–60. doi:10.1037/0022-006X.75.1.52

Tiwari, A., Cheung, D. S. T., Chan, K. L., Fong, D. Y. T., Yan, E. C. W., Lam, G. L. L., & Tang, D. H. M. (2014). Intimate partner sexual aggression against Chinese women: A mixed methods study. *BMC Women's Health*, *14*, 1–10. doi:10.1186/1472-6874-14-70

Tlapek, S. M. (2015). Women's status and intimate partner violence in the Democratic Republic of Congo. *Journal of Interpersonal Violence*, *30*, 2526–2540. doi:10.1177/0886260514553118

Umana, J. E., Fawole, O. I., & Adeoye, I. A. (2014). Prevalence and correlates of intimate partner violence towards female students of the University of Ibadan, Nigeria. *BMC Women's Health*, *14*, 1–8. doi:10.1186/1472-6874-14-131

Umubyeyi, A., Mogren, I., Ntaganira, J., & Krantz, G. (2014). Women are considerably more exposed to intimate partner violence than men in Rwanda: Results from a population-based, cross-sectional study. *BMC Women's Health*, *14*, 1–12. doi:10.1186/1472-6874-14-99

Vagi, K. J., Olsen, E. O., Basile, K. C., & Vivolo-Kantor, A. M. (2015). Teen dating violence (physical and sexual) among US high school students: Findings from the 2013 National Youth Risk Behavior Survey. *JAMA Pediatrics*, *169*, 474–482. doi:10.1001/jamapediatrics.2014.3577

Valdovinos, M. G., & Mechanic, M. B. (2017). Sexual coercion in marriage: Narrative accounts of abused Mexican-American women. *Journal of Ethnic & Cultural Diversity in Social Work*, *26*, 326–345. doi:10.1080/15313204.2017.1300437

Vatnar, S. K. B., & Bjørkly, S. (2008). An interactional perspective of intimate partner violence: An in-depth semi-structured interview of a representative sample of help-seeking women. *Journal of Family Violence*, *23*, 265–279. doi:10.1007/s10896-007-9150-7

Walker, K., & Sleath, E. (2017). A systematic review of the current knowledge regarding revenge pornography and non-consensual sharing of sexually explicit media. *Aggression and Violent Behavior*, *36*, 9–24. doi:10.1016/j.avb.2017.06.010

Wandera, S. O., Kwagala, B., Ndugga, P., & Kabagenyi, A. (2015). Partners' controlling behaviors and intimate partner sexual violence among married women in Uganda. *BMC Public Health*, *15*, 1–9. doi:10.1186/s12889-015-1564-1

Weaver, T. I., Allen, J. A., Hopper, E., Maglione, M. L., McLaughlin, D., McCullough, M. A., . . . Brewer, T. (2007). Mediators of suicidal ideation within a shelter sample of raped and battered women. *Health Care for Women International*, *28*, 478–489. doi:10.1080/07399330701226453

Weiss, K. G. (2010). Too ashamed to report: Deconstructing the shame of sexual victimization. *Feminist Criminology*, *5*, 286–310. doi:10.1177/1557085110376343

Wilson, L. C., & Miller, K. E. (2016). Meta-analysis of the prevalence of unacknowledged rape. *Trauma, Violence, & Abuse*, *17*, 149–159. doi:10.1177/1524838015576391

# 16

# DOMESTIC VIOLENCE AND ABUSE WITHIN MALE SAME-SEX RELATIONSHIPS

*Ada R. Miltz, Ana Maria Buller and Loraine J. Bacchus*

## Introduction

Domestic violence and abuse within intimate relationships, also known as intimate partner violence (IPV), affects individuals of all sexual identities. Sexual minorities include individuals who identify as monosexual (gay/homosexual) or plurisexual (bisexual, pansexual, fluid, queer, etc.) (Galupo, Davis, Grynkiewicz, & Mitchell, 2014). The definition of IPV for sexual minorities is the same as that for the heterosexual majority: physical, sexual, or psychological harm by a current or former partner or spouse (CDC, 2016). IPV may be experienced as a victim or perpetrator, or as both, often referred to as reciprocal IPV (Melander, Noel, & Tyler, 2010). There are factors unique to a sexual minority status that may increase the risk of experiencing and perpetrating IPV, and reduce help-seeking for IPV. This forms the rationale for separating out sexual minority men from their heterosexual counterparts in this chapter.

Historically, IPV was not acknowledged among sexual minorities for whom same-sex relationships were not accorded legal recognition, a practice that today persists in some countries. In the US, following a period of greater visibility of gay neighbourhoods and communities in the mid- to late '80s, anti-gay violence programmes that were originally designed to respond to hate crimes also began to respond to reported incidences of IPV (Herek & Sims, 2008). Due to the concurrency of these events with the emergence of the HIV epidemic, which placed the lives of sexual minority men at the forefront of the medical and social research agenda, IPV within male same-sex couples and its impact on men's health was for the first time widely recognised. Around this time, the term men who have sex with men, with the abbreviation MSM, was coined to acknowledge that behaviours not identities conferred risk for HIV (Young & Meyer, 2005). MSM includes gay and bisexual (plurisexual) identified men, heterosexual identified men who have sex with men, male sex workers and men who have sex with men in all male settings such as prisons. Scholarship on sexual minority men is predominantly based on this broader category of MSM. The term GBMSM (gay, bisexual and other men who have sex with men) will be used when reviewing research throughout this chapter. This is in order to acknowledge that the vast majority of MSM participants identify as gay, and to a lesser extent as bisexual, and may engage in long-term committed relationships with men. Today there is a growing body of research reporting the prevalence of IPV victimisation, and to a lesser extent IPV perpetration, among samples of GBMSM, although the majority of studies remain within the US context. Evidence suggests that the prevalence of IPV among GBMSM is higher than that among men in opposite-sex partnerships, and as high as or higher than that among women in opposite-sex partnerships (Goldberg & Meyer, 2013; Tjaden, Thoennes, & Allison, 1999).

One aspect of the new medical and social research agenda in the '80s was the investigation of the impact of sexual minority status itself on health. This was in order to assess the profound burden of HIV in these communities. The most widely used theoretical framework to culminate from this work is Meyer's minority stress theory (Meyer, 1995). Meyer's model describes the psychosocial consequences of being in continual conflict with a discriminatory social environment. Perpetual negative feedback from others is thought to lead to a process of self-stigmatisation termed internalised homophobia, whereby negative antigay social values/attitudes are directed towards the self. Internalised homophobia often results in deep conflict and poor self-regard with negative consequences such as pervasive expectations of rejection in one's life and concealment of one's identity. Concealment adds to mental distress by disallowing individuals to affiliate with people of the same sexual identity. Evidence is accumulating that suggests that internalised homophobia is strongly associated with increased risk of IPV perpetration and IPV victimisation among GBMSM (Bartholomew, Regan, Oram, & White, 2008; Finneran, Chard, Sineath, Sullivan, & Stephenson, 2012; Finneran & Stephenson, 2014; Miltz et al., 2019; Stephenson & Finneran, 2016; Suarez et al., 2018). A large number of studies have also found that experiences of IPV are associated with increased sexual risk-taking and HIV infection among GBMSM (Beymer et al., 2017; Buller, Devries, Howard, & Bacchus, 2014; Davis et al., 2015; Duncan et al., 2018; Finneran & Stephenson, 2014; Liu et al., 2018; Tomori et al., 2018; H. Y. Wang et al., 2018; Zalla, Herce, Edwards, Michel, & Weir, 2019).

Sexual minority men are not only subject to social norms surrounding masculinity that impinge on men's capacity to disclose experiences of victimisation, but also to heteronormative discourse that results in the downplaying of violence between men and to homophobic discrimination by health care providers (Huntley et al., 2019; Rolle, Giardina, Caldarera, Gerino, & Brustia, 2018). These factors form additional and profound obstacles to seeking help for IPV. In this context, there is a severe lack of data on the effectiveness of interventions to prevent/reduce IPV among sexual minority men. What works for men in same-sex relationships remains unclear.

The overall aim of this chapter is to present the evidence that IPV among sexual minority men may be a relatively common experience and that factors unique to a sexual minority status may also lead to IPV and form substantial barriers to seeking help. The specific objectives are to present among sexual minority men: (1) prevalence estimates of IPV, (2) factors associated with IPV within an ecological framework, (3) the association of IPV with substance use, depression, sexual risk behaviour, and HIV, (4) help-seeking behaviour among those who experience IPV, (5) evidence for responding to IPV and (6) the challenges to researching and responding to IPV, and key debates.

## Analysing the data on IPV among GBMSM

The terms IPV and domestic violence and abuse have been used interchangeably in the literature. In this chapter, the term IPV will be used across studies. Measures of IPV may also differ across research studies, for instance some measures capture experiences of stalking behaviours while others do not. This chapter presents a summary of the literature, thus all experiences of IPV captured on survey questionnaires are broadly compared across studies, according to recall period, as physical, sexual and/or psychological IPV victimisation or perpetration. For instance, stalking would be classified as psychological IPV and its prevalence compared to data from other

Ada R. Miltz et al.

studies that investigated stalking and/or other forms of psychological IPV. Finally, the studies reviewed in this chapter deal with cis-gender males whose gender identity is the same as their biological sex assigned at birth.

## Prevalence of IPV among sexual minority men

There is no definitive way of identifying all GBMSM members of a population. There is no GBMSM population list to recruit from such that random sampling would result in a representative sample. Therefore, it is difficult to produce valid estimates of IPV prevalence for the GBMSM population as a whole. Six general population-based studies, nationally or regionally representative surveys, have presented the prevalence of IPV among a sub-sample of GBMSM participants. These studies were conducted in the US or Canada. Comparison across studies is complicated by inter-city differences, varying socio-demographic profiles of samples and/or differing measures of IPV. For GBMSM participants, the prevalence of any (physical, psychological and/or sexual) lifetime IPV victimisation varied from 15.4% (95% confidence interval [CI]: 10.9%, 19.9%) (Tjaden et al., 1999) to 79.0% (95% CI: 71.6%, 85.3%) for gay men and 83.3% (95% CI: 76.1%, 88.8%) for bisexual men (M. L. Walters, Chen, & Breiding, 2013). IPV perpetration was asked about in one study. The prevalence of perpetrating physical IPV was 38.2% (95% CI: 31.2%, 45.6%) and psychological IPV was 96.8% (95% CI: 93.1%, 98.8%) over one's lifetime (Bartholomew et al., 2008). With the exception of one study that included in the sampling frame neighbourhoods known to be of high sexual minority residential density (resulting in 2674 GBMSM participants) (Paul, Catania, Pollack, & Stall, 2001; Stall et al., 2003), the sample sizes of GBMSM in the remaining studies were very small (≤415) (Bartholomew et al., 2008; Goldberg & Meyer, 2013; Hughes, McCabe, Wilsnack, West, & Boyd, 2010; Tjaden et al., 1999; M. L. Walters et al., 2013). A small sample size may undermine the validity of prevalence estimates, as there is a greater potential for sampling error.

In most studies related to IPV within male same-sex relationships, researchers identify a location in which large numbers of GBMSM are conveniently available for recruitment. A common approach is the recruitment of men who have contact with sexual health services. Another approach is to recruit men from gay cafes, bars, clubs, saunas and other venues on the gay scene, or from events/venues associated with sexual minority communities. Advertisement online provides another common way of recruiting GBMSM to participate in health research.

In order to synthesise findings on IPV among GBMSM and produce more precise prevalence estimates, and associations of IPV with health conditions and risky behaviour, a systematic review and meta-analysis was conducted (Buller, Devries, et al., 2014). The review included studies published up to November 2013. Prevalence of any lifetime IPV victimisation was reported in six US studies of GBMSM recruited from gay venues/events, with 3355 participants in total (Feldman, Diaz, Ream, & El-Bassel, 2007; Houston & McKirnan, 2007; Koblin et al., 2006; Mustanski, Garofalo, Herrick, & Donenberg, 2007; Nieves-Rosa, Carballo Dieguez, & Dolezal, 2000; C. F. Wong, Weiss, Ayala, & Kipke, 2010). This includes two samples of Latino men (Feldman et al., 2007; Nieves-Rosa et al., 2000) and three samples of young men (Koblin et al., 2006; Mustanski et al., 2007; C. F. Wong et al., 2010). Estimates ranged from 32% (N=817 GBMSM (Houston & McKirnan, 2007)) to 82% (N=526 GBMSM (C. F. Wong et al., 2010)). The pooled prevalence was 48% (95% CI: 31.23%, 64.99%). Although seven studies investigated the prevalence of IPV perpetration, each reported different types of IPV and utilised different recall periods, prohibiting a meta-analysis of prevalence estimates.

The database PubMed was searched in order to identity relevant studies published since 2014 (up to September 2020), see Appendix table. The reference lists of eligible studies were also searched and further papers were identified via consultation with experts in the field. Thirty-nine studies of IPV in convenience samples of GBMSM were identified that have been conducted since the meta-analysis reported by Buller, Devries, Howard, & Bacchus (2014). Findings are presented by recruitment site/strategy in Table 16.1. For nine of the 17 studies that reported on this measure, the prevalence of any lifetime IPV victimisation fell within the confidence interval of the pooled meta-analysis estimate (95% CI: 31.23%, 64.99%). For the remaining eight studies, the prevalence was mostly between 10% and 20%. In the five studies that recruited GBMSM from gay venues/events, the prevalence of IPV was similar to the pooled estimate. However, there was no obvious pattern across recent studies whereby a prevalence lower than the pooled estimate was observed in samples that recruited men from sexual health clinics or online, nor was this the case by country, study period, sample size or socio-demographic profile. Differing IPV measures may possibly explain the differences in prevalence observed. The prevalence of IPV perpetration has been reported in a small number of recent studies with estimates of any lifetime IPV perpetration ranging from 16.3% (Bacchus et al., 2017) to 35.1% (Wu et al., 2015, Table 16.1).

Convenience sampling only reaches men who visit specific venues/online sites and is more likely to recruit those who are regular users. Therefore, estimates of IPV prevalence from convenience samples may only be truly generalisable to that specific GBMSM population group (i.e. to men visiting venues on the gay scene) (Bailey & Handu, 2013).

## Risk factors for IPV among sexual minority men

Although all relationships in which violence and abuse is present are unique, it is important to understand IPV within a comprehensive framework that considers all possible risk factors and social systems, as well as their intersections. Experiences of abuse in childhood, particularly childhood sexual abuse (CSA), insecure attachments formed with primary caregivers, and socio-cultural norms that perpetuate the subjugation of certain groups, may play an important role in the manifestation of both IPV victimisation and IPV perpetration (Fang & Corso, 2007; Herek & Sims, 2008; Jennings, Richards, Tomsich, & Gover, 2015; C. L. Whitfield, Anda, Dube, & Felitti, 2003). In an ecological framework, it is the interaction between factors at the individual, relationship, community and/or societal level that is thought to predict vulnerability towards IPV (Heise, 1998; WHO, 2019). This section is focused on findings published after the meta-analysis of IPV correlates in studies published up to November 2013. Table 16.2 presents recent findings (unadjusted and adjusted associations with IPV) according to the level of each risk factor: individual (age, ethnicity, socio-economic factors, abuse in childhood and HIV status), relationship, community or societal. Pooled meta-analysis findings from the Buller et al. review are presented and discussed in the next section of this chapter in the context of the health-related and behavioural consequences of IPV. This includes the relationship between IPV and substance use.

There is consistent evidence that younger GBMSM, particularly men aged 18–25 years, are more likely to experience and perpetrate IPV (see Table 16.2). There is some evidence to suggest that Black, Asian and minority ethnic migrants and men reporting lower levels of educational attainment are more likely to have been a victim of IPV, including after adjusting for other socio-demographic factors. Findings from studies published prior to 2014 are commensurate; GBMSM of Black ethnicity in South Africa and mixed ethnicity in Brazil were more likely to report IPV victimisation compared to white GBMSM, adjusting for age, sexual orientation, education and HIV status (Finneran et al., 2012). One recent study found that men who reported unstable housing were more likely to

Table 16.1 Prevalence of IPV measures in studies of GBMSM published since 2014, by recruitment site

| Study | Location | Sample size | Measure of IPV | Prevalence of IPV % (95% CI) |
|---|---|---|---|---|
| **Participants recruited from sexual health clinics** | | | | |
| Cross-sectional study (Bacchus et al., 2017), 2010–2011 | London | N=532 gay/bisexual men | Lifetime physical/psychological/sexual IPV victimisation<br>Past year physical/psychological/sexual IPV victimisation<br>Lifetime physical/psychological/sexual IPV perpetration<br>Past year physical/psychological/sexual IPV perpetration | 33.9% (29.4%, 37.9%)<br>9.4% (7.1%, 12.2%)<br>16.3% (13.0%, 19.8%)<br>5.7% (3.8%, 8.0%) |
| The PROUD trial (Miltz et al., 2019), 2012–2014 (baseline) – two years follow-up | England | N=540 at baseline<br>N=410 at month-12<br>N=333 at month-24 (data on IPV collected at follow-ups only) | Lifetime physical/psychological/sexual IPV victimisation<br>Past year physical/psychological/sexual IPV victimisation<br>Lifetime physical/psychological/sexual IPV perpetration<br>Past year physical/psychological/sexual IPV perpetration | At 12-month:<br>44.9% (40.1%, 49.7%)<br>15.6% (12.4%, 19.5%)<br>19.5% (15.9%, 23.7%)<br>7.8% (5.6%, 10.8%) |
| Longitudinal study (Beymer et al., 2017; Beymer et al., 2016), 2009–2015 | US | N=1771 HIV-negative GBMSM (2011)<br>N=176 HIV-positive GBMSM (2011)<br>N=2944 HIV-negative Latino GBMSM<br>N=167 HIV-positive Latino GBMSM | Lifetime physical/psychological/sexual IPV victimisation<br>Lifetime physical/psychological/sexual IPV victimisation<br>Lifetime physical/psychological/sexual IPV victimisation<br>Lifetime physical/psychological/sexual IPV victimisation | 5.9% (4.8%, 7.1%)<br>14.8% (9.9%, 20.9%)<br>10.2% (9.1%, 11.3%)<br>18.6% (13.0%, 25.3%) |
| The PrEP Brasil demonstration project (De Boni et al., 2018), 2014–2015 | Brazil | N=421 | Lifetime physical/sexual IPV victimisation | 7.4% (5.1%, 10.3%) |
| Cross-sectional study (Liu et al., 2018), 2015 | China | N=732 | Lifetime physical/psychological/sexual IPV victimisation<br>Lifetime physical IPV victimisation<br>Lifetime sexual IPV victimisation | 24.3% (43.6%, 57.9%)<br>6.6% (4.9%, 8.6%)<br>5.5% (3.9%, 7.4%) |
| Cross-sectional study (Castro et al., 2019), 2014–2016 | Brazil | N=569 GBMSM living with HIV and attending HIV clinics | Lifetime physical IPV victimisation | 11.4% (8.9%, 14.3%) |

| Study | Country | N | Measure | Result |
|---|---|---|---|---|
| Cross-sectional study (Jiang et al., 2019), 2017 | China | N=976 | Lifetime physical/psychological/sexual IPV victimisation | 13.2% (11.2%, 15.5%) |
| Cohort study (Safren et al., 2018), study period not reported (published 2018) | US | N=197 | Lifetime physical/psychological/sexual IPV victimisation | 50.3% (43.1%, 57.4%) |
| **Participants recruited (predominantly) from gay venues/events** | | | | |
| Intervention study (Wu et al., 2015), 2004–2005 | US | N=74 men and 37 couples: Black GBMSM with a primary/main male partner (or men with a Black male partner) and reported meth use (past two months) | Lifetime physical/psychological/sexual IPV victimisation (main partner) | 35.1% (24.4%, 47.1%) |
| | | | Past month physical/psychological/sexual IPV victimisation (main partner) | 25.7% (16.2%, 37.2%) |
| | | | Lifetime physical/psychological/sexual IPV perpetration (main partner) | 35.1% (24.4%, 47.1%) |
| | | | Past month physical/psychological/sexual IPV perpetration (main partner) | 27.0% (17.4%, 38.6%) |
| The Brothers Project (Williams et al., 2015), 2009–2010 | US | N=1522 Black GBMSM | Lifetime physical/psychological/sexual IPV victimisation | 51.8% (49.2%, 54.3%) |
| | | | Lifetime physical IPV victimisation | 27.5% (25.3%, 29.8%) |
| | | | Lifetime sexual IPV victimisation | 22.3% (20.3%, 24.5%) |
| Project 18 (P18) (Stults, Javdani, Greenbaum, Kapadia, & Halkitis, 2015), 2009–2011 (baseline data), ages 18–19 | US | N=528 | Lifetime physical/psychological/sexual IPV victimisation | 39.2% (35.0%, 43.5%) |
| | | | Lifetime physical/psychological/sexual IPV perpetration | 30.5% (26.6%, 34.6%) |
| Project Let Us Stand Together (LUST) (Stephenson & Finneran, 2016), 2011 | US | N=1075 | Past year physical/psychological/sexual IPV victimisation | 47.8% (44.8%, 50.8%) |
| | | | Past year physical/psychological/sexual IPV perpetration | 33.6% (30.8%, 36.5%) |
| The Young Men's Relationship (YMR) Study (Kubicek et al., 2016), 2012 | US | N=101 | Past year physical IPV victimisation | 67.3% (57.3%, 76.3%) |
| | | | Past year psychological IPV victimisation | 86.1% (77.8%, 92.2%) |
| | | | Past year sexual IPV victimisation | 64.4% (54.2%, 73.6%) |
| | | | Past year physical IPV perpetration | 66.3% (56.2%, 75.4%) |
| | | | Past year psychological IPV perpetration | 84.2% (75.6%, 90.7%) |
| | | | Past year sexual IPV perpetration | 58.4% (48.2%, 68.1%) |

*(Continued)*

*Table 16.1* (Continued)

| Study | Location | Sample size | Measure of IPV | Prevalence of IPV % (95% CI) |
|---|---|---|---|---|
| **Participants recruited (predominantly) from gay venues/events** | | | | |
| Cohort study (H. Y. Wang et al., 2018), 2014 | China | N=476 HIV-negative GBMSM at baseline | Past three months physical/psychological/sexual IPV victimisation | 18.7% (15.3%, 22.5%) |
| | | | Past three months physical IPV victimisation | 9.9% (7.3%, 12.9%) |
| | | | Past three months psychological IPV victimisation | 13.7% (10.7%, 17.1%) |
| | | | Past three months sexual IPV victimisation | 9.5% (7.0%, 12.4%) |
| Cross-sectional survey (Wei et al., 2019), 2018–2019 | China | N=431 | Lifetime physical/psychological/sexual IPV victimisation | 35.5% (31.0%, 40.2%) |
| | | | Lifetime physical/psychological/sexual IPV perpetration | 27.6% (23.4%, 32.1%) |
| Cross-sectional study (Peng et al., 2020), 2019 | China | N=578 | Lifetime physical/psychological/sexual IPV victimisation | 32.7% (28.9%, 36.7%) |
| | | | Lifetime physical IPV victimisation | 9.5% (7.2%, 12.2%) |
| | | | Lifetime sexual IPV victimisation | 11.6% (9.1%, 14.5%) |
| Cross-sectional study (Wei et al., 2020), 2019 | China | N=578 | Lifetime physical/psychological/sexual IPV perpetration | 32.5% (28.7%, 36.5%) |
| **Participants recruited (predominantly) online** | | | | |
| Cross-sectional study (Finneran & Stephenson, 2014), 2010 | US | N=1575 | Past year physical IPV victimisation | 8.8% (7.5%, 10.3%) |
| | | | Past year sexual IPV victimisation | 3.6% (2.8%, 4.7%) |
| | | | Past year physical IPV perpetration | 4.3% (3.4%, 5.4%) |
| | | | Past year sexual IPV perpetration | 0.8% (0.4%, 1.4%) |
| RCT (Wall, Sullivan, Kleinbaum, & Stephenson, 2014), 2010–2011 | US | N=190 (95 couples) HIV-negative GBMSM with a male partner | Past three months physical/sexual IPV victimisation (current partner) | 7.4% (4.1%, 12.1%) |
| | | | Past three months physical IPV victimisation (current partner) | 6.3% (3.3%, 10.8%) |
| | | | Past three months sexual IPV victimisation (current partner) | 2.1% (0.6%, 5.3%) |
| The "Shanghai's Men Study" (Ibragimov et al., 2017), 2008–2012 | China | N=1335 | Past five years physical/psychological/sexual IPV victimisation | 46.3% (43.6%, 49.0%) |
| Cross-sectional study (Mimiaga et al., 2015), 2012 | Latin America | N=19772 | Past five years physical/psychological/sexual IPV victimisation | 35.7% (35.0%, 36.4%) |

**Participants recruited (predominantly) online**

| Study | Country | Participants | Outcome | Prevalence |
|---|---|---|---|---|
| Cross-sectional study (Davis, Kaighobadi, Stephenson, Rael, & Sandfort, 2016), 2013 | US | N=189 GBMSM with a current regular partner or regular partner in the past year | Past year physical/psychological/sexual IPV victimisation (regular partner) | 54.5% (47.1%, 61.7%) |
| | | | Past year physical/psychological/sexual IPV victimisation (casual partner) | 24.3% (18.4%, 31.1%) |
| | | | Past year physical/sexual IPV victimisation (regular partner) | 21.7% (16.0%, 28.3%) |
| | | | Past year physical/sexual IPV victimisation (casual partner) | 12.2% (7.9%, 17.7%) |
| | | | Past year physical/psychological/sexual IPV perpetration (regular partner) | 48.7% (41.4%, 56.0%) |
| | | | Past year physical/psychological/sexual IPV perpetration (casual partner) | 17.5% (12.3%, 23.6%) |
| | | | Past year physical/sexual IPV perpetration (regular partner) | 16.9% (11.9%, 23.1%) |
| | | | Past year physical/sexual IPV perpetration (casual partner) | 5.8% (2.9%, 10.2%) |
| RCT (Brown, Serovich, & Kimberly, 2016), 2009–2014 | US. | N=340 HIV-positive GBMSM (at baseline) | Past month physical/psychological/IPV victimisation (after disclosure of HIV serostatus) | 6.2% (3.9%, 9.3%) |
| ISHKonnect (Wilkerson et al., 2018), 2013–2014 | India | N=433 | Past year physical/psychological/sexual IPV victimisation | 56.3% (51.5%, 61.1%) |
| Intervention study (N. S. Wong et al., 2017), 2014 | China | N=624 at baseline (never tested GBMSM) | Lifetime physical/psychological/sexual IPV victimisation (current male partner) | 11.9% (9.4%, 14.7%) |
| Baseline data from RCT (Wu, 2018), 2009–2015 | US | N=1002 Black GBMSM | Past month physical/psychological/sexual IPV victimisation | 23.5% (20.9%, 26.2%) |
| | | | Past month physical IPV victimisation | 10.4% (8.6%, 12.4%) |
| | | | Past month sexual IPV victimisation | 6.1% (4.7%, 7.8%) |
| China MP3 Project (N. Wang et al., 2020), 2013–2015 | China | N=367 GBMSM newly diagnosed with HIV | Lifetime physical/psychological/sexual IPV victimisation | 23.7% (19.4%, 28.4%) |
| | | | Lifetime physical IPV victimisation | 16.6% (13.0%, 20.8%) |
| | | | Lifetime psychological IPV victimisation | 7.4% (4.9%, 10.5%) |
| | | | Lifetime sexual IPV victimisation | 5.2% (3.1%, 8.0%) |
| Cross-sectional study (Davis et al., 2015), study period not reported (published 2015) | China | N=610 GBMSM with current male sexual partner(s) | Lifetime physical/psychological IPV victimisation (current male partner) | 29.8% (26.2%, 33.6%) |
| | | | Lifetime physical IPV victimisation (current male partner) | 16.1% (13.2%, 19.2%) |

*(Continued)*

*Table 16.1* (Continued)

| Study | Location | Sample size | Measure of IPV | Prevalence of IPV % (95% CI) |
|---|---|---|---|---|
| **Participants recruited (predominantly) online** | | | | |
| Project Stronger Together (Suarez et al., 2018), 2015 | US | N=320 at baseline survey | Past year physical/psychological/sexual IPV victimisation (current partner) | 45.6% (40.1%, 51.3%) |
| | | | Past year physical/sexual IPV victimisation (current partner) | 9.7% (6.7%, 13.5%) |
| Cross-sectional study (Duncan et al., 2018), 2015 | US | N=175 | Lifetime physical/psychological/sexual IPV victimisation | 37.7% (30.5%, 45.3%) |
| | | | Lifetime physical IPV victimisation | 10.3% (6.2%, 15.8%) |
| | | | Lifetime sexual IPV victimisation | 11.4% (7.1%, 17.1%) |
| Sex positive intervention (S. M. Walters et al., 2020), 2015 | US | N=1461 GBMSM living with HIV | Lifetime physical/psychological IPV victimisation | 46.4% (42.7%, 50.1%) |
| Cross-sectional study (Goldberg-Looney et al., 2016), study period not reported (published 2016) | US | N=89 | Lifetime physical IPV victimisation | 38.2% (28.1%, 49.1%) |
| | | | Lifetime psychological IPV victimisation | 69.7% (59.0%, 79.0%) |
| | | | Lifetime sexual IPV victimisation | 34.8% (25.0%, 45.7%) |
| PrEP-AWARE Project (Braksmajer et al., 2020), study period not reported (published 2020) | US | N=863 | Past six months physical IPV victimisation | 23.3% (20.5%, 26.3%) |
| | | | Past six months sexual IPV victimisation | 20.7% (18.1%, 23.6%) |
| **Snowball sampling (participant referral)** | | | | |
| Cross-sectional study (Klingelschmidt et al., 2017), 2012 | French Antilles and French Guiana | N=733 | Lifetime physical/psychological IPV victimisation | 26.4% (23.2%, 29.8%) |
| **Respondent-driven sampling (structured form of participant referral)** | | | | |
| The Mpumalanga Men's Study (MPMS) (Lane et al., 2014), 2012–2013 | South Africa | N=605 | Past six months physical/sexual IPV victimisation | 29.6% (26.0%, 33.4%) |

**Respondent-driven sampling (structured form of participant referral)**

| | | | | |
|---|---|---|---|---|
| Cross-sectional study (Tomori et al., 2016), 2012–2013 | India | N=11788 | Lifetime physical IPV victimisation | 16.1% (15.5%, 16.8%) |
| Longitudinal study (Garofalo, Hotton, Kuhns, Gratzer, & Mustanski, 2016), 2009–2015 | US | N=355 young HIV-negative GBMSM (16–20 years) | Lifetime physical IPV victimisation | 15.2% (11.6%, 19.4%) |

**Venue-based sampling (random time-space sampling)**

| | | | | |
|---|---|---|---|---|
| National HIV Behavioral Surveillance System (Phillips et al., 2014), 2008 | US | N=451 | Past year physical IPV victimisation | 5.5% (3.6%, 8.1%) |
| Priorities for Local AIDS Control Efforts (PLACE) study (Zalla et al., 2019), 2015 | Haiti | N=520 | Past year physical IPV victimisation | 15.8% (12.7%, 19.2%) |

experience IPV victimisation. No relationship has been observed between employment status and IPV in recent studies (see Table 16.2). No association has been observed between financial insecurity and IPV in recent studies (see Table 16.2); however, the small number of studies that investigated this relationship were limited in size. Qualitative work indicates that age, nationality, education, employment and income differentials are means by which power dynamics may be established within male same-sex couples, with implications for IPV (Goldenberg, Stephenson, Freeland, Finneran, & Hadley, 2016).

Very few studies have investigated the impact of living with HIV on experiences of IPV. Findings from one study suggest that testing for HIV may be a risk factor for IPV victimisation (Table 16.2). Men may test for HIV if they are concerned about the HIV status of their partner or they have engaged in sex with a new partner(s). Both circumstances could potentially heighten the risk of abuse within a violent partnership. Studies that have investigated HIV as an outcome of IPV are described in the next section of this chapter.

Six recent studies have investigated the association between CSA and IPV in unadjusted and/or adjusted analysis among GBMSM (Table 16.2). The measurement of CSA differed across studies; some investigated unwanted/forced sexual experiences before age 16, while others also considered the age of the sexual partner; for instance CSA was considered to have occurred if the partner was more than ten years older. In five studies, the prevalence of lifetime/past year IPV victimisation was substantially elevated among men who reported CSA and the association remained after adjustment for socio-demographic and/or psychosocial factors (Table 16.2). One study did not find an association; however the sample size was greatly limited (N=139). There is a lack of data on the link between experiences of physical and psychological abuse in childhood and IPV in adulthood among GBMSM.

There is a dearth of data on associations of relationship-level factors with IPV in studies of GBMSM. One recent study investigated the association of levels of perceived emotional support from family, friends and colleagues with IPV perpetration, finding a slightly elevated risk for men with lower levels of perceived support (Table 16.2). A small number of studies have investigated the impact of gay community norms on the occurrence of IPV victimisation and perpetration. Findings from two studies indicate that sexualised drug use and group sex may be important in the context of IPV (Table 16.2). In one study, the vast majority of participants who reported sexualised drug use also indicated having practiced 'chemsex' (Miltz et al., 2019). Chemsex is a cultural phenomenon within gay communities that was first described in the UK (Bourne, Reid, Hickson, Torres Rueda, & Weatherburn, 2014). It is the intentional use of psychoactive substances (mephedrone, gamma-hydroxybutyrate/gamma-butyrolactone [GHB/GBL] and methamphetamine) to stimulate sexual arousal, facilitate different sexual practices and prolong sexual episodes. The phenomenon of chemsex emerged as a means by which to facilitate enjoyment of gay sexuality against the backdrop of a heteronormative and homophobic social environment. Chemsex typically occurs in private homes or commercial sex-on-premises venues as a group sexual activity and is often organised/facilitated via use of dating apps. In another recent study, men who sought sexual partners online versus in gay bars/clubs were more likely to report IPV victimisation (Table 16.2). Group sex environments may leave some individuals vulnerable to mistreatment particularly if drugs are used given their impact on inhibition and self-regulation. The emotional backlash from the knowledge/witnessing of a partner's sexual activity with others may also heighten the risk of IPV. In two qualitative studies, a common theme was that jealousy, particularly in the context of substance use, may serve as a catalyst for IPV within same-sex male couples (Goldenberg et al., 2016; Kubicek, McNeeley, & Collins, 2016).

There is recent evidence that homophobic discrimination (perceived and enacted) may be linked to IPV victimisation (Table 16.2). Men who reported internalised homophobia were much more likely to experience and perpetrate IPV (Table 16.2). Evidence from one recent study also suggests that men are particularly vulnerable to IPV victimisation if they experience internalised homophobia but their partner does not (Suarez et al., 2018). The association with concealment of sexual identity was investigated in one recent study, which did not find any link with IPV measures (Table 16.2). However, this study may have lacked statistical power to detect small differences. Qualitative work indicates that dyadic differences in 'outness' contribute to IPV since being out may be either a source of tension/conflict or used as a means to exert control over a partner whose identity is more concealed (Goldenberg et al., 2016; Kubicek et al., 2016).

These findings may be explained by psychodynamic theories suggesting that experiences of abuse from significant individuals during formative years can manifest in persistent feelings of unworthiness and an inability to regulate emotional responses and recognise/avoid abuse in adult intimate partnerships (Crittenden & Ainsworth, 1989). Furthermore, drawing from the literature on masculinities/gender, men experiencing internalised homophobia may perpetrate IPV in an attempt to reconstruct a contested masculinity, or as a result of conflicting desires of both partners to fulfil traditional patriarchal roles in the household (Goldenberg et al., 2016). Integrating theories across different disciplines within an ecological framework of IPV may be highly informative (Heise, 1998). For instance, understanding the interaction with degree of exposure to abuse in childhood and cultural definitions of manhood may provide further insight into why some men who experience internalised homophobia have violent partnerships while others do not. There is an urgent need to collect this data, although in some cultures that strongly define manhood in terms of dominance and aggression, this may be a very difficult task given the possible existence of punitive anti-gay laws and/or presence of violent conflict.

Research on GBMSM is increasingly being understood through the lens of intersectional feminism (D. L. Whitfield, Coulter, Langenderfer-Magruder, & Jacobson, 2018). Intersectional feminism represented a break from traditional feminist theories that focused on inequalities between men and women by emphasising the intersection of gender and ethnicity, and the multidimensionality of Black women's experiences (Choo & Myra, 2010; Crenshaw, 1991). The intersectional paradigm is useful for understanding IPV risk factors among same-sex couples as it moves beyond gender binary constructions of victim/perpetrator and related discourses of power and control. It draws upon the complexities of intersecting social statuses and systems of oppression. Systems of oppression may be operating at a structural level on the basis of gender (non-conformity), ethnicity, sexuality, income, social class, migrant status, HIV status and other dimensions of subordination across various social settings. Intersectionality suggests that multiple oppressed populations are at increased risk of experiencing IPV (Subirana-Malaret, Gahagan, Parker, & Crowther-Dowey, 2019).

Evidence from recent studies suggests that sexual minority men experience discrimination on the basis of socio-cultural factors including ethnicity with implications for increased vulnerability to IPV (Table 16.2). The intersection of homophobia with racism may form a complex web of discrimination and social oppression. There is also some evidence from recent qualitative studies (Dickerson-Amaya & Coston, 2019; Rolle et al., 2018) and a previous online survey of GBMSM (Finneran et al., 2012) suggesting that bisexual people are at greater risk of experiencing IPV than gay-identified individuals. Bisexual people may be subject to the additional stress of not fitting in with the gay or heterosexual community; experiencing homophobia and binegativity. In line with an intersectionality perspective, these findings indicate that taking a

*Table 16.2* Factors associated with IPV measures in studies of GBMSM, by individual-, relationship-, community- and society-level factors

| Study, recruitment period, location, sample size | Measure of IPV (outcome variable) – recall period | Associations investigated (exposure variable), PR/OR [95% CI] | Variables adjusted for |
|---|---|---|---|
| **Individual-level factors** | | | |
| Cross-sectional study (Finneran & Stephenson, 2014), 2010, US, N=1575 | Physical IPV victimisation – past year | Age 18–20 vs. 40–44, **AOR 4.17 [1.37, 12.50]** <br> Age 18–20 vs. 45–49, **AOR 2.50 [1.02, 6.25]** <br> Age 18–20 vs. 50+, **AOR 3.70 [1.33, 10.00]** <br> No high school diploma vs. university degree level education, **AOR 4.35 [1.45, 8.33]** <br> No high school diploma vs. some college/two-year degree, **AOR 3.13 [1.47, 6.67]** <br> Unemployed, AOR 0.85 [0.57, 1.27] <br> Black ethnicity vs. white ethnicity, AOR 0.97 [0.54, 1.77] <br> Latino ethnicity vs. white ethnicity, AOR 0.97 [0.52, 1.78] <br> HIV+ vs. never tested/unknown HIV status, AOR 1.74 [0.82, 3.72] <br> HIV- vs. never tested/unknown HIV status, AOR 1.16 [0.70, 1.90] | Age, ethnicity, sexual identity, educational attainment, employment status and HIV status |
| | Physical IPV perpetration – past year | Age 18–20 vs. 40–44, AOR 5.88 [0.71, 50.00] <br> Age 18–20 vs. 45–49, AOR 1.25 [0.41, 3.70] <br> Age 18–20 vs. 50+, AOR 6.25 [0.77, 50.00] <br> No high school diploma vs. university degree level education, **AOR 1.30 [1.18, 3.85]** <br> No high school diploma vs. some college/two-year degree, **AOR 4.00 [1.47, 11.11]** <br> Unemployed, AOR 0.67 [0.38, 1.18] <br> Black ethnicity vs. white ethnicity, APR 1.08 [0.48, 2.42] <br> Latino ethnicity vs. white ethnicity, APR 1.32 [0.61, 2.89] <br> HIV+ vs. never tested/unknown HIV status, APR 1.59 [0.56, 4.47] <br> HIV- vs. never tested/unknown HIV status, APR 1.08 [0.55, 2.12] | |
| | Sexual IPV victimisation – past year | Age 18–20 vs. 40–44, AOR 2.44 [0.50, 12.50] <br> Age 18–20 vs. 45–49, AOR 1.85 [0.50, 7.14] <br> Age 18–20 vs. 50+, AOR 1.64 [0.42, 6.25] | |

| Study | Outcome | Results | Adjustment |
|---|---|---|---|
| RCT (Wall et al., 2014), 2010–2011, US, N=190 (95 couples) HIV-negative GBMSM with a male partner | Physical/sexual IPV victimisation (current partner) – past three months | No high school diploma vs. university degree level education, AOR 2.22 [0.64, 7.69]<br>No high school diploma vs. some college/two-year degree, AOR 2.70 [0.83, 8.33]<br>Unemployed, AOR 0.95 [0.53, 1.72]<br>Black ethnicity vs. white ethnicity, APR 1.17 [0.50, 2.73]<br>Latino ethnicity vs. white ethnicity, APR 0.73 [0.27, 2.00]<br>HIV+ vs. never tested/unknown HIV status, APR 0.75 [0.24, 2.40]<br>HIV- vs. never tested/unknown HIV status, APR 0.90 [0.43, 1.87] | Ethnicity and education |
| | | Younger age (continuous variable), OR 0.95 [0.92, 1.00]<br>Black/African American vs. other ethnicity, **AOR 0.24 [0.08, 0.67]**<br>High school or less vs. education post high school, **AOR 5.01 [1.23, 20.45]**<br>HIV-positive vs. HIV-negative, AOR 0.64 [0.11, 3.70]<br>Partner younger age (continuous variable), **OR 0.95 [0.91, 0.99]**<br>Partner Black/African American vs. other ethnicity, OR 0.88 [0.32, 2.43]<br>Partner high school or less vs. education post high school, **AOR 5.14 [1.26, 20.92]** | Partner education |
| | | Partner HIV-positive vs. HIV-negative, OR 0.64 [0.20, 1.61]<br>Both partners report same ethnicity vs. different ethnicities, OR 1.20 [0.32, 4.46]<br>Both partners report same education levels vs. different levels, OR 2.36 [0.65, 8.70] | Unadjusted |
| Project Let Us Stand Together (LUST) (Stephenson & Finneran, 2016), 2011, US, N=1075 | Physical/psychological/ sexual IPV victimisation – past year | Age 18–24 vs. 25-34, **AOR 1.64 [1.12, 2.38]**<br>Age 18–24 vs. 25-44, **AOR 2.94 [0.22, 1.96, 6.51]**<br>Age 18–24 vs. 45+, **AOR 4.17 [2.63, 6.25]**<br>High school or less vs. university degree level of education, AOR 1.32 [0.88, 1.96]<br>High school or less vs. some university, **AOR 1.49 [1.01, 2.22]**<br>Unemployed, AOR 1.21 [0.87, 1.68]<br>Black/African American ethnicity vs. white ethnicity, AOR 0.72 [0.50, 1.04]<br>Latino/other ethnicity vs. white ethnicity, AOR 0.91 [0.58, 1.43]<br>HIV+ vs. HIV-, AOR 0.94 [0.68, 1.31]<br>HIV- vs. unknown HIV status/never tested, **AOR 1.75 [1.02, 3.03]** | Age, ethnicity, sexual identity, HIV status, employment status and educational attainment |

*(Continued)*

*Table 16.2* (Continued)

| Study, recruitment period, location, sample size | Measure of IPV (outcome variable) – recall period | Associations investigated (exposure variable), PR/OR [95% CI] | Variables adjusted for |
|---|---|---|---|
| | Physical/psychological/ sexual IPV perpetration – Past year | Age 18–24 vs. 25–34, **AOR 1.85 [1.28, 2.70]**<br>Age 18–24 vs. 25–44, **AOR 3.23 [2.13, 5.00]**<br>Age 18–24 vs. 45+, **AOR 4.17 [2.63, 6.67]**<br>High school or less vs. university degree level of education, AOR 1.32 [0.88, 1.96]<br>high school or less vs. some university, AOR 1.35 [0.92, 2.00]<br>Unemployed, AOR 0.91 [0.64, 1.28]<br>Black/African American ethnicity vs. white ethnicity, APR 0.94 [0.65, 1.36]<br>Latino/other ethnicity vs. white ethnicity, APR 1.13 [0.71, 1.78]<br>HIV+ vs. HIV-, APR 1.38 [0.99, 1.94]<br>HIV- vs. unknown HIV status/never tested, AOR 1.16 [0.67, 2.04] | |
| The PROUD trial (Miltz et al., 2019), 2012–2014 (baseline) – two years follow-up, England, N=436 (month 12/24) | Physical/psychological/ sexual IPV victimisation – lifetime | Age <25 vs. 45+, APR 1.27 [0.75, 2.15]<br>Non-university degree level of education, APR 1.01 [0.77, 1.32]<br>Unemployed, APR 0.85 [0.62, 1.18]<br>Not born in the UK and BAME vs. UK born and white ethnicity, APR 0.84 [0.54, 1.31]<br>Age <13 years at anal sex debut, APR 1.15 [0.72, 1.84] | Age, born in the UK, sexual identity, university education and clinic site. |
| | Physical/psychological/ sexual IPV victimisation – past year | Age <25 vs. 45+, APR 1.61 [0.73, 3.59]<br>Non-university degree level of education, APR 0.84 [0.55, 1.29]<br>Unemployed, APR 0.85 [0.52, 1.43]<br>Not born in the UK and BAME vs. UK born and white ethnicity, APR 1.83 [1.04, 3.20]<br>Age <13 years at anal sex debut, APR 1.49 [0.74, 3.03] | |
| | Physical/psychological/ sexual IPV perpetration – lifetime | Age <25 vs. 45+, **APR 2.12 [1.04, 4.30]**<br>Non-university degree level of education, APR 1.31 [0.87, 1.96]<br>Unemployed, APR 1.47 [0.83, 2.56]<br>Not born in the UK and BAME vs. UK born and white ethnicity, APR 0.92 [0.47, 1.78]<br>Age <13 years at anal sex debut, APR 1.01 [0.48, 2.13] | |

| Study | Outcome | Findings | Adjustment |
| --- | --- | --- | --- |
| | Physical/psychological/sexual IPV perpetration – past year | Age <25 vs. 45+, **APR 5.53 [1.80, 17.0]**, Age 25–29 vs. 45+, **APR 5.89 [2.30, 15.10]**, Non-university degree level of education, APR 1.28 [0.73, 2.25], Unemployed, APR 1.67 [0.75, 3.70], Not born in the UK and BAME vs. UK born and white ethnicity, APR 1.13 [0.49, 2.61] | Age, income and marital status |
| Cohort study (H. Y. Wang et al., 2018), 2014, 2015, China, N=476 HIV-negative GBMSM at baseline | Physical/psychological/sexual IPV victimisation – past three months | Age <13 years at anal sex debut, APR 1.06 [0.33, 3.44], Han Chinese ethnicity, AOR 1.70 [1.00, 3.10], Senior high school and below vs. college and above, **AOR 1.80 [1.10, 3.00]** | |
| China MP3 Project (N. Wang et al., 2020), 2013–2015, China, N=367 GBMSM newly diagnosed with HIV | Physical/psychological/sexual IPV victimisation – lifetime | Age (p=0.24): ≤30 (25.6%); >30 (20.2%), Ethnicity (p=0.97): Han (23.7%); other (24.0%), Education (p=0.12): <high school (30.0%); high school (34.3%); college (21.3%), Income (p=0.14): <5000 (26.4%); ≥5000 (19.7%), Employment (p=0.38): employed (23.7%); unemployed (18.0%); student (33.3%) | Unadjusted |
| Cross-sectional study (Liu et al., 2018), 2015, China, N=732 | Physical/psychological/sexual IPV victimisation – lifetime | Age 18–25 vs. 26–35, AOR 1.11 [0.75, 1.67], Age 18–25 vs. 36–74, AOR 1.69 [0.87, 3.33], Middle school vs. high school education, AOR 0.90 [0.41, 1.96], Middle school vs. college or above education, AOR 1.27 [0.62, 2.56] | Age, education, marital status and sexual identity |
| Project Stronger Together (Suarez et al., 2018), 2015, US, N=320 at baseline survey (160 couples) | Physical/psychological/sexual IPV perpetration – past year (current partner) | Younger age (continuous variable), **APR 1.01 [1.00, 1.02]**, Cohabiting with partner, **APR 1.74 [1.23, 2.45]** | Age, cohabiting and internalised homophobia |
| | Physical/psychological/sexual IPV perpetration – past year (current partner) | Younger age (continuous variable), **APR 1.02 [1.01, 1.03]**, Cohabiting with partner, **APR 1.68 [1.21, 2.33]** | |

*(Continued)*

*Table 16.2* (Continued)

| Study, recruitment period, location, sample size | Measure of IPV (outcome variable) – recall period | Associations investigated (exposure variable), PR/OR [95% CI] | Variables adjusted for |
|---|---|---|---|
| | Physical/psychological/sexual IPV victimisation and IPV perpetration – past year (current partner) | Younger age (continuous variable), **APR 1.03 [1.01, 1.04]**<br>Cohabiting with partner, **APR 1.64 [1.10, 2.45]** | Unadjusted |
| Cross-sectional survey (Wei et al., 2019), 2018–2019, China, N=431 | Physical/psychological/sexual IPV victimisation – lifetime | Age ≤30 vs. >30, **AOR 2.00 [1.25, 3.33]**<br>Ethnicity Han vs. other, AOR 1.70 [0.40, 6.30]<br>University education or above vs. other, AOR 1.50 [1.00, 2.20]<br>Full-time job vs. other, AOR 0.80 [0.50, 1.10] | Unadjusted. |
| Cross-sectional study (Peng et al., 2020), 2019, China, N=578 | Physical/psychological/sexual IPV victimisation – lifetime | Age (p=0.140): 18–25 (35.9%); 26–45, (31.3%); >45 (13.3%)<br>Ethnicity (p=0.250): Han (32.0%); other (40.0%)<br>Education (p=0.904): below university (33.0%); university or above (32.5%)<br>CNY Income (p=0.233): ≤1000 (26.4%); 1001–3000 (34.5%); 3001–6000 (36.1%); >6000 (27.7%)<br>Employment (p=0.802): full-time (31.9%); part-time (37.8%); student (31.9%); unemployed/retired (37.5%) | Unadjusted |
| Cross-sectional study (Wei et al., 2020), 2019, China, N=578 | Physical/psychological/sexual IPV perpetration – lifetime | Age <30 vs. ≥30, OR 1.18 [0.82, 1.69]<br>Ethnicity Han vs. other, OR 0.93 [0.50, 1.72]<br>Other education vs. university or above, OR 0.75 [0.53, 1.08]<br>Other vs. full time job, OR 1.28 [0.89, 1.85] | Unadjusted |
| National HIV Behavioral Surveillance System (Phillips et al., 2014), 2008, US, N=451 | Physical IPV victimisation – past year (exposure variable) | CSA, **AOR 3.54 [1.41, 8.92]** (outcome variable) | HIV status, depression and arrested (past 12 months) |
| Cross-sectional study (Mimiaga et al., 2015), 2012, Latin America, N=19772 | Physical/psychological/sexual IPV victimisation – past five years | CSA, **OR 1.65 [1.56, 1.75]** | Clustering by country using generalised estimating equations (GEEs) |

| Study | Type of abuse | Results | Adjusted for |
|---|---|---|---|
| Cross-sectional study (Tomori et al., 2016), 2012–2013, India, N=11788 | Physical/psychological/sexual IPV victimisation – lifetime | CSA vs. no CSA: **33.8% vs. 3.1%** | Unadjusted |
| Baseline data from RCT (Wu, 2018), 2009–2015, US, N=1002 Black GBMSM | Physical/psychological/sexual IPV victimisation – past month | CSA, **AOR 1.70 [1.20, 2.30]** | Age and HIV status |
| Cross-sectional study (Jiang et al., 2019), 2017, China, N=976 | Physical/psychological/sexual IPV victimisation – lifetime | CSA, **Beta coefficient 0.129 (p<0.001)** from structural equation modelling (SEM) | Sexual partner-seeking behaviour |
| Cross-sectional study (Lee et al., 2020), 2017, US, N=139 Latino GBMSM (18–29 years) | Physical/psychological IPV victimisation (main partner) – past month | CSA, polychoric correlation (network analysis) 0.03 (p>0.05) Poverty, polychoric correlation (network analysis) 0.07 (p>0.05) Unstable housing, **polychoric correlation (network analysis) 0.39 (p<0.001)** | CLS, recreational drug use, injection drug use, alcohol use, depression, CSA, poverty, unstable housing and prison history |
| **Community-level factors** | | | |
| The PROUD trial (Miltz et al., 2019), 2012–2014 (baseline) – two years follow-up, England, N=436 (month 12/24) | Physical/psychological/sexual IPV victimisation – lifetime | Group sex, APR 1.10 [0.88, 1.38] Had sex after using recreational drugs (past three months), **APR 1.36 [1.08, 1.71]** | Age, born in the UK, sexual identity, university education and clinic site |
| | Physical/psychological/sexual IPV victimisation – past year | Group sex, **APR 1.87 [1.25, 2.79]** Had sex after using recreational drugs (past three months), **APR 1.92 [1.28, 2.90]** | |
| | Physical/psychological/sexual IPV perpetration – lifetime | Group sex, **APR 1.38 [1.00, 1.91]** Had sex after using recreational drugs (past three months), **APR 1.75 [1.23, 2.50]** | |
| | Physical/psychological/sexual IPV perpetration – past year | Group sex, APR 1.42 [0.82, 2.46] Had sex after using recreational drugs (past three months), **APR 2.16 [1.17, 3.96]** | |

*(Continued)*

Table 16.2 (Continued)

| Study, recruitment period, location, sample size | Measure of IPV (outcome variable) – recall period | Associations investigated (exposure variable), PR/OR [95% CI] | Variables adjusted for |
|---|---|---|---|
| **Community-level factors** | | | |
| Cohort study (H. Y. Wang et al., 2018), 2014, China, N=476 HIV-negative GBMSM at baseline | Physical/psychological/ sexual IPV victimisation – past three months | Internet vs. gay venues as main venue to seek male sex partners, **AOR 3.00 [1.50, 6.00]** | Age, income and marital status |
| Cross-sectional study (Wei et al., 2020), 2019, China, N=578 | Physical/psychological/ sexual IPV perpetration – lifetime | Drug use during sex within the past six months, **OR 2.23 [1.46, 3.42]** Lower levels of perceived emotional support from family, friends/colleagues, **OR 1.10 [1.03, 1.18]** | Unadjusted |
| **Society-level factors** | | | |
| Cross-sectional study (Finneran & Stephenson, 2014), 2010, US, N=1575 | Physical IPV victimisation – past year Sexual IPV victimisation – past year Physical IPV perpetration – past year | Internalised homophobia, AOR 1.01 [0.99, 1.03] Homophobic discrimination, **AOR 1.25 [1.14, 1.37]** Racist discrimination, AOR 1.02 [0.93, 1.11] Internalised homophobia, AOR 1.00 [0.98, 1.02] Homophobic discrimination, **AOR 1.28 [1.11, 1.47]** Racist discrimination, **AOR 1.19 [1.06, 1.34]** Internalised homophobia, AOR 1.01 [0.99, 1.03] Homophobic discrimination, AOR 1.13 [0.99, 1.28] Racist discrimination, AOR 1.02 [0.90, 1.16] | Age, ethnicity, sexual identity, educational attainment, employment status and HIV status |
| China MP3 Project (N. Wang et al., 2020), 2013–2015, China, N=367 GBMSM newly diagnosed with HIV | Physical/psychological/ sexual IPV victimisation – lifetime | GBMSM-related stigma (perceived and enacted), **AOR 1.99 [1.18, 3.36]** | Age, marital status, health insurance and place of birth |
| Cross-sectional study (Wei et al., 2020), 2019, China, N=578 | Physical/psychological/ sexual IPV perpetration – lifetime | Perceived social discrimination towards gay sexuality medium vs. low, OR 1.66 [0.83, 3.32] Perceived social discrimination towards gay sexuality high vs. low, **OR 3.11 [1.64, 5.91]** Internalised homophobia, OR 1.04 [1.00, 1.07] | Unadjusted |

238

**Society-level factors**

| Study | IPV type | Findings | Adjusted for |
|---|---|---|---|
| Project Let Us Stand Together (LUST) (Stephenson & Finneran, 2016), 2011, US, N=1075 | Physical/psychological/sexual IPV victimisation – past year | Internalised homophobia, **AOR 1.02 [1.01, 1.03]**; Homophobic discrimination, **AOR 1.11 [1.05, 1.17]**; Racist discrimination, **AOR 1.10 [1.04, 1.17]** | Age, ethnicity, sexual identity, HIV status, employment status and educational attainment |
| | Physical/psychological/sexual IPV victimisation – past year | Internalised homophobia, **AOR 1.01 [1.00, 1.02]**; Homophobic discrimination, **AOR 1.08 [1.02, 1.15]**; Racist discrimination, AOR 1.02 [0.96, 1.08] | |
| The PROUD trial (Miltz et al., 2019), 2012–2014 (baseline) – two years follow-up, England, N=436 (month 12/24) | Physical/psychological/sexual IPV victimisation – lifetime | Internalised homophobia, **APR 1.31 [1.05, 1.64]**; Not 'out' to all/almost all friends, work mates and close family, APR 0.93 [0.74, 1.16] | Age, born in the UK, sexual identity, university education and clinic site |
| | Physical/psychological/sexual IPV victimisation – past year | Internalised homophobia, **APR 2.00 [1.36, 2.94]**; Not 'out' to all/almost all friends, work mates and close family, APR 0.80 [0.54, 1.18] | |
| | Physical/psychological/sexual IPV perpetration – lifetime | Internalised homophobia, **APR 1.33 [0.97, 1.83]**; Not 'out' to all/almost all friends, work mates and close family, APR 1.27 [0.89, 1.79] | |
| | Physical/psychological/sexual IPV perpetration – past year | Internalised homophobia, **APR 2.10 [1.21, 3.65]**; Not 'out' to all/almost all friends, work mates and close family, APR 1.08 [0.62, 1.89] | |
| Project Stronger Together (Suarez et al., 2018), 2015, US, N=320 at baseline survey (160 couples) | Physical/psychological/sexual IPV victimisation – past year (current partner) | Both partners report internalised homophobia, APR 1.26 [0.82, 1.94]; Internalised homophobia and partner does not report it, **APR 1.67 [1.31, 2.14]**; Only partner reported internalised homophobia, APR 0.90 [0.60, 1.35] | Age, cohabiting and internalised homophobia |

(*Continued*)

*Table 16.2* (Continued)

| Study; recruitment period, location, sample size | Measure of IPV (outcome variable) – recall period | Associations investigated (exposure variable), PR/OR [95% CI] | Variables adjusted for |
|---|---|---|---|
| | Physical/psychological/ sexual IPV perpetration – past year (current partner) | Both partners report internalised homophobia, APR 1.27 [0.86, 1.90] | |
| | | Internalised homophobia and partner does not report it, **APR 1.59 [1.23, 2.06]** | |
| | | Only partner reported internalised homophobia, APR 1.17 [0.85, 1.63] | |
| | Physical/psychological/ sexual IPV victimisation and IPV perpetration (same partner) – Past year (current partner) | Both partners report internalised homophobia, APR 1.58 [0.98, 2.53] | |
| | | Internalised homophobia and partner does not report it, **APR 1.79 [1.27, 2.51]** | |
| | | Only partner reported internalised homophobia, APR 0.97 [0.59, 1.57] | |

APR = adjusted prevalence ratio (modified Poisson regression)
AOR = adjusted odds ratio (Logistic regression)
BAME = Black, Asian and minority ethnic
CSA = Childhood sexual abuse
The associations that are statistically significant (i.e. the confidence interval does not cross 1) are shown in bold.

homogenised view of sexual minority communities may conceal the experiences of less privileged members, reinforcing other power structures.

The studies described in this section were all cross-sectional (data were collected/analysed at one point in time). For risk factors that were not predetermined at birth or early on in life, it is not possible to make inferences about causal associations. The relationships described here may operate in the opposite direction; for instance IPV may lead to lower levels of educational attainment and internalised homophobia.

## IPV health and risky behaviour correlates among sexual minority men

Substance use may be a coping mechanism used by people who experience IPV, as it can induce a state of cognitive release from rational self-awareness (McKirnan, Ostrow, & Hope, 1996). In the meta-analysis (Figure 16.1), exposure to any IPV victimisation was associated with increased odds of substance use in nine studies (N=9607 GBMSM in total): pooled OR 1.88 (95% CI: 1.59, 2.22) (Buller, Devries, et al., 2014). Any IPV perpetration was also associated with increased odds of substance use in two studies (N=1910 GBMSM in total): pooled OR 1.99 (95% CI: 1.33, 2.99). Similar findings were observed in ten recent studies (Table 16.3). A significant and independent association with heavy drinking and/or recreational drug use was consistently observed across American studies (N=7), whereas Chinese studies (N=5) failed to find such a relationship. It is possible that country specific factors may affect the relationship between IPV and substance use.

IPV may distort one's perceived self-worth and capacity to influence important outcomes in one's life, which may lead to poor mental health symptoms (Fife & Schrager, 2012). In the meta-analysis (Figure 16.1), exposure to any IPV victimisation was associated with increased odds of reporting clinically significant depressive symptoms in three studies (N=3999 GBMSM in total): pooled OR 1.52 (95% CI: 1.24, 1.86). Similar findings were observed in eight recent studies (Table 16.4). One recent study failed to find an association; however it specifically examined experiences of IPV following disclosure of an HIV status (as the outcome variable), in which case depression may not be an important risk factor. The sample size was also small (N=340).

Physical acts of violence directed towards an intimate partner often do not occur in isolation, and frequently there is overlap with other forms of violence, including sexual abuse (M. L. Walters et al., 2013). Experiences of IPV with a previous partner may also lead to unwanted sex and condomless sex (CLS) with other partners since IPV can distort one's perception of self-worth and ability to recognise dysfunctional relationship dynamics (Fife & Schrager, 2012). In the meta-analysis (Figure 25.1), exposure to any IPV victimisation was associated with CLS in eight studies (pooled OR 1.72 [95% CI: 1.44, 2.05], N=4447 GBMSM in total) and a positive HIV status in ten studies (pooled OR 1.46 [95% CI: 1.26, 1.69], N=8835). IPV perpetration was not associated with CLS across two studies (pooled OR 1.88 [95% CI: 0.22, 16.03]) or HIV positivity across three studies (pooled OR 0.93 [95% CI: 0.49, 1.78]). Five recent studies found an association of IPV victimisation (N=4) or IPV perpetration (N=1) with measures of CLS or sexually transmitted infection (STI) diagnosis (see Table 16.5). One study found an inverse relationship between IPV perpetration and STI diagnosis. This may be due to the fact that the survey was conducted in a sexual health clinic where men attend for prevention as well as treatment interventions. Potentially lower levels of CLS among men who perpetrated IPV

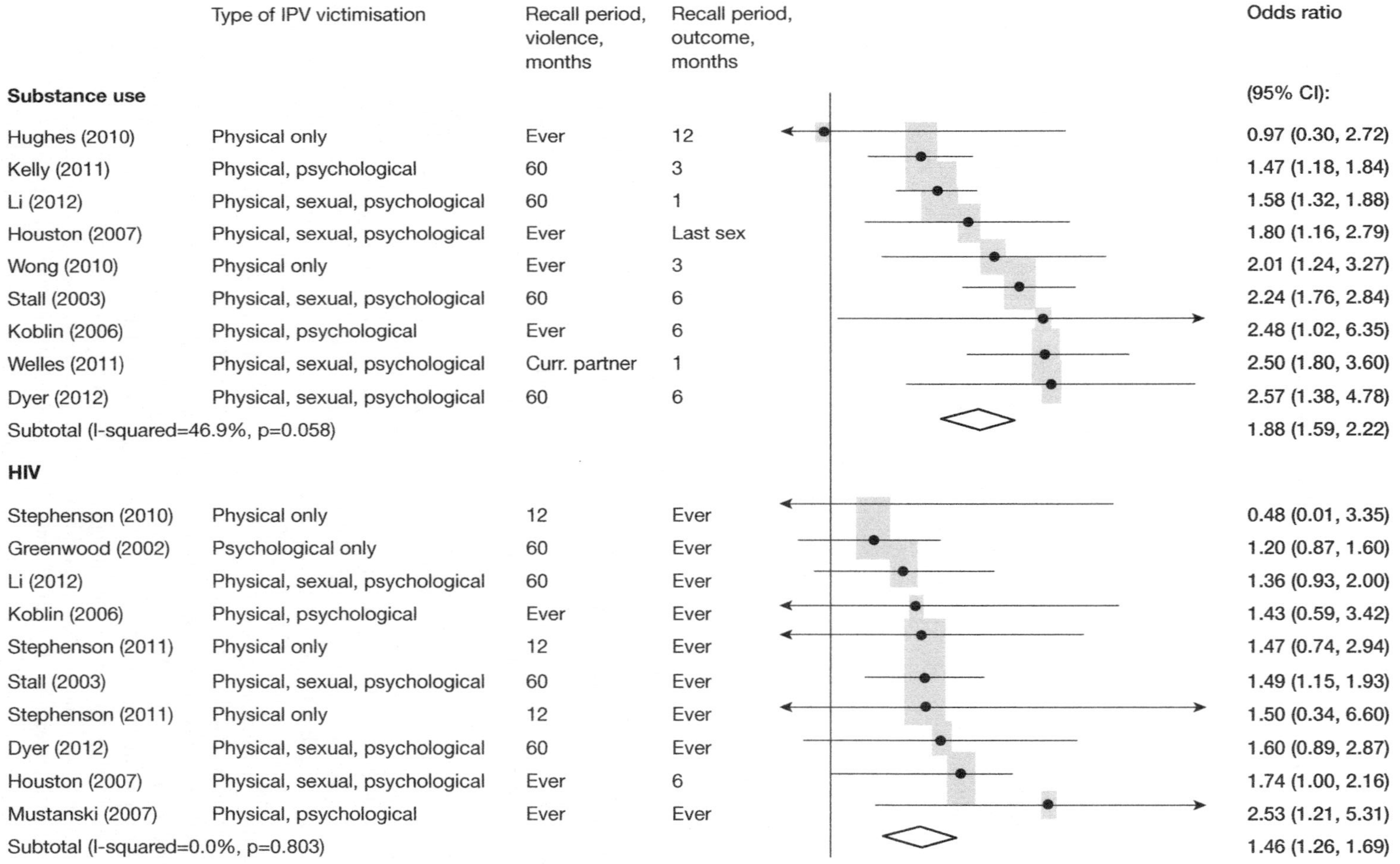

| | Type of IPV victimisation | Recall period, violence, months | Recall period, outcome, months | Odds ratio (95% CI): |
|---|---|---|---|---|
| **Substance use** | | | | |
| Hughes (2010) | Physical only | Ever | 12 | 0.97 (0.30, 2.72) |
| Kelly (2011) | Physical, psychological | 60 | 3 | 1.47 (1.18, 1.84) |
| Li (2012) | Physical, sexual, psychological | 60 | 1 | 1.58 (1.32, 1.88) |
| Houston (2007) | Physical, sexual, psychological | Ever | Last sex | 1.80 (1.16, 2.79) |
| Wong (2010) | Physical only | Ever | 3 | 2.01 (1.24, 3.27) |
| Stall (2003) | Physical, sexual, psychological | 60 | 6 | 2.24 (1.76, 2.84) |
| Koblin (2006) | Physical, psychological | Ever | 6 | 2.48 (1.02, 6.35) |
| Welles (2011) | Physical, sexual, psychological | Curr. partner | 1 | 2.50 (1.80, 3.60) |
| Dyer (2012) | Physical, sexual, psychological | 60 | 6 | 2.57 (1.38, 4.78) |
| Subtotal (I-squared=46.9%, p=0.058) | | | | 1.88 (1.59, 2.22) |
| **HIV** | | | | |
| Stephenson (2010) | Physical only | 12 | Ever | 0.48 (0.01, 3.35) |
| Greenwood (2002) | Psychological only | 60 | Ever | 1.20 (0.87, 1.60) |
| Li (2012) | Physical, sexual, psychological | 60 | Ever | 1.36 (0.93, 2.00) |
| Koblin (2006) | Physical, psychological | Ever | Ever | 1.43 (0.59, 3.42) |
| Stephenson (2011) | Physical only | 12 | Ever | 1.47 (0.74, 2.94) |
| Stall (2003) | Physical, sexual, psychological | 60 | Ever | 1.49 (1.15, 1.93) |
| Stephenson (2011) | Physical only | 12 | Ever | 1.50 (0.34, 6.60) |
| Dyer (2012) | Physical, sexual, psychological | 60 | Ever | 1.60 (0.89, 2.87) |
| Houston (2007) | Physical, sexual, psychological | Ever | 6 | 1.74 (1.00, 2.16) |
| Mustanski (2007) | Physical, psychological | Ever | Ever | 2.53 (1.21, 5.31) |
| Subtotal (I-squared=0.0%, p=0.803) | | | | 1.46 (1.26, 1.69) |

*Figure 16.1* Meta-analysis of the association of IPV victimisation with health outcomes and sexual risk behaviour in GBMSM

*Source:* Adapted from Buller, Devries et al. (2014)[1]

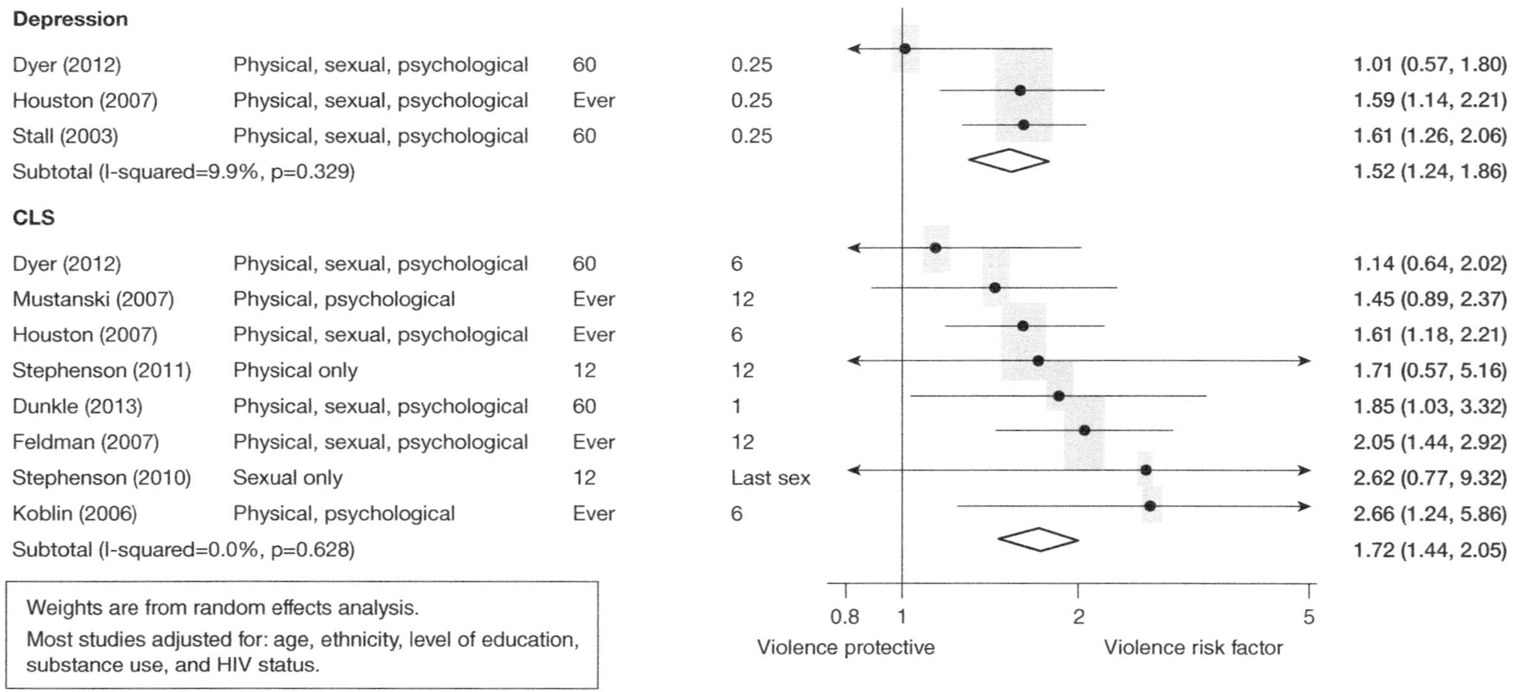
Depression
Dyer (2012) Physical, sexual, psychological 60 0.25 1.01 (0.57, 1.80)
Houston (2007) Physical, sexual, psychological Ever 0.25 1.59 (1.14, 2.21)
Stall (2003) Physical, sexual, psychological 60 0.25 1.61 (1.26, 2.06)
Subtotal (I-squared=9.9%, p=0.329) 1.52 (1.24, 1.86)
CLS
Dyer (2012) Physical, sexual, psychological 60 6 1.14 (0.64, 2.02)
Mustanski (2007) Physical, psychological Ever 12 1.45 (0.89, 2.37)
Houston (2007) Physical, sexual, psychological Ever 6 1.61 (1.18, 2.21)
Stephenson (2011) Physical only 12 12 1.71 (0.57, 5.16)
Dunkle (2013) Physical, sexual, psychological 60 1 1.85 (1.03, 3.32)
Feldman (2007) Physical, sexual, psychological Ever 12 2.05 (1.44, 2.92)
Stephenson (2010) Sexual only 12 Last sex 2.62 (0.77, 9.32)
Koblin (2006) Physical, psychological Ever 6 2.66 (1.24, 5.86)
Subtotal (I-squared=0.0%, p=0.628) 1.72 (1.44, 2.05)
Weights are from random effects analysis.
Most studies adjusted for: age, ethnicity, level of education, substance use, and HIV status.
0.8
1
2
5
Violence protective
Violence risk factor

*Figure 16.1* Continued

*Table 16.3* Associations of IPV with substance use measures in studies of GBMSM

| Study, recruitment period, location, sample size | Outcome measure | Associations investigated with IPV measures (exposure variable) | Variables adjusted for |
|---|---|---|---|
| Intervention study (Wu et al., 2015), 2004–2005, US, N=74 Black GBMSM with a primary/main male partner (or men with a Black male partner) and reported meth use (past two months) | Heavy drinking (five or more drinks in a single period) | Lifetime physical/psychological/sexual IPV victimisation (main partner), **AOR 3.40 [1.00, 11.80]**<br>Lifetime physical/psychological/sexual IPV perpetration (main partner), **AOR 5.10 [1.30, 19.90]** | Age, education, recent homelessness, income, length of relationship, HIV status and CLS with main partner |
| | Marijuana use (past month) | Lifetime physical/psychological/sexual IPV victimisation (main partner), AOR 4.20 [0.40, 41.0]<br>Lifetime physical/psychological/sexual IPV perpetration (main partner), AOR 1.70 [0.30, 11.00] | |
| | Cocaine use (past month) | Lifetime physical/psychological/sexual IPV victimisation (main partner), AOR 2.50 [0.70, 9.50]<br>Lifetime physical/psychological/sexual IPV perpetration (main partner), AOR 2.20 [0.60, 8.00] | |
| | Crack cocaine use (past month) | Lifetime physical/psychological/sexual IPV victimisation (main partner), **AOR 3.70 [1.10, 13.10]**<br>Lifetime physical/psychological/sexual IPV perpetration (main partner), AOR 3.00 [0.80, 11.50] | |
| | Methamphetamine use (past month) | Lifetime physical/psychological/sexual IPV victimisation (main partner), **AOR 9.70 [1.40, 65.6]**<br>Lifetime physical/psychological/sexual IPV perpetration (main partner), **AOR 22.90 [2.10, 248.1]** | |
| | Heroin use (past month) | Lifetime physical/psychological/sexual IPV victimisation (main partner), AOR 1.10 [0.20, 7.90]<br>Lifetime physical/psychological/sexual IPV perpetration (main partner), AOR 5.00 [0.70, 33.90] | |
| Project 18 (P18) (Stults et al., 2015), 2009–2011 (baseline data), US, N=528, ages 18–19 | 1 instance of alcohol vs. none in the last 30 days | Lifetime physical/psychological/sexual IPV victimisation, AOR 0.96 [0.52, 1.80]<br>Lifetime physical/psychological/sexual IPV perpetration, AOR 0.89 [0.46, 1.74] | Ethnicity and socio-economic status |

244

*(Continued)*

| | |
|---|---|
| 2+ instances of alcohol vs. none in the last 30 days | Lifetime physical/psychological/sexual IPV victimisation, AOR 1.58 [0.99, 2.51] |
| | Lifetime physical/psychological/sexual IPV perpetration, AOR 1.57 [0.96, 2.56] |
| 1 instance of cannabis vs. none in the last 30 days | Lifetime physical/psychological/sexual IPV victimisation, AOR 0.86 [0.46, 1.61] |
| | Lifetime physical/psychological/sexual IPV perpetration, AOR 1.01 [0.52, 1.97] |
| 2+ instances of cannabis vs. none in the last 30 days | Lifetime physical/psychological/sexual IPV victimisation, **AOR 1.62 [1.10, 2.38]** |
| | Lifetime physical/psychological/sexual IPV perpetration, **AOR 1.62 [1.08, 2.44]** |
| 1 instance of stimulant drug use vs. none in the last 30 days | Lifetime physical/psychological/sexual IPV victimisation, **AOR 2.24 [1.04, 4.84]** |
| | Lifetime physical/psychological/sexual IPV perpetration, **AOR 3.05 [1.42, 6.58]** |
| 2+ instances of stimulant drug use vs. none in the last 30 days | Lifetime physical/psychological/sexual IPV victimisation, AOR 1.34 [0.64, 2.84] |
| | Lifetime physical/psychological/sexual IPV perpetration, **AOR 2.45 [1.15, 5.24]** |
| 1 instance of other substances vs. none in the last 30 days | Lifetime physical/psychological/sexual IPV victimisation, AOR 1.48 [0.29, 7.51] |
| | Lifetime physical/psychological/sexual IPV perpetration, AOR 2.32 [0.45, 11.96] |
| 2+ instances of other substances vs. none in the last 30 days | Lifetime physical/psychological/sexual IPV victimisation, **AOR 4.14 [1.07, 16.12]** |
| | Lifetime physical/psychological/sexual IPV perpetration, **AOR 5.03 [1.41, 17.95]** |

*Table 16.3* (Continued)

| Study, recruitment period, location, sample size | Outcome measure | Associations investigated with IPV measures (exposure variable) | Variables adjusted for |
|---|---|---|---|
| Cross-sectional study (Bacchus et al., 2017), 2010–2011, London, N=532 gay/bisexual men | Cannabis use (past year) | Past year physical/psychological/sexual IPV victimisation, **AOR 1.5 [1.1, 1.9]**<br>Past year physical/psychological/sexual IPV perpetration, AOR 1.5 [0.8, 3.1] | Age, ethnicity, income, educational attainment and clinic site |
| | Class A drug use (past year) | Past year physical/psychological/sexual IPV victimisation, **AOR 1.7 [1.16, 2.47]**<br>Past year physical/psychological/sexual IPV perpetration, AOR 1.27 [0.66, 2.46] | |
| | Alcohol dependence/abuse (AUDIT-C test) | Past year physical/psychological/sexual IPV victimisation, **AOR 1.7 [1.5, 1.8]**<br>Past year physical/psychological/sexual IPV perpetration, AOR 1.3 [0.3, 5.1] | |
| Cross-sectional study (Chen et al., 2019), 2011–2012, Taiwan, N=120 MSM living with HIV | Recreational drug use (past week) | Lifetime physical/psychological/sexual IPV victimisation, **AOR 1.25 [CI not reported]; p<0.05** | Age, education, socio-economic status, years since diagnosis, viral load, physical quality of life, anxiety and social support |
| Cross-sectional study (Mimiaga et al., 2015), 2012, Latin America, N=19772 | Hazardous alcohol use (CAGE scale) | Past five years physical/psychological/sexual IPV victimisation, **OR 2.06 [1.87, 2.27]** | Clustering by country using generalised estimating equations (GEEs) |
| Cross-sectional study (Davis et al., 2016), 2013, US, N=189 GBMSM with a regular partner in the past year (n=155 with a casual partner) | Higher levels of alcohol use (AUDIT) | Past year physical/sexual IPV victimisation (regular partner), **AOR 1.11 [1.03, 1.20]**<br>Past year physical/sexual IPV victimisation (casual partner), **AOR 1.27 [1.13, 1.43]**<br>Past year physical/sexual IPV perpetration (regular partner), **AOR 1.13 [1.04, 1.22]**<br>Past year physical/sexual IPV perpetration (regular partner), **AOR 1.23 [1.08, 1.40]** | Age, ethnicity and education |
| RCT (Brown et al., 2016), 2009–2014, US, N=340 HIV-positive GBSMSM (at baseline) | Substance abuse (SAMISS) (exposure variable) | Past month physical/psychological IPV victimisation (after disclosure of HIV serostatus), **AOR 1.09 [1.01, 1.16]** (outcome variable) | Age and income |

| Study | Variable | Outcome | Adjusted for |
|---|---|---|---|
| ISHKonnect (Wilkerson et al., 2018), 2013–2014, India, N=433 | Alcohol dependence/abuse (AUDIT-C test) | Past year physical/psychological/sexual IPV victimisation, AOR 1.50 [0.88, 2.57] | Income, being married to a woman, 'outness', number of sexual partners and HIV testing |
| | Illicit drug use (past year) | Past year physical/psychological/sexual IPV victimisation, **AOR 2.21 [1.12, 4.38]** | Being married to a woman, being in a long-term relationship with a man, 'outness', number of sexual partners and anal CLS. |
| | Polysubstance use (two or more drugs used in the past year or one illicit drug and alcohol dependence/abuse) | Past year physical/psychological/sexual IPV victimisation, **AOR 6.33 [2.13, 18.83]** | Being married to a woman, 'outness', number of sexual partners, HIV testing, anal CLS and transactional sex |
| Cohort study (H. Y. Wang et al., 2018), 2014, China, N=476 HIV-negative GBMSM at baseline | Recreational drug use (past three months) (exposure variable) | Past three months physical/psychological/sexual IPV victimisation, OR 1.50 [0.70, 3.00] (outcome measure) | Unadjusted |
| China MP3 Project (N. Wang et al., 2020), 2013–2015, China, N=367 GBMSM newly diagnosed with HIV | Illicit drug use (past three months) (exposure variable) | Lifetime physical/psychological/sexual IPV victimisation (outcome measure): Drug use vs. no drug use: 21.5% vs. 24.8% (p=0.48) | Unadjusted |
| The PrEP Brasil demonstration project, (De Boni et al., 2018) 2014–2015, Brazil, N=421 | Polysubstance use (two or more of marijuana, crack/cocaine, non-prescription benzodiazepines, amphetamines, inhalants and hallucinogens; past three months) | Lifetime physical/sexual IPV victimisation, OR 1.68 (0.76, 3.71) | Unadjusted |

*(Continued)*

247

*Table 16.3* (Continued)

| Study, recruitment period, location, sample size | Outcome measure | Associations investigated with IPV measures (exposure variable) | Variables adjusted for |
|---|---|---|---|
| Cross-sectional study (Davis et al., 2015), study period not reported (published 2015), China, N=610 GBMSM with current male sexual partner(s) | Ever consumed recreational drugs (past year) | Lifetime physical/psychological IPV victimisation (current male partner), AOR 1.48 [0.98, 2.19] | Age, ethnicity, urban/rural location, region, education and income |
| Cross-sectional study (Liu et al., 2018, 2015, China, N=732 | Ever used illicit drugs (exposure variable) | Lifetime physical/psychological/sexual IPV victimisation, AOR 0.95 [0.53, 1.69] (outcome measure) | Age, education, marital status and sexual identity |
| Cross-sectional study (Duncan et al., 2018), 2015, US, n=175 | Recreational drug use (including marijuana) (past month) | Lifetime physical/psychological/sexual IPV victimisation, **AOR 1.78 [0.97, 1.06]** | Age, ethnicity, sexual orientation, education and income |
| Cross-sectional study (Lee et al., 2020), 2017, US, N=139 Latino GBMSM (18–29 years) | Frequency of recreational drug use (past month; responses ranging from no use to about every day) | Past month physical/psychological IPV victimisation (main partner), **polychoric correlation (network analysis) 0.59 (p<0.001)** | CLS, recreational drug, use, injection drug use, alcohol use, depression, CSA, poverty, unstable housing and prison history |
| | Frequency of injection drug use (past month; responses ranging from no use to about every day) | Past month physical/psychological IPV victimisation (main partner), **polychoric correlation (network analysis) 0.44 (p<0.001)** | CLS, recreational drug, use, injection drug use, alcohol use, depression, CSA, poverty, unstable housing and prison history |
| | Highest number of alcoholic drinks consumed on any one occasion in the past month | Past month physical/psychological IPV victimisation (main partner), **polychoric correlation (network analysis) –0.25 (p<0.05)** | CLS, recreational drug, use, injection drug use, alcohol use, depression, CSA, poverty, unstable housing and prison history |
| Cross-sectional survey (Wei et al., 2019), 2018–2019, China, N=431 | Recreational drug use (lifetime) | Lifetime physical/psychological/sexual IPV victimisation, OR 1.50 [1.00, 2.30] | Unadjusted |

AOR = adjusted odds ratio (Logistic regression)

*Table 16.4* Associations of IPV measures with mental health symptoms in studies of GBMSM

| Study, recruitment period, location, sample size | Outcome measure | Associations investigated with IPV measures (exposure variable) | Variables adjusted for |
|---|---|---|---|
| Cross-sectional study (Bacchus et al., 2017), 2010–2011, London, N=532 gay/bisexual men | Depression (Hospital and Anxiety Scale, HADS score of ≥8)<br><br>Anxiety (Hospital and Anxiety Scale, HADS score of ≥8) | Past year physical/psychological/sexual IPV victimisation, APR 1.4 [0.8, 2.4]<br>Past year physical/psychological/sexual IPV perpetration, **APR 1.8 [1.0, 3.3]**<br>Past year physical/psychological/sexual IPV victimisation, APR 0.8 [0.3, 2.0]<br>Past year physical/psychological/sexual IPV perpetration, **APR 3.7 [1.0, 14.6]** | Age, ethnicity, income, educational attainment and clinic site |
| Cross-sectional study (Mimiaga et al., 2015), 2012, Latin America, N=19772 | Depression (CES-D 10 score of ≥10) | Past five years physical/psychological/sexual IPV victimisation, **OR 1.76 [1.57, 1.96]** | Clustering by country using generalised estimating equations (GEEs) |
| RCT (Brown et al., 2016), 2009–2014, US, N=340 HIV-positive GBSMSM (at baseline) | Depression (CES-D score of ≥16) (exposure variable) | Past month physical/psychological IPV victimisation (after disclosure of HIV serostatus), AOR 1.27 [0.43, 4.27] (outcome variable) | Age and income |
| The PROUD trial (Miltz et al., 2019), 2012–2014 (baseline) – two years follow-up, England, N=436 (month 12/24) | Depression (Patient Health Questionnaire, PHQ-9 score of ≥10) | Lifetime physical/psychological/sexual IPV victimisation, **APR 2.57 [1.71, 3.86]**<br>Past year physical/psychological/sexual IPV victimisation, **APR 2.93 [1.96, 4.40]**<br>Lifetime physical/psychological/sexual IPV perpetration, **APR 2.87 [1.91, 4.32]**<br>Past year physical/psychological/sexual IPV perpetration, **APR 3.47 [2.13, 5.64]** | Age, born in the UK, sexual identity, university education and clinic site |
| Cohort study (H. Y. Wang et al., 2018), 2014, China, N=476 HIV-negative GBMSM at baseline | Depression (CES-D score of ≥16) (exposure variable) | Past three month physical/psychological/sexual IPV victimisation, **AOR 2.80 [1.70, 4.50]** (outcome measure) | Age, income and marital status |

*(Continued)*

*Table 16.4* (Continued)

| Study, recruitment period, location, sample size | Outcome measure | Associations investigated with IPV measures (exposure variable) | Variables adjusted for |
|---|---|---|---|
| The PrEP Brasil demonstration project, (De Boni et al., 2018) 2014–2015, Brazil, N=421 | Depression (PHQ-2 score of ≥3) | Lifetime physical/sexual IPV victimisation, **OR 9.34 [3.56, 24.5]** | Unadjusted |
| Cross-sectional study (Jiang et al., 2019; Jiang et al., 2020), 2017, China, N=976 | Depression (Zung self-rating depression scale SDS score of ≥0.5) | Lifetime physical/psychological/sexual IPV victimisation, **OR 1.67 [1.15, 2.42]** | Unadjusted |
| | | Lifetime physical/psychological/sexual IPV victimisation, **Beta coefficient 0.113 (p<0.001)** from structural equation modelling (SEM) | Education, income, sexual partner-seeking behaviour and childhood sexual abuse. |
| Cross-sectional study (Lee et al., 2020), 2017, US, N=139 Latino GBMSM (18–29 years) | Depression (PHQ-8, continuous) | Past month physical/psychological IPV victimisation (main partner), **polychoric correlation (network analysis) 0.26 (p<0.001)** | CLS, recreational drug, use, injection drug use, alcohol use, depression, CSA, poverty, unstable housing and prison history |
| Cross-sectional study (Peng et al., 2020), 2019, China, N=578 | Depression (CES-D-10, continuous) | Lifetime physical/psychological/sexual IPV victimisation, indirect Beta coefficients from SEM: **0.031 (p<0.001) via self-stigma 0.084 (p<0.001) via self-efficacy 0.033 (p<0.001) via self-stigma and then self-efficacy** | Age and income |

APR  = adjusted prevalence ratio (modified Poisson regression)

AOR  = adjusted odds ratio (Logistic regression)

perhaps as a result of their relationship having ended, may also explain this finding. However, this is unclear, as information on sexual behaviour was not collected. Three studies failed to find an association between IPV and measures of sexual risk behaviour. In two such studies, the very high numbers of CLS partners reported may explain these findings. The sample size was also limited in two studies (N=139 and N=436). Six recent studies have investigated the link between IPV victimisation and HIV, four of which found a strong link with HIV prevalence or HIV incidence (see Table 16.5). There is some evidence to suggest that GBMSM experiencing IPV are more likely to think that their partner would not support their use of pre-exposure prophylaxis (PrEP) medication to prevent HIV infection or not know if their partner would support their PrEP use (Kahle, Sharma, Sullivan, & Stephenson, 2020), and are less likely to use PrEP (Braksmajer, Walters, Crean, Stephenson, & McMahon, 2020).

The relationships described here may operate in the opposite direction. For instance, substance use and depression may act as a catalyst for enactment of violence or heighten vulnerability to dysfunctional relationship dynamics as adaptive coping mechanisms are distorted (Beck, 2008; Goldenberg et al., 2016; Herek & Sims, 2008). As described by syndemic theory, these psychosocial factors (depression, drug use and IPV) may influence each other in a cyclical pattern, with implications for an exaggerated risk of poor health outcomes including STI/HIV transmission. There is some evidence in favour of supporting this theory (Jie, Ciyong, Xueqing, Hui, & Lingyao, 2012; Mimiaga et al., 2015; Parsons, Grov, & Golub, 2012).

There is a lack of data on the link between IPV and chronic health conditions other than HIV. However, it is clear that a substantial proportion of GBMSM experiencing IPV may acquire physical injuries as a result: 20% to 30% (Bacchus et al., 2017; Goldberg-Looney, Perrin, Snipes, & Calton, 2016; Kubicek et al., 2016). No data is available on homicides related to partner violence among sexual minority men.

## Help-seeking behaviour among sexual minority men who experience IPV

Two recent literature reviews have synthesised qualitative findings on barriers to help-seeking among male victims of IPV, one of which focused on sexual minorities (Rolle et al., 2018) and the other on men regardless of sexual identity (Huntley et al., 2019). The vast majority of studies reviewed were conducted in the US. All men reported social pressure to adhere to masculine ideals of being tough and violent. Experiencing abuse contradicted these ideals. This was a key factor in non-disclosure of IPV as were fears about not being believed or being falsely accused of perpetrating the abuse. Factors commonly described by female victims were also, albeit to a lesser degree, barriers to seeking help: threat of retaliation from the perpetrator, commitment to the relationship, cultural norms, and diminished confidence and symptoms of post-traumatic stress disorder.

For sexual minority men, there may be an additional obstacle to seeking help. Violence between men was often considered admissible and normalised since men were assumed to have comparable physical strength and violent tendencies. This further prevented men from recognising abusive behaviours. In one study, 64% of sexual minority men who experienced abuse from a partner at least once reported that they had never been in a domestically violent or abusive partnership. Interviews with a sub-sample of men reiterated these findings, whereby abusive behaviours were described as "par for the course" and "just aggression in the house" (Bacchus, Buller, Ferrari, Brzank, & Feder, 2016).

Furthermore, even when sexual minority men identified IPV some reported ignoring the abuse in order to protect themselves from what was perceived as a heteronormative and

Table 16.5 Associations of IPV with measures of sexual risk behaviour and HIV in studies of GBMSM

| Study, recruitment period, location, sample size | Outcome measure – recall period | Associations investigated with IPV measures (exposure variable) | Variables adjusted for |
|---|---|---|---|
| The Brothers Project (Williams et al., 2015), 2009–2010, US, N=1522 Black GBMSM | Insertive CLS – past six months; Receptive CLS – past six months | Lifetime physical IPV victimisation, AOR 1.17 [0.68, 2.01]; Lifetime sexual IPV victimisation, AOR 0.73 [0.44, 1.21]; Lifetime physical IPV victimisation, AOR 1.02 [0.56, 1.86]; Lifetime sexual IPV victimisation, AOR 1.35 [0.76, 2.41] | Age, sexual identity, education, type of last partner at sex (casual, etc.), enrolment HIV status, non-injection drug use and study site |
| Cross-sectional study (Finneran & Stephenson, 2014), 2010, US, N=1575 | CLS at last sex | Past year physical IPV victimisation (outcome variable), AOR 1.00 [0.64, 1.57]; Past year sexual IPV victimisation (outcome variable), AOR 0.28 [0.47, 1.66]; Past year physical IPV perpetration (outcome variable), **AOR 2.08 [1.12, 3.85]** | Age, ethnicity, sexual identity, educational attainment, employment status and HIV status |
| Cross-sectional study (Bacchus et al., 2017), 2010–2011, London, N=532 gay/bisexual men | STI diagnosis – past year | Past year physical/psychological/sexual IPV victimisation, APR 0.7 [0.4, 1.2]; Past year physical/psychological/sexual IPV perpetration, **APR 0.7 [0.5, 0.9]** | Age, ethnicity, income, educational attainment and clinic site |
| Cross-sectional study (Tomori et al., 2018), 2012–2013, India, N=11771 | CLS – past six months; Active syphilis infection (based on blood samples provided) | Lifetime physical IPV victimisation, **APR 1.39 [1.16, 1.67]**; Lifetime physical IPV victimisation, APR 1.38 [0.99, 1.91] | Age, sexual identity, city and educational attainment |
| The PROUD trial (Miltz et al., 2019), 2012–2014 (baseline) – two years follow-up, England, N=436 (month 12/24) | CLS with 2+ partners – past three months | Lifetime physical/psychological/sexual IPV victimisation, APR 1.03 [0.87, 1.23]; Past year physical/psychological/sexual IPV victimisation, APR 1.11 [0.89, 1.39]; Lifetime physical/psychological/sexual IPV perpetration, APR 1.01 [0.81, 1.27]; Past year physical/psychological/sexual IPV perpetration, APR 0.98 [0.70, 1.36] | Age, born in the UK, sexual identity, university education and clinic site |

| Study | Measure | Results | Adjustments |
|---|---|---|---|
| Cohort study (H. Y. Wang et al., 2018), 2014, China, N=476 HIV-negative GBMSM at baseline | CLS with an HIV+ partner not known to be on antiretroviral treatment – past three months | Lifetime physical/psychological/sexual IPV victimisation, APR 1.28 [0.83, 1.97] Past year physical/psychological/sexual IPV victimisation, APR 1.13 [0.64, 1.97] Lifetime physical/psychological/sexual IPV perpetration, APR 0.95 [0.53, 1.70] Past year physical/psychological/sexual IPV perpetration, APR 0.86 [0.34, 2.14] | Age, income and marital status |
| | Receptive CLS – past three months (exposure variable) Insertive CLS – past three months (exposure variable) HIV incidence (based on 12 months of follow-up, survey every three months) | Past three months physical/psychological/sexual IPV victimisation, AOR 1.50 [0.90, 2.50] (outcome measure) Past three months physical/psychological/sexual IPV victimisation, **AOR 1.80 [1.10, 2.90]** (outcome measure) Past three months physical/psychological/sexual IPV victimisation, **AHR 4.1 [1.50, 11.60]** | Age, income, educational attainment and marital status |
| Longitudinal study (Beymer et al., 2017; Beymer et al., 2016), 2009–2015, US | HIV diagnosis (2011, N=1947) HIV incidence (during follow-up, 2011–2015 N=936) HIV incidence (during follow-up, 2009–2014 N=2653 Latino GBMSM) | Lifetime physical/psychological/sexual IPV victimisation, **AOR 2.39 [1.35, 4.23]** Lifetime physical/psychological/sexual IPV victimisation, **AHR 3.33 [1.47, 7.55]** Lifetime physical/psychological/sexual IPV victimisation, **AHR 1.73 [1.13, 2.64]** | Age, ethnicity, substance use, STI diagnosis, receptive CLS at last sex, and number of partners (past three months) Age, country of birth, substance use, STI diagnosis, receptive CLS with last sex partner, ethnicity and age of last sex partner, and number of partners (past three months) |

*(Continued)*

Table 16.5 (Continued)

| Study, recruitment period, location, sample size | Outcome measure – recall period | Associations investigated with IPV measures (exposure variable) | Variables adjusted for |
|---|---|---|---|
| Cross-sectional study (Davis et al., 2015), study period not reported (published 2015), China, N=610 GBMSM with current male sexual partner(s) | CLS at last sex | Lifetime physical/psychological IPV victimisation (current male partner), AOR 1.49 [0.99, 2.23] | Age, ethnicity, urban/rural location, region, education and income |
|  | Ever been diagnosed with an STI | Lifetime physical/psychological IPV victimisation (current male partner), AOR 1.35 [0.77, 2.36] |  |
|  | HIV diagnosis | Lifetime physical/psychological IPV victimisation (current male partner), **AOR 2.79 [1.31, 5.95]** |  |
| Cross-sectional study (Liu et al., 2018), 2015, China, N=732 | Ever had sex with casual male partner(s) (exposure variable) | Lifetime physical/psychological/sexual IPV victimisation, **AOR 1.72 [1.15, 2.57]** (outcome measure) | Age, education, marital status and sexual identity |
|  | Ever been diagnosed with a STI (exposure variable) | Lifetime physical/psychological/sexual IPV victimisation, **AOR 1.80 [1.12, 2.88]** (outcome measure) |  |
|  | HIV diagnosis | 1 type of IPV victimisation ever vs. none, AOR 2.01 [0.94, 4.32] 2+ types of IPV victimisation ever vs. none, AOR 0.74 [0.38, 1.43] |  |
| Cross-sectional study (Duncan et al., 2018), 2015, US, N=175 | Number of receptive CLS partners – past three months | Lifetime physical/psychological/sexual IPV victimisation, **AIRR 1.80 [1.03, 3.14]** | Age, ethnicity, sexual orientation, education and income |
|  | Number of insertive CLS partners – past three months | Lifetime physical/psychological/sexual IPV victimisation, **AIRR 2.10 [1.12, 3.93]** |  |
| Priorities for Local AIDS Control Efforts (PLACE) study (Zalla et al., 2019), 2015, Haiti, N=488 | HIV prevalence | Past year physical IPV victimisation, **PR 51.58 [20.47, 129.98]** | Unadjusted |

| | | | |
|---|---|---|---|
| Cross-sectional study (Jiang et al., 2019; Jiang et al., 2020), 2017, China, N=976 | Any CLS – past six months; Frequency of condom use during anal sex in the past three months (response options range from never to always); HIV prevalence | Lifetime physical/psychological/sexual IPV victimisation, **OR 1.60 [1.10, 2.33]**; Lifetime physical/psychological/sexual IPV victimisation, **Pearson's correlation – 0.09 (p<0.01)**; Lifetime physical/psychological/sexual IPV victimisation, OR 1.14 [0.57, 2.30] | Unadjusted |
| Cross-sectional study (Lee et al., 2020), 2017, US, N=139 Latino GBMSM (18–29 years) | CLS (past three months): Zero partners; One partner; Two or more partners | Past month physical/psychological IPV victimisation (main partner), polychoric correlation (network analysis) –0.15 (p>0.05) | CLS, recreational drug use, injection drug use, alcohol use, depression, CSA, poverty, unstable housing and prison history |

CLS = condomless sex

APR = adjusted prevalence ratio (modified Poisson regression)

AOR = adjusted odds ratio (Logistic regression)

AHR = adjusted hazard ratio (Cox regression)

AIRR = adjusted incidence rate ratio (negative binomial regression) homophobic health care and legal system. Specifically, some men described potential discomfort in disclosing IPV to a male service provider and general practitioner (GP). Sexual health clinics may be more conducive environments in which to be asked about IPV since sensitive issues including sexual identity and sexual partners are already discussed, and as a result of a greater sense of confidentiality. It was suggested in a UK study that health advisors in sexual health clinics are best placed to offer support to men experiencing IPV (Bacchus et al., 2016).

## Responding to IPV within male same-sex couples

In a recent literature review of qualitative studies, common misconceptions among service providers were that violence is always mutual between men and that gay men can more easily leave an abusive relationship as they frequently move from one partner to another (Rolle et al., 2018). The impact of these myths was the minimising of violence and abuse experienced by men in same-sex relationships and, therefore, ineffectual responses to IPV. Findings from the literature review also indicate that police often do not take reports of IPV within male same-sex couples seriously given the involvement of two men or do not recognise partners as members of a couple, particularly if men defined themselves as roommates (Rolle et al., 2018). When police did respond appropriately they were often inept in identifying the perpetrators of violence. This may be as a result of training that relies on sex as the sole criteria for identifying the aggressor. Police frequently arrested both partners, the victim, or did not follow through in terms of applying the law to the abusive partner. In a UK community/online sample (N=6861) of gay and bisexual men, of those who reported incidents of IPV to the police, 53% were not happy with how the police dealt with the situation (Guasp, 2013). This is reflected in one participant's statement;

> It is very hard to talk to them [the police] about domestic violence and I was made to feel I was wasting their time. They didn't keep me updated, failed to deal with my complaint and didn't see that the arrest of my partner was important to me and that the delay in doing it added to my worry.

The UK National Institute for Health and Care Excellence recommends that trained staff in sexual health services ask about IPV as part of good clinical practice, even where there are no indicators of violence and abuse (NICE, 2014). Sexual health care providers, those in a health advisory role in particular, may also be better equipped to navigate IPV among sexual minority men. In a UK study of gay and bisexual men (N=522), 34.7% of participants felt that sexual health professionals should ask all patients whether they have been hurt/frightened by a partner, whereas 62.6% felt only some patients should be asked based on symptoms (Bacchus et al., 2016). In a parallel study (HEalthcare Responding to MEn for Safety, HERMES), interviews with providers in a sexual health service for sexual minorities revealed a preference among some for routinely asking all men about IPV as opposed to being prompted by symptoms, which they found difficult to remember and judge (Buller, 2019). Additionally, there was some evidence from the interviews with health care providers and an audit of medical records to indicate that men who disclosed IPV were reluctant to accept a referral to the external service (Buller, Bacchus, Brzank, & Feder, 2014). These findings suggest that at the very least sexual health services should display information on IPV within male same-sex couples, as well as train staff to recognise indicators of abuse, enquire sensitively about violence and refer sexual minority men to further support within and outside of the health care setting. Similar recommendations have been made in a number of US studies of GBMSM (Rolle et al., 2018).

## Researching and responding to IPV within male same-sex couples: challenges and key debates

In countries with state-sanctioned anti-gay violence and discrimination, collecting data on male same-sex relationships is deeply challenging, and often impossible. In all countries, challenges to researching IPV among sexual minority men include the absence of a population list from which to collect a representative sample, the need to collect data over time in a longitudinal study to unpick the temporal sequence of events, and the need to collect a wider range of data on sensitive topics including experiences of abuse in childhood and emotional ties with primary caregivers.

There is also a dearth of data on the dynamics of IPV within male same-sex relationships. Four distinct categories of IPV have been observed in opposite-sex couples (Johnson, 2008). The category 'intimate terrorism', perpetrated by one partner only, describes the phenomenon of escalating control and violence to induce fear and exert power over a partner. Intimate terrorism has been linked to the social construct of hegemonic masculinity (Hester, 2012). For the remaining categories of IPV, violence/abuse is mutual, an act of self-defence, or not attached to a pattern of escalating control. Evidence suggests that violence perpetrated by women is much more likely to be an act of self-defence than an unsolicited attempt to exert control over a partner (Hester, 2012). Knowledge of the gendered dynamics of IPV is often utilised by police when assessing whether an individual in an opposite-sex partnership is a victim or perpetrator of violence (Hester, 2012; M. L. Walters et al., 2013). Data are lacking on the prevalence and circumstances of unidirectional and reciprocal IPV within male same-sex couples. In a recent study of 160 US male same-sex couples recruited online, 54 (33.8%) reported reciprocal IPV (each partner reported experiencing IPV with their partner) and 40 (25.0%) reported unidirectional IPV in the past year (Suarez et al., 2018). In this study, there was some evidence to suggest that younger men and men living with their partners were more likely to have both experienced and perpetrated IPV with the same partner in the past year. Similarly, in another US study of 26 couples (Black GBMSM methamphetamine users), 16 (61.5%) reported reciprocal IPV (each partner reported experiencing and perpetrating IPV with their partner) (Wu et al., 2015). There is an urgent need to better understand these dynamics in order to help police and other service providers avoid incorrectly blaming victims of IPV. Intersectionality may be an important theoretical framework for understanding the dynamics of IPV in same-sex couples (Subirana-Malaret et al., 2019).

Even if this data were available the challenge remains how to translate research findings into interventions in the context of downplaying of violence between male partners and the additional perpetration of homophobic abuse by service providers. Educational campaigns or smart phone applications are needed to encourage sexual minorities to identify abuse, assess their risk of danger, develop safety plans and navigate available resources. This may include apps such as myPlan (myPlan, 2019), which has been tested with women experiencing IPV in heterosexual relationships (Glass et al., 2017; Koziol-McLain et al., 2018). In parallel, adequate training for health care providers on homophobia and heterosexism will likely be highly beneficial. Once these issues have been tackled, attention can be turned to the question of how best to respond to IPV within male same-sex couples.

In the UK, a key debate is whether to screen all sexual minority men attending health care services for IPV. Given the absence of evidence for effective interventions among GBMSM – in a 2019 review no studies of IPV interventions aimed at LGBT+ populations were found in peer-reviewed academic articles (published in English) (Subirana-Malaret et al., 2019) – a case-finding approach based on symptoms that are consistent with experiences of IPV may be more pragmatic. Domestic violence training programmes for health care providers should also raise awareness of intersecting socio-cultural statuses rendering people more vulnerable to IPV. If GBMSM are reluctant to be referred to external organisations for support after disclosure, resources could be directed towards upskilling of appropriate health care providers in the principles of basic counselling or a trauma-informed response. This has also been recommended for women subjected to IPV (WHO, 2014). In the context of UK sexual health services, health care advisors who provide counselling and advice may be the most appropriate professionals to assume this role (Bacchus et al., 2016). Evaluation studies are urgently needed to investigate which interventions work for sexual minority men; however before this can be achieved, more formative research is needed to explore what kinds of interventions may work in sexual health settings. Sexual minority men are not a homogenous group. Therefore, an additional challenge is to understand the different needs of ethnic and cultural groups.

Alongside these necessary steps, we believe it is important to emphasise the need to intervene with sexual minority individuals at a young age, that is in schools and/or in LGBT+ youth groups. This may prevent the internalising of homophobic attitudes and normalising of violence in male same-sex relationships, with implications for curtailing experiences of IPV in adulthood.

## Conclusions

When addressing IPV, there is an urgent need to also acknowledge and bring to the fore the prevalence of violence and abuse in same-sex male couples. IPV is strongly associated with sexualised drug use, internalised homophobia, substance use, depression, CLS and HIV positivity among GBMSM. The cumulative effects of different forms of discrimination and oppression may also increase vulnerability to IPV. There is a need for further data to be collected over time in order to better understand the temporal sequence of events. A key challenge is how to translate research findings into effective interventions given social norms surrounding violence between men and homophobic discrimination. There is an urgent need to develop and test culturally competent interventions.

# Appendix

# SEARCH STRATEGIES TO IDENTIFY GBMSM STUDIES OF IPV PUBLISHED SINCE 2014[a]

| Database | Description[b] | MeSH terms | Fields (i.e. title, abstract) | Limits |
|---|---|---|---|---|
| PubMed | MSM sexual lifestyles/ behaviour search | ("men who have sex with men" AND ("HIV acquisition" OR "unsafe sex" [MeSH Terms] OR "HIV testing" OR "Pre-Exposure Prophylaxis" OR "Post-Exposure Prophylaxis" | All fields | Publication date from 2014/01/01 Humans, Male |
| PubMed | MSM IPV search | ([Intimate partner violence] OR IPV) AND MSM | All fields | Publication date from 2014/01/01 Humans, Male |

[a] Results from all studies identified as eligible were reviewed. All eligible studies were organised and summarised according to their recruitment setting. If a mixed method approach to recruitment was utilised, for instance if men were recruited from sexual health clinics, gay venues and online, then studies were described under the site at which the largest proportion of the sample was recruited. For studies that used mixed approaches to recruitment and did not report the proportion recruited from each site, the following rules were considered to be appropriate: (1) if online sampling was reported, this method of recruitment was assumed to have generated the largest number of men for study participation and (2) if a number of community/commercial gay venues were sited together with sexual health clinics as sites of recruitment, the former was assumed to have generated the largest number of men for study participation. Studies that recruited only from sexual health clinics were described in the clinic section.

[b] Two separate searches were undertaken. The 'MSM sexual lifestyles/behaviour search' was part of an existing review carried out by ARM. All studies identified in this search were screened to determine if data on IPV was presented. The second ('MSM IPV search') was implemented in order to specifically search for studies investigating violence within intimate partnerships among MSM.

## Critical findings

- In a meta-analysis of US studies, the pooled prevalence of any lifetime IPV victimisation among GBMSM was very high at 48%.
- The prevalence of any lifetime IPV perpetration has been reported in a number of recent studies of GBMSM, with estimates ranging from 16% to 34%.

- Younger age, minority ethnicity, lower socio-economic status, sexualised drug use (chem-sex), group sex, internalised homophobia, homophobic discrimination, concealment of sexual identity, identifying as bisexual and racist discrimination have been linked to IPV in studies of GBMSM.
- There is consistent evidence that experiencing and perpetrating IPV is strongly associated with substance use, depressive symptoms, CLS and HIV positivity.
- Social norms regarding masculinity, heteronormative discourse and homophobic discrimination negatively impacts on sexual minority men's capacity to recognise IPV and seek help. A key challenge is how to translate research findings into effective interventions in this context.
- Addressing these issues may require educational campaigns and enhanced training for health care providers.
- A better understanding of which interventions work for sexual minority men is essential in addressing IPV.

## Implications for policy, practice and research

- When addressing IPV, there is an urgent need to also acknowledge and bring to the fore the prevalence of violence and abuse in same-sex male couples.
- There is a need to collect data over time in a longitudinal study in order to explore the causal relationships between exposure to IPV and health outcomes and inform effective interventions.
- There is a need to collect a wider range of data, including experiences of abuse in child-hood, in order to inform the design of complex interventions targeting multiple levels of risk/vulnerability.
- A better understanding of IPV dynamics within male same-sex couples is needed in order to help police and other service providers avoid incorrectly charging/blaming victims of IPV.
- Educational campaigns that encourage sexual minorities to identify abuse and navigate available resources and training for service providers that attends to the issues of heterosex-ism and homophobia, is needed to address barriers to help-seeking for men experiencing IPV from a male partner.
- Sexual minority men may favour selective enquiry about IPV in health care settings, but further evidence is needed to address this issue.
- In health care settings where it is not possible to refer sexual minority men to IPV services tailored to same-sex couples, there is a need to direct resources towards upskilling of appropriate health care providers.
- There is a need to intervene with sexual minority individuals at a young age in order to prevent the internalising of homophobic attitudes and normalising of violence in male same-sex relationships, which may curtail experiences of IPV.
- Formative research to develop and test interventions, particularly in sexual and mental health settings, is needed in order to investigate which interventions work for sexual minority men experiencing IPV.

## Note

1 This work has been adapted from the original article "Associations between intimate partner violence and health among men who have sex with men: a systematic review and meta-analysis" by Buller, A.

M., Devries, K. M., Howard, L. M., & Bacchus, L. J. (2014). *PLoS Med, 11*(3), e1001609 (https://journals.plos.org/plosmedicine/article?id=10.1371/journal.pmed.1001609). The original article is an open access article distributed under the terms of the Creative Commons Attribution License (http://creativecommons.org/licenses/by/2.0), which permits unrestricted use, distribution and reproduction in any medium, provided the original work is properly cited. Of note, the chief lead and senior author of this paper are co-authors of this chapter.

# References

Bacchus, L. J., Buller, A. M., Ferrari, G., Brzank, P., & Feder, G. (2016). "It's always good to ask": A mixed methods study on the perceived role of sexual health practitioners asking gay and bisexual men about experiences of domestic violence and abuse. *Journal of Mixed Methods Research.* doi:10.1177/1558689816651808

Bacchus, L. J., Buller, A. M., Ferrari, G., Peters, T. J., Devries, K., Sethi, G., . . . Feder, G. S. (2017). Occurrence and impact of domestic violence and abuse in gay and bisexual men: A cross sectional survey. *International Journal of STD & AIDS, 28*(1), 16–27. doi:10.1177/0956462415622886

Bailey, S. L., & Handu, D. (2013). *Introduction to epidemiologic research methods in public health practice.* Burlington, MA: Jones & Bartlett Learning.

Bartholomew, K., Regan, K. V., Oram, D., & White, M. A. (2008). Correlates of partner abuse in male same-sex relationships. *Violence and Victims, 23*(3), 344–360.

Beck, A. T. (2008). The evolution of the cognitive model of depression and its neurobiological correlates. *American Journal of Psychiatry, 165*(8), 969–977. doi:10.1176/appi.ajp.2008.08050721

Beymer, M. R., Harawa, N. T., Weiss, R. E., Shover, C. L., Toynes, B. R., Meanley, S., & Bolan, R. K. (2017). Are partner race and intimate partner violence associated with incident and newly diagnosed HIV infection in African-American men who have sex with men? *Journal of Urban Health, 94*(5), 666–675. doi:10.1007/s11524-017-0169-7

Beymer, M. R., Weiss, R. E., Halkitis, P. N., Kapadia, F., Ompad, D. C., Bourque, L., & Bolan, R. K. (2016). Disparities within the disparity-determining HIV risk factors among latino gay and bisexual men attending a community-based Clinic in Los Angeles, CA. *Journal of Acquired Immune Deficiency Syndrome, 73*(2), 237–244. doi:10.1097/qai.0000000000001072

Bourne, A., Reid, D., Hickson, F., Torres Rueda, S., & Weatherburn, P. (2014). *The Chemsex Study: Drug use in sexual settings among gay and bisexual men in Lambeth, Southwark & Lewisham.* Retrieved from https://researchonline.lshtm.ac.uk/id/eprint/2197245/1/report2014a.pdf

Braksmajer, A., Walters, S. M., Crean, H. F., Stephenson, R., & McMahon, J. M. (2020). Pre-exposure prophylaxis use among men who have sex with men experiencing partner violence. *AIDS Behaviour.* doi:10.1007/s10461-020-02789-2

Brown, M. J., Serovich, J. M., & Kimberly, J. A. (2016). Depressive symptoms, substance use and partner violence victimization associated with HIV disclosure among men who have sex with men. *AIDS Behaviour, 20*(1), 184–192. doi:10.1007/s10461-015-1122-y

Buller, A. M. (2019, September 13). [Personal communication: HERMES findings].

Buller, A. M., Bacchus, L. J., Brzank, P., & Feder, G. (2014). *HERMES [HEalth professionals Responding to MEn for Safety]. Multi-method evaluation of a pilot domestic violence and abuse (DVA) training and support intervention in a sexual health clinic for lesbian, gay, bisexual and transgender people.* Paper presented at the PROVIDE conference United Kingdom.

Buller, A. M., Devries, K. M., Howard, L. M., & Bacchus, L. J. (2014). Associations between intimate partner violence and health among men who have sex with men: A systematic review and meta-analysis. *PLoS Med, 11*(3), e1001609. doi:10.1371/journal.pmed.1001609

Castro, R., De Boni, R. B., Luz, P. M., Velasque, L., Lopes, L. V., Medina-Lara, A., . . . Veloso, V. G. (2019). Health-related quality of life assessment among people living with HIV in Rio de Janeiro, Brazil: A cross-sectional study. *Quality of Life Research, 28*(4), 1035–1045. doi:10.1007/s11136-018-2044-8

CDC. (2016). *Intimate partner violence.* Retrieved from www.cdc.gov/violenceprevention/intimatepartner violence/

Chen, W. T., Shiu, C., Yang, J. P., Chuang, P., Berg, K., Chen, L. C., & Chi, P. C. (2019). Tobacco, alcohol, drug use, and intimate partner violence among MSM living with HIV. *Journal of the Association of Nurses AIDS Care, 30*(6), 610–618. doi:10.1097/jnc.0000000000000090

Choo, H. Y., & Myra, M. F. (2010). Practicing intersectionality in sociological research: A critical analysis of inclusions, interactions, and institutions in the study of inequalities. *Sociological Theory, 28*, 129–149.

Crenshaw, K. W. (1991). Mapping the margins: Intersectionality, identity politics, and violence against women of color. *Stanford Law Review, 43*, 1241–1299.

Crittenden, P. M., & Ainsworth, M. (1989). Child maltreatment and attachment theory. In D. Cicchetti & V. Carlson (Eds.), *Child maltreatment, theory and research on the causes and consequences of child abuse and neglect.* New York, NY: Cambridge University Press.

Davis, A., Best, J., Wei, C., Luo, J., Van Der Pol, B., Meyerson, B., . . . Tucker, J. (2015). Intimate Partner violence and correlates with risk behaviors and HIV/STI diagnoses among men who have sex with men and men who have sex with men and women in China: A hidden epidemic. *Sexually Transmitted Diseases, 42*(7), 387–392. doi:10.1097/olq.0000000000000302

Davis, A., Kaighobadi, F., Stephenson, R., Rael, C., & Sandfort, T. (2016). Associations between alcohol use and intimate partner violence among men who have sex with men. *LGBT Health, 3*(6), 400–406. doi:10.1089/lgbt.2016.0057

De Boni, R. B., Machado, I. K., De Vasconcellos, M. T. L., Hoagland, B., Kallas, E. G., Madruga, J. V., . . . Luz, P. M. (2018). Syndemics among individuals enrolled in the PrEP Brasil Study. *Drug Alcohol Depend, 185*, 168–172. doi:10.1016/j.drugalcdep.2017.12.016

Dickerson-Amaya, N., & Coston, B. M. (2019). Invisibility is not invincibility: The impact of intimate partner violence on gay, bisexual, and straight men's mental health. *American Journal of Men's Health, 13*(3), 1557988319849734. doi:10.1177/1557988319849734

Duncan, D. T., Goedel, W. C., Stults, C. B., Brady, W. J., Brooks, F. A., Blakely, J. S., & Hagen, D. (2018). A study of intimate partner violence, substance abuse, and sexual risk behaviors among gay, bisexual, and other men who have sex with men in a sample of geosocial-networking smartphone application users. *American Journal of Men's Health, 12*(2), 292–301. doi:10.1177/1557988316631964

Fang, X., & Corso, P. S. (2007). Child maltreatment, youth violence, and intimate partner violence: Developmental relationships. *American Journal of Preventive Medicine, 33*(4), 281–290.

Feldman, M. B., Diaz, R. M., Ream, G. L., & El-Bassel, N. (2007). Intimate partner violence and HIV sexual risk behavior among Latino gay and bisexual men. *Journal of LGBT Health Research, 3*(2), 9–19. doi:10.1300/J463v03n02_02

Fife, R. S., & Schrager, S. S. (2012). *Family violence. What health care providers need to know.* Sudbury, MA: Jones & Bartlett Learning, LLC.

Finneran, C., Chard, A., Sineath, C., Sullivan, P., & Stephenson, R. (2012). Intimate partner violence and social pressure among gay men in six countries. *Western Journal of Emergency Medicine, 13*(3), 260–271. doi:10.5811/westjem.2012.3.11779

Finneran, C., & Stephenson, R. (2014). Intimate partner violence, minority stress, and sexual risk-taking among U.S. men who have sex with men. *Journal of Homosexuality, 61*(2), 288–306.

Galupo, P., Davis, K. S., Grynkiewicz, A. L., & Mitchell, R. C. (2014). Conceptualization of sexual orientation identity among sexual minorities: Patterns across sexual and gender identity. *Journal of Bisexuality, 14*(3–4), 433–456.

Garofalo, R., Hotton, A. L., Kuhns, L. M., Gratzer, B., & Mustanski, B. (2016). Incidence of HIV infection and sexually transmitted infections and related risk factors among very young men who have sex with men. *Journal of Acquired Immune Deficiency Syndrome, 72*(1), 79–86. doi:10.1097/qai.0000000000000933

Glass, N. E., Perrin, N. A., Hanson, G. C., Bloom, T. L., Messing, J. T., Clough, A. S., . . . Eden, K. B. (2017). The longitudinal impact of an internet safety decision aid for abused women. *American Journal of Preventive Medicine, 52*(5), 606–615. doi:10.1016/j.amepre.2016.12.014

Goldberg, N. G., & Meyer, I. H. (2013). Sexual orientation disparities in history of intimate partner violence: Results from the California health interview survey. *Journal of Interpersonal Violence, 28*(5), 1109–1118. doi:10.1177/0886260512459384

Goldberg-Looney, L. D., Perrin, P. B., Snipes, D. J., & Calton, J. M. (2016). Coping styles used by sexual minority men who experience intimate partner violence. *Journal of Clinical Nursing, 25*(23–24), 3687–3696. doi:10.1111/jocn.13388

Goldenberg, T., Stephenson, R., Freeland, R., Finneran, C., & Hadley, C. (2016). "Struggling to be the alpha": Sources of tension and intimate partner violence in same-sex relationships between men. *Culture, Health & Sexuality, 18*, 875–889.

Guasp, A. (2013). *Gay and bisexual men's health survey.* Retrieved from www.stonewall.org.uk/system/files/Gay_and_Bisexual_Men_s_Health_Survey__2013_.pdf

Heise, L. L. (1998). Violence against women: An integrated, ecological framework. *Violence Against Women, 4*(3), 262–290. doi:10.1177/1077801298004003002

Herek, G. M., & Sims, C. (Eds.). (2008). *Sexual orientation and violent victimization: Hate crimes and intimate partner violence among gay and bisexual males in the United States.* New York, NY: Oxford University Press.

Hester, M. (2012). Portrayal of women as intimate partner domestic violence perpetrators. *Violence Against Women, 18*(9), 1067–1082. doi:10.1177/1077801212461428

Houston, E., & McKirnan, D. J. (2007). Intimate partner abuse among gay and bisexual men: Risk correlates and health outcomes. *Journal of Urban Health, 84*(5), 681–690. doi:10.1007/s11524-007-9188-0

Hughes, T., McCabe, S. E., Wilsnack, S. C., West, B. T., & Boyd, C. J. (2010). Victimization and substance use disorders in a national sample of heterosexual and sexual minority women and men. *Addiction, 105*(12), 2130–2140. doi:10.1111/j.1360-0443.2010.03088.x

Huntley, A. L., Potter, L., Williamson, E., Malpass, A., Szilassy, E., & Feder, G. (2019). Help-seeking by male victims of domestic violence and abuse (DVA): A systematic review and qualitative evidence synthesis. *BMJ Open, 9*(6), e021960. doi:10.1136/bmjopen-2018-021960

Ibragimov, U., Harnisch, J. A., Nehl, E. J., He, N., Zheng, T., Ding, Y., & Wong, F. Y. (2017). Estimating self-reported sex practices, drug use, depression, and intimate partner violence among MSM in China: A comparison of three recruitment methods. *AIDS Care, 29*(1), 125–131. doi:10.1080/09540121.2016.1201191

Jennings, W. G., Richards, T. N., Tomsich, E., & Gover, A. R. (2015). Investigating the role of child sexual abuse in intimate partner violence victimization and perpetration in young adulthood from a propensity score matching approach. *Journal of Child Sexual Abuse, 24*(6), 659–681.

Jiang, H., Chen, X., Li, J., Tan, Z., Cheng, W., & Yang, Y. (2019). Predictors of condom use behavior among men who have sex with men in China using a modified information-motivation-behavioral skills (IMB) model. *BMC Public Health, 19*(1), 261. doi:10.1186/s12889-019-6593-8

Jiang, H., Li, J., Tan, Z., Chen, X., Cheng, W., Gong, X., & Yang, Y. (2020). Syndemic factors and hiv risk among men who have sex with men in Guangzhou, China: Evidence from synergy and moderated analyses. *Archives of Sex Behaviour, 49*(1), 311–320. doi:10.1007/s10508-019-01488-x

Jie, W., Ciyong, L., Xueqing, D., Hui, W., & Lingyao, H. (2012). A syndemic of psychosocial problems places the MSM (men who have sex with men) population at greater risk of HIV infection. *PLoS One, 7*(3), e32312. doi:10.1371/journal.pone.0032312

Johnson, M. P. (2008). *A typology of domestic violence. Intimate terrorism, violent resistance, and situational couple violence.* Lebanon, NH: Northeastern University Press.

Kahle, E. M., Sharma, A., Sullivan, S., & Stephenson, R. (2020). The influence of relationship dynamics and sexual agreements on perceived partner support and benefit of PrEP use among same-sex male couples in the U.S. *AIDS Behaviour.* doi:10.1007/s10461-020-02782-9

Kelly, B. C., Izienicki, H., Bimb, D. S., & Parsons, J. T. (2011). The intersection of mutual partner violence and substance use among urban gays, lesbians, and bisexuals. *Deviant Behavior, 32*(5), 379–404.

Klingelschmidt, J., Parriault, M. C., Van Melle, A., Basurko, C., Gontier, B., Cabie, A., . . . Nacher, M. (2017). Transactional sex among men who have sex with men in the French Antilles and French Guiana: Frequency and associated factors. *AIDS Care, 29*(6), 689–695. doi:10.1080/09540121.2016.1234680

Koblin, B. A., Torian, L., Xu, G., Guilin, V., Makki, H., Mackellar, D., & Valleroy, L. (2006). Violence and HIV-related risk among young men who have sex with men. *AIDS Care, 18*(8), 961–967. doi:10.1080/09540120500467182

Koziol-McLain, J., Vandal, A. C., Wilson, D., Nada-Raja, S., Dobbs, T., McLean, C., . . . Glass, N. E. (2018). Efficacy of a web-based safety decision aid for women experiencing intimate partner violence: Randomized controlled trial. *Journal of Medical Internet Research, 19*(12), e426. doi:10.2196/jmir.8617

Kubicek, K., McNeeley, M., & Collins, S. (2016). Young men who have sex with men's experiences with intimate partner violence. *Journal of Adolescent Research, 31*, 143–175.

Lane, T., Osmand, T., Marr, A., Shade, S. B., Dunkle, K., Sandfort, T., . . . McIntyre, J. A. (2014). The Mpumalanga Men's Study (MPMS): Results of a baseline biological and behavioral HIV surveillance survey in two MSM communities in South Africa. *PLoS One, 9*(11), e111063. doi:10.1371/journal.pone.0111063

Lee, J. S., Safren, S. A., Bainter, S. A., Rodriguez-Diaz, C. E., Horvath, K. J., & Blashill, A. J. (2020). Examining a syndemics network among young Latino men who have sex with men. *International Journal of Behavioral Medicine, 27*(1), 39–51. doi:10.1007/s12529-019-09831-1

Liu, Y., Zhang, Y., Ning, Z., Zheng, H., Ding, Y., Gao, M., . . . He, N. (2018). Intimate partner violence victimization and HIV infection among men who have sex with men in Shanghai, China. *Bioscience Trends, 12*(2), 142–148. doi:10.5582/bst.2018.01035

McKirnan, D. J., Ostrow, D. G., & Hope, B. (1996). Sex, drugs and escape: A psychological model of HIV-risk sexual behaviours. *AIDS Care*, 8(6), 655–669. doi:10.1080/09540129650125371

Melander, L. A., Noel, H., & Tyler, K. A. (2010). Bidirectional, unidirectional, and nonviolence: A comparison of the predictors among partnered young adults. *Violence & Victims*, 25(5), 617–630.

Meyer, I. H. (1995). Minority stress and mental health in gay men. *Journal of Health and Social Behaviour*, 36(1), 38–56.

Miltz, A. R., Lampe, F. C., Bacchus, L. J., McCormack, S., Dunn, D., White, E., . . . Gafos, M. (2019). Intimate partner violence, depression, and sexual behaviour among gay, bisexual and other men who have sex with men in the PROUD trial. *BMC Public Health*, 19(1), 431. doi:10.1186/s12889-019-6757-6

Mimiaga, M. J., Biello, K. B., Robertson, A. M., Oldenburg, C. E., Rosenberger, J. G., O'Cleirigh, C., . . . Safren, S. A. (2015). High prevalence of multiple syndemic conditions associated with sexual risk behavior and HIV infection among a large sample of Spanish- and Portuguese-speaking men who have sex with men in Latin America. *Archives of Sex Behaviour*, 44(7), 1869–1878. doi:10.1007/s10508-015-0488-2

Mustanski, B., Garofalo, R., Herrick, A., & Donenberg, G. (2007). Psychosocial health problems increase risk for HIV among urban young men who have sex with men: Preliminary evidence of a syndemic in need of attention. *Annals of Behavioral Medicine*, 34(1), 37–45. doi:10.1007/bf02879919

myPlan. (2019). *Empowering decisions for a safe path forward*. Retrieved from www.myplanapp.org/home#home

NICE. (2014). *Domestic violence and abuse: How health services, social care and the organisations they work with can respond effectively*. London: NICE.

Nieves-Rosa, L. E., Carballo Dieguez, A., & Dolezal, C. (2000). Domestic abuse and HIV-risk behavior in Latin American men who have sex with men in New York City. *Journal of Gay Lesbian Social Services*, 11, 77–90.

Parsons, J. T., Grov, C., & Golub, S. A. (2012). Sexual compulsivity, co-occurring psychosocial health problems, and HIV risk among gay and bisexual men: Further evidence of a syndemic. *American Journal of Public Health*, 102(1), 156–162. doi:10.2105/ajph.2011.300284

Paul, J. P., Catania, J., Pollack, L., & Stall, R. (2001). Understanding childhood sexual abuse as a predictor of sexual risk-taking among men who have sex with men: The urban men's health study. *Child Abuse & Neglect*, 25(4), 557–584.

Peng, L., She, R., Gu, J., Hao, C., Hou, F., Wei, D., & Li, J. (2020). The mediating role of self-stigma and self-efficacy between intimate partner violence (IPV) victimization and depression among men who have sex with men in China. *BMC Public Health*, 20(1), 2. doi:10.1186/s12889-019-8125-y

Phillips, G., 2nd, Magnus, M., Kuo, I., Rawls, A., Peterson, J., Montanez, L., . . . Greenberg, A. E. (2014). Childhood sexual abuse and HIV-related risks among men who have sex with men in Washington, DC. *Archives of Sex Behaviour*, 43(4), 771–778. doi:10.1007/s10508-014-0267-5

Rolle, L., Giardina, G., Caldarera, A. M., Gerino, E., & Brustia, P. (2018). When intimate partner violence meets same sex couples: A review of same sex intimate partner violence. *Frontiers in Psychology*, 9, 1506. doi:10.3389/fpsyg.2018.01506

Safren, S. A., Blashill, A. J., Lee, J. S., O'Cleirigh, C., Tomassili, J., Biello, K. B., . . . Mayer, K. H. (2018). Condom-use self-efficacy as a mediator between syndemics and condomless sex in men who have sex with men (MSM). *Health Psychology*, 37(9), 820–827. doi:10.1037/hea0000617

Stall, R., Mills, T. C., Williamson, J., Hart, T., Greenwood, G., Paul, J., . . . Catania, J. A. (2003). Association of co-occurring psychosocial health problems and increased vulnerability to HIV/AIDS among urban men who have sex with men. *American Journal of Public Health*, 93(6), 939–942.

Stephenson, R., & Finneran, C. (2016). Minority stress and intimate partner violence among gay and bisexual men in Atlanta. *American Journal of Men's Health*, 11(4), 952–961.

Stults, C. B., Javdani, S., Greenbaum, C. A., Kapadia, F., & Halkitis, P. N. (2015). Intimate partner violence and substance use risk among young men who have sex with men: The P18 cohort study. *Drug Alcohol Depend*, 154, 54–62.

Suarez, N. A., Mimiaga, M. J., Garofalo, R., Brown, E., Bratcher, A. M., Wimbly, T., . . . Stephenson, R. (2018). Dyadic reporting of intimate partner violence among male couples in three U.S. cities. *American Journal of Men's Health*, 12(4), 1039–1047. doi:10.1177/1557988318774243

Subirana-Malaret, M., Gahagan, J., Parker, R., & Crowther-Dowey, C. (2019). Intersectionality and sex and gender-based analyses as promising approaches in addressing intimate partner violence treatment programs among LGBT couples: A scoping review. *Cogent Social Sciences*, 5(1). doi:10.1080/23311886.2019.1644982

Tjaden, P., Thoennes, N., & Allison, C. J. (1999). Comparing violence over the life span in samples of same-sex and opposite-sex cohabitants. *Violence & Victims, 14*(4), 413–425.

Tomori, C., McFall, A. M., Solomon, S. S., Srikrishnan, A. K., Anand, S., Balakrishnan, P., . . . Celentano, D. D. (2018). Is there synergy in syndemics? Psychosocial conditions and sexual risk among men who have sex with men in India. *Social Science & Medicine, 206*, 110–116. doi:10.1016/j.socscimed.2018.03.032

Tomori, C., McFall, A. M., Srikrishnan, A. K., Mehta, S. H., Nimmagadda, N., Anand, S., . . . Celentano, D. D. (2016). The prevalence and impact of childhood sexual abuse on HIV-risk behaviors among men who have sex with men (MSM) in India. *BMC Public Health, 16*. doi:10.1186/s12889-016-3446-6

Wall, K. M., Sullivan, P. S., Kleinbaum, D., & Stephenson, R. (2014). Actor-partner effects associated with experiencing intimate partner violence or coercion among male couples enrolled in an HIV prevention trial. *BMC Public Health, 14*, 209. doi:10.1186/1471-2458-14-209

Walters, M. L., Chen, J., & Breiding, M. J. (2013). *The national intimate partner and sexual violence survey (NISVS): 2010 findings on victimization by sexual orientation*. Atlanta, GA: National Center for Injury Prevention and Control, Centers for Disease Control and Prevention.

Walters, S. M., Braksmajer, A., Coston, B., Yoon, I., Grov, C., Downing, M. J., Jr., . . . Hirshfield, S. (2020). A syndemic model of exchange sex among HIV-positive men who have sex with men. *Archives of Sex Behaviour*. doi:10.1007/s10508-020-01628-8

Wang, H. Y., Wang, N., Chu, Z. X., Zhang, J., Mao, X., Geng, W. Q., . . . Xu, J. J. (2018). Intimate partner violence correlates with a higher HIV incidence among MSM: A 12-month prospective cohort study in Shenyang, China. *Scientific Reports, 8*(1), 2879. doi:10.1038/s41598-018-21149-8

Wang, N., Huang, B., Ruan, Y., Amico, K. R., Vermund, S. H., Zheng, S., & Qian, H. Z. (2020). Association between stigma towards HIV and MSM and intimate partner violence among newly HIV-diagnosed Chinese men who have sex with men. *BMC Public Health, 20*(1), 204. doi:10.1186/s12889-020-8259-y

Wei, D., Cao, W., Hou, F., Hao, C., Gu, J., Peng, L., & Li, J. (2020). Multilevel factors associated with perpetration of five types of intimate partner violence among men who have sex with men in China: An ecological model-informed study. *AIDS Care*, 1–12. doi:10.1080/09540121.2020.1734523

Wei, D., Hou, F., Hao, C., Gu, J., Dev, R., Cao, W., . . . Li, J. (2019). Prevalence of intimate partner violence and associated factors among men who have sex with men in China. *Journal of Interpersonal Violence*. doi:10.1177/0886260519889935

Whitfield, C. L., Anda, R. F., Dube, S. R., & Felitti, V. J. (2003). Violent childhood experiences and the risk of intimate partner violence in adults. *Journal of Interpersonal Violence, 18*(2).

Whitfield, D. L., Coulter, R. W. S., Langenderfer-Magruder, L., & Jacobson, D. (2018). Experiences of intimate partner violence among lesbian, gay, bisexual, and transgender college students: The intersection of gender, race, and sexual orientation. *Journal of Interpersonal Violence*. doi:10.1177/0886260518812071

WHO. (2014). *Health care for women subjected to intimate partner violence or sexual violence. A clinical handbook*. Switzerland. Retrieved from https://apps.who.int/iris/bitstream/handle/10665/136101/WHO_RHR_14.26_eng.pdf;jsessionid=5E4B2242526A367D0CDBCE5C65FB2A49?sequence=1

WHO. (2019). *Violence prevention alliance. Global campaign for violence prevention. The ecological framework*. Retrieved from www.who.int/violenceprevention/approach/ecology/en/

Wilkerson, J. M., Di Paola, A., Rawat, S., Patankar, P., Rosser, B. R. S., & Ekstrand, M. L. (2018). Substance use, mental health, HIV testing, and sexual risk behavior among men who have sex with men in the state of Maharashtra, India. *AIDS Education and Prevention, 30*(2), 96–107. doi:10.1521/aeap.2018.30.2.96

Williams, J. K., Wilton, L., Magnus, M., Wang, L., Wang, J., Dyer, T. P., . . . Cummings, V. (2015). Relation of childhood sexual abuse, intimate partner violence, and depression to risk factors for HIV among Black men who have sex with men in 6 US cities. *American Journal of Public Health, 105*(12), 2473–2481. doi:10.2105/ajph.2015.302878

Wong, C. F., Weiss, G., Ayala, G., & Kipke, M. D. (2010). Harassment, discrimination, violence, and illicit drug use among young men who have sex with men. *AIDS Education and Prevention, 22*(4), 286–298. doi:10.1521/aeap.2010.22.4.286

Wong, N. S., Tang, W., Han, L., Best, J., Zhang, Y., Huang, S., . . . Tucker, J. D. (2017). MSM HIV testing following an online testing intervention in China. *BMC Infectious Diseases, 17*(1), 437. doi:10.1186/s12879-017-2546-y

Wu, E. (2018). Childhood sexual abuse among Black men who have sex with men: A cornerstone of a syndemic? *PLoS One, 13*(11), e0206746. doi:10.1371/journal.pone.0206746

Wu, E., El-Bassel, N., McVinney, L. D., Hess, L., Fopeano, M. V., Hwang, H. G., . . . Mansergh, G. (2015). The association between substance use and intimate partner violence within Black male same-sex relationships. *Journal of Interpersonal Violence, 30*(5), 762–781. doi:10.1177/0886260514536277

Young, R. M., & Meyer, I. H. (2005). The trouble with "MSM" and "WSW": Erasure of the sexual-minority person in public health discourse. *American Journal of Public Health, 95*(7), 1144–1149. doi:10.2105/ajph.2004.046714

Zalla, L. C., Herce, M. E., Edwards, J. K., Michel, J., & Weir, S. S. (2019). The burden of HIV among female sex workers, men who have sex with men and transgender women in Haiti: Results from the 2016 Priorities for Local AIDS Control Efforts (PLACE) study. *Journal of International AIDS Society, 22*(7), e25281. doi:10.1002/jia2.25281

17

# DOMESTIC VIOLENCE AND ABUSE WITHIN FEMALE SAME-SEX RELATIONSHIPS

*Laura Badenes-Ribera and Amparo Bonilla-Campos*

## Introduction

Domestic violence and abuse (DVA) within female same-sex relationships, which in certain contexts is called "intimate partner violence and abuse" (Nicolson, 2019; Walker & Bowen, 2019), is a relatively new research area. It began to be studied in the late 1980s and early 1990s, when the first books and studies on DVA in lesbian females appeared (e.g. Brand & Kidd, 1986; Lobel, 1986). Since then the number of studies analyzing DVA has increased considerably (Badenes-Ribera, Bonilla-Campos, Frias-Navarro, Pons-Salvador, & Monterde-i-Bort, 2016). The purpose of this chapter is thus to review and summarize the current body of scientific knowledge on DVA within female same-sex relationships, including its limitations.

## Characteristics of the studies

Most studies on DVA between female same-sex couples have been carried out in the United States of America (USA), although other studies have been conducted in the United Kingdom (UK) (e.g. Donovan & Hester, 2014), Canada (e.g. Barrett & St. Pierre, 2013), China (e.g. Chong, Mak, & Kwong, 2013), Spain (e.g. Longares, Escartín, Barrientos, & Rodríguez-Carballeira, 2018a), and Latin American countries (e.g. Barrientos, Escartín, Longares, & Rodríguez-Carballeira, 2018).

Most of these studies have used cross-sectional and non-probabilistic sampling methods and small sample sizes, given the stigmatized nature of sexual minority identity, which makes it difficult to conduct studies with randomized samples. Overall, the samples have mainly been composed of volunteer participants contacted by telephone or email, listservs, websites of organizations dedicated to men's or women's issues, universities, pride events, local libraries, or using snowball sampling. Few studies have used representative probability samples (e.g. Coston, 2017; Goldberg & Meyer, 2013; Halpern, Young, Waller, Martin, & Kupper, 2004; Messinger, 2011; Tjaden, Thoennes, & Allison, 1999; Walters, Chen, & Breiding, 2013).

Studies have primarily focused on younger and midlife adults rather than adolescents and older people and on White females rather than females from minority ethnic backgrounds, including Black, Asian and Latin populations (Arlee, Cowperthwaite, & Ostermeyer, 2019; Badenes-Ribera et al., 2016). However, DVA also occurs in adolescents and older lesbian and bisexual females (e.g. Westwood, 2019; Whitton, Dyar, Mustanski, & Newcomb, 2019) and in sexual minority females from racial minorities (e.g. Hill, Woodson, Ferguson, & Parks, 2012).

## Definition and assessment of domestic violence and abuse

Researchers have used different definitions of domestic violence and partner abuse and different measurement instruments. Most studies have used the Revised Conflict Tactics Scales (CTS2, Straus, Hamby, Boney-McCoy, & Sugarman, 1996), while others have used their own definition of DVA (e.g. Carvalho, Lewis, Derlega, Winstead, & Viggiano, 2011): "Have you ever been a victim of domestic violence?" and "Have you ever been a perpetrator of domestic violence?" They also used a checklist of abusive behaviours based on standardized instruments (e.g. Lie & Gentlewarrier, 1991), lists compiled by other authors, which ask participants to report any "experience" with partner abuse that combines victimization and perpetration (e.g. Eaton et al., 2008), lists from battered women shelters (e.g. Turell, 2000), a community survey to evaluate the needs of LG people (e.g. Rose, 2003) or the authors' own lists (e.g. Schilit, Lie, Bush, Montagne, & Reyes, 1991). Other authors have used a DVA measure adapted from Greenwood et al. (2002) (e.g. Kelly, Izienicki, Bimbi, & Parsons, 2011) or from the WHO Multi-country Study on Women's Health and Domestic Violence Against Women by Garcia-Moreno, Jansen, Ellsberg, Heise, and Watts (2005) (e.g. Hellemans, Loeys, Buysse, Dewaele, & De Smet, 2015). Finally, other studies linked violence to the existence of abusive inter-couple behaviours (e.g. Miller, Greene, Causby, White, & Lockhart, 2001).

Few studies have included the evaluation of partner abuse behaviour that is relevant/specific to sexual minority groups (e.g. Balsam & Szymanski, 2005; Eaton et al., 2008; Scherzer, 1998; Turell, 2000). Such behaviours include outing or threatening to out (disclosing identity to family, friends, employer, and/or landlord), closeting (forcing concealment of identity), forcing the partner to show real and sexual affection in public, telling a bisexual partner repeatedly they should be lesbian, telling a partner repeatedly they are not a real lesbian female and that nobody else would want them (Arlee et al., 2019; Badenes-Ribera et al., 2016; Messinger, 2017; Ristock, 2002), or threatening to make reports to authorities to jeopardize the partner's child custody arrangements, resulting in fear of loss of children. Children may be used to control partner females in this way (Hardesty, Oswald, Khaw, & Fonseca, 2011; Head & Milton, 2014; Turell, 2000). Such tactics may serve to "discredit them as a mother" during custody disputes in same-sex relationships where one mother has legal parental rights and the other does not (Bermea, van Eeden-Moorefield, & Khaw, 2018; Hardesty et al., 2011). These behaviours reflect the discriminatory context in which the diverse sexualities live (Badenes-Ribera et al., 2016; Ristock, 2002).

Animal abuse in the context of abusive relationships has also received scarce attention (Taylor, Riggs, Donovan, Signal, & Fraser, 2019) and greater attention has been directed to abuse victimization rather than perpetration or bi-directional abuse (Mason et al., 2014).

Many researchers have employed multiple time frames to assess DVA rates (Badenes-Ribera et al., 2016), often asking participants about lifetime experiences (e.g. Carvalho et al., 2011) and otherwise, such as the past six months, year (e.g. Kelley et al., 2014), five years (e.g. Kelly et al., 2011) or during the current or most recent relationship (e.g. Lie, Schilit, Bush, Montagne, & Reyes, 1991).

There is therefore great variability of the proportion of DVA within female same-sex couples due to different sampling methods and research design.

# Rates of domestic violence and abuse within female same-sex relationships

The evidence suggests that females in same-sex relationships tend to experience DVA at similar or somewhat higher rates than females in opposite-sex couples (Badenes-Ribera et al., 2016; Edwards, Sylaska, & Neal, 2015; Murray & Mobley, 2009; Stiles-Shields & Carroll, 2015). For instance, Graham, Jensen, Givens, Bowen, and Rizo (2016) analyzed the prevalence of partner abuse in a sample of US college students (i.e. CTS2) across four groups of participants: males reporting on a relationship with a female, females reporting on a relationship with a male, male–male relationships and female–female relationships. They found that females in same-sex relationships reported a higher prevalence of physical assault (45%), injuries (24%), psychological aggression (85%) and injury victimization (27%), and the highest frequency of overall victimization (89%) than the other three groups. They also found that people in same-sex relationships were more likely to perpetrate and experience partner violence resulting in injury than those in mixed-sex couples.

Other studies on DVA within female couples, also using CTS2, found a prevalence of 18% for sexual abuse (Pepper & Sand, 2015), 22.5–25.4% for physical abuse (Milletich, Gumienny, Kelley, & D'Lima, 2014; Pepper & Sand, 2015), and 72.5% for psychological abuse (Pepper & Sand, 2015). In addition, the prevalence of partner victimization was 12.8% for sexual abuse, 20% for physical abuse, and 67.5% for psychological abuse (Pepper & Sand, 2015).

Sutter et al. (2019) recently used the CTS2 (short-form) on a cisgender sample (i.e. individuals whose sex assigned at birth aligns with their gender identity [APA, 2020]) of US sexual minority females and found a prevalence of lifetime partner victimization of 25.3% for sexual abuse, 34% for physical abuse, 76% for psychological abuse, and 29.3% for suffering an injury as a result of partner abuse. In terms of perpetration, the prevalence was 10.7% for sexual abuse, 26.7% for physical abuse, 72% for psychological abuse, and 21.3% for having injured a partner as a result of partner abuse. However, as Sutter et al. did not ask the participants to identify whether the violence reported occurred in a same-sex or opposite-sex relationship or to identify the sex of the victims' partners or perpetrators, so that the prevalence reported could be inflated by including violence by opposite-sex and same-sex partners (Murray & Mobley, 2009).

# Domestic violence and abuse in female same-sex relationships from an intersectional frame

Some studies suggest that experiencing DVA may not be the same for people from different sexual, gender, and racial identities (Barrett & St. Pierre, 2013; Hill et al., 2012; Langhinrichsen-Rohling, Misra, Selwyn, & Rohling, 2012). For instance, Whitfield, Coulter, Langenderfer-Magruder, and Jacobson (2018) found that partner abuse in a sample of US college students disproportionately affects students who have a minority sexual orientation, gender identity, or racial/ethnic identity. In a sample of self-identified LGB and heterosexual individuals from the USA, Goldberg and Meyer (2013) found that regardless of sexual orientation Latinas were less likely and Black women were more likely to experience lifetime and one-year partner abuse than White women. Whitton, Newcomb, Messinger, Byck, and Mustanski (2016), in sample of young LGBT people from the USA, found that racial-ethnic minorities were more likely to experience physical partner abuse than Whites and the prevalence of physical abuse remained stable with age. Likewise, Whitton et al. (2019), in a sample of young sexual and gender minority people assigned female at birth, found that racial minority young people had higher rates of most DVA types than White participants. In these cases, immigration status, limited language skills, and lack of knowledge of the legal system may be used by an abusive partner to threaten deportation or incarceration (Arlee et al., 2019).

As regards females of different sexual identities, some studies found that bisexual females are at higher risk of DVA victimization than either heterosexual females or members of other sexual minority groups (Balsam & Hughes, 2013; Balsam & Szymanski, 2005; Barrett & St. Pierre, 2013; Freedner, Freed, Yang, & Austin, 2002; Lewis, Milletich, Kelley, & Woody, 2012; Roberts, Austin, Corliss, Vandermorris, & Koenen, 2010). For instance, Walters et al. (2013), using data from the National Intimate Partner and Sexual Violence Survey, estimated the lifetime prevalence of partner abuse victimization at 61% for bisexual females, 44% for lesbian females, and 35% for heterosexual females. They also estimated that 49.3% of bisexual females compared to 29.4% of lesbian females and 24.3% of heterosexual females had experienced severe physical violence by an intimate partner. Roberts et al. (2010) observed a higher prevalence of partner abuse victimization in bisexual females (20.2%) than in lesbian females (16.1%). While Freedner et al. (2002), using an adolescent sample, found that bisexual females reported higher rates of abuse. Compared with lesbian females, bisexual females had 4.3 times higher odds of having been threatened with outing by a partner. Compared with heterosexual females, lesbian females had 2.4 times the odds of reporting that a partner had made them scared about their safety, and bisexual females had 2.0 times the odds of reporting sexual abuse by a partner. Goldberg and Meyer (2013) found a prevalence of lifetime partner violence of 31.9% among lesbian females, 52.0% among bisexual females, and 32.1% among females who had sex with other females; all three groups had greater odds of having a history of DVA than heterosexual women, but this was statistically significant only for bisexual women. Similarly, Messinger (2011), using data from the US National Violence Against Women Survey, found a prevalence of physical violence victimization of 25% among lesbian females, 42.9% among bisexual females, and 36.4% among a combined sample of lesbian and bisexual females. Each of these studies found that bisexual females were more likely than lesbian females to have experienced intimate partner violence in their lifetimes.

These findings suggest that the prevalence of DVA may be higher among lesbian and bisexual females than heterosexual females and that bisexual females experience more DVA than females belonging to other sexual identities. However, most of these studies did not examine the intersecting role of gender and/or sex when estimating prevalence rates of DVA victimization and perpetration (Badenes-Ribera, Frias-Navarro, Bonilla-Campos, Pons-Salvador, & Monterde-i-Bort, 2015; McKay, Lindquist, & Misra, 2019). That is, they do not report on the sex of the victims' partners or perpetrators or identify whether the violence reported occurs in same-sex versus opposite-sex relationships (Badenes-Ribera et al., 2016; Messinger, 2014). It is therefore not possible to draw conclusions from these data regarding the prevalence of same-sex victimization or perpetration of violence (Barret & St. Pierre, 2103). In these cases, particularly in bisexual women, but also in other sexual minority females, the prevalence of reported violence may be inflated by including violence perpetrated by opposite-sex and same-sex partners (Badenes-Ribera et al., 2016; Murray & Mobley, 2009).

As Brown and Herman (2015) pointed out, in the studies that ask for the sex of the perpetrator of violence or whether the abuse occurred in same-sex relationships, the intimate partners of sexual minority females were not all females; some were males (Bernhard, 2000; Goldberg & Meyer, 2013; McLaughlin & Rozee, 2001; Morris & Balsam, 2003; Carvalho et al., 2011; Messinger, 2011; Walters et al., 2013). For instance, Carvalho et al. (2011) found that 11.6% of a sample of self-identified lesbian females reported experiencing abuse in an opposite-sex relationship, 17.2% reported experiencing abuse in a same-sex relationship, and 7.8% reported abuse in both types of relationships. Goldberg and Meyer (2013) found that among bisexual females who had experienced partner abuse, 95% of the most recent one-year partner abuse incidents were perpetrated by males. Messinger (2011) also found that bisexual females were far more likely to be victimized by an opposite-sex abuser by verbal, controlling, and physical partner violence (45.6%, 43.2%, and 34.7%, respectively) and all the sexual violence they experienced was perpetrated by men. McLaughlin et al. (2001) found that 25% of a sample of lesbian and bisexual females reported experiencing abuse in an opposite-sex relationship and 34% in a same-sex relationship. Walters et al. (2013) noted that 67.4% of lesbian females reported only female perpetrators and 89.5% of bisexual females reported only male perpetrators of intimate partner physical violence, rape, and/or stalking. Hequembourg, Livingston, and Parks (2013) found that nearly one-third (28.8%) of the participants in a sample of self-identified lesbian and bisexual females reported between one and four over-lifetime male sexual partners, so that females and males both contribute to the prevalence of DVA among sexual minority females.

DVA should thus be analyzed separately for females of different sexual identities and the sex of the partner considered (Badenes-Ribera et al., 2016; Badenes-Ribera et al., 2015; Mason et al., 2014). In this regard a meta-analysis of the prevalence of violence in self-identified lesbian females in same-sex relationships (Badenes-Ribera et al., 2015) found that the pooled prevalence for any lifetime victimization was 48%, while psychological abuse was 43%, physical abuse 18%, and sexual abuse 13%. For lifetime perpetration, the pooled prevalence for any abuse was 43%, for psychological abuse 27%, for physical abuse 12%, and for sexual abuse 7%. For victimization in the current or most recent relationship, the pooled prevalence for any victimization was 15%, 11% for psychological abuse, 16% for physical abuse, and 4% for sexual abuse.

In a sample of self-identified lesbian females in same-sex relationships in Spain and several Latin American countries, Barrientos et al. (2018) found that the prevalence of psychological abuse victimization was 33.3% for Venezuelans, 17.4% for Mexicans, 8.8% for Spaniards, and 5.5% for Chileans. Latin American countries thus show higher levels of victimization than Spain. Finally, in a sample of self-identified lesbian females in same-sex relationships in Spain, Longares et al. (2018a) examined victimization by psychological abuse by three different estimation methods of its prevalence. The first method found a dichotomous criterion of self-labelled victims with a total of 55% victimization. The second and third methods identified a coercive systematic behaviour control pattern over a period of time (Johnson, 1995; Kelly & Johnson, 2008), while 37.1% reported occasional victimization and 18.6% reported continuous victimization.

## Bi-directional partner abuse in female same-sex partners

Some studies suggest that bi-directional partner abuse may be a common partner violence pattern within same-sex relationships in general (e.g. Bartholomew, Regan, White, & Oram, 2008; Carvalho et al., 2011; Edwards & Sylaska, 2013; Frankland & Brown, 2014; Kelly et al., 2011; Langhinrichsen-Rohling et al., 2012; Longobardi & Badenes-Ribera, 2017) and within female same-sex relationships in particular (Balsam & Szymanski, 2005; Badenes-Ribera et al., 2016; Lewis et al., 2015; Lewis, Mason, Winstead, & Kelley, 2017; Schilit, Lie, & Montagne, 1990). For instance, in a sample of lesbian and bisexual females Balsam and Szymanski (2005) found that 31% reported both partner abuse and victimization during their lifetime, while 10% reported only victimization and 7% reported only perpetration. In a sample of lesbian females Carvalho et al. (2011) found that 9% of the respondents reported they had been both victims and perpetrators of partner abuse. In a sample of LGBT people Kelly et al. (2011) found that a quarter (23.4%) reported having been both the victim and perpetrator of violence during the previous five years. Of the individuals who reported mutual partner violence, most (78.4%) indicated both physical and psychological violence between partners, 6.9% reported solely mutual psychological violence and 4.7% reported solely mutual physical violence. Likewise, Lewis et al. (2015) found that 12% of samples of self-identified lesbian females identified themselves as both perpetrators and victims of physical violence in the past year, and Lewis et al. (2017) found that the paths for perpetration and victimization of physical violence were significant in both directions, but not for psychological aggression. Lie and Gentlewarrier (1991) found that two-thirds of a sample of lesbian females reported both victimization and perpetration in a former same-sex relationship. In a sample of cisgender females identified as sexual minorities Sutter et al. (2019) found that psychological, physical, and sexual partner abuse were bi-directional. In a sample of sexual and gender minority youth assigned female at birth (FAB), including sexual minority females, transgender males, and non-binary youth, Whitton et al. (2019) found high rates of bi-directionality: 86.2% for minor psychological partner abuse and 54–67% of the severe psychological partner abuse, minor and severe physical partner abuse, injury, and coercive control was bi-directional.

## Correlates for domestic violence and abuse in female same-sex relationships shared with opposite-sex couples

Research suggests same-sex and opposite-sex couples share many DVA correlates (Badenes-Ribera et al., 2016; Kaukinen, 2014). For instance, Kimmes et al. (2017), using meta-analysis, found that alcohol abuse, anger, psychological abuse perpetration, and psychological abuse victimization are cross-sectionally related to physical partner abuse perpetration and victimization within female same-sex relationships.

Other DVA correlates identified in cross-sectional studies, mainly using data from US samples, are controlling behaviours, prior physical violence by an intimate partner (male or female), dependency, animal abuse, family history of violence, relationship satisfaction, insecure attachment style, depression, jealousy, low self-esteem, need to control, and ending the relationship (Badenes-Ribera et al., 2016; Kaukinen, 2014; Kimmes et al., 2017; Lockhart, White, Causby, & Isaac, 1994; Miller et al., 2001; Schilit et al., 1990; Taylor et al., 2019). For instance, Goldberg and Meyer (2013) found that self-identified lesbian, bisexual, and heterosexual females who reported psychological distress were more likely to report physical and sexual relationship violence. Glass et al. (2008) found that constant jealousy or possessiveness of the abuser was predictive of participants' reporting threats or actual physical or sexual violence. In a sample of UK LGBT people, Donovan and Hester (2014) found that just over 4% reported ever having been in a relationship where their pet was abused and 1.5% reported this in the previous 12 months. Renzetti (1992) found that 38% of a sample of battered lesbian females reported their pet had been abused.

With regard to relationship satisfaction and DVA, in a sample of lesbian and bisexual females Balsam and Szymanski (2005) found that lower relationship quality is related to physical or sexual violence and psychological aggression in the previous year. Kelley, Lewis, and Mason (2015) found that poorer relationship adjustment was related to higher levels of partner psychological aggression (i.e. emotional/verbal aggression and dominance/isolation) in a sample of self-identified lesbian females. Lewis, Milletich, Derlega, and Padilla (2014) also found a strong negative association between relationship satisfaction and psychological violence among self-identified lesbian females. Similarly, Matte and Lafontaine (2011) found that relationship satisfaction was inversely correlated with psychological violence perpetration, but was not correlated with psychological violence victimization in a sample of Canadian self-identified lesbian and bisexual females.

Insecure attachment styles (i.e. anxious or avoidant) has also been linked to psychological and physical violence perpetration and victimization in same-sex relationships (Craft, Serovich, McKenry, & Lim, 2008; Gabbay, & Lafontaine, 2017; Longares, Escartín, Barrientos, & Rodríguez-Carballeira, 2018b; Matte & Lafontaine, 2011; McKenry, Serovich, Mason, & Mosack, 2006; Renzetti, 1992; Stiles-Shields & Carroll, 2015). In female same-sex relationships, Matte and Lafontaine (2011) found that attachment anxiety was positively correlated with psychological violence perpetration and victimization.

Finally, a relation between alcohol and drug use and DVA was also observed in same-sex relationships (Bimbi, Palmadessa, & Parsons, 2008; Eaton et al., 2008; Goldberg & Meyer, 2013; Kelley et al., 2015; Lockhart et al., 1994; Renzetti, 1992). Both individual and partner alcohol use and drinking problems have been implicated in the risk of partner violence (Glass et al., 2008; Renzetti, 1988). For instance, in a sample of lesbian females Fortunata and Kohn (2003) compared batterers (defined as engaging in at least one act of physical violence in the past year) and nonbatterers and found that the former had higher rates of alcohol problems. Goldberg and Meyer (2013) found that females who reported daily or weekly binge drinking were more likely to report physical and sexual relationship violence. Kelly et al. (2011) found that both alcohol use and previous substance abuse treatment were associated with mutual partner violence (including physical and psychological aggression) in a sample of lesbian and bisexual females. In a sample of self-identified lesbian females Schilit et al. (1990) also found that the frequency of drinking was significantly related to both committing and being the victim of abusive acts. While several studies identified alcohol use as a predictor of partner abuse (Lewis et al., 2015, Lewis et al., 2017; Mason, Lewis, Gargurevich, & Kelley, 2016).

A relation between discrepant drinking (i.e. different alcohol use between partners) and experiencing physical assault and psychological violence in the relationship was also found in samples of self-identified lesbian females in same-sex relationships in cross-sectional (Kelley et al., 2015) and longitudinal studies (Lewis, Winstead, Braitman, & Hitson, 2018). In this regard, Lewis et al. (2018) found that discrepant drinking was related to subsequent psychological, but not physical, aggression six months later. In turn, partner abuse in same-sex relationships predicted discrepant drinking.

## Sexual minority correlates for domestic violence and abuse in female same-sex relationships

Other potential psychosocial risk factors for DVA that may be unique to, or particularly salient for, sexual minority females in same-sex relationships (e.g. internalized homophobia, outness, etc.) have been cross-sectionally associated with partner abuse (Edwards & Sylaska, 2013; Graham et al., 2016; Kimmes et al., 2017; Longobardi & Badenes-Ribera, 2017).

Several studies, mainly using data from US samples, have documented an association between internalized homophobia and partner abuse in same-sex relationships (Balsam & Szymanski, 2005; Bartholomew et al., 2008; Carvalho et al., 2011; Edwards & Sylaska, 2013; Kelley et al., 2014; Lewis et al., 2014; Milletich et al., 2014; Pepper & Sand, 2015). For instance, using a meta-analysis methodology Badenes-Ribera, Sánchez-Meca, and Longobardi (2019) found a positive association between internalized homophobia and: any partner violence perpetration ($r = .147$, 95% CI [.079, .214]), any partner abuse victimization ($r = .102$, 95% CI [.030, .173]), psychological partner abuse perpetration ($r = .145$, 95% CI [.073, .216]), and physical/sexual partner violence perpetration (*r* = .166, 95% CI [.109, .221]). Higher levels of internalized homophobia are linked to more partner abuse perpetration and victimization in same-sex couples. It is possible that people with negative feelings about themselves may project their negative self-concept through violent acts toward their same-sex partners, and in turn victims with negative feelings about themselves may believe that they deserve to be treated abusively and see the abuse as a natural consequence of their LGB identity (Stiles-Shields & Carroll, 2015).

However, there are inconsistent results regarding the link between internalized homophobia and partner abuse victimization in female same-sex relationships (Longobardi & Badenes-Ribera, 2017). Some studies found a positive relationship between internalized homophobia and physical and sexual partner abuse victimization among sexual minority females (Balsam & Szymanski, 2005), but other studies did not (Carvalho et al., 2011; Pepper & Sand, 2015). For instance, Kimmes et al. (2017) did not find a relationship between internalized homophobia and physical partner abuse victimization (*r* = .11, 95% CI [-.02, .24]; *k* = 4); however, it should be noted that the effect size was small and the confidence interval for the effect size suggests marginal statistical significance.

With regard to partner abuse perpetration in female same-sex relationships, Pepper and Sand (2015) found a positive association between internalized homophobia and sexual coercion perpetration. Kimmes et al. (2017) also found a positive relationship between internalized homophobia and physical partner abuse perpetration (*r* = .09, 95% CI [.00, .18]).

It is noteworthy that the association between internalized homophobia and partner abuse could be mediated by overall relationship quality and by the levels of rumination and fusion experienced by the partners (Badenes-Ribera et al., 2019; Balsam & Szymanski, 2005; Lewis et al., 2014; Longobardi & Badenes-Ribera, 2017; Milletich et al., 2014). Internalized homophobia has been associated with the frequency of past-year psychological abuse in lesbian females' intimate relationships through its effect on rumination and relationship satisfaction (Lewis et al., 2014). In female same-sex relationships the link between internalized homophobia and past-year partner abuse, both as perpetration and victimization, has also been fully mediated by relationship quality. The experience of internalized homophobia could therefore drive to poorer perception of relationship quality, which in turn could drive to partner abuse (Balsam & Szymanski, 2005). Finally, fusion mediated the relationship between internalized homophobia and partner abuse perpetration in women's same-sex relationships (Milletich et al., 2014).

With regard to outness, several studies have shown an association between the participants' degree of outness and partner abuse within same-sex relationships, mainly in data from US samples (Bartholomew et al., 2008; Carvalho et al., 2011; Edwards & Sylaska, 2013; Kelley et al., 2014), who found that being more "out" was associated with an increased risk for lifetime partner abuse victimization among LG people (Carvalho et al., 2011) and that lower levels of disclosure of one's sexual orientation were related to an increased risk of physical partner abuse perpetration in current relationships among LGBTQ youth (Edwards & Sylaska, 2013). However, in female same-sex couples, Balsam and Szymanski (2005) did not find a relationship between outness and victimization or perpetration of violence in a sample of self-identified lesbian and bisexual females, but they did find that outness was related to some aspects of the quality of the relationship. Kimmes et al. (2017) did not find an association between the participant's degree of outness and physical partner abuse victimization (*r* = .09, 95% CI [-.33, .48]). As Balsam and Szymanski (2005) have pointed out, it might be that levels of outness influence the quality of the relationship and then the quality of the relationship influences victimization or perpetration of violence. Longares et al. (2018b) found that outness moderated the relationship between an insecure attachment style and the perpetration of psychological abuse in a sample of LGB people from Spanish-speaking countries.

Carvalho et al. (2011) found that the participants' degree of stigma consciousness was associated positively with the perpetration and victimization of same-sex partner violence among LG people. However, Edwards and Sylaska (2013) did not find this association between both variables.

On the other hand, social constraints with friends (difficulty in talking to others about one's minority sexual identity) did not predict female's same-sex partner abuse, but it was indirectly associated with the frequency of past-year psychological aggression in female same-sex relationships through the intervening mechanisms of rumination and relationship satisfaction (Lewis et al., 2014).

Finally, using meta-analytic methodology, Kimmes et al. (2017) found an association between being a victim of homophobic controlling behaviours and physical partner abuse in female same-sex relationships.

## Discussion and analysis

The purpose of this chapter is to synthesize the current body of knowledge on DVA within female same-sex couples. Comparing the DVA rates across studies is rather difficult due to differences in sample design, DVA conceptualization, and the timeframe recalled, and these differences led to large discrepancies in the prevalence estimates. Although exact prevalence rates are difficult to determine, the evidence suggests that females in same-sex relationships tend to experience partner abuse at similar or somewhat higher rates than females in opposite-sex couples (Badenes-Ribera et al., 2015; Badenes-Ribera et al., 2016; Edwards et al., 2015; McKay et al., 2019; Murray & Mobley, 2009; Stiles-Shields & Carroll, 2015). In addition, female same-sex relationships also experienced all forms of partner abuse, with psychological abuse being the most prevalent form of victimization and perpetration of violence compared with physical and sexual abuse (Badenes-Ribera, et al., 2016; Matte & Lafontaine, 2011; Lewis et al., 2012; Messinger, 2017), while the highest rates of abuse are for milder or minor forms of violence (Badenes-Ribera et al., 2016; Sutter et al., 2019; Whitton et al., 2019).

Regarding the difference in partner abuse by sexual identity, as Barrett and St. Pierre (2013) have pointed out, despite the growing body of research examining partner abuse in female same-sex couples, even less is known about the experiences of bisexual females. How the experiences of bisexual females are different from or similar to those of lesbian females remains underinvestigated, especially outside the USA, where the research is still focused on lesbian females (e.g. Barrientos et al., 2018). Although the evidence suggests that bisexual females are at a higher risk of partner abuse than lesbian and heterosexual females, the prevalence of this violence has not been clearly determined, given that most studies that analyzed this phenomenon did not specifically ask for the sex of the perpetrator of the abuse or if the abuse occurred within same-sex relationships. Several studies have pointed out that bisexual females appear to be particularly likely to be victimized by their male partners (Hequembourg et al., 2013; Messinger, 2014). The evidence also suggests that there may be cultural differences in partner abuse within female same-sex relationships. Barrientos et al. (2018) showed that in Latin American countries self-identified lesbian females experience higher levels of partner abuse than in Spain. As these authors have pointed out, it is possible that this difference may be caused by the legal context of these countries. Spanish law recognizes LGBTI rights more fully than in many Latin American countries. These differences highlight the need for future cross-cultural studies to further analyze their possible causes.

Some studies also suggest the existence of bi-directional partner abuse within female same-sex relationships, which is consistent with the presence of reciprocal patterns of violence and control in male same-sex relationships (Bartholomew et al., 2008; Stanley, Bartholomew, Taylor, & Oram, 2006). The high rates of bi-directional violence among same-sex couples and low rates among heterosexual couples suggest that gender may be a crucial factor (Frankland & Brown, 2014). However, as Renzetti (1988, 1992) has pointed out, these studies did not differentiate between the desire to exert power over one's partner and self-defensive behaviour. As Badenes-Ribera et al. (2016) found, the comparison of rates of partner abuse might not be able to clarify to what degree the relationship is based on the dynamics of control and domination, or what factors are influential in the use or experience of abuse. Measuring partner abuse without measuring the control context could thus cause an individual who acts in self-defence against partner abuse to be labelled as a "perpetrator" and the partner as a "victim". There is still a debate about the intent of partner abuse perpetration, but conclusive supporting evidence is still lacking as to the intention of this bi-directionality (Messinger, 2014).

Some partner abuse correlates in female same-sex relationships are shared by females in opposite-sex relationships (e.g. substance use, dependence, incompatibility, stress, jealousy, etc.). However, there are unique or specific factors linked to partner abuse in same-sex relationships, in particular in female same-sex couples. These correlates stem from the homophobic/biphobic context in which sexual minority females are immersed, or that are characteristics of the relationship dynamics that may be established between them (e.g. fusion). Sexual minority females thus experience dynamics unique to them and their relationships that cannot be understood through examining partner abuse in opposite-sex relationships and cannot be effectively addressed through existing partner abuse prevention programmes developed to prevent abuse in opposite-sex relationships. This shows there is a need to develop and implement violence prevention programmes in same-sex relationships.

However, because most of the studies that analyze risk factors of partner abuse have used exclusively cross-sectional data they cannot indicate the direction of the effects. This lack of longitudinal research limits the ability to identify risk factors and the consequences of partner abuse. As it is impossible to know the order of events between risk factors and partner abuse without temporal precedence, it is therefore imperative to the understanding of these associations that data are collected longitudinally to determine directionality as well as the temporal correlates of the events.

## Conclusions

The prevalence of DVA in female same-sex couples has not been clearly determined due to across-study methodological differences. However, it is known that females in same-sex relationships experience all forms of DVA in a similar way to opposite-sex relationships and they share some DVA correlates. However, female same-sex couples have specific forms of violence (e.g. threatening to out) and unique DVA risk factors related to sexual minority status (e.g. internalized homophobia) and their relationship (e.g. fusion). DVA in same-sex couples therefore cannot be completely understood by examining DVA in opposite-sex relationships. The research should include more nuanced exploration of the role sexual minority stress can play in increasing the risk of DVA within female same-sex intimate partnerships.

## Critical findings

- All forms of DVA occur within female same-sex relationships.
- Psychological abuse and middle and minor forms of violence are the most prevalent forms of partner abuse.

- Bi-directional violence seems to be a common pattern.
- Partner abuse experience might not be the same for people from different sexual, gender, and racial identities.
- Partner abuse victimization might be higher among lesbian and bisexual females than heterosexual females.
- Bisexual females might be at higher risk for partner abuse victimization than either heterosexual or lesbian females.
- Both female and male partners may contribute to the prevalence of partner abuse in sexual minority females.
- Many correlates related to partner abuse are shared by same-sex and opposite-sex couples.
- There are unique risk factors for partner abuse in sexual minority females: relationship dynamics, internalized homophobia, outness, stigma consciousness, and being a victim of homophobic controlling behaviours.

## Implications for policy, practice, and research

- There is a need for research on DVA outside the USA and among adolescents and older females in same-sex relationships and females from minority ethnic backgrounds.
- Researchers should ask for the sex of the victims' partners to identify whether the reported violence occurs in same-sex versus opposite-sex relationships. Research should include whether the experiences and DAV risk factors in female couples differs according to sexual identity.
- Cross-cultural studies should analyze the causes of differences in DVA prevalence in female couples, including the legal context of LGTB rights, along with cultural attitudes such as risk factors and barriers to help-seeking.
- Research should explore the role of sexual minority stress as a DVA risk factor within female same-sex relationships and outing as a vulnerability factor in disclosing partner violence.
- Patterns of bi-directional partner abuse, considering types of violence, intentionality and control context, as well as dynamics unique to female couples still have to be clarified in order to understand and develop violence prevention programmes.

## References

American Psychological Association. (2020). *Publication manual of the American Psychological Association* (7th ed.). Washington, DC: American Psychological Association.

Arlee, L., Cowperthwaite, R., & Ostermeyer, B. K. (2019). Facing Stigma and discrimination as both a racial and a sexual minority member of the LGBTQ+ community. *Psychiatric Annals, 49,* 441–445. doi:10.3928/00485713-20190910-02

Badenes-Ribera, L., Bonilla-Campos, A., Frias-Navarro, D., Pons-Salvador, G., & Monterde-i-Bort, H. (2016). Intimate partner violence in self-identified lesbians: A systematic review of its prevalence and correlates. *Trauma, Violence, & Abuse, 17,* 284–297. doi:10.1177/1524838015584363

Badenes-Ribera, L., Frias-Navarro, D., Bonilla-Campos, A., Pons-Salvador, G., & Monterde-i-Bort, H. (2015). Intimate partner violence in self-identified lesbians: A meta-analysis of its prevalence. *Sexuality Research & Social Policy, 12,* 47–59. doi:10.1007/s13178-014-0164-7

Badenes-Ribera, L., Sánchez-Meca, J., & Longobardi, C. (2019). The relationship between internalized homophobia and intimate partner abuse in same-sex relationships: A meta-analysis. *Trauma, Violence, & Abuse, 20,* 331–343. doi:10.1177/1524838017708781

Balsam, K. F., & Hughes, T. (2013). Sexual orientation, victimization, and hate crimes. In C. J. Patterson, A. R. D'Augelli, C. J. Patterson, & A. R. D'Augelli (Eds.), *Handbook of psychology and sexual orientation* (pp. 267–280). New York, NY: Oxford University Press.

Balsam, K. F., & Szymanski, D. M. (2005). Relationship quality and domestic violence in women's same-sex relationships: The role of minority stress. *Psychology of Women Quarterly, 29*, 258–269. doi:10.1111/j.1471-6402.2005.00220.x

Barrett, B. J., & St. Pierre, M. (2013). Intimate partner violence reported by lesbian-, gay-, and bisexual-identified individuals living in Canada: An exploration of within-group variations. *Journal of Gay & Lesbian Social Services, 25*, 1–23. doi:10.1080/10538720.2013.751887

Barrientos, J., Escartín, J., Longares, L., & Rodríguez-Carballeira, A. (2018). Sociodemographic characteristics of gay and lesbian victims of intimate partner psychological abuse in Spain and Latin America. *Revista de Psicología Social, 33*, 240–274. doi:10.1080/02134748.2018.1446393

Bartholomew, K., Regan, K. V., White, M. A., & Oram. (2008). Patterns of abuse in male same-sex relationships. *Violence & Victims, 23*, 617–636. doi:10.1891/0886-6708.23.5.617

Bermea, A. M., van Eeden-Moorefield, B., & Khaw, L. (2018). A systematic review of research on intimate partner violence among bisexual women. *Journal of Bisexuality, 18*, 399–424. doi:10.1080/1529 9716.2018.1482485

Bernhard, L. A. (2000). Physical and sexual violence experienced by lesbian and heterosexual women. *Violence Against Women, 6*, 68–79. doi:10.1177/10778010022181714

Bimbi, D. S., Palmadessa, N. A., & Parsons, J. T. (2008). Substance use and domestic violence among urban gays, lesbians and bisexuals. *Journal of LGBT Health Research, 3*, 1–7. doi:10.1300/J463v03n02_01

Brand, P. A., & Kidd, A. H. (1986). Frequency of physical aggression in heterosexual and female homosexual dyads. *Psychological Reports, 59*, 1307–1313. doi:10.2466/pr0.1986.59.3.1307

Brown, T. N. T., & Herman, J. L. (2015). *Intimate partner violence and sexual abuse among LGBT people: A review of existing research.* Los Angeles, CA: The Williams Institute.

Carvalho, A. M., Lewis, R. J., Derlega, V. J., Winstead, B. A., & Viggiano, C. (2011). Internalized sexual minority stressors and same-sex intimate partner violence. *Journal of Family Violence, 26*, 501–509. doi:10.1007/s10896-011-9384-

Chong, E. S. K., Mak, W. W. S., & Kwong, M. M. F. (2013). Risk and protective factors of same-sex intimate partner violence in Hong Kong. *Journal of Interpersonal Violence, 28*, 1476–1497. doi:10.1177/0886260512468229

Coston, B. M. (2017). Power and inequality: Intimate partner violence against bisexual and non-monosexual women in the United States. *Journal of Interpersonal Violence.* Advance on-line publication. doi:10.1177/0886260517726415

Craft, S. M., Serovich, J. M., McKenry, P. C., & Lim, J. Y. (2008). Stress, attachment style, and partner violence among same-sex couples. *Journal of GLBT Family Studies, 4*, 57–73. doi:10.1080/15504280802084456.

Donovan, C., & Hester, M. (2014). Questionnaire survey of domestic abuse in same sex relationships: Part of the final report to the Economic and Social Research Council for a project. In *Comparing love and violence in heterosexual and same sex relationships* (Award No. RES-000–23–0650). Swindon, ESRC Research Report.

Eaton, L., Kaufman, M., Fuhrel, A., Cain, D., Cherry, C., Pope, H., & Kalichman, S. C. (2008). Examining factors coexisting with interpersonal violence in lesbian relationships. *Journal of Family Violence, 23*, 697–705. doi:10.1007/s10896-008-9194-3

Edwards, K. M., & Sylaska, D. M. (2013). The perpetration of intimate partner violence among LGBTQ college youth: The role of minority stress. *Journal of Youth and Adolescence, 42*, 1721–1731. doi:10.1007/ s10964-012-9880-6

Edwards, K. M, Sylaska, K. M, & Neal, A. M. (2015). Intimate partner violence among sexual minority populations: A critical review of the literature and agenda for future research. *Psychology of Violence, 5*, 112–121. doi:10.1037/a0038656

Fortunata, B., & Kohn, C. S. (2003). Demographic, psychosocial, and personality characteristics of lesbian batterers. *Violence & Victims, 18*, 557–568. doi:10.1891/vivi.2003.18.5.557

Frankland, A., &. Brown, J. (2014). Coercive control in same-sex intimate partner violence. *Journal of Family Violence, 29*, 15–22. doi:10.1007/s10896-013-9558-1

Freedner, N., Freed, L. H., Yang, Y. W., & Austin, S. B. (2002). Dating violence among gay, lesbian, and bisexual adolescents: Results from a community survey. *Journal of Adolescent Health, 31*, 469–474.

Gabbay, N., & Lafontaine, M. F. (2017). Understanding the relationship between attachment, caregiving, and same sex intimate partner violence. *Journal of Family Violence, 32*, 291–304. doi:10.1007/ s10896-016-9897-9

García-Moreno, C., Jansen, H. A. F. M., Ellsberg, M., Heise, L., & Watts, C. (2005). *Multi-country study from the WHO on women's health and domestic violence against women: Initial results on prevalence, health-related events and women's responses to this violence.* Geneva: World Health Organization. Retrieved from www.who.int/gender/violence/who_multicountry_study/en/

Glass, N., Perrin, N., Hanson, G., Bloom, T., Gardner, E., & Campbell, J. C. (2008). Risk for reassault in abusive female same-sex relationships. *American Journal of Public Health, 98,* 1021–1027. doi:10.2105/AJPH.2007.117770

Goldberg, N. G., & Meyer, I. H. (2013). Sexual orientation disparities in history of intimate partner violence: Results from the California health interview survey. *Journal of Interpersonal Violence, 28,* 1109–1118. doi:10.1177/0886260512459384

Graham, L. M., Jensen, T. M., Givens, A. D., Bowen, G. L., & Rizo, C. F. (2016). Intimate partner violence among same-sex couples in college: A propensity score analysis. *Journal of Interpersonal Violence,* 1–28. doi:10.1177/0886260516651628

Greenwood, G. L., Relf, M. V., Huang, B., Pollack, L. M., Canchola, J. A., & Catania, J. A. (2002). Battering victimization among a probability-based sample of men who have sex with men. *American Journal of Public Health, 92,* 1964–1969. doi:10.2105/ajph.92.12.1964

Halpern, C. T., Young, M. L., Waller, M. W., Martin, S. L., & Kupper, L. L. (2004). Prevalence of partner violence in same-sex romantic and sexual relationships in a national sample of adolescents. *Journal of Adolescent Health, 35,* 124–131. doi:10.1016/j.jadohealth.2003.09.003

Hardesty, J. L., Oswald, R. F., Khaw, L., & Fonseca, C. (2011). Lesbian/bisexual mothers and intimate partner violence: Help seeking in the context of social and legal vulnerability. *Violence Against Women, 17,* 28–46. doi:10.1177/107780120934763

Head, S., & Milton, M. (2014). Filling the silence: Exploring the bisexual experience of intimate partner abuse. *Journal of Bisexuality, 14,* 277–299. doi:10.1080/15299716.2014.903218

Hellemans, S., Loeys, T., Buysse, A., Dewaele, A., & De Smet, O. (2015). (2015). Intimate partner violence victimization among non-heterosexuals: Prevalence and associations with mental and sexual well-being. *Journal of Family Violence, 30,* 171–188. doi:10.1007/s10896-015-9669-y

Hequembourg, A. L., Livingston, J. A., & Parks, K. A. (2013). Sexual victimization and associated risks among lesbian and bisexual women. *Violence Against Women, 19,* 634–657. doi:10.1177/1077801213490557

Hill, N. A., Woodson, K. M., Ferguson, A. D., & Parks, C. W. (2012). Intimate partner abuse among African American lesbians: Prevalence, risk factors, theory, and resilience. *Journal of Family Violence, 27,* 401–413. doi:10.1007/s10896-012-9439-z

Johnson, M. P. (1995). Patriarchal Terrorism and common couple violence: Two forms of violence against women. *Journal of Marriage & the Family, 57,* 283–294. doi:10.2307/353683

Kaukinen, C. (2014). Dating violence among college students: The risk and protective factors. *Trauma, Violence & Abuse, 15,* 283–296. doi:10.1177/1524838014521321

Kelley, M. L, Lewis, R. J., & Mason, T. B. (2015). Discrepant alcohol use, intimate partner violence, and relationship adjustment among lesbian women and their relationship partners. *Journal of Family Violence, 30,* 977–986. doi:10.1007/s10896-015-9743-5

Kelley, M. L., Milletich, R. J., Lewis, R. J., Winstead, B. A., Barraco, C. L., & Padilla, M. A. (2014). Predictors of perpetration of men's same-sex partner violence. *Violence & Victims, 29,* 784–796. doi:10.1891/0886-6708.VV-D-13-00096

Kelly, B. C., Izienicki, H., Bimbi, D. S., &. Parsons, J. T. (2011). The intersection of mutual partner violence and substance use among urban gays, lesbians, and bisexuals. *Deviant Behaviour, 32,* 379–404. doi:10.1080/01639621003800158

Kelly, J. B., & Johnson, M. P. (2008). Differentiation among types of intimate partner violence: Research update and implications for interventions. *Family Court Review, 46,* 476–499. doi:10.1111/j.1744-1617.2008.00215.x

Kimmes, J. G., Mallory, A. B., Spencer, C., Beck, A. R., Cafferky, B., & Stith, S. M. (2017). Meta-Analysis of risk markers for intimate partner violence in same-sex relationships. *Trauma, Violence, & Abuse.* Advance on-line publication. doi:10.1177/1524838017708784

Langhinrichsen-Rohling, J., Misra, T. A., Selwyn, C., & Rohling, M. L. (2012). Rates of bidirectional versus unidirectional intimate partner violence across samples, sexual orientations, and race/ethnicities: A comprehensive review. *Partner Abuse, 3,* 199–230. doi:10.1891/1946-6560.3.2.19

Lewis, R. J., Mason, T. B., Winstead, B. A., & Kelley, M. L. (2017). Empirical investigation of a model of sexual minority specific and general risk factors for intimate partner violence among lesbian women. *Psychology of Violence, 7,* 110–119. doi:10.1037/vio0000036

Lewis, R. J., Milletich, R. J., Derlega, V. J., & Padilla, M. A. (2014). Sexual minority stressors and psychological aggression in lesbian women's intimate relationships: The mediating roles of rumination and relationship satisfaction. *Psychology of Women Quarterly, 38,* 535–550. doi:10.1177/0361684313517866

Lewis, R. J., Milletich, R. J., Kelley, M. L., & Woody, A. (2012). Minority stress, substance use, and intimate partner violence among sexual minority women. *Aggression & Violent Behaviour, 17,* 247–256. doi:10.1016/j.avb.2012.02.004

Lewis, R. J., Padilla, M. A., Milletich, R. J., Kelley, M. L., Winstead, B. A., Lau-Barraco, C., & Mason, T. B. (2015). Emotional distress, alcohol use, and bidirectional partner violence among lesbian women. *Violence Against Women, 21,* 917–938. doi:10.1177/1077801215589375

Lewis, R. J., Winstead, B. A., Braitman, A. L., & Hitson, P. (2018). Discrepant drinking and partner violence perpetration over time in lesbians' relationships. *Violence Against Women, 24,* 1149–1165. doi:10.1177/1077801218781925

Lie, G., & Gentlewarrier, S. (1991). Intimate violence in lesbian relationships: Discussion of survey findings and practice implications. *Journal of Social Services Research, 15,* 41–59. doi:10.1300/J079v 15n01_03

Lie, G., Schilit, R., Bush, J., Montagne, M., & Reyes, L. (1991). Lesbians in currently aggressive relationships: How frequently do they report aggressive past relationships? *Violence & Victims, 6,* 121–135.

Lobel, K. (Ed.). (1986). *Naming the violence: Speaking out about lesbian battering.* Seattle: Seal Press.

Lockhart, L. L., White, B. W., Causby, V., & Isaac, A. (1994). Letting out the secret: Violence in lesbian relationships. *Journal of Interpersonal Violence, 9,* 469–492. doi:10.1177/088626094009004003

Longares, L., Escartín, J., Barrientos, J., & Rodríguez-Carballeira, A. (2018a). Psychological abuse in Spanish same-sex couples: Prevalence and relationship between victims and perpetrators, *Innovation: The European Journal of Social Science Research, 31,* 125–141. doi:10.1080/13511610.2017.1326304

Longares, L., Escartín, J., Barrientos, J., & Rodríguez-Carballeira, A. (2018b). Insecure attachment and perpetration of psychological abuse in same-sex Couples: A relationship moderated by outness. *Sexuality Research & Social Policy.* Advance on-line publication. doi:10.1007/s13178-018-0363-8

Longobardi, C., & Badenes-Ribera, L. (2017). Intimate partner violence in same-sex relationships and the role of sexual minority stressors: A Systematic Review of the past 10 years. *Journal of Child Family Studies, 26,* 2039–2049. doi:10.1007/s10826-017-0734-4

Mason, T. B., Lewis, R. J., Gargurevich, M., & Kelley, M. L. (2016). Minority stress and intimate partner violence perpetration among lesbians: Negative affect, hazardous drinking, and intrusiveness as mediators. *Psychology of Sexual Orientation & Gender Diversity, 3,* 236–246. doi:10.1037/sgd0000165

Mason, T. B., Lewis, R. J., Milletich, R. J., Kelley, M. L., Minifie, J. B., & Derlega, V. J. (2014). Psychological aggression in lesbian, gay, and bisexual individuals' intimate relationships: A review of prevalence, correlates, and measurement issues. *Aggression &Violent Behaviour, 19,* 219–234. doi:10.1016/j. avb.2014.04.001

Matte, M., & Lafontaine, M-F. (2011). Validation of a measure of psychological aggression in same-sex couples: Descriptive data on perpetration and victimization and their association with physical violence. *Journal of GLBT Family Studies, 7,* 226–244. doi:10.1080/1550428x.2011.564944.

McKay, T., Lindquist, C. H., & Misra, S. (2019). Understanding (and acting on) 20 years of research on violence and LGBTQ + communities. *Trauma, Violence, & Abuse, 20,* 665–678. doi:10.1177/1524838017728708

McKenry, P. C., Serovich, J. M., Mason, T. L., & Mosack, K. (2006). Perpetration of gay and lesbian partner violence: Disempowerment perspective. *Journal of Family Violence, 21,* 233–243. doi:10.1007/ s10896-006-9020-8.

McLaughlin, E. M., & Rozee, P. D. (2001). Knowledge about heterosexual versus lesbian battering among lesbians. *Women & Therapy, 23*(3), 39–58.

Messinger, A. M. (2011). Invisible victims: Same-sex IPV in the national violence against women survey. *Journal of Interpersonal Violence, 26,* 2228–2243. doi:10.1177/0886260510383023.

Messinger, A. M. (2014). Marking 35 years of research on same-sex intimate partner violence: Lessons and new directions. In D. Peterson & V. R. Panfil (Eds.), *Handbook of LGBT communities, crime, and justice* (pp. 65–85). New York, NY: Springer Science Business Media.

Messinger, A. M. (2017). *LGBT intimate partner violence: Lessons for policy, practice, and research*. Oakland: University of California Press.

Miller, D. H., Greene, K., Causby, V., White, B. W., & Lockhart, L. L. (2001). Domestic violence in lesbian relationships. *Women & Therapy, 23*, 107–127. doi:10.1300/J015v23n03_08

Milletich, R. J., Gumienny, L. A., Kelley, M. L., & D'Lima, G. M. (2014). Predictors of women's same-sex partner violence perpetration. *Journal of Family Violence, 29*, 653–664. doi:10.1007/s10896-014-9620-7

Morris, J. F., & Balsam, K. F. (2003). Lesbian and bisexual women's experiences of victimization: Mental health, revictimization, and sexual identity development. *Journal of Lesbian Studies, 7*(4), 67–85. doi:10.1300/J155v07n04_05

Murray, C. E., & Mobley, K. A. (2009). Empirical research about same-sex intimate partner violence: A methodological review. *Journal of Homosexuality, 56*, 361–368. doi:10.1080/00918360902728848

Nicolson, P. (2019). *Domestic violence and psychology. Critical Perspectives on Intimate Partner Violence and Abuse* (2nd ed.). London and New York, NY: Routledge.

Pepper, B. I., & Sand, S. (2015). Internalized homophobia and intimate partner violence in young adult women's same-sex relationships. *Journal of Aggression, Maltreatment & Trauma, 24*, 656–673. doi:10.1080/10926771.2015.1049764

Renzetti, C. M. (1988). Violence in lesbian relationship: A preliminary analysis of causal factors. *Journal of Interpersonal Violence, 3*, 381–399.

Renzetti, M. C. (1992). *Violent betrayal: Partner abuse in lesbian relationship*. Newbury Park: Sage.

Ristock, J. L. (2002). *No more secrets: Violence in lesbian relationships*. New York, NY: Routledge.

Roberts, A., Austin, B., Corliss, H., Vandermorris, A., & Koenen, K. (2010). Pervasive trauma exposure among US sexual orientation minority adults and risk of posttraumatic stress disorder. *American Journal of Public Health, 100*, 2433–2441. doi:10.2105/AJPH.2009.168971

Rose, S. M. (2003). Community interventions concerning homophobic violence and partner violence against lesbians. *Journal of Lesbian Studies, 7*, 125–139. doi:10.1300/J155v07n04_08

Scherzer, T. (1998). Domestic violence in lesbian relationships: Findings of the lesbian relationships research project. *Journal of Lesbian Studies, 2*, 29–47. doi:10.1300/J155v02n01_03

Schilit, R., Lie, G. Y., Bush, J., Montagne, M., & Reyes, L. (1991). Intergenerational transmission of violence in lesbian relationships. *Affilia, 6*, 172–182. doi:10.1177/088610999100600105

Schilit, R., Lie, G. Y., & Montagne, M. (1990). Substance use as a correlate of violence in intimate lesbian relationships. *Journal of Homosexuality, 19*, 51–66. doi:10.1300/J082v19n03_03

Stanley, J. L., Bartholomew, K., Taylor, T., & Oram, D. (2006). Intimate violence in male same-sex relationships. *Journal of Family Violence, 2*, 31–41. doi:10.1007/s10896-005-9008-9

Stiles-Shields, C., & Carroll, R. A. (2015). Same-sex domestic violence: Prevalence, unique aspects, and clinical implications. *Journal of Sex & Marital Therapy, 41*, 636–648. doi:10.1080/0092623X.2014.958792

Straus, M. A., Hamby, S. L., Boney-McCoy, S., & Sugarman, D. B. (1996). The revised conflict tactics scales (CTS2). *Journal of Family Issues, 17*, 283–316. doi:10.1037/t02126-000

Sutter, M. E., Rabinovitch, A. E., Trujillo, M. A., Perrin, P. B., Goldberg, L. D., Coston, B. M., & Calton, J. M. (2019). Patterns of intimate partner violence victimization and perpetration among sexual minority women: A latent class analysis. *Violence Against Women, 25*, 572–592. doi:10.1177/1077801218794307

Taylor, N., Riggs, D. W., Donovan, C., Signal, T., & Fraser, H. (2019). People of diverse genders and/or sexualities caring for and protecting animal companions in the context of domestic violence. *Violence Against Women, 25*, 1096–1115. doi:10.1177/107780121880994

Tjaden, P., Thoennes, N., & Allison, C. (1999). Comparing violence over the lifespan in samples of same-sex and opposite-sex cohabitants. *Violence & Victims, 14*(4), 1–14.

Turell, S. C. (2000). A descriptive analysis of same-sex relationship violence for a diverse sample. *Journal of Family Violence, 15*, 281–293. doi:10.1023/A:1007505619577

Walker, K., & Bowen, E. (2019). The psychology of intimate partner violence and abuse. In D. L. L. Polaschek, A. J. D. Day, & C. R. Hollin (Eds.), *The Wiley international handbook of correctional psychology* (pp. 206–220). Hoboken, NJ: John Wiley & Sons, Inc.

Walters, M. L., Chen, J., & Breiding, M. J. (2013). *The national intimate partner and sexual violence survey (NISVS): 2010 findings on victimization by sexual orientation*. Atlanta, GA: National Center for Injury Prevention and Control, Centers for Disease Control and Prevention.

Westwood, S. (2019). Abuse and older lesbian, gay bisexual, and trans (LGBT) people: A commentary and research agenda. *Journal of Elder Abuse & Neglect, 31*, 97–114. doi:10.1080/08946566.2018.1543624

Whitfield, D. L., Coulter, R. W. S., Langenderfer-Magruder, L., & Jacobson, D. (2018). Experiences of intimate partner violence among lesbian, gay, bisexual, and transgender college students: The intersection of gender, race, and sexual orientation. *Journal of Interpersonal Violence*, 1–25. Advance on-line publication. doi:10.1177/0886260518812071

Whitton, S. W., Dyar, C., Mustanski, B., & Newcomb, M. E. (2019). Intimate partner violence experiences of sexual and gender minority adolescents and young adults assigned female at birth. *Psychology of Women Quarterly*. Advance on-line publication. doi:10.1177/0361684319838972

Whitton, S. W., Newcomb, M. E., Messinger, A. M., Byck, G., & Mustanski, B. (2016). A longitudinal study of IPV victimization among sexual minority youth. *Journal of Interpersonal Violence*, *34*, 912–945. doi:10.1177/0886260516646093

# 18

# DOMESTIC VIOLENCE AND ABUSE WHEN SURVIVORS IDENTIFY AS TRANS OR NON-BINARY

*Michaela Rogers*

## Introduction

Since the 1960s the majority of domestic violence and abuse (DVA) discourse has been domi-nated by a paradigm in which violence results from hegemonic masculinity (Connell, 2005) and promotes gender normative constructions about a particular type of 'victim' or 'survivor' and a particular type of 'perpetrator'. In other words, this 'public story' disseminates and maintains the myth that DVA is the perpetration of heterosexual men's violence against heterosexual women (Donovan & Hester, 2014, p. 9). The 1980s and 1990s saw debates about DVA contest this pub-lic story with an emerging literature about violence and abuse in lesbian relationships and, to a lesser extent, in those of gay men (Kelly, 1991; Letellier, 1994). Whilst decades of research has helped to dispel the myth that DVA only occurs in heterosexual relationships, the public story continues to be reproduced in mainstream research, policy and practice serving to exclude or marginalise survivors, as well as perpetrators, who do not identify within this typology (Walker, 2015; Rogers, 2017a). This chapter offers an alternative lens by focussing on the phenomenon of DVA when one or both partners identify as trans or non-binary gender ('trans' will be used as a catchall to include people who identify as trans and non-binary, both terms are defined in the next section of this chapter). Whilst there is literature that explores trans people as both victims and perpetrators (see Brown, 2011), this is a very modest body of work and, therefore, here the focus is on trans and non-binary people as survivors.

Some writers use academic literature or research on DVA across lesbian, gay, bisexual and trans (LGBT) communities to explore those experiences and perspectives of trans and non-binary people. Unquestionably during the last ten years there has been an upsurge in the body of work exploring the prevalence and experiences of DVA across LGBT communities, but locating and conceptualising a trans perspective in this way is problematic as trans identity is often subsumed into the LGBT umbrella (and in actuality, trans people are frequently absent from this literature, or in quantitative studies their numbers are nominal) (Rogers, 2016; Wirtz et al., 2018). The cogence of this, in an analysis of trans people's experiences of DVA, concerns the important distinction that gender identity and sexuality are *not* synonymous. Indeed, whilst there are similarities in terms of DVA and the experiences of people belonging to LGBT com-munities (which are illustrated later in this chapter), there are also very significant differences for trans people in the forms of abuse perpetrated in their relationships, in the ways in which power and control are exerted, and in terms of the impacts of DVA in everyday life. There are additional reasons to focus on trans survivors given the historical exclusion from feminist anti-violence activism and the women's sector and, in particular, considering the escalating levels of lethal violence used against trans women (Serano, 2013; Waters & Yacka-Bible, 2017; Jordan et al., 2019).

This chapter will enable the reader to see beyond the 'public story' of DVA to explore trans and non-binary people's experiences. The discussion will highlight ecological, contextual and structural issues and illuminate micro-level phenomena (such as the limits to help-seeking behaviour by trans people), meso-level factors (issues concerning service provision) and macro-level factors (in particular, the workings of gender norms and ideology) in relation to trans-identified survivors. In particular, the influence and persistence of cisgenderism (a prejudicial ideology) will be highlighted and shown to operate at various levels in problematic ways affecting trans and non-binary people.

## Understanding trans and the workings of gendered ideology

Clarity about the terminology pertaining to trans people helps to illuminate the multiplicity, complexity and dynamic nature of trans identity (Dargie et al., 2014). In essence, the term 'trans', or 'transgender', operates as an umbrella term to signify a person whose gendered self-identity differs to that which was assigned to them at birth. Gender identity pertains to one's sense of belonging to the category of man/woman or other gender (Schilt & Westbrook, 2009). Trans identities are manifold and include trans man/trans woman, transsexual man/transsexual woman, MtF/FtM, and a woman or man with a transgender history (Bachmann & Gooch, 2018). Such identities tend to align with a binary conception of gender (as a man or woman) whereas the term 'non-binary' is increasingly adopted to signify a spectrum of gender identities including genderqueer, genderfluid, agender, bi-gender, pangender, androgynous, androgyne, neutrois and other identities that do not conform to the male/female binary (Bachmann & Gooch, 2018).

It is important to note that the body of work on trans identity is tied to a shifting terrain as identity terms are constantly evolving. Trans and non-binary people reflect the dynamic and multi-dimensional nature of identity and can simultaneously identify with one or more gender labels; for example, as genderqueer/trans male. In this chapter, an ontological stance is taken in that an individual's experience of gender identity is subjective and should not be reduced to a checklist of socially defined characteristics, expression or aesthetics (Serano, 2016). Another important term in an analysis of trans and gender is 'cisgender', or 'cis', which refers to a person whose gender identity remains the same as that which was ascribed at birth (Schilt & Westbrook, 2009). Finally, whilst gender and sexuality are different elements of identity, for some trans and non-binary people, their sexual identity is similarly complex and bound up with their gender identity as well as being outside of the norm (that is, not heterosexual). It can be difficult to partition gender from sexuality in such cases (Dargie et al., 2014; Rogers & Ahmed, 2017).

It is unsurprising that minority people's experiences of DVA, as well as other forms of abuse, are often underpinned by prejudices and discriminatory perspectives. In the case of trans people, the concept of cisgenderism enhances an ecological analysis that explores DVA in micro-level settings (that is, within intimate or familial relationships) as well as in relation to macro-level influences (for example, social and cultural gender norms). Cisgenderism is a prejudicial ideology that upholds the construct of gender normativity invoking a paradigm in which social constructions of binary gender operate as the norm and, as such, position any divergence from this as abnormal (Blumer et al., 2013). Fundamentally, gender normativity is built upon beliefs about cisgender identities as natural and fixed, with heterosexual marriage and procreation between a cisgender man and a cisgender woman viewed as 'normal'.

Cisgenderist ideology reflects this paradigm of social life and rejects people who do not identify as cisgender classifying them as abnormal or deviant (Ansara & Hegarty, 2011, 2014; Rogers, 2017a, 2017b, 2020). This is related to another prejudicial ideology, heterosexism, which views heterosexuality as the norm and same-sex relationships as deviant and aberrant (Schilt & Westbrook, 2009). Cisgenderism and heterosexism operate multi-dimensionally across micro, meso and macro levels of influence as each can undergird an individual's or organisation's norms and culture, and both can be systemic and structural in nature (Ansara & Hegarty, 2014; Rogers, 2017a, 2017b).

Finally, intentionality is an important factor in this discussion as any enactment of cisgenderism can be deliberate or unintentional. Cisgenderism as an unintended, passive act can have a very different impact compared to circumstances in which it is intentional and active; it is the latter which can be experienced as oppressive, discriminatory and, in some instances, abusive. Whilst there is a growing recognition of trans and gender diversity, there is the potential for cisgenderism in countless situations as almost everyone has grown up in communities that are predominantly (and seemingly) cisgender and, until more recently, there has been a distinct lack of recognition and acceptance for identities, behaviour and experiences which are not cisgender. The point is that cisgenderism, whether subtle or overt, intended or not, can have significant harmful impacts and it is the way in which cisgenderist language or actions are perceived and experienced that is important.

## Mapping the scale of trans and non-binary people's experiences of DVA

A UK-focussed lens draws attention to the very limited research detailing prevalence rates apropos of trans or non-binary people's experiences of DVA. This dearth of data does curtail a comprehensive analysis and results from a range of issues including a lack of recognition and naming of experiences as abusive; extensive under-reporting; and/or problems in capturing a trans perspective due to survey practices, design and methodologies (Ristock, 2005, 2011; Rogers, 2016). Most existing studies have been conducted with small sample sizes but nonetheless these have produced significant findings that have policy and practice implications. For example, one of the first published studies conducted in Scotland indicated that 80% of trans people ($n = 60$) had experienced some form of emotional, sexual or physical abuse from a partner or ex-partner (Roch et al., 2010). The most common form was emotional abuse (73%), 60% of respondents had experienced controlling behaviour, 47% of respondents had experienced some form of sexual abuse and 45% had experienced physically abusive behaviour. Respondents were asked about forced sexual activity with 37% of respondents reporting that someone had forced, or tried to force them, to have sex when they were under the age of 16 and 46% of respondents said that someone had forced, or tried to force them, to engage in some other form of sexual activity when under the age of 16. Finally, 10% of respondents stated that someone had forced, or tried to force them, to engage in sexual activity for money.

More recent studies have supported Roch et al.'s main findings (that abuse is common) and a study completed by UK organisation Stonewall found that of 800+ trans and non-binary people, 28% reported to have experienced DVA from an intimate partner with similar proportions reporting abuse from family members (Bachmann & Gooch, 2018). Similarly, an analysis of the case files of LGBT survivors ($n = 626$) receiving advocacy support from Galop (a London-based charity), reported that 16% (*n* = 100) identified as trans or non-binary and that intimate partner abuse was more widespread (in 79% of the total cases) (Magić & Kelley, 2018). Concerningly, 60% of survivors identifying as trans women disclosed abuse from a male perpetrator. They were the group deemed to be at most risk of violence with the highest levels of self-reported physical, sexual and financial abuse. Of those survivors identifying as trans men, 75% reported abuse from a male perpetrator and were equally most at risk of DVA from an intimate partner. They reported the highest levels of harassment, stalking, verbal and emotional abuse.

International research reflects this picture with high levels of prevalence reported in other countries. For example, there is a growing body of work that suggests that the scale of DVA from perpetrators towards their trans partners is at a rate similar to, or higher, than that for cisgender people (Langenderfer-Magruder et al., 2016; Dyar et al., 2019). Concerningly, when scrutinising lethal violence, whilst homicides involving trans victims often go unreported or unexplained, existing data suggests that DVA plays a significant role in the reported deaths of trans and non-binary people (Waters & Yacka-Bible, 2017). The US leads the way in capturing data on trans people's experiences of DVA as this is collected comparatively frequently. Such efforts mostly focus on DVA as intimate partner violence (IPV). For example, in 2015 the US Transgender Survey gathered 27,715 responses from all 50 states. Over half (54%) of respondents experienced some form of IPV in their lifetime including acts involving coercive control and physical harm (James et al., 2016). In addition, compared to 18% of the general US population, 24% had experienced severe physical violence by an intimate partner, 47% had experienced sexual violence and 10% reported sexual violence in the past year (James et al., 2016). Prevalence is equally concerning when comparing rates for adolescents with those of adults. In studies of LGBT young people, those who identified as trans reported the highest rates of physical, psychological, cyber and sexual victimisation from an intimate or romantic partner (Dank et al., 2014; Whitton et al., 2016).

Elsewhere across the globe, prevalence is not routinely collected for trans, or even LGBT, communities. In Australia, Campo and Tayton (2015) collated the available empirical data on LGBT DVA to conclude that it exists at similar rates to those who identify as heterosexual. In addition, they noted that cisgenderism and heterosexism frequently underpin the experiences of LGBT people. In Europe limited information exists as there is no singular source of data on DVA and trans communities. In 2015 the Fundamental Rights Agency (FRA, 2015) published a report detailing findings of a survey of 6,771 trans people across 28 European member states highlighting that respondents reported a high level of violence, hate-motivated attacks and harassment as one in three trans respondents (34%) experienced violence or was threatened with violence in the five years preceding the survey. It was not clear how many incidents occurred within a domestic setting, or how many were perpetrated by a person known to the victim (that is, a partner or family member) as most incidents were located in outdoor public space.

## Gender and sexual identities: similarities and differences when accounting for DVA

Acknowledged by the World Health Organization (WHO, 2017), DVA can be found in people's relationships irrespective of their gender and/or sexuality and, as noted, there is a growing body of global literature which describes the prevalence and nature of DVA for LGBT communities. This work highlights how heterosexual and LGBT people might experience similar patterns and types of DVA, but there are additional dynamics and forms of abuse for people with non-heterosexual identities. Whilst this chapter is not concerned with DVA in same-sex relationships per se, it is important to acknowledge the overlaps in LGBT people's experiences of DVA as such forms of abuse are often underpinned by similar tactics and dynamics (such as threats to out a person, or utilising heterosexist and/or cisgenderist constructs). These tactics include:

- Forms of outing: disclosure of gender identity or sexuality to family, friends or work colleagues or to officials (for example, social workers for people with children).
- The 'double disclosure' bind: disclosing DVA may concurrently (and, potentially, problematically) result in disclosing minority status in relation to gender identity/sexuality.
- Undermining someone's sense of gender or sexual identity and exploiting a person's internalised negative self-beliefs (internalised transphobia).
- Practices of 'gaslighting': manipulating survivors into questioning their own perception, and even sanity, as the perpetrator convinces them that no one would believe the abuse is real (exploiting heterosexist or cisgenderist myths based on the public story).
- Manipulating survivors into believing that abuse is a 'normal' part of same-sex relationships.
- Social isolation through limiting or controlling access to spaces and networks that are helpful when coming out or when coming to terms with gender and/or sexual identity.
- Pressuring survivors into submission by minimalising abuse in the name of protecting the image of the LGBT community (adapted from Rogers, 2020).

Despite these overlaps in terms of the dynamics and forms of abuse, it is important to resist homogenising across the LGBT umbrella as Seelman (2015) points out that trans people may be at greater risk than others who identify as LG or B. In addition, there are various trans-specific abuses which target a person's identity and these have been articulated in recent studies. Indeed, trans and non-binary people frequently describe identity-related abuse in their narratives of everyday experience. Identity abuse refers to violence and abuse which targets a survivor's sense of self or social characteristics (see, for example, Ristock, 2011). An example is the act of restricting access to or hiding gender signifiers (clothing, accessories, wigs) that are needed to express gender identity (Rogers, 2013, 2017a). In addition, abusers may use coercion or prevent someone from pursuing medical treatment or intervention (for example, hormone therapies, speech therapy, sex reassignment procedures), or prevent and restrict someone's access to treatment or medication, effectively interfering with or preventing the transitioning process. Identity abuse can occur through misgendering when an abuser refuses to use somebody's preferred name or the correct pronouns or by threatening to out a person by disclosing their trans history (active forms of cisgenderism) (Rogers, 2020).

An abuser might use derogatory names and 'body shaming' tactics (being derisory or ridiculing a person's body image) or monitoring a person's gender expression to judge whether they 'pass' as a non-trans person (Guadalupe-Diaz & Anthony, 2017). Conversely, they may also fetishise or reject bodily boundaries (Brown & Herman, 2015). These cisgenderist, gender-specific behaviours are not uncommon, as a small-scale survey (*n* = 71) found that almost half of respondents (46%) reported intimate partner violence that was cisgenderist and transphobic in nature (Scottish Transgender Alliance, 2008). More recently, a study by Galop found misgendering, withholding medication or preventing treatment was commonly reported by trans and non-binary survivors (Magić & Kelley, 2018). Such identity-related abuses reflect the power and control dynamics that underpin abuse experiences. Moreover, trans-specific abuses have trans-specific impacts (such as restricted ability or an inability to express their gender identity, or internalised transphobia) reflecting the workings of coercion and manipulation within the context of gender monitoring, scrutiny and surveillance by an abusive partner or family member.

## Identity, intersectionality and DVA

Whilst identity-targeted abuses frequently characterise trans and non-binary people's experiences of DVA, most people do not experience the world from one social location or in relation to a singular personal characteristic; rather the interplay of different aspects of identity determines a person's life experience. By promoting the notion that identity is multi-faceted, an intersectionality framework encourages an analysis of contexts as well as a critical examination of the interlocking nature of systems of privilege and oppression. This approach to analysis has potential to illuminate how categories of gender, ethnicity, age and so on, rely on each other to function within systems of domination (Crenshaw, 1989). As such, the analytical approach to trans and non-binary people's experiences of DVA is not one of an 'additive' nature where we simply add trans identity to what is already understood in relation to DVA (Ristock, 2005); it is an approach which explores the multiplexity of identity in relation to dominant and hegemonic gender norms, ideology and stereotypes to understand the workings of power and control in micro-, meso- and macro-level contexts for trans survivors.

Beemyn and Rankin (2011) argue that intersectional aspects of identity undergird the lived experiences of discrimination and victimisation for many trans people. Moreover, an intersectional analysis has proved useful in explorations of DVA at the junctures of race, class and gender (Sokoloff & Dupont, 2005; Hassouneh & Glass, 2008). In the UK and US, for example, studies show that Black and ethnic minority (BME) trans people are victimised more generally than White trans people (Beemyn & Rankin, 2011; Grant et al., 2011) and, concerningly, it is claimed that they have a higher risk of victimisation in their intimate and familial relationships (Browne, 2007; Magić & Kelley, 2018).

The modest body of empirical studies that explore other intersectional identities (including trans and non-binary identity in relation to youth and sexuality) has important findings. For example, Reuter et al. (2017) surveyed LGBT young people to explore IPV and found demographic differences in that trans and non-binary young people, as well as youth who identified as Black/African American, are at a higher risk of victimisation than young people who identified as lesbian, gay, bisexual or White. Whitton et al. (2016) revealed similar results in a longitudinal study of LGBT young people ($n = 248$), aged 16–20 at the study outset, in an ethnically diverse community-based study. At the end of the five-year study, Whitton et al.'s study found that overall, 45.2% of LGBT youth were physically abused with the likelihood of physical victimisation to be 2.46 times higher for trans than for cisgender young people, and 2 to 4 times higher for racial-ethnic minorities than for White youth. The odds of sexual victimisation were 3.42 times higher for trans young people.

## Context, outcomes and risk

In terms of outcomes, the social, financial, relational, health and mental health impacts of DVA are widely reported in literature. In addition to prevalence and forms of abuse, the interplay of contexts, outcomes and risks associated with DVA are critical to an informed understanding of trans and non-binary people's victimhood. Moreover, both scholarship and activism have been central in highlighting the heightened vulnerability to DVA as grounded in the social, cultural and political conditions that systematically devalue and invalidate LGBT lives and relationships more generally, and this is especially the case for trans and non-binary people (Ristock, 2005,

2011; Jordan et al., 2019). The workings of these conditions in conjunction with other processes, such as the public story of DVA, can result in the invisibilisation of trans people as victims and survivors of violence. More concerningly, this can result in the ways in which trans people do not recognise violence and abuse when perpetrated against them as the very contexts for DVA, as propagated by the public story, are unrecognisable.

Exemplifying the interplay of social and cultural conditions and dominant structures (gender normativity) and the different contexts for DVA, Rogers (2017c) describes the parallels of IPV and family violence with 'honour'-based ideology in her proposal of a specific type of abuse termed *transphobic 'honour'-based abuse*. This is enacted when a person is deemed to have brought shame and embarrassment to the relationship or family by transgressing gender norms and troubling normative configurations of the family or partnership. This highlights the interplay of differing ecological contexts: the micro-setting of the home and associated roles, stereotypes and relationship expectations, as well as community-based and structural frameworks which are underpinned by gender normative expectations and notions of identity, status and belonging. This draws attention to the need to consider these different levels of influence and context in relation to assessments of risk and vulnerability.

An intersectionality lens also requires an extended analysis to explore how other, or intersecting, aspects of a person's identity can add to these levels of influence, risk and vulnerability. For example, an analysis of DVA as a problem for White populations highlights structural issues, such as gender inequality (Stark, 2007), but when turning the lens to BME populations in White-dominant societies, DVA can be explained as resulting from cultural differences or from a lack of acculturation (the process of adapting to or borrowing traits from a different culture). Dustin (2016) provides a word of caution in her analysis of gender-based violence when noting the limitations of cultural arguments which serve as a means of *othering* and distract from the gendered structural and systemic bases of DVA. Notwithstanding, there are additional risk factors for BME trans people if a person does not have asylum or refugee status and, therefore, no recourse to public funds and, as noted earlier, BME trans and non-binary people are at an even greater risk of DVA (Browne, 2007; Magić & Kelley, 2018).

Other aspects of social location or background increase risk and vulnerability to DVA. Research into the mental health outcomes of DVA shows that LGBT survivors are twice as likely to have self-harmed and almost twice as likely to have attempted suicide (SafeLives, 2018). In Roch et al.'s (2010) study, 15% of the sample reported at least one suicide attempt as a consequence of their experiences of abuse, and a national survey of trans people in North America found an increased risk of suicide among trans and non-binary survivors of DVA (Grant et al., 2011). Risk factors, as well as social and structural inequalities, are amplified and multiple for trans survivors and include an increased likelihood of social isolation, housing precarity and homelessness, substance abuse, work and economic insecurity and repeat victimisation (Stotzer, 2009; Grant et al., 2011; James et al., 2016; Wirtz et al., 2018). Browne describes this configuration of risk succinctly by noting that 'multiple marginality increases vulnerability to violence' (Browne, 2007, p. 373). However, the interrelationship between DVA and such factors (homelessness, substance misuse and so on) is complex as there is a mutual causality and reinforcing circularity that exists between DVA and other risk/vulnerability factors.

## Barriers to help-seeking

The barriers to help-seeking for all survivors are wide-ranging. However, for trans people there are additional mechanisms (as there are for other minority groups) that serve to impede help-seeking. In particular, the enactment of cisgenderism and heterosexism operating at micro, meso or macro levels, results in very specific barriers (Donovan & Hester, 2014; Rogers, 2016, 2017a, 2017b). This chapter helps to illuminate the dynamics of these barriers which can emanate from various discourses and structures; for example, dynamics associated with the public story of DVA, or those underpinned by gender normative ideology. To explore this further, it is useful to employ a theoretical model that breaks down the process of help-seeking. Liang et al. (2005) offer such a model constituted by three stages: (1) problem recognition, (2) making the decision to seek out and access help and (3) the selection of a help provider. This model explores help-seeking from the perspective of the survivor.

Firstly, the issues of problem recognition and naming abuse are fundamentally troublesome in an exposition of trans and non-binary people's experience of abuse. This was explicitly demonstrated in the narratives of Roch et al.'s participants who described their experiences as 'just something that happened' or 'wrong but not a crime' (Roch et al., 2010, p. 5). This lack of naming abuse may exemplify the power of the 'public story' which results in abuse experiences being eclipsed or invalidated where people's experiences do not meet the basic conditions of the public narrative (that is, that perpetrators are cisgender, heterosexual men using violence against cisgender, heterosexual women). There are more fundamental challenges, however, when survivors experience identity-related abuses which result in fear, shame, internalised transphobia, embarrassment, low self-confidence, lacking self-belief and the reduced capacity for decision-making, to name a few. All these are toxic, but typical, factors that impede help-seeking behaviour.

Secondly, earlier in this chapter different forms of abuse were depicted for trans people and non-binary people including the potential of outing and the threat of being outed which concurrently serve as barriers to help-seeking. Additionally, the danger of outing oneself to family, friends, the community or others when disclosing abuse, the *double disclosure* bind, may represent a significant factor in the decision-making process in relation to help-seeking for those people who are not 'out' (Brown & Herman, 2015; Seelman, 2015). A more fundamental challenge to decision-making may result from a lack of knowledge about existing support for DVA survivors and about trans-specific or trans-friendly (or LGBT-specific/friendly) services (if these exist locally) or a belief that only people who 'fit' the public story are eligible for such support.

Thirdly, in an analysis of the interaction between micro- and meso-level elements, Donovan and Hester (2014, p. 157) describe the relationship between survivors and service providers as characterised by 'a gap of trust'. In her research, Rogers (2013, 2016) found that this 'gap of trust' was often attached to the expectations that trans and non-binary people held in that they anticipated a heterosexist, cisgenderist response from service providers. Such expectations were often rooted to previous experiences of discrimination, being refused a service, being questioned in relation to eligibility on the grounds of gender (or perceived gender) or the misidentification of victims for perpetrators (Donovan & Hester, 2014; Jordan et al., 2019). Participants in Rogers' (2013) study reflected the lack of entitlement felt by trans people; again, suggestive of the powerful workings of the public story.

Amongst service providers, Rogers (2013, 2016) found: a lack of knowledge or misunderstandings about trans people's needs and the barriers to accessing mainstream services, a distinct hetero- and gender normative bias of existing services with practitioner attitudes fixed to notions about gender as a binary conception, a lack of clear referral pathway and/or links between DVA and LGBT services. Another study found that DVA services, specifically refuge accommodation, directed resources at cisgender, heterosexual women, thereby marginalising trans and non-binary people (as well as lesbian and bisexual women) (Hester et al., 2012). The dearth of explicitly trans-friendly service provision and lack of visibility in DVA discourse results in support that is inevitably ill-equipped to meet the specificity of trans and non-binary survivors (Tesch & Bekerian, 2015; Riggs et al., 2016; Walker, 2015; Kattari & Begun, 2017). Experiences of the criminal justice system are also problematic as trans and non-binary people have described patterns of discrimination and mistreatment such as the failure to intervene or take victim statements, doubts about witness credibility, and unwarranted arrests and/or detention (Goodmark, 2013; James et al., 2016).

## Best practice to support trans and non-binary survivors

The multiplicity of factors that prevent trans and non-binary survivors from accessing support are clearly articulated across the literature. These can be categorised as the interaction of individual and interpersonal factors, organisational and policy challenges or gaps, as well as the persistence of systemic and structural influences (Rogers, 2013; Wirtz et al., 2018). Therefore, an ecological approach to policy and practice is required as this bridges the gap between the individual, organisation and broader social structures. Frameworks such as *cultural competence* and *cultural humility* exist to support best practice with minority populations enabling a fair attempt to address this gap. Cultural humility requires a practitioner (whatever the professional discipline) to have a sophisticated level of reflection in order to suspend existing norms, values and stereotyping (what you think you know) in order to adopt cultural competence, which is the ability to identify and value the social characteristics, backgrounds, practices and experiences of a person in need of support knowing that these constitute an important part of their sense of self and experiences of everyday life (Birkenmaier et al., 2014). Adopting cultural competence with a trans or non-binary survivor relies on the ability to put aside norms and stereotypes that are, in essence, gender normative beliefs and constructs, in order to learn about gender diversity and a person's background, culture and gender identity. This philosophical approach positions the survivor as the *expert by experience* and represents best practice whilst simultaneously adopting an intersectional framework recognising that people do not experience the world merely from one social location (Rogers & Allen, 2019).

To counter the problematic and dominant nature of cisgender-based authoritative discourses (Ansara & Hegarty, 2011) such as those embedded in research, policy and practice, it is argued that another concept holds greater potential than a cultural competence approach; this is termed *structural competence* (Metzl & Hansen, 2014; Willging et al., 2019). This model evolved in healthcare as a means of advancing the cultural competence model, which Metzl and Hansen (2014, p. 127) argued does not go far enough and, as such, cultural competence needs to be redefined in 'structural terms'. The cultural competence model has been criticised for operating at a micro level recognising individual bias and prejudice, rather than that held and reflected in meso-level organisational policy and practice and wider social structures. Therefore, the proposition of a structural competency model, which acknowledges the entrenched nature of inequality that results from social institutions and structures, is more effective in understanding the processes of marginalisation, discrimination and vulnerability which are systemic and much more difficult to tackle than individual biases (Willging et al., 2019).

On a daily basis, practitioners can adopt specific practices to reflect non-discriminatory and trans-inclusive values. Such practices can also be integrated at meso (organisational) and macro (state) levels through policy and guidance. As dynamics of abuse are inevitably entwined with power and control, best practice can only be achieved when practitioners acknowledge, rather than elide, micro-, meso- and macro-level constraints and factors that affect trans and non-binary people's experiences of and access to services. A structural competency approach in individual practice would be reflected in language choice and respectful communication, asking a person how they wish to be named and ensuring the use of appropriate pronouns. Organisations clearly evidencing their 'trans-friendly' or 'trans-inclusive' policy would be a step towards openly trans-inclusive practice. Increased voice, representation and leadership by trans and non-binary survivors working in the field would help to address structural and political challenges (Jordan et al., 2019). Similarly, integrating trans justice values in service delivery needs to include trans survivors to establish a more sophisticated understanding about DVA for trans and non-binary people and their needs in terms of accommodation, advocacy and support more generally (Jordan et al., 2019). Whilst societal and culture change is taking place across the globe with regard to gender diversity, restrictions in developing adequate policy and practice for trans and non-binary survivors will persist until inclusion measures are widespread, not piecemeal.

## Chapter summary

This chapter has explored the phenomenon of domestic violence and abuse when survivors identify as trans or non-binary. Whilst there is a modest, but growing, body of work on this topic, there are clear implications that can be extrapolated to justify the development of current and future research, policy and practice to enable accessible and inclusive support for this population. For example, the empirical findings of existing research contest the 'public story' of DVA to show significant prevalent rates of and vulnerability to abuse experienced by trans and non-binary people. In terms of the nature of DVA for trans and non-binary people, an ecological analysis which considers micro-, meso- and macro-level factors is helpful as this illuminates the complexities of DVA and the persistence of normative ideologies and attitudes in relation to gender and their operation within interpersonal relationships. It is important to consider these complexities as the barriers to help-seeking for trans and non-binary are plentiful. Moreover, the extant body of work, albeit this is modest, does suggest that trans and non-binary survivors of DVA do not all require the same kind of help and that services must acknowledge and respond to the differences in contexts, circumstances and needs of trans and non-binary people.

## Critical findings

- Whilst a modest body of literature exists, studies to date illustrate that domestic violence and abuse occurs at the same, or higher, rates for trans and non-binary people.
- In terms of the nature and dynamics of abuse, there are similarities across the communities of people with diverse gender and sexual identities; however, there are some trans-specific forms of abuse that target a person's gender identity and prevent the expression of that identity or the transitioning process.
- Trans and non-binary people experience high rates of mental ill-health, housing precarity, homelessness, economic discrimination to name a few, and such inequalities increase risk and vulnerability to violence and abuse.
- Trans and non-binary people's experiences of abuse are often tied to the pernicious and entrenched nature of cisgenderism (a prejudicial ideology that is built upon ideas of gender as fixed at birth, male/female, and represented in heterosexual marriage).
- The workings of cisgenderism also underpins many of the barriers that prevent trans and non-binary people from recognising and naming their experiences of abuse and from seeking help.

- Barriers to help-seeking are also tied to previous or anticipated experiences of cisgenderism and heterosexism which are reportedly common when trans and non-binary people encounter public services and support.

## Implications for policy, practice and research

- Best practice with trans and non-binary survivors requires an acknowledgement and counterbalance of the structural and systemic barriers within everyday life as the values of empowerment and self-determination that underpin the field of DVA will have limited impact for trans and non-binary survivors until these are addressed.
- Policy and practice responses need to reflect the heterogeneity of identities, needs and experiences of trans and non-binary people.
- Additional research could provide a more comprehensive understanding of the ways in which policy and practice could address these structural and systemic barriers.
- Increasing voice, representation and leadership for trans and non-binary people within the field of DVA is key to the review, design and delivery of research, policy and practice.
- An intersectional framework to understanding the barriers and experiences of trans and non-binary people is important as there is evidence to suggest that marginalisation and discrimination increase when accounting for additional social characteristics such as ethnicity and age.
- Greater awareness of the myths and stereotypes associated with the 'public story' is needed across mainstream services (for instance, healthcare, social work, criminal justice agencies) working in the field of DVA to improve interactions and relations with trans and non-binary survivors.
- Routine enquiry and pathways to support should be used by practitioners, enquiring about gender and sexual identity before screening for DVA, recognising the higher risk and vulnerability to violence and abuse.
- Bridging the gap between DVA organisations and LGBT organisations may help to improve the policy and practice response in collaborations which involve knowledge and expertise transfer, as multi-agency working has long been advocated as the best approach to DVA.

## References

Ansara, Y. G., & Hegarty, P. (2011). Cisgenderism in psychology: Pathologising and misgendering children from 1999 to 2008. *Psychology and Sexuality*, *3*(2), 137–160. doi:10.1080/19419899.2011.576696

Ansara, Y. G., & Hegarty, P. (2014). Methodologies of misgendering: Recommendations for reducing cisgenderism in psychological research. *Feminism & Psychology*, *24*(2), 259–270. doi:10.1177/0959353514526217.

Bachmann, C. L., & Gooch, B. (2018). *LGBT in Britain: Trans report*. London: Stonewall.

Beemyn, B. G., & Rankin, S. (2011). *The lives of transgender people*. New York, NY: Columbia University Press.

Birkenmaier, J., Berg-Weger, M., & Dewees, M. P. (Eds.). (2014). *The practice of generalist social work* (3rd ed.). London: Routledge.

Blumer, M. L. C., Ansara, Y. G., & Watson, C. M. (2013). Cisgenderism in family therapy: How everyday clinical practices can delegitimize people's gender self-designations. *Journal of Family Psychotherapy*, *24*, 267–285. doi:10.1080/08975353.2013.849551.

Brown, N. (2011). Holding tensions of victimization and perpetration: Partner abuse in trans communities. In J. Ristock (Ed.), *Intimate partner violence in LGBTQ lives*. New York, NY: Routledge.

Brown, T. N. T., & Herman, J. L. (2015). *Intimate violence and sexual abuse among LGBT people: A review of existing research*. Retrieved from https://williamsinstitute.law.ucla.edu/wp-content/uploads/Intimate-Partner-Violence-and-Sexual-Abuse-among-LGBT-People.pdf

Browne, K. (2007). *Domestic violence and abuse: Additional findings report*. Brighton: University of Brighton, Spectrum.

Campo, M., & Tayton, S. (2015). *Intimate partner violence in lesbian, gay, bisexual, trans, intersex, and queer communities: Key issues*. Melbourne: Australian Institute of Family Studies.

Connell, R. W. (2005). *Masculinities* (2nd ed.). Cambridge: Polity Press.

Crenshaw, K. (1989). Demarginalizing the intersection of race and sex: A black feminist critique of antidiscrimination doctrine: Feminist theory and antiracist politics. *University of Chicago Legal Forum*, 138–167.

Dank, M., Lachman, P., Zweig, J. M., & Yahner, J. (2014). Dating violence experiences of lesbian, gay, bisexual, and transgender youth. *Journal of Youth and Adolescence*, *43*, 846–857. doi:10.1007/s10964-013-9975-8

Dargie, E., Blair, K. L., Pukall, C. F., & Coyle, S. M. (2014). Somewhere under the rainbow: Exploring the identities and experiences of trans persons. *The Canadian Journal of Human Sexuality*, *23*(2), 60–74. doi:10.3138/cjhs.2378

Donovan, C., & Hester, M. (2014). *Domestic violence and sexuality: What's love got to do with it?* Bristol: Policy Press.

Dustin, M. (2016). Culture or masculinity? Understanding gender-based violence in the UK. *Journal of Poverty and Social Justice*, *24*(1), 51–62. doi:10.1332/175982716X14525979706964

Dyar, C., Messinger, A. M., Newcomb, M. E., Byck, G. R., Dunlap, P., & Whitton, S. W. (2019). Development and initial validation of three culturally sensitive measures of intimate partner violence for sexual and gender minority populations. *Journal of Interpersonal Violence*. doi:886260519846856.

FRA. (2015). *Being trans in the European Union comparative analysis of EU LGBT survey data*. Vienna, Austria: The European Union Agency for Fundamental Rights.

Goodmark, L. (2013). Transgender people, intimate partner abuse, and the legal system. *Harvard Civil Rights-Civil Liberties Law review*, *48*, 51–104.

Grant, J. M., Mottet, L., Tanis, J. E., Harrison, J., & Keisling, M. (2011). *Injustice at every turn: A report of the national Transgender Discrimination Survey*. Washington, DC: National Center for Transgender Equality.

Guadalupe, X. L., & Anthony, A. K. (2017). Discrediting identity work: Understandings of intimate partner violence transgender survivors. *Deviant Behavior*, *38*, 1–16. doi:10.1080/01639625.2016.1189757

Hassouneh, D., & Glass, N. (2008). The influence of gender role stereotyping on women's experiences of female same-sex intimate partner violence. *Violence Against Women*, *14*(3), 310–325. doi:10.1177/1077801207313734

Hester, M., Williamson, E., Regan, L., Coulter, M. Chantler, K., Gangoli, G., & Green, L. (2012). *Exploring the service and support needs of male, lesbian, gay, bi-sexual and transgendered and black and minority ethnic victims of domestic and sexual violence*. Bristol: University of Bristol.

James, S. E., Herman, J. L., Rankin, S., Keisling, M., Mottet, L., & Anafi, M. (2016). *The report of the 2015 U.S. transgender survey*. Washington, DC: National Center for Transgender Equality.

Jordan, S. P., Mehrota, G. R., & Fujikawa, K. A. (2019). Mandating inclusion: Critical trans perspectives on domestic and sexual advocacy. *Violence Against Women*, 1–12. doi:10.1177/1077801219836728

Kattari, S. K., & Begun, S. (2017). On the margins of marginalized: Transgender homelessness and survival sex. *Affilia: Journal of Women and Social Work*, *32*, 92–103. doi:10.1177/0886109916651904

Kelly, L. (1991). Unspeakable acts: Women who abuse. *Trouble and Strife: The Radical Feminist Magazine*, *21*, 13–20.

Langenderfer-Magruder, L., Whifield, D. L., Walls, N. E., Kattari, S. K., & Ramos, D. (2016). Experiences of intimate partner violence and subsequent police reporting among lesbian, gay, bisexual, transgender, and queer adults in Colorado: Comparing rates of cisgender and transgender victimization. *Journal of Interpersonal Violence*, *31*(5), 855–871. doi:10.1177/0886260514556767

Letellier, P. (1994). Gay and bisexual male domestic victimization: Challenges to feminist theory and responses to violence. *Violence and Victims*, *9*(2), 95–106.

Liang, B., Goodman, L., Tummala-Narra, P., & Weintraub, S. (2005). A theoretical framework for understanding help-seeking processes among survivors of intimate partner violence. *American Journal of Community Psychology*, *36*, 71–84.

Magić, J., & Kelley, P. (2018). *LGBT+ people's experiences of domestic abuse: A report on Galop's domestic abuse advocacy service*. London: Galop.

Metzl, J., & Hansen, M. (2014). Structural competency: Theorizing a new medical engagement with stigma and inequality. *Social Science & Medicine, 103*, 126–133. doi:10.1016/j.socscimed.2013.06.032

Reuter, T. R., Newcomb, M. E., Whitton, S. W., & Mustanski, B. (2017). Intimate partner violence victimization in LGBT young adults: Demographic differences and associations with health behaviors. *Psychology of Violence, 7*(1), 101–109. Web.

Riggs, D., Fraser, H., Taylor, N., Signal, T., & Donovan, C. (2016). Domestic violence service providers' capacity for supporting transgender women: Findings from an Australian workshop. *British Journal of Social Work, 46*, 2374–2392. doi:10.1093/bjsw/bcw110

Ristock, J. (2005). *Relationship violence in lesbian/gay/bisexual/transgender/queer[LGBTQ] communities: Moving beyond a gender-based framework*. Roehampton: University of Roehampton.

Ristock, J. (Ed.). (2011). *Intimate partner violence in LGBTQ lives*. New York, NY: Routledge.

Roch, A., Ritchie, G., & Morton, J. (2010). *Out of sight, out of mind? Transgender people's experiences of domestic abuse*. Scotland: LGBT Youth Scotland and the Equality Network.

Rogers, M. (2013). *Transforming practice: Trans people's experiences of domestic abuse* (PhD thesis). University of Sheffield, UK.

Rogers, M. (2016). Breaking down barriers: The potential for social care practice with trans survivors of domestic abuse. *Health and Social Care in the Community, 24*(1), 68–76. doi:10.1111/hsc.12193

Rogers, M. (2017a). Challenging cisgenderism through trans people's narratives of domestic violence and abuse. *Sexualities*. doi:10.1177/1363460716681475

Rogers, M. (2017b). The intersection of cisgenderism and hate crime: Learning from trans people's narratives. *The Journal of Family Strengths, 17*(2). Retrieved from http://digitalcomMons.library.tmc.edu/jfs/vol17/iss2/5

Rogers, M. (2017c). Transphobic 'honour'-based abuse: A conceptual tool. *Sociology, 51*(2), 225–240. doi:10.1177/0038038515622907

Rogers, M. (2020). Exploring trans men's experiences of intimate partner violence through the lens of cisgenderism. In L. Gottzén, M. Bjørnholt, & F. Boonzaier (Eds.), *Men, masculinities and intimate partner violence*. London: Routledge.

Rogers, M., & Ahmed, A. (2017). Interrogating trans and sexual identities through the conceptual lens of translocational positionality. *Sociological Research Online, 22*(1). doi:10.5153/sro.4169

Rogers, M., & Allen, D. (2019). *Applying critical thinking and analysis in social work*. London: Sage.

SafeLives. (2018). *Free to be safe: LGBT people experiencing domestic abuse*. Bristol: SafeLives.

Schilt, K., & Westbrook, L. (2009). Doing gender, doing heteronormativity: 'Gender normals', transgender people, and the social maintenance of heterosexuality. *Gender and Society, 23*(4), 440–464. doi:10.1177/0891243209340034

Scottish Transgender Alliance. (2008). *Transgender experiences in Scotland*. Retrieved from www.scottish-trans.org/Uploads/Resources/staexperiencessummary03082.pdf

Seelman, K. L. (2015). Unequal treatment of transgender individuals in domestic violence and rape crisis programs. *Journal of Social Service Research, 41*, 307–325. doi:10.1080/01488376.2014.987943

Serano, J. (2013). *Excluded: Making feminist and queer movements more inclusive*. Berkeley: Seal Press.

Serano, J. (2016). *Whipping girl: A transsexual woman on sexism and the scapegoating of femininity* (2nd ed.). Berkeley, CA: Seal Press.

Sokoloff, H. J., & Dupont, I. (2005). Domestic violence at the intersections of race, class and gender. *Violence Against Women, 11*(1), 38–64. doi:10.1177/1077801204271476

Stark, E. (2007). *Coercive control: How men entrap women in personal life*. New York, NY: Oxford University Press.

Stotzer, R. L. (2009). Violence against transgender people: A review of United States data. *Aggression and Violent Behavior, 14*, 170–179. doi:10.1016/j.avb.2009.01.006

Tesch, B. P., & Bekerian, D. A. (2015). Hidden in the margins: A qualitative examination of what professional in the domestic violence field know about transgender domestic violence, *Journal of Gay & Lesbian Social Services, 27*, 391–411. doi:10.1080/10538720.2015.1087267

Walker, J. (2015). Investigating trans people's vulnerabilities to intimate partner violence/abuse. *Partner Abuse, 6*(1). doi:10.1891/1946–6560.6.1.107

Waters, E., & Yacka-Bible, S. (2017). *A crisis of hate: A midyear report on lesbian, gay, bisexual, transgender and qeer hate violence homicides*. National Coalition of Anti-Violence Programs. Retrieved from https://avp.org/wp-content/uploads/2017/08/NCAVP-A-Crisis-of-Hate-Final.pdf

WHO. (2017). *Violence against women: Key facts*. Retrieved from www.who.int/en/news-room/fact-sheets/detail/violence-against-women

Whitton, S., Newcomb, M. E., Messinger, A. M., Byck, G., & Mustanski, B. (2016). A longitudinal study of IPV victimization among sexual minority youth. *Journal of Interpersonal Violence, 34*, 912–945. doi:10.1177/0886260516646093

Willging, C., Gunderson, L., Shattuck, D., Sturm, R., Lawyer, A., & Crandall, C. (2019). Structural competency in emergency medicine services for transgender and gender non-conforming patients. *Social Science & Medicine, 222*, 67–75. doi:10.1016/j.socscimed.2018.12.031

Wirtz, A. L., Poteat, T. C., Malik, M., & Glass, N. (2018). Gender-based violence against transgender people in the United States: A call for research and programming. *Trauma, Violence, & Abuse*, 1–15. doi:10.1177/1524838018757749

# 19

# ECONOMIC ABUSE WITHIN INTIMATE RELATIONSHIPS

*Laura Johnson*

## Introduction

Economic abuse, also referred to as financial abuse, is a form of intimate partner violence in which an individual controls their partner's ability to acquire, use, and maintain economic resources as a means to isolate their partner and promote economic dependency (Adams, Sullivan, Bybee, & Greeson, 2008; Anderson et al., 2003). While economic abuse is similar to psychological and/or emotional abuse in that abusers use these behavioural tactics to control their partner's activities, it has been found to be a unique form of intimate partner violence (Stylianou, Postmus, & McMahon, 2013). The overall aim of this chapter is to present an overview of economic abuse in intimate relationships. This chapter will begin with a summary of the three tactics most commonly used by perpetrators of economic abuse: economic control, employment sabotage, and economic exploitation. This will be followed by a description of the research around the prevalence and impact of economic abuse within intimate relationships, and then a discussion of some of the main theories and measures used in studies that include economic abuse. Lastly, this chapter will briefly highlight some of the interventions used with survivors of economic abuse, as well as the impact these interventions have on survivors' experiences with intimate partner violence. This chapter concludes with an overview of critical findings and implications for practice, policy, and research.

## Definitions of economic abuse and associated tactics

Within the field of economic abuse, three primary tactics have been identified: economic control, employment sabotage, and economic exploitation (Postmus, Plummer, & Stylianou, 2016; Stylianou et al., 2013). Examples of each of these three tactics are presented in Table 19.1. Economic control occurs when an abuser prevents their partner from participating in financial decision-making, even when such decisions directly impact the survivor (Stylianou, 2018b). This may also involve restricting access to necessities such as household utilities like heat and electric, food, clothing, or medication (Anderson et al., 2003; Stylianou, 2018a), which may impact a survivors' ability to engage in work activities as well.

Employment sabotage refers to a range of behaviours engaged in by abusers to prevent survivors from obtaining or maintaining work or employment (Postmus et al., 2016; Adams,

*Table 19.1* Examples of economic abuse tactics

| Economic abuse tactic | Definition | Examples |
| --- | --- | --- |
| Economic control | Abuser prevents survivor from participation in financial decision-making | • Withholding financial information.<br>• Restricting access to money, credit cards, chequebooks.<br>• Strictly monitoring spending. |
| Economic sabotage | Abuser prevents survivor from obtaining or maintaining employment or work | • Preventing the survivor from going to work by threatening, injuring, or physically restraining them.<br>• Demanding the survivor quit their job.<br>• Making frequent and harassing phone calls while the survivor is at work. |
| Economic exploitation | Intentional utilization and/ or damaging of a survivor's economic resources to the abuser's advantage | • Gambling with the survivors' money.<br>• Stealing or pawning the survivors' money or property.<br>• Using money that was allocated to bills for other purposes. |

Greeson, Littwin, & Javorka, 2019). Abusers may also interfere with other activities intended to increase employment prospects, such as pursuing educational opportunities (Anderson et al., 2003), as well as disrupt receipt of other income-generating benefits like child support, public assistance, and disability payments (Stylianou, 2018a).

Lastly, economic exploitation involves the intentional utilization and/or damaging of a partner's economic resources to the abuser's advantage (Adams et al., 2019). Coerced debt has become an increasingly commonly used economic exploitation mechanism, particularly because credit has become paramount to consumer culture (Littwin, 2012). Examples of coerced debt include building up debt under the survivors' name without their knowledge, tricking victims into signing fiscally related documents, and forcing victims to open lines of credit (Littwin, 2012; Postmus et al., 2016).

## Prevalence of economic abuse

Compared with other forms of intimate partner violence, less is known about the prevalence of economic abuse. Research suggests that the prevalence of economic abuse among service-seeking survivor samples is high. Adams et al. (2008) found that 99% of the 103 survivors they surveyed had experienced economic abuse as part of their relationships. Postmus, Plummer, McMahon, Murshid, and Kim (2012) found that 94% of service-seeking survivors in their study of 120 women reported economic abuse. Similarly, Adams and colleagues (2019) found that 96% of survivors in their sample reported experiencing at least one economic abuse tactic. One of the largest studies to examine economic abuse in the lives of survivors, conducted by Stylianou et al. (2013), found that 76% of the 457 service-seeking women in the sample reported this form of violence.

In community samples prevalence rates have been lower. While economic abuse has not been measured in US-based violence prevalence studies, prevalence studies have been conducted in the United Kingdom and Australia. Notably, both of these studies also included men in their samples. In Australia researchers found that almost 11.5% of the sample reported experiencing economic abuse; of this 15.7% were women and 7.1% were men (Kutin, Russell, & Reid, 2017). Sharp-Jeffs (2015) found that one in five British adults have experienced economic abuse in an intimate relationship in their lifetime. A higher proportion of heterosexual women reported economic abuse than men. Sharp-Jeffs also found that men in same-sex relationships reported higher rates of economic abuse than women in same-sex relationships. Voth Schrag (2015) used data from the Fragile Families and Child Well-Being Study and had similar findings, with 14% of women reporting this form of violence. Voth Schrag and Ravi (2020) also found that 43.5% of 435 women attending community college reported experiencing at least one economic abuse tactic in the past 12 months.

## Impact of economic abuse on survivor well-being

While there are a range of factors that survivors must consider when deciding whether to stay in or leave an abusive relationship, one of the most significant is access to finances and other resources (Anderson et al., 2003; Fugate, Landis, Riordan, Naureckas, & Engel, 2005; Meyer, 2012). Financial independence is a predictor of whether a survivor will attempt to leave their abuser (Anderson & Saunders, 2003; Bornstein, 2006). In addition to the direct effects of economic abuse, the financial status of survivors may also be influenced by other forms of intimate partner violence, which can also increase financial dependency. For example, isolation is a common tactic used by abusers to maintain control over their partners. In some instances this can also include restricting survivors' ability to move freely about in the community. As a result, survivors may become even more emotionally and financially dependent on their abusers and also have fewer opportunities to connect with their social networks, thereby severing potential support systems and help-seeking opportunities (Fugate et al., 2005).

Survivors from diverse populations may be even more vulnerable as a result of economic abuse and intimate partner violence more broadly. For example, immigrant women face additional barriers to help-seeking which may include fear of deportation, lack of language proficiency for the country they find themselves in, and increased isolation if they recently left their country of origin (Bauer, Rodriguez, Quiroga, & Flores-Ortiz, 2000; Dutton, Orloff, & Hass, 2000; Erez, Adelman, & Gregory, 2009; Raj & Silverman, 2002). Immigrant women may also be financially dependent on their abusers due to employment ineligibility as a result of their immigration status, a limited understanding of the financial system in their country of relocation, and decreased accesses to public assistance (Dutton et al., 2000; Orloff, 1999; Postmus, 2010).

The financial impacts of intimate partner violence on survivors are particularly concerning because survivors may continue to face financial insecurity for years even after the relationship has ended. Voth Schrag (2015) found an association between past economic abuse and material hardship, even among women who have been out of the abusive relationship for years. However, this is not surprising, as it can take years for individuals to repair financial damages, such as poor credit scores, incurred due to economic abuse (Financial Industry Regulatory Authority, 2015).

In addition to the financial impact of economic abuse, this form of intimate partner violence is also associated with mental health issues. Research has found that economic abuse is associated with depression (Stylianou, 2018b; Voth Schrag, Robinson, & Ravi, 2019; Postmus, Huang, & Stylianou, 2012; Nancarrow, Lockie, & Sharma, 2009), post-traumatic stress disorder (Voth Schrag et al., 2019), psychological distress, suicide attempts (Antai, Oke, Braithwaite, & Lopez, 2014), and overall poor quality of life (Adams & Beeble, 2018). Kutin and colleagues (2017) found that for women, having a disability or a self-reported health status of fair or poor were both associated with increased odds of experiencing economic abuse. However, a study by Davila, Johnson and Postmus (2017) conducted with a Latina-only sample did not find economic abuse to uniquely predict mental health outcomes after controlling for other forms of intimate partner violence and survivor demographics.

Economic abuse has also been linked to parenting practices and youth behaviours. Postmus, Huang, and Stylianou (2012) found that economic abuse impacted women's parenting styles over the long term, with survivors less likely to engage in parent-child activities and more likely to use spanking as a form of punishment. Early childhood exposure to economic abuse was found to be significantly associated with childhood delinquency at age 9 (Huang, Vikse, Lu, & Yi, 2015). Adolescent girls in the child welfare system who were exposed to economic abuse within the home had increased rates of post-traumatic stress disorder and depression (Voth Schrag, Edmond, Tlapek, & Auslander, 2017).

## Theoretical frameworks for understanding economic abuse

Scholars have drawn on a range of theories for framing the issue of economic abuse. According to coercive control theory (Stark, 2007) abusers methodologically use a variety of tactics to maintain power and control over their partner with the goal of creating an "invisible cage" for the purpose of entrapment. As such, economic abuse is a coercive control tactic used strategically by abusers to restrict the financial freedom of their partners in order to foster dependency.

Gendered resource theory (Atkinson, Greenstein, & Lang, 2005) expands upon resource theory by suggesting that the impact of resources on the perpetration of intimate partner violence is moderated by the abuser's perceptions of gender norms. For example, if an abuser believes it is his responsibility as a man to be the breadwinner, then the financial empowerment of his female partner may increase the likelihood of violence. While this theory could be applied to same-sex couples based on the gender norms of the abusive partner, its origins are heteronormative in nature. Marital dependency theory (Vyas & Watts, 2009) suggests that the more financially dependent a survivor is on their partner, the greater their risk for intimate partner violence, as they have less bargaining power within the relationship. Following this theory, economic abuse interventions that increase survivors' resources should decrease their risk for abuse.

## Measurement of economic abuse in research

Compared to physical, sexual, and psychological and/or emotional abuse, economic abuse has been largely under researched until recent years (Stylianou, 2018a). While scholarship acknowledged linkages between intimate partner violence and financial self-sufficiency, much of this work was grounded in research about poverty more broadly. During these early studies, intimate partner violence survivors reported that their abusers were unsupportive of their employment, sometimes preventing them from going to work altogether (Riger, Ahrens, Blickenstaff, & Camacho, 1998). Women who experienced intimate partner violence were more likely to have periods of unemployment, and had higher rates of job turnover (Lloyd & Taluc, 1999). There were also concerns that female recipients of public assistance were unable to meet the work requirements due to their partner sabotaging their work opportunities (Raphael, 1995). However, the term "economic abuse" was still used sparingly, at least in research, until the first measure of economic abuse, the Scale of Economic Abuse (SEA; Adams et al., 2008), was established.

Prior to the creation of the SEA, studies sometimes included economic abuse-related items into their scales, but economic abuse was not the central focus of the work (Postmus, Hoge,

Breckenridge, Sharp-Jeffs, & Chung, 2020). For example, the Abusive Behaviour Inventory (ABI; Shepard & Campbell, 1992) contained three items related to economic abuse: "Prevented you from having money for your own use," "Put you on an allowance," and "Stopped you or tried to stop you from going to work or school." However, these items were included as part of their psychological abuse subscale. Similarly, the Index of Spouse Abuse (Hudson & McIntosh, 1981) and Psychological Maltreatment of Women Inventory (PMWI; Tolman, 1989) included questions on economic abuse as part of non-physical or psychological abuse measures, respectively.

The first measure to include an economic abuse subscale was the Domestic Violence-Related Financial Issues Scale (DV-FI), developed by Weaver, Sanders, Campbell, and Schnabel (2009) as part of their evaluation of a financial literacy curriculum with survivors of intimate partner violence. The DV-FI's economic abuse subscale included five items: "Credit card debt has played a role in my previous experiences of partner violence," "My partner prevented me from having access to money," "My partner negatively affected my credit rating," "My partner negatively affected my credit card debt," and "My partner prevented me from obtaining necessary skills or education to obtain adequate employment." However, three of these items focused specifically on consumer credit, thus excluding a wide range of economic abuse tactics (Postmus et al., 2020).

Another measure containing economic abuse as a subscale was the Checklist of Controlling Behaviours (CCB; Lehmann, Simmons, & Pillai, 2012), an 84-item intimate partner violence instrument that can be used to assess for a range of abusive tactics. The economic abuse subscale in the CCB contained seven items: "Did not allow me equal access to the family money," "Told me or acted as if it was his money, his house, his car, etc.," "Threatened to withhold money from me," "Made me ask for money for the basic necessities," "Used my fear of not having access to money to control my behaviour," "Made me account for the money I spent," and "Tried to keep me dependent on him for money."

As noted, the SEA (Adams et al., 2008) was the first to comprehensively measure economic abuse. The SEA included 28 items that asked survivors about the frequency in which their intimate partners engaged in a range of behaviours that were economically damaging to survivors. The SEA contained two subscales: economic control (17 items) and economic exploitation (11 items). Scale construction included a rigorous process from which the authors reduced a preliminary measure consisting of 120 items down to the 28 included in the final measure. Postmus, Plummer, and Stylianou (2016) used the SEA as part of a longitudinal, exploratory study evaluating a financial literacy programme. However, they conducted additional psychometric testing on the scale and reduced it from 28 items to 12. This new scale, named the Scale of Economic Abuse-12 (SEA-12), was not only shorter than the original SEA, it also identified a new factor structure. The three subscales in the SEA-12 were: economic control (five items), employment sabotage (four items), and economic exploitation (three items).

In 2019, Adams and colleagues revised the SEA, creating the SEA2. Adams and colleagues suggested that both the SEA and the SEA-12 had two primary limitations that needed to be addressed: (1) they do not adequately reflect that economic abuse is a coercive control tactic, and (2) they inadequately capture abusers' use of the consumer credit system. As part of the initial scale development process, a pool of 46 items was generated. This pool included the 28 original items from the SEA, as well as an additional eight items that improved upon the wording of questions from the original scale. Another ten items were newly created based on conversations with survivors and advocates. The final SEA2 scale contains 14 items of which five were from the original SEA, two were modified items from the original scale, and seven were newly developed. The modified items were changed to incorporate gender neutral language (e.g. "Make you ask him or her for money"). There are still two subscales; however they are now different: economic restriction (seven items) and economic exploitation (seven items).

Postmus and colleagues (2020) conducted a multi-country review to examine how economic abuse is being measured globally. Overall, the authors found 46 peer-reviewed articles in which economic and/or financial abuse was measured in the context of violence against women and a clear definition of the abuse was provided. While the majority of articles came from North America, and more specifically the United States ($n = 17$), six continents were represented in total. Economic control was the economic abuse tactic most frequently described in articles, followed by economic exploitation, and employment sabotage. Only 14 of the articles discussed all three forms of economic abuse in tandem. Of note, the authors highlighted the need for economic measures to be tested across cultural contexts to determine their validity in light of cultural and linguistic nuances. The SEA-12, for example, is currently being tested in Hong Kong, Taiwan, Australia, and New Zealand.

## Protective and intervention strategies for survivors of economic abuse

While there is a growing body of literature on the protective strategies that survivors use to promote their safety while navigating abusive relationships, this literature rarely focuses on economic abuse. Many of these strategies transcend any one particular form of violence, as most victims experience multiple coercive control tactics in the context of their relationships. However, some of these strategies are directly applicable to survivors experiencing economic abuse. Hamby's (2014) book provides one of the most comprehensive resources for understanding the protective strategies used by survivors. According to Hamby, survivors may mitigate the impact that their abusers have on their employment by asking their co-workers or bosses to rearrange work schedules, explaining how the abuse is contributing to performance and attendance issues, or developing workplace safety plans. Survivors may also engage in a range of protective strategies to increase their financial stability and self-sufficiency. These may include hiding emergency funds from the abuser, opening new bank accounts that the abuser does not have access to, seeking additional work, or paying down debts.

While much of the work conducted on intimate partner violence protective strategies has been conducted in high-income countries, researchers are beginning to look at the strategies used by survivors in low- and middle-income countries. As an example, Gillum, Doucette, Mwanza, and Munala (2018) examined the protective strategies of women in Nairobi, Kenya. Women also viewed secretly earning money as one of the primary ways to take action, either to minimize financial-driven conflicts or as part of a plan for eventually leaving their abuser. While the strategies used by Kenyan women were generally the same as those described in high-income countries, these strategies sometimes looked different in application. For example, when seeking external supports, the village chief was cited as a potential resource and relationship mediator.

Recognizing that economic abuse serves as a significant barrier to survivor safety, there has been a move to identify interventions that increase survivors' tangible resources (Dichter & Rhodes, 2011). As such, most interventions designed for survivors who have experienced economic abuse have that goal in mind. Interventions that address economic abuse include financial literacy, asset building, and resource transfer programmes. While a brief summary of these interventions are provided later, additional information can be found in the chapter on economic empowerment.

Financial literacy refers to an individual's ability to "read, analyse, manage, and communicate about the personal financial conditions that affect material well-being" (Vitt et al., 2000, p. 2). As such, financial literacy programmes educate individuals on effective financial management strategies. While several financial literacy programmes have been evaluated for use with survivors of intimate partner violence, only one has been evaluated through a randomized controlled trial (Postmus, Hetling, & Hoge, 2015). Results of this study showed that survivors in the treatment group had higher scores on financial attitudes, knowledge, self-efficacy, self-sufficiency, intentions, and behaviours as compared to the control group and these changes remained statistically significant over time. Johnson (2018) also found this intervention to be effective at increasing survivors' overall economic empowerment over time.

Asset building involves a targeted effort to help support individuals to increase their economic resources (Vyas & Watts, 2009). Examples of these programmes include microfinance and individual development accounts. Microfinance programmes provide survivors with financial resources like credit and savings, and support them in developing income-generating projects (Kim et al., 2007). Microfinance programmes for women have been found to increase self-confidence, decision-making power within the home, and status within the community (Cheston & Kuhn, 2002). Individual development accounts provide a mechanism for families with limited financial resources to save money without being penalized by public assistance programmes for having these additional assets (Hoge, Stylianou, Postmus, & Johnson, 2019). As part of these programmes, survivors are encouraged to save funds, which are then matched by the programme. Matching rates range from 1:1 to as high as 7:1 (Richards & Thyer, 2011). While individual development account programmes embedded in domestic violence organizations have not been rigorously evaluated, preliminary research suggests they are successful at increasing assets by promoting savings (Sanders, 2014). Other asset building programmes include job readiness, professional development, and access to education (Hoge et al., 2019).

Lastly, resource transfer programmes involve a direct transfer in the form of tangible resources like cash or food vouchers; these transfers can be unconditional, meaning survivors do not need to do anything to receive them, or conditional, meaning receipt is contingent on a particular behaviour or outcome like HIV testing (Gibbs, Jacobson, & Wilson, 2017). Cash transfer programmes are often used with women, in particular, because some believe that women are more likely to reinvest the resources into their families. However, results on the effectiveness of cash transfers have been mixed (Gibbs et al., 2017).

## Relationship between economic abuse interventions and intimate partner violence

While evaluations of economic abuse interventions have generally been favourable, showing positive outcomes for survivors, research has been mixed with regard to whether financial empowerment programmes increase or decrease survivors' experiences with intimate partner violence (Vyas & Watts, 2009). For example, Kim and colleagues (2007) evaluated a microfinance programme for women in South Africa and found a decrease in intimate partner violence over time for the treatment group. Ahmed (2005) conducted an evaluation of a micro-credit programme in Bangladesh and found increases in violence when the women first joined the programme, but the violence decreased over time. Hidrobo and Fernald (2013) found that the effectiveness of cash transfer programmes for survivors differed based on survivors' education level relative to their partners' education level. Specifically, the cash transfer programme increased emotional abuse in relationships when the survivor was female and her education level was equal to or greater than that of her male partner. Findings from a randomized controlled trial of an economic empowerment intervention in Cote d'Ivoire showed a reduction in economic abuse for both the intent-to-treat and per protocol analytic samples (Gupta et al., 2013). Finally, a study in India about the relationship between women's employment and intimate partner violence found that employment was not a protective factor for intimate partner violence, but women who were employed were more likely to seek help for their abuse (Dalal, 2011). Taken together, these intervention strategies may be effective at increasing survivors' financial assets and empowering them to be financially self-sufficient, but they should also be coupled with comprehensive safety planning.

## Policy responses to economic abuse and associated impacts

Few policies specifically related to economic abuse exist. The United Nations has released various declarations and conventions to address violence against women. These include the Convention on the Elimination of All Forms of Discrimination Against Women, adopted by the General Assembly in 1979, and then the Declaration on the Elimination of Violence Against Women, a resolution intended to strengthen the Convention, proclaimed by the General Assembly in 1993. However, not all countries have ratified the Convention.

In 2015, England and Wales became the first countries to criminalize coercive control behaviours within intimate relationships, and in 2019 Scotland followed. This legislation is notable, as it marks the first time that the criminal law acknowledges intimate partner violence to comprise of a pattern of behaviours that include tactics like emotional or economic abuse (Candela, 2016). However, as Stark (2016) points out, in order to hold offenders accountable, resources will need to be allocated for training law enforcement on how to investigate a course-of-conduct, rather than incident-based crime. While it is too soon to tell what the implications of such a policy will have for survivors of intimate partner violence, preliminary data suggests that intimate partner violence cases have doubled from 2017 to 2018, which may be attributed to the increased use of the law (United Kingdom Office for National Statistics, 2018).

In the US, early observations about the associations between intimate partner violence and public assistance receipt prompted the addition of the Family Violence Option (FVO) to the Personal Responsibility and Work Opportunity Reconciliation Act (PRWORA) of 1996 (Holcomb et al., 2017). As evidenced by its name, states may choose to adopt the FVO, which is a policy that permits states to waive certain Temporary Assistance for Needy Families (TANF) requirements for survivors. The FVO is an important policy because it acknowledges that survivors may be unable to meet TANF requirements either as a result of the physical and mental health impacts of intimate partner violence or because it may place survivors at increased risk for future violence (Holcomb et al., 2017). As of 2020, all but two states have either adopted the FVO or a similar policy for survivors.

Finally, employment protection policies have been implemented in some countries to protect survivors. In the US federal laws do not protect against the discrimination of survivors experiencing intimate partner violence, but some states have been enacting policies to offer such protections (Stylianou, 2018a). For example, in Connecticut employers with three or more personnel are prohibited from terminating or penalizing an employee because they are a survivor of intimate partner violence or because they have to take time off to engage in court activities. In New Mexico, survivors are entitled to "domestic abuse leave" which is paid or unpaid leave for up to 14 days to allow survivors to engage in safety-promoting activities such as obtaining protection orders or attending court proceedings. In Australia, the Fair Work Act 2009 provides survivors the right to request flexible working arrangements, although survivors may not utilize this resource because they do not wish to disclose their abuse experiences (Australian Human Rights Commission, 2014).

## Conclusions

While economic abuse has gained increased attention over time, there is still a significant need for research and intervention in this area. Although scholarship has advanced the field's understanding of the types of behaviours that constitute economic abuse (i.e. economic control, economic exploitation, employment sabotage) the body of this work has emerged from high-income countries. As such, there is a need for research in low- and middle-income countries that explores commonalities and differences in the types of behaviours that survivors experience, as well as the prevalence of economic abuse across diverse populations. Similarly, measures of economic abuse must be adapted to different cultural contexts and then tested for validity.

Globally, there are a range of interventions that aim to increase the economic self-sufficiency of survivors of economic abuse. However, it is unclear what impact these interventions have on survivors' experiences of economic abuse, and intimate partner violence more broadly. Longitudinal research is needed to better understand the short- and long-term impact of economic empowerment programmes across diverse settings.

Further, while safety planning is an intervention strategy frequently used with survivors, it rarely has a specific focus on economic abuse. Given that financial literacy has been found to be effective at increasing survivors' financial empowerment over time, Johnson (2018) suggests economic-specific safety planning may be beneficial for survivors, particularly because not all survivors may be able to attend financial literacy education programmes that occur over multiple sessions. Comprehensive safety planning should also be used in conjunction with other economic empowerment interventions, given the overall impact of these interventions on survivors' victimization is still unclear.

Lastly, policies that have the potential to address economic abuse need to be enacted globally. This may include expanding current domestic violence laws to include coercive control strategies that can be used to prosecute economic abuse cases and anti-discrimination laws that offer employment protection to survivors. As a mechanism for prevention, additional federal funding should be allocated for financial empowerment interventions both within domestic violence organizations but also to the broader community. Financial literacy has the potential to aid in the prevention of intimate partner violence by both promoting positive financial management skills and enabling all individuals to identify unhealthy financial behaviours within their relationships.

In the United Kingdom and Australia, financial institutions have identified survivors of intimate partner violence as a vulnerable population. To better serve survivors, these banks are providing staff with training on identifying signs of financial abuse, examining how their policies may impact survivors, providing specialized financial assistance to survivors, and connecting survivors to service providers specialized in intimate partner violence and trauma. Financial institutions can also play an important role in the identification of economic abuse by monitoring fiscal interactions. As such, financial institutions are encouraged to develop policies and procedures that are sensitive to experiences of survivors (Postmus et al., 2020).

In conclusion, economic abuse is an emerging area of study within the field of intimate partner violence. While preliminary research suggests that economic abuse is prevalent across the globe, additional work is needed to better understand the ways in which survivor experiences differ by intersectional factors such as socioeconomic status, geographic locale, culture, and race/ethnicity, both in terms of tactics used and the physical and mental health consequences that emerge as a result. On a practical level, a first step in intervening is helping survivors to identify their experiences as a form of intimate partner violence so that they can safety plan accordingly. This must be followed by coordinated efforts to address economic abuse across sectors such as criminal justice and banking, as such collaborations may be critical to holding abusers accountable.

## Critical findings

- Three primary economic abuse tactics have been identified in the literature: economic control, employment sabotage, and economic exploitation.
- Prevalence of economic abuse among female service-seeking samples has been found to be high, ranging from approximately 76% to 99%.
- Economic abuse has been linked to a range of mental health outcomes including depression, post-traumatic stress disorder, suicide attempts, and overall quality of life.
- Interventions that address economic abuse include financial literacy, asset building, and resource transfer programmes.
- There is debate as to whether financial empowerment interventions increase or decrease survivors' experiences with intimate partner violence over time.
- Few policies exist that address economic abuse; one of the most promising may be the establishment of coercive control laws in the United Kingdom.

## Implications for policy, practice, and research

### *Policy*

- Economic abuse interventions need to be implemented universally by organizations providing services to intimate partner violence survivors.
- Financial literacy should be made available to all as to promote positive financial management practices and help individuals identify unhealthy behaviours within their relationships.
- Training on economic abuse should be provided to domestic violence service providers so that they can work with survivors around financial literacy and financial safety planning.

### *Practice*

- Economic abuse and/or coercive control laws that encompass economic abuse should be implemented as part of domestic violence policy.
- Financial institutions should play a more significant role in addressing economic abuse by offering survivor-specific services and playing a more active role in the identification of economic abuse by monitoring fiscal activities.
- Policies should protect survivors of intimate partner violence from work time lost as a result of their victimization.

### *Research*

- Measures should continue to be adapted and tested for use with culturally diverse samples.
- Longitudinal research is needed to examine the relationship between financial empowerment interventions and intimate partner violence experiences over time.

- Economic abuse should be measured along with other forms of intimate partner violence in national prevalence studies.
- Research on the characteristics of perpetrators of economic abuse are needed to support the development of interventions that target this population.

# References

Adams, A. E., & Beeble, M. L. (2018). Intimate partner violence and psychological well-being: Examining the effect of economic abuse on women's quality of life. *Psychology of Violence, 9*(5), 517–525. doi:10.1037/vio0000174

Adams, A. E., Greeson, M. R., Littwin, A. K., & Javorka, M. (2019, online). The revised scale of economic abuse (SEA2): Development and initial psychometric testing of an updated measure of economic abuse in intimate relationships. *Psychology of Violence.* doi:10.1037/vio0000244

Adams, A. E., Sullivan, C. M., Bybee, D., & Greeson, M. R. (2008). Development of the scale of economic abuse. *Violence Against Women, 14*(5), 563–588. doi:10.1177%2F1077801208315529

Ahmed, S. M. (2005). Intimate partner violence against women: Experiences from a woman-focused development programme in Matlab, Bangladesh. *Journal of Health, Population, and Nutrition, 23*(1), 95–101.

Anderson, D. K., & Saunders, D. G. (2003). Leaving an abusive partner: An empirical review of predictors, the process of leaving, and psychological well-being. *Trauma, Violence, & Abuse, 4*(2), 163–191. doi:10.1177%2F1524838002250769

Anderson, M. A., Gillig, P. M., Sitaker, M., McCloskey, K., Malloy, K., & Grigsby, N. (2003). "Why doesn't she just leave?": A descriptive study of victim reported impediments to her safety. *Journal of Family Violence, 18*(3), 151–155. doi:10.1023/A:1023564404773

Antai, D., Oke, A., Braithwaite, P., & Lopez, G. B. (2014). The effect of economic, physical, and psychological abuse on mental health: A population-based study of women in the Philippines. *International Journal of Family Medicine, 2014,* 1–11. doi:10.1155/2014/852317

Atkinson, M. P., Greenstein, T. N., & Lang, M. M. (2005). For women, breadwinning can be dangerous: Gendered resource theory and wife abuse. *Journal of Marriage and Family, 67,* 1137–1148. doi:10.1111/j.1741-3737.2005.00206.x

Australian Human Rights Commission. (2014). *Fact sheet: Domestic and family violence – A workplace issue, a discrimination issue.* Retrieved from www.humanrights.gov.au/our-work/sex-discrimination/publications/fact-sheet-domestic-and-family-violence-workplace-issue

Bauer, H. M., Rodriguez, M. A., Quiroga, S. S., & Flores-Ortiz, Y. G. (2000). Barriers to health care for abused Latina and Asian immigrant women. *Journal of Health Care for the Poor and Underserved, 11*(1), 33–44. doi:10.1353/hpu.2010.0590

Bornstein, R. F. (2006). The complex relationship between dependency and domestic violence: Converging psychological factors and social forces. *American Psychologist, 61*(6), 595–606. doi:10.1037/0003-066X.61.6.595

Candela, K. (2016). Protecting the invisible victim: Incorporating coercive control in domestic violence statutes. *Family Court Review, 54*(1), 112–125. doi:10.1111/fcre.12208

Cheston, S., & Kuhn, L. (2002). Empowering women through microfinance. In S. D. Harris (Ed.), *Pathways out of poverty: Innovations in microfinance for the poorest families.* Bloomfield, CT: Kumarian Press.

Dalal, K. (2011). Does economic empowerment protect women from intimate partner violence? *Journal of Injury and Violence Research, 3*(1), 35–44. doi:10.5249/jivr.v3i1.76

DaVila, A. L., Johnson, L., & Postmus, J. L. (2017, online). Examining the relationship between economic abuse and mental health among Latina intimate partner violence survivors in the United States. *Journal of Interpersonal Violence,* 1–24. doi:10.1177/0886260517731311

Dichter, M. E., & Rhodes, K. V. (2011). Intimate partner violence survivors' unmet social service needs. *Journal of Social Service Research, 37*(5), 481–489. doi:10.1080/01488376.2011.587747

Dutton, M. A., Orloff, L. E., & Hass, G. A. (2000). Characteristics of help-seeking behaviors, resources and service needs of battered immigrant Latinas: Legal and policy implications. *Georgetown Journal on Poverty Law & Policy, 7*(2), 245–305.

Erez, E., Adelman, M., & Gregory, C. (2009). Intersections of immigration and domestic violence: Voices of battered immigrant women. *Feminist Criminology, 4*(1), 32–56. doi:10.1177%2F1557085108325413

Financial Industry Regulatory Authority. (2015). *How your credit score impacts your financial future*. Retrieved from www.finra.org/investors/how-your-credit-score-impacts-your-financial-future

Fugate, M., Landis, L., Riordan, K., Naureckas, S., & Engel, B. (2005). Barriers to domestic violence help seeking: Implications for intervention. *Violence Against Women, 11*(3), 290–310. doi:10.1177 %2F1077801204271959

Gibbs, A., Jacobson, J., & Wilson, A. K. (2017). A global comprehensive review of economic interventions to prevent intimate partner violence and HIV risk behaviours. *Global Health Action, 10*(2), 87–102. doi :10.1080/16549716.2017.1290427

Gillum, T. L., Doucette, M., Mwanza, M., & Munala, L. (2018). Exploring Kenya women's perceptions of intimate partner violence. *Journal of Interpersonal Violence, 33*(13), 2130–2145. doi:10.1177 %2F0886260515622842

Gupta, J., Falb, K. L., Lehmann, H., Kpebo, D., Xuan, Z., Hossain, M., Zimmerman, C., Watts, C., & Annan, J. (2013). Gender norms and economic empowerment intervention to reduce intimate partner violence against women in rural Cote d'Ivoire: A randomized controlled pilot study. *BMC International Health and Human Rights, 13*(46), 1–12. doi:10.1186/1472-698X-13-46

Hamby, S. (2014). *Battered women's protective strategies: Stronger than you know*. Oxford, UK: Oxford University Press.

Hidrobo, M., & Fernald, L. (2013). Cash transfers and domestic violence. *Journal of Health Economics, 32*(1), 304–319. doi:10.1016/j.jhealeco.2012.11.002

Hoge, G. L., Stylianou, A. M., Postmus, J. L., & Johnson, L. (2019). Domestic violence/intimate partner violence and issues of financial abuse and control: What does financial empowerment look like? In C. Callahan, J. J. Frey, & R. Imboden (Eds.), *The Routledge handbook on financial social work*. New York, NY: Routledge.

Holcomb, S., Johnson, L., Helting, A., Postmus, J. L., Steiner, J., Braasch, L., & Rirodan, A. (2017). Implementation of the family violence option 20 years alter: A review of state welfare rules for domestic violence survivors. *Journal of Policy Practice, 16*, 415–431. doi:10.1080/15588742.2017. 1311820

Huang, C. C., Vikse, J. H., Lu, S., & Yi, S. (2015). Children's exposure to intimate partner violence and early delinquency. *Journal of Family Violence, 30*(8), 953–965. doi:10.1007/s10896-015-9727-5

Hudson, W. W., & McIntosh, S. R. (1981). The assessment of spouse abuse: Two quantifiable dimensions. *Journal of Marriage and Family, 43*(4), 873–885. Retrieved from www.jstor.org/stable/351344

Johnson, L. (2018). *Increasing financial empowerment for survivors of intimate partner violence: A longitudinal evaluation of financial knowledge* (Publication No. 2203805613) (Doctoral dissertation). Rutgers, The State University of New Jersey. ProQuest Dissertations Publishing. doi:10.7282/T3TM7FKD

Kim, J. C., Watts, C. H., Hargreaves, J. R., Ndhlovu, L. X., Phetla, G., Morison, L. A., . . . Pronyk, P. (2007). Understanding the impact of a microfinance-based intervention on women's empowerment and the reduction of intimate partner violence in South Africa. *American Journal of Public Health, 97*(10), 1794–1802. doi:10.2105/AJPH.2006.095521

Kutin, J., Russell, R., & Reid, M. (2017). Economic abuse between intimate partners in Australia: Prevalence, health status, disability and financial stress. *Australian and New Zealand Journal of Public Health, 41*(3), 269–274. doi:10.1111/1753-6405.12651

Lehmann, P., Simmons, C. A., & Pillai, V. K. (2012). The validation of the Checklist of Controlling Behaviors (CCB): Assessing coercive control in abusive relationships. *Violence Against Women, 18*(8), 913–933. doi:10.1177%2F1077801212456522

Littwin, A. (2012). Coerced debt: The role of consumer credit in domestic violence. *California Law Review, 100*(4), 951–1026.

Lloyd, S., & Taluc, N. (1999). The effect of male violence on female employment. *Violence Against Women, 5*(4), 370–392. doi:10.1177%2F10778019922181275

Meyer, S. (2012). Why women stay: A theoretical examination of rational choice and moral reasoning in the context of intimate partner violence. *Australian & New Zealand Journal of Criminology, 45*(2), 179–193. doi:10.1177%2F0004865812443677

Nancarrow, H., Lockie, S., & Sharma, S. (2009). *Intimate partner abuse of women in a Central Queensland mining region* (Trends and Issues in Crime and Criminal Justice No. 378). Canberra, Australia: Criminology Research Council, Australian Institute of Criminology, Australian Government.

Orloff, L. (1999). Access to public benefits for battered immigrant women and children. *Clearinghouse Review, 33*, 237–256.

Postmus, J. L. (2010). *Economic empowerment of domestic violence survivors.* Harrisburg, PA: VAWnet, a project of the National Resource Center on Domestic Violence, Pennsylvania Coalition Against Domestic Violence.

Postmus, J. L., Hetling, A., & Hoge, G. L. (2015). Evaluating a financial education curriculum as an intervention to improve financial behaviors and financial well-being of survivors of domestic violence: Results from a longitudinal randomized controlled study. *Journal of Consumer Affairs, 49*(1), 250–266. doi:10.1111/joca.12057

Postmus, J. L., Hoge, G. L., Breckenridge, J., Sharp-Jeffs, N., & Chung, D. (2020). Economic abuse as an invisible form of domestic violence: A multicountry review. *Trauma, Violence, & Abuse, 21*(2), 261–283. doi:10.1177%2F1524838018764160

Postmus, J. L., Huang, C. C., & Stylianou, A. M. (2012). The impact of physical and economic abuse on maternal mental health and parenting. *Children and Youth Services Review, 34*(9), 1922–1928. doi:10.1016/j.childyouth.2012.06.005

Postmus, J. L., Plummer, S. B., McMahon, S., Murshid, N. S., & Kim, M. S. (2012). Understanding economic abuse in the lives of survivors. *Journal of Interpersonal Violence, 27*(3), 411–430. doi:10.1177%2F0886260511421669

Postmus, J. L., Plummer, S. B., Stylianou, A. M. (2016). Measuring economic abuse in the lives of survivors: Revising the Scale of Economic Abuse. *Violence Against Women, 22*(6), 692–703. doi:10.1177%2F1077801215610012

Raj, A., & Silverman, J. (2002). Violence against immigrant women: The roles of culture, context, and legal immigrant status on intimate partner violence. *Violence Against Women, 8*(3), 367–398. doi:10.1177%2F10778010222183107

Raphael, J. (1995). Domestic violence and welfare receipt: The unexplored barrier to employment. *Georgetown Journal on Fighting Poverty, 3*(1), 29–34.

Richards, K. V., & Thyer, B. A. (2011). Does individual development account participation help the poor? A review. *Research on Social Work Practice, 21*(3), 348–362. doi:10.1177%2F1049731510395609

Riger, S., Ahrens, C., Blickenstaff, A., & Camacho, J. (1998). *Obstacles to employment of welfare recipients with abusive partners.* Unpublished manuscript, University of Illinois at Chicago.

Sanders, C. K. (2014). Savings for survivors: An Individual Development Account program for survivors of intimate-partner violence. *Journal of Social Service Research, 40*(3), 297–312. doi:10.1080/01488376.2014.893950

Sharp-Jeffs, N. (2015). *Money matters: Research into the extent and nature of financial abuse within intimate relationships in the UK.* London, UK: The Cooperative Bank.

Shepard, M. F., & Campbell, J. A. (1992). The abusive behavior inventory: A measure of psychological and physical abuse. *Journal of Interpersonal Violence, 7*(3), 291–305. doi:10.1177%2F088626092007003001

Stark, E. (2007). *Coercive control: How men entrap women in personal life.* New York, NY: Oxford University Press.

Stark, E. (2016). Policing partner abuse and the new crime of coercive control in the United Kingdom. *Family & Intimate Partner Violence Quarterly, 8*(4), 345–353.

Stylianou, A. M. (2018a). Economic abuse within intimate partner violence: A review of the literature. *Violence and Victims, 31*(1), 3–22. doi:10.1891/0886-6708.VV-D-16-00112

Stylianou, A. M. (2018b). Economic abuse experiences and depressive symptoms among victims of intimate partner violence. *Journal of Family Violence, 33*, 381–392. doi:10.1007/s10896-018-9973-4

Stylianou, A. M., Postmus, J. L., & McMahon, S. (2013). Measuring abusive behaviors: Is economic abuse a unique form of abuse? *Journal of Interpersonal Violence, 28*(16), 3186–3204. doi:10.1177%2F0886260513496904

Tolman, R. M. (1989). The development of a measure of psychological maltreatment of women by their male partners. *Violence and Victims, 4*(3), 159–177. doi:10.1891/0886-6708.4.3.159

United Kingdom Office for National Statistics. (2018). *Statistical bulletin: Crime in England and Wales: Year ending March 2018.* Retrieved from www.ons.gov.uk/peoplepopulationandcommunity/crimeandjustice/bulletins/crimeinenglandandwales/yearendingmarch2018

Vitt, L. A., Anderson, C., Kent, J., Lyter, D. M., Siegenthaler, J. K., & Ward, J. (2000). *Personal finance and the rush to competence: Financial literacy education in the U.S.* Middleburg, VA: Institute for Socio-Financial Studies.

Voth Schrag, R. J. (2015). Economic abuse and later material hardship: Is depression a mediator? *Affilia: Journal of Women and Social Work, 30*(3), 341–351. doi:10.1177%2F0886109914541118

Voth Schrag, R. J., Edmond, T., Tlapek, S. M., & Auslander, W. (2017). Exposure to economically abusive tactics among girls in the child welfare system. *Child and Adolescent Social Work Journal, 34*, 127–136. doi:10.1007/s10560-016-0450-8

Voth Schrag, R. J., & Ravi, K. (2020). Measurement of economic abuse among women not seeking social or support services and dwelling in the community. *Violence and Victims, 35*(1), 3–19.

Voth Schrag, R. J., Robinson, S. R., & Ravi, K. (2019). Understanding pathways within intimate partner violence: Economic abuse, economic hardship, and mental health. *Journal of Aggression, Maltreatment, & Trauma, 28*(2), 222–242. doi:10.1080/10926771.2018.1546247

Vyas, S., & Watts, C. (2009). How does economic empowerment affect women's risk of intimate partner violence in low and middle income countries? A systematic review of published evidence. *Journal of International Development, 21*(5), 577–602. doi:10.1002/jid.1500

Weaver, T. L., Sanders, C. K., Campbell, C. L., & Schnabel, M. (2009). Development and preliminary psychometric evaluation of the Domestic Violence-Related Financial Issues Scale (DV-FI). *Journal of Interpersonal Violence, 24*(4), 569–585. doi:10.1177%2F0886260508317176

# 20

# DOMESTIC VIOLENCE AND DISABILITY IN INDIA EXPLORED IN RELATION TO THE SUSTAINABLE DEVELOPMENT GOALS

*Sonali Shah, Ashwini Deshmukh and Caroline Bradbury-Jones*

## Introduction

Our purpose in this chapter is to expand the current body of knowledge in relation to how domestic violence and abuse (DVA) and disability intersect, and we do this in the context of India. We have chosen India because it is the home country of one of the authors (Deshmukh) and it has been the site of research projects that deal with DVA conducted by one of the other authors (Bradbury-Jones). The third author identifies as a disabled woman and second generation Indian, or British Indian. She has published research on disability and DVA over the life-course (Shah, Tsitsou, & Woodin, 2016a, 2016b; Shah & Bradbury-Jones, 2018), primarily in the Global North.

We endorse the view of Crenshaw (1994) who argues that, when writing about DVA of disabled women in India, it is inadequate to focus on one identity (be it gender, disability or ethnicity) as each triggers unique experiences of discrimination and disadvantage. Rather, an intersectional analysis is necessary to understand how the combination of self-identities shapes the social, cultural and political structures that perpetrate violence against disabled women in general and in the context of our chapter, India specifically. Adopting such a framework allows us to understand the unique meanings of DVA, how people with different identities experience and respond to violence and abuse, how they construct particular consequences of DVA and what safety means to them. For instance, although disabled women may experience similar types of DVA to non-disabled women, they are also likely to experience disablist violence or impairment-specific violence, which will not be experienced by non-disabled women. Such acts of abuse include those which simultaneously increase the powerfulness of the perpetrators and the powerlessness of the disabled women. An example of disablist violence would include the misuse of medication, isolating individuals from family and friends, and removing the battery from the woman's power wheelchair (Shah et al., 2016a; Curry, Hassouneh-Phillips, & Johnston-Silverberg, 2001). With an intersectional lens, this chapter can also offer an understanding of how an individual's positionality and interaction with social structures influences their different levels of vulnerability to DVA and also access to support services and the responses received when disclosing DVA or seeking help.

In the first part of the chapter we visit some of the wider literature about DVA and disability for contextualisation and then explore these in the context of India. Nearer the end of the chapter we continue with the focus on India but use the United Nations Sustainable Development Goals (SDGs) as a framework to explore how DVA and disability are being addressed. This adds a fresh perspective to some of the current discussions and debates about DVA and disability in India. As we will explore, the SDGs are relevant to resource rich and resource poor countries, but the most pressing needs are in low- and middle-income countries (LMICs), such as India. We hope that the chapter will illuminate some of the important aspects of DVA and disability in India and provide insights into the SDGs for readers who are less familiar with them. Crucially, we want to provide insights into their place in tackling DVA and disability, not only in India, but globally.

## Thinking about disability

The concept of disability is culturally constructed and socially produced. It has evolved over time and space, shaped and assigned value by various cultural and social structures of a given society. In Indian society for instance, disability has not been seen as positive, and thus not been given equal value to class or gender (Daruwalla et al., 2013).

Traditionally, research in relation to people with impairments, health issues and illnesses drew largely on the powerful discourse of biological determinism which focused on a bodily or cognitive imperfection that needed curative and rehabilitative medical intervention (Barnes & Mercer, 2010; Shah & Priestley, 2011; Kudlick, 2003, 2018). This view has long governed the definition of disability and it was termed the medical or individual model of disability (Oliver, 2013). If rehabilitation fails or is not accessible, the 'disability problem' remains within the person. Focusing only on the bodily deficiency, studies based on medical models neglected the role of societal structures in shaping the choices and experiences for people with impairments.

However, disability is not just a pathological condition located within the individual. It is also influenced by environmental factors that create barriers of physical as well as attitudinal kinds that hinder people's choices and participation in society. Environmental factors and attitudes can differ depending on the time and space, and thus influence the construction of disabling behaviours or attitudes. This interpretation of disability, coined the 'social model of disability' (Oliver, 1990) was prompted by disabled people's activism, encouraging scholars to view it as a human rights issue, and find out how and why surrounding barriers are created, deconstructed or persist, and how they impact people with and without impairments. Such knowledge is useful so strategies can be put in place for their removal to enable a more equal society for all. However, the assumption that 'society' is the sole determinant of disabled people's experiences is also unhelpful. The authors of this chapter believe disability is an interplay of the individual and the social, as recognised by the United Nations Convention for the Rights of Persons with Disabilities (UNCRPD) (United Nations, 2006). We draw on the definition used in the World Report of Disability (WHO, 2011, p. 4):

> Disability results from the interaction between persons with impairments and attitudinal and environmental barriers that hinder their full and effective participation in society on an equal basis with others.

With 50 binding articles, the UNCRPD (United Nations, 2006) is the first international treaty to afford disabled people full civil rights and fundamental freedoms in all aspects of life. Three of these articles are particularly relevant to this chapter: Article 6 which pays particular attention to the situation of disabled women and girls and calls for actions to ensure they are able to exercise and enjoy their human rights; Article 15 which seeks to protect disabled persons from abuse, violence, torture or scientific experimentation by taking appropriate measures (administrative, legal and judicial); and Article 16 which also aims to protect disabled people from abuse, exploitation and violence, including gender-based violence – inside and outside the home.

There is a great deal of conceptual and definitional content in this book as regards the differences between the many forms of violence which sit under the broad term DVA. They do not need repeating here, so we move straight into a discussion about disability. When thinking and talking about disability, it is important to use language that reflects a social model of disability, as a purposeful move away from other pervasive (and in our view unhelpful) orientations, such as the medical model (Mays, 2006). Using the term 'disabled people' and 'disabled women' as opposed to 'people *with* disabilities' and 'women *with* disabilities' is consistent with this approach.

An estimated 15% of the world's population live with some form of impairment (WHO, 2018) and the percentage is increasing due to many factors, but principally an increase in chronic health conditions and ageing populations. Like DVA though, an accurate picture is difficult due to variable reporting and recording across countries. According to the Department of Economic and Social Affairs (DESA) (2018), disabled people and especially women and girls, experience disproportionate levels of poverty; lack of access to education, health services and employment; and underrepresentation in decision-making and political participation. Moreover, the report goes on to say that access to health-care services remains a challenge for many disabled people, who are more than three times as likely to be unable to get health care when they need it. Importantly, DESA do not merely problematise the issue: they lay out a number of ways to address such inequalities. Table 20.1 is adapted from the DESA report and shows what needs to be done to achieve gender equality for disabled women and girls.

*Table 20.1* Achieving gender equality and empowerment of disabled women and girls

1 Address the needs and perspectives of disabled women and girls in national strategies or action plans on disability and on gender.
2 Develop policies and programmes focused on disabled women and girls aiming at their full and equal participation in society.
3 Support the empowerment of disabled women and girls by investing in their education and work.
4 Raise awareness on the needs of disabled women and girls and eliminate stigma and discrimination against them.
5 Identify and eliminate obstacles and barriers to accessibility in health-care facilities for disabled women and girls.
6 Train health-care personnel on disability inclusion and improving service delivery for disabled women and girls.
7 Empower disabled women and girls to take control over their own health-care decisions.
8 Make sexual and reproductive health-care facilities and information accessible for disabled women and girls.

Source: Adapted from DESA (2018)

## The intersection of disability and DVA

A growing body of evidence suggests that disabled women are at a higher risk of DVA than non-disabled women, with an estimated 50% of disabled women having experienced DVA in some form across their lives (Shah et al., 2016a; Nosek, Hughes, Taylor, & Taylor, 2006; Hague, Thiara, & Magowan, 2007; Barranti & Yuen, 2008; Martin et al., 2008; Nixon, 2009; Slayter, 2009; Hague, Thiara, & Mullender, 2011). They are likely to experience prolonged periods of violence by multiple perpetrators including paid and unpaid carers. There is evidence that they are at risk of severe physical violence (Brownridge, 2006) and sexual violence. Though several forms of violence (i.e. physical, psychological and sexual violence) are not unique to disabled women and girls, this population is considered at increased risk of exposure to such violence due to their dependency on others, reduced physical and emotional defences, experience of communication barriers, stigma and discrimination (Hughs et al., 2012). Further they may be restricted in their ability to leave an abusive situation/relationship due to, for example, reliance on families and caregivers (Nixon, 2009; Human Rights Watch, 2018).

The dependent status of some disabled women can suggest, to the outside eye, that they are incompetent and powerless to resist perpetrators' advances or report them, making them an 'easy' victim. Perceptions that disabled women are powerless, lack agency to report or disclose, and are unlikely to retaliate are created by structural inequalities in different societies which exclude them from certain social processes and impede their access to support and resources to facilitate life choices and opportunities on par to non-disabled women. Galtung (1969) refers to this as structural violence, and argues how it has the potential to underpin acts of DVA. This is particularly pervasive in countries such as India where disabled women are seen as 'flawed' and their inequalities to structures and processes is seen as a social norm (Daruwalla et al., 2013).

Several authors report on the particular forms of impairment-related abuse that can take place. For example, withholding assistive devices is a common mechanism of control and abuse (Nosek et al., 2006; Radford, Harne, & Trotter, 2006; Hague et al., 2011). Impairment-specific violence was also evidenced in a four European country comparative study involving the UK, Austria, Germany and Iceland. The study was conducted between 2013–2015 (Mandl et al., 2014) and Shah led the UK team. The study evidenced the different types of violence experienced by disabled women across the life-course, sometimes motivated by specific aspects of their identity. The study showed how, often, impairment-specific violence is not recognised as violence, but as a normal part of the disabled person's life, and the perpetrator was often someone who the women was reliant on, who exploited their position (Shah, Woodin, & Tsitou, 2014, 2016). This is exemplified by the following quote from a participant named Adele (self-selected pseudonym) who recounts how she experienced abuse for a good part of a decade starting when she was a young teenager. The perpetrator, who was in their 20s at the time, was Adele's carer and sexual partner who, she believes, exploited his role as her carer to control and isolate her:

> They would purposefully give me the strongest painkillers when my friends were coming, and they couldn't come then obviously because I was asleep. [They] would cancel care shifts, they would then say that I'd cancelled them, because again when you've had them tablets you're not good at remembering anything – even what your name is.

Similarly, the refusal to provide basic care has been reported (Kroll, Jones, Kehn, & Neri, 2006; Lightfoot & Williams, 2009; Public Health England, 2015). Bowen and Swift (2019) suggest that individuals with intellectual disabilities are at heightened risk of DVA due to a number of reasons; for example, not always being able to identify and read social cues and misinterpreting inappropriate/abusive behaviour as friendship or love.

As regards disabled women and girls, abuse that violates their reproductive and sexual rights is a considerable problem and really brings to the fore the gendered aspects of abuse. Disabled women have been victims of involuntary sterilisation in a number of countries (DESA, 2018). There is a pervasive and inaccurate discourse that disabled women are a-sexual and hence their disclosures of sexual violence against them may not be taken seriously. It is why point 8 in Table 20.1 is so important: making sexual and reproductive health-care facilities and information accessible for disabled women and girls.

Pregnancy is a high-risk time for DVA, and many women experience DVA for the first time during pregnancy, or existing abuse escalates in terms of frequency and severity. There is some evidence that for disabled women, the risks are even higher. Almost 10% of women giving the birth in the UK each year have one or more long-term impairment (Redshaw, Malouf, Gao, & Gray, 2013) and approximately half of these women will experience DVA (Šumilo, Kurinczuk, Redshaw, & Gray, 2012). In 2012, one of the authors (Bradbury-Jones) led on a UK study that investigated how disabled women with experiences of DVA are able to navigate maternity services. The study highlighted multiple barriers to access and utilisation of services. Some barriers were identified as physical/environmental, but a significant obstacle to accessing much-needed maternity care was found to be women's previous experiences of treatment by health-care staff (Bradbury-Jones et al., 2015a, 2015b; Breckenridge et al., 2014). In Table 20.2, we have presented one of the quotes from a disabled woman who took part in the study. It illustrates well the multiple discrimination that we referred to earlier in the chapter.

## Disability and DVA in India

In this next section, we move the discussion to thinking about DVA and disability in India and as we have done earlier in the chapter, we explore their intersection. In India, the lifetime prevalence of DVA in general is reported by 40% of all women (Kalokhe et al., 2015). Although global estimates do vary from somewhere between 15% and 71% (WHO, 2009), this is relatively high. Moreover, it is important to recognise its distinct manifestations, attributable to prominent religious and cultural aspects of much of life in India. For example, the 'traditional' Indian family is a joint family where abuse can extend to perpetration by in-laws in addition to that perpetrated by a spouse. Daruwalla and colleagues (2013, p. 8) reported that disabled women face 'violence in the form of neglect, control, restricted mobility, forced marriages, and lack of autonomy'. Sexual abuse and forced sterilisation by family members are also risks (Mohapatra & Mohanty, 2005). Moreover, its perpetration is from multiple potential sources such as partners,

*Table 20.2* Disabled woman's perception of discrimination

---

It's really easy to put a stereotype on someone, like "Oh, well, this person cannot make good decisions for themselves because a) they're disabled or b) they made such horrible decisions to put themselves in an abusive situation", which the two don't have anything to do with each other a lot of times. I think it's understood in society that if a woman is in an abusive situation, she can't make good decisions for herself.

---

Source: Taken from Bradbury-Jones et al. (2015b)

family members and paid carers. Drawing on the work of Ahmed-Ghosh (2004) and Kalokhe et al. (2018) it is possible to identify some prominent forms of DVA in India:

1 Eviction from the house if a woman does not agree to a demand of dowry or other material.
2 Preference for a male child and abuse if a woman gives birth to a female child by physical violence and passing scathing comments.
3 Burning or beating the woman with kitchen utensils, misuse of religion and making her change her dietary preferences.

The fact that many women and girls are not literate and have not experienced the same benefits of education as many boys and men (UN (India) 2020), is another pervasive challenge around their understandings of DVA as a human rights issue. This has been a hurdle for many years in India. Within this societal and contextual environment, often girls and women do not realise that they are experiencing abuse because the acts of dominance and oppression in the household and broader society become normalised.

In India, normative judgements as regards meaningful contribution to society are based on factors such as productivity, property ownership, family as a social unit, marriage, religion and patriarchy (Daruwalla et al., 2013). Having explored the double impacts of DVA and disability on women generally it could be argued that the context of India adds yet another discrimina-tory layer. Ghai's (2001) book titled *Marginalisation and Disability: Experiences from the Third World* explores how even though disability is a global issue, in India its implications differ as regards contexts and cultures. For example, in the Hindu religion, it is widely believed that disabled people are suffering from the wrath of God: punished from misdeeds of either them or their family members. Another notion is that of disability perceived as an eternal childhood where survival depends on constant care and protection. These conceptualisations focus on disability as a negative cultural identity. Difficulty in access to education for disabled girls and women can also lead to increased susceptibility to divorce, DVA and sexual violation (Buckingham, 2011).

Financial dependence often worsens the situation (Dutta, 2015) and as Ghai points out, when families are living in extreme poverty, the birth of a disabled girl can add a significant additional financial stress on the family. Salian (2018) reported the case of a young woman with cerebral palsy who was raped by three neighbours in an Indian village in 2014. Rather than express outrage at the plight of this young woman, the villagers were reported to be angry at the decision to sentence the men to imprisonment on the grounds that it wasted their productivity as young, healthy men. This shocking account highlights well the misplaced societal responses and the shame and stigma faced by disabled women in India.

Moreover, taking the viewpoints of Padte (2013) and Deepak et al. (2014), there are a number of problems in the specific context of India. Violence towards those who are perceived as being weak in some way is part of society and is often seen in family and community rela-tionships. Sexual violence is a taboo topic in much of society and hence not discussed widely by many people. Additionally, sometimes the authorities and police who are supposed to help victims exploit them in the form of sexual favours or bribes, making the risk even greater for disabled women. There is also the pervasive problem of normalisation, with many women believing that domestic violence/beating is okay because they deserve it, owing to the low self-esteem caused by the disability and societal misconceptions (SNEHA, 2020).

Although the issue of DVA is a major concern in Indian society, there are certain barriers that hamper disclosure of sexual assault amongst disabled women (Dawn, 2014). Whilst fear of disclosure applies to most women, disabled women experiencing DVA face the fear of double disclosure; they not only worry about the stigma surrounding DVA, but also about how health professionals' misconceptions about disability may affect their care (Bradbury-Jones et al., 2015a, 2015b). Referring back to Table 20.2, we can see how the disabled woman would be anxious to talk about either of these aspects of her life. In the context of India there may be additional complexities. Barriers to disclosure of DVA among disabled women and girls act at multiple levels including societal, organisational and personal. In a society, if sexual violence is regarded as acceptable and justifiable, as it may be in some Indian contexts, then disabled women may be disinclined to report. At an organisational level, there may be barriers in communicating the violence due to ineffective or limited aids required for a disabled woman. As we explored earlier, there are physical barriers to access and utilisation of services for disabled women generally, but the development and accessibility of services in India means that the situation is more problematic. Points 4–8 in Table 20.1 point to some of the important strategies to overcome this problem. On a personal level, often violence of any type might be considered as a shameful act and an act of stigma and hence may not be disclosed and reported. Women with physical impairments may find it more difficult to escape from violent situations due to limited mobility. Because of the lack of accessible information, disabled women and girls, particularly those with intellectual disabilities, may not know that non-consensual sexual acts are a crime and should be reported.

Another factor in relation to barriers to disclosure lies in the perceptions of how a complaint will be managed and this is illustrative of the simultaneous oppression that we have already discussed. Police and court officials have a poor level of understanding about issues related to DVA and issues related to disability and when these are combined, they are likely to be even less prepared to respond appropriately. Access to justice, access to health care and dealing with the issue in the court systems are all problematic (Barriga, 2016; Salian, 2018). Salian (2018) details how the police and other officials do not have enough training in dealing with such situations. Police may not know how to speak properly and to handle the issue sensitively. So, it is important to train police officials, health-care workers and other personnel dealing with such cases about handling the issues sensitively and communicating with different forms of disabled persons effectively. The same can be said of the need to train health personnel and other workers and professionals in the context of health and social care.

## Addressing DVA and disability in India

When the women's rights movement gained momentum in India, there was a focus on poverty, education, caste discrimination, employment, dowry, population control, female feticide and domestic violence. The issue of disability was not even highlighted.

In 2007, the United Nations Convention on the Rights of People with Disabilities was signed and acknowledged by India. It recognised that disabled women and girls may be exposed to increased risk of DVA, requiring gender perspectives to be incorporated into discourses and policies about human rights; and thus, provisions were made from that point (Badjena, 2014). In 1983, DVA was recognised as a criminal act and punishable offence in India. In recent years, the government of India has taken measures to develop and improve the situation by making laws for the protection of women and girls. In 2005, the government of India passed the 2005 Protection of Women from Domestic Violence Act (PWDVA) which included experts from different committees coming together to develop policy and action. With the traditional structure of Indian families based on patriarchy, it is difficult to expect a major change in Indian society in a short span of time. However, several measures have been taken and continue to be taken by the Indian government and various non-governmental organisations (NGOs) to work towards awareness about DVA and women empowerment.

An important framework for implementing such measures is the United Nations Sustainable Development Goals (SDGs). Before exploring how these link specifically to DVA and disability in India, we will say a few words about the SDGs generally. They were adopted in 2015 by all United Nations Member States as a blueprint for ensuring wellbeing, peace and security for people all over the world. The blueprint is focused on 17 SDGs for all countries – resource rich and resource poor – to pull together as a global partnership to tackle the 17 most pressing challenges faced by the world now and in the future.

As Abu Al-Ghaib and Wilm (2020) point out, the SDGs differ in many ways from their predecessor, the Millennium Development Goals (MDGs). One crucial difference in the context of this chapter is that the MDGs were silent on the issue of disability. This is important because as we have already discussed, the issue of disability was not part of prominent policy within India until relatively recently. As a consequence, disabled people have been excluded from development initiatives and funding streams (Abu Al-Ghaib & Wilm, 2020). The SDGs on the other hand, *do* take account of disability. But, according to DESA (2020), disabled people are at a disadvantage regarding most SDGs. DESA's viewpoint is that it is critical to ensure the full and equal participation of disabled persons in all spheres of society and create enabling environments in line with the Convention on the Rights of Persons with Disabilities (DESA, 2020). Abu Al-Ghaib and Wilm (2020) make the point that it is important to bear in mind that the commitment to 'leave no one behind' means that the SDGs cannot be considered a success unless they are met for everyone – including disabled women and girls.

Unlike disability, gender equality *did* feature in the MDGs. Out of the eight MDGs, Goal 3 was to 'Promote Gender Equality and Empower Women'. The SDGs have a number of related goals as regards gender and violence, most directly Goal 5 (Gender Equality) and Goal 16 (Peace and Justice). Butchart (2020) provides a clear presentation of how the SDGs and violence intersect that makes an extremely useful resource for exploring the issue in greater depth. He suggests that there are two goals that have direct relevance to tackling violence (Goals 5 and 16) and a further six goals that help to address the risk factors for violence. These are shown in Table 20.3. It is important to remember that all the goals are inter-linked and with this in mind,

*Table 20.3* Linking the SDGs to gender and violence

---

**Achieving Gender Equality (Goal 5)**
Eliminate all forms of violence against women and girls.
Eliminate all harmful practices, such as child, early and forced marriage and female genital mutilation.
**Achieving Peace and Justice (Goal 16)**
Significantly reduce all forms of violence and related death rates everywhere.
End abuse, exploitation, trafficking, and all forms of violence against children.
**Addressing the risk factors for violence**
No Poverty (Goal 1)
Good Health (Goal 3)
Good Education (Goal 4)
Reduced Inequalities (Goal 10)
Sustainable Cities and Communities (Goal 11)
Partnerships for the Goals (Goal 17)

---

there are also several goals that can be regarded as being relevant to addressing some of the risk factors for violence as shown in Table 20.3.

One critical element of the SDGs was highlighted by DESA (2018), who made the point that many countries still address gender and disability issues separately, without focusing on the intersection between the two (DESA, 2018). Hence the relevance of this chapter where we have attempted to draw the issues together. In order to achieve Goal 5, United Nations India has a comprehensive programme to map their progress and development (Table 20.4).

Although there are several laws in India to address the intersection of DVA and disability, often women are not aware of such laws. Lack of awareness among disabled women can be due to the socialisation which truncates and limits formal and informal learning, opportunities including peer group exposure owing to their impairments. As Badjena (2014, p. 55) observed: 'The social role or absence of the role attributed to women with disabilities, in conjunction with the stereotypes that exist, contribute to their vulnerability, and lead to violation of their rights'. Thus, it is imperative for governments and relevant institutions to enact the law and to provide a mechanism for justice. An important step would be to consult with the relevant communities, particularly girls and disabled women about these laws and ways of implementation, and training of relevant officials (Barriga, 2016). This could be achieved by spreading awareness about these laws amongst the community and affected individuals in the form of advertisements on TV, newspapers, schools, primary health centres and other places of community gatherings.

Returning to Ghai's (2019) writings on the re-thinking of disability, some interesting reflections arise as regards where India has been and where it is heading in terms of addressing inequalities pertaining to gender and disability. In exploring the marginalisation of disabled people's lives and their right to a full life, Ghai talks of how India is going through rapid economic expansion and social change, which creates significant opportunities (and of course, some challenges). For example, several multinational companies across India have developed policies and practices that include disabled people, including women, proactively tackling the barriers that

*Table 20.4* UN targets for achieving gender equality and empowerment of women in India

- End all forms of discrimination against all women and girls everywhere.
- Eliminate all forms of violence against all women and girls in the public and private spheres, including trafficking and sexual and other types of exploitation.
- Eliminate all harmful practices, such as child, early and forced marriage and female genital mutilation.
- Recognise and value unpaid care and domestic work through the provision of public services, infrastructure and social protection policies and the promotion of shared responsibility within the household and the family as nationally appropriate.
- Ensure women's full and effective participation and equal opportunities for leadership at all levels of decision-making in political, economic and public life.
- Ensure universal access to sexual and reproductive health and reproductive rights. Undertake reforms to give women equal rights to economic resources, as well as access to ownership and control over land and other forms of property, financial services, inheritance and natural resources, in accordance with national laws.
- Enhance the use of enabling technology, in particular information and communications technology, to promote the empowerment of women.
- Adopt and strengthen sound policies and enforceable legislation for the promotion of gender equality and the empowerment of all women and girls at all levels.

*Source*: Adapted from https://in.one.un.org/page/sustainable-development-goals/sdg-5/

might otherwise exclude them. Given time, such initiatives can have significant impacts on the lives of many disabled women in India, lifting them out of poverty and moving them forward with an empowering agenda. For those disabled women whose lives are marred by an abusive relationship, the ability to be empowered to recognise, disclose and seek help for the abuse are far more likely to be realised.

Education and empowerment of girls increases the chances of improvement in the economy, thereby reducing poverty and population burden, achieving SD Goals 1, 3, 4, 10 and 16. Ending violence against women is a key national priority as identified by the Government of India, which aligns with SDG 5 on gender equity. As discussed, for years women in India have seen degradation and deprivation of basic human rights in their family and society. Measures taken to achieve the SDGs have raised hopes for women's empowerment and equality. That is for *all* women and girls. There is further to go for disabled women and girls where DVA exists, but in this chapter, we have provided insights into some of the policies and frameworks that may assist with this endeavour.

## Conclusions

Disabled women and girls across the world are at heightened risk of violence and abuse in myriad forms in comparison to their non-disabled counterparts. In addition to the types of violence that can be perpetrated against all women and girls, they can experience impairment-targeted abuse and/or their impairment is used as a mechanism to enhance their vulnerability in some way. India is one of the poorest countries in the world. Its poverty creates opportunities for structural violence against disabled women to be embedded within its community, which underpins other forms of DVA.

In India, both DVA and disability rates are high, yet there is a great deal being done to tackle DVA and to better support disabled women and girls. Discrimination and oppression experienced by individual disabled women will not lessen purely through interventions aimed at the individual – it requires structural change to enact attitudinal and societal change. We have explored how the SDGs come together as potential levers for change, and how an intersectional lens is critical to understand and address experiences of DVA for disabled women in India. This gives hope that in India, the enduring challenges of multiple discrimination experienced by disabled women and girls can be reduced, if not (ideally) eradicated. We have focused on India, but many of the issues discussed are transferable to other jurisdictions, particularly low- and middle-income countries.

## Critical findings

- Cultural and religious barriers, patriarchal dominance amongst Indian society act as major contributing factors for the prevalence of violence and discrimination against disabled women and girls.
- Sexuality of disabled women and girls is often not recognised and hence abuse takes place and goes unreported.
- Raising societal awareness about gender and disability rights is imperative.
- Proper training to tackle the issue of DVA with disabled women effectively amongst police personnel, health-care workers and other related officials is necessary.
- In India progress has been made to tackle many human rights issues, including saving girl children, educating women and overall women empowerment.
- The SDGs provide a framework to drive change, to tackle both DVA and disability.

# Keys implications for policy, practice and research

## *Practice*

- Public education and proper interventions are required to increase awareness among disabled women and girls regarding their rights to live free of violence.
- Health Care Practitioners (HCPs) and workers of the criminal justice system need to be trained to work with DVA related issues and disabled victims with sensitivity, care and consideration.
- Governmental organisations, various agencies, and donors are to work together to make prevention possible and provide protection services for the affected.

## *Policy*

- Under-reporting of violence is a significant problem and it is imperative for the police and lawmakers to address the issue and to enact their legal duties to protect disabled women and girls.

## *Research*

- Published literature on DVA and disability in India are primarily focused on urban populations as opposed to rural areas. Studies that include both urban and rural populations would provide useful comparisons and would ensure that a broader range of perspectives and needs are captured.
- While several policies are in place in India for women empowerment, it will be useful to know whether or not these are working and the degree to which the targets for achieving the SDGs in relation to both violence and disability are likely to be met.

## References

Abu Al-Ghaib, O., & Wilm, S. (2020). *Disability inclusion and the sustainable development goals: Practices and challenges. A report.* Leonard Cheshire Disability. Retrieved April 5, 2020, from www.leonardcheshire.org/sites/default/files/2019-10/disability-inclusion-sustainable-development.pdf

Ahmed-Ghosh, H. (2004). Chattels of society: Domestic violence in India. *Violence Against Women, 10*(1), 94–118.

Badjena, S. S. (2014). Sexual violence against women with disabilities and the legislative measures in India. *Odisha Review*, 46–57.

Barnes, C., & Mercer, G. (2010). *Exploring disability.* Cambridge: Polity Press.

Barranti, C. C., & Yuen, F. K. (2008). Intimate partner violence and women with disabilities: Toward bringing visibility to an unrecognized population. *Journal of Social Work in Disability & Rehabilitation, 7*(2), 115–130.

Barriga, S. R. (2016). Article *on 'dispatches: "Who can save me?"- Domestic violence and disability.* Retrieved May 23, 2020, from www.hrw.org/news/2016/03/08/dispatches-who-can-save-me-domestic-violence-and-disability

Bowen, E., & Swift, C. (2019). The prevalence and correlates of partner violence used and experienced by adults with intellectual disabilities: A systematic review and call to action. *Trauma, Violence, & Abuse, 20*(5), 693–705.

Bradbury-Jones, C., Breckenridge, J. P., Devaney, J., Duncan, F., Kroll, T., Lazenbatt, A., & Taylor, J. (2015a). Priorities and strategies for improving disabled women's access to maternity services when they are affected by domestic abuse: A multi-method study using concept maps. *BMC Pregnancy & Childbirth, 15*, 350.

Bradbury-Jones, C., Breckenridge, J. P., Devaney, J., Duncan, F., Kroll, T., Lazenbatt, A., & Taylor, J. (2015b). Priorities and strategies for improving disabled women's access to maternity services when they are affected by domestic abuse: A multi-method study using concept maps. *BMC Pregnancy and Childbirth, 15*(1), 350.

Breckenridge, J. P., Devaney, J., Kroll, T., Lazenbatt, A., Taylor, J., & Bradbury-Jones, C. (2014). Access and utilisation of maternity care for disabled women who experience domestic abuse: A systematic review. *BMC Pregnancy and Childbirth, 14*(1), 234.

Brownridge, D. A. (2006). Partner violence against women with disabilities: Prevalence, risk, and explanations. *Violence Against Women, 12*(9), 805–822.

Buckingham, J. (2011). Writing histories of disability in India: Strategies of inclusion. *Disability & Society, 26*(4), 419–431.

Butchart, A. (2020). *The sustainable development goals (SDG) and violence prevention: How do they connect?* World Health Organization. Retrieved April 20, 2020, from www.who.int/violence_injury_prevention/violence/7th_milestones_meeting/Butchart_SDGs_and_violence_prevention.pdf?ua=1

Crenshaw, K. W. (1994). Mapping the margins. *The Public Nature of Private Violence*, 93–118.

Curry, M. A., Hassouneh-Phillips, D., & Johnston-Silverberg, A. J. (2001). Abuse of women with disabilities: An ecological model and review. *Violence Against Women, 7*, 60–79.

Daruwalla, N., Chakravarty, S., Chatterji, S., Shah More, N., Alcock, G., Hawkes, S., & Osrin, D. (2013). Violence against women with disability in Mumbai, India: A qualitative study. *Sage Open, 3*(3), 2158244013499144.

Dawn, R. (2014). "Our lives, our identity": Women with disabilities in India. *Disability and rehabilitation, 36*(21), 1768–1773.

Deepak, S., Kumar, J., Santosh, B., Gornalli, S., Manikappa, P., Vyjantha, U., & Giriyappa, R. (2014). Violence against persons with disabilities in Bidar District, India. *Disability, CBR & Inclusive Development, 25*(2), 35–53.

Department of Economic and Social Affairs (DESA). (2018). *Disability and Development Report: Realizing the sustainable development goals by, for and with persons with disabilities.* Retrieved May 29, 2020, from https://social.un.org/publications/UN-Flagship-Report-Disability-Final.pdf

Department of Economic and Social Affairs (DESA). (2020). *UN flagship report on disability and sustainable development goals.* United Nations. Retrieved May 29, 2020, from www.un.org/development/desa/disabilities/publication-disability-sdgs.html

Dutta, S. (2015). Discrimination generated by the intersection of gender and disability. *Journal of Dental and Medical Sciences, 14*, 33–36.

Galtung, J. (1969). Violence, peace and peace research. *Journal of Peace Resolution, 6*, 167–191. doi:10.1177/002234336900600301

Ghai, A. (2001). Marginalisation and disability: Experiences from the third world. *Disability and the life course: Global Perspectives, 26.*

Ghai, A. (2019). *Rethinking disability in India.* Taylor & Francis.

Hague, G., Thiara, R. K., & Magowan, P. (2007). Disabled women and domestic violence: Making the links. *An Interim Report for the Women's Aid Federation of England.* Retrieved from www. bris. ac. uk/sps/research/projects/current/rj4502/rj4502interim. pdf

Hague, G., Thiara, R. K., & Mullender, A. (2011). Disabled women, domestic violence and social care: The risk of isolation, vulnerability and neglect. *British Journal of Social Work, 41*(1), 148–165.

Hughes, K., Bellis, M. A., Jones, L., Wood, S., Bates, G., Eckley, L., . . . Officer, A. (2012). Prevalence and risk of violence against adults with disabilities: A systematic review and meta-analysis of observational studies. *The Lancet, 379*(9826), 1621–1629.

Human Rights Watch. (2018). *Invisible victims of sexual violence: Access to justice for women and girls with disabilities in India.* Retrieved March 23, 2020, from www.hrw.org/report/2018/04/03/invisible-victims-sexual-violence/access-justice-women-and-girls-disabilities

Kalokhe, A. S., Iyer, S. R., Kolhe, A. R., Dhayarkar, S., Paranjape, A., del Rio, C., . . . Sahay, S. (2018). Correlates of domestic violence experience among recently-married women residing in slums in Pune, India. *PLoS One, 13*(4).

Kalokhe, A. S., Potdar, R. R., Stephenson, R., Dunkle, K. L., Paranjape, A., del Rio, C., & Sahay, S. (2015). How well does the World Health Organization definition of domestic violence work for India? *PLoS One, 10*(3).

Kroll, T., Jones, G. C., Kehn, M., & Neri, M. T. (2006). Barriers and strategies affecting the utilisation of primary preventive services for people with physical disabilities: A qualitative inquiry. *Health & Social Care in the Community, 14*(4), 284–293.

Kudlick, C. J. (2003). Disability history: Why we need another 'other'. *The American Historical Review*, *108*(3), 763–793.

Kudlick, C. J. (2018). Social history of medicine and disability history. In M. A. Rembis, C. J. Kudlick, & K. E. Nielsen (Eds.), *The Oxford handbook of disability history* (pp. 10–123). Oxford: Oxford University Press.

Lightfoot, E., & Williams, O. (2009). The intersection of disability, diversity, and domestic violence: Results of national focus groups. *Journal of Aggression, Maltreatment & Trauma*, *18*(2), 133–152.

Mandl, S., Sprenger, C., Schachner, A., Traustadottir, R., Woodin, S., Shah, S., & Schröttle, M. (2014). Access to specialised victim support services for women with disabilities who have experienced violence. *Journal of Applied Research in Intellectual Disabilities*, *27*(4).

Martin, S. L., Rentz, E. D., Chan, R. L., Givens, J., Sanford, C. P., Kupper, L. L., . . . Macy, R. J. (2008). Physical and sexual violence among North Carolina women: Associations with physical health, mental health, and functional impairment. *Women's Health Issues*, *18*(2), 130–140.

Mays, J. M. (2006). Feminist disability theory: Domestic violence against women with a disability. *Disability & Society*, *21*(2), 147–158.

Mohapatra, S., & Mohanty, M. (2005). Abuse and activity limitation: A study on domestic violence against disabled women in Orissa, India. *Orissa: Swabhiman*, 6–5.

Nixon, J. (2009). Domestic violence and women with disabilities: Locating the issue on the periphery of social movements. *Disability & Society*, *24*(1), 77–89.

Nosek, M. A., Hughes, R. B., Taylor, H. B., & Taylor, P. (2006). Disability, psychosocial, and demographic characteristics of abused women with physical disabilities. *Violence Against Women*, *12*(9), 838–850.

Oliver, M. (1990). *Politics of disablement*. Basingstoke: Macmillan International Higher Education.

Oliver, M. (2013). The social model of disability: Thirty years on. *Disability & Society*, *28*(7), 1024–1026.

Padte, R. (2013). *Report on, "violence and disabled women"*. Retrieved March 2, 2020, from www.infochangein-dia.org/disabilities/382-disabilities/disabled-sexualities/9338-violence-and-disabled-women

Public Health England. (2015). *Report on disability and domestic abuse: Risk, impacts and response*. Retrieved February 24, 2020, from https://assets.publishing.service.gov.uk/government/uploads/system/uploads/attachment_data/file/480942/Disability_and_domestic_abuse_topic_overview_FINAL.pdf

Radford, J., Harne, L., & Trotter, J. (2006). Disabled women and domestic violence as violent crime. *Practice*, *18*(4), 233–246.

Redshaw, M., Malouf, R., Gao, H., & Gray, R. (2013). Women with disability: The experience of maternity care during pregnancy, labour and birth and the postnatal period. *BMC Pregnancy and Childbirth*, *13*(1), 174.

Salian, P. (2018). 'Give her a voice': Activists say women with disabilities in India need independence. *GlobalPost*. Retrieved March 22, 2020, from www.pri.org/stories/2018-08-14/india-invisibility-prevents-women-disabilities-having-their-metoo-moment

Shah, S., & Bradbury-Jones, C. (Eds.). (2018). *Disability, gender and violence over the life course: Global perspectives and human rights approaches*. New York, NY: Routledge.

Shah, S., & Priestley, M. (2011). *Disability and social change: Private lives and public policies*. Bristol: Policy Press.

Shah, S., Tsitsou, L., & Woodin, S. (2016a). 'I can't forget': Experiences of violence and disclosure in the childhoods of disabled women. *Childhood*, *23*(4), 521–536.

Shah, S., Tsitsou, L., & Woodin, S. (2016b). Hidden voices: Disabled women's experiences of violence and support over the life course. *Violence Against Women*, *22*(10), 1189–1210.

Shah, S., Woodin, S., & Tsitou, L. (2014). *Access to specialised victim support services for women with disabilities who have experienced violence*. National Empirical Report UK, EC Daphne.

Shah, S., Woodin, S., & Tsitou, L. (2016). *Access to specialised victim support services for women with disabilities who have experienced violence*. National Empirical Report UK. Retrieved from https://www.gla.ac.uk/media/Media_394354_smxx.pdf

Slayter, E. (2009). Intimate partner violence against women with disabilities: Implications for disability service system case management practice. *Journal of Aggression, Maltreatment & Trauma*, *18*(2), 182–199.

SNEHA. (2020). (Team of counsellors). *Article on 'domestic violence'*. Retrieved May 23, 2020, from https://sexualityanddisability.org/violence/domestic-violence/

Šumilo, D., Kurinczuk, J. J., Redshaw, M. E., & Gray, R. (2012). Prevalence and impact of disability in women who had recently given birth in the UK. *BMC Pregnancy and Childbirth*, *12*(1), 31.

United Nations. (2006). *Convention on the rights of persons with disabilities.* New York: United Nations General Assembly.

United Nations. (2007). *United Nations: Convention on the rights of people with disabilities.* UN. Retrieved May 29, 2020, from www.un.org/esa/socdev/enable/rights/convtexte.html

United Nations India. (2020). *Sustainable development goal, report on SDG 5: Gender equality.* Retrieved March 22, 2020, from https://in.one.un.org/page/sustainable-development-goals/sdg-5/

World Health Organization. (2009). *Women and health: Today's evidence tomorrow's agenda.* Geneva: World Health Organization.

World Health Organization. (2011). *World report on disability. WHO Library Cataloguing-in-Publication Data.* Geneva: World Health Organization.

World Health Organization. (2018). *Disability and health: Key facts.* Retrieved February 24, 2020, from www.who.int/news-room/fact-sheets/detail/disability-and-health

# 21

# DOMESTIC VIOLENCE AND ANIMAL ABUSE

*Amy J. Fitzgerald, Betty Jo Barrett, Rochelle Stevenson and Patti A. Timmons Fritz*

## Introduction

Despite efforts to reduce domestic violence (DV), victimization rates have remained stubbornly stable, prompting Caman and colleagues to remark, "these tendencies putatively highlight the need for novel approaches in combating gender-based violence" (2017, p. 19). Reducing barriers to formal help-seeking has been a key target for intervention (see Barnett, 2000, 2001; Sauve & Burns, 2009), and valuable work has been undertaken to minimize barriers encountered by transgender individuals, racialized women, and undocumented women, among others.

Another sizeable population group that warrants focused attention is victims/survivors with pets. For instance, over half of Canadian (57%) and US (65%) homes contain pets (American Pet Products Association, 2017; Canadian Pet Market Outlook, 2014).[1] Moreover, the vast majority consider their animal companions family: in the 2018 US General Social Survey, 93% of respondents reported they consider their dogs members of the family, as did 83% of those with cats (Ingraham, 2019).

As such, companion animals are vulnerable to violence perpetrated within the family, and this vulnerability is increasingly being acknowledged by scholars, practitioners, policy makers and the general public (evidenced by an article in *People Magazine* [2019]). Research on the subject is relatively new (originating approximately 25 years ago) and has focused on documenting rates of animal maltreatment within DV, the predictive power of animal maltreatment perpetration vis-à-vis the use of controlling behaviours, traits of perpetrators and the consequences of these co-occurring forms of victimization for adult and child victims/survivors of DV. New policies and legislation continue to be introduced with the goal of mitigating these consequences. Research contributions in relation to these themes are explored in this chapter, and discussion of the limitations of this relatively new body of literature weaved throughout. This scholarship constitutes a novel approach of the type called for by Caman and colleagues (2017) and is beginning to have promising impacts on policy and law.

## Discussion and analysis

Although research on the subject is relatively new, acknowledging pets in discussions of DV is not. The victimization of animals within DV was mentioned in the academic literature beginning in the 1970s (e.g., Walker, 1979). The abuse of pets was also included in interventions, notably in the well-known Power and Control Wheel (Pence & Paymar, 1993), wherein "abusing pets" is included in the Using Intimidation category, right after "smashing things; destroying her property". It was not until the late 1990s that research attention became concentrated on the prevalence, aetiology and implications of the co-occurrence of animal abuse and DV.[2]

## Documenting the co-occurrence of animal maltreatment and domestic violence

The earliest research examining animal abuse within DV utilized samples of women in DV shelters in the US. The documented proportions of women reporting that their partner also mistreated their pet have ranged from 25%–86% (Ascione, 1998; Carlisle-Frank, Frank, & Nielsen, 2004; Collins et al., 2018; Faver & Cavazos Jr, 2007; Faver & Strand, 2003; Flynn, 2000a, 2000b; Simmons & Lehmann, 2007; Strand & Faver, 2005). Studies in other countries, including Australia (Volant, Johnson, Gullone, & Coleman, 2008), Ireland (Allen, Gallagher, & Jones, 2006) and New Zealand (Roguski, 2012) have also documented similar ranges. Recent research with 16 shelters in Canada documented a slightly higher proportion (89%) of women reporting their partner also mistreated their pet (Barrett, Fitzgerald, Stevenson, & Cheung, 2017; Fitzgerald, Barrett, Stevenson, & Cheung, 2019).

This wide range of reported co-occurrence of animal abuse and DV in shelters is likely due to several factors. Some samples have been relatively small and, as such, might be influenced more by outlying values; many of the samples are drawn from one community, and a variety of community-specific factors could impact the relationship observed; and the way that animal maltreatment is measured has varied, with some researchers operationalizing it strictly as physical abuse and others including threats and non-physical abuse. The Partners' Treatment of Animals Scale (PTAS; Fitzgerald, Barrett, Shwom, Stevenson, & Chernyak, 2016) was developed to mitigate this latter issue. The instrument is a 21-item scale, with five sub-scales, that measures reports of physical and emotional animal abuse, threats and neglect by intimate partners.

Another limitation of the early work was uncertainty that the amount of animal abuse documented among shelter samples was different from the proportion in the general population. Two key studies demonstrated that animal mistreatment reported by shelter samples is dramatically higher than that reported by women in the community not exposed to DV. In Ascione and colleagues' (2007) study, women in shelter were 11 times more likely to report their partner had mistreated their pets compared to their community sample of women. Of Volant and colleagues' (2008) shelter sample, 46% reported their partner made threats regarding the pets and 53% reported pet abuse. This was significantly higher than what they found among their community sample: no one reported animal abuse and only 6% reported threats against their pets.

Collectively, these studies provided evidence that reports of partner-perpetrated animal abuse are common among shelter samples – significantly more so than among the general population. However, it was unclear if the relationship between animal abuse and DV could be generalized from women in shelters to abuse victims/survivors in the community not accessing shelter services. DV research indicates that a small fraction of those abused by a partner seek out shelter services (see Barrett & St. Pierre, 2011). In order to assess the degree of generalizability to victims/survivors in the community, Fitzgerald, Barrett, Gray, and Cheung (2020) analyzed the Canadian General Social Survey, which included a question about animal maltreatment for the first time in 2014. Threatening and abusive behaviour towards pets was significantly more common among those who report DV perpetration by their partner (13%) than among respondents who were not abused (0.84%). After controlling for socio-demographic correlates of DV, those who report animal maltreatment by their partner have an 11% increased probability of also experiencing physical and/or sexual DV and 39% increased probability of experiencing emotional abuse. Moreover, animal maltreatment was a much stronger predictor of intimate partner violence (IPV) than the socio-demographic variables included in the models.

## What animal abuse can tell us about domestic violence

Animal maltreatment has commonly been perceived to be a form of coercive control and/or psychological abuse, which are broad patterns of behaviours aimed at displaying and exerting power over a partner (see Stark, 2007; Centers for Disease Control and Prevention, 2019). Carol Adams (1995) was among the first to suggest that there are numerous ways in which animal maltreatment contributes to coercive control: by harming animals the perpetrator demonstrates and confirms his/her power, teaches submission (further) isolates the victim and perpetuates an environment of terror and fear. Animal maltreatment may also be used to show victims what might happen to them if they attempt to act independently and to cause victims to experience guilt, fear and grief (Adams, 1995; Faver & Strand, 2007). Consistent with these claims, researchers have shown that animal maltreatment perpetration is related to greater use of controlling behaviours (Simmons & Lehmann, 2007) and psychological aggression (Ascione et al., 2007; Febres et al., 2014; Haden, McDonald, Booth, Ascione, & Blakelock, 2018). In qualitative research victims/survivors have similarly described control as motivation for animal maltreatment by their abuser (Allen et al., 2006; Flynn, 2000a, 2000b; Newberry, 2017).

Researchers have found that the stronger the victim-pet bond, the greater the use of animal maltreatment by perpetrators (Faver & Strand, 2007; Strand & Faver, 2005). This is consistent with feminist DV theories and theories of coercive control in that perpetrators are known to create and exploit victims' vulnerabilities (Adams, 1995; Dutton & Goodman, 2005; Johnson, 2008; Pence & Paymar, 1993). It is as if the animals become extensions of the victims such that harming the animals also brings harm to the (human) victims (Adams, 1994; Fitzgerald et al., 2019; Flynn, 2000a); this might be even more likely in cases where the animals are emotional support or service animals, although targeted research is needed.

Recent research disaggregating forms of animal maltreatment into several types (i.e., physical, emotional, threats and neglect) found that while participants perceived their abuser's neglect of their pets and emotional and threatening behaviour directed towards them as motivated by a desire to secure and maintain power and control, they did not perceive physical animal abuse perpetration as having the same motivations (Fitzgerald et al., 2019). While further research is needed, possible explanations for this finding include victims/survivors may more easily interpret neglect/emotional abuse/threats as motivated by power and control compared to physical abuse; (severe) physical abuse may not be used as a tool of power and control because it risks irrevocably harming the animal and making him/her no longer useful instrumentally; as abuse escalates, coercive control and physical abuse may become focused on the woman herself instead of the pets; and different types of abusers might harm animals for different reasons (see Fitzgerald et al., 2019).

These and other studies are increasingly demonstrating that those who report animal abuse by a partner are more likely to also be subjected to varied, frequent and severe DV (Ascione et al., 2007; DeGue & DiLillo, 2009; Simmons & Lehmann, 2007; Walton-Moss, Manganello, Frye, & Campbell, 2005). Simmons and Lehmann (2007) found in their Texas shelter sample that those who reported their abuser mistreated their pets were more likely to also report multiple forms of DV perpetration. Ascione and colleagues (2007) documented a significant relationship between severe physical DV and animal maltreatment among their Utah shelter sample. Among their Canadian shelter sample, Barrett and colleagues (2017) found women who reported animal maltreatment by their partner were significantly more likely to report more chronic and severe psychological, physical and sexual victimization than those who reported minimal or no animal maltreatment, even compared to those who did not have companion animals. Finally, in a study of risk factors for severe DV and intimate homicide, animal maltreatment was one of the most significant risk factors identified (Walton-Moss et al., 2005).

One study using a shelter sample of primarily Hispanic American women found a negative relationship between DV severity and animal maltreatment. Hartman and colleagues (2015) found that although respondents who reported animal maltreatment by their partner were significantly more likely to report severe psychological abuse, they were *less* likely to report severe physical DV. To explain the finding, they raise the possibility that cultural differences in affective relationships may make instrumentalizing the abuse of animals to harm human victims less effective in some cultures, and therefore less likely to be employed. Other studies have documented racial/ethnic differences in pet ownership and affective relations with animals (e.g., Brown, 2002; Siegel, 1995); however, small and homogeneous samples have precluded drawing conclusions about the possibility that culture can influence the relationship between animal maltreatment and DV.

Analysis of the Canadian GSS data described earlier (Fitzgerald et al., 2020) also found that animal maltreatment is a significant predictor of DV severity, net of several socio-demographic control variables. Specifically, animal maltreatment is associated with increases in the probability of reporting physical abuse (by 5.2%), injuries (by 16.1%) and fear for one's life (by 24.7%). The proportion of those who identified as white and reported animal maltreatment was higher than those who were non-white; however, statistical significance was not quite reached. Further investigation into potential differences across racial/ethnic groups is needed. Significant differences were found for other socio-demographic groups: animal maltreatment by a partner was more likely to be reported by those who were younger, had a lower income and reported a disability or daily limitation.

## Impact of animal maltreatment on victims/survivors and their children

### *Impact on victims/survivors*

Extensive research has documented the often long-lasting deleterious effects of DV (Bacchus, Ranganathan, Watts, & Devries, 2018; Simmons, Knight, & Menard, 2018) and children's experiences of DV (Howell, Barnes, Miller, & Graham-Bermann, 2016; Vu, Jouriles, McDonald, & Rosenfield, 2016). Much less research has investigated the impact of exposure to animal maltreatment on victims of DV. Animal maltreatment is particularly impactful for victims who have close emotional bonds with their pets and, in turn, many victims report experiencing intense feelings of guilt, rage, hopelessness, fear and grief following incidents of pet abuse (Adams, 1995; Faver & Strand, 2007). For instance, 86.4% of women in Ascione et al.'s (2007) shelter sample reported feeling "terrible" after their pets had been harmed. Similarly, harm to pets has been described as causing terror and intimidation (Flynn, 2000a); psychological trauma (Adams, 1995; Faver & Strand, 2007); anguish (Adams, 1995); and, primarily in cases of coercive sex with animals, humiliation, demoralization and disgust (Adams, 1995; Faver & Strand, 2007). Negative emotional responses are also often experienced by victims who must leave their pets with their abusive partners upon fleeing for their own safety, including worry, concern and fear for their pets as well as guilt and remorse (Faver & Strand, 2007; Flynn, 2000b; Hardesty, Khaw, L., & Ridgway, 2013; Strand & Faver, 2005). For some victims (especially those who experience social isolation), having their pet maltreated or killed is devastating. This was the case for one woman in Fitzgerald's (2005) qualitative study of abused women's experiences with animal maltreatment who overdosed after her kitten was killed. The woman explained, "That cat was my last lifeline, and that was it – I snapped" (Fitzgerald, 2005, p. 121).

Less quantitative research has examined the impact of animal maltreatment on victims, and future research should explore the potential additive and/or interactive effects of concomitant DV victimization and threatened/actual harm to pets on victims and examine other outcomes in addition to emotional and psychological ones. It would also be important to assess whether exposure to different forms of animal maltreatment have differential effects on victims. Such research would provide a greater understanding of the extent to which animal maltreatment impacts victims' well-being and functioning across multiple domains.

## *Impact on children*

Given the strong bond many children have with their pets, experience of threatened or actual harm to their pets can be traumatizing for children. Similar to their mothers' negative emotional responses, children in Ascione et al.'s (2007) shelter sample reported either being "very upset" (59.3%) or "sort of upset" (33.3%) by the animal maltreatment they observed. Similarly, in a qualitative study conducted in a western US state, mothers of children who experienced animal maltreatment and DV indicated that their children "felt extreme emotional distress and/ or experienced negative emotions (e.g., sadness) when coping with maltreatment of their pet" and "responded physiologically to the emotional stress by crying during or after such incidents" (McDonald et al., 2019, p. 2638). Some children become so distressed by the abuse against their pets, they intervene during beatings to protect the animals, often putting themselves in danger (Flynn, 2000a; McDonald & Ascione, 2018; McDonald et al., 2015; McDonald et al., 2019). Given these reactions, it has been recommended that children who have experienced animal maltreatment be assessed for posttraumatic stress disorder (Schaefer, 2007).

When considering children's socioemotional functioning, children in Ascione et al.'s (2007) shelter sample were found to display more symptoms of internalizing and externalizing behaviours than children in the non-shelter sample. McDonald and colleagues (McDonald, Graham-Bermann, Maternick, Ascione, & Williams 2016; McDonald et al., 2016) similarly found that children recruited from shelters who had experienced both DV and animal maltreatment were 3.22 times more likely to exhibit subclinical levels of internalizing and externalizing behaviours and 5.72 times more likely to exhibit clinical levels of these problems compared to children who experienced DV only. Despite this fact, the authors found most children (66%) were resilient and did not display significant levels of symptomatology.

In a second study by McDonald et al. (2018) using the same sample, qualitative descriptions of their experiences with animal maltreatment were compared between children who demonstrated resiliency on the socioemotional functioning measures (i.e., "asymptomatic" children) and children who exhibited some elevated level of socioemotional difficulties (i.e., children with emotional/behavioural difficulties [EBD]). Comparison of themes showed that "Asymptomatic-classified children were exposed to less severe animal-directed violence and threats than were EBD-classified children" (McDonald et al., 2018, p. 361), suggesting that animal maltreatment severity may relate to greater psychological and behavioural problems among DV-exposed children. EBD children also tended to normalize and/or justify the animal maltreatment whereas asymptomatic children did not. This suggests that exposure to animal maltreatment may also influence children's attributions and/or beliefs. Other researchers using this same dataset found that having a positive relationship with their pet reduced the likelihood of developing internalizing problems when controlling for exposure to animal maltreatment (Hawkins et al., 2019).

Lastly, childhood experiences of animal maltreatment can also increase children's risk of perpetrating animal maltreatment (Baldry, 2003; Hawkins, Hawkins, & Williams, 2017; Plant, van Schaik, Gullone, & Flynn, 2016; Volant et al., 2008). Animal maltreatment perpetration prevalence among children in DV samples has ranged from 7% (Flynn, 2000b) to 32% (Ascione, 1998). Given that animal abuse may be a precursor to human-directed violence or part of a larger pattern of antisocial behaviour, children displaying such behaviours should be recommended for treatment (Becker & French, 2004; McPhedran, 2009).

## Animal abuse and help-seeking

It is well documented that leaving an abuser is often a long, multifaceted process for survivors that is influenced by myriad psychological, structural and socio-cultural factors. Survivors' bonds with pets further complicates the relationship termination process, particularly if pets are also the targets of violence by the abuser. In their Canadian shelter samples, Barrett and colleagues (2018) found that controlling for socio-demographic factors, relationship length and physical abuse victimization, women whose pets had been severely physically abused by their partner had a significantly higher number of previous unsuccessful attempts at leaving the relationship compared to women whose pets had not been severely harmed. Further, 56% indicated that concern for their pets prevented them from leaving earlier, and 68% believed their partner's mistreatment of their pets impacted their final decision to terminate the relationship (Barrett et al., 2018). Similarly, a shelter-based survey in New Zealand (n=203) found that 33% remained with their abuser for fear that their pets would be harmed, 40% remained due to challenges accessing safe housing that would accommodate pets and approximately 27% would have left their partner earlier if they did not have a pet (Roguski, 2012). Importantly, the author found that participants who delayed leaving due to concerns for their pets remained in the abusive relationship a median of two years longer than they would have had they not had pets. Recent qualitative studies with both heterosexual (Newberry, 2017) and gender and sexually diverse populations (Rosenberg, Riggs, Taylor, & Fraser, 2020; Taylor, Riggs, Donovan, Signal, & Fraser, 2018) of DV survivors have also documented the powerful role that animal abuse plays in increasing motivation to leave a violent relationship. Concern for the safety and well-being of animal companions often increases one's desire to terminate a violent relationship while simultaneously creating barriers that may hamper this process given that the vast majority of DV shelters do not have pet programmes in place. Researchers have identified numerous barriers to facilitating safe housing for survivors and their pets. Research with US DV service providers conducted by O'Neil Hageman et al. (2018) identified four key challenges: (1) survivors view pets as family members and therefore do not want to leave them behind, (2) there are inconsistencies in screening for pets during assessments and intakes, (3) safety planning for survivors with animal companions is complicated and (4) there is difficulty finding shelters and permanent housing post-shelter that allow pets. Additional barriers identified by Wuerch and colleagues (2017) in their Canadian study include challenges arranging for the transport of animals, difficulty arranging emergency housing for pets outside of regular business hours, the short-term nature of some off-site pet programmes, some programmes requiring vet and/or ownership records, the inability of women and/or DV agencies to pay for placement of animals with facilities that require fees, and a general lack of awareness of available programmes. They also identified barriers specific to rural populations, including confidentiality concerns (i.e., a pet often identifies the survivor in small communities), limited safe housing options for larger animals, the need for protection for a multitude of animals when violence occurs in farming families, and financial dependency of farming families on animals can result in reluctance to report for fear that the animals will be removed.

Quantitative surveys have further underscored a range of barriers to effectively serving victims/survivors and their pets. In a survey of staff at 16 DV shelters in Canada, Stevenson, Fitzgerald and Barrett (2018) found over 75% of staff were aware of women in the community who had refused to come to the shelter because they could not bring their pets, yet 72% of staff indicated their organization had no questions about animals on their intake forms. Further, only one-third of staff (33.6%) stated the shelter they worked at had an official pet policy. Similarly, a national survey of 767 US DV shelters found that 45% enquired about pets during intake and 66% routinely included pets in safety planning, even though 95% of shelter staff had been made aware of pet maltreatment in shelter residents' abusive relationships (Krienert, Walsh, Matthews, & McConkey, 2012).

DV survivors with pets may also be deterred from accessing needed services due to the lack of easily accessible information. Analysis of 337 Canadian emergency DV shelter websites found that 45.9% made any mention of animals/pets (Gray, Barrett, Fitzgerald, & Peirone, 2019). Only 3% explicitly stated that pets were welcome at the shelter, and less than 30% made any direct mention of the possibility of facilitating off-site sheltering services. Moreover, only 35% mentioned pets in the context of safety planning. This is a critical omission, as research with DV survivors with pets has identified numerous complexities that pets can pose in the safety planning process (Collins et al., 2017).

Easily accessible information about support for survivors with pets is critical because isolation is often a tactic used by DV perpetrators. In a study of 503 gender and sexually diverse respondents, DV victims/survivors who reported animal abuse had significantly lower levels of social support (Riggs, Taylor, Fraser, Donovan, & Signal, 2018). For survivors experiencing isolation, pets may be the only form of emotional support available to them. Indeed, numerous studies have documented that survivors often rely on their animal companions for comfort in dealing with their experiences of violence (Newberry, 2017; Rosenberg et al., 2020), with some even crediting their pets with giving them "reason to live" (Fitzgerald, 2007). Service providers have also identified the therapeutic benefits that animal companions afford DV survivors (O'Neil Hageman et al., 2018; Strand & Faver, 2005; Wuerch et al., 2017), leading some providers to conclude that separating women in shelter from their animal companions may be detrimental to survivors' healing (O'Neil Hageman et al., 2018). In a Canadian sample of shelter staff, on average, participants were very supportive of pets being designated as emotional support animals in order to assist abused women, with the number of pets a staff member had during their lifetime being positively associated with increased support (Stevenson et al., 2018).

Although service providers have recognized the therapeutic value to co-housing families fleeing violence with their pets, they have also noted numerous concerns that have impeded the development of on-site co-sheltering programmes. Specific challenges include concerns that such programming may limit the ability to provide services to a greater number of survivors (families with pets may remain in temporary shelter longer due to lack of affordable and available pet-friendly housing), health and safety concerns, animal-specific fears, and possibly triggering survivors who had been traumatized by animals via their abuser (O'Neil Hageman et al., 2018). Financial and spatial barriers to programme development are also common concerns (Krienert et al., 2012). Despite being cognizant of challenges to safely co-housing pets, shelter providers have also identified numerous benefits, including removing the leverage abusers have over their victims, decreasing the likelihood that survivors will prematurely exit the shelter due to pet care concerns and building on the therapeutic effects of the human-animal bond (Stevenson et al., 2018).

## Perpetrators of DV and animal abuse

Although there is extensive literature examining the perpetrators of DV generally, this literature shrinks dramatically when considering concomitant animal abuse. Studies show that perpetrators of DV and animal abuse are predominantly men (Conroy, Burczycka, & Savage, 2019; Flynn, 2001; Gerbasi, 2004). Most of the research addressing the motivations and actions of perpetrators has relied on reports from victims/survivors. One of the few studies of perpetrators surveyed DV offenders (n=307) in batterer intervention programmes and found that their perpetration of animal abuse dramatically outpaced that among the general population of men (41% versus 1.5% respectively; Febres et al., 2014).

In qualitative interviews with 31 male DV perpetrators, Stevenson (2012, 2018) interrogated their relationships with their partners and pets. Participants related motives of control and dominance for their violence against their partners, including explaining that their actions were needed to respond to challenges to their masculinity. By contrast, they frequently described their relationships with companion animals as positive and valuable. Only three of the men shared that, by their own definition, they mistreated their animals. Nearly all the men reported that their companion animals represented a source of unconditional love, trust and support within their conflict-ridden relationship with their partner. Stevenson's (2012, 2018) research illustrates the complicated nexus of DV and animal abuse in relation to the perpetrators of abuse, including that abusers can have positive relationships with animals. This may be related to ownership; all the men considered the animals 'theirs' as opposed to belonging to their partner. Fitzgerald (2005) raised the idea of ownership of the companion animal as a protective factor for the animal, in that abusers are less likely to target something they consider theirs. Another possible explanation for the valued nature of the animals is that the animals supported the men's performance of masculinity, such as having a perfectly obedient dog or being a good provider or father for a companion animal, which are socially encouraged roles for men. Further research into the perceptions of perpetrators and the potential relationship to batterer sub-types is needed.

## Conclusions

Although the body of literature is relatively young, there is now sufficient empirical evidence to suggest that animal abuse and DV commonly co-occur, at least in some national contexts (e.g., Canada, the US). While early studies focused on shelter samples were unable to draw comparisons with the general population, more recent research indicates that the level of animal maltreatment reported by women in DV shelters is significantly greater than that reported among community-based comparison groups. Moreover, recent examination of a representative sample of the Canadian population (i.e., not in DV shelters) has documented not only a relationship between animal maltreatment and DV, but also identified animal maltreatment as a significant predictor of DV severity, injury and fearing for one's life.

There is also now substantial evidence that the presence of pets can impact help-seeking. This research has documented a consistent proportion (one-third to one-half) of participants from shelter samples reporting they delayed leaving their abuser due to concern for their pets' well-being combined with a dearth of services for DV victims'/survivors' pets. One study has provided evidence that those who are at greatest risk of severe DV are also most likely to report they delayed leaving their abuser because of their pets. These findings raise significant safety concerns, which are compounded by findings documenting a desire among human victims/survivors to return to their abuser because the pets are still there. Collectively, this scholarship indicates that while the abuse of pets can be a motivator to leave an abuser, it can also be a deterrent to doing so and an incentive to returning when animals are left behind. Perhaps most troubling, some may never leave an abusive relationship because they cannot escape with their pet. Establishing how common this scenario is poses a methodological challenge and will require sampling outside of DV shelters to ascertain what can be done to mitigate barriers to help-seeking among these individuals.

Other suggestions for future lines of enquiry include pursuing larger, more representative samples to provide better insight into intersectional differences among survivors. This information would be valuable for identifying where services for sheltering the pets of DV victims/survivors are most needed and should be prioritized. Furthermore, research is needed to assess the advantages and disadvantages of the pet programme models that shelters are increasingly implementing, including on-site co-sheltering, off-site fostering, and off-site boarding. Specific questions worth exploring include: what benefits, and drawbacks, do these programmes have for the adult, child and animal victims/survivors of DV? What demands do these programmes place on staff? How does on-site programming impact those at the shelter who do not have pets for various reasons (e.g., allergies, fear, religious reasons)? Are individuals who leave with their pets able to secure long-term housing?

Additional information about perpetrators is also needed to address the following questions: are specific sub-type(s) of abusers more likely to abuse animals? Do motivations for this abuse vary by sub-type of abuser? Might abuser sub-type mediate the observed relationship between animal maltreatment and controlling, frequent and severe DV? Lastly, what is grounding the positive relationship some abusers report having with animals?

These questions notwithstanding, the work done to date is beginning to have applied impacts, including providing empirical support for the need to attend to pets when offering services to human victims/survivors. It has also been used as supportive evidence in favour of legislative interventions (e.g., changes enabling the inclusion of pets in protection orders). Examining the growing body of legal developments and providing an assessment of how they are being employed and whether an ideal model of legal protections exists constitutes another challenge to be tackled.

The most persistent challenge researchers in this area have, however, arguably faced – and continue to face – has not been an empirical one; it is, instead, confronting critiques grounded in the contention that attending to the co-occurrence of animal abuse and DV detracts from the human victims/survivors. We offer four responses to this critique as we close this chapter. First, this is not a zero-sum proposition. Spending time on the intersection of violence against animals and people does not detract from time spent on the human victims/survivors of DV – we see it as doing service to both. Second, as discussed earlier, a large and growing proportion of the population has pets, and most consider them family members. Focusing attention here is therefore not a fanciful expenditure of resources on a small proportion of the population. Third, we suggest that research in this area can, and indeed is, having positive impacts on human victims/survivors. This empirical work has prompted policy and legislative developments to assist human victims/survivors leave abusive relationships and reduce incentives for returning – it is the type of novel work that has been called for. Finally, drawing on intersectional feminist insights about the intersection and interdependence of forms of oppression and victimization, we suggest that attending to the ways animals are also vulnerable to DV perpetrators is not only a necessary part of engendering a greater understanding of the significance and complexities of "multispecies living" (Haraway, 2008, p. 3) – now the norm in many countries – but given that the perpetration of violence does not respect species lines, neither should research. Analyses that are truncated at the species line overlook and undertheorize the socially meaningful relationships people can have with other species, and in so doing can also render understandings of human victimization – particularly DV – incomplete.

## Critical findings

- Perpetration of animal maltreatment by abusive intimate partners is commonly reported in DV shelter samples, and at a rate significantly greater than among those not exposed to DV.
- An increasing number of studies demonstrate a relationship between animal maltreatment and more frequent and severe DV.
- While some studies have found that DV perpetrators score higher on measures of controlling behaviour (as reported by human victims/survivors), a study that disaggregated forms of animal maltreatment found that while victims/survivors perceived animal neglect, emotional animal abuse and threats related to the pets as motivated by a desire to enact power/control by their perpetrator, they did not see physical animal abuse as having this same underlying motivation.
- Studies with DV shelter samples indicate that approximately one-third to two-thirds of survivors report they delayed leaving their abuser out of concern for their pets. Further, there is some evidence that those most likely to delay leaving are those most at risk for severe DV and leaving a pet with an abuser can provide incentive for returning to the relationship.
- Studies have documented significant emotional, psychological and behavioural impacts on women and children who have witnessed animal maltreatment in conjunction with DV.
- While quantitative research indicates that DV perpetrators are significantly more likely to report abusing animals as an adult compared to men in the community, qualitative interviews with perpetrators reveal self-reports of positive relationships with companion animals (primarily those 'owned' by them and not by others in the home).

## Implications for policy, practice and research

- DV shelters should enquire about pets when contacted by victims/survivors and screen for pets during intake.
- Service providers should engage in pet-inclusive safety planning; we suggest that survivors have pet medications and vaccine records secured and accessible, have a way to safely transport pets (e.g., a carrier for cats), and have documentation of ownership and care (e.g., adoption contracts/bill of sale, copies of veterinary bills, pet food receipts).
- DV service providers should have content on their website about animal abuse and DV to reaffirm what the victims/survivors may be experiencing and to flag it for concerned bystanders. It is critical to include information about available pet care resources, and in the absence of programmes, it would be helpful to add the following: (1) a statement for concerned family/friends suggesting that they offer to care for a friend/family member's pet if they are in a position to do so, and (2) organizations in Canada and the US could provide a link to https://safeplaceforpets.org/, a searchable map of DV shelters in Canada and the US that offer pet programmes.

- In all communications, it is important not to frame the abuse of animals as a form of property abuse. Doing so minimizes the relationship people have with their pets and stigmatizes those who delay leaving an abusive relationship due to their pets.
- Ideally, DV shelters should develop an on-site pet programme so that abuse victims/survivors can bring their pets with them, as well as an off-site programme to accommodate pets that cannot be kept on-site, such as large animals. We recommend the allocation of government funding for setting up these programmes (the recent passage of the Pets and Women Safety [PAWS] Act in the US is a step in this direction).
- Given the common co-occurrence of animal maltreatment and DV, cross-reporting between human-focused and animal-focused organizations would be prudent.
- Information about the warning signs of DV should include animal maltreatment (and not just physical animal abuse) as a warning sign. Given the growing body of research documenting a connection between animal maltreatment and DV frequency and severity, it would also be advisable to include animal maltreatment in risk assessments for DV.
- Further development of legislation aimed at assisting DV victims/survivors leave with and protect their pets would be prudent (e.g., the ability to include pets in personal protection orders).

## Notes

1 Pet ownership among particularly vulnerable sub-groups has also been documented. For survivors of IPV in need of housing, rates of animal companionship have ranged from 40% to 92% in US DV shelter samples (Ascione, 1998; Flynn, 2000; Faver & Cavazos, 2007; Simmons & Lehmann, 2007) and 64% in a Canadian shelter sample (Barrett et al., 2017, 2018; Fitzgerald et al., 2019). Animal companions are also common among shelter-seeking homeless populations, with animal companionship reported between 5% and 25% of those without permanent housing (Kerman, Gran-Ruaz, & Lem, 2019).
2 We acknowledge that there is research related to the co-occurrence of animal maltreatment and DV that would likely also be of interest to readers, such as studies of shelter staff and childhood histories of animal abuse among perpetrators of DV; however, due to space constraints we have had to limit our discussion here largely to the contemporaneous co-occurrence of animal maltreatment and DV.

## References

Adams, C. J. (1994). Bringing peace home: A feminist philosophical perspective on the abuse of women, children, and pet animals. *Hypatia, 9*(2), 63–84.

Adams, C. J. (1995). Woman-battering and harm to animals. In C. J. Adams & J. Donovan (Eds.), *Animals and women: Feminist theoretical explorations* (pp. 55–84). Durham, NC: Duke University Press.

Allen, M., Gallagher, B., & Jones, B. (2006). Domestic violence and the abuse of pets: Researching the link and its implications in Ireland. *Practice, 18*(3), 167–181. doi:10.1080/09503150600904060

American Pet Products Association. (2017). *Pet industry market size & ownership statistics.* Retrieved from www.americanpetproducts.org/press_industrytrends.asp

Ascione, F. (1998). Battered women's reports of their partner's and their children's cruelty to animals. *Journal of Emotional Health, 1*, 119–133.

Ascione, F., Weber, C., Thompson, T., Heath, J., Maruyama, M., & Hayashi, K. (2007). Battered pets and domestic violence: Animal abuse reported by women experiencing intimate violence and by nonabused women. *Violence Against Women, 13*, 354–373.

Bacchus, L. J., Ranganathan, M., Watts, C., & Devries, K. (2018). Recent intimate partner violence against women and health: A systematic review and meta-analysis of cohort studies. *BMJ Open, 8*(7), e019995. doi:10.1136/bmjopen-2017-019995

Baldry, A. C. (2003). Animal abuse and exposure to interparental violence in Italian youth. *Journal of Interpersonal Violence, 18*(3), 258–281.

Barnett, O. W. (2000). Why battered women do not leave, part 1: External inhibiting factors within society. *Trauma, Violence, and Abuse, 1*(4), 343–371.

Barnett, O. W. (2001). Why battered women do not leave, part 2: External inhibiting factors- social support and internal inhibiting factors. *Trauma, Violence, and Abuse, 2*(1), 3–35.

Barrett, B. J., Fitzgerald, A., Peirone, A., Stevenson, R., & Cheung, C. H. (2018). Help-seeking among abused women with pets: Evidence from a Canadian sample. *Violence and Victims, 33*(4), 604–626. doi:10.1891/0886–6708.VV-D-17–00072

Barrett, B. J., Fitzgerald, A. J., Stevenson, R., & Cheung, C. H. (2017). Animal maltreatment as a risk marker of more frequent and severe forms of intimate partner violence. *Journal of Interpersonal Violence.* doi:10.1177/0886260517719542

Barrett, B. J., & St. Pierre, M. (2011). Variations in women's help seeking in response to intimate partner violence. Findings from a Canadian population-based study. *Violence Against Women, 17*(1), 47–70. doi:10.1177/1077801210394273

Becker, F., & French, L. (2004). Making the links: Child abuse, animal cruelty and domestic violence. *Child Abuse Review, 13*(6), 399–414.

Brown, S. E. (2002). Ethnic variations in pet attachment among students at an American school of veterinary medicine. *Society & Animals, 10,* 249–266.

Caman, S., Kristiansson, M., Granath, S., & Sturup, J. (2017). Trends in rates and characteristics of intimate partner homicides between 1990a and 2013. *Journal of Criminal Justice, 49,* 14–21.

Canadian Pet Market Outlook. (2014). *Canadian pet market outlook, 2014.* Retrieved from Rockville, MD.

Carlisle-Frank, P., Frank, J., & Nielsen, L. (2004). Selective battering of the family pet. *Anthrozoos, 17,* 26–42.

Centers for Disease Control and Prevention. (2019). *Preventing intimate partner violence.* Retrieved from www.cdc.gov/violenceprevention/intimatepartnerviolence/fastfact.html

Collins, E. A., Cody, A. M., McDonald, S. E., Nicotera, N., Ascione, F. R., & Williams, J. H. (2017). A template analysis of intimate partner violence survivors' experiences of animal maltreatment: Implications for safety planning and intervention. *Violence Against Women, 24*(4), 452–476. doi:10.1177/1077801217697266

Collins, E. A., Cody, A. M., McDonald, S. E., Nicotera, N., Ascione, F. R., & Williams, J. H. (2018). A template analysis of intimate partner violence survivors' experiences of animal maltreatment: Implications for safety planning and intervention. *Violence Against Women, 24*(4), 452–476. doi:10.1177/1077801217697266

Conroy, S., Burczycka, M., & Savage, L. (2019). *Family violence in Canada: A statistical profile, 2018.* Ottawa, ON: Juristat, Canadian Centre for Justice Statistics.

DeGue, S., & DiLillo, D. (2009). Is animal cruelty a "red flag" for family violence? Investigating co-occurring violence toward children, partners, and pets. *Journal of Interpersonal Violence, 24,* 1036–1056. doi:10.1177/0886260508319362

Dutton, M. A., & Goodman, L. A. (2005). Coercion in intimate partner violence: Toward a new conceptualization. *Sex Roles, 52,* 743–756. doi:10.1007/s11199-005-4196-6

Faver, C. A., & Cavazos Jr, A. M. (2007). Animal abuse and domestic violence: A view from the border. *Journal of Emotional Abuse, 7*(3), 59–81. doi:10.1300/J135v07n03-04

Faver, C. A., & Strand, E. B. (2003). To leave or to stay? Battered women's concern for vulnerable pets. *Journal of Interpersonal Violence, 18,* 1367–1377.

Faver, C. A., & Strand, E. B. (2007). Fear, guilt, and grief: Harm to pets and the emotional abuse of women. *Journal of Emotional Abuse, 7*(1), 51–70.

Febres, J., Brasfield, H., Shorey, R. C., Elmquist, J., Ninnemann, A., Schonbrun, Y. C., & Stuart, G. L. (2014). Adulthood animal abuse among men arrested for domestic violence. *Violence Against Women, 20,* 1059–1077. doi:10.1177/1077801214549641

Fitzgerald, A. J. (2005). *Animal abuse and family violence: Researching the interrelationships of abusive power.* Lewistown, NY: Mellen.

Fitzgerald, A. J. (2007). "They Gave Me a Reason to Live": The protective effects of companion animals on the suicidality of abused women. *Humanity & Society, 31*(4), 355–378.

Fitzgerald, A. J., Barrett, B. J., Gray, A., & Cheung, C. H. (2020). The connection between animal abuse, emotional abuse, and financial abuse in intimate relationships: Evidence from a nationally representative sample of the general public. *Journal of Interpersonal Violence.* doi:10.1177/0886260520939197

Fitzgerald, A. J., Barrett, B. J., Shwom, R., Stevenson, R., & Chernyak, E. (2016). Development of the partner's treatment of animals scale. *Anthrozoös, 29*(4), 611–625.

Fitzgerald, A. J., Barrett, B. J., Stevenson, R., & Cheung, C. H. (2019). Animal maltreatment in the context of intimate partner violence: A manifestation of power and control? *Violence Against Women, 25*(15), 1806–1828. doi:10.1177/1077801218824993

Flynn, C. P. (2000a). Battered women and their animal companions: Symbolic interaction between human and nonhuman animals. *Society and Animals, 8*, 99–127. doi:10.1163/156853000511032

Flynn, C. P. (2000b). Women's best friend: Pet abuse and role of companion animals in the lives of battered women. *Violence Against Women, 6*, 162–177. doi:10.1177/10778010022181778

Flynn, C. P. (2001). Acknowledging the "zoological connection": A sociological analysis of animal cruelty. *Society & Animals, 9*(1), 71–87.

Gerbasi, K. C. (2004). Gender and nonhuman animal cruelty convictions: Data from pet-abuse.com. *Society & Animals, 12*(4), 359–365.

Gray, A., Barrett, B. J., Fitzgerald, A., & Peirone, A. (2019). Fleeing with Fido: An analysis of information communication via Canadian domestic violence shelter websites. *Journal of Family Violence, 34*(4), 287–298. doi:10.1007/s10896–018–0023-z

Haden, S. C., McDonald, S. E., Booth, L. J., Ascione, F. R., & Blakelock, H. (2018). An exploratory study of domestic violence: Perpetrators' reports of violence against animals. *Anthrozoös, 31*, 337–352. doi: 10.1080/08927936.2018.1455459

Haraway, D. (2008). *When species meet.* Minneapolis, MN: Minnesota University Press.

Hardesty, J., Khaw, L., & Ridgway, M. (2013). Coercive control and abused women's decisions about their pets when seeking shelter. *Journal of Interpersonal Violence, 28*(13), 2617–2639.

Hartman, C. A., Hageman, T., Williams, J. H., & Ascione, F. R. (2015). Intimate partner violence and animal abuse in an immigrant-rich sample of mother – Child dyads recruited from domestic violence programs. *Journal of Interpersonal Violence*, 1–18. doi:10.1177/0886260515614281

Hawkins, R. D., Hawkins, E. L., & Williams, J. M. (2017). Psychological risk factors for childhood non-human animal cruelty: A systematic review. *Society & Animals: Journal of Human-Animal Studies, 25*(3), 280–312. https://doi.org/10.1163/15685306-12341448

Hawkins, R. D., McDonald, S. E., O'Connor, K., Matijczak, A., Ascione, F. R., & Williams, J. H. (2019). Exposure to intimate partner violence and internalizing symptoms: The moderating role of positive relationships with pets and animal cruelty exposure. *Child Abuse and Neglect, 98*, Article 104166. doi:10.1016/j.chiabu.2019.104166

Howell, K. H., Barnes, S. E., Miller, L. E., & Graham-Bermann, S. A. (2016). Developmental variations in the impact of intimate partner violence exposure during childhood. *Journal of Injury & Violence Research, 8*(1), 43–57. doi:10.5249/jivr.v8i1.663

Ingraham, C. (2019, April 5). Dog owners are much happier than cat owners, survey finds. *Washington Post.* Retrieved from www.washingtonpost.com/business/2019/04/05/dog-owners-are-much-happier-than-cat-owners-survey-finds/?noredirect=on&utm_term=.2f37f4eb714b

Johnson, M. P. (2008). *A typology of domestic violence: Intimate terrorism, violent resistance, and situational couple violence.* Boston, MA: Northeastern University Press.

Kerman, N., Gran-Ruaz, S., & Lem, M. (2019). Pet ownership and homelessness: A scoping review. *Journal of Social Distress and Homelessness, 28*(2), 106–114. doi:10.1080/10530789.2019.1650325

Krienert, J. L., Walsh, J. A., Matthews, K., & McConkey, K. (2012). Examining the nexus between domestic violence and animal abuse in a national sample of service providers. *Violence and Victims, 27*(2), 280–296. doi:10.1891/0886-6708.27.2.280

McDonald, S. E., Cody, A. M., Collins, E. A., Stim, H., Nicotera, N., Ascione, F. R., & Williams, J. H. (2018). Concomitant exposure to animal abuse and socioemotional adjustment among children exposed to intimate partner violence: A mixed methods study. *Journal of Child & Adolescent Trauma, 11*(3), 353–365. https://doi.org/10.1007/s40653-017-0176-6

McDonald, S. E., Collins, E. A., Maternick, A. M. S., Nicotera, N., Graham-Bermann, S., Ascione, F. R., & Williams, J. H. (2019). Intimate partner violence survivors' reports of their children's exposure to companion animal maltreatment: A qualitative study. *Journal of Interpersonal Violence, 34*(14), 2627–2652. doi:10.1177/0886260516689775

McDonald, S. E., Graham-Bermann, S., Maternick, A., Ascione, F., & Williams, J. H. (2016). Patterns of adjustment among children exposed to intimate partner violence: A person-centered approach. *Journal of Child and Adolescent Trauma, 9*(2), 137–152. doi:10.1007/s40653-016-0079-y

McDonald, S. E., Shin, S., Corona, R., Maternick, A., Graham-Bermann, S., Ascione, F., & Williams, J. H. (2016). Children exposed to intimate partner violence: Identifying differential effects of family environment on children's trauma and psychopathology symptoms through regression mixture models. *Child Abuse & Neglect, 58*, 1–11. doi:10.1016/j.chiabu.2016.06.01

McDonald, S. E., Collins, E. A., Nicotera, N., O'Hageman, T., Ascione, F. R., Williams, J. H., & Graham-Bermann, S. A. (2015). Children's experiences of companion animal maltreatment in households characterized by intimate partner violence. *Child Abuse & Neglect, 50,* 116–127. doi:10.1016/j. chiabu.2015.10.005

McPhedran, S. (2009). Animal abuse, family violence, and child wellbeing: A review. *Journal of Family Violence, 24,* 41–52. doi:10.1007/s10896-008-9206-3

Newberry, M. (2017). Pets in danger: Exploring the link between domestic violence and animal abuse. *Aggression and Violent Behavior, 34*(5), 273–281. doi:10.1016/j.avb.2016.11.007

O'Neil Hageman, T., Langenderfer-Magruder, L., Greene, T., Williams, J. H., St. Mary, J., McDonald, S. E., & Ascione, F. R. (2018). Intimate partner violence survivors and pets: Exploring practitioners' experiences in addressing client needs. *Families in Society: The Journal of Contemporary Social Services, 99*(2), 134–145. doi:10.1177/1044389418767836

Pence, E., & Paymar, M. (1993). *Education groups for men who batter: The Duluth model.* New York, NY: Springer.

People Magazine. (2019, May 21). *Russell Wilson working to protect both people and their pets from domestic violence.* Kelli Bender. Retrieved from https://people.com/pets/russell-wilson-banfield-foundation-domestic-violence-pets/

Plant, M., van Schaik, P., Gullone, E., & Flynn, C. (2016). It's a dog's life: Culture, empathy, gender, and domestic violence predict animal abuse in adolescents: Implications for societal health. *Journal of Interpersonal Violence, 34*(1), 2110–2137. doi:10.1177/0886260516659655

Riggs, D., Taylor, N., Fraser, H., Donovan, C., & Signal, T. (2018). The link between domestic violence and abuse and animal cruelty in the intimate relationships of people of diverse genders and/or sexualities: A binational study. *Journal of Interpersonal Violence.* Advance online publication. doi: 10.1177/0886260518771681

Roguski, M. (2012). *Pets as pawns: The co-existence of animal cruelty and family violence.* Prepared for the Royal New Zealand Society for the Prevention of Cruelty to Animals and The National Collective of Independent Women's Refuges. Retrieved from http://nationallinkcoalition.org/wp-content/uploads/2013/01/DV-PetsAsPawnsNZ.pdf

Rosenberg, S., Riggs, D. W., Taylor, N., & Fraser, H. (2020). 'Being together really helped': A Australian transgender and non-binary people and their animal companions living through violence and marginalization. *Journal of Sociology.* Advanced on-line publication. doi:10.1177/1440783319896413

Sauve, J., & Burns, M. (2009). Residents of Canada's abused shelters for women, 2008. *Juristat, 29.*

Schaefer, K. D. (2007). Cruelty to animals and the short- and long-term impact on victims. *Journal of Emotional Abuse, 7*(3), 31–57. doi:10.1080/10926798.2007.10766831

Siegel, J. M. (1995). Pet ownership and the importance of pets among adolescents. *Anthrozoos, 8,* 217–223.

Simmons, C. A., & Lehmann, P. (2007). Exploring the link between pet abuse and controlling behaviors in violent relationships. *Journal of Interpersonal Violence, 22*(9), 1211–1222. doi:10.1177/0886260507303734

Simmons, S. B., Knight, K. E., & Menard, S. (2018). Long-term consequences of intimate partner abuse on physical health, emotional well-being, and problem behaviors. *Journal of Interpersonal Violence, 33*(4), 539–570. doi:10.1177/0886260515609582

Stark, E. (2007). *Coercive control: How men entrap women in personal life.* New York: Oxford University Press.

Stevenson, R. (2012). *Pets, intimate partner violence, and the abuser's perspective* (MA Thesis). University of Ottawa, Ottawa, Ontario.

Stevenson, R. (2018). *Men's voices: Masculinities, companion animals, and intimate relationships* (PhD dissertation). University of Windsor, Windsor, ON.

Stevenson, R., Fitzgerald, A., Barrett, B. J., & Cheung, C. (2018). Keeping pets safe in the context of intimate partner violence: Insights from domestic violence shelter staff in Canada. *Affilia: Journal of Women and Social Work, 33*(2), 236–252. doi:10.1177/0886109917747613

Strand, E. B., & Faver, C. A. (2005). Battered women's concerns for their pets: A closer look. *Journal of Family Social Work, 9*(4), 39–58. doi:10.1300/J039v09n04_04

Taylor, N., Riggs, D., Donovan, C., Signal, T., & Fraser, H. (2018). People of diverse genders and/or sexualities caring for and protecting animal companions in the context of domestic violence. *Violence Against Women, 25*(9), 1096–1115. doi:10.1177/1077801218809942

Volant, A. M., Johnson, J. A., Gullone, E., & Coleman, G. J. (2008). The relationship between domestic violence and animal abuse: An Australian study. *Journal of Interpersonal Violence, 23*(9), 1277–1295. doi:10.1177/0886260508314309

Vu, N. L., Jouriles, E. N., McDonald, R., & Rosenfield, D. (2016). Children's exposure to intimate partner violence: A meta-analysis of longitudinal associations with child adjustment problems. *Clinical Psychology Review, 46,* 25–33. doi:10.1016/j.cpr.2016.04.003

Walker, L. E. (1979). *The battered woman*. New York, NY: Harper & Row.

Walton-Moss, B. J., Manganello, J., Frye, V., & Campbell, J. C. (2005). Risk factors for intimate partner violence and associated injury among urban women. *Journal of Community Health, 30*(5), 377–389. doi:10.1007/s10900-005-5518-x

Wuerch, M. A., Giesbrecht, C. J., Price, J. A. B., Knutson, T., & Wach, F. (2017). Examining the relationship between intimate partner violence and concern for animal care and safekeeping. *Journal of Interpersonal Violence*. Advance on-line publication. doi:10.1177/0886260517700618

# 22

# TRANSNATIONAL MARRIAGE ABANDONMENT

## A new form of domestic violence and abuse in transnational spaces

*Sundari Anitha, Anupama Roy and Harshita Yalamarty*

### Introduction

This chapter addresses the issue of domestic violence and abuse within transnational spaces by focusing on the abandonment of wives as a form of domestic violence against women who marry across national borders. Transnational marriage abandonment has been recently recognised as a form of domestic violence following activism by feminist organisations. This chapter draws from our 2013–16 study conducted in India and the existing research and policy developments on this emerging theme in South Asia, Canada, Australia, England and Wales, to outline the specificity of this form of violence and its implications for understanding violence against women through the lens of intersectionality.

### What is transnational marriage abandonment?

The experience of transnational migration has been seen as a risk factor for domestic violence, which is exacerbated by factors including language barriers and social isolation (Williams & Yu, 2006). The difficulties of women facing domestic violence are heightened by the challenges of migration, and immigration sometimes shapes the nature and impact of the violence and abuse (Anitha, 2011; Erez, Adelman, & Gregory, 2009). Structural barriers such as immigration regulations, lack of access to housing, welfare benefits and right to work impedes migrant women's capacity to leave an abusive relationship; and have been scrutinised in relation to diverse jurisdictions such as the US (Raj & Silverman, 2002; Clark, 2007), Canada (Henderson, Thurston, & Roy, 2014; Okeke-Ihejirika et al., 2018; Alaggia, Regehr, & Rishchynski, 2009; Abraham & Tastsoglou, 2016; Shirwadkar, 2004), Australia (Ghafournia, 2011; Odhiambo-Abuya, 2003) and member states of the European Union (Hagemann-White, 2008). For those who migrate for the purpose of marriage without appropriate documentation, precarious immigration status exacerbates power differentials between the resident spouse and the marriage migrant, thereby increasing women's vulnerability to abuse and barriers to help-seeking, leaving women with limited options (Vishnuvajjala, 2012; Salcido & Adelman, 2004).

In many countries, marriage migrants whose immigration status is dependent on their spouse, which is often the case in the first few years of the marriage, are at risk of destitution and deportation if their marriage breaks down. In the UK, prior to 2002, marriage migrants abandoned following domestic violence were routinely deported to their country of origin, often to face further abuse from their families for not 'making the marriage work'. Following campaigns from women's organisations in the UK, the Labour government passed the Domestic Violence Rule in 2002 making it possible for a woman to apply for Indefinite Leave to Remain (ILR) in the UK *if she could prove that her marriage had broken down because of domestic violence*. However, women with insecure immigration status were prohibited from accessing public funds, resulting in many women being unable to be accommodated in refuges as the refuge provider was not entitled to claim the costs associated with providing accommodation. This rule also left women destitute while they were expected to apply for ILR (Anitha, 2011) as they were not eligible to claim welfare benefits. Southall Black Sisters (SBS) and allied organisations campaigned to change this, resulting in the Destitute Domestic Violence (DDV) Concession of 2010, which gives women access to limited support in the UK in the form of housing and welfare benefits while they apply for secure immigration status (SBS, 2010). In April 2017, after concerted campaigns, Canada announced the elimination of Conditional Permanent Residence (2012), which compelled sponsored spouses or partners of Canadian citizens and permanent residents to live with their sponsor for two years to keep their permanent resident status – a condition which could force them to stay in abusive situations.

Research indicates that for women who have migrated as dependent spouses, these barriers persist despite the existence of formal provisions such as self-petitioning under the Violence Against Women Act (VAWA) in the case of the US, the DDV Concession in the UK and similar provisions in Australia and Canada, due to the restrictive nature of concessions or high evidential requirements. Statements made by politicians, media representations about migrants as well as state immigration policies create a hostile environment towards migrants which perpetrators utilise to control their foreign national wives – who may be unaware of their rights – with threats of deportation and separation from children (Anitha, 2011; Gray, Easteal, & Bartels, 2014).

In the context of increasing provisions for marriage migrants experiencing domestic violence, activists and researchers have begun to document a growing form of violence and abuse that enables perpetrators to bypass these provisions by crossing national borders. Abandonment of wives is a form of violence and abuse that takes place in transnational marriages whereby the resident spouse – usually the husband – deliberately abandons his wife across national borders in order to deprive her of her financial and other rights.

In our research (Anitha, Roy, & Yalamarty, 2016, 2018a, 2018b), we found that there are three main contexts within which abandonment in transnational marriages takes place:

1 A woman migrates upon marriage to join her husband in another country and is subjected to a period of neglect, abuse and exploitation, following which she is thrown out of the marital home under risk of being deported to her country of origin; or less commonly, leaves to escape violence and abuse.
2 Following marriage migration and abuse, the woman is taken back to her country of origin either coercively or deceptively (e.g., on the pretext of a holiday) and abandoned there while the husband returns and revokes her visa.
3 After marrying a local woman, a visitor from another country returns to his country of residence with assurances to sponsor his wife's spouse visa without any intention to do so. The woman is left in her natal home or with her in-laws and is eventually thrown out or leaves because of domestic violence.

Manavi, a South Asian women's organisation in the US, first highlighted this problem by drawing upon their organisational experience, and argued that abandonment "constitutes an emerging face of violence against women, both by its intent and effect" (Rudra & Dasgupta, 2011, p. 7). Though subsequent research has largely focused on South Asia, different dimensions of this problem are beginning to be explored among other diasporic communities. For example, Liversage (2013) studied the power of sponsoring husbands within the Turkish community in Denmark, who married women from Turkey but dispossessed or divorced them before the period to acquire a residency permit elapsed, forcing the women to return to Turkey. Focusing on the transnational abandonment of Moroccan children, De Bree, Storms, and Bartels (2011) document how men withhold passports and resident permits from their wives and children while in Morocco, and return to the Netherlands alone. Existing research indicates that such abandonment is a gendered problem; there is little evidence from research and case law of similar forms of abandonment of male marriage migrants.

The problem of abandonment of wives by non-resident husbands has come to be recognised by government agencies in India, following media attention to this problem (Kahol, 2012; Kumar, 2018; Singh, 2006; Westhead, 2009). In 2008, the Indian government nominated the National Commission for Woman (NCW) to respond to issues pertaining to Non-Resident Indian (NRI)[1] marriages. The NCW estimates that this problem affects approximately 25,000 women, suggesting that two out of ten transnational marriages end in abandonment (NCW, 2011). Media reports and anecdotal accounts from women's organisations in the West (Rudra & Dasgupta, 2011), exploratory studies based on surveys and interviews with affected women in India (Jabbi, 2005) and scholarship based on analysis of case law in India (Bhattacharjee, 2013; Kapur, 2019; Lodhia, 2010) suggests that this is a growing problem. This chapter draws upon the limited scholarship on this issue in recent years, and presents the findings of our first ever systematic study on this issue.

## Our study

Our study explored the nature and patterns of abuse and abandonment in transnational marriages, and documented women's experience of the legal and judicial apparatus in the UK and India in their quest for justice. Conducted between 2013 and 2016, it drew upon life-history interviews with 57 abandoned wives in Delhi, Punjab and Gujarat, states in India which have a long history of outward-migration to the UK and other countries in the West. Most participants were accessed through police, women's/community organisations and lawyers, while others were accessed through snowball sampling. Additionally, semi-structured interviews were also conducted with a purposive sample of 21 practitioners including lawyers, representatives of women's organisations and police officers engaged with this issue in India and the UK. Twenty-eight of the 57 women we interviewed had been married to UK residents, eight to men resident in Italy, and four each to men resident in Australia and USA, and the remainder to men from other countries. About two-fifths of the women we interviewed had migrated after marriage while the rest stayed in India with their in-laws while they awaited a spousal visa.

## Histories of violence and abuse

Transnational abandonment of women encompasses a range of violence including physical and sexual violence, economic abuse and denial of reproductive rights, which are commonly documented forms of domestic violence, as well as specific aspects of abuse such as purposive immobilisation.

Most of the women we interviewed reported a hastily arranged marriage, exchange of dowry and lavish celebrations, all paid for by the bride's family. In the case of transnational marriages, the gendered imbalances in the norms that govern marriage negotiations between the two families (Dube, 2001) are exacerbated by global hierarchies and time constraints. Men and their families took advantage of these circumstances to negotiate the most advantageous marriage, while women and their families had limited opportunities to minimise the risk, as they would normally do in a local marriage.

## Neglect, violence and abuse

Soon after the marriage, about a quarter of the research participants realised that their husband had agreed to the marriage because of parental pressure. If the men had prior romantic relationships that their family considered unsuitable, the arranged marriage served to preserve the status of their family within their community. Often, the men had negotiated with their families to continue their prior heterosexual, or in three cases, same-sex relationships. The women's role was that of a domestic servant and care giver for elderly relatives.

> Soon after I came here, I realised that the marriage was a sham. He stayed away from home for days at a time. When I questioned him, he said, "You are nothing to me. I married you for my parents, your job is to look after them." When I complained to his parents, they said it was up to me to make him want to stay at home.
>
> (Bina, 26)[2]

In all cases – whether or not the men were pressurised into the marriage – the men and often their families acted purposively to control and dominate the women to secure benefits from these relationships. They used a combination of surveillance, degradation and isolation to exercise coercive control, with devastating effects on women's individual liberty, agency and autonomy (Stark, 2007, p. 131). They controlled the women's appearance, restricted their movement, prevented them from speaking to their family or monitored calls to their family, and restricted their access to money (Chaudhuri, Morash, & Yingling, 2014), thereby isolating women from any sources of support.

While all women were subjected to coercive control, about three-quarters of the research participants – both women who had migrated following marriage and those who were left behind with their in-laws – also experienced physical violence. Fifteen women faced physical violence from their husbands only, 11 from their in-laws only, while 16 women were subjected to physical abuse from both their husbands and his relatives. This corroborates research on domestic violence in South Asia and the South Asian diaspora which indicates that the perpetrators of domestic violence can also include members of the husband's family (Kandiyoti, 1988; Fernandez, 1997; Gangoli & Rew, 2011). In line with findings from previous studies, we found that perpetrators exploited migrant women's unfamiliarity with the sources of support available in other countries. State immigration policies exacerbate the power imbalance in these relationships and become part of the matrix of control that enables abuse to continue (Anitha, 2011; Menjivar & Salcido, 2002; Thiara, 2010).

One of the respondents, a 29-year-old woman from Gujarat who had been brought to Kenya after her marriage, recounted her experiences:

> His harassment escalated over the months. Eventually, I told him, "Now our relationship is about to come to an end. You get me a ticket for India and give me back my

passport which you have hidden somewhere." At this, he started beating me in the presence of our landlord. I was very frightened. I went to his friend for help but he told me, "You can't go anywhere. You are staying here illegally; they (police) will put you in jail straightaway." I learnt that he had not brought me there as his wife but as a visitor. The time limit for my stay was over, so I was in deep trouble. . . . When he came home, he beat me badly that night. He threatened me, "If I cut you into pieces and bury you, no one will know about it." From his behaviour, I felt that he was capable of killing me. Over the next few months the beatings continued, even escalated. I knew that I was staying there illegally. So, I didn't know what to do.

(Shiva, 29)

Where women lived with their in-laws in India, social norms against divorce and gender norms, which dictate that married women have no place in their parents' home, created a context where in-laws were able to subjugate the women and abuse them with impunity.

## Financial abuse: exploitation of domestic labour and paid work

A common form of abuse – one that is often underexplored in research on domestic violence – was the exploitation of women's unpaid and paid labour (Anitha, 2019; Sharp-Jeffs, 2017). In keeping with the gendered expectations about domestic work within all societies, all the women interviewed accepted their responsibility for domestic labour after marriage, and had indeed been socialised into such a role. What they did not expect was that this would be their only or primary role following marriage, in a context where they were not treated with the affection, reciprocity or familiarity accorded to family members.

About two weeks after our wedding, the domestic servant who used to clean and sweep the house was asked to give up that work. I had to sweep and mop the floor, remove the curtains daily and dust them. The ceiling fans, windows and doors had to be cleaned daily. After all this work, if my mother-in-law found any dust anywhere, she would shout at me and rebuke me. At times, she wouldn't give me anything to eat, or just give stale, leftover food or only chappati (bread). I . . . was not allowed to enter the kitchen, a bottle of water was kept for me outside. I was like this full-time maid who never had any days off, never had to be paid.

(Manju, 31)

Many women also recounted systematic humiliation designed to erode their sense of self – including being barred from parts of the house, having separate and inferior plates and cups reserved for their use. In keeping with the subordinate status accorded to domestic servants, a majority of women who were left with their in-laws were prohibited from using certain furniture, denied adequate food and lodgings (e.g., bed, warm clothes), denied medical care (Wittenburg, 2008) and restricted within the family home, whether by being physically locked in their rooms or within the house, or by taking away their means to communicate with their family or friends outside the house. The small minority of marriage migrants and women who lived in cities in India and undertook paid work were deprived of any control over their earnings or the hours they worked. Women initially tolerated this abuse and exploitation, as they expected to eventually migrate and join their husbands or hoped that the abuse would diminish over time. Having little access to or understanding of the visa process, it was much later that many women who were left in India realised that their husbands had never intended to sponsor them.

## *Dowry abuse*

Dowry was an important factor that contributed to the abuse. Dowry is the transfer of money, jewellery or goods to the groom's family from the family of the bride at the point of the wedding and beyond. The giving and taking of dowry is prohibited under the Dowry Prohibition Act 1961 and Sections 304B and 498A of the Indian Penal Code but continues to be a common practice. Demand for dowry where the bride's family is unable to meet the requirement is a significant (but not the sole) factor in violence against wives in India (Rastogi & Therly, 2006; Rudd, 2001). Not all women experience dowry as a repressive practice and some may consider dowry their rightful share of their parents' wealth, in a context where daughters do not commonly inherit property. However, dowry is a practice that simultaneously reflects and reinforces the devaluation of women. In transnational marriages, dowry serves to subsidise global capital, where it becomes an investment in the husband's education or business (Palriwala & Uberoi, 2008, p. 39).

The women in our study reported demands for dowry immediately before the wedding. For some it continued afterwards. All women reported the theft of dowry upon abandonment. Many research participants reported that their dowry was used to fund men's migration process, higher education or business ventures abroad. Women's parents often incurred debts to make payments to enhance men's financial security in their country of residence, expecting their daughters to join the men at a later date. Once they were entitled to secure immigration status, some men initiated ex parte divorce proceedings. While deception was a common means of securing additional dowry payments in the first few months following the marriage, consistent with other research findings (Bloch & Rao, 2002), threats were also utilised purposefully and strategically to extract payments.

> He started threatening me, saying, "Give me Rs.20 lakhs (£20,000) to open a restaurant here, then I will bring you to Germany. Otherwise I will divorce you."
>
> (Sharanjit, 28)

In a few cases, meticulous planning and careful strategising enabled men's families to secure a dowry. One woman from a poor family in a small town in Gujarat recounted the circumstances of her marriage:

> He contacted us in response to an [matrimonial] ad my father had put out in a newspaper. He was good looking, had a good job in a hotel in a Gulf state, so we decided to proceed. Their main condition was that the marriage would have to take place in their native town because his mother was too ill to travel – my dad was a bit hesitant but they said they would host the ceremony [a highly unusual offer in a context where the bride's family hosts and pays for the wedding]. So we agreed. When we reached groom's house with our extended family, we did not see any sign of celebrations there. They informed us that their uncle was on his death bed, he could die any day now. It would have to be a simple affair, out of respect for him. So, next day, we went to a temple and performed the ceremony, and I moved into my husband's place. Even the neighbours did not know about our marriage! I later found out from the neighbours that he had married twice earlier under similar circumstances. He soon left India and his sister-in-law took the gold that I got as dowry – since there were no wedding expenses, my parents had given me a dowry that was larger than would have otherwise been the case.
>
> (Arti, 36)

Over the coming months, continued harassment by her in-laws compelled Arti to return to her natal home. After a few months, she made her way to her husband's country of residence to salvage her marriage but faced domestic violence. She returned home and is now seeking the return of her dowry through the legal process.

This systematic and purposeful dowry abuse took place alongside other forms of violence (Anitha et al., 2018b) within the marriage in the case of most women we interviewed. However, a few women's narratives indicate that the sole purpose of the marriage was to extract dowry and few other aspects of marriage, such as the establishment of a conjugal home together, were ever intended to be realised. In these cases, the men and their families absconded with the dowry, leaving their 'wives' to live with the social stigma and the liminal status attached to an abandoned woman in the Indian context.

## Sexual violence and denial of reproductive rights

A third of the women reported a continuum of sexual coercion (Kelly, 1988) whereby their husband determined whether or not there were sexual relations in the marriage, and when, where and how sex took place.

> In the beginning, my husband hardly ever came home at night. He used to tell me that he had to work two to three shifts. Later, when he did come home, we used to be in the same room but he would be . . . watching horror films. I used to get frightened by such films . . . but he would pressurise me to watch and indulge in sexual acts as seen in the films. A few months later, when he went to parties, he would come back with his girlfriend. If I questioned him, he would just laugh it off. His parents never said anything to him about this. When I saw all this I was truly depressed.
>
> (Asha, 38)

Where men had been pressurised into the marriage and did not show any interest in pursuing a relationship with their wife, women were blamed by their in-laws and in some cases, were pressurised to become pregnant, in the belief that this would change men's attitude towards them.

> He never stayed at home – he was out most nights, and I thought, maybe he was with someone else. I refused to have any relations with him, but his parents wanted a grandchild. He complained to his mother, "It seems that this girl does not like me. She does not even allow me to touch her!" When my mother-in-law talked to me about it, I told her, "We haven't even spoken to each other properly yet. How can we have any relations with each other?" After that, one night when I came home from work, my mother-in-law gave me food and milk to drink and I fell asleep. I don't know what happened, what was in it, but when I got up in the morning, I found bite marks on my shoulders, breast, neck, thighs and stomach. I had pain all over my body and in my stomach. I called out but no one was home. When I called up my husband, he told me that he had (sexual) relations with me.
>
> (Chandni, 35)

The collusion of the mother-in-law in drugging her made this rape a particularly traumatic experience for Chandni. A third of the women were denied their reproductive rights:

11 women were coerced to undergo abortions and eight were pressurised to get pregnant. Consistent with previous research (Campbell, Garcia-Moreno, & Sharps, 2004; Jasinski, 2004), women reported that both verbal and physical violence escalated during pregnancy.

> As soon as I got pregnant, he started saying, "We have to have a son. If you have a daughter I will give you a divorce, that's that, and send you back."
>
> (Satinder, 34)

Although research universally associates pregnancy with the escalation of existing abuse, in our study this seemed to be particularly prevalent where women were pregnant with a female child. The preference for sons derives in part from cultural practices like dowry that create economic disincentives for having daughters. Analysing female 'deficit' in the sex ratios, Sen (1990) argues that this is a consequence of sex-selective abortions and the gender-biased allocation of resources leading to lower survival rates of girls in India. Socio-logical evidence also points to a continued preference for sons among some diasporic South Asian communities (Purewal, 2003), including among Punjabi Canadians (Mucina, 2018; Srinivasan, 2018).

Women left with their in-laws were also vulnerable to sexual harassment/violence from men in the husband's family, as they were perceived to have lost the protection that derives from the husband's claim to exclusive sexual access. Thirteen women recounted ongoing sexual harass-ment, primarily from their father-in-law. One woman, who was left with her in-laws in Gujarat for several years while her husband returned to the US, recounted:

> My father-in-law began coming to the room where I used to sleep with my son to watch me sleeping. When he began to touch me, I used to get up and get angry. Once, I even slapped him. When I told my husband about it, he did not believe me. Instead, he threatened me. Then I told my mother-in-law, and she said, "Are you going to disgrace your god-like father-in-law?". . . . My parents were not able to accommodate me. I had my own room at my in-laws' place, so I found a way out – I started sleeping with my bedroom locked.
>
> (Okhaben, 42)

This kind of abuse from other men in the family, and the lack of support from their hus-bands, compelled some women to leave the in-laws' home. Women often returned to their natal homes for a period of respite; but they also renewed their efforts to migrate abroad and establish their conjugal family lives with their husbands.

## *The deception and violence of abandonment*

Despite the violence they suffered, most women sought to keep their marriages intact. They tried to placate their husband and in-laws through silence and avoidant behaviour and lived with what they deemed an 'acceptable level' of violence. Socio-cultural norms against divorce made it very difficult for women to leave abusive relationships.

For marriage migrants, the vulnerabilities arising from insecure immigration status limited their options. In the context of some countries, including the UK, Canada and the USA, which have introduced entitlements for immigrant women who experience domestic violence, men have taken recourse to restrictive immigration policies that operate across transnational spaces to treat their wives as disposable women. Hira, who belonged to a middle class peasant family in rural Gujarat and migrated to the UK following marriage to a highly educated man, reported:

> He often used to hit me. He would tell me that he had much better girls to choose from. After three years like this, we came to India for a holiday. . . . After two to three days, he left me at my mother's place. We had return tickets – we were planning to go back together after two months. But he phoned me and said he was returning to the UK that very night and I should come back later. I was surprised, but I thought, he must have got some new project at work. We all went to the airport to see him off and he left. Later on, he suggested that I stay on to attend English classes so I could pass some exams that I was planning to take in the UK, so I extended my return ticket. It was only later that I realised that he was waiting for my visa to expire. As soon as the deadline passed, he called to say he was going to divorce me.
>
> (Hira, 32)

Of the 23 research participants who migrated upon marriage, 16 were taken back to India and abandoned and their visa revoked, thus depriving them of their right to be represented in any divorce proceedings in the country where the man resided, to claim financial settlement or secure the return of dowry. Abandonment across transnational borders meant that women were unable to initiate any criminal proceedings against the men for domestic violence, and unable to claim the rights to settlement to which they were entitled in some countries. Of the 34 women who were left with their in-laws, a majority were eventually thrown out, or less commonly, fled the marital home when the violence became unbearable. Once other options such as mediation were exhausted, some women also sought criminal sanctions against their husbands and/or in-laws, but to no avail. Men and their families were able to dominate, abuse and exploit women, secure in the knowledge that the women would not be protected by the legal frameworks in India and across transnational spaces.

## Impact of abandonment and access to justice for transnationally abandoned women

The impact of abandonment documented in several studies and in media reports include difficulty in securing employment, women's financial dependence on their natal families where they may be considered a burden, loss of relationships with extended family and friends, a detrimental impact on the social standing of their family, and the loss of good marriage prospects of younger sisters (Anitha et al., 2018a; Bajpai, 2013; Lodhia, 2010; Stewart, 2013). Women abandoned in their country of origin are often left at risk of poverty and destitution, social stigma, shame, a loss of status, and domestic abuse. In a context where marriage remains the primary marker of social status and identity for women, abandoned women have limited means of living independently or undertaking paid work, particularly in rural areas. In the absence of formal divorce proceedings, women are left in a legal limbo (Kapur, 2019) and lack the option of securing their future by marrying again in a context where the only socially acceptable position for a woman is under the 'protection' of a father, husband or son (Gandhi, Bhasin, Mander, & Jha, 2016). Our study also documented how the loss of dowry upon abandonment and having to return to their parental home placed some women in a precarious position as a potential threat to the inheritance of their brothers (Anitha et al., 2018b).

> Things are not easy here – all I can say is that I stay here. But my brother tells me all the time that I should give up my share in my father's property. My father possesses two

houses and receives a considerable pension. But my brother says he will look after me and get my daughter married only if I renounce my inheritance. If I give up my right and my relations with my brother and his wife deteriorate, where will I go.

(Jasma, 38)

Studies based on analysis of case law (Bhattacharjee, 2013; Lodhia, 2010; Kapur, 2019) reveal the difficulties women face in securing an equitable financial settlement, regular maintenance for children or the return of their dowry. Due to inadequate transnational legal mechanisms, some women are also separated from their children who are retained by the father in his country of residence. While the European Convention on Human Rights (ECHR) enables women abandoned by spouses resident in Council of Europe member states to access some remedies (Jahangir, Anitha, Patel, & Handa, 2016), these rights elude abandoned women who often lack the financial means to access legal advice and representation. Kapur (2019) draws attention to the interplay of factors including the breakdown of traditional social institutions, globalisation, and gendered policy frameworks which shape the unique nature of challenges experienced by transnationally abandoned women. Beyond the deprivation of meaningful access to family law and child custody laws, the realities and consequences of transnational abandonment require us to recognise not just that these patterns of desertion are often accompanied by other forms of abuse as noted by Lodhia (2010, pp. 735–736), but that abandonment in transnational marriages itself constitutes a form of domestic violence and abuse (Anitha et al., 2018a).

## Conceptualising transnational marriage abandonment as domestic violence and abuse

The issue of transnational marriage abandonment sheds light on violence against women in transnational spaces and thereby broadens the lens through which domestic violence and abuse is understood by drawing attention to the power asymmetries at local and transnational contexts. The gendered inequalities within the institution of marriage are exacerbated by the geopolitical inequalities, whereby the groom's family is able to command resources and mobility through access to state and legal institutions. Gender intersects with disadvantages arising from the relative poverty of women's families, state immigration policies and bordering regimes to create conducive contexts for violence (Kelly, 2016). Transnational mobility associated with the husband's 'flexible citizenship' leads to a corresponding disentitlement of the abandoned wife.

In the West, abandonment within the context of marriage is generally not considered a form of violence against women. However, in the case of transnational marriages, abandonment is embedded within a pattern of domestic violence and coercive control exercised over the woman and is intended to deprive her rights. Research shows that beyond the various processes of control and individual acts of harm that lead to and outlast the act of abandonment in transnational marriages, abandonment itself constitutes a form of violence against women. It is rooted in and results in gendered devaluation of women and is enabled by gender-blind transnational formal-legal frameworks, which construct abandoned women as an inferior class of citizens and as a category of women who can be abused and exploited with impunity.

## Recent steps towards recognition of and redress for transnational marriage abandonment

Recently, the first steps have been taken in recognising transnational marriage abandonment as a form of domestic violence and abuse. Following our study and campaigning by Southall Black

Sisters and lawyers working in the area of international family law, the family justice system in England and Wales have recognised this issue through its amended Practice Direction 12J, which came into effect from 2 October 2017. PD12J sets out what the Family Court should do in cases where it is alleged/admitted, or there is other reason to believe, that the child or a party has experienced or is at risk of domestic violence or abuse. The definition of domestic abuse is thereby expanded to incorporate "dowry-related abuse and transnational marriage abandonment" and that

> 'abandonment' refers to the practice whereby a husband, in England and Wales, deliberately abandons or 'strands' his foreign national wife abroad, usually without financial resources, in order to prevent her from asserting matrimonial and/or residence rights in England and Wales. It may involve children who are either abandoned with, or separated from, their mother.
>
> (Practice Direction 12J, 2010, para 3)

This extension of the definition of domestic abuse has important implications for abandoned women's access to Legal Aid. In February 2019, the Court of Appeal (A (Children) Re [2019] EWCA Civ 74) utilised PD12J to successfully overturn a fact-finding judgement in private law proceedings to set out the law in respect of transnational marriage abandonment and recognised the many ways in which a spouse is prevented from returning to the UK. This is a significant development, but further changes are needed within the family justice system, to child protection mechanisms where women are abandoned with or following separation from their children, to the immigration system and in frontline practice to ensure that women's rights in national and international law are realised.

These recent measures represent the beginning of policy recognition of this issue in one jurisdiction, though this problem arguably effects women in transnational marriages across the world. In a context where justice evades the vast majority of victims of transnational marriage abandonment, addressing these issues will require a range of mechanisms in local, national and transnational arenas including domestic violence services which cater to the particular vulnerabilities and needs of migrant women. However, it is only by addressing the very structures, including gender-blind bordering regimes, that enhance women's vulnerabilities that a lasting solution can be found. We urgently need better protection of women's human rights within and across national boundaries. Not only will this enable perpetrators to be held to account, it will also help dismantle the structures and processes because of which some men perceive transnational wives as disposable women whose abuse is not a matter of concern.

## Conclusion

The gendered phenomenon of transnational marriage abandonment highlights the erosion of nation-state boundaries in the emergence of violence against women in transnational spaces. Recent scholarship in this emerging area of research documents South Asian women's experiences of abandonment in transnational marriages, whereby men resident in countries in the global north exercise violence, deception, and coercive and controlling behaviour to abandon their wives across national borders in order to deprive them of their rights. Gender-blind transnational formal-legal mechanisms combine with hostile bordering regimes operated by countries in the global north to exacerbate gendered power differentials between a resident and a migrant spouse to create conducive contexts for such violence and impede any remedies for the abandoned women. We are at the very early stages of recognising transnational marriage abandonment as a form of domestic violence and abuse and there is an urgent need for further research in order to gather evidence that will drive subsequent activist efforts and make the case for policy change.

## Acknowledgements

Our study was funded by British Academy (PM120051). We would like to thank Nalini Trivedi (Ahmedabad Women's Action Group) and Anjali Chahal for their help with the data collection.

## Critical findings

- Abandonment within the context of marriage is not commonly considered a form of violence against women. In the case of transnational marriages, an emerging body of research, including our study, documents how abandonment is embedded within a pattern of domestic violence and coercive control over women which gets exacerbated by the power asymmetries that operate in transnational contexts. This study focuses on the manner in which these asymmetries unfold in contexts where women are abandoned by their husbands in their countries of origin.
- Disadvantages arising from gender inequalities, global hierarchies between nations, relative poverty of women's families compared to their transnationally resident husband, immigration policies and bordering regimes intersect to create conducive contexts for new forms of domestic violence and abuse. The transnational mobility enjoyed by husbands undermines the protection afforded to the abandoned wife by national laws and her access to international protection.
- As documented in existing research, men resident in countries in the global north are able to exercise violence, deception, and coercive and controlling behaviour to abandon their wives across national borders with impunity. By strategically abandoning the wife in her home country and then filing for divorce in the men's country of residence, transnationally mobile men can make it almost impossible for their wives to participate in legal proceedings to secure rights including financial settlement, maintenance and in some cases contact with children. The impact of abandonment also creates contexts for further forms of violence against women due to the stigma associated with divorce, women's vulnerability within natal families and issues related to inheritance and residence arrangements within the natal home after divorce.
- Research indicates that, beyond the various processes of control and individual acts of harm that lead to and outlast the act of abandonment in transnational marriages, abandonment itself constitutes a form of violence against women. It is rooted in and results in gendered devaluation of women and is enabled by gender-blind transnational formal-legal frameworks, which construct abandoned women as subordinate citizens.

## Implications for policy, practice and research

- Transnational marriage abandonment represents what was hitherto a hidden facet of domestic violence and abuse affecting transnationally married women. Specific forms of domestic violence and abuse enacted across national borders has been hitherto invisible from the practice and policy communities which are based in particular countries and have not been equipped to recognise forms of violence against women in transnational spaces. This issue has considerable implications for practitioners working to support marriage migrants experiencing domestic violence. The policies that grant residence rights to immigrant women on the basis of the domestic violence they have experienced in various jurisdictions are effectively evaded by abusive men and their families through transnational marriage abandonment.

- Awareness of this problem and the nature and forms of abandonment can enable effective pro-active support from services. For example, the period when a woman is in her husband's country of residence and in contact with services because of the domestic violence she is facing represents a crucial window of opportunity for making her aware of the very real risk of abandonment. This is also the opportunity to alert her to the risk of appropriation of her dowry. Any documentary evidence of her dowry might be crucial to any legal proceedings at a later date. However, recovery of women's dowries remains difficult in many jurisdictions including England and Wales in the context of the lack of recognition of dowry as a special form of pre-marital asset (Patel, Handa, Anitha, & Jahangir, 2016). In case of abandonment in the UK, returning before her visa has been revoked often represents her best chance of availing the Destitute Domestic Violence Concession. Both the passage of time, and abandonment with her child(ren) – in contrast to abandonment which entails separation from her child(ren) – creates particularly difficult contexts for obtaining justice and security. Where a woman has been separated from her children in the process of abandonment, Article 8 of the Human Rights Act 1998 (Right to respect for your family and private life) has previously been invoked to secure her rights (Jahangir et al., 2016) in the UK. However, this is a complicated area of law, and few remedies exist in other jurisdictions (Bhattacharjee, 2013; Lodhia, 2010; Kapur, 2019).
- The recognition of transnational marriage abandonment as a form of domestic abuse through the recent amendment to Practice Direction 12J in England and Wales opens up the possibility of Legal Aid, as well as other avenues for abandoned women. However, these are the first steps in what needs to be a package of policy measures at the national level and within transnational mechanisms to protect women's human rights.
- There is also an urgent need for more research on the problem of transnational marriage abandonment in other jurisdictions, and among marriage migrants from different countries. It is important to document the commonalities in the forms of abuse that result from the exacerbation of gender inequalities by bordering regimes as well as any specificities in the nature and manifestations of domestic violence and abuse that arise in different contexts.

## Notes

1 A Non-Resident Indian (NRI) is a citizen of India who holds an Indian passport and has temporarily emigrated to another country. However, in popular parlance, NRI denotes any person of Indian origin who lives in another country, which is how this term is used here.
2 All names have been changed to protect women's identities and a pseudonym has been allocated to each woman in accordance with regional and religion-specific naming conventions.

## References

Abraham, M., & Tastsoglou, E. (2016). Addressing domestic violence in Canada and the United States: The uneasy co-habitation of women and the state. *Current Sociology, 64*(4), 568–585.

Alaggia, R., Regehr, C., & Rishchynski, G. (2009). Intimate partner violence and immigration laws in Canada: How far have we come? *International Journal of Law and Psychiatry, 32*(6), 335–341.

Anitha, S. (2011). Legislating gender inequalities: The nature and patterns of domestic violence experienced by South Asian women with insecure immigration status in the United Kingdom. *Violence Against Women, 17*(10), 1260–1285.

Anitha, S. (2019). Understanding economic abuse through an intersectional lens: Financial abuse, control and exploitation of South Asian women's productive and reproductive labours. *Violence Against Women, 25*(15), 1854–1877.

Anitha, S., Roy, A., & Yalamarty, H. (2016). *Disposable women: Abuse, violence and abandonment in transnational marriages: Issues for policy and practice in the UK and India.* Lincoln: University of Lincoln. Accessible at http://eprints.lincoln.ac.uk/20091

Anitha, S., Roy, A., & Yalamarty, H. (2018a). Gender, migration, and exclusionary citizenship regimes: Conceptualizing transnational abandonment of wives as a form of violence against women. *Violence Against Women, 24*(7), 747–774.

Anitha, S., Roy, A., & Yalamarty, H. (2018b). Changing nature and emerging patterns of domestic violence in global contexts: Dowry abuse and the transnational abandonment of wives in India. *Women's Studies International Forum, 69*, 67–75.

Bajpai, A. (2013). Across the high seas: Abuse, desertion, and violence in transnational marriages in India, *Violence Against Women, 19*(10), 1246–1262.

Bhattacharjee, S. (2013). Distant silences and default judgments: Access to justice for transnationally abandoned women. *University of Pennsylvania Journal of Law and Social Change, 16*(1), 95.

Bloch, F., & Rao, V. (2002). Terror as a bargaining instrument: A case study of dowry violence in rural India. *American Economic Review, 92*(4), 1029–1043.

Campbell, J., Garcia-Moreno, C., & Sharps, P. (2004). Abuse during pregnancy in industrialized and developing countries. *Violence Against Women, 10*(7), 770–789.

Chaudhuri, S., Morash, M., & Yingling, J. (2014). Marriage migration, Patriarchal bargains and wife abuse: A study of South Asian women, *Violence Against Women, 20*(1), 121–161.

Clark, M. B. (2007). Falling through the cracks: The impact of VAWA 2005's unfinished business on immigrant victims of domestic violence. *University of Maryland Law Journal of Race, Religion, Gender and Class, 7*(1), 37–57.

De Bree, J., Storms, O., & Bartels, E. (2011). In between the Netherlands And Morocco: 'Home' and belonging of Dutch Moroccan return migrant and abandoned children in Northeast Morocco. In S. Evers, C. Notermans, & E. van Ommering (Eds.), *Not just a victim: The child as catalyst and witness of contemporary Africa* (pp. 173–195). Leiden: Brill.

Dube, L. (2001). On the construction of gender: Socialization of Hindu girls in patrilineal India. In *Anthropological explorations in gender: Intersecting fields* (pp. 87–118). New Delhi: Sage.

Erez, E., Adelman, M., & Gregory, C. (2009). Intersections of immigration and domestic violence: Voices of battered immigrant women. *Feminist Criminology, 4*(1), 32–56.

Fernandez, M. (1997). Domestic violence by extended family members in India: Interplay of gender and generation. *Journal of Interpersonal Violence, 12*(3), 433–455.

Gandhi, K., Bhasin, A., Mander, H., & Jha, R. (2016). Living single: Being a single woman in India. In Centre for Equity Studies (Ed.), *India exclusion report 2015* (pp. 165–188). New Delhi: Yoda Press.

Gangoli, G., & Rew, M. (2011). Mothers-in-laws against daughters-in-laws: Domestic violence and legal discourses around mother-in-law violence against daughters-in-law in India. *Women's Studies International Forum, 34*, 420–429.

Ghafournia, N. (2011). Battered at home, played down in policy: Migrant women and domestic violence in Australia. *Aggression and Violent Behavior, 16*(3), 207–213.

Gray, L., Easteal, P., & Bartels, L. (2014). Immigrant women and family violence: Will the new exceptions help or hinder victims? *Alternative Law Journal, 39*(3), 167–171.

Hagemann-White, C. (2008). Measuring progress in addressing violence against women across Europe. *International Journal of Comparative and Applied Criminal Justice, 32*(2), 149–172.

Henderson, R. I., Thurston, W. E., & Roy, A. (2014). Systematic violence and immigrant women having escaped domestic abuse: Meaningfully reducing structural barriers to leaving intimate partner and familial violence. In M. Taylor, J. A. Pooley, & R. Taylor (Eds.), *Overcoming domestic violence: Creating a dialogue around vulnerable populations* (pp. 87–104). New York, NY: Nova Science Publishers.

Jabbi, M. (2005). *A diagnostic study of wives deserted by NRIs.* New Delhi: Council for Social development. Retrieved from www.jeywin.com/wp-content/uploads/2009/12/A-Diagnostic-Study-of-Wives-Deserted-by-NRIs.pdf

Jahangir, S., Anitha, S., Patel, P., & Handa, R. (2016). Emerging issues for international family law. Part 2: Possibilities and challenges to providing effective legal remedies in cases of transnational marriage abandonment. *Family Law Journal, 46*(11), 1352–1356.

Jasinski, J. L. (2004). Pregnancy and domestic violence: A review of the literature. *Trauma, Violence, & Abuse, 5*(1), 47–64.

Kahol, V. (2012, May 30). Punjab govt cracks down on NRI grooms who abandon brides. *India Today.* Retrieved from www.indiatoday.in/india/story/punjab-govt-cracks-down-on-nri-grooms-who-abandon-brides-103900-2012-05-30

Kandiyoti, D. (1988). Bargaining with patriarchy. *Gender and Society, 2,* 274–290.

Kapur, S. (2019). Holiday brides and policy concerns: The perils of being in "no-man's" land. *Gender and Women's Studies, 2*(3), 2.

Kelly, L. (1988). *Surviving sexual violence.* Cambridge: Polity Press.

Kelly, L. (2016, March 1). The conducive context of violence against women and girls. *Discover Society, 30.* Retrieved from https://discoversociety.org/2016/03/01/theorising-violence-against-women-and-girls/

Kumar, C. (2018, February 5). One NRI wife calls home for help every 8 hours – Times of India. *The Times of India.* Retrieved from https://timesofindia.indiatimes.com/nri/other-news/one-nri-wife-calls-home-for-help-every-8-hours/articleshow/62782501.cms

Liversage, A. (2013). Gendered struggles over residency rights when Turkish immigrant marriages break up. *Onati Socio-Legal Series, 3*(6), 1070–1090.

Lodhia, S. (2010). Brides without borders: New topographies of violence and the future of law in an era of transnational citizen-subjects. *Columbia Journal of Gender and Law, 19*(3), 703–746.

Menjivar, C., & Salcido, O. (2002). Immigrant women and domestic violence: Common experiences in different countries. *Gender & Society, 16*(6), 898–920.

Mucina, M. K. (2018). Exploring the role of "honour" in son preference and daughter deficit within the Punjabi diaspora in Canada. *Canadian Journal of Development Studies/Revue canadienne d'études du développement, 39*(3), 426–442.

NCW (National Commission for Women). (2011). Issues relating to NRI marriages. In *Proceedings of a seminar.* Delhi: National Commission for Women and Ministry of Overseas Indian Affairs. Retrieved from http://ncwapps.nic.in/pdfReports/Background_Note_Seminar_Issues_Relating_to_NRI_Marriages.pdf

Odhiambo-Abuya, E. E. (2003). The pain of love: Spousal immigration and domestic violence in Australia a regime in chaos. *Pacific Rim Law Policy Journal, 12*(3), 673–708.

Okeke-Ihejirika, P., Yohani, S., Muster, J., Ndem, A., Chambers, T., & Pow, V. (2018). A scoping review on intimate partner violence in Canada's immigrant communities. *Trauma, Violence, & Abuse.* doi:10.1177/1524838018789156

Palriwala, R., & Uberoi, P. (2008). Exploring the links: Gender issues in marriage and migration. In R. Palriwala & P. Uberoi (Eds.), *Marriage, migration and gender* (pp. 23–63). New Delhi: Sage.

Patel, P., Handa, R., Anitha, S., & Jahangir, S. (2016). Emerging issues for international family law. Part 3: Transnational marriage abandonment and the dowry question. *Family Law Journal, 46*(12), 1443–1449.

Practice Direction 12j. (2010). *Child arrangements & contact orders: Domestic abuse and harm.* Retrieved from www.justice.gov.uk/courts/procedure-rules/family/practice_directions/pd_part_12j

Purewal, T. (2003). Re-producing South Asian Wom(b)en: Female feticide and the spectacle of culture. In N. Puwar & P. Raghuram (Eds.), *South Asian women in the diaspora* (pp. 137–156). New York, NY: New York University Press.

Raj, A., & Silverman, J. (2002). Violence against immigrant women: The roles of culture, context, and legal immigrant status on intimate partner violence. *Violence Against Women, 8*(3), 367–398.

Rastogi, M., & Therly, P. (2006). Dowry and its link to violence against women in India: Feminist psychological perspectives. *Trauma, Violence & Abuse, 7,* 66–77.

Rudd, J. (2001). Dowry-murder: An example of violence against women. *Women's Studies International Forum, 24*(5), 513–522.

Rudra, U., & Dasgupta, S. D. (2011). *Transnational abandonment of South Asian women: A new face of violence against women.* Manavi. Retrieved from www.scribd.com/document/105885203/Transnational-Abandonment-of-South-Asian-Women-A-New-Face-of-Violence-against-Women-Rudra-Dasgupta

Salcido, O., & Adelman, M. (2004). "He has me tied with the blessed and damned papers": Undocumented-immigrant battered women in Phoenix, Arizona. *Human Organization, 63,* 162–172.

Sen, A. (1990). More than 100 million women are missing. *The New York Review of Books, 37*(20), 61–66.

Sharp-Jeffs, N. (2017). *Money matters: Research into the extent and nature of financial abuse within intimate relationships in the UK.* London: Co-operative Bank.

Shirwadkar, S. (2004). Canadian domestic violence policy and Indian immigrant women. *Violence Against Women, 10*(8), 860–879.

Singh, K. (2006, February 8). Hopes fade for Punjab's holiday brides. *The Times of India.* Retrieved from https://timesofindia.indiatimes.com/india/Hopes-fade-for-Punjabs-holiday-brides/articleshow/1406914.cms

Southall Black Sisters. (2010, July 16). *Victory on no recourse to public funds.* [Web Log Post]. Retrieved from https://southallblacksisters.org.uk/news/victory-on-no-recourse-to-public-funds/

Srinivasan, S. (2018). Transnationally relocated? Sex selection among Punjabis in Canada. *Canadian Journal of Development Studies/Revue canadienne d'études du développement, 39*(3), 408–425.

Stark, E. (2007). *Coercive control: The entrapment of women in personal life.* New York, NY: Oxford University Press.

Stewart, A. (2013). Abuse, danger, and security in transnational marriages: Polity and community in India and the United Kingdom. *Violence Against Women, 19*(10), 1263–1281.

Thiara, R. K. (2010). Continuing control: Child contact and post separation violence. In R. K. Thiara & A. K. Gill (Eds.), *Violence against women in South Asian communities: Issues for policy and practice* (pp. 156–181). London: Jessica Kingsley Publishers.

Vishnuvajjala, R. (2012). Insecure communities: How an immigration enforcement program encourages battered women to stay silent. *Boston College Journal of Law Social Justice, 32*(1), 185–214.

Westhead, R. (2009, November 15). Lost brides: When arranged marriages go quickly awry. *Toronto Star.* Retrieved from www.thestar.com/news/world/2009/11/15/lost_brides_when_arranged_marriages_go_quickly_awry.html

Williams, L., & Yu, M-K. (2006). Domestic violence in cross-border marriage – A case study from Taiwan. *International Journal of Migration, Health and Social Care, 2*(3/4), 58–69.

Wittenburg, V. (2008). *The new bonded labour? The impact of proposed changes to the UK immigration system on migrant domestic workers* (Report). London: Kalayaan and Oxfam.

# 23

# TECHNOLOGY-ASSISTED ABUSE WITHIN INTIMATE RELATIONSHIPS

*Karlie E. Stonard*

## Introduction

Advancements in technology and the availability of the Internet has created numerous types of cyberspaces (e.g. social networking sites (SNS), chatrooms, etc.) as well as new methods of digital communication facilitated by the use of smartphones (e.g. instant messenger, video chat, etc.) allowing us to develop and maintain social and interpersonal relationships using such tools. While such technologies provide us with instant, accessible and affordable methods of communication, they have also brought risks in terms of providing a new method in which abusive behaviour within intimate relationships can occur. Drawing on published research this chapter aims to provide an overview of the role technology plays in intimate partner violence (IPV). Consideration will be given to the nature, prevalence and impact of technology-assisted abuse within intimate relationships, including the role that gender plays in such experiences. The chapter will be organised in two main sections, focusing on technology-assisted IPV that occurs in adult intimate relationships and that which occurs within adolescent romantic relationships. Finally, the implications of the research reviewed will be discussed in terms of policy, practice and research.

## Technology-assisted abuse in adult intimate relationships

IPV in adult relationships is often referred to as domestic violence or abuse and may include elements of stalking and harassment. While traditionally understandings of IPV has focused on physical, psychological, emotional, sexual and financial forms of abusive and controlling/coercive behaviour (Home Office, 2012), research has recognised that IPV may also be communicated digitally (Dragiewicz et al., 2019; Duerksen & Woodin, 2019; Harris & Woodlock, 2019; Woodlock, 2014). Unlike the government definition of domestic violence in England, the definition of stalking includes the use phone calls as a method through which stalking behaviours can be experienced (Home Office, 2011), while definitions of cyberstalking recognise a broader range of technologies such as email and other computer-based communication tools that can be used to monitor, threaten, insult or harass a person (including a current/former intimate partner), as well as infect an individual's computer with viruses (Southworth, Finn, Dawson, Fraser, & Tucker, 2007). The term obsessive relational intrusion has been used to define the unwanted pursuit of intimacy through the repeated invasion of a person's sense of physical or symbolic privacy (Spitzberg & Hoobler, 2002). Additionally, 'technology-facilitated stalking' (Woodlock, 2017), 'digital coercive control' (Harris & Woodlock, 2019), 'technological IPV' (Duerksen & Woodin, 2019) and 'technology-facilitated coercive control' (Dragiewicz et al., 2019) have been used to refer to the use of digital media to control and abuse intimate partners/ ex-partners within the context of IPV. For the purpose of this chapter, the term technology-assisted IPV will be used.

## Nature of abusive, coercive and controlling behaviours

Drawing on rational actor theory, Frisby and Westerman (2010) found that partners who had dominating conflict styles preferred computer-mediated channels of control such as text messaging, phones, instant messenger, SNS and emails, due to the proximity such methods offered, the technological advantages of convenience and because they offered opportunities for immediate contact with a partner by any means necessary in order to exert their control. Technology therefore offers many opportunities for access to a victim, in addition to a lack of deterrence due to its hidden nature.

Technology-assisted IPV has been described as being unique due to its spacelessness, meaning this method of abuse transcends fixed spatial boundaries and borders (Harris, 2018; Harris & Woodlock, 2019). As a result of this, perpetrators are able to contact, harass, abuse, control and monitor their victims 24 hours a day, seven days a week, instantly, from a distance, and repetitively, both during the relationship and after it has ended (Woodlock, 2014, 2017). Southworth et al.'s (2007) seminal paper describes the use of a broad range of technologies in intimate partner stalking including cordless and cellular telephones, fax machines, email, global positioning systems (GPS), spyware, keystroke logging hardware, video/hidden cameras, caller identification, calling cards, computer and Internet technology, and online databases. A recent study by Dragiewicz et al. (2019) reported that the most commonly described technology-assisted IPV behaviours were repetitive texting, emailing, stalking and harassment via Facebook, as well as abusers using cloud-based storage (e.g. iCloud and Google) and GPS data and devices as a method to monitor a partner.

Woodlock (2014) reports on findings from the SmartSafe Project in Australia that explored the use of technology in IPV and stalking using surveys with 152 IPV professionals and 46 victims/survivors. Woodlock (2014) found three main ways that perpetrators were using technology to facilitate their stalking including causing fear, having an omnipresence (e.g. through using GPS tracking devices/software and monitoring social media accounts) and punishing and humiliating (e.g. by publicly shaming women, often in sexualised ways). Omnipresence was described as enabling perpetrators to create the sense that they are present in every aspect of the victim's life meaning the victim had no privacy, security or sense of safety, and served to isolate victims further (Woodlock, 2014, 2017). Perpetrators threatened to share sexualised content online to humiliate the victim (Woodlock, 2017), which may result in victims becoming targets of revenge porn and harassment by others.

The use of technology in IPV can be used in combination with physical, psychological, sexual and financial abuse and control offline (George & Harris, 2014; Harris & Woodlock, 2019; Southworth et al., 2007; Woodlock, 2014). Indeed, Dragiewicz et al. (2019) emphasise that the use of technology by abusers has become interwoven within the pattern of IPV, comprised of numerous controlling, abusive, threatening and violent tactics. It is therefore argued that technology-assisted IPV is an extension of offline violence (Harris & Woodlock, 2019). In research with young adults, it was found that involvement in technology-assisted IPV increased the odds of offline IPV (Marganski & Melander, 2018). Traditional IPV perpetration has also been reported to predict technology-assisted IPV perpetration (Duerksen & Woodin, 2019). The co-occurrence of technology-assisted IPV has also been noted. For example, 35.8% of female and 26.5% of male university students in Spain reported being a victim and a perpetrator of technology-assisted IPV at the same time (Villora, Yubero, & Navarro, 2019a, 2019b).

Southworth et al. (2007) provide some examples of the use of technology in IPV and stalking from news stories and anecdotal experiences of victims in the United States (US). One example describes how a man murdered his former girlfriend after using a caller ID service to track her down, while another describes how a woman's violent husband killed her following her plan to escape to a new home after he found a deleted email that she had sent to a friend asking for help moving. These examples highlight how technology can provide perpetrators of IPV with an extensive range of tools that can be used to monitor and control a current or former intimate partner, as well as highlighting the intrusiveness of technology-assisted IPV and its devastating impact. Leaving an abusive partner does not ensure that the abusive behaviour will desist and in fact the level of technology-assisted IPV can increase. For example, all of the survivors interviewed by Dragiewicz et al. (2019) reported technology-assisted IPV began or escalated at separation. This is a crucial factor that may deter victims from leaving an abusive relationship as the perpetrator can stay connected through digital devices (Dimond, Fiesler, & Bruckman, 2011).

## *Prevalence*

A number of studies have documented the prevalence of technology-assisted IPV as being substantial, and recognised its diverse nature among both young adults and adults. It is worth noting however, that due to the increased availability and development of both digital devices and technological capabilities, seeking to measure prevalence is challenging. Woodlock (2014) identified that 97% of 152 professionals working with victims of IPV reported that perpetrators used technology to stalk women, with mobile phones being the most commonly reported device used followed by social media (such as Facebook), email and GPS tracking. This was echoed in a later study in which 98% of practitioners reported this knowledge (Woodlock, McKenzie, Western, & Harris, 2019). Depending on the behaviour measured, 6–78% of victims reported some form of technology-facilitated IPV ranging from a partner/ex-partner contacting them via a mobile/text message to call them names, harass them or put them down (78%), to a partner/ex-partner giving their children a phone/device as a way of creating further opportunities to contact them against their wishes (6%) (Woodlock, 2014). George and Harris (2014) similarly highlighted that the most commonly reported technology-assisted IPV behaviour by survivors was receiving frequent and repeated abusive messages, voice calls and harassment via their social media profiles. Harris and Woodlock (2019) contend that technology-assisted IPV must be considered as a form of gendered violence, that effects women disproportionally compared to men. However, at times research has reported mixed findings regarding gender differences in experiences of technology-assisted IPV. That is not to say however, that experiences of violence are not very different for females compared to males, as evidenced in feminist perspectives of IPV (Dobash & Dobash, 1979; Walker, 1989; Ylló & Bograd, 1990).

In their study of 804 undergraduates in the US, Burke, Wallen, Vail-Smith and Knox (2011) found that half of both females and males reported the use of technology to monitor partners, either as the perpetrator or victim. A range of monitoring or controlling behaviours were examined including sending excessive emails or making excessive phone calls; checking call and email histories; checking phone bills; monitoring partner's Facebook accounts;

making inappropriate Facebook postings/posting inappropriate pictures; using a GPS device, a webcam, hidden camera or spyware to monitor partners; and using partners' passwords to monitor them. Although both sexes reported a considerable amount of technology-assisted IPV behaviour, females were significantly more likely than males to monitor the email accounts of their partners (25% vs. 6%) and to regard doing so as appropriate behaviour (Burke et al., 2011).

Borrajo, Gámez-Guadix, Pereda, and Calvete (2015) found that in a sample of 788 young adults (aged 18–30) in Spain, a significant number reported technology-assisted IPV in the form of controlling behaviour (75% victimisation and 82% perpetration) and direct aggression such as insults and threats (14% victimisation and 10.6% perpetration). Borrajo, Gámez-Guadix and Calvete (2015) similarly found that in a sample of 656 18–30 year olds in Spain, the prevalence of online control perpetration was 88.4%, although females were significantly more likely than males to report engaging in this behaviour (90.3% vs. 81.2%). The perpetration of online direct aggression was 20.3% (26.1% females vs. 18.7% males), although gender differences were not significant. Hassett-Walker (2019) examined technology-assisted IPV in a sample of 476 young adults (aged 18–30) in the US. They found that males were significantly more likely than females (28.7% vs. 18.5%) to report being monitored or controlled by a partner via social media or technology, and experiencing emotional or verbal aggression via social networking (14.8% vs. 6.9%). Although not statistically significant, males were also more likely than females to report monitoring or controlling a partner for all technologies except for a mobile phone. A similar pattern was found for the perpetration of emotional or verbal aggression with the exception of the mobile phone and text message method (in which females reported a slightly higher percentage).

## The role of attachment

Some authors have argued that the perpetration of technology-assisted IPV (i.e. monitoring and controlling behaviours and the surveillance of a partner) is associated with attachment anxiety explained as a means to establish/re-establish proximity (Marshall, Bejanyan, Di Castro, & Lee, 2013; Reed, Tolman, & Safyer, 2015). The high prevalence of controlling or monitoring technology-assisted IPV behaviours may be explained by such attachment characteristics. However, further research is needed to explore this in more detail. It could be that our extensive use of technology in daily communication, as well as the accessibility of communication tools and personal information online has resulted in increased opportunities to use it for abusive and controlling purposes as well as to blur the boundaries between what is considered as acceptable behaviour within relationships. Indeed, Duerksen and Woodin (2019) found that technology use (especially social media use) and technological disinhibition (i.e. behaving differently online/ digitally than one would normally behave offline) uniquely predicted technology-assisted IPV perpetration.

## Impact

Although the impact of technology-assisted IPV has been viewed as being less harmful than offline IPV, and in particular physical violence, due to the perceived distance separating the victim from immediate physical harm (Hand, Chung, & Peters, 2009; McCall, 2004), the impact of such abuse can be devastating for victims. It has been argued that constantly receiving harassing messages from an intimate partner may heighten perceptions of vulnerability, potentially escalating the threat of physical violence (Dimond et al., 2011; Melander, 2010). Survivors of technology-assisted IPV report serious, pervasive and persistent negative outcomes, highlighting that technology magnifies the harms of IPV and provides opportunities for new forms of abuse (Dragiewicz et al., 2019). For example, nearly 90% of participants in Maple, Short and Brown's (2011) survey said that the harassment had actually caused a change in their lives in work, personal relationships, or financially. Similarly, the impact of technology-assisted IPV and stalking has been reported to have a significant impact on victim's mental and physical wellbeing (84%), day-to-day routines (74%), employment (66%), parenting (26%) and relationships (63%) (Woodlock, 2014). Indeed, research has highlighted a number of negative impacts of technology-assisted IPV and cyberstalking including increased fear for safety, stress, anxiety, feeling sick, insomnia, post-traumatic stress syndrome/disorder, depression, distress, distrust, anger, paranoia, frustration, helplessness, an erosion of trust in the self and other people, economic and social costs (e.g. changing phone numbers, addresses, jobs, schools, hobbies, restricting social activities, investing in protective technologies for home security and bodyguards) and physical injury (Maple et al., 2011; Logan, 2010; Spitzberg & Hoobler, 2002; Truman, 2007; Woodlock et al., 2019). Such impacts can increase the isolation of victims, which may be exacerbated for some populations in vulnerable positions. For example, research has highlighted that those living in rural locations and those from culturally and linguistically diverse backgrounds are at increased risk for IPV, including technology-assisted IPV, in addition to experiencing enhanced barriers to safety, accessing support and justice, and increased social isolation (George & Harris, 2014; Woodlock et al., 2019).

Victims of partner stalking have also paid the price of their life, or have endured attempts to kill them by their partner/ex-partner. McFarlane et al. (1999) examined intimate partner stalking that occurred within 12 months of attempted and actual partner femicide, finding that 76% of victims who were killed by an intimate or former partner and 85% of victims whose partner or former partner attempted to kill them, were stalked by that partner in the 12 months before their murder/attempted murder. This echoes the examples of cyberstalking reported by Southworth et al. (2007), in which technology was used by ex-partners to track down victims resulting in their murder.

Experiencing technology-assisted IPV can have many impacts for victims' own technology use such as having to change phone numbers and close social media accounts, consequences of the coercive tactics used by perpetrators to isolate and intimate victims (Woodlock, 2017). However, such distancing and avoidance actions could actually be more risky and unpredictable for victims as the perpetrator might try to contact them directly as a result of losing that ability to contact and control them (Woodlock et al., 2019). Some survivors have found that disconnecting a telephone line or email account in an attempt to thwart a stalker results in the abuser escalating to a new method of control or access (Southworth, Dawson, Fraser, & Tucker, 2005). This may also raise some practical challenges for women/survivors. Women who are separated from and share children with a perpetrator may not be able to disengage from digital communication channels because of shared parenting (Woodlock et al., 2019). Indeed, 13/14 survivors with children in Dragiewicz et al.'s (2019) study reported technology-assisted IPV during post-separation parenting. Additionally, Harris and Woodlock (2019) have been critical of the victim-blaming attitudes that burden victims/survivors with the responsibility of managing their technological use in terms of ensuring their own safety and digital privacy or from refraining from using technology completely. It is argued that there is a major dilemma faced by practitioners in how to promote and facilitate client safety from technology-assisted IPV while still enabling safe use of technology so clients can remain connected to family, friends and community (Woodlock et al., 2019).

## Attitudes

Research has highlighted that technology-assisted IPV may be viewed as less serious compared to traditional offline IPV among the general public. For example, Messinger, Birmingham and DeKeseredy (2018) found that intimate partner cyber monitoring was less likely to be defined as abuse and was perceived as being less serious and less deserving of survivor support than that of physical violence in a sample of young adult undergraduate students. Harris, Honey, Webster, Diemer and Polito (2015) also found that older adolescents and young adults are less likely to identify non-physical behaviours as violence than they are to recognise physical violence and forced sex, and at times, expressed that they would excuse partner violence depending on the scenario. Furthermore, 46% agreed that tracking a partner electronically was acceptable to some degree; despite the majority (84%) recognising that covert tracking of a partner electronically was a serious behaviour. Tolerant attitudes may mean technology-assisted IPV is potentially normalised in some relationships meaning its seriousness and impact is not always recognised.

## Help-seeking and the role of technology in intervention

Victims are often reluctant to seek help due to feeling embarrassed or fearful that they will not be believed, as represented by less than half of victims seeking help in Woodlock's (2014) study. Tarza, Iyer, Thrower and Hegarty (2017) highlight that delivering an IPV intervention online or via a smartphone has the potential to overcome some of these barriers such as reluctance to access services and its associated stigma. Indeed, a range of technological and Internet-based tools are now available for victims of IPV. Technology can be used to help victims in terms of raising awareness; access to information, resources and service providers; crisis support; reducing feelings of isolation by maintaining contact with social networks; provision of online/social media-based peer support groups; equipping victims with safety devices and help with safety planning; recording and collecting evidence of abuse for criminal justice agencies; wearable technology solutions; and empowering victims (Al-Alosi, 2020; Think Social Tech, Snook, & SafeLives, 2019). There are websites and helplines (e.g. nationaldahelpline.org.uk) to support victims of IPV and professionals working with survivors. Techsafety.org, a US organisation, provides a list of apps for smartphones and tablets that address the issue of IPV including screening tools to recognise abuse and find resources and safety planning and advice (e.g. myplanapp.org). However, the provision and awareness of digital services for support in the UK remains patchy and fragmented (Think Social Tech, Snook, & SafeLives, 2019).

Importantly, technology may be the only feasible way for some victims to overcome barriers from seeking help, such as time, geography, disability and communication barriers (Al-Alosi, 2020). However, factors such as age, disability, education, ethnicity and poverty may affect a victim's understanding or familiarity with technology and act as barriers due to difficulty with Internet connection and accessibility/affordability (Al-Alosi, 2020; Tarza et al., 2017). Furthermore, these authors highlight that such interventions need to be mindful of issues such as safety, privacy and the accuracy of information online.

Technology has also been reported to provide benefits for survivors of IPV, particularly those who have had to relocate to shelters for safety. Technology can offer victims opportunities for communication, help-seeking, and provide advocacy, support and administration of justice for victims/survivors (Harris, 2018; Dragiewicz et al., 2019). Dimond et al. (2011) interviewed ten women who were residents at a shelter in the US and found that mobile phones and SNS offered glimpses of support, such as feeling and staying connected with family and friends, especially when they have had to cut ties in order to move on. Additionally, IPV survivors used technology in order to find housing, jobs and resources to support themselves and their children, meaning survivors had to weigh up the risks and benefits of their continued use of technology and social networking applications. Technology has also been used to support victims to stay in their own homes once separated from an abusive partner. For example, a scheme in Wolverhampton called Safer Homes provides additional security including CCTV or digital door cameras to ensure the safety of victims. A similar approach has been used in Australia (Mikakos, 2017). Finn and Atkinson (2009) argue that technology safety issues and online privacy should be a regular part of assessment and safety training for victims/survivors and advocacy staff both in shelters and community victim services due to its practical benefits in addressing safety in addition to empowering survivors.

## Technology-assisted abuse in adolescent romantic relationships

Adolescents have been referred to as a 'digital generation' or 'digital natives' due to technologies, like the Internet and (smart) mobile phones, becoming an essential and integral part of adolescents' lives and social interactions (van der Hof & Koops, 2011). Adolescents may therefore be particularly vulnerable to experiences of technology-assisted IPV, especially as they may lack relationship experience and knowledge of what is healthy and acceptable relationship behaviours (Wekerle & Wolfe, 1999; Barter et al., 2017). The first definition of adolescent partner violence to acknowledge the role of technology is that provided by the Centers for Disease Control and Prevention (2012):

> Physical, sexual, or psychological/emotional violence between two people within a close or dating relationship, as well as stalking. It can occur in person or electronically such as repeated texting or posting sexual pictures of a partner online and may occur between a current or former dating partner.

Several studies have explored the role of technology in adolescent experiences of partner violence or what has been termed 'cyber dating violence' (Yahner, Dank, Zweig, & Lachman, 2015), 'cyber dating abuse' (Zweig, Dank, Yahner, & Lachman, 2013), 'digital dating abuse' (Reed, Tolman, & Ward, 2017), 'electronic dating aggression' (Cutbush, Williams, Miller, Gibbs, & Clinton-Sherrod, 2012) and 'technology-assisted adolescent dating violence' (Stonard, 2020). For the purpose of this chapter, the term technology-assisted adolescent dating violence (ADV) will be used.

## *Nature of abusive, coercive and controlling behaviours*

As with technology-assisted IPV among adults, technology is thought to influence the dynamics of ADV by redefining the boundaries of romantic relationships in ways that provide a fertile ground for conflict and abuse (Draucker & Martsolf, 2010). Studies have examined the use of several technologies such as mobile phone calls or texting, instant messaging, SNS, emails, picture messages, video calls, web chats/chat rooms, and websites/blogs as methods to perpetrate ADV behaviours (Cutbush et al., 2012; Stonard, 2019a). A review of technology-assisted ADV studies found the typical behaviours measured include the sending of insults, threats, humiliating or spreading rumours about a partner; non-consensual distribution of personal information or images; sexual/sexting pressure; frequently or excessively checking up on a partner's whereabouts; monitoring a partner's messages; demanding a partner's passwords to phones or online accounts; deleting or 'unfriending' a partner's contacts or friends from social media; making a partner feel afraid to not respond to communication; and preventing a partner from using technology to talk to others (Stonard, Bowen, Lawrence, & Price, 2014). Hellevik (2018) explored adolescents' experiences of technology-assisted ADV and identified four categories of victimisation including the use of technology to harass, control, monitor and sexually coerce a partner. Adolescents identified that online partner harassment was facilitated by the availability of social networks and the direct and rapid communication that at times enhanced the severity and cruelness of the harassment and provided new avenues for abusive behaviour (Hellevik, 2018).

## Prevalence

The prevalence of technology-assisted ADV in the studies reviewed by Stonard et al. (2014) ranged from 12–56% for victimisation and 12–54% for perpetration depending on the type of behaviours and technologies measured. The prevalence of technology-assisted ADV reported in these studies varies widely; however recent research suggests that the prevalence of such abuse is increasing. Studies published since this review report prevalence rates ranging from 13–73% for victimisation and 12–70.5% for perpetration (Barter et al., 2015; Dick et al., 2014; Cutbush, Williams, Miller, Gibbs, & Clinton-Sherrod, 2018; Doucette et al., 2018; Muñoz-Fernández & Sánchez-Jiménez, 2020; Morelli, Bianchi, Chirumbolo, & Baiocco, 2017; Temple et al., 2016; Stonard, 2020; van Ouytsel, Ponnet, & Walrave, 2017) depending on the type of behaviours measured and the research design used. For example, studies vary in whether they ask about current or recent relationships and the timeframe in which respondents are asked to report on their ADV experiences. Research has found that adolescents' experiences of technology-assisted ADV often include multiple abusive and controlling behaviours via a range of technology methods, highlighting its extent and intrusiveness (Stonard, 2019a). Research has also found a high co-occurrence of technology-assisted ADV victimisation and perpetration (Smith et al., 2018; Stonard, 2020).

Importantly, technology-assisted ADV has been associated with psychological, controlling, physical and/or sexual ADV that occurs offline (Doucette et al., 2018; Morelli et al., 2017; Stonard, 2020; Temple et al., 2016), emphasising the intrusive and inescapable nature of ADV. However, for some adolescents, their experience of ADV was limited to that which was technology-assisted, as they did not experience ADV in the offline context (Stonard, 2020), meaning such experiences may have unique risk factors and impacts. Hellevik (2018) also found that for the majority of the 14 Norwegian adolescents interviewed, technology-assisted ADV was experienced alongside offline ADV of a similar nature; however, for two of the adolescents, only technology-assisted ADV victimisation was experienced and the partner was viewed as behaving completely differently online than they were offline. This supports the concept of online disinhibition outlined by Suler (2004) which attempts to explain how people behave differently in the online context compared to offline as a result of factors such as dissociative anonymity, invisibility, asynchronicity, solipsistic introjection, dissociative imagination and minimisation of authority.

Although both genders report a notable amount of technology-assisted ADV involvement as a victim or perpetrator; for example, Stonard (2020) found that out of 277 adolescents (aged 12–18) surveyed in England, 68% of males and 76% of females reported experience of technology-assisted ADV victimisation and 45% of males and 53% of females reported experience of perpetration; some studies have reported notably higher percentages of victimisation for females than males. In a large five country comparative study in Europe surveying 4,500 adolescents aged 14–17, Barter et al. (2015) found that 48% of females and 25% of males had experienced emotional technology-assisted ADV consisting of six different behaviours. This echoed some earlier research with 1,353 adolescents aged 13–16 by Barter, McCarry, Berridge and Evans (2009) in the UK that found that 12% of females and 4% of males reported that a partner had used mobile phones or the Internet to humiliate and threaten them, and that 42% of females and 29% of males reported that partners had frequently checked up on their movements by phone or text. Similarly, in surveys in the US, Zweig et al. (2013) reported that in a sample of 3,745 school students, 26% of females and 12% of males reported being a victim of technology-assisted ADV, and Dick et al. (2014) identified that in a sample of 1,008 14–19-year-olds seeking care at school-based health centres, more female than male participants reported technology-assisted ADV victimisation (44.6% vs. 31.0%). Cutbush et al. (2018) however, found that victimisation was more prevalent for boys (42%) than for girls (31%), at baseline only, among 795 seventh-grade students. In a sample of 632 Spanish adolescents aged 12–18, Muñoz-Fernández and Sánchez-Jiménez (2020) found that females also reported significantly more technology-assisted ADV perpetration than males. Research has been consistent in finding that adolescent females report more victimisation of sexual technology-assisted ADV such as sexting pressure, the receiving of unwanted sexual images and the non-consensual sharing of sexting images (Stonard, 2020; Wood et al., 2015; Zweig et al., 2013).

The prevalence of technology-assisted ADV is evidently substantial among young people. However, Cutbush et al. (2018) did report that both perpetration and victimisation experiences each decreased significantly from the beginning of seventh grade to the end of eighth grade, with boys' experiences of victimisation and perpetration decreasing significantly over the two years. More research is needed to examine the trajectories of technology-assisted ADV throughout adolescence in order to assess changes over young, middle and older adolescence.

## *The role of attachment and jealousy*

Adolescents have discussed the nature of technology-facilitated communication with a dating partner as enhancing feelings of jealousy, obsession and insecurity that may lead to technology-assisted ADV behaviours such as monitoring and controlling a partner (Stonard, Bowen, Walker, & Price, 2017). For example, adolescents discussed the potential for anxiety to be felt about seeing when a partner was online but not replying to their messages and feeling anxious and obsessed with a partner's frequency or response to their communication. Females were also reported to monitor their partner's messages or Facebook accounts, demand passwords to accounts and delete female friends on Facebook due to jealousy or anxiety about a partner's fidelity (Stonard et al., 2017). Other studies have also found that unique features of technology such as increased visibility of a partner's activities and communication with others (particularly those of the opposite sex) online can exacerbate feelings of jealousy and subsequent harassment, surveillance, controlling and monitoring behaviours (Girlguiding, 2013; Baker & Carreño, 2016; Rueda, Lindsey, & Williams, 2015; van Ouytsel, Walrave, Ponnet, Willems, & Van Dam, 2019).

In terms of attachment, Reed, Tolman, Ward and Safyer (2016) found that higher levels of attachment anxiety were associated with more frequent perpetration of technology-assisted ADV and that females reported higher levels of anxiety than males and more frequent technology-assisted ADV. Bhogal and Howman (2018) also found that attachment anxiety was associated with high levels of technology-assisted ADV. Reed et al. (2016) suggest that social media may create a 'cycle of anxiety' whereby social media plays a role in triggering relationship anxiety as well as being a tool to monitor a partner online in an attempt to alleviate anxiety. However, the nature of adolescent attachment is less well understood, meaning more research in this area is needed (Brown & Wright, 2001; Crittenden, 2000). It is also important that the implications of such an approach to explaining technology-assisted ADV is considered in more detail so such explanations are not perceived as victim blaming in the sense that a perpetrator can justify their behaviour based on a need to re-establish proximity as a result of, for example, a victim's lack of communication in response to a partner's messages.

## Impact

The impact of technology-assisted ADV can be devastating for victims, especially for those who are already in violent and controlling relationships. Barter et al. (2009) identified that technology provided an extra mechanism by which partners could exert control for young people (aged 13–17) who were already in a violent relationship and that this control extended into every aspect of adolescents' social lives both online and offline. The negative impact of ADV, including technology-assisted emotional abuse, has been identified by Barter et al. (2015) to include being upset, scared, embarrassed, unhappy, humiliated; feeling bad about oneself, angry, annoyed and shocked, particularly for females. However, affirmative or no effect responses were also found which were defined as feeling loved, feeling good about oneself, wanted, protected; thinking it was funny; and it having no effect (Barter et al., 2015). Reed et al. (2017) also found that girls reported being more upset by technology-assisted ADV behaviours and expressed more negative emotional responses than boys. Technology-assisted ADV has been associated with higher levels of depression, anxiety, worse dyadic adjustment, low self-esteem and psychological/emotional distress in both adolescents and young adults (Borrajo & Gámez-Guadix, 2016; Hancock, Keast, & Ellis, 2017; Smith et al., 2018).

In a qualitative study exploring adolescents' perceptions of the role and impact of technology-assisted IPV, Stonard (2019b) found that technology was viewed as disenabling victims in addition to enabling both victims and perpetrators as a result of its unique features. For example, technology use in ADV was viewed as disenabling victims as a result of its public nature, the permanence and loss of control over abusive comments or behaviours that were posted online, as a result of the misinterpretation and confusion caused by the loss of verbal cues, the loss of privacy and a deeper invasion of personal freedom, and as a result of online abuse developing into offline abuse. Technology was viewed as enabling perpetrators by facilitating technology-assisted ADV due to its availability, immediacy, anonymity, and providing increased confidence to abuse from behind a screen. Victims were also viewed as being enabled through avoidance opportunities, the provision of proof/evidence of abuse motivating response, resilience, and/or providing a coping mechanism. Some of these findings were echoed in an earlier study by Stonard et al. (2017) which found that adolescents viewed technology-assisted ADV as inescapable. Hellevik (2018) also found some victims described the effect of permanence as a result of re-reading abusive messages from a dating partner that may be stored on a mobile phone resulting in a sense of re-victimisation each time these were viewed. One adolescent female discussed how the lack of emotional cues in text messages increased the level of derogatory emotional abuse between her and her boyfriend (Hellevik, 2018). Technology-assisted ADV therefore appears to result in some unique impacts, as well impacts that would also be present in offline ADV.

## Attitudes

Despite the potential negative impact of technology-assisted ADV, some adolescents view technology-facilitated abuse (as has been found with offline ADV) to be a relatively normative and acceptable behaviour with romantic relationships. Adolescents and young adults in both Draucker and Martsolf's (2010) and Barter et al.'s (2009) studies sometimes viewed technology-assisted ADV such as excessive contact and monitoring or controlling behaviours to be motivated by care or concern rather than being viewed as intrusive or as a result of relationship insecurity. Girlguiding (2013) found that a notable portion of female adolescents reported attitudes that were accepting of technology-assisted ADV. For example, 39% of girls believed it was acceptable for a partner to make you tell them where you are all the time; 22% said that checking up on you and reading your phone could sometimes be ok, and 17% thought it was ok to send photos or videos of you to friends without your permission. Rueda et al. (2015) similarly identified that in some cases, adolescents viewed overt monitoring such as forbidding texting with peers of the opposite sex and looking at a partner's messages as acceptable. Likewise, adolescents in Lucero, Weisz, Smith-Darden and Lucero's (2014) study indicated that some technology-assisted ADV behaviours were only problematic when they occurred outside of dating relationships (e.g. when a sexually explicit picture is shared in person or forwarded to others, or a previous partner hacks into the other's Facebook account without the implicit consent of the account owner). Furthermore, some female adolescents reported that sharing passwords shows a sign of trust and a healthy, committed relationship and is therefore not perceived as a problematic behaviour (Lucero et al., 2014).

## Help-seeking

Views that technology-assisted ADV is sometimes acceptable may explain the low levels of reporting and help-seeking among adolescents with such experiences. Less than 10% of victims of technology-assisted ADV reported seeking help in Zweig et al.'s (2013) study. Picard (2007) similarly found that the majority of young people who had been asked to engage in sexual activity (82%), been harassed or embarrassed on a SNS (78%), or been repeatedly checked up on via email or text messaging (72%) by a dating partner report that they did not tell their parents. The most common reasons reported for this were that the young people did not believe that the behaviours were serious enough to justify telling an adult or because of fears that parents may limit or take away their computer, mobile phone or prevent them from seeing their partner (Picard, 2007). As adolescents under the age of 16 are not recognised in the UK government definition of domestic violence (Home Office, 2012), they may feel deterred from help-seeking and excluded from formal support.

Nevertheless, as for adult victims of IPV, there are various websites that offer information on relationship abuse, resources and support for victims that may provide adolescents with alternative routes to in-person help-seeking such as loveisrespect.org and breakthecycle.org, although these are typically developed in the US. An app and website was developed by young people for young people as part of the Safeguarding Teenagers Intimate Relationships project where adolescents can get information about healthy relationships, explore their own attitudes and behaviours and assess risks using interactive technology (STIRitApp, 2020). The use of technology has also been developed in the form of serious game-based primary interventions to raise awareness and change attitudes towards dating violence in adolescents (Bowen et al., 2014). Adolescents have also highlighted that technology can be used to record or capture evidence of technology-assisted abuse (which could also capture offline abuse), enabling victims to report it and provide authors with proof of the incident(s) (Stonard, 2019b).

## Policy recommendations in the literature

Technology-assisted IPV and stalking has been recognised as a serious offence that must be responded to as such by professionals with effective practice, policy and legal responses needing to be developed (Woodlock, 2014, 2017). If the role of technology in IPV/ADV is not recognised, this inhibits a full understanding of the issue and the subsequent responses to help-seeking and support offered, both practical and legal. Further training is needed for professionals who work with victims of technology-assisted IPV/ADV, in addition to cooperation with the telecommunications industry and smartphone developers to assist women to use technologies safely (Woodlock, 2014). This may require innovative cybersecurity responses and the development of new tools to combat the issue (Dragiewicz et al., 2019). It has been argued that there needs to be more clarity regarding what technological platforms are currently doing to combat technology-assisted IPV, in addition to a need for a shared understanding and international consensus about what platforms should be doing to address the issue and whether such responsibilities should be required by law, given the difficulties surrounding jurisdictional differences (Dragiewicz et al., 2018). There would then be a need for more regulation to monitor and enforce such standards as a requirement of laws and policies that aim to address the issue (Dragiewicz et al., 2019). Women's Aid (2017) suggest that there is a need for criminal and civil measures to address technology-assisted IPV, along with improvements and clearer guidelines in how online providers prevent, prohibit, and respond to such crimes. The difficulty is that even if perpetrators were targeted by social media platforms (e.g. by suspending accounts. etc.), the ease in creating new accounts and disguising one's identity due to the anonymity afforded by online communication tools means perpetrators may find another way to reach their victims and continue their abusive and controlling behaviour.

## Conclusion

This chapter has provided an overview of the nature and role of technology use in IPV that occurs within both adult and adolescent romantic relationships, its prevalence, unique features, attitudes towards it, and its impact, while considering the influence of gender in such experiences. Consideration for the role of technology in prevention and intervention has also been given, along with attention towards recommendations in the literature for moving forward in tackling the issue. A detailed summary of some of the key implications for policy, practice and research arising from this chapter are summarised next.

## Critical findings

- A range of technologies and digital communication tools are used in the perpetration of abusive, controlling, and monitoring IPV/ADV behaviours such as with mobile phones, social networking applications and tracking devices/software.
- Technology-assisted IPV/ADV is often experienced alongside offline IPV/ADV.
- The prevalence of technology-assisted IPV/ADV is substantial and might be explained by the accessibility, affordability and instantaneous nature of technology-facilitated methods of communication as well as the availability of personal information online.
- Technology-assisted IPV/ADV is thought to be gendered, with experiences of victimisation and its impact being worse for females than for males, although some research findings have been mixed.
- Attachment anxiety is thought to influence the perpetration of technology-assisted IPV/ADV behaviours in an attempt to re-establish proximity.
- Technology-assisted IPV/ADV is sometimes viewed as being less serious than offline IPV/ADV and may be normalised or tolerated in intimate relationships.
- Technology-assisted IPV/ADV can have a devastating impact on victims physically, psychologically, socially, relationally and financially, as well as affecting their daily routines,

employment and parenting. At the most extreme, it can result in the death/murder of the victim. Its impact can also result in some unique consequences for victims as a result of the technology used.

- Victims of technology-assisted IPV/ADV often do not seek help.
- Technology may provide intervention opportunities in terms of help-seeking and recovery but victims and professionals must be trained on how to use technology safely.

## Implications for policy, practice and research

- A need for governments, legal responses, and practitioners to take technology-assisted IPV/ADV seriously and for this to be recognised in official definitions.
- Recognition of (technology-assisted) ADV among young people below the age of 16.
- Awareness campaigns for victims to educate about technology-assisted IPV/ADV and to encourage help-seeking.
- Training for professionals working with victims of (technology-assisted) IPV/ADV in order to understand the nature of this method of abuse, identify potential victims, and to respond effectively in supporting victims safely.
- Requirement for the technological platforms, telecommunications industry and smart-phone developers to take responsibility for the abuse that occurs via their services/products, and to support and assist victims to use technologies safely.
- A need for more consistent and comprehensive measures of technology-assisted IPV/ADV in order to make comparisons between studies.
- Further research into the impact of and attitudes towards technology-assisted IPV/ADV.
- Consideration of race, class, geographical location (i.e. rurality), sexuality and disability in the experiences and impact of technology-assisted IPV/ADV.
- Research regarding how technology can be used in reporting, help-seeking, accessing support and gathering evidence in order to inform future practical and legal responses of technology-assisted IPV/ADV.

## References

Al-Alosi, H. (2020). Fighting fire with fire: Exploring the potential of technology to help victims combat intimate partner violence. *Aggression and Violent Behavior.* doi:10.1016/j.avb.2020.101376

Baker, C. K., & Carreño, P. K. (2016). Understanding the role of technology in adolescent dating and dating violence. *Journal of Child and Family Studies, 25*(1), 308–320. doi:10.1007/s10826-015-0196-5

Barter, C., McCarry, M., Berridge, D., & Evans, K. (2009). *Partner exploitation and violence in teenage intimate relationships.* London: NSPCC.

Barter, C., Stanley, N., Wood, M., Lanau, A., Aghtaie, N., Larkins, C., & Överlien, C. (2017). Young people's online and face-to-face experiences of interpersonal violence and abuse and their subjective impact across five European countries. *Psychology of Violence, 7*(3), 375

Barter, C., Wood, M., Aghtaie, N., Larkins, C., Stanley, N., Apostolov, G., . . . Hellevik, P. (2015). *Safeguarding teenage intimate relationships (STIR): Connecting online and offline contexts and risks – Briefing paper 2: Incidence rates and impact of experiencing interpersonal violence and abuse in young people's relationships.* Funded by DAPHNE III European Commission. Retrieved from http://stiritup.eu/wp-content/uploads/2015/02/STIR-Briefing-Paper-21.pdf

Bhogal, M. S., & Howman, J. H. (2018). Mate value discrepancy and attachment anxiety predict the perpetration of digital dating abuse. *Evolutionary Psychological Science, 5*(1), 113–120

Borrajo, E., & Gámez-Guadix, M. (2016). Cyber dating abuse: Its link to depression, anxiety and dyadic adjustment. *Behavioural Psychology, 24*(2), 221–235.

Borrajo, E., Gámez-Guadix, M., & Calvete, E. (2015). Justification beliefs of violence, myths about love and cyber dating abuse. *Psicothema, 27*(4), 327–333.

Borrajo, E., Gámez-Guadix, M., Pereda, N., & Calvete, E. (2015). The development and validation of the cyber dating abuse questionnaire among young couples. *Computers in Human Behavior, 48*, 358–365. doi:10.1016/j.chb.2015.01.06

Bowen, E., Walker, K., Mawer, M., Holdsworth, E., Sorbring, E., Helsing, B. et al. (2014). "It's like you're actually playing as yourself": Development and preliminary evaluation of 'Green Acres High', a serious game-based primary intervention to combat adolescent dating violence. *Psychosocial Intervention, 23*(1), 43–55.

Brown, L. S., & Wright, J. (2001). Attachment theory in adolescence and its relevance to developmental psychopathology. *Clinical Psychology and Psychotherapy, 8*(1), 15–32.

Burke, S. C., Wallen, M., Vail-Smith, K., & Knox, D. (2011). Using technology to control intimate partners: An exploratory study of college undergraduates. *Computers in Human Behavior, 27*(3), 1162–1167. doi:10.1016/j.chb.2010.12.010

Centers for Disease Control and Prevention. (2012). *Understanding teen dating violence*. Retrieved from www.cdc.gov/violenceprevention/pdf/teen-dating-violence-factsheet-a.pdf

Crittenden, P. M. (2000). Introduction. In P. M. Crittenden & A. H. Claussen (Eds.), *The organization of attachment relationships: Maturation, culture, and context* (pp. 1–10). Cambridge: Cambridge University Press

Cutbush, S., Williams, J., Miller, S., Gibbs, D., & Clinton-Sherrod, M. (2012). *Electronic dating aggression among middle school students: Demographic correlates and associations with other types of violence*. Poster presented at the American Public Health Association, annual meeting, San Francisco, CA. Retrieved from www.rti.org/pubs/apha12_cutbush_poster.pdf

Cutbush, S., Williams, K., Miller, S., Gibbs, D., & Clinton-Sherrod, M. (2018). Longitudinal patterns of electronic teen dating violence among middle school students. *Journal of Interpersonal Violence*. doi: 10.1177%2F0886260518758326

Dick, R. N., McCauley, H. L., Jones, K. A., Tancredi, D. J., Goldstein, S., Blackburn, S., . . . Miller, E. (2014). Cyber dating abuse among teens using school-based health centers. *Pediatrics, 134*(6), e1560-e1576

Dimond, J. P., Fiesler, C., & Bruckman, A. S. (2011). Domestic violence and information communication technologies. *Interacting with Computers, 23*(5), 413–421. doi:10.1016/j.intcom.2011.04.006.

Dobash, R. E., & Dobash, R. P. (1979). *Violence against wives: A case against patriarchy*. New York, NY: The Free Press.

Doucette, H., Collibee, C., Hood, E., Gittins Stone, D. I., DeJesus, B., & Rizzo, C. J. (2018). Perpetration of electronic intrusiveness among adolescent females: Associations with in-person dating violence. *Journal of Interpersonal Violence*. doi:10.1177/0886260518815725.

Dragiewicz, M., Burgess, J., Matamoros-Fernández, A., Salter, M., Suzor, N. P., Woodlock, D., & Harris, B. (2018). Technology facilitated coercive control: Domestic violence and the competing roles of digital media platforms. *Feminist Media Studies, 18*(4), 609–625. doi:10.1080/14680777.2018. 1447341

Dragiewicz, M., Harris, B., Woodlock, D., Salter, M., Easton, H., Lynch, A., . . . Milne, L., (2019). *Domestic violence and communication technology: Survivor experiences of intrusion, surveillance, and identity crime*. Sydney, Australia: Australian Communications Consumer Action Network.

Draucker, C. B., & Martsolf, D. S. (2010). The role of electronic communication technology in adolescent dating violence. *Journal of Child and Adolescent Psychiatric Nursing, 23*, 133–142. doi:10.1111/ j.1744–6171.2010.00235.x

Duerksen, K. N., & Woodin, E. M. (2019). Technological intimate partner violence: Exploring technology-related perpetration factors and overlap with in-person intimate partner violence. *Computers in Human Behavior*. doi:10.1016/j.chb.2019.05.001

Finn, J., & Atkinson, T. (2009). Promoting the safe and strategic use of technology for victims of intimate partner violence: Evaluation of the technology safety project. *Journal of Family Violence, 24*(1), 53–59. doi:10.1007/s10896-008-9207-2

Frisby, B. N., & Westerman, D. (2010). Rational actors: Channel selection and rational choices in romantic conflict episodes. *Journal of Social and Personal Relationships, 27*(7), 970–981. doi:10.1177/026540751 0378302

George, A., & Harris, B. (2014). *Landscapes of violence: Women surviving family violence in regional and rural Victoria*. Geelong, Australia: Centre for Rural and Regional Law and Justice, Deakin University.

Girlguiding. (2013). *Care verses control: Healthy relationships. A report from Girlguiding*. London: Girlguiding. Retrieved from http://girlsattitudes.girlguiding.org.uk/pdf/2025_Care_Versus_Control.pdf

Hancock, K., Keast, H., & Ellis, W. (2017). The impact of cyber dating abuse on self-esteem: The mediating role of emotional distress. *Cyberpsychology: Journal of Psychosocial Research on Cyberspace, 11*(2), article 2. doi:10.5817/CP2017–2–2.

Hand, T., Chung, D., & Peters, M. (2009). *The use of information and communication technologies to coerce and control in domestic violence and following separation.* Stakeholder paper, 6, Canberra: Australian Domestic & Family Violence Clearinghouse. Retrieved from www.adfvc.unsw.edu.au/PDF%20files/Stakeholder%20Paper_6.pdf.

Harris, A., Honey, N., Webster, K., Diemer, K., & Polito, V. (2015). *Young Australians' attitudes to violence against women: Findings from the 2013 national community attitudes towards violence against women survey for respondents 16–24 years.* Melbourne, Australia: Victorian Health Promotion Foundation.

Harris, B. A. (2018). Spacelessness, spatiality and intimate partner violence: Technology-facilitated abuse, stalking and justice. In K. Fitz-Gibbon, S. Walklate, J. McCulloch, & J. Maher (Eds.), *Intimate partner violence, risk and security: Securing women's lives in a global world* (pp. 52–70). London: Routledge.

Harris, B. A., & Woodlock, D. (2019). Digital coercive control: Insights from two landmark domestic violence studies. *British Journal of Criminology, 59*(3), 530–550. doi:10.1093/bjc/azy052

Hassett-Walker, C. (2019). Gender differences in intimate partner violence via electronic communication technology: An exploratory study of older adolescents and young adults. *Psychology, 10*, 1663–1687. doi:10.4236/psych.2019.1012110

Hellevik, P. M. (2018). Teenagers' personal accounts of experiences with digital intimate partner violence and abuse. *Computers in Human Behavior.* doi:10.1016/j.chb.2018.11.019

Home Office. (2011). *Consultation of stalking.* London: Home Office. Retrieved from www.gov.uk/government/uploads/system/uploads/attachment_data/file/157898/consultation.pdf

Home Office. (2012). *Cross-government definition of domestic violence: A consultation summary of responses.* London: Home Office. Retrieved from https://www.gov.uk/government/uploads/system/uploads/attachment_data/file/157800/domestic-violence-definition.pdf

Logan, T. K., & Supported by the National Institute of Justice. (2010). *Research on partner stalking: Putting the pieces together.* Lexington, KY: University of Kentucky, Department of Behavioral Science & Center on Drug and Alcohol Research. Retrieved from www.cdar.uky.edu/CoerciveControl/docs/Research%20on%20Partner%20Stalking%20Report.pdf

Lucero, J. L., Weisz, A. N., Smith-Darden, J., & Lucero, S. M. (2014). Exploring gen- der differences: Socially interactive technology use/abuse among dating teens. *Affilia, 29*(4), 478–491.

Maple, C., Short, E., & Brown, A. (2011). *Cyberstalking in the United Kingdom an analysis of the ECHO pilot study.* University of Bedfordshire: National Centre for Cyberstalking Research

Marganski, A., & Melander, L. (2018). Intimate partner violence victimization in the cyber and real world: Examining the extent of cyber aggression experiences and its association with in- person dating violence. *Journal of Interpersonal Violence, 33*(7), 1071–1095.

Marshall, T. C., Bejanyan, K., Di Castro, G., & Lee, R. A. (2013). Attachment styles as predictors of Facebook-related jealousy and surveillance in romantic relationships. *Personal Relationships, 20*(1), 1–22.

McCall, R. (2004). *Online harassment and cyberstalking: Victim access to crisis, referral and support services in Canada concepts and recommendations.* Victim Assistance Online Resources. Retrieved from www.vaonline.org/Cyberstalking%20Concepts%20and%20Recommendations%20(e).pdf

McFarlane, J. M., Campbell, J. C., Wilt, S., Sachs, C. J., Ulrich, Y., & Xu, X. (1999). Stalking and intimate partner femicide. *Homicide Studies, 3*(4), 300–316.

Melander, L. A. (2010). College students' perceptions of intimate partner cyber harassment. *Cyberpsychology, Behavior and Social Networking, 13*(3), 263–268. doi:10.1089/cyber.2009.0221

Messinger, A. M., Birmingham, R. S., & DeKeseredy, W. S. (2018). Perceptions of same-gender and different-gender intimate partner cyber-monitoring. *Journal of Interpersonal Violence.* doi:10.1177%2F0886260518787814

Mikakos, J. (2017). *Keeping women and children safe.* Media release, Victoria State Government. Retrieved from www.premier.vic.gov.au/wp-content/uploads/2017/04/170429-KeepingWomenAndChildren-Safe.pdf

Morelli, M., Bianchi, D., Chirumbolo, A., & Baiocco, R. (2017). The cyber dating violence inventory: Validation of a new scale for online perpetration and victimization among dating partners. *European Journal of Developmental Psychology, 15*(4), 464–471. doi: 10.1080/17405629.2017.1305885

Muñoz-Fernández, N., & Sánchez-Jiménez, V. (2020). Cyber-aggression and psychological aggression in adolescent couples: A short- term longitudinal study on prevalence and common and differential predictors. *Computers in Human Behavior, 104.* doi:10.1016/j.chb.2019.106191

Picard, P. (2007). *Tech abuse in teen relationships*. Chicago: Teen Research Unlimited. Retrieved from www.loveisrespect.org/wp-content/uploads/2009/03/liz- claiborne-2007-tech-relationship-abuse.pdf

Reed, L. A., Tolman, R. M., & Safyer, P. (2015). Too close for comfort: Attachment insecurity and electronic intrusion in college students' dating relationships. *Computers in Human Behavior, 50*, 431–438.

Reed, L. A., Tolman, R. M., & Ward, L. M. (2017). Gender matters: Experiences and consequences of digital dating abuse victimization in adolescent dating relationships. *Journal of Adolescence, 59*, 79–89.

Reed, L. A., Tolman, R. M., Ward, L. M., & Safyer, P. (2016). Keeping tabs: Attachment anxiety and electronic intrusion in high school dating relationships. *Computers in Human Behavior, 58*, 259–268.

Rueda, H. A., Lindsey, M., & Williams, L. R. (2015). "She posted it on Facebook": Mexican American adolescents' experiences with technology and romantic relationship conflict. *Journal of Adolescent Research, 30*(4), 419–445.

Smith, K., Cénata, J. M., Lapierrea, A., Dionb, J., Héberta, M., & Côtéb, K. (2018). Cyber dating violence: Prevalence and correlates among high school students from small urban areas in Quebec. *Journal of Affective Disorders, 234*, 220–223.

Southworth, C., Dawson, S., Fraser, C., & Tucker, S. (2005). *A high-tech twist on abuse: Technology, intimate partner stalking, and advocacy*. Safety Net: National Safe & Strategic Technology Project at the National Network to End Domestic Violence Fund. Retrieved from www.acesdv.org/wp-content/uploads/2014/06/NNEDV_HighTechTwist_PaperAndApxA_English08.pdf

Southworth, C., Finn, J., Dawson, S., Fraser, C., & Tucker, S. (2007). Intimate partner violence, technology, and stalking. *Violence Against Women, 13*(8), 842–856. doi:10.1177/1077801207302045

Spitzberg, B. H., & Hoobler, G. (2002). Cyberstalking and the technologies of interpersonal terrorism. *New Media & Society, 4*(1), 71–92. doi:10.1177/14614440222226271

STIRitApp. (2020). *STIRitApp*. Retrieved from https://altraformacomunicazione.it/stiritapp/

Stonard, K. E. (2018). Technology-assisted adolescent dating violence and abuse: A factor analysis of the nature of electronic communication technology used across 12 types of abusive and controlling behaviour. *Journal of Child and Family Studies, 28*(1), 105–115. doi:10.1007/s10826-018-1255-5

Stonard, K. E. (2019). "Technology was designed for this": Adolescents' perceptions of the role and impact of the use of technology in cyber dating violence. *Computers in Human Behavior.* doi:10.1016/j.chb.2019.106211

Stonard, K. E. (2020). The prevalence and overlap of technology-assisted and offline adolescent dating violence. *Current Psychology, 1*(2), 61–78. doi:10.37256/ser.122020180.61-78

Stonard, K. E., Bowen, E., Lawrence, T. R., & Price, S. A. (2014). The relevance of technology to the nature, prevalence and impact of adolescent dating violence and abuse: A research synthesis. *Aggression and Violent Behavior, 19*, 390–417. doi:10.1016/j.avb.2014.06.005

Stonard, K. E., Bowen, E., Walker, K., & Price, S. A. (2017). "They'll always find a way to get to you": Technology use in adolescent romantic relationships and its role in dating violence and abuse. *Journal of Interpersonal Violence, 32*(14), 2083–2117

Suler, J. (2004). The online disinhibition effect. *Cyberpsychology and Behavior, 7*(3), 321–326.

Tarza, L., Iyer, D., Thrower, E., & Hegarty, K. (2017). "Technology doesn't judge you": Young Australian women's views on using the Internet and smartphones to address intimate partner violence. *Journal of Technology in Human Services, 35*(3), 199–218.

Temple, J. R., Choi, H. J., Brem, M., Wolford- Clevenger, C., Stuart, G. L., Peskin, M. F., & Elmquist, J. (2016). The temporal association between traditional and cyber dating abuse among adolescents. *Journal of Youth and Adolescence, 45*, 340–349. doi:10.1007/s10964-015-0380-3

Think Social Tech, Snook, and SafeLives. (2019). *Tech vs. abuse: Research findings*. Retrieved from https://d1c4e1f2-14ed-423b-8bab-01c0ad397d8f.filesusr.com/ugd/464d6d_b465be597dee4e04b8fa-c09363e4ef62.pdf

Truman, J. L. (2007). *Examining intimate partner stalking and use of technology in stalking victimization*. Sociology PhD. Florida: Department of Sociology in the College of Sciences at the University of Central Florida. Retrieved from http://etd.fcla.edu/CF/CFE0003022/Truman_Jennifer_L_201005_PhD.pdf

van der Hof, S., & Koops, B-J. (2011). Adolescents and cybercrime: Navigating between freedom and control. *Policy & Internet, 3*(2), article 4. doi:10.2202/1944–2866.1121

van Ouytsel, J., Ponnet, K., & Walrave, M. (2017). Cyber dating abuse: Investigating digital monitoring behaviors among adolescents from a social learning perspective. *Journal of Interpersonal Violence.* doi:10.1177/0886260517719538.

van Ouytsel, J., Walrave, M., Ponnet, K., Willems, A. S., & Van Dam, M. (2019). Adolescents' perceptions of digital media's potential to elicit jealousy, conflict and monitoring behaviors within romantic relationships. *Cyberpsychology: Journal of Psychosocial Research on Cyberspace, 13*(3), article 3. doi:10.5817/CP2019-3-3

Villora, B., Yubero, S., & Navarro, R. (2019a). Associations between feminine gender norms and cyber dating abuse in female adults. *Behavioral Sciences, 9*(4), 35–47. doi:10.3390/bs9040035

Villora, B., Yubero, S., & Navarro, R. (2019b). Cyber dating abuse and masculine gender norms in a sample of male adults. *Future Internet, 11*(4), 84–94. doi:10.3390/fi11040084

Walker, L. E. A. (1989). Psychology and violence against women. *American Psychologist, 44*(4), 695–702. doi:10.1037/0003–066X.44.4.695

Wekerle, C., & Wolfe, D. A. (1999). Dating violence in mid-adolescence: Theory, significance, and emerging prevention initiatives. *Clinical Psychology Review, 19*(4), 435–456.

Women's Aid. (2017). *Tackling domestic abuse in a digital age: A recommendations report on online abuse by the All-Party Parliamentary Group on Domestic Violence.* Bristol: Women's Aid.

Wood, M., Barter, C., Stanley, N., Aghtaie, N., & Larkins, C. (2015). Images across Europe: The sending and receiving of sexual images and associations with interpersonal violence in young People's relationships. *Children and Youth Services Review, 59,* 149–160.

Woodlock, D. (2014). *Technology-facilitated stalking: Findings and resources from the SmartSafe project.* Victoria: Domestic Violence Resource Centre.

Woodlock, D. (2017). The abuse of technology in domestic violence and stalking. *Violence Against Women, 23*(5), 584–602. doi:10.1177/1077801216646277

Woodlock, D., McKenzie, M., Western, D., & Harris, B. (2019). Technology as a weapon in domestic violence: Responding to digital coercive control. *Australian Social Work.* doi:10.1080/0312407X.2019.1607510

Yahner, J., Dank, M., Zweig, J. M., & Lachman, P. (2015). The co-occurrence of physical and cyber dating violence and bullying among teens. *Journal of Interpersonal Violence, 30*(7), 1079–1089. doi:10.1177%2F0886260514540324

Yllö, K., & Bograd, M. (Eds.). (1990). *Feminist perspectives on wife abuse.* London: Sage.

Zweig, J. M., Dank, M., Yahner, J., & Lachman, P. (2013). The rate of cyber dating abuse among teens and how it relates to other forms of teen dating violence. *Journal of Youth and Adolescence, 42,* 1063–1077. doi:10.1007/s10964-013-9922

# 24

# INTIMATE PARTNER HOMICIDE

*Solveig Karin Bø Vatnar, Christine Friestad and Stål Bjørkly*

## Intimate partner homicide

Intimate partner homicides (IPH) are fatal violent attacks perpetrated by intimate partners, usually defined as current or former spouses or common-law partners. A systematic review of the global prevalence of IPH indicated that one in seven homicides is committed by an intimate partner (Stöckl et al., 2013). IPH is the most common type of domestic homicide, and is the only homicide category in which the majority of victims are women (e.g., Liem & Roberts, 2009; Matias, Goncalves, Soeiro, & Matos, 2020). Women are far more likely to be killed by an intimate partner than by anyone else (e.g., Campbell, Webster, & Glass, 2009; Campbell, Glass, Sharps, Laughon, & Bloom, 2007; Matias et al., 2020), while the opposite is true for men. The ratio between men and women as perpetrators of IPH is 6:1 (Stöckl et al., 2013). In this chapter, we summarize existing scientific knowledge about intimate partner homicide, focusing on recent theoretical developments in the field, as well as empirically supported risk factors for IPH victimization and perpetration.

## Theoretical framework: interactional perspectives on intimate partner homicide

Current comprehension of intimate partner violence (IPV) and IPH can be categorized into sociocultural theories and individual theories. Recent research from a sociocultural perspective finds that the relationship between masculinity and femicide has been ignored, and that new conceptions of masculinities are applicable to intimate partner femicide and "honour" femicides (Johnson, Eriksson, Mazerolle, & Wortley, 2019; Messerschmidt, 2017). New theoretical frameworks including both structural and individual aspects have been proposed in order to make IPV and IPH theories more comprehensive by taking into consideration the perspectives of both victims and perpetrators, and integrating views from multiple academic disciplines (e.g., Bell & Naugle, 2008; Dixon, Hamilton-Giachritsis, & Browne, 2008; Emery, 2011; Winstok, 2007; Vatnar & Bjørkly, 2008; Vatnar, Friestad, & Bjørkly, 2017a). The traditional person-situation dichotomy is replaced by an emphasis on the mutual impact of the two variables (Funder, 2006). The main idea within an interactional perspective is that violence involves an influential and continuous interaction between individuals and the various situations and contexts they encounter. The *situation* is defined as an actual situation and how it is perceived, interpreted, and assigned meaning in the minds of those involved (Magnusson, 1981). Correspondingly, theoretical IPV and IPH perspectives and research should address the situation and proximal events associated with IPV (Bell & Naugle, 2008; Dixon & Graham-Kevan, 2011; Emery, 2011; Vatnar & Bjørkly, 2008; Vatnar et al., 2017a; Winstok, 2007). These authors have encouraged investigation of "the violence process", examining the nature of the violent relationship, events, motivations, and conditions including structural factors preceding an IPV episode, and outcomes of violent acts. Applied to IPH, an interactional perspective involves investigating the intimate partner homicide process, by examining the wider set of events and incidents that preceded and ended with the homicide (Vatnar et al., 2017a). To determine who have the greatest need for services and which services are most needed, criminal justice and health and victim support professionals need information about, for example, which subgroups are most likely to assault their partners or commit life-threatening violence (Kropp & Hart, 2015).

## Previous intimate partner violence

According to Dobash, Dobash, and Cavanagh (2009), research from the United States, Canada, and the United Kingdom (UK) reveals numerous similarities but also some differences concerning the role of previous IPV in cases of IPH. Studies have found that 65 to 80% of IPH victims had been *previously* abused by the partner who killed them (Campbell et al., 2007, 2009; Matias et al., 2020; Nicolaidis et al., 2003; Vatnar et al., 2017a). *Repeated* violence against the victim was present in 25% to 65% of the relationships that ended with the murder of a female partner (Aldridge & Browne, 2003; Campbell et al., 2007, 2009; Dobash et al., 2009; Vatnar et al., 2017a). In one study, nearly half of the perpetrators of IPH had previously been violent towards their victim, but had no prior conviction for intimate partner violence (Dobash et al., 2009). Research from the United States, primarily limited to cases with a history of previous IPV, suggests that significant risk factors for IPH may include repeated occurrences of severe IPV, stalking, sexual assault, attempts to strangle, intoxication, threats to kill, a firearm in the home, and threats with or use of a firearm (Campbell et al., 2007; Nicolaidis et al., 2003; Shields, Corey, Weakley-Jones, & Stewart, 2010). Research from the UK, including cases *without* a history of previous IPV, found that previous sexual assault, previous strangulation, and the use of sharp or blunt instruments were important risk factors, but not intoxication or the use of firearms (Dobash & Dobash, 2011; Dobash et al., 2009).

## Sociodemographic, contextual, and clinical factors

Research has identified sociodemographic characteristics that differentiate between victims of IPH and victims of nonfatal IPV (Eliason, 2009; Garcia & Hurwitz, 2007; Liem, 2010; Matias et al., 2020). The risk of intimate partner homicide is higher in cohabiting than in marital relationships and during separation or break up of the intimate relationship (Aldridge & Browne, 2003; Campbell et al., 2007, 2009; Eke, Hilton, Harris, Rice, & Houghton, 2011). Evidence suggests that at the time of a murder, one-third to one half of women killed by a partner were either separated or had expressed an intention to leave the relationship (Dobash et al., 2009; Nicolaidis et al., 2003).

Compared to nonfatal partner violence, IPH occurs more frequently among women and men who are under the age of 40, have a low level of education, are unemployed, and/or have financial and other problems associated with social and economic disadvantage (Barrett & St Pierre, 2011; Dobash & Dobash, 2015; Dobash et al., 2009; Goodman, Smyth, Borges, &

Singer, 2009). In the United States, ethnicity is considered an important risk factor, although it may be that social and economic disadvantage, rather than ethnicity per se, are the actual, underlying issues (Barrett & St Pierre, 2011; Dobash et al., 2009; Vatnar, Friestad, & Bjørkly, 2017b). The context of pregnancy and childbirth has also been associated with IPH (Campbell et al., 2007; Garcia et al., 2007; Martin, Macy, Sullivan, & Magee, 2007; Shadigian & Bauer, 2005). A population-based study of children bereaved by fatal intimate partner violence in the Netherlands showed that on average, the children were 7 years old at the time of the homicide, most lost their mother, and immigrant children were overrepresented. The majority of the children were present when the killing took place (Alisic, Groot, Snetselaar, Stroeken, & van de Putte, 2017). Alcohol and drug intoxication increase the risk both for perpetrating and for becoming a victim of IPH (Aldridge & Browne, 2003; Eliason, 2009). Some IPH perpetrators, especially homicide-suicide perpetrators, suffer from mental illness, with depression being the most commonly cited disorder (Liem, 2010).

## Help-seeking prior to IPH

The common image of a "battered woman" is often grounded in stereotypical representations of learned helplessness. However, empirical findings indicate that survivors of IPV are most commonly actively engaged in a myriad of strategies to cope with their victimization experiences (Barrett & St Pierre, 2011; Martin et al., 2007; Vatnar & Bjørkly, 2014). Recent findings highlight the complexities of help-seeking. Women who have experienced severe forms of IPV were most likely to have sought help through both formal and informal avenues (Barrett & St Pierre, 2011; Nurius, Macy, Nwabuzor, & Holt, 2011; Vatnar & Bjørkly, 2014). Frequency and seriousness of exposure to violence increased the likelihood of help-seeking. Research indicates that the strongest independent predictor of women's use of supports is fear of their lives being in danger (Barrett & St Pierre, 2011). Studies have also found that women who end up being killed by their partner have sought help from informal sources such as family and friends (e.g., Vatnar et al., 2017a). Help-seeking from both victims and perpetrators had raised concerns and led to several attempts from the bereaved to get help (Vatnar et al., 2017a). Vatnar and colleagues found that concerns were rarely conveyed to professional agencies, but when they actually were, the general experience of the bereaved was that the agencies failed to realize the seriousness and urgency of the reported situations.

Although it is far less focused upon in research, there is some evidence that IPV perpetrators have sometimes sought help before committing fatal violence (e.g., Askeland, Evang, & Heir, 2011; Dobash & Dobash, 2015; Eliason, 2009; Hester et al., 2015; Martin et al., 2007; Vatnar et al., 2017a).

## IPH and substance use

Substance use appears to be an important risk factor in IPH, although we currently lack a clear understanding of its explanatory role. Studies of IPH measuring the link between substance use and IPH have typically examined either alcohol use or drug use, but not both or combinations of the two (Aldridge & Browne, 2003; Campbell et al., 2007, 2009; Dobash, Dobash, & Cavanagh, 2009; Dobash & Dobash, 2015; Nicoladis et al., 2003). However, there are recent studies measuring several dimensions of the link between substance use and IPH (e.g., Ontario Death Review Committee in Canada, Lucas et al., 2016; Vatnar, Friestad, & Bjørkly, 2019a). Among the shortcomings in the literature are the lack of consistent definitions of such terms as *use* and *misuse*. As well as legal and illegal substances, ongoing versus previous use, perpetrator's versus victim's substance use, and, in particular, the role of substance use in the IPH incident itself.

A recent review of male perpetrators of IPH (Kivisto, 2015) suggested that most of them, despite generally high substance misuse rates, were not under the influence of drugs or alcohol at the time of the IPH. However, another often-quoted study (Campbell et al., 2007) found that 80% of the male perpetrators had been drinking at the time of the murder; two-thirds were described as intoxicated, and one quarter had consumed both alcohol and drugs. Also Garcia and Hurwitz (2007) in their literature review found that in two-thirds of IPH, including IPH attempts, the perpetrator had consumed alcohol, drugs, or a combination of both. As well, a review of perpetrators of spousal homicide found that 22% of the male perpetrators believed their partner had consumed alcohol prior to being killed, and 44% characterized their partner as having had a drug problem at the time she was killed (Aldridge & Browne, 2003). In summary, reviews and recent original studies of IPH vary considerably in their estimates (4%–80%) of the percentage of perpetrators being intoxicated at the time of an IPH incident. Furthermore, in these same reviews and studies, the results are mixed and inconclusive pertaining to the *role* of substance use in IPH (Aldridge & Browne, 2003; Campbell et al., 2007; Garcia & Hurwitz, 2007; Kivisto, 2015; Vatnar et al., 2019a).

It is generally difficult to identify perpetrators' substance misuse at the time of IPH without laboratory analyses of blood or saliva samples taken at the time of the crime (Campbell et al., 2007). As reviews and recent original studies of IPH indicate, such data are generally lacking, and those studies that do include accurate identification of perpetrators' substance use at the time of the IPH are most often based on small and selected samples (Kivisto, 2015). However, a 22-year cohort study found few differences and many similarities between IPH perpetrated under the influence of substances or not (Vatnar et al., 2019a). Still, the following findings from this study need further investigation: biological traces of substance use were found in more than half of the perpetrators and in 40% of the victims; perpetrators' and victims' substance influence at time of crime was positively associated; IPH perpetrators' type of influence at the time of the homicide was positively associated with their substance abuse in general (Vatnar et al., 2019a). These findings parallel results from a study finding victim–offender similarity in police-reported violent crimes in general (Aaltonen, 2016). This indicates a positive association between socioeconomic/criminal background and victimization being enhanced by the intensity of the perpetrator's criminal background (Aaltonen, 2016). Equally, a longitudinal cohort study examining the link between crime and drug misuse and social inclusion and exclusion in adult life showed that drug misuse is central both to processes of continuity and desistance from crime and to life chances and mortality in adulthood (Nilsson, Estrada, & Bäckman, 2014). These findings of IPH and other violent crimes concur with research indicating that established psychological and criminological theories of IPH should be expected to generalize across population groups (Skardhamar, Aaltonen, & Lehti, 2014).

A recent study conducted in Sweden indicated decreasing prevalence of alcohol influence among both perpetrator and victim in the period from 1990 to 2013 (Caman, Kristiansson, Granath, & Sturup, 2017). This pattern was not significant in a Norwegian IPH cohort study (Vatnar et al., 2019a). Campbell and collaborators' (2007) review of IPH indicated that males are more likely to be chronic alcohol misusers as victims than as perpetrators. Moreover, male victims or perpetrators are more likely to chronically misuse alcohol than females in either category. This concurs with the Caman and coworkers' (2017) findings indicating a declining trend over time in the proportion of male-perpetrated IPHs involving alcohol at the time of the crime or being preceded by a known history of IPV. However, the majority of female-perpetrated

IPHs involved alcohol and a history of known IPV. In addition, Campbell and colleagues' review indicated that alcohol use was not a unique risk factor for IPH for women as victims, but rather a common risk factor for female victims across homicide categories. A review of IPV and homicide from 2007 reported data indicating that male offenders were more likely than their female victims to drink alcohol or use drugs at the time of incidents (Garcia & Hurwitz, 2007). However, this research did not distinguish between IPH, attempted IPH, or the most severe incident of IPV. A recent study found no significant differences for sex and substance use at time of crime after controlling for other group differences (Vatnar et al., 2019a).

The great majority of studies on IPH and substance use did not have joint operational definitions and measures pertaining to variables, such as *intoxicated, under the influence of, substance use*, and *alcohol use*, or *drinking*. Accordingly, some of the mixed findings might result from applying different measures of substance use.

## IPH and immigration

Systematic reviews of the literature show that IPH committed by immigrants is *not* a major contributor to the overall prevalence of IPH, as most IPHs are committed by and toward the majority population. Still, because several studies have shown that immigrants are proportionally overrepresented in the IPH statistics (see, e.g., Echeburua, Fernandez-Montalvo, de Corral, & Lopez-Goni, 2009; Edelstein, 2016; Garcia & Hurwitz, 2007; Matias et al., 2020; Sabri, Campbell, & Dabby, 2016), empirical knowledge about IPH among immigrants is important to consider.

Some researchers have raised concerns that focusing on crime among immigrants might increase stigmatization of this group of people (e.g., Sarnecki, 2006). Others assert that established psychological and criminological theories of IPH should be expected to generalize across population groups, covering both immigrant and native populations (e.g., Skardhamar et al., 2014). To be sure, if certain groups are proportionally overrepresented with registered crime, then increased attention to those groups is warranted. Otherwise, a possible risk factor would be neglected, leaving a vulnerable group of IPV victims at increased risk. However, a higher risk among foreign citizens, both as perpetrators and as victims, might be due to contextual factors such as barriers to help-seeking faced by both perpetrators and victims, which may be due to fear of involving the police and potentially jeopardizing their immigration status. It may also be caused by sociodemographic and contextual factors of being an immigrant. The finding of perpetrator's source of income (unemployed) as a risk factor in IPH by foreign and naturalized citizen perpetrators concur with studies indicating that social and economic disadvantage, rather than ethnicity or immigration per se, are the actual, underlying issues and risk factors for IPH (Barrett & St Pierre, 2011; Dobash & Dobash, 2015; Dobash et al., 2009; Vatnar, Friestad, & Bjørkly, 2017b). However, IPV as a major risk factor for IPH is true for immigrants as well – for both foreign and naturalized citizen perpetrators (e.g., Vatnar et al., 2017b). At the same time, there might be some specific risk factors associated with immigrants or some immigrant groups, even after adjusting for other group differences. It has been asserted that IPHs committed by immigrants (mainly from patriarchal cultures) have unique characteristics such as jealousy-oriented triggers, methods of killing and use of excessive force ("overkilling") that differentiate them from other low SES groups (e.g., Campbell et al., 2007; Edelstein, 2013; Sabri et al., 2016). However, findings showing that immigrants were ascribed different motives and received longer sentences than majority population perpetrators in IPH cases, call for research into how the formal sanctioning system interprets crime committed by minority groups (Vatnar et al., 2017b). In addition, the finding indicating identical sex distribution among native and foreign perpetrators is intriguing (Vatnar et al., 2017b), signifying that the proportion of native perpetrators of female IPH were identical with foreign or immigrant perpetrators.

## IPH-suicide

Homicide-suicide incidents make up a relatively small proportion of homicides overall, but occur more frequently in IPH (Dobash & Dobash, 2015; Galta, Olsen, & Wik, 2010; Knoll & Hatters-Friedman, 2015; Liem, 2010; Liem, Barber, Markwalder, Killia, & Nieuwbeerta, 2011; Malphurs & Cohen, 2005; Marzuk, Tardiff, & Hirsch, 1992; Matias et al., 2020; Salari & Sillito, 2016). Homicide-suicide refers to a homicide of one or several individuals immediately followed by the perpetrator dying by suicide (e.g., Dobash & Dobash, 2015; Knoll & Hatters-Friedman, 2015). Commonly, cases are included in which the homicide(s) and the suicide are likely parts of the same action (Galta et al., 2010), as operationalized in terms of a time interval between homicide(s) and suicide ranging from the typical 24 hours (Dobash & Dobash, 2015; Knoll & Hatters-Friedman, 2015) to as long as one week (Eliason, 2009; Marzuk et al., 1992). Findings from Sweden and Norway showed that 24% and 25% respectively, of perpetrators of IPH with a female victim died by suicide after the homicide. This is about four times the rate of suicides completed after lethal violence under other circumstances (Belfrage & Rying, 2004; Vatnar, Friestad, & Bjørkly, 2019b). Studies from the United States have found that 27% to 32% of IPH was IPH-suicide (IPHS) (Bossarte, Simon, & Barker, 2006; Campbell et al., 2007).

There is a widespread perception borne out by prior research that homicide-suicide perpetrators differ from the prototypical "killer". Instead of emphasizing more general homicide risk factors, some researchers have argued that perpetrators of IPHS suffer from reactions to situational circumstances, such as distress over relationship termination (e.g., Galta et al., 2010; Eliason, 2009). Research has described these perpetrators as less socially marginalized, better educated, and more often employed compared to other homicide perpetrators (Campbell et al., 2007; Dobash, Dobash, Cavanagh, & Lewis, 2004; Eliason, 2009; Galta et al., 2010; Panczak et al., 2013). Common risk factors for IPH such as previous IPV, alcohol or substance use, family problems, mental illness, or a criminal record are less likely to apply to perpetrators of IPHS (Banks, Crandall, Sklar, & Bauer, 2008; Dobash et al., 2004; Eliason, 2009; Knoll & Hatters-Friedman, 2015; Panczak et al., 2013). Homicide-suicide studies have shown that substance involvement was about half of that found in homicide alone (Eliason, 2009). However, Panczak et al.'s (2013) meta-analysis indicated the influence of alcohol, history of IPV, and unemployment as common risk factors in both IPH and IPHS. Campbell et al. (2007) also emphasized unemployment as the strongest demographic risk factor for both IPH and IPHS. Previous suicide attempts were more common among perpetrators of homicide-suicide than among homicide perpetrators (Panczak et al., 2013). Across cultures, however, a high prevalence of previous physical IPV has been reported in IPHS, supporting this as an important risk factor also for this IPH subgroup (Eliason, 2009; Knoll & Friedman, 2015; Liem, 2010; Malphurs & Cohen, 2005; Vatnar et al., 2017a).

The statement that homicide-suicide perpetrators are different from the typical profile of a "killer" has also been supported by interviews with the bereaved (Vatnar et al., 2019b). However, even if perpetrators of IPHS are less likely than perpetrators of IPH to have a criminal record, qualitative data indicated previous violations of the law that were undetected or that did not incur criminal consequences (Vatnar et al., 2019b). Some bereaved have pointed out that linking the homicides to ordinary stressful situations like a heavy workload or the termination of a partnership caused anxiety and concern, at least in the local community (Vatnar et al., 2019b).

On the contrary, interviews with the bereaved indicated that the IPHS was perceived as intentional and planned, not an accidental reaction to situational circumstances (Vatnar et al., 2019b). In addition, the bereaved felt that the loss of hope or loss of a future in combination with an inability to cope with severe life disappointments was an important risk factor. This finding adds some perspective to previous findings that homicide-suicide perpetrators are commonly more depressed and their motives are failure and loss compared to homicide perpetrators (Campbell et al., 2007; Eliason, 2009; Holland, Brown, Hall, & Logan, 2018; Knoll & Hatters-Friedman, 2015; Liem, 2010; Salari & Sillito, 2016).

Within the IPHS group, there is a subgroup of ailing spouses, for which research have emphasized the role of economic strain, as well as changing health in one or both of the partners (Liem, 2010). Perpetrators of IPHS often experience mental illness, with depression being the most prevalent disorder, and were more likely than perpetrators of IPH to have been seen in health or mental health services due to depression or threats of suicide in the year prior to the incident (Campbell et al., 2007; Eliason, 2009; Knoll & Friedman, 2015; Salari & Sillito, 2016).

A comparison of IPHS perpetrators by age found that a known history of IPV was most common in young dyads (Salari & Sillito, 2016). In terms of personality characteristics, men who commit IPHS are described as over-controlling and dependent (Marzuk et al., 1992; Liem, 2010). It has also been suggested that when the continuation of a relationship is threatened, a breakthrough of aggression can take the shape of IPHS (Liem, 2010). These circumstances share jealousy as a motive, the trigger leading up to the event being the perceived rejection by the female partner and an immediate threat of separation and estrangement. Perpetrators of IPHS are hypothesized to be unable to cope with life's disappointments, such as a terminated relationship, illness, and financial difficulties (Knoll & Hatters-Friedman, 2015; Liem, 2010; Salari & Sillito, 2016; Vatnar et al., 2019b). Others have suggested that suicidal men who commit IPHS may do so because they view their partners and children as part of an "extended self" (Bossarte et al., 2006; Knoll & Hatters-Friedman, 2015; Salari & Sillito, 2016). To speculate, IPH could be interpreted as the Caucasian male's version of honour-based homicide (Vatnar et al., 2019b). However, studies are claiming that homicide-suicide cannot be categorized either as homicide or as suicide, but is actually a distinct behaviour (Eliason, 2009; Knoll & Hatters-Friedman, 2015; Marzuk et.al., 1992; Panczak et al., 2013). Nevertheless, it seems naive to assume that homicide-suicide shares no characteristics with other forms of fatal violence or that its typology is exhaustive (Marzuk et al., 1992; Vatnar et al., 2019b).

Perpetrators of IPHS seem less socially marginalized and more often employed, compared to perpetrators of homicide generally (Campbell, et al., 2007; Dobash et al., 2004; Eliason, 2009; Galta et al., 2010; Panczak et al., 2013; Vatnar et al., 2019b). Still, IPHS perpetrators emerged as more similar to, than different from, IPH perpetrators in findings from multivariate analysis comparing other sociodemographic characteristics in a recent study (Vatnar et al., 2019b). Research has found that perpetrators of IPHS were more likely than perpetrators of IPH to have used health or mental health services due to depression or threats of suicide in the year prior to the incident (Campbell et al., 2007). Yet, a recent study found that compared to that of perpetrators of IPH, information on IPHS perpetrators' previous contact with police, health, and social services was more often absent in the court case documents (Vatnar et al., 2019b). Hence, we need more research before this issue can be settled.

## Differentiating female and male IPH perpetrators

Consistent with the heavily skewed sex distribution, most research on IPH has solely studied male perpetrators and male-perpetrated IPHs with female victims (Caman, Howner, Kristiansson, &

Sturup, 2016; Weizmann-Henelius et al., 2012). This leaves a gap in our knowledge concerning potential differences between IPHs committed by female and male perpetrators. It has been suggested that female and male IPH perpetrators are distinct groups (e.g., Campbell et al., 2007; Caman et al., 2016; Weizmann-Henelius et al., 2012), but the empirical evidence is weak due to few studies and mixed results. We are currently unable to conclude whether IPH committed by women is qualitatively and interactionally different from those perpetrated by men. The lack of research and clarity concerning potential sex-specific risk factors for IPH is a serious shortcoming in the IPH literature and a potential obstacle to targeting preventive interventions.

Studies investigating the phenomenon of IPH across genders have suggested both differences and similarities between female and male perpetrators. With regard to marginalized population groups, economic disadvantage, and ethnicity, no significant sex differences have emerged (Campbell et al., 2007; Weizmann-Henelius et al., 2012). One study reported no significant sex difference regarding abuse of alcohol (Weizmann-Henelius et al., 2012). However, a recent investigation suggested that female perpetrators are more likely to be unemployed, to have suffered from a substance abuse disorder at some point in their lives and to have been subjected to violence by the victim of the IPH (Caman et al., 2016). Another study identified sex differences in four risk factors that increased the risk for female-perpetrated IPH: the victim being intoxicated, the perpetrator being unemployed at the time of offence, quarrels due to intoxication, and self-defence being the motivating circumstance of the crime (Weizmann-Henelius et al., 2012).

Several studies have suggested that male perpetrators are more often motivated by jealousy and involuntary break-up, separation, or divorce (e.g., Belfrage & Rying, 2004; Dobash & Dobash, 2015). Female perpetrators' motives are more often linked to self-defence after being systematically victimized by IPV (Caman et al., 2016; Campbell et al., 2007; Serran & Firestone, 2004; Swatt & He, 2006; Walker & Browne, 1985). Furthermore, Campbell and colleagues (2007) found that the risk of female-perpetrated IPH increased when the male victims had abused the women or their mutual children.

Recent findings indicated that female-perpetrated IPHs occurred in the most marginalized segments of this generally disadvantaged group (Caman et al., 2016; Vatnar, Friestad, & Bjørkly, 2018; Weizmann-Henelius et al., 2012). Previous studies have argued that mental illness is more often an important risk factor in female-perpetrated IPHs than in male-perpetrated IPHs (e.g., Flynn & Graham, 2010). However, recent studies (Caman et al., 2016; Vatnar et al., 2018) did not find sex differences concerning diagnosis. Previous findings have been conflicting regarding demographic characteristics and substance abuse (Weizmann-Henelius et al., 2012). Substance abuse problems have been found to be less likely among males perpetrating IPH than other types of homicide (Dobash & Dobash, 2015). In this same study, neither drug use nor alcohol abuse by the victim was independently associated with the risk of being a victim of IPH. However, a recent study found that female-perpetrated IPHs more often involved a substance-addicted *victim* (Vatnar et al., 2018). The most striking sociodemographic difference in Vatnar et al.'s study was that no female perpetrators had mutual children with their victims, in contrast to 56.4% of the male perpetrators. One hypothesis may be that female-perpetrated IPH occurs in different kinds of partnerships and in other contexts (substance misuse) than the majority of male-perpetrated IPHs. In relation to this, a systematic literature review found that familicides were almost exclusively committed by men, that relationship problems, mental health problems, and financial difficulties often precede the offence. About half of the familicide cases led to the suicide of the offender (Karlsson et al., 2019).

The empirical literature on IPH characteristics and perpetrators of IPH, based mainly on research on males, indicates that previous IPV is a major risk factor for IPH. Some studies have found that when females used lethal violence, they did so in self-defence and as a result of having been victimized by the IPH victim (Aldridge & Browne, 2003; Bailey et al., 1997; Caman et al., 2016; Campbell et al., 2007; Swatt & He, 2006; Weizmann-Henelius et al., 2012). Accordingly, it has been suggested that there are motivational sex differences related to the dynamics of the relationships (Caman et al., 2016; Liem & Roberts, 2009; Serran & Firestone, 2004; Weizmann-Henelius et al., 2012). A recent study using multivariate analyses did not find support for sex differences concerning previous IPV in the IPH relationship (Vatnar et al., 2018). However, there were bivariate findings indicating that mutual IPV was more often present in the cases of female-perpetrated IPH, 87.5% compared to 51.8% (Vatnar et al., 2018).

Recent research has revealed that women do not commit IPHs solely in self-defence, as has often been supposed previously (Dutton & Nicholls, 2005; Weizmann-Henelius et al., 2012). Quarrelling when drinking was also often reported, and a majority of female perpetrators were alcohol dependent (Weizmann-Henelius et al., 2012). This is consistent with findings of quarrelling as the most prevalent motive for female-perpetrated IPHs as well (Vatnar et al., 2018). By and large, establishing *motives* is complex and may be subject to bias. Because no exact criteria exists regarding how to measure *the motive for IPH*, it is easy to find results that converge with long-held myths and previous findings, and to ignore or overlook findings diverging from a priori interpretations and expectations. Previous research has suggested that female and male perpetrators of IPHs are distinct groups (Caman et al., 2016; Campbell et al., 2007; Eriksson & Mazerolle, 2013; Serran & Firestone, 2004; Weizmann-Henelius et al., 2012). However, the current empirical evidence for this conclusion is weak due to mixed results.

## Discussion and analysis

Previous IPV is seen in 65% to 80% of IPHs, and *repeated* previous intimate partner violence is seen in 25% to 65% of IPHs (Campbell et al., 2007, 2009; Nicolaidis et al., 2003; Vatnar et al., 2017a). This means that in the majority of cases at-risk individuals could be identified and interventions employed by multi-agency, coordinated community responses, and structured professional risk assessment and management, with considerable preventive potential (Contini & Wilson, 2019; Kropp & Hart, 2015; Robinson & Tregidga, 2007).

IPH is very rare compared to non-lethal intimate partner violence, and because of the low base rate, it is not possible to obtain valid results by using the traditional "risk prediction" format to IPH. The only scope of risk prediction is to identify a context-free risk of future violence for the actual person. In contrast to this, multi-agency, coordinated community responses, and structured professional risk assessment has two main aims: (1) to identify violence risk as an interactional or situational/contextual phenomenon and (2) to develop measures that can mitigate this risk. Instigating preventive efforts is an integrated part of this approach.

In the challenging task of identifying individuals in contexts at high risk of either perpetrating or being a victim of IPH, sociodemographic, contextual and clinical factors are relevant (Matias et al., 2020). Research shows that IPHs follow a socially biased pattern, with socially and economically marginalized groups being at highest risk (Aldridge & Browne, 2003; Dobash et al., 2009; Garcia et al., 2007; Vatnar et al., 2017a). Then, in addition to individual factors, IPH needs to be addressed at a societal level, as well. This is consistent with research on recorded crime and homicide in general. Thus, the news media's well-documented tendency to present IPH as happening out of the blue is at odds with the evidence (Peelo, Francis, Soothill, Pearson, & Ackerley, 2004; Taylor, 2009).

The socially biased distribution of IPH presents several prevention challenges. First of all, people with complex and accumulated problems are among the most challenging groups to reach effectively with adequate and sufficient preventive interventions (Whitfield, Anda, Dube, & Felitti, 2003). Furthermore, risk factors such as mutual partner violence, criminal involvement, substance abuse, and mental health problems are often misinterpreted. Rather than being correctly regarded as indicators of heightened vulnerability, they may be used to underestimate the severity of a violent episode (Vatnar et al., 2017a).

If victims and bereaved have somewhat similar thresholds for help-seeking from official sources (police, health services, etc.), it is relevant to emphasize that studies investigating help-seeking have shown that the most important independent predictor is the victim's fear of being killed. Research indicates that the actual threshold for help-seeking in IPH populations is *high* (e.g., Vatnar et al., 2017a). Still, even if helping agencies believe that they have a low threshold for individuals to access help, this appears not yet realized. It is very important for help-providing agencies to be aware of this discrepancy in order to avoid misinterpreting reports of risk and running the risk of fatal outcomes. When concerns about intimate partner violence are actually conveyed to official help-seeking resources, urgent action is often required.

Most IPH cases end in court. If different IPH perpetrator subgroups are systematically ascribed different motives, and the motives influence the length of sentences, then such perceptions might be interpreted as indicating racial or gender bias in the justice system (Vatnar et al., 2017b, 2018).

## Conclusions

The majority of IPHs do not occur without warning signs. In the majority of IPHs, risk and vulnerability factors, such as previous IPV, sociodemographic, contextual, and clinical factors, have been observed by professionals as well as by friends and family. As IPH is very rare compared to other IPV, it is important to emphasize the difference between conducting valid risk assessment of IPV to prevent repeat episodes and the complexity in accurate prediction of IPH. Further research on IPH and clinical work within this field should focus on two strongly associated issues: risk identification *and* prevention of IPH. First, this means to prioritize research and clinical work on assessments of *situations, contexts, persons,* and *the interactions/interplay* that may increase risk of IPH; and second, to implement multi-agency, structured professional risk assessment and coordinated community interventions to mitigate this risk.

## Critical findings

- Empirical research indicates that the majority of IPHs have identifiable warning signs.
- Previous intimate partner violence is the best-documented risk factor for IPH.
- The IPH distribution is biased toward low socioeconomic status, with marginalized groups characterized by accumulated welfare deficiencies being at highest risk.
- In the majority of IPHs, risk and vulnerability factors have been observed by professionals as well as by friends and family. However, there is a void of communication to health care, police, or support services and between the services. Research indicates that the actual threshold for help-seeking in IPH populations is *high*.
- A significant number of IPHs are IPH-suicide. Studies claim that homicide-suicide cannot be categorized either as homicide or as suicide, but is actually a distinct behaviour. Nevertheless, it would be naive to assume that homicide-suicide is unique and shares no characteristics with other forms of fatal violence.
- The empirical evidence to conclude that females who commit IPHs are qualitatively and clinically different from their male counterparts is weak due to mixed results.

# Implications for policy, practice, and research

## *Policy*

• The actual threshold for help-seeking in IPH populations appears to be high. Increased efforts are thus needed in order to realize the officially stated intent of providing low threshold services to this vulnerable group.

## *Practice*

• If certain groups are found to have greater involvement in IPH, then increased attention to those groups is warranted. The alternative would be to neglect possible risk factors and leave a vulnerable group of intimate partner violence (IPV) victims at increased risk.

## *Research*

• Further research on IPH and clinical work within this field should focus on two strongly associated issues: risk identification *and* prevention of IPH. This means prioritizing research and clinical work on assessments of *situations, contexts, persons*, and *the interactions/interplay* that may increase risk of IPH, and implementing interventions to mitigate this risk. Uniform operational definitions of supporting/opposing mandatory reporting and validated instruments are prerequisites for reliable and valid findings.

# References

Aaltonen, M. (2016). To whom do prior offenders pose a risk? Victim–offender similarity in police-reported violent crime. *Crime & Delinquency, 63*(11), 1410–1433. doi:10.1177/0011128716654713

Aldridge, M. L., & Browne, K. (2003). Perpetrators of spousal homicide. A review. *Trauma, Violence & Abuse, 4*, 265–276.

Alisic, E., Groot, A., Snetselaar, H., Stroeken, T., & van de Putte, E. (2017). Children bereaved by fatal intimate partner violence: A population-based study into demographics, family characteristics and homicide exposure. *PLoS One, 12*(10), e0183466. doi:10.1371/journal.pone.0183466

Askeland, I. R., Evang, A., & Heir, T. (2011). Association of violence against partner and former victim experiences: A sample of clients voluntarily attending therapy. *Journal of Interpersonal Violence,* 1095–1110.

Bailey, J. E., Kellermann, A. L., Somes, G. W., Banton, J. G., Rivara, F. P., & Rushforth, N. P. (1997). Risk factors for violent death of women in the home. *Archives of Internal Medicine, 157*(7), 777–782.

Banks, L., Crandall, C., Sklar, D., & Bauer, M. (2008). A comparison of intimate partner homicide to intimate partner homicide-suicide: One hundred and twenty-four New Mexico cases. *Violence Against Women, 14*(9), 1065–1078.

Barrett, B. J., & St Pierre, M. (2011). Variation in women's help seeking in response to intimate partner violence: Findings from a Canadian population-based study. *Violence Against Women, 17*, 47–70.

Belfrage, H., & Rying, M. (2004). Characteristics of spousal homicide perpetrators: A study of all cases of spousal homicide in Sweden 1990–1999. *Criminal Behaviour & Mental Health, 14*(2), 121–133.

Bell, K. M., & Naugle, A. E. (2008). Intimate partner violence theoretical considerations: Moving towards a contextual framework. *Clinical Psychology Review, 28*, 1096–1107.

Bossarte, R. M., Simon, T. R., & Barker, L. (2006). Characteristics of homicide followed by suicide incidents in multiple states, 2003–04. *Injury Prevention, 12*(Suppl 2), ii33–ii38. doi:10.1136/ip.2006.012807

Caman, S., Howner, K., Kristiansson, M., & Sturup, J. (2016). Differentiating male and female intimate partner homicide perpetrators: A study of social, criminological and clinical factors. *International Journal of Forensic Mental Health, 15*(1), 26–34.

Caman, S., Kristiansson, M., Granath, S., & Sturup, J. (2017). Trends in rates and characteristics of intimate partner homicides between 1990 and 2013. *Journal of Criminal Justice, 49*, 14–21. doi:10.1016/j.jcrimjus.2017.01.002

Campbell, J. C., Glass, N., Sharps, P., Laughon, K., & Bloom, T. (2007). Intimate partner homicide. Review and implications of research and policy. *Trauma, Violence & Abuse, 8*, 246–269.

Campbell, J. C., Webster, D. W., & Glass, N. (2009). The danger assessment. Validation of a lethality risk assessment instrument for intimate partner femicide. *Journal of Interpersonal Violence, 24*, 653–674.

Contini, M., & Wilson, B. (2019). *Multi-agency risk assessment conferences in the UK and Canada.* Retrieved from https://atrium2.lib.uoguelph.ca/xmlui/bitstream/handle/10214/17415/Contini_Wilson_CanadianMARACmodel_2019.pdf?sequence=1&isAllowed=y drawn 2020 01 02

Dixon, L., & Graham-Kevan, N. (2011). Until death do us part. *The Psychologist, 24*(11), 820–823. Retrieved from http://ovidsp.ovid.com/ovidweb.cgi?T=JS&CSC=Y&NEWS=N&PAGE=fulltext&D=psyc8&AN=2011-26540-003

Dixon, L., Hamilton-Giachritsis, C., & Browne, K. (2008). Classifying partner femicide. *Journal of Interpersonal Violence, 23*(1), 74–93.

Dobash, E. R., & Dobash, R. P. (2011). What were they thinking? Men who murder an intimate partner. *Violence Against Women, 17*(1), 111–134.

Dobash, E. R., & Dobash, R. P. (2015). *When men murder women.* Oxford: Oxford university Press.

Dobash, E. R., Dobash, R. P., Cavanagh, K., & Lewis, R. (2004). Not an ordinary killer – Just an ordinary guy: When men murder an intimate woman partner. *Violence Against Women, 10*(6), 577–605.

Dobash, E. R., Dobash, R. P., & Cavanagh, K. (2009). "Out of the blue". Men who murder an intimate partner. *Feminist Criminology, 4*, 194–225.

Dutton, D. G., & Nicholls, T. (2005). The gender paradigm in domestic violence research and theory: Part 1 – The conflict of theory and data. *Aggression and Violent Behavior, 10*, 680–674.

Echeburua, E., Fernandez-Montalvo, J., de Corral, P., & Lopez-Goni, J. J. (2009). Assessing risk markers in intimate partner femicide and severe violence: A new assessment instrument. *Journal of Interpersonal Violence, 24*(6), 925–939.

Edelstein, A. (2013). Culture transition, acculturation and intimate partner homicide. *Springerplus, 2*, 338. doi:10.1186/2193-1801-2-338

Edelstein, A. (2016). Intimate partner jealousy and femicide among former Ethiopians in Israel. *International Journal of Offender Therapy and Comparative Criminology.* doi:10.1177/0306624x16652453

Eke, A. W., Hilton, N. Z., Harris, G. T., Rice, M. E., & Houghton, R. E. (2011). Intimate partner homicide: Risk assessment and prospects for prediction. *Journal of Family Violence, 26*, 211–216.

Eliason, S. (2009). Murder-suicide: A review of the recent literature. *Journal of the American Academy of Psychiatry and the Law, 37*(3), 371–376.

Emery, C. R. (2011). Disorder or deviant order? Re-theorizing domestic violence in terms of order, power and legitimacy. A typology. *Aggression & Violent Behavior, 16*, 525–540.

Eriksson, L., & Mazerolle, P. (2013). A general strain theory of intimate partner homicide. *Aggression and Violent Behavior, 18*(5), 462–470. doi:10.1016/j.avb.2013.07.002

Flynn, A., & Graham, K. (2010). "Why did it happen?" a review and conceptual framework for research on perpetrators' and victims' explanations for intimate partner violence. *Aggression & Violent Behavior*, 239–251.

Funder, D. C. (2006). Towards a revolution of the personality triad: Persons, situations, and behaviors. *Journal of Research in Personality, 40*, 21–34.

Galta, K., Olsen, S. L., & Wik, G. (2010). Murder followed by suicide: Norwegian data and international literature. *Nordic Journal of Psychiatry*, 397–401.

Garcia, L., & Hurwitz, E. L. (2007). Homicides and intimate partner violence. A literature review. *Trauma, Violence & Abuse, 8*, 370–383.

Goodman, L., Smyth, K. F., Borges, A. M., & Singer, R. (2009). When crises collide. How intimate partner violence and poverty intersect to shape women's mental health and coping? *Trauma, Violence & Abuse, 10*, 306–329.

Hester, M., Ferrari, G., Jones, S., Williamson, E., Peters, T. J., Bacchus, L., & Feder, G. S. (2015). Occurrence and impact of negative behaviour, including domestic violence and abuse in men attending UK primary care health clinics: A cross-sectional survey. *British Medical Journal Open.* Retrieved from http://bmjopen.bmj.com/content/5/5/e007141

Holland, K. M., Brown, S. V., Hall, J. E., & Logan, J. E. (2018). Circumstances preceding homicide-suicides involving child victims: A qualitative analysis. *Journal of Interpersonal Violence, 33*(3), 379–401. doi:10.1177/0886260515605124

Johnson, H., Eriksson, L., Mazerolle, P., & Wortley, R. (2019). Intimate femicide: The role of coercive control. *Feminist Criminology, 14*(1), 3–23

Karlsson, L. C., Antfolk, J., Putkonen, H., Amon, S., da Silva Guerreiro, J., de Vogel, V., . . . Weizmann-Henelius, G. (2019). Familicide: A systematic literature review. *Trauma, Violence, & Abuse*. doi:10.1177/1524838018821955

Kivisto, A. J. (2015). Male perpetrators of intimate partner homicide: A review and proposed typology. *Journal of the American Academy of Psychiatry and the Law, 43*(3), 300–312.

Knoll, J. L., & Hatters-Friedman, S. (2015). The homicide-suicide phenomenon: Findings of psychological autopsies. *Journal of Forensic Sciences, 60*(5), 1253–1257. doi:10.1111/1556-4029.12819

Kropp, P. R., & Hart, S. D. (2015). *Manual for the spousal assault risk assessment guide* (3rd ed.) (SARA-V3). Sydney, Australia: Proactive Resolutions.

Liem, M. (2010). Homicide followed by suicide: A review. *Aggression & Violent Behavior, 15*, 153–161.

Liem, M., Barber, C., Markwalder, N., Killias, M., & Nieuwbeerta, P. (2011). Homicide-suicide and other violent deaths: An international comparison. *Forensic Science International, 207*(1–3), 70–76. doi:10.1016/j.forsciint.2010.09.003

Liem, M., & Roberts, D. W. (2009). Intimate partner homicide by presence or absence of a self-destructive act. *Homicide Studies, 13*(4), 339–354.

Magnusson, D. (1981). *Towards a psychology of situations: An interactional perspective*. Hillsdale, NJ: Erlbaum.

Malphurs, J. E., & Cohen, D. (2005). A statewide case-control study of spousal homicide-suicide in older persons. *American Journal of Geriatric Psychiatry, 13*(3), 211–217.

Martin, S. L., Macy, R. J., Sullivan, K. l., & Magee, M. L. (2007). Pregnancy-associated violent deaths. The role of intimate partner violence. *Trauma, Violence & Abuse, 8*, 135–148.

Marzuk, P. M., Tardiff, K., & Hirsch, C. S. (1992). The epidemiology of murder-suicide. *JAMA, 267*(23), 3179–3183.

Matias, A., Goncalves, M., Soeiro, C., & Matos, M. (2020). Intimate partner homicide: A meta-analysis of risk factors. *Aggression and Violent Behavior*. doi:10.1016/J.AVB.2019.101358

Messerschmidt, J. W. (2017). Masculinities and femicide. *Qualitative Sociology Review, 13*(3).

Nicolaidis, C., Curry, M. A., Ulrich, Y., Scarps, P., McFarlane, J., Campbell, D., . . . Campbell, J. C. (2003). Could we have known? A qualitative analysis of data from women who survived an attempted homicide by an intimate partner. *Journal of General Internal Medicine, 18*, 788–794.

Nilsson, A., Estrada, F., & Backman, O. (2014). Offending, drug abuse and life chances – A longitudinal study of a Stockholm birth cohort. *Journal of Scandinavian Studies in Criminology and Crime Prevention, 15*(2), 128–142. doi:10.1080/14043858.2014.939452

Nurius, P. S., Macy, R. J., Nwabuzor, I., & Holt, V. L. (2011). Intimate partner survivor's help-seeking and protection efforts: A person-oriented analysis. *Journal of Interpersonal Violence, 26*, 539–566.

Ontario Death Review Committee in Canada. (2016). Retrieved from www.mcscs.jus.gov.on.ca/english/Deathinvestigations/OfficeChiefCoroner/Publicationsandreports/2016DomesticViolenceDeathReviewCommitteeAnnualReport.html.

Panczak, R., Geissbuhler, M., Zwahlen, M., Killias, M., Tal, K., & Egger, M. (2013). Homicide-suicides compared to homicides and suicides: Systematic review and meta-analysis. *Forensic Science International, 233*(1–3), 28–36. doi:10.1016/j.forsciint.2013.08.017

Peelo, M., Francis, B., Soothill, K., Pearson, J., & Ackerley, E. (2004). Newspaper reporting and the public construction of homicide. *British Journal of Criminology, 44*(2), 256–275. doi:10.1093/bjc/44.2.256

Robinson, A. L., & Tregidga, J. (2007). The perceptions of high-risk victims of domestic violence to a coordinated community response in Cardiff, Wales. *Violence Against Women, 13*(11), 1130–1148. doi:10.1177/1077801207307797

Sabri, B., Campbell, J. C., & Dabby, F. C. (2016). Gender differences in intimate partner homicides among ethnic sub-groups of Asians. *Violence Against Women, 22*(4), 432–453. doi:10.1177/1077801215604743

Salari, S., & Sillito, C. L. (2016). Intimate partner homicide – Suicide: Perpetrator primary intent across young, middle, and elder adult age categories. *Aggression and Violent Behavior, 26*, 26–34. doi:10.1016/j.avb.2015.11.004

Sarnecki, J. (Ed.). (2006). *SOU 2006:30 Är rättvisan rättvis Tio perspektiv på diskriminering av etniska ochreligiösa minoriteter inom rättssystemet* [White paper Sweden, 2006. Is justice fair ten perspectives on discrimination of ethnic and religious minorities in the judicial system]. ISBN 91–38–22547. Retrieved October 12, 2017, from www.fritzes.se

Serran, G., & Firestone, P. (2004). Intimate partner homicide: A review of the male proprietariness and the self-defense theories. *Aggression and Violent Behavior, 9*(1), 1–15. doi:10.1016/s1359-1789(02)00107-6

Shadigian, E., & Bauer, S. T. (2005). Pregnancy-associated death: A qualitative systematic review of homicide and suicide. *Obstetrical & Gynecological Survey, 60*(3), 183–190.

Shields, L. B. E., Corey, T. S., Weakley-Jones, B., & Stewart, D. (2010). Living victims of strangulation. A 10-year review of cases in a metropolitan community. *American Journal of Forensic Medical pathology, 31*, 320–325.

Skardhamar, T., Aaltonen, M., & Lehti, M. (2014). Immigrant crime in Norway and Finland. *Journal of Scandinavian Studies in Criminology and Crime Prevention, 15*(2), 107–127. doi:10.1080/14043858.201 4.926062

Stöckl, H., Devries, K., Rotstein, A., Abrahams, N., Campbell, J., Watts, C., & Moreno, C. G. (2013). The global prevalence of intimate partner homicide: A systematic review. *The Lancet, 382*(9895), 859–865. doi:10.1016/S0140-6736(13)61030-2

Swatt, M. L., & He, N. (2006). Exploring the difference between male and female intimate partner homicides: Revisiting the concept of situated transactions. *Homicide Studies: An Interdisciplinary & International Journal, 10*(4), 279–292.

Taylor, R. (2009). Slain and slandered: A content analysis of the portrayal of femicide in crime news. *Homicide Studies, 13*(1), 21–49.

Vatnar, S. K. B., & Bjørkly, S. (2008). An interactional perspective of intimate partner violence: An in-depth semi-structured interview of a representative sample of help-seeking women. *Journal of Family Violence, 23*, 265–279.

Vatnar, S. K. B., & Bjørkly, S. (2014). An interactional perspective on coping with intimate partner violence: Counterattack, call for help, or give in and obey him? *Journal of Aggression, Maltreatment & Trauma, 23*(9), 881–900. doi:10.1080/10926771.2014.953716

Vatnar, S. K. B., Friestad, C., & Bjørkly, S. (2017a). Intimate partner homicide in Norway 1990–2012: Identifying risk factors through structured risk assessment, court documents, and interviews with bereaved. *Psychology of Violence, 17*, 395–405.

Vatnar, S. K. B., Friestad, C., & Bjørkly, S. (2017b). Intimate partner homicide, immigration, and citizenship: Evidence from Norway 1990–2012. *Journal of Scandinavian Studies in Criminology and Crime Prevention, 18*(2), 103–122.

Vatnar, S. K. B., Friestad, C., & Bjørkly, S. (2018). Differences in intimate partner homicides perpetrated by men and women: Evidence from a Norwegian National 22-year cohort, *Psychology, Crime & Law.* doi:10.1080/1068316X.2018.1438433

Vatnar, S. K. B., Friestad, C., & Bjørkly, S. (2019a). The influence of substance use on intimate partner homicide: Evidence from s Norwegian national 22-year cohort. *International Journal of Forensic Mental Health.* doi:10.1080/14999013.2018.1525777

Vatnar, S. K. B., Friestad, C., & Bjørkly, S. (2019b). A comparison of intimate partner homicide with intimate partner homicide-suicide: Evidence From a Norwegian national 22-year cohort. *Journal of Interpersonal Violence.* doi:10.1177/0886260519849656. Online ahead of print.

Walker, L. E., & Browne, A. (1985). Gender and victimization by intimates. *Journal of Personality, 53*(2), 179–195.

Weizmann-Henelius, G., Gröroos, M., Putkonen, H., Eronen, M., Lindberg, N., & Häkkänen-Nyholm, H. (2012). Gender-specific risk factors for intimate partner homicide – A nationwide register-based study. *Journal of Interpersonal Violence, 27*(8), 1519–1539.

Whitfield, C. L., Anda, R. F., Dube, S. R., & Felitti, V. J. (2003). Violent childhood experiences and the risk of intimate partner violence in adults. Assessment in a large health maintenance organization. *Journal of Interpersonal Violence, 18*, 166–185.

Winstok, Z. (2007). Toward an interactional perspective on intimate partner violence. *Aggression & Violent Behavior, 12*, 348–363.

# 25

# COERCIVE CONTROL

*Amanda Robinson and Andy Myhill*

## Introduction

The aims of the chapter are three-fold. First, we discuss the origins and emergence of the concept of coercive control. We then present international evidence from qualitative interviews with victims and national population surveys that coercive control is a distinctive manifestation of domestic violence and abuse (DVA). Debates related to the operationalisation and measurement of this concept are discussed, including the extent to which it helps to reveal the harms associated with DVA and how these disproportionately affect women. The final section provides information about policy and legal reforms that have taken place in recent years to criminalise coercive control, drawing primarily from England and Wales. The difficulties involved in recognising and responding to such offending behaviour are discussed, with findings from recent mixed methods empirical studies offering some insights into how these may be overcome.

## Conceptualising coercive control

Coercive control as a specific concept has come to prominence in public policy and practice relatively recently, yet dynamics of power and control in intimate relationships have been recognised since the earliest advocacy work with survivors of DVA in the 1970s (see for example Dobash & Dobash, 1979; Schechter, 1982). The term 'coercive control' in fact pre-dates the study of domestic violence. In what Stark (2007, p. 200) describes as the 'definitive' chapter on coercive control, Okun (1986) describes how the tactics employed by many domestic abusers – isolating the victim, distorting their subjective reality, imposing unpredictable rewards and punishments, inducing debility and exhaustion and so on – are analogous to those used on prisoners subject to 'thought reform' in communist China. Activists have also recognised the experience of victims of coercive and controlling DVA in the tactics listed in a 'chart of coercion' published by Amnesty International in 1973 and based on the works of Alfred D. Biderman who studied the experiences of prisoners of war, political prisoners, hostages and concentration camp survivors (see Jones, 1994).

To these descriptions of the basic tactics used to coerce and control, feminist advocates and scholars added the notion of power imbalances in intimate relationships caused by structural inequality between men and women. In the global north, patriarchal control of the family was codified historically in law and capitalist modes of production afforded women part-time/low-paid work that was compatible with their disproportionate responsibility for household work, children and other forms of caring. Though the socio-economic position of (some) women has improved to some extent over time, there remain gender orders and regimes that place men in a dominant position at both macro levels of society and in specific locations like the workplace and the family (Connell, 2009). Indeed, advocacy work with survivors of DVA in Duluth, Minnesota that informed development of the well-known 'power and control wheel' suggested 'using male privilege' is a core element of DVA that is coercive and controlling.

Evan Stark's 2007 book *Coercive Control: How Men Entrap Women in Personal Life* is arguably the single most significant work marking the rise to prominence of coercive control in policy and practice around DVA. Stark sought to position coercive control as a 'liberty crime', defining it as 'a strategic course of oppressive conduct' intended to 'intimidate, degrade, isolate, and control victims' (Stark, 2012, p. 18). Stark sub-divides the tactics deployed by abusers into those relating to coercion (physical and sexual violence; intimidation, threats and degradation) and those relating to control (isolation; exploitation and deprivation; micro-regulation of everyday behaviour). He suggests that while physical violence in the context of coercive control can be severe, it is more frequently less severe but repeated, and that there are a significant minority of cases in which there will be little or no physical violence. This position is consistent with the Duluth model which positions (the threat of) physical and sexual violence as framing and reinforcing the core non-physical behaviours of coercive control. Stark (2012) also suggests coercive control is a highly personalised form of DVA, with intimacy and proximity affording the perpetrator the opportunity to refine abusive tactics to target a victim's personal vulnerabilities. He suggests further that the abusive tactics employed in coercive control operate frequently through the lens of gender inequality, focusing on how women 'perform gender roles they inherit by default' (Stark, 2012, p. 207).

Crucially, then, coercive control presents an alternative to what Stark (2012, p. 200) calls the 'violent incident model'. The theory recognises victim-survivors' experiences of their abuse as continuous and multi-faceted, as opposed to a series of discrete or time-bound acts of physical assault or psychological aggression. Kirkwood (1993, p. 58) described a 'web' of abuse where 'the components are interwoven in such a way that they comprise a whole which has properties beyond merely the sum of those individual components'. Similarly, Pitman (2017) presented a model called 'the trap' which involves multiple and overlaying strands of abuse. Coercive control recognises that abuse can be a course of conduct, traversing time and space, rather than a time-bound incident or series of incidents of abusive acts. It recognises the range of abusive tactics and behaviours experienced by victims, and acknowledges that, for some, the harm associated with multiple non-physical abusive behaviours is more severe than the harm inflicted by discrete physical assaults (see the next section). It is a theory borne out of advocacy and support work with female victim-survivors and thus reflects their lived experiences of DVA.

## Evidencing coercive control

### 1 Prevalence and measurement

It is widely accepted that data from criminal justice sources undercounts significantly the prevalence and incidence of DVA. Many victims choose not to report their abuse to the police (see Office for National Statistics, 2018), and feminist scholars have questioned the ability of traditional crime codes to represent thoroughly the breadth of the abuse suffered by many victims (though see Walby & Towers, 2018). There have also been issues historically around the quality of police record-keeping in relation to DVA (see Myhill & Johnson, 2016).

Measurement of the prevalence of domestic violence has been hotly contested since the first sample surveys were introduced in the 1970s (see Walby & Myhill, 2001; Myhill, 2015, 2017). These debates around the measurement of DVA have rested largely on the issue of whether headline prevalence estimates from population surveys obscure the gendered nature of abuse reflected in data from specialist support services and criminal justice and other agencies. In more general terms, however, there is little consensus on the best way to measure DVA, or on whether it is possible to measure a highly personalised, multi-faceted form of DVA like coercive control in the context of a (cross-sectional) population survey. Some surveys dedicated to measuring DVA have adapted the Conflict Tactics Scale (Straus, 1979; Straus, Hamby, Boney-McCoy, & Sugarman, 1996) to add additional questions relating to coercive and controlling behaviour (see Walby & Myhill, 2001), but there has been little consistency in approaches.

Numerous attempts have been made to operationalise the concept of coercive control in more comprehensive ways. Qualitative interviews and advocacy work with survivors has informed measurement scales such as the Women's Experiences of Battering Scale (Smith, Earp, & DeVellis, 1995), the Mediators Assessment of Safety Issues and Concerns (Pokeman et al., 2014), the Checklist of Controlling Behaviors (Lehmann, Simmons, & Pillai, 2012) and the Coercive Control UK scale (Sharp-Jeffs, Kelly, & Klein, 2018). Dutton, Goodman and Schmidt (2006) report on a large-scale attempt to produce a theoretical model of coercive control and comprehensive measurement framework, which involved a literature review and input from a panel of subject experts. That measurement framework stretched to more than 100 indictors and, according to Hamberger, Larsen and Lehrner (2017), while some elements of the framework have been developed into (briefer) published measures, others have not.

Despite the extensive work that has taken place internationally, there remains no agreed definition of coercive control for the purpose of measurement, nor any single instrument that has been fielded consistently in population surveys. In a review of the literature, Hamberger et al. (2017, p. 3) suggest three 'major facets' have emerged in relation to the construct of coercive control: intentionality and motivation to obtain control, perception of the behaviour as negative by the victim and the ability of the perpetrator to make a credible threat. They caution, though, that existing measurement constructs have tended to focus on 'behaviors or tactics purported to gain control', and only indirectly or infrequently on intentionality or negative perception (Hamberger et al., 2017). In conclusion, a key problem for the measurement of coercive control in national population surveys is representing the concept in a robust and comprehensive way within the space confines of the survey. Many of the existing measurement scales have multiple items that are not practical to field in many surveys, yet reducing these to a briefer set of core indicators risks identifying cases as coercive control that may not reach what practitioners would regard as a 'clinical' level (i.e. that which produces demonstrable deleterious effects necessitating intervention).

## 2 Gender and intersectionality

Perhaps the most contentious aspect of measurement of DVA has been the issue of 'gender symmetry'. While some general population surveys report prevalence estimates that are similar for men and women (see Straus, 2011), agency samples tend to show women are far more frequently the victims of DVA. In a landmark paper, Michael Johnson (1995) suggested the explanation was that population surveys measured 'situational' violence, while agency samples featured victims of coercive control ('intimate terrorism', in Johnson's terminology). Johnson argued situational violence – acts of physical violence or verbal aggression that may be one-off or infrequent and have little or no impact on the recipient in terms of physical or psychological harm – is more gender-symmetrical at the level of basic prevalence, while coercive control is highly gendered. He also suggested that victims of coercive control would likely be prevented from participating in population surveys.

More recently, researchers (including Johnson, see Johnson, Leone, & Xu, 2014) have recognised that victims of coercive control may be found in general population samples and have attempted to identify and compare these cases with those of situational violence. Myhill (2015) used two indicators from the Crime Survey for England and Wales (CSEW) to reflect the ongoing and denigrating nature of coercive control: the respondent reported 'suffering abuse that involved frightening threats' and 'repeated belittling that made them feel worthless'. He found that respondents who reported suffering this type of abuse were overwhelmingly women. Ansara and Hindin (2010) used latent class analysis on data from the Canadian General Social Survey and found that a wider range of abuse types were present for women. Notably, they found a class particular to female victims characterised by extremely high levels of controlling behaviour and verbal abuse, but no physical violence.

Though the distinction between situational violence and coercive control is fairly widely accepted (Langhinrichsen-Rohling, 2010), an important exception is the recent work of Sylvia Walby and colleagues. Walby and Towers (2018) are critical of the concept of coercive control and propose a model of 'Domestic Violent Crime' to reveal the gendered nature of DVA. Walby and Towers (2018) suggest capturing the frequency of acts of DVA within existing crime codes is the most consistent and theoretically coherent way to demonstrate gender difference in prevalence. Critics of this approach (see Myhill & Kelly, 2019; Donovan & Barnes, 2019) argue that while measuring frequency of acts of abuse reveals the gendered nature of DVA to some degree it obscures it in other respects, principally through excluding salient elements of non-physical coercion and counting as victims those primary perpetrators who experience resistive violence. Donovan and Barnes (2019) also highlight the 'cisnormative' nature of the Domestic Violent Crime model, arguing that its neglect of sexuality overlooks important dynamics concerning lesbian, gay, bisexual and/or transgender people's victimisation. It has been suggested that coercive control can be a helpful lens through which to explore dynamics of power and control and 'intersectionality' in LGBT intimate relationships (see Stark & Hester, 2019). Following their review of the literature on measurement, Hamberger et al. (2017, p. 2) concluded that:

> without understanding of overall context of violence in relationships, including the pattern of control and violence (as opposed to a single behavior viewed in isolation), it is very difficult, if not impossible, to isolate sex differences or similarities in [DVA].

So while the theory of coercive control does not exclude the possibility of male victims and female perpetrators, the best available evidence suggests coercive control is gendered. Stark provides a useful summary of this position:

> When women deploy coercive control in heterosexual relationships, or men or women use it in same sex relationships, it is rooted in forms of privilege other than sex-based inequality . . . including social class, income, age, race, or homophobia. Since each of these characteristics may converge with systemic inequalities, they can reinforce an abuser's power in much the same way as sex-based privilege. However, since the vast

majority of intimate relationships involve racially homogeneous, same cohort hetero-sexual partnerships, sexual inequality is the primary context for coercive control and the source of the vast majority of cases police will encounter.

(Stark, 2012, p. 206)

## 3 Harm

The empirical evidence indicating that coercive control is more harmful to victims than other forms of DVA continues to grow. Proponents of coercive control suggest that the theory better accounts for and explains the harm experienced by some victim-survivors. Though the physical and emotional harm inflicted by physical assaults can be severe, the complex range of psychological and behavioural disorders seen frequently in survivors of coercive control reflects '*the cumulative result of all previous abuse*' (Stark, 2017, p. 19, emphasis in original). Narrative accounts suggest that victims perceive non-physical forms of coercion to be more harmful than discrete physical assaults (see for example Kirkwood, 1993; Williamson, 2010), and that victims who experience only non-violent coercion display the same levels of fear and use the same coping and help-seeking strategies as those who suffer both physical violence and non-violent coercion (Crossman, Hardesty, & Raffaelli, 2016; Pitman, 2017).

Though it is difficult to capture complex harms in the context of surveys, Myhill's (2015) re-analysis of CSEW data found that victims – predominantly women – who suffered abuse that involved ongoing denigration and frightening threats were more likely to suffer physical and emotional injury as a result of the abuse, and were more likely to engage with external agencies. Scott et al. (2015) reported similar findings in relation to mental health in another nationally representative sample in England and Wales. Findings from the Adult Psychiatric Morbidity Survey, which involved in-depth interviews with 7,400 adults, suggested those who had experienced 'extensive' physical and sexual violence in the context of coercive control were five times more likely than those with little experience of violence to have a common mental disorder (such as depression or anxiety), and 15 times more likely to have multiple common disorders. Post-traumatic stress disorders and eating disorders were also associated with these experiences of coercive and controlling violence.

The ultimate harm suffered by some victims of DVA is that they are killed by a current or former intimate partner, or other family member. Though prevalence estimates of DVA have been contested by some in relation to gender, domestic homicide is undeniably gendered. In England and Wales, there were a total of 400 domestic homicides recorded by the police between April 2014 and March 2017. The majority of victims were women killed by men who were their partners or ex-partners (Office for National Statistics, 2018). There is a growing evidence-base positioning coercive control as the most prominent precursor to domestic homicide, for cases involving intimate partners (Campbell et al., 2003; Dobash & Dobash, 2015; Home Office, 2013; Sharp-Jeffs & Kelly, 2016; Johnson, Eriksson, Mazerolle, & Wortley, 2019; Monckton Smith, 2019). This evidence has been drawn both from interviews with perpetrators, and multi-agency case reviews.

Coercive control can also have a devastating impact on those close to or connected with the primary victim, especially children. Using in-depth interviews with mothers and children, Katz (2016) found father's controlling behaviour isolated and disempowered children which could hamper their development and lead to emotional and behavioural problems, while Jouriles and McDonald (2015) found evidence of children exposed to coercive control externalising and internalising problems, after accounting for the frequency of physical violence and psychological abuse. In addition, Callaghan, Alexander, Sixsmith and Fellin (2018) suggest children affected by coercive control experience constrained use of space and exhibit constrained self-expression as a way of managing abuse, in much the same way as mothers. The impact of coercive control on children can continue after the end of a relationship, if child contact is used by the perpetrator as a means of continuing the abuse (see Mackay, 2017).

## Responding to coercive control

### *1 Legal and policy context*

As has been discussed, the scholarship on coercive control has evolved substantially over the years. Although not lacking contention and debate, this has clearly informed recent reform efforts designed to improve the response of agencies to those experiencing DVA as either victims or perpetrators. Most notably, the cross-governmental policy definition of DVA in England and Wales was expanded in 2012 in two important ways: (1) extending from legal adults aged 18 and over to also include those aged 16–17 years old, and (2) including coercive and controlling behaviour as a named feature. The official term was changed to 'domestic violence and abuse', in recognition of its broadened scope and to highlight the importance of non-physical and often chronic forms of abuse. The current definition is: 'any incident or pattern of incidents of controlling, coercive, threatening behaviour, violence or abuse between those aged 16 or over who are, or have been, intimate partners or family members regardless of gender or sexuality' (Home Office, 2013). Thus, this definition covers a wide range of different types of violence and behaviours, including intimate partner violence, elder abuse, sibling abuse and adolescent-to-parent violence, as well as so-called 'crimes of honour', a category that can also include female genital mutilation and forced marriage. As will be discussed later, this broad definition poses many challenges to the various practitioners that are expected to apply it in their everyday practice. However, the definition is also considered to have raised awareness of the need to support vulnerable victims and tackle other crime types, helping practitioners to 'join the dots' HMIC (2014).

Building on this policy reform, new laws have been implemented to criminalise coercive control. In England and Wales this took place with the passage of Section 76 of the Serious Crime Act 2015: Controlling or coercive behaviour in an intimate or family relationship (Home Office, 2015). Ireland and Scotland followed suit shortly thereafter by introducing similar offences (Section 39 of the Domestic Violence Act 2018 (IR) and Section 1 of the Domestic Abuse (Scotland) Act 2018, respectively). Such legal reforms are intended to align the law more closely with the 'lived reality' of DVA, and criminalise behaviour which culminates in a substantial adverse effect on victims, thereby allowing for the possibility that perpetrators will be held to account for actions for which they were previously considered 'untouchable'. As one officer put it, 'We have got a piece of law that now lets us deal with some of the most nasty people that you could come across' (Wiener, 2017, p. 502). Examples of perpetrator behaviour from the statutory guidance in England and Wales include: isolating a person from their friends and family; depriving them of their basic needs; monitoring their time; taking control over aspects of their everyday life, such as where they can go, who they can see, what to wear and when they can sleep; repeatedly putting them down such as telling them they are worthless; enforcing rules and activity which humiliate, degrade or dehumanise the victim; and threatening to hurt or kill (Home Office, 2015).

Such laws have the potential to improve the way that criminal justice agencies deal with DVA. For example, as is explored in more detail in the next section, it is likely that a focus on coercive control could assist police in better understanding the degree and nature of the risk to which victims are exposed, allowing them to make more informed decisions about risk assessment. This, in turn, has implications for how agencies attempt to manage risk in terms of actions taken to safeguard victims and respond to perpetrators. Recognising the harmful impacts of coercive control also helps police and other practitioners better understand, and therefore address, the challenges facing victims who are attempting to engage with the criminal justice process (e.g. by providing statements to police, attending court, etc.).

Recent changes to the legal and policy context surrounding DVA are widely viewed as progressive, especially when compared to what was in place in living memory. However, there are still aspects of these reforms that have been subject to convincing critique. For example, Bishop and Bettinson (2018) question the extent to which both members of the public and criminal justice practitioners will be able to recognise these behaviours as criminal, since they are also consistent with normative expectations of male and female behaviour. Further concerns include the possibility that the new legislation will increase the potential for 'legal systems abuse' and/or women being criminalised as a result of counter allegations or attempting to restrict an abuser's access to children (Burman & Brooks-Hay, 2018), and that it will increase difficulties around which charges to lay and distract from pursuing established crimes of physical assault and breach of protective orders (Walklate, Fitz-Gibbon, & McCulloch, 2018).

Arguably the most important criticism of the new law in England and Wales, however, is in relation to its gender-neutral wording, which refers to 'any incident or pattern of incidents'. As Kelly and Westmarland (2016) argue:

> This is not an academic, linguistic quibble: the notion that 'domestic violence' can be broken down into single standalone 'incidents' has skewed not only knowledge, since any incident counts the same as repetition in prevalence surveys, but also which interventions are deemed appropriate, and who should be prioritised to receive support.
>
> (Kelly & Westmarland, 2016, p. 114)

Through reference to their recent research with abusive men, they go on to make the point that an incident-based understanding of DVA represents the way perpetrators talk about their behaviours rather than how victims explain it as their 'everyday reality'. Thus, the language of the law obscures both its features as well as its highly gendered nature. In contrast, the Scottish law is situated in a policy context that recognises domestic abuse as a product of gender inequality and requires proof of 'a course of behaviour which is abusive', which better reflects the reality of DVA and its impacts on women (Burman & Brooks-Hay, 2018).

## 2 Coercive control in the criminal justice system

The extent to which these high-level reforms have resulted in change 'on the ground' has recently become the focus of empirical scrutiny. According to Stark (2012) and others, coercive control is the form of abuse most likely to be reported to the police. Indeed, a recent analysis of data from one English police force found controlling and coercive behaviour to be the dominant case profile (Myhill & Hohl, 2019). A total of 17,616 offences of controlling or coercive behaviour were recorded by the police in England and Wales in the year ending March 2019 (ONS, 2019), a number which a recent overview by Brennan (2020) shows has doubled every year since the new law was passed in England and Wales (see Figure 25.1).[1] Yet the number of crimes of coercive control recorded *prima facie* still represent a very small percentage of the number of incidents reported to the police overall. Research by Barlow, Johnson, Walklate and

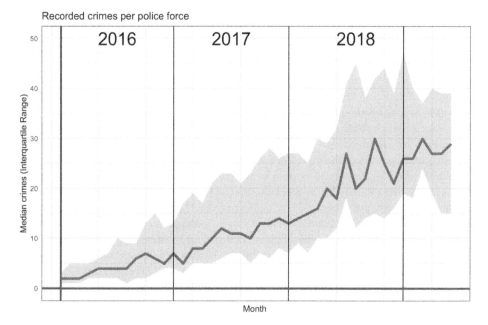

*Figure 25.1* Recorded crimes per police force

Humphreys (2020) suggested officers continued to record traditional crimes such as assault even when coercive control was evident (and should have taken precedence). Many cases of coercive control are also likely remaining recorded as non-crime incidents.

As with all officially recorded crime data, it is difficult to definitively determine whether changes in the crime rate represent true changes in prevalence rather than changes in the willingness to report (by members of the public and practitioners) and/or to record (by police) such behaviour as a criminal offence. Public awareness may have increased due to media attention following the passage of the new law, as well as popular dramatisation (e.g. the storyline in the BBC Radio 4 programme *The Archers*).[2] HMIC inspections on crime integrity may have also played a role in changing police behaviour. Overall, it seems reasonable to suggest that yearly increases in the rate of coercive control offences are due to the implementation of a series of macro-level policy and legal reforms during the past decade, which have shaped the micro-level interactions between police and victims. The police, as 'gatekeepers' to the criminal justice system, hold the 'key' as to whether perpetrators are eventually held to account for their harmful behaviour and therefore whether victims are able to lead safer lives.

However, the extent to which those instances of coercive control that come to police attention translate into the desired outcomes just described is far less certain. Brennan (2020) found around half as many coercive control crimes result in arrest in comparison with DVA (25% vs 50%) and, of those criminal investigations that begin, a far higher proportion are eventually discontinued. It is striking that only 1,177 prosecutions commenced at Magistrates courts for offences of controlling or coercive behaviour in the year ending March 2019 (ONS, 2019), and only 308 resulted in a conviction.

McGorrery and McMahon (2019) analysed media reports of 107 individuals convicted under the new law in England and Wales. Limitations of the data source aside, the findings are useful for highlighting the gendered nature of the prosecutions (all but one involved a male perpetrator and a female victim) as well as the overlap between non-physical coercion and violence (with 82 perpetrating physical or sexual violence against the victim, resulting in an additional 47 offences charged). Other reported features of these crimes reflect the multi-faceted nature of coercive control, which included the use of tactics such as intimidation and threats, isolation, regulation and surveillance of the victim's daily activities. Consistent with national criminal justice data (ONS, 2019), this study found that offenders pleading guilty and receiving custodial sentences were the most common criminal justice outcomes, positively interpreted to mean that the system, once engaged, is effective in holding offenders to account for their actions. However, as previously discussed, the number of cases coming to police attention and then proceeding through prosecution and ultimately sentencing represents a tiny fraction of the overall volume.

It is unfortunate, but not entirely surprising, that the long-standing and seemingly intractable problem of attrition through the criminal justice system for offences associated with DVA (see Hester, 2006; Robinson & Cook, 2006) is even more pernicious for the specific offence of coercive control. Some likely explanations for this can be found at the level of the individual practitioners involved (e.g. their knowledge, skills, understanding, etc.) as well as the organisational contexts in which they operate (e.g. the provision of suitable training, appropriate tools and policy guidance, etc.). These challenges to effective agency responses, and some ways they can be addressed, are discussed in the following sections.

## 3 Challenges for effective agency responses to coercive control

A substantial body of scholarship has documented a lack of understanding on the part of police and other criminal justice professionals about DVA in general, which has often translated into responses towards victims characterised as lacking empathy, respect and professionalism (see Robinson, 2018). The historical root of these problems is frequently attributed to the negative impact of the police occupational culture on the policing of DVA, and in particular how this has shaped officers' interactions with victims (Bourlet, 1990; Edwards, 1989; Hanmer, Griffiths, & Jerwood, 1989). A negative mind-set towards DVA and those experiencing it can stem from police frustration with being repeatedly called to what they perceive to be 'minor issues' at the same address. Offences such as harassment, malicious communications and criminal damage make up a significant proportion of 'domestics' coming to the attention of police, which can lead to unwarranted trivialisation of DVA as 'rubbish' work by police officers under pressure to respond quickly and effectively to a large volume of incidents on a busy shift (Myhill & Johnson, 2016). As recounted by one officer, there have been 'women dying' from the police not doing their job properly due to a lack of understanding of the dynamics of DVA leading them, on occasion, to prejudge incidents as likely to be 'sh★t on sh★t' or 'horse sh★t' (Robinson, Myhill, Wire, Roberts, & Tilley, 2016). These more negative attitudes may represent the 'received wisdom' gained from experience and handed down from officer to officer, which is one explanation for why they appear in early studies (e.g. Hoyle, 1998) as well as recent research (e.g. Myhill, 2019).

Previous research has highlighted the challenges associated with correctly interpreting and applying the broad national definition of DVA (Myhill & Johnson, 2016). Officers are required both to interpret whether the people involved satisfy the definition in relation to their age and relationship to each other, and whether the behaviour involved is in any sense abusive. This research highlighted officers' lack of understanding of coercive control as potentially a significant obstacle to recognising abuse, which is further stymied by victims who are liable to minimise the abuse they have suffered and perpetrators who manipulate their account of the circumstances of the specific incident (Kelly et al., 1999; Stark, 2007). Coercive controlling behaviour can go 'under the radar' (Robinson, Pinchevsky, & Guthrie, 2016) as it constitutes a pattern of often subtle behaviours, which is inherently more difficult to recognise than a physical assault. The dog bowl example in Wiener's (2017) study neatly illuminates how seemingly innocuous behaviours must be understood within the context of the specific relationship before they can be identified as tactics of coercive control, and therefore worthy of police investigative resources under the new laws previously mentioned. The dog bowl is from where the victim was made to eat her meals; the punishment for her not doing so was to be raped by her partner. The officer's 'professional curiosity' about the reason for having a dog bowl (when there was no dog at the premises) created the opportunity for this information to be disclosed by the victim. Such examples clearly challenge the 'black and white thinking' police have come to rely upon when dealing with incidents involving physical DVA and signal the need to overcome this 'mindshift challenge' in order to effectively identify and respond to coercive control (Wiener, 2017).

A range of negative implications follows from police (in)ability to recognise coercive and controlling patterns of abusive behaviour when responding to calls for assistance. Most notably, it can result in a failure to apply the relevant policies and protocols designed to govern how they respond to victims. The review of the national risk model for DVA in England and Wales carried out by Robinson, Myhill et al. (2016) demonstrated that whether and how police take 'positive action' during these calls, such as completing a risk assessment with the victim, depended in large part on their working knowledge of coercive control. For example, it was apparent that some frontline officers had adopted the *de facto* policy of not completing a risk assessment for 'verbal only' incidents (those that did not appear to involve physical violence or criminal offences). The analysis of case file data reinforced the finding that not all eligible incidents were put through the risk assessment process. In particular, non-crime incidents were significantly less likely to have an assessment completed, and even when one was completed, they were significantly less likely to be graded as high risk. This research revealed how DVA that manifests as a 'low-level' incident can be improperly exempted from the relevant police procedures because frontline officers do not recognise this behaviour as a possible expression of coercive control.

Furthermore, problems stemming from the under-appreciation of risk markers for coercive control were not only apparent at the frontline but also when initial assessments were reviewed by specialists in central units. Here as well, police tended to view risk factors associated with physical violence as particularly important to their evaluation of risk: injury at the current incident, threats to kill, attempts to strangle/choke, and use of weapons. Conversely, risk factors potentially indicative of coercive control (e.g. jealous and controlling behaviour, conflict over child contact, victim isolated from family/friends, perpetrator has threatened suicide, etc.) were seen as less important for understanding the risk faced by the victim. Robinson, Myhill and Wire (2018) showed how the extent to which coercive control is identified relies to some degree upon whether other (violent) offending is part of the case profile. When practitioners are assessing risk in cases devoid of other high risk markers to 'prime' them to identify coercive control, it can be missed, and the level of risk therefore underestimated (see also Barlow et al., 2020).

In most UK police forces, the risk level dictates the type and degree of intervention and safety planning with victims. As risk level increases, so too does the investment of police time and resources. But if risk levels are based on partial information and/or the de-prioritisation of important information then the safeguarding and protection afforded to victims will be less than it ought to be. Thus, these are not just measurement errors or defects in bureaucratic paperwork, but can and do have real consequences for the victims who are (incorrectly) considered by police to be suitable for a standard rather than an enhanced response. Activities such as attempting to make follow-up contact with the victim, providing referrals to partner agencies (e.g. specialist domestic abuse services), and undertaking safety planning interventions are preserved for higher risk cases. Most forces in the UK concentrate their resources on high-risk victims, for example by participating in the MARAC process (see Robinson, 2006). Problems previously described at both the initial and secondary stages of risk assessment raise concerns as to whether the correct cases are always referred to MARAC. Victims identified as suitable for a standard response have been identified in a number of domestic homicide reviews where coercive control was found to be present (Brennan, Burton, Gormally, & O'Leary, 2016; Home Office, 2013; Sharp-Jeffs & Kelly, 2016), revealing the tragic consequences that can stem from errors in risk-related decision-making.

## 4 Improving practitioner responses to coercive control

Recent research reveals that the recognition of coercive control improves when practitioners are better trained, use tools designed with explicit reference to coercive control and the harm caused by abuse which may or may not be physical, and are 'primed' to identify and effectively respond through the use of novel methods and interventions (e.g. from assessing known offender cohorts) that help to embed and centralise a concern with coercive control into their daily practice.

Her Majesty's Inspectorate of Constabulary and Fire & Rescue Service, the body tasked with assessing independently the effectiveness of police forces in England and Wales, suggested officers require a framework of systematic training, supervision and performance review in order to improve their ability to 'identify dangerous patterns of behaviour', especially where there is little physical violence but significant 'psychological intimidation and control' (HMIC, 2014, p. 9). Partly in response, the College of Policing, in collaboration with the domestic abuse charity SafeLives, designed and tested a one-day training input for first responders titled 'Domestic Abuse Matters'. The classroom-based training features coercive control prominently, with an emphasis on enhancing the skill of officers to recognise and respond effectively, thereby helping to improve the police response to DVA 'across the piece'. The training involves a mixture of videos, PowerPoint presentations and group discussions. Specific sessions include the debriefing of video footage from an actual domestic abuse incident, the types of controlling behaviours and tactics used by perpetrators, the challenges associated with leaving an abusive partner, and how perpetrators behave when the police are called. An early evaluation showed a small positive impact on officers' knowledge of coercive control and attitudes to DVA (Brennan & Myhill, 2017). Recent analysis has shown a significant increase in arrests for coercive control in forces that adopted DA Matters, compared with those who have not (Brennan, Myhill, Tagliaferri, & Tapley, in press). Although the DA Matters training is not compulsory, it has been implemented by around half of police forces in England and Wales, as well as by Police Scotland.

A sound understanding of the gendered dynamics of DVA and coercive control, reinforced through the use of properly designed risk assessment tools, is one of the principles underpinning a recently prepared evidence-based guide circulated to police in all EU member states (EIGE, 2019). The national review of police risk assessment described earlier (Robinson, Myhill et al., 2016) produced convincing evidence of the need for a revised risk assessment to help frontline practitioners to identify, document and respond more effectively to coercive control. A revised tool was developed by the College of Policing, in consultation with key stakeholders, to explicitly prompt officers to gather information about a range and frequency of coercive and controlling behaviours and the extent to which these are evidence of a pattern of abuse. Evaluation of its use in three police forces indicated promising results. Specifically, victims disclosed coercive behaviour at greater rates and officers recorded proportionately more crimes of coercive control, suggesting the new tool was better at bringing subtle and often hidden forms of abuse into the spotlight of relevant agencies (Wire & Myhill, 2018). The potential of bespoke tools that 'nudge' practitioners towards better decision-making is clear from research on new initiatives to tackle perpetrators. Prompting practitioners to evaluate the harmful consequences of both psychological and/or physical abuse, and explicitly asking them to consider whether coercive control is a feature of the case, was shown to facilitate practitioners making more informed judgements about the risk posed by perpetrators and how this can be most effectively managed by police and partner agencies (Robinson & Clancy, 2020). In conclusion, promising interventions with perpetrators have made coercive control a prominent organising feature in order to effectively reduce their harmful offending behaviour (Hester et al., 2019; Kelly & Westmarland, 2015).

## Conclusion

Coercive control has become prominent in policy and practice, in the UK at least. However, there remains little consensus on how to measure, or even define, the concept, which poses problems for criminal justice practitioners tasked with operationalising it. As such, scholars have warned of potential unintended consequences of 'coercive control creep' (Walkate & Fitz-Gibbon, 2019). Yet concerns about the potential criminalisation of women have not been realised, and convictions for controlling and coercive behaviour have risen year-on-year in England and Wales serving justice to abusers who previously would have received little or no punishment. A criminal justice response delivered through the lens of coercive control better reflects the lived experiences of victim-survivors, and there is emerging evidence that training may equip practitioners with the knowledge and understanding necessary to recognise controlling and coercive behaviour and the devastating impact it can have on those exposed to it.

## Critical findings

- Coercive control is a distinctive manifestation of domestic violence and abuse, which includes tactics deployed by abusers relating to coercion (physical and sexual violence; intimidation, threats and degradation) and those relating to control (isolation; exploitation and deprivation; micro-regulation of everyday behaviour). It has been characterised as a liberty crime and a violation of human rights.
- Research indicates this form of abuse is highly gendered, with men disproportionately perpetrating coercive and controlling behaviour against women.
- Coercive control is particularly harmful in and of itself as well as being correlated with more serious physical and sexual violence, including homicide.
- Operationalising the concept of coercive control into professional practice requires knowledge, skills and understanding on the part of those working in criminal justice and partner agencies. This is necessary to effectively respond to both the victims and the perpetrators of coercive control.

## Implications for policy, practice and research

- In recognition of the wealth of scholarship highlighting the multi-faceted nature of DVA, including both physical and non-physical forms of abuse, policy definitions of DVA have been expanded to include coercive control and new legislation in several countries has been passed to criminalise this type of behaviour. These reforms are often gender-neutral although coercive control itself is highly gendered.

- Understanding the significance of coercive control is critical for effective responses by criminal justice and partner agencies. Failure to identify and respond to coercive control results in inaccurate risk assessments, insufficient safeguarding and perpetrators not held to account for the full range of their harmful behaviours.
- The practice of police and other practitioners can be improved through bespoke training programmes designed to increase their knowledge and understanding of coercive control. Supervision and performance monitoring are necessary to reinforce these skills.
- Tools should be used which explicitly prompt practitioners to evaluate patterns (rather than incidents) of abusive behaviour and the extent to which coercive and controlling tactics are evident. This information should be shared and acted upon within multi-agency interventions designed to respond to all forms of DVA, especially coercive control.
- Emerging evidence which points to positive results from the use of specially designed tools and interventions needs to be bolstered by replication studies carried out in other settings and jurisdictions, as well as with more diverse samples (e.g. those in same-sex relationships and members of ethnic minority communities).

## Notes

1  Brennan (2020). Recorded crimes of Controlling and Coercive Behaviour by police force per month in England and Wales, 2016–2019. Figshare. doi:10.6084/m9.figshare.11932164
2  See www.bbc.co.uk/news/magazine-35961057 (accessed 04 July 2020).

## References

Ansara, D., & Hindin, M. (2010). Exploring gender differences in the patterns of intimate partner violence in Canada: A latent class approach. *Journal of Epidemiology and Community Health*, 64(10), 849–854.

Barlow, C., Johnson, K., Walklate, S., & Humphreys, L. (2020). Putting coercive control into practice: Problems and possibilities. *British Journal of Criminology*, 60, 160–179.

Bishop, C., & Bettinson, V. (2018). Evidencing domestic violence, including behaviour that falls under the new offence of 'controlling or coercive behaviour'. *International Journal of Evidence & Proof*, 22(1), 3–29.

Bourlet, A. (1990). *Police intervention in marital violence*. Milton Keynes: Open University Press.

Brennan, I. R. (2020). Recorded crimes of controlling and coercive behaviour by police force per month in England and Wales, 2016–2019. *Figshare*. doi:10.6084/m9.figshare.11932164

Brennan, I. R., Burton, V., Gormally, S., & O'Leary, N. (2016). *An exploration of domestic abuse patterns and service provision in Humberside*. Hull, England: University of Hull. Retrieved from https://hydra.hull.ac.uk/resources/hull:14106

Brennan, I. R., & Myhill, A. (2017). *Domestic abuse matters 2.0: Evaluation of first responder training*. Ryton-on-Dunsmore: College of Policing.

Brennan, I. R., Myhill, A., Tagliaferri, G., & Tapley, J. (in press). *Policing a new domestic abuse crime: Effects of force-wide training on arrests for coercive control*. Policing and Society. doi:10.1080/10439463.2020.1862838.

Burman, M., & Brooks-Hay, O. (2018). Aligning policy and law? The creation of a domestic abuse offence incorporating coercive control. *Criminology & Criminal Justice*, 18(1), 67–83. doi:10.1177/1748895817752223

Callaghan, J., Alexander, J., Sixsmith, J., & Fellin, L. (2018). Beyond "witnessing": Children's experiences of coercive control in domestic violence and abuse. *Journal of Interpersonal Violence*, 33(10), 1551–1581.

Campbell, J., Webster, D., Koziol-McLain, J., Block, C., Campbell, D., Curry, M., . . . Laughon, K. (2003). Risk factors for femicide in abusive relationships: Results from a multisite case control study. *American Journal of Public Health*, 93(7), 1089–1097.

Connell, R. (2009). *Gender*. Cambridge: Polity Press.

Crossman, K., Hardesty, J., & Raffaelli, M. (2016). "He could scare me without laying a hand on me": Mothers' experiences of nonviolent coercive control during marriage and after separation. *Violence Against Women, 22*(4), 454–473.

Dobash, R., & Dobash, R. (1979). *Violence against wives.* New York, NY: The Free Press.

Dobash, R., & Dobash, R. (2015). *When men murder women.* Oxford: Oxford University Press.

Donovan, C., & Barnes, R. (2019). Re-tangling the concept of coercive control: A view from the margins and a response to Walby and Towers (2018). *Criminology and Criminal Justice.* doi:10.1177/1748895819864622.

Dutton, M., Goodman, L., & Schmidt, R. (2006). *Development and validation of a coercive control measure for intimate partner violence*: Final technical report. Bethesda, MD: Cosmos Corporation.

Edwards, S. (1989). *Policing 'domestic' violence: Women, the law and the state.* London: Sage.

European Institute for Gender Equality. (2019). *A guide to risk assessment and risk management of intimate partner violence against women for police.* Luxembourg: Publications Office of the European Union.

Hamberger, L. K., Larsen, S., & Lehrner, A. (2017). Coercive control in intimate partner violence. *Aggression and Violent Behavior, 37*, 1–11.

Hanmer, J., Griffiths, S., & Jerwood, D. (1999). *Arresting evidence: Domestic violence and repeat victimisation.* London: Home Office.

Her Majesty's Inspectorate of Constabulary. (2014). *Everyone's business: Improving the police response to domestic abuse.* London: HMIC.

Hester, M. (2006). Making it through the criminal justice system: Attrition and domestic violence. *Social Policy and Society, 5*(1), 79–90. doi:10.1017/S1474746405002769

Hester, M., Eisenstadt, N., Ortega-Avila, A., Morgan, K., Walker, S-J., & Bell, J. (2019). *Evaluation of the drive project: A three-year pilot to address high-risk, high-harm perpetrators of domestic abuse.* University of Bristol. Retrieved from http://driveproject.org.uk/wp-content/uploads/2020/01/Drive-Evaluation-Report-Final.pdf

Home Office. (2013). *Domestic homicide reviews: Common themes identified as lessons to be learned.* London: Home Office.

Home Office. (2015). *Controlling or coercive behaviour in an intimate or family relationship: Statutory guidance framework.* London: Home Office.

Hoyle, C. (1998). *Negotiating domestic violence: Police, criminal justice and victims.* Oxford: Oxford University Press.

Johnson, H., Eriksson, L., Mazerolle, P., & Wortley, R. (2019). Intimate femicide: The role of coercive control. *Feminist Criminology, 14*(1), 3–23.

Johnson, M. (1995). Patriarchal terrorism and common couple violence: Two forms of violence against women. *Journal of Marriage and the Family, 57*, 283–294.

Johnson, M., Leone, J., & Xu, Y. (2014). Intimate terrorism and situational couple violence in general surveys: Ex-spouses required. *Violence Against Women, 20*(2), 186–207.

Jones, A. (1994). *Next time, she'll be dead: Battering and how to stop it.* Boston, MA: Beacon Press.

Jouriles, E., & McDonald, R. (2015). Intimate partner violence, coercive control, and child adjustment problems. *Journal of Interpersonal Violence, 30*(3), 459–474.

Katz, E. (2016). Beyond the physical incident model: How children living with domestic violence are harmed by and resist regimes of coercive control. *Child Abuse Review*, (25), 46–59.

Kelly, L., Bindel, J., Burton, S., Butterworth, D., Cook, K., & Regan, L. (1999). *Domestic violence matters.* London: Home Office.

Kelly, L., & Westmarland, N. (2015). *Domestic violence perpetrator programmes: Steps towards change.* Project Mirabal Final Report. London and Durham: London Metropolitan University and Durham University. Retrieved from www.dur.ac.uk/criva/projectmirabal

Kelly, L., & Westmarland, N. (2016). Naming and defining 'domestic violence': Lessons from research with violent men. *Feminist Review, 112*(1), 113–127. doi:10.1057/fr.2015.52

Kirkwood, C. (1993). *Leaving abusive partners: From the scars of survival to the wisdom for change.* London: Sage.

Langhinrichsen-Rohling, J. (2010). Controversies involving gender and intimate partner violence in the United States. *Sex Roles, 62*, 179–193.

Lehmann, P., Simmons, C., & Pillai, V. (2012). The validation of the Checklist of Controlling Behaviors (CCB): Assessing coercive control in abusive relationships. *Violence Against Women, 18*, 913–933.

Mackay, K. (2017). Child contact as a weapon of control. In J. Lombard (Ed.), *The Routledge handbook of gender and violence* (pp. 145–157). Abingdon, Oxford: Routledge.

McGorrery, P., & McMahon, M. (2019). Prosecuting controlling or coercive behaviour in England and Wales: Media reports of a novel offence. *Criminology & Criminal Justice.* doi:10.1177/1748895819880947

Monckton Smith, J. (2019). Intimate partner femicide: Using Foucauldian analysis to track an eight stage progression to homicide. *Violence Against Women.* doi:10.1177/1077801219863876.

Myhill, A. (2015). Measuring coercive control: What can we learn from national population surveys? *Violence Against Women, 21*(3), 355–375.

Myhill, A. (2017). Measuring domestic violence: Context is everything. *Journal of Gender-based Violence, 1*(1), 33–44.

Myhill, A. (2019). Renegotiating domestic violence: Police attitudes and decisions concerning arrest. *Policing and Society, 29*(1), 52–68. doi:10.1080/10439463.2017.1356299

Myhill, A., & Hohl, K. (2019). The 'golden thread': Coercive control and risk assessment for domestic violence. *Journal of Interpersonal Violence, 34*(21–22), 4477–4497.

Myhill, A., & Johnson, K. (2016). Police use of discretion in response to domestic violence. *Criminology & Criminal Justice, 16*(1), 3–20.

Myhill, A., & Kelly, L. (2019). Counting with understanding? What is at stake in debates on researching domestic violence. *Criminology and Criminal Justice.* doi:10.1177/1748895819863098.

Office for National Statistics. (2018). *Domestic abuse: Findings from the crime survey for England and Wales: Year ending March 2018.* Report, Office for National Statistics, UK.

Office for National Statistics. (2019). *Domestic abuse and the criminal justice system, England and Wales: November 2019.* Report, Office for National Statistics, UK.

Okun, L. (1986). *Woman Abuse: Facts replacing myths.* Albany: State University of New York Press.

Pitman, T. (2017). Living with coercive control: Trapped within a complex web of double standards, double binds and boundary violations. *British Journal of Social Work, 47*(1), 143–161.

Pokeman, V., Rossi, F., Holtzworth-Munroe, A., Applegate, A., Beck, C., & D'Onofrio, B. (2014). Mediator's Assessment of Safety Issues and Concerns (MASIC): Reliability and validity of a new intimate partner violence screen. *Assessment, 21*, 529–542.

Robinson, A., Myhill, A., Wire, J., Roberts, J., & Tilley, N. (2016). *Risk-led policing of domestic abuse and the DASH risk model.* Ryton-on-Dunsmore, England: College of Policing.

Robinson, A., Pinchevsky, G., & Guthrie, J. (2016). Under the radar: Policing non-violent domestic abuse in the US and the UK. *International Journal of Comparative and Applied Criminal Justice, 40*(3), 195–208.

Robinson, A. L. (2006). Reducing repeat victimisation among high-risk victims of domestic violence: The benefits of a coordinated community response in Cardiff, Wales. *Violence Against Women, 12*(8), 761–788.

Robinson, A. L. (2018). Police responses to intimate partner violence. *Oxford Bibliographies in Criminology.* doi:10.1093/OBO/9780195396607–0252

Robinson, A. L., & Clancy, A. (2020). Systematically identifying and prioritising domestic abuse perpetrators for targeted intervention. *Criminology & Criminal Justice.* doi:10.1177/1748895820914380

Robinson, A. L., & Cook, D. (2006). Understanding victim retraction in cases of domestic violence: Specialist courts, government policy, and victim-centred justice. *Contemporary Justice Review, 9*(2), 189–213. doi:10.1080/10282580600785017

Robinson, A. L., Myhill, A., & Wire, J. (2018). Practitioner (mis)understandings of coercive control in England and Wales. *Criminology & Criminal Justice, 18*(1), 29–49. doi:10.1177/1748895817728381

Schechter, S. (1982). *Women and male violence: The visions and struggles of the battered women's movement.* Boston, MA: South End Press.

Scott, S., Williams, J., MacNaughton Nicholls, C., McManus, S., Brown, A., Harvey, S., . . . Lovett, J. (2015). *Violence, abuse and mental health in England: Population patterns. Responding effectively to violence and abuse (REVA project) Briefing 1.* Retrieved from https://natcen.ac.uk/media/1057987/REVA_Brief-1_Population-patterns_FINAL_071015.pdf

Sharp-Jeffs, N., & Kelly, L. (2016). *Domestic homicide review (DHR): Case analysis.* London: Standing Together/London Metropolitan University.

Sharp-Jeffs, N., Kelly, L., & Klein, R. (2018). Long journeys toward freedom: The relationship between coercive control and space for action – Measurement and emerging evidence. *Violence Against Women, 24*(2), 163–185.

Smith, P., Earp, J., & DeVellis, R. (1995). Measuring battering: Development of the Women's Experience with Battering (WEB) Scale. *Women's Health, 1*(4), 273–288.

Stark, E. (2007). *Coercive control: How men entrap women in personal life.* Oxford: Oxford University Press.

Stark, E. (2012). Looking beyond domestic violence: Policing coercive control. *Journal of Police Crisis Negotiations, 12*(2), 199–217.

Stark, E. (2017). Coercive control as a framework for responding to male partner abuse in the UK: Opportunities and challenges. In J. Lombard (Ed.), *The Routledge handbook of gender and violence*. Abingdon, Oxford: Routledge, pp. 15–27.

Stark, E., & Hester, M. (2019). Coercive control: Update and review. *Violence Against Women, 25*(1), 81–104.

Straus, M. (1979). Measuring intrafamily conflict and violence: The conflict tactics scales. *Journal of Marriage and the Family, 41*, 75–88.

Straus, M. (2011). Gender symmetry and mutuality in perpetration of clinical-level partner violence: Empirical evidence and implications for prevention and treatment. *Aggression and Violent Behavior, 16*, 279–288.

Straus, M., Hamby, S., Boney-McCoy, S., & Sugarman, D. (1996). The revised Conflict Tactics Scale (CTS2): Development and preliminary psychometric data. *Journal of Family Issues, 17*, 283–316.

Walby, S., & Myhill, A. (2001). New survey methodologies in researching violence against women. *British Journal of Criminology, 41*(3), 502–522.

Walby, S., & Towers, J. (2018). Untangling the concept of coercive control: Theorizing domestic violent crime. *Criminology and Criminal Justice*. doi:10.1177/1748895817743541.

Walkate, S., & Fitz-Gibbon, K. (2019). The criminalisation of coercive control: The power of law? *International Journal for Crime, Justice, and Social Democracy, 8*(4), 94–108.

Walklate, S., Fitz-Gibbon, K., & McCulloch, J. (2018). Is more law the answer? Seeking justice for victims of intimate partner violence through the reform of legal categories. *Criminology and Criminal Justice, 18*, 115–131.

Wiener, C. (2017). Seeing what is 'invisible in plain sight': Policing coercive control. *The Howard Journal, 56*(4), 500–515.

Williamson, E. (2010). Living in the world of the domestic violence perpetrator: Negotiating the unreality of coercive control. *Violence Against Women, 16*(12), 1412–1423.

Wire, J., & Myhill, A. (2018). *Piloting a new approach to domestic abuse frontline risk assessment: Evaluation report. College of policing.* Retrieved from https://whatworks.college.police.uk/Research/Documents/DA_risk_assessment_pilot.pdf

# 26

# MURDER IN THE FAMILY

## Why culture is an insufficient explanation for 'honour'-based violence

*Aisha K. Gill*

### The prevalence of 'honour'-based violence

The United Nations Population Fund estimates that between 5,000 and 12,000 women are murdered in the name of 'honour' each year, primarily in the Middle East and Asia (Manjoo, 2011; Gill, 2014; Gill & Walker, 2020), though according to women's advocacy groups, the figure could be as high as 20,000; given the difficulty in obtaining accurate data because of under-reporting and poor recording, official statistics are understood to be grossly underestimated (see A/HRC/20/16). As a result, it is impossible to determine the true number of 'honour' killings that occur globally, or the full extent of 'honour'-based violence (HBV) more generally. Family members often try to conceal HBV, while many victims are abducted and never reported missing (Manjoo, 2011).

Western countries with large multi-ethnic immigrant communities, such as Britain, began recognising HBV as a significant and growing domestic issue in the late twentieth century. Understanding and awareness of HBV has shifted accordingly, prompting concerted national and international efforts to counter it. In Europe, most reported honour killings occur in South Asian, Turkish or Kurdish communities; however, there have also been cases involving Roman Catholic perpetrators, with varied ethnic backgrounds, in Brazil, Italy and America (Chesler, 2010; Kaplanian & Gill, 2020).

Perpetrators are often part of minority groups even in countries where HBV is prevalent among the majority population; this underscores the significance of economic and social marginalisation as aggravating factors (Kulczycki & Windle, 2011). For example, Sheeley (2007) surveyed a stratified convenience sample from Jordan, a nation with deeply embedded socio-cultural notions of 'honour'. A third of respondents knew someone who had been threatened with HBV, and 28 per cent knew someone who had died as a result of it. While incidence data do not explain the mechanisms through which cultural concerns with 'honour' come to motivate HBV, media reporting too often treats such data as explanatory, attributing responsibility for HBV to specific cultures and minority groups rather than exploring the numerous other factors that lead to these crimes (Begikhani, Gill, & Hague, 2015).

## Defining honour and shame

'Honour' is a pervasive concept that means different things depending on the time, place and cultural context in which it is used. As a result, attempting to define honour in an all-encompassing manner is highly problematic; the meaning and practical implications of honour are not the same across times or cultures. The issue is further complicated because, today, the term has become synonymous with notions such as fame, reputation and virtue, and is often used as a generic cross-cultural translation for subtly nuanced terms that include *ird* (Arabic Bedouin term = honour), *izzat* (Urdu = honour), *namus* (Arabic = virtue), *zina* (Urdu), *sharam* (Urdu) and *sharaf* (Arabic). However, in all contexts the term – and its antonym, 'shame' – remains evaluative (Pitt-Rivers, 1966), dictating appropriate and inappropriate behaviours within a given community (Gill, 2006; Sennett, 2004; Gill & Walker, 2020).

In a broad sense, honour is a social process that determines and designates social value. Honouring is an action involving two or more parties; it occurs both between individuals, and within groups and subgroups. Thus, any examination of honour requires analysis of the full context. Socialisation into cultural codes, norms and traditions involving honour relies on the idea that maintaining the behavioural expectations embedded in these leads to honour; this, in turn, defines the formation and dynamics of relationships among individuals, as well as between larger groups, shaping broader processes and understandings of honour up to the national and even international level. This process establishes behavioural norms, ways of conferring honour on those who uphold them and also disciplinary actions to punish transgressors. For instance, gaining and maintaining 'prestige' involves a group bestowing honour on an individual or subgroup for attributes, characteristics and actions the group values, elevating the individual's hierarchal standing in relation to others in the group as a reward (Stewart, 1994).

As honour is a dynamic process, it can be both increased and decreased; a decrease or loss of honour is seen to result in 'shame'. It follows then that honour and shame are not only intimately connected, but form part of a complex system that functions as a powerful motiving force for individuals and groups (Walker, 2018). For instance, shame – which Schliesmann (2012, pp. 48–49) defines as a complex emotion that embodies "feelings of humiliation, embarrassment, and a sense of failure" – occurs largely as a result of an individual failing to measure up to his/her community's standards and expectations (Miller, 1993). While fear of public judgement and the subsequent loss of honour is often enough to enforce adherence to social norms (Welsh, 2008), violence (or at least the threat of it) is often used as an alternative means of enforcing conformity in order to 'protect' honour (Gill & Walker, 2020).

## The consequences of losing honour

In cultures centred around notions of honour, aggression is an acceptable reaction to insults and threats to honour. Ethnographic and sociological research on diverse honour cultures, such as Iraqi Kurdistan (Begikhani et al., 2015), Spain (Gilmore, 1987), rural Greece (Safilios-Rothschild, 1969) and Turkey (Oner-Ozkan & Gencoz, 2006), suggests that members of honour cultures consider retaliation a duty when a family member or other associated individual is insulted. Failure to retaliate connotes acceptance of the insult and thus an admission of being unworthy of honour. According to Pitt-Rivers (1966), losing honour by accepting humiliation cannot be repaired by demonstrating excellence. Thus, when someone does not take appropriate action when their honour is threatened, he or she will be subjected to shame by the group. The most effective way to restore tarnished honour is to repudiate the insult by demonstrating a willingness to engage in physical aggression.

Honour killings embody the most extreme form of such aggression (Faqir, 2001; Gill, 2014). The perpetrators' willingness to take such radical measures offers insight into how seriously the loss of honour is taken; the consequences of not taking action when honour is threatened can include shaming, ridiculing, loss of respect, loss of social resources and even complete ostracism from a family or wider social group (Gill, 2014). In traditional societies, where social mobility is limited and individuals' social, psychological and material prospects are closely interwoven with those of their family, tribe or clan, ostracism not only means losing social support, but also the material resources necessary for survival. As a result, susceptibility to shame is considered a positive quality, as illustrated by phrases such as 'having a sense of shame' (Abu-Lughod, 2011). Thus, shame is not only an emotional consequence of losing honour, but also an important behavioural regulator. This demonstrates how shame and honour represent interlinked dynamic social processes, rather than static attributes, and why the avoidance of shame, and preservation of honour, are key concerns for individuals, families and whole communities.

## Honour killing

Gendered violence encompasses HBV, 'crimes of honour', 'crimes related to honour conflict', 'crimes of tradition' and 'culture-based violence'. The term 'honour killing' is used to refer to HBV that results in a person's death. Some scholars and activists reject the use of these designations altogether, categorising such crimes as domestic violence (Terman, 2010), while others place HBV under the umbrella of violence against women and girls (VAWG). Although most victims are female, HBV is sometimes committed against young men (Oberwittler & Kasselt, 2011). Like women, young men are expected to respect and heed the wishes of more senior, usually older, male relatives (Abu-Lughod, 2011). Subordinate men are most likely to cause dishonour as a result of (1) choosing the 'wrong' dating or sexual partner, (2) refusing an arranged marriage, (3) coming out as gay, bisexual or transgender (Ozturk, 2013) and/or (4) refusing to commit an act of HBV (Roberts, Campbell, & Lloyd, 2014). Nevertheless, the majority of HBV victims are female and the majority of perpetrators are male.

Honour killings take many different forms and names; these are often specific to certain cultures and communities. For example, 'bride burning' in India (Ahmad, 2008), 'crimes of passion' in Latin America (Brinks, 2007) and 'honour killings' in Islamic nations (Hellgren & Hobson, 2008). However, all share the same dynamic: women are killed by male family members in an act deemed socially acceptable, understandable, excusable and even desirable. Nevertheless, there are key distinctions between these three forms of violence. In a 'crime of passion', the woman's husband or lover commits the murder in 'heated' response to a sense of personal betrayal or anger, whereas honour killings are carried out on a premeditated basis as a symbolic rejection of a perceived dishonourable action in order to prevent the family from being shamed by the group (Sen, 2005).

As 'honour' covers a broad variety of concepts and behaviours (Gill, 2009), the violations that may trigger violence are also wide-ranging. Honour killings are most commonly committed against a woman for actual or perceived immoral behaviour deemed in breach of a family and/or community's honour (Jiwani & Hoodfar, 2012; Gill, 2014); usually this behaviour involves intimate relations with a man, whether that be adultery, sex outside marriage or simply close companionship. As even accusations of immoral behaviour lead to the loss of honour, the truth is often irrelevant and proof is rarely required. Indeed, rumours and gossip are the community's greatest weapons for instilling shame in men who cannot 'preserve the purity and chastity' of their female relatives (Shalhoub-Kevorkian & Daher-Nashef, 2013). As it is seen as the responsibility of male family members to do so, 'misbehaviour' on the part of female relatives tarnishes the honour of the whole family.

Even women who have been raped and/or sexually assaulted can become targets for honour killings. This is because the norms and values of honour cultures focus on maintaining women's sexual 'purity' to ensure that only certain bloodlines are allowed to blend, preventing wealth from becoming diluted by marriage, for instance by ensuring that women from the landed class do not form family bonds with individuals of lower social status. Other common ways honour is seen to be lost such that it can only be restored by HBV include a woman or girl (1) being in the presence of a male who is not a relative, (2) refusing an arranged marriage, (3) falling in love with someone who is unacceptable to the family, (4) seeking a divorce, (5) trying to escape marital violence, (6) presenting herself in a 'Western manner' in terms of clothing and/or makeup, (7) staying out late (Papp, 2010) and (8) perceived "defiance and disobedience" (Schliesmann, 2012, p. 48).

Compared to their white counterparts, for whom shame tends to have a more personal character as it is not seen to 'tarnish' other family members or the wider community, BME victims living in cultures and communities centred on notions of honour and shame often see themselves as responsible for damaging their loved ones through the real or perceived actions that led to the loss of honour (Feldman, 2010). Thus, many victims feel that they deserve to suffer HBV as punishment for their 'misbehaviour'. This complicates the issue of speaking out or seeking help. Other cultural norms, including not speaking to outsiders about family affairs, and women being expected to smooth over difficulties through self-sacrifice and repressing their own desires and feelings, also play a role in the low rate of reporting of HBV and other forms of VAWG by BME victims. However, just as negative family and community responses encourage victims to remain silent about abuse, positive responses are integral to enabling them to discuss their experiences of violence (Gill, 2014). Thus, policies and practices geared towards providing support and justice for victims must take account of the specialised needs of BME victims if they are to have equal access to help and redress.

The following sections apply these concepts to the murder of Shafilea Ahmed to examine how culture came to be seen as the key explanation for this crime. However, a critical analysis of racialised interpretations of such murders demonstrates that acceptance of 'honour' as the sole justification for the brutal murder of young women perceived to have shamed family members fails to grasp the importance of individual and family dynamics and, critically, how this specific form of violence relates to the broader issue of VAWG, which affects all communities and countries (Gill, 2014).

## Shafilea Ahmed

Shafilea Ahmed was born in Bradford, England, on 14 July 1986, shortly after her parents emigrated to the UK from Pakistan. From the age of 15, Shafilea frequently reported suffering domestic violence (Gill, 2014). She attended Great Sankey High School in Warrington until her father removed her from school temporarily in February 2003 for a trip to Pakistan. Shafilea was murdered in the UK in September 2003 at the age of 17. In the year prior to her death, tensions over clashing 'traditional' versus 'Western' values had intensified between Shafilea and her parents, Farzana and Iftikhar. One of her parents' complaints was that Shafilea's circle of friends consisted of mostly Caucasian peers from school, with only a small percentage from minority ethnic backgrounds.

Shafilea's case was first referred to Warrington social services on 3 October 2002 after another pupil told teachers that Shafilea's parents had physically assaulted her and prevented her from attending school. Following this first referral, Shafilea's social services file notes a mark on her face and the fact that she believed she was going to be sent to Pakistan for an arranged marriage. When Shafilea returned to school five days later, she revealed to her best friend that her mother had threatened a forced marriage. According to the friend, Shafilea's mother said, "I can't wait till you go to Pakistan to teach you a lesson" (Gill, 2014), prompting school staff to refer Shafilea to social services again. This time, Shafilea's social services file noted that her father had forced her to withdraw savings from her bank account, indicating an attempt on his part to exert control over her.

Late in November 2002, one of Shafilea's friends saw her in a park, carrying her belongings and wearing only a "thin sari"; Shafilea indicated that she was running away from home "because her parents would not let her be" (Gill, 2014). Although the school reported the incident to social services, there is no record of this on file. In a meeting subsequently arranged between Shafilea and her parents by her teacher, Shafilea spoke "quite openly" about wanting "to be able to work and have money and go out" (Gill, 2014). By the end of the meeting, Iftikhar had agreed that Shafilea would be allowed more freedom. However, things did not improve and teachers continued referring Shafilea to social services and suggesting that she should contact Childline (Gill, 2012).

On 18 February 2003, Shafilea's parents drugged her and took her to Pakistan (Gill, 2014). The trip was cut short in May when Shafilea swallowed bleach (or a similar caustic liquid) and required treatment at a local hospital. The family then returned to the UK. Her mother later told the British police that Shafilea had accidentally ingested the bleach, mistaking it for mouthwash. However, medical practitioners reported that Shafilea's mouth injury was inconsistent with the action of gargling mouthwash, but was consistent with a deliberate act of swallowing. The most likely explanation is that this was a conscious act of self-harm by Shafilea to frustrate her parents' plans to force her into marriage. As a result of this injury, Shafilea was no longer considered marriageable and was thus deemed to have shamed her family.

Despite her injury, Shafilea was determined to continue her education and become a lawyer. In September 2003, she commenced a series of courses at Priestly College in Warrington. On the evening of 11 September, she worked at her part-time job until the end of her shift at 9pm, when another employee observed her leaving the premises. She spent the evening at her family's home in Warrington with her parents and four younger siblings. Her father claims that she was alive, though asleep, when he and the rest of the family went to bed at 11pm. Although Shafilea was due to receive hospital treatment the following day, she was not seen alive again after that night.

Shafilea's former teacher reported her missing on 18 September 2003, prompting an extensive police investigation into her disappearance. At the time, the primary sources of information were Shafilea's family, friends and teachers, but significant inconsistencies soon emerged in their accounts. The investigation also revealed the history of school, social services and law enforcement involvement with Shafilea and her family. In December 2003, Shafilea's parents were arrested on suspicion of abduction. They denied any involvement in their daughter's disappearance and were released on police bail (see Gill, 2014). On 4 February 2004, the decomposed remains of a human body were found on the banks of the River Kent near Force Bridge. A DNA match to Shafilea was made on 23 February 2004.

Shafilea's parents gave a number of press interviews in March 2004, including one broadcast on *Newsnight* on 2 March. Whereas Farzana remained silent throughout the interview, Iftikhar appeared attentive and focused, distancing himself from Shafilea by referring to her as "the daughter" or "the girl". When asked about Shafilea's suicide attempt, he contradicted the medical evidence, stating that his daughter "took a sip" of poisonous liquid. He claimed, "I'm not a strict parent in any way. . . . I'm as English as anybody can picture me, right. But obviously the police portrayal of me is different . . . we have not been treated fairly" (Gill, 2014). He complained that his family was misunderstood by the police and the public, and feigned being hurt by the suspicion that they were responsible for the death of "the girl". Rather than making a plea to those responsible for his daughter's death, he defended his "Englishness", illustrating the importance he placed on saving face and maintaining honour in the eyes of others. Iftikhar used the word "normal" many times in the *Newsnight* interview when describing Shafilea, his family, the "holiday" to Pakistan during which Shafilea swallowed bleach, and the night of her disappearance (Gill, 2014). He continuously sought to present his family in a positive light and focused less on the loss of his daughter and more on what he perceived as the unfair treatment directed at him and his family.

## Building a legal case

In September 2004, the police submitted a file of evidence to the Crown Prosecution Service (CPS) to determine whether to pursue a case against Shafilea's parents. Six months later, Mr Robin Spencer QC advised the police that there was insufficient evidence to demonstrate guilt beyond a reasonable doubt and secure a conviction. On 11 January 2008, a coroner's inquest into the circumstances of Shafilea's death found that she had been "unlawfully killed" (*Warrington Guardian*, 11 June 2009). The situation changed in August 2010 when Shafilea's sister "Alesha" (a pseudonym) was taken into custody on suspicion of having arranged a robbery at her parents' home. Having requested to speak to officers about another matter, she was interviewed in the presence of her solicitor. During the interview, Alesha claimed that, when she was 15, she and her three surviving siblings had witnessed their parents killing Shafilea on the night of 11 September 2003. "Both of my parents were very controlling and tried to bring us up in the Pakistani Muslim way", she said, before explaining that Shafilea was the one who was "picked on" the most by their parents (Gill, 2014, p. 185).

One of Alesha's earliest childhood memories was seeing her mother hitting Shafilea. She stated that her parents attacked her and her sisters on countless occasions, both verbally and physically, and that her parents' abuse of Shafilea escalated over time. Alesha explained that between the ages of 14 and 17, Shafilea was attacked virtually every day for the most trifling reasons – if she received a text message or phone call from a boy, wore 'inappropriate' clothes or associated with white friends at school, Farzana would claim that Shafilea had shamed the family. Alesha described one incident in which her mother hit Shafilea and then shut her in a room without food for two days, only allowing her out to use the toilet: "They knew that they could control us completely through fear" (Gill, 2014, p. 186). Alesha's testimony allowed the CPS to advance a convincing case against Shafilea's parents. In September 2011, both were charged with murder. Their trial commenced on 21 May 2012 at Chester Crown Court.

## The trial

During the trial, Shafilea's parents insisted that they had not been involved in their daughter's disappearance or murder; they also denied claims that they had repeatedly beaten her over a prolonged period.

As a witness for the prosecution, Alesha was called on to describe the night of Shafilea's disappearance. She recalled going with her mother and brother to collect Shafilea from work. When Shafilea reached the car, they saw that she was wearing a lilac t-shirt and white trousers made from stretchy material, with ties at each hip. As soon as Farzana saw Shafilea, she complained that her clothes were too revealing. Alesha stated that, when they arrived home, the whole family assembled in the kitchen, with Farzana demanding that they collectively search Shafilea's bags; this practice was not unusual. Finding some money in Shafilea's handbag increased Farzana's anger and she accused Shafilea of hiding the money and pushed her, placing both hands on her daughter's chest and shoulders to shove her onto the settee in the sitting room. Alesha stated that Shafilea, still weak from her injuries as a result of the bleach, had a small frame and weighed not much more than five or six stone (31–38 kg). Alesha then heard her mother say "*Etay khatam kar saro*", Punjabi for "just finish it here". Iftikhar went to Shafilea and pulled her into a lying position on the settee. Shafilea began to struggle as both parents hit her and held her down. One of them said, "Get the bag". Alesha saw her mother grab a thin white carrier bag from the stool next to the settee; she and Iftikhar together forced the entire bag into Shafilea's mouth. Each placed a hand over her mouth and nose. Shafilea's legs kicked, but Iftikhar put his knee on the settee to pin her down until she stopped struggling (Gill, 2014, pp. 186–187).

Despite having seen her sister die the night before, Alesha told the court that the following morning she asked her mother where Shafilea was. Alesha and her siblings were sternly instructed that, if anyone asked, they were to say that Shafilea came home from work, went to bed, then ran away during the night. Alesha and her siblings were sent to school as normal, where Alesha broke down and told some friends what had occurred; she described being very upset and confused at the time and, as a result, spontaneously blurted out that her father had killed her sister. When her teachers asked her about this, she recanted out of fear of reprisal from her parents. Questions remain as to why those who witnessed Alesha's breakdown at school did not take further action to investigate Shafilea's disappearance; why did the teachers only contact the police on 18 September 2003, days after Alesha's admission?

Eight weeks into the trial, Farzana changed her defence in what the judge described as a "significant" development (Gill, 2014, p. 187). On 8 July 2012, she admitted that an incident of "violence" involving Shafilea took place on 11 September 2003 at the family home (Gill, 2014, p. 187). Up until then she had denied having any knowledge of what had happened to her daughter. Now, Farzana's defence counsel stated that, on the night in question, Iftikhar was very angry, "hitting [Shafilea], slapping her with his hands towards the facial area and punching her two to three times to the upper part of her body. [Farzana] tried to intervene but she was told to go away" (author's personal notes, 2012). The defence counsel went on to explain that when Farzana tried, again, to help her daughter, she was "pushed away by both hands and also punched with a clenched fist" (Gill, 2014, p. 187). Contrary to Alesha's account, Farzana claimed that only her third eldest daughter, then aged 12, was present. "Extremely scared" and fearing for her younger child's safety, Farzana took her upstairs. Some twenty minutes later, she heard a car leave and came downstairs to find Shafilea and Iftikhar gone, along with her car. At 6:30am the next day, her husband returned without Shafilea (author's personal notes, Gill, 2012).

However, there was even more damning evidence for Farzana's complicity in Shafilea's murder than Alesha's testimony. This evidence came from a covert listening device that had been installed in the Ahmed home by the police in November 2003 after Alesha's teachers had contacted them to report her story about Shafilea's murder. On one recording, Farzana, in conversation with her other children, can be heard warning them not to say anything at school about what happened to Shafilea, telling her son, "If the slightest thing comes out of your mouth, we will be stuck in real trouble. Remember that". In another exchange, Farzana scolded her children, saying, "Today is not a day to be beaten up, okay. Are you listening to me? I'm talking to you", demonstrating that abuse and violence were a normal part of family life in the Ahmed home.

Farzana's treatment of Shafilea is illuminated by Kandiyoti's seminal 1988 study of the phenomenon of abuse of daughters by their mothers in South Asian families; Kandiyoti saw this as a culturally specific form of "patriarchal bargain" between the mother and the extended household (Walker & Gill, 2019). Kandiyoti's discussion of 'classic patriarchy' explains how family dynamics between younger and older women in South Asian familial systems are structured according to a patriarchal model that stresses "corporate male-headed entities rather than more autonomous mother and child units" (1988, p. 275): "Different forms of patriarchy present women with distinct 'rules of the game' and call for different strategies to maximize security and optimize life options with varying potential for active or passive resistance in the face of oppression". In other words, men make the rules, but, if women play by them, they can gain a form of symbolic capital; specifically, they can present themselves as 'conforming women', enabling their survival under the patriarchal system. Where one woman's misbehaviour is seen to dishonour the entire patriarchal familial unit, to ensure their survival and security, women, as much as men, monitor one another's behaviour and enact punishment for transgressions. As such, Farzana's behaviour can be partly understood as an attempt to preserve the honour of her family, to ensure that her other children avoided shame, and to protect herself against potential accusations from her husband of complicity in Shafilea's behaviour.

Ultimately, the jury accepted Alesha's version of events. On 3 August 2012, Shafilea's parents were convicted of her murder: both received life sentences.

## Cultural predicaments

In sentencing Shafilea's parents, the judge, Mr Justice Roderick Evans, described Shafilea as a determined, able and ambitious girl "squeezed between two cultures, the culture and way of life that she saw around her and wanted to embrace and the culture and way of life her parents wanted to impose upon her" (Gill, 2014, p. 195). However, the causal factors behind Shafilea's murder were far more complex than this or the British media's tale of backward parents acting against modern Britain's progressive social values. While the true facts of the case may never be known, all the accounts of what happened on 11 September 2003 circle back to the key role of honour, while demonstrating that a purely cultural explanation for Shafilea's death is insufficient; her murder was a product of many factors, including the relationship between honour, gender and power inequalities within the Ahmed household.

The Ahmed family lived in a context that was both British and Pakistani, in what Homi Bhabha (1994) refers to as a "third space". This notion applies to both generations of the Ahmed family, albeit in different ways. For instance, Iftikhar's defence of his Englishness is particularly interesting in this context – it reveals how his own claims that he was sufficiently influenced by the UK's cultural practices to consider himself English indicate that his actions were not simply caused by cultural conflict or adherence to notions of honour derived from his Pakistani upbringing (Brah, 1996). Indeed, Iftikhar had been married before to a Danish woman with whom he had a child (Keaveny, 2012) and led a "creolized-Western" lifestyle (Grillo, 2003). If Iftikhar considered himself English to the extent of taking great pains to insist on this as an important part of his identity, then it does not make sense that he murdered his daughter purely as a result of notions of 'honour' and 'shame'; his pride in having a high degree of English values sits at odds with the notion that he would kill to demonstrate his 'honour' under Pakistani-derived values. While cognitive dissonance is a possible explanation for this contradiction, or the idea that he might have felt torn between two different sets of cultural values, it is clear that his position in relation to notions of honour was not simple and straightforward. Moreover, given that he lived a different life with his first wife, the dynamics of his marriage to Farzana must have played at least some role in Shafilea's murder. While culture and 'honour' were clearly key factors, they do not offer a sufficient explanation.

The fact that the various members of the Ahmed family did not occupy a single, shared, intersectionally configured space helps explain why the Ahmed children reacted to Shafilea's murder in such different ways. Alesha's brother spoke against her testimony, denying all of her claims about Shafilea's murder. By contrast, Alesha initially behaved as if the murder had never happened, then told friends and teachers at school about it, and then recanted, only coming forwards again when she, herself, was accused of a crime involving her parents. As a child and domestic abuse victim who suffered trauma and coercion, Alesha had nowhere to go in the wake of Shafilea's murder. She was still living at home and facing abuse in August 2010, when she finally told the police the full story of what she had seen on the night of 11 September 2003. Her situation was complicated by the fact that giving evidence against her parents had serious repercussions for her within Warrington's tight-knit Pakistani community, which is why she had been too afraid to discuss Shafilea's disappearance previously. Although her testimony proved crucial to securing her parents' conviction, Alesha was too afraid to attend court again afterwards and was not present to hear the verdict.

Shafilea and Alesha's social location was determined partly by being born in the 1980s in postcolonial Britain, and partly by the fact that their parents had immigrated from a rural area of Pakistan. The patriarchal system in which Shafilea and Alesha were ensnared did not derive simply from the Ahmeds' 'backward' rural roots in opposition to enlightened British culture. Rather, they lived under the constraints imposed by both the patriarchal values to which all British women are subject, and the patriarchal values of their parents' rural Pakistani upbringing. In struggling to make their own life choices, Alesha and Shafilea were continuously confronted with the contradictions between their internalised need to conform to their family's values and, in doing so, avoid bringing shame upon themselves and their family, and their own desire to pursue greater personal freedom as British citizens living in the UK. While culture was a major factor, complex family dynamics, intersectional intergenerational differences and general issues of gender all played their part in Shafilea's murder.

## Critical findings

Culture is a major factor in 'honour'-based violence, but it is not sufficient to explain the phenomenon. While individual and family dynamics also play a role, it is critical to understand HBV as part of the broader problem of violence against women and girls, which affects all communities and sectors of society. Only once the general issue of gendered violence is recognised can the specific forms that VAWG takes in different communities and cultures be properly understood and tackled through effective policy, practice and law. The following key findings exemplify these issues:

- In cultures and communities with a strong sense of family and community honour, rather than just notions of personal standing, the behaviour of one member can seriously affect all the others in terms of social status, access to resources and even inclusion in the community. Real or perceived 'misbehaviour' against social norms, values and traditions must be punished to alleviate 'shame', as this is the only way to restore the group's standing.

- Codes of behaviour concerned with honour and shame are rigid and highly gendered in that they are focused around control of female members' sexual 'purity'. This restricts the lives of women and girls in these communities in stringent ways.
- When a family or community that holds such notions of shame and honour is based in the UK, there is often significant conflict between these family and/or community expectations and rules, and the rights that women and girls hold under British law. Intergenerational factors and family dynamics further complicate these conflicts.
- South Asian women are socialised to believe that they are to blame for any violence they experience if it stems from real or perceived misbehaviour, as this shames and damages their entire family and only punishment can alleviate it. As a result, victims are reluctant to seek help or redress, especially from statutory agencies, and are often highly conflicted even when they do.
- While acknowledging that cultural concepts of honour do play a powerful role in violence and domestic abuse against black and minority women, this is by no means the only factor at play in such cases. Ignoring how forms of violence specific to these communities relate to broader patterns of VAWG is vital in creating effective policy and laws while avoiding stigmatising communities and cultures in racialised ways.

## Implications for policy, practice and research

The police refused to call Shafilea's murder an 'honour' killing because they wanted to stress that no licence should be granted to those who claim that their cultural rights excuse acts of brutality. At the same time, however, those charged with protecting the public must be able to identify and understand the risk factors associated with all forms of VAWG in order to respond effectively. Achieving this goal will rely on the following:

- Debates about HBV and VAW must explore the intersection of culture with gender and other axes of differentiation; tackling violence against females in society is not just a question of culture, but also one of equity.
- More training for police officers based on case studies of successful and unsuccessful prosecutions, and the processes employed to successfully bring offenders to trial, is needed. In other words, training programmes must take account of what works and what does not work if the police are to be more effective in identifying, investigating and supporting the prosecution of HBV and other forms of VAWG.
- Knowledge about best practice must be disseminated and shared if governments, statutory agencies and NGOs are to develop effective policy, law and practical guidelines to tackle and prevent VAWG nationally and internationally.
- The need for a holistic intersectional approach both to achieve successful prosecutions and to better support victims needs to be recognised. This understanding must also be carried forward in better inter-agency cooperation and more effective engagement with specialist providers; only with the requisite knowledge can all victims receive equal treatment.
- Increasing the number of female officers from BME communities, and promoting their engagement in work to develop training, policy and practice, will help ensure that the police service has a wide range of lived experience within its own ranks to draw on.

Understanding the violence experienced by BME women in Britain requires a criminal justice approach that not only considers the links between all forms of gender-based violence, but also addresses the specificity of particular forms of VAWG, such as HBV. A distinction must be drawn between condemning the culture of a specific social group and condemning a particular cultural practice, while recognising that culture is never a sufficient or complete explanation for an individual act of VAWG.

# References

Abu-Lughod, L. (2011). Seductions of honor crime. *Differences: Journal of Feminist Cultural Studies, 22*(1), 17–63.

Ahmad, N. (2008). Dowry deaths in India and abetment of suicide: A socio-legal appraisal. *Journal East Asia International Law, 1*(2), 275–289.

Begikhani, N., Gill, A. K., & Hague, G. (2015). *"Honour"-based violence: Experiences and counter strategies in Iraqi Kurdistan and the UK Kurdish diaspora.* Aldershot: Ashgate.

Bhabha, H. (1994). *The location of culture.* London: Routledge.

Bhagdin, A. (2012). *Transcript of sections of audio from covert recordings with audio file and real timings.* (Case notes on file with author)

Brah, A. (1996). *Cartographies of diaspora/contesting identities.* New York, NY: Routledge.

Brinks, D. (2007). *The judicial response to police killings in Latin America: Inequality and the rule of law.* New York, NY: Cambridge University Press.

Chesler, P. (2010, Spring). Worldwide trends in honor killings. *Middle East Quarterly, 17*(2), 3–11.

Faqir, F. (2001). Intrafamily femicide in defence of honour: The case of Jordan. *Third World Quarterly, 22*(1), 65–82.

Feldman, S. (2010). Shame and honour: The violence of gendered norms under conditions of global crisis. *Women's Studies International Forum, 33*(4), 305–315.

Gill, A. K. (2006). Patriarchal violence in the name of 'honour'. *International Journal of Criminal Justice Sciences, 1*(1), 1–12.

Gill, A. K. (2009). "Honour" killings and the quest for justice in black and minority ethnic communities in the UK. *Criminal Justice Policy Review, 20*(4), 475–494.

Gill, A. K. (2012). Author's personal notes related to expert court attendance of this case at. *Chester Crown Court.*

Gill, A. K. (2014). "All they think about is honour": The murder of Shafilea Ahmed. In A. K. Gill, C. Strange, & K. Roberts (Eds.), *"Honour" killing and violence: Theory, policy and practice* (pp. 177–199). London: Palgrave Macmillan.

Gill, A. K., & Walker, S. (2020). On honour, culture and violence against women in black and minority ethnic communities. In S. Walklate & K. Fitz-Gibbon (Eds.), *Emerald handbook of criminology, feminism and social change.* Bingley: Emerald.

Gilmore, D. (1987). *Aggression and community: Paradoxes of Andalusian culture.* New Haven: Yale University Press.

Grillo, R. (2003). Cultural essentialism and cultural anxiety. *Anthropological Theory, 3*(2), 157–173.

Hellgren, Z., & Hobson, B. (2008). Cultural dialogues in the good society: The case of honour killings in Sweden. *Ethnicities, 8*(3), 385–400.

Jiwani, Y., & Hoodfar, H. (2012, January 30). Should we call it 'honour killing'? No. It's a false distancing of ourselves from a too-common crime: The murders of females. *The Montreal Gazette* [online]. Retrieved from http://www.violenceisnotourculture.org/News-and-Views/should-we-call-it-%E2%80%98honour-killing%E2%80%99-no

Kandiyoti, D. (1988). Bargaining with patriarchy. *Gender and Society, 2*(3), 274–290.

Kaplanian, C., & Gill, A. K. (2020). Honour killings in Jordan. *International Journal of Criminal Justice Sciences, 14.*

Keaveny, P. (2012, August 3). Murderer Iftikhar Ahmed abandoned son and Danish first wife to follow through with arranged marriage to Shafilea's mother Farzana. *Independent.* Retrieved from www.independent.co.uk/news/uk/crime/murderer-iftikhar-ahmed-abandoned-son-and-danish-first-wife-to-follow-through-with-arranged-marriage-to-shafileas-mother-farzana-8005441.html

Kulczycki, A., & Windle, S. (2011). Honor killings in the middle east and North Africa: A systematic review of the literature. *Violence Against Women, 17*(11), 1442–1464.

Manjoo, R. (2011). *UN Doc. A/HRC/17/26. United nations human rights council HRC (2012) report of the special rapporteur on violence against women, its causes and consequences, Rashida Manjoo.* UN Doc A/HRC/20/16. United Nations Human Rights Council.

Miller, W. (1993). *Humiliation: And other essays on honor, social discomfort, and violence*. Ithaca, NY: Cornell University.

Oberwittler, D., & Kasselt, J. (2011). *Ehrenmorde in Deutschland: Eine Untersuchung auf der Basis von Prozessakten [Honor killings in Germany: A study based on prosecution files] (Polizei +Forschung, Bd. 42, hrsg. vom Bundeskriminalamt)*. Cologne: Wolters Kluwer.

Oner-Ozkan, B., & Gencoz, T. (2006). Gurur toplumu bakis acisiyla Turk kulturunun incelenmesi [the importance of the investigation of Turkish culture from the point of view of cultural pride]. *Kriz Dergisi*, *14*, 19–25.

Ozturk, S. (2013, August 8). Sydney's killer: The gay-hate epidemic that claimed 80 men. *Star Observer*. Retrieved from www.starobserver.com.au/news/local-news/new-south-wales-news/sydneys-624 killer-the-gay-hate-epidemic-that-claimed-80-men/107657

Papp, A. (2010). *Culturally driven violence against women: A growing problem in Canada's immigrant communities*. FCPP Policy Series No. 92. Winnipeg, MB: Frontier Centre for Public Policy.

Pitt-Rivers, J. (1966). *Honour and social status. Honour and shame: The values of Mediterranean society*. Cambridge: Cambridge University Press.

Roberts, K., Campbell, G., & Lloyd, G. (2014). *Honor-based violence: Policing and prevention, advances in police theory and practice*. London: Routledge.

Rose, J. (2012, August 6). Shafilea Ahmed's murder is a crime meshed in migration and modernity. *The Guardian*, p. 22. Retrieved from www.guardian.co.uk/commentisfree/2012/aug/05/shafilea-ahmed-murder-migration-modernity

Safilios-Rothschild, C. (1969). Honour crimes in contemporary Greece. *British Journal of Sociology, 20*, 205–218.

Schliesmann, P. (2012). *Honour on trial: The Shafia murders and the culture of honour killings*. Toronto, ON: Fitzhenry and Whiteside.

Sen, P. (2005). Crimes of honour: Value and meaning. In L. Welchman & S. Hossain (Eds), *Honour: Crimes, paradigms and violence against women* (pp. 42–64). London: Zed Books.

Sennett, R. (2004). *Respect: The formation of character in an age of inequality*. London: Penguin Books.

Shalhoub-Kevorkian, N., & Daher-Nashef, S. (2013). Femicide and colonization between the politics of exclusion and the culture of control. *Violence Against Women, 19*(3), 295–315.

Sheeley, E. (2007). *Reclaiming honor in Jordan: A national public opinion survey on "honor" killings*. Amman: Black Iris.

Stewart, F. (1994). *Honour*. Chicago: Chicago University Press.

Terman, R. (2010). To specify or single out: Should we use the term "honour killing"? *Muslim World Journal of Human Rights*, *7*(2), 1642.

Walker, S. (2018). *De-culturalising honour and violence: Exploring 'victims' experiences of 'honour'-based violence in rural England* (PhD thesis). Keele University, Keele, UK.

Warrington Guardian. (2009, June 12). Shafilea Ahmed's father fails to overturn verdict that she was "unlawfully killed". *Warrington Guardian*. Retrieved from www.warringtonguardian.co.uk/news/644 4436238.print/

Welsh, A. (2008). *What is honor? A question of moral imperatives*. New Haven, CT: Yale University Press.

# 27

# INTIMATE PARTNER VIOLENCE AGAINST WOMEN IN FORCED MIGRATION

*Karin Wachter and Laurie Cook Heffron*

## Introduction

The contemporary salience of forced migration and the need for robust and principled international, national, and local responses are evident. In recent history, the world has borne witness to mass migrations of Afghans, South Sudanese, Rohingya, and Venezuelans, among many others. In 2018, over 70 million people migrated due to persecution, conflict, violence, or human rights violations (UNHCR, 2019). In spite of the millions of Syrian refugees seeking refuge in the Middle East, tensions in the West erupted in 2015 following the migration of tens of thousands of people who risked harrowing journeys to reach Europe. Similarly, in 2014, continuing decades of northbound migration, adults and children fleeing gang violence and economic strife in Central America refueled a debate in the United States (US) on the criminalization of migrants, use and conditions of detention centers, denial of asylum claims, deportation, and border security. Similar patterns of conflict, human rights violations, and structural oppression spur migrations around the world.

Recent re-escalations in anti-immigrant rhetoric and policies, reflective of global resurgences of nationalism, have served to deny the humanity of people fleeing inhumane circumstances and hinder short-term responses and long-term change. Structural solutions for entrenched conflicts and political impasses appear elusive. The universally recognized right for people to seek asylum has become increasingly tenuous. The enormity of unmet basic needs – shelter, food, water, and security – coupled with faltering political will to launch and maintain adequate responses, obscures additional concerns. The violence women experience at the hands of a partner or spouse is one such concern relegated to the "private" sphere and frequently overlooked in forced migration discourse. With the aim of shining light on the complexity of human experiences of forced migration, this chapter examines how intimate partner violence (IPV) and forced migration intersect in women's lives.

## Forced migration

Broadly, forced migration refers to the physical movement of individuals, families, and communities due to circumstances that threaten people's security and well-being. Circumstances that incite forced migration, or displacement, may include persecution, armed conflict and war, political instability, repression, environmental disasters, famine, ecological degradation, large-scale development initiatives, and other situations that put people's rights, lives, and livelihoods in danger (Fiddian-Qasmiyeh, Loescher, Long, & Sigona, 2014). People whose migrations are deemed voluntary or primarily driven by economic concerns are protected under international human rights law, but do not automatically have access to specific protections defined under international and regional refugee law (UNHCR, 2016). In contrast, legally constructed categories of forced migrants who are potentially eligible to claim specific protections under international law include refugees, asylum seekers, internally displaced persons, stateless persons, and returnees (UNHCR, 2016).

It is important to consider the language used in narratives of forced versus voluntary migration. "Forced" evokes compulsory and coerced physical movement spurred by circumstances beyond people's control and against their will, which render living conditions and the possibility of staying untenable. In contrast, "voluntary" implies an individual's choice to leave behind acceptable or "livable" circumstances in pursuit of personal, educational, professional, and/or economic goals in another geographic location. In reality, the motivations spurring migration ("push" and "pull" factors) and the degree to which people are able to exercise agency exist along a spectrum or continuum (Nawyn, Reosti, & Gjokaj, 2009; Snyder, 2012). Subjective and "objective" assessments of circumstances as tenable exist along a similar continuum, complicating notions of "forced" and "voluntary" migrations. The term "forced" can obscure the myriad ways in which people as individuals, families, and groups decide when, how, where, and whether or not to migrate (Turton, 2003), even in what might appear to the external world as clear-cut life or death situations (i.e. Rohingya fleeing persecution in Myanmar or Haitians displaced by a magnitude 7.0 earthquake). Scholarship challenging rigid categorizations of forced and voluntary migration notes that these delineations fuel notions of more or less "deserving" migrants, with "forced" migrants often considered more worthy of protection and humanitarian assistance than "voluntary" or "economic" migrants (Gibney, 2014; Turton, 2003).

This chapter employs an understanding of forced migration as a dynamic process and lived experience in which people, exercising varying degrees of agency, uproot under difficult circumstances to seek safety and the opportunity to care for themselves and their families. We emphasize the importance of situating forced migration processes within specific contexts, simultaneously recognizing the diversity and variation of people's experiences within given contexts. The consideration of historical and contemporary structural forces that create the conditions for, and shape responses to, forced migration are paramount to understanding lived experiences of individuals, families, and communities in conjunction to macro dynamics (Wachter & Snyder, 2018). Migratory processes are often more complex than linear trajectories of leaving home and arriving to fixed destinations. The distances and directions people travel in search of respite and safety can vary dramatically. Some migrate in close proximity to their home in order to avoid endangerment on a regular and even seasonal basis. Others cross an international border, apply for asylum or register as refugees on the other side, and regularly return home to assess the situation. Some cross multiple international borders only to be apprehended, detained, and deported to their country of origin, while others flee their countries of origin, never to return.

## Intimate partner violence

The chapter focuses on IPV as defined by behaviors that inflict physical, sexual, or psychological harm on an intimate partner or spouse (past or present), including acts of physical aggression, sexual coercion, psychological abuse, economic abuse, and controlling behaviors (World Health

Organization, 2017). Although the definition is gender-neutral, women and girls are globally disproportionately the target of IPV by a male partner (World Health Organization, 2012).[1] In acknowledgment of this reality and inherent limitations in the scope of this chapter, we focus exclusively on IPV experienced by women.

As in any context, IPV in forced migration does not occur in isolation of other interpersonal and familial dynamics, which may also involve violence and abuse. Broader definitions of domestic violence are more inclusive of the violence women face by immediate and extended members of the family, and/or within a domestic sphere, and are an important reminder of the range and spectrum of violence against women across the life cycle, inclusive of child sexual abuse, non-partner sexual violence and exploitation, stalking, and harassment. In considering IPV in relation to forced migration, it is critical to examine the intersecting roles that race, class, nationality, and other positionalities play in shaping migrating women's experiences. An intersectional lens recognizes that race, gender, religion, ethnicity, age, sexual orientation, and class co-exist to shape social identity, behavior, opportunities, and access to rights (Crenshaw, 1991). Women who face systematic discrimination, such as Black, Brown, and Indigenous women, and women whose gender identities and sexual orientations do not align with cisgender and heterosexual norms, are frequent targets of persecution and also can be disproportionately affected by IPV (Black et al., 2011; Rosay, 2016; Walters, Chen, & Breiding, 2013).

The chapter examines literature from various disciplinary traditions that increasingly study IPV in forced migration, and highlights examples from diverse regions around the world that are by no means exhaustive. Guided by feminist perspectives (Mohanty, 2003), the chapter seeks to examine women's experiences of IPV in forced migration in their deserved complexity and to call attention to the myriad ways IPV affects women across distinct phases of forced migration. Although conceptualized as a complex, varied, and dynamic process, for heuristic purposes it is helpful to situate forced migratory trajectories within time and space. As such, the chapter begins with an overview of IPV within the pre-migration context of armed conflict, followed by considerations of IPV as a catalyst or motivation for migration. We then examine the literature related to IPV during migration and displacement. The subsequent section reviews IPV in post-migration contexts and considers IPV in relation to immigration detention.

## Intimate partner violence in armed conflict

Armed conflict – inclusive of warfare, widespread gang violence, and acts of terrorism – is a significant precipitator of forced migration and an important factor to consider in understanding women's past, present, and future experiences of IPV and its consequences. In armed conflict, civilians are indiscriminately or deliberately threatened, extorted, tortured, murdered, and disappeared. Armed factions punish individuals or any combination of groups based on perceptions of disloyalty. Regardless of motivation, armed groups carry out inhumane acts against civilians to maximize power and control. Local and international efforts brought long overdue acknowledgment and condemnation of the pervasive use of sexual violence in the Guatemalan, the former Yugoslavian, Rwandan, and Democratic Republic of Congo conflicts, among others. Yet, the rise in international attention on conflict-related (non-partner) sexual violence inadvertently obscured the violence and abuse women and girls experience at home, prior to, during, and in the aftermath of armed conflict (Stark & Ager, 2011).

A growing body of evidence, policy, and practice has highlighted the extent to which women and girls experience violence in the home during armed conflict. Studies included in a systematic review of gender-based violence in complex emergencies indicated higher rates of physical IPV than most reports of non-partner sexual violence, which suggest that even at times of political instability women are at greatest risk for violence at home (Stark & Ager, 2011). In the war-affected context of Côte d'Ivoire in West Africa, IPV may have been more widespread than sexual violence perpetrated by armed actors (Hossain et al., 2014). In a study of gender-based violence in Somalia – a context affected by decades of war, natural disasters, and mass population displacement – 35.6% of women reported adult lifetime experiences of physical or sexual IPV (Wirtz et al., 2018). However, capturing an accurate picture of IPV in settings marked by armed conflict and displacement is inherently difficult due to challenges associated with access, and heightened fear and stigma; moreover, inconsistencies in measurement hinder direct comparisons between studies that measure rates of violence against women (Stark & Ager, 2011).

Exposure to armed conflict over time contributes to cumulative stress, which strains family relationships (Al-Krenawi, Graham, & Sehwail, 2007) and exacerbates risks of violence against women at home (Annan & Brier, 2010). Adding to Heise's (1998) ecological model of violence against women as operating across personal, situational, and sociocultural factors of the social environment, Usta and Singh's (2015) conceptual framework highlights key factors contributing to domestic violence in armed conflict at different levels of the social ecology. Factors at the structural level include deepening of gender inequalities, displacement, breakdown of legal systems, impunity, and widespread poverty and unemployment (Usta & Singh, 2015). Community- and social-level factors include altered sex ratio, changing norms, and civilian adoption of violence (Usta & Singh, 2015). Relationship-level factors include shifting gender roles and relationship dynamics, and women's loss of intra-household bargaining power (Usta & Singh, 2015). Factors operating at the individual level include trauma, physical insecurity, lack of resources, death of loved ones, and displacement (Usta & Singh, 2015). Furthermore, men's responses to stressors may involve using violence against women in attempts to regain power and control, and turning to alcohol and drugs as a negative coping mechanism (Usta & Singh, 2015).

With a focus on El Salvador, Mo Hume (2008) reports that women's fears of reporting the abuse they experience is related to the broader context of public and gang violence in the country. She suggests that men use this wider context as a way to threaten and control the women they abuse. Hume describes the outcry against "public" violence (gang violence) amidst a simultaneous silence around "private" violence (IPV). Cecilia Menjívar (2011) also relates interpersonal violence to larger and multiple structural inequalities and state violence. Consistent with Hume's work, Menjívar argues for recognizing interconnections of various forms of violence, stating that violence experienced within intimate relationships is connected to violence perpetrated against indigenous communities. Menjívar asserts that the current state of violence against women in Guatemala, in particular, is rooted in the atrocities committed during the political conflict.

Compelling research in occupied Palestinian territories underscores the intersection between armed conflict and IPV. A nationally representative survey of married women in the West Bank and Gaza Strip generated 12-month prevalence estimates of IPV that showed high rates of psychological aggression and physical assault (Haj-Yahia & Clark, 2013). Risk factors associated with psychological, physical, and sexual IPV included stressful life events, political violence, community resources, and locality-level acceptance of spousal abuse, among other variables (Haj-Yahia & Clark, 2013). Findings from a mixed methods study conducted in the Gaza Strip indicated that an Israeli military operation in 2014 increased domestic violence, even at relatively low levels of destruction (Müller & Tranchant, 2019). This analysis suggests that the effects were due to displacement, decreased married women's abilities to contribute to household decision-making, and reduced social support networks caused by the military operation (Müller & Tranchant, 2019). Another study with Palestinians affected by armed conflict showed significantly higher odds of physical and sexual IPV among women whose husbands experienced political violence (Clark et al., 2010).

## Intimate partner violence as a catalyst for migration

IPV often plays a role in motivations to migrate and in migration-related decision-making. In addition to recognizing IPV as a precipitating factor in forced migration, evidence points to migration as a strategy to escape or resist violence and related oppression (Salcido & Adelman, 2004; Nawyn et al., 2009; Upegui-Hernández, 2012). Parson (2010) demonstrates the co-existing elements of force, choice, and agency in the life history of Antonia, who migrated from Peru to Chile, fleeing an abusive husband in order to provide a better life for her children. Antonia's migration is "one of the many instances in her life when she resisted intimate abuse and the structural violence of poverty and asserted her agency" (p. 888). Analysis of data collected at migrant shelters participating in the Kino Border Initiative in the Southwest region of the US demonstrates that migrating women experienced multiple episodes of violence from the time of childhood until the present, and that in this chronic context of violence, migration is a strategy for survival (Conrad, 2013).

In addition to the immediate risks to safety experienced by survivors, scholars attend to the multiple structures of oppression that contribute to relationships of unequal power and control. An ecological perspective recognizes that in addition to the role IPV may play as a motivating factor to migrate, it is important to consider the ways in which racism and poverty act as interrelated factors influencing migration-related decision-making (Parson, 2010). Salcido and Adelman (2004) found that Mexican survivors of IPV might cross the border to seek both safety from violence and economic security. In addition, Belanger and Rahman (2013) found that IPV, in concert with economic issues, functions as a motivation for women to migrate in search of employment. Pre-migration decision-making involves interrelated problems of domestic violence, financial predicaments, social status, underemployment and/or limited employment opportunities in the home country (Belanger & Rahman, 2013).

## Intimate partner violence during migration and displacement

Whether people suddenly flee their homes or decide to migrate because the costs of remaining become untenable, they face dramatic changes in all aspects of life. Whatever degree of stability and security their home and community had afforded them dissipates. In forced migration, people suffer the loss of financial assets and material goods. Some have to choose whom to leave behind; for others, the circumstances under which they flee relinquish any semblance of choice in that regard. Forced migration frequently separates loved ones from one another, temporarily or permanently. The journey, whether by foot, car, train, boat, or plane, can be harrowing and fraught with danger and the possibility of exploitation. In transit, women are vulnerable to violence, abuse, and exploitation (Freedman, 2016). At some point, people reach a destination and the physical journey ceases, temporarily for some and indefinitely for others. People face the possibility of being unable to move forward to an intended destination and unable to return home. Some journey to an area of relative safety within the political borders of their country of origin, others cross one or more international borders in their search of safety and respite. If they are able to avoid detention and deportation, people will journey to and ultimately remain where they can receive some assistance and protection, and/or make an asylum claim. In this state of displacement, people cobble together resources to survive and the cycle of daily life – including IPV – persists, often under dire circumstances.

Studies in displacement contexts in the past decade have provided important insights into the scope of IPV. A study conducted with Somali women in Ethiopian refugee camps and host communities indicated that gender-based violence was widespread and largely domestic, prevalence was higher in town than in the camp, and women faced a higher risk of violence in the camp compared with in flight (Parcesepe, Stark, Roberts, & Boothby, 2016). In a camp for displaced persons in the Kurdistan region of Iraq, over 58% of women who formed part of a non-representative sample of married couples (n=46) reported past-year experiences with IPV (Goessmann, Ibrahim, Saupe, Ismail, & Neuner, 2019). Results from a study that spanned three refugee camps on the Thai-Burma border indicated that close to 8% of women reported experiencing IPV in the past year (Falb, McCormick, Hemenway, Anfinson, & Silverman, 2013). Research points to an association between experiences of non-partner violence (i.e. sexual violence by an armed actor in war or another form of conflict-related violence) and IPV in displacement (Wako et al., 2015; Falb et al., 2013), although other studies have failed to demonstrate a relationship (Sipsma et al., 2015). In displacement contexts associated with natural disasters, women who screened positive for mental health symptoms post-Hurricane Katrina (2005) in the US were 2.7 times more likely to have also reported post-disaster gender-based violence (Anastario, Larrance, & Lawry, 2008).

A robust body of research has brought to light key factors associated with the perpetration and experience of IPV in displacement, which bear close resemblance to Usta and Singh's (2015) ecological framework of domestic violence against women in war and armed conflicts, in which displacement forms both structural- and individual-level factors in women's experience of IPV. As in any context, people carry with them entrenched ideas, beliefs, and attitudes about gender when they migrate despite everything left behind. Pre-existing social norms that sanction IPV to greater or lesser degrees do not dissipate in displacement and in fact can reconfigure and strengthen as people struggle for stability, identity, and any semblance of power and control over a situation marked by loss of agency. Global and culturally specific norms that excuse and/or encourage violence against women in the home by an intimate partner and other family members – for instance, as a mechanism of instruction, discipline, and punishment – are well researched, play a significant role in empirical explanations of IPV, and point to significant areas for intervention (Heise & Kotsadam, 2015; Jewkes, Flood, & Lang, 2015). At the same time, displacement disrupts, challenges, and destabilizes entrenched ideas and norms stipulating and regulating the roles delegated to women and men.

Research with displaced persons has identified the connection between such changes in social roles and marital conflict (Okello & Hovil, 2007; Ondeko & Purdin, 2004). Displacement can make it exceedingly difficult for some to fulfill traditional roles and compel people to push the boundaries of prescribed gender roles, creating tensions between new and old roles (Cardoso et al., 2016). Displacement often sparks dramatic shifts in social status and roles (Hynes et al., 2016). In qualitative research with displaced women in Colombia, changes to the roles women and men filled brought about by conditions of displacement – such as men's underemployment and women's employment outside the home – stood in stark contrast with entrenched gender norms held by both women and men, and were understood by participants to spark conflict (Hynes et al., 2016). Similarly, a qualitative study in three refugee camps spanning South Sudan, Kenya, and Iraq highlighted partners' unmet expectations of one another across a spectrum of gender roles, and particularly related to who provides and controls financial resources (Wachter et al., 2018).

The significant economic hardships for people displaced from their homes are intrinsically interrelated with changing gendered social norms. A qualitative study with people displaced by the armed conflict in Colombia highlighted how war and the resulting economic insecurity and stress exacerbated IPV against women (Wirtz et al., 2014). In a qualitative study with internally displaced persons in northern Uganda, participants systematically pointed to economic deprivation as contributing to all forms of gender-based violence, including IPV (Ager, Bancroft, Berger, & Stark, 2018). In Côte d'Ivoire, urban poverty characterized by unemployment, food insecurity, and housing instability contributed to IPV among people displaced by conflict (Cardoso et al., 2016). Among Syrian refugees who fled to Lebanon, women reported IPV, as well as harassment and community violence, difficult living conditions marked by crowding and lack of privacy, and unemployment (Usta, Masterson, & Farver, 2019).

Marriages that take place in the context of displacement may carry a high risk of IPV against women. In Colombia for instance, women displaced by the conflict noted patterns of successive abusive marriages, in which women sought help with supporting themselves and their children in a new urban context and were frequently significantly younger than their spouses (Wirtz et al., 2014). In Côte d'Ivoire, the absence of supportive networks, and changing gender roles and norms, were salient factors contributing to IPV among people displaced by the conflict (Cardoso et al., 2016). Across three refugee camps, participants emphasized women's separation from their parents and extended families, and resulting loss of potential protection and support, as contributing to women's experiences of IPV (Wachter et al., 2018). Finally, research has highlighted how even the humanitarian infrastructure set up to address IPV in displacement can inadvertently contribute to women's experiences of violence in the home. Official responses that destabilize community structures, instead of encouraging them to work on behalf of women and girls, can exacerbate vulnerabilities by forcing women to choose between their community and safety (Horn, 2010a).

## Post-migration intimate partner violence

The threat and experience of IPV may traverse time and space alongside women who migrate, or may emerge for the first time post-migration. Post-migration implies an arrival to a particular destination, when the physical migration ceases or pauses and people take steps to settle in a new community with or without legal protections. In the post-migration phase, additional socially and legally constructed labels are applied to categories of newcomers – such as documented or undocumented immigrants, resettled refugees, and asylees – implying varying degrees of welcome and unwelcome. However, the post-migration phase is not always easily distinguishable from contexts of long-term displacement (e.g. generations of Somalis or Palestinians living in camps with no solution, such as permanent settlement or repatriation, in sight). To be "post" migration – that is, to arrive and settle – implies a release from dynamics that compel migration, and being safe enough to carry on with the business of life and providing for oneself and one's family. Arguably, "post" migration is a matter of subjectivity, a state of mind, which only the subjects of any forced migration can define for themselves. Similar to experiences of IPV, forced migration processes may not have a definitive end; the ongoing effects and lived experiences of forced migration do not end simply when the physical migration ceases. People may settle, only to migrate again. In the post-migration phase, however fluid, women with previous or current exposure to IPV often contend with policies and practices that both promote and hinder social integration and exclusion, further shaping the impact of IPV on their lives.

While crossing borders may be an avenue to escape public and private violence, women face ongoing and new risks of violence upon arrival and post-migration (Cook Heffron, 2018; Freedman, 2016; Salcido & Adelman, 2004). Studies have reported women experiencing an escalation or initiation of violence and abuse by their partners after migrating (Guruge,

Khanlou, & Gastaldo, 2010; Kiwanuka, 2008). Amanor-Boadu and colleagues (2012) found that immigrant women experiencing IPV face greater physical, financial, legal, and social risk associated with leaving abusive relationships, in comparison to non-immigrant women. Yet, estimating the prevalence of IPV among immigrant populations is challenging. Language and social marginalization are barriers to participating in research, especially among undocumented newcomers. Immigrants are underrepresented in crime statistics, due to low rates of formal reports to law enforcement. Rates reported by immigrant survivors of violence may be lower in comparison to other survivors, given fears of deportation. It is generally considered that the risks of abuse are potentially higher among undocumented immigrants (Bhuyan, Shim, & Velagapudi, 2010), and immigrant women face higher risks of intimate partner homicide (Sabri, Campbell, & Messing, 2018). Studies in the US, however, report conflicting estimates of IPV rates among immigrant groups (Runner, Yoshihama, & Novick, 2009), complicating the discourse that immigrant women experience higher rates of abuse than their non-immigrant counterparts.

Intersecting aspects of post-migration experiences related to language proficiency, acculturation, gender roles and expectations, employment, immigration status, discrimination, and knowledge of laws and services are factors associated with the perpetration and experience of IPV (Menjívar & Salcido, 2002). Post-migration risk factors for IPV mirror and interrelate with barriers limiting women's access to services (Bauer, Rodriguez, Quiroga, & Flores-Ortiz, 2000; Reina, Lohman, & Maldonado, 2014). Again, shifting gender power dynamics is a salient factor (McIlwaine, 2010). While migrating may serve to challenge traditional gender inequalities and offer some protections to women (Hirsch, 1999), it can conversely recreate or intensify pre-migration gender norms. Studies have also highlighted intersections between violence against women post-migration and sending remittances to countries of origin in support of partners, families, and community projects (Erez, Adelman, & Gregory, 2009; Upegui- Hernández, 2012). In particular, Erez et al. (2009) found that the economic marginalization of immigrant survivors of abuse, combined with the continued responsibility for sending remittances home, contributed to batterers' justification for abuse. Bui and Morash (2008) also found that IPV survivors reported experiencing IPV in connection with conflicts about sending remittances as they relate to gendered interpretations of economic responsibilities and disagreement over the amounts and recipients of remittances.

Fear of law enforcement and deportation create significant barriers for immigrant women experiencing IPV, particularly among those with precarious legal status (Levine & Peffer, 2012). Survivors in the US, for instance, often fear that reporting crimes, seeking shelter, or requesting help will lead to their deportation, and they may lack familiarity with or access to available social service or criminal justice systems, albeit systems that possess limited immigrant-related cultural and linguistic competencies (Becerra, Wagaman, Androff, Messing, & Castillo, 2017; Erez et al., 2009). Abusers may take advantage of precarious immigration status and constructed "illegality" as a mechanism of maintaining power and control in an intimate relationship, threatening to report their partners to immigration officials, feeding legitimate fears of deportation, separation from children, and loss of financial support (Erez et al., 2009; Parson & Heckert, 2014).

Discrimination, racism, and anti-immigrant or xenophobic sentiments also serve to restrict access to services among immigrant survivors (Bauer et al., 2000; Crandall, Senturia, Sullivan, & Shiu-Thornton, 2005), thereby contributing to women's vulnerability to IPV in post-migration contexts. For instance, recent policy changes in the US have restricted access to legal remedies for asylum-seekers fleeing IPV; as of June 2018, IPV as a basis for asylum claims in the US has come into question and become increasingly restricted (Smith, 2020).

## Intimate partner violence and immigration detention

A largely unexplored area of research is the risk of violence women face during and following apprehension and incarceration in immigration detention systems. Researchers have identified immigration detention practices in Australia as incurring negative mental health outcomes among asylum-seekers (Silove, Austin, & Steel, 2007; Steel et al., 2011) and the US serves as another relevant example. On any given day, US Immigration and Customs Enforcement detains as many as 55,000 individuals accused of violating US immigration laws, the majority seeking asylum from El Salvador, Guatemala, Honduras, and Mexico (Transactional Records Access Clearinghouse, 2019). Anecdotal evidence suggests that an overwhelming number of women in immigration detention are survivors of violence, abuse, and trauma.

Detention facilities rely on control, coercion, and containment, and exacerbate the lack of stability women feel, by creating a persistent state of alertness, heightened fear, and hyper-vigilance, replicating tactics used by abusers, traffickers, and other perpetrators (Cook Heffron, Serrata, & Hurtado, 2019). These include restricting mobility; disrupting sleep with bed checks; insults and humiliation; withholding information; ever-changing rules and expectations; restricting access to support; isolating women from one another, from their own children, and from the community; intimidation; and threats (Cook Heffron, 2018; Cook Heffron et al., 2019). This context may re-trigger negative mental health outcomes associated with IPV. While there is little empirical evidence on post-release risk, advocates anticipate that these compounding and multi-level factors contribute to increased vulnerability to exploitation and other abuses (Canning, 2019; Cook Heffron et al., 2019).

## Conclusions

This chapter calls attention to the myriad ways in which IPV affects women across diverse geographies at various phases and contexts prior to, during, and following migration. The discussion highlights the importance of understanding the intersections of forced migration and IPV as lived experiences and processes marked by complexity and heterogeneity, in which people exercise varying degrees of agency. Other perspectives not included here, legal and otherwise, are also important. While numerous challenges impede knowledge production with migrating populations, a growing body of research shines light on the scope of IPV across global contexts and the multiple levels across the social ecology at which factors associated with exposure to and consequences of IPV persist. Together, these elements of complex stories serve as a reminder of the shifting landscapes of forced migration, and how, across time and space, IPV both shapes migration and is shaped by migration.

Research highlights the importance of expanding current understandings of suffering in armed conflict to include violence perpetrated by an intimate partner (Miller & Rasmussen, 2010; Usta & Singh, 2015). However, gaps remain regarding the consequences of and needs associated with IPV throughout various stages of forced migration. Cycles of abuse and physical, emotional, and economic consequences of IPV can traverse transnational geographies and complicate efforts to rebuild life and home. Temporal considerations complicate understandings of needs as women may continue to suffer consequences of IPV they no longer experience, or live with the continuous threat of violence because they migrated with an abusive partner or remain connected to an abusive partner, transnationally (Wachter, Dalpe, & Cook Heffron, 2019).

The ecological perspective highlighted in this chapter helps to elucidate IPV in relation to forced migration and serves as a useful tool to inform approaches for IPV prevention and intervention throughout migration. By formulating solutions as individual-level and IPV-only interventions, however, we risk failing to respond to structural factors that not only foster IPV against women but also are associated with other forms of oppression. By tackling community-, systemic-, and structural-level factors, and moving beyond the temptation to respond to IPV at a purely individual level, we expand possibilities for shifting inequalities related to socio-economics, health and wellness, overall living conditions, and access to rights. Examples from field-based work point to important avenues for interventions, community organizing, and macro-level structural change (see Bhuyan, Osborne, Zahraei, & Tarshis, 2014; Cook Heffron et al., 2019; Horn, 2010b; Michau, Horn, Bank, Dutt, & Zimmerman, 2015; Usta & Singh, 2015). Feminist community-based organizations and activists play vital roles in addressing violence against women at multiple levels of the social ecology. Collaborative partnerships between community-based activist groups, domestic violence and sexual assault agencies, immigrant-led organizations, and agencies serving asylum seekers, refugees, and marginalized immigrants form the foundation for developing meaningful action across geographic settings. In addition, local and international humanitarian organizations play an important role in advancing policy, practice, and research to mitigate vulnerabilities associated with IPV in armed conflict and forced migration.[2]

It is important to bear in mind that formal acknowledgment of IPV in times of armed conflict, as a catalyst of forced migration, during migration and displacement, and post-migration is relatively new. Indeed, recognition of women as forced migrants with valid claims for asylum on their own terms is only a recent development (Fiddian-Qasmiyeh, 2014). The literature from which this chapter draws to present facets of the intersection of IPV and forced migration points to positive developments in this regard, as it represents an energized and growing body of knowledge with significant potential for informing policy and practice, ongoing research, and advocacy. At the same time, it bears highlighting inherent limitations in perspectives presented here, which draw almost exclusively from academic scholarship and thus do not capture the courageous and revolutionary efforts of women and allies on the ground who have long strove to dismantle structures, practices, and norms that condone violence against women and girls in all spheres of life. Likewise, while this chapter has reflected researchers' efforts to explain and describe the risks, vulnerabilities, and consequences of IPV on migrating women, it also reveals the paucity of attention to women's individual and collective resistance to IPV at multiple levels. Alongside the contributions of academic scholars referenced here, migrating and immigrant women must be at the center of formulating an understanding of IPV and of deciding when and how to address IPV at every phase of forced migration.

## Acknowledgment

We thank Cherra Mathis, MSW, a social work doctoral student at Arizona State University, for her judicious and thoughtful assistance with this project.

## Critical findings

- Intimate partner violence (IPV) affects women across diverse geographies at various phases and contexts prior to, during, and post-migration.
- IPV plays a role in motivations to migrate and in migration-related decision-making. The threat and experience of IPV may traverse time and space alongside women who migrate, or may emerge for the first time in displacement or post-migration.
- While numerous challenges impede knowledge production with migrating populations, a growing body of research shines light on the scope of IPV across global contexts and the

multiple levels across the social ecology at which factors associated with exposure to and consequences of IPV persist.

• Key factors associated with IPV in forced migration include pervasive poverty and unemployment, early and quick (re)marriages, shifts in gender roles, changing norms around violence, and deepening inequalities.

## Implications for policy, practice, and research

• Although existing evidence points to high rates of violence within private spheres of life, IPV is likely under-reported due to challenges with measuring violence against women in contexts shaped by forced migration. Ongoing research is necessary to bring the full scale of the problem to light.

• Gaps remain regarding the consequences of and needs associated with IPV throughout various stages of forced migration.

• An unexplored area of research is the risk of violence migrating women face during and following apprehension by immigration officials and incarceration in federal immigration detention systems.

• Collaborative partnerships between community-based activist groups, domestic violence and sexual assault agencies, immigrant-led organizations, and agencies serving forced migrants are fundamental to addressing IPV among forced migrant groups across geographic settings.

• Women with relevant lived experiences must be at the center of advocacy, intervention, and research efforts to address and mitigate intersections of forced migration and IPV.

## Notes

1 In armed conflict and forced migration, men face various manifestations of violence and children are especially vulnerable to abuse and exploitation.
2 Examples include the International Rescue Committee GBV Responders' Network (gbvresponders.org); the World Health Organization (https://www.who.int/health-topics/violence-against-women#tab=tab_1); UN Women (https://www.unwomen.org/en/what-we-do/ending-violence-against-women); and the Women's Refugee Commission (womensrefugeecommission.org).

## References

Ager, A., Bancroft, C., Berger, E., & Stark, L. (2018). Local constructions of gender-based violence amongst IDPs in northern Uganda: Analysis of archival data collected using a gender- and age-segmented participatory ranking methodology. *Conflict and Health, 12*(1), 1–10. https://doi.org/10.1186/s13031-018-0140-6

Al-Krenawi, A., Graham, J., & Sehwail, M. (2007). Tomorrow's players under occupation: An analysis of the association of political violence with psychological functioning and domestic violence among Palestinian youth. *The American Journal of Orthopsychiatry, 77,* 427–433. doi:10.1037/0002-9432.77.3.427

Amanor-Boadu, Y., Messing, J. T., Stith, S. M., Anderson, J. R., O'Sullivan, C. S., & Campbell, J. C. (2012). Immigrant and nonimmigrant women: Factors that predict leaving an abusive relationship. *Violence Against Women, 18*(5), 611–633. https://doi.org/10.1177/1077801212453139

Anastario, M. P., Larrance, R., & Lawry, L. (2008). Using mental health indicators to identify postdisaster gender-based violence among women displaced by Hurricane Katrina. *Journal of Women's Health, 17*(9), 1437–1444. https://doi.org/10.1089/jwh.2007.0694

Annan, J., & Brier, M. J. (2010). The risk of return: Intimate partner violence in northern Uganda's armed conflict. *Social Science & Medicine, 70*(1), 152–159. doi: 10.1016/j.socscimed.2009.09.027

Bauer, H. M., Rodriguez, M. A., Quiroga, S. S., & Flores-Ortiz, Y. G. (2000). Barriers to health care for abused Latina and Asian immigrant women. *Journal of Health Care for the Poor and Underserved, 11*(1), 33–44. https://doi.org/10.1353/hpu.2010.0590

Becerra, D., Wagaman, M. A., Androff, D., Messing, J., & Castillo, J. (2017). Policing immigrants: Fear of deportations and perceptions of law enforcement and criminal justice. *Journal of Social Work, 17*(6), 715–731. https://doi.org/10.1177/1468017316651995

Bélanger, D., & Rahman, M. (2013). Migrating against all the odds: International labour migration of Bangladeshi women. *Current Sociology, 61*(3), 356–373. https://doi.org/10.1177/0011392113484453

Bhuyan, R., Osborne, B., Zahraei, S., & Tarshis, S. (2014). *Unprotected, unrecognized: Canadian immigration policy and violence against women, 2008–2013.* Publications and Scholarship. https://source.sheridancollege.ca/fahcs_publications/5

Bhuyan, R., Shim, W., & Velagapudi, K. (2010). Domestic violence advocacy with immigrants and refugees. In L. L. Lockhart & F. S. Danis (Eds.), *Domestic violence* (pp. 155–182). New York, NY: Columbia University Press.

Black, M. C., Basile, K. C., Breiding, M. J., Smith, S. G., Walters, M. L., Merrick, M. T., Chen, J., & Stevens, M. R. (2011). *The national intimate partner and sexual violence survey (NISVS): 2010 summary report.* Atlanta, GA: National Center for Injury Prevention and Control, Centers for Disease Control and Prevention. Retrieved from www.cdc.gov/violenceprevention/pdf/nisvs_report2010-a.pdf

Bui, H., & Morash, M. (2008). Immigration, masculinity, and intimate partner violence from the standpoint of domestic violence service providers and Vietnamese-origin women. *Feminist Criminology, 3*(3), 191–215. https://doi.org/10.1177/1557085108321500

Canning, V. (2019). Degradation by design: Women and asylum in northern Europe. *Race & Class, 61*(1), 46–63. https://doi.org/10.1177/0306396819850986

Cardoso, L. F., Gupta, J., Shuman, S., Cole, H., Kpebo, D., & Falb, K. L. (2016). What factors contribute to intimate partner violence against women in urban, conflict-affected settings? Qualitative findings from Abidjan, Côte d'Ivoire. *Journal of Urban Health, 93*(2), 364–378. https://doi.org/10.1007/s11524-016-0029-x

Clark, C. J., Everson-Rose, S. A., Suglia, S. F., Btoush, R., Alonso, A., & Haj-Yahia, M. M. (2010). Association between exposure to political violence and intimate-partner violence in the occupied Palestinian territory: A cross-sectional study. *Lancet, 375*(9711), 310–316. https://doi.org/10.1016/S0140-6736(09)61827-4

Conrad, M. (2013). *Women's testimonios of life and migration in el cruce.* MA: Arizona State University. Retrieved from http://search.proquest.com/docview/1355757315/abstract/B57CD4CC3C064753PQ/1

Cook Heffron, L. (2018). "Salía de uno y me metí en otro:" Exploring the migration-violence nexus among Central American women. *Violence against Women, 25*(6), 677–702. doi:10.1177/1077801218797473

Cook Heffron, L., Serrata, J. V., & Hurtado, G. (2019). *Latina immigrant women & children's well-being & access to services after detention.* Casa de Esperanza's National Latino Network. Retrieved from https://nationallatinonetwork.org/images/Family_Detention_Report_English.pdf

Crandall, M., Senturia, K., Sullivan, M., & Shiu-Thornton, S. (2005). Latina survivors of domestic violence: Understanding through qualitative analysis. *Hispanic Health Care International, 3*(3), 179.

Crenshaw, K. (1991). Mapping the margins: Intersectionality, identity politics, and violence against women of color. *Stanford Law Review, 43*(6), 1241–1299. JSTOR. https://doi.org/10.2307/1229039

Erez, E., Adelman, M., & Gregory, C. (2009). Intersections of immigration and domestic violence: Voices of battered immigrant women. *Feminist Criminology, 4*(1), 32–56. https://doi.org/10.1177/1557085108325413

Falb, K. L., McCormick, M. C., Hemenway, D., Anfinson, K., & Silverman, J. G. (2013). Violence against refugee women along the Thai-Burma border. *International Journal of Gynecology & Obstetrics, 120*(3), 279–283. https://doi.org/10.1016/j.ijgo.2012.10.015

Fiddian-Qasmiyeh, E. (2014). Gender and forced migration. In E. Fiddian-Qasmiyeh, G. Loescher, K. Long, & N. Sigona (Eds.), *The Oxford handbook of refugee and forced migration studies* (pp. 176–197). Oxford, England: Oxford University Press.

Fiddian-Qasmiyeh, E., Loescher, G., Long, K., & Sigona, N. (Eds.). (2014). Introduction: Refugee and forced migration studies in transition. In *The Oxford handbook of refugee and forced migration studies* (pp. 1–17). Oxford, England: Oxford University Press.

Freedman, J. (2016). Sexual and gender-based violence against refugee women: A hidden aspect of the refugee "crisis". *Reproductive Health Matters, 24*(47), 18–26.

Gibney, M. (2014). Political theory, ethics, and forced migration. In E. Fiddian-Qasmiyeh, G. Loescher, K. Long, & N. Sigona (Eds.), *The Oxford handbook of refugee and forced migration studies*. Oxford, England: Oxford University Press.

Goessmann, K., Ibrahim, H., Saupe, L. B., Ismail, A. A., & Neuner, F. (2019). The contribution of mental health and gender attitudes to intimate partner violence in the context of war and displacement: Evidence from a multi-informant couple survey in Iraq. *Social Science & Medicine, 237*, 112457. https://doi.org/10.1016/j.socscimed.2019.112457

Guruge, S., Khanlou, N., & Gastaldo, D. (2010). Intimate male partner violence in the migration process: Intersections of gender, race and class. *Journal of Advanced Nursing, 66*(1), 103–113. https://doi.org/10.1111/j.1365-2648.2009.05184.x

Haj-Yahia, M. M., & Clark, C. J. (2013). Intimate partner violence in the occupied Palestinian territory: Prevalence and risk factors. *Journal of Family Violence, 28*(8), 797–809. https://doi.org/10.1007/s10896-013-9549-2

Heise, L. L. (1998). Violence against women: An integrated, ecological framework. *Violence Against Women, 4*(3), 262–290.

Heise, L. L., & Kotsadam, A. (2015). Cross-national and multilevel correlates of partner violence: An analysis of data from population-based surveys. *The Lancet Global Health, 3*(6), e332–e340. https://doi.org/10.1016/S2214-109X(15)00013-3

Hirsch, J. S. (1999). En el Norte la Mujer Manda: Gender, generation, and geography in a Mexican transnational community. *American Behavioral Scientist, 42*(9), 1332–1349. https://doi.org/10.1177/00027649921954930

Horn, R. (2010a). Responses to intimate partner violence in Kakuma refugee camp: Refugee interactions with agency systems. *Social Science & Medicine, 70*(1), 160–168. doi:10.1016/j.socscimed.2009.09.036

Horn, R. (2010b). Exploring the impact of displacement and encampment on domestic violence in Kakuma refugee camp. *Journal of Refugee Studies, 23*(3), 356–376. https://doi.org/10.1093/jrs/feq020

Hossain, M., Zimmerman, C., Kiss, L., Kone, D., Bakayoko-Topolska, M., Manan, K. A. D., . . . Watts, C. (2014). Men's and women's experiences of violence and traumatic events in rural Côte d'Ivoire before, during and after a period of armed conflict. *BMJ Open, 4*(2), e003644. https://doi.org/10.1136/bmjopen-2013-003644

Hume, M. (2008). The myths of violence: Gender, conflict, and community in El Salvador. *Latin American Perspectives, 35*(5), 59–76. https://doi.org/10.1177/0094582X08321957

Hynes, M. E., Sterk, C. E., Hennink, M., Patel, S., DePadilla, L., & Yount, K. M. (2016). Exploring gender norms, agency and intimate partner violence among displaced Colombian women: A qualitative assessment. *Global Public Health, 11*(1–2), 17–33. https://doi.org/10.1080/17441692.2015.1068825

Jewkes, R., Flood, M., & Lang, J. (2015). From work with men and boys to changes of social norms and reduction of inequities in gender relations: A conceptual shift in prevention of violence against women and girls. *Lancet, 385*(9977), 1580–1589. https://doi.org/10.1016/S0140-6736(14)61683-4

Kiwanuka, M. (2008). *The effect of migration on urban migrant women's perceptions of domestic violence*. Thesis submitted in 2008 to Graduate School for the Humanities and Social Sciences – University of the Witwatersrand, Johannesburg, South Africa

Levine, H., & Peffer, S. (2012). Quiet casualties: An analysis of U non-immigrant status of undocumented immigrant victims of intimate partner violence. *International Journal of Public Administration, 35*(9), 634–642. https://doi.org/10.1080/01900692.2012.661191

McIlwaine, C. (2010). Migrant machismos: Exploring gender ideologies and practices among Latin American migrants in London from a multi-scalar perspective. *Gender Place and Culture, 17*(3), 281–300. doi:10.1080/09663691003737579

Menjivar, C. (2011). *Enduring violence: Ladina women's lives in Guatemala*. Berkeley, CA: University of California Press.

Menjívar, C., & Salcido, O. (2002). Immigrant women and domestic violence: Common experiences in different countries. *Gender & Society, 16*(6), 898–920. https://doi.org/10.1177/089124302237894

Michau, L., Horn, J., Bank, A., Dutt, M., & Zimmerman, C. (2015). Prevention of violence against women and girls: Lessons from practice. *Lancet, 385*(9978), 1672–1684. https://doi.org/10.1016/S0140-6736(14)61797-9

Miller, K. E., & Rasmussen, A. (2010). War exposure, daily stressors, and mental health in conflict and post-conflict settings: Bridging the divide between trauma-focused and psychosocial frameworks. *Social Science & Medicine, 70*(1), 7–16. https://doi.org/10.1016/j.socscimed.2009.09.029

Mohanty, C. T. (2003). *Feminism without borders: Decolonizing theory, practicing solidarity*. Durham, NC: Duke University Press.

Müller, C., & Tranchant, J.-P. (2019). Domestic violence and humanitarian crises: Evidence from the 2014 Israeli military operation in Gaza. *Violence Against Women*. https://doi.org/10.1177/1077801218818377

Nawyn, S. J., Reosti, A., & Gjokaj. L. (2009). Gender in motion: How gender precipitates international migration. In M. T. Segal & V. Demos (Eds.), *Perceiving gender locally, globally, and intersectionally: Advances in gender research* (Vol. 13, pp. 175–202). Bingley, UK: Emerald Press.

Okello, M., & Hovil, L. (2007). Confronting the reality of gender-based violence in Northern Uganda. *International Journal of Transitional Justice, 1*. doi:10.1093/ijtj/ijm036

Ondeko, R., & Purdin, S. (2004). Understanding the causes of gender-based violence. *Forced Migration Review, 19*, 30.

Parcesepe, A., Stark, L., Roberts, L., & Boothby, N. (2016). Measuring physical violence and rape against Somali women using the neighborhood method. *Violence Against Women, 22*(7), 798–816. https://doi.org/10.1177/1077801215613852

Parson, N. (2010). "I Am Not [Just] a Rabbit who has a bunch of children!" Agency in the Midst of suffering at the intersections of global inequalities, gendered violence, and migration. *Violence Against Women, 16*(8), 881–901. https://doi.org/10.1177/1077801210376224

Parson, N., & Heckert, C. (2014). The golden cage: The production of insecurity at the nexus of intimate partner violence and unauthorized migration in the United States. *Human Organization, 73*(4), 305–314. doi:10.17730/humo.73.4.9v34586u28354l12

Reina, A. S., Lohman, B. J., & Maldonado, M. M. (2014). "He said they'd deport me": Factors influencing domestic violence help-seeking practices among Latina immigrants. *Journal of Interpersonal Violence, 29*(4), 593–615. https://doi.org/10.1177/0886260513505214

Rosay, A. B. (2016). *Violence against American Indian and Alaska native women and men*. National Institute of Justice. Retrieved January 9, 2020, from https://nij.ojp.gov/topics/articles/violence-against-american-indian-and-alaska-native-women-and-men

Runner, M., Yoshihama, M., & Novick, S. (2009). *Intimate partner violence in immigrant and refugee communities: Challenges, promising practices, and recommendations*. Family Violence Prevention Fund for the Robert Wood Johnson Foundation. Retrieved November 5, 2020, from https://www.futureswithoutviolence.org/userfiles/file/ImmigrantWomen/IPV_Report_March_2009.pdf

Sabri, B., Campbell, J. C., & Messing, J. T. (2018). Intimate partner homicides in the United States, 2003–2013: A comparison of immigrants and nonimmigrant victims. *Journal of Interpersonal Violence*. doi:10.1177/0886260518792249

Salcido, O., & Adelman, M. (2004). "He has me tied with the blessed and damned papers": Undocumented-immigrant battered women in Phoenix, Arizona. *Human Organization, 63*(2), 162–172.

Silove, D., Austin, P., & Steel, Z. (2007). No refuge from terror: The impact of detention on the mental health of trauma-affected refugees seeking asylum in Australia. *Transcultural Psychiatry, 44*(3), 359–393. doi: 10.1177/1363461507081637

Sipsma, H. L., Falb, K. L., Willie, T., Bradley, E. H., Bienkowski, L., Meerdink, N., & Gupta, J. (2015). Violence against Congolese refugee women in Rwanda and mental health: A cross-sectional study using latent class analysis. *BMJ Open, 5*(4). https://doi.org/10.1136/bmjopen-2014-006299

Smith, H. R. (2020). *Asylum and related protections for aliens who fear gang and domestic violence*. Congressional report service report (No. LSB10207). Retrieved November 5, 2020, from https://fas.org/sgp/crs/homesec/LSB10207.pdf

Snyder, S. (2012). *Asylum-seeking, migration and church*. Farnham, UK: Ashgate Publishing.

Stark, L., & Ager, A. (2011). A systematic review of prevalence studies of gender-based violence in complex emergencies. *Trauma, Violence, & Abuse, 12*(3), 127–134. https://doi.org/10.1177/1524838011404252

Steel, Z., Momartin, S., Silove, D., Coello, M., Aroche, J., & Tay, K. W. (2011). Two year psychosocial and mental health outcomes for refugees subjected to restrictive or supportive immigration policies. *Social Science & Medicine, 72*(7), 1149–1156. doi: 10.1016/j.socscimed.2011.02.007

Transactional Records Access Clearinghouse (2019). *Immigration and Customs Enforcement detention: ICE data snapshots*. Syracuse University. https://trac.syr.edu/phptools/immigration/detention/

Turton, D. (2003). *Conceptualising forced migration refugee studies Centre*. Working Paper Series 12, University of Oxford, Oxford. Retrieved November 5, 2020 from https://www.rsc.ox.ac.uk/files/files-1/wp12-conceptualising-forced-migration-2003.pdf

United Nations High Commissioner for Refugees (UNHCR). (2017). *'Refugees' and "migrants' – frequently asked questions.* Retrieved November 5, 2020, from https://www.unhcr.org/en-us/news/latest/2016/3/56e95c676/refugees-migrants-frequently-asked-questions-faqs.html#_ftn3

United Nations High Commissioner for Refugees (UNHCR). (2019). *Global trends: Forced displacement in 2018.* Retrieved from www.unhcr.org/globaltrends2018/

Upegui-Hernández, D. (2012). I. What is missing in the transnational migration literature? A Latin American feminist psychological perspective. *Feminism & Psychology, 22*(2), 228–239. https://doi.org/10.1177/0959353511415831

Usta, J., Masterson, A. R., & Farver, J. M. (2019). Violence against displaced Syrian women in Lebanon. *Journal of Interpersonal Violence, 34*(18), 3767–3779. https://doi.org/10.1177/0886260516670881

Usta, J., & Singh, S. (2015). Domestic violence against women in war and armed conflicts. In M. Taylor, J. Pooley, & R. S. Taylor (Eds.), *Overcoming domestic violence creating a dialogue around vulnerable populations* (pp. 205–244). Hauppauge, NY: Nova Science Publishers.

Wachter, K., Dalpe, J., & Cook Heffron, L. (2019). Conceptualizations of domestic violence-related needs among women who resettled to the U.S. as refugees. *Social Work Research, 43*(4), 207–219. doi:10.1093/swr/svz008

Wachter, K., Horn, R., Friis, E., Falb, K., Ward, L., Apio, C., Wanjiku, S., Puffer, E. (2018). Drivers of intimate partner violence against women in three refugee camps. *Violence Against Women, 24*(3), 286–306. https://doi.org/10.1177/1077801216689163

Wachter, K., & Snyder, S. (2018). Centering subjectivities: Theoretical considerations for practice with women in forced migration. *Affilia, 33*(3), 395–409. https://doi.org/10.1177/0886109918766620

Wako, E., Elliott, L., De Jesus, S., Zotti, M. E., Swahn, M. H., & Beltrami, J. (2015). Conflict, displacement, and IPV: Findings from two Congolese refugee camps in Rwanda. *Violence Against Women, 21*(9), 1087–1101. https://doi.org/10.1177/1077801215590669

Walters, M. L., Chen, J., & Breiding, M. J. (2013). *The national intimate partner and sexual violence survey (NISVS): 2010 findings on victimization by sexual orientation.* Atlanta, GA: National Center for Injury Prevention and Control, Centers for Disease Control and Prevention. Retrieved from www.cdc.gov/violenceprevention/pdf/nisvs_sofindings.pdf

Wirtz, A. L., Perrin, N. A., Desgroppes, A., Phipps, V., Abdi, A. A., Ross, B., . . ., Glass, N. (2018). Lifetime prevalence, correlates and health consequences of gender-based violence victimisation and perpetration among men and women in Somalia. *BMJ Global Health, 3*(4), e000773. https://doi.org/10.1136/bmjgh-2018-000773

Wirtz, A. L., Pham, K., Glass, N., Loochkartt, S., Kidane, T., Cuspoca, D., . . . Vu, A. (2014). Gender-based violence in conflict and displacement: Qualitative findings from displaced women in Colombia. *Conflict and Health, 8*(1), 1–14. doi:10.1186/1752-1505-8-10

World Health Organization. (2012). *Understanding and addressing violence against women.* Retrieved from https://apps.who.int/iris/bitstream/handle/10665/77432/WHO_RHR_12.36_eng.pdf;jsessionid=7D0AD35B13409CE0ABC2CD635C3813F7?sequence=1

World Health Organization. (2017). *Intimate partner violence.* Retrieved from http://apps.who.int/violence-info/intimate-partner-violence

# PART 5

# Responding to domestic violence and abuse

28

# INTERNATIONAL REVIEW OF THE LITERATURE ON RISK ASSESSMENT AND MANAGEMENT OF DOMESTIC VIOLENCE AND ABUSE

*Stephanie Holt and Lynne Cahill*

## Introduction

The criminal justice system is tasked with responsibility for protecting victims of domestic violence and abuse (DVA), and at the same time safeguarding the rights of the accused at different stages in the criminal justice process, such as bail, sentencing, and parole. A clear rationale for the implementation of risk assessment and management processes includes an acknowledgement of the role such processes can play in protecting victims and preventing future victimisation, including intimate partner homicide. With global rates estimating more than one-third of female homicides perpetrated by an intimate partner (Stockl et al., 2013) and a history of DVA considered the most robust risk indicator for intimate partner homicide[1] (Dawson, 2017; Graham, Sahay, Rizo, Messing, & Macy, 2019; Holt, 2007), international strategies to address DVA and reduce homicide risk include the introduction of standardised risk assessment and management tools. These are currently utilised in many states across Europe (EIGE, 2019), the United Kingdom (Robinson, 2006), the United States (Dutton & Kropp, 2000), Canada (Millar, Code, & Ha, 2013), China (Chan, 2012), and Australia (Lauria, McEwan, Luebbers, Simmons, & Ogloff, 2017). However, the absence of systematic and robust processes for defining and understanding the dynamics, nature, and impact of DVA; for responding to the complex needs of victims and perpetrators; for identifying, assessing, and managing risk, has also been compounded by debates about terminology and disputes about gender. It is worth noting, albeit briefly, some debates critical to any risk assessment and management process, before moving on to the main body of the chapter where the risk assessment tools themselves will be critically presented.

While the emergence and recognition of the concept of coercive control as central to the phenomena of DVA has only been established in policy and legislation in the past decade or so (Robinson, Myhill, & Wire, 2018), it should be noted that the centrality of power and control to the experience of DVA has been fundamental to feminist-advocate understanding of this issue since the 1970s (Schechter, 1982; Sheppard & Pence, 1988). With reference to Myhill and Hohl's (2016) analysis of risk assessments in England and Wales, Robinson et al. (2018, p. 32) further note that factors correlating with coercive control, including perpetrators' controlling, stalking, and sexually coercive behaviour, in addition to victim experiences of isolation and fear, formed the most constant pattern of abuse. As such, while an in-depth understanding of the significance of coercive controlling behaviour would seem critical to effective responses, Robinson et al. (2018, p. 33) conclude that "the evidence establishing whether practitioners do in fact 'get it' is relatively scant".

This chapter presents an extensive review of the available international literature regarding the design, implementation, and evaluation of risk assessment and management tools. Set against the backdrop of the Council of Europe Convention on preventing and combating violence against women and domestic violence (the 'Istanbul Convention', 2011), this chapter is grounded in the evidence that gender, specifically being female, intersects with multiple adversities – including but not limited to domestic, sexual, and gender-based violence – and that this discrimination and marginalisation can occur across a woman's lifespan.

The chapter commences with an overview of the methodological approach employed to gather data for inclusion in the chapter before moving on to highlight some of the nuances and complexities requiring consideration in any discussion on risk assessment and management in the context of DVA. The main body of the chapter then focuses on risk assessment both as a process and as a tool, providing a critical overview of the main approaches to, and models of, risk assessment.

## Methodology

The identification of literature for inclusion in this chapter comprised of a systematic search of seven identified databases (BMJ Journals Online, CINAHL, Internurse, Web of Science, Psychological and Behavioral Sciences Collection, PsycINFO, and Scopus). The search was conducted using all possible combinations of the following terms: 'risk assessment', 'risk management', and 'risk factors' were combined with 'domestic violence', 'intimate partner abuse', 'domestic homicide', and 'front line responders'. An additional search was conducted to retrieve literature related to known risk assessment instruments based on the following names and acronyms: 'Danger Assessment', 'DA', 'Brief Spousal Assault', 'B-SAFER', 'Domestic Violence Risk Assessment Guide', 'DVRAG', 'Domestic Violence Screening Instrument', 'DVSI', 'Ontario Domestic Assault Risk Assessment', 'ODARA', and 'Spousal Assault Risk Assessment', 'SARA'. Studies included in the review were English language, accessed from scholarly peer-reviewed journals, with an unspecified date range. The database search was subsequently augmented with a review of the bibliographies of related articles. Using the citation indexes (Kugley et al., 2016) of previously identified studies was especially useful in the identification of seminal texts and key authors in the field. This search strategy complemented the searches conducted in the database searches and provided an alternative way of accessing relevant studies. This search aimed to capture a geographical spread of the empirical material cognisant of the fact that evidence from Canada, the UK, USA, Australia, and New Zealand dominates this field.

## Analysis and discussion

Starting from the premise that DVA is a complex issue, risk assessment processes must have as their starting point a clearly grounded understanding of the dynamics of DVA, in particular the centrality of power and coercive control to the abusive experience. Reflecting on pilot risk assessment processes in England and Wales, however, Robinson, Myhill, and Wire (2018) noted that police officers often failed to identify coercive controlling behaviours, instead prioritising physical abuse at call-outs. Similarly, Wire and Myhill (2018) advised that a risk tool will not, by itself, result in officers making appropriate risk assessments. Rather, having an in-depth appreciation of the complex dynamics of DVA, with a sophisticated understanding of the nuanced nature of coercive control is an integral requirement of appropriate risk assessment. Stated simply, any professional responding to DVA needs to know what they are looking for. We argue therefore that risk identification is the first step in a three-step process that involves secondly, risk assessment and thirdly, risk management.

Risk instruments are not precise enough to reliably discriminate among different types of risk (e.g., who will commit homicide vs. who will commit less serious violence). Therefore, some professional discretion will likely always be necessary. However not everyone can or should perform risk assessments. Such evaluations require specialised knowledge and experience. Those conducting risk assessments should understand the dynamics of DVA, and they should have experience working with perpetrators and victims (Wire & Myhill, 2018). Proper risk assessment training is extremely important and should include issues regarding report writing and communication (Robinson et al., 2018).

We would also argue for the need for clarity and agreement about a number of further questions. For example, what is the purpose of the risk assessment? Is it to reduce the number of police call-outs and therefore reduce the draw on police time and/or reduce the incidence of serious harm? What risk is being assessed and whose risk is being assessed? Are we assessing the risk of current and future victimisation, either adult or child, or the risk of current and future harm perpetrated by the perpetrator? Given the research evidence that adult victims report negatively on police call-outs, experiencing this intervention as simultaneously being blamed for the problem and held responsible for the solution to the problem (Anderson et al., 2003), we argue for the risk assessment process to focus on the risk the perpetrator presents. Adapting this focus would work towards lifting the responsibility from the victim, particularly given that the perpetrator might pose risks to more than one victim, including children, other family members of the victim, and any other current/future partners of the perpetrator. More recent research focusing on children's experiences of police call-outs should also usefully inform policing practices (Millar, Devaney, & Butler, 2019; Elliffe & Holt, 2019).

Researchers argue that it is insufficient to report the level of risk posed by the alleged perpetrator without attention being paid to how the individual's risk is managed (Kropp, 2002, 2004; Heilbrun, 1997). As such, it is important to make a clear distinction between risk assessment and risk management. Thompson and Thompson (2008) contrast risk assessment, which they identify as the process of identifying risk, to risk management where actions are taken in response to the identification and assessment of the risk. With risk considered a "complex practice and policy issue" (Kemshall & Pritchard, 1996, p. 2), caution is also advised against seeing these two as distinct stand-alone stages. Rather they are intertwined and interactive, taking into account both static and dynamic factors and features of individual cases. Static risk factors are risk factors that are fixed and unchangeable, for example demographic factors (age, gender), childhood history, and criminal history. As such they are not changeable through intervention. Dynamic risk factors on the other hand are defined by their ability to change throughout the life-course. Examples of these factors include unemployment, substance abuse, and negative peer associations.

## Risk assessment

Heilbrun (1997) asserts that it is useful to distinguish two major goals of risk assessment (RA): prediction (with an emphasis on accuracy) and management (with an emphasis on risk reduction). The former approach assesses the likelihood of recidivism of a person of concern while the latter is concerned with a person being further victimised. The origins of the development and use of RA tools in cases of DVA increased as a result of policy change and research in Canada and the United States (Douglas & Otto, 2010; Roehl & Guertin, 2000). Roehl and Guertin (2000, p. 172) suggest that reform in the criminal justice system regarding DVA in the 1970s, and in the mental health field where "legal requirements and professional concerns have encouraged clinicians to develop feasible estimates of a person's potential for violence", spurred research in the field, leading to a growing body of scientific knowledge examining risk predictors for violence. In Canada, the UK and the US in the early 1990s, pro-arrest policies in cases of DVA led to an increase in cases presenting in the criminal justice system (Bowen, 2011; Cattaneo & Goodman, 2003). Roehl and Guertin (2000) argue that this increase created the need to develop a mechanism to ensure scarce resources were directed to those most at risk. Furthermore, this change was happening against a backdrop of a series of court decisions that held clinicians negligent for inadequate predictions of danger, not protecting victims, or providing warnings to potential clients (Hart, 1988).

Comprised of questions that assess risk factors for intimate partner homicide (IPH) and DVA re-assault, RA tools are designed to assist a range of professionals responding to DVA – advocates, criminal justice personnel, nurses, social workers, and other first responders in identifying those individuals at particular risk for ongoing danger and lethality in the context of intimate partnerships (Heilbrun, Yasuhara, & Shah, 2010; Messing & Thaller, 2012).[2] Common risk factors include past abusive, controlling, or threatening behaviour; a history of mental health and/or substance misuse; unemployment; prior use of a weapon; and separation or threats of self-harm (Graham et al., 2019).

Examining domestic homicide case reviews in Canada between 2003 and 2015, Dawson (2017) highlights that more than 70% of the 261 cases were found to have seven or more risk factors, with only four cases reviewed revealing no known risk factors. Dawson cautions however against a simplistic linear correlation between the presence of multiple risk factors and higher levels of preventability, as some risk factors are considered more lethal than others. Dawson (2017, p. 73) also highlights that little research has established the lethality of "risk factor clusters or combinations".

## Models of risk assessment

Before outlining the models of available risk assessments, it is important to highlight some key limitations. Firstly, risk assessment for DVA is largely focused on a 'violence model' (Gelles, 1997, p. 14) where abuse is defined as "an act carried out with the intention or perceived intention of causing physical pain or injury to another person". Consequently, DVA risk assessment is primarily concentrated on predicting individual risk factors and the statistical validity of instruments that predict future re-victimisation and reoffending of physical assault, using case examples from the police. The focus on violence prediction and recidivism may be redundant in contexts of coercive control where severe acts of violence may not be either present at all or present initially, and the perpetrator surveillance of everyday life comprises threats and low-level but routinised coercion without any physical assault (Stark, 2007).

We also note that the choice of a method of risk assessment is complicated, with one clear limitation of risk assessment tools is that they have all been substantially informed by an understanding of domestic violence perpetration by males against females in intimate partner relationships (current and former). As such, their applicability to other intimate partnerships is unknown. The most recent systematic review investigating risk assessment and intimate partner violence (Graham et al., 2019) found that while the reviewed studies primarily examined DVA/ IPH RA tools in the context of relationships with a male perpetrator and female victim, many other studies reviewed had not specified either perpetrator or victim gender. Less is known about other types of perpetrator-victim dyads, with researchers calling for the expansion of cross-validation studies to include diverse samples that are inclusive of the lesbian, gay, bisexual, and transgender populations, and male victims and female perpetrators (Glass et al., 2008; Nicholls, Pritchard, Reeves, & Hilterman, 2013). However, the limited empirical evidence that exists assessing and managing female DVA perpetration suggests that women present with fewer risk factors than men (Storey & Strand, 2013).

With these limitations in mind, an examination of the literature reveals four models of violence risk assessment: unstructured clinical decision-making, actuarial risk assessment, structured professional judgement, and victim appraisal (victim's perception of their own risk).

*Unstructured clinical decision-making* is possibly the most commonly used approach in the risk assessment of DVA (Dutton & Kropp, 2000; Kropp, 2008). With this approach, the professional collects and assesses information and produces a risk assessment based on their professional judgement (Helmus & Bourgon, 2011), without guidelines or pre-determined constraints.

One strength of this approach is that it allows for an idiographic analysis of offender behaviour which permits the professional to develop a person- and context-specific risk assessment and violence prevention strategy (Kropp, 2008). However, there are multiple issues identified with this approach. The model has been described as an "informal, in the head, impressionistic, subjective conclusion, reached (somehow) by a human clinical judge" (Grove & Meehl, 1996, p. 294). Researchers argue the major weaknesses include the limited accountability, replicability, transparency, validity, and the heavy emphasis on professional discretion (Helmus & Bourgon, 2011; Kropp, 2008; Nicholls, Desmarais, Douglas, & Kropp, 2006; Nicholls et al., 2013). Further, because this model is heavily influenced by professional opinion and discretion, the approach is vulnerable to missing important known risk factors. Secondly, recommendations for management strategies by professionals may be influenced by training, preferences, and biases of the assessor rather than crime-relevant risk factors and empirically validated intervention strategies. Finally, the approach includes consideration of issues such as suicidal behaviour that are not strong predictors of domestic violence (Hilton & Harris, 2005).[3] Consequently, those involved in risk assessment strategies are moving away from this practice (Dutton & Kropp, 2000; Nicholls et al., 2013), concluding that "unstructured clinical judgement by itself is no longer a useful or necessary approach to appraising violence risk" (Heilbrun et al., 2010, p. 5).

In an effort to improve clinical accuracy and the structure of risk appraisals, the field moved toward the application of the second model, *actuarial risk assessment* (Nicholls et al., 2013), also described as "nondiscretionary" approaches (Hart & Logan, 2011). The actuarial approach to risk assessment is strongly aligned with the predictive paradigm in the literature on violence (Heilbrun, 1997).[4] The method utilises statistical models and empirical research on recidivism and risk factors to (1) create formulas that provide a probability that future violence will occur (Nicholls et al., 2013), and (2) to predict specific behaviours within a specific time period compared to a norm-based reference group (Kropp, 2004, 2008). Risk factors are combined using explicit rules, such as an algorithm or equation (Grove & Meehl, 1996). The assessment is based on counting and scoring of empirically validated risk factors (Wheller & Wire, 2014). Risk factors are assigned a numerical value and a total is generated through an algorithm (Singh, Grann, & Fazel, 2011). The assessor indicates if risk factors are present or absent, and then adds up the values to get a total score (Nicholls et al., 2013). The total score estimates the probability that the individual will reoffend within a specific time frame (Singh et al., 2011). Examples of Actuarial Risk Assessment models include the Ontario Domestic Assault Risk Assessment (ODARA), the Domestic Violence Risk Assessment Guide (DVRAG), and the Domestic Violence Screening Instrument (DVSI) – the DVSI-R.

Several strengths have been identified with the actuarial approach. For example there is consensus in the literature that the key strength associated with the actuarial approach is that it improves upon the poor reliability and validity of unstructured clinical assessments (Grove & Meehl, 1996; Kropp, 2008; Nicholls et al., 2013). Actuarial risk assessment uses the same criteria, and therefore findings can be easily replicated, while independent tests of the model show that it has the ability to predict violent outcomes (Kropp, 2008). An important advantage of actuarial assessments for police officers and the courts system is that each score corresponds to a percentile rank in the referent population, thus, providing the ability to estimate the probability of an outcome (Hilton et al., 2004). For example, using scores from an actuarial assessment can inform the decision to deny bail based on the probability of recidivism within a certain time period or in the identification of the most dangerous perpetrators. Because actuarial RAs are based on a fixed set of risk factors, they can be used by professionals who are not clinically qualified, or trained in the area of DVA (EIGE, 2019; Northcott, 2008).[5]

An examination of the literature reveals that the limitations to this approach include a focus on prediction rather than risk management and violence prevention (Heilbrun et al., 2010), and a dependence on static risk factors that cannot capture how risk can fluctuate over time (Kropp, 2004; Nicholls et al., 2013).[6] Because this method removes professional discretion in the analysis of risk, practitioners are reluctant to engage with the model, creating a "schism between science and practice" (Kropp, 2008, p. 206).[7] Similarly, Nicholls et al. (2013) describe assessors being uncomfortable using the tool to inform a decision about risk because of the lack of attention to case specific factors. Actuarial approaches limit the assessor to a fixed set of factors, which one could assert is a strength of the approach as it reduces the evidence to the fewest possible factors required to make the most likely prediction of future outcomes. Therefore, it has a practical utility, alongside validity and reliability. However, one might also question why they do not consider 'low base' (Nicholls et al., 2013) factors that do not occur frequently, such as homicidal ideation, that may be relevant to a case and have been found to correlate modestly with violence (Kropp, 2008; Nicholls et al., 2006).

Kropp (2008) argues that while the approach can tell us about the overall level of risk management required, there is less information available about violence prevention strategies. Heilbrun (1997) compared predictions vs. management models of risk assessment, proposing that risk assessment based on prediction lacks the capacity to capture sensitivity to change, and that this likely results in minimal implications for management. The focus on predicting rather than preventing and managing violence, has been found to impact professional non-engagement with such tools. Researchers suggest that a possible explanation for this might be that professionals see themselves in a preventive rather than predictive role (Douglas & Kropp, 2002; Heilbrun, 1997). Another limitation identified with the approach is that it may not be compatible with offender treatment programmes as actuarial tools do not consider 'attitudes toward violence' or 'denial and minimisation' and 'victim empathy' (Kropp, 2004, 2008).[8] As such, researchers advocate for risk assessment tools where professional judgement is a necessary component of any risk related decision-making process (Nicholls et al., 2013). Finally, actuarial risk assessment tools with their focus on violence prediction and recidivism may not be designed to capture the nuances of ongoing coercive controlling behaviours. The counting and scoring of empirically validated individual risk factors, targeting discrete violent acts, cannot account for the continuous nature of abuse attributed to coercive control with studies demonstrating that where there is effort to 'count' abuse, the option of 'daily' is not enough for victims of coercive control (Evans et al., 2016).

The third type of risk assessment model is the *structured professional approach*, also known as the 'guided professional approach' or the 'guided clinical approach' (Kropp, 2004).[9] The primary goal of this model is to prevent violence (Douglas & Kropp, 2002). The term 'professional' is significant as it recognises the reality that many professionals are involved in the conduct of risk assessment outside of the clinical professions. Examples include the Spousal Assault Risk Assessment Guide (SARA) and the Brief Spousal Assault Form for the Evaluation of Risk (B-SAFER).

The risk assessment is based on guidelines that reflect current theoretical, clinical, and empirical knowledge, where the assessor follows guidelines that include both static and dynamic risk factors (Kropp, 2004). The guidelines further allow the assessor to "include recommendations for information gathering, communicating opinions, and implementing violence prevention strategies" (Kropp, 2004, p. 683). This approach is considered as a professional guideline that allows evaluators to integrate their own judgement, while also providing a list of factors garnered from consultation, theory, and the literature for consideration. The model suggests risk factors to consider; however assessors do not add up those factors to determine a final score (Nicholls et al., 2013). Unlike the actuarial approach, there are no restrictions on the inclusion, weighting, or combining of risk factors; rather the model is dependent on the evaluator for the final decision (Kropp, 2004). The final step in combining risk factors is not done by algorithm and this aspect of the model facilitates flexibility.

There are a number of strengths associated with this approach. Kropp (2004) argues that the model's ability to systematically identify both static and dynamic risk factors creates the opportunity to tailor management strategies to prevent violence. The structured professional approach relies on risk factors culled from the empirical evidence base, which means the tools are more generalisable than tools developed for a specific population, as is often the case with the actuarial approach (Helmus & Bourgon, 2011). Interestingly, while it would appear that SARA has been outperformed by other RAs of generic violence risk (Bowen, 2011), the results of these studies need to be interpreted with caution as in the majority of cases (except Kropp & Hart, 2000), the SARA was not used as intended due to the reliance on file information rather than the comprehensive perpetrator and victim assessment that is recommended. Consequently, it is possible that the actual performance of the complete SARA assessment is better, and that the predictive accuracy is greater (Bowen, 2011, p. 220).

However, a study exploring intimate partner abuse risk assessment and the role of female victim risk appraisals reported that actuarial instruments outperform those based on structured professional judgement. Like the issues identified with the earlier model of unstructured clinical decision-making, Bowen (2011) argued that the reliability of evaluator-identified critical items are not particularly effective in predicting violence particularly problematic.

There are several limitations associated with the model. It is vulnerable to the same criticism as the unstructured clinical decision-making in terms of the emphasis on professional judgement (Kropp, 2004, 2008). The approach involves professional subjectivity rather than basing the risk assessment decision on a total score derived from an empirically validated tool (Helmus & Bourgon, 2011). Other research has highlighted that the model includes risk factors, such as suicidal behaviour, that are reported as not strong predictors of intimate partner violence (Hilton & Harris, 2005).

The final model of risk assessment is described in the literature as *victim risk appraisals* (Bowen, 2011).[10] Authorities in the field recommend that risk assessment should be victim-informed (Kropp, 2004), while those who developed SARA (a structured professional risk assessment), caution that risk assessment should never be performed without the inclusion of victim-informed data (Kropp, Hart, Webster, & Eaves, 1999 cited in Kropp, 2004). Unlike risk assessment in cases of domestic homicide and general violence, the evaluator has access to the victim who can provide critical information pertaining to dynamic risk factors such as the perpetrator's violent history, personality, attitudes, and mental health (Dutton & Kropp, 2000; Kropp, 2004). Kropp (2004) argues for the importance of 'collateral informants' in the conduct of risk assessment as there is a danger with evaluations of risk that rely on perpetrator self-report data. Not only do perpetrators deny or minimise their responsibility for violence, they are also reluctant to disclose information that may affect their outcomes in the criminal justice system.

Previous research indicates that female predictions of re-assault are empirically validated. Weisz, Tolman, and Saunders's (2000) examination of severe physical violence assessed following a four month follow-up, reported that for the 177 female victims, their survivor predictions of re-assault were significantly associated with the reoccurrence of severe violence. Examining continued abuse assessed at a three month follow-up with a sample of 169 women, Bennett Cattaneo and Goodman (2003) reported that victim assessments were significant predictors of abuse. A later study by Bennett and colleagues (2007) examining re-abuse, defined as physical assault, injury, and attempts to kill at an 18-month follow-up, reported that of the sample of 276 women, 182 (66%) accurately assessed their own risk. Another study explored psychological abuse at an 18-month follow-up and reported that of a sample of 244 women, 151 (62%) accurately assessed their risk, and furthermore, the study found that victims were equally skilled in predicting re-assault and non-re-assault (Bell, Cattaneo, Goodman, & Dutton, 2008). The empirical data concerning female victim risk appraisal assessed over different time periods, and taking account physical, psychological, and continued non-assault abuse, indicates that victims provide important information that should be factored into the risk assessment process.

All of this stated, studies also reveal the limitations of victim-informed risk assessment. Weisz et al. (2000) cautioned that victims' perceptions of their risk are not always accurate. Depending solely on victims' assessment is not recommended. Victims have been reported to both under- and over-estimate their risk, and may be reluctant to share information for fear of their safety and their children's safety, fear of losing their children, or to protect their abuser. It is also worth noting here that not all DVA victims may be likely to participate in such assessments and may be unwilling to engage with the criminal justice system (Kropp, 2008; Nicholls et al., 2006). For example, victims of colour may not provide information about their partners to law enforcement for fear of policing bias or indiscriminate incarceration, and other groups of victims (LGBTQ+, and victims with limited resources) may be systematically disadvantaged and prevented from participating in the criminal justice system.

Although structural professional approaches to risk assessment continue to lean toward general violence recidivism risk factors, they are inclusive of specific DVA factors (Bowen, 2011). Structured professional approaches to risk assessment and victim appraisal tools present more opportunities for the assessor to capture coercive controlling behaviours. Unlike actuarial risk assessments, the assessor has the opportunity to capture victim-informed data by considering the victim statements, and cross-referencing the perpetrator report with the victim report, by interviewing the victim where possible. This creates the ability to assess for impact of abuse, a critical component in assessing for coercive control as Myhill (2015, p. 360) forewarns, "Without considering impact, even comprehensive scales risk summating controlling behaviors without being able to assess whether or not a *state* of coercive control has been achieved". Furthermore, structured professional approaches reflect a move away from counting discrete incidents of abuse to assessing the continuous nature of abuse attributed to coercive control, with some instruments, the B-SAFER for example, appraising past and current behaviours within the past four weeks (Bowen, 2011).

## Managing risk

Risk management requires familiarity and cooperation across multiple stakeholders and agencies with different skill sets and mandates (Kropp, 2008). Moreover, the design and implementation of a "comprehensive, integrated, multidisciplinary risk management plan" (ibid., p. 214) should be supported with a policy to guide the plan and an accompanying manual for procedures (Kropp, Hart, Lyon, & LePard, 2002). Kropp (2008) suggests that risk assessment evaluators should initiate four risk management activities: monitoring, treatment, supervision, and victim safety planning.

The day-to-day reality of risk assessment and management practice also needs to account for the organisational culture and individual practices of professionals' involvement in the tasks. This highlights the need for inter-/multi-disciplinary risk management strategies. Robinson (2006) contends that in cases of DVA, accurate risk assessments provide structure for responding police officers to gather detailed and relevant information from victims, to share information between agencies that can lead to an improved service response, and the creation of a paper trail of evidence to be used by prosecutors should the victim decide not to proceed with a case.

Communicating risk effectively plays an integral role in the prevention of violence, and can greatly affect how information is received and utilised (Heilbrun, O'Neill, Strohman, Bowman, & Philipson, 2000; Kropp, 2008). Heilbrun et al. (2000, p. 159) assert that "risk communication is the link between risk assessment and decision making about risk", with risk assessments that are not effectively communicated on a multi-disciplinary level to decision-makers, specialist practitioners, and victims essentially considered useless. The crucial role of risk communication in the risk assessment process is evident from reviews of domestic homicide, where despite the presence of risk indicators, this information was not recorded or communicated to those who needed this information (including victims, criminal justice agencies, offender treatment programmes, and the police) (Sharp-Jeffs & Kelly, 2016; Websdale, 1999).

Kropp (2008) proposes several principles of "sound risk communication". Firstly, professional opinions about risk must be supported concisely and grounded in evidence. Guidelines and checklists associated with the DA, ODARA, DVSI, and SARA assist with structuring opinion and instincts about risk. Secondly, communicating risk to victims allows for an understanding of their overall level of risk and the precautions needed (Kropp, 2008). Educating victims about specific risk factors is important as studies indicate that victims can interpret risk factors such as unemployment, mental health problems, and substance abuse as sympathy factors rather than causal factors for violence (Kropp et al., 2002). Communicating risk to victims can also inform an effective safety plan. Thirdly, risk assessment opinions must be qualified and any limitations with the collection of information must be made clear. For example, in the absence of a victim interview, those contributing information to the risk assessment must be made aware that the information they provide could seriously affect the validity (the extent to which the scale can be said to measure what it claims to measure) of the risk assessment. As Kropp (2008, p. 213) forewarns, "there is nothing more dangerous than a risk assessment based on inadequate information that does not include adequate qualifications", which can lead to underestimating risk and the provision of inaccurate information to victims and other relevant agencies.

While the research evidence on risk assessment has expanded significantly in recent years, evidence concerning risk management is relatively thin, with no empirical evidence available on the ability of violence risk assessment instruments to aid in the management and the prevention of violence until very recently (Belfrage et al., 2012; Storey, Kropp, Hart, Belfrage, & Strand, 2014).

In the UK, Wire and Myhill's (2018) review concluded that the evidence base for the usefulness of Multi-agency Risk Assessment Conferences (MARAC)[11] is thin (Steel, Blakeborough, & Nicholas, 2011), and that furthermore, longitudinal evaluation of outcomes for victims following police engagement was largely non-existent. Commenting on the process of conducting primary and secondary risk assessment,[12] the authors also highlight the variability in secondary risk assessment and management by the police, particularly when it comes to multi-agency and partnership working. Concurring with Robinson, Myhill, Wire, Roberts, and Tillwy's (2016) recommendation that police involvement in secondary risk assessment processes should be minimised in favour of specialist support services involvement, Wire and Myhill (2018) conclude that specialist support workers are best placed to undertake a thorough risk assessment.

## Conclusion

This chapter has provided an overview of the four main risk assessment models, highlighting their strengths and weaknesses in respect of DA and linking those models with risk instruments, all of which have similar content and some of which have established psychometric reliability and validity.

Although the risk factors for DVA are well established in the literature, these are grounded in an intersectional and gender-based understanding of male-perpetrated violence and abuse against women, with further research needed to understand the applicability of risk assessment tools for more diverse samples. Furthermore, we would argue, risk assessment tools do not always translate easily into risk assessment practice and tools, particularly regarding the issue of coercive behaviours, and the misuse of power and control. With no validated measure of coercive control (Stark, 2012) and risk factors associated with coercive controlling behaviour featuring less frequently in standardised risk assessment, we would concur with Stark (2012) that "the level of control an offender is exercising is a far better way to ration scarce police resources than the level of violence". The evidence consistently demonstrates that the existence of control predicts a range of harms, physical, sexual, and fatal violence, more so than prior assault (Glass et al., 2008).

While the concept of coercive control should therefore forefront any risk assessment tool, it should also be noted however that a risk tool will not, by itself, result in appropriate risk assessments. Having an in-depth appreciation of the complex dynamics of DVA, with a sophisticated understanding of the nuanced nature of coercive control is an integral requirement of appropriate risk assessment.

Furthermore it is important for those conducting risk assessments to not rely solely on self-reported information from the offender. It is also critical to use victim-based information somehow. This must be done sensitively and respectfully with attention paid to ethical and safety issues. Finally, it is important to recognise that risk management involves far more than just DVA programming. Other specialised treatments might be necessary, as well as proper monitoring and supervision. Moreover, victim safety planning is crucial, as offender intervention is far from perfect for preventing future violence. The principle of 'interventions should restrict opportunities for harm' should underpin the identification–assessment–management of risk processes.

## Critical findings

- The risk factors for domestic violence are well established in the literature but do not always translate easily into risk assessment tools, particularly the issue of coercive behaviours and power and control.
- A risk tool will not, by itself, result in appropriate risk assessments. Having an in-depth appreciation of the complex dynamics of domestic violence, with a sophisticated understanding of the nuanced nature of coercive control is an integral requirement of appropriate risk assessment.
- Given the centrality of coercive control to the experience of domestic violence, the concept of coercive control should forefront any risk assessment tool, representing the "thread" from identification to assessment and through to risk management.
- Existing RA tools are primarily focused on statistical precision when predicting future physical assault and re-victimisation. As such they have limited ability to accurately assess for coercive control.

## Implications for policy, practice, and research

- Not everyone can or should perform risk assessments. Such evaluations require specialised knowledge and experience. Those conducting risk assessments should understand the dynamics of domestic violence, and they should have experience working with offenders and victims. Proper risk assessment training is extremely important.
- One clear limitation of risk assessment tools is that they have all been substantially informed by an understanding of domestic violence perpetration by males against females in intimate partner relationships (current and former). As such, their applicability to other intimate partnerships is unknown.
- This presents a clear gap in the literature examining IPA predictors for same-sex relationships, and a lack of research focused on female perpetrators.
- While the research evidence base on risk assessment has expanded significantly in recent years, evidence concerning risk management is relatively thin.

## Notes

1 Dawson's 2017 review of Canadian Homicide Reviews between 2013 and 2015 concluded that the top four risk factors included a history of domestic violence in the couple's relationship (71%), actual or pending separation (67%), obsessive behaviour by the perpetrator (48%), and a victim who had an intuitive sense of fear towards the perpetrator (44%).
2 One clear limitation of risk assessment tools is that they have all been substantially informed by an understanding of domestic violence perpetration by males against females in intimate partner relationships (current and former). As such, their applicability to other intimate partnerships is unknown.
3 Suicidal behaviour is a strong risk indicator for domestic homicide but not domestic violence.
4 Ontario Domestic Abuse Risk Assessment (ODARA) and the Domestic Violence Risk Appraisal Guide (DVRAG) are examples of actuarial models of RA.
5 A note of caution however is advised that professionals including first responders receive adequate training in using the tool appropriately and in identifying and responding to domestic violence cases (Graham et al., 2019; Robinson, Myhill, Wire, Roberts, & Tillwy, 2016).

6 Static risk factors are risk factors that are fixed and unchangeable, for example demographic factors (age, gender), childhood history, and criminal history.

7 Anecdotal evidence from the UK suggests that statutory professionals are resisting training and education around domestic violence, expressing a preference for a tool only (consultation with Davina James-Hanman).

8 Most perpetrator programmes in Ireland have been trained in the use of the B-SAFER risk assessment tool and continue to develop systems for using this information to improve safety for women and inform work with men. This is a tool developed by Randall Kropp and others from the original Spousal Assault Risk Assessment (SARA) tool. One service providing support to women experiencing domestic violence (Sonas Housing) utilises the CAADA Dash in risk assessment processes.

9 SARA and B-SAFER risk assessment instruments are examples of the structured professional approach to RA.

10 Campbell's Danger Assessment (DA) is designed entirely for use with victims.

11 The Multi-agency Risk Assessment Conference (MARAC) is a monthly meeting of agencies such as the local police, health and housing practitioners, shelter workers and other government and nongovernmental specialists, including Independent Domestic Violence Advisors (IDVAs) providing services to domestic violence survivors identified as being at the highest risk (defined as a pattern of abuse which presents a risk of serious harm or femicide).

12 Primary assessments can be conducted by both responding officer(s) attending a domestic abuse incident and by their supervisors (sergeants) who review the circumstances of the incident, using professional judgement. They may or may not perform background intelligence checks on force systems.

Secondary risk assessments are undertaken by the police on all or a proportion of cases by a central unit, using professional judgement, and drawing on the primary risk assessment, information contained on force systems, and, in some cases, the Police National Computer and data from partner agencies.

# References

Anderson, M., Gillig, P., Sitaker, M., McCloskey, K., Malloy, K., & Grigsby, N. (2003). "Why doesn't she just leave?": A descriptive study of victim reported impediments to her safety. *Journal of Family Violence, 18*(3), 151–155.

Belfrage, H., Strand, S., Storey, J. E., Gibas, A. L., Kropp, P. R., & Hart, S. D. (2012). Assessment and management of risk for intimate partner violence by police officers using the spousal assault risk assessment guide. *Law and Human Behavior, 36*(1), 60–67. https://doi.org/10.1037/h0093948

Bell, M., Cattaneo, L., Goodman, L., & Dutton, M. (2008). Assessing the risk of future psychological abuse: Predicting the accuracy of battered women's predictions. *Journal of Family Violence, 23*(2), 69–80. https://doi.org/10.1007/s10896-007-9128-5

Bennett Cattaneo, L., Bell, M., Goodman, L., & Dutton, M. (2007). Intimate partner violence victims' accuracy in assessing their risk of re-abuse. *Journal of Family Violence, 22*(6), 429–440. https://doi.org/10.1007/s10896-007-9097-8

Bennett Cattaneo, L., & Goodman, L. A. (2003). Victim-reported risk factors for continued abusive behavior: Assessing the dangerousness of arrested batterers. *Journal of Community Psychology, 31*(4), 349–369. https://doi.org/10.1002/jcop.10056

Bowen, E. (2011). An overview of partner violence risk assessment and the potential role of female victim risk appraisals. *Aggression and Violent Behavior, 16*(3), 214–226. https://doi.org/10.1016/j.avb.2011.02.007

Cattaneo, L. B., & Goodman, L. A. (2003). Victim-reported risk factors for continued abusive behavior: Assessing the dangerousness of arrested batterers. *Journal of Community Psychology, 31*(4), 349–369. https://doi.org/10.1002/jcop.10056

Chan, K. L. (2012). Predicting the risk of intimate partner violence: The Chinese risk assessment tool for victims. *Journal of Family Violence, 27*(2), 157–164. https://doi.org/10.1007/s10896-012-9418-4

Dawson, M. (2017). *Domestic homicides and death reviews: An international perspective.* London: Palgrave Macmillan.

Douglas, K. S., & Kropp, P. R. (2002). A prevention-based paradigm for violence risk assessment: Clinical and research applications. *Criminal Justice and Behavior, 29*(5), 617–658. https://doi.org/10.1177/009385402236735

Douglas, K. S., & Otto, R. K. (2010). Introduction and overview. In R. K. Otto & K. S. Douglas (Eds.), *Handbook of violence risk assessment* (pp. ix–x). New York, NY: Routledge Taylor & Francis Group.

Dutton, D. G., & Kropp, P. R. (2000). A review of domestic violence risk instruments. *Trauma, Violence, & Abuse, 1*(2), 171–181. https://doi.org/10.1177/1524838000001002004

EIGE. (2019). *Draft guidelines for risk assessment by police of intimate partner violence against women* [Draft report]. Vilnius, Lithuania: European Institute for Gender Equality.

Elliffe, R., & Holt, S. (2019). Reconceptualizing the child victim in the police response to domestic violence. *Journal of Family Violence, 34*, 589–600.

Evans, M., Gregory, A., Feder, G., et al. (2016). 'Even "daily" is not enough': How well do we measure domestic violence and abuse? A think-aloud study of a commonly used self-report scale. *Violence and Victims, 31*(1), 3–26.

Gelles, R. J. (1997). Intimate violence in families. Newbury Park, CA: Sage.

Glass, N., Perrin, N., Hanson, G., Bloom, T., Gardner, E., & Campbell, J. C. (2008). Risk for reassault in abusive female same-sex relationships. *American Journal of Public Health, 98*(6), 1021–1027.

Graham, L. M., Sahay, K. M., Rizo, C. F., Messing, J. T., & Macy, R. J. (2019). The validity and reliability of available intimate partner homicide and reassault risk assessment tools: A systematic review. *Trauma, Violence, & Abuse*, 1–23.

Grove, W. M., & Meehl, P. E. (1996). Comparative efficiency of informal (subjective, impressionistic) and formal (mechanical, algorithmic) prediction procedures: The clinical – statistical controversy. *Psychology, Public Policy, and Law, 2*(2), 293–323. https://doi.org/10.1037/1076-8971.2.2.293

Hart, B. (1988). Beyond the 'duty to warn': A therapist's 'duty to protect' battered women and children. In K. Yllo & M. Bograd (Eds.), *Feminist perspectives on wife abuse* (pp. 234–248). Newbury Park, CA: Sage.

Hart, S. D., & Logan, C. (2011). Formulation of violence risk using evidence-based assessments: The structured professional judgement approach. In P. Sturmey & M. McMurran (Eds.), *Forensic case formulation* (pp. 83–106). Chichester, UK: Wiley-Blackwell.

Heilbrun, K. (1997). Prediction versus management models relevant to risk assessment: The importance of legal decision-making context. *Law and Human Behavior, 21*(4), 347–359.

Heilbrun, K., O'Neill, M. L., Strohman, L. K., Bowman, Q., & Philipson, J. (2000). Expert approaches to communicating violence risk. *Law and Human Behavior; Southport, 24*(1), 137–148.

Heilbrun, K., Yasuhara, S., & Shah, S. (2010). Violence risk assessment tools: Overview and critical analysis. In R. Otto & K. Douglas (Eds.), *Handbook of violence risk assessment* (pp. 1–17). New York, NY: Routledge and Taylor & Francis.

Helmus, L., & Bourgon, G. (2011). Taking stock of 15 years of research on the spousal assault risk assessment guide (SARA): A critical review. *International Journal of Forensic Mental Health, 10*(1), 64–75. https://doi.org/10.1080/14999013.2010.551709

Hilton, N. Z., & Harris, G. T. (2005). Predicting wife assault: A critical review and implications for policy and practice. *Trauma, Violence, & Abuse, 6*(1), 3–23. https://doi.org/10.1177/1524838004272463

Hilton, N. Z., Harris, G. T., Rice, M. E., Lang, C., Cormier, C. A., & Lines, K. J. (2004). A brief actuarial assessment for the prediction of wife assault recidivism: The Ontario domestic assault risk assessment. *Psychological Assessment, 16*(3), 267–275. doi:10.1037/1040-3590.16.3.267

Holt, S. (2007). A matter of life and death: Intimate partner homicide in Ireland. *Irish Journal of Family Law, 10*(4), 12–20.

Kemshall, H., & Pritchard, J. (1996). *Good practice in risk assessment and risk management.* London: Jessica Kingsley Publishers.

Kropp, P., Hart, S., Lyon, D., & LePard, D. (2002). Managing stalkers: Coordinating treatment and supervision. In L. Sheridan & J. Boon (Eds.), *Stalking and psychosexual obsession: Psychological perspectives for prevention, policing and treatment* (pp. 141–163). Chichester, UK: Wiley.

Kropp, P., Hart, S., Webster, C., & Eaves, D. (1999). *Manual for the spousal assault risk assessment guide* (3rd ed.). Toronto, Canada: Multi Health Systems.

Kropp, P. R. (2004). Some questions regarding spousal assault risk assessment. *Violence Against Women, 10*(6), 676–697. https://doi.org/10.1177/1077801204265019

Kropp, P. R. (2008). Intimate partner violence risk assessment and management. *Violence and Victims; New York, 23*(2), 202–220. http://dx.doi.org/10.1891/0886-6708.23.2.202

Kropp, P. R., & Hart, S. D. (2000). The spousal assault risk assessment (SARA) guide: Reliability and validity in adult male offenders. *Law and Human Behavior, 24*(1), 101–118.

Kugley, S., Wade, A., Thomas, J., Mahood, Q., Jørgensen, A., Hammerstrøm, K., & Sathe, N. (2016). *Searching for studies: A guide to information retrieval for Campbell systematic reviews*. Oslo: The Campbell Collaboration.

Lauria, I., McEwan, T. E., Luebbers, S., Simmons, M., & Ogloff, J. R. P. (2017). Evaluating the Ontario domestic assault risk assessment in an Australian frontline police setting. *Criminal Justice and Behavior, 44*(12), 1545–1558. https://doi.org/10.1177/0093854817738280

Messing, J. T., & Thaller, J. (2012). The average predictive validity of intimate partner violence risk assessment instruments. *Journal of Interpersonal Violence, XX*(X), 1–22.

Millar, A. M., Code, R., & Ha, L. (2013). *Inventory of spousal violence risk assessment tools used in Canada*. Retrieved from Department of Justice website: www.justice.gc.ca/eng/rp-pr/cj-jp/fv-vf/rr09_7/index.html

Millar, A. M., Devaney, J., & Butler, M. (2019). Emotional intelligence: Challenging the perceptions and efficacy of 'soft skills' in policing incidents of domestic abuse involving children. *Journal of Family Violence, 34*, 577–588.

Myhill, A. (2015). Measuring coercive control: What can we learn from national population surveys? *Violence Against Women, 21*(3), 355–375. doi:10.1177/1077801214568032

Myhill, A., & Hohl, K. (2016). The 'golden thread': Coercive control and risk assessment for domestic violence. *Journal of Interpersonal Violence, Epub Ahead of Print*, 1–21.

Nicholls, T. L., Desmarais, S., Douglas, K., & Kropp, P. (2006). Violence risk assessments with perpetrators of intimate partner abuse. In J. Hamel & T. Nicholls (Eds.), *Family interventions in domestic violence: A handbook of gender-inclusive theory and treatment* (pp. 275–301). New York, NY: Springer Publishing Company.

Nicholls, T. L., Pritchard, M. M., Reeves, K. A., & Hilterman, E. (2013). Risk assessment in intimate partner violence: A systematic review of contemporary approaches. *Partner Abuse; New York, 4*(1), 76–168. http://dx.doi.org/10.1891/1946-6560.4.1.76

Northcott, M. (2008). *Intimate partner violence risk assessment tools: A review* (No. rr12–8e). Canada: Research and Statistics Division, Department of Justice Canada.

Robinson, A. L. (2006). Reducing repeat victimization among high-risk victims of domestic violence: The benefits of a coordinated community response in Cardiff, wales. *Violence Against Women, 12*(8), 761–788. https://doi.org/10.1177/1077801206291477

Robinson, A. L., Myhill, A., & Wire, J. (2018). Practitioner (mis) understandings of coercive control in England and wales. *Criminology & Criminal Justice, 18*(1), 29–49.

Robinson, A. L., Myhill, A., Wire, J., Roberts, J., & Tillwy, N. (2016). *What works: Crime reduction research. Risk-led policing of domestic abuse and the DASH risk model*. Wales: Cardiff University, College of Policing and UCL Department of Security and Crime Science.

Roehl, J., & Guertin, K. (2000). Intimate partner violence: The current use of risk assessments in sentencing offenders. *The Justice System Journal, 21*(2), 171–199.

Schechter, S. (1982). *Women and male violence: The visions and struggles of the battered women's movement*. Boston, MA: South End Press.

Sharp-Jeffs, N., & Kelly, L. (2016). *Domestic homicide reviews case analysis*. London: Metropolitan University and Standing Together.

Sheppard, M., & Pence, E. (1988). The effects of battering on the employment status of women. *Affilia, 3*(2), 55–61.

Singh, J. P., Grann, M., & Fazel, S. (2011). A comparative study of violence risk assessment tools: A systematic review and metaregression analysis of 68 studies involving 25,980 participants. *Clinical Psychology Review, 31*(3), 499–513. https://doi.org/10.1016/j.cpr.2010.11.009

Stark, E. (2007). *Coercive control: How men entrap women in personal life*. New York, NY: Oxford University Press.

Stark, E. (2012). Looking beyond domestic violence: Policing coercive control. *Journal of Police Crisis Negotiations, 12*(2), 199–217.

Steel, N., Blakeborough, L., & Nicholas, S. (2011). *Supporting high-risk victims of domestic violence: A review of multi-agency risk assessment conferences (MARACs)*. London: Home Office.

Stockl, H., Devries, K., & Rotstein, A., et al. (2013). The global prevalence of intimate partner homicide: A systematic review. *Lancet, 382*(9895), 859–865.

Storey, J. E., Kropp, P. R., Hart, S. D., Belfrage, H., & Strand, S. (2014). Assessment and management of risk for intimate partner violence by police officers using the brief spousal assault form for the evaluation of risk. *Criminal Justice and Behavior, 41*, 256–272, 275.

Storey, J. E., & Strand, S. (2013). Assessing violence risk among female IPV perpetrators: An examination of the B-SAFER. *Journal of Aggression, Maltreatment & Trauma, 22*(9), 964–980.

Thompson, N., & Thompson, S. (2008). *The social work companion*. Hampshire: Palgrave Macmillan.

Websdale, N. (1999). Understanding domestic homicide. Boston, MA: Northeastern University Press.

Weisz, A. N., Tolman, R. M., & Saunders, D. G. (2000). Assessing the risk of severe domestic violence: The importance of survivors' predictions. *Journal of Interpersonal Violence, 15*(1), 75–90. https://doi.org/10.1177/088626000015001006

Wheller, L., & Wire, J. (2014). *Domestic abuse risk factors and risk assessment: Summary of findings from a rapid evidence assessment*. London, UK: College of Policing.

Wire, J., & Myhill, A. (2018). *Piloting a new approach to domestic abuse frontline risk assessment* [Evaluation]. London, UK: College of Policing.

# 29

# INTERVENTIONS FOR CHILDREN AND YOUNG PEOPLE WHO HAVE EXPERIENCED DOMESTIC VIOLENCE AND ABUSE

*Åsa Källström*

## Introduction

Children exposed to domestic violence are at heightened risk of developing problems such as post-traumatic stress, anxiety, depression, other emotional or behavioural problems, and difficulties in school or with social relationships (e.g. Kitzmann, Gaylord, Holt, & Kenny, 2003; Wolfe, Crooks, Lee, McIntyre-Smith, & Jaffe, 2003). Furthermore, children exposed to domestic violence are at increased risk of physical abuse and other forms of maltreatment (e.g. Appel & Holden, 1998). Hence, limiting the consequences of such exposure is of utmost importance.

However, children's reactions to being exposed to domestic violence vary widely. Some muster the resilience to deal with it and overcome their experiences without suffering long-term harm (Howell, 2011; Levendosky, Huth-Bocks, & Semel, 2002). Others are affected to a greater extent, but are subsequently able to recover using their own resources. As an example, domestic violence seems to affect the psychosocial well-being of teenagers less than that of younger children, perhaps because teenagers are better able to avoid the violence, or have greater emotional distance to their parents (Levendosky et al., 2002). There are, however, indications that experiencing domestic violence in early childhood can have consequences such as emotional and/or behavioural problems also in one's teenage years and even early adulthood (Cater, Miller-Graff, Howell, & Graham-Bermann, 2015; Moylan et al., 2010).

In addition, in Norway, witnessing domestic violence during childhood has been found to increase the risk of later being violently victimized by a teenage partner (Hellevik & Øverlien, 2016). In the USA, witnessing violence between parents has been found to predict dating violence among black, but not white, adolescents (Foshee, Ennett, Bauman, Benefield, & Suchindran, 2005). Given the diversity of children's and young people's experiences of and reactions to domestic violence, the need for professional intervention varies among them. This chapter focuses on how well interventions match the needs of children and young people.

Although children who have been exposed to domestic violence and abuse are sometimes described as witnesses, they are rarely mere (passive) victims. Rather, their understanding of the situation may shape the impact the violence has in their lives (Graham-Bermann, Cater,

Miller-Graff, & Howell, 2017). How children and young people interpret and understand their experiences of domestic violence can be influenced by talking to other people. One way to prevent or reduce some of the problems is therefore to provide them with an opportunity to talk about their experiences (Cohen, Mannarino, & Iyengar, 2011; Graham-Bermann, Kulkarni, & Kanukollu, 2011). But what specifically do they need to talk to professionals about? And how should such talk be designed?

This chapter aims to discuss and analyze (1) how varying experiences of domestic violence affect children's and young people's need for professional support and interventions, (2) particular needs to be addressed in interventions, (3) the intervention models currently available, (4) what we can learn from children and young people about what they value in support interventions, and (5) challenges to developing and implementing interventions for them.

## How children's and young people's varying experiences of domestic violence affect their need for professional support and interventions

The risk of children's and young people's health, well-being, and development being adversely affected increases with the seriousness of the domestic violence they have experienced and the length of time that it has persisted (Kitzmann et al., 2003); however there are other characteristics of the violence that also seem crucial for children's and young people's needs.

So-called intimate terrorism, typically male-perpetrated, frequent and severe physical assaults combined with power, domination and control tactics, tends to instil in victims a constant sense of imminent danger (e.g. Johnson, 2008). Children living with intimate terrorism perpetrators may be used as tools in the violence, with the attachment between mother and child being used as a means of controlling them (Johnson, 2008). For children, fathers' unidirectional violence entails a risk that it is particularly severe, including more serious threats, damage, and neglect of the child's basic needs (Miller, Cater, Howell, & Graham-Bermann, 2014). In contrast, so-called situational couple violence is typically not embedded in a pattern of control, but occurs in particular situations that are experienced as provoking and/or of one or both partners using violence to handle conflicts (Stith et al., 2001; Johnson, 2008). For children, bidirectional domestic violence may entail a longer duration of exposure (Miller et al., 2014). Thus, coercive control, including tactics intending to intimidate, humiliate, and exploit an intimate partner, seems central to what domestic violence means for children and young people.

To understand how such patterns are related to children's and young people's needs, however, it is important to also understand variations in how they perceive such violence. For children, a strong and supportive relationship with a non-abusive mother supports their resilience to domestic violence. Lower levels of coercive control within a perpetrator's/father's use of domestic violence seem to enable mothers and children to stay closer to each other (Katz, 2019). Thus, controlling behaviour is an important factor in screening and assessing the quality of mother–child relationships and what harms them, and tailoring interventions to reverse such harms.

Furthermore, although the typologies of domestic violence briefly described have been widely utilized and validated in the literature on adults, and much is known about the impact of domestic violence on children, few empirical studies have linked these typologies to children's exposure. One study that links these typologies to a child perspective is Øverlien's (2013) analysis of interviews with children expressing strong feelings of fear in relation to the characteristics of intimate terrorism. The study found that this approach to categorizing domestic violence generated a more nuanced understanding of how and why children are differently affected by it.

Øverlien thus contributed a new perspective that illustrates the importance of identifying differences in children's descriptions of violence and categorizing patterns of violence in relation to children's experiences.

Another qualitative study (Cater & Sjögren, 2016) uses the typologies described earlier as an analytical framework for exploring patterns in children's descriptions of the violence they have experienced. Three main types of children's experiences of domestic violence were identified. For children experiencing "obedience-demanding violence", occurring because the father does not get his way, the violence becomes closely connected with the necessity of complying with the father's demands. Thus, they may particularly need help handling feelings of guilt about not being able to prevent the violence, despite constantly trying to act in accordance with the father's wishes. Other children described experiencing "chronic and mean violence", which consists of severe and escalating violence that is a result of the father's malicious personality and thus is impossible for them to avoid. These children may particularly need help to handle living in constant fear. Yet other children described "parenthood-embedded violence", which was particularly closely related to the perpetrator being their father, as the violence seemed overshadowed by the positive role their father plays – or could play – in their lives. These children may particularly need help to avoid sympathizing with the perpetrator's viewpoint and minimizing his violence, and handling the difference between the father they have and the one they wish they had.

Thus, understanding differences in domestic violence from children's perspectives can tell us something about their needs when it comes to professional intervention. Additional research on what different types of domestic violence mean for children's and young people's needs could be a next step in developing services.

## Particular needs to be addressed in interventions

In designing interventions for these children and young people, it is also important to consider what factors mediate the relationship between exposure to domestic violence and developing emotional and/or behavioural problems. Recovery is generally easier if parental contact is safe and the child experiences adequate physical and emotional security, structure and boundaries that provide some predictability, strong ties to a parent or sibling, and a sense of not having to care for or be responsible for a parent (Bancroft & Silverman, 2004). In other words, ending conflicts and violence is of central importance for children's recovery opportunities and favours their development. However, intervention programmes cannot always guarantee that the violence will end.

Psychological stability, good social skills, respect and empathy for others, and being able to manage stress seem to be beneficial for children's resilience (Geffner, Igelmann, & Zellner, 2003). It also benefits from positive self-confidence, and a sense of control over their life and of hope for the future (Geffner et al., 2003; Guille, 2004). Further, it may be easier for children to recover if they have developed an understanding of the experience that is coherent, not distorted and not self-pathologizing or characterized by guilt (Gorell Barnes, 1999; Papadopoulos & Byng-Hall, 1997). Feelings of responsibility, guilt, and self-blame may hamper children's and young people's resiliency (Geffner et al., 2003; Grych, Fincham, Jouriles, & McDonald, 2000; Guille, 2004). Nevertheless, some children and young people are blamed for the violence in their families (Ablow, Measelle, Cowan, & Cowan, 2009; Kim, Jackson, Conrad, & Hunter, 2008). Graham-Bermann et al. (2017) found that young people subjected to domestic violence who believed during childhood that the perpetrator used violence in a cruel or sadistic manner or to punish the child had greater problems later in life with anxiety, traumatic stress, and use of aggression than those who believed that the violence was due to the perpetrator being distressed or concerned about finances, or debilitated in some way.

While the importance of parental warmth may be an aspect to convey to parents when working with them, children's and young people's beliefs about the reasons behind the violence and their own role in relation to it seem particularly central to interventions aimed directly at the children.

## The intervention models currently available

A key factor for resilience and coping is social support, for example in the form of access to a non-abusive parent or other adult support person with whom one has a positive relationship (Geffner et al., 2003; Guille, 2004; Osofsky, 2003). One important aspect that interventions sometimes can address is the quality of child-parent relationships. Domestic violence tends to disrupt those relationships (Letourneau et al., 2007). When possible, however, warm mother–child and father–child interactions have been found to play a key role in long-term resilience for those subjected to domestic violence during childhood (Collishaw et al., 2007; Miller, Cater, Howell, & Graham-Bermann, 2016). A systematic review of the literature examining the effects of interventions designed to address parenting among women affected by domestic violence suggested, however, that it is not yet clear what interventions or intervention components are most effective in addressing the unique needs of these women (Austin, Shanahan, Barrios, & Macy, 2017.)

However, children and young people may need opportunities to talk with a professional about their experiences (Broberg et al., 2011). In recent decades, different support programmes have been developed to offer children and young people access to social support. These often focused on helping them achieve a reasonable understanding of the domestic violence they have experienced. Being able to tell about their experiences can reduce or prevent symptoms such as behavioural problems (Jouriles et al., 2009) and post-traumatic stress syndrome (Graham-Bermann, 2001). Many programmes have common components or themes like education about domestic violence, promotion of open discussion of the children's experiences, development of coping and problem-solving skills, exploration of attitudes about domestic violence, safety planning, reducing trauma symptoms, and improving psychological well-being and self-esteem (Anderson & van Ee, 2018; Rizo, Macy, Ermentrout, & Johns, 2011).

Based on a comprehensive literature review and a critical analysis of the literature on interventions that either directly or indirectly target children exposed to domestic violence, Rizo et al. (2011) identified four categories of interventions: counselling/therapy, crisis/outreach, parenting, and multicomponent intervention programmes. Many of these can be considered secondary preventive support programmes. Secondary preventive interventions are aimed at individuals who have been exposed to some type of hazard – like domestic violence – associated with an increased risk of negative development (Weisz, Sandler, Durlak, & Anton, 2005). The aims of these programmes are to promote healthy development despite the children's experiences and to reduce the risk for future problems. This means that the programmes are offered to a wide variety of children and young people with different or no symptoms. A few intervention approaches for children who have been exposed to domestic violence have been relatively rigorously assessed and are more or less considered evidence-based.

One of these is Child Parent Psychotherapy (CPP), developed by Lieberman and Van Horn, which is aimed at preschool-aged children traumatized by, for example, domestic violence. A therapist helps the child and parent/s with their interactions. Findings have provided evidence of the efficacy and durability of CPP after one year of the intervention for traumatized

3–5-year-olds, compared to case management plus community referral for individual treatment (Lieberman, Ippen, & Van Horn, 2006).

Project Support (PS), an intensive home-based intervention targeting parenting and maternal distress, was developed by Jouriles and McDonald to support mothers subjected to domestic violence whose children (3–9 years) have developed conduct problems. Families who received PS services, which included teaching mothers child-management skills and providing them with instrumental and emotional support, showed greater reductions in mothers' perceived inability to manage childrearing responsibilities, mothers' reports of harsh parenting, and observations of ineffective parenting practices than families who received the usual services offered for child-conduct problems (Jouriles et al., 2009).

Trauma-focused cognitive behavioural therapy (TF-CBT) is a psychotherapeutic intervention for children suffering from post-traumatic stress. Developed by Cohen, Deblinger, and Mannarino, it includes strengthening of the parent's ability to support the child in parallel with therapeutic conversations with the child. It comprises 12–16 sessions with nine components designed to gradually expose the child to the traumatic situation. It has been found effective in significantly reducing symptoms of post-traumatic stress and other emotional problems in children aged 3–11 years (e.g. Mannarino, Cohen, Deblinger, Runyon, & Steer, 2012; Scheeringa, Weems, Cohen, Amaya-Jackson, & Guthrie, 2011).

Kids' Club is a group format programme for children exposed to domestic violence, and their mothers. The method was developed by Graham-Bermann and consists of ten 60-minute weekly sessions for groups of children 6–12 years of age and their mothers. The children's intervention is designed to strengthen their sense of safety and help them manage emotions and conflicts. The programme for mothers focuses on building empowerment and safety by educating them about power and control and discussing ways to break cycles of domination. It has been found to be successful in reducing children's externalizing and internalizing of problems, particularly when the children's programme is combined with parallel sessions for the victimized mother (e.g. Graham-Bermann & Miller, 2013).

In the USA and Canada, the development of programmes has been going on the longest, but more and more activities are emerging in Europe (see Humphreys et al., 2000; Humphreys & Mullender, 2000; Mullender & Morley, 1994). However, the conducting of evaluations (especially RCT studies) of services targeting this specific group of children is surrounded by many practical and ethical challenges, which is why strong evidence is still limited. Furthermore, careful consideration is needed when transferring programmes between cultures that differ when it comes to such things as expectations on fathers, child custody legislation and traditions after separation, and whether NGOs or public services typically provide such support.

## The nature of the intervention models currently available – and possible ways forward

Mullender et al. (2002) identify some key factors in support efforts that can help children cope with their situation: (1) that they are listened to, kept informed, and taken seriously; and (2) that they are invited to actively take part in finding solutions and making decisions. Such interventions can be done individually or in groups, be more or less structured, and getting children involved can be done through games, role playing, or conversation.

Talking in groups is a common form of support intervention. McAlister Groves (1999) points out that groups can break children's (perceived) isolation and give them the opportunity to share their experiences with others who have similar experiences. For older children and teenagers, groups may be particularly suitable, as peer relationships are especially important, and it is possible to discuss violence in dating relationships as well as attitudes to sexism, power, and control. Jaffe, Wolfe, and Wilson (1990) suggest that a group method is best for children who have more highly developed reflective capabilities. For preschoolers, McAlister Groves (1999) instead recommends individual intervention models combined with parenting efforts.

However, group interventions may not be sufficient for these children. First, it can be difficult to offer group interventions. In small municipalities, it may be difficult to gather enough children of suitable ages. Furthermore, language difficulties can inhibit group conversations. Factors pertaining to some children may also require special consideration. For example, children who have experienced violence from their mothers or who have been subjected to sexual abuse may perceive the group as yet another arena for exclusion, similar to what children with a different cultural background than the other children and group leaders may experience. There may also be other risks associated with group dynamics; for instance children with more difficulties may influence children who have held up better despite having experienced similar events, children may be "forced" to relive a potentially traumatizing event before they are ready, and children's experiences may be pathologized by tacitly or openly conveying the assumption that they "should" lead to worry or ill health. Therefore, it is necessary to assess these risks before offering group interventions to a child.

When assessing a child's support needs, it may be important to find out the specific experiences the child has had and to use a trauma-screening tool. Some of these children's problems come to the knowledge of adults and professionals in direct connection with the mother's actions, for example, reporting the father, moving to a domestic violence shelter, or otherwise seeking help. Other problems only come to the knowledge of adults and professionals after long periods of trying to deal with the children's problems within the family and with the help of their natural network. Therefore, many researchers have pointed out that "one size does not fit all" (Jaffe et al., 1990; Prinz & Feerick, 2003). In other words, when we have a particular support model in front of us, we have to ask ourselves: what children do we think this particular intervention model can suit? Is it those children who are suffering from traumatization, or those showing other signs of emotional difficulties? Should the same programme be offered to children who (also) display controlling and aggressive behaviours? Should children who do not show feelings or behaviours that can be consequences of violence be offered the same intervention (cf. Silvern, Karyl, & Landis, 1995)? Further, for the sake of further practice development, studies are needed of the value of any specific intervention method's characteristics in relation to common therapeutic factors, such as the group leader's warmth, empathy and judgement, and in relation to other interventions and forms of support for these children and their mothers.

Research consistently finds that common (or general) therapeutic factors (rather than method-specific ones) are crucial for intervention success (Bohart et al., 2002). One central common factor is the quality of the relationship between helper and helped (Bohart et al., 2002; Norcross, 2010). This seems also to be relevant for children exposed to domestic violence, because the children expressed the most appreciation for aspects of treatment that are not intervention-specific, but rather curative components of treatment in their own right (Pernebo & Almqvist, 2016). Similarly, Källström and Thunberg (2019) found that young people who had experienced domestic violence described how important it was to them that the adult counsellor listened to them and accommodated their wishes and needs. Thus, such common factors may constitute important conditions that enable these children and young people to benefit from specific interventions or techniques, but which so far have been overlooked in practice-development and research. However, communicating acceptance of the helped person's experiences may be particularly difficult when the experiences have to do with family violence. Eriksson (2003) found that for some family-law social workers, professional ideals prescribing distance, objectivity, and (gender) neutrality made it seem partial to take a victim at face value and (initially) act upon statements about subjection to violence, but impartial to (initially) take the accused fathers' denial of violence at face value and let it be the basis for (non)action (to protect). Hence, they handled fathers' violence within norms that make a certain level of violence from fathers acceptable, and distrusted mothers' narratives of child sexual abuse.

Some argue that although not all children and young people exposed to domestic violence are traumatized, interventions offered to them must be *trauma-informed*. Trauma-informed services or programmes are ones that recognize and respond to the impact of traumatic stress on children, caregivers, and service providers, understand how trauma shapes a client's fundamental beliefs about the world and affects his or her psychosocial functioning, and incorporate principles to avoid reproducing unhealthy interpersonal dynamics in the helping relationship. They can be integrated into models of evidence-based services across populations and agency settings to strengthen the therapeutic alliance and facilitate post-traumatic growth (Levenson, 2017). However, Berliner and Kolko (2016) remind us that it is still not proven that trauma-informed practice actually makes a difference, that is, improves the lives of the children subjected to harm.

Despite the previously described interventions' positive results for most children, other children do not improve, and their trauma symptoms may even increase during or after an intervention (Broberg et al., 2011). This can possibly be explained by variations in the needs of children exposed to domestic violence (cf. Prinz & Feerick, 2003; Wolfe et al., 2003). It could also be a result of some children being hesitant to talk about their experiences of domestic violence because they have been explicitly or implicitly silenced, think they should protect their mothers, or simply do not want to speak (cf. Mullender, 2006). Encouraging and facilitating the disclosure of shameful symptoms and related behaviours has been found to have positive implications for the effectiveness of treatment (Hook & Andrews, 2005). Specifically, Graham-Bermann et al. (2011) found that children who spontaneously disclosed traumatic events exhibited a significantly greater change in both their internalization of problems and their understanding of the unacceptability of family violence after intervention, and that children who were actively involved and engaged during the intervention were more likely to disclose their experiences. Based on these findings, Graham-Bermann et al. (2011) call for research that sheds light on whether intervention programmes should help children to better engage with therapeutic activities.

## What we can learn from what children and young people value in support interventions

For children and young people willingly to engage in intervention activities, the activities must appear meaningful to them. Yet, we know only a little about what children and young people exposed to domestic violence value in support interventions and themselves judge that they need. This section outlines what we can learn from children and young people about how to design and set up such programmes.

Preschool-aged children who had participated in group programmes for children exposed to domestic violence described the treatment sessions as a safe place to have fun and meet others, and a place where they can talk about distressing matters and gain new abilities (Pernebo & Almqvist, 2016). Pernebo and Almqvist suggest the experience of joy being evident in all interviews may be because the group format offers a setting that normalizes experiences and reactions as well as participation in treatment, and furthermore prevents alienation from peers while offering training in social skills. The intervention programme had taken precautions to avoid destructive interaction between the children by having only 4–6 children and two experienced group leaders in each group. Pernebo and Almqvist stress that the aspects which the children expressed the greatest appreciation of – joy, security, and relatedness – are not specific to the intervention programmes, but rather conditions that permit the children to benefit from specific interventions or techniques.

Among children aged 7 to 10, issues of agency, choice, and intersecting identities seem central to how they experience recovery after domestic violence (Beetham, Gabriel, & James, 2019). Power relations that "infantilize" children, treat them as "objects" or position them in a "needs" discourse can be (re)negotiated by children. Thus, children play an active role in how they negotiate relational encounters and contexts in their recoveries. These children's experiences of activities, and their articulations of agency and choice were relational, which shows that having experienced domestic violence is not the only foundation of the children's sense of self. Beetham et al. therefore suggest that it is crucial to offer children a means by which to explore and express feelings about their experiences of violence and make decisions about how and when they want to talk about their experiences, as well as to explore and value other aspects of their identities. They further argue that "readiness to engage" must be evaluated contextually, and choice and consent must be treated as relational, ongoing and open to the possibility of change. It is thus crucial that children are consulted in inclusive ways in order to contribute to the development and accessibility of services designed to support them when they have been affected by domestic violence.

Children between 9 and 13 years of age who described the domestic violence they had experienced as a horrifying experience perceived talking about the violence as a positive, if sometimes distressing, experience that made a real difference in their lives; whereas children who preferred not to think about the violence did not see much need to talk about it or benefit in talking about it (Izaguirre & Cater, 2018). Thus, even if talking to professionals is an important source of support, not all children feel they need or want to do so. Izaguirre and Cater stress, however, that it is crucial that professionals distinguish between those children who are so severely affected by the violence that they cannot talk about it and those who do not want to talk about it because they were not very strongly affected by it.

Among young people between 12 and 19 years of age, the most valuable aspect of a counselling relationship was to feel equal to other people (Källström & Thunberg, 2019). The young people valued having the right to influence sessions, to have healthy relationships, and to feel a sense of normality and pride. This is understandable, given that subjection to violence is an extreme form of an unequal power balance and subordination, and being treated as an equal could be seen as a direct contrast to what it is like to live under conditions of pervasive and continuous control. The younger teenagers more commonly valued having the opportunity to rest from talking about the violence, while the older ones more commonly described valuing being treated almost like adults. They described how important it was to them that the adult counsellor listened to them and accommodated their wishes and needs, and that the counselling relationship was flexible and empathic. Källström and Thunberg suggest that counsellors need to be particularly flexible with young people exposed to violence, in order to enable them to exercise their autonomy and thereby reduce the power inequality built into the counsellor-client relationship, and in order to counteract their narrowed space for action.

Taken together, these studies suggest that younger children exposed to domestic violence may value relationships with other children in counselling, while older children and young people may value being treated as equals by the adult providing the support. How can these requests be met in practice? Children and young people aged 4–19 years who had received interventions for children exposed to domestic violence describe how participation processes in the different phases of the intervention are related to three prerequisites for children actually to receive the intervention offered, namely that the child must (1) get in contact with the unit, (2) start the intervention process, and (3) actually talk about the violence (Cater, 2014). For some children and young people, being provided with information about services, receiving opportunities to participate in the decision to start an intervention, and being able to inform themselves about it step by step, may be crucial for their willingness to talk about the violence and for their retrospective experience of the intervention. In addition, if counsellors limit children's opportunities to influence how the counselling is carried out, they may take the (more drastic) choice of dropping out. Thus, while children's and young people's experiences of domestic violence may call for particular flexibility, individual adaptation and attention to common factors, it may be particularly important that groups arranged for younger children provide positive child–child relationships and that counselling for teenagers provides a sense of equality in the youth–adult relationship.

## Challenges to interventions for children and young people with experiences of domestic violence

The development and implementation of intervention programmes for children and young people exposed to domestic violence are affected by several specific challenges. First of all, some mothers who seek help and support on behalf of their children remain with the violent man, and it can be difficult to determine if the threat – whether actual or as perceived by the child – has really ended. And if the violence or threat of violence remains part of the children's lives, they may not be able to make use of the intervention offered to them (Broberg et al., 2011).

Another significant challenge is the fact that many children and young people hide their "secret" from everyone because if others found out the shame would be devastating. One possible result of living with the shame that domestic violence entails for many children is that their self-esteem is damaged (Holt, Buckley, & Whelan, 2008; Kitzmann et al., 2003). This is a challenge in two ways. First, it means that children and young people may refrain from seeking the help they need. As an example, Howell, Cater, Miller-Graff, and Graham-Bermann (2015) found that that roughly half of young Swedish adults retrospectively reported confiding in someone about the domestic violence they had witnessed as children. This rate is in line with findings of the only other study to examine domestic violence disclosure among youth (Graham-Bermann et al., 2011). Secondly, as described earlier, this may mean that children do not talk about the violence while in a programme.

The research on the effectiveness of intervention programmes would benefit from more uniform effect measures to enable comparisons of results from studies of different types of interventions. Such studies need to have sufficient numbers of participants, control groups, and longer follow-up times than are normally used. Further, studies of dropout and of change moderators are warranted. More studies are also needed about children's and young people's experiences of interventions. Questions to which we particularly need to find answers are: when do children need an intervention? As soon as possible, before thought structures that lead to incomprehension, fear, and guilt become established in the child's consciousness? Is it more important that the child's life situation is stabilized, for example after moving away from the perpetrator? And is it more important for a child receiving intervention, individually or in groups, that the perpetrator is involved in and participates in the treatment, so that – through personal development and in the best case by taking the blame – the perpetrator can help the child through the process? Or is it better for the child to avoid the threat posed by the perpetrator, because treatment is only meaningful when you can guarantee that the child will not be confronted with the perpetrator during the treatment period?

It is possible that these questions must be answered using intersectional analyses to bring attention to possible differences in race, gender, (dis)ability, and age among children and young people who have experienced domestic violence. The research on which this chapter is based is largely limited to North American, Canadian, and European settings. It is likely that interventions have been developed and tested, and important knowledge developed, that has only been published in a language other than English, and hence is not included in this chapter. The field would benefit from also being able to draw conclusions from such studies. Finally, it is likely that support is not equally available to all children within societies. Some parents have limited knowledge about the availability of support and how society works, and some fear deportation or intervention by the child protection services. Research about the impact of financial and social resources on the availability of services for children and young people who have experienced domestic violence could possibly help us develop more inclusive systems for support provision.

## Conclusions

Several conclusions can be drawn from this chapter. Some aspects reported warrant practical as well as academic attention. First, because children who have experienced violence may particularly need help to overcome perceptions that a relative perpetrated the violence out of hatred toward the child or as punishment, to become free from feelings of guilt and self-blame, and to be able to feel warmth from a parent, these aspects need to be included in programme development and addressed in evaluations. Secondly, because typologies of domestic violence can help us understand the differing needs among children and young people, empirical studies linking children's exposure to violence with such typologies as well as programmes actively and explicitly addressing children's varied experiences of domestic violence are warranted. On a more general note, because common factors may constitute important conditions that enable these children and young people to benefit from specific interventions or techniques, they need to be included in practice development and research about these children. Programme development and research on how the needs of children exposed to domestic violence can best be met in services would plausibly also benefit from learning from evaluations of services and programmes directed at children subjected to direct physical abuse or other forms of maltreatment in their family.

This chapter shows that understanding differences in domestic violence from children's perspectives can tell us something about their need for professional intervention. Assuming that for children and young people willingly to engage in intervention activities the activities must appear meaningful to them, the chapter suggests that the next steps for programme development include balancing a child's need to talk against the value of respecting the child's integrity and matching interventions with individual needs. Balancing a child's need to talk about the violence against the value of respecting the child's personal motivation and preferences is an especially delicate task for adult practitioners, and is necessary if they are to achieve the most beneficial outcome in interventions with this particular group. Because many currently available programmes are devoted to a wide variety of children and young people with different or no symptoms, particular attention needs to be paid to matching interventions to individual needs. In addition, a particular challenge for services is that they cannot always guarantee that the violence will end. Based on the research in this chapter, I suggest that the next steps for programme development should include finding additional ways to acknowledge young people's demands for flexibility and their need (and right) to make their own decisions; help service providers/staff protect children from domestic violence, use common factors to stimulate children and young people to disclose/talk about the violence without pressuring them, deal with group dynamics, and match interventions to the individual needs in rural areas.

Finally, many questions remain that need to be answered. Specifically, more research is needed that addresses which interventions or intervention components, including common factors, are most effective in addressing the unique parenting needs of women subjected to domestic violence, as well as the varying individual needs of their children. It is also worth empirically investigating whether manuals that strike a different balance between techniques on the one hand, and common factors such as flexibility, acceptance, and empathy on the other, suit different service-providing settings. Future research should include empirical investigations of how programmes developed and evaluated as supported by good evidence in North America can be transferred to other cultural settings. In addition, programmes developed in Europe, for example, should be disseminated in English, in order to enable cross-cultural learning.

## Critical findings

- Typologies of domestic violence can help us understand the different needs of children and young people.
- A particular challenge for services is that they cannot always guarantee that the violence will end.
- Children who have experienced violence may particularly need help to overcome perceptions that a relative perpetrated the violence out of hatred towards the child or as punishment, to become free from feelings of responsibility and self-blame, and to be able to feel warmth from a parent.
- Programmes evaluated as having robust designs and good results are available, but strong evidence is still limited outside North America, and transferring programmes between cultures requires careful consideration.

## Implications for policy, practice, and research

The next steps for programme development should include finding additional ways to:

- Acknowledge young people's demand for flexibility and their need (and right) to make their own decisions.
- Help service providers/staff protect children from domestic violence.
- Use common (or general) therapeutic factors to stimulate children and young people to disclose/talk about the violence without pressuring them, and deal with group dynamics.
- Match interventions to the individual needs of children and young people in rural areas.
- More research is needed that addresses which interventions or intervention components are most effective in addressing the unique parenting needs of women subjected to domestic violence, as well as the varying individual needs of their children.

## References

Ablow, J. C., Measelle, J. R., Cowan, P. A., & Cowan, C. P. (2009). Linking marital conflict and children's adjustment: The role of young children's perceptions. *Journal of Family Psychology, 23*(4), 485–499. doi:10.1037/a0015894

Anderson, K., & Van Ee, E. (2018). Mothers and children exposed to intimate partner violence: A review of treatment interventions. *International Journal of Environmental Research and Public Health, 15.*

Appel, A. E., & Holden, G. W. (1998). The co-occurrence of spouse and physical child abuse: A review and appraisal. *Journal of Family Psychology, 12*(4), 578–599.

Austin, A. E., Shanahan, M. E., Barrios, Y. V., & Macy, R. J. (2017). A systematic review of interventions for women parenting in the context of intimate partner violence. *Trauma, Violence and Abuse.* Advance online publication. doi:10.1177/1524838017719233

Bancroft, L., & Silverman, J. G. (2004). Assessing Abusers' Risks to children. In P. G. Jaffe, L. L. Baker, & A. J. Cunningham (Eds.), *Protecting children from domestic violence: Strategies for community intervention* (pp. 101–119). New York, NY: Guildford Publications.

Beetham, T., Gabriel, L., & James, H. (2019). Young children's narrations of relational recovery: A school-based group for children who have experienced domestic violence. *Journal of Domestic violence.* doi:10.1007/s10896-018-0028-7

Berliner, L., & Kolko, D. J. (2016). Trauma informed care: A commentary and critique. *Child Maltreatment, 21*(2), 168–172. doi:10.1177/1077559516643785

Bohart, A. C., Elliott, R., . . . Watson, J. C. (2002). Empathy. In *Psychotherapy relationships that work: Therapist contributions and responsiveness to patients.* New York, NY: Oxford University Press.

Broberg, A., Almqvist, K., Axberg, U., Cater, Å. K., Eriksson, M., Forssell, A. M., . . . Sharifi, U. (2011). *Stöd till barn som bevittnat våld mot mamma. Resultat från en nationell utvärdering. [Support for children who have witnessed violence against their mothers. Results from a national evaluation study].* Gothenburg: Psykologiska institutionen, Göteborg University.

Cater, Å. K. (2014). Children's descriptions of participation processes in intervention for children exposed to intimate partner violence. *Child & Adolescence Social Work, 31*(5), 455–473. doi:10.1007/s10560-014-0330-z

Cater, Å. K., Miller-Graff, L. E., Howell, K. H., & Graham-Bermann, S. A. (2015). Childhood exposure to intimate partner violence (IPV) and adult health: Age, gender and violence characteristics. *Journal of Family Violence, 30*, 875–886. doi:10.1007/s10896-015-9703-0

Cater, Å. K., & Sjögren, J. (2016). Child witnesses to intimate partner violence describe their experiences – a typology-based qualitative analysis. *Child & Adolescence Social Work 33*(6), 473–486. doi:10.1007/s10560-016-0443-7

Cohen, J. A., Mannarino, A. P., & Iyengar, S. (2011). Community treatment of post-traumatic stress disorder for children exposed to intimate partner violence. *Archives of Pediatric and Adolescent Medicine, 165*(1), 16–21.

Collishaw, S., Pickles, A., Messer, J., Rutter, M., Shearer, C., & Maughan, B. (2007). Resilience to adult psychopathology following childhood maltreatment: Evidence from a community sample. *Child Abuse & Neglect, 31*, 211–229. doi:10.1016/j.chiabu.2007.02.004

Eriksson, M. (2003). *I skuggan av Pappa: Familjerätten och hanteringen av fäders våld [In the shadow of daddy: Family law and the handling of father's violence].* Stehag: Förlags AB Gondolin.

Foshee, V. A., Ennett, S. T., Bauman, K. E., Benefield, T., & Suchindran, C. (2005). The association between family violence and adolescent dating violence onset: Does it vary by race, socioeconomic status, and family structure? *The Journal of Early Adolescence, 25*(3), 317–344. doi:10.1177/0272431605277307

Geffner, R., Igelmann, R. S., & Zellner, J. (2003). *The effects of intimate partner violence on children.* Binghamton, NY: Haworth.

Gorell Barnes, G. (1999). Operationalizing the uncertain: Some critical reflections. *Journal of Family Therapy, 21*(2), 145–153.

Graham-Bermann, S. A. (2001). Designing intervention evaluations for children exposed to domestic violence: Applications of theory and research. In S. Graham-Bermann & J. L. Edleson (Eds.), *Domestic violence in the lives of children: The future of research, intervention, and social policy* (1st ed.). Washington, DC: American Psychological Association.

Graham-Bermann, S. A., Cater, Å. K., Miller-Graff, L., & Howell, K. (2017). Adults' explanations for intimate partner violence (IPV) during childhood and associated effects. *Journal of Clinical Psychology, 73*(6), 652–668. doi:10.1002/jclp.22345

Graham-Bermann, S. A., Kulkarni, M. R., & Kanukollu, S. N. (2011). Is disclosure therapeutic for children following exposure to traumatic violence? *Journal of Interpersonal Violence, 26*(5), 1056–1076. doi:10.1177/0886260510365855

Graham-Bermann, S. A., & Miller, L. E. (2013). Intervention to reduce traumatic stress following intimate partner violence: An efficacy trial of the moms' empowerment program (MEP). *Psychodynamic Psychiatry, 41*, 329–350. doi:10.1521/pdps.2013.41.2.329

Grych, J. H., Fincham, F. D., Jouriles, E. N., & McDonald, R. (2000). Interparental conflict and child adjustment: Testing the mediational role of appraisals in the cognitive–contextual framework. *Child Development, 71,* 1648–1661.

Guille, L. (2004). Men who batter and their children: An integrated review. *Aggression and Violent Behavior, 9,* 129–163. doi:10.1016/S1359-1789(02)00119-2

Hellevik, P., & Øverlien, C. (2016). Teenage intimate partner violence: Factors associated with victimization among Norwegian youths. *Scandinavian Journal of Public Health, 44*(7), 702–708. doi:10.1177/1403494816657264

Holt, S., Buckley, H., & Whelan, S. (2008). The impact of exposure to domestic violence on children and young people: A review of the literature. *Child Abuse & Neglect, 32,* 797–810. doi:10.1016/j.chiabu.2008.02.004

Hook, A., & Andrews, B. (2005). The relationships of non-disclosure in therapy to shame and depression. *British Journal of Clinical Psychology, 44*(3), 325–438.

Howell, K. H. (2011). Resilience and psychopathology in children exposed to family violence. *Aggression and Violent Behavior, 16,* 562–569. doi:10.1016/j.avb.2011.09.001

Howell, K. H., Cater, Å. K., Miller-Graff, L. E., & Graham-Bermann, S. A. (2015). The process of reporting and receiving support following exposure to intimate partner violence during childhood. *Journal of Interpersonal Violence, 30*(6), 2886–2907. doi:10.1177/0886260514554289

Humphreys, C., Hester, M., Hague, G., Mullender, A., Abrahams, H., & Lowe, P. (2000). *From good intentions to good practice: Working with families where there is domestic violence.* Bristol: Policy Press.

Humphreys, C., & Mullender, A. (2000). *Children and domestic violence: A research overview of the impact on children.* Bristol: The Policy Press.

Izaguirre, A., & Cater, Å. K. (2018). Child witnesses to intimate partner violence (IPV): Their descriptions of talking about the violence. *Journal of Interpersonal Violence, 33*(24), 3711–3731. doi:10.1177/0886260516639256

Jaffe, P. G., Wolfe, D. A., & Wilson, S. K. (1990). *Children of battered women.* Thousand Oaks, CA: Sage.

Johnson, M. P. (2008). *Typology of domestic violence: Intimate terrorism, violent resistance, and situational couple violence.* Boston, MA: Northeastern University Press.

Jouriles, E. N., McDonald, R., Rosenfield, D., Stephens, N., Corbitt-Shindler, D., & Miller, P. C. (2009). Reducing conduct problems among children exposed to intimate partner violence: A randomized clinical trial examining effects of project support. *Journal of Consulting and Clinical Psychology, 77,* 705–717. doi:10.1037/a0015994

Källström, Å., & Thunberg, S. (2019). "As equal in a way" – What young people exposed to domestic violence value in counselling. *Journal of Family Violence.* doi:10.1007/s10896-018-00032-0

Katz, E. (2019). Coercive control, domestic violence, and a five-factor framework: Five factors that influence closeness, distance, and strain in mother – Child relationships. *Violence Against Women, 25*(15), 1829–1853. doi:10.1177/1077801218824998

Kim, K. L., Jackson, Y., Conrad, S. M., & Hunter, H. L. (2008). Adolescent report of interparental conflict: The role of threat and self-blame appraisal on adaptive outcome. *Journal of Child and Family Studies, 17*(5), 735–751. doi:10.1007/s10826-007-9187-5

Kitzmann, K. M., Gaylord, N. K., Holt, A. R., & Kenny, E. D. (2003). Child witnesses to domestic violence: A meta-analytic review. *Journal of Consulting and Clinical Psychology, 71,* 339–352. doi:10.1037/0022-006X.71.2.339

Letourneau, N. L., Fedick, C. B., & Willms, J. D. (2007). Mothering and domestic violence: A longitudinal analysis. *Journal of Family Violence, 22,* 649–659. doi:10.1007/s10896-007-9099-6

Levendosky, A. A., Huth-Bocks, A. C., & Semel, M. A. (2002). Adolescent peer relationships and mental health functioning in families with domestic violence. *Journal of Clinical Child Psychology, 31*(2), 206–218. doi:10.1207/S15374424JCCP3102_06

Levenson, J. (2017). Trauma-informed social work practice. *Social Work, 62*(2).

Lieberman, A. F., Ippen, C. G., & Van Horn, P. (2006). Child-parent psychotherapy: 6-month follow-up of a randomized controlled trial. *Journal of the American Academy of Child & Adolescent Psychiatry, 45,* 913–918. doi:10.1097/01.chi.0000222784.03735.92

Mannarino, A. P., Cohen, J. A., Deblinger, E., Runyon, M. K., & Steer, R. A. (2012). Trauma-focused cognitive-behavioral therapy for children: Sustained impact of treatment 6 and 12 months later. *Child Maltreatment, 17*(3), 231–241. doi:10.1177/1077559512451787

McAlister Groves, B. (1999). Mental health services for children who witness domestic violence. *The Future of Children, 9*(3).

Miller, L. E., Cater, Å. K., Howell, K. H., & Graham-Bermann, S. A. (2014). Perpetration patterns and environmental contexts of IPV in Sweden: Relationships with adult mental health. *Child Abuse and Neglect, 38*, 147–158. doi:10.1016/j.chiabu.2013.10.023

Miller-Graff, L. E., Cater, Å. K., Howell, K. H., & Graham-Bermann, S. A. (2016). Parent-child warmth as a potential mediator of childhood exposure to intimate partner violence and positive adulthood functioning. *Anxiety, Stress & Coping, 29*(3), 259–273. doi:10.1080/10615806.2015.1028030

Moylan, C. A., Herrenkohl, T. I., Sousa, C., Tajima, E. A., Herrenkohl, R. C., & Russo, M. J. (2010). The effects of child abuse and exposure to domestic violence on adolescent internalizing and externalizing behavior problems. *Journal of Family Violence, 25*(1), 53–63. doi:10.1007/s10896-009-9269-9

Mullender, A. (2006). What children tell us: 'He said he was going to kill our mom'. In C. Humphreys & N. Stanley (Eds.), *Domestic violence and child protection – Directions for good practice* (pp. 53–68). London: Jessica Kingsley Publishers.

Mullender, A., Hague, G., Imam, U., Kelly, L., Malos, E., & Regan, L. (2002). *Children's perspectives on domestic violence*. London: Sage.

Mullender, A., & Morley, R. (Eds.). (1994). *Children living with domestic violence – Putting men's abuse of women on the child care agenda*. London: Whiting & Birch.

Norcross, J. C. (2010). The therapeutic relationship. In *The heart and soul of change: Delivering what works in therapy* (2nd ed.). Washington, DC: Am Psychological Ass.

Osofsky, J. D. (2003). Prevalence of children's exposure to domestic violence and child maltreatment: Implications for prevention and intervention. *Clinical Child and Family Psychology Review, 3*(6), 161–170.

Øverlien, C. (2013). The children of patriarchal terrorism. *Journal of Family Violence, 28*, 277–287. doi:10.1007/s10896-013-9498-9

Papadopoulos, R., & Byng-Hall, J. (Eds.). (1997). *Multiple voices: Narrative in systemic family psychotherapy*. London: Duckworth.

Pernebo, K., & Almqvist, K. (2016). Young children's experiences of participating in group treatment for children exposed to intimate partner violence: A qualitative study. *Clinical Child Psychology and Psychiatry*, 1–14. doi:10.1177/1359104514558432

Prinz, R. J., & Feerick, M. M. (2003). Next steps in research on children exposed to domestic violence. *Clinical Child and Family Psychology Review, 6*(3).

Rizo, C. F., Macy, R. J., Ermentrout, D. M., & Johns, N. B. (2011). A review of family interventions for intimate partner violence with a child focus or child component. *Aggression and Violent Behavior, 16*, 144–166.

Scheeringa, M. S., Weems, C. F., Cohen, J. A., Amaya-Jackson, L., & Guthrie, D. (2011). Trauma-focused cognitive-behavioral therapy for posttraumatic stress disorder in three-through six year-old children: A randomized clinical trial. *Journal of Child Psychology and Psychiatry, 52*(8), 853–860. doi:10.1111/j.1365-2885.2010.01243.x

Silvern, L., Karyl, J., & Landis, T. (1995). Individual psychotherapy for the traumatized children of abused women. In E. Peled, P. G. Jaffe, & J. L. Edleson (Eds.), *Ending the cycle of violence: Community responses to children of battered women* (pp. 43–76). Newberry Park: Sage.

Stith, S. M., Amanor-Boadu, Y., Strachman Miller, M., Menhusen, E., Morgan, C., & Few-Demo, A. (2001). Vulnerabilities, stressors, and adaptations in situationally violent relations. *Family Relations, 60*, 73–89. doi:10.1111/j.1741-3729.2010.00634.x

Weisz, J. R., Sandler, I. N., Durlak, J. A., & Anton, B. S. (2005). Promoting and protecting youth mental health through evidence-based prevention and treatment. *American Psychologist, 60*, 628–648.

Wolfe, D. A., Crooks, C. V., Lee, V., McIntyre-Smith, A., & Jaffe, P. G. (2003). The effects of children's exposure to domestic violence: A meta-analysis and critique. *Clinical Child and Family Psychology Review, 6*, 171–187. doi:10.1023/A:1024910416164

# 30

# MOTHERING IN THE CONTEXT OF DOMESTIC VIOLENCE

*Simon Lapierre*

## Introduction

Since the 1990s, concerns regarding abused women's mothering have been raised alongside concerns regarding the situation of children living with domestic violence. Research, policies and practices in this area have focused on women's ability (or inability) to protect and care for their children, and have generally failed to address their complex experiences as mothers in such circumstances. For a long time, women's mothering has also been invisible in the feminist literature on violence against women (Krane & Davies, 2002). In 2001, Radford and Hester argued that

> Despite almost thirty years of research into and activism against violence against women, little has been written about mothering in the context of abuse, whether from the viewpoint of women's experiences, of children's experiences, or on the basis of review of social policy and academic discourses.
>
> (Radford & Hester, 2001, p. 135)

Over the last two decades, a growing number of feminist scholars have investigated women's experiences as mothers in the context of domestic violence (Krane & Davies, 2007; Radford & Hester, 2006). They have argued that these experiences need to be understood in relation to both the particular conditions created by men's violence and the institution of motherhood (see Lapierre, 2008). Drawing upon Rich's (1976) work, motherhood can be understood as a patriarchal institution that constrains, regulates and dominates women and their mothering. It ensures that women perform their mothering in particular ways, according to high (and often unrealistic) standards of 'good' mothering.

This chapter focuses on mothering and domestic violence, drawing primarily upon the work of feminist scholars in Australia, Canada, New Zealand, the United Kingdom and the United States. It is divided into five sections. The first section considers domestic violence as an attack on women's mothering and mother-child relationships. The second section focuses on abused women's experiences as mothers, looking at the difficulties and challenges they face, which often lead to self-blame and mother-blame. This section also highlights the multiple strategies women develop in order to protect and care for their children. The following section examines how abused women's mothering has been addressed in policies and practices in the domestic violence sector, child protection services and family courts. The final section identifies directions for future research in this area.

## Domestic violence as an attack on mothering and mother-child relationships

Domestic violence perpetrators use various strategies in order to control their female partners (Lehmann, Simmons, & Pillai, 2012; Morris, 2009; Stark, 2007), and some of these strategies specifically target their partners' mothering and relationships with their children. Such attacks often start early in women's experiences as mothers, and some women can even be forced into motherhood against their will. Indeed, women can become pregnant as a result of their partners' control over contraception, sexual coercion and sexual violence (Campbell, Pugh, Campbell, & Visscher, 1995; Coggins & Bullock, 2003). In this regard, data from the National Intimate Partner and Sexual Violence Survey revealed that almost 2.9 million American women experience rape-related pregnancies during their lifetime (Basile et al., 2018). Three-quarters (77.3%) of these women reported that the perpetrator had been a current or former intimate partner, and rape perpetrated by an intimate partner was more likely to lead to pregnancy, compared with rape perpetrated by an acquaintance or a stranger. Some women reported that their partners had tried to get them pregnant and stop them from using birth control, and had refused to use condoms.

Moreover, pregnancy has been identified as an important period in many women's history of domestic violence (Izaguirre & Calvete, 2014). In a review of the literature in this area, Bailey (2010) noted that violence during pregnancy is associated with numerous negative outcomes, including low birth weight and preterm delivery. Men's violent behaviours can also influence some women's decision to terminate their pregnancies (Côté & Lapierre, 2014).

Men who use violence towards their partners are likely to also use violence towards their children (Bancroft, Silverman, & Ritchie, 2012; Mbilinyi, Edleson, Hagemeister, & Beeman, 2007), and to control all family members (Morris, 2009; Mullender et al., 2002; Stark, 2007). In this regard, Kelly (1994) pointed out the need to account for the perpetrators' double level of intentionality, which means that acts directed towards children can also be intended to affect their mothers, just as acts directed towards women can also be intended to affect their children. Examples of this include abusing women in front of their children or abusing children in front of their mothers in order to control both, or making women watch, or participate in, the abuse of their children. Such strategies affect women's and children's safety and well-being, as well as mother-child relationships. They are likely to also undermine women's confidence in their ability to protect their children, and send children the message that their mothers are not able to protect them.

In addition, abusive men use more subtle manipulation strategies in order to disrupt their children's routine, criticize their partners' education methods, and undermine their authority and confidence as mothers (Bancroft et al., 2012; Lapierre, 2010a; Radford & Hester, 2006). They also tend to blame their partners and portray them as 'bad' mothers (Heward-Belle, 2017; Lapierre, 2010a; Radford & Hester, 2006). In a study conducted with 17 men who had perpetrated domestic violence in Australia, Heward-Belle (2017) showed that men's attacks on women's mothering was a distinct tactic of coercive control, which had occurred alongside physical, psychological, sexual and financial abuse. Findings from this study also demonstrated that these men had used women's mental health and women's behaviours, particularly with regard to alcohol and drug use, to portray them as 'bad' or even 'mad' mothers. According to this author, 'It was obvious that many men understood and indeed exploited the power of women's desires to be good mothers to meet their own needs' (p. 384).

Furthermore, research evidence has shown that domestic violence, including attacks on women's mothering and mother-child relationships, tends to continue in the post-separation period (Brownridge et al., 2008; Radford & Hester, 2006; Humphreys & Thiara, 2003; Lapierre, 2010a; Zeoli, Rivera, Sullivan, & Kubiak, 2013). In this context, abusive men can use their children to control their ex-partners, and violent incidents, including homicides, often take place during father-child contact arrangements (Coy, Scott, Tweedale, & Perks, 2015; Harrison, 2008; Holt, 2011; Saunders & Oglesby, 2016; Stanley, Chantler, & Robbins, 2019). In a study on post-separation violence, which was conducted with 19 women in the United States, Zeoli et al. (2013) pointed out that these women's ex-partners 'made use of opportunities presented to them by child custody and parenting time arrangement to further abuse mothers and children' (p. 556).

Finally, these men can threaten to report their children's situation to child protection services and use family court proceedings in order to control their ex-partners (Harrison, 2006, 2008; Radford & Hester, 2006). In this regard, Elizabeth (2017) recently proposed the concept of 'custody stalking', which refers to

> a malevolent course of conduct involving the use or threatened use of legal and other bureaucratic proceedings by fathers to obtain, or attempt to obtain, care time with their children far in excess of their involvement with them prior to separation.
>
> (p. 187)

Drawing upon interviews conducted with 12 women in New Zealand, she explains that custody stalking is a tactic used by violent and controlling men to 'fracture the mother-child relationship and produce maternal loss' (p. 189). She revealed three main narratives in relation to custody stalking: 'payback for crashing his dream of a happy little family' (p. 191), 'retaliation for pursuing child support' (p. 193), and 'hurting me and winning' (p. 195).

## Women's experiences as mothers in the context of domestic violence

While abused women perform their mothering in the adverse conditions that have been described earlier, their experiences are complex and can change over time. Women's experiences also vary according to their social locations and access to resources (Barrios et al., 2020; Lippy, Jumarali, Nnawulezi, Williams, & Burk, 2020). In order to understand these experiences, it is essential to take into account, on the one hand, the difficulties and challenges they face, which often lead to mother-blame and self-blame. On the other hand, it is crucial to acknowledge the multiple strategies that women put in place in their attempts to protect and care for their children – and to be 'good' mothers.

### *Difficulties and challenges*

Abused women have limited control over how they perform their mothering. In the context of domestic violence, women's freedom and choices are limited, which means that their actions as mothers often take place within narrow boundaries that have been established by their partners (Lapierre, 2010a; Radford & Hester, 2006). Perpetrators can even limit women's interactions and communication with their children (Humphreys, Mullender, Thiara, & Skamballis, 2006;

Lapierre et al., 2018; Mullender et al., 2002). Moreover, the impacts of men's violence on women's physical and mental health are likely to make it more challenging for them to perform the hard and time-consuming work involved in looking after their children (Lapierre, 2010a; Radford & Hester, 2006).

At the same time, children living with domestic violence need additional protection and support, and may display behaviours that require more attention from their mothers (Lapierre, 2010a). Children's needs vary according to their age, and findings from a study conducted with 16 women in Australia shed light on the particular challenges involved in looking after babies in the context of domestic violence (Buchanan, Power, & Verity, 2013). They demonstrated that fear had significantly influenced these women's relationships with, and responses to, their babies' needs. Some children can also be manipulated by their fathers into blaming their mothers for the situation, and older children can even end up reproducing the perpetrators' violent behaviours towards their mothers (Bancroft et al., 2012).

Even though there is no clear evidence regarding the negative impacts of domestic violence on children through its impacts on women's mothering (Greeson et al., 2014) – and some studies suggest that abused women tend to compensate to overcome the impacts of violence on their children (Levendosky, Huth-Bocks, Shapiro, & Semel, 2003) – the issues that have been noted put a strain on mother-child relationships (Katz, 2019; Lapierre, 2010a; Radford & Hester, 2006). In this regard, findings from a recent study, which was conducted with 59 children who had experienced domestic violence in Canada, showed that women's and children's victimizations had been inextricably linked, and that men's violence had affected both their communication and their relationships (Lapierre et al., 2018). In this study, several children described difficult relationships with their mothers while going through domestic violence, even though they saw their mothers as significant individuals with whom they had close relationships.

In a study conducted with 15 women and 16 children in England, Katz (2019) identified five main factors that had influenced closeness, distance and strain in mother-child relationships in the context of coercive control. The first factor referred to the perpetrators' behaviours towards their children. When their fathers had almost always displayed hostility and indifference towards them, children had very negative views of their fathers and very positive views of their mothers. The second factor was the perpetrators' use of domestic violence, particularly the levels of coercive control and the frequency and severity of physical violence. On the one hand, lower levels of coercive control had allowed women and children to remain close to each other, whereas higher levels of coercive control had limited their interactions. On the other hand, children who had been exposed to the perpetrators' regular use of physical violence towards their mothers had a clearer sense that these behaviours were wrong, and had closer relationships with their mothers. In contrast, children who had been less aware of their fathers' use of physical violence had been closer to them. The third factor was the perpetrators' undermining of mother-child relationships, which had led to more strenuous relationships. With regard to the fourth factor, women who had been harmed in ways that had left them less able to emotionally connect with their children had more strenuous relationships with them. Finally, children's views of their parents, including who they wanted to talk to, spend time with and be close to, were identified as important factors influencing mother-child relationships.

Several difficulties and challenges remain when women leave their abusive partners. In addition to the violence and its impacts, women and children have to cope with multiple changes, which may include moving into a new home, a new school and a new community (Abrahams, 2007; Lapierre, 2010a). In this regard, findings from a study conducted with 25 women in the United States revealed that this process is influenced by the intersections of various factors that shape women's access to resources (Barrios et al., 2020). They demonstrated that racialized women face additional challenges when leaving their abusive partners, and the situation is even more complex when considering the intersections between gender, ethnicity and social class.

At the same time, women may have to go through family court proceedings, and they often feel that they are left on their own to manage father-child contact arrangements (Harrison, 2008; Zeoli et al., 2013). In a study conducted with 45 women and 52 children in the United Kingdom, Thiara and Humphreys (2017) referred to the 'absent presence' to acknowledge the fact that men's violence continues to affect women's and children's lives in the post-separation period. While perpetrators continue to be present in their lives through father-child contact arrangements and harassing behaviours, these authors also argued that past trauma, erosion of self-esteem and the undermining of mother-child relationships 'continue to create a shadow across the present relationship' (p. 140). They demonstrated that, for women and children who have experienced domestic violence, the past continually surfaces in the present: 'There was slippage in the language about the present and the past. Even though women were separated, they often spoke as though the past experience of domestic violence was ongoing' (p. 140).

## *Mother-blame and self-blame*

In the context of domestic violence, women often consider that they have not been 'good' or 'good enough' mothers (Lapierre, 2010a, 2010c; Moulding, Buchanan, & Wendt, 2015; Radford & Hester, 2001, 2006). In a recent study conducted in the United Kingdom, which involved 15 abused women who had been in contact with child protection services, Stewart (2020) reported that these women had internalized high expectations with regard to their mothering. These expectations included keeping children safe and meeting their basic needs, as well as doing their best to put children first, spending time with them, showing them that they are loved, nurturing their emotions, and being warm, caring and supportive with them. In another study conducted with 25 women in England, Lapierre (2010a) demonstrated that the particular conditions created by men's violence are at odds with the high and often unrealistic expectations that the institution of motherhood places upon women as mothers. As a result,

> These women tend to experience an increased sense of responsibility in regard to their children, as well as a loss of control over their mothering. This creates a tension by which women are required to achieve more with less control over means and resources, which is likely to result in feelings of failure, self-blame and guilt.
>
> (Lapierre, 2010a, p. 1446)

The women who took part in this study reported that, even though they had generally managed to protect their children and care for their basic needs, they had felt guilty about their 'failure' to care for their children's more emotional needs. In this regard, some women stated that they had 'emotionally neglected' their children.

Such feelings can be reinforced by the fact that mother-blame is a strategy commonly used by perpetrators to undermine their partners' confidence as mothers. Moreover, women can be blamed by their children, even though research evidence has shown that children can also recognize the difficulties and challenges faced by their mothers (Buchanan, Wendt, & Moulding, 2015; Mullender et al., 2002). In an Australian study conducted with nine mothers and 16 individuals who had experienced domestic violence during their childhood, Moulding et al. (2015) noted that mother-blame and self-blame were common themes in the participants' accounts.

These authors showed that mother-blame was rooted in contemporary discourses on mother-hood, and linked in a cyclic way with both domestic violence and maternal protectiveness:

> When women act protectively by remaining silent or taking the blame, they risk incurring mother-blame from children. More broadly, taking the blame in order to protect could also exacerbate the already unequal power relations between women and their violent partners, inadvertently providing men with self-justifications for blame and violence, and ongoing risks for women and children. Thus, the web of mother-blame that characterizes domestic violence more generally, together with more specific blame for 'failure to protect', could work to further entangle women and children in violence, undermining their choices, safety and mother-child relationships.
>
> (p. 257)

Findings from another Australian study, which was conducted with 14 women and two men who had experienced domestic violence during their childhood, revealed complex interactions between children's perceptions of their own needs and their understanding of their mothers' vulnerability (Buchanan et al., 2015). These authors noted a shift in children's views as they developed a deeper insight into the impacts of violence on their mothers and on themselves.

## Strategies to protect and care for their children

Despite the difficulties and challenges that have been presented, research evidence has shown that abused women generally want to be 'good' mothers, and develop a wide range of strategies in order to protect and care for their children (Buchanan et al., 2013; Lapierre, 2010b; Nixon, Bonnycastle, & Ens, 2017; Radford & Hester, 2001, 2006; Wendt, Buchanan, & Moulding, 2015). In the study conducted with 25 women in England, Lapierre (2010b) identified diverse strategies, which included predicting the violent incidents through the monitoring of their partners' moods and behaviours, and preventing such incidents by behaving in ways that would not upset their partners. During the incidents, women can keep children away, or avoid them overhearing the violence from another room or seeing the bruises or injuries caused by the violence. They can also challenge their partners' behaviours and, in some circumstances, use violence towards their partners in order to protect their children. The women who took part in this study had also developed strategies to care for their children's physical, emotional and educational needs. Finally, findings from this study revealed that children's safety and well-being had been important factors in their decisions to both stay with their partners and leave their partners.

Based on findings from a study conducted with nine women in Australia, Wendt et al. (2015) also pointed out that these women's protective strategies had included attempts to 'please' their partners and to preserve their partner's image as a father in the eyes of their children. These authors argued that maternal protectiveness should be understood as a continuum:

> More obvious and overt forms such as preventing physical harm of children were located at one end, with more subtle and convert ways at the other, such as emotional protection through creating routines for children to prevent the escalation of violence.
>
> (p. 537)

Women also need to develop diverse strategies in the post-separation period, particularly when there is ongoing violence (Archer-Kuhn, 2018; Lapierre, 2010b; Zeoli et al., 2013). In this regard, findings from a study that investigated women's responses to abuse perpetrated by their ex-partners, which was conducted with 19 women in the United States, revealed that their strategies had included setting boundaries to limit interactions with their ex-partners (Zeoli et al., 2013). These women had turned to family courts for assistance in setting such boundaries, even though they reported that courts had not responded in ways that had protected their children. Moreover, findings from a study that investigated the role of supported and supervised contact arrangements in the United Kingdom revealed that abused women had agreed to such father-child contact arrangements despite concerns for their children's safety and for their own safety, due to fears that contestations would lead to courts imposing even less safe custody or contact arrangements (Harrison, 2008).

Furthermore, research evidence has shown that children generally see their mothers as their main source of protection and support, and often recognize the multiple strategies that have been developed by their mothers (Buchanan et al., 2015; Lapierre et al., 2018; Mullender et al., 2002; Overlien, 2014). Moreover, recent studies have revealed that these children can act to protect their mothers (Lapierre et al., 2018; Overlien, 2014), and Buchanan et al. (2015) talked about 'mutual protectiveness' involving women and children living with domestic violence. Children's attempts to protect their mothers tend to provide them with feelings of pride and efficacy, which challenges discourses that see these behaviours as inherently damaging for children (Buchanan et al., 2015; Katz, 2016; Lapierre et al., 2018).

## Policies and practices with mothers in the context of domestic violence

Shelter workers have been the first to raise concerns regarding the situation of children living with domestic violence, and to provide accommodation and support to both abused women and their children (Jaffe et al., 1990; Mullender et al., 1998). Over the last few decades, there has been a more general recognition of the negative impacts of children's exposure to domestic violence, but this has led to inconsistent and sometimes contradictory responses, particularly in child protection services and family court proceedings. Hester (2010, 2011) referred to the 'three planets' to illustrate and explain the inconsistencies and contradictions in these different sectors: 'In each of the three "planets" of domestic violence work, child protection, and child contact/visitation, there are distinct "cultural histories" underpinning practices and outcomes' (Hester, 2010, p. 517). These responses have important implications for women's mothering, which are addressed in this section.

### *Invisibility, surveillance and support in the domestic violence sector*

Even though domestic violence shelters have always provided accommodation and support to both women and children, women's complex experiences as mothers have not necessarily been addressed in shelter practices. In a case study that involved a combination of participant observation and interviews with five workers and 12 women in one shelter in Canada, Krane and Davies (2002) argued that women's mothering had been largely invisible and taken for granted due to the dominant perspective that had been adopted in that shelter:

> Feminist intervention in the shelter centered on the emancipation of women from oppressive, violent relations. Although this goal is both understandable and admirable,

failing to shape intervention to respond to women as mothers is to risk failing to end the violence in their lives. This practice begs the question of the place of mothering in rethinking feminist intervention in this arena.

(p. 187)

A few years later, Krane and Davies (2007) conducted another case study, which involved both participant observation and interviews with 11 workers in one domestic violence shelter. The findings suggested that while women's mothering had remained largely invisible, their interactions with their children had become more visible and had been understood through 'a lens of heightened sensitivity to abusive relationships that are marked by the unacceptable use of power and control' (p. 24). The authors argued that this lens was distorted and that practices with women and children require a better understanding of the complexities and challenges of everyday mothering.

In a recent study conducted with 12 women in four domestic violence shelters in the United States, Fauci and Goodman (2019) demonstrated that these women had experienced 'parenting surveillance' through the workers' monitoring, evaluating and controlling practices. The women who took part in this study described the negative impacts of such practices on their mothering, their mother-child relationships and their children's well-being. These authors argued that, even though shelter practices are committed to supporting women's autonomy and empowerment, this surveillance may echo the abusive dynamics from which they are attempting to escape. Moreover, the obligation to report to child protection services has particular implications for women from poor and marginalized communities, where 'the threat of state intrusion into family life casts a long shadow, profoundly affecting individual and community safety, trust in social institutions, the quality of social relationships, and parental control' (Goodman & Fauci, 2020, p. 217).

At the same time, there have been attempts to support women's mothering and mother-child relationships (Anderson & Van Ee, 2018; Austin et al., 2019; Humphreys et al., 2006; Thiara & Humphreys, 2017). Based on a review of 19 programmes, Anderson and Van Ee (2018) concluded that programmes generate more successful recovery when women and children work both separately and jointly across sessions. However, Austin et al. (2019) argued that, given the limitations of the current research base, more research is required in order to identify which programmes or intervention components are the most effective to support women's mothering in the context of domestic violence.

## Child protection services and the 'failing' mothers

Over the last few decades, most Western countries have adopted policies that recognize children's exposure to domestic violence as a form of child abuse or as a threat to children's safety (Nixon et al., 2007; Rivett & Kelly, 2006; Stanley & Humphreys, 2015). Given that responses to children's needs have been primarily seen as women's responsibility (Scourfield, 2003), concerns regarding the situation of children living with domestic violence have been raised alongside concerns regarding their mothers' ability (or inability) to protect and care for them (Douglas & Walsh, 2010; Strega & Janzen, 2013). Based on a review of 13 academic studies that have been conducted in four different countries over several decades, Humphreys and Absler (2011) examined how domestic violence had been addressed in the history of child protection services, and identified 'mother-blaming' as the dominant response in this area. Their work revealed a repeating history where abused women have been seen as 'inadequate' mothers who 'fail to protect' their children, while abusive men have been ignored.

In this context, abused women, and particularly those from poor and marginalized communities, tend to fear child protection services, and to experience their interventions as punitive (Goodman & Fauci, 2020; Hughes, Chau, & Poff, 2011; Johnson & Sullivan, 2008; Lapierre, 2010c). In a study conducted with 64 women in Canada, only a few respondents mentioned that child protection services had been helpful to them (Hughes et al., 2011). Most respondents reported that they had been provided with little or no concrete assistance, and that they had been required to attend programmes that had not adequately addressed their situation. In the same sense, findings from a study conducted with 20 women in the United States showed that, while some respondents had found child protection interventions helpful, most women had felt misunderstood and unsupported by their child protection workers (Johnson & Sullivan, 2008). Some respondents even stated that child protection interventions had harmed them and their children. Moreover, research evidence has demonstrated that immigrant women face additional risks in such circumstances, given that child protection workers may not understand the cultural issues associated with domestic violence and the implications related to their immigration status (Earner, 2010).

Similar findings have emerged in studies conducted with shelter workers, who have reported tenuous collaborations with child protection services (Douglas & Walsh, 2010; Mills et al., 2000). Based on a study that involved five focus groups with domestic violence workers in Australia, Douglas and Walsh (2010) reported that child protection workers tended to misunderstand domestic violence, which had led to inappropriate responses and negative outcomes for both women and children. According to these authors, 'child protection workers appeared, first, to construct women as the one with the responsibility to care for children, and then to blame women for the domestic violence in the home and the consequent failure to protect their children' (p. 493). Many workers who took part in this study also talked about the 'ultimatum' that had been given to abused women, who had to either leave their violent partners or have their children removed from their care.

Practices that frame these situations in terms of women's 'failure to protect' are grounded in the assertion that women have a duty to protect their children from avoidable harm, and that those who fail to fulfil this duty are thus liable for the resulting harm to their children (Nixon et al., 2017; Strega et al., 2013). Such practices inevitably blame women for their partners' violence and shift the focus away from men's violence, allowing perpetrators to avoid accountability for their behaviours (Archer-Kuhn & Villiers, 2019; Featherstone & Peckover, 2007; Strega et al., 2008). In this regard, Stewart (2020) rightly pointed out that 'it is pertinent to remember that these mothers were being assessed due to someone else's violence and behaviour; that they were being held accountable for something and someone they cannot, and should not be expected to, control' (p. 18).

Overall, these research findings suggest that child protection workers cannot protect and support women and children living with domestic violence unless they adequately address the ongoing dynamics of power and control, the trauma of past abuse, as well as the difficulties and challenges involved in mothering under such circumstances (Bourassa et al., 2008; Hughes et al., 2011; Humphreys, 2010; Johnson & Sullivan, 2008; Stanley & Humphreys, 2015). Recent initiatives have provided promising frameworks for child protection practices in domestic violence cases, focusing on the perpetrators' patterns of behaviours and promoting partnerships with abused women in order to achieve children's safety and well-being (Humphreys et al., 2018; Mandel et al., 2017).

## Family court proceedings and the 'hostile' or 'alienating' mothers

Despite the fact that the violence and its impacts often continue during the post-separation period, research evidence shows that domestic violence is not necessarily identified and taken into account in decisions regarding custody and contact arrangements (Harrison, 2008; Jaffe et al., 2003; Jeffries, 2016; Macdonald, 2016; Silberg & Dallam, 2019). This happens in a context where the priority is to maintain children's contact with both parents (Harrison, 2008; Macdonald, 2016), and where domestic violence is often misunderstood, minimized and framed in terms of 'high conflict' (Archer-Kuhn, 2018; Harrison, 2006; Jaffe et al., 2003). In this regard, findings from a study conducted with five women in Canada showed that 'violence and control can be masked as poor communication and conflict when people experiencing high conflict and those experiencing physical violence are combined in the analysis' (Archer-Kuhn, 2018, p. 224). As a result, men tend to be seen as 'good enough' fathers despite their violent behaviours (Eriksson & Hester, 2001; Harrison, 2008; Macdonald, 2016).

In a recent study conducted in the United States, which involved an analysis of 27 court cases, Silberg and Dallam (2019) reported that the judges had initially been highly suspicious of women's and children's allegations of abuse by fathers. As a result, 59% of perpetrators had been given sole custody of their children, and the rest had been given joint custody or unsupervised contact arrangements. In a study conducted in the United Kingdom, which involved an analysis of 70 custody evaluation reports, Macdonald (2016) reported that father-child contact had been considered desirable and inevitable in the vast majority of these cases, despite evidence of violence and concerns for the children's safety and well-being. The author pointed out that this had also been the case when the children had expressed fears regarding contact with their fathers. Based on these findings, Macdonald (2016) argued that,

> Despite policy developments, practice directives, and improved professional knowledge, in practice the presumption of contact continues to usurp this knowledge in all but exceptional cases. Therefore, although some progress related to recognition and understanding of domestic violence has undoubtedly been made, the unrelenting influence of deeply embedded ideologies regarding relationships with fathers continues to have the effect of marginalizing issues of safeguarding in the majority of cases.
>
> (p. 847)

In this regard, it should be noted that shared parenting arrangements create significant challenges for women who have experienced domestic violence, even though they generally wish for their children to have a meaningful relationship with both parents (Archer-Kuhn, 2018; Lapierre, 2010a; Radford & Hester, 2006). In their study conducted in the United States, Zeoli et al. (2013) explained that women who had turned to family courts for assistance in setting boundaries with their ex-partners reported that courts had not responded in ways that had protected their children. In the same sense, findings from a study of supported and supervised child contact centres in the United Kingdom, showed that accessing such resources had not significantly reduced the levels of post-separation violence and harassment (Harrison, 2008). Some women even described how violence had been perpetrated during contact sessions within the centres.

In a context where allegations of abuse have been treated with suspicions, and where the priority has been to maintain children's contact with both parents, women who express concerns or oppose father-child contact arrangements are likely to be seen as 'hostile' mothers (Harrison, 2006). Moreover, recent studies have revealed that, in such circumstances, women can be seen as 'alienating' mothers (Barnett, 2020; Lapierre et al., 2020; Neilson, 2018; Rathus, 2020). Children's refusal to see their fathers is also likely to be interpreted as a consequence of their mothers' alienating behaviours. Even though these women may have well-grounded reasons to express concerns or even oppose father-child contact arrangements, accusations of 'parental alienation' can result in women losing custody of their children. In this regard, Sheehy and Boyd (2020) argued that,

> A mother who has experienced IPV may be terrified and re-traumatized at the prospect of having to cooperate with a violent father in relation to child rearing. Yet a powerful ideological expectation prevails – reinforced by legislation, lawyers, mediators, social workers and judges – that mothers should suppress their rational fears in relation to their children and ensure their relationship with fathers, no matter the quality of the relationship.
>
> (p. 89)

In recent years, initiatives have been developed in order to improve family courts' responses in cases with a history of domestic violence, including specialized and integrated domestic violence courts (Birnbaum, Sinai, Bala 2017; Koshan, 2018). These initiatives have the potential to improve practices and ensure a more coordinated responses to families living with domestic violence.

## Directions for future research

While several studies explore women's diverse experiences as mothers in the context of domestic violence, there is a need to address more fully the experiences of women from marginalized and poor communities, as well as the intersections between gender, ethnicity, social class and (dis)ability. Future research should also account for women's complex experiences, including issues such as mental health problems, substance misuse and homelessness. Moreover, more attention needs to be given to children's experiences and perspectives. Furthermore, large-scale quantitative studies could provide additional data on the challenges that women and children face in such circumstances, and on the strategies that mothers put in place in order to protect and care for their children.

Future research should also investigate policies and practices in shelters, child protection services and family courts. Researchers should continue to document persistent problems in policies and practices, and their impacts on women's mothering and mother-child relationships. They should also be able to identify new trends at local, national and international levels. Finally, evaluative studies ought to be conducted in order to identify the most effective policies, programmes and practices to support women's mothering and mother-child relationships in the context of domestic violence.

## Conclusion

This chapter has focused on mothering and domestic violence, accounting for women's complex experiences as mothers in this context. It has been argued that these experiences need to be understood in relation to both the particular conditions created by men's violence and the patriarchal institution of motherhood, which constrains, regulates and dominates women and their mothering. In fact, as Heward-Belle (2017) rightly pointed out,

> Assaulting women as mothers and their mothering is effective because of the hegemonic construction of the good mother and the institutional practices that result from this construction. Such practices produce and reproduce normative benchmarks against which women are unfairly judged and serve as fertile ground for domestically violent men to exploit.
>
> (p. 385)

While addressing women's mothering and mother-child relationships is important to improve women's and children's safety and well-being, it should not shift the focus away from men's violence and control over women and children.

## Critical findings

- Abused women's experiences as mothers need to be understood in relation to both the particular conditions created by men's violence and the patriarchal institution of motherhood, which constrains, regulates and dominates women and their mothering.
- Domestic violence ought to be considered as an attack on women's mothering and mother-child relationships, as perpetrators use strategies that specifically target their partners' mothering and relationships with their children.
- While abused women face several difficulties and challenges, they also develop multiple strategies in order to protect and care for their children.
- Mother-blame and self-blame emerge as important themes in women's experiences as mothers in the context of domestic violence.
- The recognition of the negative impacts of children's exposure to domestic violence in research, policies and practices has led to inconsistent and sometimes contradictory responses, particularly in child protection services and family court proceedings. In these contexts, abused women are likely to be seen either as 'failing to protect' their children or as 'hostile' or 'alienating' mothers.

## Key implications for policy, practice and research

- Professionals in domestic violence shelters, child protection services and family courts need to better understand women's complex experiences as mothers in the context of domestic violence.
- Professionals need to take into account both the difficulties and challenges they face in such circumstances and the multiple strategies they develop in order to protect and care for their children.
- Policies and practices should support women's mothering and mother-child relationships, taking into account women's social locations and access to resources.
- While addressing women's mothering and mother-child relationships is important to improve women's and children's safety and well-being, it should not shift the focus away from men's violence and control over women and children.
- Policies and practices should address the inconsistencies and contradictions that abused women face when going through child protection and family court proceedings.

# References

Abrahams, H. (2007). *Supporting women after domestic violence: Loss, trauma and recovery*. London: Jessica Kingsley.

Anderson, K., & Van Ee, E. (2018). Mothers and children exposed to intimate partner violence: A review of treatment interventions. *International Journal of Environmental Research and Public Health, 15*, 1–25.

Archer-Kuhn, B. (2018). Domestic violence and high conflict are not the same: A gendered analysis. *Journal of Social Welfare and Family Law, 40*(2), 216–233.

Archer-Kuhn, B., & Villiers, S. (2019). Gendered practices in child protection: Shifting mother accountability and father invisibility in situations of domestic violence. *Social Inclusion, 7*(1), 228–237.

Austin, M. E., Shanahan, M. E., Barrios, Y. V., & Macy, R. J. (2019). A systematic review of interventions for women parenting in the context of intimate partner violence. *Trauma, Violence & Abuse, 20*(4), 498–519.

Barnett, A. (2020). A genealogy of hostility: Parental alienation in England and wales. *Journal of Social Welfare and Family Law, 42*(1), 18–29.

Barrios, V. R., Khaw, L. B. L., Bermea, A., & Hardesty, J. L. (2020). Future directions in intimate partner violence research: An intersectionality framework for analyzing women's processes of leaving abusive relationships. *Journal of Interpersonal Violence*, 1–26.

Bailey, B. A. (2010). Partner violence during pregnancy: Prevalence, effects, screening, and management. *International Journal of Women's Health, 2*, 183–198.

Bancroft, L., Silverman, J. G., & Ritchie, D. (2012). *The batterer as parent: Addressing the impact of domestic violence on family dynamics*. Thousand Oaks, CA: Sage.

Basile, K. C., Smith, S. G., Liu, Y., Kresnow, M. J., Fasula, A. M., Gilbert, L., & Chen, J. (2018). Rape-related pregnancy and association with reproductive coercion in the US. *American Journal of Preventive Medicine, 55*(6), 770–776.

Birnbaum, R., Sinai, M., & Bala, N. (2017). Canada's first integrated domestic violence court: Examining family and criminal court outcomes at the Toronto I.D.V.C. *Journal of Family Violence, 32*, 621–631.

Bourassa, C., Lavergne, C., Damant, D., Lessard, G., & Turcotte, P. (2008). Child welfare workers' practice in cases involving domestic violence. *Child Abuse Review, 17*, 174–190.

Brownridge, D., Chan, K. L., Hiebert-Murphy, D., Ristock, J., Tiwari, A., Leung, W. C., & Santos, S. C. (2008). The elevated risk for non-lethal post-separation violence in Canada: A comparison of separated, divorced, and married women. *Journal of Interpersonal Violence, 23*(1), 117–135.

Buchanan, F., Power, C., & Verity, F. (2013). Domestic violence and the place of fear in mother/baby relationships: 'What was I afraid of? Of making it worse'. *Journal of Interpersonal Violence, 28*(9), 1817–1838.

Buchanan, F., Wendt, S., & Moulding, N. (2015). Growing up in domestic violence: What does maternal protectiveness mean? *Qualitative Social Work, 14*(3), 399–415.

Campbell, J. C., Pugh, L. C., Campbell, D., & Visscher, M. (1995). The influence of abuse on pregnancy intention. *Women's Health Issues, 5*, 214–223.

Coggins, M., & Bullock, L. F. C. (2003). The wavering line in the sand: The effects of domestic violence and sexual coercion. *Issues in Mental Health Nursing, 24*, 6–7.

Côté, I., & Lapierre, S. (2014). Abortion and domestic violence: Women's decision-making process. *Affilia: Journal of Women and Social Work, 23*(9), 285–297.

Coy, M. C., Scott, E., Tweedale, R., & Perks, K. (2015). 'It's like going through the abuse again': Domestic violence and women and children's (un)safety in private law contact proceedings. *Journal of Social Welfare and Family Law, 37*(1), 53–69.

Douglas, H., & Walsh, T. (2010). Mothers, domestic violence, and child protection. *Violence Against Women, 16*(5), 489–508.

Earner, I. (2010). Double risk: Immigrant mothers, domestic violence and public child welfare services in New York City. *Evaluation and Program Planning, 33*, 288–293.

Elizabeth, V. (2017). Custody stalking: A mechanism of coercively controlling mothers following separation. *Family Legal Studies, 25*, 185–201.

Eriksson, M., & Hester, M. (2001). Violent men as good enough fathers? A look at England and Sweden. *Violence against Women, 7*(7), 779–798.

Fauci, J. E., & Goodman, L. A. (2019). "You don't need nobody else knocking you down": Survivor-mothers' experiences of surveillance in domestic violence shelters. *Journal of Family Violence*. Published online.

Featherstone, B., & Peckover, S. (2007). Letting them get away with it: Fathers, domestic violence and child welfare. *Critical Social Policy, 27*(2), 181–202.

Goodman, L. A., & Fauci, J. E. (2020). The long shadow of family separation: A structural and historical introduction to mandated reporting in the domestic violence context. *Journal of Family Violence, 35*, 217–223.

Greeson, M. R., Kennedy, A. C., Bybee, D. I., Beeble, M., Adams, A. E., & Sullivan, C. (2014). Beyond deficits: Intimate partner violence, maternal parenting, and child behavior over time. *American Journal of Community Psychology, 54*(1–2), 46–58.

Harrison, C. (2006). Damned if you do and damned if you don't? The contradictions between private and public law. In C. Humphreys & N. Stanley (Eds.), *Domestic violence and child protection: Directions for good practice* (pp. 137–154). London: Jessica Kingsley.

Harrison, C. (2008). Implacably hostile or appropriately protective? Women managing child contact in the context of domestic violence. *Violence against Women, 14*(4), 381–405.

Hester, M. (2010). Commentary on 'Mothers, domestic violence, and child protection' by heather Douglas and tamara Walsh. *Violence Against Women, 16*(5), 516–523.

Hester, M. (2011). The three planet model: Towards an understanding of contradictions in approaches to women and children's safety in contexts of domestic violence. *British Journal of Social Work, 41*, 837–853.

Heward-Belle, S. (2017). Exploiting the 'good mother' as a tactic of coercive control: Domestically violent men's assaults on women as mothers. *Affilia: Journal of Women and Social Work, 32*(3), 374–389.

Holt, S. (2011). Domestic abuse and child contact: Positioning children in the decision-making process, *Child Care in Practice, 17*(4), 327–346.

Hughes, J., Chau, S., & Poff, D. C. (2011). "They're not my favourite people": What mothers who have experienced intimate partner violence say about involvement in the child protection system. *Children & Youth Services Review, 33*, 1084–1089.

Humphreys, C. (2010). Crossing the great divide: Response to Douglas and Walsh. *Violence Against Women, 16*(5), 509–515.

Humphreys, C., & Absler, D. (2011). History repeating: Child protection responses to domestic violence. *Child and Family Social Work, 16*, 464–473.

Humphreys, C., Healey, L., & Mandel, D. (2018). Case reading as a practice and training intervention in domestic violence and child protection. *Australian Social Work, 71*(3), 277–291.

Humphreys, C., Mullender, A., Thiara, R., & Skamballis, A. (2006). 'Talking to my mum': Developing communication between mothers and children in the aftermath of domestic violence. *Journal of Social Work, 6*(1), 53–63.

Humphreys, C., & Thiara, R. K. (2003). Neither justice nor protection: Women's experiences of post-separation violence. *Journal of Social Welfare and Family Law, 25*(3), 195–214.

Izaguirre, A., & Calvete, E. (2014). Intimate partner violence during pregnancy: Women's narratives about their mothering experiences. *Psychosocial Intervention, 23*, 209–215.

Jaffe, P. G., Lemon, N., & Poisson, S. (2003). *Child custody and domestic violence: A call for safety and accountability*. Thousand Oaks, CA: Sage.

Jaffe, P. G., Wolfe, D. A., & Wilson, S. K. (1990). *Children of battered women*. London: Sage.

Jeffries, S. (2016). In the best interests of the abuser: Coercive control, child custody proceedings and the 'expert' assessments that guide judicial determinations, *Laws, 5*(14). Published online.

Johnson, S. P., & Sullivan, C. M. (2008). How child protection workers support or further victimize battered mothers. *Affilia: Journal of Women and Social Work, 23*(3), 242–258.

Katz, E. (2016). Beyond the physical incident model: How children living with domestic violence are harmed by and resist regimes of coercive control. *Child Abuse Review, 25*, 46–59.

Katz, E. (2019). Coercive control, domestic violence, and a five-factor framework: Five factors that influence closeness, distance, and strain in mother-child relationships. *Violence Against Women, 25*(15), 1829–1853.

Kelly, L. (1994). The interconnectedness of domestic violence and child abuse: Challenges for research, policy and practice. In A. Mullender & R. Morley (Eds.), *Children living with domestic violence* (pp. 43–56). London: Whiting and Birch.

Koshan, J. (2018). Specialised domestic violence courts in Canada and the United States: Key factors in prioritising safety for women and children. *Journal of Social Welfare and Family Law, 40*(4), 512–532.

Krane, J., & Davies, L. (2002). Sisterhood is not enough: The invisibility of mothering in shelter practice with battered women. *Affilia: Journal of Women and Social Work, 17*(2), 167–190.

Krane, J., & Davies, L. (2007). Mothering under difficult circumstances: Challenges to working with battered women. *Affilia: Journal of Women and Social Work, 22*, 23–38.

Lapierre, S. (2008). Mothering in the context of domestic violence: The pervasiveness of a deficit model of mothering. *Child & Family Social Work, 13*(4), 454–463.

Lapierre, S. (2010a). More responsibilities, less control: Understanding the challenges and difficulties involved in mothering in the context of domestic violence. *The British Journal of Social Work, 40*(5), 1434–1451.

Lapierre, S. (2010b). Striving to be 'good' mothers: Abused women's experiences of mothering. *Child Abuse Review, 19*, 342–357.

Lapierre, S. (2010c). Are abused women 'neglectful' mothers? A critical reflection based on women's experiences. In B. Featherstone, C. A. Hooper, J. Scourfield, & J. Taylor (Eds.), *Gender and child welfare in society* (pp. 121–148). London: John Wiley & Sons.

Lapierre, S., Côté, I., Lambert, A., Buetti, D., Lavergne, C., Damant, D., & Couturier, V. (2018). Difficult but close relationships: Children's perspectives on relationships with their mothers in the context of domestic violence. *Violence Against Women, 24*(9), 1023–1038.

Lapierre, S., Ladouceur, P., Frenette, M., & Côté, I. (2020). The legitimization and institutionalization of 'parental alienation' in the province of Quebec. *Journal of Social Welfare and Family Law, 42*(1), 30–44.

Lehmann, P., Simmons, C. A., & Pillai, V. K. (2012). The validation of the checklist of controlling behaviors (CCB): Assessing coercive control in abusive relationships. *Violence Against Women, 18*(8), 913–933.

Levendosky, A. A., Huth-Bocks, A. C., Shapiro, D. L., & Semel, M. A. (2003). The impact of domestic violence on the maternal-child relationship and preschool-age children's functioning. *Journal of Family Psychology, 17*(3), 275–287.

Lippy, C., Jumarali, S. N., Nnawulezi, N. A., Williams, E. P., & Burk, C. (2020). The impact of mandatory reporting laws on survivors of intimate partner violence: Intersectionality, help-seeking and the need for change. *Journal of Family Violence, 35*, 255–267.

Macdonald, G. S. (2016). Domestic violence and private family court proceedings: Promoting child welfare or promoting contact? *Violence against Women, 22*(7), 832–852.

Mandel, D., Humphreys, C., & Healey, L. (2017). *The PATRICIA project: Summary of the safe and together case reading*. Sydney: ANROWS.

Mbilinyi, L. F., Edleson, J. L., Hagemeister, A. K., & Beeman, S. K. (2007). What happens to children when their mothers are battered? Results from a four city anonymous telephone survey. *Journal of Family Violence, 22*, 309–317.

Mills, L. G., Friend, C., Conroy, K., Fleck-Henderson, A., Krug, S., Magen, R., & Thomas, R. (2000). Child protection and domestic violence: Training, practice, and policy issues, *Children and Youth Services Review, 22*(5), 315–332.

Morris, A. (2009). Gendered dynamics of abuse and violence in families: Considering the abusive household gender regime. *Child Abuse Review, 18*(6), 414–427.

Moulding, N. T., Buchanan, F., & Wendt, S. (2015). Untangling self-blame and mother-blame in women's and children's perspectives on maternal protectiveness in domestic violence: Implications for practice. *Child Abuse Review, 24*, 249–260.

Mullender, A., Debbonaire, T., Hague, G., Kelly, L., & Malos, E. (1998). Working with children in women's refuges. *Child and Family Social Work, 3*, 87–98.

Mullender, A., Hague, G., Imam, U. F., Kelly, L., Malos, E., & Regan, L. (2002). *Children's perspectives on domestic violence*. London: Sage.

Neilson, L. C. (2018). *Parental alienation empirical analysis: Child best interests or parental rights?* Fredericton: Muriel McQueen Fergusson Centre for Family Violence Research.

Nixon, K. L., Bonnycastle, C., & Ens, S. (2017). Challenging the notion of failure to protect: Exploring the protective strategies of abused mothers living in urban and remote communities and implications for practice. *Child Abuse Review, 26*, 63–74.

Nixon, K. L., Tutty, L. M., Weaver-Dunlop, G., & Walsh, C. A. (2007). Do good intentions beget good policy? A review of child protection policies to address intimate partner violence. *Children and Youth Services Review, 29*, 1469–1486.

Overlien, C. (2014). 'He didn't mean to hit mom, I think': Positioning, agency and point in adolescents' narratives about domestic violence. *Child and Family Social Work, 19*, 156–164.

Radford, L., & Hester, M. (2001). Overcoming mother blaming? Future directions for research on mothering and domestic violence. In S. A. Graham-Bermann & J. L. Edleson (Eds.), *Domestic violence in the lives of children: The future of research, intervention, and social policy* (pp. 135–155). Washington, DC: American Psychological Association.

Radford, L., & Hester, M. (2006). *Mothering through domestic violence.* London: Jessica Kingsley.

Rathus, Z. (2020). A history of the use of the concept of parental alienation in the Australian family law system: Contradictions, collisions and their consequences. *Journal of Social Welfare and Family Law, 42*(1), 5–17.

Rich, A. (1976). *Of woman born: Motherhood as experience and institution.* London: Virago Press.

Rivett, M., & Kelly, S. (2006). 'From awareness to practice': Children, domestic violence[†] and child welfare. *Child Abuse Review, 15*, 224–242.

Saunders, D. G., & Oglesby, K. H. (2016). No way to turn: Traps encountered by many battered women with negative child custody experiences. *Journal of Child Custody, 13*(2–3), 154–177.

Scourfield, J. (2003). *Gender and child protection.* London: Palgrave Macmillan.

Sheehy, E., & Boyd, S. B. (2020). Penalizing women's fear: Intimate partner violence and parental alienation in Canadian child custody cases. *Journal of Social Welfare and Family Law, 42*(1), 80–91.

Silberg, J., & Dallam, S. (2019). Abusers gaining custody in family courts: A case series of over turned decisions. *Journal of Child Custody, 16*(2), 140–169.

Stanley, N., Chantler, K., & Robbins, R. (2019). Children and domestic homicides. *British Journal of Social Work, 49*(1), 59–76.

Stanley, N., & Humphreys, C. (2015). Domestic violence and protecting children: The new landscape. In N. Stanley & C. Humphreys (Eds.), *Domestic violence and protecting children: New thinking and approaches* (pp. 13–16). London: Jessica Kingsley.

Stark, E. (2007). *Coercive control: The entrapment of women in personal life.* New York, NY: Oxford University Press.

Strega, S., Fleet, C., Brown, L., Dominelli, L., Callahan, M., & Walmsley, C. (2008). Connecting father absence and mother blame in child welfare policies and practice. *Children and Youth Services Review, 30*(5), 705–716.

Strega, S., & Janzen, C. (2013). Asking the impossible of mothers: Child protection systems and intimate partner violence. In S. Strega, J. Krane, S. Lapierre, C. Richardson, & R. Carlton (Eds.), *Failure to protect: Moving beyond gendered responses* (pp. 49–76). Winnipeg: Fernwood Publishing.

Stewart, S. (2020). A mother's love knows no bounds: Exploring 'good mother' expectations for mothers involved with children's services due to their partner violence. *Qualitative Social Work.* Published online.

Thiara, R. K., & Humphreys, C. (2017). Absent presence: The ongoing impact of men's violence on the mother-child relationship. *Child and Family Social Work, 22*, 137–145.

Wendt, S., Buchanan, F., & Moulding, N. (2015). Mothering and domestic violence: Situating maternal protectiveness in gender. *Affilia: Journal of Women and Social Work, 30*(4), 533–545.

Zeoli, A. M., Rivera, E. A., Sullivan, C. M., & Kubiak, S. (2013). Post-separation abuse of women and their children: Boundary-setting and family court utilization among victimized mothers. *Journal of Family Violence, 28*, 547–560.

# 31

# FATHERING IN THE CONTEXT OF DOMESTIC VIOLENCE AND ABUSE

*Katreena Scott*

## Introduction

Efforts to understand and address the serious harm to children exposed to domestic violence (DV) have been oddly silent on the topic of fathers (Kimball, 2016; Murray & Powell, 2009). Within women's shelter and advocacy services, the effects of DV on children are recognized; however, most work is focused on meeting women's immediate needs for safety, services, and empowerment; children's relationships with their fathers tend to be considered only as a safety concern (Hester, 2011). Children and family mental health services, when they recognize and address DV, tend to do so through the lens of addressing child trauma and strengthening mother-child relationships (MacMillan et al., 2009). Child protective services (CPS) also work primarily with mothers and children, focusing more on mothers' protection of their children from DV than on any actions fathers may (or may not) be taking to end abusive behaviour (Bourassa, Lavergne, Damant, Lessard, & Turcotte, 2008; Hughes & Chau, 2013; Jenney, Mishna, Alaggia, & Scott, 2014; Lapierre & Côté, 2016). Men appearing in criminal court on charges related to DV may be ordered to attend a perpetrator-focused intervention program that includes one or two sessions on the effects of DV on children; however, the primary focus of these programmes is men's behaviour in intimate relationships, not their role as a parent. Thus, across this landscape of typical services, the importance of fathers' relationships with their children has often fallen through the gaps, rendering domestically violent fathers' role with, and influence on, their children largely invisible (Heward-Belle, Humphreys, Healey, Toivonen, & Tsantefski, 2019; Scott & Crooks, 2004).

Fortunately, in recent years the role of fathering in the context of DV has been increasingly recognized in child protection services and family courts. Interventions have been developed to address fathering in the context of DV. Slowly, the broader links between gender-based violence and maltreatment of children are being recognized (Guedes, Bott, Garcia-Moreno, & Colombini, 2016). This chapter explores this developing research and service landscape.

## How big a problem is fathering in the context of domestic violence?

There is overwhelming evidence that child exposure to DV is harmful and that children who experience multiple or chronic forms of adversity are likely to show the most compromised social, emotional, psychological, and physical outcomes (Felitti et al., 2019; Finkelhor, Shattuck, Turner, Ormrod, & Hamby, 2011; Ford, Elhai, Connor, & Frueh, 2010). There are many studies exploring mechanisms by which early adversity may translate into later dysfunction and on factors that protect against harms, such as the quality of the mother-child relationship. Surprisingly, studies of child victimization have only recently included a focus on *who has caused* this harm as part of conceptualization and analyses. Even when data on perpetrators of harm against children is collected, it is often aggregated in such a way that makes delineating which parent perpetrated the harm impossible. For example, results from a recent national survey of child victimization in the UK reports results by four categories of perpetrators: parents/caregivers, siblings, peers, and youth dating partners, with no differentiation of mothers, fathers, and other caregivers within the parent category (Radford, Corral, Bradley, & Fisher, 2013). Similarly, in most national incidence reports on investigated child abuse and neglect, perpetrators of harm are categorized into parents and non-parents or into all males and all females, which in both cases obscures the relative importance of mothers and fathers (US Department of Health & Human Services, 2019).

When data on perpetration of harm against children can be disaggregated, it becomes clear that fathers are perpetrators in a majority of cases of children's exposure to DV as well as in at least half of cases of child physical abuse. One of the most comprehensive analyses of child victimization, that National Survey of Children's Exposure to Violence in the US, showed that in 78% of incidents of child exposure to DV, males were identified as perpetrators, with fathers making up the clear majority, followed by non-cohabiting boyfriends of mothers (Finkelhor et al., 2011). Rates of reported exposure to DV dually perpetrated by both mothers and fathers were low (8.6%). More severe forms of DV exposure (e.g., exposure to a parent being kicked, choked, or beaten) had even higher proportions of male (88%) versus female (12%) perpetrators. This general pattern of results is echoed in disaggregated child protection data and police data (Lee, Bellamy, & Guterman, 2009).

Addressing fathering in the context of DV also has the potential to counteract an overreliance on "separation as solution" practice, which is based in the assumption that once men's DV is adequately recognized, "good" mothers will protect their children by leaving their abusive partners thereby preventing further exposure of their children to DV. There are major flaws to such approaches (Jenney et al., 2014; Thiara & Humphreys, 2017). Although cessation of contact between fathers and children is an important goal in some cases, a majority of children and mothers will continue to have contact with fathers. For many complex reasons including the desire of couples to stay together, practical and financial challenges of single parenting, limited and/or ineffective consideration of DV in family court, mothers' concerns about their children's safety, and children's wish to maintain a connection with their fathers, many children will continue to have contact with their fathers following exposure to DV (Forssell & Cater, 2015; Humphreys et al., 2019). Relying on, monitoring, and pressuring mothers to be "protective" of their children's exposure to DV by preventing father-child contact is unfair and unrealistic (Brown, Tyson, & Arias, 2014; Kopels & Sheridan, 2002). The separation as solution model also fails to engage men in addressing the harms associated with their exposure of children to DV or in developing healthier father-child relationships (Scott & Crooks, 2004).

## Discussion and analysis

Once we recognize the importance of considering the father-child relationship in men who have been domestically violent, what do we do next? Part of the response to this question requires consideration of aspects of men's parenting that are likely to be compromised (Bancroft,

Silverman, & Ritchie, 2011). Research in this area was recently summarized by Scott, Thompson-Walsh, and Nsiri (2018) who identified a number of aspects of men's fathering that are particularly important to child outcomes.

## What do we know about the parenting of men who perpetrate domestic violence?

### *Domestic violence perpetration* as parenting

First, it is important to understand and conceptualize father's perpetration of DV *as parenting*. Historically, and to some extent today, thinking about children's exposure to DV starts and ends with the incident of violence. For example, one might ask if the child had direct (i.e., saw or heard) or indirect (e.g., was told about) exposure and about whether children experienced the event as a potential trauma (i.e., did impact include worry about the safety of self or caregiver?). Following this line of thinking, protecting children against harm focuses on shielding them from the "adult issue" of DV. Scholars, commentators, and practitioners have been clear that, although attention to DV incidents is important, for children living in families where fathers abuse mothers, exposure to DV is more accurately described as a condition relevant to all aspects of children's lives (Cunningham & Baker, 2007). This is, in part, because DV often occurs in the context of coercive control – a pattern of acts of assault, threats, humiliation, and other abuses that instil fear and control of an intimate partner (Stark, 2007). Children are thus not only exposed to specific acts of verbal, emotional, or physical abuse, but also often live in a home in which their fathers coercively control their mothers (Callaghan, Alexander, Sixsmith, & Fellin, 2018). Worsening this situation, mothering is often a focus of men's abusive and coercively controlling behaviour. Fathers may disparage mothers' parenting, blame her for difficult child behaviour, and try to control the amount of time and attention she gives to him as compared to their children (Hardesty, Khaw, Chung, & Martin, 2008; Holt, 2015; Lapierre, 2010; Morrison, 2015). Fathers may also create strain in the mother–child relationship by deliberately undermining mothers, corrupting children's views of their mothers, and creating and reinforcing narratives of mother-blaming (Katz, 2019; Moulding, Buchanan, & Wendt, 2015).

In situations where women's parenting and responses to children are part of fathers' abuse and coercive control, children cannot help but feel involved and often responsible for problems. Children rely on their parents to support them when they feel worried or scared and cannot separate their relationships with their parents from abuse experiences. How does one seek support from a mother who is herself dealing with victimization? Or from a father who has caused this harm? Minimization or denial of abuse can further compound harms by leading children to question the validity of their distress, fear, and anger or learn to attribute these reactions to a flaw in themselves rather than as a reasonable reaction to their situation (Cicchetti & Rogosch, 1994). In these ways, the impact of child exposure to DV goes well beyond the fear and helplessness that children may feel in response to DV "incidents" and become an integral part of children's experience of their parents. As described by Mandal (n.d.) as part of the Safe and Together model, fathers' perpetration of DV is a *parenting* choice (https://safeandtogetherinstitute.com/about-us/founders-statement/).

### *Men's co-parenting*

Beyond ongoing DV and associated patterns of coercive control, men's co-parenting is also emerging as a critical predictor of outcomes for children. Co-parenting is defined as the extent to which parents are invested in caregiving, are able to communicate with each other about parenting, and value and respect the other parent (Feinberg, 2003; McHale, Waller, & Pearson, 2012). Meta-analytic work in general population samples has found a consistent relationship between co-parenting and child internalizing, externalizing, and social difficulties, with greater effects in separated as opposed to intact families (Teubert & Pinquart, 2010). Some of the effects of co-parenting dysfunction are indirect, through parenting. In particular, there is evidence that for fathers especially, co-parenting conflict is associated with declines in emotional availability, sensitivity and with increased paternal psychological control (Davies, Sturge-Apple, Woitach, & Cummings, 2009; Sturge-Apple, Davies, & Cummings, 2006). Moreover, there is a growing body of literature suggesting that co-parenting is an important area of change for fathers with a history of perpetrating DV (Hardesty, Crossman, Khaw, & Raffaelli, 2016; Scott et al., 2018; Stover, Easton, & McMahon, 2013). For example, in an examination of predictors of child outcomes of 123 fathers with confirmed histories of DV perpetration and 101 fathers without such histories, Thompson-Walsh, Scott, Lishak, and Dyson (submitted) found that fathers' co-parenting difficulties significantly mediated the relationship between exposure to DV and child internalizing problems.

## *Rejection, hostility, over-reactivity and co-occurring physical abuse*

There is also evidence for increased risk of a number of parenting problems in men who perpetrate DV. Some of these difficulties may reflect an extension of men's coercive controlling behaviour to their children. Children interviewed about their thoughts and feelings about their domestically violent fathers often describe them as over-reactive and frequently rejecting (Holt, 2015; Øverlien, 2013, 2014). Consistent with these descriptions, meta-analytic work has confirmed that men who have been violent in their intimate relationships have higher levels of general anger and hostility on self-report and observational measures than men who have not (Birkley & Eckhardt, 2015; Norlander & Eckhardt, 2005), with many studies confirming that such traits translate to greater over-reactivity and more rejection in parenting (Francis & Wolfe, 2008; Scott & Lishak, 2012; Stover & Kiselica, 2015). High rates of anger and hostility are also likely contributors to the co-occurrence between perpetration of DV and child physical abuse (Herrenkohl, Sousa, Tajima, Herrenkohl, & Moylan, 2008; Stith et al., 2009). Although estimated co-occurrence varies, child physical abuse appears to be present in at least one-third to one half of families in which men are domestically violent (Appel & Holden, 1998; Hamby, Finkelhor, Turner, & Ormrod, 2010; Tajima, 2000).

## *Lack of emotional responsivity and positive involvement*

Emotional responsivity and positive involvement of domestically violent fathers with their children is another area of parenting that has been the focus of research (Bancroft & Silverman, 2011; Scott & Crooks, 2004). Children who have been exposed to DV often describe their fathers as being emotionally and psychologically absent and express a desire to have their fathers "know" them (Holt, 2015). Research on domestically violent fathers' level of responsivity has found that they have limited capacity to think about the thoughts and feelings of their children and generally have less emotionally close relationships (Francis & Wolfe, 2008; Smith Stover & Spink, 2012). Although emotional closeness may be a concern for many domestically violent fathers, in their review of the literature on potential intervention targets for this group, Scott et al. (2018) advise caution in focusing intervention on this aspect of fathering in the absence of ongoing monitoring of abuse, pointing to studies that suggest having a warm and emotionally responsive father who is also abusive, disparaging, and frightening may be more confusing and detrimental to children than a parent who is predictably harsh and unavailable.

## Co-occurring substance use, criminality, and depression

Finally, it is important to consider other problems that frequently co-occur in domestically violent fathers that have established impact on children. Three problems are emerging as particularly important: substance abuse, criminality, and depression. All three of these problems occur considerably more often in domestically violent than non-domestically violent fathers (Foran & O'Leary, 2008; Oram, Trevillion, Feder, & Howard, 2013; Stith et al., 2009; Trevillion et al., 2015). There is also evidence of synergistic effects of problem co-occurrence – that men's parenting and children's outcomes are dually compromised in fathers with co-occurring difficulties (Coley, Carrano, & Lewin-Bizan, 2011). Stover and colleagues (2013), for example, examined parenting and child outcomes in fathers with recent histories of substance abuse, DV, both or neither. They found that those fathers with co-occurring substance abuse and DV had the least positive co-parenting, the most negative parenting, and had children with more emotional and behavioural problems.

## How might we address fathering in the context of DV?

We have so far established that fathering in the context of DV should be a major concern for those seeking to improve outcomes for children. Fathers are responsible for a large proportion of harm to children in families as a result of exposure to DV and men's use of DV often co-occurs with compromised parenting, co-parenting, and other problems. Improvements necessary to address domestically violent fathers in courts, child protection, specialist intervention, and generalist service are outlined.

## Better recognition of domestically violent fathers in family court

Separation is a time of increased risk for DV. It may also be a time where, as a result of custody arrangements, men spend more time parenting their children independently, which may convey additional risks to children if men's fathering is compromised. Recognizing these and other concerns, there are consistent calls to better recognize, and give sufficient weight to, past and ongoing harms related to DV perpetration in family court decisions (Godbout, Parent, & Saint-Jacques, 2015; Hans, Hardesty, Haselschwerdt, & Frey, 2014; Rivera, Zeoli, & Sullivan, 2012; Trinder, Firth, & Jenks, 2009). Despite significant legislative changes in a number of countries to require consideration of DV in post-separation parenting plans, reviews of practice find that family law continues to give inadequate regard to the potentially harmful past and ongoing impact of DV (Macdonald, 2016; MacKay, 2018). Court and judicial decisions based on assessments of DV including the nature, context, and ongoing impact of domestically violent fathers on their children through ongoing abuse, disrespectful co-parenting, and DV-related deficits in parenting has significant potential to shift these patterns. A number of models have been developed to guide such assessments. A particularly strong and well-developed model is SAFeR, presented by the Battered Women's Justice Project (www.bwjp.org/our-work/projects/safer.html). The SAFeR approach to decision making consists of four well-developed steps: (1) screening for DV,

(2) assessing the full nature and context of DV, (3) focusing on past and ongoing effects of DV, and (4) responding to DV across all recommendations, decisions, and interventions. With such assessments, the responsibility of fathers for harms caused and for acting to address these harms is highlighted.

There have also been a number of recommendations for improving broader family court processes around DV, in part to ensure that such assessments are completed and available. One recommendation is for better sharing of information across criminal and family courts under "one family, one judge" models, also sometimes referred to as DV or unified courts. It is argued that such models are both more efficient and effective in recognizing and responding to patterns of abuse perpetration over the life of a case (Jaffe, Johnston, Crooks, & Bala, 2008; Jaffe, Crooks, & Bala, 2009; Martinson, 2010; Shdaimah & Summers, 2013). Others recommend models that include early screening for DV and differential processing of cases with and without DV concerns (Jaffe et al., 2009). The Family Safety Model developed by the Victorian branch of Relationships Australia, for example, diverts mediation clients assessed as having been affected by family violence to an in-house family safety practitioner to conduct a comprehensive assessment, make referrals to intervention and support services, guide transitions between services, and manage the case for up to one year (Hunter & Choudhry, 2018). Taking another approach, Scotland expanded the options for courts to take a more inquisitorial approach when the welfare of the child is a paramount consideration (MacKay, 2018). Within the Scottish model, the court can appoint a solicitor to act as a child welfare reporter to the court who could investigate and present information they deemed relevant including prior criminal convictions, record and pattern of police involvement, and past and present child protection investigations and concerns. The hope for these models (as of yet, mostly unevaluated) is for improved recognition of DV, greater consideration of potential harms in cases in which ongoing contact could place children at risk, and ultimately, for better and safer outcomes for families.

## Better recognition of domestically violent fathers in CPS

A second key location for better recognition and response to fathers who have perpetrated DV is within child protection. CPS have been frequently criticized for failing to hold men accountable for their abuse, not intervening to address men's parenting, and for blaming mothers for failures to ensure child safety and well-being (Humphreys & Absler, 2011; Radford & Hester, 2001). There have been a number of system-level interventions aimed at improving practice. Examples include collaborative agreements between violence against women and CPS, the creation of DV teams within child protection, and the provision of specialized training. Only a few of these have been evaluated, with results generally showing more consistent changes in knowledge and attitude than in practice, and with evidence that the changes in practice that are achieved are often site-specific and difficult to maintain (Turner et al., 2017). Perhaps unsurprisingly then, recent reviews of child welfare work in Australia, Canada, and the UK have all noted that fathers who perpetrate violence are seldom included as a focus in child protection assessment, monitoring, or intervention (Alaggia, Gadalla, Shlonsky, Jenney, & Daciuk, 2015; Macvean, Humphreys, & Healey, 2018). Efforts continue to shift practice. Some of the most interesting current work is associated with the Safe and Together model (Humphreys, Healey, & Mandel, 2018). This model includes multi-level, multi-day training and follow-up along with the implementation of a range of tools and resources to help guide child protection practice in cases of child exposure to DV. Ongoing studies of this model are occurring in various sites in Australia, Canada, and the US (Heward-Belle, Laing, Humphreys, & Toivonen, 2018).

# Developments in intervention programmes addressing fathering in the context of DV

It is clear that a spectrum of programmes, services, and initiatives should be available to respond to DV perpetrators of varying forms and risk level of family violence and that fathering should be included as one important nexus of risk to be considered (Scott, Heslop, David, & Kelly, 2017; State of Victoria, 2014–16). Intervention programmes developed to target fathers have significant potential to improve collaboration and connection with child protection and other child- and family-focused services, thereby increasing the reach of intervention. Having intervention focused on fathering may also assist with initial engagement and leverage of men's motivation, both of which are consistent challenges for the field (Bourassa, Turcotte, Lessard, & Labarre, 2013; Fleck-Henderson & Areán, 2004; Perel & Peled, 2008). Having programmes and services focused on fathering is also deemed important by families. Based on extensive interviews with key stakeholders for perpetrator programmes including men, women partners/ex-partners, programme staff and funders in the UK, Westmarland and Kelly (2012) identified six key determinants of whether or not a DV perpetrator programme "works." One was cessation of violence and abuse against women and children. Three other outcomes directly concerned men's roles as fathers: (1) shared positive and safe parenting; (2) men's awareness of the impact of their perpetration of DV on children, as well as partners; and (3) for children, safe and healthier childhoods where they feel heard and cared about.

There have now been a number of intervention programmes developed to specifically address fathering in the context of DV. Priorities and guiding principles for such programmes were outlined in the mid 2000s by Scott and colleagues (Scott & Crooks, 2004, 2007; Scott, Francis, Crooks, Paddon, & Wolfe, 2007; Scott, Kelly, Crooks, & Francis, 2014). Consistent with these recommendations, interventions for fathers in the context of DV generally prioritize children's safety and well-being, recognize that children's safety is integrally connected to the safety of their mothers, and prioritize changing *fathers'* behaviour, including improving their co-parenting and reducing hostility and over-reactivity in parenting. These programs are generally offered collaboratively with DV services, particularly women's advocacy services, men's perpetrator programmes, and child protection services. To various extents, programmes endorse the need for a web of accountability for fathers in which intervention around men's role as fathers is viewed as one part of an ongoing commitment to monitor, address, and contain risk with men who have perpetrated violence. Three general approaches that have been taken include integrating fathering material into DV perpetrator programmes, stand-alone interventions, and integrating within non-specialist DV services (Labarre, Bourassa, Holden, Turcotte, & Letourneau, 2016).

## *Integrating fathering material into DV perpetrator programmes*

A first approach is to integrate materials on fathering into existing programmes for men who have perpetrated intimate partner violence (i.e., beyond the one or two sessions on the effects of DV on children that have traditionally been part of this work). Innovation possibilities are limited, to some extent, by the length of programming. In a typical 12- to 20-week DV perpetrator programme, incorporating sufficient material to address the challenges of parenting in DV fathers would require a major reconceptualization of content and priorities (Alderson, Westmarland, & Kelly, 2013). However, such work can be feasibly done in longer perpetrator programmes. Interventions for DV perpetrators that last between six and 12 months could expand, and in some cases have expanded, their mandate to include more fulsome intervention on fathering.

Various curriculum materials have been developed to support such work. The *Fathering After Violence* programme developed by the Family Violence Prevention Fund (Areán & Davis, 2006; Fleck-Henderson & Areán, 2004) focuses on empathy, role modelling, and rebuilding the father-child relationship in sessions intended to be delivered over four to six weeks. Another excellent resource is the digital stories of DV-exposed children addressing their fathers developed at the University of Melbourne with funding from the Luke Batty Foundation (Lam, 2017). A third well-known resource designed to be run as part of perpetrator services is the *Addressing Fatherhood with Men Who Batter* (Scaia, Connelly, & Downing, 2010) program, which provides many exercises that can be integrated into intervention or offered as supplemental programming to men who have completed intervention for intimate partner abuse. Major aims of these exercises are to ensure freedom from abuse for women and children, help men better understand themselves as fathers, develop men's empathy for their children, foster father-child engagement and improve men's co-parenting skills and support of children's mothers.

## Stand-alone intervention for fathers in the context of DV

A second approach to working with fathers at the intersection of DV is to develop "stand-alone" intervention programmes within the DV specialist service sector. Stand-alone programmes have potential advantages for referrers concerned primarily with outcomes for children. Because these programmes emphasize child safety and well-being, they also often address father's perpetration of other forms of child maltreatment (i.e., physical abuse, emotional abuse, neglect) alongside child exposure to DV and some accept referrals for fathers who have perpetrated other forms of abuse.

A number of stand-alone programmes for domestically violent fathers have been developed, though some are small and community specific. Two manualized, published and evaluated programmes currently available are *Strong Fathers* and *Caring Dads*. *Strong Fathers* was developed by the Center for Child and Family Health in Durham, North Carolina drawing on materials from *Caring Dads* and *Fathering After Violence*. Some preliminary research on *Strong Fathers* has explored referral pathways and documented father's positive experience of the programme (Pennell & Brandt, 2017). *Caring Dads: Helping Fathers Value Their Children* (Crooks, Scott, Francis, Kelly, & Reid, 2006; Scott et al., 2007) was developed as a result of a collaboration between men's services, women's advocates, child and family services, child protection, and university researchers in Canada in the early 1980s. It consists of a 17-week combined group and individual intervention for fathers, systematic outreach to mothers to ensure safety and freedom from coercion, and ongoing, collaborative case management of fathers with referrers and with other professionals involved with men's families. *Caring Dads* currently runs in many locations in Canada, the US, the UK, Australia, and Europe and has been translated into French, Spanish, German, Swedish, and Arabic and adapted for cross-cultural use with Muslim communities. Research conducted on *Caring Dads* to date is promising. Evaluation conducted by the NSPCC in the UK with 504 fathers, 132 partners, and 38 children found that completion of *Caring Dads* is associated with pre- to post-group reductions in parenting stress and in level of hostility, indifference, and rejection as reported by fathers and reductions in DV victimization (emotional abuse, isolation, violence, injury, use of children), depression, and anxiety as reported by mothers. Changes in identified domains persisted over six months and were well in excess of changes made by comparison group fathers over a similar time period (McConnell, Barnard, & Taylor, 2017). A recent study by the Child Welfare Institute and Scott in Canada found that enrolment in *Caring Dads* was associated with substantially higher levels of contact between men and child protection workers and lower rates of re-referral over two years for men enrolled in the programme as compared to those referred but not enrolled in service (Scott et al., submitted).

Other examples of stand-alone programmes include those developed by and within Indigenous communities. In a 2017 scoping review, Gallant and colleagues (2017) identified 11 programmes addressing Aboriginal men's family violence, all from Australia, Canada, or New Zealand. An important feature of these programmes is recognition of colonization and associated systemic social, economic, health, well-being, and intergenerational traumas as important contributors to Aboriginal men's use of violence. Building from this foundation, programmes most often used a holistic approach to men's issues, aiming to address men's violence against women, children, and community together, rather than separately. In other programmes, intervention on men's violence was paired with the provision of support for developing employment skills or addressing substance misuse. Programmes developed within Indigenous contexts also consistently build cultural strengths and healing into intervention models. For example, the Yarra model uses a culturally appropriate river metaphor to integrate thinking about addressing socio-economic, political, and psychological aspects of men's journey towards change, using gendered accountability, healing, intersectionality, and culture as foundational practice elements towards safety for women and children (Andrews et al., 2018).

## Integrating within non-specialist DV services

A third approach to intervention with fathers in the context of DV is to integrate programming into non-specialist family-based services, such as supervised visitation centres, support centres for young men, substance use programmes, and services to incarcerated populations. One of the most promising models of integrated intervention is *Fathers for Change (F4C)* (Stover et al., 2013; Stover, 2015), used primarily with fathers accessing services for substance abuse. *F4C* consists of a series of topics to be delivered across four intervention phases. The first two phases, pre-treatment and individual intervention, involve fathers alone. Fathers who are successful in these sessions move into dyadic intervention sessions with mothers (phase 3) and children (phase 4) where appropriate, safe, and necessary. *F4C* was originally delivered in outpatient substance use treatment settings and a small randomized trial within that setting found greater reductions in DV and significantly improved father–child interactions among fathers completing *F4C* as compared to individual drug counselling (Stover, 2015). *F4C* has also been adapted for use in residential substance abuse treatment, with pilot implementation studies demonstrating significant reductions in hostility and affect regulation difficulties among men who participated (Stover, Carlson, Patel, & Manalich, 2018).

## Addressing DV and child maltreatment together in low- and middle-income countries

Finally, there is some innovative international development of intervention to address child maltreatment and intimate partner violence together. A scoping review by Bacchus and colleagues (2017) identified four programmes in low- and middle-income countries with this combined aim. One of these programmes, REAL (responsible, engaged, and loving), specifically targets fathers. REAL is a six-month mentoring programme that includes a community awareness campaign to improve fathers' knowledge and skills in positive parenting, conflict resolution, and reflection on gender roles. Mentors nominated from within the community are trained to support individual or small groups of fathers in developing relationship skills, dealing with stress, and managing emotions. REAL has been shown to have positive effects, reducing corporal punishing and intimate partner violence and increasing positive parenting (Ashburn, Kerner, Ojamuge, & Lundgren, 2017). Fewer changes, to date, have been shown in men's view of the roles and expectations of women and men in the family.

## Ongoing challenges and future directions

Although there have been promising developments in courts, child protection, and in intervention specifically for fathers who have perpetrated DV, there are also a number of settings in which consideration of fathering in the context of DV needs to be more robust. One of these areas is within the responsible fathering programmes. The role of a father within a family has changed rapidly over the past 50 years. Population-level messaging around the importance of fathers' positive involvement with their children and policies in support of shared parenting (e.g., parental leave for fathers) reflect these changes. There has been substantial growth in programmes and services in support of fathers and fatherhood. Some major examples are Dads4Kids (www.fatherhood.org.au/), National Responsible Fatherhood Clearinghouse (www.fatherhood.gov/about-us), National Fatherhood Initiative (www.fatherhood.org/about-us), Dads Central (www.dadcentral.ca/), and the Fatherhood Institute (www.fatherhoodinstitute. org/) network of service providers. Further, parenting programmes are slowly beginning to include and target fathers (see review by Panter-Brick et al., 2014). Notable examples include the *Family Foundations* programme (Feinberg & Kan, 2008), a series of eight classes, delivered before and after birth, to mothers and fathers and the *Supporting Father Involvement* programme (Pruett, Pruett, Cowan, & Cowan, 2017; Pruett, Cowan, Cowan, Gillette, & Pruett, 2019) for high-risk couples without current issues pertaining to intimate partner violence, child abuse, or child neglect. Although these and other fatherhood programmes and services are clear about the need for fathers to be non-abusive in their families, they rarely include materials explicitly on DV and sometimes exclude fathers for whom violence is a concern. Given national US data that as many as one in seven children report being exposed to their father's violence, fatherhood services likely need more services and programmes targeting domestic violence along with stronger alignments with programmes that do work with fathers who have perpetrated DV so that referrals could be facilitated.

Problems recognizing and responding to fathers' violence are even greater in child and family mental health services where work is still ongoing to involve fathers *at all*, let alone higher-risk fathers and fathers who have perpetrated DV. Programmes for new mothers, supports for early years parents, and community-based parenting programmes are all examples of services that are accessed mostly by mothers and in which father involvement is too often viewed as an optional "add-on." Such services rarely include robust efforts to screen for DV or involve men in interventions to address DV.

Turning the mirror around to reflect on work to address fathering in the context of DV, efforts to date would benefit from a greater consideration of intersectionality and its implications. Part of such work involves ensuring that programmes are culturally safe and provide space for discussions of how intersectional dimensions of class, race, and culture play out in men's experiences of being fathers and in their use of violence (Andrews et al., 2018). At a deeper level, consideration is also needed on the extent to which racialized and poor fathers are identified and referred to programmes addressing fathering in the context of DV, often via involvement with criminal justice or child protection, both systems which disproportionally include fathers facing structural disadvantages. One might rightfully question this over-representation, ask why opportunities to avoid abuse and violence were not provided earlier, and push for efforts to address the societal and structural factors including racism, colonialism, historic, and intergenerational trauma that perpetuate inequity in education, housing, employment, health, and opportunity, and contribute in multiple and complex ways to increased risk of perpetrating DV. This approach to understanding and supporting fathers has been adopted by some parts of the fatherhood movement. In particular, there has been work to consider the multiple structural disadvantages facing young African American fathers and to develop programmes and services that reflect and address their needs (Julion, Breitenstein, & Waddell, 2012). Programmes adopting strong intersectional analyses emphasize community ownership, concentrate on being accessible and attractive to fathers, and generally take holistic, empowering, and healing approaches. Such approaches contrast with the more accountability- and gender-focused perspective of "mainstream" DV work and can lead to questions about whether men's abuse and violence is adequately recognized and the safety needs of men's partners and children are given enough priority (e.g., fatherhood programmes seldom include partner contact). It is important and useful to engage with this tension. Ongoing work is needed to combine intersectional and DV thinking to develop culturally safe ways to promote change, and ideally, find ways to work with men *before* they cause harm in their families.

## Conclusions

In summary, there is growing attention to the need to intervene with men at the nexus of DV and parenting; however, much still needs to be done. Increased recognition of the role of domestically violent fathers in their children's lives is needed within courts, child protection, and child and family services. Such recognition should also include a fulsome understanding of the range of challenges that often co-occur with DV and on intersecting societal influences on fathering. As programmes and policies in this area continue to develop, there is a need to continue to involve specialist service providers, multiple stakeholders, and to develop in ways that empower and give ownership to those communities and populations facing structural disadvantages. With such models, partnerships are needed with professionals who work with children, who understand the need to "listen" to children's voices, and who appreciate the complexities of keeping children safe and helping them recover and heal from past trauma. Contributions of women's advocates, who are acutely sensitive to the multiple ways that men's desire to control women intersects with men's parenting decisions are also needed, as are those with professionals from men's behaviour change programmes who are skilled at engaging men and in monitoring fluctuating levels of dynamic risk. This is a rapidly developing area of research and practice that has significant potential to improve intervention for perpetrators of DV and to increase the safety and well-being of their children and families.

## Critical findings

- Part of meeting the needs of children exposed to DV is recognizing and responding to fathers who have perpetrated this abuse.
- Fathers who perpetrate DV often have difficulties in other aspects of parenting, especially over-reactivity, hostility, and respectful co-parenting. Parenting difficulties associated with men's substance use, depression, and general antisocial behaviour also need to be considered.
- A range of approaches to intervention have been developed to address fathering in the context of DV including those that involve integration of materials into programmes for perpetrators of intimate partner violence, stand-alone programmes for fathers within the

specialist DV sector, and programmes designed as part of other mental health or child and family services. Research on these programmes is promising but more rigorous testing is needed.

## Implications for policy, practice, and research

- Continued work is needed within family court and child protective services to adequately recognize fathering risks associated with men's perpetration of DV.
- Continued research and development is needed on approaches to intervention with fathers who are perpetrators of DV. Such work should include the perspectives of those working with women survivors and children exposed to DV, as well as DV specialist service providers with experience working with men.

## References

Alaggia, R., Gadalla, T. M., Shlonsky, A., Jenney, A., & Daciuk, J. (2015). Does differential response make a difference: Examining domestic violence cases in child protection services. *Child & Family Social Work, 20*, 83–95. https://doi.org/10.1111/cfs.12058

Alderson, S., Westmarland, N., & Kelly, L. (2013). The need for accountability to, and support for, children of men on domestic violence perpetrator programmes. *Child Abuse Review, 22*, 182–193. https://doi.org/10.1002/car.2223

Andrews, S., Gallant, D., Humphreys, C., Ellis, D., Bamblett, A., Briggs, R., & Harrison, W. (2018). Holistic programme developments and responses to Aboriginal men who use violence against women. *International Social Work*. https://doi.org/10.1177/0020872818807272

Ashburn, K., Kerner, B., Ojamuge, D., & Lundgren, R. (2017). Evaluation of the responsible, engaged, and loving (REAL) fathers initiative on physical child punishment and intimate partner violence in Northern Uganda. *Prevention science, 18*, 854–864. doi:10.1007/s11121-016-0713-9

Areán, J. C., & Davis, L. (2007). Working with fathers in batterer intervention programs. In J. Edleson & O. Williams (Eds.), *Parenting by men who batter: New directions for assessment and intervention* (pp. 118–130). New York, NY: Oxford University Press.

Bacchus, L. J., Colombini, M., Contreras Urbina, M., Howarth, E., Gardner, F., Annan, J., . . . Watts, C. (2017). Exploring opportunities for coordinated responses to intimate partner violence and child maltreatment in low and middle income countries: A scoping review. *Psychology, Health & Medicine, 22*, 135–165. https://doi.org/10.1080/13548506.2016.1274410

Bancroft, L., Silverman, J. G., & Ritchie, D. (2011). *The batterer as parent: Addressing the impact of domestic violence on family dynamics*. Thousand Oaks: Sage.

Birkley, E. L., & Eckhardt, C. I. (2015). Anger, hostility, internalizing negative emotions, and intimate partner violence perpetration: A meta-analytic review. *Clinical Psychology Review, 37*, 40–56. https://doi.org/10.1016/j.cpr.2015.01.002

Bourassa, C., Lavergne, C., Damant, D., Lessard, G., & Turcotte, P. (2008). *Child welfare workers' practice in cases involving domestic violence*. John Wiley & Sons. doi:10.1002/car.1015

Bourassa, C., Turcotte, P., Lessard, G., & Labarre, M. (2013). La paternité en contexte de violence conjugale. *La Revue Internationale De L'Éducation Familiale, 1*, 149–167. https://doi.org/10.3917/rief.033.0149

Brown, T., Tyson, D., & Arias, P. F. (2014). Filicide and parental separation and divorce. *Child Abuse Review, 23*, 79–88. https://doi.org/10.1002/car.2327

Callaghan, J. E., Alexander, J. H., Sixsmith, J., & Fellin, L. C. (2018). Beyond "witnessing": Children's experiences of coercive control in domestic violence and abuse. *Journal of Interpersonal Violence, 33*, 1551–1581. https://doi.org/10.1177/0886260515618946

Cicchetti, D., & Rogosch, F. A. (1994). The toll of child maltreatment on the developing child: Insights from developmental psychopathology. *Child and Adolescent Psychiatric Clinics of North America, 3*, 759–776. https://doi.org/10.1016/S1056-4993(18)30469-3

Coley, R. L., Carrano, J., & Lewin-Bizan, S. (2011). Unpacking links between fathers' antisocial behaviors and children's behavior problems: Direct, indirect, and interactive effects. *Journal of Abnormal Child Psychology, 39*, 791–804. doi:10.1007/s10802-011-9496-4

Crooks, C. V., Scott, K. L., Francis, K. J., Kelly, T., & Reid, M. (2006). Eliciting change in maltreating fathers: Goals, processes, and desired outcomes. *Cognitive and Behavioral Practice, 13*, 71–81. https://doi.org/10.1016/j.cbpra.2004.10.002

Cunningham, A. J., & Baker, L. L. (2007). *Little eyes, little ears: How violence against a mother shapes children as they grow*. London, ON: Centre for Children & Families in the Justice System.

Davies, P. T., Sturge-Apple, M. L., Woitach, M. J., & Cummings, E. M. (2009). A process analysis of the transmission of distress from interparental conflict to parenting: Adult relationship security as an explanatory mechanism. *Developmental Psychology, 45*, 1761–1773. http://dx.doi.org/10.1037/a0016426

Devine, C., Colquhoun, C., Webb, S., & Goodman, D. (2018). *Caring dads final report 2014–2016*. Child Welfare Institute, Toronto, Canada. Retrieved October 1, from www.childwelfareinstitute.torontocas.ca/node/201

Feinberg, M. E. (2003). The internal structure and ecological context of coparenting: A framework for research and intervention. *Parenting: Science and Practice, 3*, 95–131. https://doi.org/10.1207/S15327922PAR0302_01

Feinberg, M. E., & Kan, M. L. (2008). Establishing family foundations: Intervention effects on coparenting, parent/infant well-being, and parent–child relations. *Journal of Family Psychology, 22*, 253–263. http://dx.doi.org/10.1037/0893-3200.22.2.253

Felitti, V. J., Anda, R. F., Nordenberg, D., Williamson, D. F., Spitz, A. M., Edwards, V., . . . Marks, J. S. (2019). Relationship of childhood abuse and household dysfunction to many of the leading causes of death in adults: The adverse childhood experiences (ACE) study. *American Journal of Preventive Medicine, 56*, 774–786. https://doi.org/10.1016/j.amepre.2019.04.001

Finkelhor, D., Shattuck, A., Turner, H. A., Ormrod, R., & Hamby, S. L. (2011). Polyvictimization in developmental context. *Journal of Child & Adolescent Trauma, 4*, 291–300. https://doi.org/10.1080/19361521.2011.610432

Fleck-Henderson, A., & Areán, J. C. (2004). *Fathering after violence: Curriculum guidelines and tools for batterer intervention programs*. San Francisco, CA: Family Violence Prevention.

Foran, H. M., & O'Leary, K. D. (2008). Alcohol and intimate partner violence: A meta-analytic review. *Clinical Psychology Review, 28*, 1222–1234. https://doi.org/10.1016/j.cpr.2008.05.001

Ford, J. D., Elhai, J. D., Connor, D. F., & Frueh, B. C. (2010). Poly-victimization and risk of posttraumatic, depressive, and substance use disorders and involvement in delinquency in a national sample of adolescents. *Journal of Adolescent Health, 46*, 545–552. https://doi.org/10.1016/j.jadohealth.2009.11.212

Forssell, A. M., & Cater, Å. (2015). Patterns in child – Father contact after parental separation in a sample of child witnesses to intimate partner violence. *Journal of Family Violence, 30*, 339–349. https://doi.org/10.1007/s1089

Francis, K. J., & Wolfe, D. A. (2008). Cognitive and emotional differences between abusive and nonabusive fathers. *Child Abuse & Neglect, 32*, 1127–1137. https://doi.org/10.1016/j.chiabu.2008.05.007

Gallant, D., Andrews, S., Humphreys, C., Diemer, K., Ellis, D., Burton, J., . . . Torres-Carne, S. (2017). Aboriginal men's programs tackling family violence: A scoping review. *Journal of Australian Indigenous Issues, 20*, 48–68.

Godbout, E., Parent, C., & Saint-Jacques, M. (2015). Positions taken by judges and custody experts on issues relating to the best interests of children in custody disputes in Quebec. *International Journal of Law, Policy and the Family, 29*, 272–300. https://doi.org/10.1093/lawfam/ebv007

Guedes, A., Bott, S., Garcia-Moreno, C., & Colombini, M. (2016). Bridging the gaps: A global review of intersections of violence against women and violence against children. *Global Health Action, 9*, 31516. https://doi.org/10.3402/gha.v9.31516

Hans, J. D., Hardesty, J. L., Haselschwerdt, M. L., & Frey, L. M. (2014). The effects of domestic violence allegations on custody evaluators' recommendations. *Journal of Family Psychology, 28*, 957. http://dx.doi.org/10.1037/fam0000025

Hardesty, J. L., Crossman, K. A., Khaw, L., & Raffaelli, M. (2016). Marital violence and coparenting quality after separation. *Journal of Family Psychology, 30*, 320–330. http://dx.doi.org/10.1037/fam0000132

Hardesty, J. L., Khaw, L., Chung, G. H., & Martin, J. M. (2008). Coparenting relationships after divorce: Variations by type of marital violence and fathers' role differentiation. *Family Relations, 57*, 479–491. https://doi.org/10.1111/j.1741-3729.2008.00516.x

Herrenkohl, T. I., Sousa, C., Tajima, E. A., Herrenkohl, R. C., & Moylan, C. A. (2008). Intersection of child abuse and children's exposure to domestic violence. *Trauma, Violence, & Abuse, 9*, 84–99. https://doi.org/10.1177/1524838008314797

Heward-Belle, S., Humphreys, C., Healey, L., Toivonen, C., & Tsantefski, M. (2019). Invisible practices: Interventions with men who use violence and control. *Affilia: Journal of Women and Social Work*, 369–382. https://doi.org/10.1177/0886109919848750

Heward-Belle, S., Laing, L., Humphreys, C., & Toivonen, C. (2018). *Intervening with children living with domestic violence: Is the system safe?* Routledge. doi:10.1080/0312407X.2017.1422772

Holt, S. (2015). Post-separation fathering and domestic abuse: Challenges and contradictions. *Child Abuse Review*, *24*, 210–222. https://doi.org/10.1002/car.2264

Hughes, J., & Chau, S. (2013). *Making complex decisions: Child protection workers' practices and interventions with families experiencing intimate partner violence*. https://doi-org.myaccess.library.utoronto.ca/10.1016/j.childyouth.2013.01.003

Humphreys, C., & Absler, D. (2011). History repeating: Child protection responses to domestic violence. *Child & Family Social Work*, *16*, 464–473. https://doi.org/10.1111/j.1365-2206.2011.00761.x

Humphreys, C., Diemer, K., Bornemisza, A., Spiteri-Staines, A., Kaspiew, R., & Horsfall, B. (2019). More present than absent: Men who use domestic violence and their fathering. *Child & Family Social Work*, *24*, 321–329. https://doi.org/10.1111/cfs.12617

Humphreys, C., Healey, L., & Mandel, D. (2018). Case reading as a practice and training intervention in domestic violence and child protection. *Australian Social Work*, *71*(3), 277–291. https://doi.org/10.1080/0312407X.2017.1413666

Hunter, R., & Choudhry, S. (2018). Conclusion: International best practices. *Journal of Social Welfare and Family Law*, *40*, 548–562. doi:10.1080/09649069.2018.1519658

Jaffe, P. G., Crooks, C. V., & Bala, N. (2009). A framework for addressing allegations of domestic violence in child custody disputes. *Journal of Child Custody*, *6*, 169–188. https://doi.org/10.1080/15379410903084517

Julion, W. A., Breitenstein, S. M., & Waddell, D. (2012). Fatherhood intervention development in collaboration with African American non-resident fathers. *Research in Nursing & Health*, *35*, 490–506. doi:10.1002/nur.21492

Jenney, A., Mishna, F., Alaggia, R., & Scott, K. (2014). Doing the right thing? (re) considering risk assessment and safety planning in child protection work with domestic violence cases. *Children and Youth Services Review*, *47*, 92–101. https://doi-org.myaccess.library.utoronto.ca/10.1016/j.childyouth.2014.07.015

Katz, E. (2019). Coercive control, domestic violence, and a five-factor framework: Five factors that influence closeness, distance, and strain in mother – Child relationships. *Violence Against Women*, *25*, 1829–1853. https://doi.org/10.1177/1077801218824998

Kimball, E. (2016). Edleson revisited: Reviewing children's witnessing of domestic violence 15 Years later. *Journal of Family Violence*, *31*, 625–637. doi:10.1007/s10896-015-9786-7

Kopels, S., & Sheridan, M. C. (2002). Adding legal insult to injury: Battered women, their children, and the failure to protect. *Affilia: Journal of Women and Social Work*, *17*, 9–29. https://doi.org/10.1177/0886109902017001002

Labarre, M., Bourassa, C., Holden, G. W., Turcotte, P., & Letourneau, N. (2016). Intervening with fathers in the context of intimate partner violence: An analysis of ten programs and suggestions for a research agenda. *Journal of Child Custody*, *13*, 1–29. https://doi.org/10.1080/15379418.2016.1127793

Lamb, K. (2017). *Seen and heard: Embedding the voices of children and young people who have experienced family violence in programs for fathers* (Doctoral dissertation), University of Melbourne, Victoria, Australia.

Lapierre, S. (2010). Striving to be 'good' mothers: Abused women's experiences of mothering. *Child Abuse Review*, *19*, 342–357. https://doi.org/10.1002/car.1113

Lapierre, S., & Côté, I. (2016). Abused women and the threat of parental alienation: Shelter workers' perspectives. *Children and Youth Services Review*, *65*, 120–126. https://doi.org/10.1016/j.childyouth.2016.03.022

Lee, S. J., Bellamy, J. L., & Guterman, N. B. (2009). Fathers, physical child abuse, and neglect: Advancing the knowledge base. *Child Maltreatment*, *14*, 227–231. https://doi.org/10.1177/1077559509339388

Macdonald, G. S. (2016). Domestic violence and private family court proceedings: Promoting child welfare or promoting contact? *Violence Against Women*, *22*, 832–852. https://doi.org/10.1177/1077801215612600

MacKay, K. M. (2018). The approach in Scotland to child contact disputes involving allegations of domestic abuse. *Journal of Social Welfare and Family Law*, *40*, 477–495. doi:10.1080/09649069.2018.1519654

MacMillan, H. L., Wathen, C. N., Barlow, J., Fergusson, D. M., Leventhal, J. M., & Taussig, H. N. (2009). Interventions to prevent child maltreatment and associated impairment. *The Lancet*, *373*, 250–266. https://doi.org/10.1016/S0140-6736(08)61708-0

Macvean, M. L., Humphreys, C., & Healey, L. (2018). *Facilitating the collaborative interface between child protection and specialist domestic violence services: A scoping review.* Routledge. doi:10.1080/0312407X.2017.1415365

Martinson, D. J. (2010). One case – One specialized judge: Why courts have an obligation to manage alienation and other high-conflict cases. *Family Court Review, 48,* 180–189. https://doi.org/10.1111/j.1744-1617.2009.01297.x

McConnell, N., Barnard, M., & Taylor, J. (2017). Caring dads safer children: Families' perspectives on an intervention for maltreating fathers. *Psychology of Violence, 7,* 406–416. http://dx.doi.org/10.1037/vio0000105

McHale, J., Waller, M. R., & Pearson, J. (2012). Coparenting interventions for fragile families: What do we know and where do we need to go next? *Family Process, 51,* 284–306. https://doi.org/10.1111/j.1545-5300.2012.01402.x

Morrison, F. (2015). 'All over now?' The ongoing relational consequences of domestic abuse through children's contact arrangements. *Child Abuse Review, 24,* 274–284. https://doi.org/10.1002/car.2409

Moulding, N. T., Buchanan, F., & Wendt, S. (2015). Untangling self-blame and mother-blame in women's and children's perspectives on maternal protectiveness in domestic violence: Implications for practice. *Child abuse review, 24,* 249–260. https://doi.org/10.1002/car.2389

Murray, S., & Powell, A. (2009). *"What's the problem?": Australian public policy constructions of domestic and family violence.* Sage. doi:10.1177/1077801209331408

Norlander, B., & Eckhardt, C. (2005). Anger, hostility, and male perpetrators of intimate partner violence: A meta-analytic review. *Clinical Psychology Review, 25,* 119–152. https://doi.org/10.1016/j.cpr.2004.10.001

Oram, S., Trevillion, K., Feder, G., & Howard, L. M. (2013). Prevalence of experiences of domestic violence among psychiatric patients: Systematic review. *The British Journal of Psychiatry, 202,* 94–99. https://doi.org/10.1192/bjp.bp.112.109934

Øverlien, C. (2013). The children of patriarchal terrorism. *Journal of Family Violence, 28,* 277–287. doi:10.1007/s10896-013-9498-9

Øverlien, C. (2014). 'He didn't mean to hit mom, I think': Positioning, agency and point in adolescents' narratives about domestic violence. *Child & Family Social Work, 19,* 156–164. https://doi.org/10.1111/j.1365-2206.2012.00886.x

Panter-Brick, C., Burgess, A., Eggerman, M., McAllister, F., Pruett, K., & Leckman, J. F. (2014). Practitioner review: Engaging fathers – Recommendations for a game change in parenting interventions based on a systematic review of the global evidence. *Journal of Child Psychology and Psychiatry, 55,* 1187–1212. https://doi.org/10.1111/jcpp.12280

Pennell, J., & Brandt, E. (2017). Men who abuse intimate partners: Their evaluation of a responsible fathering program. In *Innovations in interventions to address intimate partner violence* (pp. 227–243). Routledge.

Perel, G., & Peled, E. (2008). The fathering of violent men: Constriction and yearning. *Violence Against Women, 14,* 457–482. https://doi.org/10.1177/1077801208314846

Pruett, M. K., Cowan, P. A., Cowan, C. P., Gillette, P., & Pruett, K. D. (2019). Supporting father involvement: An intervention with community and child welfare – Referred couples. *Family Relations, 68,* 51–67. https://doi.org/10.1111/fare.12352

Pruett, M. K., Pruett, K., Cowan, C. P., & Cowan, P. A. (2017). Enhancing father involvement in low-income families: A couples group approach to preventive intervention. *Child Development, 88,* 398–407. https://doi.org/10.1111/cdev.12744

Radford, L., Corral, S., Bradley, C., & Fisher, H. L. (2013). The prevalence and impact of child maltreatment and other types of victimization in the UK: Findings from a population survey of caregivers, children and young people and young adults. *Child Abuse & Neglect, 37,* 801–813. https://doi.org/10.1016/j.chiabu.2013.02.004

Radford, L., & Hester, M. (2001). Overcoming mother blaming? future directions for research on mothering and domestic violence. In S. A. Graham-Bermann & J. L. Edleson (Eds.), *Domestic violence in the lives of children: The future of research, intervention, and social policy* (pp. 135–155). Washington, DC: American Psychological Association. http://dx.doi.org/10.1037/10408-007

Rivera, E. A., Zeoli, A. M., & Sullivan, C. M. (2012). Abused mothers' safety concerns and court mediators' custody recommendations. *Journal of Family Violence, 27,* 321–332. doi:10.1007/s10896-012-9426-4

Scaia, M., Connelly, L., & Downing, J. (2010). *Addressing fatherhood with men who batter: A curriculum for working with men as fathers in a batterer intervention program (BIP).* Grand Rapids, MN: Advocates for Family Peace.

Scott, K. L., & Crooks, C. V. (2004). Effecting change in maltreating fathers: Critical principles for intervention planning. *Clinical Psychology: Science and Practice, 11*, 95–111. https://doi.org/10.1093/clipsy. bph058

Scott, K. L., Dubov, V. Devine, C., Colquhoun, C. Hoffelner, C. Niki, I. Webb, S., & Goodman, D. (submitted). *Caring Dads intervention program for fathers who have caused harm: Quasi-experimental evaluation of child protection outcomes over two years.*

Scott, K. L., Francis, K. J., Crooks, C., Paddon, M., & Wolfe, D. A. (2007). Guidelines for intervention with abusive fathers. In J. Edleson & O. Williams (Eds.), *Parenting by men who batter: New directions for assessment and intervention* (pp. 102–117). New York, NY: Oxford University Press.

Scott, K. L., Heslop, L., David, R., & Kelly, T. (2017). Justice-linked domestic violence intervention services: Description and analysis of practices across Canada. In *Innovations in interventions to address intimate partner violence* (pp. 51–74). Routledge.

Scott, K. L., & Lishak, V. (2012). Intervention for maltreating fathers: Statistically and clinically significant change. *Child Abuse & Neglect, 36*, 680–684. https://doi.org/10.1016/j.chiabu.2012.06.003

Scott, K. L., Thompson-Walsh, C., & Nsiri, A. (2018). Parenting in fathers who have exposed their children to domestic violence: Identifying targets for change. *International Journal on Child Maltreatment: Research, Policy and Practice, 1*, 51–75. https://doi.org/10.1007/s42448-018-0004-0

Shdaimah, C., & Summers, A. (2013). Baltimore city's model court: Professional stakeholders' experience with Baltimore city's one family, one judge docketing. *Family Court Review, 51*, 286–297. https://doi. org/10.1111/fcre.12027

Stark, E. (2007). *Coercive control: How men entrap women in personal life*. Oxford: Oxford University Press.

State of Victoria, Royal Commission into Family Violence: Report and recommendations, Vol III, Parl Paper No 132. (2014–16). Retrieved October 1, 2019 from www.rcfv.com.au/MediaLibraries/ RCFamilyViolence/Reports/Final/RCFV-Vol-III.pdf

Stith, S. M., Liu, T., Davies, L. C., Boykin, E. L., Alder, M. C., Harris, J. M., . . . Dees, J. (2009). Risk factors in child maltreatment: A meta-analytic review of the literature. *Aggression and Violent Behavior, 14*, 13–29. https://doi.org/10.1016/j.avb.2006.03.006

Stover, C. S. (2015). Fathers for change for substance use and intimate partner violence: Initial community pilot. *Family Process, 54*, 600–609. https://doi.org/10.1111/famp.12136

Stover, C. S., Carlson, M., Patel, S., & Manalich, R. (2018). Where's dad? the importance of integrating fatherhood and parenting programming into substance use treatment for men. *Child Abuse Review, 27*, 280–300. https://doi.org/10.1002/car.2528

Stover, C. S., Easton, C. J., & McMahon, T. J. (2013). Parenting of men with co-occurring intimate partner violence and substance abuse. *Journal of Interpersonal Violence, 28*, 2290–2314. https://doi. org/10.1177/0886260512475312

Stover, C. S., & Kiselica, A. (2015). Hostility and substance use in relation to intimate partner violence and parenting among fathers. *Aggressive Behavior, 41*, 205–213. https://doi.org/10.1002/ab.21548

Stover, C. S., & Spink, A. (2012). Affective awareness in parenting of fathers with co-occurring substance abuse and intimate partner violence. *Advances in Dual Diagnosis, 5*, 74–85. https://doi. org/10.1108/17570971211241903

Sturge-Apple, M. L., Davies, P. T., & Cummings, E. M. (2006). Hostility and withdrawal in marital conflict: Effects on parental emotional unavailability and inconsistent discipline. *Journal of Family Psychology, 20*, 227. http://dx.doi.org/10.1037/0893-3200.20.2.227

Tajima, E. A. (2000). The relative importance of wife abuse as a risk factor for violence against children. *Child Abuse & Neglect, 24*, 1383–1398. https://doi.org/10.1016/S0145-2134(00)00194-0

Teubert, D., & Pinquart, M. (2010). The association between coparenting and child adjustment: A meta-analysis. *Parenting: Science and Practice, 10*, 286–307. https://doi.org/10.1080/15295192.2010. 492040

Thiara, R. K., & Humphreys, C. (2017). Absent presence: The ongoing impact of men's violence on the mother – child relationship. *Child & Family Social Work, 22*, 137–145. https://doi.org/10.1111/ cfs.12210

Thompson-Walsh, C. A., Scott, K. L., Lishak, V., & Dyson, A. (submitted). *Examining the relationship between fathers' domestic violence perpetration and child social-emotional development: Psychological features, parenting, and co-parenting mediators.*

Trevillion, K., Williamson, E., Thandi, G., Borschmann, R., Oram, S., & Howard, L. M. (2015). A systematic review of mental disorders and perpetration of domestic violence among military populations. *Social Psychiatry and Psychiatric Epidemiology, 50*, 1329–1346. doi:10.1007/s00127-015-1084-4

Trinder, L., Firth, A., & Jenks, C. (2009). 'So presumably things have moved on since then?' The management of risk allegations in child contact dispute resolution. *International Journal of Law, Policy and the Family, 24,* 29–53. https://doi.org/10.1093/lawfam/ebp010

US Department of Health & Human Services, Administration for Children and Families, Administration on Children, Youth and Families, Children's Bureau. (2019). *Child maltreatment 2017.* Retrieved from www.acf.hhs.gov/cb/research-data-technology/statistics-research/child-maltreatment.

Westmarland, N., & Kelly, L. (2012). Why extending measurements of 'success' in domestic violence perpetrator programmes matters for social work. *British Journal of Social Work, 43,* 1092–1110. https://doi.org/10.1093/bjsw/bcs049

# 32

# ADOLESCENT INTIMATE PARTNER VIOLENCE PREVENTION AND INTERVENTION

## A developmental, intersectional perspective

*Heather L. McCauley and Taylor A. Reid*

### Introduction

Adolescence is a dynamic developmental period characterized by intense physical, neurological, psychological, and psychosocial changes spanning from approximately age 10 through the late 20s (Luna, Padmanabhan, & O'Hearn, 2010). Related to this rapid period of development, adolescents experience elevated risk for physical and sexual violence and psychological abuse in their romantic and dating relationships, called adolescent intimate partner violence (IPV). Here, we present the social epidemiology of adolescent IPV and highlight strategies for prevention and intervention to mitigate this significant social, economic, public health, and human rights concern. However, given the relatively stable prevalence of IPV over time, current prevention efforts are not enough. Thus, we employ developmental and intersectional lenses to emphasize need for developmentally relevant prevention and intervention strategies that consider the unique experiences of adolescents with marginalized identities, including sexual and gender minority youth, racial and ethnic minority youth, and youth with disabilities, who are disproportionately affected by IPV.

### The social epidemiology of adolescent intimate partner violence

Adolescent IPV comprises physical violence, sexual violence, and/or psychological abuse in romantic or dating relationships during adolescence, a developmental period spanning ages 10 through the late 20s (Luna et al., 2010; Miller, Jones, & McCauley, 2018). A robust body of literature has documented IPV as a significant problem, with adolescents at highest risk (Abramsky et al., 2011; Romans et al., 2007; Smith et al., 2018). Indeed, a study of men ages 15 to 19 across four countries – China, India, South Africa, and the United States – found that past year physical or sexual IPV perpetration ranged from 9% to 40% (Peitzmeier et al., 2016). Another study of male and female adolescents ages 10 to 18 in Tanzania and South Africa found that 10%–38% of youth had been victims of IPV, while 3.1%–21.8% had been perpetrators

(Wubs et al., 2009). Findings from the 2013 United States (US) Centers for Disease Control and Prevention's (CDC) Youth Risk Behavior Survey (YRBS) indicated that one in five female youth ages 14 to 18 (95% Confidence Interval (CI) 19.0%–23.0%) and one in ten male youth ages 14 to 18 (95% CI 9.0%–11.7%) experienced physical or sexual IPV in the previous year (Vagi, Olsen, Basile, & Vivolo-Kantor, 2015). Among college and university students, a study of almost 16,000 participants from 22 countries found that 17% to 44% reported physical IPV perpetration and 14% to 39% reported physical IPV victimization in the past year. Sexual IPV was also common with 8% to 34% of participants reporting perpetrating this form of abuse, while 9% to 46% reported being victims of sexual IPV (Chan, Straus, Brownridge, Tiwari, & Leung, 2008). Findings from the most recent Association of American Universities (AAU) campus climate survey indicate that approximately one in ten partnered students will experience IPV in college (Cantor et al., 2019). Adolescents who experience IPV also report the presence of controlling behaviors, verbal insults, and threats (Ybarra, Espelage, Langhinrichsen-Rohling, Korchmaros, & Boyd, 2016). Indeed, psychological abuse has been found to occur more frequently than physical or sexual IPV (Coker et al., 2014; Cuevas, Sabina, & Bell, 2014).

Adolescence is the one of the most dynamic periods of physical, neurological, psychological, and psychosocial human development, which provides important context for understanding how IPV manifests in adolescent relationships. With the onset of puberty, adolescents become aware of and explore their sexual desires, arousal, attraction, and intimate relationships (Fortenberry, 2013; Tulloch & Kaufman, 2013). Studies conducted in global settings have found that between one-third and one half of adolescents have had sex, with adolescent men more likely than adolescent women to report sexual behavior. Moreover, adolescent men are more likely than adolescent women to have sex outside of the context of legal marriage, highlighting how social norms, including those about gender roles, shape the contexts of adolescents' sexualities and relationships (Singh, Samara, & Cuca, 2000). Findings from the CDC support this research with approximately 40% of US adolescents having sexual intercourse, with 10% of these adolescents having more than four partners (Kann et al., 2018). Among sexually active youth, slightly more than half report using condoms the last time they engaged in sexual intercourse (Kann et al., 2018).

In a related developmental milestone, adolescents are recognizing and negotiating dimensions of their sexual orientations (e.g. attractions, identities), which can be stressful (and exploited by others) for those with non-heteronormative sexualities (Floyd & Stein, 2002). Indeed, a US study of adult men found that earlier "gay-related development" (e.g. recognizing a non-heterosexual sexuality, coming out to others) was associated with elevated risk for forced sex (Friedman, Marshal, Stall, Cheong, & Wright, 2008). Youth who identify as lesbian, gay, bisexual, or transgender (LGBT) may endure ridicule from their peers and lack support from their family (Goodenow, Watson, Adjei, Homma, & Saewyc, 2016; Poteat, Espelage, & Koenig, 2009; Ryan, Russell, Huebner, Diaz, & Sanchez, 2010), during a time when adolescents yearn for social acceptance (McElhaney, Antonishak, & Allen, 2008). For racial and ethnic minority youth, this period of identity development unfolds in racist and xenophobic societies that exert pressure (and use violence) on youth to conform to norms of their White peers (Brittian, 2012; Spiegler, Wölfer, & Hewstone, 2019). A qualitative study with transgender youth of color highlights the ways that sexual identities, gender identities, and racial/ethnic identities are simultaneously evolving and, importantly, shaped by the ways that adults in their lives use power to affirm or deny adolescents' intersecting identities and experiences (Singh, 2013).

Further compounding the adolescents' vulnerability to IPV during identity development, most adolescents, regardless of minority status, have limited experiences with romantic and/or sexual relationships. Adolescents develop relationship attitudes and behaviors via social learning processes, modeling behaviors they witness in their parents or caregivers (Kuo et al., 2017; Langhinrichsen-Rohling, Hankla, & Stormberg, 2004), in the media (Bleakley, Hennessy, Fishbein, & Jordan, 2008; J. D. Brown & L'Engle, 2009), and among their peers (Whitaker & Miller, 2000). Youth who do not have models of healthy relationships may perceive violence as normative behavior in dating relationships. This may be especially the case for coercive relationship behaviors and psychological abuse. A recent study of online discourse about IPV found that social media users expressed that they wished they had learned early that psychological abuse was a form of IPV, as it was central to their experiences in adolescence and young adulthood (McCauley, Bonomi, Maas, Bogen, & O'Malley, 2018). During a period of rapid socioemotional learning, adolescents are also testing the limits of their independence from caregivers (Koepke & Denissen, 2012). With the establishment of new boundaries during a process of individuation, adolescents may hesitate to discuss their romantic relationships with their caregivers, preventing caregivers from recognizing signs of unhealthy relationship behaviors.

Finally, many digital native adolescents explore their identities and relationships in online spaces (Davis, 2013). In high-income countries, almost half of teens admit to "almost constant" online usage, mostly notably through social media (Anderson & Jiang, 2018). Studies in low-income communities have found adolescents to report high online use, even among those who do not personally own a mobile device (Kreutzer, 2009). A growing body of research has illustrated the ways in which IPV emerges in these online spaces. Abusive partners may isolate and control partners by monitoring online behavior, insist on constant contact, and stalk partners online (Draucker & Martsolf, 2010; Øverlien, Hellevik, & Korkmaz, 2019). Adolescent girls often report a higher prevalence of cyber dating violence than adolescent boys (Barter et al., 2017; Dick et al., 2014; Felmlee & Faris, 2016; Zweig, Dank, Yahner, & Lachman, 2013; Zweig, Lachman, Yahner, & Dank, 2014), while LGB adolescents experience cyber IPV rates that are four times higher than that of completely heterosexual adolescents (Felmlee & Faris, 2016). Adolescent girls are also more likely to have a partner share a sexually explicit image of them to others without their consent, a type of IPV called image-based sexual abuse (Branch, Hilinski-Rosick, Johnson, & Solano, 2017; Henry, Powell, & Flynn, 2017). Studies suggest that these online forms of IPV overlap with and are extensions of IPV in face-to-face adolescent relationships (Barter et al., 2017; Choi, Van Ouytsel, & Temple, 2016; Dick et al., 2014; Morelli, Bianchi, Chirumbolo, & Baiocco, 2018; Temple et al., 2016).

## Marginalization and IPV risk

Adolescents with marginalized identities experience elevated risk for IPV. Populations experiencing marginalization are defined as those who are excluded from mainstream social, economic, cultural, or political life, and/or those who experience exploitation, inequity, and harm because of discrimination and injustice. In the context of IPV, such adolescents include sexual and gender minorities, youth with disabilities, and youth of color, among other populations. Further, drawing on intersectionality theory, many adolescents hold multiple marginalized identities resulting in unique social locations that confer even greater risk for IPV, such as transgender youth of color (Coulter et al., 2017; Crenshaw, 1991; McCauley, Campbell, Buchanan, & Moylan, 2019). Here, we outline findings regarding the prevalence and impacts of IPV among adolescents, paying particular attention to the ways that IPV differentially affects youth who experience marginalization.

## Gender

Research on IPV has focused primarily on the experiences of cisgender women and to a lesser extent, cisgender men. The most recent YRBS (2017) found that adolescent women were more likely than adolescent men to experience both physical and sexual IPV (Kann et al., 2018). However, an analysis of YRBS data from 1999–2011 found that adolescent women and men experienced physical IPV at approximately the same rates (Rothman & Xuan, 2014). Data regarding perpetration suggest that adolescent women are more likely than men to perpetrate *physical IPV* but are also significantly more likely to fear sustaining injury from a partner (Carroll, Raj, Noel, & Bauchner, 2011; Swahn, Simon, Arias, & Bossarte, 2008). Adolescent men are more likely than women to perpetrate *sexual IPV* and are more likely to inflict physical injury or harm on their partner (Swahn et al., 2008). Together, this work highlights that adolescent women and men use and experience different types of violence in their dating relationships related to the differing structural contexts in which women and men negotiate their relationships (Anderson, 2005).

Data illustrating the experiences of gender minority youth – those whose sex assigned at birth and gender identities do not align (e.g. transgender, nonbinary youth) – are comparatively scarce. However, findings from the National College Health Assessment (NCHA) suggest that transgender college students have elevated odds of experiencing sexual violence in their dating relationships compared with cisgender college students (Griner et al., 2017). The AAU Campus Climate survey reiterated these findings, with evidence that gender minority students reported IPV at higher rates than their cisgender peers but extended these findings with evidence that they were more likely to experience IPV with multiple partners (Cantor et al., 2019). Transgender adolescents experience elevated risk for violence because of stigma and discrimination in their communities related to their gender identities (White Hughto, Reisner, & Pachankis, 2015). Evidence from the Growing Up Today Study suggests that gender nonconformity increases risk for IPV among adolescent men, but not adolescent women (Adhia et al., 2018), independent of sexual orientation. Researchers have found "masculine discrepancy stress" or distress related to not conforming to hegemonic masculinity norms, to be associated with IPV perpetration (Berke, Reidy, Gentile, & Zeichner, 2019), which may help explain findings regarding gender nonconformity and IPV exposure among adolescent men.

## Sexual orientation

There is growing evidence regarding elevated risk for IPV among sexual minority youth, including youth who identify as lesbian, gay, bisexual, or queer; experience same-gender attraction; or engage in same-gender sexual behavior (Dank, Lachman, Zweig, & Yahner, 2014; Edwards, 2018; Luo, Stone, & Tharp, 2014; Martin-Storey, 2015; McCauley et al., 2015; Reuter, Sharp, & Temple, 2015). According to the 2017 YRBS, 21.9% of LGB adolescents reported being physically forced to have sex at some point during their lives, compared with 5.4% of heterosexual adolescents (Kann et al., 2018). Specific to their dating relationships, 15.8% of LGB students and 5.5% of heterosexual students had experienced sexual IPV in the 12 months prior to the survey, while 17.2% of LGB students and 6.4% of heterosexual students experienced physical IPV in the 12 months prior to the survey (Kann et al., 2018). IPV among sexual minority youth is often understood using a minority stress framework, which highlights the ways that heterosexist discrimination and inequity related to holding a minority sexual orientation "gets under the skin," manifesting in maladaptive coping behaviors, victimization, and reduced help-seeking (Edwards, Sylaska, & Neal, 2015; Gillum & DiFulvio, 2012; Krieger,

2005). For example, studies have found internalized minority stressors (e.g. homonegativity, identity concealment) to be associated with both IPV victimization and perpetration (Edwards et al., 2015).

## Disability

Adolescents with disabilities are a heterogeneous population that has also received limited attention in the research literature. Findings from the 2005 US YRBS and the 2009 Massachusetts Youth Health Survey suggest that adolescents (both cisgender girls and boys) with disabilities report higher rates of IPV than their peers without a disability (Alriksson-Schmidt, Armour, & Thibadeau, 2010; Mitra, Mouradian, & McKenna, 2013). Findings from the NCHA suggest that university students with disabilities are also more likely to experience violence in their dating relationships (Scherer, Snyder, & Fisher, 2013). Specifically, one in five (20.4%) adolescent women with disabilities reported any form of IPV in the previous year, compared with approximately one in ten (11.1%) of adolescent women without disabilities. Differences in IPV victimization were noted for adolescent men, too, with 11.7% of adolescent men with disabilities and 6.7% of adolescent men without disabilities reporting this outcome (Scherer, 2013). Another study using these data found that university students with mental disabilities and multiple disability types, specifically, are at greatest risk for IPV (Scherer, Snyder, & Fisher, 2016). There is also evidence to suggest that the intersection of disability status, sexual orientation, and gender identity confers greater risk for IPV. A study of more than one thousand US college students found that sexual and gender minority students who identified as deaf or hard of hearing had greatest risk for IPV, compared with their heterosexual and hearing peers (Porter & McQuiller Williams, 2013). Notably, a study of university students highlighted the ways that perpetrators may exploit their partners' disabilities, reporting that abusive partners interfered with taking medication or completing tasks such as bathing or dressing (Findley, Plummer, & McMahon, 2016).

## Race and ethnicity

There is inconsistent evidence in the scientific literature regarding whether adolescents of color are more likely than White adolescents to have relationships characterized by violence. In the 2017 US YRBS, 6.9% of White adolescents, 6.9% of Hispanic adolescents, and 4.8% of Black adolescents experienced sexual IPV in the previous year, while 7.0% of White adolescents, 7.6% of Hispanic adolescents, and 10.2% of Black adolescents experienced physical IPV in the previous year (Kann et al., 2018). This finding regarding physical IPV is supported by pooled YRBS data from 1999–2011, which found that Black and multiracial adolescents had a higher prevalence of physical dating violence, compared with their White, Hispanic, and Asian counterparts (Rothman & Xuan, 2014). However, a study of 2,895 middle school students in four US cities found no racial differences in IPV perpetration (Niolon et al., 2015). Studies highlight racial differences in correlates of IPV perpetration, suggesting key contextual differences in the experiences of White youth and youth of color. For example, a longitudinal study of adolescents in grades 8 and 9 at baseline found that key modifiable factors mediated the relationship between IPV perpetration among youth of color, including communication skills, IPV acceptance, inequitable gender attitudes, and exposure to family violence (Foshee et al., 2008). Research on reproductive coercion, a type of IPV common among adolescents where abusive partners manipulate contraception, condom use, and pregnancy, has documented racial disparities in this outcome, though these appear to manifest in later adolescence and young adulthood

(Hill et al., 2019; Holliday et al., 2017). Qualitative research has highlighted the impact of systemic oppression on reproductive coercion with evidence to suggest that Black women's higher rates of reproductive coercion may be partially explained by male desires to establish a legacy in the face of concerns about mass incarceration, neighborhood violence, or premature death (Holliday et al., 2018; Nikolajski et al., 2015). These findings suggest that, similar to understanding gender differences in IPV, racial disparities in adolescent IPV must be conceptualized understanding how structural inequality, power, and oppression are relevant to the prevalence, impact, and prevention of IPV.

## IPV and associated health and education outcomes

IPV confers multiple adverse health, educational, and interpersonal outcomes for survivors and yields a population economic burden of nearly $3.6 trillion over survivors' lifetimes (Peterson, Kearns et al., 2018). Youth exposed to IPV consistently report more depression symptoms, anxiety, PTSD, suicidal ideation, and eating disorders, amongst other mental and behavioral health concerns (Banyard & Cross, 2008; Brown et al., 2009; Choi et al., 2017; Haynie et al., 2013; Howard, Debnam, & Wang, 2013; McCauley, Breslau, Saito, & Miller, 2015; Nahapetyan, Orpinas, Song, & Holland, 2014; Sabina, Cuevas, & Cotignola-Pickens, 2016; Van Ouytsel, Ponnet, & Walrave, 2017; Wolitzky-Taylor et al., 2008). Youth in relationships characterized by IPV are also more likely to report sexual behaviors (e.g. condom non-use) that increase their risk for health outcomes including unintended pregnancy and sexually transmitted infections (Alleyne-Green, Coleman-Cowger, & Henry, 2012; Howard et al., 2013; Shorey et al., 2015). Studies have found that those who experience IPV are more likely to fear negotiating condom use and experience negative consequences of asking a male partner to use a condom, which precludes youth from negotiating whether, when, and how they engage in sexual behavior (Ferguson, Vanwesenbeeck, & Knijn, 2008; Teitelman, Ratcliffe, Morales-Aleman, & Sullivan, 2008; Wingood & DiClemente, 1997).

The impacts of IPV also extend to educational outcomes. IPV victims experience a decreased desire to attend school and demonstrate poorer academic performance compared to their non-abused peers (Banyard & Cross, 2008). Poorer academic performance manifests as lower grades and a greater likelihood of dropping out of school altogether (Hagan & Foster, 2001). Due to feelings of being unsafe at school, these adolescents also suffer from decreased attendance overall (Vivolo-Kantor, Olsen, & Bacon, 2016). Within the school context, IPV victims experience more bullying and are more likely to perpetrate bullying behaviors towards their peers (Orpinas, Nahapetyan, Song, McNicholas, & Reeves, 2012; Vivolo-Kantor et al., 2016). A longitudinal study by Adams and colleagues (2013) demonstrates the lasting impact of adolescent IPV on educational attainment. Adolescents who have experienced IPV are less likely to graduate high school, precluding their ability to seek higher education. Consequently, IPV victims earn lower incomes than their non-abused counterparts and report smaller growth in their income over time (Adams, Greeson, Kennedy, & Tolman, 2013). For example, a study of ethnically diverse victims of physical IPV found that this population was less likely to be engaged in paid employment nearly five years after the abuse occurred (Lindhorst, Oxford, Gillmore, 2007). In addition, survivors of IPV are at elevated risk for revictimization in adolescence and adulthood, compounding the potential for long-term social and economic outcomes (Cuevas et al., 2014; Cui, Ueno, Gordon, & Fincham, 2013; Exner-Cortens, Eckenrode, Bunge, & Rothman, 2017). It is likely these outcomes differ by gender and sexual orientation, with women more likely than men to be economically dependent on their partners and experience poverty after leaving an abusive relationship, while sexual minorities may face employment discrimination after an abusive partner "outs" them to an employer (Anderson, 2005). Indeed, adolescents with marginalized identities report lower well-being outcomes and more negative social reactions, compared with White, heterosexual, cisgender youth (Moschella, Potter, & Moynihan, 2020). Despite this robust body of literature documenting the prevalence and impacts of IPV and mounting evidence that adolescents with marginalized identities are disproportionately burdened by adverse outcomes associated with IPV, our prevention efforts have failed to consider the ways IPV manifests differently vis-à-vis youths' identities and social locations, warranting attention to the ways that we can promote equity with our IPV work.

## Evidence-based prevention strategies for IPV among adolescents

The World Health Organization and the US Centers for Disease Control and Prevention have outlined strategies for preventing intimate partner violence over the life-course, emphasizing the need to focus on multiple levels of the social ecology (Niolon et al., 2017; WHO, 2010). These recommendations are informed by global research documenting risk factors for the perpetration of abusive behavior such as peer attitudes and behaviors, gender- and violence-related cognitions, and structural/environmental factors (Tharp et al., 2013; WHO, 2010). Later, we present evidence of programs that have been rigorously evaluated for their effectiveness in reducing IPV perpetration and victimization, before we apply a developmental, intersectional lens to interrogate whether and how these programs address the needs of adolescents with marginalized identities.

## Teaching safe and healthy relationship skills

Given the social, behavioral, and health outcomes associated with IPV, researchers have evaluated programs aiming to promote individual-level healthy relationship behaviors, including communication, empathy, respect, and conflict resolution (Niolon et al., 2017). The programs most rigorously evaluated in this domain include *Safe Dates*, *Fourth R*, *Dating Matters to Promote Healthy Teen Relationships*, and *Stepping Stones* (Crooks et al., 2019; Jewkes et al., 2008; Niolon et al., 2017). *Safe Dates* is a ten-session program that aims to shift IPV norms, gender-role norms, and conflict management skills. Evidence from a randomized controlled trial among 8th and 9th graders in the United States indicated that the program was associated with reductions in the perpetration of psychological, moderate physical, and sexual dating violence perpetration and moderate physical dating violence victimization (Foshee et al., 2005).

School-based program *Fourth R* comprises 21 lessons taught by classroom teachers. The manualized program is incorporated into health and physical education curricula and weaves content about healthy relationship behaviors into related topics, such as substance use and healthy sexuality. Broader school-level efforts include teacher training and providing parents information about the program (Wolfe et al., 2009). Rigorous evaluation of the program identified a relative reduction in IPV perpetration, with youth in the control schools reporting greater perpetration than youth in the intervention schools at follow-up (Wolfe et al., 2009).

*Dating Matters to Promote Healthy Teen Relationships* is an IPV prevention program that targets middle school youth in high-risk urban communities. This seven-session, school-based curriculum focuses on healthy relationships and teaching social-emotional learning skills, with additional curricula for parents and teachers. It has been evaluated for its effectiveness compared with the *Safe Dates* program, finding statistically significant reductions in IPV perpetration and victimization among adolescents participating in *Dating Matters* (Niolon et al., 2017). It also shows evidence of reducing violence with shared risk factors, including bullying (Vivolo-Kantor et al., 2019).

Finally, *Stepping Stones* is an HIV prevention program originally developed in 1994 for rural Uganda that has been adapted and implemented across the globe (Lundgren & Amin, 2015). Given the links between sexual health and IPV, it is perhaps unsurprising that exposure to the program, which aims to promote more equitable gender norms, was associated with reductions in IPV perpetration among adolescent men ages 15 to 25 in South Africa (Jewkes et al., 2008).

## Engaging influential adults and peers

Educational institutions have implemented bystander intervention programs to reduce IPV victimization and perpetration among adolescent male athletes (Miller et al., 2020; Miller et al., 2013), high school students (Coker et al., 2017), and college and university students (Coker et al., 2016). Generally, these programs prompt adolescents to notice a situation as potentially harmful, recognize the need to take action, take responsibility for helping someone vulnerable to harm, know how to help, and take action to interrupt (e.g. distract, step in to prevent) abusive behavior (Darley & Latane, 1968). Such community responsibility for violence prevention is an alternative to strategies that consider participants as either victims or perpetrators of abusive behavior (such as the healthy relationships programs, described previously). Indeed, bystander intervention approaches engage community members as potential witnesses and allies to shape social norms and reduce victim-blaming attitudes and defensiveness, rather than focusing on individual-level risk (Banyard, Plante, & Moynihan, 2004). A meta-analysis of bystander intervention programs on university campuses found that youth participating in such programs demonstrated greater pro-social attitudes/beliefs about sexual violence and intervening to prevent it, and engaged in more bystander behavior (Jouriles, Krauss, Vu, Banyard, & McDonald, 2018).

Importantly, bystander intervention programs to prevent IPV are often rooted in Social Norms theory, which posits that individual behavior is informed by perceptions and misperceptions of others' attitudes and behaviors (Berkowitz, 2002; Fabiano, Perkins, Berkowitz, Linkenbach, & Stark, 2003). Indeed, such programs rely on key influencers in a community to model prosocial, bystander intervention and relationship behaviors. Programs have differed regarding *which influencers* they choose to engage. For example, the *Coaching Boys into Men* program, developed by Futures Without Violence, is a coach-delivered intervention for male student-athletes, which aims to raise awareness about the scope of IPV while promoting respectful alternatives, promoting gender-equitable attitudes, and encouraging positive bystander intervention when witnessing disrespectful behaviors among peers. Research has demonstrated the effectiveness of *Coaching Boys into Men* in reducing IPV perpetration among middle (Miller et al., 2020) and high school male student-athletes in the United States (Miller et al., 2013; Miller et al., 2012). The program has also been adapted for cricket athletes in India. An evaluation of this adapted program, *Parivartan*, found that adolescent boys exposed to the program demonstrated greater improvements in gender-equitable attitudes, compared with athletes who were not exposed to the program (Miller et al., 2014). Notably, the adaptation involved more extensive training with coaches (program implementers), compared with the program as originally designed for US settings, and resulted in positive outcomes including more gender-equitable attitudes and increased positive bystander behavior (Das et al., 2015).

*Green Dot* is an evidence-based bystander intervention program that has been tested in high school (Coker et al., 2017) and college settings (Coker et al., 2016). This program purposely engages mixed gender groups of students and trains popular opinion leaders, youth who are identified by school staff as having influence over their peers. Findings suggest that youth exposed to the intervention are less likely to report IPV perpetration and victimization over time (Coker et al., 2017, 2016).

Finally, *Bringing in the Bystander* is an evidence-based program rooted in community responsibility that teaches youth how to intervene safely and effectively to interrupt IPV with strangers, acquaintances, or friends. In addition to evidence with general samples of college students (Peterson, Sharps et al., 2018), this program has been evaluated for its engagement of student leaders (Banyard, Moynihan, & Crossman, 2009), student-athletes (Moynihan, Banyard, Arnold, Eckstein, & Stapleton, 2010), and sororities (Moynihan, Banyard, Arnold, Eckstein, & Stapleton, 2011). Findings suggest that youth exposed to the program demonstrate more prosocial attitudes and greater self-efficacy and intentions to intervene.

## Creating protective environments

Addressing the need for interventions at multiple levels of the social ecology, *Shifting Boundaries* is perhaps the most well-known example of a multi-level IPV intervention intended to create protective environments for youth. Specifically, the *Shifting Boundaries* program for middle school youth focuses on preventing sexual harassment and precursors to IPV via a classroom-based curriculum and school-wide intervention, which aims to modify the physical and social environments of schools. Youth complete "hot spot" maps to identify unsafe areas of their school communities that can then be monitored by teachers and administrators. Moreover, they employ building-based restraining orders for students at risk of IPV. Studies have demonstrated the effectiveness of the building-level component of *Shifting Boundaries* in reducing IPV and sexual harassment perpetration and victimization among middle school youth (Taylor, Mumford, & Stein, 2015; Taylor, Stein, Mumford, & Woods, 2013).

## Applying a developmental, intersectional framework to strengthen prevention

Despite studies documenting the effectiveness of prevention efforts to reduce IPV, the prevalence of this phenomenon has remained stable over time, warranting greater attention to what might be missing from our work to prevent IPV. We suggest that prevention scientists would benefit from applying a developmental, intersectional lens to expand our prevention strategies to consider the unique experiences of adolescents with marginalized identities, including sexual and gender minority youth, racial and ethnic minority youth, and youth with disabilities, who are disproportionately affected by violence.

## Shifting prevention earlier in the life-course

First, let us consider whether and how our programs employ a *developmental* lens. IPV is rooted in social norms, including those about gender. Researchers have found that awareness of gender begins in infancy, with gender stereotypes, including those about the use of aggression, beginning as early as 4 years old (Martin & Ruble, 2009). Moreover, evidence suggests that gender-based, sexual harassment increases in middle adolescence (Bentley, Galliher, & Ferguson, 2007;

Manganello, 2008; McMaster, Connolly, Pepler, & Craig, 2002; Pellegrini, 2001) with studies identifying such experiences as early as 10 years old (Callahan, Tolman, & Saunders, 2003; Eaton et al., 2010; O'Keefe, 1997; Taylor et al., 2013). Collectively, these studies emphasize the necessity to begin IPV prevention efforts early as programs for middle and high school settings may be too late. Our evidence base would benefit from additional focus on how programs like *Coaching Boys into Men* were adapted for early adolescence, a developmental period during which youth are establishing romantic or sexual relationships for the first time (Noonan & Charles, 2009; Stein, 1995).

We would also benefit from efforts to dismantle silos that inhibit prevention programs from drawing on lessons learned from related phenomena. For example, research has documented the links between perpetration of homophobic teasing, bullying, and subsequent perpetration of sexual violence (Espelage, Basile, & Hamburger, 2012; Espelage, Basile, Leemis, Hipp, & Davis, 2018; Espelage & Holt, 2007). Indeed, perpetrators of bullying behavior use this form of aggression to assert power and gain social status (Espelage, 2014), much like perpetrators of IPV (Anderson, 2005). With schools wary of implementing programs focused on sexual violence among younger adolescents, framing efforts in the context of bullying may be an effective strategy to address related risk and protective factors with downstream benefits of reduced IPV perpetration.

## Centering the margins in prevention

Another important limitation of the current literature includes the lack of attention to whether and how IPV prevention addresses the unique experiences of adolescents with marginalized identities. To date, rigorously evaluated prevention strategies have been tested in predominately White, cisgender, presumably heterosexual samples (Banyard et al., 2007; Coker et al., 2017, 2016; Miller et al., 2020). There are two notable exceptions, with differing implications. An evaluation of *Safe Dates* found that the program worked equally well for White students as it did for students of color (Foshee et al., 2005), which is promising. However, given inconsistencies in the evidence base regarding the relative risk for IPV among adolescents of color and a robust body of research that documents the ways that racial discrimination exacerbates trauma, disclosure of IPV, and related care-seeking (McCauley, Campbell, Buchanan, & Moylan, 2019), IPV prevention efforts would be strengthened by intentionally using intersectionality to inform the development and implementation of IPV prevention programs.

The second example of research that has considered how prevention differentially affects adolescents includes a recent study that assessed the effectiveness of the *Green Dot* program in US high schools. This study was the first of its kind, comparing outcomes among sexual minority versus heterosexual youth. It found that *Green Dot* worked best to reduce IPV perpetration and victimization primarily among heterosexual adolescents. In other words, it did not work for sexual minority adolescents (Coker, Bush, Clear, Brancato, & McCauley, 2020). As we previously described, bystander intervention approaches often use popular opinion leaders to normalize prosocial behavior. Central to this approach is an individual's willingness to intervene, which is shaped by cultural assumptions of what attributes or behaviors "deserve" to be punished and whom deserves to be protected (Katz & Moore, 2013). Taken together, these findings suggest that sexual minority youth may not benefit from their peers intervening on their behalf because of homophobia and cooccurring attitudes regarding the acceptance of violence towards sexual minorities. Efforts to build empathy and connection and improve climate for adolescents with marginalized identities may be critical supplemental efforts to current bystander intervention programs (Abbott & Cameron, 2014; Coulter & Rankin, 2017; Dessel, Goodman, & Woodford, 2017).

## Complicating our prevention paradigms

Tensions between competing theoretical frameworks in the field may also hinder the ability of our prevention programs to make tangible reductions in IPV. As we have emphasized, IPV is shaped by structural inequality, warranting attention to the ways that IPV manifests differently by gender, race, sexual orientation, and other intersecting domains. Globally, communities have developed their IPV prevention efforts using a gender transformative lens, which have an explicit focus on complicating hegemonic gender attitudes and engaging men and boys in violence prevention, given evidence that gender-inequitable attitudes are modifiable risk factors for IPV perpetration (Casey, Carlson, Two Bulls, & Yager, 2018; McCauley et al., 2013; Pederson, Greaves, & Poole, 2014). These programs aim to move beyond shaping individual-level attitudes to influence outer levels of the social ecology (Kato-Wallace et al., 2019). However, critics of gender-transformative programs caution against approaches that privilege gender over ones that highlight oppression at the intersection of gender, race, sexual orientation, ability, and other domains of difference (Dworkin, Fleming, & Colvin, 2015). The alternative to gender-transformative programs are gender-neutral approaches, which emphasize that perpetrators and victims can be of any gender, allowing adolescents to see themselves in program content (Katz, Heisterkamp, & Fleming, 2011). However, critics of gender-neutral programs counter that, given the systems of power that underpin IPV, prevention programs that assume equity in the ability to negotiate consent or intervene to disrupt abusive behavior may be insufficient to promote sustained reductions in IPV and other forms of violence (Hong, 2017).

From a developmental, intersectional perspective, prevention efforts would be strengthened by being explicitly power-conscious (McCauley et al., 2019). Power-conscious prevention strategies would identify the ways that multiple stakeholders in a system (e.g. peers, adults) create "nets of accountability" against which adolescents negotiate and police their own gender and that of their peers (Brush & Miller, 2019). These programs, though, must recognize the ways that gender cannot be divorced from an adolescent's race or sexual orientation, and explicitly address structural oppression to prevent IPV (McCauley et al., 2019).

## Moving beyond school-based prevention

Finally, the focus of many of our prevention efforts to teach safe and healthy relationship skills, engage influential adults and peers, and create protective environments have been on individual programs in school-based settings. While school environments are central to the lives and experiences of adolescents, overlapping systems of families, neighborhoods, and broader cultural communities inevitably shape risk for and protection from IPV, complicating what sustained reductions school-based programs can reasonably achieve. Could we more effectively reduce IPV by changing the social contexts that shape adolescents' physical and social-emotional development, as has been recommend (but not yet achieved) in sexual violence prevention (DeGue et al., 2012)? Policy interventions are one strategy to consider. For example, a study by Hoefer and colleagues found that stricter laws (assessed as the availability of civil protection orders for IPV) were associated with lower rates of IPV (Hoefer, Black, & Ricard, 2015). Policy interventions might be a particularly salient strategy to promote safety among adolescents with marginalized identities, given the structural roots of marginalization. Indeed, research has found that LGBT youth in school districts with anti-violence policies experience less violence victimization and experience more positive school climates (Kull, Greytak, Kosciw, & Villenas, 2016). Comprehensive IPV prevention strategies would also strive to work across community systems, as school environments are inevitably shaped by surrounding local and national contexts (McCauley et al., 2019).

## Conclusion

IPV remains a significant social, economic, public health, and human rights problem despite efforts to develop prevention strategies that address risk and protective factors across the social ecology. Given adolescents with marginalized identities bear a disproportionate burden of IPV, our prevention work would be strengthened by employing a developmental, intersectional lens to explicitly address the ways that discrimination and injustice manifest in violence perpetration and victimization among adolescents. Prevention programs would ideally move beyond individual-level risk to shape the social contexts in which adolescents are developing their identities and romantic relationships. To move in this direction, we encourage violence prevention scholars to engage with adolescents, who are experts in their own lives, to inform next steps in research and practice (Goldman et al., 2016).

## Critical findings

- Globally, adolescents are at greatest risk for intimate partner violence (IPV), which comprises physical, psychological, and sexual abuse in intimate relationships.
- Adolescents with marginalized identities, such as sexual and gender minorities, youth of color, and youth with disabilities have increased risk for experiencing IPV.
- Evidence-based programs have been implemented in communities globally to prevent adolescent IPV focused on teaching healthy relationship skills, engaging influential adults and peers, and shaping environments.
- Evaluation of IPV prevention efforts have largely focused on the experiences of White, heterosexual, cisgender adolescents in high-income countries.

## Implications for policy, practice, and research

- Prevention scientists would benefit from applying a developmental, intersectional lens to more explicitly incorporate the needs of adolescents with marginalized identities into prevention programs.
- Prevention efforts and evaluation of these efforts must begin earlier in childhood before gender-based conflicts occur.
- Prevention programs must be as rigorously tested for students with marginalized identities as they are for White, cisgender, heterosexual adolescents.
- Prevention efforts should adapt a power-conscious approach that allows for the identification of ways in which multiple stakeholders in a system create "nets of accountability" against which adolescents negotiate their own identities and those of their peers.
- Policy interventions should be utilized to promote safety amongst youth with marginalized identities and should extend into the community, rather than remaining solely in school settings.

## References

Abbott, N., & Cameron, L. (2014). What makes a young assertive bystander? The effect of intergroup contact, empathy, cultural openness, and in-group bias on assertive bystander intervention intentions. *Journal of Social Issues, 70*(1), 167–182. doi:10.1111/josi.12053

Abramsky, T., Watts, C. H., Garcia-Moreno, C., Devries, K., Kiss, L., Ellsberg, M., . . . Heise, L. (2011). What factors are associated with recent intimate partner violence? Findings from the WHO multi-country study on women's health and domestic violence. *BMC Public Health, 11*, 109.

Adams, A. E., Greeson, M. R., Kennedy, A. C., Tolman, R. M. (2013). The effects of adolescent intimate partner violence on women's educational attainment and earnings. *Journal of Interpersonal Violence, 28*, 3283–3300.

Adhia, A., Gordon, A. R., Roberts, A. L., Fitzmaurice, G. M., Hemenway, D., & Austin, S. B. (2018). Childhood gender nonconformity and intimate partner violence in adolescence and young adulthood. *Journal of Interpersonal Violence*. Epub ahead of print.

Alleyne-Green, B., Coleman-Cowger, V. H., & Henry, D. B. (2012). Dating violence perpetration and/or victimization and associated sexual risk behaviors among a sample of inner-city African American and Hispanic adolescent females. *Journal of Interpersonal Violence, 27*(8), 1457–1473. doi:10.1177/0886260511425788

Alriksson-Schmidt, A. I., Armour, B. S., Thibadeau, J. K. (2010). Are adolescent girls with physical disability at increased risk for sexual violence? *Journal of School Health, 80*(7), 361–367.

Anderson, K. L. (2005). Theorizing gender in intimate partner violence research. *Sex Roles, 52*(11/12), 853–865.

Anderson, M., & Jiang, J. (2018). *Teens, social media, & technology 2018*. Washington, DC: Pew Research Center.

Banyard, V. L., & Cross, C. (2008). Consequences of teen dating violence: Understanding intervening variables in ecological context. *Violence Against Women, 14*(9), 998–1013. doi:10.1177/1077801208 322058

Banyard, V. L., Moynihan, M. M., & Crossman, M. T. (2009). Reducing sexual violence on campus: The role of student leaders as empowered bystanders. *Journal of College Student Development, 50*(4), 446–457.

Banyard, V. L., Moynihan, M. M., & Plante, E. G. (2007). Sexual violence prevention through bystander education: An experimental evaluation. *Journal of Community Psychology, 35*(4), 463–481.

Banyard, V. L., Plante, E. G., & Moynihan, M. M. (2004). Bystander education: Bringing a broader community perspective to sexual violence prevention. *Journal of Community Psychology, 32*, 61–79.

Barter, C., Stanley, N., Wood, M., Lanau, A., Aghtaie, N., Larkins, C., & Øverlien, C. (2017). Young people's online and face-to-face experiences of interpersonal violence and abuse and their subjective impact across five European countries. *Psychology of Violence, 7*(3), 375–384.

Bentley, C. G., Galliher, R. V., & Ferguson, T. J. (2007). Associations among aspects of interpersonal power and relationship functioning in adolescent romantic couples. *Sex Roles, 57*(7–8), 483–495.

Berke, D. S., Reidy, D. E., Gentile, B., & Zeichner, A. (2019). Masculine discrepancy stress, emotion-regulation difficulties, and intimate partner violence. *Journal of Interpersonal Violence, 34*(6), 1163–1182. doi:10.1177/0886260516650967

Berkowitz, A. (Ed.). (2002). *Fostering men's responsibility for preventing sexual assault*. Washington, DC: American Psychological Association.

Bleakley, A., Hennessy, M., Fishbein, M., & Jordan, A. (2008). It works both ways: The relationship between exposure to sexual content in the media and adolescent sexual behavior. *Media Psychology, 11*(4), 443–461. doi:10.1080/15213260802491986

Branch, K., Hilinski-Rosick, C. M., Johnson, E., & Solano, G. (2017). Revenge porn victimization of college students in the united states: An exploratory analysis. *International Journal of Cyber Criminology, 11*(1), 128–142.

Brittian, A. S. (2012). Understanding African American adolescents' identity development: A relational developmental systems perspective. *Journal of Black Psychology, 38*(2), 172–200. doi:10.1177/ 0095798411414570

Brown, A., Cosgrave, E., Killackey, E., Purcell, R., Buckby, J., & Yung, A. R. (2009). The longitudinal association of adolescent dating violence with psychiatric disorders and functioning. *Journal of Interpersonal Violence, 24*(12), 1964–1979. doi:10.1177/0886260508327700

Brown, J. D., & L'Engle, K. L. (2009). X-Rated: Sexual attitudes and behaviors associated with U.S. early adolescents' exposure to sexually explicit media. *Communication Research, 36*(1), 129–151. doi:10.1177/0093650208326465

Brush, L. D., & Miller, E. (2019). Trouble in paradigm: "Gender transformative" programming in violence prevention. *Violence Against Women, 25*(14), 1635–1656.

Callahan, M. R., Tolman, R. M., & Saunders, D. G. (2003). Adolescent dating violence victimization and psychological well-being. *Journal of Adolescent Research, 18*(6), 664–681. doi:10.1177/0743558403254784

Cantor, D., Fisher, B. S., Chibnall, S., Harps, S., Townsend, R., Thomas, G., . . . Madden, K. (2019). *Report on the AAU campus climate survey on sexual assault and misconduct.* Rockville, MD: Westat.

Carroll, B. C., Raj, A., Noel, S. E., & Bauchner, H. (2011). Dating violence among adolescents presenting to a pediatric emergency department. *Archives of Pediatrics & Adolescent Medicine, 165*(12), 1101–1106.

Casey, E., Carlson, J., Two Bulls, S., & Yager, A. (2018). Gender transformative approaches to engaging men in gender-based violence prevention: A review and conceptual model. *Trauma, Violence, & Abuse, 19*(2), 231–246. doi:10.1177/1524838016650191

Chan, K. L., Straus, M. A., Brownridge, D. A., Tiwari, A., & Leung, W. C. (2008). Prevalence of dating partner violence and suicidal ideation among male and female university students worldwide. *Journal of Midwifery and Women's Health, 53,* 529–537.

Choi, H., Van Ouytsel, J., & Temple, J. R. (2016). Association between sexting and sexual coercion among female adolescents. *Journal of Adolescence, 53,* 164–168. https://doi.org/10.1016/j.adolescence.2016.10.005

Choi, H. J., Weston, R., & Temple, J. R. (2017). A three-step latent class analysis to identify how different patterns of teen dating violence and psychosocial factors influence mental health. *Journal of Youth and Adolescence, 46*(4), 854–866. doi:10.1007/s10964-016-0570-7

Coker, A. L., Bush, H. M., Clear, E. R., Brancato, C. J., & McCauley, H. L. (2020). Bystander program effectiveness to reduce violence and violence acceptance within sexual minority male and female high school students using a cluster RCT. *Prevention Science.* Advance online publication.

Coker, A. L., Bush, H. M., Cook-Craig, P. G., DeGue, S. A., Clear, E. R., Brancato, C. J., . . . Recktenwald, E. A. (2017). RCT testing bystander effectiveness to reduce violence. *American Journal of Preventive Medicine, 52*(5), 566–578. https://doi.org/10.1016/j.amepre.2017.01.020

Coker, A. L., Bush, H. M., Fisher, B. S., Swan, S. C., Williams, C. M., Clear, E. R., & DeGue, S. (2016). Multi-college bystander intervention evaluation for violence prevention. *American Journal of Preventive Medicine, 50*(3), 295–302. https://doi.org/10.1016/j.amepre.2015.08.034

Coker, A. L., Clear, E. R., Garcia, L. S., Asaolu, I. O., Cook-Craig, P. G., Brancato, C. J., . . . Fisher, B. S. (2014). Dating violence victimization and perpetration rates among high school students. *Violence Against Women, 20*(10), 1220–1238. doi:10.1177/1077801214551289

Coulter, R. W. S., Mair, C., Miller, E., Blosnich, J. R., Matthews, D. D., & McCauley, H. L. (2017). Prevalence of past-year sexual assault victimization among undergraduate students: Exploring differences by and intersections of gender identity, sexual identity, and race/ethnicity. *Prevention Science, 18*(6), 726–736. doi:10.1007/s11121-017-0762-8

Coulter, R. W. S., & Rankin, S. R. (2017). College sexual assault and campus climate for sexual- and gender-minority undergraduate students. *Journal of Interpersonal Violence,* 1–16. Advance online publication.

Crenshaw, K. (1991). Mapping the margins: Intersectionality, identity politics, and violence against women of color. *Stanford Law Review, 43,* 1241–1299.

Crooks, C. V., Jaffe, P., Dunlop, C., Kerry, A., & Exner-Cortens, D. (2019). Preventing gender-based violence among adolescents and young adults: Lessons from 25 years of program development and evaluation. *Violence Against Women, 25*(1), 29–55.

Cuevas, C. A., Sabina, C., & Bell, K. A. (2014). Dating violence and interpersonal victimization among a national sample of Latino youth. *Journal of Adolescent Health, 55*(4), 564–570. https://doi.org/10.1016/j.jadohealth.2014.04.007

Cui, M., Ueno, K., Gordon, M., & Fincham, F. D. (2013). The continuation of intimate partner violence from adolescence to young adulthood. *Journal of Marriage and Family, 75*(2), 300–313. doi:10.1111/jomf.12016

Dank, M., Lachman, P., Zweig, J. M., & Yahner, J. (2014). Dating violence experiences of lesbian, gay, bisexual, and transgender youth. *Journal of Youth and Adolescence, 43*(5), 846–857. doi:10.1007/s10964-013-9975-8

Darley, J. M., & Latane, B. (1968). Bystander intervention in emergencies: Diffusion of responsibility. *Journal of Personality and Social Psychology, 4,* 377–383.

Das, M., Verma, R., Ghosh, S., Ciaravino, S., Jones, K., O'Connor, B., & Miller, E. (2015). Community mentors as coaches: Transforming gender norms through cricket among adolescent males in urban India. *Gender & Development, 23,* 61–75.

Davis, K. (2013). Young people's digital lives: The impact of interpersonal relationships and digital media use on adolescents' sense of identity. *Computers in Human Behavior, 29*(6), 2281–2293. https://doi.org/10.1016/j.chb.2013.05.022

DeGue, S., Holt, M. K., Massetti, G. M., Matjasko, J. L., Tharp, A. T., & Valle, L. A. (2012). Looking ahead toward community-level strategies to prevent sexual violence. *Journal of Women's Health, 21*(1), 1–3.

Dessel, A. B., Goodman, K. D., & Woodford, M. R. (2017). LGBT discrimination on campus and heterosexual bystanders: Understanding intentions to intervene. *Journal of Diversity in Higher Education, 10*(2), 101–116.

Dick, R. N., McCauley, H. L., Jones, K. A., Tancredi, D. J., Goldstein, S., Blackburn, S., . . . Miller, E. (2014). Cyber dating abuse among teens using school-based health centers. *Pediatrics, 134*(6), e1560–e1567. doi:10.1542/peds.2014-0537

Draucker, C. B., & Martsolf, D. S. (2010). The role of electronic communication technology in adolescent dating violence. *Journal of Child and Adolescent Psychiatric Nursing, 23*(3), 133–142. doi:10.1111/j.1744-6171.2010.00235.x

Dworkin, S. L., Fleming, P. J., & Colvin, C. J. (2015). The promises and limitations of gender-transformative health programming with men: Critical reflections from the field. *Culture, Health, & Sexuality, 17*.

Eaton, D. K., Kann, L., Kinchen, S., Shanklin, S., Ross, J., Hawkins, J., . . . Wechsler, H. (2010). Youth risk behavior surveillance – United States, 2009. *MMWR Surveillance Summaries, 59*(5), 1–142. Retrieved from www.cdc.gov/mmwr/pdf/ss/ss5905.pdf

Edwards, K. M. (2018). Incidence and outcomes of dating violence victimization among high school youth: The role of gender and sexual orientation. *Journal of Interpersonal Violence, 33*(9), 1472–1490. doi:10.1177/0886260515618943

Edwards, K. M., Sylaska, K. M., & Neal, A. M. (2015). Intimate partner violence among sexual minority populations: A critical review of the literature and agenda for future research. *Psychology of Violence, 5*(2), 112–121.

Espelage, D. L. (2014). Ecological theory: Preventing youth bullying, aggression, and victimization. *Theory into Practice, 53*, 257–264.

Espelage, D. L., Basile, K. C., & Hamburger, M. E. (2012). Bullying perpetration and subsequent sexual violence perpetration among middle school students. *Journal of Adolescent Health, 50*(1), 60–65. https://doi.org/10.1016/j.jadohealth.2011.07.015

Espelage, D. L., Basile, K. C., Leemis, R. W., Hipp, T. N., & Davis, J. P. (2018). Longitudinal examination of the bullying-sexual violence pathway across early to late adolescence: Implicating homophobic name-calling. *Journal of Youth and Adolescence, 47*(9), 1880–1893. doi:10.1007/s10964-018-0827-4

Espelage, D. L., & Holt, M. K. (2007). Dating violence and sexual harassment across the bully-victim continuum among middle and high school students. *Journal of Youth and Adolescence, 36*, 799–811.

Exner-Cortens, D., Eckenrode, J., Bunge, J., & Rothman, E. (2017). Revictimization after adolescent dating violence in a matched, national sample of youth. *Journal of Adolescent Health, 60*(2), 176–183. https://doi.org/10.1016/j.jadohealth.2016.09.015

Fabiano, P. M., Perkins, H. W., Berkowitz, A., Linkenbach, J., & Stark, C. (2003). Engaging men as social justice allies in ending violence against women: Evidence for a social norms approach. *Journal of American College Health, 52*(3), 105–112. doi:10.1080/07448480309595732

Felmlee, D., & Faris, R. (2016). Toxic ties: Networks of friendship, dating, and cyber victimization. *Social Psychology Quarterly, 79*(3), 243–262. doi:10.1177/0190272516656585

Ferguson, R. M., Vanwesenbeeck, I., & Knijn, T. (2008). A matter of facts . . . and more: An exploratory analysis of the content of sexuality education in the Netherlands. *Sex Education, 8*(1), 93–106. doi:10.1080/14681810701811878

Findley, P. A., Plummer, S. B., & McMahon, S. (2016). Exploring the experiences of abuse of college students with disabilities. *Journal of Interpersonal Violence, 31*(17), 2801–2823.

Floyd, F. J., & Stein, T. S. (2002). Sexual orientation identity formation among gay, lesbian, and bisexual youths: Multiple patterns of milestone experiences. *Journal of Research on Adolescence, 12*(2), 167–191. doi:10.1111/1532-7795.00030

Fortenberry, J. D. (2013). Puberty and adolescent sexuality. *Hormones and Behavior, 64*(2), 280–287. https://doi.org/10.1016/j.yhbeh.2013.03.007

Foshee, V. A., Bauman, K. E., Ennett, S. T., Suchindran, C., Benefield, T., & Linder, G. F. (2005). Assessing the effects of the dating violence prevention program "safe dates" using random coefficient regression modeling. *Prevention Science, 6*(3), 245. doi:10.1007/s11121-005-0007-0

Foshee, V. A., Karriker-Jaffe, K. J., Reyes, H. L. M., Ennett, S. T., Suchindran, C., Bauman, K. E., & Benefield, T. S. (2008). What accounts for demographic differences in trajectories of adolescent dating violence? An examination of intrapersonal and contextual mediators. *Journal of Adolescent Health, 42*(6), 596–604. https://doi.org/10.1016/j.jadohealth.2007.11.005

Friedman, M. S., Marshal, M. P., Stall, R., Cheong, J., & Wright, E. R. (2008). Gay-related development, early abuse and adult health outcomes among gay males. *AIDS and Behavior, 12*(6), 891–902. doi:10.1007/s10461-007-9319-3

Gillum, T. L., & DiFulvio, G. (2012). "There's so much at stake": Sexual minority youth discuss dating violence. *Violence Against Women, 18*(7), 725–745. doi:10.1177/1077801212455164

Goldman, A. W., Mulford, C. F., & Blachman-Demner, D. R. (2016). Advancing our approach to teen dating violence: A youth and professional defined framework of teen dating relationships. *Psychology of Violence, 6*(4), 497–508.

Goodenow, C., Watson, R. J., Adjei, J., Homma, Y., & Saewyc, E. (2016). Sexual orientation trends and disparities in school bullying and violence-related experiences, 1999–2013. *Psychology of Sexual Orientation and Gender Diversity, 3*(4), 386–396.

Griner, S. B., Vamos, C. A., Thompson, E. L., Logan, R., Vázquez-Otero, C., & Daley, E. M. (2017). The intersection of gender identity and violence: Victimization experienced by transgender college students. *Journal of Interpersonal Violence.* Advance online publication. doi:10.1177/0886260517 723743

Hagan, J., & Foster, H. (2001). *Youth violence and the end of adolescence.* Washington, DC: American Sociological Association. doi:10.2307/3088877

Haynie, D. L., Farhat, T., Brooks-Russell, A., Wang, J., Barbieri, B., & Iannotti, R. J. (2013). Dating violence perpetration and victimization among U.S. adolescents: Prevalence, patterns, and associations with health complaints and substance use. *Journal of Adolescent Health, 53*(2), 194–201. https://doi.org/10.1016/j.jadohealth.2013.02.008

Henry, N., Powell, A., & Flynn, A. (2017). *Not just 'revenge pornography': Australians' experiences of image-based abuse: A Summary Report.* Melbourne: RMIT University.

Hill, A. L., Jones, K. A., McCauley, H. L., Tancredi, D. J., Silverman, J. G., & Miller, E. (2019). Reproductive coercion and relationship abuse among adolescents and young women seeking care at school health centers. *Obstetrics & Gynecology, 134*(2), 351–359.

Hoefer, R., Black, B., & Ricard, M. (2015). The impact of state policy on teen dating violence prevalence. *Journal of Adolescence, 44*, 88–96.

Holliday, C. N., McCauley, H. L., Silverman, J. G., Ricci, E., Decker, M. R., Tancredi, D. J., . . . Miller, E. (2017). Racial/ethnic differences in women's experiences of reproductive coercion, intimate partner violence, and unintended pregnancy. *Journal of Women's Health, 26*(8), 828–835.

Holliday, C. N., Miller, E., Decker, M. R., Burke, J. G., Documet, P. I., Borrero, S. B., . . . McCauley, H. L. (2018). Racial differences in pregnancy intention, reproductive coercion, and partner violence among family planning clients: A qualitative exploration. *Women's Health Issues, 28*(3), 205–211.

Hong, L. (2017). Digging up the roots, rustling the leaves: A critical consideration of the root causes of sexual violence and why higher education needs more courage. In J. C. Harris & C. Linder (Eds.), *Intersections of identity and sexual violence on campus: Centering minoritized students experiences* (pp. 23–41). Sterling, VA: Stylus.

Howard, D. E., Debnam, K. J., & Wang, M. Q. (2013). Ten-year trends in physical dating violence victimization among us adolescent females. *Journal of School Health, 83*(6), 389–399. doi:10.1111/josh.12042

Jewkes, R., Nduna, M., Levin, J., Jama, N., Dunkle, K., Puren, A., & Duvvury, N. (2008). Impact of stepping stones on incidence of HIV and HSV-2 and sexual behavior in rural South Africa: Cluster randomised controlled trial. *BMJ, 337*, a506.

Jouriles, E. N., Krauss, A., Vu, N. L., Banyard, V. L., & McDonald, R. (2018). Bystander programs addressing sexual violence on college campuses: A systematic review and meta-analysis of program outcomes and delivery methods. *Journal of American College Health, 66*(6), 457–466. doi:10.1080/074 48481.2018.1431906

Kann, L., McManus, T., Harris, W. A., Shanklin, S. L., Flint, K. H., Queen, B., . . . Ethier, K. A. (2018). Youth risk behavior surveillance – United States, 2017. *MMWR Surveillance Summaries, 67*(8), 1–114.

Kato-Wallace, J., Barker, G., Garg, A., Feliz, N., Levack, A., Ports, K., & Miller, E. (2019). Adapting a global gender-transformative violence prevention program for the U.S. community-based setting for work with young men. *Global Social Welfare, 6*, 121–130.

Katz, J., Heisterkamp, H. A., & Fleming, W. M. (2011). The social justice roots of the mentors in violence prevention model and its application in a high school setting. *Violence Against Women, 17*(6), 684–702.

Katz, J., & Moore, J. (2013). Bystander education training for campus sexual assault prevention: An initial meta-analysis. *Violence and Victims, 28*, 1054–1067.

Koepke, S., & Denissen, J. J. A. (2012). Dynamics of identity development and separation – Individuation in parent – Child relationships during adolescence and emerging adulthood – A conceptual integration. *Developmental Review, 32*(1), 67–88. https://doi.org/10.1016/j.dr.2012.01.001

Kreutzer, T. (2009). *Generation mobile: Online and digital media usage on mobile phones among low-income urban youth in south Africa.* Cape Town: Center for Film & Media Studies.

Krieger, N. (2005). Embodiment: A conceptual glossary for epidemiology. *Journal of Epidemiology and Community Health, 59*(5), 350–355. doi:10.1136/jech.2004.024562

Kull, R. M., Greytak, E. A., Kosciw, J. G., & Villenas, C. (2016). Effectiveness of school district antibullying policies in improving LGBT youths' school climate. *Psychology of Sexual Orientation and Gender Diversity, 3*(4), 407–415.

Kuo, S. I. C., Wheeler, L. A., Updegraff, K. A., McHale, S. M., Umana-Taylor, A. J., & Perez-Brena, N. J. (2017). Parental modeling and deidentification in romantic relationships among mexican-origin youth. *Journal of Marriage and Family, 79*, 1388–1403.

Langhinrichsen-Rohling, J., Hankla, M., & Stormberg, C. D. (2004). The relationship behavior networks of young adults: A test of the intergenerational transmission of violence hypothesis. *Journal of Family Violence, 19*(3), 139–151. doi:10.1023/B:JOFV.0000028074.35688.4f

Lindhorst, T., Oxford, M., & Gillmore, M. R. (2007). *Longitudinal effects of domestic violence on employment and welfare outcomes.* Los Angeles, CA: Sage. doi:10.1177/0886260507301477

Luna, B., Padmanabhan, A., & O'Hearn, K. (2010). What has fMRI told us about the development of cognitive control through adolescence? *Brain and Cognition, 72*(1), 101–113. https://doi.org/10.1016/j.bandc.2009.08.005

Lundgren, R., & Amin, A. (2015). Addressing intimate partner violence and sexual violence among adolescents: Emerging evidence of effectiveness. *Journal of Adolescent Health, 56*, S42–S50.

Luo, F., Stone, D. M., & Tharp, A. T. (2014). Physical dating violence victimization among sexual minority youth. *American Journal of Public Health, 104*(10), e66–e73. doi:10.2105/ajph.2014.302051

Manganello, J. A. (2008). Teens, dating violence, and media use – A review of the literature and conceptual model for future research. *Trauma Violence Abuse, 9*(1), 3–18. doi:10.1177/1524838007309804

Martin-Storey, A. (2015). Prevalence of dating violence among sexual minority youth: Variation across gender, sexual minority identity and gender of sexual partners. *Journal of Youth and Adolescence, 44*(1), 211–224. doi:10.1007/s10964-013-0089-0

Martin, C. L., & Ruble, D. N. (2009). Patterns of gender development. *Annual Review of Psychology, 61*, 353–381.

McCauley, H. L., Bonomi, A. E., Maas, M. K., Bogen, K. W., & O'Malley, T. L. (2018). #MaybeHeDoesntHitYou: Social media underscore the realities of intimate partner violence. *Journal of Women's Health, 27*(7), 885–891.

McCauley, H. L., Breslau, J. A., Saito, N., & Miller, E. (2015). Psychiatric disorders prior to dating initiation and physical dating violence before age 21: Findings from the National comorbidity survey replication (NCS-R). *Social Psychiatry and Psychiatric Epidemiology, 50*(9), 1357–1365. doi:10.1007/s00127-015-1044-z

McCauley, H. L., Campbell, R., Buchanan, N., & Moylan, C. A. (2019). Advancing theory, methods, and dissemination in sexual violence research to build a more equitable future: An intersectional, community-engaged approach. *Violence Against Women, 25*(16), 1906–1931.

McCauley, H. L., Silverman, J. G., Decker, M. R., Agenor, M., Borrero, S., Tancredi, D. J., . . . Miller, E. (2015). Sexual and reproductive health indicators and intimate partner violence victimization among female family planning clinic patients who have sex with women and men. *Journal of Women's Health, 24*(8), 621–628.

McCauley, H. L., Tancredi, D. J., Silverman, J. G., Decker, M. R., Austin, S. B., McCormick, M., . . . Miller, E. (2013). Gender-equitable attitudes, bystander behavior, and recent abuse perpetration against heterosexual dating partners of male high school athletes. *American Journal of Public Health, 103*(10), 1882–1887.

McElhaney, K. B., Antonishak, J., & Allen, J. P. (2008). "They like me, they like me not": Popularity and adolescents' perceptions of acceptance predicting social functioning over time. *Child Development, 79*(3), 720–731.

McMaster, L. E., Connolly, J., Pepler, D., & Craig, W. M. (2002). Peer to peer sexual harassment in early adolescence: A developmental perspective. *Development and Psychopathology, 14*(1), 91–105. doi:10.1017/s0954579402001050

Miller, E., Das, M., Tancredi, D. J., McCauley, H. L., Virata, M. C. D., Nettiksimmons, J., . . . Verma, R. (2014). Evaluation of a gender-based violence prevention program for student athletes in Mumbai, India. *Journal of Interpersonal Violence, 29*, 758–778.

Miller, E., Jones, K. A., & McCauley, H. L. (2018). Updates on adolescent dating and sexual violence prevention and intervention. *Current Opinion in Pediatrics, 30*(4), 466–471.

Miller, E., Jones, K. A., Ripper, L., Paglisotti, T., Mulbah, P., & Abebe, K. Z. (2020). An athletic coach-delivered middle school gender violence prevention program. *JAMA Pediatrics*. Advance online publication.

Miller, E., Tancredi, D. J., McCauley, H. L., Decker, M. R., Virata, M. C. D., Anderson, H. A., . . . Silverman, J. G. (2013). One-year follow-up of a coach-delivered dating violence prevention program: A cluster randomized controlled trial. *American Journal of Preventive Medicine, 45*(1), 108–112. https://doi.org/10.1016/j.amepre.2013.03.007

Miller, E., Tancredi, D. J., McCauley, H. L., Decker, M. R., Virata, M. C. D., Anderson, H. A., . . . Silverman, J. G. (2012). "Coaching boys into men": A cluster-randomized controlled trial of a dating violence prevention program. *Journal of Adolescent Health, 51*(5), 431–438. https://doi.org/10.1016/j.jadohealth.2012.01.018

Mitra, M., Mouradian, V. E., & McKenna, M. (2013). Dating violence and associated health risks among high school students with disabilities. *Maternal and Child Health Journal, 17*(6), 1088–1094. doi:10.1007/s10995-012-1091-y

Morelli, M., Bianchi, D., Chirumbolo, A., & Baiocco, R. (2018). The cyber dating violence inventory. Validation of a new scale for online perpetration and victimization among dating partners. *European Journal of Developmental Psychology, 15*(4), 464–471.

Moschella, E. A., Potter, S. J., & Moynihan, M. M. (2020). Disclosure of sexual violence victimization and anticipated social reactions among lesbian, gay, and bisexual community college students. *Journal of Bisexuality*, 1–20. doi:10.1080/15299716.2020.1715910

Moynihan, M. M., Banyard, V. L., Arnold, J. S., Eckstein, R. P., & Stapleton, J. G. (2010). Engaging intercollegiate athletes in preventing and intervening in sexual and intimate partner violence. *Journal of American College Health, 59*(3), 197–204. doi:10.1080/07448481.2010.502195

Moynihan, M. M., Banyard, V. L., Arnold, J. S., Eckstein, R. P., & Stapleton, J. G. (2011). Sisterhood may be powerful for reducing sexual and intimate partner violence: An evaluation of the bringing in the bystander in-person program with sorority members. *Violence Against Women, 17*(6), 703–719. doi:10.1177/1077801211409726

Nahapetyan, L., Orpinas, P., Song, X., & Holland, K. (2014). Longitudinal association of suicidal ideation and physical dating violence among high school students. *Journal of Youth and Adolescence, 43*(4), 629–640. doi:10.1007/s10964-013-0006-6

Nikolajski, C., Miller, E., McCauley, H. L., Akers, A., Schwarz, E. B., Freedman, L., . . . Borrero, S. (2015). Race and reproductive coercion: A qualitative assessment. *Women's Health Issues, 25*(3), 216–223.

Niolon, P. H., Kearns, M., Dills, J., Rambo, K., Irving, S., & Armstead, T. L. (2017). *Preventing intimate partner violence across the lifespan: A technical package of programs, policies, and practices*. Atlanta, GA: U.S. Centers for Disease Control and Prevention.

Niolon, P. H., Vivolo-Kantor, A. M., Latzman, N. E., Valle, L. A., Kuoh, H., Burton, T., . . . Tharp, A. T. (2015). Prevalence of teen dating violence and co-occurring risk factors among middle school youth in high-risk urban communities. *Journal of Adolescent Health, 56*(Suppl. 2), S5–S13. https://doi.org/10.1016/j.jadohealth.2014.07.019

Noonan, R. K., & Charles, D. (2009). Developing teen dating violence prevention strategies formative research with middle school youth. *Violence Against Women, 15*(9), 1087–1105. doi:10.1177/1077801209340761

O'Keefe, M. (1997). Predictors of dating violence among high school students. *Journal of Interpersonal Violence, 12*(4), 546–568. doi:10.1177/088626097012004005

Orpinas, P., Nahapetyan, L., Song, X., McNicholas, C., & Reeves, P. M. (2012). Psychological dating violence perpetration and victimization: Trajectories from middle to high school. *Aggressive Behavior, 38*(6), 510–520. doi:10.1002/ab.21441

Øverlien, C., Hellevik, P. M., & Korkmaz, S. (2019). Young women's experiences of intimate partner violence – Narratives of control, terror, and resistance. *Journal of Family Violence*. Advance online publication. doi:10.1007/s10896-019-00120-9

Pederson, A., Greaves, L., & Poole, N. (2014). Gender-transformative health promotion for women: A framework for action. *Health Promotion International, 30*(1), 140–150.

Peitzmeier, S. M., Kågesten, A., Acharya, R., Cheng, Y., Delany-Moretlwe, S., Olumide, A., . . . Decker, M. R. (2016). Intimate partner violence perpetration among adolescent males in disadvantaged neighborhoods globally. *Journal of Adolescent Health, 56*, 696–702.

Pellegrini, A. D. (2001). A longitudinal study of heterosexual relationships, aggression, and sexual harassment during the transition from primary school through middle school. *Journal of Applied Developmental Psychology, 22*(2), 119–133. doi:10.1016/s0193-3973(01)00072-7

Peterson, C., Kearns, M. C., McIntosh, W. L., Estefan, L. F., Nicolaidis, C., McCollister, K. E., . . . Florence, C. (2018). Lifetime economic burden of intimate partner violence among U.S. adults. *American Journal of Preventive Medicine, 55*(4), 433–444.

Peterson, K., Sharps, P., Banyard, V., Powers, R. A., Kaukinen, C., Gross, D., . . . Campbell, J. (2018). An evaluation of two dating violence prevention programs on a college campus. *Journal of Interpersonal Violence, 33*(23), 3630–3655. doi:10.1177/0886260516636069

Porter, J. L., & McQuiller Williams, L. (2013). Dual marginality: The impact of auditory status and sexual orientation on abuse in a college sample of women and men. *Journal of Aggression, Maltreatment & Trauma, 22*(6), 577–589.

Poteat, V. P., Espelage, D. L., & Koenig, B. W. (2009). Willingness to remain friends and attend school with lesbian and gay peers: Relational expressions of prejudice among heterosexual youth. *Journal of Youth and Adolescence, 38*(7), 952–962.

Reuter, T. R., Sharp, C., & Temple, J. R. (2015). An exploratory study of teen dating violence in sexual minority youth. *Partner Abuse, 6*, 8–28.

Romans, S., Forte, T., Cohen, M. M., Du Mont, J., & Hyman, I. (2007). Who is most at risk for intimate partner violence? *Journal of Interpersonal Violence, 22*(12), 1495–1514.

Rothman, E. F., & Xuan, Z. (2014). Trends in physical dating violence victimization among U.S. high school students, 1999–2011. *Journal of School Violence, 13*(3), 277–290. doi:10.1080/15388220.2013. 847377

Ryan, C., Russell, S. T., Huebner, D., Diaz, R., & Sanchez, J. (2010). Family acceptance in adolescence and the health of LGBT young adults. *Journal of Child and Adolescent Psychiatric Nursing, 23*(4), 205–213.

Sabina, C., Cuevas, C. A., & Cotignola-Pickens, H. M. (2016). Longitudinal dating violence victimization among Latino teens: Rates, risk factors, and cultural influences. *Journal of Adolescence, 47*, 5–15. https:// doi.org/10.1016/j.adolescence.2015.11.003

Scherer, H. L., Snyder, J. A., & Fisher, B. S. (2016). Intimate partner victimization among college students with and without disabilities: Prevalence of and relationship to emotional well-being. *Journal of Interpersonal Violence, 31*(1), 49–80. doi:10.1177/0886260514555126

Scherer, H. L., Snyder, J. A., & Fisher, B. S. (2013). A gendered approach to understanding intimate partner victimization and mental health outcomes among college students with and without disability. *Women & Criminal Justice, 23*, 209–231.

Shorey, R. C., Fite, P. J., Choi, H., Cohen, J. R., Stuart, G. L., & Temple, J. R. (2015). Dating violence and substance use as longitudinal predictors of adolescents' risky sexual behavior. *Prevention Science, 16*(6), 853–861. doi:10.1007/s11121-015-0556-9

Singh, A. A. (2013). Transgender youth of color and resilience: Negotiating oppression and finding support. *Sex Roles, 68*(11), 690–702. doi:10.1007/s11199-012-0149-z

Singh, S., Wulf, D., Samara, R., & Cuca, Y. P. (2000). Gender differences in the timing of first intercourse: Data from 14 countries. *International Family Planning Perspectives, 26*(1), 21–28 & 43.

Smith, S. G., Zhang, X., Basile, K. C., Merrick, M. T., Wang, J., Kresnow, M., & Chen, J. (2018). *The national intimate partner and sexual violence survey (NISVS): 2015 data brief – Updated release.* Atlanta, GA: U.S. Centers for Disease Control and Prevention.

Spiegler, O., Wölfer, R., & Hewstone, M. (2019). Dual identity development and adjustment in Muslim minority adolescents. *Journal of Youth and Adolescence, 48*(10), 1924–1937. doi:10.1007/s10964-019-01117-9

Stein, N. (1995). Sexual harassment in school – The public performance of gendered violence. *Harvard Educational Review, 65*(2), 145–162. Retrieved from <Go to ISI>://WOS:A1995RC04900003

Swahn, M. H., Simon, T. R., Arias, I., & Bossarte, R. M. (2008). Measuring sex differences in violence victimization and perpetration within date and same-sex peer relationships. *Journal of Interpersonal Violence, 23*(8), 1120–1138. doi:10.1177/0886260508314086

Taylor, B. G., Mumford, E. A., & Stein, N. D. (2015). Effectiveness of "shifting boundaries" teen dating violence prevention program for subgroups of middle school students. *Journal of Adolescent Health*, *56*(Suppl. 2), S20–S26. https://doi.org/10.1016/j.jadohealth.2014.07.004

Taylor, B. G., Stein, N. D., Mumford, E. A., & Woods, D. (2013). Shifting boundaries: An experimental evaluation of a dating violence prevention program in middle schools. *Prevention Science*, *14*(1), 64–76. doi:10.1007/s11121-012-0293-2

Teitelman, A. M., Ratcliffe, S. J., Morales-Aleman, M. M., & Sullivan, C. M. (2008). Sexual relationship power, intimate partner violence, and condom use among minority urban girls. *Journal of Interpersonal Violence*, *23*(12), 1694–1712. Doi:10.1177/0886260508314331

Temple, J. R., Choi, H. J., Brem, M., Wolford-Clevenger, C., Stuart, G. L., Peskin, M. F., & Elmquist, J. (2016). The temporal association between traditional and cyber dating abuse among adolescents. *Journal of Youth and Adolescence*, *45*(2), 340–349. doi:10.1007/s10964-015-0380-3

Tharp, A. T., DeGue, S., Valle, L. A., Brookmeyer, K. A., Massetti, G. M., & Matjasko, J. L. (2013). A systematic qualitative review of risk and protective factors for sexual violence perpetration. *Trauma, Violence, & Abuse*, *14*, 133–167.

Tulloch, T., & Kaufman, M. (2013). Adolescent sexuality. *Pediatrics in Review*, *34*(1), 29–38. doi:10.1542/pir.34-1-29

Vagi, K. J., Olsen, E. O., Basile, K. C., & Vivolo-Kantor, A. M. (2015). Teen dating violence (physical and sexual) among us high school students: Findings from the 2013 national youth risk behavior survey. *JAMA Pediatr*, *169*(5), 474–482.

Van Ouytsel, J., Ponnet, K., & Walrave, M. (2017). The associations of adolescents' dating violence victimization, well-being and engagement in risk behaviors. *Journal of Adolescence*, *55*, 66–71. https://doi.org/10.1016/j.adolescence.2016.12.005

Vivolo-Kantor, A. M., Niolon, P. H., Estefan, L. F., Le, V. D., Tracy, A. J., Latzman, N. E., . . . Tharp, A. T. (2019). Middle school effects of the dating matters® comprehensive teen dating violence prevention model on physical violence, bullying, and cyberbullying: A cluster-randomized controlled trial. *Prevention Science*. Doi:10.1007/s11121-019-01071-9

Vivolo-Kantor, A. M., Olsen, E. O. M., & Bacon, S. (2016). Associations of teen dating violence victimization with school violence and bullying among US high school Students. *Journal of School Health*, *86*(8), 620–627. doi:10.1111/josh.12412

Whitaker, D. J., & Miller, K. S. (2000). Parent-adolescent discussions about sex and Condoms: Impact on peer influences of sexual risk behavior. *Journal of Adolescent Research*, *15*(2), 251–273. doi:10.1177/0743558400152004

White Hughto, J. M., Reisner, S. L., & Pachankis, J. E. (2015). Transgender stigma and health: A critical review of stigma determinants, mechanisms, and interventions. *Social Science & Medicine*, *147*, 222–231. https://doi.org/10.1016/j.socscimed.2015.11.010

Wingood, G. M., & DiClemente, R. J. (1997). The effects of an abusive primary partner on the condom use and sexual negotiation practices of African-American women. *American Journal of Public Health*, *87*(6), 1016–1018. doi:10.2105/ajph.87.6.1016

Wolfe, D. A., Crooks, C., Jaffe, P., Chiodo, D., Hughes, R., Ellis, W., . . . Donner, A. (2009). A school-based program to prevent adolescent dating violence. *Arch Pediatr Adolesc Med*, *163*(8), 692–699.

Wolitzky-Taylor, K. B., Ruggiero, K. J., Danielson, C. K., Resnick, H. S., Hanson, R. F., Smith, D. W., . . . Kilpatrick, D. G. (2008). Prevalence and correlates of dating violence in a national sample of adolescents. *Journal of the American Academy of Child & Adolescent Psychiatry*, *47*(7), 755–762. https://doi.org/10.1097/CHI.0b013e318172ef5f

World Health Organization/London School of Hygiene and Tropical Medicine. (2010). *Preventing intimate partner and sexual violence against women: Taking action and generating evidence*. Geneva: World Health Organization.

Wubs, A. G., Aarø, L. E., Flisher, A. J., Bastien, S., Onya, H. E., Kaaya, S., & Mathews, M. (2009). Dating violence among school students in Tanzania and South Africa: Prevalence and sociodemographic variations. *Scandinavian Journal of Public Health*, *37*, 75–86.

Ybarra, M. L., Espelage, D. L., Langhinrichsen-Rohling, J., Korchmaros, J. D., & Boyd, D. (2016). Lifetime prevalence rates and overlap of physical, psychological, and sexual dating abuse perpetration and victimization in a national sample of youth. *Archives of Sexual Behavior*, *45*, 1083–1099.

Zweig, J. M., Dank, M., Yahner, J., & Lachman, P. (2013). The rate of cyber dating abuse among teens and how it relates to other forms of teen dating violence. *Journal of Youth and Adolescence, 42*(7), 1063–1077. doi:10.1007/s10964-013-9922-8

Zweig, J. M., Lachman, P., Yahner, J., & Dank, M. (2014). Correlates of cyber dating abuse among teens. *Journal of Youth and Adolescence, 43*(8), 1306–1321. doi:10.1007/s10964-013-0047-x

# 33

# COMMUNITY-BASED SAFETY PARTNERSHIPS TO REDUCE GENDER-BASED VIOLENCE IN UGANDA

## The Anti-Domestic Violence and Abuse Center (ADOVIC) approach

*Maria T. Clark, Kyemba Rosemary Wakesho, Recheal Silvia Bonsuk, Shiella Nabunya, Bugonzi Margaret Kyemba Kulaba and Julie Taylor*

### Introduction

Reducing the incidence and prevalence of gender-based violence (GBV) in low- and middle-income countries is a United Nations (UN) sustainable development goal (SDG 5; Signorelli et al., 2018). The UN Women's annual report (UN Women, 2017) showed that in the East and Southern African Regions it is a particularly serious problem. In these regions, violence against girls is one of the major contributing factors for high school dropout rates for girls. Physical and sexual violence affects one in three women and bears a significant threat to life. However, it is also normalised. United Nations Women (2017) reported that 51% of African women suggested that beatings by their husbands are justified in certain circumstances. As such:

> Accurate statistics on the higher prevalence of physical and sexual violence against women and girls in African countries is difficult to determine due to stigma and under-reporting.
>
> (WHO, 2013)

The Ugandan Demographic Health Survey (USAID, 2012) reported that 56% of women aged between 15 and 49 years have experienced physical violence at some point in life, while 22% have experienced sexual violence. More than one million Ugandan women suffer sexual abuse every year. The USAID Evaluation of Africa's Health report (USAID, 2010) suggested that among all married women who had experienced physical violence, 70–80% reported their husband as the perpetrator. In the eastern region of Uganda, 75% of women were abused before the age of 45 (UBOS, 2019). A review of gender-based violence research in humanitarian settings highlighted that intimate partner violence (IPV) is the most common form of violence

(Hossain & McAlpine, 2017). The authors concluded that the gendered impacts of violence in African countries needs to be better researched, by adopting a wider range of methodologies and involving local participants in research. We use the broader term GBV here to encompass women and girls' experience of all types of abuse in *all* settings, across the life-course. Here, we report on a small-scale research collaboration between the Anti-Domestic Violence and Abuse Center (ADOVIC) in Jinja, Uganda and the Institute of Global Innovation at the University of Birmingham (UK).

## *The Anti-Domestic Violence and Abuse Center (ADOVIC)*

ADOVIC describes itself as a community-based organisation (CBO; ADOVIC, 2019). It is a local non-governmental organisation (NGO) that aims to "prevent domestic abuse and reduce the impact of violence on individuals and families living in the region" (ADOVIC, 2020). Based in the Amber Court District of Jinja, the wooden office is accessible by foot, bicycle, taxi scooter (*boda boda*) or car. Jinja is located in the east of Uganda, on the northern shore of Lake Victoria. Historically, the town was a small fishing village and trading post, with a developing industrial infrastructure, mainly the growth and supply of cotton, coffee, subsistence agriculture and crafts, involving open-air markets. The current estimated population is 93,061 (UBOS, 2019). The capital of Uganda, Kampala, is 82 kilometres (54 miles) by road. The nearest airport is Entebbe, approximately 116 kilometres (72 miles) from Jinja. A major engineering development of a main highway aims to better link Jinja to Kampala and Entebbe.

A popular tourist destination because of its abundant natural environment, river trips and water sports across the Nile are commonplace in season. Emergent stories suggest that Jinja is a colonial name for 'stone' or 'rock', attributed to the governor Hesketh Bell in 1906; representing the place from where small boats launched, to cross the river from the Busoga to Buganda regions. Jinja is a developing, complex and diverse urban society, living through a postcolonial legacy of urbanisation, displacement and political unrest (Byerley, 2013).

From the outset, ADOVIC campaigned for the eradication of domestic violence "in order to create a conducive environment in families where women and girls would live healthy lives free from fear of violence, able to exploit their full potential to the benefit of their families" (ADOVIC, 2020). Co-founded by Ben Kulaba and Bugonzi Margaret Kyemba Kulaba it aimed to provide shelter for victims of domestic violence while negotiating cases with families and other authorities. When the demand for the shelter far exceeded capacity to respond, the shelter closed. ADOVIC re-strategised to concentrate on training and advocacy; sensitising communities to the causes and effects of domestic violence. ADOVIC also trained local council courts to handle cases under the Ugandan Domestic Violence Act (2010), including by training police within child and family protection departments, as well as health workers on how to handle domestic violence victims referred to their care. The services included direct mediation and counselling, legal advice, and some health and social support delivered in a range of settings.

The long-term organisational vision is to have families free from all forms of GBV, by "promoting positive social norms that prevent GBV and challenging norms that support violence and a culture of impunity" (ADOVIC, 2020). Three work-based approaches involve:

1   **Rights-based approach:** to analyse and address the root causes of discrimination and inequality to ensure that everyone, regardless of their gender, age, ethnicity or religion, has the right to live with freedom and dignity, safe from violence, exploitation and abuse, in accordance with principles of human rights law.

2 **Community-based approach:** to ensure that affected populations are actively engaged as partners in developing strategies related to their protection and the provision of humanitarian assistance. This approach involves direct consultation with women, girls and other at-risk groups at all stages in the humanitarian response, to identify protection risks and solutions and build on existing community-based protection mechanisms.

3 **'Do no harm' approach:** to take all measures necessary to avoid exposing a victim to further harm because of our actions.

The ADOVIC programme aims to increase:

- Human rights awareness among populations to improve response and prevention of domestic violence.
- Women empowerment to improve response and prevention of domestic violence.
- Gender engagement for dismantling patriarchy to improve response and prevention of domestic violence.
- Institutional development to facilitate response and prevention of domestic violence.

The Ugandan Domestic Violence Act (2010) was an important legal lever for ADOVIC service development; criminalising domestic violence and abuse (DVA) is a practical forward step, although it is not always clear how the law operates in local contexts. The strategic aim of the organisation is "to mobilize women and men in Uganda to review all customs, norms, cultures, policies and practices which perpetuate inequality and violence against women" (ADOVIC, 2019, p. 13). ADOVIC has well-established international development partnerships; these include Irish Aid, UNICEF, UN Women, UN Trust Fund and others, financing GBV activities including the drive to end early child marriages and female genital mutilation. Locally, however, ADOVIC staffing is not stable and retention is a problem. During our visits, ADOVIC relied upon continued donations and funding to sustain their work within communities.

To build capacity for raising awareness of the scale and impact of GBV, ADOVIC trains women and men volunteers to identify and respond to the issue. ADOVIC describes the people they train as 'key workers' and 'duty bearers' who may be asked to undertake visits (with the ADOVIC workers) in people's homes, communities, places of worship, civic organisations and schools. On a weekly basis, ADOVIC receives three to five survivors who seek counselling, psychosocial support and guidance on various legal issues. Complex legal issues range from reporting life-threatening or disabling critical events, involving violence and abuse against women and sexual abuse of children. Victims often need immediate access to essential medical and psychological care, as well as safe housing in a context that does not always recognise a woman's rights to independent ownership of land and property.

The UK team connected with ADOVIC during two field visits to Jinja in 2018/9 (Clark, 2018). The first was partly serendipitous – we were there on another project – but ADOVIC welcomed our visit and in discussion, we agreed joint priorities to take forward as a precursor to a fuller outcomes evaluation. Public involvement and engagement work before and during a research application (as well as throughout the research) is expected in many countries now. As follows, we present the descriptive findings from our small-scale research engagement, which aimed to explore the social and political factors that influenced community engagement with ADOVIC services. We particularly wanted to find out more about the ADOVIC approach to partnership working with other organisations and agencies to protect women and children from GBV.

## Methods

We used the principles of 'participatory action research' (PAR) to guide our academic engagement with ADOVIC. PAR is a social research method, usually involving a co-learning process (Schulz, Krieger, & Galea, 2002; Sullivan, Bhuyan, Senturia, Shiu-Thornton, & Ciske, 2005; Tighe, Peters, & Skirton, 2013). Continuous cycles of planning, acting, observing and reflecting inform the data collection and analysis, which includes action plans to enable social transformation (Benjamin-Thomas, Corrado, McGrath, Rudman, & Hand, 2018). In this case, the first visit to ADOVIC prepared the groundwork through face-to-face sharing about our respective experiences of GBV prevention. During this visit we agreed shared research priorities for a follow-up visit (Clark, 2018).

The second visit involved advance planning for structured research activities, within the context of co-learning about ADOVIC's approach to community engagement to reduce GBV in the region. We undertook interim email and phone call conversations to help prepare for our arrival. ADOVIC shared their reports and strategies to enable us to undertake exploratory data collection and analysis. The five days of community engagement activities included (1) documentary analysis, (2) community worker interviews and (3) a stakeholder focus group.

Other studies in Africa (Bradbury-Jones, 2018; Lund, Standing Voice, & Advantage Africa, 2017) found that when people are very enthusiastic and engaged in the topic, interviews and focus groups can be arranged very rapidly, in the field, and often beyond expectations. Here too, a series of semi-structured individual face-to-face interviews with nine ADOVIC-linked stakeholders included a survivor, police officer, community social worker in a local health clinic and six volunteer workers. This was supplemented by an hour-long focus group with 18 wider stakeholders, including representatives from religious, civic and community groups. The interviews took place securely in ADOVIC mediated settings, with the assistance of ADOVIC facilitating recruitment and translation. In 2019, the University of Birmingham (UK) research ethics committee gave ethical approval for the study. ADOVIC secured all local permissions, helped construct the broad questions for the interviews and arranged the practical, logistic elements of hosting the participants and obtaining consent.

Descriptive thematic analysis of the interviews identified plural, intersecting factors that helped build local community-based partnerships to steer women and children towards personal safety. Next, we present these descriptive findings.

## Findings

### *1 Legal, religious and civic pluralism*

Uganda is a diverse society, with various legal, religious and civil responses to GBV, including domestic abuse. Local participants spoke about ADOVIC's capacity to respond to overwhelming needs in the context of extreme poverty. Working within this impoverished context involves sensitivity to the gross inequities in women's legal recourse to paid employment and independent land or property ownership (see Table 33.1 for an overview of plural legal influences). Whitehead and Tsikata (2003) note that most Ugandan women have limited understanding of the legal code and also lack access to legal advocacy, especially those women living in remote rural areas. Where legal structures do exist, local leaders might unfairly favour customary laws. Women's education and pathways to paid work in Uganda are very limited. Relatively few women are included in 'land boards' despite the Land Act of 2010 which encouraged greater diversity.

Extreme poverty, exploitation and homelessness affect how ADOVIC addresses GBV locally. ADOVIC workers showed their local knowledge of women's experience of adversity by harnessing wide-ranging legal, religious and civic supports from various community leaders, organisations and agencies, sensitising individuals and communities to the need for GBV reduction. In this way, ADOVIC provided examples of the 'contextual safeguarding' approach advocated by Firmin (2017) and others as a means to critical place-based reporting of localised problems and practices. Here, participants spoke about how ADOVIC workers 'knowing' of the intra and extra familial context is integral to place-based responses to survivors of DVA, using well-situated volunteer supports and multi-agency resources to help prevent its re-occurrence in local families and communities. Unusually, working together with victims and perpetrators in and outside of the familial home environment is an element of ADOVIC's approach:

> So when this person reports to ADOVIC the other people write a letter to the community support office explaining the issue that is happening between this victim and the perpetrator and then sets a date that you meet these two people. First, they listen to the victim and then they listen to the perpetrator. After they have listened to the both sides ADOVIC and the chairperson now bring out ideas they speak themselves. When they agree on something these two people write down something they have agreed on. Therefore, if they follow what they have written down, they end there. But just in case one of them decides to not do what was written down by the both of them they then take the issue to a different place, maybe the police or somewhere else.
>
> [Participant 2 – Social Worker]

> I know that ADOVIC works and is supportive, consisting of counselling and home visits. I have a cousin who home visits. ADOVIC tried to find out the victims and then they listened to them. That's how ADOVIC works. After finding the victims ADOVIC sits with the victim and listens to her, then after listening to her they consult the victim and implements. . . . When I receive someone who has issues I have to find a police office and then the office [ADOVIC] has to connect back to the court. . . . So it's the office here [ADOVIC] that connects everything.
>
> [Participant 1 – Health Worker]

Extending place-based supports is a challenge. The personal safety of ADOVIC staff was a concern raised by two participants, including the police:

> Sometimes the workers needs protection. I want you to note that. Where you go to the house and the husband is very hostile. She needs to travel with the security people but in plain clothing. That is how I have been working with this office.
>
> [Participant 3 – Police Worker]

A complex case, discussed by a number of participants, involved working with health services (medical), police and social work, alongside the mother of a child victim of serious sexual assault:

> I arrest this man. I take him to the council and there is not enough evidence. . . . So they came ADOVIC they saw, they asked me what happened and then they went

to the police. So at the police station, they said whatever evidence you have it is not enough. . . . So with ADOVIC . . . we looked for the doctor who wrote in the book and then in the hospital. . . . Because of their help, the person was arrested and finally taken to prison. I felt I had failed my daughter and I was not going to make it through, but ADOVIC helped me.

[Participant 5 – Mother of Child Victim of Sexual Assault]

---

## A CASE EXAMPLE

Alara [pseudonym] was 19 years old when she presented to ADOVIC and reported a case of land grabbing. She narrated her story to one of the counsellors.

"My late father passed on and left behind property. My uncle convinced me to sell the property so that we can purchase land that is in a better environment. My uncle went ahead and sold my late father's home at seven million and five hundred thousand Ugandan shillings [$US 2000] and then he bought land in my names at two million Uganda shillings [$US 529]. The balance was used to construct rental units. This made me happy and I felt important that my uncle and I were working closely to see that I have a bright future, and being a girl, rarely do such incidences happen where a girl is allowed to inherit the father's property when he passes away. In most cases, they will either look at the close relatives like uncles, or sons born to the uncles. Recently when I returned to settle in my home, my uncle used his power over me and he beat me up badly and chased me away claiming that I did not own any property."

The counsellor asked, "Do you have the documents of transaction?"

"No they are with my grandmother who is also working hand in hand with my uncle to confiscate my property."

ADOVIC worked with local 'duty bearers' to resolve the issue. Duty bearers are ADOVIC activists who have a particular responsibility "to respect, promote and realize human rights and to abstain from human rights violation". They may be parents, teachers, police, community leaders and all these can be neighbours to the victim or relatives. ADOVIC visited the community where Alara claimed that she was denied her property. Local people who knew Alara confirmed that the property belonged to her. In most cases if not all ADOVIC use a community engagement approach to decision making about how to resolve the situation.

If the people around you are 'in the know', they can be the ones to help you out when all is not well. After all this we had to go visit the grandmother and also hear her view since she is the one who had the document of the transactions of the property. She complained that Alara was disrespectful, and they were scared to let her stay alone as she is still a young girl. We as ADOVIC agreed to talk to Alara about her behaviours and she agreed to adjust accordingly. Together grandmother and uncle finally gave back the document and property to Alara. She is since living happily and appreciates that ADOVIC responded positively to her.

[Participant 6 – Social Worker]

*Figure 33.1* Addressing GBV in the context of 'land grabbing' in a local community

The case study shows the ways in which gender, poverty and land ownership intersect with GBV against women in this region. Women's rights to property and land assets in Uganda are a continued struggle. First, there is a distinction (and often a conflict) between state and customary laws in Uganda. Here, we show how ADOVIC identifies and responds to this conflict through its community engagement approach, particularly when women victims find their rights to state protection intersect with plural customary religious and local laws.

Alara's case shows how ADOVIC is often involved in supporting women's rights to property. Many women have fled their communities due to violence and abuse, and they are sexually and financially vulnerable to exploitation on the streets. When a woman is assaulted or rendered homeless, legal levers can help secure criminal justice and a place of safety. To ensure a woman can remain in or return to the family home, the Ugandan Constitution of 1995, the Employment Act 2006, the Occupational Safety and Health Act of 2006 might help her argue her case (Nabwiiso, 2018). Bajpai (2014) suggested that even relatively able and successful African women (such as those who work as entrepreneurs) are likely to receive only a fraction of the available profit. The plural factors that influenced ADOVIC's community-based approach to GBV reduction are shown in Table 33.1. While discrete, these factors also intersect with each other. This is analysed in the remaining text.

The law offers a starting point or lever to address the problem of violent behaviours, wife abandonment and polygamy within intimate relationships.

> There is of course violence through marriage in the community . . . most of their homes are full of violence.
>
> [Participant 2 – Social Worker]

*Table 33.1* Influencing factors impacting ADOVIC's community-based safety partnerships

| | CONTEXT | INFLUENCING FACTORS |
|---|---|---|
| 1 | Legal, religious and civic pluralism | • Criminalisation of DVA (Ugandan Domestic Violence Act, 2010).<br>• The Customary Marriage (Registration) Act (1978) of Uganda.<br>• The 1995 Constitution and 1998 Land Act.<br>• The Employment Act 2006, and the Occupational safety and Health Act of 2006.<br>• Local policing arrangements/duty-bearer relationships.<br>• Personal safety concerns (all workers).<br>• Access to healthcare (securing funding for emergency care).<br>• Local marriage rituals – polygamy, land and property.<br>• Family relationships – spousal and intergenerational conflicts, displacement of women and children, homelessness and abuse.<br>• Access to 'duty bearers' and other (local influencers) to resolve conflicts – often involving outreach home visits and advocacy. |
| 2 | Multi-agency advocacy | • Statutory agencies involved – supporting funders, healthcare agencies, schools, police, religious institutions and duty bearers in communities. ADOVIC meetings/advocacy/training. |
| 3 | Volunteer training and education | • Volunteer unpaid and/or nominally paid key workers – social workers, counsellors, international volunteers (interns).<br>• Training, knowledge, skills of ADOVIC workers derived from education and lived experience/ADOVIC programmes. |

Seeley (2012) discussed the ways in which women's relationships necessarily intersect with other women who subsequently marry their husbands. Conjugal arrangements are complex. Co-wives and 'outside' wives may live alongside and these relationships change over time. Supportive relationships may develop as women age, but the level of conflict and tension between wives and children is also high. Illness is a feature – rape, HIV, AIDS and pregnancy profoundly affect women's capacity to care for themselves and others, especially in rural Uganda. ADOVIC partner with advocates who are male and engaging local leaders was a core element of the work. The role of male 'duty bearers' trained by ADOVIC is to raise awareness about the legal issues and negotiate with victims in local communities through ADOVIC link-making. A male community leader from a rural village described how he referred an abused woman to ADOVIC; to support behavioural change towards women who have been beaten, raped and abandoned by their husbands. He noted how the ADOVIC workers needed his support to meet with the woman and men in his village.

> When I saw the address [for ADOVIC] I went and asked them if the ADOVIC project would come in my village. So when ADOVIC came I gathered some of the residents to have the ADOVIC project in this area.
>
> [Participant 7 – Duty Bearer]

> The weakness also is because you know in Uganda a woman cannot do well without a man . . . so she needs to be in a combination . . . when they are together . . . they can work better than a female alone. . . . I devised the project to have some males in the group so they come together they can fight together . . . [against the abuse].
>
> [Participant 7 – Duty Beare]

Relatedly, the Customary Marriage (Registration) Act (1978) of Uganda allows for polygamy and privileges male dominance by customarily destabilising women's ownership of land through kinship and marriage. Ugandan wedding celebrations are notably extravagant, exorbitant and popular (BBC, 2018), involving patrilineal exchange of land for a traditional 'brideprice' and/or dowry exchange. Constitutionally allowed, this has, in some cases, been legally challenged (Goitom, 2015). The customary 'rule of law' system is traditionally gender biased against women (Ikdahl, Hellum, Kaarhus, Benjaminsen, & Kameri-Mbote, 2005), paradoxically attributed to the transient nature of women's relationships.

Uganda's land laws are additionally complex. Both the 1995 Constitution and 1998 Land Act recognise customary laws that allow women's rights to land. The statutory land tenure laws legalise women's property rights by embedding customary laws, in a plural fashion, within marriage (Whitehead & Tsikata, 2003). Joireman (2008) asserts that discrimination against women remains rife in Uganda, due to corruption and weak legal structures for implementing change. Critical perspectives on women's access to land ownership in Uganda suggest that women's land rights have weakened due to land commercialisation.

Tripp (2015) demonstrated that modern and traditional matrimonial practices in postcolonial Africa contribute to gendered inequities, by dispossessing women of jointly acquired land in the event of abandonment, violent hounding out or displacement by another woman. Even when a man dies, if a Ugandan woman has no land, she will have no source of subsistence (Tripp, 2004). The intergenerational impacts of GBV on women and children exposed to violence is recognised but weakly addressed in its own right. Next, we show how the problems prompted multi-agency advocacy – by mobilising ADOVIC responses in a range of settings.

## 2 Multi-agency advocacy

Legal frameworks such as the Ugandan Domestic Violence Act (2010) have helped deliver criminal justice for some victims. An ADOVIC worker explains how the legal reforms helped them to work proactively with the police:

> When the police has a case and they think it is too much for them to handle they will call in ADOVIC. We have a plan for police to come and help us so we can intervene, we work closely with this family or that couple and advise them accordingly, so we have a good relationship with different police stations.
>
> [Participant 2 – Social Worker]

ADOVIC workers identified different forms of local policing partnerships:

> We work with the central police, we have a good relationship with them, thus we work with them, also 'mama police' she sits in the office of Family and Child Protection Unit and in most cases she handles violence cases for children and women.
>
> [Participant 2 – Social Worker]

The police reported that this is a good partnership;

> The law helps ADOVIC. . . . If they the victim has gone to ADOVIC for safety the law helps ADOVIC in prosecuting the offender.
>
> [Participant 8 – Police]

The police headquarters is located at some distance from the ADOVIC office. Working closely with them required good relationship-building over time. Utilising the Domestic Violence Act (2010) was important because the law provided a structural framework for confidently informing the police about their new responsibilities. Evolving relationships suggested that ADOVIC workers were developing and influencing policing responses.

> We work closely with the police and also the local leaders because we derive our mandates to work with these people from our law, that is the Domestic Violence Act. So our work together with them is we empower them because most of the time the local community the local council does not know the law. Unfortunately our government brings out the law but does not invest into sensitising people. All the duty bearers do is about the law so that they can use it to do their work. So ADOVIC will tell them it is a duty.
>
> [Participant 4 – Social Worker]

ADOVIC workers and participants from various agencies realised their role as advocates and 'duty bearers'. Ellen [pseudonym] worked as an ADOVIC social worker in a busy health clinic, situated in a rural community outside Jinja. Attendant women and children appeared malnourished and emaciated. Chronic and acute disease was evident in the way they lay passively on walkways, some feverish and with oozing wounds.

"There are many ways to explain the way ADOVIC works", Ellen said. The point she emphasised, often, is "working together":

> ADOVIC works directly with the people in the exercise of home visits. Then there is the outreach and the meeting when they come for family planning . . . they can see

the women complaining. . . . They complain about . . . "my husband, I was beaten by my husband because I done the family planning", "my husband doesn't want to buy anything at home because I did the family planning", "he is abusing me so that I don't want to produce children or deliver any children to him" . . . so something along those lines.

[Participant 5 – Social Worker]

Ellen called for more community workers visiting at home, while noting ADOVIC capacity is limited and transport to rural clinics and services is difficult.

You cannot base those issues on what someone tells you so, you have to go and see the situation and anyway when you do home visiting it makes sense with ADOVIC because you can see which home you can support and which home you cannot support.

Other volunteer(s) suggested the importance of outreach home visiting.

The times I've travelled in the field, even though my work has been so much online, I think, because there is a problem the community, as time goes on, we start to welcome member of ADOVIC because of oppressing challenges.

I remember one time when we met men without women and realised the actual oppression and violence as well in their families. At the end of the session they were more than happy to welcome back ADOVIC. That means the community has a problem or there is a problem in the community and when they see someone actually tackling the problem they are more willing to collaborate.

Some may not understand what they are going through. . . . There are the local leaders, like CDO (community development officers), local chairmen, they help in mobilising people, telling them about the cause and the opportunity to interact with things . . . like church. . . . So social gatherings around the community is a good way to tell people we are here to help and this is what we do.

[Participant 5 – Social Worker]

Engaging communities is integral to the ADOVIC approach. Community participation with the interviews and the focus group showed wider community engagement with ADOVIC.

Much of the ADOVIC service response is enabled through direct self-referral to the office and in follow-up visits that involve voluntary face-to-face meetings with victims, families and communities. Those affected are increasingly coming out of their villages to seek help that was previously not available to them. Volunteer workers aim to enable victims, mainly women and children, to safely leave abusive relationships. Monthly, at Jinja Central Police Station, approximately 39 cases of violence against women are registered. The biggest percentage of women and girls that report to authorities are victims of physical violence. Increasingly, women come to seek services after the police recommend them to ADOVIC for assistance. As follows, many participants in this study were volunteer activists who had used the ADOVIC service at some point, and/or helped others within their communities to address the problem of GBV. This reflects the contextual safeguarding approach advocated by Firmin (2017), which suggests a more place-based means of including those affected in determining the response. Also recognising the opportunity for researchers and community members to learn from each other, through research, in order to advance or transform a shared social aim.

## 3 Volunteer training and education

Volunteer training and education is part of the ADOVIC community-based partnership approach, drawing from youth communities where GBV was recognised. Jeremiah [pseudonym] is a young volunteer who talked about his experience of ADOVIC training and education, particularly awareness-raising in local communities. He was keen to express how he understood the role of the Domestic Violence Act (2010) in enforcing protection, and although he did not cite the Act he gave examples of how ADOVIC developed a localised outreach strategy to tackle the issue.

> From what I understand from the local community since I joined is that some people are ignorant about the law and they don't know how it's actually protecting them. I've met men, fathers who actually are going through domestic violence but they didn't have a platform where they could share . . . so if I could talk about the strategy, the approach ADOVIC is taking in going to communities. . . . I think it makes sense because that's where the victims are and that's where you meet and you understand what's actually happening.
> [Participant 2 – Social Worker]

Volunteers are an essential element of service provision. The organisation has scaled up to a number of core community activities that include: Capacity Building; Mentorship; Mediation and Counselling; Income Generation; Youth Empowerment; Resettlement. These core areas involve diverse fundraising activities, including creative craft and jewellery-making to enable women's recovery, socialisation and employment. Furthermore, through community outreach, at the end of face-to-face meetings, ADOVIC workers call upon individuals that have an interest in working against GBV and abuse in their distinct communities. Thus ADOVIC intervention also serves as a recruitment exercise in civic participation, to garner support from young men in particular.

> We start engaging the interested individuals by availing them with all the necessary materials and information preparing them as activists against domestic violence. Those individuals that show full commitment to learn and become fully equipped throughout the training period graduate into our community activists. Since we are still operating on a small scale and do not have branches in various communities, the activists become our eyes and ears in their different locations. Through this approach as we engage the community activists and the different stakeholders we partner with, we engage communities in supporting, developing and implementing prevention strategies that target reducing domestic violence and abuse in individuals, communities, and society.
> [Participant 4 – Social Worker]

Volunteer activism enabled ADOVIC to operationalise its community-based safety partnership approach through engaging social workers, police, health workers, community activists, local and religious leaders along with other NGOs to reduce GBV. Their community mobilisation approach bears some resemblance to another regional initiative to reduce violence against women and HIV prevention in the region. Starmann et al. (2017) reported on the SASA! (domestic abuse prevention) intervention in neighbouring Kampala, which showed that volunteer and community engagement with SASA! led to positive changes in some couples' relationships, reducing conflict over time. Multi-level prevention included the fostering of more reflective couple relationships – linking to the wider social communities where women lived with their partners. Figure 33.2 illustrates ADOVIC's processes for reaching out to diverse communities. Subsequent strategic actions developed by ADOVIC extend their localised approach (ADOVIC, 2019, 2020).

- Responding to referrals
- Face to face metings
- Follow up in local communities, villages, schools, health centres, homes.
- Creative crafts for women's recovery (and employment)

- Policing
- Medical care
- Religious leaders
- Volunteers and Community Leaders ('duty bearers')
- Counselors

**Community Engagement**

**Partnerships**

GBV Reduction

- Victims
- Perpetrators
- Villages
- Schools
- Homes

**Awareness Raising and Training**

**Advocacy & Volunteer Recruitment**

- Young people
- Women and Men
- Community Leaders
- Support workers
- Duty bearers
- Counselors

*Figure 33.2*   GBV reduction strategies and processes: the ADOVIC approach

ADOVIC leads a co-ordinated volunteer strategy for community engagement to reduce GBV in the region. The interviews and focus groups helped identify the community engagement elements of the ADOVIC approach, demonstrating active stakeholder participation in how the service operates and responds to GBV. Women and men contribute to volunteer service development and become multi-agency advocates for GBV reduction in their local communities. This is an important example of local activism to address the problem, involving rural outreach home visiting.

## Conclusion

This chapter elucidates the social and political factors that influenced ADOVIC's capacity to address GBV reduction in Uganda, through developing local community-based safety partnerships. The findings are small scale, necessarily bound to time and place, and limited as such. Reynolds and Sariola (2018) remind us that critical perspectives on community engagement show not just 'who' is involved in participatory research, but how. This chapter offers a descriptive qualitative introduction to the ADOVIC approach, introducing the different stakeholders within the reach of the study. The global researcher privilege cannot be underestimated (Sullivan et al., 2005). ADOVIC's engagement with research activities is the means through which we can report its place in GBV reduction. Sullivan et al. (2005) discussed how the participatory research process helps further relationships in communities, including those affected by domestic violence. These researcher relationships shaped our findings, negotiated as it was by academic interest in ADOVIC's approach to GBV reduction in this Ugandan setting. ADOVIC's approach highlighted the gendered economic nature of the challenges they face. The legal frameworks (Table 33.1) enabled them to structure their multi-agency response. Legal, religious and civic pluralism is significant here, allowing a breadth of community responses to the structural, relational problems associated with GBV. Sustaining these responses over the longer term is challenging. There is hope, however, with ADOVIC extending their strategic reach and vision (ADOVIC, 2019). This is an important outcome of their participatory relational process, showing how community-based safety partnerships can advance stakeholder roles in GBV reduction. The ADOVIC approach offers a model of micro and macro community engagement, mobilising some women's emancipation from GBV. Gaps remain, particularly in identifying and responding to the children affected by DVA, and differentiating the plural, intersecting elements of abused women's lives as Ugandan girls, mothers and wives in a complex, rapidly developing society. Women and men identify as ADOVIC service users, volunteers, duty bearers, workers, victims and survivors. There is a continuing need to evaluate the short- and longer-term actions arising from the ADOVIC approach. Future GBV reduction strategies could aim towards this, extending co-researcher capacity in this local context.

## Critical findings

- GBV against women is a significant problem in Uganda, as it is in East Africa as a whole.
- ADOVIC is a non-government organisation that aims to reduce GBV in Jinja, Uganda.
- Legal, religious and civic pluralism enables ADOVIC to co-ordinate its multi-agency response.
- ADOVIC's community engagement involves recruitment and training of volunteer activists.
- ADOVIC works with both victims and perpetrators, and seeks written agreement between them, with local community supporting the implementation.

## Implications for policy, practice and research

- ADOVIC's 'best practice' is building local community-based partnerships for GBV reduction.
- Outreach home visiting and community engagement takes place in plural social contexts.
- GBV reduction strategies address women's intersecting lives as girls, mothers and wives.
- Service gaps include identifying and responding to impoverished children affected by GBV.
- Future GBV reduction strategies could encompass and build participatory research capacity.

## References

ADOVIC. (2019). *5-year Strategic Plan 2019–2024*. Jinja, Uganda: ADOVIC.

ADOVIC. (2020). *Anti domestic violence coalition*. Retrieved January 30, 2020, from www.givingway.com/organization/anti-domestic-violence-coalition

Bajpai, G. C. (2014). African women entrepreneur: Problems, challenges and future opportunities. *International Journal of Managerial Studies and Research, 2*(5), 17–22.

BBC. (2018, June 21). *The true cost of a dream ugandan wedding*. Retrieved January 30, 2020, from www.bbc.co.uk/news/av/world-africa-44551616/the-true-cost-of-a-dream-ugandan-wedding

Benjamin-Thomas, T. E., Corrado, A. M., McGrath, C., Rudman, D. L., & Hand, C. (2018). Working towards the promise of participatory action research: Learning from ageing research exemplars. *International Journal of Qualitative Methods, 17*(1). doi:10.1177/1609406918817953

Bradbury-Jones, C., Ogik, P., Betts, J., Taylor, J., & Lund, P. (2018). Beliefs about people with albinism in Uganda: A qualitative study using the common-sense model. *PLoS One, 13*(10). doi:10.1371/journal. pone.0205774

Byerley, A. (2013). Displacement in the name of (re)development: The contested rise and contested demise of colonial 'African' housing estates in Kampala and Jinja. *Planning Perspectives, 28*(4), 547–570.

Clark, M. (2018, November 11). Promoting global knowledge exchange about domestic abuse prevention in the UK and Uganda. *Blog: Evidence Based Nursing.* Retrieved from https://blogs.bmj.com/ebn/2018/11/11/ enabling-global-knowledge-exchange-about-domestic-abuse-prevention-in-the-uk-and-uganda/

Firmin, C. (2017). *Contextual safeguarding an overview of the operational, strategic and conceptual framework.* Luton: University of Bedfordshire.

Goitom, H. (2015, August 12). Uganda: Court declares refund of bride-price under customary law uncon-stitutional. *Global Legal Monitor.* Retrieved January 30, 2020, from www.loc.gov/law/foreign-news/ article/uganda-court-declares-refund-of-bride-price-under-customary-law-unconstitutional/

Hossain, M., & McAlpine, A. (2017). *Gender based violence research methodologies in humanitarian settings: An evidence review and recommendations.* Retrieved March, 17 2018, from www.elrha.org/wp-content/ uploads/2017/06/ElrhaR2HC-Gender-Based-Violence-Research-Methodologies-in-Humanitarian-Settings_2017.pdf

Ikdahl, I., Hellum, A., Kaarhus, R., Benjaminsen, T. A., & Kameri-Mbote, P. (2005, July). Human rights, formalisation and women's land rights in southern and eastern Africa *Studies in Women's Law No. 57.* Retrieved from https://docs.escr-net.org/usr_doc/noradrapport.pdf

Joireman, S. F. (2008). The mystery of capital formation in sub-saharan africa: Women, property rights and customary law. *World Development, 36*(7), 1233–1246. doi:10.1016/j.worlddev.2007.06.017

Lund, P., Standing Voice, & Advantage Africa. (2017). *An investigation into the impact of stigma on the educa-tion and life opportunities available to children and young people with albinism in tanzania and uganda.* Coven-try: International Foundation of Applied Disability Research.

Nabwiiso, S. (2018, December 10). *Allocate enough resources to expedite gender based violence cases.* Retrieved Jan-uary 30, 2020, from www.busiweek.com/allocate-enough-resources-to-expedite-gender-based-cases/

Reynolds, L., & Sariola, S. (2018). The ethics and politics of community engagement in global health research. *Critical Public Health, 28*(3), 257–268. doi:10.1080/09581596.2018.1449598

Schulz, A. J., Krieger, J., & Galea, S. (2002). Addressing social determinants of health: Community-based participatory approaches to research and practice. *Health Education & Behavior, 29*(3), 287–295. doi:10.1177/109019810202900302

Seeley, J. (2012). The changing relationships of co-wives over time in rural southern uganda. *The Journal of Development Studies, 48*(1), 68–80. doi:10.1080/00220388.2011.629651

Signorelli, M. C., Hillel, S., de Oliveira, D. C., Ayala Quintanilla, B. P., Hegarty, K., & Taft, A. (2018). Voices from low-income and middle-income countries: A systematic review protocol of primary healthcare interventions within public health systems addressing intimate partner violence against women. *BMJ Open, 8*(3), e019266. doi:10.1136/bmjopen-2017-019266

Starmann, E., Collumbien, M., Kyegombe, N., Devries, K., Michau, L., Musuya, T., . . . Heise, L. (2017). Exploring couples' processes of change in the context of SASA!, a violence against women and HIV prevention intervention in uganda. *Prevention Science, 18*(2), 233–244. doi:10.1007/s11121-016-0716-6

Sullivan, M., Bhuyan, R., Senturia, K., Shiu-Thornton, S., & Ciske, S. (2005). Participatory action research in practice: A case study in addressing domestic violence in nine cultural communities. *Journal of Interpersonal Violence, 20*(8), 977–995. doi:10.1177/0886260505277680

Tighe, M., Peters, J., & Skirton, H. (2013). Advancing social research relationships in postnatal support settings. *Public Health Nursing, 30*(3), 266–276. doi:10.1111/phn.12028

Tripp, A. M. (2004). Women's movements, customary law and land rights in Africa: The case of uganda. *African Studies Quarterly, 7*(4), 1–19.

Tripp, A. M. (2015). *Women and power in postconflict Africa.* Cambridge: Cambridge University Press.

UBOS. (2019). *Gender Issues in uganda: An analysis of gender based violence, asset ownership and employment.* Retrieved January 30, 2020, from www.ubos.org/wp-content/uploads/publications/03_2019UBOS_ Gender_Issues_Report_2019.pdf

UN Women, A. (2017). *Stepping up for gender equality – UN women east and southern Africa 2016 annual report.* Retrieved May 17, 2018, from https://africa.unwomen.org/en/digital-library/publications/2018/01/ stepping-up-for-gender-equality – un-women-east-and-southern-africa-2016-annual-report

USAID. (2010). *Evaluation of Africa's health*. Retrieved 2010, from http://ghpro.dexisonline.com/sites/default/files/resources/legacy/sites/default/files/Final%20Report%20of%20Africa%202010%20Evaluation%20508%204_27_2010.pdf

USAID. (2012). *Ugandan demographic health survey 2011*. Retrieved January 30, 2020, from www.usaid.gov/sites/default/files/documents/1860/Uganda_Demographic_and_Health_Survey_2011.pdf

Whitehead, A., & Tsikata, D. (2003). Policy discourses on women's land rights in sub-Saharan Africa: The Implications of the re-turn to the customary. *Journal of Agrarian Change 3*(1–2). doi:10.1111/1471-0366.00051

WHO. (2013). *Global and regional estimates of violence against women: Prevalence and health effects of intimate partner violence and non-partner sexual violence*. Geneva: World Health Organization Department of Reproductive Health and Research, London School of Hygiene and Tropical Medicine, South African Medical Research Council.

# 34

# HEALTHCARE-BASED VIOLENCE AGAINST WOMEN STRATEGIES TO ADDRESS THE PROBLEM IN ARGENTINA

*Lorena Saletti-Cuesta*

## Introduction

### *Violence against women as a public health problem*

Violence against women (VAW) is an extreme manifestation of gender inequity, targeting women and girls because of their subordinate social status in society. According to United Nations (1993), VAW, a broad umbrella term, is any act of gender-based violence that results in, or is likely to result in, physical, sexual or mental harm or suffering to women, including threats of such acts, coercion or arbitrary deprivation of liberty, whether occurring in public or in private life. One of the most common forms of VAW is intimate partner violence (IPV) which includes physical, sexual and emotional abuse by an intimate partner.

VAW is an important public health problem and human right concern rooted in gender inequalities. Therefore, there are a number of reasons to focus on healthcare systems for addressing VAW. It is well known that healthcare providers (physicians, nurses, psychologists, etc.) are often women's first point of professional contact. Moreover, all women are likely to seek health services at some point in their lives, and women and girls experiencing violence are more likely to use health services (World Health Organization (WHO), 2016).

According to the WHO (2016) the roles of the health system within a national multisectoral response to address VAW are to advocate for a public health perspective; identify those who are experiencing VAW and provide them with comprehensive health services at all levels of health service delivery; develop, implement and evaluate VAW prevention programmes as part of its population-level prevention and health promotion activities; and document the magnitude of the problem, its causes and its health and other consequences, as well as effective interventions.

### *Health-sector responses to VAW*

Providing supportive care for women and children facing the consequences of VAW is also an essential role for healthcare providers. The evidence suggests that women-centred health interventions, such as first-line responses, risk assessment, safety planning, counselling and support, all provide some health benefits to women (Ramsay, Rivas & Feder, 2005; Rivas et al., 2015;

Spangaro, 2017; Trabold, McMahon, Alsobrooks, Whitney, & Mittal, 2018; Rivas et al., 2019), even in low- and low-middle-income countries (Kirk, Terry, Lokuge, & Watterson, 2017). However, the evidence for the effectiveness of such health interventions to reduce women's re-victimisation is weak (Ellsberg et al., 2015).

Globally, there are growing calls among VAW prevention advocates, healthcare providers and policymakers for universal, IPV screening by healthcare providers for all women. Accordingly, IPV screenings during women's routine healthcare visits are likely the most widespread VAW intervention across all health systems globally. Nonetheless, to date the overall evidence suggests that while universal IPV screening or routine enquiry increases the identification of such violence, it may be ineffective in reducing VAW and/or improving women's health outcomes (World Health Organization, 2013b; Ellsberg et al., 2015; O'Doherty et al., 2015; Spangaro, 2017). However, more research needs to be conducted to study the complex relationship between screening and improvement in quality of life and/or a reduction in the recurrence of IPV.

Specifically, one area for further research is in the education and training of healthcare staff to improve their identification and responses for VAW, which has been found to be a promising practice (World Health Organization, 2013b). Relatedly, several studies showed improvements in knowledge of providers following a VAW training intervention. Interventions involving interactive techniques (i.e., role playing, discussions simulations) and training in VAW identification, care and referral appear to improve detection and changes in providers' attitudes. However, evidence also suggest that training programmes in isolation are ineffective to create sustainable change. Instead, personnel training in conjunction with system changes (i.e., standardised documentation), may be the most valuable approaches for bringing about beneficial changes for identification (Ellsberg et al., 2015; García Moreno et al., 2015; Ansari & Boyle, 2017; Spangaro, 2017).

Notably, mother-child interventions, that is, those that strengthen the mother–child relationship in the aftermath of violence, offered in the context of healthcare systems may improve children's behaviours, self-esteem and anxiety, as well as reduce traumatic stress levels in both children and their mothers. Although such interventions are resource intensive, the severe long-term effects on children from exposure to violence and associated health costs suggest this is likely to be a cost-effective endeavour (World Health Organization, 2013b; Spangaro, 2017).

Furthermore, some healthcare systems offer treatment programmes for those who perpetrate violence that aim to reduce or stop abusive behaviour. However, and again, there is little evidence of the effectiveness of healthcare-based programmes for perpetrators of violence (Ellsberg et al., 2015; Spangaro, 2017).

Prevention of violence is another important role of the healthcare system. Several studies show that it is possible to prevent VAW and that the healthcare sector may be helpful in this regard. Specifically, multisectoral programmes that engage with multiple stakeholders seem to be the most successful to change attitudes and behaviours that support and enable VAW (Ellsberg et al., 2015).

### *Elements needed for a robust health-sector response to VAW*

After an expert meeting to develop guidelines for strengthening the health-sector response, the WHO (2010) identified 13 key elements of a health-sector response to VAW, focusing on resource-poor settings (Table 34.1). The first element is an enabling environment of national policies and guidelines to recognise and underscore VAW as a pressing healthcare problem. Moreover, according to García Moreno and collaborators (2015) the necessary core elements in

*Table 34.1* WHO's recommendations for health-sector responses to violence against women

1 Enabling environments
2 Training
3 Systems and services
4 Accountability and monitoring
5 Research and surveillance
6 Approaches to psychosocial and emotional support
7 Non-negotiable issues and principles (ethical and safety issues, documentation)
8 Screening
9 Network development
10 Linking VAW with child protection in the guidelines
11 Mandatory reporting
12 Responding to men as victims and perpetrators
13 Prevention and health promotion

the delivery of effective women-centred responses come not only from the healthcare system itself but also from a societal level that supports health systems through child protection, laws and criminal justice, social services and community-based services.

Training providers is another recommendation that should include these minimum components: raise clinicians' awareness to sensitise to them to VAW; build clinicians' capacities to ask about VAW and listen to women; build clinicians' skills to support and validate women's disclosures; enhance clinicians' attention to ethical issues (i.e., safety and confidentiality); build clinicians' awareness of legal issues (i.e., women's rights); build clinicians' awareness to child protection in the context of VAW; and provide guidance to clinicians concerning documentation and record keeping. In addition, health-sector organisations should strive to build and enhance their VAW care pathways within and external to their systems.

Other elements of a robust health-sector response to VAW include organisation of the systems and services to provide response and support, accountability and monitoring to demonstrate that the problem exists and provide data on the number of cases, as well as additional VAW research and surveillance (WHO, 2010). To distinguish the different approaches to psychosocial and emotional support that victims will need at different points in time (e.g., psychosocial support given by a healthcare professional that has first contact with the woman relative to longer-term support that comes later from other professionals) along with non-negotiable issues and principles (i.e., ethical issues, safety concerns, documentation) are also crucial recommendations.

In addition, the WHO (2010) recommended: asking women about violence if they present with certain health conditions (e.g., injuries); the development of network and multi-agency collaboration, since the healthcare facility will not be able to meet women's multiple and complex needs; linking VAW with child protection including in mandatory reporting if there is a real risk to the woman's life, a child is being abused or a person discloses that they intend to harm or kill someone else, while also taking into account local legislation; responding to men as both victims and perpetrators; and primary prevention and health promotion (i.e., integrated messages about VAW as part of routine health-promotion activities).

## Identified barriers

Although VAW has been accepted as a critical public health problem, it is still not included in the public health policies of many countries. The crucial role that the healthcare systems play, in a multisector response, is poorly understood and/or not well accepted within many of the national health programmes and policies of various countries and territories (World Health Organization, 2013b). Unfortunately, health systems' integration of policy and practical attention to VAW is slow and incremental (García Moreno et al., 2015). Although some countries have guidelines to address VAW, generally they are only gradually adopted and then in often haphazard ways due to cultural barriers and limited resources for implementation (García-Moreno et al., 2015).

Despite the fact that healthcare systems have a crucial role in detecting, referring and caring for women affected by violence, there are significant barriers experienced by primary care providers in addressing VAW (Saletti-Cuesta, Aizenberg, & Ricci-Cabello, 2018). At an organisational level, barriers include (1) little or no training for healthcare staff in providing comprehensive care, empathic communication skills, as well as helping staff better understand the social and gendered roots of VAW; (2) high workloads, which in turn, means limited consultation time, competing priorities, limited resources and high staff turnover; (3) healthcare staff's limited understanding of their legal responsibilities regarding VAW; (4) absence of guidelines to address VAW within the healthcare system; (5) limited supervision or debriefing facilities for healthcare staff and (6) insufficient resources and a fragmented network of community-based VAW services outside of healthcare systems (Saletti-Cuesta et al., 2018).

Furthermore, traditional biomedical approaches, which are often used in healthcare, constitutes an important barrier in understanding, identifying and offering compassionate care in VAW situations because biomedical approaches reinforce the division of biological and biopsychosocial needs. Moreover, this approach values technical, clinical skills and laboratory investigations, while also regarding communication skills and emotional/subjective information as less important (García Moreno et al., 2015; Briones-Vozmediano et al., 2015; Saletti-Cuesta et al., 2018).

## *The importance of the context*

As discussed earlier in the chapter, there is insufficient evidence that particular policies, protocols or models of care are more effective than others in responding to VAW. Accordingly, countries should develop responses and services that take into account country-specific resources that are available, as well as the availability of specialised violence-support services (World Health Organization, 2013b; García-Moreno et al., 2015). Health intervention efforts typically used in high- and/or middle-income countries may not translate to low-resource areas effectively due to social, cultural and economic differences. Moreover, when research on healthcare interventions has been limited to high-income countries, little is known about the evidence base of intervention efforts in other countries and contexts (Schwab-Reese & Renner, 2018). For example, women-centred counselling as well as community-based advocacy and support have shown to be helpful for VAW in high-income countries. However, a recent review shows that psychotherapeutic counselling, other forms of counselling and/or support for accessing services (e.g., through crisis centres) may not be helpful in preventing future IPV in low- and low-middle-income countries (Kirk et al., 2017). Because no one model works in all contexts, national leaders who are working to prevent and address VAW in the context of healthcare should develop country-specific policies and programmes, while keeping in mind the availability of resources, current national policies and procedures, as well as other available support services.

In addition, low- and middle-income countries often face the challenge of a growing burden of VAW, while not having sufficient resources and/or healthcare personnel who are skilled in addressing VAW (World Health Organization, 2013b). For example, while research shows that the global prevalence of IPV among all ever-partnered women is 30.0%, the prevalence was higher in low- and middle-income countries than in high income ones, with women in the Americas reporting the second highest prevalence globally (World Health Organization, 2013a). A recent review and reanalysis of national, population-based VAW estimates from 1998 to 2017 confirms that violence in the Americas remains a crucial problem, which in turn calls for additional prevention, response and research in these parts of the world (Bott, Guedes, Ruiz-Celis, & Mendoza, 2019).

In addition to VAW being a significant problem in this part of the globe, Latin America is one of the world's most unequal regions. Although health and disease indicators have improved in the past decade, significant and relative inequalities and gaps continue to exist between classes, ethnic groups and geographic areas. While there have been increases in public and private health spending, equitable access to health services for the poorest sectors has yet to be achieved. Public health spending remains insufficient and varies greatly between countries. For example, in 2014, Uruguay assigned more than 6% of their Gross Domestic Product to public health spending while Argentina spent only 2.7% (Benza & Kessler, 2020).

Taking into account the high prevalence of VAW of the region, the inequitable access to healthcare, which is exacerbated by the weak and fragmented Latin America health systems, research on the implementation of VAW health-based strategies are timely and important. For all these reasons, this chapter next presents research that aims to add evidence concerning healthcare intervention efforts that address VAW in a middle-income country, specifically Argentina.

## Argentinian context

The Argentine Republic covers an area of 3,761,274 km$^2$ and consists of 23 provinces. Nearly 65% of the population is concentrated in the Centro region, particularly in the province of Buenos Aires. In 2010, the country's population was 40,117,096, of which 91% lived in urban areas (Pan American Health Organization, 2017).

The proportion of women who reported physical and/or sexual violence ever in the majority of Latin American countries, including Argentina, ranged from one-fourth to one-third (Bott et al., 2019). In 2015 Argentina carried out a telephone survey to estimate VAW using the International Violence Against Women Survey. The percentage of women, aged 18 to 69, who reported physical and/or sexual violence ever was 41.6% (Ministerio de Justicia y Derechos Humanos, 2017).

Since the 1990s, Argentina, similar to other Latin American countries, has passed laws to protect and promote women's rights mainly in the private sphere. The Inter-American Convention on the Prevention, Punishment and Eradication of VAW (Convention of Belém do Pará) adopted in 1994, represents an important milestone in the area of state responsibility to address this problem. By 2016, the Convention of Belém do Pará had been adopted and ratified by the majority of states, including Argentina. Thanks to the adherence to Belém do Pará, as well as the political efforts and advocacy of civil society organisations – especially feminists – as in other countries, Argentina have made progress in legislation to address VAW (Essayag, 2017). For example, the law N°26.485 titled, "Comprehensive Protection to Prevent, Punish and Eradicate Violence against Women in Areas Where They Develop Their Interpersonal Relations" (Senate and Chamber of Deputies of the Argentine Nation, 2009). The policy included forms of VAW that are not only perpetrated in private and domestic ways but also in the public sphere, including domestic violence, institutional violence, obstetric violence, mediatic violence, violence at the workplace and violence against the reproductive rights. Furthermore, this law emphasises the comprehensive care of the victims through the implementation of prevention, service and response, as well as in punishment and reparation measures, in coordination with various actors including the education and health governmental sector. Although Argentina is one of the few countries of Latin America that mentioned the health sector in VAW legislation (Ortiz-Barreda & Vives-Cases, 2013), its integration, within the multisectoral commitment to response to VAW, is still a challenge.

A series of violent attacks against women and girls in 2015 generated massive protests nation-wide called *Ni una Menos* (Not One Less; The Guardian, 2016; Terzian, 2017). After a violent murder against a teenager activist from the *Not One Less* movement (El Pais, 2017), a recently approved national law required mandatory training in gender and VAW for all state officials and workers.

Moreover, in 2018 the legislative debate towards legal abortion reform caused the "green wave", which in turn, strengthened the feminist movement and situated women' rights onto the public agenda (Booth, 2018). However, the debate has also impacted on the growing role of anti-rights sectors, who are strongly advocating against a sexual and reproductive rights agenda for Argentina (Vaggione, 2018).

## Argentinian healthcare system

According to the Pan American Health Organization (2017), Argentina's health system, which includes public, private and social security sectors, is one of the most fragmented and segmented in Latin America. Such fragmentation is largely due to the country's federal structure, in that each of the 23 provinces functions independently and has constitutional responsibility for the leadership, financing and delivery of health services. The public sector comprises the national and provincial Health Ministries, hospitals and primary healthcare centres. This sector is decentralised from the federal level to provincial or local administrations. Therefore, differences in infrastructure, budget and administration, as well as uneven and unclear distribution of their legally assigned part of the federal budget, result in important regional inequalities (Novick, 2017).

The Pan American Health Organization (2017) concluded that the Argentinian health system's fragmentation falls into: coverage problems, since not all the population has access to the same health benefits and services; geographic disparities, given the extreme economic-development differences; and differing regulatory functions, since leadership and regulatory authority are diffuse.

In addition, in 2018, the National Ministry of Health lost a level of authority in the institutional hierarchy and was downgraded to a Secretariat. Furthermore, health and educational programmes have been cut, closed and/or emptied due to deepening budget cuts, which in turn, create even more health inequities across regions.

Taking into account the Argentine context, this chapter next presents a study that investigated healthcare-based services and responses for VAW within the public health sector. In the first study phase, the national and provincial Health Ministries' websites and policies were reviewed between August and September 2019. For each website and set of policy documents, a search of terms and phrases related to VAW was conducted. Once relevant documents were identified, specific content was analysed and classified with focus on the content's main aim, objectives and target audience and/or participants. In a second study phase, semi-structured interviews were conducted by phone with key informants from provincial Health Ministries in seven provinces of different regions. Snowball techniques were used to recruit participants. Informed consent was given. All the interviews were digitally audio-recorded and transcribed. The main focus of the interviews concerned the response for VAW withing the healthcare sector, experiences in local communities, as well as response barriers and facilitators. A thematic analysis was used to identify, analyse and report patterns (i.e., qualitative themes) within data (Braun & Clarke, 2006). The analysis of both data sources were the basic inputs for the preparation of the Argentinian mapping of health-based VAW strategies.

## Discussion and analysis

The presentation of the findings is linked to the study's phases. In the first phase, the national and provincial Health Ministries' websites and policies were reviewed. According to the national Health Ministry website a health-based strategy to address VAW, specifically, a protocol to assist victims of sexual violence (Chejter, 2011, 2015), has been developed. The document focused both on emergency assistance after sexual violence, as well as provided a legal framework underscoring the crucial role that healthcare providers should play in addressing VAW. In its second edition of the document, medical, legal and bioethics information was elucidated. Another identified practice carried out by the national Health Ministry was in the training of primary healthcare providers (Pierina Juarez et al., 2012). However, no information concerning its implementation was offered on the website. Only a few informative resources were available on the national Health Secretariat's website, which were part of the promotion and prevention actions.

As a result of fragmentation, the national Health authority and leadership are limited. Therefore, each of the provinces developed their own approach to respond to VAW, though there were some national standards and resources that all provinces used. Taking into account the number of health-based strategies implemented in each province, Figure 34.1 shows the disparities across the country.

As described earlier, the Argentinian healthcare system is highly decentralised and each of the governments of the 23 provinces are in charge of managing health services, which are offered through a network of hospitals, primary healthcare centres and specialised services (i.e., mental health). Table 34.2 presents the healthcare-based VAW strategies developed in each province according to the website review. The identified strategies across the provinces included having protocols or standard procedures to address VAW; training of providers to understand VAW and provide a comprehensive response (e.g., health workforce development and capacity building); having a health information system for documenting and monitoring VAW; developing primary prevention activities; providing supportive care to survivors of VAW; and creating VAW-focused units or networks within the healthcare management organisation to advocate for transforming institutional cultures to prioritise the tackling of VAW (i.e., by a training plan for providers).

According to the websites, 11 provinces from different regions (47.8%) had offered training to their providers. However, there was no training plan published. Only eight provinces had enacted healthcare protocols to address VAW. However, the majority of the protocols were not available online and information about their contents was difficult to find. Prevention programmes were carried out in only seven provinces (30.4%). According to the websites reviewed, the majority of actions were short term, focused mainly on women, and were offered on key women' rights dates (i.e., 25th of November and/or 8th of March). Examples of such interventions included mass, public awareness-raising campaigns, recreational actions and/or VAW awareness talks in public spaces or within healthcare institutions. Information regarding the available resources to assist women with violence had been published in the websites of only four provinces (17.4%) (i.e., national or provincial hotlines). Such findings suggest the need to reinforce collaborative intersectoral efforts.

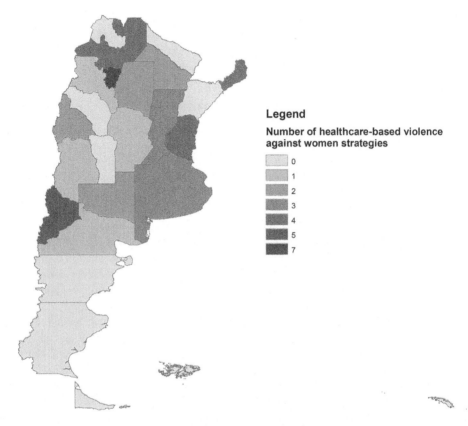

*Figure 34.1*   Number of healthcare-based VAW strategies by province

Although Argentinian policy also underscores the importance of developing information systems to document and research VAW, only two provinces mentioned this strategy on their websites. In this regard, only one province had online guidelines available, which focused on improving healthcare providers' abilities to document, register and record accurately practices related to VAW within their health information system.

By law, all Regional Ministries must include service provision for women who are experiencing violence victimisation, as well as their children. However, only five province websites provided information about the availability of specialised care or programmes within their healthcare services.

The website review also showed, from five provinces, that a potentially promising practice was the creation of units, commissions and/or professionals' networks to address VAW. These units or networks provided support, coordinated actions, developed trainings and/or assessed healthcare practices.

With the "big picture" of the healthcare-based strategies from the first study phase as a foundation, a second phase was carried out to investigate specific, local healthcare-based services and responses for VAW within the public health sector. Via in-depth interviews, key informants highlighted a growing engagement of some providers from different regions, who despite the lack of political will, supported women who experienced IPV victimisation. Many of these key informants reported relying on informal or personal networks and relationships for advice or

Table 34.2 Healthcare-based violence against women strategies in Argentina

| Provinces | Protocol or standard procedures to address VAW | Training of providers | Health information system | Primary prevention activities | Information on available resources for VAW | Provision of supportive care to survivors of VAW | Violence units/networks within the healthcare system |
|---|---|---|---|---|---|---|---|
| Misiones | Yes | Yes | No | Yes | No | No | Yes |
| Corrientes | No | No | No | No | No | No | No |
| Chaco | Yes | Yes | No | No | No | No | No |
| Formosa | No | No | No | No | No | No | No |
| Salta | Yes | Yes | No | Yes | No | No | Yes |
| Jujuy | No | No | No | No | No | No | No |
| Santiago del Estero | Yes | Yes | No | No | No | No | No |
| Tucumán | Yes | Yes | Yes | Yes | Yes | Yes | Yes |
| Catamarca | Yes | No | No | No | No | No | No |
| La Rioja | No | No | No | No | No | No | No |
| Mendoza | No | Yes | No | No | No | No | No |
| San Juan | No | Yes | No | No | No | Yes | No |
| San Luis | No | No | No | No | No | No | No |
| Buenos Aires | Yes | No | No | No | Yes | No | Yes |
| Santa Fe | No | No | Yes | Yes | No | Yes | No |
| Entre Rios | No | Yes | No | Yes | No | Yes | Yes |
| Córdoba | No | Yes | No | No | No | No | No |
| Chubut | No | No | No | No | No | No | No |
| Rio Negro | No | No | No | Yes | No | No | No |
| La Pampa | No | Yes | No | No | Yes | No | No |
| Neuquen | Yes | Yes | No | Yes | Yes | Yes | No |
| Santa Cruz | No | No | No | No | No | No | No |
| Tierra del Fuego | No | No | No | No | No | No | No |

referral women. One key informant mentioned that despite the political will to introduce VAW into the health agenda, the financial resources allocated to the creation of units, commissions and/or professionals' networks to address VAW were scarce (i.e., only one professional assigned to the unit). In another province, an additional key informant reported the same limitation: specifically, a providers' network was implemented in a hospital without any financial support. Likewise, other key informants described how, in some provinces, primary, violence prevention activities were organised mainly by motivated healthcare providers without any institutionalisation of these programmes.

Some key informants mentioned that, compared to physicians, providers from social and mental health areas of professional practice were the most interested in attending the few VAW courses offered. Likewise, one key informant described how VAW information is under-recorded within existing health information systems conceived mainly for mortality and morbidity information.

Notably, the study results suggest that, in Argentina, there is a growing commitment among healthcare providers to address VAW, which could be related to feminist movement-based activism, especially after the *Not One Less* movement as well as the country's 2018 abortion legislative debate. Such developments are encouraging and suggest that anti-VAW activism has the potential to improve healthcare prevention and care, as well as challenge unequal gender norms, shape policy agendas and inform interventions (Michau, Horn, Bank, Dutt, & Zimmerman, 2015; Shiffman & Smith, 2007).

This study findings also suggest that women-centred interventions should be strengthened since their effectiveness has been demonstrated in low- and low-middle-income countries (Kirk et al., 2017). In addition, according to the law, prevention and awareness-raising activities should be prioritised, in order to change the gender *status quo*. Moreover, rather than limit such activities to certain times of the year and/or audiences, VAW prevention and awareness-raising programmes should be delivered throughout the year, as well as to diverse audiences and targets. Notably research from other countries, specifically Spain, has described similar challenges in which prevention and awareness-raising – supposedly a priority within healthcare services – has not been prioritised in practice (Goicolea et al., 2013).

Training for healthcare staff is strongly recommended as an important strategy to ensure that the healthcare sector can address VAW effectively and meaningfully (World Health Organization, 2013b). As first steps, trainings could aim to strengthen healthcare staff members' understanding of VAW, as well as aim to address the prejudices and hostile attitudes of some healthcare providers (Saletti-Cuesta, 2018). Therefore, training actions should include all the healthcare professions, not only those related to mental health and social work, and should be developed in all the provinces throughout Argentina.

According to this study's findings, accurate records were not a priority within the health services, despite the well-known fact that properly collected, managed and analysed data from records can both improve the services provided to women and help inform primary prevention (World Health Organization, 2013b; García Moreno et al., 2015). However, as the World Health Organization (2013b) underscored, such data collection is easier to implement in high-income countries with well-functioning electronic health information systems, compared to the paper-based systems that are currently used in most low- and middle-income countries.

## Conclusions

Healthcare systems have a crucial role in preventing, detecting, referring, caring for women affected by VAW, and leading efforts to address this problem. This work provides an overview of the health-based interventions being implemented within the Argentinian public sector.

Despite the positive legislative advances made in the country, the highlighted role of the healthcare systems within a multisector response to VAW, as well as the highlighted role of healthcare in the existing legislation, the study findings revealed important differences in how different Argentine regions both developed and implemented VAW prevention and response strategies. Only a few provinces were actively seeking to respond to the problem. Among those provinces offering VAW strategies, training and healthcare protocols were the most implemented. Thus, there is a clear need to strengthen prevention actions, as well as specialised care services to assist VAW throughout Argentina. In addition, local data from the key informants showed the extent of the problems and challenges. For example, accurate data collection to monitor and assess VAW, which should be prioritised in Argentina, could help strengthen the health system's response to VAW considerably.

Encouragingly, a promising practice was the creation of VAW units in some provinces. This strategy allowed the coordination of VAW actions within the healthcare system, as well as across the sectors in order to improve VAW prevention and response. In light of this strategy's promise, the creation of VAW units could be interesting to implement in other communities and contexts. Moreover, other important study findings highlighted how some healthcare providers' commitment to addressing VAW, as well how the inclusion of VAW in a broader social agenda point to potential strengths within the health sector that could be fruitfully developed and reinforced throughout Argentina and beyond. The study findings also underscore how healthcare providers should be supported in providing appropriate and comprehensive care through political commitment and institutionalisation of their actions.

Despite the effort made in Argentina to address VAW in the healthcare context, there are some points that are interesting to discuss in order to inform the broader context. The consequences of the decentralisation and fragmentation of the healthcare system are crucial. For example, there is no VAW national health protocol that includes the various forms of VAW incorporated in the Argentinian legislation, and the only existing national protocol is focused only on sexual violence. At the same time, some provinces have designed protocols focused on some types of violence (i.e., sexual violence or IPV).

Therefore, each of the provinces have implemented their own approach and strategies to respond VAW, with great disparities across the region that need to be addressed. Undoubtedly, Argentina is not the only country challenged with a fragmented healthcare system. Accordingly, future research could help address how VAW prevention and response might be implemented and sustained in such complex and dynamic systems.

In addition, the study findings highlighted how the Argentine VAW policies and laws, which are quite meaningful and robust, could be better implemented in the health sector throughout Argentina. Health-sector leadership and political commitment need to be strengthened in order to effectively involve health sectors within a multisectoral response to VAW and to provide a platform for effective and collaborative interventions across the region. Further research should include contextual factors and processes that influence services' integration of VAW interventions in order to better understand the disparities across the region.

## Critical findings

- Despite a strong legal framework, which includes the healthcare system as a central element, the Argentinian health sector has not been actively involved in comprehensive responses to VAW.
- There are important differences of the implemented strategies between regions. Only a few Argentinian provinces are actively seeking to respond to the problem. Training and protocols are the most implemented strategies. There is a need of strength prevention actions and specialised care services. Also, local data collection shows the extent of the VAW problem remains a challenge throughout Argentina.
- The commitment of some healthcare providers and the inclusion of VAW on the social agenda are encouraging and suggest potential strategies to improve, not only healthcare prevention and response, but also to challenge unequal gender norms more broadly throughout Argentina.

## Implications for policy, practice and research

- There is sufficient evidence that VAW is a public health problem and that addressing it in healthcare services is important.
- Health-sector leadership and commitment needs to be increased in order to effectively engage this sector within a multisectoral response to VAW according to the legislation.

- Primary, secondary and tertiary prevention are essential public health interventions and should be developed.
- The importance of the strength of the providers involved with this problem should be supported by political commitment, actions and resources.
- Further research should include contextual factors and processes that influence services' integration of VAW interventions in order to understand the inequalities across the region.

# References

Ansari, S., & Boyle, A. (2017). Emergency department-based interventions for women suffering domestic abuse: A critical literature review. *European Journal of Emergency Medicine, 24,* 13–18. doi:10.1097/MEJ.0000000000000416

Benza, G., & Kessler, G. (2020). *Uneven trajectories.* Cambridge: Cambridge University Press. doi:10.1017/9781108775489

Booth, A. (2018). Argentina votes on bill to legalise abortion up to 14 weeks. *Lancet.* Published online June 11, 2018. http://dx.doi.org/10.1016/S0140-6736(18)31321-7

Bott, S., Guedes, A., Ruiz-Celis, A. P., & Mendoza, J. A. (2019). Intimate partner violence in the Americas: A systematic review and reanalysis of national prevalence estimates. *Revista Panamericana de Salud Pública, 43,* e26. https://doi.org/10.26633/RPSP.2019.26

Braun, V., & Clarke, V. (2006). Using thematic analysis in psychology. *Qualitative Research in Psychology, 3*(2), 77–101. doi:10.1191/1478088706qp063oa

Briones-Vozmediano, E., Maquibar, A., Vives-Cases, C., Ohman, A., Hurtig, A. K., & Goicolea, I. (2015). Health-sector responses to intimate partner violence: Fitting the response into the biomedical health system or adapting the system to meet the response? *Journal of Interpersonal Violence, 33,* 1653–1678. https://doi.org/10.1177/0886260515619170

Chejter, S. (2011). *Protocolo para la atención integral de personas víctimas de violaciones sexuales. Instructivo para equipos de salud.* Buenos Aires: Ministerio de Salud de la Nación.

Chejter, S. (2015). *Protocolo para la atención integral de personas víctimas de violaciones sexuales. Instructivo para equipos de salud.* Buenos Aires: Ministerio de Salud de la Nación.

El País. (2017). *Argentina rocked by murder of activist who fought sexist violence.* Retrieved March 4, 2020, from https://english.elpais.com/elpais/2017/04/10/inenglish/1491830225_471455.html

Ellsberg, M., Arango, D. J., Morton, M., Gennari, F., Kiplesund, S., Contreras, M., & Watts, C. (2015). Prevention of violence against women and girls: What does the evidence say? *Lancet, 385,* 1555–1566. doi:10.1016/S0140-6736(14)61703-7

Essayag, S. (2017). *From commitment to action: Policies to end violence against women in Latin America and the Caribbean. Regional Analysis Document.* Panama: UNDP and UN Women.

García-Moreno, C., Hegarty, K., Lucas d'Oliveira, A. F., Koziol-McLain, J., Colombini, M., & Feder, G. (2015). The health-systems response to violence against women. *Lancet, 385,* 1567–1579. doi:10.1016/S0140-6736(14)61837-7

Goicolea, I., Briones-Vozmediano, E., Öhman, A., Edin, K., Minvielle, F., & Vives-Cases, C. (2013). Mapping and exploring health systems' response to intimate partner violence in Spain. *BMC Public Health, 13*(1162). Retrieved from www.biomedcentral.com/1471-2458/13/1162

The Guardian. (2016). *The guardian view on NiUnaMenos: Challenging misogyny and murder editorial.* Retrieved March 5, 2020, from www.theguardian.com/commentisfree/2016/oct/19/the-guardian-view-on-niunamenos-challenging-misogyny-and

Kirk, L., Terry, S., Lokuge, K., & Watterson, J. L. (2017). Effectiveness of secondary and tertiary prevention for violence against women in low and low-middle income countries: A systematic review. *BMC Public Health, 17,* 622. doi:10.1186/s12889-017-4502-6.

Michau, L., Horn, J., Bank, A., Dutt, M., & Zimmerman, C. (2015). Prevention of violence against women and girls: Lessons from practice. *Lancet, 385,* 1672–1684. doi:10.1016/S0140-6736(14)61797-9.

Ministerio de Justicia y Derechos Humanos. (2017). *Primer estudio nacional sobre violencias contra la mujer 2015, basado en la international violence against women survey (IVAWS). [First national study on violence against women 2015, based on the international violence against women survey].* Buenos Aires: Ministerio de Justicia y Derechos Humanos de la Nación. Retrieved August 18, 2019, from www.saij.gob.ar/primer-estudio-nacional-sobre-violencias-contra-mujer-basado-international-violence-against-women-survey-ivaws-ministerio-justicia-derechos-humanos-nacion-lb000215–2017–07/123456789–0abc-defg-g51–2000blsorbil

Novick, G. (2017). Health care organization and delivery in Argentina: A case of fragmentation, inefficiency and inequality. *Global Policy*, *8*, 93–96. https://doi.org/10.1111/1758-5899.12267

O'Doherty, L., Hegarty, K., Ramsay, J., Davidson, L. L., Feder, G., & Taft, A. (2015). Screening women for intimate partner violence in healthcare settings. *Cochrane Database Systematic Review*, *7*, CD007007. doi:10.1002/14651858.CD007007.pub3

Ortiz-Barreda, G., & Vives-Cases, C. (2013). Legislation on violence against women: Overview of key components. *Revista Panamericana de Salud Publica*, *33*, 61–72.

Pan American Health Organization. (2017). *Argentina. Overall context*. Retrieved August 28, 2019, from www.paho.org/salud-en-las-americas-2017/?p=2706

Pierina Juarez, D., Bagnasco, M. E., Candal, W., Gygli, M. S., Quiroga, M., & Santandrea, C. (2012). *Violencia sobre las Mujeres. Capacitación en servicio para trabajadores de la salud en el primer nivel de atención*. Buenos Aires: Ministerio de Salud de la Nación.

Ramsay, J., Rivas, C., & Feder, G. (2005). *Interventions to reduce violence and promote the physical and psychological well-being of women who experience partner violence: A systematic review of controlled evaluations*. London: Barts and The London. Queen Mary's School of Medicine and Dentistry.

Rivas, C., Ramsay, J., Sadowski, L., Davidson, L. L., Dunne, D., Eldridge, S., Hegarty, K., Taft, A., & Feder, G. (2015). Advocacy interventions to reduce or eliminate violence and promote the physical and psychosocial well-being of women who experience intimate partner abuse. *Cochrane Database Systematic Review*, *3*(12), CD005043. doi:10.1002/14651858.CD005043.pub3

Rivas, C., Vigurs, C., Cameron, J., & Yeo, L. (2019). A realist review of which advocacy interventions work for which abused women under what circumstances. *Cochrane Database Systematic Review*, *29*(6), CD013135. doi:10.1002/14651858.CD013135.pub2

Saletti-Cuesta, L. (2018). Violencia contra las mujeres: definiciones del personal sanitario en los centros de atención primaria de Córdoba, Argentina. *Revista de Salud Pública*, *22*, 66–76.

Saletti-Cuesta, L. Aizenberg, L., & Ricci-Cabello, I. (2018). Opinions and experiences of primary healthcare providers regarding violence against women: A systematic review of qualitative studies. *Journal of Family Violence*, *33*, 405–420. https://doi.org/10.1007/s10896-018-9971-6

Schwab-Reese, L. M., & Renner, L. M. (2018). Screening, management, and treatment of intimate partner violence among women in low-resource settings. *Womens Health (Lond)*, *14*. doi:10.1177/1745506518766709

Senate and Chamber of Deputies of the Argentine Nation. (2009). *Law N°26.485 Comprehensive protection to prevent, punish and eradicate violence against women in areas where they develop their interpersonal relations*. Retrieved May 12, 2020, from http://servicios.infoleg.gob.ar/infolegInternet/anexos/150000-154999/152155/norma.htm

Shiffman, J., & Smith, S. (2007). Generation of political priority for global health initiatives: A framework and case study of maternal mortality. *Lancet*, *370*, 1370–1379. https://doi.org/10.1016/S0140-6736(07)61579-7

Spangaro, J. (2017). What is the role of health systems in responding to domestic violence? An evidence review. *Australian Health Review*, *41*, 639–645. doi:10.1071/AH16155

Terzian, P. (2017). *The Ni Una Menos movement in 21st century argentina: Combating more than femicide* (Dickinson College Honors Theses). Carlisle. Paper 288.

Trabold, N., McMahon, J., Alsobrooks, S., Whitney, S., & Mittal, M. (2018). A systematic review of intimate partner violence interventions: State of the field and implications for practitioners. *Trauma Violence Abuse*, *1*. doi:10.1177/1524838018767934. [Epub ahead of print]

United Nations. (1993). *Declaration on the elimination of violence against women*. New York, NY: United Nations.

Vaggione, Juan Marco. (2018). (Re)acciones conservadoras [Conservative (Re)actions]. In P. Bergallo, J. Sierra, I. Cristina, & J. M. Vaggione (comp.), *El aborto en América Latina. Estrategias jurídicas para luchar por su legalización y enfrentar las resistencias conservadoras. [Abortion in Latin America. Legal strategies to fight for its legalization and face the conservative resistance]* (pp. 327–332). Buenos Aires: Siglo XXI Editores Argentina.

World Health Organization. (2010). *Expert meeting on health-sector responses to violence against women, 17–19 March 2009*. Geneva, Switzerland. Geneva: World Health Organization.

World Health Organization. (2016). *Draft global plan of action on violence* (69th ed.). Geneva: World Health Assembly.

World Health Organization. (2013a). *Global and regional estimates of violence against women: Prevalence and health effects of intimate partner violence and nonpartner sexual violence*. Geneva: World Health Organization.

World Health Organization. (2013b). *Responding to intimate partner and sexual violence against women: WHO clinical and policy guidelines*. Geneva: World Health Organization.

# 35

# DOMESTIC VIOLENCE SURVIVORS' EMOTIONAL AND MENTAL HEALTH

*Jeongsuk Kim and Rebecca J. Macy*

## Introduction

Domestic violence (DV) victimization is a significant trauma that can result in both short-term and long-term emotional and mental health problems. DV survivors (also referred to as survivors of intimate partner violence) may frequently suffer from psychological symptoms associated with stress and trauma (O'Brien & Macy, 2016). A cohort study in the UK found that women who experienced intimate partner violence (IPV) had 2.62 times the odds of mental illness, including depression and anxiety, than unexposed women (Chandan et al., 2019). In addition, a cross-sectional survey showed that the posttraumatic stress disorder (PTSD) scores for the majority of DV survivors were above the clinical threshold (i.e., they would likely be diagnosable in a treatment setting), and that their depression and anxiety levels were also close to clinical thresholds (Ferrari et al., 2016).

Among survivors of DV, emotional health problems and mental health disorders can co-occur and overlap (e.g., a survivor might struggle with both depression and PTSD; Macy, Jones, Graham, & Roach, 2018). Thus, this entire set of emotion health problems may be described as "trauma-related mental health symptoms and illnesses," referring to the comorbidity of multiple mental disorders often associated with the experience of trauma from DV victimization (Macy, Jones et al., 2018, p. 36). Researchers have reported that the severity of such psychological symptoms is often closely associated with survivors' individual characteristics, relational situations, and sociocultural context (Goodman, Smyth, Borges, & Singer, 2009; Sasseville, Maurice, Montminy, Hassan, & St-Pierre, 2020). That is, the disadvantaged and oppressive context in which some survivors live (e.g., having few economic resources, previous exposure to violence, racism, and other forms of oppression) can contribute to and/or exacerbate survivors' emotional and mental health issues, as well as impede their help-seeking efforts for DV (Goodman et al., 2009). Accordingly, survivors' mental health problems should be assessed and addressed within the context of the abusive relationship, as well as in the other personal, situational, and sociocultural contexts which compose and influence women's coping with the trauma of DV.

For all these reasons, this chapter first aims to overview the major emotional and mental health problems faced by DV survivors, attending specifically to the problems of depression, posttraumatic stress disorder (PTSD), suicide intentions, and substance abuse. The chapter will then discuss mental health service delivery settings. Finally, the chapter will present key intervention approaches for DV survivors' emotional and mental health problems, including cognitive behaviour therapy (CBT), mindfulness interventions, advocacy, and trauma-informed substance abuse treatments. Throughout, the chapter will attend to the evidence on which these topics and issues are based, including the limits of the research, and note on how cultural context intersects with these issues, as well as discuss the key challenges for the DV field concerning how best to address survivors' emotional and mental health (Goodman et al., 2009).

## Discussion and analysis

### Major emotional and mental health problems among domestic violence survivors

#### Depression

Depression is characterized by persistent sadness, loss of interest in activities once enjoyed, and lethargy that impairs the individual's ability to function in both social and work settings (WHO, 2019). The findings of a meta-analysis suggest that DV survivors have 2 to 3 times the odds of incident depressive disorder and 1.5 to 2 times the odds of incident elevated depressive symptoms and postpartum depression in comparison with women who have not experienced DV (Devries et al., 2013). The degree of depression is often closely associated with sexual violence experiences, previous trauma, pregnancy and childbearing, and living situations, such as poverty. For example, experiencing sexual violence from an intimate partner increases both the probability and the severity of depressive symptoms (Chen, Rovi, Vega, Jacobs, & Johnson, 2009; Dillon, Hussain, Loxton, & Rahman, 2013; Garcia, Stoever, Wang, & Yim, 2019). Prior traumas and pregnancy and childbearing experiences also exacerbate such psychological difficulties as depression in women facing DV (Kendall-Tackett, 2007; Ludermir, Lewis, Valongueiro, de Araújo, & Araya, 2010; Warshaw, Sullivan, & Rivera, 2013; Jordan, Nietzel, & Walker, 2004).

Research also indicates that the relationship between violence victimization and depression appears to be bidirectional (Devries et al., 2013). Women who experience violence victimization are more prone to depressive symptoms; and conversely, women with existing depressive symptoms are more likely to experience subsequent DV. There are various possible explanations for this relationship. For instance, women struggling with depression may be less sensitive to signals of incipient partner abuse, and/or they may be less likely to seek help because depression might dampen their capacities toward active coping (Devries et al., 2013; Iverson et al., 2013; White & Satyen, 2015). Moreover, the relationship between depression and re-victimization is also likely potentiated by women's situational context, with challenges such as discrimination and racism, poverty, and other oppressions also playing roles in the continuation of depression and violence. Regardless of the causal factor, unresolved mental disorders may play a role in DV re-victimization.

#### Posttraumatic stress disorder (PTSD)

PTSD shows four core symptoms: "intrusive recollections of the event, avoidance of reminders of the event, negative alterations in cognition or mood, and alterations in physiological arousal and reactivity" (Wortmann, Larson, Lubin, Jordan, & Litz, 2015, p. 192). Along with depression, PTSD has been identified as a one of the most prevalent mental health issues among DV survivors (Allen, 2013). In cross-sectional studies, around 25–50% of the survivor women showed moderate to severe PTSD symptoms (Coker, Weston, Creson, Justice, & Blakeney,

2005; Woods, 2000). Researchers have reported that chronic and severe DV victimization (Pill, Day, & Mildred, 2017), multiple victimization experiences, including sexual abuse (Coker et al., 2005), as well as recent partner abuse and recent interpersonal trauma (Khadra, Wehbe, Fiola, Skaff, & Nehme, 2015) all increase the risk of PTSD symptoms. Moreover, PTSD symptoms among violence survivors might differ from symptoms resulting from a one-time traumatic event. Researchers have noted that multiple or chronic traumatic events in which the perpetrator and receiver of the violent victimization have ongoing contact are associated with more complicated and multifaceted PTSD symptoms than symptoms resulting from a one-time traumatic event (Pill et al., 2017).

## Suicide intention

Suicide intention is another serious mental health issue often associated with DV victimization. One systematic review found that, with only one exception, all of the studies showed a strong and consistent association between intimate partner abuse and suicidality (McLaughlin, O'Carroll, & O'Connor, 2012). Not surprisingly, the relationship between DV victimization and suicidality can be influenced by other mental health problems. For example, a cross-sectional study showed that the presence of PTSD and depression mediated the relationship between sexual abuse and suicidal ideation among sheltered women (Weaver et al., 2007). In a study of African American survivors' suicidality, Kaslow and colleagues (1998) found that psychological distress, hopelessness, and drug use were risk factors that increased the women's suicidality; and social support was a protective factor that decreased their risk.

Notably, some research shows that abused women who seek shelter and abused women who are pregnant should perhaps be considered at heightened risk of suicidal ideation. As an example, Martin and colleagues (2007) reported that abused women were more likely than non-abused women to have attempted suicide while pregnant. Likewise, one-third of shelter-seeking women reported suicidal ideation or suicide attempts (Golding, 1999). These findings may suggest that for abused women in specific circumstances such as pregnancy and homelessness, seeking safety comes with practical difficulties (e.g., finding employment and housing, and engaging in healthcare and legal processes) that increase distress, which may in turn, increase vulnerability to suicidal ideation.

## Substance abuse

Women who experience DV victimization may also be more likely to use drugs or alcohol to cope with their trauma and distress (Macy & Goodbourn, 2012). Research has shown that the rates of substance problems are five times higher among women victimized by DV than among non-exposed women (Logan, Walker, Cole, & Leukefeld, 2002). However, a meta-analysis of longitudinal studies found a bidirectional relationship between substance abuse and victimization (Devries et al., 2013). In particular, when substance abuse co-occurs with other problems such as depression or PTSD, women may be less able to detect warning signs of emerging violence and may be less likely to access safety resources (Iverson et al., 2013; Weaver, Gilbert, El-Bassel, Resnick, & Noursi, 2015). Furthermore, alcohol use among women is likely to be confounded by their partners' alcohol use, as women and men may drink together; and men's alcohol use is strongly linked with DV perpetration (Devries et al., 2013). Overall, women who use drugs and suffer from violent victimization are more likely to continue using drugs and to have more substance abuse relapses (Weaver et al., 2015).

## *Intersectionality*

As discussed, DV survivors' individual, relational, and sociocultural circumstances can intensify their mental health problems. Research has indicated that racially marginalized and socio-economically disadvantaged women experiences stress, powerlessness, and social isolation in cumulative contexts; and that this vulnerability produces and exacerbates depression, PTSD, and other emotional difficulties (Goodman et al., 2009; Sasseville et al., 2020). For example, abused women in poverty are disadvantaged not only by the traumas of violence and subsequent feelings of powerlessness, but also by the scarcity of resources that might be used to cope with these conditions (Goodman et al., 2009). Immigrant women are at especially heighted risk of experiencing depressive symptoms (White & Satyen, 2015). The stress of acculturation, including language barriers and lack of social support, might place significant additional stress on relationships that already involve DV victimization (White & Satyen, 2015). It also should be noted that such situations and contexts may lead to disparities in the services available for DV intervention and safety. In turn, such disparities may lead to re-victimization, as well as further mental health problems.

## Approaches and challenges to service provision for violence survivors' mental health

DV survivors struggling with mental health problems may be reluctant to seek help or utilize relevant services due to feelings of shame, fear, isolation, and distrust of others. Thus, a survivor-centred, trauma-focused approach is needed to identify women struggling with DV and to deliver appropriate services. This section is an overview of service settings for survivors' safety and mental health, and a discussion of challenges to such service delivery.

### *Community domestic violence (DV) service setting*

In general and in some parts of the world, community-based organizations (CBO) and non-governmental organizations (NGO) DV agencies are on the frontlines of delivering mental health and safety services to violence survivors (Macy, Martin, Nwabuzor Ogbonnaya, & Rizo, 2018). Although such CBOs and NGOs tend to offer a range of services to survivors and their families, DV agencies generally provide services such as 24-hour crisis lines and emergency response, counselling, support groups, court and legal advocacy, shelter services, as well as referrals to other services in their communities (Van Deinse, Wilson, Macy, & Cuddeback, 2019). In particular, individual/group counselling and support group services that are delivered in such agencies can provide mental health care and emotional support for violence survivors. Nonetheless, counselling provided by DV agencies typically focuses on supportive assistance and help, which does not necessarily include mental health treatment and which may be delivered by staff or volunteers without mental health expertise (Macy, Giattina, Montijo, & Ermentrout, 2010). Such an approach is often associated with the historical development of DV response services, which tended to have community-based, grassroots origins emphasizing social justice and empowerment (Macy et al., 2010; Macy, Rizo, Johns, & Ermentrout, 2013).

### *Service Barriers*

DV agency leaders have often reported that their staff lack mental health expertise, which in turn, prohibits counselling services that include a focus on women's mental health, especially when women are struggling with serious mental illnesses such as major depression (Macy et al., 2010; Van Deinse et al., 2019). Even though DV agency directors recognize the benefits of offering mental health services on site (Macy et al., 2010), they are often unable to offer such services due to lack of funding for mental health professionals, inadequate staffing, and insufficient training for employees (Macy et al., 2010; Mengo, Beaujolais, Kulow, Ramirez, Brown, & Nemeth, 2020). These agencies gaps and needs also presents challenges in helping violence survivors with substance abuse. For instance, DV agencies do not always allow violence survivors with substance problems to access their shelter services both to ensure other survivors' safety and because they lack agency staff to address substance abuse issues (Van Deinse et al., 2019). As violence survivors might use alcohol or drugs to cope with distress or at the coercion of their partners (Weaver et al., 2015), such policies might prohibit survivors with urgent needs from accessing safety services (Van Deinse et al., 2019). Given these challenges, staff at DV agencies may refer violence survivors with mental health problems to local mental health and substance abuse agencies in their communities, if such services are available.

## Mental health setting

The mental health system has a part to play in the prevention of DV and women's re-victimization through identifying violence survivors, providing clinical care for mental illness, and coordinating advocacy with other services sectors (e.g., child care, housing and shelter, and legal advocacy; García-Moreno et al., 2015). As discussed earlier, mental health professionals encounter violence survivors not only through referral systems but also through diagnosis and self-disclosure of DV among their patients. For example, a survey of mental health clients in London discovered that 70% of female service recipients had been victims of DV and abuse as adults (Khalifeh et al., 2015). Because mental health professionals frequently encounter violence survivors, international organizations such as the World Health Organization (WHO) recommend that mental health professionals encourage disclosure of abuse as part of routine clinical assessments and to provide appropriate referrals and treatment in the context of violence and trauma (Oram, Khalifeh, & Howard, 2016).

## Service Barriers

Research indicates that mental health agencies face individual and systemic barriers in providing services to violence survivors, including a scarcity of services overall, few qualified mental health professionals, and high staff turnover (García-Moreno et al., 2015). Globally, the availability of mental health services is highly variable with some countries and communities offering mental health care freely, other countries offering such services in a way that is personally costly for those seeking care, and with some countries and communities not able to offer mental health care at all to anyone (Alegría et al., 2000; Ngui, Khasakhala, Ndetei, & Roberts, 2010). Even when such services are available, violence survivors referred to mental health settings often experience long wait times before intake and/or changes in counsellors. In this context, García-Moreno and colleagues (2015) suggest that referral to mental health agencies might not always be effective, especially in low-income and middle-income countries that lack an adequate workforce of mental health professionals. In addition, it is worth noting here that even when both DV safety services and mental health services are available in a given community, there have historically been and may continue to be tensions between these two service sectors given their significantly different treatment and services approaches and philosophies (Chandan et al., 2019; Van Deinse et al., 2019).

Another challenge at the intersection of DV and mental health is that mental health professionals often lack trauma-informed practice training and guidance. This lack, in turn, results in mental health professionals being unable to identify violence survivors or provide trauma-focused services to survivors in consistent and high-quality ways (Oram et al., 2016). As violence survivors might tend not to seek outside help for their abuse and trauma, professional identification of DV can be a significant early step in providing help and services. In addition, mental health professionals often respond primarily with individual-focused psychotherapeutic solutions designed to help victims and may miss the particular impact of DV on survivors' mental health and well-being (Goodman & Epstein, 2008). Likewise, pathologizing survivors' mental illness obscures understanding of inter-correlated trauma symptoms and hampers implementation of comprehensive treatments (Oram et al., 2016).

## Future directions for service delivery

As discussed, organizational service gaps and service providers' limited skills might be barriers to providing timely, effective mental health services. Thus, dedicated training to ensure meaningful and safe responses is necessary. Many researchers and practitioners have emphasized the importance of trauma-informed care training for DV agency staff and mental health professionals (Macy et al., 2010; García-Moreno et al., 2015; Mengo et al., 2020). As a specific approach, DV agencies and mental health settings' inclusion of substance abuse providers could implement cross-training guided by trauma-informed principles (Macy & Goodbourn, 2012; Van Deinse et al., 2019). This cross-training could focus on building service providers' understanding of the interrelationship between trauma, DV, mental health, substance use, and other comorbid problems and could foster a mental health/ substance abuse-focused counselling approach (Macy & Goodbourn, 2012; Van Deinse et al., 2019).

In addition, poor service coordination between mental health providers and DV agencies creates a critical gap in mental health service delivery (Mengo et al., 2020). Thus, it is essential to reduce service gaps between DV agencies, mental health care, and substance abuse treatment settings. As one strategy, multisector service providers could create protocols for referral networks and systems and other collaborative service provision (Mengo et al., 2020). Protocols and guidelines can support multisector providers by letting them know what actions to take as well as what services on which to collaborate (Mengo et al., 2020). For example, such service protocols should include clear guidance on specific referral processes, how best to attend to survivors' service priorities and needs, how best to monitor survivors' progress, as well as how best to assess survivors' service outcomes and completion.

## Key intervention approaches for survivors' emotional and mental health

This section will introduce four major intervention approaches for improving survivors' emotional and mental health, as well as review empirical evidence for the effectiveness of these interventions. It should be noted here that these interventions are not always distinct approaches. Rather, these interventions are often interdependent and overlapping in their theoretical grounding, in how they have been investigated in research studies, and in how they are implemented in practice.

### *Cognitive behaviour therapy*

Cognitive behaviour therapy (CBT) is a treatment that has been widely used and validated across many clinical settings among violence survivors with mental health disorders – in particular, PTSD. The central principle of CBT is that DV survivors' cognitions, the process by which individuals understand incoming information, determines their emotions and behaviours. Thus, CBT posits that modifying women' cognitions will lead them to desired changes in their corresponding emotions and behaviour (Macy, 2006). CBT includes a wide range of individual and group interventions that use cognitive and behavioural components such as exposure therapy, motivational interviewing, and/or problem-solving techniques which focus on positively changing existing unhelpful cognition (Tirado-Muñoz, Gilchrist, Farré, Hegarty, & Torrens, 2014).

## Effectiveness

CBT has generally shown benefits for violence survivors' mental health. For example, Kar (2011) reviewed 31 randomized control trials to evaluate the effectiveness of CBT in treating patients with PTSD. The review suggested that CBT methods such as exposure therapy are effective treatments for both acute and chronic PTSD, having both short-term and long-term benefits. The review also suggested that CBT is effective for clients dealing with comorbidity of PTSD and other severe mental illness. As for the effectiveness of specific types of CBT, Diehle and colleagues (2014) conducted a meta-analysis to determine which CBT methods are most effective in reducing trauma-related cognition among people with PTSD symptoms, including survivors of DV. Using 16 randomized controlled trial studies, the author found that trauma-focused CBT interventions led to the greatest reduction in PTSD and trauma-related cognitions.

Despite such promising findings, readers are encouraged to keep in mind the limits of this body of research. Although review research has found positive effects of CBT for violence survivors, the articles used for these reviews were limited in some key ways (Diehle, Schmitt, Daams, Boer, & Lindauer, 2014; Kar, 2011). For example, CBT interventions are generally short term. In addition, the majority of studies reviewed involved racially homogeneous samples of mostly white women (Schmidt, 2014) even though some studies found validated findings of CBT for culturally diverse populations (e.g., Kubany et al., 2004).

## Further considerations

Careful consideration is necessary in applying CBT to DV. For example, CBT interventions are most often recommended for women who are no longer experiencing violence and may not be as helpful for women who are still struggling with violent victimization and needing to secure their safety (Tirado-Muñoz et al., 2014). In addition, because CBT emphasizes individuals' thoughts, it focuses on changing beliefs – a fact which might conflict with individuals' cultural and/or personal values. Therefore, practitioners should understand patients' cultural values and how they relate to survivors' cognitions and emotions before undertaking CBT.

## *Mindfulness interventions*

Mindfulness-based interventions include meditation, mindfulness movement such as yoga, mantras repeating a word or phrase to help in meditation, and individual body scans exploring physical sensations (Shapero, Greenberg, Pedrelli, de Jong, & Desbordes, 2018). These mindfulness practices commonly focus on self-regulation of attention to the present moment and acceptance of previous experiences (Dutton, Bermudez, Matas, Majid, & Myers, 2013; Shapero et al., 2018). Mindfulness-based practices can be used not only as solitary interventions, but also as part of a broader treatment program (Niles et al., 2017). Even though mindfulness-based interventions are used frequently with CBT, they differ from CBT in that they focus not on changing cognitions, but rather on learning to experience thoughts as internal events which a violence survivor can accept or let go (Kahl, Winter, & Schweiger, 2012). Notably, mindfulness interventions show high retentions rates among clients and service users, and practitioners report that mindfulness intervention is suitable in cases where other treatments may be inappropriate (Lang et al., 2012).

## Effectiveness

Although mindfulness-based interventions are a relatively newly researched therapeutic area, researchers have found promising results for survivors' mental health. For example, Kelly and Garland (2016) examined the effectiveness of a trauma-informed, mindfulness intervention. Using a randomized study design, DV survivors attended an eight-week intervention involving meditation, gentle movement exercise, didactic lecture, and group discussion. Study findings showed significant decreases in PTSD, depression, and anxiety among the treatment group relative to the control group. However, this study was limited by a small sample, use of a waitlist control group, and lack of follow-up observations. More recently, Macy and colleagues (2018a) reviewed studies of the benefits of yoga for DV survivors. This review found that yoga may have generally positive and beneficial effects on survivors' psychological symptoms, including depression, anxiety, and PTSD. However, Macy, Jones et al. (2018) noted that existing studies have serious, universal methodological issues, including a lack of randomization and control groups, lack of validated measurements, poor quality baseline data, and lack of long-term follow-up.

## Further considerations

Mindfulness intervention should be used cautiously and with a consideration of individuals' characteristics and unique situations. Research suggests that mindfulness skills focused on self-control may be unsuitable for individuals with severe trauma. As examples, meditation might cause flashback of abuse or exacerbate psychological disorders (Longacre, Silver-Highfield, Lama, & Grodin, 2012). In addition, mindfulness movement practices should also be used carefully, considering survivors' ages, injuries, physical conditions, and prior trauma. For example, Macy, Jones et al. (2018) suggested that yoga should be used cautiously with pregnant women, older adults, and individuals with physical disabilities. Also, some yoga postures using a particular part of the body, such as the chest or groin areas, may cause discomfort or flashbacks for survivors of physical or sexual abuse (Longacre et al., 2012; Macy, Jones et al., 2018).

## Advocacy

Advocacy programs, in the context of DV services, encompass a broad range of services designed to empower survivors by connecting them with community resources. Specific activities of advocacy services include support for safety planning, legal assistance, housing and financial advice, emergency housing, informal counselling, and ongoing support (WHO, 2013). DV survivors usually access these services through a staff member – often called an advocate – at a CBO and/or NGO violence service program (Macy, Giattina, Sangster, Crosby, & Montijo, 2009). Through advocacy interventions, victims receive not only support for their safety but also the emotional support of having the advocate's companionship during stressful situations such as seeking legal remedies or testifying in court (Bell & Goodman, 2001). Advocacy may be especially critical to violence survivors who lack informal social support (e.g., family and friends), materials resources, and/or those who may face system barriers in advocating on their behalf (e.g., immigrant survivors, survivors with disabilities, survivors whose first language is not the language of the community in which they are living, youth who are survivors; Bell & Goodman, 2001).

## Effectiveness

Two systematic review studies investigated the effectiveness of advocacy interventions (Rivas et al., 2016; Tirado-Munoz et al., 2014). Overall, the findings regarding advocacy programs and emotional health issues, including quality of life, depression, self-efficacy, and psychological distress, were mixed and inconclusive. These reviews noted that the primary studies that were reviewed had considerable heterogeneity in terms of the intensity of the advocacy offered (i.e., ranging from about 30 minutes to 80 hours), the delivery methods, and outcome measurements. Accordingly, it is difficult to evaluate the effectiveness of advocacy for survivors' mental health, though the approach does appear to hold some promise for helping address survivors' emotional health and trauma.

## Further considerations

The effectiveness of advocacy as an intervention relies largely on positive, strong alliances and collaboration between advocates and violence survivors (Goodman, Fauci, Sullivan, DiGiovanni, & Wilson, 2016). However, research demonstrates that several factors may negatively influence the development and sustaining of these relationships. For example, ethnic minority groups might experience cultural misunderstanding with their advocates, which in turn, lead to significantly lower feelings of alliance (Goodman et al., 2016). Such findings point to the importance of culturally meaningful advocacy interventions that are tailored to survivors and communities.

Even though direct evidence of the effectiveness of advocacy programs on survivors' emotional health is inconclusive and limited (Rivas et al., 2016; Tirado-Munoz et al., 2014), research argues that survivors' emotional well-being is best established through a holistic approach to violence prevention that includes not only psychologically focused interventions, but also addresses survivors' safety, child care, economic well-being, and housing, as examples (Pill et al., 2017). Accordingly, whether or not advocacy interventions are effective in improving violence survivors' emotional and mental health on their own, these interventions appear essential in addressing violence survivors' safety and well-being, which in turn, may also lead to survivors' emotional well-being and mental health.

## Trauma-informed substance abuse treatments

Research has found a high co-occurrence of mental health problems (e.g., depression, PTSD) and substance use disorders among trauma survivors. For example, individuals with a diagnosis of PTSD engage in treatment for substance use disorders at a rate five times higher than the general population (Atkins, 2014). Trauma is well known to commonly play a role in mental and substance use disorders, and thus should be systematically addressed across all prevention, treatment, and recovery settings (Macy & Goodbourn, 2012). Based on this need, a trauma-informed substance abuse service framework has been developed (Elliott, Bjelajac, Fallot, Markoff, & Reed, 2005; SAMHSA, 2011). Trauma-informed substance abuse services provide therapies that are sensitive and responsive to the unique needs of trauma survivors, and they also offer trauma-specific interventions (Macy & Goodbourn, 2012; Reeves, 2015).

## *Effectiveness*

Although there is limited evidence concerning trauma-informed substance treatment overall, existing research regarding this service framework are promising. For example, randomized controlled trials of the *Seeking Safety* program focusing on co-occurring issues of PTSD and substance abuse showed positive results (Najavits, 2007). A recent meta-analysis evaluating the effectiveness of *Seeking Safety* in reducing the severity of PTSD and co-occurring substance use symptoms also yielded promising findings. Among the 12 studies identified, findings showed medium effect sizes for *Seeking Safety* for decreasing symptoms of PTSD and modest effects for decreasing symptoms of substance use (Lenz, Henesy, & Callender, 2016). However, overall, research on the efficacy of these trauma-informed treatment is nascent. More work is needed to establish the efficacy of this service framework.

## *Further considerations*

Even though trauma-informed substance abuse intervention is promising, this framework has not been widely used to deal with violence survivors' substance abuse. Macy and Goodbourn (2012) provided several recommendations to promote increased collaboration among providers in both DV service settings and substance abuse treatment settings:

> 1) dedicated case management to facilitate referral and coordination; 2) interagency case consultation to coordinate services and treatment planning; 3) co-location of providers from collaborating agencies' to promote service accessibility and foster interagency staff relationships; 4) assigning one staff member to act as an interagency liaison to facilitate collaborative efforts; and 5) developing working relationships at all agency levels.
>
> (p. 249)

In addition, a trauma-informed service approach underscores the importance of providing women with gender-specific substance abuse treatment, which attends to the pain and difficulties women have endured due to victimization, their role as parents, and the importance of their relationships with positive family members and intimates as critical components in their recovery from substance abuse (Elliott et al., 2005; SAMHSA, 2011).

## Future directions for intervention approach

In general, the interventions presented in this chapter showed promise for addressing survivors' emotional and mental health. However, the extant intervention studies reviewed here universally possess methodological limitations. Longitudinal studies with follow-up are lacking, and very little intervention research has addressed survivors' co-occurring emotional and mental health problems. The available research also lacks studies that use randomization and comparison groups. Therefore, the findings of these studies might be confounded by various factors given that the research to date has not typically considered comparison group findings for baseline or follow-up. Small sample sizes limit the generalizability of the findings, and many of the intervention studies lack robust, validated measures. Therefore, this review underscores the importance of additional, future research concerning interventions for violence survivors' emotional and mental health, including research that uses rigorous study designs and includes longitudinal follow-up.

Also importantly, survivors' history of abusive relationships, coping behaviours, and their emotional responses to victimization can be greatly influenced by their background, communities, and culture. However, existing studies suggest a lack of culturally informed approaches, as well as a lack of research examining the effectiveness of such approaches for violence survivors. Recently, a few studies have shown moderate effectiveness for culturally informed intervention (O'Brien & Macy, 2016; Kubany et al., 2004; Sokoloff & Dupont, 2005). However, the authors of this research emphasize that such approaches are still relatively new and require more evidence before being deemed effective. Accordingly, future practice and research efforts are strongly encouraged to develop and investigate approaches that are meaningful for and relevant to survivors' background, cultural heritage, and community context. In addition, it should be pointed out that most of the research presented here focused on heterosexual women. Women are highly burdened by both DV victimization and mental health problems and thus should be a continued focus for both research and treatment. In addition, practitioners and researchers are also called to attend to these issues among LGBTQ+ violence survivors, as well as male violence survivors. Last but not least, practitioners and researchers are also strongly urged to collaborate with survivors, advocates, and community workers from diverse groups in order to facilitate the development of and research on intervention approaches (O'Brien & Macy, 2016).

## Conclusions

This chapter explored the major emotional and mental health problems among DV survivors, specifically attending to the problems of depression, PTSD, suicide intentions, and substance abuse. The chapter then presented mental health service approaches and challenges to service provision, focusing on community-based DV agency settings and mental health settings. The chapter also presented key intervention approaches for DV survivors' emotional and mental health problems, including CBT, mindfulness interventions, advocacy, and trauma-informed substance abuse treatments.

Research reviewed here suggests that survivors who are struggling with their emotional and mental health may be less likely to seek help and to access relevant resources and thus may be more likely to be re-victimized. Notably, some of the factors that may exacerbate DV survivors' emotional and mental health problems (e.g., homelessness, lack of social support, poverty, pregnancy, and racism) may also present realistic challenges in accessing services. Such factors might be usefully considered social determinants of both DV and survivors' mental health. For all these reasons, safety services, as well as mental health and substance abuse treatment programs, should consider how best to engage with and encourage violence survivors to participate in programming for their mental health and emotional well-being, for example by using dedicated outreach services and trauma-informed service approaches. Likewise, service providers should also be prepared to identify and address violent victimization among people who present for economic services, housing services, and prenatal care because survivors may seek services without readily identifying the violence that is occurring in their lives. In addition, practitioners across service sectors (i.e., DV safety services, mental health treatment and substance abuse treatment programs) should use a trauma-informed, holistic approach to identity and address violence survivors' co-occurring emotional and mental health problems, as well as their safety and practical needs.

In sum, research strongly shows that many violence survivors struggle with serious emotional and mental health problems, especially survivors who have had prior experiences of violence victimization in their lives, as well as those who have experienced enduring and severe DV. Such emotional and mental health problems may be exacerbated by the challenges and realities of survivors' lives (e.g., homelessness, poverty, and pregnancy), as well as the additional injustices that they may face (e.g., racism and discrimination). Encouragingly, there is growing attention to the intersection of DV victimization and survivors' mental health. This increasing attention has led to the development of a number of intervention approaches that show promise for helping survivors with their emotional and mental health. Nonetheless, much of the intervention development and associated research is still only promising. Therefore, advocates, treatment providers, funders, and policymakers are strongly urged to continue and increase their attention to violence survivors' mental health and emotional well-being.

## Critical findings

- Domestic violence (DV) survivors often struggle with a comorbidity of emotional and mental health problems due to the trauma of victimization.
- Factors that exacerbate DV survivors' mental health problems (e.g., homelessness, lack of social support, poverty, pregnancy, and racism) may also present realistic challenges in accessing services for safety and for mental health.
- Community DV service settings, mental health settings, and substance abuse settings are on the frontlines of delivering mental health and safety services to domestic violence survivors.
- Challenges in service delivery settings include a lack of collaboration among relevant service sectors and limited training in trauma-informed, culturally sensitive service provision. Effective collaborations require multidimensional strategies at the provider, agency, and policy levels.
- The intervention approaches reviewed here show promising results for improving survivors' emotional and mental health. However, these intervention studies universally possess methodological limitations.
- Existing interventions often lack attention to or implementation of culturally informed approaches for violence survivors.

## Implications for policy, practice, and research

### *Policy*

- Policymakers should encourage DV agencies and mental health settings, including substance abuse treatment agencies, to implement cross-training guided by culturally sensitive, trauma-informed service.
- Policies should be enacted to facilitate the creation of protocols for referral to service providers and for collaboration among multisector service organizations.
- Governments and private grant makers should fund services in ways that enable and promote interagency collaboration.

### *Practice*

- Practitioners need to consider the specific precautions of major interventions before implementing any with domestic violence (DV) survivors. By considering a survivors' background, trauma experience, and current needs, the practitioner can provide appropriate, survivor-centred services.

- Practitioners across service sectors (i.e., DV safety services, mental health treatment, and substance abuse treatment) should use a trauma-informed, holistic approach to identity and address violence survivors' co-occurring emotional and mental health problems, as well as their safety and practical needs.
- DV agencies should collaborate with mental health and substance abuse treatment programs in facilitating cross-trainings and case management including service referral and coordination.

## Research

- Future research, with rigorous research designs, is needed to determine how best to provide comprehensive intervention programs for violence survivors' mental health and safety needs.
- Future research needs to focus on developing and evaluating interventions tailored to the emotional and mental health of diverse violence survivors.
- Future research should consider social determinants (e.g., homelessness, poverty, oppression, and racism) associated with DV, including how these issues may exacerbate and prolong both DV and women's mental health problems.

## References

Alegría, M., Kessler, R. C., Bijl, R., Lin, E., Heeringa, S. G., Takeuchi, D. T., & Kolody, B. (2000). Comparing data on mental health service use between countries. In B. Andrews & A. Henderson (Eds.), *Unmet need in psychiatry: Problems, resources, responses* (pp. 97–118). Cambridge: Cambridge University Press.

Allen, M. (2013). *Social work and intimate partner violence*. Hoboken: Taylor and Francis.

Atkins, C. (2014). *Co-occurring disorders: Integrated assessment and treatment of substance use and mental disorders*. Eau Claire, WI: PESI Publishing & Media.

Bell, M. E., & Goodman, L. A. (2001). Supporting battered women involved with the court system: An evaluation of a law school-based advocacy intervention. *Violence Against Women, 7*(12), 1377–1404. https://doi.org/10.1177/10778010122183919

Chandan, J. S., Thomas, T., Bradbury-Jones, C., Russell, R., Bandyopadhyay, S., Nirantharakumar, K., & Taylor, J. (2019). Female survivors of intimate partner violence and risk of depression, anxiety and serious mental illness. *The British Journal of Psychiatry*, 1–6. https://doi.org/10.1192/bjp.2019.124

Chen, P. H., Rovi, S., Vega, M., Jacobs, A., & Johnson, M. S. (2009). Relation of domestic violence to health status among Hispanic women. *Journal of Health Care for the Poor and Underserved, 20*(2), 569–582. https://doi.org/10.1353/hpu.0.0145

Coker, A. L., Weston, R., Creson, D. L., Justice, B., & Blakeney, P. (2005). PTSD symptoms among men and women survivors of intimate partner violence: The role of risk and protective factors. *Violence and Victims, 20*(6), 625–643. https://doi.org/10.1891/0886-6708.20.6.625

Dana Schmidt, I. (2014). Addressing PTSD in low-income victims of intimate partner violence: Moving toward a comprehensive intervention. *Social Work, 59*(3), 253–260. https://doi.org/10.1093/sw/swu016

Devries, K. M., Mak, J. Y., Bacchus, L. J., Child, J. C., Falder, G., Petzold, M., . . . Watts, C. H. (2013). Intimate partner violence and incident depressive symptoms and suicide attempts: A systematic review of longitudinal studies. *PLoS Medicine, 10*(5), e1001439. https://doi.org/10.1371/journal.pmed.1001439

Diehle, J., Schmitt, K., Daams, J. G., Boer, F., & Lindauer, R. J. (2014). Effects of psychotherapy on trauma-related cognitions in posttraumatic stress disorder: A meta-analysis. *Journal of Traumatic Stress, 27*(3), 257–264. https://doi.org/10.1002/jts.21924

Dillon, G., Hussain, R., Loxton, D., & Rahman, S. (2013). Mental and physical health and intimate partner violence against women: A review of the literature. *International Journal of Family Medicine, 2013*, 313909–313915. https://doi.org/10.1155/2013/313909

Dutton, M. A., Bermudez, D., Matas, A., Majid, H., & Myers, N. L. (2013). Mindfulness-based stress reduction for low-income, predominantly African American women with PTSD and a history of intimate partner violence. *Cognitive and Behavioral Practice, 20*(1), 23–32. https://doi.org/10.1016/j.cbpra.2011.08.00

Elliott, D. E., Bjelajac, P., Fallot, R. D., Markoff, L. S., & Reed, B. G. (2005). Trauma-informed or trauma-denied: Principles and implementation of trauma-informed services for women. *Journal of Community Psychology, 33*(4), 461–477. https://doi.org/10.1002/jcop.20063

Ferrari, G., Agnew-Davies, R., Bailey, J., Howard, L., Howarth, E., Peters, T. J., . . . Feder, G. S. (2016). Domestic violence and mental health: A cross-sectional survey of women seeking help from domestic violence support services. *Global Health Action, 9*(1), 29890–298910. https://doi.org/10.3402/gha.v9.29890

Garcia, E. R., Stoever, J. K., Wang, P., & Yim, I. S. (2019). Empowerment, stress, and depressive symptoms among female survivors of intimate partner violence attending personal empowerment programs. *Journal of Interpersonal Violence*. https://doi.org/10.1177/0886260519869693

García-Moreno, C., Hegarty, K., d'Oliveira, A. F. L., Koziol-McLain, J., Colombini, M., & Feder, G. (2015). The health-systems response to violence against women. *The Lancet, 385*(9977), 1567–1579. https://doi.org/10.1016/S0140-6736(14)61837-7

Golding, J. M. (1999). Intimate partner violence as a risk factor for mental disorders: A meta-analysis. *Journal of Family Violence, 14*(2), 99–132. https://doi.org/10.1023/A:1022079418229

Goodman, L. A., & Epstein, D. (2008). *Listening to battered women: A survivor-centered approach to advocacy, mental health, and justice*. Washington, DC: American Psychological Association.

Goodman, L. A., Fauci, J. E., Sullivan, C. M., DiGiovanni, C. D., & Wilson, J. M. (2016). Domestic violence survivors' empowerment and mental health: Exploring the role of the alliance with advocates. *American Journal of Orthopsychiatry, 86*(3), 286–296. https://doi.org/10.1037/ort0000137

Goodman, L. A., Smyth, K. F., Borges, A. M., & Singer, R. (2009). When crises collide: How intimate partner violence and poverty intersect to shape women's mental health and coping? *Trauma, Violence, & Abuse, 10*(4), 306–329. https://doi.org/10.1177/1524838009339754

Iverson, K. M., Litwack, S. D., Pineles, S. L., Suvak, M. K., Vaughn, R. A., & Resick, P. A. (2013). Predictors of intimate partner violence revictimization: The relative impact of distinct PTSD symptoms, dissociation, and coping strategies. *Journal of Traumatic Stress, 26*(1), 102–110. https://doi.org/10.1002/jts.21781

Jordan, C. E., Nietzel, M. T., & Walker, R. (2004). *Intimate partner violence: A clinical training guide for mental health professionals*. New York, NY: Springer Publishing Company.

Kahl, K. G., Winter, L., & Schweiger, U. (2012). The third wave of cognitive behavioural therapies: What is new and what is effective? *Current Opinion in Psychiatry, 25*(6), 522–528. https://doi.org/10.1097/YCO.0b013e328358e531

Kar, N. (2011). Cognitive behavioral therapy for the treatment of post-traumatic stress disorder: A review. *Neuropsychiatric Disease and Treatment, 7*(1), 167–181. https://doi.org/10.2147/NDT.S10389

Kaslow, N. J., Thompson, M. P., Meadows, L. A., Jacobs, D., Gibb, B., & Bornstein, H. (1998). Factors that mediate and moderate the link between partner abuse and suicidal behaviour in African American women. *Journal of Consulting and Clinical Psychology, 66*(3), 533–540. https://doi.org/10.1037/0022-006X.66.3.533

Kelly, A., & Garland, E. L. (2016). Trauma-informed mindfulness-based stress reduction for female survivors of interpersonal violence: Results from a stage I RCT. *Journal of Clinical Psychology, 72*(4), 311–328. https://doi.org/10.1002/jclp.22273

Kendall-Tackett, K. A. (2007). Violence against women and the perinatal period: The impact of lifetime violence and abuse on pregnancy, postpartum, and breastfeeding. *Trauma, Violence, & Abuse, 8*(3), 344–353. https://doi.org/10.1177/1524838007304406

Khadra, C., Wehbe, N., Fiola, J. L., Skaff, W., & Nehme, M. (2015). Symptoms of post-traumatic stress disorder among battered women in Lebanon: An exploratory study. *Journal of Interpersonal Violence, 30*(2), 295–313. https://doi.org/10.1177/0886260514534774.

Khalifeh, H., Moran, P., Borschmann, R., Dean, K., Hart, C., Hogg, J., . . . Howard, L. M. (2015). Domestic and sexual violence against patients with severe mental illness. *Psychological Medicine, 45*(4), 875–886. https://doi.org/10.1017/S0033291714001962

Kubany, E. S., Hill, E. E., Owens, J. A., Iannce-Spencer, C., McCaig, M. A., Tremayne, K. J., & Williams, P. L. (2004). Cognitive trauma therapy for battered women with PTSD (CTT-BW). *Journal of Consulting and Clinical Psychology, 72*(1), 3–18. https://doi.org/10.1037/0022-006X.72.1.3

Lang, A. J., Strauss, J. L., Bomyea, J., Bormann, J. E., Hickman, S. D., Good, R. C., & Essex, M. (2012). The theoretical and empirical basis for meditation as an intervention for PTSD. *Behavior Modification, 36*(6), 759. https://doi.org/10.1177/0145445512441200

Lenz, A. S., Henesy, R., & Callender, K. (2016). Effectiveness of seeking safety for co-occurring post-traumatic stress disorder and substance use. *Journal of Counseling & Development, 94*(1), 51–61. https://doi.org/10.1002/jcad.12061

Logan, T. K., Walker, R., Cole, J., & Leukefeld, C. (2002). Victimization and substance abuse among women: Contributing factors, interventions, and implications. *Review of General Psychology, 6*(4), 325–397. https://doi.org/10.1037/1089-2680.6.4.325

Longacre, M., Silver-Highfield, E., Lama, P., & Grodin, M. (2012). Complementary and alternative medicine in the treatment of refugees and survivors of torture: A review and proposal for action. *Torture: Quarterly Journal on Rehabilitation of Torture Victims and Prevention of Torture, 22*(1), 38–57.

Ludermir, A. B., Lewis, G., Valongueiro, S. A., de Araújo, T. V. B., & Araya, R. (2010). Violence against women by their intimate partner during pregnancy and postnatal depression: A prospective cohort study. *The Lancet, 376*(9744), 903–910. https://doi.org/10.1016/S0140-6736(10)60887-2

Macy, R. J. (2006). Cognitive therapy. In A. B. Rochlen (Ed.), *Applying counseling theories: An online, case-based approach* (pp. 157–176). Upper Saddle River, NJ: Pearson.

Macy, R. J., Giattina, M. C., Montijo, N. J., & Ermentrout, D. M. (2010). Domestic violence and sexual assault agency directors' perspectives on services that help survivors. *Violence Against Women, 16*(10), 1138–1161. https://doi.org/10.1177/1077801210383085

Macy, R. J., Giattina, M. C., Sangster, T. H., Crosby, C., & Montijo, N. J. (2009). Domestic violence and sexual assault services: Inside the black box. *Aggression and Violent Behavior, 14*(5), 359–373. https://doi.org/10.1016/j.avb.2009.06.002

Macy, R. J., & Goodbourn, M. (2012). Promoting successful collaborations between domestic violence and substance abuse treatment service sectors: A review of the literature. *Trauma, Violence, & Abuse, 13*(4), 234–251. https://doi.org/10.1177/1524838012455874

Macy, R. J., Jones, E., Graham, L. M., & Roach, L. (2018a). Yoga for trauma and related mental health problems: A meta-review with clinical and service recommendations. *Trauma, Violence, & Abuse, 19*(1), 35–57. https://doi.org/10.1177/1524838015620834

Macy, R. J., Martin, S. L., Nwabuzor Ogbonnaya, I., & Rizo, C. F. (2018b). What do domestic violence and sexual assault service providers need to know about survivors to deliver services? *Violence Against Women, 24*(1), 28–44. https://doi.org/10.1177/1077801216671222

Macy, R. J., Rizo, C. F., Johns, N. B., & Ermentrout, D. M. (2013). Directors' opinions about domestic violence and sexual assault service strategies that help survivors. *Journal of Interpersonal Violence, 28*(5), 1040–1066. https://doi.org/10.1177/1077801210383085

Martin, S. L., Macy, R. J., Sullivan, K., & Magee, M. L. (2007). Pregnancy-associated violent deaths: The role of intimate partner violence. *Trauma, Violence, & Abuse, 8*(2), 135–148. https://doi.org/10.1177/1524838007301223

Mengo, C., Beaujolais, B., Kulow, E., Ramirez, R., Brown, A., & Nemeth, J. (2020). Knowledge and perspectives of domestic violence service providers about survivors with mental health disability. *Journal of Family Violence, 35*(2), 181–190. https://doi.org/10.1007/s10896-019-00053-3

McLaughlin, J., O'Carroll, R. E., & O'Connor, R. C. (2012). Intimate partner abuse and suicidality: A systematic review. *Clinical Psychology Review, 32*(8), 677–689. https://doi.org/10.1016/j.cpr.2012.08.002

Najavits, L. M. (2007). Seeking safety: An evidence-based model for substance abuse and trauma/PTSD. In K. A. Witkiewitz & G. A. Marlatt (Eds.), *Therapists' guide to evidence-based relapse prevention: Practical resources for the mental health professional* (pp. 141–167). Amsterdam: Elsevier Press.

Ngui, E. M., Khasakhala, L., Ndetei, D., & Roberts, L. W. (2010). Mental disorders, health inequalities and ethics: A global perspective. *International Review of Psychiatry, 22*(3), 235–244. https://doi.org/10.3109/09540261.2010.485273

Niles, B. L., Mori, D. L., Polizzi, C., Kaiser, A. P., Weinstein, E. S., Gershkovich, M., & Wang, C. (2017). A systematic review of randomized trials of mind-body interventions for PTSD. *Journal of Clinical Psychology, 74*, 1485–1508. https://doi.org/10.1002/jclp.22634

O'Brien, J. E., & Macy, R. J. (2016). Culturally specific interventions for female survivors of gender-based violence. *Aggression and Violent Behavior, 31*, 48–60. https://doi.org/10.1016/j.avb.2016.07.005

Oram, S., Khalifeh, H., & Howard, L. M. (2016). Violence against women and mental health. *The Lancet Psychiatry, 4*(2), 159–170. https://doi.org/10.1016/S2215-0366(16)30261-9

Pill, N., Day, A., & Mildred, H. (2017). Trauma responses to intimate partner violence: A review of current knowledge. *Aggression and Violent Behavior, 34*, 178–184. https://doi.org/10.1016/j.avb.2017.01.014

Reeves, E. (2015). A synthesis of the literature on trauma-informed care. *Issues in Mental Health Nursing, 36*(9), 698–709. https://doi.org/10.3109/01612840.2015.1025319

Rivas, C., Ramsay, J., Sadowski, L., Davidson, L. L., Dunnes, D., Eldridge, S., . . . Feder, G. (2016). Advocacy interventions to reduce or eliminate violence and promote the physical and psychosocial well-being of women who experience intimate partner abuse: A systematic review. *Campbell Systematic Reviews, 12*(1), 1–202. https://doi.org/10.4073/csr.2016.2

Sasseville, N., Maurice, P., Montminy, L., Hassan, G., & St-Pierre, É. (2020). Cumulative contexts of vulnerability to intimate partner violence among women with disabilities, elderly women, and immigrant women: Prevalence, risk factors, explanatory theories, and prevention. *Trauma, Violence, & Abuse,* https://doi.org/10.1177/1524838020925773

Shapero, B. G., Greenberg, J., Pedrelli, P., de Jong, M., & Desbordes, G. (2018). Mindfulness-based interventions in psychiatry. *Focus, 16*(1), 32–39. https://doi.org/10.1176/appi.focus.20170039

Sokoloff, N. J., & Dupont, I. (2005). Domestic violence at the intersections of race, class, and gender: Challenges and contributions to understanding violence against marginalized women in diverse communities. *Violence Against Women, 11*(1), 38–64. https://doi.org/10.1177/1077801204271476

Substance Abuse and Mental Health Services Administration. (2011). Addressing the needs of women and girls: Developing core competencies for mental health and substance abuse service professionals (HHS Pub. No. SMA 11–4657). http://store. samhsa.gov/shin/content//SMA11–4657/SMA11–4657.pdf

Tirado-Muñoz, J., Gilchrist, G., Farré, M., Hegarty, K., & Torrens, M. (2014). The efficacy of cognitive behavioural therapy and advocacy interventions for women who have experienced intimate partner violence: A systematic review and meta-analysis. *Annals of Medicine, 46*(8), 567–586. https://doi.org/10.3109/07853890.2014.941918

Van Deinse, T. B., Wilson, A. B., Macy, R. J., & Cuddeback, G. S. (2019). Intimate partner violence and women with severe mental illnesses: Needs and challenges from the perspectives of behavioral health and domestic violence service providers. *The Journal of Behavioral Health Services & Research, 46*(2), 283–293. https://doi.org/10.1007/s11414-018-9624-9

Warshaw, C., Sullivan, C. M., & Rivera, E. A. (2013). *A systematic review of trauma-focused interventions for domestic violence survivors*: National Center on Domestic Violence, Trauma & Mental Health. Retrieved from www.nationalcenterdvtraumamh.org/wp-content/uploads/2013/03/NCDVTMH_EBPLitReview2013.pdf

Weaver, T. L., Allen, J. A., Hopper, E., Maglione, M. L., McLaughlin, D., McCullough, M. A., . . . Brewer, T. (2007). Mediators of suicidal ideation within a sheltered sample of raped and battered women. *Health Care for Women International, 28*(5), 478–489. https://doi.org/10.1080/07399330701226453

Weaver, T. L., Gilbert, L., El-Bassel, N., Resnick, H. S., & Noursi, S. (2015). Identifying and intervening with substance-using women exposed to intimate partner violence: Phenomenology, comorbidities, and integrated approaches within primary care and other agency settings. *Journal of Women's Health, 24*(1), 51–56. https://doi.org/10.1089/jwh.2014.4866

White, M. E., & Satyen, L. (2015). Cross-cultural differences in intimate partner violence and depression: A systematic review. *Aggression and Violent Behavior, 24*, 120–130. https://doi.org/10.1016/j.avb.2015.05.005

Woods, S. J. (2000). Prevalence and patterns of posttraumatic stress disorder in abuse and postabused women. *Issues in Mental Health Nursing, 21*, 309–324.

World Health Organization. (2013). *Responding to intimate partner violence and sexual violence against women: WHO clinical and policy guidelines*. Retrieved from https://apps.who.int/iris/bitstream/handle/10665/85240/9789241548595_eng.pdf;jsessionid=BDCDC7B81FDE5855510921458C59F197?sequence=1

World Health Organization. (2019). *Depression: A global public health concern*. Retrieved from www.who.int/mediacentre/factsheets/fs369/en/index.html

Wortmann, J. H., Larson, J. L., Lubin, R. E., Jordan, A. H., & Litz, B. T. (2015). Exposure therapy for posttraumatic stress disorder. *Encyclopedia of Mental Health, 2*, 192–195. https://doi.org/10.1016/B978-0-12-397045-9.00267-6

# 36

# HOUSING STRATEGIES FOR ADDRESSING DOMESTIC VIOLENCE AND ABUSE

*Nkiru Nnawulezi and Marc Dones*

## Introduction

Abusers who enact violence create inherently unstable, chaotic, and dangerous conditions which subsequently threaten survivors' fundamental housing needs. Many survivors are forced to either stay housed with their abusive partners or leave their homes. Leaving can result in either immediate placement into a housing program such as a crisis shelter or an experience of prolonged homelessness. As such, intimate partner violence (IPV) and housing instability become inextricably linked (Breiding, Basile, Klevens, & Smith, 2017). The aim of this chapter is to describe the interpersonal and community conditions that lead IPV survivors to seek out housing support across multiple sources. We discuss the best available evidence on formal housing interventions for survivors, primarily drawing on empirical studies based in North America, Australia, and the United Kingdom, as well as strategies that survivors employ to obtain housing from their informal networks. We describe the limitations of formal and informal sources and conclude with critical next steps for research, policy, and practice that will advance current housing interventions.

## What is housing instability?

Housing instability can be broadly defined as not being able to obtain and secure stable housing. It can encompass homelessness but is also distinct because a person may have a physical roof over their heads but live in an environment that is not fit for habitation. While the definitions vary across studies, researchers tend to operationalize housing instability using three shared indicators: (1) a count of the number of moves within a set period of time (i.e., the period of time varies from one year to three years); (2) current inability to meet financial obligations to maintain housing (i.e., issues of paying rent or mortgage, evictions, foreclosures); or (3) involuntary or undesirable moves to live with family or friends (i.e., also known as doubling up; Adams et al., 2018; Burgard, Seefeldt, & Zelner, 2012; Dichter, Wagner, Borrerro, Broyles, & Montgomery, 2017; Park, Fertig, & Metraux, 2014; Pavao, Alvarez, Baumrind, Induni, & Kimmerling, 2006; Sullivan, 2016; Wilson & Laughon, 2015). One national study in the United States included denial of affordable housing into their definition of housing instability. This definition included how aspects of the housing system can perpetuate housing instability (Breiding et al., 2017).

Despite the varied definitions, few researchers have asked survivors to define housing stability. Woodhall-Melnik and colleagues (2017) are an exception. They interviewed a diverse sample of 41 Canadian female survivors to understand what constitutes becoming stably housed. Survivors stated that housing stability encompassed material and structural stability, affordability, comfortability, and longevity. Achieving stability would result in security, calmness, independence, control, and freedom. Housing stability would also mean more consistency in their daily routines, an increase in the ability to build and sustain strong social networks, and opportunities to think more strategically about their future. Mother-survivors described stability as relational – they were not safe unless their children felt safe. Survivors' definition also incorporated quality of life and affordability indicators that enhance previous definitions of housing stability.

## Housing instability and intimate partner violence

IPV and housing instability are highly associated and mutually reinforcing experiences. In a national population study based in the United States, 46.3% of female IPV survivors reported that in the last year they worried about their ability to pay their housing expenses. Unstably housed women more likely to report IPV relative to women who did not report recent housing instability (Breiding et al., 2017). In a 2003 statewide study of California residents, women who experienced IPV were four times more likely to report housing instability compared to women who did not experience IPV (Pavao et al., 2006). An overwhelming majority of survivors in small qualitative, community-based research studies describe how their partners' abusive physical, sexual, and financial behaviors created uninhabitable living conditions (Phipps, Dalton, Maxwell, & Clearly, 2019; Yu et al., 2018). A recent scoping review, which included studies from across the globe, found that severe physical and sexual abuse histories significantly contributed to survivors' homelessness (Phipps et al., 2019). While multiple studies have described how IPV can contribute to housing instability, it is also possible for housing instability to increase risk of experiencing violence. Meth (2003) conducted focus groups with nine women living in shack settlements in South Africa. Survivors discussed the lack of material protection and privacy typically provided by a house increased their vulnerability to violence. Taken together, violence is a significant contributor to housing instability and vice versa, especially for women.

## Housing instability, intimate partner violence, and health

There are number of well-documented social, psychological, and physical health repercussions that arise as a consequence of having a violent partner and experiencing housing instability. When survivors were not stably housed or experienced homelessness, they were significantly more likely to be traumatized, feel depressed and anxious, experience higher rates of physical and sexual abuse compared to women who were stably housed (Gilroy, McFarlane, Maddoux, & Sullivan, 2016). The chaos inherent in involuntary moves over a short period of time also contributes negatively to health (Burgard et al., 2012). This is true for survivors, and their children. Unstably housed school-aged children, compared to children who have stable housing, are significantly more likely to report a mental health problem (Bassuk, Richard, &

Tsertsvadze, 2015). Generally, housing instability significantly lowers survivors' quality of life, places them in increased danger, and worsens overall individual and familial health (Phipps et al., 2019; Rollins et al., 2012).

## Survivors' pathways to housing instability

The pathways to housing instability and subsequent homelessness are maintained through unequal relational power dynamics and abusers' oppressive interpersonal behaviors which keep survivors without consistent access to stable housing. Many pathways begin with interpersonal relationship dynamics. For example, Canadian survivors described having their material needs met, but the abuser contributed to psychological or emotional instability (O'campo, Daoud, Wright-Hamilton, & Dunn, 2016). The abuse led survivors to strategize about how best to keep themselves and their families safe while also staying housed (Clough, Draughon, Njie-Carr, Rollins, & Gladd, 2014). In one study of 138 Australian women, 26% chose to stay with their abusive partners, while 67% relocated (Diemer, Humphreys, & Crinall, 2016). Survivors described often choosing to stay with their partners because there were no alternative housing options. For many survivors leaving meant that they would eventually end up homeless because they did not have the financial resources to live independently (O'campo et al., 2016; Clough et al., 2014). Survivors from another Australian-based study who stayed in their relationships developed strategies for saving money and actively searching for independent housing as a way to protect their children from being housing unstable. Some survivors were specifically motivated to maintain their current housing because they felt more equipped to protect their children from the trauma of abuse than from the trauma of homelessness (Meyer, 2016). Moreover, many survivors also did not want to compromise the quality of their current housing for lower-quality housing in unsafe neighborhoods (Clough et al., 2014).

## Survivor's relocation from the abusive home

Survivors are often forced to leave their housing due to the severity of their abusive partners' behaviors (O'campo et al., 2016; Zufferey, Chung, Franzway, Wendt, & Moulding, 2016). Survivors reported being severely physically assaulted, being kicked out of their homes by their partners, or being left with abuser-generated debt which made it difficult to afford their homes (Tutty, Ogden, Giurgiu, & Weaver-Dunlop, 2014). Some survivors became immediately homeless after leaving an abusive partner. They described sleeping in their cars, in parks, and on the streets (Lang, 2015; O'campo et al., 2016; Zufferey et al., 2016). Survivors who were able to move often transitioned into housing that was located in unsafe neighborhoods, provided a lower sense of safety, or was poorer quality compared to the housing they left with their abusive partners (Hetling, Dunford, & Botein, 2019; Zufferey et al., 2016). In other studies, survivors left and move into new places, but the relationship separation increased their partner's violence, resulting in survivors having to relocate multiple times in order to maintain safety (Yu et al., 2018; Zufferey et al., 2016). In addition to navigating violence from within the relationship, survivors who lived on the streets or in shelters reported being physically or sexually assaulted and believed they were at heightened risk for experiencing violence in the future (Tutty et al., 2014). Some survivors who left their partners ended up moving back because it was impossible to find a safe, permanent place to stay (Lang, 2015; Meyer, 2016).

Women who became homeless after leaving an relationship described being without a home for a prolonged period of time, and even when they were able to secure permanent or temporary housing, it took multiple years to recover from surviving homelessness and abuse (Meyer, 2016; Tutty et al., 2014).

## Economic abuse contributes to survivors' housing instability

Economic abuse contributes to housing instability for many survivors (Doud et al., 2016; Sullivan, Bomsta, & Hacskaylo, 2019). Common abusive tactics include stealing rent money from survivors, refusing to pay bills, or lying about paying bills. In a study conducted in the United States, some abusers did not tell survivors about overdue notices or simply abandoned survivors, leaving them to fulfill the financial responsibilities and pay all debts amassed during the abusive relationship (Sullivan et al., 2019; Zufferey et al., 2016). Economic abuse also compromised survivors access to income. Some survivors had to reduce their work hours or lost their jobs because their abusive partners engaged in sabotaging behaviors (O'campo et al., 2016; Sullivan et al., 2019). As a result of abuse, many survivors did not have the financial means to pay rent or mortgage. Evictions and foreclosures due to violence all contributed to survivors' housing instability and hindered survivors' ability to access housing in the future (Doud et al., 2016; Clough et al., 2014; O'campo et al., 2016). For example, if a survivor is evicted for not paying the rent, has poor credit, or is without consistent employment, landlords will label them as risky, which will lower the possibility that survivors will be considered for safe housing options.

## Survivors' informal housing options

If survivors leave their partners, they typically choose two housing options: informal and formal. Informal housing means moving in with family members or friends. This housing option requires that survivors have strong relationships with their social support networks, and that those networks can support their short- or long-term housing needs. Studies have identified this as doubling up and it is a common first step for many survivors (Baker, Billhardt, Warren, Rollins, & Glass, 2010; Zufferey et al., 2016). Some survivors create informal housing arrangements such as working in exchange for a room in a home. Informal housing can also include staying in the home where they live and removing the abuser using a personal protection order. However, the abuser often makes it difficult for the survivor to actually stay in the home due to stalking and ongoing violations of the personal protection orders (Diemer et al., 2016). Therefore, survivors may choose to seek out more formal housing options, which is described next.

## Survivors' formal housing options

Formal housing options for survivors vary significantly. One option is to rent an apartment or house at market rate. This option is difficult to access because it depends on the affordability of the housing stock. Most survivors cannot choose this option unless they, or their social networks, are well-resourced (Clough et al., 2014). Outside of the traditional housing market, housing programs are the most commonly utilized among survivors. Survivors make attempts to access immediate crisis housing from domestic violence shelters, general homeless shelters, and/or transitional housing programs (Tutty et al., 2014). Permanent supportive housing provide long-term options for survivors. And, some survivors are able to access supportive housing vouchers, rapid rehousing, or Housing First programs which allows them to transition into the traditional housing market while also receiving supportive advocacy and financial assistance from programs. All of these formal housing options are in high demand and low in quantity. There is often not enough funding for housing programs relative to the prevalence of homelessness and housing instability (Gezinski & Gonzalez-Pons, 2019).

Survivors engage in sustained outreach to multiple systems to receive housing support (Lang, 2015). Across studies in the United States and Canada, survivors commonly described how difficult it was to actually qualify for placement in housing programs. Survivors were required to disclose significant and personal details about their life in order to prove that they were abused and homeless. This burden of proof and high barrier entry policies were time consuming, unsupportive, and revictimizing (Clough et al., 2014; Jeffrey & Barata, 2017). Few survivors felt that the housing programs truly understood the urgency of their situations while trying to escape a violent partner (Yu et al., 2018). However, when survivors were able to make a connection to a formal housing program, many believed that it put them in a better position to maintain their housing stability. Housing programs helped survivors get connected to housing resources, financial assistance, and provided the time necessary to stabilize their lives (Lang, 2015).

Most of the evidence on survivors' housing needs come from women living in domestic violence shelters or transitional housing programs (Klein, Chesworth, Howland-Myers, Rizo, & Macy, 2019). These studies primarily describe what brings survivors to shelters (experiences of abuse) and relative satisfaction with shelter programs. Yet, very few studies discuss the short- and long-term outcome of using a domestic violence shelter while attempting to obtain housing stability. In addition, many studies on housing instability range from 15 to 819 participants, which makes it difficult to obtain predictive and generalizable results. There is outcome data to describe the impact of housing interventions on IPV survivors, but the evidence is limited (Klein et al., 2019). Survivors' complicated experiences with traditional housing markets and formal housing programs are discussed in greater detail in the following sections.

## Traditional housing market

Obtaining housing stability through the traditional housing market was not a viable option for many survivors because housing stock was unaffordable and/or they could not access high quality apartments in nice neighborhoods (Gezinski & Gonzalez-Pons, 2019; Meyer, 2016). Survivors across multiple studies described issues qualifying for a home due to poor credit, having evictions on their record, or experiencing other financial barriers that were a direct result of the abuse (Wilson & Laughon, 2015; Sullivan, Lopez-Zeron, Bomsta, & Menard, 2019). Landlords in the traditional housing market in the United States also discriminated against survivors by refusing to rent to them, charging additional fees, or placing them in subpar units in unsafe neighborhoods (Clough et al., 2014; Gezinski & Gonzalez-Pons, 2019). Traditional housing, while preferred by survivors because it offers the most control over housing quality, safety, and neighborhood selection, is also the most inaccessible and difficult housing option.

## Domestic violence and general homeless shelters

There are two primary sources of immediate, crisis housing support options for survivors: domestic violence (DV) shelters and general homeless shelters. DV shelters are short-term, crisis housing responses specifically designed for survivors who are actively fleeing an abusive relationship and are the most commonly studied housing response for IPV survivors (Klein et al., 2019). Survivors who are accepted into shelters tend to have immediate housing needs due to the high lethality of their abuse. Domestic violence shelters often require proof of abuse to qualify for services. This can include recent episodes of physical violence, a high score on a lethality assessment, or presence of a personal protection order. Survivors who meet shelter criteria are provided temporary stays ranging from 21 days to 60 days and offered supportive advocacy services to help them in finding long-term housing support. Many found the material resources offered by shelters to be helpful in their housing search. Yet, survivors across multiple shelter-based studies have described that the short shelter time limits do not allow enough time search for, qualify, and obtain safe and reliable long-term housing (Lang, 2015). Those who were unable to find long-term housing were forced to return home to their partners after their shelter stay (O'campo et al., 2016). In addition, violations of strict domestic violence shelter policies could also lead to survivors being removed from shelter further perpetuating their housing instability (Lang, 2015).

The transition to a domestic violence shelter can be difficult for children. In a Norwegian study, young children of survivors described how the disruption of their routines in schools or separation from their friends was difficult to process. Given the temporary nature of shelters, it was also difficult for children to make friends at the shelter and then leave them soon after. For some children, the burden of keeping the shelter a secret and being far from home contributed to their feelings of isolation. Other children simply felt shame for living in a DV shelter (Øverlien, 2011). Overall, there are significant trade-offs for families to live in a shelter. It is difficult for survivors to negotiate the conflicting emotions of their children, while also navigating individual and familial safety and trying to obtain stable housing.

Homeless shelters are designed for the general homeless population and are often segregated by gender (man versus woman) and/or familial status (single versus family). Entry into these shelters range from low to high barrier. Often these shelters allow people to stay nightly, but residents are not allowed to be there during the day. Women who enter into the general homeless shelter system often report histories of violent victimization (Phipps et al., 2019). While understudied, a few scholars have described how stays domestic violence shelters then led to stays in general homeless shelters. Evidence suggests that survivors who were not able to meet entry criteria at domestic violence shelters but were in immediate crisis sought support from general homeless shelters (Gezinski & Gonzalez-Pons, 2019). Stylianou and Pich (2019) examined how social identity and reason for discharge from a domestic violence shelter in New York City influenced future housing placements. They found that single survivors whose first language was not English, who did not have a work history or income, or who were removed from shelter based on a rule violation were most often discharged to the general homeless shelter system (Stylianou & Pich, 2019). Both sheltering options do not offer stability given its short time limits and crisis orientation; however they can provide temporary respite from relationship violence if survivors are able to access these services.

## Transitional housing

Transitional housing provides individuals and families with longer-term housing stays as they prepare for more permanent and stable housing options. Housing stays can range from 12–24 months and are typically offered to those who have been in a shelter. Case workers offer supportive housing services to residents in order to obtain stability in a permanent unit. These programs are designed to be "bridge" programs between crisis housing and permanent supportive housing to help individuals develop their "readiness" for housing. Mothers in domestic violence shelters with young children and those who had more income were likely to be discharged to a transitional housing program compared to other housing options (Stylianou & Pich, 2019). Transitional housing programs provide survivors more time being housed than emergency shelters, yet it is not entirely clear whether and how participation in these programs support long-term housing stability (Klein et al., 2019; Meyer, 2016).

## Permanent supportive housing

Permanent supportive housing provides people who are homeless a designated set of apartment units and supportive services. People are eligible for this program if they do not have the resources to obtain housing on their own, have been homeless prior to entering the program, are living in an emergency shelter or transitional housing, have a disabling condition, or are being discharged from an institution. Few studies have examined survivors' experiences with this housing option. Hetling and colleagues (2018) interviewed eight women who lived in permanent supportive housing in New York City. Survivors described the benefits of living in long-term permanent supportive housing. Specifically, they were not stressed about having to move or adhere to impending time limits. This housing option allowed survivors to care for themselves and plan for the future. Despite the benefits, the housing complex was still located in an unsafe neighborhood with violent crime. Survivors also described not being in control of their housing because they had to abide by restrictive policies and curfews. As such, permanent supportive housing provided long-term support but may not be able to offer the full scope of stability, specifically comfort, independence, and freedom.

## Subsidized housing

Subsidized housing is a governmental rental assistance program in the United States that provides housing support to individuals and families. This support encompasses housing choice vouchers, public housing, and private subsidized housing. Limited studies focus on survivors' experiences with subsidized housing. Stylianou and Pich (2019) found that survivors who exited a domestic violence shelter in New York City and went to subsidized housing were in the shelter for a longer time compared to people who went into the general homeless system. One possible explanation for this finding is the significant amount of time it takes to actually qualify for assistance. Subsidized housing provides long-term stability, yet survivors were being offered poor quality rental units and often forced to live in unsafe neighborhoods due to discrimination by landlords and stigma associated with using a voucher (Doud et al., 2016; Jeffrey & Barata, 2017; Meyer, 2016). Similar to findings about permanent supportive housing, while survivors were housed, they did not actually feel like they had much choice or control over their housing. Survivors did not believe they were able to choose better alternatives nor were they in a financial position to move (Jeffrey & Barata, 2017). Subsidized housing provided an opportunity to maintain material stability over a period of time. However, similar to permanent supportive housing, the options were limited for survivors and safety was a continued concern.

## Domestic violence Housing First programs

Housing First (HF) is an approach that immediately intervenes on threats to housing instability. Within this approach, HF advocates seek to stabilize individuals prior to loss of housing. In this model, people are immediately housed and then advocates work with residents on other issues (e.g., substance abuse, mental health issues). Traditional housing models require that case workers deem individuals "ready" for housing prior to actually being housed. Housing First has been adapted for the domestic violence field and outcome data for helping survivors achieve housing stability via this approach is in its infancy. The DV Housing First model is comprised of four components: survivor-driven, flexible funding, mobile advocacy, and community engagement (Sullivan & Olsen, 2016). Survivor-driven approaches mean that all services are based on survivors' expressed needs. Mobile advocacy is the practice of meeting survivors where they are and actively working to mobilize resources on their behalf. Community engagement requires mobilizing community as way to build support networks to increase housing stability. Flexible funding focuses on providing immediate financial assistance to survivors (Sullivan & Olsen, 2016).

Recently, researchers conducted a longitudinal evaluation of one component of DV Housing First, flexible assistance in Washington, DC. They examined how the receipt of low-barrier funding influenced survivors' housing stability (Bomsta & Sullivan, 2018; Sullivan et al., 2019). Results demonstrated that when survivors were provided with flexible assistance, 40% were able to stay in their original homes as desired. Some survivors received subsidized vouchers, others transitioned into housing after being homeless, and a few voluntarily moved in with family members. Survivors most often requested grants to directly support with rent and utilities. Other requests were for cell phone bills, transportation, and food. No matter what the request, the financial assistance supported survivors' ability to maintain safety, reduce stress, and helped maintain stability for themselves and their children (Bombsta & Sullivan, 2018; Sullivan et al., 2019). There was a notable contribution that flexible funding had on the lives of children and their mothers. Flexible funding provided an opportunity for mothers to offer their children stability – not having to relocate their children. They could keep the same routines, same friends, and same familiar environments. This made children happier and more comfortable (Bombsta & Sullivan, 2018). Some mothers have to send their children away to live with other relatives while they focus on building housing stability, this separation can have detrimental impacts on families (Wilson & Laughon, 2015). Flexible funding provides immediate support for stability which reduces the chances for involuntary separation supporting families to stay together (Bombsta & Sullivan, 2018). Components of DV Housing First improve housing stability and most align with survivors' definition of stability (Woodhall-Melnik et al., 2017).

## Limitations of current IPV and housing instability research

This brief overview describes the domestic violence field's best available evidence on housing responses designed to help survivors maintain housing stability, yet has limitations. First, much of the current literature is based on shelters and transitional housing programs. While necessary for immediate crisis intervention, these housing programs are not designed to support long-term stability. They become passthroughs to enter into other programs or, unwillingly going back to the abuser. In addition, there is very little information about survivors' experiences over time (see Sullivan et al., 2019, for exception). Most of the literature is based on correlational quantitative designs that explore associations between stability and other indicators, or qualitative exploratory designs that seek to understand how survivors' make meaning of their experiences with violence and instability. Longitudinal designs, either qualitative, quantitative, or mixed, would help researchers evaluate what actually contributes to obtaining housing stability. Also, research at the intersections of IPV and housing instability do not pay enough attention to system-level practices. The overemphasis on individual indicators of housing instability and the under-emphasis on structural indicators may contribute to why a majority of studies focus on understanding or changing survivors' behaviors and attitudes (e.g., counting the number of moves), rather than changing how the housing system itself operates (e.g., the continuous reduction in affordable housing stock).

## Housing and intersectionality

Based on their social identities, survivors do not have equal chance of experiencing housing instability or homelessness, nor an equitable ability to obtain safe housing. Being young, a person of color, being poor, or being disabled and experiencing IPV all predict instability (Pavao et al., 2006). For example, women of color were more likely to report higher rates of violence compared to White women subsequently increasing risk of housing instability (Breiding, Chen, & Black, 2014). Due to structural racism, sexism, and classism, Black people and women also tend to occupy tenuous minimum wage jobs that do not provide adequate income or benefits that allow them to easily afford market-level rent (Burgard et al., 2012). In one statewide study, young people and Black people were more likely to report having to move multiple times in a year, moving because of housing costs, living with family members or friends, or being homeless. Evictions were more commonly reported by women and Black participants than men and White participants (Burgard et al., 2012). Other social identities also influence access to housing support. Survivors with disabilities reported limited to no accessibility to traditional domestic violence shelter programs. Survivors experienced barriers related to physical access to buildings or the inability to bring personal assistants into shelters (Lightfoot & Williams, 2009).

Given the state of the evidence on housing instability among IPV survivors (mostly qualitative, smaller samples, correlational), it is difficult to determine the predictive relationships among social identities, housing instability, and violence. Researchers can employ intersectional approaches in order to understand for whom and under what conditions multiply marginalized survivors become housing unstable and subsequently gain stability. Intersectionality supposes that individuals experience simultaneous oppressions shaped by social forces that uniquely contribute to social life (Hill Collins & Blige, 2016). An intersectional analytic approach provides researchers an opportunity to build survivor-responsive housing options by exploring sociohistorical and political contexts that influence housing response, applying an analysis of power, and understanding how holding multiple social identities influences survivors' access to power. Currently, housing studies with IPV survivors often do not explicitly take into consideration the differential experiences of violence by social identity, and to our knowledge, few studies explored how the simultaneous experience of racism, sexism, ableism, classism, and other types of oppression influence the ability to reach housing stability.

## Future directions for policy, practice, and research implications

There are myriad of ways scholars and practitioners can continue to support survivors in obtaining housing stability, as well as develop and evaluate effective responses across housing systems.

Some critical opportunities for progression include developing a more inclusive definition of housing stability, consistently employing intersectionality in research methods, developing creative alternative solutions to obtaining housing stability, and building programs that increase survivor power.

## *Develop inclusive definitions of housing instability*

The development of a clear and consistent definition of housing stability/instability that is inclusive of survivors' diverse and complex experiences would be beneficial to the domestic violence field. If the act of living in a home where abuse occurs fundamentally makes survivors unstably housed, and then it would reduce the heavy burden of proof survivors experience when they seek out support from housing organizations. In addition, the indicators of housing instability are often rooted in individual characteristics and experiences, rather than systems characteristics. Many of the prominent housing instability indexes align with this perspective, and as such, create interventions that continue to require individuals change their behaviors rather than making significant changes in the housing system. For example, a system-level inclusive definition of housing instability could include the number of times that housing programs deny survivors entry, the length of time that people have been on a waiting list for housing, the number of years that the housing list has been closed in a city, the reduction in number of grants for subsidized housing, or reduction in number of landlords who accept vouchers. An incorporation of system indicators would contribute to a more expansive and equitable housing response that allows researchers to identify mutable indicators in housing systems that can be leveraged to support system-level change.

## *Incorporate intersectionality into housing responses*

Housing responses that do not focus on structural racism, structural misogyny, wealth inequality, and their intersections, are not sufficient responses to the complex problem of housing instability. As such, scholars must think clearly and purposefully about how intersectionality informs the conceptualization and response to housing instability among survivor populations. If not, it is possible that studies will reify and endorse mainstream practices that were designed primarily to help those who have the greatest access to social power and limit and create barriers for those who do not traditionally have access to social power. Currently, the housing field remains unclear about the right options for survivors of color and those who hold historically marginalized and disenfranchised identities. There is some promising evidence that demonstrates that implementing an anti-racist approach to a housing program design may improve long-term housing outcomes among Black people (Stergiopoulous et al., 2016). Innovative and culturally relevant solutions to housing that are well-researched can help build responses that are diverse, complex, and equitable.

## *Develop or identify alternative housing responses*

While domestic violence shelters are critical for immediate crisis response, they are also ripe for reimagining. Survivors should have more options to respond to crisis beyond calling the police, being displaced from their home, and potentially experiencing prolonged homelessness. One understudied alternative housing response could be to find ways to resource informal community networks. Given that friends and family are the first points of disclosure for many survivors and often the "first responders" to remedying housing instability and preventing homelessness, they could be critical points of intervention. Future housing response strategies and research about such strategies could valuably focus on the potential of informal community networks.

## *Ensure all housing responses build survivors' power*

Empowerment theory undergirds the domestic violence movement – which supposes that choice is a critical component of safety and increased power. Housing responses that increase survivor choice, at a fundamental level, is critical to how the field should move forward with future housing advocacy. Housing is a human right which means that survivors should be able to choose how they want to live, where they want to live, and what they need to obtain stability. Future research should continue to provide evidence on empowerment-based program-level, state-level, and federal policies that promote safety and increase power. Using a holistic, survivor-driven version of housing stability, researchers can incorporate attainment of freedom and choice into their evaluations of housing programs. Survivors deserve the time and space to regain dignity while achieving housing stability.

## Conclusion

In sum, IPV is a direct, or indirect, reason why many survivors experience housing instability or homelessness. While it varies in its definition, survivors who report housing instability desire a housing response that provides an opportunity to rebuild in their lives, supports them in regaining power, and promotes their long-term physical and emotional safety. The housing options for survivors vary, ranging from staying in their relationships, going to short-term shelters or longer-term housing programs, staying with friends, or entering into the traditional market with or without financial support. Both the housing and IPV fields are ripe for innovative approaches that are multi-level and intersectional with the long-term aim of severing the connection between IPV and housing instability.

## Critical findings

- Women with abusive partners are more likely than those without abusive partners to report experiencing housing instability. Abusive interpersonal dynamics create uninhabitable and unsafe living conditions.
- Housing instability is often defined at the individual level as the number of moves within a defined period, inability to meet financial obligations to maintain housing, and/or doubling up involuntarily with family or friends. This definition rarely includes structural indicators such as availability of affordable housing.
- Intimate partner violence survivors describe housing stability as security, calmness, independence, control, and freedom. Stable housing would also provide consistent daily routines, ability to build and sustain strong social networks, and an opportunity to plan for the future. They incorporated quality of life and affordability indicators that are missing from other definitions of housing stability.
- Survivors choose to stay in their homes with their abusive partners or leave their homes to get away from their partners.

- Survivors who leave their partners are at increased risk of being homeless. In order to avoid homelessness, survivors may move in with family members or friends or pursue formal housing options such as the traditional housing market, shelters, transitional housing, permanent supportive housing, rapid rehousing, or Housing First programs.

## Implications for policy, practice, and research

- Develop a housing stability definition that is inclusive of survivors' diverse and complex life experiences.
- Incorporate more system-level indicators of housing instability.
- Develop housing responses that do not require immediate displacement of survivors.
- Acknowledge that housing instability is outcome of structural racism, structural misogyny, wealth inequality, and their intersections. Develop structural interventions that directly attend to these issues.
- Given that friends and families are often first points of disclosure and sources to remedy housing instability, resource informal community networks.
- Increase available evidence about the longitudinal impact of current housing responses on survivors' housing stability.

## References

Adams, E. N., Clark, H. M., Galano, M. M., Stein, S. F., Grogan-Kaylor, A., & Graham-Bermann, S. (2018). Predictors of housing instability in women who have experienced intimate partner violence. *Journal of Interpersonal Violence*. Advanced online publication. doi:10.1177/0886260518777001

Baker, C. K., Billhardt, K., Warren, J., Rollins, C., & Glass, N. (2010). Domestic violence, housing instability, and homelessness: A review of housing policies and program practices for meeting the needs of survivors. *Aggression and Violent Behavior*, 15(6), 430–439. doi:10.1016/j.avb.2010.07.005

Bassuk, E. L., Richard, M. K., & Tsertsvadze, A. (2015). The prevalence of mental illness in homeless children: A systematic review and meta-analysis. *Journal of the American Academy of Child & Adolescent Psychiatry*, 54(2), 86–96. doi: 10.1016/j.jaac.2014.11.008

Bombsta, H., & Sullivan, C. M. (2018). IPV survivors' perceptions of how a flexible funding housing intervention impacted their children. *Journal of Family Violence*, 33(6), 371–380. doi:10.1007/s10896-018-9972-5

Breiding, M. J., Basile, K. C., Klevens, J., & Smith, S. G. (2017). Economic insecurity and intimate partner and sexual victimization. *American Journal of Preventive Medicine*, 43(4), 457–464. doi:10.1016/j.amepre.2017.03.021

Breiding, M. J., Chen, J., & Black, M. C. (2014). *Intimate partner violence in the United States – 2010*. Atlanta, GA: National Center for Injury Prevention and Control, Centers for Disease Control and Prevention.

Burgard, S. A., Seefeldt, S., & Zelner, S. (2012). Housing instability and health: Findings from the Michigan recession and recovery study. *Social Science and Medicine*, 75(12), 2215–2224. doi:10.1016/j.socscimed.2012.08.020

Clough, A., Draughon, J. E., Njie-Carr, V., Rollins, C., & Gladd, N. (2014). "Having housing made everything else possible": Affordable, safe and stable housing for women survivors of violence. *Qualitative Social Work*, 13(5), 671–688. doi:10.1177/1473325013503003

Dichter, M. E., Wagner, C., Borrerro, S., Broyles, L., & Montgomery, A. E. (2017). Intimate partner violence, unhealthy alcohol use, and housing instability among women veterans in the veteran's health administration. *Psychological Services*, 14(2), 246–249. doi:/10.1037/ser0000132

Diemer, K., Humphreys, C., & Crinall, K. (2016). Safe at home? Housing decisions for women leaving family violence. *Australian Journal of Social Issues*, 52(1), 32–47. doi:10.1002/ajs4.5

Doud, N., Matheson, F. I., Pedersen, C., Hamilton-Wright, S., Minh, A., Zhang, J., & O'Campo, P. (2016). Pathways and trajectories linking housing instability and poor health among low-income women experiencing intimate partner violence (IPV): Toward a conceptual framework. *Women and Health*, 56(2), 208–225. doi:10.1080/03630242.2015.1086465

Gezinski, L. B., & Gonzalez-Pons, K. (2019). Unlocking the door to safety and stability: Housing barriers for survivors of intimate partner violence. *Journal of Interpersonal Violence*. Advanced online publication.

Gilroy, H., McFarlane, J., Maddoux, J., & Sullivan, C. M. (2016). Homelessness, housing instability, intimate partner violence, mental health, and functioning: A multi-year cohort study of IPV survivors and their children. *Journal of Social Distress and the Homeless*, 25(2), 86–94. doi:10.1080/10530789.2016.1245258

Glendening, Z. S., McCauley, E., Shinn, M., & Brown, S. R. (2018). Long-term housing subsidies and SSI/SSDI income: Creating health-promoting contexts for families experiencing housing instability with disabilities. *Disability and Health Journal*, 11(2), 214–220. doi:10.1016/j.dhjo.2017.08.0 06

Hetling, A., Dunford, A., & Botein, H. (2019). Community in the permanent supportive housing model: Applications to survivors of intimate partner violence. *Housing Theory and Society*. Advanced online publication. doi:10.1080/14036096.2019.1624388

Hetling, A., Dunford, A., Lin, S., & Michaelis, E. (2018). Long-term housing and intimate partner violence: Journeys to healing. *Affilia: Journal of Women and Social Work*, 33(4), 526–542. doi:10.1177/0886109918778064

Hill Collins, P., & Blige, S. (2016). *Intersectionality*. Cambridge, MA: Polity Press.

Jeffrey, N. K., & Barata, P. C. (2017). When social assistance reproduces social inequality: Intimate partner violence survivors' adverse experiences with subsidized housing. *Housing Studies*, 32(7), 912–930. doi:10.1080/02673037.2017.1291912

Klein, L. B., Chesworth, B. R., Howland-Myers, J. R., Rizo, S. F., & Macy, R. J. (2019). Housing interventions for intimate partner violence survivors: A systematic review. *Trauma, Violence, and Abuse*. Advanced online publication. doi:10.1177/1524838019836284

Lang, S. M. (2015). Navigating homelessness and navigating abuse: How homeless mothers find transitional housing while managing intimate partner violence. *Journal of Community Psychology*, 43(8), 1019–1035. doi:10.1002/jcop.21729

Lightfoot, E., & Williams, O. (2009). The intersection of disability, diversity, and domestic violence: Results of national focus groups. *Journal of Aggression, Maltreatment, & Trauma*, 18, 133–152. doi:10.1080/10926770802675551

Meth, P. (2003). Rethinking the 'domus' in domestic violence: Homelessness, space and domestic violence in South Africa. *Geoforum*, 34, 317–327. doi:10.1016/S0016-7185(03)00005-8

Meyer, S. (2016). Examining women's agency in managing intimate partner violence and the related risk of homelessness: The role of harm minimization. *Global Public Health: An International Journal of Research, Policy and Practice*, 11(1–2), 198–210. doi:10.1080/17441692.2015.1047390

O'campo, P., Daoud, N., Wright-Hamilton, S., & Dunn, J. (2016). Conceptualizing housing instability: Experiences with material and psychological instability among women living with partner violence. *Housing Studies*, 31(1), 1–19. doi:10.1080/02673037.2015.1021768

Øverlien, C. (2011). Abused women with children or children of abused women? A study of conflicting perspectives at women's refuges in Norway. *Child & Family Social Work*, 16(1), 71–80. doi:10.1111/j.1365-2206.2010.00715.x

Park, J. M., Fertig, A., & Metraux, S. (2014). Factors contributing to the receipt of housing assistance by low-income families with children in twenty American cities. *Social Service Review*, 88(1), 166–193. doi:10.1086/675353

Pavao, J., Alvarez, J., Baumrind, N., Induni, M., & Kimmerling, M. (2006). Intimate partner violence and housing instability. *American Journal of Preventive Medicine*, 32(2), 143–146. doi:10.1016/j.amepre.2006.10.008

Phipps, M., Dalton, L., Maxwell, H., & Cleary, M. (2019). Women and homelessness, a complex multidimensional issue: Findings from a scoping review. *Journal of Social Distress and the Homeless*, 28(1), 1–13. doi:10.1080/10530789.2018.1534427

Rollins, C., Glass, N. E., Perrin, N. A., Billhardt, K., Clough, A., Barnes, J., . . . Bloom, T. L. (2012). Housing instability is a strong predictor of poor health outcomes as level of danger in an abusive relationship: Findings from the share study. *Journal of Interpersonal Violence*, 27(4), 623–643. doi:10.1177/0886260511423241

Stergiopoulous, V., Gozdzik, A., Misir, V., Skosireva, A., Sarang, A., Connelly, J., Whisler, A., & McKenzie, K. (2016). The effectiveness of a housing first adaptation for ethnic minority groups: Findings of a pragmatic randomized controlled trail. *BMC Public Health*, 16(1), 1110. doi:10.1186/s12889-016-3768-4

Stylianou, A. M., & Pich, C. (2019). Beyond domestic violence shelter: Factors associated with housing placements for survivors exiting emergency shelters. *Journal of Interpersonal Violence*. Advanced online publication. doi:10.1177/0886260519858293

Sullivan, C. M., Bomsta, H. D., & Hacskaylo, M. A. (2019). Flexible funding as a promising strategy to prevent homelessness for survivors of intimate partner violence. *Journal of Interpersonal Violence, 34*(14), 3017–3033. doi:10.1177/08886260516664318

Sullivan, C. M., Lopez-Zeron, G., Bomsta, H., & Menard, A. (2019). There's just all these moving parts: Helping domestic violence survivors obtain housing. *Clinical Social Work Journal, 47*(2), 198–206. doi:10.1007/s10615-018-0654-9

Sullivan, C. M., & Olsen, L. (2016). Common group, complementary approaches: Adapting the housing first model for domestic violence survivors. *Housing and Society, 43*(3), 182–194. doi:10.1080/08882746.2017.1323305

Tutty, L. M., Ogden, C., Giurgiu, B., & Weaver-Dunlop, G. (2014). I built my house of hope: Abused women and pathways into homelessness. *Violence Against Women, 19*(12), 1498–1517. doi:10.1177/1077801213517514

Wilson, P. R., & Laughon, K. (2015). House to house, shelter to shelter: Experiences of black women seeking housing after leaving abusive relationships. *Journal of Forensic Nursing, 11*(2), 77–83. doi:10.1097/JFN.0000000000000067

Woodhall-Melnik, J., Hamilton-Wright, S., Daoud, N., Metheson, F., Dunn, J. R., & O'campo, P. (2017). Establishing stability: Exploring the meaning of 'home' for women who have experienced intimate partner violence. *Journal of Housing and the Built Environment, 32*(2), 253–268. doi:10.1007/s10901-016-9511-8

Yu, B., Montgomery, A. E., True, G., Cusak, M., Sorrentino, A., Chhadra, M., & Dichter, M. E. (2018). The intersection of interpersonal violence and housing instability: Perspectives from women veterans. *American Journal of Orthopsychiatry*. Advanced online publication. doi:10.1037/ort0000379

Zufferey, C., Chung, D., Franzway, S., Wendt, S., & Moulding, N. (2016). Intimate partner violence and housing: Eroding women's citizenship. *Affilia: Journal of Women and Social Work, 31*(4), 463–4798. doi:10.1177/0886109915626213

# 37

# ECONOMIC EMPOWERMENT IN THE CONTEXT OF DOMESTIC VIOLENCE AND ABUSE

*Nadine Shaanta Murshid, Sarah Richards-Desai and Andrew Irish*

### Case vignette

The Story of Moina
Name: Moina
Location: Dhaka, Bangladesh

Moina was a study participant for research on women's experiences with microfinance, an institution purported to be an empowerment tool for women in the global South. She described her marriage as "arranged," as is the norm in rural areas like the one she came from. After getting married, her husband moved to the city of Dhaka. She only joined him there later, after a living with her in-laws, once he could secure stable housing. For them, stable housing meant a spot in a shanty town with limited access to water and sanitation facilities and almost no privacy. Despite this, perhaps the most difficult circumstance for her was the abuse that came from her husband. Although she partially excused his behaviour as a product of workplace frustrations that bled over into marital difficulty and abuse, she felt particularly dehumanised by the violence because her neighbours could see what she had to endure. Her neighbours often chided her about allowing her husband to treat her that way, but when she would speak of leaving, the hush that would fall told her that this was not a socially permissible response. A victim of poverty and violence, Moina found herself dealing with what she perceived as an ugly "fate," a conception shared by many women in such circumstances. She sought refuge through microfinance, with the aim of owning her own micro-business. After ten years, she became the owner of a tailoring shop which she runs all day.

When asked if microfinance participation had paved her way out of violence, her "both yes and no" response was a familiar one, common among many women. Yes, because she was away from their small domicile, far enough to not be hit physically. But not in other crucial ways, recalling incidents of emotional abuse and control, including accusations of infidelity associated with being out of the home at work.

When asked if she thought about leaving her husband now that she had the financial means to do so, she laughed and said no. Not because it was socially unacceptable, but because there was no guarantee that the next man wouldn't be worse. She explained that a future partner might use her first marriage as an excuse for violence against her. Moina is right. Dominant patriarchal mores govern the 'marriage market,' conceptualising women as objects of conquest and strongly favour sexual virginity as an indicator of purity and value. This means, as a divorcee, Moina would be more likely to be ill-treated, including by the use of violence, by a future husband.

Moina's description of how she dealt with the violence in her life revealed that she acted agentically when she decided that she did not want to leave her husband. "I know how to deal with this one. I have *learned* him. That protects me. He's not a bad guy." One might assume that empowerment in this case should result in a woman leaving her abusive spouse. However, her confidence in her own ability to deal with her situation was empowering in and of itself. When asked of emotional abuse, she offered, "I've accepted it as part of life. I am fortunate in other ways; I focus on that."

Moina's internalisation corroborates previous research which indicates that women who justify violence against women are less likely to report signs of mental health problems, such as depression. Moina's attitude of acceptance rather than justification may have allowed her some reprieve. "I'm not home a lot anymore; that protects me" she said, as if hearing my concerned thoughts. My last question for her was whether she was happy. Her response was *"goriber ar shukh!"* which is a sarcastic exclamation that roughly translates to: "the happiness of poor people!"

## Current debates in the economic empowerment of women:[1] what does it mean?

We know that economic disempowerment and poverty create conditions that deprive women and girls of autonomy and status. Scholars such as Duflo (2012) suggest there may be a mutually reinforcing relationship between economic development and the empowerment of women, as poverty reduction can aid in reducing inequality across genders. Meanwhile, reduction of the economic dependency of women on abusive partners is an important aspect of women's safety, as evidenced by research showing that women remain in violent relationships during economic downturn due to economic need and risk of homelessness (Renzetti, 2019). It is important to recall that women choosing to remain in abusive relationships does not mean that they are not exercising agency, but may likely mean that their choices are severely conscribed by their environment. Despite a wide variety of options for the economic empowerment of women, the most prevalent model to date has been microfinance loans.

While concern for women's economic well-being is founded, the mechanisms for achieving this are contested. Early work focused on the poverty-reducing aspects of economic empowerment programs such as microfinance, but recent research suggests scholars are concerned that programs intended to empower women fail to do so. Such programs are criticised as not appreciably fostering social and political power for women, failing to either sufficiently personally empower women, or alter structural risks for violence. In fact, the inclusion of women in microfinance during the last few decades is partly attributable to women being perceived as more likely to repay loans and invest in the well-being of their children (Shahriar, Unda, & Alam, 2020; Viswanath, 2018). This is notably unrelated to their intrinsic deservingness of empowerment for their own well-being.

It is important to recognise that empowerment of women by microfinance or other employment programs comes with a serious cost. They are then laden with the double burden of continuing to provide unpaid labour in the household as part of their gender role and now also assuming substantial paid labour duties as well. Additionally, in the absence of policies which protect their physical and emotional safety, women entering traditionally masculine work places are subject to rampant harassment. Considering the case of Moina, we can see how the neoliberal conceptualisation of microfinance as economic empowerment for women may play out, especially in the global South. Entrance to the labour force comes at a cost of additional labour hours, thrusts women into an arena of frequent violence, opens avenues to new forms of emotional abuse.

One should also be cognisant of the idea that this form of economic empowerment serves to make women more controllable and traceable within a formalised system (Deleuze & Guattari, 1988), removing them from an informal economy in which they enjoy freedom from institutional oversight. In fact, being tied to microfinance products encases them in a sphere dominated by neoliberal ideology of hard work and personal responsibility. As micro-business owners, for example, they are subject to market pressures forcing them to compete not only with corporations, but also with each other. The rhetorical presentation of economic empowerment against a backdrop of powerlessness lures women to consent to this model on the obvious appeal of poverty alleviation. However, this often occurs only in the short run, whereby in the long run they merely incur more debt, rendering them dependent on this system (Karim, 2011). So, we observe a neoliberal contradiction (Murshid & Murshid, 2018) – the loans represent crucial sustenance which may contribute to poverty alleviation or reductions in violence in the short term, but often perpetuate a cycle of poverty while exposing women to other risks and drastically increasing extraction of labour. Without addressing this, women's economic empowerment may only go as far as making women consumers of financial products.

Despite variations in definition and conceptualisation, scholars agree that economic empowerment programs are not a "magic bullet" (Kabeer, 2005). A growing body of literature identifies that participation in such programs is connected to disempowering effects including experiences of violence inside and outside the home (Murshid, Akincigil, & Zippay, 2016; Murshid & Murshid, 2018). Questions of whether programs actually empower, rather than reify power imbalances (Bay-Cheng, Lewis, Stewart, & Malley, 2006) through a financial technological fix (Harvey, 2003), are particularly important considerations.

## *Types of economic interventions*

Economic empowerment interventions come from different sources and in different forms. Some interventions are instituted through governmental welfare programs, especially in the global North. Poverty alleviation programs geared towards women and children, especially from non-governmental organisations (NGOs), are another common source of intervention in developing countries of the global South, often operating in a 'small government' political culture that relies on non-government sources to provide social welfare. These intervention programs primarily include microfinance and cash transfers, but also investments in education and working skills, and skill-building in finance and banking. The rationale of these intervention programs has been to further women's earnings and access to capital as a pathway to lifting their households out of poverty (Mehra, 1997). However, most of these empowerment interventions are at the level of individual economic participation, burdening women to bring their families out of poverty, rather than invoking macro-level institutional change to combat poverty-generating mechanisms. While women participating in microfinance are able to meet some of their needs in the short run, they often accrue long-term debt moving from microfinance organisations to money lenders to repay loans, predatory loans which they had no power to negotiate.

## Defining economic empowerment

Spurred by the UN push for gender equity, the last few decades have focused on economic empowerment, particularly of women, as an antidote to poverty in both the global South and North. However, there is no uniform agreement over what economic empowerment entails, with vastly different conceptions of empowerment in general, and economic empowerment particularly. Some scholars focus on individual agency, while others conceptualise empowerment with individual constructs such as self-efficacy, knowledge, and literacy; relational ones such as gender roles, decision-making power, and autonomy; or outcomes including, choice, balance, and agency in economic, social, and political spheres (Malhotra, Schuler, & Boender, 2002). Empowerment notions can be roughly described using Hartsock's (1983) categorisation of power – power as an individual attribute; power as a relationship of domination wherein someone has power over another; and power as capability, such that individuals have the power to challenge oppressive social conditions.

## Power as an individual attribute

International organisations such as the Organization for Economic Cooperation and Development (OECD) (2011) define economic empowerment as the:

> capacity of individuals to participate in, contribute to and benefit from growth processes in ways that recognise the value of their contributions, respect their dignity and make it possible to negotiate a fairer distribution of the benefits of growth,

adding further that "economic empowerment increases women's access to economic resources and opportunities including jobs, financial services, property and other productive assets, skills development and market information" (p. 6). This conceptualisation views empowerment as a constellation of personal opportunities that can lead to income generation. Contrastingly, a substantial portion of the implemented economic empowerment programs have been microfinance programs alone. These programs are well short of the more inclusive OECD conception and have been criticised as including exploitative practices from lending institutions (Kratzer & Kato, 2013); being poorly tailored for implementation, especially to specific populations (Leach & Sitaram, 2002); and failing to align with important principles of empowerment such as socially cohesive cooperation, or to convincingly demonstrate effectiveness (Mayoux, 2000). While the adoption of microfinance and similar interventions does provide them with short-term income, and addresses gender-based disparities at this social level (Malhotra et al., 2002), we should also note that such programs reflect the failure of governments to provide for basic social welfare and guarantee the economic well-being of their citizens.

## Power as a relationship of domination (power over)

While women's participation in these economic interventions is individual, it reinforces the power held by governments and NGOs. Through micro-entrepreneurship, women must participate in the public sphere even when it is not physically safe for them to do so. Moreover, they take on new risks and commitments as they commonly become part of solidarity groups with other borrowers in which they share responsibility for loan repayment. This also introduces relations of dominance between groups members. Likewise, women are subordinated to loan officers — street level bureaucrats — who wield direct authority and control over them.

Gender role ideology, specifically regarding the permissibility of male violence, as well as male control of both resources and decision making, also represents substantial risk for domestic violence against women. Women's traditionally limited access to social connections outside the home constrains their opportunities to seek help in cases of violence or abuse. Programs which serve to aid them in this regard could be advantageous. For example, Granovetter's (1973) conceptualisation of the "strength of weak ties" can be used to illustrate why microfinance models could lead to greater safety from violence and abuse. Entrance to the workforce can serve to expand social networks, and may allow women to seek help when they experience abuse. Contrastingly however, previous microfinance research has shown that while the social networks of participating women may increase, this does not necessarily translate to help-seeking social networks (Murshid & Zippay, 2017), suggesting that the relationship of domination that men have over their wives can persist even when women's social networks and social capital expand.

## *Power as capability (to challenge oppression) (power to)*

Hartsock (1983) conceptualised this form of power as the ability to challenge oppressive structures such as racism and sexism. While this form of power is vitally important, we also recognise that women of low socioeconomic status may not in fact *have* the power to meaningfully challenge systemic oppression even if they *feel* personally empowered. Bay-Cheng (2012) advocates for "depersonalizing and re-politicizing" empowerment, highlighting how empowerment can serve a "regulatory and disciplinary function" (p. 76) where those who need to be empowered are empowered by 'empowerers.' As a top-down imposition which furthers notions of individualised responsibility, this is inconsistent with empowerment principles. In the same way, current economic empowerment models often stand in self-contradiction to the notion of empowerment, permitting only limited forms of individual opportunity. We suggest that empowerment, in its true sense, can only happen from below.

Amartya Sen's (1999) capabilities approach to human development emphasises a person's *functionings* – actions and ways of being; *capabilities* – things which one has the opportunity to accomplish; and *agency* – one's ability to self-advocate or enact change. Sen also speaks of substantive freedoms, which are meaningful opportunities for people to have the functionings they desire in a context that supports their capabilities. An individual's resources and well-being impact their capabilities and freedom to use the resources available in order to act on those capabilities (Sen, 2000).

Nussbaum (2001) focuses the capabilities approach on examining a relationship between economic and gender-based disparities. She identifies a positive correlation between poverty and gender inequality, stating that their combination often results in a loss of basic human rights such as health, nutrition, access to education and literacy, as well as the underreporting of violent crime. Nussbaum argues for the inclusion of a feminist lens in all global development projects arguing that while women suffer from the effects of poverty unrelated to their sex, they are also impacted by gender-based discrimination that calls for a gendered approach to poverty reduction programs (Nussbaum, 2001). Nussbaum and others urge that women's access to institutions, such as formal education at an equal level to men is not only necessary to find work and become literate, but in order to access information about broader society including their own rights. Without these institutional changes, individual-level empowerment attempts leave women cut off from crucial capacities in society.

## Which comes first: economic empowerment or domestic violence?

Economic empowerment programs do not consistently prove to be an overall aid to women or women experiencing violence. Individual and family microeconomic factors are both causes of and affected by domestic violence. In addition, macroeconomic structural factors also play a substantial role in domestic violence. The economic empowerment of women has been proposed as a measure to reduce domestic violence. However, the role and effects of economic empowerment programs on domestic violence vary substantially based on a number of factors including socioeconomic status (Kessler, Molnar, Feurer, & Appelbaum, 2001; Koenig, Ahmed, Hossain, & Mozumder, 2003), community characteristics (Benson, Wooldredge, Thistlethwaite, & Fox, 2004), and the location of the individual or population in the context of the global North or South.

In the United States, research indicates that economic empowerment programs may lead to positive outcomes such as economic self-efficacy and financial literacy when it is part of domestic violence programming, particularly when women experience economic abuse (Postmus, 2010). However, it is often observed that economic empowerment precedes negative domestic violence outcomes across geographic locations. For example, Nam and Tolman (2002) show that women accessing welfare in the United States are at higher risk of experiencing domestic violence, similar to research from Bangladesh finding that women above the lowest socioeconomic strata were more likely to report domestic violence than their counterparts when accessing economic empowerment tools such as microfinance (Murshid, Akinzicigil, & Zippay, 2016). Researchers continue working to uncover the micro- and macroeconomic correlates of domestic violence, but the picture is far from complete.

### *Domestic violence has economic repercussions*

The economic repercussions of domestic violence with regard to individuals, families, and societies at large are noteworthy. The National Coalition Against Domestic Violence (2019) reports that 21 to 60 percent of US domestic violence victims lose their jobs due to abuse. Collectively, victims in the US miss approximately 8 million days of work each year and the total cost to the economy is greater than $8.3 billion (Max, Rice, Finkelstein, Bardwell, & Leadbetter, 2004; Rothman, Hathaway, Stidsen, & de Vries, 2007). The Centers for Disease Control and Prevention similarly estimates the total cost of intimate partner rape, assault, and stalking of women in the US to be at least $5.8 billion annually, which they note as an underestimate due to unavailability of data (National Center for Injury Prevention and Control, 2003). In addition, losses are not limited to short-term costs. Lindhorst et al. (2007) found that domestic violence has a negative effect on economic capacity many years after its occurrence and that violence in combination with associated psychological distress may undermine women's ability for economic self-sufficiency.

Outside the US, the economic picture is also bleak. A World Bank report noted that Vietnam loses 1.41 percent of GDP to domestic violence, a figure equal to approximately one-quarter of annual expenditures on education, or the cost of starting 24,000 businesses. In fact, the problem is severe throughout the world, with the costs of domestic violence as a percentage of GDP greater than 1 percent in Australia, the United Kingdom, Nicaragua, Chile, Uganda, Morocco, Vietnam, and Bangladesh (Duvvury, Callan, Carney, & Raghavendra, 2013).

The economic toll of domestic violence on individuals is also stark. Greater than one-quarter of all intimate partner assaults in the US resulted in medical treatment, which can lead to burdensome debt, even among persons with health insurance. Additionally, nearly 13 percent of stalking victims incur personal, out-of-pocket costs over $1,000. Victims of this violence also suffer greater rates of homelessness, work fewer days than non-abused peers, and often are strapped to the debt of abusive partners (McLean & Gonzalez Bocinski, 2017).

## *Economic empowerment may lead to domestic violence*

Some prior research has examined domestic violence through models based on *rational choice theory*, conceptualising a 'threat point' – a point at which the abused partner perceives that enduring abuse is no longer worth the cost and leaves the relationship. From this perspective, an increase in the financial holdings of women should generally correspond with reductions in the level of violence enacted toward them. Several studies of women across different regions of the US have found evidence for this hypothesis. For example, Farmer and Tiefenthaler (1997) conclude that increases in women's incomes or other means of access to resources will reduce the level of violence in abusive relationships. Results are often substantially mixed, however.

An analysis of the *Oportunidades* program in Mexico found that physical abuse of women who were beneficiaries of the program declined by 40 percent, but violent threats without accompanying physical abuse increased (Bobonis, Gonzalez-Brenes, & Castro, 2013). Other studies have presented mixed results which may depend on a variety of key variables including the relative social status of partners, known as *status inconsistency theory* (Hornung, McCullough, & Sugimoto, 1981). A study of Ecuadorian mothers found that receipt of cash transfers tended to decrease violence; however, among women with primary school education or less, violence increased with transfers if the woman had equal or greater education than her partner (Hidrobo & Fernald, 2013). These models do have drawbacks however. For example, Yick (2001) reviewed status inconsistency theory finding it helpful in noting the power dynamics in relationships; however, it was lacking in accounting for larger structural factors and differentiation between types of power, which vary between cultures and with gender roles, among other factors.

Highlighting these mixed results, a systematic review of research on economic empowerment and domestic violence in low- and middle-income countries concluded that greater household wealth and greater female education were generally protective factors, but that women having a role in wealth generation was both a risk factor in some studies and a protective factor in others. The alleviation of poverty seems to be a protective factor for domestic violence; however, women's financial participation and autonomy is not clearly risky, nor protective (Vyas & Watts, 2009).

Other research has found little evidence for the protective value of economic empowerment alone. Dalal's (2011) investigation into the economic empowerment of Indian women found that working women had higher rates of exposure to domestic violence leading to the conclusion that economic empowerment alone was insufficient to protect from violence, but rather concurrent improvement in women's level of education as well as modification of cultural norms of violence against women may collectively serve to protect. Likewise, analysis of a nationally representative survey in Bangladesh found that women's microfinance participation generally was not related to experiencing domestic violence, but may increase risk among women with higher socioeconomic status (Murshid et al., 2016).

The mixture of findings in this research may be attributable to both the multitude of factors that determine domestic violence, and how empowerment and indeed, violence, are defined and measured. In addition to rational choice 'threat point', and status inconsistency explanations, there are also models based on *resource-exchange theory* which posits that every social system at its most fundamental level is partly rooted in the threat of force (Goode, 1971), and therefore violence may be exercised when rewards of doing so outweigh costs (Gelles, 1983). From this perspective domestic violence is a predictable occurrence and specially fostered by mechanisms such as norms of privacy or patriarchy which reduce the 'cost' of violence. Recent research contrasting the numerous theories on domestic violence collectively reviewed more than a dozen conceptions of individual-, family-, cultural-, and structural-level violence (Arthur & Clark, 2009; Lawson, 2012). Considering the variety of approaches to understanding domestic violence, it is important to understand that economic empowerment has had troubling mixed results, and that economic intervention alone is insufficient.

## Is domestic violence structurally produced?

Examining domestic violence and abuse through an economic structural lens can shed light on the ways in which the vulnerabilities and inequities in societies share in its production. These factors in domestic violence are important in that they can be targets for policy reform as it is policy that contributes to their presence. Recalling the case study of Moina, we can see that there are many factors making her vulnerable to domestic violence which fall far beyond her scope of control.

One relevant economic characteristic of many societies is a wage gap – the gender-based difference in financial compensation between women and men, especially when holding equivalent employment positions. Aizer (2010) conducted a study of a 13-year period in the US and concluded that "in addition to more equitable redistribution of resources, policies that serve to narrow the male-female wage gap also reduce violence and the costs associated with it" (p. 1858). An Inter-American Development Bank study in Uruguay also found that the wage gap increased the frequency of domestic violence in both rich and poor urban areas (Munyo & Rossi, 2015). Peter (2006) similarly suggests that the lower wage gap in Sweden relative to the US is part of a network of political and economic inequalities which account for a greater rate of domestic violence in the US.

A growing body of research also reports a link between domestic violence and unemployment. Jewkes (2002) argues that both male and female unemployment can pose an increased risk for domestic violence through the onset of poverty or financial distress and that male unemployment specifically may be an additional risk factor because of associated identity crisis and perceived gender role failure. Other research has found that male unemployment is a risk factor for both female-to-male and male-to-female partner violence among persons employed in the construction industry (Cunradi, Todd, Duke, & Ames, 2009). A study of domestic violence in the UK found that male unemployment was associated with less intimate partner violence while female unemployment corresponded with greater partner violence (Anderberg, Rainer, Wadsworth, & Wilson, 2015). In the context of refugee resettlement, a reshuffling of gender roles around employment and economic participation has also been linked to domestic violence (James, 2010).

These factors are nested in capitalism, an economic system based on the private ownership of goods, services, and production of a society. This system, by definition, does not manage resource scarcity with an egalitarian approach, and artificially creates scarcity and deprivation when it would not otherwise be present naturally. Predicated on status competition, differential monetary compensation, and denial of the provision of basic living needs as a right, but rather supplying them conditionally (Chang, 2012), a capitalist economy intrinsically represents multiple risk factors for domestic violence (Weissman, 2015).

The source of much violence lies within institutional structures. These institutions are frequently constructed in a manner that cloaks the oppression of marginalised populations and individuals. Relatedly, narratives about women's incompetence, and the need to control them, cast them into a vulnerable position where their concerns and experiences are obscured because they are deemed inferior. The interaction of marginalising narratives with non-egalitarian institutions allows the maintenance of violence and other forms of oppression against women.

## The way forward

### *Cultural context and intersectionality*

The pervasiveness of women's subordination calls for an *intersectional* framework (Crenshaw, 1990) to elucidate key differences between groups and allow for a contextual understanding of how women can be empowered. Because empowerment as a construct contains culturally specific content for people with diverse locations and identities, programs designed to empower women, economically or otherwise, must account for and reflect the norms and characteristics of their cultural and personal context. For example, some perceive physical mobility as a key component of empowerment because they are often not allowed to leave their homes without permission (Murshid & Ball, 2018). Alternatively, some scholars have focused on psychological attributes such as self-efficacy (Sanders, Weaver, & Schnabel, 2007). Regardless, interventions should be carried out in a way that does not further subordinate women to men or to economic control, and effort should be concentrated on institutional reform that meets the needs of women and generates egalitarian systemic change.

As we would expect, different types of empowerment programs have different effects. For example, a social welfare program is not likely to affect women's autonomy in the same way as entrepreneurship does. Regardless, participation in such programs is not sufficient alone. More attention should be given to understanding how women fare beyond the strictly economic ramifications of such participation. In fact, we need to recognise that women may have histories of trauma that can be exacerbated in employment settings where women are more vulnerable to harassment and violence, compounding their risk for violence at home. The pervasiveness of abuse has recently found the public eye in the form of the #metoo movement. In light of this, we advise trauma-informed intervention and programming. Economic empowerment, in any location, is futile without pillars of safety, collaboration, trust, choice, and the employment of an intersectional lens to determine what would best serve marginalised groups (Bowen & Murshid, 2016). If we have learned anything from Moina, it is this: empowerment means different things to different people. As such, a transnational approach to understanding violence, broadly, and domestic violence in particular, is crucial to make sense of this global social problem.

### *Supporting financial capability for all*

As discussed previously, a substantial body of work focuses on capabilities as empowerment. Nussbaum acknowledges both that the basis for many decisions may involve ethnic or religious factors and the role of bias or "value imperialism" in determining human rights (Nussbaum, 2003, p. 107). In line with Nussbaum's approach, we forward the idea that empowerment programs need to be cognisant of the violence that is produced as a result, such as changes in status. We also see that some women access loans for their husbands, which runs counter to the intended goal and potentially limits the women's ability to flourish.

While women may suffer from effects of poverty unrelated to their gender, the combination of poverty and gender inequality results in a loss of basic human capabilities (Nussbaum, 2001). Additionally, capability need not be limited to financial capability; we can think of capability in terms of healthy relationships, as well. As such, programs could include education modules and offer relationship counselling and mental health support as appropriate. From a feminist perspective, equality defined and achieved by mirroring a masculine economic norm, does not confer empowerment. Reductions in the inequalities that permit and encourage abuse and violence should be the focus. Achieving economic equality is only a limited success where it is a success at all, treating the symptoms rather than evaluating, challenging, and reshaping attitudes, behaviours, and underlying structures that breed these symptoms.

## Feminism under neoliberalism – are we back to square one?

In conclusion, from the authors' perspectives, microfinance represents an expansion of the global financial market to include women in the global South. This model can be melded with patriarchal norms such that both are ideologically and materially enhanced, intertwined, and constitutive of each other. In this way, violence against women is accepted as an economic externality, and leaves women vulnerable and responsibilised. As Spivak (2016) points out, there is an *orientalist* (Said, 1978) approach embedded in such empowerment projects, rooted in ideas of Euro-centric supremacy, leaving 'saved' women torn between their new reality and tradition.

Alongside these ideological pitfalls, we also observe a concerning feminist schism. A middle-class feminism has emerged that has abandoned the concerns of the working class, despite the substantial number of low-income working women (Roesch, 2019). This vogue, middle-class feminism endorses the belief that proffered economic solutions will pave the way to women's independence. Meanwhile, low-income women's employment and asset ownership foments violence at home and fails to bring them out of poverty. Facebook COO Sheryl Sandberg's lean-in feminism, for example, has gained traction in some developing countries among the upper classes. This rebranding of feminisms eclipses the needs of billions in the working class and renders their issues marginal.

Jobs and finance alone do not empower women. Women do not want to be mere economic actors, but individuals with real economic power. Mohanty's work on 'third world feminism' has not been utilised (Mohanty, 1988; Mohanty, Russo, & Torres, 1991). We are back to square one where women in 'third world' locations of the global North or South bear the brunt of exploitation under the ideological cover of economic empowerment. The ignorance of this exploitation shows a failure of solidarity between third- and first-world feminists, lacking transnational sisterhood. A generation of women are being 'empowered' by programs of constrained choices, that enhance their debt, accumulate capital to the wealthy, and keep them at risk of violence without any increase in power to create substantive change.

The situation in the 'first world' is also unsettlingly problematic. As Dáil (2012) notes in her book on poverty among women in the United States, "the concepts of free-enterprise, profit-motive capitalism, social justice, and moral obligation should be the three legs of the stool upon which the social economy rests . . . however, today's economic realities do not offer much indication that this is true" (p. 214). Describing poverty as a "social disaster" resulting from profit-motive capitalism, she recognises the failure of policy and social welfare programs to qualitatively improve not only poor women's economic power, but also society's ambivalence toward persistent economic inequality across gender (Dáil, 2012, p. 229). Migrant women in the United States are told that they are now liberated and free to work outside the home, where they find precarious jobs that "meet the social reproductive needs [of the United States] rather than liberate these women in any way" (Kumar, 2019, p. 23). We find ourselves in a place where neoliberal feminism "presents the markets as the solution to precisely the problems created by the market" (Kumar, 2019, p. 22). This is wholly insufficient to meaningfully address Moina's economic or other empowerment needs.

# Critical findings

- Economic and other costs of domestic violence to individuals and societies are extensive. Because women disproportionately experience poverty throughout the world, economic empowerment has been suggested as a broad solution to many gendered problems including domestic violence.

- However, economic and social interventions such as microfinance may produce violence at home and in public spaces.

- Economic empowerment interventions have tended to take two broad forms: social welfare programs in the 'global North' nations, and microfinance loans and programming in the 'global South'. These interventions have had some success in short term poverty alleviation and/or domestic violence reduction.

- However, reductions in poverty and domestic violence may be temporary and other forms of abuse may be substituted for physical violence.

- Further, these forms of intervention, even when successful in increasing financial holdings, fall far short of the fundamental principles of empowerment. Such intervention may involve women significantly adding to their work burden by taking on employment, but retaining their domestic responsibilities as well. They are also thrust into unsafe workplaces where further violence often occurs, and shifting gender roles often precipitate greater domestic violence or other domestic difficulties.

- Finally, entering the formal economic sphere does not provide women with fundamental economic or other power to alter the institutions that fundamentally place them at greater risk of violence and abuse. Rather, such interventions primarily serve the economic needs of neoliberal economies through expansion into a highly disempowered and precarious workforce.

# Implications for policy, practice, and research

- A broad range of theories review the important considerations in examining economic empowerment and domestic violence. As we think about how to pave a path out of domestic violence through economic empowerment, we must honour the principles of empowerment (such as power and capabilities) discussed throughout the chapter and address the basic structural risk factors for violence.

- Narrowly focused, individualist interventions that extend neoliberal economies and ideology to women show limited effectiveness and counterproductivity.

- Empowerment strategies should focus on development of women's capabilities and opportunities across a broad range of domains, including but not limited to economic empowerment.

- Stakeholder direction and participation should be a cornerstone of the development and design of empowerment programs and interventions, so as to ensure the needs of appropriate parties are addressed.

- Patriarchal social structures and ideologies that provide psychological and environmental space for the perpetration of domestic violence should be undermined. Legal and ideological change is needed whereby men do not abuse women, and violence from any party is minimised.

- Economic structures that as a matter of design and operation render large swaths of the global population impoverished and disempowered should be dismantled. Patriarchy and capitalism, especially the latter's neoliberal form, are dangerous structures which inherently produce disempowerment and a form of violence.

- Interventions thus far may have done more to perpetuate than to overcome these risks. Moving forward, we recommend practice, policy, and research that are aimed at fundamental egalitarian structural change, according to the economic and other needs of all – planned, governed, directed, and enacted with representative input from women and the historically disempowered.

## Glossary

**Neoliberalism**          Neoliberalism, the current stage of capitalism, is market-oriented reform policies characterised by free market trade, deregulation of financial markets, privatisation, individualisation, and a shift away from state welfare provision.

**Neoliberal ideology**    An ideology that centres free-market capitalism as a governing mechanism through mantras of personal responsibility, individual choice, efficiency, meritocracy, and hard work, among others.

**Neoliberal feminism**    An individualised version of feminism that centres the market (e.g., lean-in feminism)

**Small government**       An economic and political system in which there is minimal government involvement in the provision of public goods and social welfare (e.g., education, health care)

## Note

1 Authors' note: Though heterosexual and cis gender normativity are significant factors in many sex and gender outcomes, these relationships are beyond the scope of this chapter. We here use terms such as masculine, female, and women with reference to majority occurrence rather than all-inclusively.

## References

Aizer, A. (2010). The gender wage gap and domestic violence. *American Economic Review, 100*(4), 1847–1859.

Anderberg, D., Rainer, H., Wadsworth, J., & Wilson, T. (2015). Unemployment and domestic violence: Theory and evidence. *The Economic Journal, 126*(597), 1947–1979.

Arthur, C., & Clark, R. (2009). Determinants of domestic violence: A cross-national study. *International Journal of Sociology of the Family, 35*(2), 147–167.

Bay-Cheng, L. Y. (2012). Recovering empowerment: De-personalizing and re-politicizing adolescent female sexuality. *Sex Roles, 66*(11–12), 713–717.

Bay-Cheng, L. Y., Lewis, A. E., Stewart, A. J., & Malley, J. E. (2006). Disciplining "girl talk" the paradox of empowerment in a feminist mentorship program. *Journal of Human Behaviour in the Social Environment, 13*(2), 73–92.

Benson, M. L., Wooldredge, J., Thistlethwaite, A. B., & Fox, G. L. (2004). The correlation between race and domestic violence is confounded with community context. *Social Problems, 51*(3), 326–342.

Bobonis, G. J., González-Brenes, M., & Castro, R. (2013). Public transfers and domestic violence: The roles of private information and spousal control. *American Economic Journal: Economic Policy, 5*(1), 179–205.

Bowen, E. A., & Murshid, N. S. (2016). Trauma-informed social policy: A conceptual framework for policy analysis and advocacy. *American Journal of Public Health, 106*(2), 223–229.

Chang, H. J. (2012). *23 Things they don't tell you about capitalism*. New York, NY: Bloomsbury Publishing.

Crenshaw, K. (1990). Mapping the margins: Intersectionality, identity politics, and violence against women of colour. *Stanford Law Review, 43*, 1241–1300.

Cunradi, C. B., Todd, M., Duke, M., & Ames, G. (2009). Problem drinking, unemployment, and intimate partner violence among a sample of construction industry workers and their partners. *Journal of Family Violence, 24*(2), 63–74.

Dáil, P. W. (2012). *Women and poverty in 21st century America*. Jefferson, NC: McFarland.

Dalal, K. (2011). Does economic empowerment protect women from intimate partner violence? *Journal of Injury and Violence Research, 3*(1), 35.

Deleuze, G., & Guattari, F. (1988). *A thousand plateaus: Capitalism and schizophrenia*. Minneapolis: University of Minnesota Press.

Duflo, E. (2012). Women empowerment and economic development. *Journal of Economic Literature, 50*(4), 1051–1079.

Duvvury, N., Callan, A., Carney, P., & Raghavendra, S. (2013). *Intimate partner violence: Economic costs and implications for growth and development*. Washington, DC: World Bank Group.

Farmer, A., & Tiefenthaler, J. (1997). An economic analysis of domestic violence. *Review of Social Economy, 55*(3), 337–358.

Gelles, R. J. (1983). *An exchange/social control theory*. In D. Finkelhore, R. J. Gelles, G. T. Hotaling, M. A. Straus (Eds.), *The dark side of families: Current family violence research*. Thousand Oaks, CA: Sage.

Goode, W. J. (1971). Force and violence in the family. *Journal of Marriage and the Family, 33*(4), 624–636.

Granovetter, M. S. (1973). The strength of weak ties. *American Journal of Sociology, 78*(6), 1360–1380.

Hartsock, N. C. (1983). *Money, sex, and power: Toward a feminist historical materialism*. Boston, MA: Northeastern University Press.

Harvey, D. (2003). The fetish of technology: Causes and consequences. *Macalester International, 13*(1), 3–30.

Hidrobo, M., & Fernald, L. (2013). Cash transfers and domestic violence. *Journal of Health Economics, 32*(1), 304–319.

Hornung, C. A., McCullough, B. C., & Sugimoto, T. (1981). Status relationships in marriage: Risk factors in spouse abuse. *Journal of Marriage and the Family*, 675–692.

James, K. (2010). Domestic violence within refugee families: Intersecting patriarchal culture and the refugee experience. *Australian and New Zealand Journal of Family Therapy, 31*(3), 275–284.

Jewkes, R. (2002). Intimate partner violence: Causes and prevention. *The Lancet, 359*(9315), 1423–1429.

Kabeer, N. (2005). Is microfinance a 'magic bullet' for women's empowerment? Analysis of findings from South Asia. *Economic and Political Weekly*, 4709–4718.

Karim, L. (2011). *Microfinance and its discontents: Women in debt in Bangladesh*. Minneapolis: University of Minnesota Press.

Kessler, R. C., Molnar, B. E., Feurer, I. D., & Appelbaum, M. (2001). Patterns and mental health predictors of domestic violence in the United States: Results from the national comorbidity survey. *International Journal of Law and Psychiatry, 24*(4–5), 487.

Koenig, M. A., Ahmed, S., Hossain, M. B., & Mozumder, A. K. A. (2003). Women's status and domestic violence in rural Bangladesh: Individual- and community-level effects. *Demography, 40*(2), 269–288.

Kratzer, J., & Kato, M. P. (2013). Empowering women through microfinance: Evidence from Tanzania. *ACRN Journal of Entrepreneurship Perspectives, 2*, 31–59.

Kumar, D. (2019). Imperialist feminism. *International Socialist Review, 102*.

Lawson, J. (2012). Sociological theories of intimate partner violence. *Journal of Human Behavior in the Social Environment, 22*(5), 572–590.

Leach, F., & Sitaram, S. (2002). Microfinance and women's empowerment: A lesson from India. *Development in Practice, 12*(5), 575–588.

Lindhorst, T., Oxford, M., & Gillmore, M. R. (2007). Longitudinal effects of domestic violence on employment and welfare outcomes. *Journal of Interpersonal Violence, 22*(7), 812–828.

Malhotra, A., Schuler, S. R., & Boender, C. (2002). Measuring women's empowerment as a variable in international development. In *Background paper prepared for the world bank workshop on poverty and gender: New perspectives* (Vol. 28). Washington, DC: The World Bank.

Max, W., Rice, D. P., Finkelstein, E., Bardwell, R. A., & Leadbetter, S. (2004). The economic toll of intimate partner violence against women in the United States. *Violence and Victims, 19*(3), 259.

Mayoux, L. (2000). *Micro-finance and the empowerment of women: A review of the key issues* (No. 993441343 402676). Geneva, Switzerland: International Labour Organization.

McLean, G., & Gonzalez Bocinski, S. (2017). *The economic cost of intimate partner violence, sexual assault, and stalking* (IWPR #B367). Retrieved from https://iwpr.org/wp-content/uploads/2017/08/B367_Economic-Impacts-of-IPV-08.14.17.pdf

Mehra, R. (1997). Women, empowerment, and economic development. *The Annals of the American Academy of Political and Social Science, 554*(1), 136–149.

Mohanty, C. T. (1988). Under Western eyes: Feminist scholarship and colonial discourses. *Feminist Review, 30*(1), 61–88.

Mohanty, C. T., Russo, A., & Torres, L. (1991). *Third world women and the politics of feminism* (Vol. 632). Bloomington, IN: Indiana University Press.

Munyo, I., & Rossi, M. A. (2015). *The effects of real exchange rate fluctuations on the gender wage gap and domestic violence in Uruguay* (No. IDB-WP-618). IDB Working Paper Series.

Murshid, N. S., Akinzicigil, A., & Zippay, A. (2016). Microfinance participation and domestic violence in Bangladesh: Results from a nationally representative survey. *Journal of Interpersonal Violence, 31*(9), 1579–1596. doi:10.1177/0886260515569065

Murshid, N. S., & Ball, A. (2018, July). Examining women's physical mobility and microfinance participation in Bangladesh: Results from a nationally representative sample. *Women's Studies International Forum, 69*, 33–39. Pergamon.

Murshid, N. S., & Murshid, N. (2018). Women's experiences with microfinance in urban Bangladesh: Results from a qualitative study. *Journal of Sociology & Social Welfare, 45*, 113.

Murshid, N. S., & Zippay, A. (2017). Social networks in the context of microfinance and intimate partner violence in Bangladesh: A mixed-methods study. *Journal of Sociology & Social Welfare, 44*, 147–172.

Nam, Y., & Tolman, R. (2002). Partner abuse and welfare receipt among African American and Latino women living in a low-income neighborhood. *Social Work Research, 26*(4), 241–251.

National Center for Injury Prevention and Control. (2003). *Costs of intimate partner violence against women in the United States*. Atlanta, GA: Centers for Disease Control and Prevention.

National Coalition Against Domestic Violence. (2019). *Domestic violence*. Retrieved from www.speakcdn.com/assets/2497/domestic_violence2.pdf

Nussbaum, M. C. (2001). *Women and human development: The capabilities approach* (Vol. 3). Cambridge: Cambridge University Press.

Nussbaum, M. C. (2003). Capabilities as fundamental entitlements: Sen and social justice. *Feminist Economics, 9*(2–3), 33–59.

Organization for Economic Cooperation and Development. (2011). *Women's economic empowerment (Issues paper)*. Retrieved from www.oecd.org/dac/gender-development/47561694.pdf

Peter, T. (2006). Domestic violence in the United States and Sweden: A welfare state typology comparison within a power resources framework. *Women's Studies International Forum, 29*(1), 96–107.

Postmus, J. L. (2010, October). Economic empowerment of domestic violence survivors. In *VAWnet applied research forum: National resource center on domestic violence.* (The production and dissemination of this publication was supported by Cooperative Agreement Number 1U1VCE001742-01 from the Centers for Disease Control and Prevention. Its contents are solely the responsibility of the authors and do not necessarily represent the official views of the CDC, VAWnet, or the Pennsylvania Coalition Against Domestic Violence)

Renzetti, C. M. (2019). Economic stress and domestic violence. *CRVAW Faculty Research Reports and Papers, 1*, 1–15. Retrieved from https://uknowledge.uky.edu/crvaw_reports/1

Roesch, J. (2019). The new women's movement. *International Socialist Review, 112*. Retrieved from https://isreview.org/issue/112/new-womens-movement on 5/10/2020

Rothman, E. F., Hathaway, J., Stidsen, A., & de Vries, H. F. (2007). How employment helps female victims of intimate partner violence: A qualitative study. *Journal of Occupational Health Psychology, 12*(2), 136.

Said, E. (1978). *Orientalism*. New York, NY: Pantheon.

Sanders, C. K., Weaver, T. L., & Schnabel, M. (2007). Economic education for battered women: An evaluation of outcomes. *Affilia: Journal of Women and Social Work, 22*(3), 240–254.

Sen, A. (1999). *Commodities and capabilities*. New York: Oxford University Press Catalogue and Oxford University Press, number 9780195650389.

Sen, A. (2000). *Social exclusion: Concept, application, and scrutiny*. Social Development Papers 1. Office of Environment and Social Development, Asian Development Bank.

Shahriar, A. Z. M., Unda, L. A., & Alam, Q. (2020). Gender differences in the repayment of microcredit: The mediating role of trustworthiness. *Journal of Banking & Finance, 110*, 105685.

Spivak, G. C., & Riach, G. (2016). *Can the subaltern speak?* London: Macat International Limited.

Viswanath, P. V. (2018). Microfinance and the decision to invest in children's education. *International Journal of Financial Studies*, 6(1), 16.

Vyas, S., & Watts, C. (2009). How does economic empowerment affect women's risk of intimate partner violence in low and middle income countries? A systematic review of published evidence. *Journal of International Development*, 21(5), 577–602.

Weissman, D. M. (2015). Countering neoliberalism and aligning solidarities: Rethinking domestic violence advocacy. *Southwestern Law Review*, 45, 915–958.

Yick, A. G. (2001). Feminist theory and status inconsistency theory: Application to domestic violence in Chinese immigrant families. *Violence Against Women*, 7(5), 545–562.

# 38

# GENDER JUSTICE ADVOCATES AND THE MAKING OF THE *DOMESTIC ABUSE (SCOTLAND) ACT 2018*

*Marsha Scott and Emma Ritch*

## Introduction

In February 2018, the Scottish Parliament passed the Domestic Abuse (Scotland) Bill 2018, called the "new gold standard" for domestic abuse law by Professor Evan Stark, author of the seminal book *Coercive Control: How Men Entrap Women in Everyday Life* (2007). After the vote, parliamentarians in the Debating Chamber gave a standing ovation to the domestic abuse survivors and advocates sitting in the public gallery. For the first time, Scotland had a specific offence defining and criminalising domestic abuse. The definitions in the law were framed by feminist theory and informed by extensive engagement with children and women survivors of domestic abuse.

The feminist political and social discourse that produced the Act rested on decades of feminist activism and the Women's Aid movement in Scotland (see Speaking Out – 40 Years of the Women's Aid Movement in Scotland, 2018). The savvy politicking from an established feminist infrastructure (i.e., feminist organisations supported by strong relationships between feminists inside and outside government and Parliament) injected the powerful stories of survivors into policymaking and changed policy processes.

The development and passage of the new law offers a template for progressive feminist domestic abuse policy specifically and violence against women more generally. This chapter examines the gendering of the policy process in the two decades preceding the law's passage. The chapter discusses the importance of gender infrastructure and feminist civil society, the notable features of the law, and the impact of an unprecedented engagement by officials with victim-survivors and their advocates in the law's development and passage.

## Gender justice

Women and men and girls and boys live very different lives. Any analysis, research, policy, or legislation can be said to be 'gender competent' when it reflects that principle. Familiarity with the dynamics of gender in our gendered world enables the development of policy and laws that disrupt the unequal distribution of power, prosperity, and safety in our families, communities, and institutions and promote social justice. Gender competence is thus required for activists, governments, and state institutions to develop and deliver policy and practice that sees oppression, understands how it works, and then dismantles it.

The interaction of feminist activists, policy machineries within government, and legislatures is complex (Mackay, 2015). Gender justice advocates seek to advance women's equality and rights both by influencing specific policy outcomes and by transforming the institutions in which policy and law are made. If legislatures and governments are currently gendered, then a possibility exists for what Karen Beckwith (2005) describes as "regender[ing]," by which process these institutions can be reoriented to the realisation of women's equality.

The work of feminist gender justice advocates is predicated on the notion that inequalities persist between the sexes and that the unequal distribution of power, resources, and safety fundamentally shapes the lives of women and girls. There are emblematic issues for women's equality and rights and usually include women's representation in political and public life, anti-discrimination law (e.g., the US Civil Rights Act of 1964 and the UK Equality Act of 2010), and access to justice, violence against women, participation in the labour market and the gender pay gap, publicly funded childcare, maternity and parental leave, abortion and reproductive justice, and divorce and family law.

The interaction of all these elements of women's inequality acts as a feeder system for how and why men practice domestic abuse and women and children experience (and resist) it. Men's privileged position enables abuse, and children's and women's relative poverty of power and money form the constraints on women's space for action that enforce abuse. This is Scotland's 'causal story' and a critical feature of the feminist argument that women's inequality is the cause and consequence of violence against women. (See Bacchi, 1999 for helpful discussion of problem definition and causal stories.) It is no accident that the Scottish Government's Violence Against Women and Girls department is located in the government's Equality Unit.

## A feminist theory of change

In one of the most systematic and wide-ranging analyses of the impact of state responses to the call for gender justice, Htun and Weldon (2018) mapped and analysed gender equality-promoting policies (including legislation) in 70 countries at four points in time between 1975 and 2005. The authors found a high level of variability in the types of gender equality policy adopted across countries.

Although all gender justice advocacy challenges existing cultural and social norms, Htun and Weldon conclude that feminist actors have been more effective in challenging dominant discourses relating to women's 'status.' Status here includes violence against women and the creation of gender quotas for elected bodies and boardrooms, rather than on what the authors delineate as 'gender-class' issues such as the gendered division of labour. In other words, challenging *how* the system works has been more successful than confronting the structure of the system itself.

In some policy areas the work of gender justice advocates has been decisive in enabling shifts. Htun and Weldon find that, with regard to the global development of policies on violence against women from 1975 to 2005, "the autonomous mobilization of feminists in domestic and transnational contexts – not Left parties, women in parliament, or national wealth – is the critical factor accounting for policy change" (p. 29). *It is feminist activism, more than any other single factor, that has introduced and improved policy on violence against women.* Echoing Htun and Weldon's analysis, Cavaghan (2017, p. 27) points out that the "single most significant factor [in the uptake of gender mainstreaming] was the presence and participation of transnational women's NGOs arguing the relevance of gender/women's interests across a range of policy areas," including violence against women.

## Making policy work for women in Scotland

Scotland, like many European nations and states, requires its public bodies – including the Scottish Government – to mainstream a gendered analysis within policymaking and legislating. The gender equality duty (GED) came into force in 2007 and placed a range of reporting, equal pay, and gender impact assessment requirements on public bodies. Subsequent legislation in the UK Parliament moved coverage of the GED into an omnibus Equality Act 2010, thus removing the focus on gender and replacing it with an integrated public sector equality duty (PSED).

The duties have acted as a hook on which to hang the advocacy work of feminist civil society organisations in Scotland. Burman and Johnstone (2015, p. 45) observed that

> devolution [of powers to Scotland from the UK Government in 1999] led to new principles and accountability mechanisms, more gender balance in political institutions and significant new opportunities for women's groups to shape and inform the policy and legislative process.

The authors conclude that this context of newness "rendered Scotland particularly receptive to the gender equality duty, which in turn accelerated the progress of legal and policy reform" despite "low levels of awareness of the duty and its underlying principles" (p. 45).

The 20 years since devolution in Scotland have seen gender justice advocates "animated by the possibility of newness," as the Scottish Parliament was reconvened with gender-sensitive features as diverse as a creche, a standing Equal Opportunities Committee, and almost 40% female parliamentarians (Ritch, 2019, p. 337). This sense of the possible was refreshed during the debate about Scottish independence between 2012 and 2014, as women's organisations entered "a bold period of imagining those [new] powers and institutions as shaped, directed, and delivering to meet the needs of women and girls, as well as boys and men" (Ritch, 2019, p. 337).

## The *Domestic Abuse (Scotland) Act 2018*

In the devolution settlement agreed with the Westminster government prior to the re-opening of the Scottish Parliament in 1999, the latter held 'devolved' authority for policy and law relating to violence against women in all areas with a few exceptions that intersected with matters reserved to Westminster (chiefly immigration issues). Policing and the criminal and civil justice system are distinctively autonomous Scottish institutions. Some examples of distinctly Scottish initiatives include the establishment of a specialist domestic abuse court in 2004, the promotion of national training strategies, the creation of a National Domestic Abuse Taskforce within Police Scotland in 2013, and, most significant, the development of the *Equally Safe* strategy on violence against women and girls (VAWG) (Scottish Government, 2015).

A critical enabler for the innovative policy and practice work was Scotland's sustained investment in feminist 'strategic intermediaries' in civil society – the women's sector NGOs and, specifically, Scottish Women's Aid (SWA). ('Strategic intermediaries' are defined thus by Scottish Government: "These bodies play an important role in the policymaking process by supporting and engaging communities, and informing understanding of the issues experienced by equality groups. In a number of cases they also provide support to frontline services" [www.

gov.scot/publications/equality-national-intermediary-bodies-funding-2017-2020/]. Scottish Women's Aid is an explicitly feminist domestic abuse umbrella organisation with 36 member services around Scotland.) As Htun and Weldon (2018) demonstrated, investment in feminist civil society delivered effective and innovative policy advocacy and a progressive policymaking collaboration with government.

In this context, an appetite was growing in civil society for legislative reform to match the progressive VAWG strategy and give it teeth. At the time, Scotland had no specific offence of domestic abuse. A number of other offences, most often breach of the peace or threatening or abusive behaviour, were in place. Domestic abuse law and national (VAWG) policy developed in parallel but often non-congruent processes that allowed for different definitions of domestic abuse in national strategies, policing, and prosecution.

The definition of domestic abuse in policy documents was from the beginning linked to UN documents such as the 1993 *Declaration on the Elimination of Violence Against Women* and was gendered. Domestic abuse was restricted to partners and ex-partners. The following definition was agreed by the Scottish Partnership on Domestic Abuse in 2000:

> Domestic abuse can be perpetrated by partners or ex-partners and can include physical abuse (assault and physical attack involving a range of behaviour), sexual abuse (acts which degrade and humiliate women and are perpetrated against their will, including rape) and mental and emotional abuse (such as threats, verbal abuse, withholding money and other types of controlling behaviour such as isolation from family or friends). Children are witness to and subjected to much of this abuse; there is a correlation between domestic abuse and the mental, physical and sexual abuse of children.

Domestic abuse is associated with broader inequalities in society, is part of a range of behaviours constituting male abuse of power, and is linked to other forms of male violence, such as rape and child abuse. Domestic abuse occurs in all social groups, is not caused by stress, unemployment, poverty, alcohol or mental illness, nor by the women who experience the abuse (Scottish Centre for Crime and Justice Research, 2015).

The definition covered a broad range of harms and linked abuse with broad social inequalities. Although a similar definition was adopted by police and prosecution officials (the Crown Office Procurator Fiscal Service of Scotland), it would take 18 years for the criminal law to give effect to this definition.

Despite Scotland's reliable cross-party consensus on violence against women policy, activists were concerned that debate over a new law would endanger Scotland's existing definition and reignite debates about the role of gender in domestic settings (Scott, 2006). However, commitment to the gendered analysis of domestic abuse had solidified over the ten years since the first domestic abuse policy, and the need for a specific offence was strongly supported by the evidence from a 30-year, 70-country study:

> [r]egardless of national context, attempts to address violence against women under the rubric of more general laws against violence or assault have generally been unsuccessful. . . . Obtaining an effective response from the law enforcement bureaucracy has generally required both legal reform and training of law enforcement officials from police officers to judges.
>
> (Weldon, 2002, p. 13)

## Early adoption of Stark's theory of coercive control in Scotland

Evan Stark's 2007 critique of the 'violent-incident' model of domestic violence and his paradigm of coercive control were taken up in Scotland as early as 2006–7. The women's sector was the first and strongest advocate for challenging the old paradigm. In April 2006, the *Women's Support Project* in Glasgow brought Stark to Scotland to present at a seminar, and in September 2007, just as Stark's (2007) book was being published, Scottish Women's Aid (an explicitly feminist women's rights organisation and Scotland's national domestic abuse service and policy advocacy organisation) brought Stark to Edinburgh for the organisation's annual national conference. That appearance by Professor Stark was the first of many, including three months at the University of Edinburgh as the Leverhulme Visiting Professor in 2013.

Both academics and practitioners were keenly aware that the 'domestic violence' described in various laws bore little resemblance to its reality in women's and children's lives. Survivors' accounts of their experiences over the 40-plus years of the Women's Aid movement in Scotland eloquently described the trauma and harm caused by domestic abuse generally and emotional/psychological violence specifically (Speaking Out – 40 Years of the Women's Aid Movement in Scotland, 2018). Stark's (2007) critique of existing constructions of domestic violence highlighted three 'myths' in the dogma:

1 That domestic violence occurs as discrete incidents of physical violence (rather than as a 24/7 ongoing pattern of coercion and control that is sometimes enforced by physical violence).
2 That domestic violence is 'domestic,' and occurs only in the home where a perpetrator and victim live together (whereas health and criminal justice data indicate that in many cases perpetrators are no longer living with their partners when victims come to the attention of services, and that separation does not bring safety).
3 That the most salient aspect of the 'violence' is physical assault (however, physical violence, when present, is most often used instrumentally to enforce the perpetrator's control, along with other acts of humiliation, coercion, degradation, and threats to children, other family members and pets; rather than only physical violence, domestic abuse is a violation of the victim's human rights, a liberty crime).

Stark's critique was translated for officials and politicians through survivors' accounts of their own experiences. In turn, these accounts were to form the backbone of Scotland's new law.

## Gender (a)symmetry

While SWA highlighted Stark's gendered coercive control paradigm in its policy work, the gender symmetry debate raged in academia. Many academics, police, and practitioners argued that domestic abuse was primarily male-perpetrated (Dobash, Dobash, Wilson, & Daly, 1992), but others (Straus, 1999) claimed that women were as violent as men in intimate relationships. Adoption of the new, intrinsically gendered coercive control paradigm, depended on a resolution of this debate in policy circles. The Scottish Government commissioned research (Gadd, Farrall, Dallimore, & Lombard, 2002) and sponsored academic debates, hoping to establish a policy consensus.

Meanwhile, SWA and sister organisations were making the case for asymmetry and defending the gendering of policy in Scotland. Reframing the gender asymmetry debate was critical to progress on developing law to match Scotland's policy documents (Lombard & Whiting,

2018). In addition to Stark's work on coercive control, campaigners' arguments were supported robustly by the publication of Michael Johnson's (2008) work. Johnson argued that discussions of gender symmetry in domestic abuse often conflated a number of distinct phenomena:

- Intimate terrorism (involving violence and control), experienced predominantly by women and perpetrated predominantly by men.
- Violent resistance, perpetrated mostly by women with mostly male victims.
- Mutual violent control.
- Situational couple violence, largely gender symmetrical.

Like Stark, Johnson highlighted the role of power and control in violence between partners and ex-partners and demonstrated that failing to distinguish among these different phenomena produced ostensibly contradictory findings in the literature.

Johnson's analysis had particular resonance in the criminal justice system and especially the prosecution service (COPFS), which needed to understand the growing number of cases going through Scotland's courts. In particular, Johnson's analysis explained why official figures, which conflated situational couple violence (one-off incidents of violence) with intimate terrorism, had significant numbers of female perpetrators. Separating those one-off incidents from the course-of-conduct offence of intimate terrorism allowed a very different picture of offending to emerge. In 2015 the COPFS invited Johnson to speak to attendees at its Prosecution College, and references to 'situational couple violence' can be found in numerous COPFS (2014) speeches and protocols.

Gender justice advocates used the theoretical and empirical evidence offered by Stark and Johnson to challenge government and justice agencies, calling for improved foundations for policy and practice. The advocates' power to influence change derived from their status as strategic intermediaries and their growing voice as the 'content experts' on domestic abuse in Scotland. The perception by officials and parliamentarians that the sector's expertise reflected both traditional academic evidence and practice-based, survivor-informed evidence, would be critical in the debates of a new law.

## The road to a specific offence

In early 2015, after a number of years of advocacy by the women's sector and growing interest in policy change from the Crown Office, the Scottish Government consulted on whether a specific offence was needed. Officials' questions included the extent to which existing laws were adequate and whether a new specific offence concerning domestic abuse should be introduced. Reponses reflected strong agreement (93%) that current laws were not adequate and that a specific offence would be an improvement (96%). A majority of respondents (67%) thought that any specific offence of 'domestic abuse' should be restricted to people who are partners or ex-partners, supporting the case made by the women's sector that domestic abuse was an intrinsically gendered form of abuse (Scottish Government, 2015).

In September 2015, the government's Programme for Government committed to publishing a draft of a specific offence. During the drafting period, members of the Government's Bill Team corresponded regularly with policy experts in SWA and other victims service organisations. SWA offered to test proposed language with survivors, service users, and staff working directly with women and children. Scottish Women's Aid ran focus groups to gather survivors' expert input, and the Bill Team responded by making language changes in the draft Bill.

Survivors were particularly keen that explicit references be made to constraints on their autonomy. Section 2 of the Bill describes what constitutes abusive behaviour. This section, and the related explanatory notes, are peppered with phrases from service users and advocates, including "regulating day-to-day activities" and "restricting freedom of action." The explanatory note for this section is one of a number that use language that came from consultation with survivors:

> Section 2(3)(b) provides that behaviour which has the effect of isolating the victim from friends, relatives or other sources of support can be considered to have a relevant effect. This could include, for example, controlling the victim's movements or access to their phone or other forms of communication, not allowing visits from or to the victim's friends or family, or deliberately failing to pass on messages from friends or family.

In December 2015, the draft law was released for consultation, and on 17 March 2017 Cabinet Secretary for Justice Michael Matheson, Member of the Scottish Parliament (MSP), introduced the Bill. The Justice Committee conducted a number of public evidence sessions, and a subgroup of the Committee held private sessions with survivors (who were supported by a number of victim support agencies, including SWA and one of its member services, Shakti Women's Aid). The significant impact of these meetings with survivors was reflected in Michael Matheson reading out statements from two of them (one of whom was in the public gallery) during the final debate on the Bill. Matheson concluded debate on the Bill by noting that "the very heart of this legislation is the voices of those women who have experienced domestic abuse" (Wilson & Hutchison, 2018).

The Bill was amended as it passed through Parliament. Amendments included:

- New language to provide for extraterritorial jurisdiction to comply with the Council of Europe's *Convention on Action Against Violence Against Women and Domestic Abuse* (the 'Istanbul Convention'), which the Scottish Government has committed to (Westminster Parliament has signed but not yet ratified this Convention).
- New elements added to the section dealing with aggravation involving children.
- Changes to the drafting regarding non-harassment orders. The original Bill included provisions requiring courts to consider making non-harassment orders when sentencing for the offence of domestic abuse. Amendments extended consideration of the making of these orders to also cover children, and created a presumption in favour of making such orders.

The *Domestic Abuse (Scotland) Act 2018* was passed in February 2018 with an implementation date to be announced once plans were in place.

## Notable elements of the Act

The new law is notable in a number of ways. The law focuses on the behaviour of the perpetrator rather than that of the victim, requires a course of behaviour rather than a discrete incident, uses human rights language (autonomy, freedom from fear and coercion), and reflects what women and children account.

## *Course of behaviour*

Moving away from constructing domestic abuse as an incident to a pattern of behaviour is one of the central tenets of the new offence in Scotland. The elements of the offence are contained in section 1:

### 1. *Abusive behaviour towards partner or ex-partner*

(1)  A person commits an offence if –

    (a)  the person ("A") engages in a course of behaviour which is abusive of A's partner or ex-partner ("B"), and

    (b)  both of the further conditions are met.

(2)  The further conditions are –

    (a)  that a reasonable person would consider the course of behaviour to be likely to cause B to suffer physical or psychological harm,

    (b)  that either –

        (i)  A intends by the course of behaviour to cause B to suffer physical or psychological harm, or

        (ii)  A is reckless as to whether the course of behaviour causes B to suffer physical or psychological harm.

(3)  In the further conditions, the references to psychological harm include fear, alarm and distress.

A course of behaviour, defined in section 10(4) of the Act, "involves behaviour on at least two occasions." Additionally, "psychological harm" expressly includes "fear, alarm and distress" (s 1(3)).

The offence is committed against a partner or ex-partner: "partner" is defined in section 11 to include spouses, civil partners, parties living together as if spouses of each other, and persons in an intimate relationship; an ex-partner is a person who had previously been in such a relationship.

The Act provides that prosecution must demonstrate *either* that the defendant intended to harm the victim, or that they were "reckless" about potential harm. These two legal constructions were especially welcome to those who were familiar with victim-survivor stories, which typically are filled with details that would lead a "reasonable person" to understand that harm was an expected outcome of the offender's course of behaviour.

The Act describes in some detail (extensive but "not exhaustive") what constitutes abusive behaviour. This section of the Act reflected consultation with survivors, sometimes using their words to describe the offence.

### *Abusive behaviour*

What constitutes abusive behaviour is non-exhaustively defined in section 2.

## 2. What constitutes abusive behaviour

(1)  Subsections (2) to (4) elaborate on section 1(1) as to A's behaviour.

(2)  Behaviour which is abusive of B includes (in particular) –

    (a)  behaviour directed at B that is violent, threatening or intimidating,

    (b)  behaviour directed at B, at a child of B or at another person that either –

        (i)  has as its purpose (or among its purposes) one or more of the relevant effects set out in subsection (3), or

        (ii)  would be considered by a reasonable person to be likely to have one or more of the relevant effects set out in subsection (3).

(3)  The relevant effects are of –

    (a)  making B dependent on, or subordinate to, A,

    (b)  isolating B from friends, relatives or other sources of support,

    (c)  controlling, regulating or monitoring B's day-to-day activities,

    (d)  depriving B of, or restricting B's, freedom of action,

    (e)  frightening, humiliating, degrading or punishing B.

(4)  In subsection (2) –

    (a)  in paragraph (a), the reference to violent behaviour includes sexual violence as well as physical violence,

    (b)  in paragraph (b), the reference to a child is to a person who is under 18 years of age.

'Violent' behaviour directed at B is not restricted to physical violence and includes sexual violence (s 2(4)) as well as behaviour that has a "relevant effect." The *Explanatory Notes* prepared by the Scottish Government provide numerous examples of relevant abusive behaviours and effects. For example, the notes indicate that behaviour which makes a victim dependent on, or subordinate to, a perpetrator can be considered to have a relevant effect under section 2(3) (a) where such behaviour prevents the victim from having access to money, forces the victim to leave their job, takes charge of household decision-making to the exclusion of the victim, or treats the victim as a domestic slave.

## 'Is the behaviour harmful?' versus 'How much did she suffer?'

The new law shifts the focus of prosecution from evidence of injury experienced by the victim to evidence of perpetration. Indeed, prosecutors need not prove that the victim actually did suffer harm or experience any relevant effect (although such evidence may be presented). Instead, the prosecution must establish that a reasonable person would consider that the course of behaviour would be likely to cause physical and/or psychological harm to the victim (taking into account the particular characteristics of the victim).

## 4. Evidence of impact on victim

(1)  The commission of an offence under section 1(1) does not depend on the course of behaviour actually causing B to suffer harm of the sort mentioned in section 1(2).

(2)  The operation of section 2(2)(b) does not depend on behaviour directed at someone actually having on B any of the relevant effects set out in section 2(3).

(3)  Nothing done by or mentioned in subsection (1) or (2) prevents evidence from being led in proceedings for an offence under section 1(1) about (as the case may be) –

(a)  harm actually suffered by B as a result of the course of behaviour, or
(b)  effects actually had on B of behaviour directed at someone.

Shifting the focus from the victim and onto the offending behaviour opens up the possibility for dramatically changing victims' experiences, especially in court. Notions of 'deserving victims,' questions about 'why didn't she just leave,' and the relentless pressure to present in court as traumatised and broken have made testifying a necessary evil at best, and a form of re-victimisation at worst. Although courts will interpret and implement these provisions in their own ways, this framing of the offence offers hope to victims and their supporters that a trial might be harder on the accused than on the victim, which Shakespeare might refer to as a "consummation devoutly to be wished."

## Children are not 'witnesses' but victims

The new Act reframes the experience of children and young people living with domestic violence, constructing them as *experiencing* the abuse rather than merely *witnessing* it. This is achieved through section 5 of the Act, which deals with "aggravation in relation to a child."

Prior to passage of the new Act, victim advocates, children's rights organisations, and researchers had begun to challenge the notion that children who are not direct targets experience domestic violence merely as 'witnesses'; that is, that the harm that a child experiences is solely a consequence of witnessing incidents of violence directed at the non-offending parent (the mother in the vast majority of cases), rather than a product of the child's own experience of control and coercion (Callaghan, Alexander, Sixsmith, & Chiara Fellin, 2018; Katz, 2015, 2016; Morrison, 2015; Morrison & Tisdall, 2013; Morrison & Wasoff, 2012).

Moreover, linked to increasing evidence that separation from an abusive ex-partner does not bring safety for adult victims is the widespread acknowledgement of the continuation of abuse through child contact arrangements. The most visible evidence of harm to children was in the context of court-ordered contact with the offending parent. Scottish Women's Aid, the Centre for Research on Families and Relationships at the University of Edinburgh, and the office of the Commissioner for Children and Young People in Scotland (CCYPS) collaborated on numerous pieces of work in an effort to generate change.

The CCYPS commissioned two pieces of research: one investigated child contact proceedings, and recommended that a common definition of domestic abuse be adopted and that service providers receive more extensive training in relation to children affected by domestic abuse and contact (Morrison & Tisdall, 2013; Mackay, 2013). Scottish Women's Aid led on a joint participation project with the Children and Young People's Commission in Scotland – *Power Up/Power Down* – that focused specifically on how the views of children were treated in contact disputes (Scottish Women's Aid, *Power Up/Power Down: Changing the Story, Hearing Children and Young People's Voices.* https://womensaid.scot/project/power-up-power-down). The study involved 27 children and young people aged between 6 and 17 years old. A series of sessions explored themes of power, children's rights, making their voices heard in court, and how to improve the experience and outcomes for children affected by domestic abuse in family court actions relating to contact decisions.

During the consultation process prior to launch of the new Act, a new coalition of children's charities and women's charities was formed, and the coalition delivered a powerful voice for children. The primary concern of this coalition was the gap between criminal and civil proceedings. Sheriffs and judges often had no information about the behaviour of the offending parent when making contact decisions. Advocates believed that creating a status for children as co-victim with the non-offending parent would improve the likelihood that abusive behaviours discussed in criminal cases would be considered relevant in linked civil cases where child contact discussions were being made. This was a step too far for the drafters of the Bill, and the language in the first version of the Bill reflected this:

## 5. *Aggravation in relation to a child*

(1)  This subsection applies where it is, in proceedings for an offence under section 1(1) –

  (a)  specified in the complaint or libelled in the indictment that the offence is aggravated by reason of involving a child, and
  (b)  proved that the offence is so aggravated.

(2)  The offence is so aggravated if –

  (a)  at any time in the commission of the offence –

    (i)   A directs behaviour at a child, or
    (ii)  A makes use of a child in directing behaviour at B.

  (b)  a child sees or hears, or is present during, an incident of behaviour that A directs at B as part of the course of behaviour.

Ministers, Members of the Scottish Parliament, and government officials were lobbied extensively to change this language, replacing it with language that provided children with co-victim status. The government retained the original language but offered a subsequent amendment that was a significant improvement. The final language, negotiated with the powerful coalition of children's and women's organisations, included the following additional subsections.

## 5. *Aggravation in relation to a child*

. . .

(3)  The offence is so aggravated if a child sees or hears, or is present during, an incident of behaviour that A directs at B as part of the course of behaviour.
(4)  The offence is so aggravated if a reasonable person would consider the course of behaviour, or an incident of A's behaviour that forms part of the course of behaviour, to be likely to adversely affect a child usually residing with A or B (or both).
(5)  For it to be proved that the offence is so aggravated, there does not need to be evidence that a child –

  (a)  has ever had any –

    (i)   awareness of A's behaviour, or
    (ii)  understanding of the nature of A's behaviour, or

  (b)  has ever been adversely affected by A's behaviour.

When aggravation in relation to a child is established, the court must note this when stating and recording the conviction and must take the matter into account when imposing sentence (s 7).

## The future

On 20 March 2017, the new Domestic Abuse Bill was announced by First Minister Nicola Sturgeon. Cabinet Secretary for Justice Michael Matheson commented that, in his experience, development of the Bill had involved "an unprecedented amount of engagement with stakeholders"; the First Minister replied, "That's how the best laws are made" (personal communication). Just over a year later, the *Domestic Abuse (Scotland) 2018 Act* passed virtually unanimously and, as mentioned, was hailed by Professor Evan Stark as "a new gold standard."

Mirroring Stark's concept of "coercive control" and Johnson's "intimate terrorism," the new law frames domestic abuse as a crime that violates basic human rights to autonomy, to lives free from fear and coercion, to space for action denied women for so long by the constraints of patriarchy and women's inequality. For the first time in Scotland, domestic abuse legislation is congruent with national policy as expressed in government documents. For the first time Scotland has domestic abuse legislation that offers an opportunity to operationalise what has become the mantra of the Women's Aid movement in Scotland – that domestic abuse is a cause and consequence of women's inequality.

A number of problems remain. For example, the divide between civil and criminal cases is not addressed sufficiently in this legislation. However, the language in section 5 (dealing with aggravation in relation to a child) does remove the requirement for children to witness abuse and acknowledges that a reasonable person might assume that if children are in a family where abuse occurs, they are victims. This is a positive development. The Government launched a significant consultation on the *Children (Scotland) Act 1995*, which looks specifically at provisions in existing law relating to court decisions about child contact (Scottish Government, 2018b). Children's and women's charities continue to coordinate consistent messages to officials that this is a critical issue and that positive developments are expected in any forthcoming legislation. Inadequate application of the child aggravator raises the spectre that perpetrators will use the absence of an aggravator as demonstration that the criminal court established that the offence did not harm children in the family and that contact is therefore safe.

Another problem not addressed in the Act was the issue of emergency orders. During the progress of the *Domestic Abuse Bill* through Parliament, Scottish Women's Aid urged the Justice Committee to instruct the government to include emergency barring orders (EBOs) in the new law. Various forms of EBOs are in place across Europe, and they are required for compliance with Article 52 of the Council of Europe's *Istanbul Convention* which requires parties to the convention to have in place:

> measures to ensure that the competent authorities are granted the power to order, in situations of immediate danger, a perpetrator of domestic violence to vacate the residence of the victim or person at risk for a sufficient period of time and to prohibit the perpetrator from entering the residence of or contacting the victim or person at risk.

These orders empower authorities (usually police) to immediately remove a suspected perpetrator of abuse from the family home, enabling victims to stay in their own homes. Women and children forced to leave their homes because of domestic abuse are the third largest source of homelessness applications in Scotland, and robust short-term orders protecting their right to stay would reduce harm as well as serve natural justice. The Government responded to this call for amendment with a commitment to launch a consultation process in parallel with the review of the *Children (Scotland) 1995 Act*. The consultation was launched (Scottish Government, 2018a), and First Minister Nicola Sturgeon announced in October 2019 that EBO legislation would be introduced in the current legislative session (www.gov.scot/news/protecting-people-from-domestic-abuse).

Gender justice advocates continue to argue that policy and programmes that lack gender competence are simply incompetent, ineffective, and costly. The policy landscape in Scotland has shifted profoundly as a consequence of the new Act. The salience of gender, the influence and expertise of survivors and advocates, and early moves to reflect children's human rights in the State's response to domestic abuse are milestones delivered by the development, debate, and discourse surrounding the Act. Implementation of the Act heralds a new stage in which Scotland has the opportunity to transform institutional responses and demonstrate the difference legislation can make in the lives of the Scottish people.

## Critical findings

- Policy advocacy by feminist non-governmental organisations (NGOs) can produce 'gold standard' domestic abuse legislation that rests on a sound gendered analysis. This analysis reflects the profoundly different lives of women and men and reveals the inextricable link between systemic and structural sexism and the dynamics and prevalence of coercive control and domestic abuse.
- The voices and views of children and women with experience of domestic abuse tell powerful stories that can shape progressive legislation to criminalise coercive control and domestic abuse.
- Government investment in feminist civil society can establish a gender infrastructure that enables progressive influencing on policy makers by gender justice advocates.

## Implications for policy, practice, and research

- Gender justice advocates can improve law and policymaking when their infrastructure is resourced adequately and sustainably.
- Linking domestic abuse with the other elements of women's and children's inequality supports development of gender-competent policy and law that reflects the intrinsically gendered nature of domestic abuse and other forms of gender-based violence.
- Alliances between women's rights and children's rights organisations can provide a powerful influence on policy and law to criminalise coercive control.
- When resourced and supported properly, feminist non-governmental organisations (NGOs) can support survivors' voices to be heard and heeded in law making.
- Governments interested in improving violence against women policy must invest in their local gender infrastructure generally and feminist NGOs working with survivors in particular.

## References

Bacchi, C. L. (1999). *Women, policy and politics: The construction of policy problems*. London: Sage.
Beckwith, K. (2005). "A common language of gender?" *Politics & Gender, 1*(1), 128–137. doi:10.1017/S1743923X05211017

Burman, M., & Johnstone, J. (2015). High hopes? The gender equality duty and its impact on responses to gender-based violence. doi:10.1332/030557312X655846

Callaghan, J. E. M., Alexander, J. H., Sixsmith, J., & Chiara Fellin, L. (2018). Beyond "witnessing": Children's experiences of coercive control in domestic violence and abuse. *Journal of Interpersonal Violence*, *33*(10), 1551–1581.

Cavaghan, R. (2017). *Making gender equality happen: Knowledge, change and resistance in Eu gender mainstreaming*. London: Routledge.

Crown Office Procurator Fiscal Service. (2014). *Challenging abuse together (COPFS Conference on domestic abuse, Glasgow, 8 May 2014)*. Retrieved from www.copfs.gov.uk/images/Documents/Our%20Priorities/Domestic%20abuse/Speech%20by%20PF%20Domestic%20Abuse%20at%20COPFS%20Conference%208%20May%202014.pdf

Dobash, R. P., Dobash, R. E., Wilson, M., & Daly, M. (1992). The myth of sexual symmetry in marital violence. *Social Problems*, *39*(1), 71–91.

Gadd, D., Farrall, S., Dallimore, D., & Lombard, N. (2002). *Domestic abuse against men in Scotland*. Retrieved from https://www2.gov.scot/Publications/2002/09/15201/9609

Htun, M., & Laurel Weldon, S. (2018). *The logics of gender justice: State action on women's rights around the world*. Cambridge: Cambridge University Press.

Johnson, M. P. (2006). Conflict and control: Gender symmetry and asymmetry in domestic violence. *Violence Against Women*, *12*(11), 1003–1018.

Johnson, M. P. (2008). *A typology of domestic violence: Intimate terrorism, violent resistance, and situational couple violence*. Boston, MA: Northeastern University Press.

Katz, E. (2015). *Surviving together: Domestic violence and mother-child relationships* (PhD thesis). University of Nottingham, Nottingham.

Katz, E. (2016). Beyond the physical incident model: How children living with domestic violence are harmed by and resist regimes of coercive control. *Child Abuse Review*, *25*(1), 46–59.

Lombard, N., & Whiting, N. (2018). What's in a name? The Scottish government, feminism and the gendered framing of domestic abuse. In N. Lombard (Ed.), *The Routledge handbook of gender and violence*. New York, NY: Routledge.

Mackay, F. (2015). *Gender, politics and institutions: Towards a feminist institutionalism* (M. Krook, Ed., 1st ed.). Basingstoke and New York, NY: Palgrave Macmillan.

Mackay, K. (2013). *The treatment of the views of children in private law child contact disputes where there is a history of domestic abuse: A report to Scotland's commissioner for children and young people*. Retrieved from www.cypcs.org.uk/publications/domestic-abuse

Morrison, F. (2015). 'All over now?' The ongoing relational consequences of domestic abuse through children's contact arrangements. *Child Abuse Review*, *24*(4), 274–284.

Morrison, F., & Tisdall, E. K. (2013). *Child contact proceedings for children affected by domestic abuse: A report to Scotland's commissioner for children and young people*. Retrieved from www.cypcs.org.uk/publications/domestic-abuse.

Morrison, F., & Wasoff, F. (2012). Child contact centers and domestic abuse: Victim safety and the challenge to neutrality. *Violence Against Women*, *18*(6), 711–720.

Ritch, E. (2019). Foreboding newness: Brexit and feminist civil society in Scotland. In M. Dustin, N. Ferreira, & S. Millns (Eds.), *Gender and queer perspectives on Brexit. Gender and politics*. Cham and London: Palgrave Macmillan.

Scott, M. (2006). *Partnership, power and policy: A case study of the Scottish partnership on domestic abuse* (PhD thesis). University of Edinburgh, Edinburgh.

Scottish Centre for Crime and Justice Research. (2015). *Violence against women and girls*, p. 1. Retrieved from www.sccjr.ac.uk/wp-content/uploads/2015/10/SCCJR-Violence-against-women-and-girls.pdf

Scottish Government. (2015). *Equally safe: Reforming the criminal law to address domestic abuse and sexual offences – Analysis of consultation responses*. Retrieved from https://www2.gov.scot/Publications/2015/03/4845/4

Scottish Government. (2018a). *Protective orders for people at risk of domestic abuse: Consultation*. Retrieved from www.gov.scot/publications/consultation-protective-orders-people-risk-domestic-abuse/pages/2/

Scottish Government. (2018b). *Review of part 1 of the children (Scotland) act 1995 and creation of a family justice modernisation strategy: A consultation*. Retrieved from www.gov.scot/publications/review-part-1-children-scotland-act-1995-creation-family-justice/

Scottish Women's Aid. *Power up/power down: Changing the story, hearing children and young people's voices*. Retrieved from https://womensaid.scot/project/power-up-power-down/

Speaking Out – 40 Years of the Women's Aid Movement in Scotland. (2018). Retrieved from https://womenslibrary.org.uk/gwl_wp/wp-content/uploads/2017/12/Speaking-Out-40-years-of-Womens-Aid-1.pdf

Stark, E. (2007). *Coercive control: How men entrap women in personal life*. Oxford: Oxford University Press.

Straus, M. A. (1999). The controversy over domestic violence by women: A methodological, theoretical, and sociology of science analysis. In X. B. Arriaga & S. Oskamp (Eds.), *Violence in intimate relationships*. Thousand Oaks, CA: Sage.

Weldon, L. (2002). *Protest, policy, and the problem of violence against women: A cross-national comparison*. Pittsburgh, PA: University of Pittsburgh Press.

Wilson, L., & Hutchison, C. (2018, February 2). MSPs pass domestic abuse bill. *The Guardian*. Retrieved from www.bbc.com/news/live/uk-scotland-scotland-politics-42858902

# 39

# TRAUMA-INFORMED AND OPPRESSION-SENSITIVE INTERVENTION FOR THOSE WHO ENGAGE IN INTIMATE PARTNER VIOLENCE

*Casey T. Taft, Maxine Davis, Hannah E. Cole, Molly R. Franz*
*and Gabrielle Johnson*

## Introduction

Trauma-informed intervention approaches have long been advocated for a range of problems because trauma is pervasive, life-altering, impacts many life domains, and may hinder the development of therapeutic relationships and a positive therapeutic process (Harris & Fallot, 2001). There is seemingly universal acknowledgment that exposure to trauma and abuse contributes to aggression and other problem behaviors in children, with some of the most effective interventions based on a trauma-informed social information processing model addressing the abused child's faulty ways of interpreting the world (Dodge, Godwin, & Conduct Problems Prevention Research Group, 2013). These difficulties resulting from early trauma often do not resolve when abused children reach adulthood, and not surprisingly, there is an extensive research base indicating that both childhood and adult trauma are linked with abusive and violent behavior in intimate relationships (Capaldi, Knoble, Shortt, & Kim, 2012; Davis et al., 2018).

There is an increasing recognition that models of IPV that do not take trauma into consideration are incomplete and may impede the success of prevention and treatment of violent behavior. Research demonstrates that models of IPV that incorporate trauma are relevant for both military and civilian populations and linked with the most effective interventions (see Taft, Murphy, & Creech, 2016), and there has been some movement in the general IPV intervention field to better train counselors on trauma and its impacts.

In this chapter we also highlight that in order for an IPV intervention to be truly intersectional and inclusive, and meet the needs of the general population, it must also be trauma-informed. To effectively intervene with diverse clients who experience racism, sexism, and other forms of ongoing and historical trauma, it is important that the provider work to understand their experience so that they can assist clients in developing insight and collaborative therapeutic relationships. We do not view trauma-informed intervention as relevant for only a subset of IPV perpetrators, because no abusive client is without any prior trauma or other prior life event(s) that have shaped the way that they view others and that impacts their behavior in interpersonal relationships.

## Defining trauma

As defined in the DSM-5, traumatic stress involves "exposure to actual or threatened death, serious injury, or sexual violence" (APA, 2013, p. 271), and the diagnostic criterion allows for exposure through witnessing such events in person, finding out that a traumatic event has occurred to a close family member or friend, or being exposed in a repeated or extreme fashion to the unpleasant details of a traumatic event (i.e. vicarious traumatization).

We have previously argued that this definition of trauma is too limited and doesn't capture non-physical forms of abuse that are strongly linked to PTSD and other trauma reactions, such as emotional abuse, in which a child or adult is denigrated, humiliated, devalued, or intimidated; significant abandonment and detachment experiences; emotional neglect; and physical neglect (Taft, Murphy, & Creech, 2016). Similar to physical and sexual violence exposure, psychological abuse and neglect can alter core beliefs and emotions regarding safety, closeness, trust, power, and control, which are linked with abusive behavior in adulthood (Lamotte, Taft, & Weatherill, 2016).

Based on empirical evidence, scholars have also called for DSM-5 criteria to be expanded to include experiences of oppression (Holmes, Facemire, & DaFonseca, 2016) because it is too narrow in relation to "threat to life," when "threat to life" is a constant for particular racial/ethnic groups. Black and Latino men in particular encounter disturbingly high levels of race-based trauma (i.e. racial discrimination) in the US, which has a significant impact on their psychosocial well-being (Myers et al., 2015). These daily experiences trigger pains from the past, intensifying ones survived in the present. Experiencing oppression and racism at the individual, institutional, and structural level is traumatic. Trauma is comprised not only of one-time events, but can be insidious, and Black and Latinx people in America are especially vulnerable to daily instances of race-based trauma. Ultimately, racism is not time-specific, but perpetual.

Of the many forms of trauma that have been examined as predictors of IPV perpetration, one factor that has not been explored sufficiently is race-based trauma. Indeed, "In the US . . . racism and racist structures, as they determine access to land, wealth, and labor, have maintained inequality and perpetuated trauma quite literally from the country's birth as the US" (Leisey & Lewis, n.d., p. 38). Conceptually and theoretically, historical trauma has only recently been included in public health literature as a way of explaining various health disparities (Brave Heart, 1995; Leary, 2001; Sotero, 2006). According to Leisey and Lewis (p. 31, n.d.), "Historical trauma is the result of human actions and/or human-made systems and structures; in other words, there is a group that directly or indirectly caused the collective trauma of another group."

## Trauma-informed social information processing model of IPV

Trauma-informed IPV intervention is supported by the trauma-informed social information processing model (see Taft, Macdonald, Creech, Monson, & Murphy, 2016). As is the case with those exhibiting a variety of problem behaviors, how one perceives and interprets their social world is of central importance, and helping individuals to view others and their environment in a less hostile or threatening way is a key goal for therapy. With respect to individuals with histories of trauma, this process typically involves helping them to make more positive, and fewer negative, interpretations of their social world, because trauma exposure can produce biases and deficits in social information processing that place individuals at risk for engaging in violence (Taft et al., 2015). Thus, it follows that developing a better understanding of how the client's processing of social information has been impacted by trauma, and helping the client unlearn biases and interpret various social situations in a more accurate fashion, should lead to healthier relationships and a reduction in IPV.

McFall (1982) developed a highly influential model that involves three sequential stages through which elements of social information are transformed into responses or task performances. During the first step, the encoding stage, incoming information is received, perceived, and interpreted in relation to meaning structures available to the individual. Difficulties at this stage may be caused by inattention or distraction, as well as misinterpretation of social information. The second step, the decision-making stage, involves generating possible responses and evaluating response options. Response choice is influenced by the individual's understanding of what is expected in the situation, appraisals of one's ability to carry out various responses, and potential costs and benefits of the response options. The final step is the enactment stage, during which the individual carries out the selected response and monitors and evaluates its impact. A number of factors can influence social information processing at any stage, such as mood state, stress level, and substance use.

A very large research base demonstrates social information processing deficits among those who engage in IPV (Anglin & Holtzworth-Munroe, 1997; Clements, Holtzworth-Munroe, Schweinle, & Ickes, 2007; Eckhardt, Barbour, & Davison, 1998; Eckhardt & Jamison, 2002; Eckhardt & Kassinove, 1998; Holtzworth-Munroe & Anglin, 1991; Holtzworth-Munroe & Hutchinson, 1993; Marshall & Holtzworth-Munroe, 2010). Researchers have long argued that trauma and PTSD are strongly linked with aggressive behavior in part because those with PTSD are more likely to perceive threats in their environment due to their prior experience of trauma and life threat (e.g. Novaco & Chemtob, 1998; Taft, Vogt, Marshall, Panuzio, & Niles, 2007). In other words, these individuals become physiologically and cognitively wired to misperceive social cues and inappropriately respond with aggression. Consistent with this notion, our group has shown PTSD "hyperarousal" symptoms to be most strongly linked with IPV (Taft, Street, Marshall, Dowdall, & Riggs, 2007; Taft, Schumm, Marshall, Panuzio, & Holtzworth-Munroe, 2008), and our work also demonstrates indirect effects of PTSD through social information processing deficits (Taft et al., 2008, 2015). Other researchers have found that those with PTSD may be more likely to misperceive ambiguous partner behaviors as rejecting and this may contribute to social information processing deficits and IPV (Sippel & Marshall, 2011).

Several other problems can result from trauma, such as depression, alcohol use problems, and traumatic brain injury, that may also elevate IPV risk through their impact on social information processing (see Heyman, Taft, Howard, Macdonald, & Collins, 2012). Further, the experience of trauma can have a profound effect on the way that individuals view the world, and even absent a psychiatric diagnosis, there are several core themes affected by trauma that may have an impact on how one processes social information, such as difficulties with trust, power and control, self- and other-esteem (Monson et al., 2006; Resick & Schnicke, 1992). These themes may be particularly important to address in trauma-informed IPV interventions as they may represent core beliefs that underlie and maintain abusive behavior.

Racial discrimination is connected to biases in social information processing, insomuch that survivors of race-based trauma are more likely to be leery or suspect malicious intentions of others in order to maintain their own safety and survival (Taft, Murphy, Elliott, & Keaser, 2001). However, when those perceptions of threat transfer to how one views their intimate partner, the sequence may transform from a protective mechanism to one behaving harmfully against their partners (Holtzworth-Munroe, 1992). This is especially important to take into account when working with men of color who may face chronic trauma by way of repeated daily ethnoracial discrimination.

Scholars have posited a relationship between structural racism and IPV perpetration, with various mediators such as stress or unemployment further explaining the connection. Powell (2008) suggested more than ten years ago that experiencing racial discrimination and oppression impacts social information processing, which may thereby partially explain higher rates of IPV perpetration among Black men. Though few studies have moved beyond theory into testing these ideas, Reed et al. (2010) was the first to examine this relationship empirically. She and her colleagues found that Black men who survived high levels of racial discrimination were almost twice as likely to perpetrate IPV than those who experienced low levels of race-based discrimination. Another recent study confirmed that there is indeed an indirect effect between racial discrimination and IPV perpetration via attributional biases. Using longitudinal data, Sutton and colleagues (2019) found that racial discrimination experienced in adolescence was indirectly linked to IPV perpetration in young adulthood through anger and hostile attribution bias. Simply put, racial discrimination predicts greater anger and stronger appraisals of others as malicious (due to deficits in social information processing), which in turn are linked to IPV perpetration. Furthermore, the tested model explained nearly 18% of the variance in IPV perpetration, meaning that a substantial portion of IPV perpetration that occurs amongst Black men can be explained by surviving racial discrimination.

## Process considerations

Process factors refer to the nonspecific factors that may influence treatment outcomes beyond the use of specific therapy techniques, such as the therapeutic alliance, motivational readiness for change, and group cohesion. Some in the field have argued that standard IPV programs downplay the importance of process factors shown to promote success in other areas of directed behavior change (Daniels & Murphy, 1997; Jennings, 1987; Murphy & Baxter, 1997), and these programs may resort to confrontational tactics that are anti-therapeutic (Mankowski, Haaken, & Silvergild, 2002; Murphy & Baxter, 1997; Taft & Murphy, 2007) and that reinforce negative core themes around issues related to power and control (Murphy & Baxter, 1997; Safran & Muran, 1996). This is concerning because across a range of populations, process factors are often more influential in determining successful outcome than type of intervention employed (Krupnick et al., 1996).

Trauma histories can significantly impact the process of therapy, and it may require greater effort on the part of the provider to facilitate a positive therapeutic environment. Previously discussed themes that may be affected by trauma, such as difficulties with trust, self-esteem, or power and control often play out in therapeutic relationships. Therefore, our efforts to facilitate a positive alliance take on even greater importance when working with a highly traumatized population.

The most heavily studied process factor in IPV intervention research has been the therapeutic alliance, which refers to agreement on the goals and tasks related to therapy, as well as the bond formed between client and therapist (Bordin, 1979). Though it is admittedly often difficult to form a positive therapeutic alliance with abusive clients, a strong alliance is crucial in motivating these individuals for changing their behavior. If abusive clients do not believe the therapist is there to help them, and do not agree with the goals and tasks of treatment, they will not work towards developing new coping strategies and better ways to handle their anger. Further, clients will have difficulty in exploring how prior unresolved trauma may impact their current abusive behavior if they do not have a positive therapeutic relationship (Sonkin & Dutton, 2003). Multiple studies have now shown that a positive therapeutic alliance is associated with reductions in abusive behavior in IPV intervention programs (Brown & O'Leary, 2000; Rosenberg, 2003; Santiago, del Castillo, Carbajosa, & Marcuello, 2013; Taft, Murphy, King, Musser, & DeDeyn, 2003), as well as greater program compliance (Brown, O'Leary, & Feldbau, 1997; Cadsky, Hanson, Crawford, & Lalonde, 1996; Rondeau, Brodeur, Brochu, & Lemire, 2001).

Prochaska and DiClemente's transtheoretical model (1982, 1992) has been used extensively across a range of clinical fields to describe how individuals undergo intentional behavior change (Evers et al., 2012; Heather, Honekopp, & Smailes, 2009; Levesque, Gelles, & Velicer, 2000; Prochaska, Johnson, & Lee, 2009). One key element of the model focuses on five stages of change (pre-contemplation, contemplation, preparation, action, maintenance) representing distinct cognitive markers which individuals pass through in order to undergo successful behavior change. This model may be particularly relevant with regard to those pressured or mandated to receive IPV intervention, considering they are particularly likely to be in earlier stages of change (O'Hare, 1996) and lack accountability for abusive behavior. Confrontational therapist tactics with other "resistant" populations are associated with higher client resistance and poorer outcomes, whereas higher therapist expressions of support and empathy are predictive of less resistance and better outcomes (Miller, Benefield, & Tonigan, 1993; Miller, Taylor, & West, 1980). In IPV intervention, more confrontational provider behaviors may lead the client to negatively react and not join with the provider in working to change behavior. In contrast, some work has shown motivational techniques to facilitate intervention compliance and enhance outcomes in IPV intervention (Alexander, Morris, Tracy, & Frye, 2010; Murphy & Maiuro, 2009; Scott, King, McGinn, & Hosseini, 2011; Taft, Murphy, Elliott, & Morrel, 2001).

Taking a trauma-informed therapeutic approach does not mean that we "collude" with clients in their victim-blaming, denial, or minimization of abuse (Corvo & Johnson, 2003; Voith, Logan-Greene, Strodthoff, & Bender, 2018). Rather, we are clear with the individual that they are responsible for their abusive behavior, but take this stance in the context of a relationship where there is genuine interest in understanding the client and recognizing how the client has learned their abusive patterns. We work to understand the prior traumas and negative life events that the client has experienced and how this impacts their current relationships, communicating to the client that we recognize they are not abusive by nature. When we work to understand them and how their problems developed, we get away from stigmatizing or labeling them simply as "batterers" and show that we are listening to their stories. Rabbi Daniel Cotzin Burg simply summarizes the point by emphasizing that, "to humanize is not to justify acts of terror . . . [in fact] . . . dehumanization removes accountability" (Burg, 2011). Spending time in early sessions to understand the client's experiences, including their trauma histories, leads our clients to more openly discuss their abusive behavior and make genuine efforts to change. Validating the client's difficulties is also very therapeutic. Again, this does not mean that we validate statements suggesting victim-blaming or minimization of IPV, but rather to validate their personal struggles and acknowledge the impacts that trauma and related problems have had on them. The provider should be careful to maintain a stance of understanding and validation while not joining the client in rejecting their own role in their problems.

Group cohesion – the connectedness of the group and the degree to which the members are able to work together constructively to further the therapeutic work – has been associated with positive therapeutic outcomes in diverse clinical populations (Ellis, Peterson, Bufford, & Benson, 2014; Gallagher, Tasca, Ritchie, Bafour, & Bissada, 2014; Joyce, Piper, & Ogrodniczuk,

Casey T. Taft et al.

2007; Schnur & Montgomery, 2010), including men in IPV intervention programs (Rosenberg, 2003; Taft et al., 2003). A primary goal of the provider in trauma-informed IPV intervention is to develop a collective sense that group members need to take positive and proactive steps to change their behavior. Facilitation of a positive group environment is likely to be especially important when working with trauma-exposed groups. Trauma-exposed individuals may have a more difficult time trusting others, and establishing and maintaining relationships may be particularly challenging. The sharing of experiences in the group context among those who have difficulty with relationships may be especially powerful given that these group members may have no other sources for advice or support. Moreover, when individuals have experienced a similar trauma, they may develop an especially powerful bond. Providers are likely to be more effective if they can facilitate an environment in which group members teach one another and process issues, rather than "teaching" the information in a more didactic format. While discussion of the myriad strategies and principles important in facilitating positive group process is beyond the scope of this chapter, we refer the reader to Yalom's (1995) work on the fundamental principles and practices for experiential group psychotherapy, and our prior discussion of how trauma relates to these principles and practices (Taft, Macdonald et al., 2016).

## Oppression-sensitive IPV intervention

Amidst the broad call for evidence-based intervention for IPV perpetration, especially ones effective among racial minorities (Babcock et al., 2016), we contend that oppression-sensitive IPV interventions which recognize oppression as historical trauma could help improve treatment outcomes for Black, Native American, and Latino men. Although culturally focused programming for African American men has been explored (Gondolf & Williams, 2001), we emphasize why implementing culturally tailored programs that are also trauma-informed is so crucial.

Dr. Oliver Williams has been writing about the potential of culturally tailored programming for Black men since the early 1990s (Williams, 1994, 1995), which, in particular, were thought to have a positive impact on Black men with higher racial pride (Gondolf & Williams, 2001). This is notable because as Kirmayer, Gone, and Moses (2014) highlight, denigration of identity may be linked to lower self-esteem, which in turn may perpetuate IPV perpetration. Perhaps racial pride needs to first be built up, or experiences of racism need to be processed before programming can have meaningful impacts. In essence, culturally sensitive programming may only be meaningful if the program and process is truly trauma-informed and guided by a humanistic approach. Though one experimental study found that, when compared to a conventional cognitive behavioral therapy intervention, culturally focused programming for Black men did not yield additional benefit (Gondolf, 2007), the expert assessing treatment integrity questioned the fidelity of the counselor who conducted the culturally focused counseling sessions (Gondolf, 2010).

Clearly, further research studies are needed to advance our knowledge on the potential of culturally specific IPV intervention for Black men. Even a small degree of intentionality could have substantial impacts. For example, in one IPV treatment study, when group facilitators sent hand-written notes to those who missed a treatment session, this reduced dropout rates among Black clients, but not white clients, suggesting that out-of-session supportive therapist communications may be particularly important for the former group (Taft et al., 2001).

Evaluation of culturally sensitive intervention for Latino men is even scarcer compared to research on Black men. Such programs have been manualized (Welland & Ribner, 2010) but

we were unable to locate any published quasi-experimental or randomized controlled trials examining treatment effects. As for programming for indigenous men, although there has been a call for tailored programming (Day, Jones, Nakata, & McDermott, 2012), we could not locate manualized publication or the results of empirical testing.

As the evidence for trauma-informed treatment for people who engage in IPV grows (Schauss, Zettler, & Russell, 2019), it is essential that these interventions address the historical and ongoing trauma of racism where applicable (Aymer, 2011). If not, the impacts of addressing childhood or other trauma alone will be limited. Leisey and Lewis (n.d.) note that social and psychological service providers "must be historical trauma-informed and fully take into account the community's history, experience of historical trauma, and ways in which intervention might be perpetuating trauma, retraumatizing, and/or increasing the effects of a historical trauma response." Moreover, "As long as systems are unchallenged by those that influence them, groups whose power appears in oppressive structures will maintain historical trauma in groups they influence" (p. 73, n.d.).

## Example of trauma-informed group intervention #1: *Strength at Home*

*Strength at Home* is a group IPV intervention based on the trauma-informed social information processing model holding that trauma may negatively impact one's ability to interpret and respond to social situations and social cues effectively, and highlights the importance of cognitive behavioral strategies to monitor one's thoughts and responses to interpersonal situations (Taft, Macdonald et al., 2016). The intervention derives from a unique fusion of interventions for trauma and IPV, integrating elements of cognitive processing therapy for PTSD (Resick, Monson, & Chard, 2008), couples therapy for PTSD (Monson et al., 2012), and a cognitive behavioral intervention for IPV (Murphy & Scott, 1996). The program consists of 12 two-hour weekly sessions, co-led by one to two providers. Throughout the program, group members complete in-session practice exercises and are provided "practice assignments" to consolidate and apply information learned in group.

The model derives from prior theory and research indicating that those who are exposed to trauma and other negative life events are more likely to exhibit irrational beliefs, problematic thinking, and faulty interpretations of others' intentions (Holtzworth-Munroe, 1992; McFall, 1982; Anglin & Holtzworth-Munroe, 1997; Eckhardt et al., 1998). Through the improvement of social information processing, conflict and risk for aggression and violence should decrease. Core themes that underlie social information processing and relationship problems, including those related to power and control conflicts, low self-esteem, and trust difficulties are also addressed throughout the program.

See Figure 39.1 for how the *Strength at Home* intervention components map onto the social information processing model. Decoding skills are developed through increased insight into how trauma-related problems and core themes underlying negative life events impact how we receive, perceive, and interpret social information from others, including intimate partners. Considerable work throughout group focuses on assisting group members in identifying and replacing negatively biased thoughts. Group members are also taught to develop more realistic expectations of outcomes and consider the costs and benefits of responses, and group leaders use the group process to assist in enhancing self-efficacy (Decision Skills Stage). To assist group members in enacting more effective responses, skills in communication, stress and anger management, and responsiveness to social feedback are emphasized.

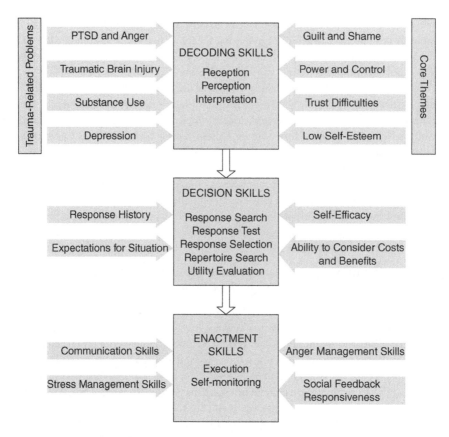

*Figure 39.1* Trauma-informed social information processing model

## *Evidence for* Strength at Home

We have published pilot studies (Taft, Macdonald, Monson, Walling, Resick, & Murphy, 2013), implementation studies (Creech, Benzer, Ebalu, Murphy, & Taft, 2018; Hayes, Gallagher, Gilbert, Creech, DeCandia, Beach, & Taft, 2015; Love, Morland, Taft, MacDonald, & Mackintosh, 2015), and a randomized controlled trial (Taft, Macdonald et al., 2016) all attesting to the effectiveness of *Strength at Home* and the feasibility of effectively implementing the program. The program is the only such IPV intervention program shown effective for a military/veteran sample in a clinical trial, and is the only program officially endorsed in a national IPV program rollout in the US Department of Veterans Affairs.

It is particularly important to highlight the randomized controlled trial funded by the Department of Defense (Taft, Macdonald et al., 2016). Controlled trials are critical for determining the efficacy of any IPV intervention program because there are so many factors that can lead to decreases in IPV (e.g. protective orders, court monitoring, shelter seeking in victims, other forms of intervention) that we must compare those who receive the active intervention with those who do not receive the intervention. Simply showing pre-intervention to post-intervention change for an IPV intervention tells us very little about whether the program is effective or not; we must compare those receiving the intervention to a comparison group who receives other (or no) intervention.

For this study of 135 veterans and service members, we compared those assigned to *Strength at Home* to those in an *enhanced treatment as usual* condition. Those in enhanced treatment as usual were free to receive any other care or abuser intervention within or outside of the treatment setting, and they were provided treatment referrals by the study staff if indicated. Results demonstrated significant time-by-condition effects such that *Strength at Home* participants evidenced relatively more reductions in physical and psychological IPV over time, as indicated by veteran/service member and partner reports of IPV on the Revised Conflict Tactics Scales (Straus, Hamby, Boney-McCoy, & Sugarman, 1996). Physical IPV recidivism (Figure 39.2) was also significantly higher in enhanced treatment as usual (43.3%) compared to *Strength at Home* (23.3%) at post-treatment. Differences remained at three-month follow-up, with 26.7% recidivism in enhanced treatment as usual and only 18.5% recidivism in *Strength at Home*.

We have published two follow-up studies of this randomized controlled trial that further attest to the effectiveness of *Strength at Home*. The first (Creech, Macdonald, Benzer, Poole, Murphy, & Taft, 2017) showed that (1) those in *enhanced treatment as usual* further reduced their IPV after receiving *Strength at Home* following the trial; (2) physical IPV was 56% less likely for those receiving *Strength at Home* overall; and (3) participants with and without PTSD benefitted from *Strength at Home*, showing that the intervention is broadly efficacious. The second follow-up study (Berke et al., 2017) demonstrated that *Strength at Home* was effective relative to enhanced treatment as usual in reducing symptoms of alexithymia (Figure 39.3), suggesting that the intervention may be impactful at least in part due to its enhancement of the identification and expression of emotions.

We have been implementing *Strength at Home* across the VA healthcare system in partnership with VA leadership and through funding from the Bob Woodruff Foundation and Blue Shield of California Foundation. Thus far, *Strength at Home* is in place at more than 50 hospitals and close to 1,000 individuals have received the intervention. Through this implementation, those receiving *Strength at Home* evidenced reductions in both physical and psychological IPV, as well as symptoms of PTSD (Creech et al., 2018).

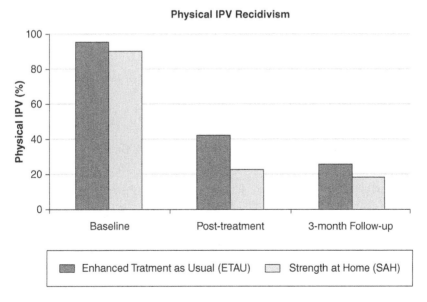

*Figure 39.2*   Physical IPV recidivism rates by condition

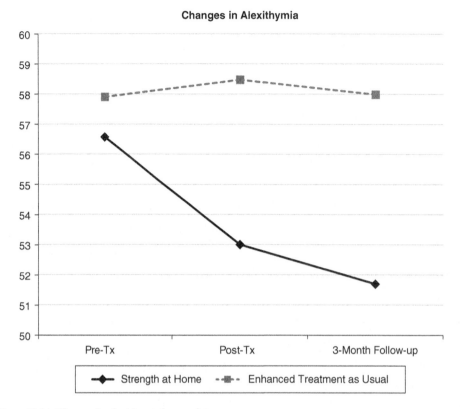

*Figure 39.3*   Changes in alexithymia by condition

We have recently conducted a NIMH pilot study to evaluate whether reductions in IPV extend to court-mandated civilians receiving *Strength at Home* in Rhode Island. Recent, as yet unpublished data from 20 participants shows large reductions in physical IPV ($t = 2.59$, $p < .05$, $r = .54$) and psychological IPV ($t = 2.48$, $p < .05$, $r = .53$). Interestingly, 88% of participants reported they would "definitely" recommend the program to a friend, and 100% reported the program helped them deal more effectively with their problems. Thus, initial data is quite promising regarding the fit and effectiveness of *Strength at Home* for the civilian population.

## Example of trauma-informed group intervention #2: "the men's group" at St. Pius V parish

The Men's Group (TMG) in Chicago, Illinois is a spirituality-based, trauma-informed, and voluntary IPV intervention that is culturally specific to Spanish-speaking Latino men. Over 400 men have participated in TMG (without court mandate), and many remain in the group for several years. The program is unique in several ways compared to most IPV intervention programs in the US (Cannon, Hamel, Buttell, & Ferreira, 2016). Here, we first explain why the program is defined as spirituality-based, then focus on the findings related to why it is defined as a trauma-informed program.

### Defining the men's group: spirituality-based versus faith-based

Given the self-reported importance of spirituality in the lives of Black, Native, and Latino men (Hubbert, 2011; Fisher-Townsend, 2018; Welland & Ribner, 2010), we highlight TMG as just one example of a program incorporating many of the considerations discussed throughout this chapter. Interview, focus group, and observational TMG data consistently indicate that TMG does not purport that reliance upon God or belief in a specific religion is required in order to change abusive behaviors. Yet, all group participants and administrators rejected the idea that TMG should be classified as a secular program. There are many ways to define "faith-based" or "spirituality-based" social service organizations. The decision in favor of the term spirituality-based was determined because explicitly religious content (i.e. proselytization, worship) was not incorporated as part of the curriculum.

### Defining the men's group: trauma-informed

We characterize TMG as trauma-informed largely based on the data collected during multiple observations of group sessions, which indicated that process considerations are paramount to the function and delivery of the program. Some of the most notable elements demonstrating sensitivity to trauma are revealed in how basic communication occurs during group sessions. For example, participants are not interrupted or spoken to in a combative manner, and are encouraged to share their experiences of ethnoracial discrimination, which are recognized as potentially traumatic and thus viewed as central to the process of addressing IPV perpetration. Furthermore, the intervention is not restricted to weekly group sessions alone, but is much more flexible to participant needs, recognizing the need for individualized, group, and extended care. As one administrator noted, "The group is not only every Wednesday . . . it's 24 hours a day, and seven days a week." While material on how men are impacted by trauma is incorporated into the content, the aforementioned process considerations were equally important in ensuring that the intervention truly operates from a trauma-informed perspective.

### Evidence for the men's group

A case study and process evaluation (Davis, Jonson-Reid, Stoops, & Sabri, in press) revealed that the reason men remain engaged in TMG over time (in tandem with peer support) was largely due to the sense of respect they experienced from group facilitators and staff, highlighting the importance of process in practice (see Figure 39.4). This factor is evidence of facilitators and the program founders establishing a commitment to creating a space and group environment that values positive therapeutic alliance. Furthermore, according to interview and observational data, the context of the community environment was noted as a significant factor that facilitated the feasibility and acceptability of this program.

While data for a longitudinal impact evaluation is currently being collected, the results of a few completed qualitative investigations shed light on why participants view the program to be beneficial and how they arrived at seeking help from TMG (Davis, Fernandez, Jonson-Reid, & Kyriakakis, 2019). Next are a few quotes illustrating the qualitative impact of TMG.

> What I like most is how my counselor responds to me . . . not in the way I want to hear, because if I wanted for him to respond with what I want to hear, well then, (laughs) I'm wasting my time there. He responds to me like a total professional. After

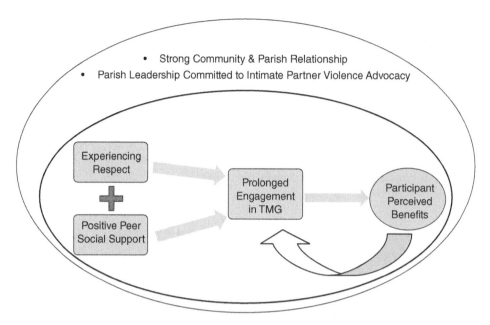

*Figure 39.4*  Emerging theoretical model for prolonged engagement of non-court mandated men in a parish-based partner abuse intervention program

he's heard me, he has all the time and the patience. Sometimes I've extended myself with him two to three hours. He has a lot of patience.

– Focus group participant

I couldn't argue with my emotions. There came a point I had given up and I knew I needed help, so I looked. My ex-mother-in-law told me about the group and that I could change. . . . Now, after two years [of being a member], I've seen it's a community of men where one helps the other and one can open oneself and without repercussions and without judgment, but they give us tools to help make our lives better and that's why I've stayed in this group because I know that in this group, I have found more than help. I have found friends.

– Focus group participant

Without the group, I don't know where I would be now, maybe in jail and she'd [my wife] be in the hospital or vice versa, or one of us in the cemetery or both of us, because the situation was just really bad. Of course, the group has had a positive impact . . . if it wasn't for the group I don't know where my life would be now.

– Interview #6

I have liked the group because of the experiences of the other men, learning from that and reflecting on my own life as well as the tips that Carlos [group facilitator] has given us and how to handle the anger, how to treat others and be more patient and calm. Reading some of the books and [discussing] our experiences with others [also helps].

– Interview #4

## Summary and conclusions

We have discussed the role of trauma in IPV etiology, outlined the importance of trauma- and oppression-informed IPV intervention, provided empirically supported examples of these interventions, and given guidance on facilitating a positive therapeutic environment. While there is increasing recognition of the importance of trauma-informed IPV programs, as of yet most state-certified programs do not address trauma in their curriculum, and there is relatively little coordination between IPV intervention programs and those offering services related to trauma. Further, almost every state in the United States has mandated intervention standards which are not based in scientific evidence, most specifying excessive program lengths, and many proscribing a focus on trauma. Another challenge in providing quality trauma-informed IPV intervention is that providers in some community-based programs have little or no training in trauma-informed care, and may have even been instructed during their training to ignore individual's histories of trauma or to interpret these experiences as irrelevant to the goals of IPV intervention. Finally, there is a general lack of adequate services for self-referred clients, and a reliance on lengthy and ineffective court-mandated "batterer" programs that are often stigmatizing and unappealing to those who are self-motivated to work on their problems related to trauma and violence.

If we are to overcome these barriers and make a true shift towards more effective trauma-informed intervention, it is critical that we stop denying the role of trauma in increasing IPV risk, and recognize that acknowledging trauma in the intervention context only serves to enhance and not diminish personal accountability. If we listen to our clients and truly hear their stories of trauma, and the client feels heard and understood, they will be more likely to take responsibility for their abusive behavior and challenge others to do the same. We need to carefully consider the fact that randomized controlled trials do not support interventions that are not trauma-informed, and rather than tinkering around the margins by trying to modify ineffective programs, we should be replacing them altogether with more effective options. It will take bold leadership on the part of many to decide that what we have been doing for so long simply is not working as it should, and at the very least, whatever guidelines are in place should encourage innovation and research on program efficacy, and should not prevent effective programs from operating. A shift to a more trauma-informed approach without stigmatizing labels on our clients should encourage more people to voluntarily seek services. We know of no more basic principle of behavior change than the fact that others will be more likely to listen to us and want to change their problematic behavior if they feel heard and understood themselves.

## Critical findings

- Trauma and trauma-related problems are among the strongest risk factors for intimate partner violence (IPV).
- A trauma-informed social information processing model has been used to explain common links between trauma and IPV and validated by numerous studies.
- This model should be expanded to incorporate the role of the experience of racism as a stressor that may impact risk for violence.
- At this time, few trauma-informed interventions for IPV perpetration have been developed, tested, and disseminated to the field.
- Even fewer interventions have been developed and tested for use in ethnic minority communities, who experience unique stressors such as racism and prejudice in addition to high rates of trauma – both personal and historical.

- However, two trauma-informed IPV interventions, *Strength at Home* and The Men's Group, have demonstrated efficacy in reducing IPV amongst trauma-exposed individuals.
- Culturally tailored, oppression-sensitive IPV interventions which recognize oppression as historical trauma could help improve treatment outcomes and are essential to robust trauma-informed care.
- Empirical research on culturally tailored, trauma-informed IPV interventions amongst Black, Latinx, and Native American communities is scarce and represents a serious gap in the literature that must be addressed.

# Implications for policy, practice, and research

## *Policy*

- The definition of trauma should be expanded to include non-physical forms of abuse and experiences of oppression (e.g. racism, sexism, homophobia/heterosexism), which have been linked to PTSD and negative psychosocial outcomes in empirical studies.
- Given the strong link between trauma-exposure and IPV use, there should be increased coordination between IPV intervention programs and those offering services related to trauma.
- IPV intervention standards at the state level must be revised in accordance with empirical evidence which suggests the efficacy of trauma-informed interventions.
- IPV intervention services should be adapted and expanded to be inclusive of and appealing to self-referred clients, who may be deterred from seeking help by stigmatizing and overly long mandated intervention programs.

## *Practice*

- Clinicians and intervention programs must be sensitive to clients' experiences of trauma and oppression, how these experiences impact risk for IPV perpetration, and how acknowledgment and validation of these experiences can promote a positive therapeutic alliance and behavior change.
- IPV intervention facilitators should receive training on trauma and its impacts, particularly its association with risk for violence.
- Facilitation of a positive and cohesive group environment is key to promoting positive behavior change and reducing violence use amongst trauma-exposed individuals.

## *Research*

- More research is needed to examine the efficacy of culturally specific, trauma-informed interventions.
- Given the stakes of partner and family safety, randomized controlled trials are essential in IPV intervention research as many non-intervention factors can lead to short-term decreases in IPV (e.g. protective orders, court monitoring, shelter seeking in victims, other forms of intervention) and can overestimate program efficacy in pre- to post-intervention studies.

# References

Alexander, P. C., Morris, E., Tracy, A., & Frye, A. (2010). Stages of change and the group treatment of batterers: A randomized clinical trial. *Violence and Victims, 25*(5), 571–587.

American Psychiatric Association. (2013). *Diagnostic and statistical manual of mental disorders* (5th ed.). Arlington, VA: Author.

Anglin, K., & Holtzworth-Munroe, A. (1997). Comparing the responses of maritally violent and nonviolent spouses to problematic marital and nonmarital situations: Are the skill deficits of physically aggressive husbands and wives global? *Journal of Family Psychology, 11*(3), 301–313.

Aymer, S. R. (2011). A case for including the "lived experience" of African American men in batterers' treatment. *Journal of African American Studies, 15*(3), 352–366.

Babcock, J., Armenti, N., Cannon, C., Lauve-Moon, K., Buttell, F., Ferreira, R., . . . Lehmann, P. (2016). Domestic violence perpetrator programs: A proposal for evidence-based standards in the United States. *Partner Abuse, 7*(4), 355–460.

Berke, D. S., Macdonald, A., Poole, G. M., Portnoy, G. A., McSheffrey, S., Creech, S. K., & Taft, C. T. (2017). Optimizing trauma-informed intervention for intimate partner violence in veterans: The role of alexithymia. *Behaviour Research and Therapy, 97*, 222–229. https://doi.org/10.1016/j.brat.2017.08.007

Bordin, E. S. (1979). The generalizability of the psychoanalytic concept of the working alliance. *Psychotherapy: Theory, Research & Practice, 16*(3), 252–260.

Brave Heart, M. Y. H. (1995). *The return to the sacred path; Healing from Historical Trauma and historical unresolved grief among the Lakota* (Unpublished dissertation), Smith College School of Social Work, Northampton, MA.

Brown, P. D., & O'Leary, K. D. (2000). Therapeutic alliance: Predicting continuance and success in group treatment for spouse abuse. *Journal of Consulting and Clinical Psychology, 68*(2), 340–345.

Brown, P. D., O'Leary, K. D., & Feldbau, S. R. (1997). Dropout in a treatment program for self-referring wife abusing men. *Journal of Family Violence, 12*(4), 365–387.

Burg, D. C. (2011, May). *Humanizing the enemy.* Retrieved from https://bethambaltimore.org/religiouslife/sermons/humanizing-the-enemy/

Cadsky, O., Hanson, R. K., Crawford, M., & Lalonde, C. (1996). Attrition from a male batterer treatment program: Client-treatment congruence and lifestyle instability. *Violence and Victims, 11*(1), 51–64.

Cannon, C., Hamel, J., Buttell, F., & Ferreira, R. J. (2016). A survey of domestic violence perpetrator programs in the United States and Canada: Findings and implications for policy and intervention. *Partner Abuse, 7*(3), 226–276.

Capaldi, D. M., Knoble, N. B., Shortt, J. W., & Kim, H. K. (2012). A systematic review of risk factors for intimate partner violence. *Partner Abuse, 3*(2), 231–280.

Clements, K., Holtzworth-Munroe, A., Schweinle, W., & Ickes, W. (2007). Empathic accuracy of intimate partners in violent versus nonviolent relationships. *Personal Relationships, 14*(3), 369–388.

Corvo, K., & Johnson, P. J. (2003). Vilification of the "batterer": How blame shapes domestic violence policy and interventions. *Aggression and Violent Behavior, 8*(3), 259–281.

Creech, S. K., Benzer, J. K., Ebalu, T., Murphy, C. M., & Taft, C. T. (2018). National implementation of a trauma-informed intervention for intimate partner violence in the department of veterans affairs: First year outcomes. *BMC Health Services Research, 18*(1), 582. https://doi.org/10.1186/s12913-018-3401-6

Creech, S. K., Macdonald, A., Benzer, J. K., Poole, G. M., Murphy, C. M., & Taft, C. T. (2017). PTSD symptoms predict outcome in trauma-informed treatment of intimate partner aggression. *Journal of Consulting and Clinical Psychology, 85*(10), 966–974. https://doi.org/10.1037/ccp0000228

Daniels, J. W., & Murphy, C. M. (1997). Stages and processes of change in batterers' treatment. *Cognitive and Behavioral Practice, 4*(1), 123–145.

Davis, K. C., Masters, N. T., Casey, E., Kajumulo, K. F., Norris, J., & George, W. H. (2018). How childhood maltreatment profiles of male victims predict adult perpetration and psychosocial functioning. *Journal of Interpersonal Violence, 33*(6), 915–937.

Davis, M., Dahm, C., Jonson-Reid, M., Stoops, C., & Sabri, B. (in press). "The men's group" at St. Pius V: A case study of a parish-based voluntary partner abuse intervention program. *American Journal of Men's Health.*

Davis, M., Fernandez, B., Jonson-Reid, M., & Kyriakakis, S. (2019). Pathways to seeking help from a partner abuse intervention program: A qualitative study of voluntary and non-court mandated Latino men's experiences. *Journal of Interpersonal Violence,* 1–25.

Day, A., Jones, R., Nakata, M., & McDermott, D. (2012). Indigenous family violence: An attempt to understand the problems and inform appropriate and effective responses to criminal justice system intervention. *Psychiatry, Psychology and Law, 19*(1), 104–117.

Dodge, K. A., Godwin, J., & The Conduct Problems Prevention Research Group. (2013). Social-information-processing patterns mediate the impact of preventive intervention on adolescent antisocial behavior. *Psychological Science, 24*(4), 456–465.

Eckhardt, C. I., Barbour, K. A., & Davison, G. C. (1998). Articulated thoughts of maritally violent and nonviolent men during anger arousal. *Journal of Consulting and Clinical Psychology, 66*(2), 259–269.

Eckhardt, C. I., & Jamison, T. R. (2002). Articulated thoughts of male dating violence perpetrators during anger arousal. *Cognitive Therapy and Research, 26*(3), 289–308.

Eckhardt, C. I., & Kassinove, H. (1998). Articulated cognitive distortions and cognitive deficiencies in maritally violent men. *Journal of Cognitive Psychotherapy, 12*(3), 231–250.

Ellis, C. C., Peterson, M., Bufford, R., & Benson, J. (2014). The importance of group cohesion in inpatient treatment of combat-related PTSD. *International Journal of Group Psychotherapy, 64*(2), 180–206.

Evers, K. E., Paiva, A. L., Johnson, J. L., Cummins, C. O., Prochaska, J. O., Prochaska, J. M., . . . Gokbayrak, N. S. (2012). Results of a transtheoretical model-based alcohol, tobacco, and other drug intervention in middle schools. *Addictive Behaviors, 37*(9), 1009–1018.

Fisher-Townsend, B. (2018). Aboriginal men, violence, and spirituality: "A big part of who we are is the spiritual part". In *Religion, gender, and family violence* (pp. 125–145). Leiden, Netherlands: BRILL.

Gallagher, M. E., Tasca, G. A., Ritchie, K., Balfour, L., & Bissada, H. (2014). Attachment anxiety moderates the relationship between growth in group cohesion and treatment outcomes in group psychodynamic interpersonal psychotherapy for women with binge eating disorder. *Group Dynamics: Theory, Research, and Practice, 18*(1), 38–52.

Gondolf, E. W. (2007). Culturally-focused batterer counseling for African-American men. *Criminology & Public Policy, 6*(2), 341–366.

Gondolf, E. W. (2010). Lessons from a successful and failed random assignment testing batterer program innovations. *Journal of Experimental Criminology, 6*(4), 355–376.

Gondolf, E. W., & Williams, O. (2001). Culturally focused batterer counseling for African American men. *Trauma, Violence and Abuse, 2(4)*, 283–295.

Harris, M., & Fallot, R. (Eds.) (2001). *Using trauma theory to design service systems. New directions for mental health services.* San Francisco, CA: Jossey-Bass.

Hayes, M. A., Gallagher, M. W., Gilbert, K. S., Creech, S. K., DeCandia, C. J., Beach, C. A., & Taft, C. T. (2015). Targeting relational aggression in veterans: The strength at home friends and family intervention. *The Journal of Clinical Psychiatry, 76*(6), e774–e778. https://doi.org/10.4088/JCP. 14m09155

Heather, N., Honekopp, J., & Smailes, D. (2009). Progressive stage transition does mean getting better: A further test of the transtheoretical model in recovery from alcohol problems. *Addiction, 104*(6), 949–958.

Heyman, R. E., Taft, C. T., Howard, J. M., Macdonald, A., & Collins, P. S. (2012). Intimate partner violence. In D. K. Snyder & C. M. Monson (Eds.), *Couple-based interventions for military and Veteran families: A practitioner's guide* (pp. 122–146). New York, NY: Guilford Press.

Holmes, S. C., Facemire, V. C., & DaFonseca, A. M. (2016). Expanding criterion a for posttraumatic stress disorder: Considering the deleterious impact of oppression. *Traumatology, 22*(4), 314–321.

Holtzworth-Munroe, A. (1992). Social skill deficits in maritally violent men: Interpreting the data using a social information processing model. *Clinical Psychology Review, 12*(6), 605–617.

Holtzworth-Munroe, A., & Anglin, K. (1991). The competency of responses given by maritally violent versus nonviolent men to problematic marital situations. *Violence and Victims, 6*(4), 257–269.

Holtzworth-Munroe, A., & Hutchinson, G. (1993). Attributing negative intent to wife behavior: The attributions of maritally violent versus nonviolent men. *Journal of Abnormal Psychology, 102*(2), 206–211.

Hubbert, P. D. (2011). Transforming the spirit: Spirituality in the treatment of the African American male perpetrator of intimate partner violence. *Journal of Religion & Spirituality in Social Work: Social Thought, 30*(2), 125–143.

Jennings, J. L. (1987). History and issues in the treatment of battering men: A case for unstructured group therapy. *Journal of Family Violence, 2*(3), 193–213.

Joyce, A. S., Piper, W. E., & Ogrodniczuk, J. S. (2007). Therapeutic alliance and cohesion variables as predictors of outcome in short-term group psychotherapy. *International Journal of Group Psychotherapy, 57*(3), 269–296.

Kirmayer, L. J., Gone, J. P., & Moses, J. (2014). Rethinking historical trauma. *Transcultural Psychiatry, 51*(3), 299–319.

Krupnick, J. L., Sotsky, S. M., Simmens, S., Moyer, J., Elkin, I., Watkins, J., & Pilkonis, P. A. (1996). The role of the therapeutic alliance in psychotherapy and pharmacotherapy outcome: Findings in the national institute of mental health treatment of depression collaborative research program. *Journal of Consulting and Clinical Psychology, 64*(3), 532–539.

LaMotte, A. D., Taft, C. T., & Weatherill, R. P. (2016). Mistrust of others as a mediator of the relationship between trauma exposure and use of partner aggression. *Psychological Trauma: Theory, Research, Practice, and Policy, 8*(4), 535.

Leary, J. D. (2001). *African American male violence: Trying to kill the part of you that isn't loved* (Unpublished dissertation), Portland State University Graduate School of Social Work, Portland, OR.

Leisey, T., & Lewis, P. (n.d.). *Historical trauma, power, and an argument for collective healing practices* (Unpublished Thesis), Brandeis University Heller School for Social Policy and Management, Boston, MA.

Levesque, D. A., Gelles, R. J., & Velicer, W. F. (2000). Development and validation of a stages of change measure for men in batterer treatment. *Cognitive Therapy and Research, 24*(2), 175–199.

Love, A. R., Morland, L. A., Taft, C. T., MacDonald, A., & Mackintosh, M. A. (2015). "Strength at home" intervention for male Veterans perpetrating intimate partner aggression: Perceived needs survey of therapists and pilot effectiveness study. *Journal of Interpersonal Violence, 30*(13), 2344–2362.

Mankowski, E. S., Haaken, J., & Silvergild, C. S. (2002). Collateral damage: An analysis of the achievements and unintended consequences of batterer intervention programs and discourse. *Journal of Family Violence, 17*(2), 167–184.

Marshall, A. D., & Holtzworth-Munroe, A. (2010). Recognition of wives' emotional expressions: A mechanism in the relationship between psychopathology and intimate partner violence perpetration. *Journal of Family Psychology, 24*(1), 21–30.

McFall, R. M. (1982). A review and reformulation of the concept of social skills. *Behavioral Assessment, 4*(1), 1–33.

Miller, W. R., Benefield, R. G., & Tonigan, J. S. (1993). Enhancing motivation for change in problem drinking: A controlled comparison of two therapist styles. *Journal of Consulting and Clinical Psychology, 61*(3), 455–461.

Miller, W. R., Taylor, C. A., & West, J. C. (1980). Focused versus broad-spectrum behavior therapy for problem drinkers. *Journal of Consulting and Clinical Psychology, 48*(5), 590–601.

Monson, C. M., Fredman, S. J., Macdonald, A., Pukay-Martin, N. D., Resick, P. A., & Schnurr, P. P. (2012). Effect of cognitive-behavioral couple therapy for PTSD: A randomized controlled trial. *JAMA, 308*(7), 700–709.

Monson, C. M., Schnurr, P. P., Resick, P. A., Friedman, M. J., Young-Xu, Y., & Stevens, S. P. (2006). Cognitive processing therapy for veterans with military-related posttraumatic stress disorder. *Journal of Consulting and Clinical Psychology, 74*(5), 898–907.

Murphy, C. M., & Baxter, V. A. (1997). Motivating batterers to change in the treatment context. *Journal of Interpersonal Violence, 12*(4), 607–619.

Murphy, C. M., & Maiuro, R. D. (2009). *Motivational interviewing and stages of change in intimate partner violence.* New York, NY: Springer.

Murphy, C. M., & Scott, E. (1996). *Cognitive-behavioral therapy for domestically assaultive individuals: A treatment manual.* Unpublished manuscript, University of Maryland, Baltimore County.

Myers, H. F., Wyatt, G. E., Ullman, J. B., Loeb, T. B., Chin, D., Prause, N., . . . Liu, H. (2015). Cumulative burden of lifetime adversities: Trauma and mental health in low-SES African Americans and Latino/as. *Psychological Trauma: Theory, Research, Practice, and Policy, 7*(3), 243.

Novaco, R. W., & Chemtob, C. M. (1998). Anger and trauma: Conceptualization, assessment, and treatment. In V. M. Follette, J. I. Ruzek, & F. R. Abueg (Eds.), *Cognitive-behavioral therapies for trauma* (pp. 162–190). New York, NY: Guilford Press.

O'Hare, T. (1996). Court-ordered versus voluntary clients: Problem differences and readiness for change. *Social Work, 41*(4), 417–422.

Powell, J. A. (2008). The impact of societal systems on Black male violence. *Journal of Aggression, Maltreatment & Trauma, 16*(3), 311–329.

Prochaska, J. O., & DiClemente, C. C. (1982). Transtheoretical therapy: Toward a more integrative model of change. *Psychotherapy: Theory, Research & Practice, 19*(3), 276–288.

Prochaska, J. O., & DiClemente, C. C. (1992). The transtheoretical approach. In J. C. Norcross & M. R. Goldfried (Eds.), *Handbook of psychotherapy integration* (pp. 300–334). New York, NY: Basic Books.

Prochaska, J. O., Johnson, S., & Lee, P. (2009). The transtheoretical model of behavior change. In S. A. Shumaker, J. K. Ockene, & K. A. Riekert (Eds.), *The handbook of health behavior change* (3rd ed., pp. 59–83). New York, NY: Springer.

Reed, E., Silverman, J. G., Ickovics, J. R., Gupta, J., Welles, S. L., Santana, M. C., & Raj, A. (2010). Experiences of racial discrimination & relation to violence perpetration and gang involvement among a sample of urban African American men. *Journal of Immigrant and Minority Health, 12*(3), 319–326.

Resick, P. A., Monson, C. M., & Chard, K. M. (2008). *Cognitive processing therapy: Therapist's manual.* Boston, MA: Department of Veterans' Affairs.

Resick, P. A., & Schnicke, M. K. (1992). Cognitive processing therapy for sexual assault victims. *Journal of Consulting and Clinical Psychology, 60*(5), 748–756.

Rondeau, G., Brodeur, N., Brochu, S., & Lemire, G. (2001). Dropout and completion of treatment among spouse abusers. *Violence and Victims, 16*(2), 127–143.

Rosenberg, M. S. (2003). Voices from the group: Domestic violence offenders' experience of intervention. *Journal of Aggression, Maltreatment & Trauma, 7*(1–2), 305–317.

Safran, J. D., & Muran, J. C. (1996). The resolution of ruptures in the therapeutic alliance. *Journal of Consulting and Clinical Psychology, 64*(3), 447–458.

Santiago, B., del Castillo, M. F., Carbajosa, P., & Marcuello, C. (2013). Context of treatment and therapeutic alliance: Critical factors in court-mandated batterer intervention programs. *The Spanish Journal of Psychology, 16*, E40.

Schauss, E., Zettler, H. R., & Russell, A. (2019). Examining ACTV: An argument for implementing neuroscience-based and trauma-informed treatment models in offender treatment programs. *Aggression and Violent Behavior, 46*, 1-7.

Schnur, J. B., & Montgomery, G. H. (2010). A systematic review of therapeutic alliance, group cohesion, empathy, and goal consensus/collaboration in psychotherapeutic interventions in cancer: Uncommon factors? *Clinical Psychology Review, 30*(2), 238–247.

Scott, K., King, C., McGinn, H., & Hosseini, N. (2011). Effects of motivational enhancement on immediate outcomes of batterer intervention. *Journal of Family Violence, 26*(2), 139–149.

Sippel, L. M., & Marshall, A. D. (2011). Posttraumatic stress disorder symptoms, intimate partner violence perpetration, and the mediating role of shame processing bias. *Journal of Anxiety Disorders, 25*(7), 903–910.

Sonkin, D. J., & Dutton, D. (2003). Treating assaultive men from an attachment perspective. *Journal of Aggression, Maltreatment, & Trauma, 7*(1–2), 105–133.

Sotero, M. (2006). A conceptual model of historical trauma: Implications for public health practice and research. *Journal of Health Disparities Research and Practice, 1*(1), 93–108.

Straus, M. A., Hamby, S. L., Boney-McCoy, S., & Sugarman, D. B. (1996). The revised conflict tactics scales (CTS2): Development and preliminary psychometric data. *Journal of Family Issues, 17*(3), 283–316.

Sutton, T. E., Gordon Simons, L., Martin, B. T., Klopack, E. T., Gibbons, F. X., Beach, S. R., & Simons, R. L. (2019). Racial discrimination as a risk factor for African American men's physical partner violence: A longitudinal test of mediators and moderators. *Violence Against Women.* doi:10.1177/1077801219830245

Taft, C. T., Macdonald, A., Creech, S. K., Monson, C. M., & Murphy, C. M. (2016). A randomized controlled clinical trial of the strength at home men's program for partner violence in military veterans. *The Journal of Clinical Psychiatry, 77*(9), 1168–1175.

Taft, C. T., Macdonald, A., Monson, C. M., Walling, S. M., Resick, P. A., & Murphy, C. M. (2013). "Strength at Home" group intervention for military populations engaging in intimate partner violence: Pilot findings. *Journal of Family Violence, 28*(3), 225–231.

Taft, C. T., & Murphy, C. M. (2007). The working alliance in intervention for partner violence perpetrators: Recent research and theory. *Journal of Family Violence, 22*, 11–18.

Taft, C. T., Murphy, C. M., & Creech, S. K. (2016). *Trauma-informed treatment and prevention of intimate partner violence.* Washington, D.C: American Psychological Association.

Taft, C. T., Murphy, C. M., Elliott, J. D., & Keaser, M. L. (2001). Race and demographic factors in treatment attendance for domestically abusive men. *Journal of Family Violence, 16*(4), 385–400.

Taft, C. T., Murphy, C. M., King, D. W., Musser, P. H., & DeDeyn, J. M. (2003). Process and treatment adherence factors in group cognitive-behavioral therapy for partner violent men. *Journal of Consulting and Clinical Psychology, 71*(4), 812–820.

Taft, C. T., Schumm, J. A., Marshall, A. D., Panuzio, J., & Holtzworth-Munroe, A. (2008). Family-of-origin maltreatment, posttraumatic stress disorder symptoms, social information processing deficits, and relationship abuse perpetration. *Journal of Abnormal Psychology, 117*(3), 637–646.

Taft, C. T., Street, A. E., Marshall, A. D., Dowdall, D. J., & Riggs, D. S. (2007). Posttraumatic stress disorder, anger, and partner abuse among Vietnam combat Veterans. *Journal of Family Psychology, 21*(2), 270–277.

Taft, C. T., Vogt, D. S., Marshall, A. D., Panuzio, J., & Niles, B. L. (2007). Aggression among combat Veterans: Relationships with combat exposure and symptoms of posttraumatic stress disorder, dysphoria, and anxiety. *Journal of Traumatic Stress, 20*(2), 135–145.

Taft, C. T., Weatherill, R. P., Scott, J. P., Thomas, S. A., Kang, H. K., & Eckhardt, C. I. (2015). Social information processing in anger expression and partner violence in returning US Veterans. *Journal of Traumatic Stress, 28*(4), 314–321.

Voith, L. A., Logan-Greene, P., Strodthoff, T., & Bender, A. E. (2018). A paradigm shift in batterer intervention programming: A need to address unresolved trauma. *Trauma, Violence, & Abuse.* doi:10.1177/1524838018791268

Welland, C., & Ribner, N. (2010). Culturally specific treatment for partner-abusive Latino men: A qualitative study to identify and implement program components. *Violence and Victims, 25*(6), 799.

Williams, O. J. (1994). Group work with African American men who batter: Toward more ethnically sensitive practice. *Journal of Comparative Family Studies, 25*(1), 91–103.

Williams, O. J. (1995). Treatment for African American men who batter. *CURA Report, 25*(3), 6–10.

Yalom, I. D. (1995). *The theory and practice of group psychotherapy* (4th ed.). New York, NY: Basic Books.

# PART 6

# Researching domestic violence and abuse

# 40

# LISTENING TO LESS-HEARD VOICES

Methodological approaches, considerations and challenges when researching domestic violence and abuse with vulnerable and marginalised women

*Siobán O'Brien Green and Sarah Morton*

## Introduction

Who are vulnerable and marginalised women, and how do research ethics committees define them? What criteria are used to craft this definition by academics, researchers and research funders, and how does it impact on subsequent research design? Potentially, is a victim/survivor of domestic violence hypothetically always contained within the parameters of the definition of 'vulnerable'? How does this categorisation within research contribute to increasing safety and supports for women, or potentially – conversely – put them a greater risk, stigmatisation, exclusion and harm? Most importantly, how do women participating in research self-define themselves and convey this to researchers? This chapter aims to address these formidable questions and draw on the experiences and knowledge of the authors, who have undertaken research that has focussed on listening to women at the periphery of social research due to numerous factors and circumstances, including women experiencing domestic violence.

### *Rationale and stimuli for undertaking inclusive research on domestic violence*

There is an increasing international mandate for conducting research and collating data on domestic violence. Yet any research must be inclusive of marginalised and vulnerable populations in order to ensure robust and pertinent resultant research data, prevalence rates and statistics, findings and recommendations. Women living in remote, rural settings, women with disabilities, women living in poverty and migrant women all need to be included in research on violence against women, to create data and evidence to effectively combat the issue. By paying attention to diversity in study sampling and recruitment, and by acknowledging the great risks and vulnerabilities that some women experience, the voices of women traditionally excluded from, or on the margins of, social research can be heard and contribute meaningfully to research-focussed and informed policy change and service responses (Bellis,

Hughes, Perkins, & Bennett, 2012; Crenshaw, 1991; Nixon & Humphreys, 2010; Sokoloff & Dupont, 2005).

There is a growing focus on public and patient involvement in research design and process and requests for more engaged research practice, to better address complex social issues and involve the communities and cohorts most impacted by them (Campus Engage, 2016). All of these stimulants in relation to research require a collaborative, inclusive and ethical approach to research design and processes that are cognisant of the needs and realties of those participating in the research. Research should seek to measure, understand, and then amend and ameliorate the situations and conditions that allow for harmful complex social issues and local and global societal challenges, such as domestic violence and abuse, especially regarding vulnerable populations.

## The contribution of intersectionality and intersecting circumstances and realities in women's lives

The contribution that intersectionality makes to a traditional feminist framework on researching violence against women is to explore the role of culture, expand definitions of abuse, look at the structural causes of partner violence, and shift from disempowering presentations of vulnerable and marginalised female victims to resourceful, active survivors of violence. The social contexts in which women live are formed and maintained by intersecting systems of power and of oppression, which modify and interact with each other to frame safety from, and responses to, domestic violence, and what this implies for individual women, their communities and contexts (Sokoloff & Dupont, 2005). Intersectional research is distinguished by the inclusion of less-heard perspectives and making the lives and experiences of marginalised groups visible. Intersectionality is also a theory that examines how individual characteristics and hierarchies of power and oppression interact, construct and reinforce each other. Fundamentally, it is located in praxis and commitment to social justice (Withaeckx, 2017). McKibbin et al. present intersectionality as a feminist discourse that acknowledges diversity and explains how different groups of women live with, and experience, disadvantage (2015). This form of discourse is helpful to enabling the voices of marginalised women to be heard, and allows for researchers and policymakers to conceptualise women's diverse range of experiences and develop potential future responses to them.

## Addressing intersectionality, marginalisation and vulnerability within research methodology

As with any research field, there are a range of research methodologies relevant to aspects of domestic violence and women's experiences, and how the inclusion of vulnerability and marginalisation needs to be considered throughout. The core assumptions of intersectionality methodology, according to Hankivsky et al. are to recognise that all members of a social group (e.g. the LGBTQI community, migrants, Travellers, ethnic-minority women) do not necessarily have the same experiences; and, therefore, humans cannot be separated into elements, or an essentialist approach taken (2014). It is proposed that researchers undertaking intersectional studies be committed to social change and social justice, and be engaging with a range of stakeholders (ibid.). This is required both to do the research and to inform and leverage subsequent action and change. Resultant research findings must empower the individuals who participated in the research, and not reproduce or reinforce the inequalities with which they live. The researcher(s) must also reflect on and acknowledge their privileged position as they undertake research with marginalised groups (Withaeckx, 2017).

## Quantitative research considerations

Quantitative research design, as a primary data collection and analysis method in relation to domestic violence and abuse, is most often utilised for surveys, to determine the prevalence of the phenomena. Prevalence aims to measure how frequently domestic violence occurs in a specific population, such as women aged between 18 and 65, during a specific time period, such as lifetime/ever, last year, last month, last week, etc. (European Institute for Gender Equality, 2017). Ensuring that surveys include demographic data collection and sufficient options for respondents to self-describe their features and characteristics in order to capture the breadth of a survey sample is vital. This is in order to ascertain if it is reflective of a population and sufficiently captures the diversity contained within populations, especially in relation to migration patterns, which can fluctuate and change at a frequency greater than census or other data sources can capture. In some cases, dynamic survey sampling and the use of purposive booster samples will ensure that sufficient variance is reached, to be representative of population diversity (Leye et al., 2017).

Self-completion surveys or online surveys may not be accessible to women with certain disabilities and/or literacy challenges, and therefore need to be optimised to include these groups of participants. In all survey approaches, pilot testing of the data collection tools with varied groups representing potential participants is recommended in advance of field research commencing.

Secondary analysis of existing data sets and administrative data collected from the relevant domestic and sexual violence services, police, courts, coroners, etc. may also be important sources of quantitative data, but they often lack sufficient disaggregation in relation to ethnicity, religion, disability, sexual orientation, etc (Goodey, 2017). As a result, they are not comprehensive enough to reflect all of the population. Caution must be also used in relation to categorising ethnicities, nationalities, or other identifying features of a study sample that exist in such low numbers to make identification within a community or population highly likely.

Regular survey data will be required at a country level to monitor progress in relation to the United Nations Sustainable Development Goals and the Council of Europe Convention on preventing and combating violence against women and domestic violence (United Nations, 2019; Walby, 2016). As a result, it is imperative that the data collection categories and sampling frames are as robust as is feasible. This may require utilisation of approaches such as snowball or time-location sampling, to ensure adequate reach into marginalised population groups (Johnson & Chang, 2014). Finally, the data, prevalence and statistics on domestic violence that emerge from quantitative research methods are often the catalyst for further research or can be used to provide a rationale for research funding and studies that specifically include vulnerable populations or groups.

## Qualitative research considerations

Qualitative research approaches are often considered the ideal route to gather data on domestic violence, as they are concerned with meaning, context and lived experiences, and potentially offer private settings to collect data, such as one-to-one interviews. How participants' experiences are recounted, interpreted and understood by the research participants themselves, together with elements of reflexivity and subjectivity on the part of the researcher, are essential to qualitative research (Guest, Namey, & Mitchell, 2013).

Some literature suggests that participation in qualitative research studies on domestic violence enables victims to use their experiences to help others, as they may find the interview a cathartic and meaningful experience, and feel valued and listened to as they recount their own personal story, reflections and opinions to a researcher (Downes, Kelly, & Westmarland, 2014). Focus groups can also create an environment for peer support, as well as generate dynamic and deep data collection through the group interactions and stimuli (O'Brien Green, 2017). However, given the importance of connection and rapport between interviewer and interviewee in qualitative research methods, it is vital to grapple with the potential for coercion, pressure and power dynamics to be explored and addressed within qualitative research design, especially concerning vulnerable groups (World Health Organization, 2016).

Action research offers the potential to understand professional judgement, lived experiences, and multiple ways of knowing when seeking to develop effective practice (Gaventa & Cornwall, 2008; Reason & Bradbury, 2012). It is particularly applicable to health and social-care settings, where there is a desire to move beyond measuring outcomes and explore processes of change and practice development based on collaboration, as well as addressing power imbalances (Donnelly & Morton, 2019). Numerous examples exist of the use of action research with regard to domestic violence and marginalisation, across different cultural settings (Sullivan, Bhuyan, Senturia, Shiu-Thornton, & Ciske, 2005).

## Mixed-method research approaches

For some research studies on domestic violence and abuse, the most effective approach is a combination of methods, to ensure that the study is as comprehensive and thorough as possible, and to compensate for when data collection may not be feasible via certain routes to reach all in a sample. In these situations, a mixed-method approach, combining aspects of qualitative and quantitative research, may be most appropriate (Lewis, 2014). For some studies, this may imply in-depth interviews, in addition to a survey questionnaire on the same topic, but to differing study cohorts (Women's Health Council, 2009). Mixed methods can also be used to verify, explain or seek corroboration of initial quantitative study findings, and therefore act as a form of data triangulation (European Institute for Gender Equality, 2015). Mixed methods may also be utilised when the sample size or population to be researched is potentially very small and hard to reach, so inputs from those working with the population maybe sought (such as domestic violence service staff), in addition to data collection from the core sample, and potentially additional data collection via case file analysis or an online survey (SAFE Ireland, 2016).

While a mixed-method approach can provide a pragmatic solution to researching complex issues with hard-to-reach populations, the study design and sequencing must be rigorous enough to ensure valid research results, and not risk the time and effort that researchers and participants have devoted to the study be dismissed (Lewis, 2014). A mixed-method approach utilising multiple data sources and respondents may be the most appropriate in cases of intimate-partner femicide, by which the fundamental research participant has been silenced through murder. This approach is in order to enhance risk identification and risk reduction measures via the analysis of data sources available to ultimately reduce the incidence of femicide (Schröttle & Meshkova, 2018).

## Research ethics, ethical research design and safety considerations

The absence of research on domestic violence that fully considers the realities that women live with and in, and the potential of research on these intersecting topics to inform professional guidelines, service delivery, screening and legislation, creates an ethical dilemma in relation to policymaking in a research vacuum without adequate, substantial and recent research to guide and inform this process. However, the ethical considerations in relation to researching domestic violence, in the context of additional vulnerabilities, such as pregnancy, migrant status, drug use, disability, etc., require considerable thought and ongoing reflection in relation to the safety, on multiple levels and contexts, of the research participants and the researcher. This is because issues can arise before, during and after data collection, and there exists the potential of re-traumatisation and re-victimisation of the interviewee and vicarious trauma for the interviewer via both the data collection processes and research write-up. There also exists the possibility of the safety and risk contexts of the research participants changing and deteriorating during the study. Effectively preparing field researchers or interviewers on how to respond to and process what they are hearing in interviews is also necessary, in addition to enacting participant safety and onward-referral protocols, and legal requirements in relation to child protection, if required (Fraga, 2016).

How women are engaged with and accessed to participate in research, are heard and listened to by researchers, have their histories documented, and where the research and reports are published in the context of potentially life-threatening past and future experiences places much responsibility on the researcher in relation to safety, confidentiality, re-victimisation and vicarious trauma (O'Brien Green, 2018). Additionally, the dimensions of pregnancy or a recent birth, current drug use, mental health issues, etc. by participants in a study adds another layer of potential safety concerns and heightened vulnerability. There exists the possibility of re-victimisation of study participants in research on domestic abuse, in particular if women are asked to repeatedly recount incidences of forms of violence that they have experienced.

Transcription and/or translation utilisation in research studies needs to take into account potential confidentially breaches, especially if the language or dialect spoken by research participants is limited to a very small population subgroup and is particularly distinguishable or identifiable. The European Commission states that the vulnerabilities of research participants can be exacerbated if the confidential information that they share with researchers can, in any way, be linked to them (2018). This is particularity the situation for research participants who are sex workers, refugees, disabled women, LGBTQI persons and victims of domestic violence.

The inclusion of women of childbearing potential in research studies and those with other perceived vulnerabilities, such as the use of substances/drugs or engagement in sex-working, may intensify the sensitivity of research ethics committees to potential harms, and, as a result, they may opt for additional safety measures or the exclusion of this population cohort in research studies. Within these committees there may also be a limited understanding of how domestic violence services are structured and operate, and the staffing arrangements and demanding, resource-limited environments in which many of these services function. Yet, overly restrictive or prescriptive study inclusion and exclusion criteria within a study designed to incorporate the most current and comprehensive considerations in relation to ethics and participant safety can result in a situation where the study participation criteria are such that recruitment is exceptionally limited and/or challenging, and/or interviewees are non-existent.

Downes et al. state that the challenges in gaining ethical approval to undertake research on domestic violence may lead to a diminishment of research occurring and policymaking taking place without evidence (2014). This situation may become even more challenging, as research-performing organisations, such as universities, become more risk aware and averse, and less open to complex research studies with vulnerable populations (Miller & Bell, 2002). However, the challenges and risks associated with researching violence against women, while great, must also be compared with the absence of survivor voices to correctly and comprehensively inform policy, service provision and legislation. Although pregnant and migrant women, women who have experienced domestic violence, women who are victims of crime, and those who have experienced trauma are generally classified as vulnerable populations in research settings, given the prevalence of these experiences in the adult female global population, they cannot be considered rare or infrequent.

## Safety considerations

In relation to research with women who have experienced domestic violence, both participant and researcher safety gains a heightened importance and emphasis (Ellsberg & Heise, 2005; Fraga, 2016; Sullivan & Cain, 2004). Any study design must be cognisant of safety issues for interviewees in the following: participant recruitment processes, risk assessment of potential interviewees, researcher contact with potential interviewees prior to and after interviews, location of interviews, and referral routes and supports identified in case of risks or needs changing in the course of the research study or during the interview. The World Health Organization (WHO) states that research interventions with women who have experienced partner violence while pregnant require special ethical considerations and referral routes for interviewees, given the increased risk of pregnancy loss due to violence (2016).

Planning the location of study interviews and/or focus groups is a key feature of the safety considerations in any domestic violence study. Sullivan and Cain recognise that the immediate safety needs of women are usually met when research interviews are conducted in domestic violence refuges, but they also acknowledge that study interviews may take place in other locations that women interviewees themselves deem safe and comfortable (2004). Domestic violence refuges and services may have pre-established professional links with local medical services and police, should these services be required during or after a study interview. Nonetheless, there are potential confidentiality issues that may arise when being interviewed in a refuge where a woman has lived or is currently living. As there is an element of mobility attached to seeking safety and protection from a violent partner, and as a woman's personal situation of risk may escalate and de-escalate rapidly (with a perpetrator being released from prison, or a barring or protection order expiring, for example), undertaking more than one interview with a woman or longitudinal studies, with multiple interviews planned, may not be feasible (Sullivan & Cain, 2004).

At the end of an interview, a researcher can leave, both physically and psychologically, the topics or issues being investigated, and the place of the interview. The researcher may not have the ongoing safety concerns and issues with which their interviewee must continue to live, and, indeed, options such as travel or where to live may not be available to the research participant for safety and child protection/access reasons (Montoya & Rolandsen Agustín, 2013; Women's Health Council, 2009). Being sensitised to this reality and acknowledging that the options and choices that researchers may have at the end of an interview or the research study are not the same as those of their participants is important, both in relation to study safety design and protocols and in terms of researcher reflexivity.

## *Study documentation and protocols*

Documents related to the research study, such as participant and gatekeeper information, must provide clear, comprehensive and accurate information on the study in a format (and, potentially, a language) that is appropriate to the research cohort. An approach to maximising the readability of the study documents for participants should be used, and this may imply proofreading documents and checking legibility by people outside of the research team. A concise research study summary may be useful, to generate interest and support and assist with recruitment from the outset. This summary can be reviewed during the consent-gathering process, to ensure that participants are cognisant of the study's aims, purpose and implications, and the topics and subjects covered in the interviews or survey. An adequate budget for translation should be part of the study design. To ensure the participation of all study documents – the summary and survey/interview questions, or, at minimum, consent forms – should be available in the languages and/or formats of relevance to potential participants. This is to ensure that women are not further marginalised and excluded from research participation.

Study documentation should also address data protection and confidentiality, and how the data storage and analysis will respect the confidentiality of study participants. Study documentation must refer to the protocols and policies for dealing with issues that can arise during research on domestic violence. The protocols need to be devised prior to fieldwork and may require legal, child protection or other relevant inputs. Any protocols must be mindful of national mandatory, legal-reporting and disclosure requirements, especially in the case of an ongoing risk of child abuse or disclosure related to potential self-harm or suicide. In relation to vulnerable populations, protocols must be even more attuned to risk potential and harm mitigation throughout the entire research process, while also providing clarity on the limits of researcher confidentiality as prescribed by law.

During data collection, unintended and unexpected issues or findings may emerge, and researchers may need to refer interviewees to a wider range of support services than originally anticipated, in particular, in cases of human trafficking, sexual and labour exploitation, and other criminal activity (European Commission, 2018). Intended or planned forced marriage or female genital mutilation may also emerge during research with particular groups of women, and although they may not necessarily be the primary focus of the study, protocols will need to be in place to respond to these situations (European Institute for Gender Equality, 2015). These unanticipated findings may have harmful current and future implications beyond the immediate study cohort, and researchers have ethical and legal responsibilities to ensure that non-maleficent aspects of their research design are upheld.

## *Safety and drug-related and/or organised crime*

Women may be directly and indirectly connected with networks of criminal activity, drug-related crime and intimidation which may have implications for the safety of the woman and the researcher, particularly in small communities (Raghavan, Mennerich, Sexton, & James, 2006). For instance, Sandberg and Copes found that researchers needed to take specific safety measures where there was a belief or concern about criminal activity, violence or drug-dealing, including always completing interviews in organisational settings and informing colleagues of their location and schedule (2013). However, it was noted that having access to such contexts in the course of the research could have both emotional and practical safety implications, and that while researchers may become privy to information and understandings that are not reportable to police or other relevant agencies, being immersed in such settings was ethically and morally challenging (ibid.). This immersion in, and exposure to, such activity could affect the researcher's world view and personal and community relationships (Morton & Hohman, 2016). It must be noted that some research with vulnerable populations simply may not be possible due to profound safety concerns, both for the researcher and/or the participant.

## Compensation

While compensation can be seen as incentivising potential interviewees to participate by means of monetary pressure, and, therefore, possibly biased study samples, it can also mitigate against interviewees' travel costs, childcare expenses and lost earnings when giving their time to participate in a study (O'Brien Green, 2018). Supporting the reality of expenses incurred in order to participate in research studies should form part of every research study design and budget. Adequate compensation upon completing a study interview that is offered in a manner that women can utilise discreetly and easily is part of responsible research, yet compensation for study participants can be problematic for research ethics committees and cause concerns about stimulating or over-incentivising research participation (O'Brien Green, 2017). If substantially higher study recruitment is observed amongst specific cohorts of the study population, a re-examination of compensation on offer and recruitment methods may be required, to ensure that undue inducement is not a factor (World Health Organization, 2016).

## Childcare needs

For some women, a lack of extended family and strong informal support networks may mean that childcare options are very limited or completely absent, and the only way that women can participate in research is with their children. This can present challenges for the researcher, as time will need to be allocated for breaks and noise from the child(ren) can be an issue for the transcription of interviews (O'Brien Green, 2017). Having a child present can also be a challenge to the participant's safety. Children should not be present in interviews if they are verbal for any research on domestic violence, for two main reasons: the interview content (both questions and responses) can be upsetting to the child, and there exists a possibility of children being later interrogated (for example, by the perpetrator of violence or other family or community members) as to what their mother has told others. As a result, having verbal children in interviews or focus groups has the potential to escalate risk and compromise participant safety (Zimmerman & Watts, 2003). When and where interviews are scheduled must try to accommodate women's childcare needs and should form a part of study design. Providing or funding childcare for women to participate in research studies is also (potentially) an enabling factor for study recruitment and a realistic aspect of robust study design.

## Consent

Documentary evidence of the voluntary, free and informed consent of research study participants is generally a requirement of research ethics committees and research funders. However, in cases of research with vulnerable and marginalised groups, the process and routes to provide a mutually agreed understanding of consent between researcher and participant, to demonstrate that consent was given, may be more challenging than with other research cohorts. This can be due to language differences between the researcher and the interviewee, literacy, disability impacting on reading, hearing, etc., mental health issues, and women being affected by their substance use or medication. Emphasising the right to withdraw consent at any time without any consequences or impact on accessing services (such those services in which the interview or focus group is being held) is very important (World Health Organization, 2016). It is also imperative to demonstrate that avoiding coercion and any misrepresentation of possible benefits of participation in the study has been addressed fully and clearly with interviewees (Miller & Bell, 2002). Additionally, study participants should be fully aware of whom is commissioning and/or funding the research and why (European Commission, 2018).

Existing evidence indicates that 50% of women experiencing domestic violence may have used, or are currently using, substances, usually as a response to their experiences of abuse (Galvani, 2004; George, Boulay, & Galvani, 2011). Beyond this, women may also be prescribed or misusing medication, the side effects of which can impact on daily living (Romans, Cohen, Forte, Du Mont, & Hyman, 2008). The risks to participants may be resolved by simply not including those who are intoxicated, but given the prevalence of substance use for women experiencing domestic violence, important narratives and data may be excluded. In addition, the opportunity to understand drug use patterns and to inform practice and policy will also be foregone (Barratt, Norman, & Fry, 2007). Rather than engage with fallible methods of assessing intoxication, Aldridge and Charles advocate focussing on the process of ensuring that the information is understood by the research participant during the consent process (2008). This may include, for instance, ensuring that information about the research is understood by the participant and excluding those who are not able to demonstrate such understanding, as well as asking participants directly if they feel that their substance or medication use may be impacting on their ability to provide consent and to fully participate in the data collection process (ibid.). Deciding not to include women who are currently using substances or intoxicated by their use assumes that there will be obvious outward and identifiable indicators of substance or medication use. It also assumes that women using substances are automatically 'vulnerable' (Aldridge & Charles, 2008). Given the level of medication use, and sometimes misuse, for women experiencing domestic violence, the effect of medication on the ability of a woman to provide informed consent and to engage in a research process requires special attention (Wuest et al., 2007).

Finally, confirming that consent is freely given and enabling consent comprehension and affirmation are the responsibilities of the researcher, not the research participant. Enabling women from marginalised and vulnerable contexts to fully consent and participate should be the aim of inclusive and representative research on domestic violence and abuse.

## Challenges and overcoming them

Ensuring that, potentially, the most vulnerable and marginalised voices get listened to and included in research in domestic violence is not without challenges. There can be resistance from research ethics committees and research funders, resource and time pressures, and immense logistical and practical challenges to overcome. As community-engaged research and utilisation of approaches that facilitate the inclusion of less-heard voices are receiving greater focus within the field, challenges have been identified with regard to both, especially as they are underpinned by principles of power-sharing and collaboration. For instance, community-engaged research can be complex, requiring the development of processes for participation and the co-creation of knowledge and action, with the aim of transforming how knowledge is produced (Stoecker, 2012). While community organisations, such as domestic violence support agencies, may be ideally placed to facilitate participation and advocate for social change, questions remain as to whether community-engaged research addresses power dynamics or lacks the ability to support societal-level change that will truly address social and health inequities (Belle-Isle, Benoit, & Pauly, 2014; Gustavsen, 2014). There is a growing focus on the meaningful involvement of including seldom-heard voices within research processes, but radical shifts in both research processes and practice are required, to ensure that this is effective (Ní Shé et al., 2019). Yet community-engaged research and practitioner partnership approaches to addressing research challenges, while not compromising the confidentiality of participants, can remain complex to negotiate.

## Participant (de)selection by gatekeepers

When gatekeepers from domestic violence services are utilised to access a study population and promote participation in a research study, the potential exists for power and control dynamics being exerted and subsequent sample selection bias (O'Brien Green, 2018). There may be efforts to frame how domestic violence supports and services are perceived, and, as a result, only particular clients are informed about the research by the gatekeepers, and then subsequently opt to take part (Vearey, Barter, Hynes, & McGinn, 2017). Recognising that there is potentially a level of study self-selection by participants and then potentially an additional layer of selective participant recruitment by gatekeepers, which ultimately may influence a study's findings, despite as broad a recruitment effort as possible, is unavoidable. Women perceived as too vulnerable to participate in a research study by gatekeepers may not be offered the possibility of having their voices heard therein (Miller & Bell, 2002). This can further exacerbate the marginalisation of vulnerable women and reduce their access and contributions to research, with an outcome of potentially silencing the voices that most need to be listened to.

## Vicarious trauma

The complex realties of women's lives and experiences of domestic violence are not easy to listen to and process, no matter how much experience a researcher has investigating challenging and complex topics. Various terms have been applied to the potentially traumatic experience of listening to or hearing the violent, abusive or harmful experiences of others (Clemens, 2005; Coles, Astbury, Dartnall, & Limjerwala, 2014; Morton & Hohman, 2016). Vicarious trauma to interviewers/researchers/transcribers can occur during the interview and while revising the data by listening to interview recordings and reviewing interview transcripts and notes repeatedly. Vicarious trauma for the researcher is an often overlooked issue when researching complex and distressing issues with participants who are exceptionally stigmatised and marginalised. Changes in world view, increased sensitisation to the issues of power and control in society, and a re-evaluation of one's own past and perceptions of violence tend to be common reactions to working with such material (Morton & Hohman, 2016). Building support, debriefing and other processes into the research design, as well as opportunities to discuss study challenges, is crucial to retaining researcher objectivity, completing the study and research study staff retention (Medical Research Council, 2015). Supports for researchers should be in place prior to the data collection commencement, in order to reduce the potential for vicarious trauma and distress and its subsequent impact on data collection and analysis. These supports need to be built into the study design and researcher supervision processes, including resourcing them from the outset. In addition, debriefing, accessing peer support and having a manageable workload and a supportive work environment can also help reduce the potential for vicarious trauma emergence and impact.

## Onward referral of research participants

Given the nature of women's experiences regarding domestic violence, especially where there are multiple/complex issues or aspects of exclusion or disadvantage, relevant and accessible support services are important. Trauma-informed responses (TIR) are being widely discussed, considered and implemented in different social and community service settings, and specialist services (such as sexual assault services) and exist in most jurisdictions. Yet lack of funding, waiting lists and a 'silo approach' to complex issues can persist. In recent research considering women experiencing a range of complex issues, including domestic violence and substance use, the lack of immediacy of service delivery was a key theme, together with women often not meeting basic criteria for access to services, such as stability in their substance use (Morton, MacDonald, & Christophers, 2020). This has implications for any research study, given the importance of ensuring adequate referral pathways for research participants, should they find that they are emotionally impacted or if re-victimisation occurs by their perpetrator during the research process.

## *Misuse of research data*

Unfortunately, when vulnerable or marginalised groups are identified as part of research cohorts, the possibility exists that the research data may be misconstrued or misused for negative and harmful political or ideological purposes. This potential particularly exists in relation to ethnic-minority, migrant and sex-working study participants, to be misused by racist and anti-migrant campaigns and movements. As a result, the published research findings, as well as the public and media presentation of any research findings, need to be carefully considered and prepared, being aware of ethical concerns and possible ulterior motives for the potential misuse of data (European Commission, 2018; European Institute for Gender Equality, 2013).

## Conclusions

Ensuring that women in vulnerable contexts and who may be considered marginalised are core to undertaking research on domestic violence, given the importance of their experiences and their trajectory and reality of living through abuse, is crucial. This is to ensure that all victims/survivors of domestic violence have equitable opportunities to contribute to the knowledge base, to inform policy, legislation and service development. It is also to ensure that women on the periphery of society, or whose voices are less amplified and heard in research, are centre-staged and acknowledged. Recognising that women can be experiencing and/or have lived through/survived domestic violence, as well as other forms of gender-based violence, in addition to discrimination and specific exploitation due to their vulnerability (disability, mental health, addiction status, pregnancy, etc.) and/or legal status, such as trafficking, etc., is crucial, to reflect the lived realties of women's lives. Furthermore, women may be participating in research studies related to their circumstances and situations, such as their migration status, pregnancy, substance use, disability, etc. Ensuring that these studies are also cognisant of the potential for the sample to have experienced gender-based violence is important, to guarantee that women receive the supports and referrals they need, but also to ensure visibility of the intersecting nature of multiple challenges and vulnerabilities with and through which women live.

How research participants are enabled to engage with the research study results, reports and publications needs to be considered, to ensure that a collaborative and appreciative approach to the research design is apparent at the end of the study. Producing and disseminating research study findings in a timely manner and in accessible formats (via open-access publications, research summaries, briefing papers, etc.) is also important, in order to optimally influence the policy and legislative changes that may follow distinctive timetables (such as national/regional parliamentary calendars or European Union directive transposition deadlines). In conclusion, researchers have a vital role to work beyond designations such as vulnerable and marginalised; to reduce power differentials between the academic/researcher and those providing the data for studies; to proactively involve, recognise and compensate all women who agree to take part in research studies while optimising safety, respect and appreciation for those who contribute to the global knowledge base on domestic violence, in order to effectively respond to it, to reduce and, ultimately, end it.

## Critical findings

- By attending to diversity, and acknowledging the great risks and vulnerabilities some women experience, those who are traditionally excluded from social research can be included and integrated into research-informed legal and policy change and service responses.
- Collaborative, inclusive and ethical approaches to research design are needed, that allow and account for the intersecting systems of power and oppression, vulnerability and exclusion that may exist in women's lives.
- Safety for participants, and the researcher, is key throughout the research process, with special attention required to safety during participant recruitment processes, during and after interviews.
- It is imperative to demonstrate that consent has been provided and that consent is mutually agreed and understood, especially where language issues, disabilities or effects of substance use may be factors.
- Researchers must work to reduce power differentials between the academic/researcher and those providing the data for studies and proactively involve, recognise and compensate all women who agree to take part in research studies while optimising safety, respect and appreciation for those contributing to the global knowledge base on domestic violence.

## Implications for policy, practice and research

- Ensuring that women in vulnerable contexts and who may be considered marginalised are core to undertaking research on domestic violence, given the importance of their experiences and their trajectories and realities of living through abuse, is crucial. This is to allow all victims/survivors of domestic violence to have equitable opportunities to contribute to the research knowledge base and to inform policy, legislation and service development.
- It is important to recognise that women can be experiencing and/or have lived through/ survived domestic violence, as well as other forms of gender-based violence, in addition to discrimination and specific exploitation due to their vulnerability (e.g. disability, mental health, addiction, pregnancy, migration/legal status, etc.).
- Where women are participating in research studies related to their circumstances and situations (e.g. migration status, pregnancy, substance use, disability, etc.) it is important to be cognisant of the potential for them to have experienced domestic violence and abuse.
- Ensuring women receive the supports and referrals they need during and after a research study is important, especially where there are complex and intersecting needs and experiences.
- Research study findings should be produced and disseminated in a timely manner and in accessible formats such as via open-access publications, research summaries, briefing papers. The research findings should also be accessible to the study participants.

# References

Aldridge, J., & Charles, V. (2008). Researching the intoxicated: Informed consent implications for alcohol and drug research. *Drug and Alcohol Dependence, 93*(3), 191–196.

Barratt, M. J., Norman, J. S., & Fry, C. L. (2007). Positive and negative aspects of participation in illicit drug research: Implications for recruitment and ethical conduct. *International Journal of Drug Policy, 18*(3), 235–238.

Belle-Isle, L., Benoit, C., & Pauly, B. (2014). Addressing health inequities through social inclusion: The role of community organizations. *Action Research, 12*(2), 177–193.

Bellis, M., A., Hughes, K., Perkins, C., & Bennett, A. (2012). *Protecting people promoting health: A public health approach to violence prevention for England*. London, UK: Department of Health and National Health Service.

Campus Engage. (2016). *Engaged research practice and principles: Society and higher education addressing grand societal challenges together*. Dublin: Irish University Association and Irish Research Council.

Clemens, S. (2005). Recognizing vicarious traumatization: A single session group model for trauma workers. *Social Work with Groups, 27*(2/3), 55–74. doi:10.1300/J009v27n02_05

Coles, J., Astbury, J., Dartnall, E., & Limjerwala, S. (2014). A qualitative exploration of researcher trauma and researchers' responses to investigating sexual violence. *Violence Against Women, 20*(1), 95–117.

Crenshaw, K. W. (1991). Mapping the margins: Intersectionality, identity politics, and violence against women of color. *Stanford Law Review, 43*(6), 1241–1299. doi:10.2307/1229039

Donnelly, S., & Morton, S. (2019). Creating organisational and practice change through the use of co-operative inquiry groups in healthcare settings. *Action Research, 17*(4), 451–468. doi:1476750319855126

Downes, J., Kelly, L., & Westmarland, N. (2014). Ethics in violence and abuse research – A Positive empowerment approach. *Sociological Research Online, 19*(1), 1–13.

Ellsberg, M., & Heise, L. (2005). *Researching violence against women: A practical guide for researchers and activists*. Washington, DC: World Health Organization.

European Commission. (2018). *Ethics in social science and humanities*. Luxembourg: Publications Office of the European Union.

European Institute for Gender Equality. (2013). *Female genital mutilation in the European union and Croatia*. Vilnius: EIGE.

European Institute for Gender Equality. (2015). *Estimation of girls at risk of female genital mutilation in the European Union*. Vilnius: EIGE.

European Institute for Gender Equality. (2017). *Glossary of definitions of rape, femicide and intimate partner violence*. Vilnius: EIGE.

Fraga, S. (2016). Methodological and ethical challenges in violence research. *Porto Biomedical Journal, 1*(2), 77–80.

Galvani, S. (2004). Responsible disinhibition: Alcohol, men and violence to women. *Addiction Research & Theory, 12*(4), 357–371.

Gaventa, J., & Cornwall, A. (2008). Power and knowledge. *The SAGE handbook of action research: Participative inquiry and practice* (pp. 172–189). London and Thousand Oaks, CA: Sage.

George, S., Boulay, S., & Galvani, S. (2011). Domestic abuse among women who misuse psychoactive substances: An overview for the clinician. *Addictive Disorders & Their Treatment, 10*(2), 43–49.

Goodey, J. (2017). Violence against women: Placing evidence from a European union-wide survey in a policy context. *Journal of Interpersonal Violence, 32*(12), 1760–1791.

Guest, G., Namey, E. E., & Mitchell, M. (2013). *Collecting qualitative data: A field manual for applied research*. London: Sage.

Gustavsen, B. (2014). Social impact and the justification of action research knowledge. *Action Research, 12*(4), 339–356.

Hankivsky, O., Grace, D., Hunting, G., Giesbrecht, M., Fridkin, A., Rudrum, S., & Clark, N. (2014). An intersectionality-based policy analysis framework: Critical reflections on a methodology for advancing equity. *International Journal for Equity in Health, 13*(1), 119. doi:10.1186/s12939-014-0119-x

Johnson, M., & Chang, S,. (2014). Sampling in quantitative research. In S. Jirojwong, M. Johnson, & Anthony Welch (Eds.), *Research methods in nursing and midwifery: Pathways to evidence-based practice* (2nd ed., pp. 165–181). Victoria: Oxford University Press.

Lewis, J. (2014). Mixed methods research. In S. Jirojwong, M. Johnson, & A. Welch (Eds.), *Research methods in nursing and midwifery: Pathways to evidence-based practice* (2nd ed., pp. 268–286). Victoria: Oxford University Press.

Leye, E., De Schrijver, L., Van Baelen, L., Andro, A., Lesclingand, M., Ortensi, L., & Farina, P. (2017). *Estimating FGM prevalence in Europe. Findings of a pilot study. Research report.* Ghent: International Centre for Reproductive Health.

McKibbin, G., Duncan, R., Hamilton, B., Humphreys, C., & Kellett, C. (2015). The intersectional turn in feminist theory: A response to Carbin and Edenheim (2013). *European Journal of Women's Studies, 22*(1), 99–103. doi:10.1177/1350506814539445

Medical Research Council. (2015). *Guidelines for the prevention and management of vicarious trauma among researchers of sexual and intimate partner violence.* Pretoria: Medical Research Council.

Miller, T., & Bell, L. (2002). Consenting to what? Issues of access, gate-keeping and 'informed' consent. In M. Mauthner, M. Birch, J. Jessop, & T. Miller (Eds.), *Ethics in qualitative research* (pp. 54–69). London: Sage.

Montoya, C., & Rolandsen Agustín, L. (2013). The othering of domestic violence: The eu and cultural framings of violence against women. *Social Politics: International Studies in Gender, State & Society, 20*(4), 534–557.

Morton, S., & Hohman, M. (2016). "That's the weight of knowing": Practitioner skills and impact when delivering psychoeducational group work for women who have experienced IPV. *Social Work with Groups, 39*(4), 277–291.

Morton, S., MacDonald, P., & Christophers, L. (2020). *Substance use, homelessness and violence: Policy and practice in regard to women with complex needs.* Dublin: Merchants Quay Ireland.

Ní Shé, E., Morton, S., Lambert, V., Ni Cheallaight, C., Lacey, V., Dunn, E., . . . Kroll, T. (2019). Clarifying the mechanisms and resources that enable the reciprocal involvement of seldom heard groups in health and social care research: A collaborative rapid realist review process. *Health Expectations, 22*(3), 298–306. doi.org/10.1111/hex.12865

Nixon, J., & Humphreys, C. (2010). Marshalling the evidence: Using intersectionality in the domestic violence frame. *Social Politics: International Studies in Gender, State & Society, 17*(2), 137–158. doi:10.1093/sp/jxq003

O'Brien Green, S. (2017). Organising focus groups: Process and logistics. In E. Leye & G. Coene (Eds.), *Researching female genital mutilation/cutting* (pp. 85–90). Brussels: Brussels University Press.

O'Brien Green, S. (2018). "I have a story to tell": Researching migrant women's experiences of female genital mutilation and gender-based violence in Ireland and Europe. *Social Work and Social Sciences Review, 19*(3), 134–151.

Raghavan, C., Mennerich, A., Sexton, E., & James, S. E. (2006). Community violence and its direct, indirect, and mediating effects on intimate partner violence. *Violence Against Women, 12*(12), 1132–1149.

Reason, P., & Bradbury, H. (2012). *The SAGE handbook of action research: Participative inquiry and practice* (2nd ed.). London and Thousand Oaks, CA: Sage.

Romans, S. E., Cohen, M. M., Forte, T., Du Mont, J., & Hyman, I. (2008). Gender and psychotropic medication use: The role of intimate partner violence. *Preventive Medicine, 46*(6), 615–621.

SAFE Ireland. (2016). *SNaP: Specific needs and protection orders. Justice Sought justice lost.* Athlone: SAFE Ireland.

Sandberg, S., & Copes, H. (2013). Speaking with ethnographers: The challenges of researching drug dealers and offenders. *Journal of Drug Issues, 43*(2), 176–197.

Schröttle, M., & Meshkova, K. (2018). Data collection: Challenges and opportunities. In S. Weil, C. Corradi, & M. Naudi (Eds.), *Femicide across Europe: Theory, research and prevention* (pp. 33–52). Bristol, UK: Policy Press.

Sokoloff, N. J., & Dupont, I. (2005). Domestic violence at the intersections of race, class, and gender: Challenges and contributions to understanding violence against marginalized women in diverse communities. *Violence Against Women, 11*(1), 38–64. doi:10.1177/1077801204271476

Stoecker, R. (2012). Community-based research and the two forms of social change. *Journal of Rural Social Sciences, 27*(2), 83.

Sullivan, C., & Cain, D. (2004). Ethical and safety considerations when obtaining information from or about battered women for research purposes. *Journal of Interpersonal Violence, 19*(5), 603–618.

Sullivan, M., Bhuyan, R., Senturia, K., Shiu-Thornton, S., & Ciske, S. (2005). Participatory action research in practice: A case study in addressing domestic violence in nine cultural communities. *Journal of Interpersonal Violence, 20*(8), 977–995. doi:10.1177/0886260505277680

United Nations. (2019). *Global indicator framework for the sustainable development goals and targets of the 2030 agenda for sustainable development.* New York, NY: United Nations.

Vearey, J., Barter, C., Hynes, P., & McGinn, T. (2017). Research ethics in practice: Lessons from studies exploring interpersonal violence in different contexts. *Families, Relationships and Societies, 6*(2), 273–289.

Walby, S. (2016). *Ensuring data collection and research on violence against women and domestic violence: Article 11 of the Istanbul convention.* Strasbourg: Council of Europe.

Withaeckx, S. (2017). Researching harmful cultural practices: Values and limits of an intersectional perspective. In E. Leye & G. Coene (Eds.), *Researching female genital mutilation/cutting: Proceedings of the 2nd international academic seminar of MAP-FGM project* (pp. 113–118). Brussels: Vubpress Brussels University Press.

Women's Health Council. (2009). *Translating pain into action: A study of gender-based violence and minority ethnic women in Ireland. Full report.* Dublin: Women's Health Council.

World Health Organization. (2016). *Ethical and safety recommendations for intervention research on violence against women. Building on lessons from the WHO publication Putting women first: Ethical and safety recommendations for research on domestic violence against women.* Geneva: World Health Organization.

Wuest, J., Merritt-Gray, M., Lent, B., Varcoe, C., Connors, A. J., & Ford-Gilboe, M. (2007). Patterns of medication use among women survivors of intimate partner violence. *Canadian Journal of Public Health, 98*(6), 460–464.

Zimmerman, C., & Watts, C. (2003). *WHO ethical and safety recommendations for interviewing trafficked women.* Geneva: World Health Organization.

# 41

# CREATIVE METHODOLOGIES

## Using digital stories to embed the voices of children within programs for men who use domestic violence

*Katie Lamb and Cathy Humphreys*

### Introduction

Historically, our insight into the impact of domestic violence on the lives of children has come from professional and adult observation (Eriksson & Nasman, 2012; Guille, 2004). However, since the advancement of the 'new sociology of childhood', children and young people are increasingly being portrayed as social actors with valid views and considered experts in their own lives (Humphreys, Houghton, & Ellis, 2008). As a result, there has been increased acknowledgement of the importance of seeking children's perspectives in research, policy, practice and decision-making that affects their lives (Cashmore, 2006; Humphreys et al., 2008). This increased focus on the importance of gaining children's perspectives has been reflected across a range of disciplines including in the emergence of qualitative research studies with children who have experienced domestic violence (Alderson, 2015; Cater & Forssell, 2014; Eriksson & Nasman, 2012; Holt, 2015, 2018; Stanley, Miller, & Richardson Foster, 2012; Swanston, Bowyer, & Vetere, 2014).

While research with children and young people who have experienced domestic violence is growing, one area where children's voices are still seldom heard is in the design, delivery and evaluation of programs for fathers who use violence (Alderson, Westmarland, & Kelly, 2013; Rayns, 2010). This is despite several authors and significant anecdotal evidence suggesting that engaging men as fathers may be a powerful lever for increasing motivation to change (Broady, Gray, Gaffney, & Lewis, 2015; Stanley, Graham-Kevan, & Borthwick, 2012). This chapter draws upon research undertaken in Victoria, Australia which sought to combine traditional research methods and digital storytelling to bring together two strands of work which rarely intersect: work with children experiencing domestic violence and programs for men who use domestic violence. This chapter will outline some of the research findings as well as the authors' reflections on the strengths and challenges of using digital technology in research with children who have experienced domestic violence.

### *Research study*

While internationally some work has been undertaken to develop specific interventions for fathers who use violence (Scott, 2010), often the development of programs for men who use violence has occurred without strong consideration of their role as parents (Broady et al., 2015; Mackay, Gibson, Lam, & Beecham, 2015). While best practice standards both in Australia and in the UK require that programs working with men who use violence maintain contact with the man's partner/ex-partner, there are not similar guidelines for how programs should interact or engage with children. Our understanding about the degree to which children would like to be engaged in their father's change process and their views about the type of parenting content they would like covered by programs is also very limited.

In recognition of these gaps, qualitative research was undertaken with children and young people who had experienced domestic violence and were aged between 9 and 19 years. Consistent with other research in this area (Morris, Hegarty, & Humphreys, 2012), young people aged over 16 years were considered competent or mature minors and able to give informed consent to participate in the research themselves. The consent of the non-offending parent was required in addition to assent from young people aged 15 years or younger. In recognition of the feminist underpinnings of this study which consider payments to participants as a principle of ethically sound research (Crivello, Camfield, & Woodhead, 2009), an honorarium was paid to all children and young people in the form of a gift voucher. Considerable work was undertaken to ensure that power imbalances between researcher and children were addressed in the interview process. This included allowing the young person to bring a support worker with them, conducting interviews in a location familiar to the young person, providing meals or snacks and using an age-appropriate format (Morris et al., 2012). A Steering Committee comprising two community organisations and the researchers was established to provide advice about the study design and also assisted in the recruitment of young people for the study.

The research comprised three stages, each guided by a research question developed iteratively with different methods of data collection. The first stage of the research used focus groups and interviews with children and young people who had lived with domestic violence to explore the question: 'What are the perspectives of children and young people on fathering in the context of domestic violence?'.

Following the interviews and focus group, the second stage of the research involved inviting children and young people who participated in the first stage to attend a two-day digital storytelling workshop at the Australian Centre for the Moving Image in Melbourne. Eight girls (aged 10–18 years) accepted the invitation to create a three-minute digital story outlining what they believed fathers who attend a program to address their violence need to know about the impact of their behaviour on their children. A range of protections was introduced to protect the identity of the children and young people. Some of the stories created can be found at www.counterpointadvisory.com.au/phd-research. The research question guiding this stage was 'What are the key messages children and young people who have experienced domestic violence have for fathers who attend a program to address his violence?'.

The third stage of the research was a series of focus groups with professionals who manage, develop or deliver programs for men who use violence. The purpose of the focus groups was to determine whether workers believed that it would be feasible to introduce the digital stories created by young people into Men's Behavioural Change Programs and what the impacts and challenges of doing this might be. A total of 21 professionals attended the digital storytelling screening and discussion. The research question guiding this stage was, 'What are the likely impacts of children and young people's digital stories on a program for fathers who use violence and its participants?'. While the results of this third stage of the research will not be presented in full in this chapter, they are found in an alternative publication (Lamb, 2017).

Data obtained from the interviews and focus groups with children and young people were transcribed and entered into NVivo software as were the written scripts children and young people wrote as part of the development of their digital story. The data was then subject to thematic analysis following the method outlined by Attride-Stirling (2001). The initial line-by-line coding indicated that the emerging themes from the first two stages of the research were similar and therefore the thematic analysis of both stages occurred across both data sets to interrogate the data for secondary themes, and emerging concepts (Attride-Stirling, 2001).

## Discussion and analysis

### *The perspectives of children and young people on fathers in the context of domestic violence*

There is now an evidence base that strongly supports the notion that fathers who use violence are having significant negative impacts on their children (Buckley, Holt, & Whelan, 2007; Holt, Buckley, & Whelan, 2008; Kitzmann, Gaylord, Holt, & Kenny, 2003). Children and young people in the study described good fathers as making their children feel safe and loved unconditionally but suggested that their own interactions with their father often resulted in verbal or emotional abuse.

In line with research which indicates that emotional abuse can lead to mental health problems (Paul & Eckenrode, 2015), a number of young people described their fathers abusive behaviour as leaving themselves or their siblings feeling depressed, anxious and undermining their self-confidence:

> My sister suffers like really bad anxiety and stuff like that. And I don't know, like probably it stems from Dad probably putting her down. Just, I don't know. She doesn't want to go anywhere because she doesn't want anyone to look at her. Like she just freaks out. Doesn't want anyone to speak to her or anything like that because whenever you'd talk to Dad or anything, like he'd make you second guess everything that you're saying, or he'd put you down with however you look or whatever you've done or anything like that. Just not nice.
>
> (Young Person 9)

The tendency for fathers who use violence to be 'quite accessible in a physical sense' but to be described by their children in terms of 'lack of care' and involvement in family life has been noted in previous research (Cater & Forssell, 2014, p. 188). One young person in the current study suggested that they believed that this is the reason that fathers who use violence do not really understand the impacts of their behaviour on their children:

> 'cause it's just like, abusive fathers generally don't talk to their kids. They don't understand that they're having an emotional impact.
>
> (Young Person 5)

Recent work has suggested that children are also impacted by their father's coercive control (Callaghan, Alexander, Sixsmith, & Fellin, 2015; Katz, 2016). This study's findings were consistent with previous work and found that children and young people described a number of ways in which their fathers used coercive control and the distress that this had caused them. Methods of control described by children and young people in the study were similar to those that have been described by adult victim survivors (Stark, 2007) and included: control of the distribution of resources, use of surveillance and isolation, and the use of fear as a means of ensuring compliance.

Previous research has found that adult victim survivors describe the psychological impacts of experiencing domestic violence as 'extensive and penetrating' and that their partners feel like they are 'omnipresent' (Stark, 2007) or 'an absent presence' (Thiara & Humphreys, 2015), a sentiment expressed in the digital story of one of the young persons in the current study:

> If I look hard enough, I can still see him in the shadows and around corners. My mind adds silhouettes of him underneath streetlights and behind windows, the figures unshakeable no matter how many times I blink.
>
> (Young Person 16)

Consistent with other research about fathers (Morman & Floyd, 2006), the current study found that children and young people believed an important role for fathers was to act as a positive role model. With only a few exceptions, the children and young people in this study felt that their own fathers were poor role models who made them feel sceptical and afraid of men in general. Several of the young women suggested that they had already had experiences of dating individuals who were like their fathers and they believed that their experiences of growing up with violence had impacted their view of relationships. Several young people also suggested that they did not plan to become involved in a relationship or have children, as they saw the world as too scary a place for children or else worried that they would become violent parents themselves.

## Key messages for fathers who attend a program to address their violence

Children's voices are very rarely heard in the design, delivery and evaluation of programs for fathers who use violence. To address this gap, the children and young people in the study were asked what they would like fathers who attend a program to address their violence to understand. They described wanting their fathers to recognise the significant impact of the violence on their lives. Expanding on this discussion, children and young people often described a desire for fathers who attend programs to address their violence to be told that they need to 'make amends' with their children. The researchers subsequently grouped these comments under the organising theme of 'reparation' which became a significant theme to emerge from the research.

While a small number of young people said that they did not want to have any further contact with their father, the majority of children and young people said they would consider having some contact if their father made substantial changes to both his behaviour and attitudes. It should be acknowledged that all participants in the study (even those young people who stated that they did not want to have an ongoing relationship with their father) still expressed a desire to receive reparation from their fathers so that they could move on with their lives and achieve closure.

Thematic network analysis of the data collected in this study showed that young people saw reparation as comprising three key stages: 'addressing the past', 'commitment to change' and then (in some cases) conditions for 'rebuilding trust' and moving forward (see Figure 41.1).

## Addressing the past

The first stage of reparation described by young people, 'addressing the past', prioritised the need for fathers to acknowledge that they had done something wrong, recognise the harm they had caused and apologise for this. A number of the young people saw the need for fathers to

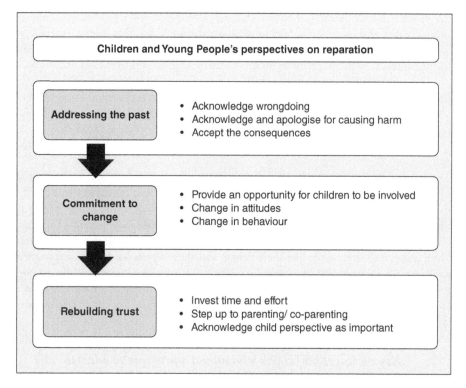

*Figure 41.1* Children and young people's perspectives on reparation

admit they had done something wrong as a significant challenge. They described their fathers as being 'deluded' and in 'denial' about their behaviour. One young person described her father as being certain that the reason his children did not want to see him was because their mother had encouraged them to feel negatively towards him. This was a source of frustration for the young person who felt her mother had been unfairly demonised within their family's social networks:

> Yeah, [our father] like, completely brainwashed himself into thinking that he is the good parent and that mum's brainwashed us. He never hit us. He never yelled at us. He was always the perfect father.
>
> (Young Person 6)

Young people were also very clear that they did not want to hear excuses from their father about why the violence had occurred. One young person said that their father often stated that he was only violent 'when they deserved it'. It took some years before she realised this was not an acceptable justification. Another young person said that her father used his history of growing up around violence as an excuse for why he was abusive. While she had some sympathy for the negative environment he had grown up in, she objected to him trying to justify his behaviour.

The young people in the study were in universal agreement about how valuable a genuine apology from their father would be. However, when questioned further, each had a different view on the necessary content and context of an apology that would be needed to be truly effective. Several young people said that their father never apologised and this was a significant issue for them:

> I'm still angry because you never even apologised, admitted the least bit of guilt and that makes me angrier still and unable to move on.
>
> (Young Person 6)

Several young people felt that an apology on its own could be important:

> Like it would be amazing for them to apologise and actually mean it, like they could apologise and like not mean it, but like they've got to mean it and then it'll just – an apology can like do a lot.
>
> (Young Person 15)

Other young people had opposing views where their father apologised all the time, but kept repeating the behaviour and therefore the apology became meaningless:

> I've seen apologies all the time and he always – he does apologise but it just always comes back to the same case, so yeah I feel a bit more relieved when he apologised but it just, it repeats itself.
>
> (Young Person 7)

These young people were very clear that an apology needed to be real and genuine and backed up with evidence of change. An apology would become meaningless if the violence or abusive behaviour occurred again. One young person also said that they wanted to be clear that just because a father apologises to his child for his behaviour did not mean that their mother automatically had to forgive him as well.

Some young people had strong feelings about the need for an apology to be followed by their father taking the consequences of his behaviour or paying 'penance'. Just what this meant varied according to different young people. One set of siblings felt strongly that their father should have had consequences from the legal system:

> He denied all the abuse and stuff. If he had of – I mean, that's what happened. And maybe if he'd done some time in prison and apologised for what he did, I'd prob-ably – you know, I might think about seeing him. But he just denies that everything happened and he refuses to apologise for anything or own up to his behaviour. He's like a child.
>
> (Young Person 6)

In the absence of criminal justice intervention, they felt that fathers should still experience the consequences of their actions:

> And sometimes the consequences don't end up being legal time. They end up – your kids are going to be weird around you for a while.
>
> (Young Person 5)

The impacts of a public statement or admission of responsibility by men who use domestic violence has been identified in the literature as having benefits for victim recovery (Hopkins,

2012). It has also been found that children who have experienced domestic violence describe 'the ability of their father to truly listen, empathise, and understand what life had been like for those living under his regime of control' as important (Alderson, 2015, p. 223). However, it also has been suggested that practices of apology and forgiveness can be dangerous in the context of domestic violence and can also be used as a powerful tool for continuing oppression and control in the family:

> Apology and forgiveness, the primary method of restorative repair, can often be anything but healing. They can be essential weapons for placing an offender in a position to inflict new wounds and reopen old ones.
>
> (Acorn, 2004, p. 74)

This is a relevant point in relation to the young people in this study who described fathers who constantly apologised but continued their violence and may explain why children and young people described the first stage of reparation 'addressing the past' as being supported by a 'commitment to change'.

## Commitment to change

The concept of 'commitment to change' was described by children and young people as a father engaging in a process of change that included his children. Once the violence and its harm has been acknowledged, an apology made and consequences follow, the next priority identified was a need to see evidence of willingness to change:

> Once I thought an apology was all you needed. But I don't think that would even be enough. I need to see your actions have changed. Because saying sorry . . . well they are just words. I need actions. Actions to prove to me you are truly sorry. I don't care about the money or the bribes to win me back. I just want a father that I am not scared to see.
>
> (Young Person 15)

Several young people suggested that one way that their father could show a commitment to change would be if he attended therapy or a program to address his violence. However, currently there is little evidence available about children's knowledge of their father's attendance at a program to address his violence. The evidence which is available suggests that children are mostly not told when their father is attending a program, nor do they have any involvement in the program or know what their father has learnt (Alderson et al., 2013; Rayns, 2010). These are potentially significant issues for accountability. The results of the current study support the notion that children currently have limited involvement in programs for fathers with only one young person being aware that her father had attended a program to address his violence.

When asked whether they believed that young people should be told when their father is attending a program, the majority of the young people answered that they believe they should be because:

> I think that way the kids could know that they're actually trying to improve, they're trying to say to – they're trying to say to their kids basically that I want our relationship to go back to normal or however they used to be. Yeah so I think it's a good thing if the kids knew.
>
> (Young Person 7)

Research has found that when programs for fathers who use violence are evaluated, children's perspectives are rarely heard (Alderson, Kelly, & Westmarland, 2015; Alderson et al., 2013). In the current study, the majority of young people were confident that their fathers could change if they wanted to and believed a father who would not change just did not care enough for his children or family:

> He can change – a dad can change. But you can also tell that he's also – if he goes there and just listens then he probably doesn't even care and then comes back and then he doesn't change – he doesn't change a bit. It's like he doesn't care.
>
> (Young Person 3)

Young people were asked about the type of changes they would like to see if their father attended a program for his violence. The changes they valued as important indicators of the program's effectiveness included changes to both attitudes and behaviours with many outcomes directly relating to their fathers' interactions and communication with their children as well as with their mothers:

> One of our father's favourite mottos was children should be seen and not heard, especially when it came to women, and his wife shouldn't be seen OR heard.
>
> (Young People 5 and 6 in conversation)

Another suggested that she would determine whether change had occurred by the way her father made her feel:

> Like be there when we do drop off and pick up for him to actually be there and for him to not get angry at me and say bad things, not to make me feel uncomfortable when I'm there, to make me feel safe, to make me feel wanted, to make me feel loved, like yeah.
>
> (Young Person 15)

In addition, several young people also spoke about wanting their father to stop their violence not only for their children and their relationships but also for themselves. They believed their fathers were having unhappy lives as a result of their violence. They also suggested that an important outcome of attending a program would be that fathers come to terms with the abuse they experienced as children:

> Because men – people like these need to change not just for their children, but for themselves emotionally as well.
>
> (Young Person 6)

The cessation of abusive behaviour is considered an essential element of any reparation between children and their fathers (Arean & Davis, 2007). In the current study, children and young people wanted violence to cease as part of the process of committing to change. They also wanted to see a change in their father's attitudes and behaviour towards themselves and their mother. These findings fit well with other recent work which found that cessation of violence alone may not make women and children safer, as once the physical violence stops it is possible women and children may continue 'to live in unhealthy atmospheres laden with tension and threat' (Westmarland & Kelly, 2013).

## *Rebuilding trust*

The third stage of the reparation process described by children and young people in this study was identified as 'rebuilding trust'. This was the stage that young people who wanted to have an ongoing relationship with their father saw as extremely important. However, they also saw it as one that was difficult to achieve. It included their fathers investing time in them, stepping up to parenting and being a reliable co-parent.

One of the areas of significant agreement was that it would take some time for children to be able to trust their fathers. One young person suggested fathers need to:

> tell them it's going to be alright and work on it. Like they're not going to trust him straight away, but he's gotta like work on it and let the kids know that nothing like that is going to ever happen again.
>
> (Young Person 15)

When children and young people were asked about what their fathers could do to make it up to them, one young person was very clear that the emphasis should be on fathers to think of ways to make it up to their children:

> I don't really know what you could do, so that I would want to see you again. How do you think you are going to change this? It's up to you.
>
> (Young Person 12)

Other young people were more willing to offer suggestions for how their father could make it up to them. This included ensuring that time with children was spent well and was quality time and not uncomfortable. Some of the suggestions for fathers included being generous, giving your child things, making them feel special and taking them places.

Another concept discussed by young people was the need for fathers who have been violent to 'step up to parenting'. In fact, one young person called their digital story *Step Up Your Game*. The young people discussed this issue when talking about what makes a good father, and then reflected on how a father who has been violent might go about making amends and rebuilding trust with his children. Another young person suggested that this would differ according to the child and their interests and fathers should make the time to find out about what interested their children.

Young people believed that fathers too often (in their experience) play the role of 'good time guy' and do not help out or get involved with parenting. Young people wanted their fathers to 'step up' and do a better job of co-parenting with their mothers. The literature suggests that 'maternal alienation' is one of the tactics deployed by fathers who use violence, with the aim to undermine the relationship between mothers and their children (Morris, 2009). In the current study, young people expressed considerable anger about how after the physical violence had ended and their parents had separated, their fathers often continued with the verbal and emotional abuse of their mothers and how damaging this was for them:

> In the emails you do not want to know what he calls our mother. 'Cause he thinks we don't read them. He's convinced that mum never shows them to us, and that, how it's all this elaborate plan of mum and she's planted these ideas that he abused us in our heads.
>
> (Young Person 6)

In fact, the way in which their fathers spoke about their mothers was a key factor that determined whether young people wanted to spend time with their fathers. One young person explained how she looked forward to her visits with her father (and even snuck out to see him at times) but how these visits often ended in frustration and disappointment because:

All he ever wanted to talk about was how bad mum was.

(Young Person 16)

Children and young people described being a reliable co-parent as respecting a child's mother and listening to what their children want from them, even if that was no ongoing contact for a period of time. This was a key element of reparation for some young people who felt that even if their fathers had admitted the harm they caused, apologised and shown a commitment to change there was still the opportunity for children to say, they were not ready to spend time their fathers. As one young person explained:

Like I never used to do school work and I was always sad at school and I never talked to anyone about anything and once I got over that it was better because I didn't see my dad and it was better for me not to see him.

(Young Person 10)

## Reflections on the strengths and challenges of using digital storytelling as part of the research method

Previous work has found visual research effective in providing opportunities to gain insight into children's lives and perspectives (Fournier, Bridge, Pritchard Kennedt, Alibhai, & Konde-Lule, 2014; Gibbs, MacDougall, & Harden, 2013; Heidelberger & Smith, 2016). For these reasons, digital storytelling was used to augment traditional research methods in the current study.

Research about the impacts of participating in a digital storytelling workshop is best described as emerging (Anderson & Cook, 2015; Moorehead, 2014; Shea, 2011; Stellavato, 2013). The insights from the literature suggest that participants who have experienced trauma describe the process of engaging in a digital storytelling workshop emotionally difficult, but also cathartic (Ferrari, Rice, & McKenzie, 2015; Loe, 2013; Moorehead, 2014; Stellavato, 2013), and the effects comparable with other forms of therapy (Shea, 2011).

For children and young people in the current study (and their workers), an interest in participating in the digital storytelling workshop was a key driver for engagement in the research process. Workers told the researchers that they viewed favourably the potential for young people to gain some tangible skills from the project.

Digital storytelling was also found to show considerable promise as a mechanism for capturing the perspectives of children and young people and acting as a valuable tool for discussing the implications of their violence on the children of men who attend a program. The majority of the program managers and facilitators could see benefits from integrating the digital stories into their programs as a way of increasing men's understanding of the impacts of domestic violence on children. One practitioner suggested that they often find it difficult to explain to fathers how their children would be feeling, and the digital stories would be one way of overcoming resistance:

It is one thing being handed a piece of paper, being asked about how do you feel about what you have done to your children. But hearing an actual story, a true story from a child it resonates better . . . it has more impact than handing them a piece of paper . . . that visual content it is really mind blowing.

(Practitioner Focus Group 3)

Digital storytelling also had the unanticipated benefit of providing an effective way for the researchers to share their research findings with a broader audience. Like all research with children in the context of domestic violence, there were a significant number of ethical considerations that needed to be made in preparing the Human Research Ethics Application. A number of studies have acknowledged that the use of visual research methods can also bring a range of additional ethical challenges for researchers (Cox et al., 2014) and this was the case for the current study. Some of the unique challenges posed by the use of digital storytelling are outlined later.

One of the most significant procedural ethical considerations for this work was ensuring participants' safety. The children and young people's workers played a role in determining which young people were invited to participate, taking into account the issues of risk, vulnerability and maturity and used a risk assessment framework developed by the researchers. The challenges around ensuring anonymity when using visual research methods with children are discussed in the literature in a range of contexts (Nutbrown, 2011).

In the current study, all of the young people were considered to be at some risk of danger from their fathers and therefore a decision was made to ensure all stories were anonymous. As one young person said in the interview:

I honestly believe if my father ever found where we lived, like I wouldn't be surprised if he came and killed us all. Because that's the sort of person he is.

(Participant 5)

In the current study, when the likelihood of their father's viewing the stories (given they were being developed for the purpose of being played within programs for men who use domestic violence) was discussed with children and young people, there was general (but not unanimous) agreement that anonymity was the safest option.

In order to ensure anonymity, the voices of all of the children and young people who completed digital stories were altered to ensure they could not be identified. This was an effective strategy in protecting identity, but did lead to the voices sounding a little 'robotic'. This was an issue that concerned some of the practitioners who attended focus groups who suggested that child actors should have been hired to read the young people's scripts. While the researchers did consider re-recording the digital stories, a decision was made not to do this, due to concerns about maintaining authenticity and respect for the considerable work already undertaken by children and young people. One practitioner suggested that they would approach this issue by informing men in their program that the reason for the voices of the children being altered was because these children are still living in significant fear of their fathers. This in itself would be a powerful message. A key learning was that this issue should have been considered in an earlier stage of research planning.

One of the key tenets of participatory research is the desire to ensure that participants 'stand on equal ground' with researchers and some commentators have asked what happens to that ground when participants' names (and voices) are removed from materials produced through a research process that was meant to be empowering (Gubrium, Hill, & Flicker, 2014, p. 1611). In the current study, as has been found in context of other digital storytelling projects, at times participants want to be identifiable and claim credit as experts in their topic and their new skills (Bagnoli & Clark, 2010; Gubrium et al., 2014). Again, this issue still sits somewhat unresolved and uncomfortably with the researchers.

Another challenge for the project was the dissemination of the digital stories once completed. While considerable effort had been invested in ensuring that the children and young people provided fully informed consent about how the stories would be used once complete, less consideration was given to how the stories would be disseminated. Previous research has suggested that some children and young people who participate in digital storytelling workshops prefer that their stories not appear on the internet particularly when of a sensitive nature (Loe, 2013; Willis et al., 2014). This issue was discussed with children and young people in the current study, with three young people giving consent for their stories to be placed on the internet. The remaining five agreed for their stories to be shared with programs and services via a USB stick. In theory this was a sound ethical procedure; however, in practice this decision significantly hampered distribution of the stories and produced a significant administrative burden.

## Conclusion

One of the significant conclusions that can be drawn from this work is that children as young as 9 years of age are often very interested in being involved in research even when the subject matter might be described as sensitive. By seeking the perspectives of children who have experienced domestic violence, a greater understanding of the interaction between children and fathers in the context of domestic violence has been gained. In particular, children and young people's views on the importance of reparation have significant implications for policy and practice for both those working with children and fathers who use violence. The use of digital storytelling provided a more interesting and enjoyable way to engage with children and young people as well as providing a useful way to disseminate research findings to a broader range of audiences than publication alone might achieve. This approach was not without its challenges and some of those encountered have been outlined throughout this chapter to provide guidance for others seeking to use digital technology to engage in participatory research with children and young people.

## Critical findings

- Digital storytelling is one potentially useful strategy for capturing the perspectives of children and young people who have experienced domestic violence and sharing those messages with fathers who attend programs to address their violence.
- Children and young people express a desire to engage in a process of reparation with their fathers after domestic violence.
- Reparation was considered important by children and young people regardless of whether they wanted a relationship with their father into the future or not.
- Key components of reparation described by children and young people included: addressing the past, making a commitment to change and rebuilding trust.

## Implications for policy, practice and research

- There are a number of additional ethical and practical considerations when using visual research methods to engage with children and young people who have experienced domestic violence and these issues should be given significant consideration in the early stages of research planning.

- There is potential for those who work with fathers who use violence to consider creative and safe options to ensure the perspectives of children and young people are brought into their work.
- Reparation has been identified by children and young people as a key principle that they would like to see inform engagement with families after domestic violence.

# References

Acorn, A. (2004). *Compulsory compassion: A critique of restorative justice.* Vancouver: UBC Press.

Alderson, S. (2015). *An investigation into the impact of domestic violence perpetrator programs on children and young people* (PhD). Durham University, Durham, UK.

Alderson, S., Kelly, L., & Westmarland, N. (2015). Expanding understandings of success: Domestic violence perpetrator programmes, children and fathering. In *Domestic violence and protecting children* (pp. 182–195). London: Jessica Kingsley Publishers.

Alderson, S., Westmarland, N., & Kelly, L. (2013). The need for accountability to, and support for, children of men on domestic violence perpetrator programmes. *Child Abuse Review, 22*(3), 182–193.

Anderson, K., & Cook, J. (2015). Challenges and opportunities of using digital storytelling as a trauma narrative intervention for children. *Advances in Social Work, 16*(1), 78–89.

Arean, J., & Davis, L. (2007). Working with fathers in batterer intervention programs. In J. Edleson & O. Williams (Eds.), *Parenting by men who batter: New directions for assessment and intervention* (pp. 118–130). New York: Oxford University Press.

Attride-Stirling, J. (2001). Thematic networks: An analytic tool for qualitative research. *Qualitative Research, 1*(3), 385–405.

Bagnoli, A., & Clark, A. (2010). Focus groups with young people: A participatory approach to research planning. *Journal of Youth Studies, 13*(1), 101–119.

Broady, T., Gray, R., Gaffney, I., & Lewis, P. (2015). 'I miss my little one a lot': How father love motivates change in men who have used violence. *Child Abuse Review, 26*(5), 328–339.

Buckley, H., Holt, S., & Whelan, S. (2007). Listen to me! Children's experiences of domestic violence. *Child Abuse Review, 16*, 296–310.

Callaghan, J., Alexander, J., Sixsmith, J., & Fellin, L. C. (2015, December). Beyond "witnessing": Children's experiences of coercive control in domestic violence and abuse. *Journal of Interpersonal Violence,* 1–31.

Cashmore, J. (2006). Ethical issues concerning consent in obtaining children's reports on their experience of violence. *Child Abuse & Neglect, 30*, 969–977.

Cater, A., & Forssell, A. M. (2014). Descriptions of fathers' care by children exposed to intimate partner violence (IPV) – Relative neglect and children's needs. *Child & Family Social Work, 2*, 185.

Cox, S., Drew, S., Guillemin, M., Howell, C., Warr, D., & Waycott, J. (2014). *Guidelines for ethical visual research methods.* Melbourne: Victoria Visual Research Collaboratory.

Crivello, G., Camfield, L., & Woodhead, M. (2009). How can children tell us about their wellbeing? Exploring the potential of participatory research approaches with young lives. *Social Indicator Research, 90*, 51–72.

Eriksson, M., & Nasman, E. (2012). Interviews with children exposed to violence. *Children & Society, 1*, 63.

Ferrari, M., Rice, C., & McKenzie, K. (2015). ACE pathways project: Therapeutic catharsis in digital storytelling. *Psychiatric Services, 66*(5), 556.

Fournier, B., Bridge, A., Pritchard Kennedt, A., Alibhai, A., & Konde-Lule, J. (2014). Hear our voices: A Photovoice project with children who are orphaned and living with HIV in a Ugandan group home. *Children and Youth Services Review, 45*, 55–63.

Gibbs, L., MacDougall, C., & Harden, J. (2013). Development of an ethical methodology for post-bushfire research with children. *Health Sociology Review, 22*(2), 114–123.

Gubrium, A., Hill, A., & Flicker, S. (2014). A Situated practice of ethics for participatory visual and digital methods in public health research and practice: A focus on digital storytelling. *American Journal of Public Health, 104*(9), 1606–1614.

Guille, L. (2004). Men who batter and their children: An integrated review. *Aggression and Violent Behavior: A Review Journal, 9,* 129–163.

Heidelberger, L., & Smith, C. (2016). Low income, urban children's perspectives on physical activity: A photovoice project. *Maternal and Child Health Journal, 20*(6), 1124–1132.

Holt, S. (2015). Focusing on fathering in the context of domestic abuse: Children's and father's perspectives. In N. Stanley & C. Humphreys (Eds.), *Domestic violence and protecting children*. London: Jessica Kingsley Publishers.

Holt, S. (2018). A voice or a choice? Children's views on participating in decisions about post-separation contact with domestically abusive fathers. *Journal of Social Welfare and Family Law, 40*(4), 459–476.

Holt, S., Buckley, H., & Whelan, S. (2008). The impact of exposure to domestic violence on children and young people: A review of the literature. *Child Abuse & Neglect, 32*(8), 797–810.

Hopkins, C. (2012). Tempering idealism with realism: Using restorative justice processes to promote acceptance of responsibility in cases of intimate partner violence [article]. *Harvard Journal of Law and Gender, 35*(2), 311–355.

Humphreys, C., & Absler, D. (2011). History repeating: Child protection responses to domestic violence. *Child and Family Social Work, 16,* 369–489.

Humphreys, C., Houghton, C., & Ellis, J. (2008). *Literature review: Better outcomes for children and young people experiencing domestic abuse- directions for good practice*. Edinburgh: The Scottish Government.

Katz, E. (2016). Beyond the physical incident model: How children living with domestic violence are harmed by and resist regimes of coercive control. *Child Abuse Review, 25*(1), 46–59.

Kitzmann, K., Gaylord, N., Holt, A., & Kenny, E. (2003). Child witnesses to domestic violence: A meta-analytic review. *Journal of Consulting and Clinical Psychology, 2,* 339.

Lamb, K. (2017). *Seen and heard: Embedding the voices of children and young people who have experienced family violence in programs for fathers* (Doctor of Philosophy), University of Melbourne, Melbourne.

Loe, M. (2013). The digital life history project: Intergenerational collaborative research. *Gerontology & Geriatrics Education, 34*(1), 26–42.

Mackay, E., Gibson, A., Lam, H., & Beecham, D. (2015). *Perpetrator Interventions in Australia: Part one- literature review*. New South Wales: Australia's National Research Organisation for Women's Safety (ANROWS).

Moorehead, V. (2014). *Digital storytelling and urban American Indians: Exploring participant experiences*. Berkeley, CA: The Wright Institute.

Morman, M., & Floyd, K. (2006). Good fathering: Father and son perceptions of what it means to be a good father. *Fathering, 4*(2), 113–136.

Morris, A. (2009). Gendered dynamics of abuse and violence in families: Considering the abusive household gender regime. *Child Abuse Review, 18,* 414–427.

Morris, A., Hegarty, K., & Humphreys, C. (2012). Ethical and safe: Research with children about domestic violence. *Research Ethics, 8*(2), 125–139.

Nutbrown, C. (2011). Naked by the pool? Blurring the image? Ethical issues in the portrayal of young children in arts-based educational research. *Qualitative Inquiry, 17*(1), 3–14.

Paul, E., & Eckenrode, J. (2015). Childhood psychological maltreatment subtypes and adolescent depressive symptoms. *Child Abuse & Neglect, 47,* 38–47.

Rayns, G. (2010). *What are children and young people's views and opinions of perpetrator programmes for the violent father/male carer?* Leeds, UK: NSPCC.

Scott, K. L. (2010). *Caring dads theory manual*. London, ON, Canada: Caring Dads.

Shea, M. (2011). *An exploration of personal experiences of taking part in a digital storytelling project* (MSc). Sheffield, UK: Sheffield Hallam University.

Stanley, N., Graham-Kevan, N., & Borthwick, R. (2012). Fathers and domestic violence: Building motivation for change through perpetrator programmes. *Child Abuse Review, 21*(4), 264–274.

Stanley, N., Miller, P., & Richardson Foster, H. (2012). Engaging with children's and parents' perspectives on domestic violence. *Child & Family Social Work, 17*(2), 192–201.

Stark, E. (2007). *Coercive control: The entrapment of women in personal life*. New York, NY: Oxford University Press.

Stellavato, M. (2013). *Tales of healing: A narrative analysis of the digital storytelling workshop experience*. Eugene, OR: University of Oregon.

Swanston, J., Bowyer, L., & Vetere, A. (2014). Towards a richer understanding of school-age children's experiences of domestic violence: The voices of children and their mothers. *Clinical Child Psychology & Psychiatry, 19*(2), 184–201.

Thiara, R. K., & Humphreys, C. (2015). Absent presence: the ongoing impact of men's violence on the mother-child relationship. *Child & Family Social Work, 22*(1), 1–9.

Westmarland, N., & Kelly, L. (2013). Why extending measurements of 'Success' in domestic violence perpetrator programmes matters for social work. *British Journal of Social Work, 43*, 1092–1110.

Willis, N., Frewin, L., Miller, A., Dziwa, C., Mavhu, W., & Cowan, F. (2014). "my story" – HIV positive adolescents tell their story through film. *Children and Youth Services Review, 45*, 129–136.

# 42

# QUALITATIVE INTERVIEWS WITH CHILDREN AND ADOLESCENTS WHO HAVE EXPERIENCED DOMESTIC VIOLENCE AND ABUSE

*Carolina Øverlien and Stephanie Holt*

## Introduction

Researchers have included children and adolescents in research for hundreds of years. Charles Darwin (1877), for example, conducted detailed observations of his ten children, documenting their biological development and emotional reactions from their first moment in life. The observations were published in the journal *Mind*, and the article, *Biographical Sketch of an Infant*, in the year 1877. Jean Piaget's theory of children's cognitive developmental phases, developed during the first part of the last century, were also based on his own children's thoughts and behaviour. His theory has had a significant impact on the Western world's understanding of children and childhood (cf. Piaget, 1964). One can conclude, however, that the main interest in these and other early studies was to conduct studies *on* children, with the aim of developing universal theories, rather than to conduct studies *about, with* or *for* children, capturing them in their situational, contextual and individual surroundings. (There are noteworthy exceptions, see for example Mead, 1930). Throughout this historical journey, the interest to describe, understand and analyse children and childhood, not only by observing them or having their caretakers answering surveys on their behalf, has grown exponentially.

Increasing attention to and focus on individual children's voices in research, as well as practice and policymaking, has become particularly evident since the early 1990s, with many countries ratifying the United Nations Convention on the Rights of the Child (UNCRC). Articles 12 and 13 of the UNCRC clearly state that children should be informed, involved and consulted on all decisions with which they and their lives are concerned. As such, the philosophical rhetoric underpinning the UNCRC reflects a construction of childhood that appreciates children as competent social actors whose thoughts and opinions are worthy of consideration (Bosisio, 2012). This theoretical and conceptual shift from viewing children as 'mere objects of enquiry' to dynamic and key participants (James, Jenks, & Prout, 1998; Powell & Smith, 2009) recognises not only their capacity to operate within 'adult-centred socially constructed meanings of citizenship', but also their capacity to influence them as well (Bacon, 2014, p. 22). In more recent years, the issue of engaging with children and involving them in research has similarly developed considerable impetus (Øverlien & Holt, 2017). This reflects an empirically grounded awareness that this involvement is not only a right, but also that such participation values the original contribution that children can make to our understanding of childhood and to how children experience their individual lives. Simultaneous considerations of children as 'experts' in their own lives (Kjorholt, 2002, p. 64) affords children the rights to hold and express an opinion, to have that opinion taken seriously and respected, to be consulted in all matters that affect them and to participate in decisions that impact on their individual lives. However, despite legal obligations under the UNCRC and an evolving consensus that recognises children as social and competent actors, adults can struggle to translate this rhetoric into meaningful research practice reality (Butler, Scanlan, Douglas, & Murch, 2002; Masson, 2003; Skjorten, 2013). In particular, barriers to children's research participation include ethical concerns for children's capacity to consent and worries over re-traumatising children who participate in research on sensitive topics, in turn potentially jeopardising and minimising their right to research participation (Øverlien & Holt, 2017). This is something we return to later in the chapter.

Today, in what Silverman (1997) calls our 'interview society', qualitative interviews as a research method have become widely used and significant to empirical studies, including studies where children are informants. Indeed, qualitative methods are often used in research to explore sensitive topics or to understand the lived experience of a person, offering an insider perspective that can inform evidence-based practice (Padgett, 2008). Whilst acknowledging that quantitative methods can be used successfully in children's research, qualitative data nonetheless provides richer meaning and context to the child's experience (Morrow & Richards, 1996; Punch, 2002) and are more appropriate when seeking to explore the subjective meaning given to experiences of abuse by survivors (Downes, Kelly, & Westmarland, 2014). Regardless of whether the study design involves an ethnographic, narrative, phenomenological or indeed case study approach, we would argue that employing qualitative methods across these designs can allow respondents to communicate their own subjective experience, which Freeman and Mathison (2009) argue is more suited to authentic research with children. Furthermore, qualitative methods, in contrast to quantitative approaches, allow for a more emotive dataset and understanding of the child's world (Grover, 2004).

Employing a range of varying research designs, the authors of this chapter have conducted qualitative research with children and adolescents who have had difficult life experiences, including living with domestic violence and abuse (DVA). However, we argue that children growing up with domestic violence are children first and foremost, and much knowledge of interviews are the same, regardless of experiences. As such, the content of this chapter can be applicable to qualitative interviews with children in general, across the range of research designs referred to earlier. Our interest and experience lies predominately with open to semi-structured interviews where the child is interviewed face to face, and the focus is on research *about* or *with* children, rather than *on* or *for*. Semi-structured interviews provide a framework for discussion while allowing for probative follow-up and affording children sufficient control to direct the discussion to issues unanticipated by the researcher (Mabry, 2008). This method also ensures that misunderstandings on the part of the interviewer or interviewee can be checked immediately (Brenner, Brown, & Canter, 1985).

In our experience, the goal of the interview has been to capture the lifeworld of the child to the best of our (adult) abilities; that is to see the world through the eyes of the child, as experienced by him or her. As such, we have aimed to cover both the factual and meaning level, that is, what happened and when, as well as what meaning the child ascribes to what has happened. Drawing on our experiences throughout this chapter, we further concur with Mantle et al. (2007, p. 792) who caution against a 'naïve positivism underlying any assumption' that the views of the child are simply 'out there waiting to be collected'. Rather, as Smart (2002) has argued, we advocate for ethical and skilful research practice that elicits children's views, involving the ability to hear what they are saying in addition to considering what they are not saying, via their silences and non-verbal messages (Houghton, 2018). It requires an adept understanding of the psychological complexity of children and an ability to understand their 'internal world', particularly where abusive experiences have rendered them confused and vulnerable (Schofield, 1998, p. 430).

We will now continue by discussing, in a processual manner, some practical and fundamental (but far from simple) issues to consider when conducting qualitative interviews with children, issues that can be found in most introductory texts on research methods. However, our focus is on interviewing children who have been victims of domestic violence and abuse. Hence, our discussion will evolve around the specificity (and at times non-specificity) of preparing for, setting the scene, and being a skilled interviewer, when conducting interviews with this specific group. As most texts on research interviews with children assume that the child is above 8 years old, or even 12 years old, we will end the chapter with a discussion on how to also include the youngest informants in qualitative research interviews. Throughout the text, the issue of research ethics underpins the narrative and will be specifically included whenever relevant (for a more thorough discussion on research ethics and children experiencing domestic violence and abuse, see Mudaly & Goddard, 2009; Øverlien & Holt, 2017; Källström Cater & Øverlien, 2014). In several places, it draws on our own experience of conducting interviews with children. It should not be perceived as a comprehensive guide on how to conduct interviews with children experiencing DVA, as each research project is unique and researchers should adopt a reflexive stance in relation to their specific project. Also, our chapter should be complemented with other methodological literature for a more comprehensive picture (such as Kvale & Brinkman, 2008). We begin by sharing some reflection on how to conduct ethically sound interviews. Next, we point to vital practical preparations before the interviews can take place. We then discuss what it takes to become a skilled interviewer, and finally, we show how young children can be meaningful and important informants. We conclude by arguing that participating in research should not only be seen as a right, but also that participation can be experienced as empowering for children, as their lived experience can contribute to research and, ultimately, to improved practice and policy.

## Discussion and analysis

### *Preparing for ethically sound interviews*

Increasingly, Research Ethics Committees (RECs) play a significant role in social research in ensuring procedural guidelines are followed (Graham, Powell, & Taylor, 2015), and have become a critical first step in the research process for researchers to manage, particularly when it involves children and sensitive topics (Campbell, 2008; Powell & Smith, 2009). In many countries, applying to ethical boards for permission to conduct the study is mandatory, and increasingly, scientific journals require authors to have their studies reviewed by such groups. Hence, in a 'hierarchy of gatekeepers', RECs can be considered at the top, at times experienced by researchers as problematic and over-paternalistic in their quest to avoid all forms of possible risks and harms (Powell et al., 2020).

There are a number of ethical issues that need to be taken seriously when conducting research that involves children, and the issue is particularly pertinent when the topic can be considered as sensitive (see Powell et al., 2018, for a discussion on 'sensitive issues' in research). Several of them, such as the issue of consent, must be dealt with when preparing for the interviews, or when applying to the ethical board. Acquiring consent before the start of data collection is perhaps the most central principal in all research, regardless of methods and research design, and the consent must be clearly informed and voluntary. That is, the potential participant must be given enough information to be able to make an informed decision, and there must be no circumstances that force or persuade him or her into agreeing to participate.

How consent is explained to a child (and indeed their parent, if parental consent is required) is critical, as is the giving of information to children in developmentally appropriate ways about the risks and benefits of participation in research. To this end, two further issues are worth highlighting for further consideration (for a more detailed discussion please see Rizo, O'Brien, Macy, Ermentrout, & Lanier, 2019). The first of these concerns the potential impact of exposure to domestic violence and abuse on the child's developmental capacity, including an acknowledgement that the child may not be functioning at their expected age and developmental stage. Related to impact, the substantial evidence concerning the overlap between living with domestic violence and abuse and child maltreatment demands that researchers consider that their child participants understand the limits to confidentiality should concerns about their safety and welfare emerge. Rizo and colleagues (2019) provide space for a detailed discussion on reporting protocols in these situations.

A child of any age must be given the opportunity for real consent or dissent, and for this to be possible, the information must be given in an age- and developmentally appropriate language. However, before we get to that point, as children under a certain age (the age limit varies depending on the country) are not deemed competent to give independent consent, rather parents, caretakers or other 'gatekeepers' must often also give their consent. In some countries, adults such as parents or teachers are always required to give consent, regardless of the child (Øverlien & Holt, 2017). There may be many layers of gatekeepers, including both formal (such as RECs) and informal (such as employees working closely with children in institutions), both groups with great power to influence whether or not a child can be considered a potential informant (Powell et al., 2020; Øverlien & Holt, 2017). Vaswani (2018, p. 504) cautions that while gatekeepers play an important role in the protection of children considering the power difference between adult researchers and child participants, the gate-keeping role paradoxically may not in fact address the power imbalance that results from adults deciding whether or not children are allowed to participate. Furthermore, gatekeepers may misunderstand or convey inaccurate or insufficient information for the child to make truly informed decisions (Wiles, Crow, Charles, & Heath, 2007; Martins, Oliveira, & Tendais, 2018). Defining these gate-keepers, and discussing the best way of approaching them, is vital in preparing for any project involving the recruitment of children for interviews. The requirement for both parents' consent in certain circumstances and in particular jurisdictions can also simultaneously raise concerns for children's safety and also exclude them from the research process (see for example, Elliffe, Holt, & Øverlien, 2019; Morris, Hegarty, & Humphreys, 2012).

Reflecting the experiences of other researchers in the field, we have found that gaining ethical approval is an onerous task, with REC concerns for children's capacity to consent and potential re-traumatisation the dominant concerns (Callaghan, Alexander, Sixsmith, & Fellin, 2016; Campbell, 2008; Katz, 2016; Øverlien, 2010; Øverlien & Holt, 2017). As researchers, we cannot absolutely eliminate this risk, and neither can we guarantee that the study we conduct will not in any way cause discomfort, upset or even harm. Reflecting on research with bereaved young people, Buckle, Dwyer and Jackson (2010, p. 117) question 'are we causing or inducing pain when we ask research participants about their experience of the death of their loved one or are we bearing witness to the pain that is already there?' This poignantly reflects our experience of research with children and young people who have experienced domestic violence and abuse and who seemingly find the interview challenging, but with few exceptions typically seize the opportunity to share, sometimes for the first time.

What we need to do through thoughtful and expert research practice is to strive to ensure that the probable gains outweigh the potential risks in our research (Øverlien & Holt, 2017). When we conduct interviews with children who have lived with domestic violence and abuse for example, the conditions we create for that interview should be the directly opposite to the abusive situation or environment the child has experienced in the past. In other words, we need to create an environment that is predictable, agreed on beforehand and clearly structured. The onus is on us, the researchers to create such an environment, ensuring that it is respectful, considerate and attentive to the child's needs, a situation that the child is in control of, can chose what to answer, when to take breaks and when to finish. Concurring with the observations of other children's researchers (Butler et al., 2002; Thomas & O'Kane, 1998), we assert that the reality of children's experience of domestic violence and abuse has been emphatically established and remains unquestioned. This experience, therefore, needs to be acknowledged and respected. Roche (1999) asserts that this respect is reflected in their right to participate, while Emond (2008, p. 192) suggests that the manner in which participation is achieved represents a 'finely balanced position between recognising and respecting the abilities of children whilst at the same time viewing them as inherently vulnerable'. The next two sections explore this further.

## Setting the scene – the importance of the research interview context

In order to be able to talk about issues that are sensitive, such as a child's experience of living with domestic violence and abuse perpetrated by one caregiver against another, we argue that there are a number of important considerations. Firstly, the location where the interview takes place needs to feel safe for the child. As argued by Hydén (2014), being able to tell about self-experienced violence and abuse demands a specific kind of context, and involves a particular interactive reality. It is the responsibility of the interviewer to create a place where it is safe enough to speak, a 'relationally safe space', to speak about issues that may have previously been forbidden to articulate. A safe space is also predictable, peaceful and undisturbed. Here we are mindful of Fargas-Malet, McSherry, Larkin and Robinson's (2010) caution that privacy and maintaining confidentiality can be an obstacle when conducting interviews with children, and may as a consequence compromise what the child will talk about during the interview. Hence, the researcher needs to find a location where the interview can be conducted without disruptions from people coming in, knocking on the door or shouting outside. A safe environment includes not only feeling safe from potential violence and abuse, but also in terms of the child being 'permitted' to speak.

Secondly, we would assert that integral to conducting meaningful research with children is the necessity for the child to feel that their involvement is essential, that they are the experts and what they have to say is important (Aubrey & Dahl, 2005; May, 2001; Mayall, 1996). Maintaining their interest throughout the research interview begins with, and is dependent on, establishing rapport and trust – this requires the development of a relationally safe space and building trust takes time. Powell et al.'s (2018, p. 657) findings highlight the significance of relationships built on trust, providing 'the medium for conveying information and addressing concerns of children, parents and other stakeholders'.

It is therefore preferable if the interviewer can spend some time together with the child, and perhaps the caregiver, prior to the interview. If possible, do some activities together, such as playing, helping out with homework or cooking. Share something of yourself, become a human being in front of the child. As most research projects have a limited budget and a strict time frame, it might not be possible to spend a vast amount of time on this. It could be enough with a day or two, or even just an afternoon. On the day of the interview, May (2001) suggests that this rapport building can involve the use of descriptive questions to stimulate conversation. To this end, before the interview commences, a small snack can be shared between the child and the researcher, with light conversation about neutral issues such as school, homework, the length of time it had taken everyone to get to the venue and so forth. Considerable time should then be spent explaining the purpose of the research, the researcher's role and why the child has been asked to participate.

Finally we would advocate for considered attention to the interview structure and format, including aids and props. Although a clearly structured interview is important, it is even more so when conducting an interview with a child who has experienced violence and abuse. A situation with structure, predictability and where the child is in control of the conversation is most likely the opposite to what many children growing up with violence have experienced. It is the responsibility of the interviewer to provide a structure for the interview, with the interview guide considered an important tool to this end. When the interviews are open or semi-structured, the guide is usually not highly scripted and is not be treated as a list of questions where each and every question needs to be answered and checked. They are, however, a good reminder of what to bring up, and in what order, helping the interviewer to move the interview forward. Other interview props such as vignettes, agony aunt letters or pictorial aids such as feeling faces and cartoon characters can used effectively and safely in ensuring the experience is sensitive to the child's age and capacity and to their comfort with different methods.

From our experience, attention to detail is not only an ethical matter of sensitivity, care and respect. It could also be the difference between an interview that is a positive experience for all, or a chaotic interview impossible to proceed with and questionably adhering to the ethical priority to do no harm. Attention to detail in creating a safe and ethically sensitive context for the child to participate in a meaningful manner requires a particular skillset. This will be explored in the next section.

## *The skilled interviewer*

Becoming a skilled interviewer takes time, practice and many hours of listening to and transcribing your own interviews, as this is an important way to learn and improve. One possible lesson to learn is that silence does not threaten the interview, but enriches it. Issues surrounding violence and abuse are complex, and depending how much the child has talked about the situation in his or her home, there is often a need for contemplation before being able to respond and/or continue talking. In this respect, we are mindful of Spyrou's (2016, p. 9) observation that 'what is recorded, transcribed, and coded is that which is uttered and heard' and Poland and Pederson's (1998, p. 293) reminder that 'what is not said may be as revealing as what is said, particularly since what is left out ordinarily exceeds what is put in'. Hence, a skilled interviewer does not fear silence, but welcomes it, and allows for time rather than interrupting. The skilled interviewer further appreciates silence as a critical component in the pursuit to ascertain the voice of the child (Spyrou, 2016) and understands Lewis's (2010, p. 19) caution that such a one-dimensional quest may result in less scrutiny to how we listen and the methods we used.

Furthermore, a skilled interviewer listens closely to what the child has to say, also taking into account what Bakhtin (1986) calls a 'multiplicity of voices', the understanding that every meaning exists among other meanings. Hence, the experience described by the child, and the meaning he or she ascribes to it, can be understood as a sort of link in a chain of meanings. The interviewer needs to be attentive both to the individual perspective of the child *and* the numerous dialogues the child has been involved in before, that together create the multiple voices of the child. Growing up in a household with violence and abuse means growing up in an environment with domination, unequal power and control. Hence, the interviewer will most likely, through the voice of the child, hear the voice of the abuser as well as 'societal voices' related to understandings in society regarding issues such as victimisation, relationships, parenthood and emotions. Growing up in a household with domestic violence and abuse can also mean that the child has been exposed to and impacted by other (at times multiple) adversities that intersect with domestic violence and abuse. The interviewer therefore needs to be cognisant of the many cumulative and overlapping ways in which adversity, discrimination, marginalisation and inequality may be experienced by these children in varying ways and contexts.

With the new era of children's rights, brought forward by many countries' ratification of the UNCRC in the early 1990s, engaging children as peer researchers has become increasingly common (Bradbury-Jones & Taylor, 2015). The adult researcher conducting interviews with children can decide to engage (or employ) a child as a researcher or co-researcher, both in terms of designing, implementing and interpreting the research findings. As argued by Bradbury-Jones and Taylor (2015), including children as researchers has great potential, as children can be a powerful conduit for other children's voices, but the approach is also challenging, as it involves a number of ethical, methodological and practical issues. For example, children lack research competence and need training, and have a right to be protected from any potential harm involved in being peer researchers. Considered reflection on how children might be ethically and safely included in the design, implementation and interpretation of research is beyond the scope of this chapter but is addressed elsewhere (Houghton, 2018; Tisdall, Davis, & Gallagher, 2009; Ward, 1997).

Returning briefly to the issue of consent, before starting the interview it is important to confirm with the child that they understand the purpose of the interview, are informed about issues such as how long it will take and that there are no right and wrong answers to the questions the researcher will ask. Just as with adult participants, children need to understand the potential risks and benefits, in an age- and maturity-appropriate language. It is important to have in mind that, as Westcott and Littleton (2005) point out, 'children may rarely be spoken to, or seriously listened to, unless they have done something "wrong"' (p. 141), and that rather than being passive receivers, they are actively trying to make sense of the interview situation, including the interviewer and his or her questions. They may, therefore, give answers that they think the researcher wants, or appreciates. However, our research experience also reflects Powell et al.'s (2018) observations on children's agency and capacity to make meaningful decisions about what and what not information they share (see also Evang & Øverlien, 2014). We have also met many children and adolescents with a strong wish to contribute with their knowledge and experiences, so that other children in similar situations can be helped. Although this is to be commended, it also needs to be addressed, so that the child is not given false hopes that their participation may lead to direct benefits in their own lives.

Moving from initial settling in questions/conversations, we suggest then transitioning to ask preferably open-ended questions regarding the child's experiences with abuse. We assert that 'closed-questions' (questions that result in 'yes' and 'no' answers), should be avoided, as should questions that are suggestive (such as 'it must have been horrible to see your father angry'). After conducting a number of studies where victims of domestic violence and abuse were interviewed, Hydén (2014) presented a method of interviewing that was open in its form, focusing on stimulating narratives and resulting in rich data. In the 'teller-focused interview', the interviewer is fully focused on the teller, asking open questions such as 'can you tell me . . .'. The goal with this form of interview is 'to find a way to facilitate and support the research participants – women, men and children – in formulating themselves in as genuine and multifaceted a narrative as possible' (Hydén, 2014, p. 796). An integrated part of this form of interview is the understanding, brought to the forefront by, for example, Mishler (1991), that qualitative interviews are co-constructed in a dialogue between interviewer and interviewee. The interview, Mishler (1999, p. xvi) argues, can be understood as a 'complex sequence of exchanges through which interviewer and interviewee negotiate some degree of agreement on what they will talk about, and how'. However, when interviewing children, although the questions can be open, the language used must be adjusted for their age and development. A 6 year old, for example, could be asked: 'If you were to describe to a friend what it is like to live in this house [a refuge for abused women and their children], what would you tell him?' An older child, on the other hand, could be asked a more specific question, including exact names and concepts, such as: 'If you know someone who had experiences with violence and abuse, and needed to seek shelter at a refuge, what would you tell him about what it is like living here?' Also, older children can be expected to structure their talk in a narrative form, to a larger extent than younger children. At the age of 9, children's narratives have been found to be causally structured and can include numerous details about both negative and positive experiences (Trabasso & Stein, 1997).

Applying this to the context of interviewing children with experiences of domestic violence and abuse, there are two issues that we in particular would like to address. The first concerns the importance of the interviewer knowing the topic at hand, when aiming for these forms of dialogic, teller-focused interviews. Without the relevant follow-up questions, there will be no in-depth knowledge produced, and very little dialogue. The example we would like to use comes from an interview with Ronny, a 20-year-old young man, interviewed by the first author, who had a childhood behind him filled with severe violence and abuse. He described how when the violent episodes happened, he would lock himself into his room, and play computer games. When the interviewer asks why he did this, he replied that he wanted to distract himself. The interviewer, who knew that children who live with violence in their homes often take on great responsibility for the abused parent and younger siblings, asks if he had the sound on the computer. When Ronny nods his head no, she asks why. 'I wanted to keep track on what was going on downstairs in the living room [where his mother was beaten]', he answers. Hence, a response that could, without the appropriate follow-up questions, be interpreted as a young person not particularly engaged in what was happening to his mother, is instead understood as a young man with a constant eye to his mother's well-being.

A second issue important to address if aiming to create an interview that is dialogic in nature is the issue of power relations. In addition to the interviewer–interviewee dichotomy, interviews with children experiencing domestic violence and abuse also involve other dichotomies such as adult–child, and exposed–(possibly) non-exposed. Children and adolescents experience unequal power relations when interacting with adults in all aspects of their everyday life, at times expressed as great domination and control over every detail of their lives. This power imbalance due to age cannot be overcome, but can be handled in constructive and creative ways before and during the interview. The age gap between interviewer and interviewee is not possible to change, but the interviewer can be attentive and sensitive to the specific age and maturity of the child or adolescent, by using age-appropriate language and references. Teenagers, for example, often react strongly against being treated and talked to as if they were younger than they are. In order to destabilise the interviewer–interviewee dichotomy, control of important details such as where the interview is taking place, and what snack to serve, can be shifted to the interviewee. Hence, without compromising on responsibility, the power must shift in so far as the adult becoming the listener in need of knowledge, while the child is the teller with expertise that needs to be shared. This child-centred approach Morris et al. (2012) assert can minimise the power differentials between the interviewer and the child, by the interviewer explicitly placing the child in the expert position, being fully attentive, interested, and asking relevant follow-up questions. Vaswani (2018) further asserts that appropriate methods can help to redress some of this power imbalance. These can involve participatory methods including interviews, vignettes and arts-based techniques (Clark & Morriss, 2017).

Finally, a skilled interviewer is not content with the written or oral consent given by the child before the start of the interview, but considers consent as an ongoing process (Källström Cater & Øverlien, 2014), rather than a 'hurdle to be overcome' (Moore, McArthur, & Noble-Carr, 2018, p. 90); that is, that the child is willing to participate until the very end of the interview and beyond. As such, gaining informed consent does not begin and end with the signing of the consent forms (Morris et al., 2012). Notwithstanding our earlier comments around silence, falling quiet for long periods of time, changing the subject, wanting to play and asking for the time may all be signals that the child no longer wants to participate. Directly asking the child if they want to continue, or offering them 'stop' and 'go' signs at the beginning of the interview are options to consider (Morris et al., 2012). Moore et al. (2018, p. 90) assert that skilful research practice involves what they call 'negotiating and renegotiating consent with participants, including children before and during data collection'. In that process of negotiation and renegotiation, Eriksson and Näsman (2012, p. 72) argue that we open up a space where children's participation 'may create opportunities for validating experiences of violence; and thereby for support to children's recovery after exposure to violence'.

## The youngest informants

Younger children are often not included in research, other than in observational studies, where for example the interaction between parents and toddlers are in focus, or preschool children observed on the playground, interacting with peers. In general, young children, to a greater extent than older, have shorter attention spans and limited language skills, and are therefore considered a challenge to include in research (Ponizovsky-Bergelson, Dayan, Wahle, & Strier, 2019). They also, in general, have less understanding of the purpose and consequences of the research interview they are consenting to participate in, and it may be more difficult to engage them in the interview process (Fleer & Li, 2016). This is one of the reasons why observation through video is a common and recommended research method when studying young children (see for example Dunphy & Farrell, 2011). However, the challenges involved with younger children do not mean that qualitative interviews are not a suitable method, but that additional methodological skills, practical adjustments and flexibility on behalf of the researcher is required. By using an excerpt from a young informant the first author interviewed a few years back, some of these additional skills and considerations will be discussed next.

Oda is 4 years old and lives at the time of the interview at a refuge for abused women and children, together with her mother. She is asked by the interviewer how things were before she came to the refuge.

*Oda:* My dad became so mean and my mom met Christian [her mother's new boyfriend]. And then he becomes so mean if my mom and me have moved to the apartment. Then he becomes so very very mean.

*Interviewer:* Is it the dad that becomes mean?

| *Oda:* | Yes, very mean |
| *Interviewer:* | mm |
| *Oda:* | Can we be calm now? |
| *Interviewer:* | Be calm? Like, be a little quiet you mean? |
| *Oda:* | Yes |
| *Interviewer:* | You want a break? |
| *Oda:* | Yes |

This is an example of a young informant who is able to share important information about her experiences, interacting with the interviewer in a dialogic manner, and setting boundaries and regulating her own engagement and involvement in the interview. The interviewer is supporting her with emotionally attuned utterances, age-appropriate language and open-ended questions. She asks relevant follow-up questions to clarify matters, and is attentive to Oda's request for a break, even though it may not be apparent that it is a break she is asking for ('can we be calm now?'). Oda needed several breaks during the 45-minute interview, and she invited the interviewer into drawing and playing on several occasions.

The second author's research involving participants as young as 4 years of age also clearly demonstrates children's capacity to hold views and articulately express them, with support from age-appropriate methodologies. For example, when asked about why her parents separated, 4-year-old Victoria recalled her mother crying all the time, and when probed about the reason for this, she used 'improv' (improvisation) to graphically act out a violent incident where her father punched her mother, stating:

Daddy hit Mom on the head – bang!

As stated earlier, researchers always have responsibility to control the interview in terms of time and structure, and to be supportive and attentive to the interviewee. However, as the evidence illustrates (Evang & Øverlien, 2014; Holt, 2018; Kyronlampi-Kylmani & Maatta, 2011), children as young as 4–5 years old can regulate, limit and even take the lead in interviews about sensitive issues such as domestic violence and abuse, if the interviewer is attentive and flexible to them and their needs. Even though a high level of dependency, limited language skills and life experience implies increased vulnerability, these findings challenge the assumption of age-related power and helplessness. Furthermore, the youngest children also have a right to have a say in all matters that affect them and their lives, according to the UNCRC.

This current chapter, therefore, supports Smith, Taylor and Tapp's (2003) criticism of the 'escape clause' against children's participation on grounds of age and maturity, and supports the view that the argument should not be one of proving the child's ability to participate, but more one of responsibility on adults to be competent enough to elicit those views in the context of a trusting relationship with the child. Similarly, both Øverlien and Holt (2017) and Thomas and O'Kane (1998) argue that when children are judged incompetent to participate, we should, perhaps, firstly question whether the methods used to elicit their views were appropriate and secondly, whether those methods were 'competently' administered. Skilful and competent research practice involves, as Smart (2002) has argued, the practice of allowing the child to speak, the skill in eliciting their views, as well as the ability to hear what they are saying, a process Schofield (1998) asserts is more complicated than simply obtaining a view from the child.

# Conclusion

This chapter has focused on the practices and principles of conducting qualitative interviews with children experiencing domestic violence and abuse, grounding the discussion in children's capacity for participation in social research whilst simultaneously acknowledging their need for protection from harm. While many textbooks on qualitative research methods start out by warning the novice researcher against thinking that interviewing is easy, or a quick and effortless way to collect data, we have argued in this chapter that conducting interviews with children, and even more so, children with experiences of violence and abuse, requires additional training, and an understanding and respect for what they have lived through. However, if the interviews are conducted in an ethically sound manner, they can be experienced as empowering for the child, and the data, the life stories of the children, should be considered as a gift to be handled with respect and care by the researcher. This gift supports our understanding about their lives and the social problems they encounter, and their participation upholds their rights, notably their right to participate in processes that affect their lives.

# Critical findings

- The interest to describe, understand and analyse children and childhood, through conducting qualitative interviews, has grown exponentially. This increasing concern in obtaining individual children's voices has become particularly evident since the early 1990s, with many countries ratifying the United Nations Convention on the Rights of the Child (UNCRC).
- Conducting interviews with children, and even more so, children with experiences of violence and abuse, requires additional training, and an understanding and respect for what they have lived through.
- If the interviews are conducted in an ethically sound manner, they can be experienced as empowering for the child, and the data, the life stories of the children, should be considered as a gift to be handled with respect and care by the researcher.

# Implications for policy, practice and research

- Children have a right to participate in research, regardless of age. Interviews with the youngest informants require additional methodological skills, practical adjustments and flexibility on behalf of the researcher.
- When planning for ethically sound interviews, the conditions we create for that interview should be the directly opposite to the abusive situation or environment the child has experienced in the past: a situation which is predictable, agreed on beforehand and clearly structured.
- Becoming a skilled interviewer takes time, practice and many hours of listening to and transcribing your own interviews. It also involves knowing the topic at hand, as this increases the chance for dialogic, teller-focused interviews.

# References

Aubrey, C., & Dahl, S. (2005). 'That child needs a good listening to!' Reviewing effective interview strategies. *Journal of Education, 35*, 99–119.

Bacon, K. (2014). Rethinking children's citizenship: Negotiating structure, shaping meanings. *International Journal of Children's Rights, 1*, 21–42.

Bakhtin, M. M. (1986). *Speech genres and other late essays* (V. W. McGee, Trans.). Austin, TX: University of Texas Press.

Bosisio, R. (2012). Children's right to be heard: What children think. *International Journal of Children's Rights, 20,* 141–154.

Bradbury-Jones, C., & Taylor, J. (2015). Engaging with children as co-researchers: Challenges, counter-challenges and solutions. *International Journal of Social Research Methodology, 18*(2), 161–173. doi:10.10 80/13645579.2013.864589

Brenner, M., Brown, J., & Canter, D. (1985). *The research interview: Uses and approaches.* London: Academic Press.

Buckle, J. L., Dwyer, S. C., & Jackson, M. (2010). Qualitative bereavement research: Incongruity between the perspectives of participants and research ethics boards. *International Journal of Social Research Methodology, 13*(2), 111–125.

Butler, I., Scanlan, L., Douglas, G., & Murch, M. (2002). Children's involvement in the parents' divorce: Implications for practice. *Children & Society, 16,* 89–102.

Callaghan, J., Alexander, J., Sixsmith, J., & Fellin, L. (2016). Beyond "witnessing": Children's experiences of coercive control in domestic violence and abuse. *Journal of Interpersonal violence, 33*(10), 1551–1581.

Campbell, A. (2008). For their own good: Recruiting children for research. *Childhood – A Global Journal of Child Research, 15*(1), 30–49.

Clark, A., & Morriss, L. (2017). The use of visual methodologies in social work research over the last decade: A narrative review and some questions for the future. *Qualitative Social Work, 16*(1), 29–43. https://doi.org/10.1177/1473325015601205

Darwin, C. (1877). A biological sketch of an infant. *Mind, 2*(7), 285–294.

Downes, J., Kelly, L., & Westmarland, N. (2014). Ethics in violence and abuse research – A positive empowerment approach. *Sociological Research Online.* Retrieved June 27, 2017, from www. socreson-line.org.uk/19/1/2.html

Dunphy, L., & Farrell, T. (2011). Indoor play provision in the classroom. In D. Harcourt, B. Perry, & T. Waller (Eds.), *Researching young children's perspectives: Debating the ethics and dilemmas of educational research with children* (pp. 128–142). London, England: Routledge.

Elliffe, R., Holt, S., & Øverlien, C. (2019). Hiding and being hidden: The marginalisation of children's participation in research and practice responses to domestic violence and abuse. *Social Work & Social Sciences Review,* 5–24.

Emond, R. (2008). Children's voices, children's rights. In A. Kendrick (Ed.), *Residential child care: Prospects and challenges* (pp. 183–195). London: Jessica Kingsley.

Eriksson, M., & Nasman, E. (2012). Interviews with children exposed to violence. *Children & Society, 26,* pp. 63–73.

Evang, A., & Øverlien, C. (2014). "If you look you have to leave" Young children regulating research interviews about experiences of domestic violence. *Journal of Early Childhood Research.* doi:10.1177/1476718X14538595

Fargas Malet, M., McSherry, D., Larkin, E., & Robinson, C. (2010). Research with children: Methodological issues and innovative techniques. *Journal of Early Childhood Research, 8*(2), 175–192. https://doi.org/10.1177/1476718X09345412

Fleer, M., & Li, L. (2016). A child-centered evaluation model: Gaining the children's perspective in evaluation studies in China. *European Early Childhood Education Research Journal, 24,* 342–356.

Freeman, M., & Mathison, S. (2009). *Researching children's experiences.* London: Guilford Press.

Graham, A., Powell, M., & Taylor, N. (2015). Ethical research involving children: Putting the evidence into practice. *Family Matters, 96,* 23–28.

Grover, S. (2004). Why won't they listen to us? On giving power and voice to children participating in social research. *Childhood-a Global Journal of Child Research, 11*(1), 81–93.

Holt, S. (2018). A voice or a choice? Children's views on participating in decisions about post-separation contact with domestically abusive fathers. *Journal of Social Welfare and Family Law, 40*(4), 459–476.

Houghton, C. (2018). Voice, agency, power: A framework for young survivors' participation in national domestic abuse policy-making. In S. Holt, C. Overlien, & J. Devaney (Eds.), *Responding to domestic violence: Emerging challenges for policy, practice and research in Europe* (pp. 77–96). London: Jessica Kingsley.

Hydén, M. (2014). The teller-focused interview: Interviewing as a relational practice. *Qualitative Social Work, 13*(4), 795–812.

James, A., Jenks, C., & Prout, A. (1998). *Theorizing childhood.* Cambridge, MA: Polity Press.

Källström Cater, Å., & Øverlien, C. (2014). Children exposed to domestic violence: A discussion about research ethics and researchers' responsibilities. *Nordic Social Work Research, 4*(1), 67–79. doi:10.1080/2156857X.2013.801878

Katz, E. (2016). Beyond the physical incident model: How children living with domestic violence are harmed by and resist regimes of coercive control. *Child Abuse Review, 25*(1), 46–59. doi:10.1002/car.2422

Kjorholt, A. T. (2002). Small is powerful: Discourses on 'children and participation' in Norway. *Childhood, 9*, 63–82.

Kvale, S., & Brinkman, S. (2008). *Interviews: Learning the craft of qualitative research interviewing* (2nd ed.). Thousand Oaks, CA: Sage.

Kyronlampi-Kylmani, T., & Maatta, K. (2011). Using children as research subjects: How to interview a child age 5–7. *Educational Research and Review, 6*(1), 87–93.

Lewis, A. (2010). Silence in the context of "child voice." *Children & Society, 24*(1), 14–23.

Mabry, L. (2008). Case study in social research. In P. Alasuutari, L. Bickman, & J. Brannen (Eds.), *The SAGE handbook of social research methods*. London: Sage.

Mantle, G., Moules, T., Johnson, K., Leslie, J., Parsons, S., & Shaffer, R. (2007). Whose wishes and feelings? Children's autonomy and parental influence in family court enquiries. *British Journal of Social Work, 37*(5), 785–805.

Martins, P. C., Oliveira, V. H., & Tendais, I. (2018). Research with children and young people on sensitive topics – The case of poverty and delinquency. *Childhood, 25*(4), 458–472.

Masson, J. (2003). Paternalism, participation and placation: Young people's experiences of representation in child protection proceedings in England and wales. In J. Dewar & S. Parker (Eds.), *Family law: Processes, practices, pressures* (pp. 79–98). Oxford: Hart Publishing.

May, T. (2001). *Social research: Issues, methods and process* (3rd ed.). Buckingham: Open University Press.

Mayall, B. (1996). *Children, health and the social order*. Buckingham: Open University Press.

Mead, M. (1930). *Growing up in New Guinea*. New York, NY: Morrow.

Mishler, E. (1991). *Research interviewing: Context and narrative*. Cambridge, MA: Harvard University Press.

Mishler, E. (1999). *Storylines. Craft artists' narratives of identity*. London: Harvard University Press.

Moore, T. P., McArthur, M., & Noble-Carr, D. (2018). More a marathon than a hurdle: Towards children's informed consent in a study on safety. *Qualitative Research, 18*(1), 88–107.

Morris, A., Hegarty, K., & Humphreys, C. (2012). Ethical and safe: Research with children about domestic violence. *Research Ethics, 8*, 125–139. doi:10.1177/1747016112445420

Morrow, V., & Richards, M. (1996). The ethics of social research with children: An overview. *Children & Society, 10*(2), 90–105.

Mudaly, N., & Goddard, C. (2009). The ethics of involving children who have been abused in child abuse research. *International Journal of Children's Rights, 17*, 261–281.

Øverlien, C. (2010). Children exposed to domestic violence. What have we concluded and challenges ahead. *Journal of Social Work, 10*, 80–97.

Øverlien, C., & Holt, S. (2017). Including children and adolescents in domestic violence research: When myths and misconceptions compromise participation. In S. Holt, C. Øverlien, & J. Devaney (Eds.), *Responding to domestic violence – Emerging challenges for policy, practice and research in Europe*. London: Jessica Kingsley Publishers.

Padgett, D. (2008). *Qualitative methods in social work research* (2nd ed.). Thousand Oaks, CA: Sage.

Piaget, J. (1964). Part I: Cognitive development in children: Piaget development and learning. *Journal of Research in Science Teaching, 2*(3), 176–186.

Poland, B., & Pedersen, A. (1998) Reading between the lines: Interpreting silences in qualitative research. *Qualitative Inquiry, 4*(2): 293–312.

Ponizovsky-Bergelson, Y., Dayan, Y., Wahle, N., & Roer-Strier, D. (2019). A qualitative interview with young children: What encourages or inhibits young children's participation? *International Journal of Qualitative Methods, 18*. doi:10.1177/1609406919840516

Powell, M. A., Graham, A., McArthur, M., Moore, T., Chalmers, J., & Taplin, S. (2020). Children's participation in research on sensitive topics: Addressing concerns of decision-makers. *Children's Geographies, 18*(3), 325–338. doi:10.1080/14733285.2019.1639623

Powell, M. A., McArthur, M. Chalmers, J. Graham, A., Moore, T., Spriggs, M., & Taplin, S. (2018). Sensitive topics in social research involving children. *International Journal of Social Research Methodology, 21*(6), 647–660. doi:10.1080/13645579.2018.1462882

Powell, M. A., & Smith, A. B. (2009). Children's participation rights in research. *Childhood, 16*, 124–142.

Punch, S. (2002). Research with children, the same or different from research with adults? *Childhood, 9*(3), 321–341.

Rizo, C. F., O'Brien, J. E., Macy, R. J., Ermentrout, D. M., & Lanier, P. (2019). Reporting maltreatment to child protective services in the context of intimate partner violence research. *Violence Against Women, 25*(2) 131–147. doi:10.1177/1077801218761604

Roche, J. (1999). Children and divorce: A private affair? In S. Slater & C. Piper (Eds.), *Undercurrents of divorce* (pp. 35–75). Aldershot: Darthmouth.

Schofield, G. (1998). Making sense of the ascertainable wishes and feelings of insecurely attached children. *Child and Family Law Quarterly, 10*(4), 429–443.

Silverman, D. (1997). *Qualitative research: Theory, method and practice.* London: Sage.

Skjorten, K. (2013). Children's voices in Norwegian custody cases. *International Journal of Law, Policy and the Family, 27*, 289–309.

Smart, C. (2002). From children's shoes to children's voices. *Family Court Review, 40*(3), 307–319.

Smith, A. B., Taylor, N. J., & Tapp, P. (2003). Rethinking children's involvement in decision making after parental separation. *Childhood, 10*, 201–216.

Spyrou, S. (2016). Researching children's silences: Exploring the fullness of voice in childhood research. *Childhood, 23*, 7–21. doi:10.1177/0907568215571618

Thomas, N., & O'Kane, C. (1998). When children's wishes and feelings clash with their 'best interests'. *The International Journal of Children's Rights, 6*(2), 137–154.

Tisdall, K., Davis, J., & Gallagher, M. (2009). *Researching with children and young people: Research design, methods and analysis.* London: Sage.

Trabasso, T., & Stein, N. L. (1997). Narrating, representing, and remembering event sequence. In T. Bourg, P. J. Bauer, & W. Paulus Van Den Broek (Eds.), *Developmental spans in event comprehension and representation. Bridging fictional and actual events* (pp. 237–270). Mahwah, NJ: Erlbaum.

Vaswani, N. (2018). Learning from failure: Are practitioner researchers the answer when conducting research on sensitive topics with vulnerable children and young people? *International Journal of Social Research Methodology, 21*(4), 499–512.

Ward, L. (1997). *Seen and heard: Involving disabled children and young people in research and development projects.* New York, NY: Joseph Rowntree Foundation.

Westcott, H. L., & Littleton, K. S. (2005). Exploring meaning in interviews with children. In S. Greene & D. Hogan (Eds.), *Researching children's experience: Approaches and methods* (pp. 141–157). London: Sage.

Wiles, R., Crow, G., Charles, V., & Heath, S. (2007). Informed consent and the research process: Following rules or striking balances? *Sociological Research Online, 12*(2), 1–12.

# 43

# DOMESTIC HOMICIDE REVIEW PROCESSES AS A METHOD OF LEARNING

*Myrna Dawson*

## Introduction

Domestic violence remains a pervasive social problem across socio-economic, geographical, age, cultural, and religious boundaries (United Nations Office of Drugs and Crime, 2018).[1] Overwhelmingly, when domestic violence turns lethal, women are killed by male partners and, globally, it is one of the leading causes of death for women (Garcia-Moreno, Jansen, Ellsberg, Heise, & Watts, 2005; UNODC, 2018). Research has developed extensively over the last several decades to understand risk and protective factors for domestic homicide (Porter & Gavin, 2010; Campbell, Glass, Sharps, Laughon, & Bloom, 2007). The findings from this research have been drawn upon to develop prevention initiatives which have led to systemic, structural transformations and increased public education and awareness about the dynamics of domestic violence and the deaths that result (Dobash & Dobash, 2015; Johnson & Dawson, 2011; Monckton-Smith & Williams, 2014; van Wormer & Roberts, 2009).

One specific mechanism for conducting research and informing prevention has been domestic violence death reviews (DVDR), originating in the United States in the 1990s, and now operating in six high-income countries (Dawson, 2017a; Websdale, Ferraro, & Barger, 2019). Following a brief discussion of the rise of these initiatives and their overall objectives, this chapter will describe how models vary across jurisdictions, including key decisions faced when establishing such initiatives which have implications for research. Key challenges that continue to face DVDRs are also discussed, including innovative responses. Finally, the opportunities that DVDRs continue to present for strengthening prevention efforts are highlighted, including actual and potential impacts for strengthening policy and practice as well as contributing to education and awareness. This chapter uses the term 'domestic violence death review' to describe the initiatives in general, but it is acknowledged that there is within- and cross-country terminology used.

## Evolution and objectives of DVDRs

The first DVDR was conducted in San Francisco into a high-profile domestic homicide-suicide in 1990. The female victim, Veena Charan, had been seeking help for months from various agencies, but her efforts were in vain. She was shot and killed by her husband in front of students and teachers at her son's elementary school. Her death resulted in an ad hoc review which is seen as a watershed moment for the beginning of domestic violence death reviews in the United States (Websdale et al., 2017). Resulting in a series of recommendations, the Charan review highlighted gaps in service delivery, communication and coordination, data collection, access to services, and training (Websdale et al., 2017). Today, between 175–200 review teams operate in the US (Websdale et al., 2017) and the National Domestic Violence Fatality Review Initiative (www.ndvfri.org) continues to provide support to these initiatives.

Canada was next to follow with the establishment of a DVDR in Ontario in 2002 after coroner's inquests into two high-profile domestic homicides of women by their male partners. Six Canadian provinces have now established DVDRs with several in progress (Dawson, Jaffe, Campbell, Lucas, & Kerr, 2017). New Zealand established its Family Violence Death Review Committee in 2008 (Tolmie, Wilson, & Smith, 2017), followed closely by Australia in 2009 with its first Domestic and Family Violence Death Review in Victoria (Butler et al., 2017). Australia currently has initiatives operating in five states and the Northern Territory. Their work is supported by the Australian Domestic and Family Violence Death Review Network. In 2011, the United Kingdom introduced legislation in England and Wales to allow for the implementation of multi-agency domestic homicide reviews (Payton, Robinson, & Brookman, 2017). Most recently, in 2017, Portugal implemented a death review mechanism focusing on domestic homicide (Websdale et al., 2019).

While variations exist across DVDRs, their overall goal is to retrospectively examine system and human factors prior to and surrounding domestic homicides with the aim of reducing similar future deaths. Most review teams compile descriptive data to identify: (1) victim, perpetrator, relationship, and incident characteristics; (2) history of system contacts and possible points of intervention; (3) gaps or failures in service delivery; (4) policy or program inadequacies; and (5) opportunities and strategies for system and legislative reform. In addressing core goals, DVDRs often differ in structure and mechanisms of governance, case inclusion criteria, review measures, and outputs. Next, some key decisions involved in establishing or operating DVDRs are discussed.

## Discussion and analysis

### *Establishment and governance of DVDRs*

The impetus for DVDRs has largely been driven by feminist and violence against women activists/advocates whose consistent voices are heard most acutely following high-profile killings of women and/or their children by male partners. The Charan review largely grew from efforts by a coalition of frontline women's organizations who pressed for a full investigation into her death and the role played by sectors who did not respond adequately to her pleas for help (Sheehy, 2017). In Canada, building on ground-breaking research on intimate femicide spearheaded by a group of feminist frontline workers in Ontario (Crawford, Gartner, & Women We Honour Action Committee, 1992; Crawford, Gartner, Dawson, & Women We Honour Action Committee, 1997), women and feminist activism/advocacy played a role in two pivotal coroner's inquests. Similarly, in Australia and New Zealand, women's advocacy groups, including frontline workers, were active in pushing for change during panel reviews and task force activities (Bugeja et al., 2013). Recommendations generated from these inquests, panels, or task forces included recommendations to establish DVDRs.

Most DVDRs typically have some type of government endorsement enabling varying types of support (i.e. funding, resources, agency engagement), however, the degree of formalized government support varies significantly (Bugeja, Dawson, McIntyre, & Poon, 2017). Some jurisdictions enacted a statute, code, or executive order to establish or mandate a review initiative. Others used already-existing legislative mechanisms in coroner or medical examiner acts (e.g. Coroner's Court of Victoria used their coroner's act). Finally, some jurisdictions had no formalized mechanism, but were able to set up initiatives using localized, regional, and national efforts of civil society members and/or organizations.

It is argued there are benefits to having a legislative framework for the reviews (Dale, Celaya, & Mayer, 2017; Sheehy, 2017). Legislation can help ensure transparency and accountability and identify an authoritative body that provides legitimacy and guidelines for governance, processes, and outputs (Dale et al., 2017; Sheehy, 2017). Statutes also provide frameworks to ensure reviews are confidential and may formalize team philosophies, membership, and protocols. However, there is no evidence-based support for the benefits of legislation, compared to those operating without such legislation, particularly for achieving social change. Regardless, a transparent, guiding framework is arguably crucial for the reasons identified and vital when bringing together a diverse set of actors with individual and group concerns about confidentiality and accountability. These concerns are significant and impact collaborations despite the 'no blame, no shame' guiding philosophy that is often foundational to review teams.

The 'no blame, no shame' philosophy has the underlying goal of achieving reviews that are collaborative and consultative, maintain independence, and ensure strict confidentiality and privacy protections. Largely universal and voluntary, this philosophy is not without its inherent challenges. In her review of 35 DVDR initiatives, Watt (2010) identified tensions between ensuring 'no blame' and achieving accountability for actions leading to domestic homicides. Her study showed 17 percent of the 35 DVDRs stated they tried to enforce accountability while simultaneously and cooperatively engaging with agencies to identify recommendations for improvement. This was done without publicly blaming those involved. New Zealand's committee reportedly adopts this approach to ensure feasibility of recommendations and to encourage a commitment to implementation by those responsible (Tolmie et al., 2017).

Sheehy (2017) questions whether the 'no blame, no shame' philosophy can produce change, however, asking "if the errors of specific individuals and agencies are not criticized, exposed to public view, and translated into consequences, is it realistic to expect change?" (p. 389). Providing some support for this argument, DVDR annual reports frequently contain recommendations that repeat the need for improvements already identified in earlier reviews (often more than once) or indicate 'no new recommendations' meaning that what would have been recommended has already been recommended. Sheehy (2017) argues that repeating recommendations highlights that change has yet to occur and the decision not to repeat recommendations may mean DVDR teams feel that it "has done its best to urge change but that the same problems persist" (p. 389).

## *Team composition of DVDRs*

Team composition varies significantly, often depending on whether there is existing legislation or an order including membership requirements. Some teams are comprised of individuals who all work within the same organization (e.g. coroner's office, Victoria, Australia); however, more often representatives from more than one agency are invited to sit on reviews. If eligibility criteria exist, they often identify government representatives (i.e. police, prosecution, corrections, parole, child welfare, and family services), but some DVDRs have requirements for domestic violence advocates, service providers, representatives from diverse communities, particularly if overrepresented among victims and perpetrators. The New South Wales team, for example, has various government representatives, but legislation stipulates that at least one member must be Aboriginal or Torres Strait Islander and one representative must be from Aboriginal Affairs in the Department of Education and Communities (Wilson, 2017). Similarly, two US jurisdictions have legislation that require representation from American Indian/Native American tribal organizations (Websdale et al., 2017). Although fewer, other DVDRs involve family members or survivors such as in the United Kingdom where, largely due to efforts by Advocacy After Fatal Domestic Violence (AAFDA), family members play a key role in review processes (Mullane, 2017).

Some committees have the capacity to grant ad hoc membership to individuals with specific expertise – important for DVDRs with limited, permanent membership. The Coroner's Court of Victoria review initiative has a permanent team located in the Violence Prevention Unit, along with a diverse advisory committee with varying expertise (Bugeja et al., 2013; Butler et al., 2017). Therefore, if a case involves immigration and there is no permanent team member with this expertise, an outside immigration expert from the advisory committee can be brought into the review. In jurisdictions without advisory committees, outside experts can and have been brought onto reviews for specific cases. If a DVDR is national in scope, its representatives may represent higher-level government peak bodies or agencies. If more regional or local in scope, it might have representation from more diverse organizations who regularly interact with those experiencing domestic violence. An initiative can have both types of teams in play simultaneously. In New Zealand, there is a two-tier system that allows for both national and regional/local reviews, each with varying team representation. The national review team has a wide range of expertise, including two Māori (the Indigenous peoples) and representation from the non-governmental family violence sector (Tolmie et al., 2017). The four regional review panels who conduct in-depth local reviews across the country provide a safe space for team members to learn from each other's experiences within a regional context (Tolmie et al., 2017).

Team composition is one of the most critical decisions in establishing a DVDR because it impacts resulting deliberations, analyses, recommendations, and, ultimately, the knowledge generated (Sheehy, 2017). A key consideration is the degree to which members represent the community in which they operate, including racial/ethnic groups, age, disability status, and religion, among other potential subgroups and populations (Dale et al., 2017). One challenge is identifying who community representatives should be, particularly at the national level, given that one or two 'token' individuals cannot speak for entire communities or minority groups (Bent-Goodley, 2013). In the United States, the New Mexico team formed a Native American subcommittee to review cases on or off tribal land involving Native American victims and/or perpetrators (Websdale et al., 2017). However, given the overrepresentation of racial/ethnic groups among domestic violence victims and perpetrators, there is still much work to be done (Bent-Goodley, 2013; Sheehy, 2017; Websdale et al., 2017).

Second, review teams must have core experts in the field of intimate partner and domestic violence with related policy, program, and practice expertise. This should include individuals with knowledge and awareness of state/provincial and national policies which is particularly relevant if the teams engage in policy reform. However, core expertise is often found in non-governmental communities as well, including those working in violence against women organizations as well as mental health and addictions agencies. These professionals and advocates often hold crucial information about domestic violence in their communities and there needs to be more effort to capture these expert voices. Without their participation only a partial understanding of the circumstances leading to the domestic homicide is possible.

## *Scope of DVDR reviews*

Review scopes vary from a narrow focus on women killed by current/former male partners to a broader focus on all domestic violence-related deaths, including children, other relatives, bystanders, and/or near-fatalities (Bugeja et al., 2017). Some DVDRs have recently broadened their scope to capture domestic violence victims who die by suicide (Bugeja et al., 2017). However, the primary focus of most teams remains intimate partner homicide (including homicide-suicide) and, specifically, women killed by male partners, but there are good reasons to go beyond such cases. There have been many 'secondary' or 'collateral' fatal victims whose deaths should be counted (Fairbairn, Jaffe, & Dawson, 2017) and others who did not die, but were targeted, which supports focusing on attempted homicides (e.g. New Jersey, Florida, and Georgia in the United States). Of specific importance are those children killed in the context of domestic violence and whether and how DVDRs operate with, or alongside of, child death reviews which have existed much longer (Jaffe, Campbell, Reif, Fairbairn, & David, 2017). While some jurisdictions are developing protocols to deal with the overlapping scope of these two types of reviews, DVDRs have developed parallel to child death reviews for the most part. However, many of the risk factors are similar and families experiencing violence are often facing similar obstacles and challenges that integrated reviews may be able to address more adequately (Jaffe et al., 2017). The review scope often depends on available resources, however.

A second consideration is whether *all* deaths meeting review criteria are examined or only a subset of cases and, if the latter, how the subset will be selected. Reviewing all deaths allows for accumulated knowledge about patterns over time and across subtypes (e.g. familicide, domestic-violence related filicide, homicide-suicide). This information is crucial to understanding emerging priorities for system improvements as well as practice, professional, and research concerns. However, breadth may mean that depth is lost (i.e. fewer details collected) which might mean vital nuances for assessing risk and safety are missed. Further, information required to understand differing contexts within which domestic homicides occur may also be missed, crucial for understanding risk and safety for marginalized or vulnerable populations (e.g. Indigenous, immigrant/refugee, and/or rural/remote victims). This approach also has the potential for prioritizing some victims over others and these more marginalized, and subsequently, vulnerable populations may be ignored, particularly if numbers are smaller. The best-case scenario, then, is to conduct both aggregate, quantitative analyses and more nuanced, context-based qualitative reviews to achieve a comprehensive understanding, which is the goal of such reviews.

## *What is reviewed and whose voices are represented?*

There are variations in what is reviewed for each death, including the types of documents accessed and, ultimately, whose voices are heard – whether on paper or in person. Victims cannot speak for themselves, so who speaks for them, if anyone, and how this is determined by review committees is crucial but has received minimal attention. This is concerning because who gets to construct these events and what materials are used to do so has significant implications for understanding what happened which informs recommendations. In England and Wales, the involvement of the victim's family, friends, and/or colleagues is specified in their review policy because it is recognized these individuals often have important information about barriers and shortfalls that contributed to the death of someone close to them (Mullane, 2017; Regan, Kelly, Morris, & Dibb, 2007). The decision to involve family and friends remains controversial, however, for at least three reasons. First, ethical issues are identified that stem from approaching and speaking with surviving family or friends who may be re-traumatized as a result, particularly if those conducting their interviews are not adequately trained (Mullane, 2017). Second, involving those close to victims requires additional time for team members, most of whom are volunteers. Finally, the time between domestic homicides and the reviews is often lengthy, meaning it can be difficult to locate surviving family members, which has both ethical and practical implications (Mullane, 2017).

Few disagree, however, that family members and friends may have the most information about the events leading to domestic homicides because victims do not always seek help from formal agencies or have access to the resources to do so even if they wished (particularly in rural and remote locations). Therefore, the voices of family and friends can be crucial to understanding a woman's decisions about seeking help or not and understanding the responses she received if she did so. DVDRs are often the only forum, apart from a criminal trial if there is one, in which those significantly impacted by the death of a loved one can participate and seek answers about the domestic homicide. While many are often interviewed by police immediately after the incident, these same people may not get another chance to speak upon recovering from shock and reflecting on the circumstances. It is only then that they may be able to think more clearly about possible contributors, including system responses (or lack thereof) of which they may be aware, and the loss of this knowledge can weaken the review and recommendations that result.

There are several issues to consider if involving family and friends in the review process. First, there may be difficulties identifying whether and whom is the most reliable person to speak for the victim. Family is often narrowly defined to include close biological/kin connections rather than the often broader 'family-like' connections valued by women experiencing violence and/or who may be estranged from their biological/kin families. Second, there are ethical and social-psychological challenges to working with those who have experienced the loss of a loved one. These may include emotions about their own perceived failure to help the victim, their potential defensiveness, and their protectiveness of formal agencies. The latter may be due, in part, to their own intimidation by state and other professionals whom they may see as more of an authority. In the UK, AAFDA responds to these issues by supporting and guiding family members involved in domestic homicide reviews and is seen as an international best practice in involving family/friends in reviews.

## *What and how is information disseminated?*

Two key types of outputs are common from DVDRs. First, descriptive data on all or a subset of domestic homicides that have occurred during the review period and, in some cases, historical statistical data from the time the DVDR was established (e.g. Ontario; Bugeja et al., 2017). The objective of doing so is to document common precursors or 'red flags' in domestic homicides which are often represented as risk factors. It is acknowledged that most initiatives do not conduct systematic research, including a comparison or reference group of non-lethal domestic violence cases, to discern whether a specific factor is a real risk or simply frequently present in cases reviewed (Websdale et al., 2017). Regardless, understanding common factors that precede killings or common characteristics of those involved can improve future responses.

The second key output of DVDRs are recommendations meant to facilitate system change, although the quality and quantity of those recommendations vary. For example, while some teams target all recommendations to specific organizations or agencies, other teams target just some or none at all. A few DVDRs direct recommendations to lead agencies who liaise with various sectors to implement recommendations. At the very least, it is recognized that DVDRs must have the capacity to make recommendations which is a necessary, but not a sufficient, condition for system and social change. They must also have the capacity to monitor recommendation uptake and implementation.

Reports produced by DVDR teams are often made available to the public and released either annually, biannually, or at varying times throughout the review process (Bugeja et al., 2017). These reports typically contain information about how the DVDR functions, the number of deaths reviewed including descriptive data summarizing the characteristics of domestic homicides and those involved. The reports also frequently contain the recommendations generated from each case or collection of cases. While information varies across reports, most recognize it is essential that lessons learned from reviews are transmitted to the broader public which is done using recommendations and public reporting mechanisms.

## *Tracking and monitoring recommendations for update and implementation*

Despite recommendations being the most concrete and tangible outcomes of DVDRs, there is a dearth of systematic research that sheds light on what improvements or changes have been recommended, how often similar recommendations are made, what sectors or organizations are tasked with implementing recommendations, or what outcomes and impacts have developed, if any, as a result. The lack of research can be attributed, in part, to the fact that few jurisdictions mandate responses to recommendations which makes monitoring implementation difficult (Bugeja, Dawson, McIntyre, & Walsh, 2015; Bugeja et al., 2017). This means that there is also a dearth of systematic knowledge about overall impacts of DVDRs, including accountability of agencies/organizations/sectors meant to improve responses.

Some DVDRs assign team members to take recommendations to organizations targeted whereas others report holding symposiums to synthesize and prioritize recommendations to facilitate the development of implementation plans. There is little information as to what are the outcomes of these two approaches or others that may be adopted. One exception is Victoria, Australia, who monitors recommendations through mechanisms in place for coronial investigations and their accompanying coroner's act. Specifically, statutory bodies and entities must provide a response to recommendations within 90 days although their response can be a refusal or a decision to put the recommendation on hold (Coroner's Court of Victoria, 2014). A second exception is the state of Iowa where legislation is enacted for this purpose. Other jurisdictions request, but do not mandate responses, including the District of Columbia and Ontario, Canada, where directors of agencies are asked to respond to recommendations within 60 days (Bugeja et al., 2017; Office of the Chief Coroner of Ontario, 2018).

One approach to increasing the uptake of recommendations by those targeted has been adopted by New Zealand (Tolmie et al., 2017). This review team reportedly undergoes extensive stakeholder engagement with agencies and sectors identified or targeted, including meetings with senior staff. The goal is to seek organizational feedback about how recommendations can be constructed to account for system constraints that may not be amenable to change because it involves multiple agencies with different processes, procedures, tools, disciplinary understandings, and resources. The philosophy of the New Zealand approach is that engaging with agencies prior to making recommendations, or during the construction of recommendations, ensures what is generated is practical and based on a solid understanding of the agency's current processes (Tolmie et al., 2017). Obtaining prior agreement to a recommendation also increases agency buy-in and subsequent uptake. It is reported that this approach has contributed to their initiative having a fair measure of success in recommendation implementation (Tolmie et al., 2017). Further, in this jurisdiction, in addition to the national recommendations, each death review results in local recommendations which are actioned at that level.

## *Key ongoing challenges facing DVDRs*

### *Accounting for and responding to intersecting oppressions*

Despite overall declines in domestic homicide in some world regions (e.g. North America), some groups of victims remain at high risk with little evidence of corresponding declines. Indigenous populations subject to historical and ongoing impacts of colonization, discrimination, and racism are disproportionately represented in domestic violence-related deaths, compared to non-Indigenous groups living in Australia, Canada, New Zealand, and the United States (Wilson, 2017). Similarly, African Americans in the United States (Bent-Goodley, 2013) and some regions of other countries, including Canada, also face high risk of domestic violence. Women living in rural and remote regions face higher risks than their urban counterparts (Dawson et al., 2018). Finally, immigrant and refugee women face unique challenges when experiencing violence which contributes to their marginalization and vulnerability (Dawson et al., 2018).

Given increased vulnerability to domestic homicide of these and other groups, it is crucial that DVDRs consider and speak to the intersecting oppressions experienced by many victims, perpetrators and their families. Specifically, Hobart (2004) argues that specific attention is needed to whether responses to varying experiences of violence are shaped by "institutional biases regarding race, poverty, literacy, language, immigration status, disability, age, culture, gender or sexual orientation" (p. 5). For example, among 43 DVDRs examined by Sheehy (2017), three required the committee composition to reflect the diversity of the jurisdiction, and another six required specific numbers of diversity appointees, sometimes naming the specific groups.

Given the vast overrepresentation of Indigenous women among victims of domestic homicide in Canada, Australia, New Zealand, and the US, more concerted efforts must be made by DVDRs to understand how colonialism and racism contributes to their increased marginalization and vulnerability. Some Indigenous communities have strategic ways of responding to domestic violence and have insights into the realities of Indigenous women's lives that will be crucial to crafting recommendations. The New Zealand committee has reported to have adopted an inter-generational approach to domestic homicide, drawing upon the expertise of Māori communities, recognizing reviews must include both historical victims and those who follow and, specifically, the children left behind (Tolmie et al., 2017).

### *The role of feminists and women's advocates*

An ongoing criticism of many DVDRs is that there is little to no representation from a core group of experts who arguably have the greatest wealth of knowledge about domestic violence – feminist and/or frontline women's advocates. In most jurisdictions, feminist and grassroots violence against women agencies were largely responsible for lobbying for the establishment of these initiatives. It is perplexing, then, their voices are not represented to a greater degree (Sheehy, 2017). Some teams recognize their actual and potential contributions and have ensured that their expert voices are at the table or, at least, in an advisory capacity. Such appointees are required in many US jurisdictions with some orders or statutes stipulating the eligibility of "a certified domestic violence center" (Alabama, 2009), "a domestic violence victim service agency" (Alaska, 2012), "domestic violence shelter service staff and battered women's advocates" (California, 2012), or a "victim advocate" (Delaware, 2013) (Sheehy, 2017). However, Sheehy (2017) has argued that the proportion of total team members who are feminists or frontline advocates/workers remains small overall, meaning review teams may not have a clear or comprehensive understanding of the root causes of male violence against women.

Women's advocates are also often better equipped than government and criminal justice representatives to speak to intersecting oppressions in women's lives because they work directly for, and with, victims/survivors. Feminists and women's advocates who work with women living in poverty and/or confronting racism are often able to underscore the role played by "class dimensions of patriarchy and white domination" (Richie, 2000). Similarly, feminist advocates can contribute to reviews' considerations of other inequalities such as women with disabilities (Healey, Howe, Humphreys, Jennings, & Julian, 2008) and immigrant and refugee women fleeing male violence (Zannettino et al., 2013). The most urgent need for DVDRs, then, is to include the voices and expertise of Indigenous and racialized populations as well as feminist women's advocates as permanent members of DVDRs so that particular cultural or community perspectives can fully inform the development of review processes and provide insight on individual reviews.

## Documenting impacts

One of the key challenges moving forward is the limited systematic research examining the impact of DVDRs on prevention (Dawson, 2017a; Websdale et al., 2017). There is little to no evidence-based research examining associations among reviews, socio-legal change, and declining rates of domestic violence or homicide. There have been no large-scale environmental scans of the large number of reports produced internationally, capturing type, frequency, and content of recommendations generated by these review teams (but see Dawson, 2017a). Further, no research has followed up with those involved with DVDRs and the communities in which they operate to determine if changes have occurred as a result. Finally, there have been no matched, case-control studies that compare jurisdictions with and without DVDRs over an extended time period to determine if there has been system or social change.

In an earlier review, Watt (2010) reported anecdotal evidence that DVDRs have produced change through increased public education, media coverage of the release or dissemination of annual reports, improved cooperation across multiple sectors involved in responding to these cases, changes in law enforcement practices, and increasing funding for services. Some countries have also witnessed new laws, growing public disapproval of domestic violence, promising agency protocols and/or practices, more intensive and/or comprehensive coordinated community responses, and the emergence of risk and safety initiatives (Dawson, 2017a; Websdale et al., 2017). Many of these changes may be attributable to DVDRs, but it is not possible to know for sure given few efforts to track their impacts.

Most DVDRs indicate reducing domestic homicide is a core goal, but few teams report whether this has been achieved (Bugeja et al., 2015, 2017). In part, this is due to the inability to establish a causal relationship between the work of DVDRs and the incidence of subsequent domestic violence-related deaths. DVDRs are only one component of a larger set of reforms that have occurred which may, in turn, contribute to reducing domestic homicide. As such, isolating the independent contribution of DVDRs is difficult which raises the question of whether such a measure of success is appropriate and should be stated in the first place. Of course, the long-term goal is to reduce such deaths, otherwise why conduct the reviews in the first place, but stating this as a primary outcome measure or overarching goal sets the initiatives up for failure if declines are not noted, or if increases are documented, particularly in the short term.

Despite this complexity, many teams feel stating this goal remains important because it demonstrates domestic violence is unacceptable by society and it is preventable (Bugeja et al., 2015). In a sense, then, one of the more crucial roles played by DVDRs is that they send the message that domestic violence is an issue that requires attention and their existence, symbolically and practically, shows that responding to domestic violence requires all sectors and members of society to work collaboratively. The fact that findings of DVDRs regularly feature in local and national news strengthens this cultural effect, underscoring the preventable nature of such crimes rather than their more common representation as 'isolated and episodic' events that defy prevention. This raises the status of domestic violence as a serious social issue (Mullane, 2017).

## Opportunities

The cultural transformation in how individuals and society think about domestic violence that led to the development of DVDRs has taken decades to achieve and, while there is much work left to be done, progress is undeniable. It may take a significant period of time before we understand the contributions of DVDRs to the prevention of domestic violence and homicide. Until then, the stated goal of DVDRs should be to strengthen domestic violence service systems through the development and implementation of recommendations and to monitor their impacts on systems over time. The research emphasis should be to describe what improvements are identified by reviews, examine uptake and implementation of recommendations, and to examine subsequent impacts on the systems they were meant to change. Only then will it be possible to determine what the impacts have been on the experiences of victims, perpetrators, and communities. In the meantime, various opportunities continue to present themselves through DVDRs which have had current and immediate impacts.

First, simply by establishing a DVDR, jurisdictions bring together a diverse set of actors who may not typically come together in a collaborative and consultative manner thereby becoming more familiar with each other and the constraints they work within. Ultimately, a better understanding of the roles they play separately and together is achieved by all involved. This educational aspect is built upon by the New Zealand team who regularly uses information from the death reviews to provide feedback to agencies on key practice issues as well as professional training (Wilson, Smith, Tolmie, & Haan, 2015). Second, DVDRs provide a unique opportunity to identify deficiencies in, and to work out mechanisms for enhancing, information. Third, the work of the DVDRs produces better data that can be disaggregated to more clearly understand the circumstances surrounding these deaths and those involved. The previous dearth of information in most countries has underscored the need for more accurate tracking of these cases and the violence prevention role that may be played by domestic violence death review teams (Bugeja et al., 2017). This need has been reiterated time and again by the United Nations Special Rapporteur on violence against women who urges countries to collect more data that can be disaggregated, especially by sex, and that can be standardized and aggregated over time (Vincent, 2014).

## Conclusion

There have been significant social, cultural, and legal transformations in recent decades in how society perceives and responds to domestic violence and the rise of DVDRs which indicate a shift from reactive to preventative approaches. Historically, criminal investigations have been perceived as the primary mechanism for responding to domestic violence and homicide and, while they continue to be crucial, it is recognized that they do not act alone. Further, the work of DVDRs means that the role of responding sectors is now enhanced by information and knowledge gained from similar preceding deaths thereby learning from patterns and trends over time.

Currently, these initiatives exist largely in high-income countries, despite domestic violence being a serious social issue in low- to middle-income countries. Although child death reviews have been implemented more extensively across the world, it is not yet clear whether DVDRs can be usefully transferred to middle- and low-income countries, to different cultural milieus, or to countries with vastly different governance structures (Dawson, Mathews, Abrahams, & Campbell, 2017; Jaffe et al., 2017). The wholesale adoption of any of the current DVDR models may not be possible, and even the applicability of the process itself may have limited utility unless certain criteria within a country's sociopolitical infrastructure are met. Perhaps the most significant factor influencing transferability is whether the systems of governance maintain and advance the philosophical position that violence against women is unacceptable. Where the systems of governance do not operate from this fundamental standpoint, individual death reviews would do little to ameliorate the experiences of domestic violence. In addition, other relevant considerations would be whether countries recognize that, as a public health problem, domestic violence is preventable; whether they have the infrastructure required to conduct such reviews (e.g. resources, means of data collection, legal governance); and whether they have the ability or power to implement any recommendations made.

Since DVDRs are largely in their infancy in terms of evolution in most of the jurisdictions in which they operate, there are valuable opportunities for international dialogues on good practices that have evolved and how we might better understand their impacts on the populations they are meant to help. Currently, DVDRs are the only mechanism available to review these deaths, particularly those ending in the suicide of the perpetrator. Arguably, however, investigations with the goal of solving a crime and proceeding to trial have different mandates than the reviews themselves – the latter of which is focused solely on prevention – and so their potential for reducing all domestic-violence related deaths is clear. Only with systematic research on their processes and impacts can DVDRs achieve their potential and this should be the research and practice priority as they head into the next decade.

## Critical findings

- Key considerations for the establishment and operation of domestic violence death reviews (DVDRs) and the research that results are governance models, team composition, review scope, whose voices are represented what and how information is disseminated, and how recommendations generated will be tracked and monitored.
- Key challenges of these initiatives are accounting for and responding to victims, perpetrators and communities experiencing violence who have intersecting oppressions; ensuring the diversity and inclusiveness of voices in the reviews; and documenting outcomes and impacts of recommendations and their ability to achieve system and social change.
- Key opportunities are the cultural transformation facilitated by the rise of these initiatives both practically and symbolically; their ability to bring together a diverse set of individuals and groups who respond to domestic violence; enhancement of information sharing across groups and sectors to allow for better responses to those experiencing violence; and better data on domestic violence-related deaths, given they are currently the only mechanism with such a mandate.

## Implications for practice, policy, and research

- While similar in many ways, DVDRs differ along important dimensions that make it difficult to identify good practices; therefore, it is imperative to begin more systematically sharing existing knowledge by expanding networks across national and international jurisdictions.
- Policy development will remain a challenge until jurisdictions begin to mandate responses to recommendations and develop mechanisms for tracking and monitoring responses to recommendations by the agencies targeted.
- Future research to provide a more comprehensive understanding of the core elements of death review initiatives, move recommendations from the development to implementation stage, and ensure systematic examination of their impacts on systems and social change is a priority.

## Note

1 The terms 'domestic violence' and 'domestic homicide' are used, given they are the most commonly referenced in related death review initiatives. It is acknowledged, however, that other terms may be more accurate such as intimate partner femicide, given that most of the cases reviewed are women killed by current or former male partners.

## References

Bent-Goodley, T. B. (2013). Domestic violence fatality reviews and the African American community. *Homicide Studies, 17*(4), 375–390.

Bugeja, L., Butler, A., Buxton, E., Ehrat, H., Hayes, M., McIntyre, S. J., & Walsh, C. (2013). The implementation of domestic violence death reviews in Australia. *Homicide Studies, 17*(4), 353–374.

Bugeja, L., Dawson, M., McIntyre, S. J., & Poon, J. (2017). Domestic/family violence death reviews: An international comparison. In M. Dawson (Ed.), *Domestic homicides and death reviews: An international perspective* (pp. 3–26). London: Palgrave Macmillan.

Bugeja, L., Dawson, M., McIntyre, S. J., & Walsh, C. (2015). Domestic/family violence death reviews: An international comparison. *Trauma, Violence, & Abuse, 16*(2), 179–187.

Butler, A., Buxton-Namisnyk, E., Beattie, S., Bugeja, L., Ehrat, H., Henderson, E., & Lambe, A. (2017). Australia. In M. Dawson (Ed.), *Domestic homicides and death reviews: An international perspective* (pp. 125–158). London: Palgrave Macmillan.

Campbell, J. C., Glass, N., Sharps, P. W., Laughon, K., & Bloom, R. (2007). Intimate partner homicide: Review and implications of research and policy. *Trauma, Violence, & Abuse, 8*, 246–269.

Coroner's Court of Victoria. (2014). Retrieved from www.coronerscourt.vic.gov.au/home/coronial+investigation+process/family+violence+investigations/

Crawford, M., Gartner, R., Dawson, M., & Women We Honour Action Committee. (1997). *Woman killing: Intimate femicide in Ontario 1990–1994*. Toronto: Women We Honour Action Committee.

Crawford, M., Gartner, R., & Women We Honour Action Committee. (1992). *Woman killing: Intimate femicide in Ontario 1974–1990*. Toronto: Women We Honour Action Committee.

Dale, M., Celaya, A., & Mayer, S. J. (2017). Ethical conundrums in the establishment and operations of domestic/family violence fatality reviews. In M. Dawson (Ed.), *Domestic homicides and death reviews: An international perspective* (pp. 229–256). London: Palgrave Macmillan.

Dawson, M. (2013). Fatality and death reviews. *Homicide Studies, 17*(4), 335–338.

Dawson, M. (2017a). *Domestic homicides and death reviews: An international perspective*. London: Palgrave Macmillan.

Dawson, M. (2017b). *An international examination of domestic violence death review outcomes: The frequency, type and content of recommendations for improvement in four countries*. Paper presented at the Sweden Symposium of Criminology, Stockholm, June.

Dawson, M., Jaffe, P., Campbell, M., Lucas, W., & Kerr, K. (2017). Canada. In M. Dawson (Ed.), *Domestic homicides and death reviews: An international perspective* (pp. 59–90). London: Palgrave Macmillan.

Dawson, M., Mathews, S., Abrahams, N., & Campbell, J. (2017). Death reviews in the context of domestic homicide in low- to middle-income countries: South Africa as a case study. In M. Dawson (Ed.), *Domestic homicides and death reviews: An international perspective* (pp. 345–372). London: Palgrave Macmillan.

Dawson, M., Sutton, D., Jaffe, P., Straatman, A., Poon, J., Gosse, M., Peters, O., & Sandhu, G. (2018). *One is too many: Trends and patterns in domestic homicides in Canada 2010–2015* (49 pages). Guelph, ON: Canadian Domestic Homicide Prevention Initiative with Vulnerable Populations.

Dobash, R. E., & Dobash, R. P. (2015). *When men murder women.* Oxford: Oxford University Press.

Fairbairn, J., Jaffe, P., & Dawson, M. (2017). Challenges in defining domestic homicide: Considerations for research and practice. In M. Dawson (Ed.), *Domestic homicides and death reviews: An international perspective* (pp. 201–228). London: Palgrave Macmillan.

Garcia-Moreno, C., Jansen, H. A. F. M., Ellsberg, M., Heise, L., & Watts, C. (2005). *WHO multi-country study on women's health and domestic violence against women: Initial results on prevalence, health outcomes and women's responses.* Geneva, Switzerland: World Health Organization.

Healey, L., Howe, K., Humphreys, C., Jennings, C., & Julian, F. (2008). *Building the evidence: A report on the status of policy and practice in responding to violence against women with disabilities in Victoria.* Victoria: Women's Health Victoria and Victorian Women with Disabilities Network.

Hobart, M. (2004). *Advocates and fatality reviews.* Seattle: Washington State Coalition Against Domestic Violence.

Jaffe, P., Campbell, M., Reif, K., Fairbairn, J., & David, R. (2017). Children killed in the context of domestic violence: International perspectives from death review committees. In M. Dawson (Ed.), *Domestic homicides and death reviews: An international perspective* (pp. 91–124). London: Palgrave Macmillan.

Johnson, H., & Dawson, M. (2011). *Violence against women in Canada: Research and policy perspectives.* Toronto: Oxford University Press.

Monckton-Smith, J., & Williams, A. (2014). *Domestic abuse, homicide and gender: Strategies for policy and practice.* London: Palgrave Macmillan.

Mullane, F. (2017). The impact of family members' involvement in the domestic violence death review process. In M. Dawson (Ed.), *Domestic homicides and death reviews: An international perspective* (pp. 257–286). London: Palgrave Macmillan.

Office of the Chief Coroner of Ontario. (2018). *Domestic violence death review committee 2017 annual report.* Toronto, ON: Office of the Chief Coroner of Ontario.

Payton, J., Robinson, A., & Brookman, F. (2017). United Kingdom. In M. Dawson (Ed.), *Domestic homicides and death reviews: An international perspective* (pp. 91–124). London: Palgrave Macmillan.

Porter, T., & Gavin, H. (2010). Infanticide and neonaticide: A review of 40 years of research literature on incidence and causes. *Trauma, Violence, & Abuse, 11*, 99–112.

Regan, L., Kelly, L., Morris, A., & Dibb, R. (2007). *'If only we'd known': An exploratory study of seven intimate partner homicides in Engleshire.* Final Report to the Engleshire Domestic Violence Homicide Review Group. London: Child and Woman Abuse Studies Unit.

Richie, B. (2000). A black feminist reflection on the antiviolence movement. *Signs, 25*(4), 1133–1137.

Sheehy, E. (2017). A feminist reflection on domestic violence death reviews. In M. Dawson (Ed.), *Domestic homicides and death reviews: An international perspective.* (pp. 373–402). London: Palgrave Macmillan.

Tolmie, J., Wilson, D., & Smith, R. (2017). New Zealand. In M. Dawson (Ed.), *Domestic homicides and death reviews: An international perspective* (pp. 169–200). London: Palgrave Macmillan.

United Nations Office of Drugs and Crime. (2018). *Global study on homicide: Gender-related killing of women and girls.* Vienna: UNODC.

van Wormer, K., & Roberts, A. R. (2009). *Death by domestic violence: Preventing the murders and murder-sucides.* London: Praeger.

Vincent, S. (2014). Child death review processes: A six-country comparison. *Child Abuse Review, 23*(2), 116–129.

Watt, K. E. (2010). *Domestic violence fatality review teams: Collaborative efforts to end intimate partner femicide* (D Phil Psychology). University of Illinois, Urbana-Champaign.

Websdale, N., Celaya, A., & Mayer, S. (2017). United States. In M. Dawson (Ed.), *Domestic homicides and death reviews: An international perspective* (pp. 27–58). London: Palgrave Macmillan.

Websdale, N., Ferraro, K., & Barger, S. D. (2019). The domestic violence fatality review clearinghouse: Introduction to a new national data system with a focus on firearms. *Injury Epidemiology, 6*(6). https://doi.org/10.1186/s40621-019-0182-2

Wilson, D. (2017). Indigenous populations and the domestic violence death review process. In M. Dawson (Ed.), *Domestic homicides and death reviews: An international perspective* (pp. 287–316). London: Palgrave Macmillan.

Wilson, D., Smith, R., Tolmie, J., & Haan, I. (2015). Becoming better helpers: Rethinking language to move beyond simplistic responses to women experiencing intimate partner violence. *Policy Quarterly, 11*(1), 25–31.

Zannettino, L., Pittaway, E., Eckert, R., Bartolomei, L., Ostapiej-Piatkowski, B., Allimant, A., & Parris, J. (2013). *Improving responses to refugees with backgrounds of multiple trauma: Pointers for practitioners in domestic and family violence, sexual assault and settlement services.* Sydney: Australian Domestic & Family Violence Clearinghouse.

# 44

# INTERVENTIONS TO PREVENT OR REDUCE ADOLESCENT DATING VIOLENCE

## Methodological considerations in randomized-controlled trials

*Ernest N. Jouriles, Kelli S. Sargent, Alison Krauss and Renee McDonald*

### Introduction

Adolescent dating violence (ADV) refers to acts of physical, sexual, psychological, or emotional violence that occur between adolescents and a current or former romantic partner (Centers for Disease Control and Prevention, 2019). Such acts include kicks or slaps, threats, insults or put-downs, sexual coercion, or stalking. Among dating adolescents in the United States (US), approximately 21% of females and 10% of males report experiencing physical or sexual ADV over the course of a year alone (Vagi, Olsen, Basile, & Vivolo-Kantor, 2015). Psychological and emotional dating violence estimates are much higher, with up to 77% of adolescents reporting verbal or emotional abuse perpetration in the past year (Niolon et al., 2015). Experiencing ADV is linked to a range of adjustment difficulties, including depressive symptoms (Ackard, Eisenberg, & Neumark-Sztainer, 2007; Exner-Cortens, Eckenrode, & Rothman, 2013), suicidal ideation (Nahapetyan, Orpinas, Song, & Holland, 2014), substance use (Ackard et al., 2007; Foshee, Reyes, Gottfredson, Chang, & Ennett, 2013), and risk for revictimization (Jouriles, Choi, Rancher, & Temple, 2017).

Developmentally, dating has been conceptualized as a novel "task" of adolescence. Through dating, youth build skills and form scripts for navigating romantic relationships (Collins, Welsh, & Furman, 2009). Almost 50% of US adolescents report a current dating relationship by age 15 (Carver, Joyner, & Udry, 2003), and the average age of first sexual intercourse in the US quickly follows at 16.5 years (Vasilenko, Kugler, & Rice, 2016). Thus, adolescence offers youth opportunities to form and crystallize romantic relationship scripts. Unfortunately, sometimes these scripts include aggression (Jouriles, McDonald, Mueller, & Grych, 2012). Given the scope and consequences of ADV, early to middle adolescence represents an ideal time period to intervene to attempt to prevent or reduce such violence.

## Interventions to prevent or reduce adolescent dating violence

Reviews of the literature suggest that over 60 programs have been developed and tested to address ADV (De La Rue, Polanin, Espelage, & Pigott, 2017; Edwards & Hinsz, 2014; Fell-meth, Heffernan, Nurse, Habibula, & Sethi, 2013; Lundgren & Amin, 2015; Ting, 2009). These programs vary in the populations they target (e.g., potential perpetrators, potential victims, witnesses or bystanders of ADV), the attitudes and behaviors they address (e.g., rape myths, bystander behaviors), and methods by which they are delivered (e.g., small group discussions, classroom lectures). However, they share the broader goal of reducing violence perpetration and victimization among adolescents.

According to reviews of the literature, ADV programs tend to have favorable effects on attitudes and knowledge pertaining to violence, yet evidence that they reduce violence perpetration and victimization is lacking. For example, a meta-analysis of school-based ADV interventions (De La Rue et al., 2017) documented favorable effects on rape myth acceptance, ADV attitudes, knowledge, and healthy conflict skills at posttest across 23 studies that utilized a control group. There were no differences, however, between intervention and control groups on ADV perpetration or victimization. In short, although ADV intervention programs show promising effects on important constructs, more work is needed to achieve and document observable reductions in actual violence and victimization. Thus, researchers will likely attempt to build upon prior ADV intervention efforts, and continue to design studies to prevent or reduce ADV.

## Current review

Prior reviews of evaluation research on ADV interventions (e.g., De La Rue et al., 2017; Edwards & Hinsz, 2014; Fellmeth et al., 2013; Lundgren & Amin, 2015; Ting, 2009) focus on whether interventions designed to address ADV influence dependent variables of interest (e.g., attitudes about ADV, ADV perpetration). Yet, there is tremendous variability in the methodological rigor of these evaluations. Rigor is an important consideration in intervention studies, as diminished rigor can contribute to biased results (Higgins, Churchill, Tovey, Lesserson, & Chandler, 2011; Kazdin, 2017), making it difficult to infer that the intervention being evaluated caused the observed effects. Lack of rigor may also exaggerate the actual effects of an intervention and obstructs one's ability to interpret promising findings (Kazdin, 2017); less rigorous studies have shown larger effect sizes than studies with greater methodological rigor (Cheung & Slavin, 2016; Wood et al., 2008). Insufficient attention to certain methodological considerations, such as sample size and measurement of key study variables (e.g., violence perpetration), can also impede the ability to detect intervention effects.

There are many challenges to conducting methodologically rigorous research evaluating effects of ADV intervention programs. Some of these are common to evaluations of interventions in general, such as the ability to recruit an adequately sized sample and to track and retain participants over time. Other challenges arise from the combination of the sensitive nature of the subject matter – especially in a population of minors – and the challenges of engaging multiple stakeholders in conducting the research, including adolescents, parents, personnel at the settings where the intervention programs are delivered, and internal review boards.

Our primary aim in this chapter is to help the field move toward greater sophistication in both the conduct and reporting of methods in randomized controlled trials (RCTs) evaluating ADV intervention programs. An RCT is a study in which units (individuals, classrooms, schools) are allocated at random, or by chance, either to receive the intervention that is being evaluated or to receive a control or comparison intervention. RCTs are often considered the gold standard design for making conclusions about effects of an intervention program in medicine, psychology, and education (Schulz, Altman, & Moher, 2010).

To organize information and describe the importance of certain features of RCTs, we used the Consolidated Standards of Reporting Trials or more simply CONSORT statements (Schulz et al., 2010) and the Clinical Trials Assessment Measure (CTAM) (Tarrier & Wykes, 2004) as guides. The CONSORT statements emanated from efforts to improve the reporting of RCTs, and were based, in part, on methodological research that can influence outcomes. The CTAM is a tool for evaluating the methodological quality of clinical interventions (e.g., treatments of a psychological disorder). Both the CONSORT statements and the CTAM include items to help evaluate studies.

We began by systematically reviewing the literature to identify randomized controlled trials of ADV intervention programs. After identifying relevant studies, we reviewed them for the purpose of providing examples of what we consider exemplary methodological practices for designing, conducting, and reporting ADV research in the domains of: (1) sample description, (2) description of treatment and control conditions, (3) allocation of participants to treatment and control conditions, (4) assessment of outcomes, (5) participant retention and missing data, (6) data analysis, and (7) considerations prior to initiating an RCT.

## Literature search

MEDLINE, ERIC, PsycINFO, PsycArticles databases were searched to identify published articles and gray literature (e.g., empirical theses and dissertations) pertaining to ADV interventions through August 2017. The following search terms were entered in factorial fashion: *Term 1)* adolescent, teen, youth, student, high school, middle school; *Term 2)* dating violence, dating abuse, relationship violence, relationship abuse, partner violence, partner abuse, intimate partner violence, sexual violence, physical violence, psychological violence, emotional violence, verbal abuse, date rape, sexual coercion, revictimization, rape, sexual assault, victimization, perpetration, relationship aggression, partner aggression, courtship violence, courtship aggression, courtship abuse, dating aggression, sexual aggression, verbal aggression; *Term 3)* intervention, program, education, training, intervention program, curriculum, prevention.

An initial screening yielded 12,835 published articles and dissertations (referred to collectively as articles), after accounting for exact duplicates. One primary rater and two additional independent raters screened titles and abstracts of all retrieved articles. Each independent rater overlapped at least 10% with the primary rater. Discrepancies were discussed and reconciled by consensus. To be included in the review, articles had to be 1) published in English, and report on a study that: 2) empirically evaluated an intervention that had been administered (not just a program description or analysis of baseline data), 3) utilized an RCT design, 4) included measures of ADV or ADV-related outcomes, such as knowledge, attitudes, efficacy, and/or bystander behavior related to ADV, and 5) sampled adolescents (youth 10–19 years old). Studies that used exclusively elementary or college student samples were excluded.

Figure 44.1 details the process of article exclusion. Of the 12,835 identified articles, 39 met inclusion criteria. Among these, 37 unique intervention programs were evaluated. Table 44.1 lists the articles that were included, and summarizes aspects of the programs evaluated (e.g., number of sessions, duration, setting of the evaluation). Most of the articles report the evaluation of a single ADV intervention using a two-group RCT design (i.e., an intervention group and a control group), but three articles evaluated two interventions separately against a control group (DePrince, Chu, Labus, Shirk, & Potter, 2015; Taylor, Stein, & Burden, 2010; Taylor, Stein, Mumford, & Woods, 2013), and are listed twice in Table 44.1.

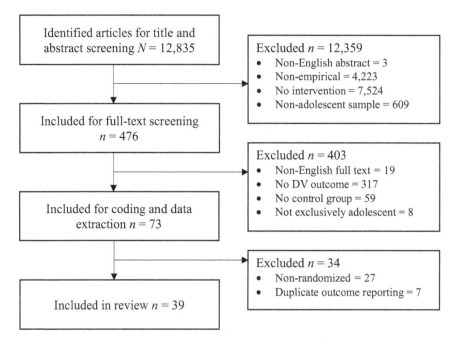

*Figure 44.1* CONSORT of article identification, screening, and included studies

## Discussion and analysis

### *Practices within methodological domains*

#### *Sample description*

Investigators commonly reported the inclusion and exclusion criteria used to determine who was eligible to participate in their studies. This is especially important in ADV research, because some programs target specific groups of adolescents, such as males or females only (e.g., *Coaching Boys into Men*, *My Voice My Choice*). Investigators also routinely provided routine descriptive information on their samples, including the sample size and demographics such as sex, age, race, and ethnicity.

ADV programs are often administered and evaluated in community settings (e.g., schools, juvenile correction facilities, inpatient treatment centers), and features of these settings may influence aspects of the program and its evaluation. Thus, it is desirable to go beyond basic sample description and provide information about the setting as well. For school-based studies, this can include socioeconomic data (e.g., percentage of students qualifying for free or reduced lunch; Sargent et al., 2017) and general academic proficiency and truancy rates (Taylor et al., 2013). Fay and Medway (2006) went a step further, situating the school within its broader community context:

> The educational setting of this project was the only high school located in a rural, primarily agricultural, town of 6600 residents within South Carolina. The town was selected because of high-risk factors of residents: 21% of the population had family

Table 44.1 Studies included in review

| Article authors (year) | Program | Sessions | Duration (min) | Approach | Presenter | Setting | Format | Study n | % Male | Mean age | Outcomes |
|---|---|---|---|---|---|---|---|---|---|---|---|
| Baiocchi et al. (2017) | IMPower | 6 | 720 | Selected | School staff | School | Group | 5,686 | 0 | | V |
| Brown et al. (2012) | PR:EPARe | 2 | 350 | Universal | Online/Indirect | School | Group | 505 | 48.9 | 13.5 | A, E |
| Coker et al. (2017) | Green Dot | | | Universal | Community professional | School | Group | 16,509 | 54.4 | | P, V |
| Connolly et al. (2015) | RISE | 2 | 90 | Universal | Community professional | School | Group | 509 | 48.6 | 12.4 | A, K, V |
| Cunningham et al. (2013) | SafERteens | 1 | 35 | Indicated | Community professional; online/indirect | Hospital | Group | 397 | 35.5 | 16.8 | V |
| DePrince et al. (2015) | Social Learning/Feminist; | 12 | 1080 | Selected | Research staff | Community | Group | 180 | 0 | 15.9 | V |
| DePrince et al. (2015) | Risk reduction & Executive Functioning | 12 | 1080 | Selected | Research staff | Community | Group | 180 | 0 | 15.9 | V |
| Espelage, Low, Polanin, and Brown (2013) | Second Step | 15 | 750 | Universal | School staff | School | Group | 3,616 | 52 | 11.2 | P, V |
| Espelage, Low, Polanin, and Brown (2015) | Second Step | 28 | 1400 | Universal | School staff | School | Group | 3,658 | 52 | 11 | P, V |
| Fay and Medway (2006) | -- | 2 | 120 | Universal | Research staff | School | Group | 154 | 43.5 | 15.5 | A |
| Foshee et al. (2004) | Safe Dates | 10 + Booster | 450+ | Universal | School staff | School | Group | 957 | 41.5 | 15.5 | P, V |
| Foshee et al. (2005) | Safe Dates | 10 | 450 | Universal | School staff | School | Group | 1,566 | 46.8 | 13.9 | A, P, V |
| Foshee et al. (2012) | Families for Safe Dates | 10 | 450 | Universal | Online/Indirect | Community | Parent-adol | 324 | 42 | 14 | A, P, V |

(Continued)

Table 44.1 (Continued)

| Article authors (year) | Program | Sessions | Duration (min) | Approach | Presenter | Setting | Format | Study n | % Male | Mean age | Outcomes |
|---|---|---|---|---|---|---|---|---|---|---|---|
| Foshee et al. (2015) | Moms and Teens for Safe Dates | 6 | | Universal | Online/Indirect | Community | Parent-adol | 409 | 25.9 | 13.6 | P, V |
| Gonzalez-Guarda et al. (2015) | Youth: Together Against Dating Violence | 6 | 540 | Selected | Research staff | School | Parent-adol | 82 | 44 | 14.3 | P, V |
| Jaycox et al. (2006) | Ending Violence | 3 | 180 | Universal | Community professional | School | Group | 2,540 | 48.3 | 14.4 | A, K, P, V |
| Joppa, Rizzo, Nieves, and Brown (2016) | Katie Brown Educational Program | 5 | 300 | Universal | Community professional | School | Group | 225 | 46 | 15.9 | A, K, P, V |
| Langhinrichsen-Rohling and Turner (2012) | Building a Lasting Love | | 360 | Selected | Community professional | Community | Group | 72 | 0 | 17.2 | P, V |
| Levesque, Johnson, Welch, Prochaska, and Paiva (2016) | Teen Choices | 3 | 90 | Universal | Online/Indirect | School | Individual | 3,901 | 46.5 | 15.4 | A, P, V |
| Macgowan (1997) | – | 5 | 300 | Universal | School staff | School | Group | 440 | 56.1 | 12.6 | A, K |
| Mathews et al. (2016) | PREPARE | 21 | 1890 | Selected | Community professional | School | Group | 3,451 | 38.7 | 13 | P, V |
| McArthur (2010) | Young Parenthood Program | 10 | | Selected | Community professional | Community | Individual | 46 | 50 | | V |
| Miller et al. (2012) | Coaching Boys into Men | 11 | 165 | Selected | School staff | School | Group | 2,006 | 100 | | A, B, K, P |
| Miller et al. (2013) | Coaching Boys into Men | 11 | 165 | Selected | School staff | School | Group | 1,513 | 100 | | A, B, K, P |
| Miller et al. (2015) | SHARP | 1 | | Universal | School staff | School | Individual | 1,011 | 23.7 | | E, B, K, V |
| Pacifici, Stoolmiller, and Nelson (2001) | Dating and Sexual Responsibility | 4 | 240 | Universal | School staff | School | Group | 458 | 48 | 15.8 | A |
| Peskin et al. (2014) | It's Your Game . . . Keep it Real | 24 | 1080 | Selected | School staff | School | Group | 766 | 40 | 13 | P, V |

(Continued)

Table 44.1 (Continued)

| Article authors (year) | Program | Sessions | Duration (min) | Approach | Presenter | Setting | Format | Study n | % Male | Mean age | Outcomes |
|---|---|---|---|---|---|---|---|---|---|---|---|
| Polanin and Espelage (2015) | *Second Step* | | 100 | Universal | School staff | School | Group | 3,616 | 47.2 | 11.2 | P, V |
| Roberts (2009) | *Expect Respect* | 4 | 186 | Universal | Community professional | School | Group | 332 | 49 | | A, P, V |
| Rothman, Stuart, Heeren, Paruk, and Bair-Merrit (n.d.) | *Real Talk* | 1 | 45 | Indicated | Community professional | Hospital | Individual | 172 | 14 | 17 | P, V |
| Rothman and Wang (2016) | *Real Talk* | 1 | 45 | Indicated | Community professional | Hospital | Individual | 27 | 26 | 17 | P, V |
| Rowe, Jouriles, and McDonald (2015) | *My Voice, My Choice* | 1 | 90 | Selected | Research staff | School | Group | 83 | 0 | 15.6 | V |
| Salazar and Cook (2006) | *Men Stopping Violence* | 5 | 390 | Indicated | Community professional | Juvenile correctional | Group | 47 | 100 | 14.9 | A, K |
| Sargent, Jouriles, Rosenfield, and McDonald (2017) | *TakeCARE* | 1 | 26 | Universal | Online/Indirect | School | Group | 1,295 | 47.5 | 15.3 | B, E |
| Taylor et al. (2010) | *Interaction* | 5 | 200 | Universal | Community professional | School | Group | 123 | 48 | 12 | A, K, P, V |
| Taylor et al. (2010) | *Law and justice* | 5 | 200 | Universal | Community professional | School | Group | 123 | 48 | 12 | A, K, P, V |
| Taylor et al. (2013) | *Shifting Boundaries: Classroom* | 6 | 240 | Universal | School staff | School | Group | 2,655 | 46.5 | 11.8 | P, V |
| Taylor et al. (2013) | *Shifting Boundaries: Classroom + Building* | 6 | 240 | Universal | Online/Indirect, school staff | School | Group | 2,655 | 46.5 | 11.8 | P, V |
| van Lieshout et al. (2016) | *Make a Move* | 8 | 720 | Selected | Research staff | Community | Group | 177 | 100 | 14.8 | A, E |
| Wolfe et al. (2003) | *Youth Relationships Project* | | 2160 | Selected | Community professional | Community | Group | 158 | 47.2 | 14.5 | P, V |
| Wolfe et al. (2009) | *Fourth R* | 21 | 225 | Universal | School staff | School | Group | 1,722 | 48 | 15.2 | V |
| Yom and Eun (2005) | CD-ROM Educational Program | 18 | 60 | Universal | Online/Indirect | School | Individual | 79 | 100 | 11.5 | A, K |

*Note:* A = Attitudes, B = Bystander, E = Efficacy, K = Knowledge, P = Perpetration, V = Victimization incomes below the poverty rate and the town's incidence of reported rape was 62% higher than national averages.

(p. 225)

Such information provides readers valuable context for thinking about study results. For studies recruiting through larger agency networks, setting descriptions like the one provided by Wolfe and colleagues (2003) are helpful:

> Youths from Child Protective Services (CPS) agencies were targeted for the study because their histories of maltreatment. . . . Seven CPS agencies participated in the study, including urban, rural, and semirural jurisdictions (whereas over 90% of the sample came from CPS agencies and were under a protection, supervision, or ward-ship order, we also included a small subset of maltreated youths attending a special needs school in the community). Social workers were provided with information on the content and requirements of the study; each agency had a volunteer coordinator to assist in identifying potential participants.
>
> (p. 281)

Many articles reporting on evaluations of ADV intervention programs do not include an explanation or rationale for the size of the sample recruited for the study. Depending on the program being evaluated, sample size could include the number of participants, classrooms, or schools, or some combination thereof, depending on the randomization and nesting procedure. In determining sample size an important consideration is power, or the ability, using statistical tests, to detect an intervention effect when one exists (Field, 2018). Power is determined by a number of factors, including sample size, the size of the anticipated between-group differ-ence (or effect size), and the statistical test used for data analysis. For instance, a larger sample is needed to detect a small effect size, compared to a large effect size. A study that is "under-powered" may lack a large enough sample to detect meaningful small effects. Reporting the reasoning for the sample size, and the extent to which the sample is sufficiently powered, gives readers a fuller understanding of the study results (or lack thereof).

An RCT of an ADV intervention should ideally be designed with sufficient power to detect small between-group effects, if such differences exist. Small intervention effects can be extremely meaningful for an ADV intervention program (Sargent et al., 2017). This is especially true for ADV intervention programs that are more universal in nature and meant to be delivered to large groups of teens, such as programs designed for dissemination to an entire school or school district. As Sargent and colleagues (2017) note, small effect sizes across an entire school can conceivably result in substantial reductions in ADV:

> [T]he average number of situations in which helpful bystander behavior was reported by students at baseline was 4.39. In a high school of over 1000 students, this translates to at least 4390 helpful bystander behaviors over a 3-month period. The average dif-ference in helpful bystander behavior between students who viewed TakeCARE and those in the control condition was 0.56 situations per student at follow-up, translating to an additional 560 helpful bystander behaviors over the follow-up period. Such an increase could make a considerable difference in reducing school victimization rates and could help contribute to changing a school's culture regarding tolerance of rela-tionship violence.
>
> (p. 640)

Under ideal circumstances, the sample size for an ADV intervention program evaluation would be determined in advance of the evaluation, and the method for determining the study's power (e.g., a power analysis) is described in the evaluation report. However, a post hoc justification of sample size is better than none at all. Coker and colleagues (2017) provide an excellent example of sample size justification:

> The sample size for the primary analysis was determined a priori based on number of regional rape crisis centers ($n = 13$) and the design in which two demographically similar public high schools were identified and randomized in each of the 13 service regions. . . . For secondary analyses using individual-level data within a single year, power calculations were provided using Stata, version 11 (sampsi), assuming 500 students participating at each school within a year, accounting for clustering of students within schools (intraclass correlation of 0.005), and a two-sided significance level of 0.05. Greater than 80% power was anticipated to test for a 50% reduction in physically forced sex, relative to 5% rate in control condition (Appendices, available online).
>
> (p. 568)

Investigators should also describe how the participants were recruited, since intervention effects may vary by recruitment method (Kazdin, 2017). For example, an ADV intervention found to be effective for students who volunteered to participate after seeing a study advertisement may have different effects (or none) on other groups of students. A clear presentation of how participants were recruited can help readers make judgments about the applicability of the intervention program to other samples. Again, in Coker and colleagues' (2017) evaluation of the *Green Dot* bystander intervention program, the investigators clearly identify the program as a universal program targeting all eligible students, and they specify that all students were included unless the student or parent opted out of the study protocol (p. 568).

## Description of intervention and control conditions

There are several key things to consider when describing ADV intervention programs. First, the description should be thorough enough to allow the reader to have a good conceptual understanding of the program's design and objectives. Such descriptions should include key content and characteristics (e.g., number of sessions, service provider, format) of the intervention. One way to do this is to provide a link to a website with all program materials, as was done by Miller and colleagues (2012) in their evaluation of *Coaching Boys into Men*. Several researchers have also provided detailed tables of session-by-session intervention content (e.g., Gonzalez-Guarda, Guerra, Cummings, Pino, & Becerra, 2015; Jaycox et al., 2006; van Lieshout, Mevissen, van Breukelen, Jonker, & Ruiter, 2016; Wolfe et al., 2009).

Second, evaluation reports should also include a detailed description of the assessment of treatment fidelity – how investigators ensured that the ADV intervention program was delivered as it was designed to be delivered. Successful implementation of an ADV intervention program involves a complex set of processes and events that unfold over time and across the individuals who provide and participate in the intervention. Documenting that the program was delivered as it was designed to be helps support conclusions about its effectiveness. On the other hand, poor treatment fidelity opens the door to alternative explanations for study results. If null results occur, a fidelity check indicating that the program was not implemented as intended can help reduce the likelihood of abandonment of a potentially useful program. Jaycox and colleagues

(2006) provide an excellent example of a fidelity check for their *Ending Violence* ADV intervention program:

> We assessed fidelity to the *Ending Violence* curriculum via two mechanisms. A single expert observed 10% of classes and rated the content and quality of the presentation. Observations were selected to obtain a variety of implementers, schools, and sessions. Delivery style, overall presentation, and interaction with participants were rated on five-point scales (poor to excellent); average ratings fell between good and very good, with one exception (the average rating of use of visual aids fell between fair and good). On average, 69% of curriculum elements were covered completely, 26% covered partially, and 5% of elements not covered. Implementers rated their own presentation for the amount of content they covered and class compliance for 153 of 165 class sessions (92%). Implementers nearly always reported covering at least 90% of the material, with only five sessions reported in the range of 76%–90%. Implementers rated the quality of the program delivered as good to excellent in all but three sessions (which were rated as fair). Classes were rated as moderately to extremely cooperative or compliant in all but 11 sessions, which were rated as "a little bit" cooperative or compliant. Classes were rated as moderately to extremely engaged and interested in all but six sessions, which were rated as "a little bit" engaged and interested.
>
> (p. 697)

Additionally, duration of the intervention, including the number of sessions and how long they last; format (e.g., group, individual, community, online vs. in person); a description of the individuals who administered the intervention, and the training and oversight they received in delivering the intervention is helpful for readers to judge whether the intervention program is feasible for administration in their desired setting. If journal restrictions (e.g., page requirements) prohibit this level of detail, such information could be made available through supplemental materials – see Taylor, Stein, Woods, & Mumford's (2011) publicly available data report. We summarize these descriptors for the RCTs we identified in Table 44.1.

Investigators should also describe the control condition thoroughly, and explain what the control condition is designed to control. In the studies we reviewed, investigators deployed a wide range of control conditions, including wait-list controls (i.e., no treatment), treatment-as-usual, and active comparison interventions. Control conditions that control for non-specific aspects of the ADV intervention (e.g., therapist/service-provider contact) are particularly rigorous. These help provide stronger evidence that any observed ADV intervention effects are attributable to the ADV intervention.

## Allocation of participants to treatment and control conditions

Random assignment to treatment and control conditions serves multiple purposes in the evaluation of ADV program effects. Perhaps the most important is to increase the likelihood that the intervention and control groups are equivalent on key study variables at the outset (Kleijnen, Gøtzshe, Kunz, Oxman, & Chalmers, 1997). Key variables include such things as demographic characteristics, the outcomes of interest (e.g., dating violence perpetration), and variables targeted by the intervention or potentially linked to the outcome of interest. The practice of random assignment involves the generation of a random allocation sequence, so that the pattern of unit (individuals, classrooms, schools) assignment to the treatment and control conditions is not predictable. Random assignment procedures range from simple to quite complex, and investigators should clearly report the methods used to generate the random allocation sequence, as well as allocation concealment procedures. To provide an example, Baiocchi and colleagues (2017) detail the specific randomization algorithm used in their supplemental material:

> The study's statistician used a nonbipartite matching algorithm to find optimal matched pairs (4). The characteristics and assignments of the matched-pairs design are summarized in Table 2. A binary vector of length 16, representing the 16 matched pairs, was created using the sample function in R. A 1 (intervention) or a 0 (SOC) was sampled for each of the 16 entries in the vector, with the probability of sampling a 1 being ½. This approach ensures that each school had an equal probability of being assigned to the intervention.
>
> (ESM 1 p. 2)

Random assignment to condition increases the likelihood of equivalent groups, but it does not guarantee it. Thus, investigators should ideally report each group's characteristics at baseline, as was done by DePrince and colleagues (2015):

> [W]e evaluated equivalence of the adolescents in the three groups (RD/EF, SL/F, and no-treatment groups) in terms of a host of demographic (e.g., age, ethnicity, placement type, school level) and individual difference (e.g., violence exposure, previous healthy relationship classes) factors. The only significant group difference noted related to witnessing domestic violence: 85% of youth in the SL/F group reported witnessing domestic violence relative to 55% in the RD/EF and 67% in the no-treatment group ($\chi^2 = 14.22$; $p = .001$).
>
> (p. S36)

## Assessment of outcome

Existing evaluations determine program efficacy across a broad range of ADV constructs, including self-reported behaviors (victimization, perpetration, bystander behaviors), attitudes about dating aggression, knowledge of ADV, and self-efficacy to manage relationship conflict in healthy or prosocial ways (see Table 44.1 for these assessments by study). Although ADV interventions broadly aim to reduce the occurrence of ADV victimization and perpetration, many also seek to influence purported precursors, maintaining factors or other variables thought to contribute to the onset and continuation of relationship violence.

An overall strength of the studies included in this review is the commitment to follow-up assessments. Most studies included assessments beyond an immediate posttest (e.g., Cunningham et al., 2013; DePrince et al., 2015), and several describe repeated assessments up to four years post-intervention (Coker et al., 2017; Foshee et al., 2005; Gardner & Boellaard, 2007). An important consideration in ADV intervention research is the timing of assessments. The assessment scheduling might be determined, in part, by what is feasible in the setting where the intervention is being tested. Scientific considerations include: (1) how quickly the intervention is expected to show effects and (2) the extent to which some constructs and behaviors are likely to change more quickly than others. Summarizing the rationale for the timing of the assessments would be beneficial.

Most investigators routinely describe their measures well, including the number of items, sample items, and some index of the reliability of the measures in the study sample. Ideally, investigators also provide evidence of convergent and/or criterion validity of measures as documented in previous literature with relevant samples. An excellent illustration of this can be found in Foshee and colleagues (2015), in which a standardized violence outcome measure is described:

> The perpetration of and the victimization from psychological dating abuse were assessed with items from the Safe Dates Psychological Dating Abuse Scales (Centers for Disease Control and Prevention 2006; Foshee 1996). The Safe Dates Dating Abuse Scales (for assessing psychological and physical dating abuse) have high internal consistency ($\alpha$ = .94) and are among the most widely used scales for assessing dating violence among adolescents (Centers for Disease Control and Prevention 2006). The scales have been found to correlate with other constructs as expected and produce prevalence estimates comparable to those produced with other dating abuse scales (Foshee et al., 2001). To assess perpetration, the adolescent was asked how many times he/she had ever (1) insulted a date in front of others, (2) not let a date do things with other people, (3) threatened to hurt a date, (4) hurt a date's feelings on purpose, and (5) said mean things to a date. Parallel questions were asked to assess victimization by asking adolescents how many times these things had been done to them. Responses were summed to create the perpetration of psychological dating abuse and the victimization from psychological dating abuse composite variables.
>
> (pp. 1000–1001)

### Participant retention and missing data

Retaining participants in the study is vital to a rigorous RCT, because it helps ensure the internal validity of the trial's experimental design. Unfortunately, many published RCTs evaluating ADV programs do not include much description of the strategies employed to retain participants. Descriptions of participant retention strategies, particularly those that are successful, can help advance knowledge on best practices for participant retention.

Strategies reported in the literature include monetary compensation (e.g., Foshee et al., 2015; Gonzalez-Guarda et al., 2015), assistance with transportation costs (e.g., DePrince et al., 2015), refreshments and small gifts at intervention sessions, and "loyalty cards" redeemable for gift cards after attending a certain number of sessions (Mathews et al., 2016). Similarly, Langhinrichsen-Rohling and Turner (2012) articulated clear efforts to retain participants in their intervention:

> Attendance incentives included: facilitating transportation to each session, weekly check-in/reminder calls from project staff, in-session snacks and drinks, optional color printed take-home copies of session materials, on-site childcare, and small incentives for an on-site store that was stocked with essential childcare items including diapers.
>
> (p. 387)

Missing data is inevitable in most RCTs, particularly those involving adolescents as participants. Missing data can occur for a number of reasons. As implied earlier, one form of missing data occurs with attrition of study participants (i.e., loss of all participant data beyond a given time point). It is often useful to examine and report on differences between participants with and without complete data (using baseline data), especially on primary variables of interest. Another form of missing data occurs when a participant provides incomplete data on certain measures, such as by not answering some items on questionnaires (loss of only some participant data at a time point).

There are several approaches to handling missing data (Baraldi & Enders, 2010). Two traditional approaches include restricting analyses only to cases with complete data (known as complete-case analysis; see Foshee et al., 1998, for example), or using different subsamples of complete data based on the analysis presented (known as pairwise deletion; see Fay & Medway, 2006). Such techniques should be used with caution, as they can produce biased estimates when data missingness is related to the variables of interest (as is often the case). Another common technique for handling missing data includes imputation methods. Such strategies infer values of missing data from available data and allow the researcher to produce a complete dataset. Single imputation (such as mean imputation or last observation carried forward; Coker et al., 2017) and multiple imputation methods (such as maximum likelihood estimation and multiple imputation; Foshee et al., 2015) are frequently used to account for bias due to missing data. Others employ data analysis techniques (regardless of number of completed assessments or questionnaire completeness) rather than imputing missing values (discussed next in the Data analysis section).

There are pros and cons to each of the various approaches to handling missing data, and it is likely that multiple methods could be appropriate for any given study. However, different methods for handling missing data can yield different findings. Therefore, researchers should clearly specify the method used for handling missing data as well as their reasoning for choosing that method.

## Data analysis

As with any study, appropriate statistical analyses – those that adequately address the research question and hypotheses – are needed for determining the effects of ADV intervention programs. For instance, an RCT that purports to examine differences between an intervention and control condition should utilize a between-groups design in analyzing data. Appropriate analytic strategies are of specific concern for evaluating ADV interventions because increasingly, researchers are using sophisticated research designs, such as cluster randomization across multiple classrooms and schools. Such designs necessitate analyses that account for dependency across subjects within the same cluster. For instance, students within the same school are likely to be similar to one another due to shared characteristics of the school. Such similarities could artificially inflate intervention effects if the dependency of students within schools is not appropriately modeled in the analyses. There are several ways in which dependent data can be appropriately modeled in statistical analyses, including the use of nesting procedures, as Taylor and colleagues (2013) detail:

> Given the nested nature of our data, variables at the student level, class level, and building level may be correlated. Because our substantive interest is in the individual outcomes, and because of the need to adjust for correlated standard errors, we do not present simple means for the treatment and control groups. We included a robust variance estimate to adjust for within-cluster correlation called the Huber/White/ sandwich estimate of variance (Froot, 1989; Huber, 1967; Rogers, 1993; White, 1980; Williams, 2000), the vce (cluster clustvar) option in Stata 8.0. For our count data, we used a negative binomial regression with a robust variance estimate. We used logistic regression with a robust variance estimate for our prevalence outcome variables.
>
> (p. 68)

A rigorous method for handling data in a RCT is an intent-to-treat analysis, in which all participants are included and modeled within the condition to which they were originally randomized, regardless of whether they participated in their assigned condition or completed all follow up assessments. That is, participants assigned to an intervention condition are analyzed with the intervention group, even if they failed to complete the intervention. Additionally, participant data from a baseline assessment is retained in analyses even if the participant was subsequently lost to attrition.

There are several statistical approaches appropriate for intent-to-treat designs; for instance, Connolly and colleagues (2015) utilize a multilevel linear model that includes all available data for participants, regardless of whether all follow-up assessments were completed:

> Multilevel linear models (MLMs; Raudenbush & Bryk, 2002; Snijders & Bosker, 1999) using Full Information Maximum Likelihood (FIML) were fitted to the data to determine the program effects on knowledge, attitudes, victimization, and emotional school adjustment. . . . A second important characteristic of MLM using FIML is that it uses all the available participant information for the analysis, even those with missing data at one of the assessments. This use of all data when conducting inference tests on groups with small sample size makes the inference more efficient and also increases accuracy of the standard error (Laird, 1988).
>
> (p. 415)

### Considerations prior to initiating an RCT

Background information on the investigators' efforts to engage and collaborate with community stakeholders and to develop/adapt an intervention that is acceptable to the unique needs of a given community can be very informative. To illustrate, we present several of the steps reported by Rothman and Wang (2016) in the development of their program, *Real Talk*:

> The Real Talk intervention development process used the Intervention Mapping protocol method, which entails six steps: (a) needs assessment, including establishing a participatory planning group; (b) identifying behavior change goals; (c) selecting a behavior change theory to guide the development of the intervention; (d) creating the program and preparing materials; (e) implementing the intervention; and (f) evaluating and refining the intervention based on results (Bartholomew, Parcel, & Kok, 1998). In addition to these steps, the intervention developer gathered background information on brief intervention and motivational interviewing by reading about them and participating in training delivered by national experts (BNI ART Institute, 2015), interviewing the staff of an existing alcohol brief intervention, using a Delphi process to vet the ADA intervention script with a panel of experts, roleplaying the intervention for a focus group of youth from the target population, and revising the intervention based on youth and expert feedback before pilot-testing . . . intervention materials were iteratively created over a year-long period. A first-draft copy of the intervention manual, intervention handouts and props, and a resource book containing referral options were put together collaboratively by the principal investigator, a brief intervention expert, research assistants, and a project advisor from a nationally funded, local youth dating violence prevention program (i.e., Start Strong). Drafts

were shared with youth peer-leaders affiliated with the Start Strong program, field-tested with several patients, and then materials were refined.

(pp. 434–436)

Human subjects protection is salient to all violence research; describing the handling of particular concerns in ADV program evaluations can help provide examples of best practices, establish practice norms, and ensure readers that research protocols are protective of human subjects. Considerations include assent practices with minors, mandated child-abuse reporting requirements (including state and setting-based restrictions around what is reported, to whom, and under what circumstances), confidentiality, and assessments of safety and risk, among others. Common publishing practices request inclusion of language around institutional review board approval and description of consent/assent procedures. However, additional information on human subjects' protections is often not reported in manuscripts describing ADV evaluations. We encourage researchers to describe specific protections, safety protocols, and checks utilized to uphold and refine ethical practices. For example, Gonzalez-Guarda et al. (2015) described informing and setting expectations among participants around confidentiality and mandated reporting during sessions:

> [Prior to treatment,] confidentiality and its limits, including the research team's role as mandated reporters, were clearly defined to the participants. The group was made aware that any suspicion or statement of physical or sexual abuse and/or neglect would be reported to ensure the child's safety and allow for appropriate assistance of the family.

(p. 5)

Baiocchi et al. (2017) described the handling of participant disclosure of sexual assault victimization:

> This intervention was a behavior modification program with a low risk of an increase in harm due to the intervention. Surveys were anonymous, so incidences of sexual assault were only identified if the participants decided to disclose to the trainers or other research staff. Ujamaa-Africa instructors and researchers are trained to link students who disclose sexual assault to organizations such as Médecins Sans Frontières and to programs and services provided by Ujamaa-Africa.

(p. 821)

## Conclusions

ADV is a sufficiently significant public health concern that a sizable body of research has accumulated to advance knowledge about it, and numerous intervention programs have been developed to try to reduce or prevent it. There is considerable variability in the methodological rigor of studies conducted to evaluate the outcomes of such programs, and further variability in the extent to which certain aspects of the methods are reported. To make clearer inferences about the outcomes of RCTs evaluating ADV intervention programs, the field will be advanced by attention to the methodological points covered in this chapter. Moreover, in addition to strengthening the ability to make inferences about the results of such RCTs, reporting fully and clearly on these areas of research design and methods can provide researchers and service providers a more nuanced understanding of the factors that give rise to successful – or unsuccessful – intervention efforts.

## Critical findings

- Reviews of the literature indicate that programs designed to prevent and reduce adolescent dating violence (ADV) tend to have favorable effects on attitudes and knowledge about violence, but evidence of their effectiveness at preventing ADV perpetration and victimization is less compelling; thus, continued intervention research is needed.
- A comprehensive search of published articles and gray literature (e.g., empirical theses and dissertations) pertaining to ADV intervention programs through August 2017 yielded 39 articles in which a randomized controlled trial (RCT) was used to evaluate an ADV intervention program.
- There is considerable variability in the methodological rigor of studies conducted to evaluate the outcomes of ADV intervention programs, and further variability in the extent to which certain aspects of the methods are reported. Increased rigor and more consistent reporting of key aspects of research methods can help strengthen research and knowledge on ADV prevention.
- Examples of exemplary methodological practices for designing, conducting, and reporting ADV research are available in the literature, and are presented in the domains of (1) sample description, (2) description of treatment and control conditions, (3) allocation of participants to treatment and control conditions, (4) assessment of outcomes, (5) participant retention and missing data, (6) data analysis, and (7) considerations prior to initiating an RCT.

## Implications for policy, practice, and research

- Additional research on adolescent dating violence (ADV) intervention programs is necessary to understand how best to prevent ADV perpetration and victimization.
- Since randomized controlled trials (RCTs) are often considered the gold standard design for making conclusions about effects of an intervention program, it is likely that researchers will be designing RCTs for the purpose of evaluating ADV intervention programs.
- To make clear inferences about the outcomes of RCTs evaluating ADV intervention programs, greater attention needs to be directed at research methodology.
- When researchers report fully and clearly on their: (1) sample, (2) treatment and control conditions, (3) the allocation of participants to treatment and control conditions, (4) the assessment of outcomes, (5) participant retention and missing data, (6) data analysis, and (7) considerations prior to initiating an RCT, researchers and other consumers of the research literature (service providers, policy makers) can gain a more nuanced understanding of the factors that give rise to successful – or unsuccessful – intervention efforts.

## References

Ackard, D. M., Eisenberg, M. E., & Neumark-Sztainer, D. (2007). Long-term impact of adolescent dating violence on the behavioral and psychological health of male and female youth. *The Journal of Pediatrics, 151*(5), 476–481. https://doi.org/10.1016/j.jpeds.2007.04.034

Baiocchi, M., Omondi, B., Langat, N., Boothroyd, D. B., Sinclair, J., Pavia, L., . . . Sarnquist, C. (2017). A behavior-based intervention that prevents sexual assault: The results of a matched-pairs, cluster-randomized study in Nairobi, Kenya. *Prevention Science, 18*(7), 818–827. https://doi.org/10.1007/s11121-016-0701-0

Baraldi, A. N., & Enders, C. K. (2010). An introduction to modern missing data analyses. *Journal School Psychology, 48*(1), 5–37. https://doi.org/10.1016/j.jsp.2009.10.001

Bartholomew, L. K., Parcel, G. S., & Kok, G. (1998). Intervention mapping: A process for developing theory- and evidence-based health education programs. *Health Education & Behavior, 25*, 545–563. https://doi.org/10.1177/109019819802500502

BNI ART Institute. (2015). *Training in SBIRT.* Retrieved from http://www.bu.edu/bniart/sbirt-training-consulting/sbirt-training/

Brown, K., Arnab, S., Bayley, J., Newby, K., Joshi, P., Judd, B., . . . Clarke, S. (2012). Tackling sensitive issues using a game-based environment: Serious game for relationships and sex education (RSE). In B. K. Wiederhold & G. Riva (Eds.), *Annual review of cybertherapy and telemedicine* (pp. 165–171). Amsterdam: IOS Press.

Carver, K., Joyner, K., & Udry, J. R. (2003). National estimates of adolescent romantic relationships. In P. Florsheim (Ed.), *Adolescent romantic relations and sexual behavior: Theory, research, and practical implications* (p. 23–56). Mahwah, NJ: Lawrence Erlbaum Associates Publishers.

Centers for Disease Control and Prevention. (2006). *Measuring intimate partner violence victimization and perpetration: A compendium of assessment tools.* Retrieved from http://stacks.cdc.gov/view/cdc/11402/

Centers for Disease Control and Prevention. (2019). *Preventing teen dating violence* [Factsheet]. Retrieved from www.cdc.gov/violenceprevention/pdf/tdv-factsheet.pdf

Cheung, A. C. K., & Slavin, R. E. (2016). How methodological features affect effect sizes in education. *Educational Researcher, 45*(5), 283–292. https://doi.org/10.3102/0013189X16656615

Coker, A. L., Bush, H. M., Cook-Craig, P. G., DeGue, S. A., Clear, E. R., Brancato, C. J., . . . Recktenwald, E. A. (2017). RCT testing bystander effectiveness to reduce violence. *American Journal of Preventive Medicine, 52*(5), 566–578. https://doi.org/10.1016/j.amepre.2017.01.020

Collins, W. A., Welsh, D. P., & Furman, W. (2009). Adolescent romantic relationships. *Annual Review of Psychology, 60*, 631–652. https://doi.org/10.1146/annurev.psych.60.110707.163459

Connolly, J., Josephson, W., Schnoll, J., Simkins-Strong, E., Pepler, D., MacPherson, A., . . . Jiang, D. (2015). Evaluation of a youth-led program for preventing bullying, sexual harassment, and dating aggression in middle schools. *The Journal of Early Adolescence, 35*(3), 403–434. https://doi.org/10.1177/0272431614535090

Cunningham, R. M., Whiteside, L. K., Chermack, S. T., Zimmerman, M. A., Shope, J. T., Raymond Bingham, C., . . . Walton, M. A. (2013). Dating violence: Outcomes following a brief motivational interviewing intervention among at-risk adolescents in an urban emergency department. *Academic Emergency Medicine, 20*(6), 562–569. https://doi.org/10.1111/acem.12151

De La Rue, L., Polanin, J. R., Espelage, D. L., & Pigott, T. D. (2017). A meta-analysis of school-based interventions aimed to prevent or reduce violence in teen dating relationships. *Review of Educational Research, 87*(1), 7–34. https://doi.org/10.3102/0034654316632061

DePrince, A. P., Chu, A. T., Labus, J., Shirk, S. R., & Potter, C. (2015). Testing two approaches to revictimization prevention among adolescent girls in the child welfare system. *Journal of Adolescent Health, 56*(2), S33–S39. https://doi.org/10.1016/j.jadohealth.2014.06.022

Edwards, S. R., & Hinsz, V. B. (2014). A meta-analysis of empirically tested school-based dating violence prevention programs. *SAGE Open, 4*(2), 1–7. https://doi.org/10.1177/2158244014535787

Espelage, D. L., Low, S., Polanin, J. R., & Brown, E. C. (2013). The impact of a middle school program to reduce aggression, victimization, and sexual violence. *Journal of Adolescent Health, 53*(2), 180–186. https://doi.org/10.1016/j.jadohealth.2013.02.021

Espelage, D. L., Low, S., Polanin, J. R., & Brown, E. C. (2015). Clinical trial of second step© middle-school program: Impact on aggression & victimization. *Journal of Applied Developmental Psychology, 37*, 52–63. https://doi.org/10.1016/j.appdev.2014.11.007

Exner-Cortens, D., Eckenrode, J., & Rothman, E. (2013). Longitudinal associations between teen dating violence victimization and adverse health outcomes. *Pediatrics, 131*(1), 71–78. https://doi.org/10.1542/peds.2012-1029

Fay, K. E., & Medway, F. J. (2006). An acquaintance rape education program for students transitioning to high school. *Sex Education, 6*(3), 223–236. https://doi.org/10.1080/14681810600836414

Fellmeth, G. L., Heffernan, C., Nurse, J., Habibula, S., & Sethi, D. (2013). Educational and skills-based interventions for preventing relationship and dating violence in adolescents and young adults: A systematic review. *Campbell Systematic Reviews, 9*(1), 1–124. https://doi.org/10.4073/csr.2013.14

Field, A. (2018). *Discovering statistics using IBM SPSS statistics* (5th ed.). Thousand Oaks, CA: Sage.

Foshee, V. (1996). Gender differences in adolescent dating abuse prevalence, types, and injuries. *Health Education Research, 11*(3), 275–286. https://doi.org/10.1093/her/11.3.275-a

Foshee, V. A., Bauman, K. E., Arriaga, X. B., Helms, R. W., Koch, G. G., & Linder, G. F. (1998). An evaluation of Safe Dates, an adolescent dating violence prevention program. *American Journal of Public Health, 88*(10), 45–50. https://doi.org/10.2105/AJPH.88.1.45

Foshee, V. A., Bauman, K. E., Ennett, S. T., Linder, G. F., Benefield, T., & Suchindran, C. (2004). Assessing the long-term effects of the Safe Dates program and a booster in preventing and reducing adolescent dating violence victimization and perpetration. *American Journal of Public Health, 94*(4), 619–624. https://doi.org/10.2105/AJPH.94.4.619

Foshee, V. A., Bauman, K. E., Ennett, S. T., Suchindran, C., Benefield, T., & Linder, G. F. (2005). Assessing the effects of the dating violence prevention program "Safe Dates" using random coefficient regression modeling. *Prevention Science, 6*(3), 245–258. https://doi.org/10.1007/s11121-005-0007-0

Foshee, V. A., Benefield, T., Dixon, K. S., Chang, L. Y., Senkomago, V., Ennett, S. T., . . . Bowling, J. M. (2015). The effects of Moms and Teens for Safe Dates: A dating abuse prevention program for adolescents exposed to domestic violence. *Journal of Youth and Adolescence, 44*(5), 995–1010. https://doi.org/10.1007/s10964-015-0272-6

Foshee, V. A., Linder, F., MacDougall, J., & Bangdiwala, S. (2001). Gender differences in the longitudinal predictors of adolescent dating violence. *Preventive Medicine, 32*, 128–141. https://doi.org/10.1006/pmed.2000.0793

Foshee, V. A., Reyes, H. L. M., Ennett, S. T., Cance, J. D., Bauman, K. E., & Bowling, J. M. (2012). Assessing the effects of Families for Safe Dates, a family-based teen dating abuse prevention program. *Journal of Adolescent Health, 51*(4), 349–356. https://doi.org/10.1016/j.jadohealth.2011.12.029

Foshee, V. A., Reyes, H. L. M., Gottfredson, N. C., Chang, L.-Y., & Ennett, S. T. (2013). A longitudinal examination of psychological, behavioral, academic, and relationship consequences of dating abuse victimization among a primarily rural sample of adolescents. *Journal of Adolescent Health, 53*(6), 723–729. https://doi.org/10.1016/j.jadohealth.2013.06.016

Froot, K. A. (1989). Consistent covariance-matrix estimation with cross-sectional dependence and heteroskedasticity in financial data. *Journal of Financial and Quantitative Analysis, 24*, 333–355. doi:10.2307/2330815.

Gardner, S. P., & Boellaard, R. (2007). Does youth relationship education continue to work after a high school class? A longitudinal study. *Family Relations: Interdisciplinary Journal of Applied Family Science, 56*(5), 490–500. https://doi.org/10.1111/j.1741-3729.2007.00476.x

Gonzalez-Guarda, R. M., Guerra, J. E., Cummings, A. A., Pino, K., & Becerra, M. M. (2015). Examining the preliminary efficacy of a dating violence prevention program for Hispanic adolescents. *The Journal of School Nursing, 31*(6), 411–421. https://doi.org/10.1177/1059840515598843

Higgins, J., Churchill, R., Tovey, D., Lasserson, T., & Chandler, J. (2011). Update on the MECIR project: Methodological expectations for Cochrane intervention reviews. *Cochrane Methods, 2*, 2–5. Retrieved from https://injuries.cochrane.org/sites/injuries.cochrane.org/files/public/uploads/Cochrane%2520Methods%2520September%25202011.pdf#page=5

Huber, P. J. (1967). *The behavior of maximum likelihood estimates under nonstandard conditions.* Paper Presented at the Fifth Berkeley Symposium on Mathematical Statistics and Probability, Berkeley, CA.

Jaycox, L. H., McCaffrey, D., Eiseman, B., Aronoff, J., Shelley, G. A., Collins, R. L., & Marshall, G. N. (2006). Impact of a school-based dating violence prevention program among Latino teens: Randomized controlled effectiveness trial. *Journal of Adolescent Health, 39*(5), 694–704. https://doi.org/10.1016/j.jadohealth.2006.05.002

Joppa, M. C., Rizzo, C. J., Nieves, A. V., & Brown, L. K. (2016). Pilot investigation of the Katie Brown educational program: A school-community partnership. *Journal of School Health, 86*(4), 288–297. https://doi.org/10.1111/josh.12378

Jouriles, E. N., Choi, H. J., Rancher, C., & Temple, J. R. (2017). Teen dating violence victimization, trauma symptoms, and revictimization in early adulthood. *Journal of Adolescent Health, 61*(1), 115–119. https://doi.org/10.1016/j.jadohealth.2017.01.020

Jouriles, E. N., McDonald, R., Mueller, V., & Grych, J. H. (2012). Youth experiences of family violence and teen dating violence perpetration: Cognitive and emotional mediators. *Clinical Child and Family Psychology Review, 15*(1), 58–68. https://doi.org/10.1007/s10567-011-0102-7

Kazdin, A. E. (2017). *Research design in clinical psychology* (5th ed.). Boston, MA: Pearson.

Kleijnen, J., Gøtzshe, P. C., Kunz, R. H., Oxman, A., & Chalmers, I. (1997). So what's so special about randomisation. In A. Maynard & I. Chalmers (Eds.), *Non-random reflections: On health services research: On the 25th anniversary of Archie Cochrane's effectiveness and efficiency* (pp. 231–249). London: BMJ.

Laird, N. M. (1988). Missing data in longitudinal studies. *Statistics in Medicine, 7*, 305–315. https://doi.org/10.1002/sim.4780070131

Langhinrichsen-Rohling, J., & Turner, L. A. (2012). The efficacy of an intimate partner violence prevention program with high-risk adolescent girls: A preliminary test. *Prevention Science, 13*(4), 384–394. https://doi.org/10.1007/s11121-011-0240-7

Levesque, D. A., Johnson, J. L., Welch, C. A., Prochaska, J. M., & Paiva, A. L. (2016). Teen dating violence prevention: Cluster-randomized trial of teen choices, an online, stage-based program for healthy, nonviolent relationships. *Psychology of Violence, 6*(3), 421–432. https://doi.org/10.1037/vio0000049

Lundgren, R., & Amin, A. (2015). Addressing intimate partner violence and sexual violence among adolescents: Emerging evidence of effectiveness. *Journal of Adolescent Health, 56*(1S), S42–S50. https://doi.org/10.1016/j.jadohealth.2014.08.012

Macgowan, M. J. (1997). An evaluation of a dating violence prevention program for middle school students. *Violence and Victims, 12*(3), 223–235. https://doi.org/10.1891/0886-6708.12.3.223

Mathews, C., Eggers, S. M., Townsend, L., Aarø, L. E., de Vries, P. J., Mason-Jones, A. J., . . . Wubs, A. (2016). Effects of PREPARE, a multi-component, school-based HIV and intimate partner violence (IPV) prevention programme on adolescent sexual risk behaviour and IPV: Cluster randomised controlled trial. *AIDS and Behavior, 20*(9), 1821–1840. https://doi.org/10.1007/s10461-016-1410-1

McArthur, L. E. (2010). *Intimate partner violence, attachment, and coparenting intervention outcomes among Latino teen parents.* Retrieved from ProQuest Dissertations Publishing (3419374).

Miller, E., Goldstein, S., McCauley, H. L., Jones, K. A., Dick, R. N., Jetton, J., . . . Tancredi, D. J. (2015). A school health center intervention for abusive adolescent relationships: A cluster RCT. *Pediatrics, 135*(1), 76–85. https://doi.org/10.1542/peds.2014-2471

Miller, E., Tancredi, D. J., McCauley, H. L., Decker, M. R., Virata, M. C. D., Anderson, H. A., . . . Silverman, J. G. (2012). "Coaching boys into men": A cluster-randomized controlled trial of a dating violence prevention program. *Journal of Adolescent Health, 51*(5), 431–438. https://doi.org/10.1016/j.jadohealth.2012.01.018

Miller, E., Tancredi, D. J., McCauley, H. L., Decker, M. R., Virata, M. C. D., Anderson, H. A., . . . Silverman, J. G. (2013). One-year follow-up of a coach-delivered dating violence prevention program: A cluster randomized controlled trial. *American Journal of Preventive Medicine, 45*(1), 108–112. https://doi.org/10.1016/j.amepre.2013.03.007

Nahapetyan, L., Orpinas, P., Song, X., & Holland, K. (2014). Longitudinal association of suicidal ideation and physical dating violence among high school students. *Journal of Youth and Adolescence, 43*(4), 629–640. https://doi.org/10.1007/s10964-013-0006-6

Niolon, P. H., Vivolo-Kantor, A. M., Latzman, N. E., Valle, L. A., Kuoh, H., Burton, T., . . . Tharp, A. T. (2015). Prevalence of teen dating violence and co-occurring risk factors among middle school youth in high-risk urban communities. *Journal of Adolescent Health, 56*(2), S5–S13. https://doi.org/10.1016/j.jadohealth.2014.07.019

Pacifici, C., Stoolmiller, M., & Nelson, C. (2001). Evaluating a prevention program for teenagers on sexual coercion: A differential effectiveness approach. *Journal of Consulting and Clinical Psychology, 69*(3), 552–559. https://doi.org/10.1037//0022-006X.69.3.552

Peskin, M. F., Markham, C. M., Shegog, R., Baumler, E. R., Addy, R. C., & Tortolero, S. R. (2014). Effects of the It's Your Game . . . Keep It Real program on dating violence in ethnic-minority middle school youths: A group randomized trial. *American Journal of Public Health, 104*(8),1471–1477. https://doi.org/10.2105/AJPH.2014.301902

Polanin, J. R., & Espelage, D. L. (2015). Using a meta-analytic technique to assess the relationship between treatment intensity and program effects in a cluster-randomized trial. *Journal of Behavioral Education, 24*(1), 133–151. https://doi.org/10.1007/s10864-014-9205-9

Raudenbush, S. W., & Bryk, A. S. (2002). *Hierarchical linear models* (2nd ed.). Thousand Oaks, CA: SAGE.

Roberts, K. E. C. (2009). *An evaluation of the Expect Respect: Preventing teen dating violence high school program.* Retrieved from OhioLINK (ohiou1242323117).

Rogers, W. H. (1993). Regression standard errors in clustered samples. *Stata Technical Bulletin, 3*, 88–94. Retrieved from http://stata-press.com/journals/stbcontents/stb13.pdf

Rothman, E. F., Stuart, G. L., Heeren, T., Paruk, J., & Bair-Merrit, M. (n.d.). *RCT of the Real Talk brief intervention to prevent dating abuse perpetration in adolescent health care settings* [Unpublished manuscript].

Rothman, E. F., & Wang, N. (2016). A feasibility test of a brief motivational interview intervention to reduce dating abuse perpetration in a hospital setting. *Psychology of Violence, 6*(3), 433–441. https://doi.org/10.1037/vio0000050

Rowe, L. S., Jouriles, E. N., & McDonald, R. (2015). Reducing sexual victimization among adolescent girls: A randomized controlled pilot trial of My Voice, My Choice. *Behavior Therapy, 46*(3), 315–327. https://doi.org/10.1016/j.beth.2014.11.003

Salazar, L. F., & Cook, S. L. (2006). Preliminary findings from an outcome evaluation of an intimate partner violence prevention program for adjudicated, African American, adolescent males. *Youth Violence and Juvenile Justice, 4*(4), 368–385. https://doi.org/10.1177/1541204006292818

Sargent, K. S., Jouriles, E. N., Rosenfield, D., & McDonald, R. (2017). A high school-based evaluation of TakeCARE, a video bystander program to prevent adolescent relationship violence. *Journal of Youth and Adolescence, 46*(3), 633–643. https://doi.org/10.1007/s10964-016-0622-z

Schulz, K. F., Altman, D. G., & Moher, D. (2010). CONSORT 2010 statement: Updated guidelines for reporting parallel group randomized trials. *Annals of Internal Medicine, 152*(11), 726–733. https://doi.org/10.7326/0003-4819-152-11-201006010-00232

Snijders, T. A. B., & Bosker, R. J. (1999). *Multilevel analysis: An introduction to basic and advanced multilevel modeling.* London, England: SAGE.

Tarrier, N., & Wykes, T. (2004). Is there evidence that cognitive behaviour therapy is an effective treatment for schizophrenia? A cautious or cautionary tale? *Behaviour Research and Therapy, 42*(12), 1377–1401. https://doi.org/10.1016/j.brat.2004.06.020

Taylor, B. G., Stein, N. D., & Burden, F. (2010). The effects of gender violence/harassment prevention programming in middle schools: A randomized experimental evaluation. *Violence and Victims, 25*(2), 202–223. https://doi.org/10.1891/0886-6708.25.2.202

Taylor, B. G., Stein, N. D., Mumford, E. A., & Woods, D. (2013). Shifting Boundaries: An experimental evaluation of a dating violence prevention program in middle schools. *Prevention Science, 14*(1), 64–76. https://doi.org/10.1007/s11121-012-0293-2

Taylor, B. G., Stein, N. D., Woods, D., & Mumford, E. (2011). *Shifting Boundaries: Final report on an experimental evaluation of a youth dating violence prevention program in New York City middle schools.* Retrieved from www.ncjrs.gov/pdffiles1/nij/grants/236175.pdf

Ting, S.-M. R. (2009). Meta-analysis on dating violence prevention among middle and high schools. *Journal of School Violence, 8*(4), 328–337. https://doi.org/10.1080/15388220903130197

Vagi, K. J., Olsen, E. O. M., Basile, K. C., & Vivolo-Kantor, A. M. (2015). Teen dating violence (physical and sexual) among US high school students: Findings from the 2013 National Youth Risk Behavior Survey. *JAMA Pediatrics, 169*(5), 474–482. https://doi.org/10.1001/jamapediatrics.2014.3577

van Lieshout, S., Mevissen, F. E., van Breukelen, G., Jonker, M., & Ruiter, R. A. (2016). Make a Move: A comprehensive effect evaluation of a sexual harassment prevention program in Dutch residential youth care. *Journal of Interpersonal Violence, 34*(9), 1–29. https://doi.org/10.1177/0886260516654932

Vasilenko, S. A., Kugler, K. C., & Rice, C. E. (2016). Timing of first sexual intercourse and young adult health outcomes. *Journal of Adolescent Health, 59*(3), 291–297. https://doi.org/10.1016/j.jadohealth.2016.04.019

White, H. (1980). A heteroskedasticity-consistent covariance-matrix estimator and a direct test for heteroskedasticity. *Econometrica, 48*, 817–838. https://doi.org/10.2307/1912934

Williams, R. L. (2000). A note on robust variance estimation for cluster-correlated data. *Biometrics, 56*, 645–646. https://doi.org/10.1111/j.0006-341X.2000.00645.x

Wolfe, D. A., Crooks, C., Jaffe, P., Chiodo, D., Hughes, R., Ellis, W., . . . Donner, A. (2009). A school-based program to prevent adolescent dating violence: A cluster randomized trial. *Archives of Pediatrics & Adolescent Medicine, 163*(8), 692–699. https://doi.org/10.1001/archpediatrics.2009.69

Wolfe, D. A., Wekerle, C., Scott, K., Straatman, A. L., Grasley, C., & Reitzel-Jaffe, D. (2003). Dating violence prevention with at-risk youth: A controlled outcome evaluation. *Journal of Consulting and Clinical Psychology, 71*(2), 279–291. https://doi.org/10.1037/0022-006x.71.2.279

Wood, L., Egger, M., Gluud, L. L., Schulz, K. F., Jüni, P., Altman, D. G., . . . Sterne, J. A. C. (2008). Empirical evidence of bias in treatment effect estimates in controlled trials with different interventions and outcomes: Meta-epidemiological study. *BMJ, 336*(7644), 601–605. https://doi.org/10.1136/bmj.39465.451748.AD

Yom, Y.-H., & Eun, L. K. (2005). Effects of a CD-ROM educational program on sexual knowledge and attitude. *CIN: Computers, Informatics, Nursing, 23*(4), 214–219. https://doi.org/10.1097/00024665-200507000-00009

45

# EVALUATING GROUP-BASED PROGRAMMES FOR INDIVIDUALS WHO USE VIOLENCE AND ABUSE IN THEIR INTIMATE RELATIONSHIPS

*John Devaney*

## Introduction

Many national policies and local strategies addressing domestic violence and abuse typically consist of three complementary strands: firstly, to introduce measures to prevent domestic violence occurring in the first instance or to limit its reoccurrence; secondly, where domestic violence does occur, to ensure that victims receive prompt and comprehensive support; and finally, to ensure that those who use violence and abuse against their current or former partner are held to account for their behaviour (Devaney & Lazenbatt, 2016). However, one of the challenges for such an objective is that "the problem targeted by preventive interventions are often complex, embedded in multiple levels of social and environmental context, and occur across the developmental lifespan" (Hassmiller-Lich, Ginexi, Osgood, & Mabry, 2013, p. 279). It is within this context that research can assist in providing a bridge between what we seek to achieve and what we could do. As with many social interventions, the goal and the intervention are framed by wider conceptualisations of what causes and sustains the behaviour we are seeking to change, and this requires unpacking and examination within the process of evaluation.

This chapter will explore these issues by focusing on what we have learnt about working with those who use violence and abuse against their intimate partner, with a particular focus on group-based programmes, and their evaluation. Drawing upon the current evidence about the effectiveness of such programmes, the chapter will explore the underpinning research methods and how our current understanding of whether group-based programmes are effective is inextricably linked to the design of studies and the methodological choices made, which in turn are framed by our broader understanding of what causes someone, typically men, to behave in an abusive manner towards those they profess to care about, most usually women and children.

Within the professional and research communities the language used to refer to those who use violence and abuse is varied – including offender (as some of the behaviour is clearly unlawful and constitutes a crime), perpetrator (as much of the behaviour of concern is directed by one individual against another) and batterer (although this term is becoming less popular as we now recognise the many varied ways that individuals can control and terrorise their adult and child victims without needing to use much actual physical violence). In this chapter I will use the term *individual who uses violence and abuse* as a more encompassing and also neutral term. This is not to lessen the concern for victims or to minimise the impact of violence and abuse on their lives, but is part of a wider debate about whether a focus on holding individuals to account, primarily through a criminal justice-focused response, is actually appropriate and effective. As Goodmark (2018) has noted, the framing of domestic violence within a criminal justice discourse has certainly brought some benefits to victims, but it has also had a number of unintended consequences for adult and child victims, such as help being predicated on keeping them safe, rather than meeting their holistic needs, of which safety is just one. This framing has resulted in significant funds being expended on trying to make the criminal justice system more efficient and effective, with little evidence that this serves the needs of victims well, and reducing the funding available for other support services.

The typical criminal justice framing also tends to homogenise individuals into a singular group, rather than recognising that individuals who use domestic violence engage in a range of different behaviours, and their motivations for doing so are often varied (Johnson, 2010). As noted elsewhere, the vast majority of those who use violence and abuse are not arrested and never convicted, let alone sentenced and mandated to attend a programme for rehabilitation (Devaney, 2014; Goodmark, 2018). An alternative view of accountability is that men should be supported and encouraged to take personal responsibility for their behaviour, and to hold themselves to account for how they have behaved in the past and will behave in the future, rather than seeking to force or shame them into change (Camp, 2018; Kaplenko et al., 2018). This perspective is rooted in a belief that personal change is more likely to be achieved and sustained when individuals make their own free choice rather than being sanctioned or coerced into change. This of course is problematic in situations where the behaviour of one individual can have such drastic consequences for others, but as we have seen in other fields, such as substance misuse, there can be a much wider benefit in thinking about how we intervene in ways which are ultimately more likely to be effective (Henninger & Sung, 2014). However, some individuals may not be willing or able to change their behaviours, regardless of the quality of supports and interventions available. In these instances, external controls to try and manage the risk that individuals pose to others need to be implemented, particularly for those who pose the greatest risks.

All this is rooted in a belief that, as Gadd and Corr (2017) note, professionals need to support individuals to imagine a different, and better future for themselves. This involves acknowledging and taking responsibility for what they have done, and the impact, but also allows them to move beyond being defined by their past behaviour. However, such an approach must be rooted in ways of working by professionals which are likely to achieve this outcome for both the individual who has used violence in their intimate relationships, as well as their former, current and future partners.

This debate is at the heart of one type of intervention aimed at those who are domestically violent – group-based programmes. The remainder of this chapter will now focus on what we know about group-based programmes for individuals who use violence in their intimate relationships, the evidence about the effectiveness of such interventions, and how this evidence has been shaped by the underlying methods used in the research.

## Discussion and analysis

### *History of the development of group-based programmes for individuals*

The first group-based programme for domestically violent men, Emerge, was created in Quincy, Massachusetts, in 1977 (Adams, 1988). Such programmes were not developed as an alternative to criminal justice interventions, but rather as an experiment to explore whether men could be engaged in a process of change, and symbolically, to highlight the importance of men being accountable for their behaviour and its impact on others (Kelly & Westmarland, 2015). The programmes were premised on the belief that violence in intimate relationships is embedded in wider structural inequalities within society. Behind men's abusive behaviour lies their need for power and control in their intimate relationships, that is, getting their own way and being in charge. These beliefs and behaviours are underpinned by a set of ideas about how the world should operate, creating high expectations for the behaviour of one's partner. These expectations are imposed on others, and when they are not met can create extreme frustration and resultant violence. As Gondolf (2012, p. 21) notes:

> Men have plenty of reinforcement for these expectations, and aggression to enact them. They learn them from the examples of their fathers, their peers, and television and movie characters, as well as from watching or playing sports, and military experience.

This is further reinforced by societal structures that preference men more widely in society. Therefore, responding to and intervening effectively with domestic violence and abuse requires change at both an individual and societal level (Laing, Humphreys, & Kavanagh, 2013).

In the mid- to late 1980s, a second wave of intervention programmes emerged to address the increasing demand for intervention services and the need to develop co-ordinated community responses, of which group-based programmes were one important element. Duluth's Domestic Abuse Intervention Project was developed in 1981 in Duluth, Minnesota, as a means to (1) change the privacy and secrecy which often surrounded domestic violence, and instead make it public, (2) make communities safer for victims and (3) hold individuals accountable for their behaviour. The Duluth model pioneered the Coordinated Community Responses (CCR) system that prioritised victim safety and advanced ideas related to that approach. The basic premise of the CCR is to bring together the different parts of the system (i.e. police, courts, victim support services, housing, social services) in order to address issues of domestic violence. The Duluth model (Pence & Paymar, 1993) is regarded as a hybrid of feminist and cognitive behavioural principles in that accountability for one's actions, challenging and changing beliefs/attitudes, and education are central to changing the violent behaviour of men who abuse their partners. The model is grounded in the belief that arrest and prosecution coupled with court-mandated intervention, primarily in the form of group work, is crucial for change. As the Duluth model views domestic violence as learnt behaviour, treating psychological problems and/or attempting to change personalities is not considered part of the process. Group facilitators typically avoid psychiatric-type diagnoses and do not consider their work to be "therapy." Instead, facilitated group work between peers is viewed as the best means for individuals to re-learn gender sensitive, non-violent behaviours (Lehmann & Simmons, 2009).

Critical to the Duluth model is the belief that male-only groups are the safest and most ethical means of helping men take responsibility for addressing and changing their behaviours. The groups typically take place over a period of six months (or more) in weekly one-and-a-half- to two-hour group sessions. The curriculum content and delivery is a manualised one. A core premise of this approach is the belief that domestic violence is a learnt pattern of intimidation, coercive control and socially sanctioned behaviour against women. Thus, the work of groups is to re-educate participants in a structured manner by challenging individuals' (1) sense of gendered entitlement and misogynistic attitudes towards women, and (2) their minimisation and denial of abusive behaviour, and challenging each man to take responsibility and to be fully accountable for his behaviour. As part of the Duluth approach participants sign a release-of-information form and a programme contract with the understanding that acts of violence and breach of court orders (i.e. for legally mandated individuals) will be reported to the court, and that noncompliance with programme rules will likely result in suspension from the group. In this model of intervention, those who participate on a voluntary non-mandated basis are treated in the same manner as those who are court mandated.

While the majority of intervention programmes base much of their curricula and policies on the feminist cognitive behavioural principles outlined in the Duluth model, a few alternatives exist. Of those developed in the last two decades, cognitive behavioural therapy (CBT) in the form of therapeutically orientated men's groups is the most prominent (Murphy & Eckhardt, 2005). In contrast to the Duluth model, a CBT approach conceptualises domestic violence as a consequence of problems with the person's thoughts, assumptions, beliefs and behaviours (Lehmann & Simmons, 2009). The underlying idea of those operating from a CBT perspective is that violence is used because it is functional for the person using it. That is, individuals use violence against their partner to reduce inner tension, to achieve victim compliance, to end an uncomfortable situation and/or to give the themselves a feeling of power and control over a situation. Therefore, CBT approaches to intervention focus on behavioural skill building/role playing with the intent of reducing anger, conflict management and increasing positive interaction (such as active listening and/or non-violent assertiveness). A range of CBT-informed group-based programmes have been developed and evaluated, such as Acceptance and Commitment Therapy (Zarling, Bannon, & Berta, 2019) and Dialectical Behaviour Therapy (Graham-Evan & Bates, 2020). However, Babcock et al. (2004, p. 1026) observe that:

> Most modern cognitive-behavioural groups also usually address perpetrator attitudes and values regarding women and the use of violence toward women. To the extent that CBT groups address patriarchal attitudes, and Duluth model groups address the learned and reinforced aspects of violence, any distinction between CBT and Duluth model groups becomes increasingly unclear.

Over the past two decades there has been a proliferation of group-based programmes for domestically violent individuals, including those in same-sex relationships, and women who are domestically violent within heterosexual relationships (Devaney & Lazenbatt, 2016). A recurring finding from reviews of studies of the effectiveness of programmes is that they are often seeking to accommodate a diverse group of participants. While in the US in particular, groups have been established for females who have used abuse within their intimate same-sex and different-sex relationships, the evidence of effectiveness is very limited due to a lack of published research (Babcock et al., 2016). At the most basic level, most groups are single gender in terms of participants; however, this might include individuals who have been violent and abusive within same-sex and different-sex relationships. While working with perpetrators from same-sex relationships in a group setting is believed to be appropriate, there is a concern over whether involving gay or lesbian individuals in groups with heterosexual participants runs the risk of creating additional dynamics due to widespread homophobia in society (Hamel, 2014).

In one of the few articles exploring work with lesbian perpetrators, Coleman (2003) argues that it is essential that the professionals involved in facilitating this work are knowledgeable about lesbian issues, and practice lesbian/gay affirmative treatment. From such a perspective, homosexuality and a lesbian lifestyle are healthy and normal cultural variations. Professionals must be knowledgeable about lesbian identity development and the impact of homophobia and heterosexism on lesbians. When working with lesbians of colour, the impact of racism and the ways in which racism can compound experiences of homophobia and heterosexism need additional consideration.

The use of group-based programmes is now common internationally (for example, see Lilley-Walker, Hester, & Turner, 2018; McCloskey, Boonzaier, Steinbrenner, & Hunter, 2016; Niaz & Tariq, 2017; Santoveña & da Silva, 2016). Programmes all have a similar set of underlying principles of which the primary goal is to increase victim safety. As noted by Lilley-Walker et al. (2018) programmes vary considerably, not just in philosophical orientation but also in format, duration, approach and who is involved. There is a tension between whether programmes should be more orientated towards rehabilitation efforts or alternatively holding individuals to account for their behaviour, drawing some programmes more in one direction than the other (Graham-Kevan & Bates, 2020). Many programmes work with individuals who are in denial about their abusive behaviour, and there is a debate about whether acceptance of responsibility should be a precursor for attendance, or part of the process of change that programmes seek to bring about (Moore, 2009; Tew, 2016). On the whole, programmes still draw upon a gender-based, cognitive behavioural approach to inform their content and mode of delivery (Maiuro & Eberle, 2008). As Gondolf (2012, p. 14) notes, "the fact that programmes have aspects of both treatment and education, and of both accountability and punishment, make them an unwieldy enterprise."

However, there does appear to be a consensus around some core objectives of programmes, which are to:

- Help individuals to stop being violent and abusive towards former, current and future partners.
- Help individuals to learn how to relate to their partners in a respectful and equal way.
- Show individuals non-abusive ways of dealing with difficulties in their relationships and cope with their anger.
- Keep their current, past or future partner safer from further violent and abusive behaviour.

One key distinction is that some individuals are externally mandated to attend the programme, for example by a court or child protection services. In such cases it is to be expected that some individuals may not acknowledge their need to attend or change. In contrast some programmes are designed for individuals who self-refer on the basis of recognising that they need help to change. Of course in practice these two groups, the mandated and non-mandated, may not be as distinct as presented here, but such a distinction reflects an important dynamic that underpins the delivery of and engagement with the intervention.

Importantly, many commentators and activists in specific communities have proposed that perpetration and justification of, and explanations for domestic violence vary significantly between different ethnic or cultural groups (Laing et al., 2013; Debbonaire, 2015). They often then conclude from this that interventions should ideally be specific to or contain specific understanding for individual cultural or ethnic groups. To date though, scant research examines the difference in effectiveness of programmes between different racial and ethnic minority groups (Babcock et al., 2016). However, such an approach runs the risk of conceptualising identity of an ethnic group or culture as singular and fixed, and that from a practical point of view it is unlikely that specific programmes dealing with specific groups is financially feasible. Rather than establish separate programmes for individuals from ethnic minorities, it is proposed that groups are inclusive, with active attention given to both explicit barriers (such as language) and implicit barriers (such as racial bias of the facilitators) (Debbonaire, 2015).

This brief history of the development of domestic violence group-based programmes is important in thinking about how we can build a body of evidence about what programmes or elements of an intervention might work for which individuals and in what circumstances. At first look, group-based programmes may appear more similar than dissimilar, but the underpinning theory of change both informs and shapes the basis on which individuals attend, the nature of programme content and the process of the group. As such, the theory of change is central to how we might understand what change we are expecting to see, and how this might be gauged (Moran, 2011; Graham-Kevan & Bates, 2020). Additionally, it can underpin the methods chosen and the conclusions drawn in evaluations of such programmes.

## Evidence of the effectiveness of group-based programmes

The effectiveness of group-based programmes for individuals who are domestically violent has been debated for years with little clear research evidence that such programmes work (Babcock et al., 2016). At best, it is argued that such programmes may have significant but very small effects, with Babcock, Green and Robie (2004) indicating that someone in such a programme is only 5% less likely to perpetrate physical aggression toward a female partner than a man who has only been arrested and sanctioned.

As with the evaluation of many social interventions there is a need to unpack such findings, to clarify whether the evidence of lack of effectiveness is robust, and a reflection of the actual utility of the intervention under investigation, or possibly an artefact of the quality of the research to date. As noted by Eckhardt et al. (2013, p. 225), "Interventions for perpetrators show equivocal results regarding their ability to lower the risk of intimate partner violence, in part because of widespread methodological flaws."

Kelly and Westmarland (2015) reviewed 49 published studies of programmes designed for individuals who use violence and abusive behaviour in their intimate relationships, and found that there have been two 'generations' of studies. 'First generation' studies concentrated on behavioural responses to interventions with success defined as a reduction in the frequency and severity of violence measured by further criminal justice convictions and/or the self-reports of the male group participants. Whilst these studies demonstrated that those who completed programmes were less likely to re-offend in the following 12 months, both in the US and the UK, the limitations of the measures of success resulted in a strong methodological critique. Studies using women's reports as an outcome measure found significant disparities in the assessment of change reported by male group participants compared to their female partners (Kelly & Westmarland, 2015). 'Second generation' studies took one of two routes to address these shortcomings: an experimental research design that randomly assigned group participants to either intervention or non-intervention conditions; or a systemic, multi-site evaluation of established programmes (Kelly & Westmarland, 2015).

Eckhardt et al. (2013) found 20 studies that were deemed adequate for their review of the effectiveness of programmes for domestically violent men – 14 of those studies were Duluth-type programmes, four were CBT-type programmes with a therapeutic focus, and two with other foci, including a culturally focused CBT group for African American males. To be included in the review, the study had to have (1) an intervention for perpetrators, (2) one or more comparisons groups, (3) a measure of recidivism and (4) to have been published since 1990. Nine of the 20 programmes showed significant reductions in partner aggression, but of the six studies that had no treatment control comparison, there were no differences in the recidivism rates and two of these six studies were Duluth-type programmes. Eckhardt et al. indicated that quasi-experimental groups are more likely to show change, but as the methodological rigour of a study increased, the likelihood of obtaining significant effects decreased.

In a review of 60 published and unpublished evaluations relating to domestic violence programmes for men across 12 European countries, involving 7,212 participants, Lilley-Walker et al. (2018) identified a range of evaluation approaches to the study of the outcomes of such programmes. Only two adopted a randomised controlled trial design, one conducted in a prison setting in Spain with 36 male prisoners convicted for domestic violence-related crimes, and one in a substance misuse clinic in the Netherlands evaluating an integrated programme for substance misuse and partner violence. Of the remaining studies, 14 employed various quasi-experimental designs, comparing intervention outcomes between either different sites, different settings, different interventions, different cohorts of men or different offender populations.

Experimental designs are often presented as the most robust in evaluation research, and have in the main found limited effect for domestic violence group-based programmes. Smedslund, Dalsbø, Steiro, Winsvold and Clench-Aas (2011) undertook a Cochrane systematic review of randomised controlled trials that evaluated the effectiveness of cognitive behavioural therapy for men who had physically abused their female partner and included a measure of the impact of the intervention on violence. Their review extended from 1950–2010. Only six trials, all from the US, involving 2,343 participants, were deemed of sufficient rigour to be included. The authors found that, at best, group-based programmes work for some men who engaged in a programme, in some circumstances, some of the time, but for whom, how and when was still very unclear. Overall they concluded that there were still too few randomised controlled trials to draw conclusions about the effectiveness of cognitive behaviour therapy for men who use violence and abuse within their intimate relationships. More recently, Nesset et al. (2019) undertook a follow-up to the Smedlund et al. (2011) review, looking at all relevant studies published between January 2010 and February 2018. Nesset et al. (2019) identified six new studies that met the inclusion criteria: four randomised controlled trials (three from the US and one from Norway) and two nonrandomised trials (from Sweden and Spain) involving 1,585 men. Three of the randomised controlled trials found a reduction in intimate partner violence after treatment. The fourth randomised trial found that a subsample of responding partners reported a reduction in violence but no changes in the men's self-reported violence after treatment. No effect could be detected in the two nonrandomised studies. Analysis of risk of bias revealed mixed results, indicating both strengths and weaknesses within and across the included studies. They concluded that there is still insufficient evidence to confirm that group-based CBT for men engaged in intimate partner violence has a positive effect. They also restated the conclusion by Smedlund and colleagues (2011) that future research should focus on randomised controlled studies, and that such studies need to distinguish between convicted and non-convicted populations where violent behaviour is the primary outcome.

A limitation of Cochrane and other forms of systematic reviews is that they are often focused on data from particular types of studies and then only if these studies have been published. The ability to conduct randomised control trials in the criminal justice system is hindered by a number of implementation challenges. The ethics of such studies – leaving women and children outside potential support for the sake of study design, and the fact that professionals may refuse to implement them 'by the book' – raises critical questions about the appropriateness and fidelity of trying to undertake traditional 'gold standard' evaluations (Kelly and Westmarland, 2015). The pivotal element are the challenges in achieving a random assignment of subjects when so many opt-out of a study, practitioners (such as judges) over-ride the assignment of individuals between intervention and comparison groups, and agencies oppose or resist assignment (Gondolf, 2012). In addition, similar to other experimental studies, they can suffer from the effects of sub-groups, insufficient monitoring of the fidelity of the intervention, compensating treatments in the control group, intention-to-treat versus treatment-received effects, simplistic outcome measures, and low or biased follow-up response (Gondolf, 2012). Such threats to internal validity can lead to experimental designs being seen more as a 'bronze standard' rather than the treasured gold (Berk, 2005, p. 416). Gondolf (2012), a proponent of group-based programmes, is less pessimistic, arguing that programmes do work in some instances. He has arrived at this conclusion based upon his own research and a review of some of the same studies in the Smedslund et al. (2011) review that meet at least a 'bronze' standard of research quality. Gondolf subscribes to the view that those who use violence and abuse within their intimate relationships are a heterogeneous group, and as such individuals are likely to be differentially responsive to treatment as they have both differing patterns of behaviour and motivations for their behaviour (Emery, 2011). Accordingly, future research might better emphasise and investigate what components of particular programmes are likely to work for particular individuals, and for certain groups of individuals.

A further criticism is the implicit presumption that programmes can be studied independent of their context, when, in fact, they are frequently delivered as part of co-ordinated local responses (Kelly & Westmarland, 2015). The alternative quasi-experimental design allows for consideration of such contextual factors. The most methodologically rigorous study to date is Gondolf's (2002) multi-site evaluation, which found that programmes situated within a co-ordinated community response can improve the safety of the majority of women. This study also found that data gathered more than a year after completion yields few new findings.

In what they call a 'third generation' evaluation, Kelly and Westmarland (2015) have studied domestic violence perpetrator programmes for men in England, Scotland and Wales. The authors identified six key measures by which such programmes should be measured:

1   An improved relationship between the programme participants and their current or previous partner underpinned by respect and effective communication.
2   Expanded 'space for action' for women which restores their voice and ability to make choices, whilst improving their well-being.
3   Safety and freedom from violence and abuse for women and children.
4   Safe, positive and shared parenting.
5   Enhanced awareness of self and others for men, including an understanding of the impact that domestic violence has had on their partner and children.
6   For children, safer, healthier childhoods in which they feel heard and cared about.

The authors report that for the majority of participants (both men and their female partners) participation in the programme and the accompanying support for partners did result in positive benefits and improvements in abusive behaviour.

The promotion of a common set of standards that programmes must adopt in order to be seen as a credible programme for those who use violence and abuse has done much to promote key elements of intervention, such as providing support for current and recent former partners (Babcock et al., 2016; Respect, 2017). However, this approach has been critiqued as the issue of domestic violence has been framed from a feminist perspective as an issue of gender inequality, rather than a source of generating hypotheses to be tested against alternatives (Graham-Kevan & Bates, 2020). It has therefore restricted the type of research that can be carried out, and has adopted the defensive position of countering findings from a range of alternative psychological and sociological viewpoints (Dixon, Archer, & Graham-Kevan, 2012).

This poses the question of whether a particular form of programme or specific elements within programmes is core to bringing about change, or, as is put forward by others, it is more about the nature and quality of the relationship between group facilitators and group participants (Mahon, Devaney, & Lazenbatt, 2009).

## Challenges and considerations for future research

### Evaluation method

As noted earlier there have been a wide range of methods used to evaluate the efficacy of programmes. More robust evaluation approaches seek to ensure that those undertaking an intervention are compared at baseline and completion with a comparable group undertaking either no intervention or a different intervention. Research with those who pose a risk to others must engage with the thorny ethical issue that once identified, those who pose such a risk should indeed be offered some sort of intervention, and that in many cases they may be subject to compulsory requirements such as probation supervision. In their review Babcock et al. (2016) highlighted that most studies using a randomised design failed to find significant differences in programme effectiveness, whereas the opposite pattern was observed among quasi-experimental studies, which were more likely to show evidence of effectiveness relative to no-treatment control groups. However, some authors, such as Gondolf (2010), highlight how various designs can helpfully use statistical controls for selection biases present in nonrandomised designs (e.g. propensity score analysis) in studying the effectiveness of programmes, and in their review Eckhardt et al. (2013) found some of the strongest evidence of a programme effect when such statistical methods were employed (e.g. Jones & Gondolf, 2002).

### Types of outcome measures

The central issue in any effectiveness evaluation is to identify the outcome(s) which the intervention is designed to bring about. For example, in the review by Smedslund and colleagues (2011) the primary outcome they were seeking to gauge was physically violent behaviour towards a man's female partner, wife or ex-partner. They also included other violent behaviour, like verbal aggression and hostile attitudes, but overlooked the many other forms of domestic abuse covered in this Handbook. Secondary outcomes were improved self-esteem, reduced substance abuse and anger management. As noted earlier, first generation studies typically sought self-reports of changes in behaviour or reports from criminal justice agencies to gauge the success or otherwise of participant change. This later moved, in second generation studies, to include reports from partners and others as men might not come to the attention of the police again, and could not be trusted to disclose their behaviour, especially if it might have serious implications such as being brought back to court. Reflecting on the positions of some women whose current or former partners were on programmes, and the utility of follow-up interviews, Westmarland and Kelly (2013) have raised questions about the now accepted orthodoxy that women's accounts should be the key benchmark of programme outcomes. Women who were no longer in a relationship with the man, especially those where the relationship ended some time ago, were not in a position to assess change on some dimensions. Other women who had separated chose not to take part since they were seeking to move on. The fact that some men at Time 2 admitted to abuse also challenged the positioning of them as inherently unreliable, untrustworthy informants. However, as the example from Smedslund et al. (2011) demonstrates, outcomes sought may go beyond the safety of others to also seek to take account of factors, such as problematic substance use, which may influence behaviour. This reflects the earlier discussion about different conceptualisations of what programmes are seeking to do, and how they do this. For example, Lilley-Walker et al. (2018) found that in the 14 studies within their review using various quasi-experimental designs, the majority (including ten from Spain) used a range of psychometric instruments to measure pre–post changes in psychopathological and psychosocial characteristics, such as hostility, anger, depression, anxiety, self-esteem, persecutory ideas, attitudes toward women and the use of violence, and levels of maladjustment to assess the extent to which the participants' current problems affected other areas of their life. Such an approach reflects an orientation to domestic violence as arising from intra-psychic difficulties as much as living within an unequal and patriarchal society. As such, it is unsurprising that reviews of extant studies might struggle to form a coherent and consistent view of whether programmes work whenever the underlying conceptualisation of what needs to change and how to measure this differ so radically.

## Heterogeneity of group participants

One key distinction in programme participation is that some individuals are externally mandated to attend the programme, for example by a court or child protection services. In such cases it is to be expected that some individuals may not acknowledge their need to attend or change. In contrast some programmes are designed for individuals who self-refer on the basis of recognising that they need help to change (for example, Stanley and colleagues, 2012; Williamson & Hester, 2009). Of course in practice these two groups, the mandated and non-mandated, may not be as distinct as presented here, but such a distinction reflects an important dynamic that underpins the delivery of and engagement with the intervention (Devaney & Lazenbatt, 2016).

In addition, as mentioned earlier, groups often do not differentiate between individuals in same-sex or different-sex relationships, or participants from different ethnic groups, assuming that wider structural inequalities such as homophobia or racism are not 'in the room' with both other group participants and even facilitators. The intersection of such issues is often not considered as part of either the design or evaluation of many programmes, yet seems so important.

In summary, some of the findings to date about the effectiveness of programmes may be as a result of programmes seeking to work with such a diverse range of participants, and therefore future studies need to be better able to capture these differences and to control for them in their analyses.

## Programme content or process

As noted earlier, the content of programmes has been developed to address the needs of participants, reflecting the underlying assumptions about what are the primary causes for individuals using abuse and violence within their intimate relationships. Yet, as with research on other types of behaviour change, there is evidence that the way a programme is delivered is as important, and maybe even more important, than the programme content. A feature of many group-based programmes is the high level of attrition or non-completion of the programme. As noted earlier, programmes require significant commitment over a period of months, and often include high expectations in respect of attendance. However, the alliance between group facilitators and participants appear to be a crucial element in whether participants move from a position of defensiveness and resistance, to one of engagement and acceptance of the need to change (Lømo, Haavind, & Tjersland, 2018). How therapist and facilitators work with resistance and respond to participants' invitation to see their perspective and engage with their narrative appears important in the process of change (Lømo, Haavind, & Tjersland, 2019). As such, it is important to consider the full range of evaluation methods to assess process, outcomes and impact.

The alliance between group facilitator and participants is likely to be influenced by a range of facilitator-related factors, such as experience, and factors that the facilitator must contend with, such as group size. For example, in a survey of programme characteristics in the United States and Canada, Cannon and colleagues (2016) found that the average number of participants per group was 8 (n = 166), with a wide range from 1 to 42. The modal number of participants in a programme at any given time was 10. No experimental studies have been conducted on group size, but Babcock et al. (2016) propose that clinical experience suggests that group cohesion and a strong client-facilitator alliance, so important for group retention and lower levels of post-treatment violence, may not be possible with larger groups of more than 10.

## Conclusions

As noted by Devaney and Lazenbatt (2016) domestic violence is a much misunderstood phenomenon. While there is an increasing recognition of the existence of violence and abuse within intimate relationships, and a growing appreciation of the different forms that it takes, there continues to be a simplistic, and at times unhelpful, conceptualisation about who uses such abuse and violence, and why. There is a tendency, amongst professionals as well as the general public, to talk about individuals who engage in domestic violence as though they are a homogenous group, behaving in similar ways, for the same reasons, and possessing common characteristics and personality traits (Holtzworth-Munroe & Meehan, 2004). The danger of such a discourse is that it is easy to assume that one approach to intervening with such individuals should work for everyone, and if it does not, it reinforces the belief, held by some, that the majority of those who are domestically violent are beyond help. Yet, there is an alternative thesis, one that proposes we need a range of ways of working with individuals reflecting their behaviour and needs, and that we need to become more discerning in assessing who might benefit from an intervention, and in which circumstances. This requires us to have a stronger evidence base of which interventions are effective, and for who and when. In doing so we can, more effectively, seek to reduce the incidence of domestic violence, and therefore create a safer society.

## Critical findings

- Considerable resources have been poured into developing and running a range of group-based programmes for individuals who use violence and abuse within their intimate relationships.
- Programmes are premised on different conceptualisations of what causes and sustains domestic violence.
- Many programmes are seeking to meet the needs of a diverse range of individuals.
- Many participants of groups have co-existing challenges in their life, including poor mental health and/or problematic substance use.
- The facilitation process of group programmes seems to be as important as the content.

- The current evidence base is inconclusive about whether such group-based programmes are effective, but this may be related to the quality of the research.
- Quasi-experimental studies appear to be more likely to identify change across a broader range of domains compared to RCTs.
- Key findings indicate that group-based programmes do work for some men in some circumstances, but the key components of change are still unclear.

## Keys implications for policy, practice and research

- There is a need to see individuals who use violence and abuse within their intimate relationships as heterogeneous.
- Consideration should be given to supporting individuals to take responsibility for their own behaviour.
- Group programmes should seek to work with individuals who are more similar rather than dissimilar to one another (e.g. mandate for attendance, sexual orientation, ethnicity).
- Greater attention should be given to designing programmes that are amenable to being evaluated across a range of domains which victims and participants rate as important.
- Greater collaboration between programme providers and evaluators on core information to be gathered and analysed would likely assist in improving the ability to make a judgement about which elements of programmes are effective, and for whom and in what circumstances.
- The role of group facilitators could be studied more closely to ascertain their influence on the outcomes achieved.
- Future research could usefully compare the efficacy of group-based versus individual interventions.

## References

Adams, D. (1988). Treatment models of men who batter: A profeminist analysis. In K. Yllo & M. Bograd (Eds.), *Feminist perspectives on wife abuse*. Newbury Park, CA: Sage.

Babcock, J. C., Armenti, N., Cannon, C., Lauve-Moon, K., Buttell, F., Ferreira, R., . . . Lehmann, P. (2016). Domestic violence perpetrator programs: A proposal for evidence-based standards in the United States. *Partner Abuse, 7*(4), 355–460.

Babcock, J. C., Green, C. E., & Robie, C. (2004). Does batterers' treatment work? A meta-analytic review of domestic violence treatment. *Clinical Psychology Review, 23*, 1023–1053.

Berk, R. A. (2005). Randomized experiments as the bronze standard. *Journal of Experimental Criminology, 1*(4), 417–433.

Camp, A. R. (2018). Pursuing accountability for perpetrators of intimate partner violence: The peril and utility of shame. *Boston University Law Review, 98*, 16771736.

Cannon, C., Hamel, J., Buttell, F., & Ferreira, R. J. (2016). A survey of domestic violence perpetrator programs in the United States and Canada: Findings and implications for policy intervention. *Partner Abuse, 7*(3), 226–276.

Coleman, V. E. (2003). Treating the lesbian batterer. *Journal of Aggression, Maltreatment & Trauma, 7*(1–2), 159–205

Debbonaire, T. (2015). *Responding to diverse ethnic communities in domestic violence perpetrator programmes*. Work with Perpetrators European Network. Retrieved July 12, 2020, from www.work-with-perpetrators. eu/fileadmin/WWP_Network/redakteure/Expert%20Essays/WWP-EN%20Expert%20Essay%20 -%20Diversity.pdf

Devaney, J. (2014). Male perpetrators of domestic violence: How should we hold them to account? *The Political Quarterly, 85*(4), 480–486.

Devaney, J., & Lazenbatt, A. (2016). *Domestic violence perpetrators – Evidence informed responses*. Oxon: Routledge.

Dixon, L., Archer, J., & Graham-Kevan, N. (2012). Perpetrator programmes for partner violence: Are they based on ideology or evidence? *Legal and Criminological Psychology, 17*(2), 196–215.

Eckhardt, C. I., Murphy, C. M., Whitaker, D. J., Sprunger, J., Dykstra, R., & Woodard, K. (2013). The effectiveness of intervention programs for perpetrators and victims of intimate partner violence. *Partner Abuse, 4*(2), 196–231.

Emery, C. R. (2011). Disorder or deviant order? Re-theorizing domestic violence in terms of order, power and legitimacy: A typology. *Aggression and Violent Behavior, 16*(6), 525–540.

Gadd, D., & Corr, M.-L. (2017). Beyond typologies: Foregrounding meaning and motive in domestic violence perpetration. *Deviant Behaviour, 38*(7), 781–791.

Gondolf, E. W. (2002). *Batterer intervention systems: Issues, outcomes, and recommendations.* Thousand Oaks, CA: Sage.

Gondolf, E. W. (2010). Lessons from a successful and failed random assignment testing batterer program innovations. *Journal of Experimental Criminology, 6*, 355–376.

Gondolf, E. W. (2012). *The future of batterer programmes. Reassessing evidence based practice.* Boston, MA: North-eastern University Press.

Goodmark, L. (2018). *Decriminalising domestic violence – A balanced policy approach to intimate partner violence.* Oakland: University of California Press.

Graham-Kevan, N., & Bates, E. A. (2020). Perpetrator programmes ideology or evidence-based practice? In J. S. Wormith, L. A. Craig, & T. E. Hogue (Eds.), *The Wiley handbook of what works in violence risk management: Theory, research, and practice.* London: Wiley Blackwell.

Hamel, J. (2014). *Gender-inclusive treatment of intimate partner violence abuse* (2nd ed.). New York, NY: Springer Publishing Company.

Hassmiller-Lich, K., Ginexi, E. M., Osgood, N. D., & Mabry, P. L. (2013). A call to address complexity in prevention science research. *Prevention Science, 14*(3), 279–289.

Henninger, A., & Sung, H. E. (2014). History of substance abuse treatment. In G. Bruinsma & D. Weisburd (Eds.), *Encyclopedia of criminology and criminal justice.* New York, NY: Springer.

Holtzworth-Munroe, A., & Meehan, J. C. (2004). Typologies of men who are martially violent: Scientific and clinical implications. *Journal of Interpersonal Violence, 19*, 1369–1389.

Johnson, M. P. (2010). *A typology of domestic violence: Intimate terrorism, violent resistance, and situational couple violence.* New England: Northeastern University Press.

Jones, A. S., & Gondolf, E. W. (2002). Assessing the effect of batterer program completion on reassault: An instrumental variables analysis. *Journal of Quantitative Criminology, 18*(1), 71–98.

Kaplenko, H., Loveland, J. E., & Raghavan, C. (2018). Relationships between shame, restrictiveness, authoritativeness, and coercive control in men mandated to a domestic violence offenders program. *Violence and Victims, 33*(2), 296–309.

Kelly, L., & Westmarland, N. (2015). *Domestic violence perpetrator programmes: Steps towards change. Project Mirabal final report.* London and Durham: London Metropolitan University and Durham University.

Laing, L., Humphreys, C., & Kavanagh, K. (2013). *Social work and domestic violence: Developing critical and reflective practice.* London: Sage.

Lehmann, P., & Simmons, C. A. (2009). The state of batterer intervention programmes: An analytical discussion. In P. Lehmann & C. A. Simmons (Eds.), *Strengths-based batterer intervention: A new paradigm in ending family violence.* New York, NY: Springer Publishing Company.

Lilley-Walker, S. J., Hester, M., & Turner, W. (2018). Evaluation of European domestic violence perpetrator programmes: Toward a model for designing and reporting evaluations related to perpetrator treatment interventions. *International Journal of Offender Therapy and Comparative Criminology, 62*(4), 868–884.

Lømo, B., Haavind, H., & Tjersland, O. A. (2018). From resistance to invitations: How men voluntarily in therapy for intimate partner violence may contribute to the development of a working alliance. *Journal of Interpersonal Violence, 33*(16), 2579–2601.

Lømo, B., Haavind, H., & Tjersland, O. A. (2019). Finding a common ground: Therapist responsiveness to male clients who have acted violently against their female partner. *Journal of Interpersonal Violence.* Online First. https://doi.org/10.1177/0886260519862271

Mahon, M., Devaney, J., & Lazenbatt, A. (2009). The role of theory in promoting social work values and its potential effect on outcomes in work with domestically violent men. *Irish Probation Journal, 6*, 151–170.

Maiuro, R. D., & Eberle, J. A. (2008). State standards for domestic violence perpetrator treatment: Current status, trends and recommendations. *Violence and Victims, 23*(2), 133–155.

McCloskey, L. A., Boonzaier, F., Steinbrenner, S. Y., & Hunter, T. (2016). Determinants of intimate part-ner violence in sub-Saharan Africa: A review of prevention and intervention programs. *Partner Abuse*, 7(3), 277–315.

Moran, D. (2011). Re-education or recovery? Re-thinking some aspects of domestic violence perpetrator programmes. *Probation Journal*, 58(1), 23–36.

Moore, S. (2009). The gold coast domestic violence male offender education and intervention program for male perpetrators. In A. Day, P. O'Leary, D. Chung, & D. Justo (Eds.), *Domestic violence: Working with men. Research, practice experiences and integrated responses.* Sydney: The Federation Press.

Murphy, C. M., & Eckhardt, C. I. (2005). *Treating the abusive partner: An individualized cognitive-behavioural approach.* New York, NY: Guildford Press.

Nesset, M. B., Lara-Cabrera, M. L., Dalsbø, T. K., Pedersen, S. A., Bjørngaard, J. H., & Palmstierna, T. (2019). Cognitive behavioural group therapy for male perpetrators of intimate partner violence: A sys-tematic review. *BMC Psychiatry*, 19(1), 11.

Niaz, U., & Tariq, Q. (2017). Situational analysis of intimate partner violence interventions in South Asian and Middle Eastern countries. *Partner Abuse*, 8(1), 47–88.

Pence, E., & Paymar, M. (1993). *Education groups for men who batter: The Duluth model.* New York, NY: Springer.

Respect. (2017). *The respect standard* (3rd ed.). London: Respect.

Santoveña, E. E. E., & da Silva, T. (2016). Domestic violence intervention programs for perpetrators in Latin America and the Caribbean. *Partner Abuse*, 7(3), 316–352.

Smedslund, G., Dalsbø, T., Steiro, A., Winsvold, A., & Clench-Aas, J. (2011). Cognitive behavioural therapy for men who physically abuse their female partner. *Cochrane Database of Systematic Reviews* Issue 2. Art. No.: CD006048.pub2

Stanley, N., Graham-Kevan, N., & Borthwick, R. (2012). Fathers and domestic violence: Building moti-vation for change through perpetrator programmes. *Child Abuse Review*, 21, 264–274.

Tew, J., Bennett, A. L., & Dixon, L. (2016). The chromis experience: An interpretative phenomenological analysis of participants' experiences of the chromis programme. *International Journal of Offender Therapy and Comparative Criminology*, 60(14), 1669–1689.

Westmarland, N., & Kelly, L. (2013). Why extending measurements of 'success' in domestic violence per-petrator programmes matters for social work. *British Journal of Social Work*, 43(6), 1092–1110.

Williamson, E., & Hester, M. (2009). *Evaluation of the south Tyneside domestic abuse perpetrator programme 2006–2008: Final report.* Bristol: University of Bristol.

Zarling, A., Bannon, S., & Berta, M. (2019). Evaluation of acceptance and commitment therapy for domestic violence offenders. *Psychology of Violence*, 9(3), 257–266.

# 46

# COMMUNITY-BASED RESEARCH IN THE DOMESTIC VIOLENCE CONTEXT

*Lisa A. Goodman and Helen P. Hailes*

## Introduction

As each of the chapters in this book conveys, intimate partner violence (IPV)[1] – including physical, psychological, sexual, and financial abuse, and stalking – is a public health epidemic (Breiding, Chen, & Black, 2014) with pervasive and sustained effects on survivors' mental and physical health (Campbell, 2002; Goodman, Smyth, Borges, & Singer, 2009), economic stability (McLean & Bocinski, 2017), and capacity to parent effectively (Pels, van Rooij, & Distelbrink, 2015). Since IPV was first recognized as a social problem rather than a private issue between two people, researchers and practitioners have used their respective skills, resources, and strategies to identify and address the dynamics of IPV and the needs of those affected by it. Yet, these two groups have often remained in their own silos, failing to integrate their complementary knowledge and skills in service of knowledge creation (Yuan et al., 2016). The cost inevitably falls on survivors and those who work with them: researchers fail to ask questions that are deeply grounded in the wisdom, perspectives, and needs of those most affected, and programs, policies, and practices cannot evolve or transform on the basis of relevant and rigorous research.

Community-based participatory research (CBPR) – an approach to research that emphasizes ongoing collaboration, joint decision-making, and shared power between researchers and relevant stakeholders – offers a critical alternative, one embraced by a growing number of researchers and community members in the IPV field (Goodman et al., 2017). By combining types of expertise, researchers and community stakeholders can produce more relevant, creative, and applicable research on IPV than could be obtained through the exclusive reliance on traditional approaches (Goodman et al., 2017). For example, in one collaboration, described in more detail later, researchers partnered with advocates and consulted with survivors to develop a DV program outcome measure now used widely across the country (Goodman, Bennett et al., 2015). Its value comes from its dual foundations in practice relevance and research rigor. Yet, distrust among IPV-affected community members, and insufficient opportunity to learn about CBPR among both researchers and potential community partners remain major obstacles. Further, scholarship on this approach remains sparse and somewhat disjointed, focused more on specific studies than on what CBPR is and how it is or could be used in the IPV context (Ragavan et al., 2019). This chapter aims to fill this gap, providing an overview of the nature and uses of CBPR in the IPV context.

## Discussion and analysis

The first part of this section reviews the historical roots of CBPR, the second describes its major principles, and the third takes a deeper dive into some recent CBPR partnerships and the findings they have generated to improve the lives of survivors.

## What are the historical roots of CBPR?

CBPR emerges from several academic and activist traditions: the *Northern tradition* promoted the idea of *action research*, with the practical goal of improving systems (Wallerstein & Duran, 2017). Kurt Lewin coined the term *action research* in the 1940s to describe a form of research that could shrink the gap between theory and action. Specifically, he wanted to solve practical problems through a research cycle that involved planning, action, and investigating the results of the action (Lewin, 1948, 1997). This process inevitably engaged the community as active participants in the research process rather than simply objects under investigation (Wallerstein & Duran, 2017). Lewin's work inspired and guided generations of researchers interested in conducting research in service of social change (Wallerstein, Duran, Oetzel, & Minkler, 2017).

By contrast, the *Southern tradition* was more frankly political, emphasizing the need to challenge the historically colonizing practices of research that produced knowledge by and for the elites (Hall, Tandon, & Tremblay, 2015). This tradition emerged in the 1970s in Latin America, Asia, and Africa as a close cousin to liberation theology, a Marxist critique of the social sciences, and the development of adult education practices with marginalized communities vulnerable to the forces of globalization (Wallerstein & Duran, 2017). At its heart, this tradition stressed the importance of knowledge that emanated from people's experience rather than from the academy. Academics and researchers had an important role as catalysts and supports of educational processes, but not as substance experts or leaders of the change process (Hall, Gillette, & Tandon, 1982). Brazilian philosopher, educator, and activist Paulo Freire (1970) was central to this movement. He critiqued authoritarian paradigms in which education was unidirectional, objective, and decontextualized, creating a "culture of silence" in which those without power simply lost the means to critically respond (Wallerstein & Duran, 2017). Instead, he developed a method of popular education that centred the critical analysis of personal lives in relation to oppressive structural forces that could control them. The goal of this emancipatory process was critical consciousness (conscientização), the capacity to perceive social, political, and economic oppression and then act against it (Ferreira & Gendron, 2011).

Although Freire focused on education, Colombian sociologist Orlando Fals Borda built on these ideas to promote the "decolonization of social sciences" (Fals-Borda, 2013, p. 157). He coined the term *participatory action research* (PAR) to describe an approach that involved a cyclical process of research, action, and reflection with communities in service of understanding the world through trying to change it. In this process the research relationship was transformed from one in which communities were objects of study to one in which community members participated centrally in the enquiry itself (Wallerstein & Duran, 2017).

Over time, multiple academic disciplines have taken up various strands of these traditions to forge their own approaches to collaborative research, using a variety of terms including participatory research, participatory action research, collaborative enquiry, feminist research, community-engaged research, research-practice partnerships, and community-based participatory research.

Although these various approaches do not share all the same assumptions, they do share certain fundamental characteristics that set them apart from traditional research paradigms. They hold, for example, that research is not value-neutral and the role of the researcher is not to be a detached expert; that research should serve to transform the world, not simply describe it; and that those who are the focus of research have extensive and unique knowledge that requires their participation in all parts of the research process (Edleson & Bible, 2001).

## What are the major tenets of a CBPR approach?

CBPR in particular is prominently associated with public health, medicine, and nursing, though researchers in psychology and sociology have begun to take it up as well (e.g. Collins et al., 2018). It is not a set of methods, but rather an approach to research that fundamentally changes the relationship between researchers and researched (Wallerstein et al., 2017).

The community of people being researched might be characterized by a shared identity or challenge, shared geography, or a common interest. In each of these cases, CBPR researchers see community stakeholders as invaluable partners, with unique expertise on the subject at hand, without whom critical research questions simply could not be addressed. Rather than remaining separate and independent of the people being researched, then, CBPR researchers emphasize the need to join with community members throughout the research process, collaborating on identifying the question to be asked, determining the methods to be used, and interpreting and disseminating the results (Israel et al., 1998; Minkler & Wallerstein, 2010). In doing so, they aim to create transformative, and sustainable change "together with, for, and in communities" (Collins et al., 2018, p. 1).

## What is the role of CBPR in the IPV context?

Although there have been many successful collaborations between researchers and community members to conduct IPV-related research, forming partnerships has also been fraught with tension and distrust (e.g. Andrews, Pepler, & Motz, 2019; Ghanbarpour et al., 2018; Murray & Smith, 2009; Murray & Welch, 2010; National Violence Against Women Prevention Research Center, 2001). In the IPV context, two sets of community stakeholders are especially salient: practitioners who work with IPV survivors, and survivors themselves. Turning first to practitioners, members of this group have raised a series of concerns about researchers, even those who have in some way attempted to consult or partner with them. They have perceived some researchers as too narrow in their focus, or interested only in the experience of certain survivors – for example White heterosexual women – ignoring the influence of race, class, sexual orientation, and other aspects of experience (Richie, 2012). Some point to researchers' insufficient concern for survivors' mental health and safety throughout the research process (Murray & Welch, 2010). Some are impatient with a research process that takes too long in the face of urgent need (Edleson & Bible, 2001). Some feel intimidated, demeaned, or taken advantage of by researchers (Burk, 2018; Murray & Smith, 2009; NVAWPRC, 2001). Some feel distrustful of researcher motives, especially when they have been burned before by "drive-by" data collectors who swoop in to collect data and are then never heard from again (Horowitz, Robinson, & Seifer, 2009). Some have seen the results of their work published in a way that renders their own contributions invisible (Goodman et al., 2017).

Although less has been written about survivor concerns about research, the first author has heard from scores of survivors that they worry about the very same things as researchers. Several have described their array of worries under the banner of feeling "unseen" by researchers who sometimes fail to see survivors as three-dimensional people, who are both strong and vulnerable, capable in some realms, and in need of support in others, valuable thought partners on how to conduct the research as well as critical reporters on the experience of abuse and how to heal from it.

These concerns are not surprising. It is easy to imagine how researchers who do not form relationships with the people about whom they are researching could fail to see survivors and those who support them as valuable experts and co-learners, just as it would be easy for them to miss the multiple forms of power, resources, and status they carry (Muhammad et al., 2015). Their power to conduct and disseminate research shapes the way a social issue is defined, understood, and responded to. Further, researchers may also hold power and privilege based on their social class, education, race/ethnicity, or other identities. They may not even realize how these forms of power shape their interactions with community members, even in subtle ways such as, for example, expecting community members to volunteer while university research assistants are paid, assuming that community partners will come to a university for a meeting without considering their expense or comfort; or failing to translate research tools into languages that would provide more opportunity for a wider range of participants (Goodman et al., 2017).

These and other dynamics may be especially important in IPV research given how much survivors and DV practitioners are attuned to the possibilities of abuses of power in their relationships. A strong CBPR partnership in the IPV context therefore requires careful work to identify and manage potential unequal power dynamics between researchers and community partners (Muhammad et al., 2015).

To provide a taste of how a CBPR partnership in the IPV context might address some of the previously described challenges, the following section describes a set of principles adapted from two sources: an online toolkit for IPV researchers interested in CBPR, which the first author co-developed (Goodman et al., 2017; Goodman et al., 2018), and a recent article discussing equitable research-practice partnerships (Burk, 2018). They are not fixed rules, nor are they comprehensive guidelines. Rather, they combine to create a flexible framework for approaching diverse types of CBPR partnerships in the IPV context.

### *Principle 1: CBPR requires honesty and mutual trust*

Although traditional researchers do not form partnerships with members of the community they aim to study, doing so is the cornerstone of CBPR. Building honest and mutually trusting relationships is not easy. It requires clear and sometimes difficult communication about expectations and goals for the research process, commitments that each party is making, and the products to come from it. Researchers may need to nurture these conditions with particular care when working with marginalized communities. Survivors and practitioners from these communities may have faced decades of discrimination and trauma and feel deep concern about whether their ways of seeing and knowing will be prioritized, especially when the researchers are not from the same community.

Whether or not they share certain identities, CBPR researchers cannot expect to gain the trust of their community partners without spending the time to learn about their varying backgrounds and contexts – not just as individuals but also as a community aligned for a common purpose. If CBPR researchers are working with practitioners in a DV program, they need to learn about the program's history, philosophy, challenges, and organizational culture, as well as the backgrounds, wishes, needs, and hopes of the survivors in it (Goodman et al., 2017). They need to learn whether and how staff and survivors at that program have worked with researchers in the past, and how they feel about research as a result. All of these things will shape how the relevant stakeholders enter into and communicate within the partnership. For example, if community stakeholders have had prior negative experiences with researchers, they may enter a new partnership with a certain level of suspicion or at least caution. CBPR researchers will be in a better position to negotiate that position with sensitivity if they understand something about these past experiences.

In particular, building trusting relationships requires attending to intersectional power dynamics within CBPR partnerships. Salient identities that may confer power include race, class, educational status, immigrant status, gender identity, and sexual orientation, just to name a few. Different members of a collaboration will almost certainly have differing combinations of privileged and marginalized identities, though it is common for researchers to have significantly more identities that confer power, just by virtue of their educational and professional backgrounds. The ability to recognize the complex ways that intersectional identities and power dynamics play out in a CBPR collaboration and affect how members relate to one another can meaningfully impact mutual honesty and trust (Hailes, Colgan, Goodman, & Thomas, under review).

To give a taste of the grainy details that go into creating good communication between researchers and their community partners, consider a recent project designed to develop guidelines for putting CBPR into practice in the IPV context (Burke et al., 2013). Academics and DV practitioners held a series of meetings to discuss what it means to build successful CBPR relationships and came up with the following recommendations:

> Define how to address each other (first names vs. titles). Develop structured way to check-in with all group members such as asking everyone to speak. . . . Routinely check in with the community as to what their needs are and what gains can be made. Disseminate information back to ALL; inform and communicate what is learned. . . . Discuss why each member is involved. Constantly make time for feedback and to address challenges. Understand [that] parts of process will make flexibility and feedback easier and some parts harder. . . . Encourage on-going communication. Identify a point person responsible for communication. Meet regularly with agreed upon frequency. Identify one person to serve as liaison from community and one from academic institution.
>
> (p. 9)

### Principle 2: CBPR entails building on each party's skills, resources, and interests

Another cornerstone of CBPR is the idea that research is best accomplished by combining the knowledge, skills, resources, and sources of power of researchers and community partners respectively (Burke et al., 2013; Minkler & Wallerstein, 2010). These assets may be held at the individual, organizational, and community levels (Minkler & Wallerstein, 2003; Banks & Armstrong, 2012). For example, at the individual level, community members may have lived experience of IPV that will lead to specific research questions that researchers could not conceive of. At the same time researchers may have a way of formulating those specific questions to make them more easily researchable. At the organizational level, each party may have something to offer so that, perhaps, a program can offer a setting in which to conduct the research while the university can offer access to important research infrastructure including software, transcription services, and other research support. And at the community level, researchers have the skills to conduct rigorous investigation into a given issue, while community stakeholders may hold the trust of the community of interest, who will look to them to determine whether or not the research is worthwhile even if rigorous. Understanding all of these nuances will enable both researchers and their community partners to leverage the strengths that each party brings to the table.

No matter what kinds of expertise each party is bringing to the table, it is important to establish as clearly as possible what roles and responsibilities each member of the collaboration will take on, how decisions will be made, and how people will be accountable to each other throughout the process. This can look different in different projects. It may be that one party has greater expertise or interest in one domain and the other party excels in another. It may be that one party does not want to participate in certain decisions but very much wants to participate in others. A variety of decision-making arrangements make sense in the CBPR context, as long as the needs and goals of each party are considered.

To ensure a robust decision-making process, many CBPR projects build on an organized, coherent, and collaboratively developed plan that is documented and shared by those involved. The plan would clearly describe mutually agreed upon (1) contributors and roles – for example who will be responsible for tasks as varied as sending communications, planning and attending meetings, and recruiting participants; (2) expectations and goals for the project; (3) processes that will be used throughout, including how meetings will be run and how disagreements or unexpected events will be navigated; and (4) how results will be shared and disseminated (Minkler, 2004; Sullivan, Price, McPartland, Hunter, & Fisher, 2017). At the same time, in any CBPR project, decisions are likely to be revisited as unexpected challenges arise (Ross et al., 2010) or as reflective researchers and community partners come to new understandings of how power can be shared more effectively.

### Principle 3: Centre survivor safety and mental health in all CBPR activities

That means, for example, that all parties in the partnership need to consider the ways that confidentiality will be upheld throughout the process, and how researcher reporting mandates might affect survivors, their family members, and others. For example, what happens if a researcher discovers that a child is currently being exposed to the survivor's partner's abuse? Under what conditions would that information have to be reported to the state and how would that affect the survivor and her family, as well as the CBPR partnership as a whole?

Second, all parties need to conduct their work with an eye towards how current and prior trauma might be shaping the research process for survivors, their family members, and program staff (Edleson & Bible, 2001; World Health Organization, 2001; Sullivan et al., 2017). All should understand the ways that interpersonal trauma affects individuals, families, and communities; how other forms of oppression might intersect with interpersonal trauma to shape individual experience; and how that experience, in turn, could be worsened or alleviated by various parts of the search process. Understanding these dynamics enables researchers and their community partners to build relationships with each other and perhaps with outside organizations to ensure that the right levels of support are available throughout the process.

### Principle 4: The products of the CBPR process belong to all partners

At the heart of CBPR is the idea that research products should be co-owned by researchers and community partners and disseminated to both practitioner, community, and scholarly audiences (Banks & Armstrong, 2012; Wilson, Kenny, & Dickson-Swift, 2018). This means that data needs to be interpreted jointly, with each party bringing its own lens to the process of understanding what a set of research findings really means. This can be a complicated undertaking. If a CBPR partnership finds that a specific intervention does not produce the expected outcomes for a group of survivors, for example, the implication could be that the intervention failed to effect change or that it was administered by the wrong people, conducted in the wrong setting, or focused on the wrong outcome. Interpretation matters a great deal and the best interpretations emerge from discussions across roles, social identities, forms of expertise, and life experiences.

In terms of actually disseminating results, although peer-reviewed publications may be critical products for researchers, policy reports, practice manuals, or op-eds may be more valuable to community partners. It is therefore critical that from the beginning, practitioners and researchers work together to interpret and frame all results jointly; and they think about who is best positioned for what kinds of dissemination, recognizing the different strengths, social locations, skills, and networks of various stakeholders.

## What does a CBPR partnership actually look like?

Having described principles of CBPR in the DV field, we now turn to a few examples of how these principles have been applied in practice. We selected these particular case studies both because they have been described in some detail in the scholarly literature and because they each represent a distinct type of partnership: the Domestic Violence Program Evaluation and Research Collaborative (DVPERC) is an ongoing regional CBPR partnership involving multiple DV organizations and research institutions collaborating on a range of projects over years. The District Alliance for Safe Housing (DASH) CBPR collaboration involved one DV organization and one research institution collaborating on a single program evaluation project. The Interconnections Project/Proyecto Interconexiones was a collaboration between one research institution and multiple community organizations to develop and pilot culturally relevant mental health interventions.

### DVPERC

The Domestic Violence Program Evaluation and Research Collaborative was developed in Massachusetts in 2011 when a small group of DV agencies came together to discuss the increasing pressure they felt to evaluate and demonstrate program effectiveness to funders (Thomas et al., 2018). Agreeing that no existing measures adequately documented the strengths of their programs, they decided to create their own measures and reached out to the first author for assistance. She introduced another researcher to the project, other DV agencies joined, and soon the group grew into a regional collaborative comprised of representatives from over 20 programs across New England. Together, the group developed a set of research priorities and a plan to achieve them, committing to include survivors in the process even though survivors themselves were not part of the DVPERC. Since then, DVPERC has developed into an ongoing collaboration, where researchers and practitioners meet on a bi-monthly basis to share recent research findings, challenges and insights from their practice, and collaborate on research projects (Thomas et al., 2018).

The initial DVPERC project developed outcome measures for DV program evaluation, involving multiple focus groups with advocates and survivors to create the measures and a survey of hundreds of survivors across agencies to validate the measures. Ultimately, DVPERC generated several measures, including the Measure of Victim Empowerment Related to Safety

(MOVERS; Goodman, Bennett et al., 2015; Goodman, Thomas, & Heimel, 2015) and the Survivor Defined Practice Scales (SDPS; Goodman, Thomas et al., 2016). Shared ownership of these research projects led to peer-reviewed academic articles as well as an online guide to implementing and scoring the MOVERS scale (Goodman, Bennett et al., 2015; Goodman, Thomas et al., 2015). This scale has been used in multiple states in the United States and in multiple countries around the world. Recently, an international group of scholars and practitioners developed an online community of practice to share experiences using the MOVERS in both research and program evaluation.

Since its inception, DVPERC has practiced the CBPR principles described above. From the outset of the collaboration, all parties were committed to transparency about their individual, organizational, and collective needs and goals (Thomas et al., 2018). Many early conversations around these needs and goals contributed to a foundational sense of honesty and trust within the group (Hailes et al., under review). Without this foundation of trusting relationships, DVPERC may not have continued to produce research on a range of other topics relevant to survivor and advocate interests, after the initial project that produced the MOVERS scale. DVPERC has also built upon the unique skills and resources of all of its members. For instance, in the development of the SDPS and MOVERS scales, the partnership relied upon both academic researchers' expertise in developing validated measurements and DV practitioners' knowledge of the challenges of communicating their work for funders (Goodman, Bennett et al., 2015; Goodman, Thomas et al., 2016). DVPERC's commitment to prioritizing survivor safety and mental health is clear even from the type of measures the collaborative has developed. The MOVERS scale operationalizes empowerment related to safety as an important outcome, and from a later project, the Trauma Informed Practice (TIP) scales help DV organizations evaluate and improve the trauma-sensitivity of their programs (Goodman, Bennett et al., 2015; Goodman, Sullivan et al., 2016). As mentioned, shared ownership of DVPERC products has led to practical user guides for the scales and a community of practice, along with academic journal articles.

## DASH

While DVPERC is an ongoing regional CBPR collaboration, many CBPR partnerships develop around a specific single project between one research institution and one DV organization. The DASH program evaluation CBPR partnership is one example of this model. The partnership developed when two researchers reached out to DASH, a community organization that provides housing, advocacy, counselling, and other supportive services in the Washington, DC area, to see if they had evaluation data for their program (Nnawulezi, Sullivan, Marcus, Young, & Hacskaylo, 2019). The researchers were interested in DASH's model because of its focus on increasing survivors' sense of power, autonomy, and well-being. While DASH leadership were interested in evaluating their program, they had not had capacity to do so yet, so, with trust already established between one of the researchers and the founding director of DASH through a prior relationship, the researchers proposed a CBPR partnership to evaluate DASH's model.

The researchers and members of the DASH leadership team collaboratively determined the study design, and the researchers developed trust and buy-in from organization staff by introducing the project during regularly scheduled staff meetings, inviting staff to participate during paid work hours, and asking staff about what kinds of findings would be useful for them and how involved they would like to be in the study. These steps demonstrated respect for staff members' time and expertise and genuine interest in their input in the research process. The study ultimately involved designing and implementing staff and resident interview protocols.

DASH staff members were involved at multiple points in the process and to varying degrees depending on their interest level. The collaborators determined that data from the study would be shared and research products decided upon collaboratively. So far, products have included a dissertation, multiple peer-reviewed articles and conference presentations, and a report to be used with partners and funders. DASH has also implemented a transformational coaching framework across the organization, based on study findings.

As in the DVPERC case study, the CBPR principles are clearly evident in the DASH program evaluation partnership. Buy-in from staff members within the organization was essential for effectively evaluating DASH's model, and the entire project would not have been possible without careful attention to establishing trusting relationships with both senior leadership and program staff at DASH (Nnawulezi et al., 2019). The evaluation relied on the expertise of all members of the partnership, for instance researcher knowledge and capacity to conduct evaluations and organization staff's expertise on practice issues and their own program. Attention to survivor safety and mental health was evidenced by the careful way that members of the partnership incorporated survivor input: researchers and DASH staff partnered on all aspects of the study but collaboratively decided to invite residents in the program (survivors) to be involved only in a limited subset of these aspects, partly out of recognition of survivors' more pressing needs (Nnawulezi et al., 2019). Like DVPERC, the DASH partnership has also shared research products among members and has created a transformational coaching framework, along with academic articles and presentations.

## The Interconnections Project/Proyecto Interconexiones

The Interconnections Project/Proyecto Interconexiones is an example of another different kind of CBPR partnership from DASH and DVPERC. The Interconnections Project/Proyecto Interconexiones partnership developed between medical researchers and multiple community programs to create culturally specific treatments for depression among DV survivors (Nicolaidis, Mejia et al., 2013; Nicolaidis, Wahab et al., 2013). Initially, the group conducted a series of focus groups with White, Latina, and African American survivors to understand their experiences, beliefs, and recommendations about depression and seeking help for depression (Nicolaidis et al., 2008, 2010, 2011). Through these focus groups, the partners determined a need for culturally specific adaptations of depression interventions for IPV survivors, tailored to African American and Latina women. Culturally specific interventions were developed and piloted in collaboration with the Bradley-Angle House, a DV agency that runs a culturally specific drop-in centre for African American women and with Familias en Acción, a community-based organization serving Latinx families.

The intervention for Latina survivors was designed and implemented by a team that consisted primarily of Latina women, including women with experiences of DV (Nicolaidis, Mejia et al., 2013). In response to focus group feedback, the intervention was led by a *promotora* (community health worker) and was hosted at the community organization, rather than in a medical setting. The intervention was based on an existing Chronic Care Model (CCM) for depression, consisted of 12 weekly group sessions, was conducted entirely in Spanish, and was adapted to incorporate creative elements, such as crafting projects and icebreaker activities. The intervention was found to be effective for decreasing depression symptoms, increasing depression self-efficacy and self-esteem, and decreasing stress. Participants reported high satisfaction with the program and expressed appreciation that the intervention was community-based and specific to Latina women. A similar intervention was designed and piloted specifically for African

American survivors and achieved similarly high levels of participant satisfaction (Nicolaidis, Wahab et al., 2013).

While the structure and aims of the Interconnections Project/Proyecto Interconexiones CBPR partnership were different to the DASH and DVPERC models, it also exemplified key CBPR principles. Researchers and practitioners collaborated on focus groups studies together for five years before piloting their culturally specific depression interventions, developing crucial relationships of trust (Nicolaidis, Wahab et al., 2013). Researchers and practitioners each played invaluable roles in the partnership, as well. Latina and African American community collaborators provided essential expertise about their racial and ethnic communities, for instance suggesting that the interventions be housed in community programs rather than medical settings and that they be led by *promotoras* and community health advocates to promote trust (Nicolaidis, Mejia et al., 2013; Nicolaidis, Wahab et al., 2013). For the White principal investigator on these studies, accessing, building trust, and effectively studying these communities would have been incredibly difficult without the expertise of collaborators of Colour. The partnership's prioritization of survivor mental health and safety was evidenced by the very decision to study and develop culturally specific interventions for survivors with depression (Nicolaidis, Mejia et al., 2013; Nicolaidis, Wahab et al., 2013). Finally, because they were conducted by *promotoras* and community health advocates and in a community setting, the interventions piloted by the Interconnections Project/Proyecto Interconexiones may also be easier for the community collaborators involved in the study and other community organizations to replicate (Nicolaidis, Mejia et al., 2013; Nicolaidis, Wahab et al., 2013).

## Conclusion

Without careful attention to forming true partnerships, grounded in trust, transparency, recognition of shared and separate strengths, and keen attention to power dynamics, it is hard to imagine that our research will reflect the true experiences, challenges, strengths, and vulnerabilities of domestic violence-affected communities. Through CBPR collaborations, researchers, practitioners, and survivors are able to co-create knowledge that each party would be unable to create alone. While CBPR collaborators may come from different backgrounds, with different experiences and expertise, the common aim to support and advocate for the needs of survivors and their communities is a powerful shared orientation, which has led partnerships to develop a wide range of tools for practitioners and survivors, along with traditional research publications. As the value of this approach is increasingly recognized, opportunities to conduct CBPR are expanding through new funding opportunities, fellowships, trainings, and journals devoted exclusively to participatory research (Horowitz et al., 2009). With these growing opportunities, we hope to see the rich tapestry of CBPR collaborations in the DV field continue to develop, deepening our collective understanding and ability to advocate for survivors.

## Critical findings

- Modern CBPR developed out of the combined influences of the Northern and Southern traditions of community-based research.
- CBPR researchers view community stakeholders as critical partners and experts.
- Four principles of CBPR research on intimate partner violence include:

    1   CBPR requires honesty and mutual trust.
    2   CBPR entails building on each party's skills, resources, and interests.

3    CBPR centres survivor safety and mental health in all CBPR activities.
4    The products of the CBPR process belong to all partners.

- Successful CBPR collaborations on intimate partner violence have taken a range of forms, from ongoing, regional partnerships to single-project-focused collaborations between a researcher and a community organization.

## Implications for policy, practice, and research

- CBPR approaches can mitigate harmful power dynamics and legacies of mistrust in the community and can be a powerful tool for researchers and community collaborators to build trusting relationships.
- More detailed recommendations for those interested in exploring CBPR partnerships on intimate partner violence can be found in the CBPR Toolkit (cbprtoolkit.org).
- Universities and funding bodies should facilitate and support researchers engaging in CBPR research with community organizations and survivors.
- Further development and study of the range different CBPR collaborations will enrich our collective understanding of the power and possibilities of this form of research.

## Note

1  Although intimate partner violence (IPV) has become the preferred term to describe abuse by an intimate partner in scholarly literature, programs that support survivors typically use the term domestic violence (DV). Thus, we use the two terms interchangeably.

## References

Andrews, N. C. Z., Pepler, D. J., & Motz, M. (2019). Research and evaluation with community-based projects: Approaches, considerations, and strategies. *American Journal of Evaluation.* https://doi.org/10.1177/1098214019835821

Banks, S., & Armstrong, A. (2012). *Ethics in community-based participatory research: Case studies, case examples and commentaries.* Durham: National Coordinating Centre for Public Engagement and the Centre for Social Justice and Community Action.

Breiding, M. J., Chen, J., & Black, M. C. (2014). *Intimate partner violence in the United States– 2010.* Atlanta: National Center for Injury Prevention and Control, Centers for Disease Control and Prevention.

Burk, C. (2018). Observer effect: Insights for building equitable community-research partnerships. *Journal of Family Violence, 33,* 515–519. https://doi.org/10.1007/s10896-018-9992-1

Burke, J. G., Hess, S., Hoffmann, K., Guizzetti, L., Loy, E., Gielen, A., & Yonas, M. (2013). Translating community-based participatory research (CBPR) principles into practice: Building a research agenda to reduce intimate partner violence. *Progress in Community Health Partnerships: Research, Education, and Action, 7*(2), 115–122. http://dx.doi.org/10.1353/cpr.2013.0025

Campbell, J. C. (2002). Health consequences of intimate partner violence. *The Lancet, 359,* 1331–1336. http://dx.doi.org/10.1016/S0140-6736(02)08336-8

Collins, S. E., Clifasefi, S. L., Stanton, J., The LEAP Advisory Board, Straits, K. J. E., Gil-Kashiwabara, E., . . . Wallerstein, N. (2018). Community-based participatory research (CBPR): Towards equitable involvement of community in psychology research. *American Psychologist, 73*(7), 884–898. http://dx.doi.org/10.1037/amp0000167

Edleson, J. L., & Bible, A. B. (2001). Collaborating for women's safety: Partnerships between research and practice. In C. Renzetti, J. Edleson, & R. Bergen (Eds.), *Sourcebook on violence against women* (pp. 73–95). Thousand Oaks, CA: Sage.

Fals Borda, O. (2013). Action research in the convergence of disciplines. *International Journal of Action Research, 9*(2), 155–167. http://dx.doi.org/10.1688/1861-9916_IJAR_2013_02_Fals-Borda

Ferreira, M. P., & Gendron, F. (2011). Community-based participatory research with traditional and indigenous communities of the Americas: Historical context and future directions. *International Journal of Critical Pedagogy, 3*(3), 153–168.

Freire, P. (1970). *Pedagogy of the oppressed.* New York, NY: Continuum International Publishing.

Ghanbarpour, S., Palotai, A., Kim, M. E., Aguilar, A., Flores, J., Hodson, A., . . . Shim, H. (2018). An exploratory framework for community-led research to address intimate partner violence: A case study of the survivor-centered advocacy project. *Journal of Family Violence, 33,* 521–535.

Goodman, L. A., Bennett Cattaneo, L., Thomas, K., Woulfe, J., Chong, S. K., & Fels Smyth, K. (2015). Advancing domestic violence program evaluation: Development and validation of the measure of victim empowerment related to safety (MOVERS). *Psychology of Violence, 5*(4), 355–366. https://doi.org/10.1037/a0038318

Goodman, L. A., Smyth, K. F., Borges, A. M., & Singer, R. (2009). When crises collide: How intimate partner violence and poverty intersect to shape women's mental health and coping? *Trauma, Violence and Abuse, 10,* 306–329. http://dx.doi.org/10.1177/1524838009339754

Goodman, L. A., Sullivan, C. M., Serrata, J., Perilla, J., Wilson, J. M., Fauci, J. E., & DiGiovanni, C. D. (2016). Development and validation of the Trauma-informed practice scales. *Journal of Community Psychology, 44*(6), 747–764. https://doi.org/10.1002/jcop.21799.

Goodman, L. A., Thomas, K., Cattaneo, L. B., Heimel, D., Woulfe, J., & Chong, S. K. (2016). Survivor-defined practice in domestic violence work: Measure development and preliminary evidence of link to empowerment. *Journal of Interpersonal Violence, 31,* 163–185. https://doi.org/10.1177/0886260514555131.

Goodman, L. A., Thomas, K. A., & Heimel, D. (2015). A guide for using the measure of victim empowerment related to safety (MOVERS). Retrieved from www.dvevidenceproject.org/evaluation-tools

Goodman, L. A., Thomas, K. A., Nnawulezi, N., Lippy, C., Serrata, J. V., Ghanbarpour, S., . . . Bair-Merritt, M. H. (2018). Bringing community based participatory research to domestic violence scholarship: An online toolkit. *Journal of Family Violence, 33*(2), 103–107.

Goodman, L. A., Thomas, K. A., Serrata, J. V., Lippy, C., Nnawulezi, N., Ghanbarpour, S., . . . Bair-Merritt, M. H. (2017). *Power through partnerships: A CBPR toolkit for domestic violence researchers.* National Resource Center on Domestic Violence. Retrieved from https://cbprtoolkit.org

Hailes, H. P., Colgan, C., Goodman, L. A., & Thomas, K. A. (Under Review). *Power and presence in community-based participatory research: A process evaluation.*

Hall, B., Gillette, A., & Tandon, R. (Eds.). (1982). *Creating knowledge: A monopoly?* New Delhi: Society for Participatory Research in Asia.

Hall, B., Tandon, R., & Tremblay, C. (Eds.). (2015). *Strengthening community university research partnerships: Global perspectives.* Victoria, BC: University of Victoria Press.

Horowitz, C. R., Robinson, M., & Seifer, S. (2009). Community-based participatory research from the margin to the mainstream: Are researchers prepared? *Circulation, 119,* 2633-2642. https://doi.org/10.1161/CIRCULATIONAHA.107.729863

Israel, B. A., Schulz, A. J., Parker, E. A., & Becker, A. B. (1998). Review of community-based research: Assessing partnership approaches to improve public health. *Annual Review of Public Health, 19,* 173–202. https://doi.org/10.1146/annurev.publhealth.19.1.173

Lewin, K., (1948). Action research and minority problems. In G. W. Lewin (Ed.), *Resolving social conflicts* (pp. 143–152). New York, NY: Harper.

Lewin, K. (1997). *Resolving social conflicts and field theory in social science.* Washington, DC: American Psychological Association. http://dx.doi.org/10.1037/10269-000

McLean, G., & Bocinski, S. G. (2017). *The economic cost of intimate partner violence, sexual assault, and stalking.* Institute for Women's Policy Research. Retrieved from https://iwpr.org/publications/economic-cost-intimate-partner-violence-sexual-assault-stalking/

Minkler, M. (2004). Ethical challenges for the "outside" researcher in community-based participatory research. *Health Education & Behavior, 31*(6), 684–709. https://doi.org/10.1177/1090198104269566

Minkler, M., & Wallerstein, N. (Eds.). (2003*). Community based participatory research for health.* San Francisco, CA: Jossey-Bass, a Wiley Brand.

Minkler, M., & Wallerstein, N. (2010). Community-based participatory research contributions to intervention research: The intersection of science and practice to improve health equity. *American Journal of Public Health, 100,* 40–46. https://doi.org/10.2105/AJPH.2009.184036

Muhammad, M., Wallerstein, N., Sussman, A. L., Avila, M., Belone, L., & Duran, B. (2015). Reflections on researcher identity and power: The impact of positionality on community-based participatory research (CBPR) processes and outcomes. *Critical Sociology*, *41*(7–8), 1045–1063. https://doi.org/10.1177/0896920513516025

Murray, C. E., & Smith, P. H. (2009). Perceptions of research and practice among domestic violence researchers. *Journal of Aggression, Conflict, and Peace Research*, *1*, 4–21.

Murray, C. E., & Welch, M. L. (2010). Preliminary construction of a service provider-informed domestic violence research agenda. *Journal of Interpersonal Violence*, *25*(12), 2279–2296.

National Violence Against Women Prevention Research Center (NVAWPRC). (2001). *Fostering collaborations to prevent violence against women integrating findings from practitioner and research focus groups*. Charleston, SC: Author.

Nicolaidis, C., Gregg, J., Galian, H., McFarland, B., Curry, M., & Gerrity, M. (2008). "You always end up feeling like you're some hypochondriac": Intimate partner violence survivors' experiences addressing depression and pain. *Journal of General Internal Medicine*, *23*(8), 1157–1163. http://dx.doi.org/10.1007/s11606-008-0606-0

Nicolaidis, C., Mejia, A., Perez, M., Alvarado, A., Celaya-Alston, R., Quintero, Y., & Aguillo, R. (2013). Proyecto Interconexiones: A pilot test of a community-based depression care program for Latina violence survivors. *Progress in Community Health Partnerships: Research, Education, & Action*, *7*(4), 395–401. http://dx.doi.org/10.1353/cpr.2013.0051

Nicolaidis, C., Perez, M., Mejia, A., Alvarado, A., Celaya-Alston, R., Galian, H., & Hilde, A. (2011). "Guardarse las cosas adentro" (keeping things inside): Latina violence survivors' perceptions of depression. *Journal of General Internal Medicine*, *26*(10), 1131–1137. http://dx.doi.org/10.1007/s11606-011-1747-0

Nicolaidis, C., Timmons, V., Thomas, M. J., Waters, A. S., Wahab, S., Mejia, A., & Mitchell, S. R. (2010). "You don't go tell White people nothing": African American women's perspectives on the influence of violence and race on depression and depression care. *American Journal of Public Health*, *100*(8),1470–1476. http://dx.doi.org/10.2105/AJPH.2009.161950

Nicolaidis, C., Wahab, S., Trimble, J., Mejia, A., Mitchell, S. R., Raymaker, D., . . . Waters, A. S. (2013b). The interconnections project: Development and evaluation of a community-based depression program for African American violence survivors. *Journal of General Internal Medicine*, *28*(4), 530–538. http://dx.doi.org/10.1007/s11606-012-2270-7

Nnawulezi, N., Sullivan, C. M., Marcus, S., Young, L., & Hacskaylo, M. (2019). Negotiating participatory research processes with domestic violence program staff to obtain ecologically valid data. *Journal of Interpersonal Violence*, *34*(23–24), 4817–4837. https://doi.org/10.1177/0886260519871535

Pels, T., van Rooij, F. B., & Distelbrink, M. (2015). The impact of intimate partner violence (IPV) on parenting by mothers within an ethnically diverse population in the Netherlands. *Journal of Family Violence*, *30*(8), 1055–1067. http://dx.doi.org/10.1007/s10896-015-9746-2

Ragavan, M. I., Thomas, K., Medzhitva, J., Brewer, N., Goodman, L. A., & Bair-Merritt, M. (2019). A systematic review of community-based research interventions for domestic violence survivors. *Psychology of Violence*, *9*(2), 139–155. http://dx.doi.org/10.1037/vio0000183

Richie, B. E. (2012). *Arrested justice: Black women, violence, and America's prison nation*. New York, NY: New York University Press.

Ross, L., Loup, A., Nelson, R., Botkin, J., Kost, R., Smith, G., & Gehlert, S. (2010). The challenges of collaboration for academic and community partners in a research partnership: Points to consider. *Journal of Empirical Research on Human Research Ethics*, *5*(1), 19–31. http://dx.doi.org/10.1525/jer.2010.5.1.19

Sullivan, T. P., Price, C., McPartland, T., Hunter, B. A., & Fisher, B. S. (2017). The researcher practitioner partnership study (RPPS): Experiences from criminal justice system collaborations. studying violence against women. *Violence Against Women*, *23*(7), 887–907. http://dx.doi.org/10.1177/1077801216650290

Thomas, K. A., Goodman, L. A., Schön Vainer, E., Heimel, D., Barkai, R., & Collins-Gousby, D. (2018). "No sacred cows or bulls": The story of the domestic violence program evaluation and research collaborative (DVPERC). *Journal of Family Violence*, *33*(8), 537–549. https://doi.org/10.1007/s10896-018-9978-z

Wallerstein, N., & Duran, B. (2017). Theoretical, historical, and practice roots of CBPR. In N. Wallerstein, B. Duran, J. G. Oetzel, & M. Minkler (Eds.), *Community-based participatory research for health* (pp. 17–30). San Francisco, CA: Jossey-Bass, a Wiley Brand.

Wallerstein, N., Duran, B., Oetzel, J., & Minkler, M. (2017). *Community based participatory research for health: Advancing social and health equity*. San Francisco, CA: Jossey-Bass, a Wiley Brand.

Wilson, E., Kenny, A., & Dickson-Swift, V. (2018). Ethical challenges in community-based participatory research: A scoping review. *Qualitative Health Research*, *28*(2), 189–199. http://dx.doi.org/10.1177/1049732317690721

World Health Organization. (2001). *Putting women first: Ethical and safety recommendations for research on domestic violence*. Geneva, Switzerland: Garcia-Moreno, C.

Yuan, N. P., Gaines, T. L., Jones, L. M., Rodriguez, L. M., Hamilton, N., & Kinnish, K. (2016). Bridging the gap between research and practice by strengthening academic-community partnerships for violence research. *Psychology of Violence*, *6*(1), 27–33. http://dx.doi.org/10.1037/vio0000026

# 47
# MIXED METHODS IN THE CONTEXT OF QUASI-EXPERIMENTAL RESEARCH DESIGNS

*Claire M. Renzetti, Diane R. Follingstad and Margaret I. Campe*

## Introduction

The combination of quantitative and qualitative data collection methods in empirical studies is commonly referred to as mixed-methods research. The use of mixed methods is growing in social science research, including research on domestic violence and abuse (Campbell, Patterson, & Bybee, 2011; Tashakkori & Teddlie, 2010). One reason for this increasing popularity is that researchers recognise that while each method alone has its own strengths, the combination of diverse methods may not only multiply the data collected, but also enrich the findings, yielding a fuller picture of a complex phenomenon of interest and more nuanced answers to research questions. Nevertheless, as Morgan (2014) points out, combining methods is no easy task and the potential benefits it may produce come at a cost to the researcher.

In fact, combining two methods often involves more than twice as much work as using a single method, since you must not only use each separate method effectively but also integrate them effectively. Simply having more results or different results does not inherently improve your work; in addition, you must bring those results together in a way that demonstrates the value of your additional effort (Morgan, 2014, p. 4).

Mixed-methods data collection, then, is not inherently better than data collection using a single method. The researcher must have a sound rationale for using multiple methods and design the study such that the multiple methods used are not simply additive but *integrated*.

In this chapter, we discuss the use of mixed methods in an evaluation of a therapeutic horticulture (TH) programme at a battered women's shelter, a programme that came to be known simply as "the farm project."[1] The quasi-experimental design of this study incorporated both quantitative and qualitative methods at various points in the data collection process, including surveys of residents, ratings of residents' behaviour and well-being by shelter staff and farm personnel, participant observation by the project manager in staff meetings, and interviews with TH programme participants. The evaluation was undertaken as a researcher-practitioner partnership in which the researchers and shelter staff collaborated to develop a plan for ongoing evaluation of the TH programme after the current project ended and also collect data that can be used in future funding requests to sustain or expand the TH programme. In the first section of the chapter, we discuss various rationales for using mixed methods, and more specifically, why we chose to use mixed methods in our evaluation, emphasising what we consider the potential benefits of combining methods in this type of study. In the second section, we describe the evaluation in detail, including the research questions and objectives; the methods and measures, both quantitative and qualitative; and the research procedure. We conclude the chapter by examining some of the challenges posed by conducting a mixed-methods, quasi-experimental programme evaluation at a battered women's shelter while adhering to the principles of the researcher-practitioner partnership, and we discuss the ways these challenges were addressed.

## Why mixed methods?

Any reader who has taken even an introductory research methods course is likely familiar with the basic differences between quantitative and qualitative methods. Quantitative studies are designed to test a set of a priori hypotheses and use measures for which the research participants' responses can be coded in numerical form and analysed using statistical tests. Qualitative studies, in contrast, are typically inductive; theory emerges from the data. Qualitative data are collected naturalistically – for example, through field observations or through semi-structured or unstructured interviews in which research participants "tell their story," thereby providing narrative data that are analysed thematically (Denzin & Lincoln, 2017; Lincoln & Guba, 1985; Miles, Huberman, & Saldana, 2019). With regard to domestic violence and abuse, quantitative studies have made significant contributions to calculating estimates of frequency and severity, identifying risk and protective factors, and testing a range of hypotheses generated from various explanatory theories. Among the many contributions of qualitative studies, with their focus on meaning-making, has been their ability to illuminate subjective experiences of domestic violence and abuse and its consequences. But as Testa, Livingston, and VanZile-Tamsen (2011) point out, while each of these methodological types independently has advanced our knowledge of domestic violence and abuse, the integration of the two in mixed-methods studies "offers perhaps the best and most thorough means" for a comprehensive understanding because domestic violence and abuse is "a complex, multifaceted phenomenon, occurring within a social context influenced by gender norms, interpersonal relationships, and sexual scripts" (p. 237).

As noted, however, the use of multiple methods in a study demands considerable time and effort, so researchers must carefully consider the relative advantages and disadvantages of combining methods as opposed to using a single method of data collection. Morgan (2014) argues that there are three basic motivations for using mixed methods: (1) the value of sequential contributions, (2) the desire for additional coverage, and (3) the need for convergent findings. All three of these goals were present in the farm project evaluation, so we will discuss each in turn.

Mixed-methods research motivated by sequential motivations uses one type of method to "enhance the performance of another method. This approach relies on a division of labour in which each method serves a different purpose and one method builds on what you learned from the other" (Morgan, 2014, p. 10). Campbell and colleagues' (2011) evaluation of how a Sexual Assault Nurse Examiner (SANE) programme affected prosecution rates of adult sexual assault cases provides an example of the sequential contributions motivation. Campbell et al. discuss this project as a sequence of six studies. They began by collecting quantitative data comparing criminal justice outcomes for adult sexual assault cases treated in county hospitals five years before implementation of the SANE programme with outcomes for cases treated in the SANE programme over seven years post-implementation. They also collected quantitative data on the characteristics of victims, assaults, and medical forensic evidence to identify factors associated with successful prosecution. They next conducted qualitative interviews with police and prosecutors about their experiences with the SANE programme to help them explain what they had learned so far about the SANE programme's effectiveness. In a fourth study, they collected quantitative data from police reports of sexual assault cases to see if police investigations differed in cases in which a SANE was involved. They subsequently conducted qualitative interviews with victims/survivors about their experiences with the SANE programme and the criminal justice system, and with SANEs about their experiences with patients and the criminal justice system. In the Campbell et al. evaluation, each method has a unique data collection purpose, but it builds on the one preceding it to eventually form a comprehensive picture of how the SANE programme impacted the prosecution of adult sexual assault cases.

Another common use of mixed methods that illustrates the sequential contributions motivation is administering a survey to identify potential participants for a qualitative study, or conducting qualitative interviews or focus groups to inform the development of a larger, quantitative study (Morgan, 2014; Noonan & Charles, 2009). It was in this way that the sequential contributions motivation was at work in our design of the TH evaluation. We began by conducting interviews with shelter staff, which provided historical data on the shelter and the development of the farm project as well as the staff's perceptions of the programme's benefits and their concerns about the future of the programme. This preliminary stage of the evaluation also helped solidify the researcher-practitioner partnership in that the staff interviews informed us about aspects of the farm project they felt should be evaluated. We provide more detail about this stage of the evaluation in the next section.

The second motivation for using mixed methods is additional coverage. It has been argued, for instance, that the effects of violent victimisation cannot be fully understood using scales or forced-response questionnaires. Rather, a comprehensive understanding of violence and abuse requires the perspectives of those who have been victimised, provided through an open-ended narrative process in which they convey, in their own words, the subjective meaning of their experiences (Testa et al., 2011). This does not mean that surveys are useless or inappropriate, but rather that they are insufficient for understanding complex, multidimensional problems, such as domestic violence and abuse. Testa and her colleagues (2011), for example, describe a study in which they initially asked women to complete the Sexual Experiences Survey (SES; Koss, Gidycz, & Wisniewski, 1987), and then followed up with interviews with women who reported a victimisation incident on the survey. The interview began by asking the woman to describe in her own words how the event happened.[2] According to Testa et al. (2011), "These descriptions of victimisation incidents, from the victim's perspective, provided a critical window into understanding sexual victimisation that could not be obtained through quantitative description alone" (p. 239). Similarly, in our evaluation we realised that while we could gauge the impact of participation in the TH programme on victims/survivors' mental health, self-view, social functioning, physical self-efficacy, and financial efficacy using a wide array of standardised quantitative measures, the women's own subjective assessments of the impact of the TH programme on their health and well-being would provide an additional dimension to the evaluation that the quantitative data could not, and thereby significantly enhance our understanding of the programme's effectiveness. In addition, we felt that a quantitative assessment alone would not likely capture the therapeutic benefits of the farm project – for example, how much improvement was made week to week – as well as the participants' subjective assessments would. Moreover, if differences among the farm project participants' subjective assessments of the programme's impact emerged, these qualitative data may help us explain our quantitative data and provide a better understanding of *which women* in the shelter population might benefit most from TH participation.

The third motivation for using mixed methods is the need for convergent findings, or what is often called triangulation or cross-validation. If different methods produce similar results, the researcher has greater confidence in the validity of their findings. Returning to Campbell et al.'s (2011) study of the effects of a SANE programme on prosecution of adult sexual assault cases, the researchers note that the quantitative data they collected in their fourth study (i.e., data from sexual assault police reports) could be used to "cross-check" the findings obtained through interviews with police and prosecutors in their third study. In our study, the shelter and farm staff's independent ratings of study participants' functioning and programme engagement can serve to "cross-check" the findings obtained through the scales on the surveys, which we discuss in more detail in the next section.

## Evaluating a therapeutic horticulture programme: methods, measures, and procedures

As noted, the primary goal of the evaluation was to determine whether participation in a TH programme (i.e., the farm project) produced physical, psychological, and functional benefits for intimate partner violence (IPV) victims residing at the shelter that exceeded the benefits of the shelter's standard programming and that were sustained following the women's shelter stay. The second major goal of the study was to make good on our promises to our practitioner partners by developing research strategies and protocols that would inevitably enable them to maintain, improve, and continue to evaluate the TH programme beyond the life of the initial evaluation. From the outset, we recognised that trying to isolate the effects of the farm project, which had been instituted rather recently within a long-standing shelter programme with multiple foci designed to benefit IPV victims, would be difficult, especially since the evaluation had to take place within the ongoing day-to-day operation of the shelter, which can often be chaotic and crisis-driven, resulting in abrupt programming changes. In this section, then, we discuss the methods, measures, and procedures we used to accomplish the study's two major goals, offering greater insight into the quasi-experimental design of the study and the various quantitative and qualitative methods we used as well as our motivations for using this mixture of methods. In the subsequent section, we discuss specific challenges that arose during the evaluation and how we addressed these challenges.

### *Preliminary researcher-practitioner partnership development*

Our partnership with the shelter staff began in the spring of 2012. Although we were already familiar with the shelter and the shelter administrators, we were interested in helping shelter staff integrate the newly instituted farm project into their existing therapeutic programming, and in generating an evidence base for the therapeutic impact of the farm project itself. In consultation with the associate director, the farm manager, and the farm activities coordinator, we developed a semi-structured, qualitative interview to assess each staff member's perceptions of the general functioning of the shelter, followed by their perceptions of the farm project and how it aligns with the shelter's mission. The interviews with all 17 staff members took place between September 2012 and January 2013. Interviews averaged 90 minutes in duration and each was audio-recorded. This process and our analysis of the interview data were instrumental in the development of our mutually beneficial researcher-practitioner partnership for the full evaluation of the farm project. Although building a researcher-practitioner partnership is time- and labour-intensive, it is a worthwhile investment for several reasons. For instance, collaborating with practitioners who work directly with the population being studied helps researchers develop better research questions and better measures to answer them. Partnering with practitioner organisations and agencies also gives researchers better access to the population of interest. Moreover, practitioners' endorsement of the research provides research participants with a level of assurance that the researchers can be trusted which, in turn, promotes participant enrolment and retention in the study. And the study findings can then be used to develop tangible and timely policy and programming recommendations (Edleson & Bible, 1998; Gondolf, 2010; Sullivan, Price, McPartland, Hunter, & Fisher, 2017). Findings from our preliminary interviews with shelter staff (see Renzetti & Follingstad, 2015) led to the proposed evaluation of the farm project's benefits and outcomes as a viable, evidence-based TH experience. The qualitative interviews were also influential in the design of the quasi-experimental evaluation and in identifying the therapeutic outcomes to be assessed, which will be discussed in more detail shortly.

At the same time, building a researcher-practitioner partnership has benefits for practitioners and their clients. Some researchers have been criticised for engaging in "drive-by research" in which they engage practitioners to gain access to the study population and even to collect the data for a study, but do not provide any real incentives or benefits to the organisation or participants (Edleson & Bible, 1998; Kaye, 1990; Riger, 1999). Community-based domestic violence advocacy organisations and shelters are often underfunded, with staff doing emotionally taxing work with large caseloads and limited resources. Staff support of a research study, therefore, rightfully requires researchers to demonstrate how the study will benefit staff, clients, and the organisation.

Concerns about limited resources, time constraints, and meeting the multiple needs of shelter residents were clearly communicated by staff in the preliminary interviews for the TH study which, in turn, influenced our decisions regarding study design and issues such as participation incentives. For example, the grant the researchers secured to fund the evaluation provided greater financial stability to the farm programme. Prior to the evaluation, stipends for farm programme participation were funded through a combination of sources including small local grants and private donations. The TH evaluation grant relieved the stress and uncertainty involved in finding funding each year for farm stipends. In addition, the grant allowed us to nearly double the weekly stipends – from US\$40 to US\$75 for each ten-hour week of farm work. We also provided incentives to all participants in the control and intervention groups to complete the surveys associated with the evaluation. Consequently, even if shelter residents did not want to participate in the farm project or could not participate for other reasons, they could still earn US\$20 for taking a pre-test survey, US\$20 for taking a post-test survey, and US\$30 for taking a post-shelter survey approximately four months after leaving the shelter, thus providing the opportunity for tangible financial benefits to all shelter residents. In addition, the evaluation grant funded a Project Manager (PM) who handled the day-to-day operations of the study, thereby relieving the shelter staff of most research tasks and demonstrating respect for their time and work priorities. The PM also served as a liaison between the shelter and the TH programme. Prior to the evaluation, farm and shelter staff had to recruit residents to work in the farm programme; during the evaluation, the PM recruited farm participants. Future potential benefits were considered as well; one of the primary goals of the evaluation was to provide the shelter administration and staff with empirical data that demonstrate the efficacy of the TH programme so that the organisation can leverage the findings to obtain sustainable funding for the programme going forward. We turn now to further discussion of the evaluation's goals, research questions, and objectives.

## *Goals, research questions, and objectives*

To determine the therapeutic and functional outcomes of participation in a TH programme during IPV victims' stay at a domestic violence shelter, our first research question was: if shelter residents participate in a TH programme that involves "working the land and being in nature" (e.g., preparing beds, planting, watering, mulching, and harvesting) *in addition to* their participation in standard therapeutic programming offered by the shelter, to what extent do they experience greater psychological and physical benefits compared with shelter residents who have no involvement in the TH programme (see Figure 47.1)? Our objective was to measure whether TH participants working in an additional six-week, 60-hour outdoor programme over and above standard therapeutic programming demonstrated significantly greater improvement than non-participating women (i.e., women receiving only the standard therapeutic programming offered by the shelter) on mental health indicators (decreased anxiety and depression), cognitive functioning (focused attention, planning, decreased rumination), self-view (self-esteem, self-acceptance), self-sufficiency and efficacy, social functioning (increased interaction, sense of belonging, increased self-disclosure), and financial efficacy (increased financial knowledge, increased financial management skills) during their shelter stay. We also wished to determine whether IPV victims in a TH programme experienced greater benefits in particular outcomes compared with other outcomes. Because it is possible that particular outcomes might be more evident, especially following six weeks of involvement in TH, we also assessed the relative benefits experienced by TH participants on the hypothesised outcomes.

To determine if any demonstrated benefits from participating in a TH programme during the women's shelter stay were sustained *after leaving the shelter*, our second research question was: are hypothesised therapeutic and functional outcomes among women who participated in the TH programme compared with women who had no TH involvement while residing at the shelter still evident *following* their shelter stay? In other words, does TH participation have lasting

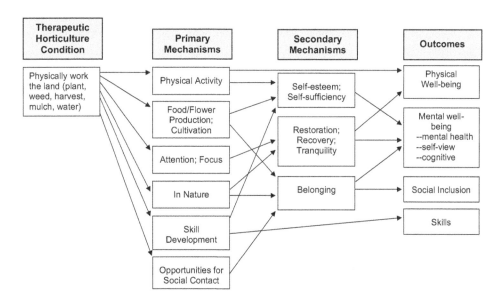

*Figure 47.1*   Model of hypothesised mechanisms and outcomes resulting from engagement in therapeutic horticulture

beneficial effects that are not only evident in the outcomes measured during shelter residency, but also potentially in lifestyle changes post-shelter, such as *positive changes in employment* and/or *intimate relationship status*? To answer this second research question, women who participated in the TH programme during their shelter stay were assessed three months after leaving the shelter in order to gauge the impact of the TH programme on the hypothesised therapeutic and functional outcomes as well as their employment and relationship status.

## Research design and methodology: experimental vs. quasi-experimental

Experimental studies, such as randomised controlled trials (RCTs), are frequently referred to as the "gold standard" for assessing causality in evaluations of clinical interventions (Handley, Lyles, McCulloch, & Cattamanchi, 2018). In experimental designs such as RCTs, individuals are *randomly* assigned to either the intervention/treatment group or the non-intervention/standard care/placebo/control group, which minimises selection bias and increases the likelihood that any measured and unmeasured confounding variables are distributed equally between the two groups. Consequently, the researchers can be more confident that any observed differences between the treatment group and the control group in terms of the outcomes being measured are the result of the intervention they are evaluating (Handley et al., 2018; Mildner, 2019). In many "real-world" settings, however, experimental methods such as RCTs are not feasible due to practical, ethical, and legal concerns. For instance, the farm programme at the battered women's shelter where we conducted our evaluation had been added to a menu of long-standing services and was underway before we established our researcher-practitioner partnership. We could not redesign the programme and roll it out according to our own specifications. In addition, we could not ethically deny women who wished to participate in what could be a beneficial intervention, the opportunity to do so. Furthermore, Kentucky, like many states, has enacted regulations that prohibit shelters and other agencies from forcing or requiring women who have experienced abuse to do any work or participate in programming, so as not to recreate the controlling environment in which they lived with their abusive partners (Kulkarni, Bell, & Rhodes, 2012).

In light of these practical and ethical constraints, we chose a quasi-experimental design that allowed us to use comparison groups to determine whether shelter residents who participated in a standardised TH experience of working the land and being in nature (the TH Programme Condition) showed greater improvement in hypothesised outcomes than women shelter residents who had no involvement in the TH programme (Non-TH or Control Condition). This design allowed us to compare women with and without the TH component added to the shelter's standard interventions over time using repeated measures during their shelter stay. Shelter residents *self-selected* into the TH Programme Condition or the Control Condition, or they could choose to participate in neither, a point to which we will return shortly.

All study participants completed a pre-test survey approximately one week after entering the shelter, and a post-test survey after they had resided at the shelter for about four months, at which time it was expected that women who had subsequently volunteered to participate in the farm project would have completed the 60-hour programme. A post-shelter assessment was conducted about three months after participants left the shelter. This assessment consisted of the same measures administered during the first two surveys, but also included items regarding employment and intimate relationship status and satisfaction.

To standardise the "dosage" of the TH component so that participants did not spend different amounts of time working on the farm, the TH programme was structured to engage participants in relatively similar outdoor activities of "working the land" over a six-week period (approximately ten hours a week for a total of 60 hours) for which they received a stipend. Thus, there is a measurable "dose" of TH: all TH programme participants engage in comparable farming tasks for a specified number of hours. Even though study participants were not randomised into the TH and Non-TH Conditions, we did not expect the two groups to differ significantly in terms of key demographic variables. We did collect demographic data to allow us to make this determination empirically. At the research design stage, however, we examined demographic data for residents that had been collected by shelter staff in years prior to the start of the TH evaluation, and these data showed that a third of the shelter's residents were married to the IPV perpetrator, only 28% were employed before coming to the shelter, and only 18% were over the age of 45.

## Outcome variable assessment

### Identical assessments for both intervention and control participants

Participants were assessed using both quantitative and qualitative methods to obtain objective and subjective information, respectively, and to triangulate participants' self-reports with data from other sources. First, quantitative measures, covering the range of physical, psychological, and functional variables we discussed earlier, were completed by both intervention and control participants at three points in time. These surveys included a small number of qualitative items as well. Second, shelter staff responsible for client intake provided initial ratings of intervention and control participants within a week of their arrival at the shelter. These ratings assessed participants' functioning at that time along with factors (e.g., initial stress and trauma levels, resilience, reporting styles) that could potentially confound research results. The intake ratings paralleled the factors measured by the scales on the surveys participants completed. Third, staff also completed ratings of all intervention and control participants at the time of the post-test survey administration (approximately three to four months into their shelter stay). These ratings paralleled the initial ratings by staff at intake, but were completed by participants' case workers who had primary contact with the women during their stay and, therefore, were in the best position to report on participants' functioning at the time of the post-test.

### Additional assessment for TH participants

Assessment of participants' experiences in the farm project was needed to understand whether participants perceived the TH programme in the way we hypothesised. In addition, we wanted to know if there were differences in these perceptions among participants and, if so, whether these differential perceptions could help us understand differential outcomes among the participants should we find any. Again, we used mixed methods for assessing the TH experience, but each method collected data to assess the range of potential impacts (e.g., a sense of belonging, a sense of accomplishment, a sense of peacefulness; see Figure 47.1). First, semi-structured interviews were conducted with participants to allow them to assess their subjective experiences of the farm project in their own words. Second, additional measures specific to the TH experience (e.g., Perceived Restorativeness Scale, Therapeutic Factors Inventory) were included in the post-test survey to obtain TH participants' self-reported quantitative assessments of the hypothesised impacts of TH. And third, farm personnel provided independent ratings of participants to assess the *physical* farm experience (e.g., use of tools, type of farming task, weather) and each participant's reaction to the farming (e.g., showed motivation and drive, took responsibility for a task, indicated or expressed pleasure in the work).

## Procedure

In this section, we describe how the mix-methods evaluation unfolded from one stage to the next to show how the design and methods were implemented over the course of the study.

### Solicitation and pre-testing of research participants

The project manager introduced the opportunity to participate in a research study to new shelter residents approximately five days after they arrived at the shelter. Women were not approached immediately after arrival in order to give them protected time to orient and adjust to their new living arrangements, and also because about nearly 13% (about one in eight) women who enter a shelter leave within a week. The PM explained her role to potential participants as the person running a research study titled "Women's Shelter Experiences" for the local university to assure them that the study was separate from the shelter and that their decision to participate in the study would not affect their shelter stay and their ability to receive services. There was no mention of evaluating the farm (TH) programme because, at that stage, women were not being solicited into the TH programme and we wished to reduce demand characteristics for the women completing the surveys.

Women who enrolled in the study were given instructions for completing the baseline survey on a dedicated computer located in a private office at the shelter after the Informed Consent (IC) document was reviewed with them. They were informed about the Privacy Certificate from the Office on Violence Against Women (OVW, US Department of Justice) that protects participants from disclosure of their self-report. The PM read survey items to participants who needed help reading, but women recorded their own responses on the computer. Spanish speakers were provided a Spanish translation of the survey, if they preferred it. At the time of the pre-test, the PM also obtained contact information for participants' family or friends who could help us locate them after their shelter stay to complete the post-shelter assessment.

### Post-testing procedures for all participants

When women enrolled in the study, they were told they would complete two surveys during their shelter stay and one after they left the shelter, and they would be compensated for each one. As noted, the second survey was completed by all participants approximately three to four months after they entered the shelter. The timing of the post-test was based on several factors: (1) women who chose to also participate in the TH programme had typically completed that aspect of the study by this time; (2) women who stay at the shelter longer than four months are often employed or have other responsibilities that preclude them from working on the farm; and (3) only a small percentage of women live at the shelter for more than six months. Women enrolled in the study who left before completing the second survey (the post-test) were contacted to ask if they were still willing to complete it and, if so, arrangements were made for them to do so conveniently and privately and to be compensated. All study participants were contacted for the post-shelter survey approximately three months after they left the shelter.

## Solicitation of the participants for the TH programme

Within two weeks of completing the pre-test, all residents who had enrolled in the study were approached by the PM to invite them to participate in the TH programme, unless shelter staff indicated a reason for exclusion from this aspect of the study (e.g., health problems, problem pregnancy). Thus, all women who initially enrolled in the study were eligible to also participate in the farm programme with only a few exceptions. The parameters of the farm programme were explained as a six-week, 60-hour commitment (i.e., ten hours of farm work per week) for which they would receive a stipend; if they completed the full six weeks, they would receive a bonus of an additional week's pay. They were also asked to consent to a 30-minute interview at the end of their six-week commitment, which, as we discussed, was designed to understand their subjective experiences of the TH programme. This interview provided additional compensation for participation. The transcribed interviews were analysed using a grounded theory approach; NVivo software was used to identify content and themes related to farm involvement and participants' perceptions of TH impacts. The deidentified interview data are expected to be useful to shelter staff in future planning to enhance the therapeutic benefits of the farm programme.

## Nonrandomisation

As noted previously, shelter residents were not randomised into the TH programme for practical, ethical, and legal reasons; they chose whether or not to work on the farm once they enrolled in the study. In our interviews preliminary to the evaluation, shelter staff reported that in the past, women who volunteered to work on the farm had varied motivations (e.g., desire or need to earn money, alleviation of boredom, distraction from worries or cravings, prior experience or interest in gardening). Our analysis plan for the quantitative data, however, included identifying any differences between TH participants and other shelter residents, which would then require statistical adjustments. Here again we see one of the benefits of a mixed-methods design: qualitative interview data informed later quantitative data analysis.

Despite careful planning and efforts to ensure programme fidelity, conducting research in the field – in this case, on site at a shelter for batted women – poses some significant challenges. These are discussed in the next section.

## Addressing challenges

As we have stated, a mixed-methods, quasi-experimental design offers researchers interested in evaluating programmes for at-risk populations, including domestic violence and abuse victims, the ability to gather quantitative data that can bolster programme validity, while also capturing situational context and subjective perceptions through descriptive qualitative data. Such was the case with our TH programme evaluation, but despite having a well-thought-out research design and a strong researcher-practitioner partnership, several challenges arose once the study got underway.

Not surprisingly, data collection at a shelter can be difficult. The nature of everyday work and life at a domestic violence shelter is not necessarily ideal for collecting time-sensitive data. Shelters are crisis-response organisations, so while stability for residents is obviously a major shelter goal, staff are often operating in crisis mode and tasks associated with a research study will have low priority. For example, although shelter staff knew that their role in the study was to provide short ratings of residents shortly after they arrived at the shelter and again when they left, this task often was not completed in a timely manner. The need to quickly respond to crises meant that staff sometimes forgot or put off completing the ratings. The data collection plan called for ratings to be done within a week of a participant's arrival and within a week on either end of a participant's exit from the shelter; these timelines were inconsistently met, posing threats to the quality of the data. Often, the PM would gently remind staff about the ratings, wanting to maintain a positive working relationship with them and respect the immediacy of the other tasks to which they must attend, while also reiterating the importance of data collection for the future of the TH programme.

The shelter at which our evaluation was conducted is relatively large with approximately 40 staff members in-house and off-site, and the shelter operates in a more egalitarian way than most businesses and government agencies. Staff are trusted to use their judgement, develop their own processes, and implement programming as they see fit. Consequently, if staff members see something they think needs to be changed, they will change it, frequently with little or no communication with other shelter staff or administrators, much less the researchers. This poses potential problems for the evaluation because the research protocol was developed around the programmes, policies, and procedures that were in place when the grant was written. Staff, however, are not thinking about how a change in programming might affect the research; their primary concern is how a change will affect clients, who, after all, are their raison d'être. Occasionally, then, programmatic changes with the potential to impact the validity of the study would occur without any notice to the researchers. In these situations, a type of mutual education about the critical issues – both client- and research-related – had to occur. Owing largely to the strong partnership between the researchers and the staff, this was accomplished through meetings with the associate director of the shelter, who had operational authority, and specific staff members, as appropriate. This method of troubleshooting preserved the integrity of the evaluation, but also ensured that the needs of shelter staff and residents were met. It also provided opportunities for shelter staff to offer feedback on how they felt the evaluation was progressing, thereby reinforcing the collaborative relationship between the staff and the researchers.

The life circumstances of the research population may also give rise to unanticipated challenges. While there are commonalities among survivors in the shelter, each arrives with some unique circumstances, barriers, and skillsets. In recent years, shelter staff have been reporting that many women arrive at the shelter with a substance use disorder. Kentucky has been particularly hard hit by the opioid crisis that has swept through the United States, and shelter staff estimate that 80–90% of women who now stay at the shelter have a substance use problem of varying severity. Residents' substance use problems can affect the evaluation research in multiple ways, including interference with residents' ability to complete the surveys and interviews accurately and coherently, their failure to arrive on time or at all for work on the farm, their ability to execute farm tasks safely and efficiently, and their ability to follow the study guidelines. Drug and alcohol use, of course, is prohibited at the shelter, but residents have the freedom to come and go largely at will, so staff cannot control the women's substance use outside of the shelter. In this study, some residents whose shelter stays were complicated by substance use problems nevertheless completed the full six-week TH programme, but many left shortly thereafter and did not complete their post-test surveys nor provide reliable follow-up contact information, making it difficult, if not impossible, to locate them.

Shelter residents may also have undiagnosed, untreated, or unacknowledged mental health disorders. Mental health disorders did not always interfere with shelter residents' ability to participate in and complete the farm project, or participate in the control group. However, residents' mental health problems did affect the evaluation in at least two ways. First, shelter staff became aware *after* some residents enrolled in the study as a control or TH programme partici-pant that they did not come to the shelter to escape intimate partner violence, but rather to get help with their mental health issues and/or homelessness. This was problematic for the evalu-ation because the study was designed to measure the effects of the TH programme on women who have experienced IPV. The TH programme may well be beneficial for those living at the shelter for other reasons, but unfortunately, that was not one of the aims of the study at the time. In these cases, the participants' data were not used in the analysis. A second way that residents' mental health problems affected the evaluation was that they manifested or worsened after arriv-ing at the shelter and enrolling in the study, making it no longer safe or feasible for them to continue their study participation. In these instances, a note was made in the participants' data files regarding when and why they were withdrawn from the study.

The research team, associate director, and shelter staff addressed these challenges as they arose. Staff, in fact, suggested a variety of workable solutions in light of their practice experi-ence. For instance, staff encouraged residents to use their income from the farm project to open an Individual Development Account (IDA)[3] or to make a financial plan for how they would like to use the money, with the goal of reducing the likelihood that the money would be used to buy drugs or alcohol. Staff also encouraged participants to develop relapse prevention plans, receive intensive outpatient treatment, or join a support programme such as Alcoholics Anonymous or Narcotics Anonymous.

The PM addressed data attrition challenges in several ways as well. For instance, she regularly attended case review meetings, where clients' individual circumstances and staff concerns about specific clients were discussed in detail. She postponed inviting residents to enrol in the study until after case review, since then she would have a better sense of residents' actual eligibility and suitability for study participation. Case review was also helpful for learning from staff which study participants were close to leaving the shelter. The PM would subsequently follow up with those participants to ensure they completed the post-test survey before leaving. In addition, she began to obtain residents' post-tests as soon as possible after they completed the farm project, even if they were expected to reside at the shelter well beyond programme completion, in order to reduce the number of participants' who left without completing the post-test survey.

Attrition and retention are common concerns when data collection occurs over an extended period of time at a field site. In our study, attrition sometimes occurred for positive reasons. For example, some study participants secured stable housing, which allowed them to leave the shelter sooner than expected. Other participants withdrew from the study because they obtained full-time employment. Still others decided to seek in-patient treatment for substance use disorders. Despite the fact that these women had to drop out of the study before complet-ing all the quantitative and qualitative measures (i.e., missing data), we appreciated these positive outcomes. But attrition also occurred for many other reasons. Study participants sometimes left the shelter sooner than expected because they were arrested, overdosed, posed a severe safety threat to other shelter residents, or they returned to their abusive partners.

Among the participants who did complete the pre-test and post-test surveys, there were nonetheless obstacles to completing the final post-shelter survey. Often, residents arrived at the shelter without a reliable phone number, and members of their social networks, includ-ing their emergency contacts, were also frequently without reliable phone numbers. Study participants who left unexpectedly sometimes had not shared their contact information or that of their social network members with staff or the PM despite having been asked to do so when they enrolled in the study. Consequently, locating these participants for the final sur-vey administration proved difficult. Occasionally, participants had provided an email address, but emails sent by the PM to participants went unanswered or "bounced" because of invalid addresses. If phone numbers, emergency contacts, and email were unsuccessful in locating a participant, the PM turned to social media sites such as Facebook to contact them. The PM used Facebook's messenger feature, for example, to locate several participants and to schedule them to complete their post-shelter survey. Clearly, persistence and resourcefulness on the part of researchers are needed for successful data collection, be it quantitative or qualitative, in these types of studies.

Additional barriers to residents' participation in the farm project included physical disabilities, pregnancy, and lack of child care during TH programme hours. To address inclusion of women with disabilities, the research team met with the farm manager, farm activities director, and associate director of the shelter to discuss the possibility of an accessible alternative to the farm project that still maintained the principal components of TH. Unfortunately, neither the budget nor staff capacity allowed for this. For pregnant women, their doctor's written approval was required for participation in the farm project. And for women with young children who either were not school-age or were on summer recess, the researchers implemented a volunteer programme in which university students provided on-site child care while mothers participated in the TH programme.

Some of the challenges that arose during this evaluation had relatively simple solutions, while others required that some ingenuity and compromise be applied, and still others had no feasible solution. In an effort to help gauge the impact that various problems may have on the reliability and validity of our findings, the PM kept detailed field notes stemming from her interactions with residents, conversations with staff, and information disclosed during case review. These field notes were indispensable for identifying potential confounders in our quantitative data, but also served as additional qualitative data points that help us explain our findings, offering a further illustration of integration in mixed-methods research.

## Conclusion

In sum, although the TH evaluation discussed in this chapter presented a variety of research challenges – many of which were unanticipated when the study began – the benefits of the researcher-practitioner partnership and the value of the data collected using mixed methods in a quasi-experimental design strongly motivated us to develop workable, if not perfect, solutions. The combination of qualitative interviews and field observations and note-taking add depth to and enrich our quantitative measures. We anticipate that the study's findings will not only make a significant contribution to the literature on therapeutic services for victims of domestic violence and abuse as well as research methodology and therapeutic horticulture more broadly, but also impact policy and practice, especially for shelter service providers considering the development of a therapeutic horticulture programme.

## Critical findings

- Mixed methods may yield not only more data, but also richer findings that give a fuller picture of a complex phenomenon, such as domestic violence and sexual assault, and more nuanced answers to research questions.
- Because a mixed-methods approach typically requires the researcher to invest considerably more time and resources than required for a single method approach, the researcher must have a sound rationale for using multiple methods in a study and must also take care to integrate these methods, rather than simply using them in an additive fashion.

- There are three major reasons for using mixed methods: (1) the value of sequential contributions, (2) the desire for additional coverage, and (3) the need for convergent findings (i.e., triangulation). These reasons are not mutually exclusive.
- Although an experimental design, particularly the randomised controlled trial (RCT), is widely considered the "gold standard" for programme evaluation, experiments may not be feasible in many "real-world" settings, such as a battered women's shelter, because of practical, ethical, or legal concerns. In such settings, a quasi-experimental design is more feasible. One type of quasi-experimental design allows participants to self-select into the intervention/treatment condition or the Control Condition (or neither), and researchers then compare the outcomes of the intervention/treatment group with those of the control group to assess the extent to which the intervention/treatment had an effect.

## Implications for policy, practice, and research

- A quasi-experimental mixed-methods design is useful for evaluating programmes in the "real-world" setting of a battered women's shelter, where the ongoing day-to-day operation of the shelter requires that responding to the needs of women in crisis takes primacy over other issues and activities.
- Researchers and practitioners seeking to evaluate the effects of a specific programme or intervention can benefit from developing a truly collaborative researcher-practitioner partnership. Among the benefits of this partnership to researchers are: (1) the development of better research questions and the measures to answer them; (2) improved access to the population of interest; and (3) help in establishing trust in the researchers by potential research participants, which, in turn, promotes study enrolment and retention. Among the benefits of this partnership to practitioners are: (1) findings that can be used to develop tangible and timely policy and programming recommendations, (2) tangible financial and resource benefits to both the organisation and clients (e.g., improved financial stability for clients through monetary payments for participation), and (3) development of research skills to sustain evaluation of a programme beyond the study period.
- Although a quasi-experimental evaluation of a shelter programme poses several challenges to the validity of the research, there are ways to address these that minimise their potentially negative impact. A key to this is developing a strong researcher-practitioner partnership that allows for ongoing problem-solving, such as mutual education meetings. These meetings help preserve the integrity of the evaluation, ensure that the needs of staff and clients/residents are met, and provide opportunities for staff to offer feedback on the evaluation, which further strengthens the collaborative nature of the project.

## Notes

1 This study was funded through a grant (Award #2016-SI-AX-0002) from the Office on Violence Against Women (OVW), US Department of Justice (DOJ). Opinions expressed in the chapter are those of the authors alone.
2 Testa et al.'s (2011) study also illustrates the sequential contributions motivation, since the initial survey was used to identify potential participants for the qualitative interview stage of the study.
3 An Individual Development Account (IDA) is a savings account specifically for people with low incomes and assets. Money saved in an IDA is matched, usually at a ratio of 2:1 or 3:1, with funds donated by government, private businesses, and local community-based organizations (VAWnet, n.d.).

# References

Campbell, R., Patterson, D., & Bybee, D. (2011). Using mixed methods to evaluate community intervention for sexual assault survivors: A methodological tale. *Violence Against Women*, *17*(3), 376–388. doi:10.1177/1077801211398622

Denzin, N. K., & Lincoln, Y. S. (Eds.). (2017). *The SAGE handbook of qualitative research* (5th ed.). Thousand Oaks, CA: Sage.

Edleson, J. L., & Bible, A. L. (1998). *Forced bonding or community collaboration? Partnerships between science and practice in research.* (NCJ 176979). Washington, DC: National Institute of Justice, Office of Justice Programs, US Department of Justice.

Gondolf, E. W. (2010). The contributions of Ellen Pence to batterer programming. *Violence Against Women*, *16*(9), 992–1006. doi:10.1177/1077801210379330

Handley, M. A., Lyles, C. R., McCulloch, C., & Cattamanchi, A. (2018). Selecting and improving quasi-experimental designs in effectiveness and implementation research. *Annual Review of Public Health*, *39*, 5–25. doi:10.1146/annurev-publhealth-040617-014128

Kaye, G. (1990). A community organizer's perspective on citizen participation research and the researcher-practitioner partnership. *American Journal of Community Psychology*, *18*(1), 151–157.

Koss, M. P., Gidycz, C. A., & Wisniewski, N. (1987). The scope of rape: Incidence and prevalence of sexual aggression and victimization in a national sample of higher education students. *Journal of Consulting and Clinical Psychology*, *55*, 162–170.

Kulkarni, S. H., Bell, H., & Rhodes, D. M. (2012). Back to basics: Essential qualities of services for survivors of intimate partner violence. *Violence Against Women*, *18*(1), 85–101. doi:10.1177/1077801212437137

Lincoln, Y. S., & Guba, E. G. (1985). *Naturalistic inquiry*. Beverly Hills, CA: Sage.

Mildner, V. (2019). Experimental research. In J. S. Damico & M. J. Ball (Eds.), *The SAGE encyclopedia of human communication sciences and disorders* (pp. 728–732). Thousand Oaks, CA: Sage. doi:10.4135/9781483380810.n242

Miles, M. B., Huberman, A. M., & Saldana, J. (2019). *Qualitative data analysis: A methods sourcebook* (4th ed.). Thousand Oaks, CA: Sage.

Morgan, D. J. (2014). *Integrating qualitative and quantitative methods: A pragmatic approach*. Thousand Oaks, CA: Sage.

Noonan, R. K., & Charles, D. (2009). Developing teen dating violence prevention strategies: Formative research with middle school youth. *Violence Against Women*, *15*, 1087–1105.

Renzetti, C. M., & Follingstad, D. R. (2015). From blue to green: The development and implementation of a therapeutic horticulture program for residents of a battered women's shelter. *Violence and Victims*, *30*(4), 676–689. doi:10:1891/0886-6708.VV-D-14-00091

Riger, S. (1999). Working together: Challenges in collaborative research on violence against women. *Violence Against Women*, *5*(10), 1099–1117.

Sullivan, T. P., Price, C., McPartland, T., Hunter, B. A., & Fisher, B. S. (2017). The researcher-practitioner partnership study (RPPS): Experiences from criminal justice system collaborations studying violence against women. *Violence Against Women*, *23*(7), 887–907. doi:10.1177/1077801216650290

Tashakkori, A., & Teddlie, C. (Eds.). (2010). *The SAGE handbook of mixed methods in social and behavioral research* (2nd ed.). Thousand Oaks, CA: Sage.

Testa, M., Livington, J. A., & VanZile-Tamsen, C. (2011). Advancing the study of violence against women using mixed methods: Integrating qualitative methods into a quantitative research program. *Violence Against Women*, *17*(2), 236–250. doi:10.1177/1077801210397744

VAWnet. (n.d.). *Individual development accounts*. Harrisburg, PA: National Resource Center on Domestic Violence. Retrieved from https://vawnet.org/sc/individual-development-accounts

# 48

# QUANTITATIVE METHODS FOR RESEARCHING DOMESTIC VIOLENCE AND ABUSE

*Christopher J. Wretman, Cynthia Fraga Rizo, Sandra L. Martin and Lawrence L. Kupper*

## What are quantitative methods?

Quantitative methods are increasingly being used by researchers to examine research questions related to domestic violence and abuse (DVA). These methods represent an interconnected family of approaches all united by one key attribute: numerical data. Quantitative research is, thus, fundamentally *numerically focused* and founded upon the collection and statistical analysis of such data. Quantitative methods are widely used to plan, conduct, analyze, interpret, and disseminate research to inform social change.

A particular strength of quantitative research is that the comparability of numerical results across samples, settings, and time frames lends the evidence generated to be potentially generalizable beyond individual research studies (Rubin & Babbie, 2016). As a result, quantitative methods manifest in research processes that focus on deductive reasoning, predetermined criteria and guidelines, and the creation of evidence that can be generalizable to other populations and settings (Creswell, 2017; McDavid, Huse, & Hawthorn, 2018; Saunders, 2015).

Without question, quantitative approaches are increasingly being embraced both for what they represent and, perhaps more importantly, for the two valuable outputs they can produce: (a) processes that are reproducible; and, (b) results that can be comparable. Such processes and results are not only intrinsically desirable and held in high esteem by quantitative researchers, but are becoming increasingly valued externally by stakeholders in the effort to build evidence that can affect widespread social change. If it can be confidently said that, within a DVA research study, a program/intervention/service was validly and precisely determined to produce a positive change to an outcome, and the evidence has been distilled into numerical results that can be understood by others, then that research stands on solid ground to inform future practice, policy, and research endeavors.

An important point should be made here. For as much as is made about the difficulty in conducting quantitative research, which increasingly requires advanced statistical expertise, one overarching goal attendant when conducting quantitative methods is simplicity. Distilling the findings of a multi-faceted research study down to a few valid and precise numerical conclusions can make for ease of understanding and interpretation. Stating, for example, that female survivors of violence had depression scores after participating in a program that were "3.88 points lower" than at program entry (Rizo, Wretman, Macy, Guo, & Ermentrout, 2018, p. 7) is a concise way of emphasizing a particular finding. Simple numerical-based statements are powerful tools that can often be understood and utilized by stakeholders in positions of power. Overall, there is much to be said for numerically quantifying results in a manner to make them useful for future practice, policy, and research endeavours.

## Chapter overview

The goal of this chapter is to provide a non-technical overview of quantitative methods for DVA research so that researchers can enhance: (1) their understanding of the value of quantitative research, (2) their skills as quantitative researchers, and (3) the validity and utility of their quantitatively focused research projects. Although conducting valid quantitative DVA research must entail very particular attention to a research study's design (e.g., research questions, sampling plans, data collection), this chapter will largely focus on quantitative data analysis methods and the interpretation of the numerical results produced from these methods.

The chapter is divided into two main sections. In the "Discussion and Analysis" section, a variety of quantitative methods will be discussed. Alongside a discussion of broad uses of quantitative methods for DVA research, the text will also briefly mention some technical points and reference published quantitative research examples for the reader. In the "Conclusions" section, important findings will be summarized and implications for practice, policy, and research will be highlighted.

## Discussion and analysis

Almost all statistical analyses, no matter how straightforward or how complicated, result in the computation of p-values and confidence intervals (CIs), the goal being to assess the *statistical significance* of research findings. P-values and CIs are computed using test statistics that involve estimates of population parameters (e.g., means, variances, correlations, regression coefficients) and their estimated standard errors. A p-value is strictly defined as the probability of observing a test statistic at least as extreme as the one actually observed, assuming that the null hypothesis under consideration is true and also assuming that the statistical model being used is valid. Crucially, this framework includes all attendant statistical assumptions and the use of reliable data. The importance of the assumption about model validity is generally not appreciated by many researchers. If this assumption is violated, the validity of any statistical finding is severely compromised. Unfortunately, for decades, it has been a standard but dubious practice to assume that p-values smaller than 0.05 in value provide valid statistical evidence of important research findings. In reality, many scholars have highlighted the many problems with relying solely on p-values, including misunderstandings of what p-values actually mean and of what can easily go wrong with their use (e.g., Branch, 2014; Greenland et al., 2016; Wasserman & Lazar, 2016). In particular, a small p-value could be due to the null hypothesis being false, to violations of assumptions made about the statistical model, and to problems with the data being used to fit the statistical model (e.g., selection bias, recall bias, misclassification, measurement error, missing data). Moreover, a large p-value does not justify the conclusion that the null hypothesis being considered is true.

Fortunately, in recent years, most research disciplines have moved away from relying solely on p-values, as evidenced by the revised publication policies of almost all respected research journals for such disciplines. More and more, confidence intervals (CIs) are a required component of all research articles accepted for publication. An approximate 95% CI has a random lower limit and a random upper limit, with the probability being roughly 0.95 that the true value of the unknown parameter of interest (e.g., a mean, the difference between two means, a correlation, a regression coefficient) is contained within this random interval. Once the data are used to compute numerical values for these lower and upper limits, the probability is either zero or one that the unknown parameter value is contained in the computed CI. Thus, a CI gives a reasonable and informative idea of the precision with which an important parameter is being estimated. In general, assuming that valid numerical information is being used correctly, the shorter the width of the computed CI, the more precisely the parameter of interest is being estimated.

Finally, it is important to mention that there can be a considerable difference between a statistically significant finding and a *meaningful* finding. As a simple example, suppose that a DVA research study is designed to compare two treatments for depression, with the key variable for each study subject being the change in a depression score from pre-treatment to post-treatment. The statistical parameter of interest would be the difference between the true (or population) average change score for each treatment group. The null hypothesis would be that this true average change score difference is equal to zero, and the two-sided alternative hypothesis would be that this true average change score difference is not equal to zero. Suppose that the data consist of large numbers of subjects in each treatment group. If the true average change score difference is not much different from zero, implying an unimportant practical finding, the large sample sizes would almost guarantee a statistically significant result (e.g., a small p-value and a CI not enclosing the null value of zero). In fact, studies with very large sample sizes almost always guarantee some statistically significant findings, even when most such findings have no practical relevance.

## Typologies of quantitative analysis

Quantitative approaches can be categorized in various ways. Two different typologies for characterizing quantitative methods include: (1) a purpose-focused typology and (2) a statistically focused typology.

The *purpose-focused* typology characterizes quantitative analyses as (1) descriptive or (2) explanatory. In other words, this framework asks "What do we want to do with our analyses?" A study by Lepistö and colleagues (2011), for example, was purely descriptive and focused on describing the experiences of different types of domestic violence among adolescents in Finland. The entire framing, implementation, and reporting of the study's details were descriptive, and the results thus focused primarily on prevalence rates. In contrast, the article by Hasan and colleagues (2014) employed a mixed methods strategy using both qualitative and quantitative methods to examine the physical and psychological suffering of Bangladesh women experiencing violence and their various coping strategies, focusing primarily on teasing out potential causal/explanatory mechanisms and pathways. Both studies were highly valuable contributions to the field, but with different purposes.

Alternatively, the *statistically focused* typology categorizes quantitative methods as comprising (1) univariate, (2) bivariate, and (3) multivariable analyses examining 1, 2, and $\geq 3$ variables, respectively. Conceptualizing one's quantitative methods in such a way is thus akin to asking "What information are we working with for our analyses?" Thinking in terms of the number of variables, and their nature, happens to be crucially important in choosing, implementing, and reporting the numerical results derived from quantitative methods. Perhaps somewhat differently than the purpose-focused typology described earlier, such variable-focused methods are almost always used in concert with one another. In fact, statistically focused analyses of this sort typically build on each other such that univariate analyses inform bivariate ones which, in turn, inform subsequent multivariable methods – typically considered to be the most definitive results presented in a quantitative DVA research article.

## Fundamentals of quantitative methods

Four components are part of any quantitative approach: (1) basic statistics related to measures of centre and spread, (2) the dependent versus independent variable framework, (3) the concept of association, and (4) levels of measurement. Each component will now be briefly reviewed.

Basic statistics for centre and spread are numerical values that help to *characterize* the sample distribution of a variable. Measures of centre, commonly the mean, median, and mode, are numerical estimates designed to determine a variable's central tendency (Weisberg, 1992). In other words, these measures seek to answer the question "What is the average or typical value for this variable among the observations in this sample?" This value can be interpreted as a measure of central tendency for that variable, a number that is the first step towards describing the sample distribution of the variable and can be seen in a published DVA research article as something akin to a statement like "the mean age for the subjects in the sample was 21.4 years." On the other hand, measures of spread determine the variability of a set of observations, asking the question "How spread out from the centre are observed values for this variable in this sample?" One simple measure of the spread of a variable is its "range," defined as the maximum observed value of the variable minus the minimum observed value of the variable. Note that the range would include all observed values of the variable, some of which might be quite extreme and represent outliers that may not be representative of a reasonable value for the variable under consideration due to coding errors and other problems. Once totally unreasonable or erroneous values of a variable are validly eliminated, the most appropriate measure of spread is the sample variance or its square root, the sample standard deviation. If a histogram of the variable under consideration suggests approximate normality (i.e., a bell-shaped histogram roughly symmetric about the sample mean), then the range of values of the variable from one sample standard deviation less than the sample mean to one sample standard deviation greater than the sample mean would very roughly encompass just over 68% of all the observed values of the variable. An estimate of spread like the sample standard deviation should always accompany one for central tendency (e.g., sample mean) and can be seen as something akin to a statement like "the standard deviation for age was 6.3." One very important thing to remember is that variables with large spread (e.g., large sample variances) can compromise the precision of statistical analyses involving these variables and so adversely affect the power of a study to identify important relationships.

Defining a variable as either dependent (i.e., related to the outcome) or independent (i.e., related to prediction of the outcome) seeks to position these variables in relation to one another. By specifying a variable Y as a dependent variable, a decision that is almost always made prior to any statistical analyses, one is effectively stating that variation in Y might be at least partially explained by variation in the independent variable X. It is important to note that the positing of variables as either dependent or independent can depend on the context in which they are studied and that different DVA studies can define the same variable as being either dependent or independent as dictated by the research questions being addressed. In the study by Rizo and colleagues (2018) noted earlier, program participation was posited to be the independent variable of interest, with depression being the dependent variable, such that the research question addressed whether participation in the program reduced depression levels. One could just as validly flip the research question to focus on program participation (e.g., perhaps it is low or inconsistent across time) by asking a research question regarding whether participants' depression reduces program participation. These two scenarios outline two different research questions using the same two variables in different ways.

Simply put, quantifying a relationship between two variables X and Y involves examining: (1) a measure of association (i.e., negative, neutral, positive), (2) the strength of that association (i.e., small, moderate, large), and (3) a statistical inference (i.e., statistically significant, not statistically significant). As an example, if it can be confidently stated that the results of a DVA study determined that participation in a program, intervention, approach, or other purposive initiative under study (X = Program participation: 0 = No, 1 = Yes) was statistically significantly linked to a positive change on some defined outcome (Y = Positive outcome change: 0 = No, 1 =Yes), it can then be claimed, with some caution, that X may have caused a positive change in Y.

There exist broad types, or *levels*, of measurement for variables in DVA research. Typically, these levels can be grouped into a typology comprising: (1) nominal, (2) ordinal, and (3) continuous designations (Weisberg, 1992). *Nominal* variables, considered the least informative or most crude, are simple groupings of response options without any order or ranking; an example would be "Shelter services = 1, Legal advocacy = 2, Crisis services = 3," where numbers are used out of statistical necessity for computer coding purposes but have no real meaning. *Ordinal* variables are also simple groupings but with the additional component of a ranking to categories such as "Disagree = 1, Neutral = 2, Agree = 3." The numbers 1, 2, 3 reflect the ordinal ranking of these three categories, but it could be a serious mistake to use these numbers directly in a statistical analysis since they assume equally spaced effects. *Continuous* variables, meanwhile, take the grouping plus ranking one step further by providing an exact numerical distance between the rankings and also feature a meaningful zero value, thus maximizing the granularity of information provided: grouping + ranking + exact numerical distance + true zero. Age, income, and certain types of psychological scales are examples of variables that can reasonably be treated as continuous variables in statistical analyses.

Our discussion now proceeds to a review of common quantitative methods, proceeding from basic to more sophisticated. The following sections will review, in turn, methods comprising (1) bivariate analyses, (2) regression analyses, (3) multilevel regression analyses, (4) factor analyses, and (5) structural equation modelling. Each method is reviewed, with specific consideration given to the basic idea behind each method, some technical points, applications to DVA research, and published examples in the DVA literature using the method.

## Bivariate analyses

Statistical analyses of bivariate associations involve quantifying the relationship between two variables X and Y. Initial bivariate analyses could simply involve descriptive examination of the data on X and Y, such as computing sample means and variances, and constructing a scatterplot with one variable on the X-axis and the other on the Y-axis. In practice, however, quantitative researchers almost always carry out additional statistical analyses to assess the statistical significance of observed characteristics of the X–Y relationship. Thus, bivariate analyses are typically characterized by two components: (1) a descriptive examination of the relationship between two variables; and, (2) the conduct of statistical tests of certain null and alternative hypotheses and the construction of CIs for important parameters of interest. Testing for statistically significant differences in the observed distributions of two variables is very frequently a fundamental starting point for analysis. So, how would such analyses be conducted? There are a variety of ways of conducting such tests, all of which are dependent upon the levels of the variables and whether the data are paired or unpaired. Paired data, for example, could consist of responses for the same subject at two different time points (e.g., depression scores at program entry and program completion). Alternatively, unpaired data could consist of individual responses from subjects in different groups (e.g., depression scores at program completion for groups of subjects that received different yet comparable interventions). Table 48.1 lists some bivariate tests of association that could be useful for quantitative DVA researchers.

Statistical analysis methods are parametric when their expected behaviour depends on the validity of assumptions about the populations from which the data emanate. For example, a two-sample t-test involves the assumption that the data consist of random samples from two normally distributed populations, each with the same variance (i.e., the so-called homogeneous variance assumption). When the normality and homogeneous variance assumptions are true, then the two-sample t-test is the best option for testing the null hypothesis that two population means are equal versus the alternative hypothesis that they are not. If these two assumptions are not true, then the use of a two-sample t-test could produce erroneous conclusions. If there is evidence (e.g., based on descriptive analyses of the available data) that these assumptions are not true, then researchers can turn to the use of a so-called nonparametric test, especially for small sample sizes.

Nonparametric tests are valid without making any assumptions about the populations from which the data come. The nonparametric alternative to the two-sample t-test is the Wilcoxon rank-sum test, where the original observations are replaced by ranks. When in doubt about the validity of assumptions underlying parametric statistical testing methods, DVA researchers should opt for the use of nonparametric tests, especially when confronted with small sample sizes. In any research setting, validity is always more important than precision – no ethical researcher should wish to promote a precise but biased research finding. It is important to mention that nonparametric methods put an emphasis on validity, at the possible expense of power and precision. Researchers should always consider whether nonparametric tests might be more appropriate for their particular data analysis situation, especially when the assumptions associated with attendant parametric methods are questionable.

Examples of bivariate analyses in DVA research are unsurprisingly abundant. Although inherently simplistic, bivariate tests of association are actually well suited to DVA research in

*Table 48.1* Common bivariate statistical tests

| Name of test | Type of test | Type of data |
| --- | --- | --- |
| Fisher's exact test | Nonparametric | Unpaired, categorical |
| McNemar's test | Nonparametric | Paired, categorical |
| Two-sample t-test | Parametric | Unpaired, continuous |
| Wilcoxon rank-sum test | Nonparametric | Unpaired, ordinal or continuous |
| Paired t-test | Parametric | Paired, continuous |
| Wilcoxon signed-rank test | Nonparametric | Paired, ordinal or continuous |
| One-way analysis of variance | Parametric | Unpaired, continuous |
| Kruskal-Wallis test | Nonparametric | Unpaired, ordinal or continuous |
| Repeated measures analysis of variance | Parametric | Paired, continuous |
| Friedman test | Nonparametric | Paired, ordinal or continuous |

a variety of ways across multiple settings and contexts. Rather than being an analytic end-point, bivariate tests are often a fundamental precursor in many DVA studies to additional, more advanced analyses. For example, Tavoli and colleagues (2016) used both one-way analysis of variance and two-sample t-tests as an initial step to determine bivariate differences in quality of life scores among 266 physically and/or psychologically abused versus non-abused pregnant women in Iran before moving to a multivariable analysis. Establishing such preliminary differences by participant sub-group status was thus the justification for a more advanced examination that controlled for women's potential confounding characteristics (e.g., age, education). Bivariate statistical tests and associated CIs can, of course, stand on their own and be the summary quantitative methods used in a DVA research study. For example, Baird and colleagues (2018) used the Wilcoxon signed-rank test to determine that, after completing a domestic violence training program in Australia, midwives had higher knowledge and preparedness to enquire about violence six months post-training as compared to baseline.

## Regression analysis

Regression analysis is a widely applicable approach that is used to describe the relationship between a dependent variable Y (e.g., a DVA research study outcome) and a set of independent variables that might help to explain variation in Y. In the simplest situation known as *simple linear regression*, the primary objective is to model a dependent variable Y as a straight-line function of an independent variable X using the equation

$$Y_i = \beta_0 + \beta_1 X_i + e_i$$

where $Y_i$ is the observed value of the dependent variable Y for the i-th subject in the data set, $\beta_0$ is the intercept of the straight line, $\beta_1$ is the slope of the straight line, and $e_i$ is the random error component of the model and accounts for the fact that X will not explain all the variation in Y. This simple linear regression model is typically not very useful in actual practice. In most research settings, researchers need to consider multiple predictors of Y, not just one predictor. Models containing more than one predictor are called multiple linear regression models. For example, if there are five predictors of Y, the multiple linear regression model would have the structure

$$Y_i = \beta_0 + \beta_1 X_{1i} + \beta_2 X_{2i} + \beta_3 X_{3i} + \beta_4 X_{4i} + \beta_5 X_{5i} + e_i$$

where $\beta_1$, for example, measures the effect of $X_1$ on Y, controlling for the other X variables in the model. In particular, for a one-unit change in $X_1$, Y changes an amount equal to $\beta_1$ assuming that all the other X values are fixed (i.e., controlling for all the other X's).

Regression models can take many different forms, sometimes within the same study, and are highly dependent upon the distribution of the dependent variable. The most basic type of regression model is the multiple linear regression model where Y is a continuous variable assumed to be approximately normally distributed. This type of model, and regression approach, is the foundation for understanding more complicated multivariable regression analysis methods. DVA researchers interested in exploring multiple regression model options should refer to any number of statistical books on the subject, such as those by Darlington and Hayes (2016), Harrell (2015), and Kleinbaum and colleagues (2014).

Extensions beyond multiple linear regression models include a whole series of models that DVA researchers can consider when the dependent variable under study is not approximately normally distributed. One common series of such models is called *generalized linear models* (McCullagh & Nelder, 1989). For a generalized linear model, the mean (i.e., expected value) of the dependent variable gets transformed via a "link function" from its original, nonlinear state into a resultant form where a linear relationship can, in fact, be assumed between this transformed mean response and the chosen set of X variables. Dependent variables requiring the use of generalized linear models are, in fact, common in DVA research because outcomes are frequently non-normal and dichotomous (e.g., presence or absence of abuse), ordinal (e.g., "Disagree," "Neutral," "Agree"), multi-categorical (e.g., multiple reasons for exiting an abusive relationship: financial, safety, children), and count-based (e.g., number of times accessing services). Such DVA dependent variables would typically be analyzed with logistic regression, ordinal logistic regression, polytomous logistic regression, and Poisson regression, respectively. Readers of this chapter are encouraged to examine the statistical books mentioned earlier for more information on the various regression models available for analyzing dependent variables that cannot be assumed to be approximately normally distributed.

DVA research is marked by hundreds, if not thousands, of applications of regression modelling to address key research questions of interest across a variety of settings, contexts, and samples. For example, Pearlman and colleagues (2016) used a series of race-specific multiple linear regression models to examine the contribution of neighbourhood conditions on the risk of domestic violence among 413,292 women in the United States, finding that (1) living in a low socioeconomic neighbourhood was associated with increased risk of violence victimization but, importantly, that (2) such risk models were quite different for black, Hispanic, and white women.

## Multilevel regression analysis

Multilevel regression analysis, or *multilevel modelling* (MLM), is an advanced regression-based quantitative method whose focus is on potential ecological clustering of observations. Often referred to as mixed effects modelling or hierarchical linear modelling, the underlying idea behind MLM is built upon important substantive and statistical concerns related to observations within a study being nested or *clustered* within levels (Raudenbush & Bryk, 2002). In DVA research, such levels can manifest in (1) cross-sectional data (e.g., survivors clustered within a group intervention) and (2) longitudinal data (e.g., data collection at multiple time points clustered within individuals). It is important that such clustering is accounted for statistically. For example, survivors in a group intervention may show similar (i.e., positively correlated) improved outcomes because of the intervention itself, or because such outcomes are a result of a specific facilitator and the associated dynamics within the group.

Some types of regression models are totally inappropriate for the analysis of such clustered data because they ignore: (1) the conceptual importance of multiple levels of data, and (2) correlations among responses within the same level (e.g., correlations among depression scores among survivors in the same treatment group; see Raudenbush & Bryk, 2002; Rose, 2018). MLM models typically use random effects (e.g., random intercepts and/or random slopes) to correct for possible bias in significance testing and confidence interval construction induced by responses being clustered (and hence mutually correlated) within levels. As an example, a very simple two-level MLM model is as follows:

Level 1: $Y_{ij} = \beta_{0j} + \beta_1 X_{ij} + e_{ij}$
Level 2: $\beta_{0j} = \gamma_{00} + u_{0j}$

where $Y_{ij}$ is the observed response for the $i$-th subject at the $j$-th level ($j = 1, 2$) and where $X_{ij}$ is the independent variable value associated with $Y_{ij}$. In the last equation, the level 1 model is augmented with a level 2 model where $\beta_{0j}$ is the intercept for the $j$-th level, and where these group-specific intercepts vary around a grand mean $\gamma_{00}$ due to the random effect $u_{0j}$. Thus, the regression line at each level has a different intercept, and there is now the same positive correlation between each pair of responses at the same level (Rose, 2018).

The levels of data in MLM analyses are typically either implicitly or explicitly numbered, with the convention being that the lowest, or the ($X_{ij}$, $Y_{ij}$) data level in the earlier example, is labelled "1," and the next higher level (group) is labelled "2," and so on. If a DVA research study has multiple observations nested within each participant, then these observations are "level 1" and the participants themselves are "level 2." Statistically, these designations do not matter much, but they are useful for DVA researchers to remember as they structure, implement, and interpret MLM analyses. Two-level MLM analyses are most common, but three-level or even higher level analyses are possible, though typically overly complicated to model and interpret, as well as being computationally demanding even for modern computers. As a simple illustration, an MLM analysis could involve three propositions:

- Micro-level proposition relating a level 1 $X_1$ to a level 1 $Y_1$.
- Multilevel proposition relating both a level 1 $X_1$ and a level 2 $X_2$ to a level 1 $Y_1$.
- Cross-level proposition describing the effect of a level 2 $X_2$ on the relationship between a level 1 $X_1$ and a level 1 $Y_1$.

These three potential propositions can be seen graphically framed as potential DVA research questions in Figure 48.1.

Since MLM is a fairly advanced modelling procedure, examples of the use of MLM methodology in DVA research studies remain somewhat sparse, although a fair number of recent DVA research studies have used MLM to answer sophisticated research questions. One longitudinal multilevel analysis by Yount and colleagues (2016) vividly illustrates the substantive and methodological power of MLM via an examination of the effect of child marriage on intimate partner violence (IPV) among 3,355 Bangladesh women. The authors modelled three research

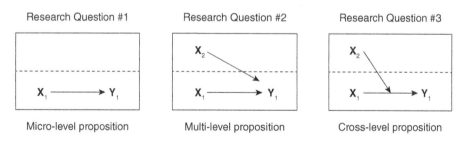

$Y_1$ = Level 1 dependent variable, $X_1$ = Level 1 independent variable,
$X_2$ = Level 2 independent variable

*Figure 48.1* Multilevel modelling research questions

questions corresponding to the earlier three possible MLM propositions. They found that, in addition to typical level 1 subject-specific variables, the characteristics of the village that a woman was from (level 2) were also important in predicting IPV victimization.

## Factor analysis

*Factor analysis* (FA) comes in both exploratory and confirmatory forms and is inherently focused on measurement of latent constructs. Briefly, FA is a method used to describe variability among observed variables that are empirically and theoretically associated, and to conceptualize them as indicators of a more parsimonious number of unobserved (i.e., unmeasured in the data) variables typically called *factors* or *latent variables* (Bollen, 1989; DeVellis, 2012).

The key substantive issue driving the potential need for FA is that some constructs in DVA research are not easy to measure and analyze and, thus, likely cannot be captured with a single variable. A variable like "Receipt of service" can be validly answered with either a "No" (0) or a "Yes" (1). But, what about a variable such as post-traumatic stress? Would any DVA researcher feel comfortable asking study participants the single question "Are you experiencing post-traumatic stress?" and being satisfied with a single yes or no answer? Such a construct like post-traumatic stress is complex, nuanced, and thus likely could only be adequately characterized via answers to multiple questions covering a range of potential experiences. Conducting FA thus entails modelling multiple observed variables (i.e., actual variables in the data often referred to as indicators, like $X_{1a}$, $X_{1b}$, and $X_{1c}$ in Figure 48.2) as manifestations of a central unobserved construct (i.e., a variable like $X_1$ in Figure 48.2) that is not directly measurable.

The number of observed variables and unobserved variables can vary widely based on the measure but, typically, a DVA researcher using FA should consider three to ten indicator variables for each latent variable, and then perhaps one to four correlated latent variables in total for a measure. As always, an overarching goal is parsimony and simplicity. FA is generally conceptualized as being either (1) *exploratory* concerning previously undetermined latent constructs such as when creating a new measurement scale, or (2) *confirmatory* concerning a previously explored measure with a new sample, translation, response array, or other altered characteristic (DeVellis, 2012). Robust development and validation of DVA measures will, of course, include both exploratory and confirmatory testing across multiple samples.

By hypothesizing a shared, underlying latent variable that causes variation in responses on observed items (i.e., indicators), one can conceptualize and model all the variation of an

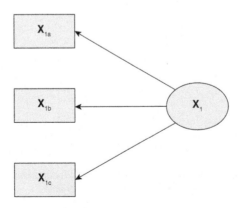

*Figure 48.2* Latent variable structure

observed variable not explained by the hypothesized latent variable as being measurement error (Bollen, 1989). This is important because it allows the analysis to, in effect, model this measurement error in ways that other quantitative methods do not. In fact, in the methods that have previously been mentioned, there is virtually no practical consideration given to measurement error at all. It is assumed that all of the variables in the regression model are measured without error. Latent variables, although built upon theoretical and somewhat subjective considerations of their own, at least present a possible advancement of thinking such that the possibility of measurement error and its effects can be considered.

Examples of FA applications in DVA research are numerous and growing. For example, Russell and Higgins (2020) used exploratory factor analysis to measure the capability of 345 Australian service providers to implement and support practices to prevent child sexual abuse, resulting in a final set of correlated latent variables measuring (1) knowledge, (2) attitudes, (3) self-efficacy, and (4) awareness that can be validly used in future research. As an example of confirmatory FA, Afifi and colleagues (2020) recently refined a measure related to adverse childhood experiences among 1,002 adolescent Canadians and their parents, finding that two latent constructs were most appropriate: (1) child maltreatment and peer victimization; and, (2) household challenges.

## Structural equation modelling

*Structural equation modelling* (SEM) refers to a fairly broad, but very powerful, family of methodologies that focus on the combination of (1) factor analyses involving multiple latent variables and (2) path analysis among variables using multiple regression equations. SEM research is typically concerned with examining hypothesized causal pathways among variables. In particular, SEM can be used to answer interesting and potentially impactful questions related to whether one or more variables *mediate* the relationship between one or more independent variables and a dependent variable, as depicted in Figure 48.3 (Baron & Kenny, 1986).

In conducting SEM analysis, DVA researchers use the variance-covariance matrix calculated from the observed data to estimate parameters that are then compared with a theoretical variance-covariance matrix specified based on theory (Bollen, 1989). In assessing appropriateness of the results of the model, SEM is perhaps unique in that is seeks a non-significant (e.g., p-value > 0.05) fit, indicative of little to no difference between the conceptual model and the data. SEM offers great flexibility in that it can be used with cross-sectional, longitudinal, single-level, or multilevel data. Although all of the major statistical software programs (i.e., R, SAS, SPSS, Stata) offer SEM capabilities, MPlus deserves particular mention as a unique and largely

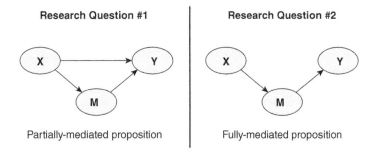

*Figure 48.3*   Mediated research questions

SEM-specific program that has a high frequency of use by DVA researchers and has powerful SEM and FA capabilities.

SEM is quite well suited to address DVA research questions and, although underutilized, has seen increased usage in recent years. As an example of the use of SEM, Herrero and colleagues (2018) examined data on 23,863 heterosexual women from the 28 countries within the European Union, testing the potential causal associations between child abuse and adult IPV incidence. Their findings demonstrated that exposure to abuse as a child was positively and significantly associated with later life violence revictimization via adult partner selection. In other words, the authors' work confirmed a theoretical model positing that, when abused girls become adults, they are more likely to be targeted by partners who are violent (Herrero, Torres, & Rodríguez, 2018).

## Conclusions

A brief comparison between quantitative and qualitative research methods is now worthwhile. Being *verbally focused*, qualitative research highlights the spoken word and written text, and seeks to analyze such data using subjective analysis and interpretation to build evidence (Hesse-Biber & Leavy, 2011). Qualitative analyses have a rich history in DVA research both past and present (e.g., Arai et al., 2019; Rose et al., 2011), and these methods are ably and extensively covered elsewhere in this volume for the interested reader. Overall, the differences between quantitative and qualitative research are both over-stated and under-stated. They are over-stated in that both approaches, when conducted rigorously, can build evidence to understand, prevent, and respond to DVA. They are under-stated in that the various assumptions, processes, and products of each are really quite different. Both forms of research, it could be said, take distinct paths on their journey towards arriving at a shared goal. Any DVA research question can be addressed by either approach, but the actual research project results will manifest quite differently using one approach compared to the other.

It is something of a misnomer, though frequently stated, to declare that quantitative research can be further characterized beyond data type and analytic approach to represent research that is "factual" or "empirical" or "scientific." The implications, of course, are that qualitative research is not characterized by such important qualities and is thus an inferior approach. Such notions should be rejected. There are many different ways of viewing the world, and individual researchers can bring unique assumptions and valid preferences to the table. The truth is that both types of research, as well as hybrid mixed methods and multi-method approaches, are characterized by similar philosophies, including, but not limited to, development of research questions and hypotheses, application of theoretical considerations, establishment of internal and external validity, and, most broadly, pursuit of valid and useful evidence to inform service delivery in DVA contexts.

## Issues with quantitative research methods

Although many DVA researchers, and social researchers in general, have recently come to widely and enthusiastically embrace the use of quantitative research methods, no form of numerical analysis is free from possible problems associated with its use. Four general issues exist with the selection, application, and inference associated with quantitative research methods, and all DVA researchers would be wise to keep these issues in mind.

First, quantitative methods are far from perfect. Generally, it is safe to say that quantitative researchers embrace the putative objectivity of numerical data. If there is one word or concept cited perhaps most frequently by quantitative researchers to identify their general research orientation and overarching research goals, it is *clarity*. Whether true or not, proponents and practitioners of quantitative research methods operate from a philosophical viewpoint that research clarity is not only possible, but achievable, via valid and precise numerical evaluation of research study data. With all that said, DVA researchers should be aware that the misuse and misinterpretation of quantitative research findings can have serious repercussions. As with all research, crucial components related to context, bias, error, interpretation, and application matter a great deal. Using sophisticated quantitative methods absolves neither the researcher nor the service provider from careful judgement regarding the utility of findings emanating from the use of such methods. Moreover, although quantitative research methods emphasize systematic processes and precise results, they are, in fact, often haphazardly conducted and so can result in erroneous and misleading conclusions.

Second, choosing what quantitative methods to use can be challenging. It is important to realize that most of the aforementioned quantitative methods can be applied across a variety of research designs. Also, complexity of design does not necessarily engender the need for complex analyses. In fact, it can be the opposite situation. For example, it is sometimes the case that one will encounter large-scale, multi-year, and very expensive randomized studies where the primary quantitative findings have relied mainly upon the use of simple two-sample t-tests and associated CIs. Conversely, the analysis of certain cross-sectional surveys may involve complicated statistical analyses requiring sophisticated statistical expertise to implement and interpret correctly. Careful application of quantitative research methods, as outlined in this chapter, can greatly enhance the quality of DVA research studies. In general, the choice of which advanced quantitative research method to use will depend on the type of study design, the method of data collection, the size of the sample, the characteristics of the dependent and independent variables being considered, the quantity and the quality of the information being obtained on these variables, and the research questions of interest. The use of advanced statistical multivariable modelling procedures should be preceded by data cleaning and the use of descriptive analyses. Establishing the validity of any research findings should be the primary objective when conducting any DVA research study, quantitative ones included.

Third, despite the advantages of quantitative research methods, and the generally high rigour with which they are applied in DVA research, findings from the use of such methods do not allow the conclusion of causality. It is typically conceptualized that there exist three criteria necessary to establish a relationship where one can confidently state that, say, a particular independent variable X "causes" changes in a particular dependent variable Y: (1) the causal relationship between X and Y must have temporal order, namely, that X must precede Y in time; (2) X and Y should be empirically significantly associated with each another; and, (3) the observed significant association between X and Y cannot be the result of a third variable Z that causes the observed relationship between X and Y (Lazarsfeld, 1959). Although quantitative research methods can often establish the second criterion, the third criterion is often difficult to determine without appropriate data. Usually, the first criterion is actually a typical characteristic of the design of a DVA study. It is only with robust longitudinal and randomized designs that causality can reasonably be established. In many research areas, strong evidence for a causal conclusion is reached once numerous, and different types of, rigorously undertaken studies involving reliable samples from different populations all lead to the same finding, an example being the causal connection between smoking and lung cancer.

Fourth, there likely exist numerous threats to the internal validity of quantitative research conclusions, or reasons why conclusions about the relationship between two variables (e.g., "X causes Y") may actually be incorrect, despite seemingly rigorous application of quantitative methods. Shadish and colleagues (2002) have outlined a widely used typology of threats to internal validity that includes: (1) ambiguous temporal precedence, (2) selection, (3) history, (4) maturation, (5) regression, (6) attrition, (7) testing, (8) instrumentation, and (9) additive and interactive effects. This list is not an exhaustive list of all the ways in which the numerical results produced from a DVA study, and the implications drawn from them, can be flawed or misleading.

## Summary

This chapter provided an introduction to quantitative research methods by highlighting some basic and advanced statistical procedures that are useful for analyzing quantitative DVA research data and for interpreting subsequent numerical findings. In particular, this chapter has considered some commonly used univariate and bivariate statistical analysis methods, as well as various advanced multivariable modelling methods that are increasingly being used in DVA research.

DVA researchers are increasingly using quantitative methods to advance their field of study and to address questions to better understand DVA, as well as to help prevent and respond to this form of violence. Quantitative research methods seek to distil complex results into parsimonious key findings, often resulting in a handful of insightful, precise, and, most importantly, valid scientific conclusions. Quantitative methods have various implications for DVA practice, policy, and research. Practitioners with a basic understanding of quantitative methods can use univariate and bivariate statistics to help evaluate their practices and organizations. Findings from such evaluations can help to ensure accountability to clients and stakeholders, and are increasingly being required by funders. Policymakers can also benefit from being educated about quantitative methods – specifically, the accurate use and interpretation of quantitative DVA research findings that result in more evidence-informed policies.

## Critical findings

- DVA researchers are increasingly using quantitative methods to promote understanding, prevention, and response to DVA.
- Quantitative methods can be used to distil complicated DVA research information into clear, precise, and valid summarizations of key findings.
- A foundational understanding of study design, significance testing and confidence interval construction, distributional characteristics of variables including centre and spread, and the dependent and independent variable modelling framework is necessary for validly and precisely analyzing and interpreting quantitative DVA research study data.
- DVA researchers commonly employ descriptive statistics, bivariate analysis methods, multiple linear regression, and factor analysis, with a slow but increasing focus on the use of more advanced statistical analysis methods such as generalized linear models, multilevel regression analysis, and structural equation modelling.

## Implications for policy, practice, and research

### *Policy*

- Educating policymakers about quantitative methods can help to avoid misinterpretation and misuse of quantitative DVA research findings.

## Practice

- DVA practitioners can use basic quantitative methods to evaluate their practices and organizations, helping to ensure accountability to clients, stakeholders, and funders.

## Research

- DVA researchers interested in applying quantitative methods are encouraged to pursue continuing education about such methods via statistical textbooks, workshops, and collaborations with methodological experts.
- DVA researchers are encouraged to consider how their research studies can benefit from the use of quantitative research methods, and to understand the strengths and limitations of different statistical analysis methods.

## References

Afifi, T. O., Salmon, S., Garcés, I., Struck, S., Fortier, J., Taillieu, T., . . . MacMillan, H. L. (2020). Confirmatory factor analysis of adverse childhood experiences (ACEs) among a community-based sample of parents and adolescents. *BMC Pediatrics, 20*, 1–14. https://doi.org.10.1186/s12887-020-02063-3

Arai, L., Heawood, A., Feder, G., Howarth, E., MacMillan, H., Moore, T. H., . . . Gregory, A. (2019). Hope, agency, and the lived experience of violence: A qualitative systematic review of children's perspectives on domestic violence and abuse. *Trauma, Violence, & Abuse*. Advance online publication. https://doi.org/10.1177/1524838019849582

Baird, K., Creedy, D. K., Saito, A. S., & Eustace, J. (2018). Longitudinal evaluation of a training program to promote routine antenatal enquiry for domestic violence by midwives. *Women and Birth, 31*, 398–406. https://doi.org/10.1016/j.wombi.2018.01.004

Baron, R. M., & Kenny, D. A. (1986). The moderator – Mediator variable distinction in social psychological research: Conceptual, strategic, and statistical considerations. *Journal of Personality and Social Psychology, 51*, 1173–1182. https://doi.org/10.1037/0022-3514.51.6.1173

Bollen, K. A. (1989). *Structural equations with latent variables*. New York: Wiley.

Branch, M. N. (2014). Malignant side effects of null hypothesis significance testing. *Theory & Psychology, 24*, 256–277. https://doi.org/10.1177/0959354314525282

Creswell, J. W. (2017). *Research design: Qualitative, quantitative, and mixed methods approaches* (4th ed.). Los Angeles: Sage.

Darlington, R. B., & Hayes, A. F. (2016). *Regression analysis and linear models: Concepts, applications, and implementation*. New York: Guilford Press.

DeVellis, R. F. (2012). *Scale development: Theory and applications* (3rd ed.). Los Angeles: Sage.

Greenland, S., Senn, S. J., Rothman, K. J., Carlin, J. B., Poole, C., Goodman, S. N., & Altman, D. G. (2016). Statistical tests, P values, confidence intervals, and power: A guide to misinterpretations. *European Journal of Epidemiology, 31*, 337–350. https://doi.org/10.1007/s10654-016-0149-3

Harrell, F. E. Jr. (2015). *Regression modeling strategies: With applications to linear models, logistic and ordinal regression, and survival analysis*. New York: Springer.

Hasan, T., Muhaddes, T., Camellia, S., Selim, N., & Rashid, S. F. (2014). Prevalence and experiences of intimate partner violence against women with disabilities in Bangladesh: Results of an explanatory sequential mixed-method study. *Journal of Interpersonal Violence, 29*, 3105–3126. https://doi.org/10.1177/0886260514534525

Herrero, J., Torres, A., & Rodríguez, F. J. (2018). Child abuse, risk in male partner selection, and intimate partner violence victimization of women of the European Union. *Prevention Science, 19*, 1102–1112. https://doi.org/10.1007/s11121-018-0911-8

Hesse-Biber, S. N., & Leavy, P. (2011). *The practice of qualitative research* (2nd ed.). Los Angeles: Sage.

Kleinbaum, D. G., Kupper, L. L., Nizam, A., & Rosenberg, E. S. (2014). *Applied regression analysis and other multivariable methods* (5th ed.). Boston: Cengage Learning.

Lazarsfeld, P. F. (1959). Problems in methodology. In R. K. Morton, L. Broom, & L. S. Cottrell, Jr. (Eds.), *Sociology today: Problems and prospects* (Vol. 1., pp. 39–72). New York: Basic Books.

Lepistö, S., Luukkaala, T., & Paavilainen, E. (2011). Witnessing and experiencing domestic violence: A descriptive study of adolescents. *Scandinavian Journal of Caring Sciences, 25,* 70–80. https://doi.org/10.1111/j.1471-6712.2010.00792.x

McCullagh, P., & Nelder, J. A. (1989). *Generalized linear models.* Boca Raton: Chapman & Hall/CRC Press.

McDavid, J. C., Huse, I., & Hawthorn, L. R. L. (2018). *Program evaluation and performance measurement: An introduction to practice* (2nd ed.). Los Angeles: Sage.

Pearlman, D. N., Zierler, S., Gjelsvik, A., & Verhoek-Oftedahl, W. (2016). Neighborhood environment, racial position, and risk of police-reported domestic violence: A contextual analysis. *Public Health Reports, 118,* 44–58. https://doi.org/10.1093/phr/118.1.44

Raudenbush, S. W., & Bryk, A. S. (2002). *Hierarchical linear models: Applications and data analysis methods* (2nd ed.). Los Angeles: Sage.

Rizo, C. F., Wretman, C. J., Macy, R. J., Guo, S., & Ermentrout, D. M. (2018). A novel intervention for system-involved intimate partner violence survivors: Changes in mental health. *The American Journal of Orthopsychiatry, 88,* 681–690. https://doi.org/10.1037/ort0000332

Rose, D., Trevillion, K., Woodall, A., Morgan, C., Feder, G., & Howard, L. (2011). Barriers and facilitators of disclosures of domestic violence by mental health service users: Qualitative study. *The British Journal of Psychiatry, 198,* 189–194. https://doi.org/10.1192/bjp.bp.109.072389

Rose, R. A. (2018). Multilevel modeling in family violence research. *Journal of Family Violence, 33,* 109–122. https://doi.org/10.1007/s10896-017-9938-z

Rubin, R., & Babbie, E. R. (2016). *Essential research methods for social work* (4th ed.). Boston: Cengage Learning.

Russell, D., & Higgins, D. (2020). Safeguarding capabilities in preventing child sexual abuse: Exploratory factor analysis of a scale measuring safeguarding capabilities in youth-serving organizations workers. *Child Maltreatment, 25,* 233–242. https://doi.org.10.1177/1077559519870253

Saunders, R. P. (2015). *Implementation monitoring and process evaluation.* Los Angeles: Sage.

Shadish, W. R., Cook, T. D., & Campbell, D. T. (2002). *Experimental and quasi-experimental designs for generalized causal inference.* Boston: Cengage Learning.

Tavoli, Z., Tavoli, A., Amirpour, R., Hosseini, R., & Montazeri, A. (2016). Quality of life in women who were exposed to domestic violence during pregnancy. *BMC Pregnancy and Childbirth, 16,* 19. https://doi.org/10.1186/s12884-016-0810-6

Wasserman, R. L., & Lazar, N. A. (2016). The ASA statement on p-values: Context, process, and purpose. *The American Statistician, 70,* 129–133. https://doi.org/10.1080/00031305.2016.1154108

Weisberg, H. F. (1992). *Central tendency and variability.* Los Angeles: Sage.

Yount, K. M., Crandall, A., Cheong, Y. F., Osypuk, T. L., Bates, L. M., Naved, R. T., & Schuler, S. R. (2016). Child marriage and intimate partner violence in rural Bangladesh: A longitudinal multilevel analysis. *Demography, 53,* 1821–1852. https://doi.org.10.1007/s13524-016-0520-8

# 49

# EXTENDING WOMEN'S VOICE THROUGH INNOVATIVE METHODS

## Lessons from struggles for democracy in Hong Kong

*Sui-Ting Kong, Petula Sik Ying Ho and Yu Te Huang*

### Introduction

The struggles for democracy and justice in Hong Kong and Taiwan have driven us towards rethinking how we do research with people (Ho, Kong, & Huang, 2018). We have witnessed and participated in the Sunflower Movement, the Umbrella Movement and the latest protests against extradition law amendment bill (anti-ELAB)[1] in Taiwan and Hong Kong. In the latest anti-ELAB movement, civilians were teargassed, beaten by batons and shot by beanbag/rubber bullets (United Nations, 13 August 2019). Amid week-on-week scenes of mounting violence and arrests, we have seen images of women protesters and passers-by being harassed by police. Women protesters' underpants/private body parts have been exposed to public gaze (Carvalho, 2019) or have experienced glove-less strip-searching without reasonable grounds or consent (Cheng, 2019). In addition to these countless incidents of sexual assault against woman protesters, a woman first aider was headshot by the police with beanbag bullets at a protest site which has led to her permanent loss of vision (Kilpatrick, 16 August 2019).

Witnessing the pervasive use of violence against women by the police, Hong Kong protesters have adopted the anti-sexual harassment rallying cry of the #MeToo movement to raise international awareness of the issue. The Hong Kong-based Women's Coalition on Equal Opportunities (WOCEO) organised a rally in Central on 28 August 2019 to draw attention to police use of sexual violence against female protesters in order to intimidate and silence women. Thousands joined the rally, all dressed in black and shouting the slogan 'stop Hong Kong police's use of sexual violence'. The rally condemned the violation of women's rights to assembly. The women involved in the high-profile cases of unreasonable strip-searching and sexual intimidation during arrest both appeared on-stage at the rally wearing masks. Attendees scrawled '#ProtestToo' on their forearms with lipstick and handed out purple ribbons (Creery, 29 August 2019).

The spectacle of cruelty on the streets and other public spaces, as well as the political crackdown on democratic struggles, has increased our awareness of the politics of 'victimhood', and of the researcher-researched distinction that underpins many conventional methodologies. This chapter attempts to capture some of our thinking regarding a number of questions: who are victims of gender-based violence and who are possibly not? How can we identify and recognise the suffering of those who cannot even claim to be victims? How can we address the overlooked injustices embedded in marginalised victimhoods? What justifications are there for violent resistance in the form of self-defence and retaliation? As researchers doing gender-based violence and sexuality studies in politically turbulent times, we also resolve to transform our academic practices for seeking ways to unsettle and challenge hierarchies and extend women's voice through democratic knowledge production.

This chapter will draw on the authors' experiences and observations made during Hong Kong's recent pro-democracy protests to examine how violence and the gender regime interrelate. Informed by the concept of intersectionality, the chapter unpacks the politics of victimhood, making the case that constructions of 'ideal victimhood' can marginalise some women's experiences of violence. The blurred boundary between victim-survivors and non-victim-survivors also challenges the researcher-researched distinction and mandates methodological innovation in favour of more 'engaged research'. At the end of the chapter, we will include some examples of our innovative methods/methodologies to demonstrate how research can be done 'care'-fully (Brannelly & Boulton, 2017) to pursue situated gender justice. Throughout the chapter, we refer to gender-based violence as 'violence that is directed against a woman because she is a woman or that affects women disproportionately'; and domestic violence as 'acts of physical, sexual, psychological or economic violence that occur within the family or domestic unit or between former or current spouses or partners' (Platek, 2019).

## Discussion and analysis: democracy and our academic practices

### *The function of fear in personal and public spheres*

Gender-based violence is a tool that both men and states use to subordinate women, as well as men performing marginalised masculinities, and hence profiting from it (Platek, 2019). Platek's work published in 2004 is useful to illustrate this point – the Polish government intentionally omitted Article IX of the Convention on the Political Rights of Women and Article 29 of CEDAW leading to barriers to realising women's equal rights to political participation, freedom from any forms of discrimination, physical and mental health and proper working conditions. The state's violation of women's rights itself is a form of violence, and it condones patriarchy which 'gives a man the right to categorise and evaluate others, and exempts him from being classified and graded and from taking responsibility' (p. 10). Therefore, violence against women is a method of 'doing gender' which, through processes of structuration (Giddens, 1984) at individual, cultural and institutional levels, reinforces existing gender inequalities (Risman, 2004). In various contexts and cases, the political level is ever-present. As Boesten (2010) demonstrates, patterns of direct state violence against women are a function of gender structure in society, which intersects with other societal hierarchies like race and class. Systematic state violence, in turn, helps reproduce those very structures and inequalities. These interlinked practices and processes of state violence, everyday violence against women and domestic violence are therefore the constituents of gender structure, which shifts from time to time, to persistently hinder women from pursuing freedom and gender equality in a given society.

One of the mechanisms by which violence can be used to reproduce gender inequality and subordinate women is by instilling fear (Pain, 2014). As Stark (2009a, 2009b, 2013) suggests, violence against women does not always involve overt physical violence, but also everyday micro-aggressions and forms of micro-regulation that erode women's self-esteem, sense of control and autonomy. This has led some to refer to covert violence in their intimate lives as 'intimate terrorism' (e.g. Johnson, 2010). Fear can sustain men's control over women by stopping women from making choices that reflect their interests and by pushing them towards performing gender stereotypes, such as around womanhood and motherhood. Fear can become chronic (Pain, 2012), routine and habitual (Vera-Gray, 2018) when women are subject to everyday violence. This fear is reasonable and justified when the invasion of personal body and space is experienced or anticipated in either/both personal and public spheres. This chronic, routine and habitual fear jeopardises women's sense of control over their time, material possessions, relationships and body.

However, since fear is learned through experiences of gender inequality and uninvited invasion of personal space by men it can also trigger acts of resistance that help women identify and mitigate such dangers (Hyden, 1999; Pain, 2012; Vera-Gray, 2018). When women resist, they might not always aim to be reclaiming their autonomy (making choice free of fear) but rather seeking to reduce levels of violence or mitigate the impact of such violence. The prolonged experience of losing control in extensive aspects of life can make women feel less of themselves (Stark, 2009a), at its worst resulting in what Králová (2015) terms 'social death' – losses of social identity, social connectedness and a sense of bodily integration.

## Fear is a cultural product in shifting social hierarchies

Fear is also cultural while culture is fluid and dynamic. Our experiences in the Umbrella Movement have reaffirmed for us how Chinese culture of paternalism holds the voices of women and youths in lower regard, at the bottom of the familial and social hierarchy. The fear of authority and the consequences of disobedience reinforces a patriarchal culture that legitimises violence against women at home and in the larger society. For example, unsettling this familial hierarchy can lead to relationship breakdown, violence and emotional blackmail (Ho, Jackson, & Kong, 2018). People in Hong Kong sometimes refer to the Central Government of the People's Republic of China (PRC) as 'grandpa', drawing on the patriarchal lineage in the Chinese family structure to make sense of the power imbalance between Hong Kong and PRC and the crackdown on the democratic struggles in Hong Kong (Kong & Ho, 2016).

After the Umbrella Movement, young people in Hong Kong continued to seek ways to destabilise the paternalistic culture through the anti-ELAB protest movement. The anti-ELAB movement is demarcated by a shift of power from the middle-aged and older elites to young front-line valiant protesters. While middle-aged pacifist protesters remain to be a huge presence in the current protests, their participation in the movement is considered 'useful'[2] only if they could join hands with the valiant camp to fight the authoritarian regime. The discourse of solidarity holds the pacifists responsible (mostly older and middle-aged citizens) for protecting and standing with the young valiant protesters despite the latter's use of violence against pro-establishment peaceful protesters and businesses. This form of solidarity taps into the cultural notion of parental protection, leaving little space for older and middle-aged pacifists to question the valiant strategies otherwise risking humiliation for not fulfilling their cultural obligation. Is an effect of Hong Kong's struggles for freedom to (re)produce a form of patriarchal authority dominated by young men that are honoured for their martyrdom? While some young women have become valiant soldiers at the front line fighting against the police, we wonder how women's participation in the movement and experience of violence is shaped by their gender position, age, class and political orientation in the shifting power relations and hierarchies.

## *Zero-tolerance of violence in a politically turbulent time?*

As a product of patriarchal cultures, tolerance of violence in the name of collective benefits is another mechanism of control over women. Campaigns for zero-tolerance of violence flourished in Canada, the US and the UK in the early '90s. These intended to challenge the taken-for-granted nature of violence against women in society, and promote a cultural and social change that would afford women more protection (Mackay, 1996; McMahon & Pence, 2003). This initiative was later taken up by governments in various countries, and yielded changes in terms of national policy on violence against women and legal changes to protect women and prosecute domestic violence (ibid.). While some feminists celebrated the endorsement of these campaigns, others became critical of their institutionalisation (McMahon & Pence, 2003). The dismissal of the relationships and contexts in which women used violence resulted in a high number of women prosecuted for using violence to resist (ibid.). For McMahon and Pence (2003), the heavy reliance on the criminal justice system to advocate for social and cultural change risks homogenising women's experiences of domestic violence and reduces intersecting inequalities into prosecutable incidents. Goodmark (2018) further advocated for decriminalising intimate partner violence. Their approach is to emphasise the importance of seeing intimate partner violence as a multidimensional problem, entailing diverse community-based and evidence-based social and service responses to prevent it and mitigate its impact.

Despite these criticisms, zero-tolerance campaigns should be promoted as an antidote to a culture of patriarchy and complicity which sustains violence against women. Notably, patriarchal norms and violent behaviours are mutually reinforcing. Some evidence shows that men who abused their children and, at the same time, endorsed patriarchal ideology and infantilised women showed more use of violence against their female intimate partners (Emery, Kim, Song, & Song, 2013). It is also well acknowledged in the literature that the use of violence against women is the means to subordinate women to a male-dominant gender regime that renders women second-class citizenship (infantilisation) (Risman, 2004). To break this vicious cycle, we not only need to seek ways to reduce public acceptability of violence against women, but to also challenge racialised, classist, ageist and gendered practices that can make women second-class citizens because of their social positions (Nixon & Humphreys, 2010).

Experiencing and witnessing the Hong Kong anti-ELAB protests, a new question emerges for us: how can we promote zero-tolerance on violence against women when state violence and violent resistance by citizens are justifying and escalating each other's indiscriminate use of force? The *Onsite Survey Findings in Hong Kong's Anti-Extradition Bill Protests* (Centre for Communication and Public Opinion Survey, 2019) shows that Hong Kongers are increasingly sympathetic towards radical violent resistance after months of anti-government unrest and police violence (Amnesty International, 2019). Most survey participants agree that, without government concessions, radical violent tactics are justifiable. Some respondents were in favour of protesters' escalating use of violence, with very few expressing a desire to see the protest movement pause their actions. Doyle and McWilliams's study (2018) on 40 years of political conflict in Northern Ireland highlights issues that could be relevant to understanding domestic violence in other politically turbulent contexts: how is women's access to protection and justice, including the police and legal support, upset or jeopardised in the context of political conflict? Northern Ireland's experiences suggest that male perpetrators of domestic violence use their political affiliations to threaten women, sustaining the perception that women have nowhere to go and intensifying women's fear of violence by showing how women can be harassed in public spaces. Erez, Ibarra, and Gur (2015) realised that the journey of reporting domestic violence to the police can be coloured by the Arab-Israeli conflict in Israel. Arab abused women could feel ashamed and an ultimate sense of betrayal for seeking help from the Israeli police, while Israeli police can uphold a stereotypical image of Arab families in doing their policing work and may hold grievances against Arabs because of the prolonged political conflicts. The intersection of the political and the private spheres in these studies suggests the possibility of perpetrators of domestic violence using everyday political violence to control their female partners. Although the experiences of Northern Ireland and Israel are not directly comparable to Hong Kong, the questions and issues raised are still critical for rethinking the legitimacy of violence and violent resistance in a politically turbulent time.

## Who are victim-survivors and who are not?

'We are all survivors (of violence).'
*– Siu Ka Chung, social worker and an imprisoned democratic*
*activist in Hong Kong, wrote in his letter to the public*

Acts of domestic violence are not aberrant behaviours of individuals (e.g. delinquent behaviours, poor anger and stress management, etc.) but rather manifestations of a culture that sanctions gendered violence (Kelly, 2002; Lombard, 2013; WHO, 29 November 2017). In places where the culture tends to accept women's subordination to men and men's ownership over women, domestic violence against women is also found to be more prevalent (WHO, 29 November 2017).

The positive correlation between a culture of gender inequality and the prevalence of intimate partner violence has raised the question of whether only those who have witnessed or experienced explicit physical violence are 'victim-survivors'. This classification of 'victim-survivor' excludes those who do not have these direct experiences of violence but are prone to violence for deviating from the dominant gender order (Ray, 2018). On the other hand, those who are deemed 'non-victim-survivor' might still confront certain trivialised, less visible forms of violence, such as psychological manipulation, name calling, social isolation and micro-regulation in their everyday life. The definition of violence and victims should be broadly informed by nature, dynamics, severity and consequence of a treatment.

These reflections on 'victimhood' highlight the importance of the continuum of violence which addresses women's experience of multiple forms of violence in everyday life, including harassment, coercion and control, which can be equally or more detrimental to women's well-being and agency when compared to overt physical and sexual assault (Kelly, 2002). Failing to understand violence against women as a continuum can render invisible the suffering of women who do not conform to 'ideal victimhood'. For example, in the case of the #ProtestToo rally and the anti-ELAB movement in Hong Kong, only civilian women and protesters who have experienced explicit physical and sexual assault by the police would be regarded as victims of gender-based violence. The construction of 'ideal victimhood' is circumscribed by the political agenda of the anti-ELAB protests, which exclusively focuses on the brutality of state and police. The consequence is the ignorance of the violence exercised by the protesters for the sake of cementing an alliance for challenging the authoritarian regime. Women activists' experiences of public humiliation and harassment on the street and in online spaces are rendered invisible for political expedience (Kong, Ho, & Jackson, 2018).

This dominant discourse of victimhood further forbids people from challenging the protesters' violence against the wives and family of the police, such as those who chanted 'Black cop, the whole family dies!' and 'Police on overtime, their wives enjoying threesome'. These bullying slogans that blame women for men's wrongdoings or confine women to gender stereotypes can be easily trivialised or dismissed when women do not fit the image of 'ideal victim', constructed at the interplay of cultural, socio-political and institutional powers in a specific context (Pain, 2014). Politics of victimhood sensitises us to the limitation of using a well-accepted construction of victimhood to guide our understanding of gender-based violence. The construction of ideal victim defines what acts are counted as violence, and it inevitably renders some violent acts against women overlooked and gender injustices unnoticed.

Furthermore, the 'worthy of sympathy' undertone of victimhood could sometimes stop us from questioning victims' use of violence. While violent resistance is widely accepted and justified on the grounds of self-defence (McColgan, 1993; McPherson, 2019), the anti-ELAB protests lead us to question the legitimacy of violent resistance when it is directed to family members and partners of perpetrators of abuse. We consider this question crucial for pursuing justice. It is clear to us in the anti-ELAB protests that people dare not criticise protesters' violence against the wives of police officers since misogynistic slogans and sexual harassment serve as resistance strategies. In a politically heterogenous movement, we have observed that violent resistance can be used against women activists who hold different stances and approaches to others. Ho, an author of this chapter, organised a peaceful rally (5 August 2019) against sexual violence against women protesters weeks before the #ProtestToo rally. It took place outside the Tin Shui Wai police station, where several male police officers had exposed the private parts of a woman protester by holding her legs open and causing her dress to ride up. During that day, 70 plus people were arrested by police. Ho was subsequently blamed by activists for the arrests, verbally attacked and physically confronted by the radical pro-confrontation factions of the movement. The fear of physical attacks and online bullying forestalled us, as academics, to raise uncomfortable questions which can potentially discredit the current anti-ELAB movement. Instead of finding support in the #ProtestToo assembly or the Pacifist factions of the social movement, bullying and harassment experienced by Ho were barely acknowledged in other rallies and public platforms. For the authors of this chapter, these experiences and observations were personally shocking, and forced us to reflect on the limitations of the way we understand gender-based violence in the context of authoritarianism and civil unrest. Accepting violent resistance, simply due to the victim status of the perpetrator, can render the injustices that it creates invisible.

## *Doing research as making change together*

Recognising everyone can be a victim-survivor in a culture of gender inequality forces us to reconsider the responsibility of researchers in the field of gender-based violence. Nissim-Sabat (2009), in her Marxist analysis of victimhood, argued that our conventional constructions of victimhood are underpinned by 'individualism' and naïve empiricism. These constructions share the understanding that victimisation is the experience of rational and self-conscious individuals who are either (1) subject to unavoidable natural disasters or social misfortune (poverty, domestic abuse and discrimination); or (2) choose to put themselves in situations of misfortune or deprivation by not resisting enough. By denying the dependencies and inter-dependencies that constitute our society, it is easy to blame the 'victim' for their sufferings rather than turning the gaze towards ourselves and those who allow these sufferings to take place or could have done something to mitigate these sufferings.

Focusing on 'who could have made a difference' speaks to a relational approach, which considers victimisation/survival as experienced and understood in relation to social context.

Victim-survivors' agency faces various constraints (Vera-Gray, 2016) including their social positions, the power relations that they are located in and their material reality. Connell (1995) and Connell and Messerschmidt (2005) argued that individual males and females are granted varied resources to claim and change a set of rules for how different genders should be performed, depending on their class, ethnicity, age and sexuality in a particular cultural and political context. The relational approach not only holds accountable those who maintain, reproduce or remain silent to the power relations that make gender violence more conducive in a particular context (Kelly, 2016) but also advocates for a shared responsibility to reduce victimisation and support survival and recovery of abused women (Pain, 2014).

The relational approach further raises questions about the legitimacy of the researcher/researched distinction which often limits the space for 'respondents' or 'participants' to have 'a voice, a vote, and a veto' (Kara, 2017, p. 289) in knowledge-making. This distinction upholds the assumption that the researchers are objective observers of victim-survivors and their experiences without recognising that researchers themselves could be exposed to a continuum of gender violence stratified by their social positions. By contesting the distinctions of victim-survivor/non-victim-survivor and researcher/researched, we acknowledge that the social positions occupied by researchers affect how they understand, experience and dismiss the experience of gender violence, hence posing questions on research design and analysis that are based on claims of neutrality and objectivity. The relational approach also highlights the moral obligation of academic researchers for acting against and challenging gendered social hierarchies through their everyday research practices. It further justifies a feminist, participatory, reflexive and action-based approach to researching gender violence (Harding & Norberg, 2005).

## Engaged feminist research

'Whose questions are we asking? And to whom do we owe an answer? Thinking about methodology in this way puts the technical details into a social and political context and considers their consequences for people's lives. It gives us a space for critical reflection and for creativity.'

*(Sprague, 2016, p. 5)*

'Engaged feminist research', as opposed to an ostensibly value-free and objective approach, can yield new knowledge by challenging the status quo and associated power imbalances that are embedded in contemporary institutional research practice (Harding & Norberg, 2005; Sprague, 2016). Feminist research advances its epistemological and political agenda by generating knowledge from the marginalised standpoints of women and by problematising the hierarchy of knowledge (i.e. that objective is better than subjective/intersubjective) (Sprague, 2016). Feminist research involves validating women's labour, experiences, values and (relational) agency which dominant modes of research practice all too readily dismiss. In the field of domestic violence, for example, Hester, Donovan, and Fahmy (2010) have found that heteronormative assumptions have shaped the development of both measurement tools and sampling in prevalence studies of intimate partner violence, adding difficulty to assessing the prevalence of intimate partner violence happening in LGBTQ relationships. The authors recalled the discussion regarding how to measure intimate partner violence in lesbian relationships in the conference of 'Violence in the Lesbian Community' held in Washington DC in September 1983, stating that some feminists had denied the existence of such abuse. One of the reasons is that they believed 'lesbian relationships were a "utopic" alternative to oppressive heterosexual relation-ships – where lesbian relationships were likely to be egalitarian compared to the inevitability of male/female inequality in heterosexual relationships' (ibid., p. 253). The assumption that power and control can be exercised only by men over women has created barriers in examining how power and control play out in same-sex relationships, resulting in difficulties in devising tools to capture these dynamics (in terms of contexts and impact of abuse). Not only has domestic vio-lence in same-sex relationships had a much more recent history compared to domestic violence in heterosexual relationships, the early literature and studies on same-sex domestic violence focused mainly on lesbian relationships, partly because lesbians became a sub-group of women seeking domestic violence or rape support services ostensibly set up for heterosexual women. Studies of intimate partner violence among gay men were not present until the late '90s and majorly linked to health research on HIV/AIDS. In addition, Ho, Chan, and Kong (2017) identify how conventional modes of knowledge production, which primarily produces textual knowledge, can hamper an understanding of women's emotional experiences of sexual harass-ment and bullying. In contrast to text-based knowledge production, they recommend the use of theatre for more engaged research with women's embodied experiences. This renewed engage-ment also engenders an ethics that works 'towards more shared forms of managing power', both within the enquiry group and in the larger social system/structure (Palacios, 2016, p. 940).

To achieve these ends, the research process itself must also be democratic and able to address the everyday as well as structural injustices *as experienced* by women. Methodological innova-tion therefore is needed for transforming everyday research practice into action that (1) creates a safe space for recognising overlooked sufferings of women and communicating socio-political differences, and (2) developing a community of care that supports non-violent resistance to gender-based and domestic violence. Methodological innovations, we suggest, are critical and radical practices in research for challenging power held by academic researchers in defining what is knowledge, for example, the culture of objectivity and the prohibition of different forms of 'knowing' in research (Heron, 1996; Kong, 2016). Ultimately, we emphasise a process of pursuing a situated ethics of justice (Bank, 2014), meaning that we negotiate and understand principles of justice in the contexts of our research. These principles inform our research pro-cesses where we prioritised people's wellbeing and feelings and shared power with 'participants' in deciding on the scope, design, process and the use of the research.

## Use of group for creating safe space: sense of community and sense of control

A space that people can talk freely, without fear of violence against them and the fear of nega-tive consequence if they challenge social hierarchies, is a requirement for achieving/pursuing/realising justice. This space can be transformative for women, since it can create an emotional break from their chronic, routine and habitual fears that intervenes and constrains them from recognising their sufferings and articulating and acting upon them (Kong & Robson, 2020). Generating this space usually involves creating and supporting relationships that are caring and non-judgemental so that women come to trust that their stories will be heard and believed.

### Example 1: Cooperative Grounded Inquiry

Cooperative Grounded Inquiry (CGI) (Kong, 2016) was developed in a project that worked with women who had separated from their abusive partners in Hong Kong. The lack of post-separation support for abused women in Hong Kong reflects a systemic failure to understand abused women's post-separation lives. CGI positions women's voice in the centre of knowledge-making and social service development, with the hope of finding practical ways to address the challenges experienced and identified by women in the post-separation context.

CGI combines techniques of Grounded Theory Methodology (Glaser & Strauss, 1967) with Cooperative Inquiry (Heron & Reason, 1997) to enable the reflection-action-reflection cycles. In practice, Kong worked with women victim-survivors for six months, meeting regularly at least once a week, to create categories and themes together to make sense of each other's post-separation challenges. They developed role play-based learning, one-on-one support sessions and group-based problem-solving practices to address problems identified in their everyday parenting and the difficulties in navigating the stigmatising 'ideal victimhood' and 'ideal survivorhood' that underpin social care support.

Underlying the knowledge-making processes was the ethic of care that helped cultivate a family-like community of practice (Kong & Hooper, 2017) for solving problems together. The ethic of care enabled women to talk about power imbalances and personal biases that surfaced in the group process. With the use of a reflective diary, diagrams, self-portrait for documentation of experiences, and constant comparative analysis for making sense of each other's behaviours, interactions and observations, the enquiry group contested the 'either victim or survivor' dichotomy that created power differences among themselves (Kong, under review). They also interrogated the impact of domestic violence on their mother-child relationships (Kong & Hooper, 2017).

## *Example 2: Collaborative Focus Group Analysis*

Collaborative Focus Group Analysis (CFGA) (Kong, Ho, & Jackson, 2020) was developed to make sense of the impact of Hong Kong's protest movement on people's intimate lives. The purpose of doing so is to expand the space for dialogue and subvert the conventional knowledge-making hierarchy. In developing this approach, we aimed to explore how we could use focus groups in more democratic and participatory ways. CFGA is operationalised through a focus group and reflecting team, both of which take it in turns to observe and analyse each other. The focus group is formed by participant-researchers from the community, diversified in terms of age, gender, sexuality and political orientation; meanwhile, the reflecting team is a group of academic researchers. It differs from the design of a conventional focus group by giving participants the opportunity to influence how their experiences, values and views are described, understood and disseminated.

CFGA is also a process that can help mend the broken relationships that arose from political differences between people in the post-Umbrella Movement context. CFGA creates a space for communicating political and social differences, reducing antagonism and generating a sense of solidarity among academic and community co-researchers. CFGA involves four stages: (1) a planning stage in which the reflecting team and focus group are formed; (2) reflecting team observing the focus group discussion; (3) a focus group observing the reflecting team discussion; and (4) dialogue between the focus group and reflecting team. Researchers in CFGA are facilitators of conversations among co-researchers and need to help set ground rules, such as mutual respect and confidentiality. They also agree to enable communication of similar and different experiences in the conversations. This methodological design recognises the situated and contingent nature of knowledge (Davids & Willemse, 2014), considering data as being generated in the interactional encounter among co-researchers in a specific setting rather than simply collected by objective, politically neutral researchers (Ellis & Berger, 2003; Nencel, 2014).

## Listening to silenced stories through alternative forms of knowing

Democratising research practices entails validating different forms of knowing. It responds to the reality that people make sense of the world not only through building theories, propositions or concepts but also, and majorly, through their experiences in and reflection on problem-solving. The approach embraces Heron and Reason's (Heron, 1996; Heron & Reason, 1997) 'extended epistemology' (i.e. experiential knowing, practical knowing, propositional knowing and presentational knowing) for guiding our knowledge production practices and methodological decisions and directions. An extended epistemology poses critical questions about the value of theories, the purpose of knowledge (know what, know that or know how) and the nature of human consciousness. The implication for academic research is that we have to reflect on how far theories/propositions/conceptual understanding are the best form of knowledge and what are their limitations in exploring emotions, embodiment, memories and intelligibility that characterise social life (Schatzki, 1996).

## *Example 3: labouring women: a devised theatre (辛苦女協作劇場, 2016)*

Devised theatre (Ho, Chan, & Kong, 2017) is a critical Arts-Based Research (ABR) methodology employing collaborative focus group analysis to understand women activists' experiences of sexual harassment and public humiliation during the protest movement in Hong Kong in 2014. While these violent incidents are often trivialised or dismissed as sacrifices 'for the bigger game (of democracy) 為大局犧牲', we seek ways to use theatrical performance to provide a democratic space for women activists and academics to collaboratively generate an understanding of personal political trauma.

Inspired by Boal's (1979) Theatre of the Oppressed, our approach views theatrical performance as bringing to the foreground our own and others' reflections on the difficulties facing women brave enough to participate in public and political spheres of life. Drawing out the complexity of people's life stories, especially the ignored and subjugated aspects of their experiences, enables theatre members and the public to see what could not previously be seen. If social science interviewing is a task of allowing participants to find words for what has previously not been said (Glesne & Peshkin, 1992), critical arts-based performance allows participants to actualise what has been previously felt but repressed (Saldaña, 2016).

At the beginning, we worked collaboratively with women activists to identify the barriers to women's political participation. Specifically, we focused on the intra-movement stigmatisation, and their experiences in the Umbrella Movement and its ensuing consequences for their body image, self-presentation, performance in the media sphere, and intimate relationships. These experiences were documented and shared in the group, and later informed the collaborative script writing. Women activists were involved in the design and development of the theatre performance to ensure authenticity and anonymity in the storytelling. Academics were involved as reflecting team members for responding to women activists' stories. Rather than offering conceptual analysis, they were encouraged to create a mini performance. When understanding was not limited to discursive practice, reflecting team members responded emotionally as they recalled how personal experiences affected their analysis of other people's stories. These emotional exchanges between academics and women activists fostered a sense of solidarity as they began to see more similarities in their experiences of gender inequality than differences in terms of researcher/research and scholar/activist distinctions (Hale, 2008).

## *Example 4: 'The Shape of Me': an arts-based approach to understanding coercive control*

'The Shape of Me' (Kong, 2019; Kong & Robson, 2020) is a pilot project that uses art to enable abused women to have more control over the ways they tell their stories. Women who have experienced coercive control, when involved in social care or legal systems, often feel the pressure to tell formulaic stories to justify their needs for social care and legal support (Guthrie & Kunkel, 2015). Proving oneself to be the ideal/pure victim, a competent mother (despite coercive control against themselves) and a credible witness in the court is hard and can be tremendously disempowering (Creek & Dunn, 2011; McDermott & Garofalo, 2004). These institutionalised stories of domestic violence restrict us from seeing the full spectrum of impacts of coercive control on women. These narratives continue to undermine women's freedom and credibility in giving an account of themselves. How can art serve as a language, alternative to institutional languages, for describing experiences of coercive control? How can we create a safe space, in terms of control and anonymity for women to explore and express the impact of coercive control on themselves? These questions informed the development of an artistic tool, 'The Shape of Me: Walking the Line, Mapping Oneself' (ibid.).

'The Shape of Me: Walking the Line, Mapping Oneself' was collaboratively developed by a number of people: an academic researcher, a creative facilitator, women who have experienced coercive control, their social workers and a counsellor. Through this artistic tool, women represent their experiences in symbols of their own choosing, at their own pace and to their chosen audience. This approach has two components: an art workshop for producing a self-portrait and a follow-up reflective conversation. In the workshop, women participants were encouraged to 'take the line through the experiences of coercive control' (see Figure 49.1) and then extend the line to create the shape of themselves (see Figure 49.2).

The 'line' does not refer to a timeline but rather a tool for revisiting the hard-to-talk-about experiences of living with coercive control. The flexibility that a line can offer, such as drawing peaks and dips, spirals, loops and shapes, enabled women to revisit different time points of their life all at once and to create suitable symbols to represent their experiences without compromising their anonymity.

The self-portrait is created by extending the 'line' to provide the visual spaces for women to reflect on how they have been shaped inside and outside their experiences of coercive control. The simultaneity of inside and outside of coercive control, as laid out on the body map, helped with exploring the connectedness between the embodied experiences of coercive control and the relational-social-historical-political context from which coercive control is performed and

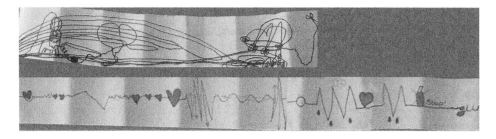

*Figure 49.1*   Examples of 'walking the line' exercise

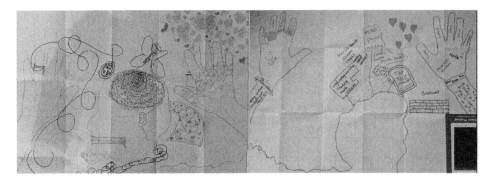

*Figure 49.2* Examples of 'mapping oneself' exercise

resisted. In the follow-up reflective conversation, the researcher did not refer to a set of pre-formulated questions but rather sought invitation into women's experiences. The researcher asked whether the participants would mind 'taking me through the line'. This approach seeks to redress the power position that academic researchers hold to excavate people's experiences, and to ensure that women take control over how they would like to explore the (un)represented experiences in the conversation.

The use of 'The Shape of Me' successfully created a safe space for translating the highly embodied experiences of coercive control into symbolic/pictorial forms (presentational knowing) and provided the dialogical space for co-creating narratives (propositional knowing) about the represented and unrepresented experiences. Women's marginalised stories about 'Dreams', 'Ghost of the perpetrator' and 'Moments in life' shed light on the impact of coercive control on women's concepts of self, time and relationship. These stories problematise linear temporality for organising experiences of coercive control, visualise fluidity of (relational) self and identify social relationships that can support women's resistance against coercive control (Kong, 2019).

## Conclusions

Our experiences of protesting against police violence in Hong Kong have led us to re-examine how state violence, everyday gender-based violence and domestic violence against women may work together to control and subordinate women in a patriarchal gender regime. We suggest that long-term exposure to violence against women, carried out at both the state and interpersonal levels, normalises fear and increases acceptability of violence against women. In a context of political conflict, perpetrators of domestic violence could also use their affiliation, either actual or fictitious, with violent groups as tools to threaten and control women. By reflecting on our encounters with political conflicts, we suggest that more research be conducted on the interrelations between political conflict on gender-based violence and domestic violence. It is especially important for research of this type to be carried out in colonial and post-colonial contexts, such as Hong Kong, to challenge the whiteness in theorising everyday and global terrorism (Pain, 2014).

Recognising that violence can be used at different levels as strategies for reinforcing a gender regime, we re-examine the distinction of 'victim-survivors and non-victim-survivors'. Rather than seeing just 'the few of them who are battered', we can now see many of us are victim-survivors of the patriarchal gender regime, and can be variably vulnerable to violence depending on our social positions. It is also in light of this relationality that a democratic methodology is needed to map the force field of power relations and to sensitise us to the problems and politics in defining victimhood – no one can be a pure victim/perpetrator. This awareness not only fosters a sense of solidarity between those who are socially constructed as 'non-victim-survivors' and 'victim-survivors', but also helps researchers to recognise their moral obligation to transform their everyday research practices. There is a need to create safe research space that is fear-free and communicative for validating women's experiences of violence. These stories are often dismissed or marginalised by 'ideal victimhood' and other formula stories of women's victimisation, used for informing political actions and legal and social care support.

Methodological innovation, therefore, supports action-oriented research that can empower women through the democratisation of knowledge-making. As academic researchers in the field of gender-based violence and sexuality studies, challenging the hierarchy of knowledge and the hierarchy of knowledge-makers is part of the process of validating women's experiences of gender-based violence and to represent them in ways that engage the community to act to respond to violence against women more sensitively and 'care'fully. The least, we seek to avoid reproducing the gender regime that undermines women and where their experiences are not believed.

## Critical findings

- Violence against women is a method of 'doing gender' which, through processes of structuration at individual, cultural and institutional levels, reinforces existing gender inequalities.
- One of the mechanisms by which violence can be used to reproduce gender inequality and subordinate women is by instilling fear. Fear is both deterrent and resource to women's participation in shaping intimate and political lives; meanwhile, fear is mediated through culture and social hierarchies where women are often disadvantaged.
- Tolerance of violence in the name of collective benefits is another mechanism to exercise control over women. The heightened acceptability of violent acts, as a result of prolonged political conflicts in a society, can normalise women's experience of violence and have impact on abused women's willingness to seek help. Women might then lose their ground for request for protection and justice when violence becomes a 'necessary evil'.
- We need to address women's experience of violence and abuse from a relational and intersectional lens (see also the continuum of violence by Liz Kelly).
- We have to be sensitive to the politics of victimhood and how a well-accepted construction of victimhood might render some violent acts against women overlooked and gender injustices unnoticed. Individual women's experiences and understandings of violence and abuse are influenced by their intersecting social positions, including gender, age, class, ethnicity and political orientation.

## Implications for policy, practice and research

- Victimisation/survival is experienced and understood in relation to social context. Recognising everyone can be a victim-survivor in a culture of gender inequality forces us to reconsider the responsibility of researchers in the field of gender-based violence.
- The relational approach raises questions about the legitimacy of researcher/researched distinction which often limits the space for 'respondents' or 'participants' to have 'a voice, a vote, and a veto' (Kara, 2017, p. 289) in knowledge-making.
- The relational approach also highlights the moral obligation of academic researchers for acting against and challenging gendered social hierarchies through their everyday research

practices. It justifies a feminist, participatory, reflexive and action-based approach to researching gender violence, namely 'engaged feminist research'.

- 'Engaged feminist research', as opposed to an ostensibly value-free and objective approach, can yield new knowledge by challenging the status quo and associated power imbalances that are embedded in contemporary institutional research practice.
- Methodological innovation therefore is needed for transforming everyday research practice into action that (1) creates a safe space for recognising overlooked sufferings of women and communicating socio-political differences, and (2) developing a community of care that supports non-violent resistance to gender-based and domestic violence.

## Notes

1  The Umbrella Movement was one of the biggest pro-democracy movements in Hong Kong's history. It took place in 2014 and developed into a 79-day occupation of main roads in the city. Five years later, in 2019, numerous protests broke out in Hong Kong against the proposed extradition law bill amendment which would allow extradition of Hong Kong citizens and foreign nationals to China for trial. Unprecedented police violence was observed, reported and recorded by international organisations, leading to more than 100 days of civil unrest in the city.
2  The terms 'useless elders' 廢老 and 'useless middle-aged' 廢中 have been used by the young protesters to criticise the older generations for not making enough effort to advocate for democracy; meanwhile, these terms are also widely adopted by the elders and middle-aged protesters to justify their unconditional support for the younger generations, especially the valiant camp, due to their political indebtedness to them.

## References

Amnesty International. (2019). *Hong Kong: Arbitrary arrests, brutal beatings and torture in police detention revealed*. Retrieved September 30, 2019, from www.amnesty.org/en/latest/news/2019/09/hong-kong-arbitrary-arrests-brutal-beatings-and-torture-in-police-detention-revealed/
Banks, S. (2014). Reclaiming social work ethics: Challenging the new public management. In S. Banks (Eds.), *Ethics: Critical and radical debates in social work* (pp. 1–24). Bristol, UK: Policy Press.
Boal, A. (1979). *Theatre of the oppressed* (C. A. McBride & M. O. Leal McBride, Trans.). New York, NY: Theatre Communications Group Inc. (Original work published 1974).
Boesten, J. (2010). *Intersecting inequalities: Women and social policy in Peru, 1990–2000*. Pennsylvania, PA: The Pennsylvania State University Press.
Brannelly, T., & Boulton, A. (2017). The ethics of care and transformational research practices in Aotearoa New Zealand. *Qualitative Research, 17*(3), 340–250.
Carvalho, R. (2019, August 28). Thousands gather at #MeToo rally to demand Hong Kong police answer accusations of sexual violence against protesters. *South China Morning Post*. Retrieved September 18, 2019, from www.scmp.com/news/hong-kong/politics/article/3024789/thousands-gather-metoo-rally-demand-hong-kong-police-answer
Centre for Communication and Public Opinion Survey. (2019). *Onsite survey findings in Hong Kong's anti extradition bill protests*. Hong Kong: The Chinese University of Hong Kong.
Cheng, K. (2019, August 23). Hong Kong police accused of indecent assault after protester strip searched days after arrest. *Hong Kong Free Press*. Retrieved September 18, 2019, from www.hongkongfp.com/2019/08/23/hong-kong-police-accused-metoo-assault-protester-strip-searched-days-arrest/
Connell, R. W. (1995). *Masculinities*. Berkeley, CA: University of California Press.
Connell, R. W., & Messerschmidt, J. (2005). Hegemonic masculinity – Rethinking the concept. *Gender and Society, 19*(6), 829–859.
Creek, S. J., & Dunn, J. L. (2011). Rethinking gender and violence: Agency, heterogeneity, and intersectionality. *Sociology Compass, 5*(5), 311–322.
Creery, J. (2019, August 29). #ProtestToo: Hongkongers adopt anti-sexual harassment rallying cry in response to police assault allegations. *Hong Kong Free Press*. Retrieved September 10, 2019, from www.hongkongfp.com/2019/08/29/protesttoo-hongkongers-adopt-anti-sexual-harassment-rallying-cry-response-police-assault-allegations/

Davids, T., & Willemse, K. (2014). Embodied engagements: Feminist ethnography at the crossing of knowledge production and representation-An introduction. *Women's Studies International Forum, 2014*(43), 1–4.

Doyle, J., & McWilliams, M. (2018). *Intimate partner violence in conflict and post-conflict societies: Insights and lessons from Northern Ireland*. Edinburgh: Political Settlements Research Programme (PSRP).

Ellis, C., & Berger, L. (2003). Their story/my story/our story. In J. Holstein & J. F. Gubrium (Eds.), *Inside interviewing: New lenses, new concerns* (pp. 467–493). Thousand Oaks, CA: Sage Publications.

Emery, C. R., Kim, J., Song, H. A., & Song, A. (2013). Child abuse as a catalyst for wife abuse? *Journal of Family Violence, 28*(2), 141–152.

Erez, E., Ibarra, P. R., & Gur, O. M. (2015). At the intersection of private and political conflict zones: Policing domestic violence in the Arab community in Israel. *International Journal of Offender Therapy and Comparative Criminology, 59*(9), 930–963.

Giddens, A. (1984). *The Constitution of society: Outline of the theory of structuration*. Berkeley, CA: University of California Press.

Glaser, B. G., & Strauss, A. L. (1967). *The discovery of grounded theory*. New Brunswick: Aldine Transaction.

Glesne, C., & Peshkin, A. (1992). Making words fly: Developing understanding from interviewing. *Becoming Qualitative Researchers*, 63–92.

Goodmark, L. (2018). *Decriminalizing domestic violence: A balanced policy approach to intimate partner violence* (Vol. 7). Oakland, CA: University of California Press.

Guthrie, J. A., & Kunkel, A. (2015). Problematizing the uniform application of the formula story: Advocacy for survivors in a domestic violence support group. *Women & Language, 38*(1), 43–62.

Hale, C. R. (2008). *Engaging contradictions: Theory, politics, and methods of activist scholarship*. Berkeley, CA: University of California Press.

Harding, S., & Norberg, K. (2005). New feminist approaches to social science methodologies: An introduction. *Journal of Women in Culture and Society, 30*(4), 2009–2015.

Heron, J. (1996). *Co-operative inquiry: Research into the human condition*. London: Sage.

Heron, J., & Reason, P. (1997). A participatory inquiry paradigm. *Qualitative Inquiry, 3*(3), 274–294.

Hester, M., Donovan, C., & Fahmy, E. (2010). Feminist epistemology and the politics of method: Surveying same sex domestic violence. *International Journal of Social Research Methodology, 13*(3), 251–263.

Ho, P. S. Y., Chan, C. H. Y., & Kong, S. T. (2017). Expanding paradigms: Art as performance and performance as communication in politically turbulent times. In M. Cahnmann-Taylor & R. Siegesmund (Eds.), *Arts-based research in education* (pp. 137–146). New York: Routledge.

Ho, P. S. Y., Jackson, S., & Kong, S. S. T. (2018). Speaking against silence: Finding a voice in Hong Kong Chinese families through the umbrella movement. *Sociology, 52*(5), 966–982.

Ho, P. S. Y., Kong, S. T., & Huang, Y. T. (2018). Democratising qualitative research methods: Reflections on Hong Kong, Taiwan and China. *Qualitative Social Work, 17*(3), 469–481.

Hydén, M. (1999). The world of the fearful: Battered women's narratives of leaving abusive husbands. *Feminism & Psychology, 9*(4), 449–469.

Johnson, M. P. (2010). *A typology of domestic violence: Intimate terrorism, violent resistance, and situational couple violence*. Hanover and London: Northeastern University Press.

Kara, H. (2017). Identity and power in co-produced activist research. *Qualitative Research, 17*(3), 289–301.

Kelly, L. (2002). The continuum of sexual violence. In K. Plummer (Ed.), *Sexualities: Some elements for an account of the social organisation of sexualities* (Vol. 2). London and New York, NY: Taylor & Francis.

Kelly, L. (2016). The conducive context of violence against women and girls. *Discover Society*, Issue 30. Retrieved August 22, 2019, from https://discoversociety.org/2016/03/01/theorising-violence-against-women-and-girls/

Kilpatrick, R. H. (2019, August 16). 'An eye for an eye': Hong Kong protests get figurehead in women injured by police. *The Guardian*. Retrieved August 21, 2019, from www.theguardian.com/world/2019/aug/16/an-eye-for-an-eye-hong-kong-protests-get-figurehead-in-woman-injured-by-police

Kong, S. T. (2016). Social work practice research innovation, implementation and implications: A case of 'cooperative grounded inquiry' with formerly abused women in Hong Kong. *Qualitative Social Work, 15*(4), 533–551.

Kong, S. T. (2019). 'The Shape of Me': Re-examining time, self and relationships in coercive control with women co-inquirers. The European Conference of Domestic Violence 2019, Oslo, Norway. Abstract. Retrieved from https://ecdv-oslo.org/files/2019/08/ECDV-Conference2019-WEB.pdf

Kong, S. T. (under review). Beyond 'safeguarding' and 'empowerment': Towards a relational model for supporting separated abused women in Hong Kong. *Journal of Family Violence*.

Kong, S. T., & Ho, P. S. Y. (2016). Struggling on: Intimacy as an emerging space of political participation. *Discover Society*, Issue 31. Retrieved September 18, 2016, from https://discoversociety.org/2016/04/05/struggling-on-intimacy-as-an-emerging-space-of-political-participation/

Kong, S. T., Ho, P. S. Y., & Jackson, S. (2020). Doing being observed: Experimenting with collaborative focus group analysis in post-umbrella movement Hong Kong. Submitted to *Sociological Research Online*.

Kong, S. T., & Hooper, C. A. (2017). Building a community of practice for transforming 'mothering' of abused women into a 'mutual care project': A new focus on partnership and mutuality. *British Journal of Social Work, 48*(3), 633–655.

Kong, S. T., & Robson, M. (2020). *Practice briefing: Re-sourcing autonomy through arts: A participatory action research for resisting coercive control*. Durham, UK: Department of Sociology, Durham University.

Králová, J. (2015). What is social death? *Contemporary Social Science, 10*(3), 235–248.

Lombard, N. (2013). 'What about the men?' Understanding men's experiences of domestic abuse within a gender-based model of violence. In N. Lombard and L. McMillan (Eds.), *Violence against women: Current theory and practice in domestic abuse, sexual violence and exploitation* (pp. 177–194). London and Philadelphia: Jessica Kingsley Publishers.

Mackay, F. (1996). The zero tolerance campaign: Setting the agenda. *Parliamentary Affairs, 49*(1), 206–221.

McColgan, A. (1993). In defence of battered women who kill. *Oxford Journal of Legal Studies, 13*(4), 508–529.

McDermott, M. J., & Garofalo, J. (2004). When advocacy for domestic violence victims backfires: Types and sources of victim disempowerment. *Violence Against Women, 10*(11), 1245–1266.

McMahon, M., & Pence, E. (2003). Making social change: Reflections on individual and institutional advocacy with women arrested for domestic violence. *Violence Against Women, 9*(1), 47–74.

McPherson, R. (2019). Battered woman syndrome, diminished responsibility and women who kill: Insights from Scottish case law. *The Journal of Criminal Law*. doi:10.1177/0022018319858506

Nencel, L. (2014). Situating reflexivity: Voices, positionalities and representations in feminist ethnographic texts. *Women's Studies International Forum, 2014*(43), 75–83.

Nissim-Sabat, M. (2009). *Neither victim nor survivor: Thinking toward a new humanity*. Plymouth, UK: Lexington Books.

Nixon, J., & Humphreys, C. (2010). Marshalling the evidence: Using intersectionality in the domestic violence frame. *Social Politics, 17*(2), 137–158.

Palacios, J. M. (2016). The sex of participatory democracy. An analysis of the theoretical approaches and experiences of participatory democracy from a feminist viewpoint. *Democratization, 23*(5), 940–959.

Pain, R. (2012). *Everyday terrorism: How fear works in domestic abuse*. Durham, UK: Centre for Social Justice and Community Action, Durham University and Scottish Women's Aid.

Pain, R. (2014). Everyday terrorism: Connecting domestic violence and global terrorism. *Progress in Human Geography, 38*(4), 531–550.

Platek, M. (2019, September). *What is specific about Eastern European gender-based violence (GBV)?* Keynote speech at the European Conference of Domestic Violence 2019, Oslo, Norway. Abstract retrieved from https://ecdv-oslo.org/keynotes/monika-platek/

Ray, L. (2018). *Violence and society*. London: Sage Publications.

Risman, B. J. (2004). Gender as a social structure: Theory wrestling with activism. *Gender & Society, 18*(4), 429–450.

Saldaña, J. (2016). *Ethnotheatre: Research from page to stage*. New York: Routledge.

Schatzki, T. R. (1996). *Social practices: A Wittgensteinian approach to human activity and the social*. Cambridge: Cambridge University Press.

Sprague, J. (2016). *Feminist methodologies for critical researchers: Bridging differences*. Lanham, MD: Rowman & Littlefield.

Stark, E. (2009a). *Coercive control: The entrapment of women in personal life*. Oxford: Oxford University Press.

Stark, E. (2009b). Rethinking coercive control. *Violence Against Women, 15*(12), 1509–1525.

Stark, E. (2013). Coercive control. Violence against women: Current theory and practice in domestic abuse, sexual violence and exploitation. In N. Lombard & L. Mcmillan (Eds.), *Violence against Women: Current theory and practice in domestic abuse, sexual violence and exploitation* (pp. 17–33). London: Jessica Kingsley Publishers.

United Nations. (2019, August 13). *Press briefing note on Hong Kong, China*. Geneva: United Nations Human rights Office of the High commissioner. Retrieve August 21, 2019, from www.ohchr.org/EN/NewsEvents/Pages/DisplayNews.aspx?NewsID=24888&LangID=E

Vera-Gray, F. (2016). *Men's intrusion, women's embodiment: A critical analysis of street harassment*. Oxon: Routledge.

Vera-Gray, F. (2018). *The right amount of panic: How women trade freedom for safety*. Bristol: Policy Press.

WHO. (2017, November 29). *Violence against women*. Retrieved August 14, 2019, from www.who.int/news-room/fact-sheets/detail/violence-against-women

# PART 7

# Concluding thoughts

# 50

# CONCLUDING THOUGHTS

*John Devaney, Stephanie Holt, Carolina Øverlien, Caroline Bradbury-Jones and Rebecca J. Macy*

### Concluding thoughts

This Handbook has brought together scholars and practitioners from across the globe, with varying practice and disciplinary backgrounds, to explore the nature of domestic violence and abuse as well as the way it presents in different places and in various forms. The contributors have also explored how society and professionals might respond in ways which are likely to be helpful to both adult and child victims, while also recognising that domestic violence requires societal change if future generations are to be spared pain and suffering. In the Handbook, while recognising that many political actors have been allies, we have sought to highlight that much of the progress made over recent decades has been led by and driven by bottom-up/ grass-roots movements, rather than the beneficence of governments and other national or global organisations.

In a previous book edited by some of us, we argue that policy, practice and research are not easily distinguishable, as they, rightfully, intertwine, connect and influence one another (Holt, Øverlien, & Devaney, 2018). Indeed, while the relationship between the three is considered complex, as editors for the Handbook, we aimed for this text to be a 'knowledge platform' that has the potential to play a 'brokering role' or a 'bridge' among the three activities (de Haas & van der Kwaak, 2017, p. 11). As noted in the introduction, our intention, as editors, has been to curate contributions that summarise the latest thinking and understanding about what causes and sustains domestic violence and abuse, while also looking at the intersection with other issues that reinforce the inequalities which are so prevalent within and between societies internationally. These inequalities, primarily relating to gender, but also linked to other issues such as sexual orientation, race, ethnicity, disability and poverty, lie at the heart of the challenge that must be faced in responding to gender-based violence more generally, and domestic violence and abuse specifically. As editors we have sought to ensure that we were inclusive about who we invited to contribute to this Handbook, mindful that we are scholars working in high-income countries, and with our own experiences and biases that have shaped how we understand these issues. We are conscious that due to space, we have made choices about what to include, and just as importantly not include. We own the choices we have made, while also acknowledging that a different editorial team may have gone in a different direction. We are immensely grateful to each of the individuals who have contributed to the Handbook, especially as the majority wrote their chapters during the recent and ongoing pandemic. In this concluding chapter we pull together some of the key themes which run through the Handbook and the implications identified by contributors for future policy, practice and research.

If you have had time to read at least a handful of the chapters in the Handbook, it will be clear that what we define as domestic violence and abuse is both wide and yet specific. It covers a range of types of behaviour, as outlined in Parts 3 and 4, but specifically this behaviour is enacted to exert power and control by one or more individuals over someone else with whom they have an ongoing or previous intimate or familial relationship. It is this issue of power and control, and its misuse, which characterises the nature and forms of domestic violence and abuse as outlined in many of the chapters in the Handbook. How we understand domestic violence and abuse can be framed in very different ways, as outlined in Part 2, and the way we understand what lies behind the thinking resulting in the behaviour, can lead to very different ideas about how society and professionals should respond, as outlined in Part 5. In Part 6 we have highlighted how research can help to shed light on these phenomena using a diverse range of methodologies and approaches. What is apparent is that our knowledge and understanding of domestic violence and abuse has developed significantly over the past thirty years as both policy makers and researchers have focused attention on the issue. We now have a much better understanding about the prevalence and incidence of many forms of domestic violence and abuse, and the impact in both the immediate and longer term for child and adult victims. More recently, the evidence of what works in helping victims, or those who use violence and abuse within their intimate relationships, has increased considerably, with notable improvements in the quality and robustness of the evidence produced. However, there is still much we do not know enough about, and the contributors to this Handbook are to be commended for identifying where those gaps are.

A common theme across many of the chapters is the gap between awareness by the public, policy makers and organisations delivering services, regarding the nature and impact of domestic violence and abuse. This applies, for example, to housing departments, health providers and the criminal justice system, where translation of this awareness into services and ways of working, needs to be attuned to the needs of victims and survivors. There are plenty of examples across the various chapters in this book of where policies and services are centred around the victim/survivor, but there are also lots of examples of this gap in both understanding and action.

In Part 2 we explored differing ways of conceptualising what causes and sustains domestic violence and abuse, and how the ways in which we think about these issues informs and influences how we respond. As noted in the introduction to this Handbook, we have adopted a socio-ecological approach in inviting contributions on both topics and perspectives. We want to avoid a simplistic approach of assuming that all perspectives are of explanatory equivalence, as it is clear that a gendered understanding of domestic violence and abuse is central to fully grasping the nature of the problem and where attention needs to be focused by policy makers, legislators and wider society. However, the chapters in Part 2 demonstrate the value of seeking to understand the phenomenon of domestic violence from different angles to recognise the nested nature of the individual's context, their interpersonal and relational context, the community context, as well as the larger social environment (Heise & Kotsadam, 2015; Krug et al., 2002). Hence later contributions in the Handbook detailing responses to domestic violence and abuse draw out how we should seek to respond in reframing the inequalities in society. This is to be achieved through using all available levers, including legislation, to rebalance the inequalities between genders which create the context within which some individuals can seek to control, coerce and abuse their current or former intimate partner, and any children they may have.

An important message from across this Handbook is the recognition that domestic violence and abuse is prevalent in all societies, and across all age groups, from those experiencing their first intimate relationships as young people, to adults in later life. We have also taken a position that children are equally victims of domestic violence and abuse (Øverlien & Holt, 2019) with the impact having the potential to last into adulthood (Radford, Richardson-Foster, Hargreaves, & Devaney, 2019). In Part 3 contributors have argued that policies and services need to acknowledge and respond to the differing presentation and impacts across the age spectrum, drawing upon theories about the lifecourse. Thinking needs to be joined-up so that transition periods across the lifespan do not mean that some groups of people, for example those in the 'middle years', are excluded from research and policy (or remain hidden), and we need to be sensitive to the language we use, so that we keep in mind the gendered nature of abuse and do not conflate different forms of harmful behaviour, such as elder abuse and domestic violence.

In Part 4 we profile some of the many ways in which domestic violence may present. A recurring theme is the need for the public and service providers to move beyond looking at incidents of abuse, to recognising that most forms of domestic violence are about patterns of behaviour over time that minimise the space for action that victims and survivors have to live full and independent lives. In recent years our understanding of particular forms of harm, such as economic abuse or the use of animals to control victims, have improved, and it is encouraging to see that in some jurisdictions both services and protections have evolved to respond to these newly recognised harms. However, across all the chapters there is a call for further research to explore how these issues present and should be responded to in ways which recognise the heterogeneity of victims' characteristics and circumstances, and the intersection of different aspects of disadvantage or discrimination.

This theme is picked up in Part 5 of the Handbook which presents the best available evidence, as well as practice and policy innovations, concerning responses to domestic violence and abuse. As seen from this section, current and innovative responses include helping address the needs of domestic violence victims and survivors (e.g., interventions with children who have experienced domestic violence and abuse in their families and interventions for violence survivors who care for these children), as well as the needs of those who are actively abusive toward their partners (e.g., trauma-informed, oppression-sensitive intervention for those who use domestic violence and abuse). In addition, current responses to domestic violence can include interventions (e.g., dating violence prevention), policy interventions (e.g., policy change-initiatives from gender-justice advocates), programmes (e.g., local community partnership to address domestic violence and abuse), services (e.g., approaches to ameliorate domestic violence victims' emotional health) and strategies (e.g., domestic violence risk assessments). Likewise, and consistent with the social ecological model, this section's chapters underscore how varied responses may be directed at individuals, relationships, families, communities and the greater social context. Two chapters, one on economic empowerment and one concerning housing responses, illustrate how important responses to domestic violence and abuse should be targeted beyond individuals and families toward communities, social groups and countries as a whole. Notably, each chapter offers important evidence-based guidance and recommendations to inform and guide responses to domestic violence and abuse. Considerable and important work has been conducted to date to develop and study a wide range of responses to domestic violence. Nonetheless, each chapter has also shown how all the responses described herein could benefit from increased research attention, particularly when such research is conducted in victim- and survivor-centred ways, in partnership with communities, and in ways that attend to the ecological validity of the research as much as the internal validity and rigour of the proposed methods.

In our final main section we showcase a diverse range of research designs and methodologies, illustrating the multiplicity of approaches to seeking answers to many of the questions raised by our chapter contributors in previous sections. As noted earlier, we have given particular attention to the often considered marginalised or less heard victims of violence and abuse, with a specific focus on children and young people dominating three of the ten chapters and marginalised women in a further two chapters. Across these five chapters we illustrate how innovative methodologies can be employed ethically and creatively to capture the lived experience, inform our understanding of that experience and contribute more robustly to the evidence base on 'what works'. Reflecting a strong 'research in practice' theme throughout this section, the evaluative power of research to inform practice in an evidence-informed manner is also palpable, as is the clear ability for the three strands of policy, practice and research to connect.

It is important to recognise the gains which have been made in recent decades in addressing domestic violence and abuse at both a national and transnational level (Holt et al., 2018). However, we must also recognise that the gains made need to be constantly protected and championed to ensure that they are not lessened by those who would attempt to maintain the status quo, or to assert their dominance. At the time of completing this Handbook we are witnessing a roll back of legislation and safeguards in some countries in Europe including Poland, Russia and Turkey (e.g., Semukhina, 2020; Szwed & Zielińska, 2017) in spite of a strong international framework in The Council of Europe Convention on preventing and combating violence against women and domestic violence (The Istanbul Convention) (Council of Europe, 2011). We are also mindful that the rights we seek to protect in respect of domestic violence and abuse are indivisible from rights associated with political freedom, structural racism, poverty and climate inequality which are so very apparent in different parts of the world at the time of compiling this Handbook. Many of these issues intersect with gender inequality and gender-based violence, and benefit from a gendered analysis that informs more sophisticated political and service responses.

Finally, at the time of writing this final chapter that reflects on the significant development in our knowledge and understanding of domestic violence over recent decades, whilst simultaneously identifying areas and issues for future concern and consideration, we must acknowledge that this Handbook was completed during a global health crisis. Characterised by the World Health Organization (WHO, 2020) as a pandemic, Coronavirus or Covid-19 has wreaked havoc in the lives of individuals, families and communities across the world, killing people, spreading human suffering and upending people's lives, resulting in a significant sense of threat and unpredictability. Globally, Covid-19 has been experienced most acutely since January 2020, with many countries imposing public health policies involving lockdown-style orders, restricting movement and human interaction.

While Covid-19 has been relentless and is attacking all segments of our populations, it has however been particularly detrimental to more vulnerable groups, including those living with domestic violence and abuse. Whilst lockdown and quarantine were and continue to be seen as essential to suppressing the virus in the community, an unintended consequence of such a policy has resulted in victims and those who abuse them being confined in close quarters for long periods of time, with subsequent sharp rises globally in the reported number of cases of domestic abuse and violence. Lockdown measures imposed by governments to help slow the spread of the virus have also altered the availability of support services, forcing professionals to find new ways of working with victims and their families through the crisis. Paradoxically, at a time of additional need, the availability of health and social services may be compromised and it may be challenging for professionals to complete accurate risk assessments with reduced access to families. Emerging empirical studies highlight the surge in demand for specialist domestic violence services and helplines (Kaukinen, 2020), the challenges faced by services in responding to the changing needs of families in an ever-changing environment (Banks et al., 2020; Øverlien, 2020), and the development of innovative practices by professionals internationally (IFSW, 2020). A full assessment of the impact may not be known for some time.

In conclusion, we hope that this Handbook can become a resource for students, practitioners and researchers in considering how we might better understand and respond to domestic violence and abuse in all its forms at a local, national and international level.

# References

Banks, S., Cai, T., de Jonge, E., Shears, J., Shum, M., Sobočan, A. M., . . . Weinberg, M. (2020). Practising ethically during COVID-19: Social work challenges and responses. *International Social Work.* doi:10.1177/0020872820949614

Council of Europe. (2011). *Convention on preventing and combating violence against women and domestic violence.* Strasbourg: Council of Europe.

de Haas, B., & van der Kwaak, A. (2017). Exploring linkages between research, policy and practice in the Netherlands: Perspectives on sexual and reproductive health and rights knowledge flow. *Journal of Health Research Policy and Systems, 15*(40), 1–13.

Heise, L. L., & Kotsadam, A. (2015). Cross-national and multilevel correlates of partner violence: An analysis of data from population-based surveys. *The Lancet Global Health, 3*(6), e332–e340.

Holt, S., Øverlien, C., & Devaney, J. (Eds.). (2018). *Responding to domestic violence: emerging challenges for policy, practice and research in Europe.* London: Jessica Kingsley Publishers.

IFSW. (2020). *The social work response to Covid-19 – Six months on: Championing changes in services and preparing for long-term consequences.* Geneva: IFSW.

Kaukinen, C. (2020). When stay-at-home orders leave victims unsafe at home: Exploring the risk and consequences of intimate partner violence during the COVID-19 pandemic. *American Journal of Criminal Justice,* 1–12.

Krug, E. G., et al. (Eds.). (2002). *World report on violence and health.* Geneva: World Health Organization. Retrieved from https://apps.who.int/iris/bitstream/handle/10665/42495/9241545615_eng.pdf

Øverlien, C. (2020). The COVID-19 pandemic and its impact on children in domestic violence refuges. *Child Abuse Review, 29*(4), 379–386.

Øverlien, C., & Holt, S. (2019). Letter to the editor: Research on children experiencing domestic violence. *Journal of Family Violence, 34*(1), 65–67.

Radford, L., Richardson-Foster, H., Hargreaves, P., & Devaney, J. (2019). *Research review: Early childhood and the 'intergenerational cycle of domestic violence'.* London: NSPCC.

Semukhina, O. (2020). The decriminalization of domestic violence in Russia. *Demokratizatsiya: The Journal of Post-Soviet Democratization, 28*(1), 15–45.

Szwed, A., & Zielińska, K. (2017). A war on gender? The roman catholic church's discourse on gender in Poland. In S. Ramet & I. Borowik (Eds), *Religion, politics, and values in Poland* (pp. 113–136). New York, NY: Palgrave Macmillan.

World Health Organisation. (2020). *WHO Director-General's opening remarks at the media briefing on COVID-19 – 11th March 2020.* Retrieved from https://www.who.int/director-general/speeches/detail/who-director-general-s-opening-remarks-at-the-media-briefing-on-covid-19---11-march-2020

# INDEX

Note: Page numbers in *italic* indicate a figure and page numbers in **bold** indicate a table on the corresponding page.